NOVEL & SHORT STORY WRITER'S MARKET

2018

Includes a one-year online subscription to **Novel & Short Story Writer's Market** on

WritersMarket.com

Where & How to Sell What You Write

THE ULTIMATE MARKET RESEARCH TOOL FOR WRITERS

To register your *Novel & Short Story Writer's Market 2018* and **start your one-year online genre-only subscription**, scratch off the block below to reveal your activation code, then go to WritersMarket.com. Find the box that says "Purchased a Deluxe Edition?" then click on "Activate Your Account" and enter the activation code. It's that easy!

UPDATED MARKET LISTINGS FOR YOUR INTEREST AREA
EASY-TO-USE, SEARCHABLE DATABASE • RECORD-KEEPING TOOLS
PROFESSIONAL TIPS & ADVICE • INDUSTRY NEWS

Your purchase of *Novel & Short Story Writer's Market* gives you access to updated listings related to this writing genre (valid through 12/31/18). For just $9.99, you can upgrade your subscription and get access to listings from all of our best-selling Market Books. Visit **WritersMarket.com** for more information.

WritersMarket.com

Where & How to Sell What You Write

Activate your WritersMarket.com subscription to get instant access to:

- **UPDATED LISTINGS IN YOUR WRITING GENRE:** Find additional listings that didn't make it into the book, updated contact information, and more. WritersMarket.com provides the most comprehensive database of verified markets available anywhere.

- **EASY-TO-USE, SEARCHABLE DATABASE:** Looking for a specific magazine or book publisher? Just type in its name. Or widen your prospects with the Advanced Search. You can also search for listings that have been recently updated!

- **PERSONALIZED TOOLS:** Store your best-bet markets, and use our popular recording-keeping tools to track your submissions. Plus, get new and updated market listings, query reminders, and more every time you log in!

- **PROFESSIONAL TIPS & ADVICE:** From pay-rate charts to sample query letters, how-to articles to Q&As with literary agents, we have all the resources writers need.

YOU'LL GET ALL OF THIS WITH THE INCLUDED SUBSCRIPTION TO

WritersMarket.com

Where & How to Sell What You Write

◄ 37TH ANNUAL EDITION ►

NOVEL & SHORT STORY WRITER'S MARKET

2018

Rachel Randall, Editor

WRITER'S DIGEST
BOOKS
WritersDigest.com
Cincinnati, Ohio

Writer's Market website: www.writersmarket.com
Writer's Digest website: www.writersdigest.com

Distributed in Canada by Fraser Direct
100 Armstrong Avenue
Georgetown, Ontario, Canada L7G 5S4
Tel: (905) 877-4411

Distributed in the U.K. and Europe by F&W Media International
Brunel House, Newton Abbot, Devon, TQ12 4PU, England
Tel: (+44) 1626-323200, Fax: (+44) 1626-323319
E-mail: postmaster@davidandcharles.co.uk

ISSN: 0897-9812
ISBN-13: 978-1-4403-5265-2
ISBN-10: 1-4403-5265-8

Attention Booksellers: This is an annual directory of F+W Media, Inc. Return deadline for this edition is December 31, 2018.

Edited by: Rachel Randall
Designed by: Alexis Estoye
Production coordinated by: Debbie Thomas

CONTENTS

FROM
THE EDITOR

"The times, they are a-changin." My father, a Bob Dylan devotee, sang me this song when I was little. It was his way of saying that the world inevitably changes, and you need to change with it. Later, I understood the deeper message: To be successful, you have to evolve.

In the rapidly shifting world of publishing, fiction writers would do well to heed this advice. Platforms like Wattpad (which boasts some *45 million* readers) and Inkvite are providing new ways for authors to reach a broader audience. New marketing and promotional opportunities are constantly cropping up, and the trends can be difficult to follow. And against all odds, short stories are hotter than ever.

But despite these changes, I believe wholeheartedly that a strong foundation in craft is essential. The celebration of writing skill is the one constant in a tumultuous industry, and while the times are indeed a-changin', the need for expertly crafted prose and compelling stories will never fade.

That's why resources like *Novel & Short Story Writer's Market* are more important than ever. To gain an edge, writers *need* to balance their skill with their business savvy.

"You better start swimming/or you'll sink like a stone." While his words may seem ominous to some, Dylan was right. But as you make your way downriver, keep that balance between craft and business in mind. It's what *NSSWM* is all about—and it will equip you for any change you may face as you navigate the currents of change.

Rachel Randall
Editorial Director, Writer's Market

P.S. Don't miss our exclusive webinar from *New York Times* best-selling author Jennifer Probst. "Say What? Create Dialogue to Hook Readers and Make Your Story Pop" can be accessed at www.writersmarket.com/2018-nsswm-webinar.

HOW TO USE *NSSWM*

To make the most of *Novel & Short Story Writer's Market*, you need to know how to use it. And with more than five hundred pages of fiction publishing markets and resources, a writer could easily get lost amid the information. This quick-start guide will help you navigate through the pages of *Novel & Short Story Writer's Market*—as well as the fiction-publishing process—and accomplish your dream of seeing your work in print.

1. READ, READ, READ. Read numerous magazines, fiction collections, and novels to determine if your fiction compares favorably with work currently being published. If your fiction is at least the same caliber as what you're reading, then move on to step two. If not, postpone submitting your work and spend your time polishing your fiction. Reading the work of others is one of the best ways to improve your craft.

You'll find advice and inspiration from best-selling authors and seasoned writers in the articles found in the first few sections of this book (**Craft & Technique**, **Interviews**, and **The Business of Fiction Writing**). *Novel & Short Story Writer's Market* also includes listings for **Literary Agents** who accept fiction submissions, **Book Publishers** and **Magazines** that publish fiction in a variety of genres, **Contests & Awards** to enter, and **Conferences & Workshops** where you can meet fellow writers and attend instructive sessions to hone your skills.

2. ANALYZE YOUR FICTION. Determine the type of fiction you write to target markets most suitable for your work. Do you write literary, genre, mainstream, or one of many other categories of fiction? For definitions and explanations of genres and subgenres, check out the **Glossary** and the **Genre Glossary** in the **Resources** section of the book. Many magazines and presses are currently seeking specialized work in each of these areas as well as numerous others.

For editors and publishers with specialized interests, see the **Category Index** in the back of the book.

3. LEARN ABOUT THE MARKET. Read *Writer's Digest* magazine; *Publishers Weekly*, the trade magazine of the publishing industry; and *Independent Publisher*, which contains information about small- to medium-size independent presses. And don't forget the Internet. The number of sites for writers seems to grow daily, and among them you'll find www.writersmarket.com and www.writersdigest.com.

4. FIND MARKETS FOR YOUR WORK. There are a variety of ways to locate markets for fiction. The periodical section in bookstores and libraries is a great place to discover new journals and magazines that might be open to your type of short stories. Read writing-related magazines and newsletters for information about new markets and publications seeking fiction submissions. Also, frequently browse bookstore shelves to see what novels and short story collections are being published and by whom. Check acknowledgment pages for names of editors and agents, too. Online journals often have links to the websites of other journals that may publish fiction. And last, but certainly not least, read the listings found here in *Novel & Short Story Writer's Market*.

5. SEND FOR GUIDELINES. In the listings in this book, we try to include as much submission information as we can get from editors and publishers. Over the course of the year, however, editors' expectations and needs may change. Therefore, it is best to obtain a copy of the submission guidelines. You can check each magazine's and press's website—they usually contain a page with guideline information. Or you can do it the old-fashioned way and send a self-addressed, stamped envelope (SASE) with a request for them.

6. BEGIN YOUR PUBLISHING EFFORTS WITH JOURNALS AND CONTESTS OPEN TO BEGINNERS. If this is your first attempt at publishing your work, your best bet is to begin with local publications or those you

KEY TO ICONS & ABBREVIATIONS

- Ⓐ market accepts agented submissions only
- ⊘ market does not accept unsolicited submissions
- award-winning market
- Canadian market
- market located outside of the U.S. and Canada
- Ⓢ market pays (in magazine sections)
- comment from the editor of *Novel & Short Story Writer's Market*
- ○ actively seeking new writers
- ◐ seeks both new and established writers
- ● prefers working with established writers, mostly referrals
- ◎ market has a specialized focus
- ◉ imprint, subsidiary, or division of larger book publishing house (in book publishers section)
- publisher of graphic novels or comics

know are open to beginning writers. After you have built a publication history, you can try submitting to the more prestigious and nationally distributed magazines. For markets most open to beginners, look for the ◯ symbol preceding listing titles. Also look for the ◑ symbol, which identifies markets open to exceptional work from beginners as well as work from experienced, previously published writers.

7. SUBMIT YOUR FICTION IN A PROFESSIONAL MANNER. Take the time to show editors that you care about your work and are serious about publishing. By following a publication's or book publisher's submission guidelines and practicing standard submission etiquette, you can increase your chances that an editor will want to take the time to read your work and consider it for publication. Remember: First impressions matter. A carelessly assembled submission packet can jeopardize your chances before your story or novel manuscript has had a chance to speak for itself.

8. KEEP TRACK OF YOUR SUBMISSIONS. Know when and where you have sent fiction and how long you need to wait before expecting a reply. If an editor does not respond in the time indicated in his or her market listing or guidelines, wait a few more weeks before following up with an e-mail or letter (with SASE) asking when the editor anticipates making a decision. If you do not receive a reply from the editor within a month or two, send a letter withdrawing your work from consideration and move on to the next market on your list.

9. LEARN FROM REJECTION. Rejection is the hardest part of the publication process. Unfortunately rejection happens to every writer, and every writer needs to learn to deal with the negativity involved. Believe it or not, rejection can be valuable when used as a teaching tool rather than a reason to doubt yourself and your work. If an editor offers suggestions with his or her rejection slip, take those comments into consideration. You don't have to agree with an editor's opinion of your work. It may be that the editor has a different perspective on the piece than you do. Or you may find that the editor's suggestions give you new insight into your work and help you improve your craft.

10. DON'T GIVE UP. The best advice we can offer you as you try to get published is to be persistent and to always believe in yourself and your work. By continually reading other writers' work, constantly working on the craft of fiction writing, and relentlessly submitting your work, you will eventually find that magazine or book publisher that's the perfect match for your fiction. *Novel & Short Story Writer's Market* will be here to help you every step of the way.

GUIDE TO LISTING FEATURES

Below is an example of the market listings contained in *Novel & Short Story Writer's Market,* with callouts identifying the various format features of the listings. (For an explanation of the icons used, see the sidebar on page 3.)

AT-A-GLANCE REFERENCE ICONS

E-MAIL AND WEBSITE INFORMATION

SPECIFIC CONTACT NAMES

DETAILED SUBMISSION GUIDELINES

TIPS FOR SUBMISSION

❶$❸ꙮ THE SOUTHERN REVIEW

Old President's House, Louisiana State University, Baton Rouge, LA 70803-5001. (225)578-5108. Fax: (225)578-5098. E-mail: southernreview@lsu.edu. **Website:** www.lsu.edu/thesouthern review.

Contact Cara Blue Adams, editor. Magazine: 6¼ × 10; 240 pages; 50 lb. Glatfelter paper; 65 lb. #1 grade cover stock. Quarterly. Circ. 3,000.

• Several stories published in *The Southern Review* were Pushcart Prize selections.

NEEDS Literary. "We select fiction that conveys a unique and compelling voice and vision." Receives approximately 300 unsolicited mss/month. Accepts 4-6 mss/issue. Reading period: September-June. Publishes ms 6 months after acceptance. Agented fiction 1%. Publishes 10-12 new writers/year. Recently published work by Jack Driscoll, Don Lee, Peter Levine, and Debbie Urbanski. Also publishes literary essays, literary criticism, poetry, and book reviews.

HOW TO CONTACT Mail hard copy of ms with cover letter and SASE. No queries. ("Prefer brief letters giving author's professional information, including recent or notable publications. Biographical info not necessary." Responds in 10 weeks to mss. Sample copy for $8. Writer's guidelines online. Reviews fiction, poetry.

PAYMENT/TERMS Pays $30/page. Pays on publication for first North American serial rights. Sends page proof to author via e-mail. Sponsors awards/contests.

TIPS "Careful attention to craftsmanship and technique combined with a developed sense of the creation of story will always make us pay attention."

MASTERING THE ART OF THE UNEXPECTED

Fred D. White

A good story takes us on a journey through a milieu that is both familiar and strange, where mystery and often danger lurk just beneath recognizable surfaces. As readers, we want our curiosity to be aroused by unexpected twists and turns of events, or by one character's unanticipated reaction to another's words or deeds. Because fiction enables us to experience vicariously what we would be unlikely to experience in ordinary life, writers need to master the techniques that fill readers with a sense of wonder about what is going to unfold next, and surprise them with unexpected incidents and disclosures.

Developing this skill can be tricky; unexpected events and disclosures also must be plausible. You don't want to risk disrupting your readers' willing suspension of disbelief with a situation that doesn't ring true or seems arbitrary. The ingredients for surprise should already be implicit in the story milieu or in the characters' natures.

The first step in becoming adept at taking your readers on a roller-coaster ride is to review the different unexpected events and revelations that can take place.

VARIETIES OF THE UNEXPECTED

There are five types of story-based unexpected elements, any or all of which can be used to transform a ho-hum story into a riveting one.

- The protagonist's goal proves tougher than expected.
- Appearances prove to be illusory.
- A character reveals his or her hidden intentions or feelings.

- Setbacks threaten to undo progress.
- A sudden insight illuminates a seemingly insurmountable problem.

In addition to the above story-based techniques for upending reader expectations, there are rhetorical techniques—clever turns of phrase, unusual metaphors, or startling witticisms—that can enhance the reader's involvement in the story.

Let's take a look at some of the ways these techniques are employed.

STORY-BASED TECHNIQUES FOR GENERATING THE UNEXPECTED

The Protagonist's Goal Proves Tougher Than Expected

Left for dead on the surface of Mars after an accident, Mark Watney, the protagonist of Andrew Weir's 2012 science fiction thriller, *The Martian,* must stay alive long enough to be rescued. The situation seems hopeless, then marginally possible, but Watney cannot at first foresee the extraordinary measures he must take for the rescue to have any chance of succeeding. The plot consists of one unexpected, life-threatening complication followed by an equally unexpected—yet plausible—solution. For example, with only a very limited supply of water left, Watney must make a crude distillery and boil his urine. Weir's novel is a textbook example of how a series of unexpected-yet-plausible incidents and outcomes drive a narrative forward from page to page.

Appearances Prove to Be Illusory

Here is how Nathanael West opens his scathing satire of 1930s Hollywood, *The Day of the Locust*:

> Around quitting time, Tod Hackett heard a great din on the road outside his office. The groan of leather mingled with the jangle of iron and over all beat the tattoo of a thousand hooves. He hurried to the window.
>
> An army of cavalry and foot was passing … its lines broken, as though fleeing from some terrible defeat. The dolmans of the hussars, the heavy shakos of the guards, Hanoverian light horse, with their flat leather caps and flowing red plumes, were all jumbled together in bobbing disorder.

A bizarre invasion? A riot? The reader wonders what on earth is going on here. Then comes this startling passage:

> While he watched, a little fat man, wearing a cork sun-helmet, polo shirt and knickers, darted around the corner of the building in pursuit of the army.
>
> "Stage Nine—you bastards—Stage Nine!" he screamed through a small megaphone.

This comic reversal of expectations—that the "invading army" was nothing more than a bunch of actors in costume marching toward the wrong sound stage—serves as a kind of prologue to West's story about the tragicomic confusion between illusion and reality both in and out of the movie studio.

A Character Reveals His or Her Hidden Intentions or Feelings

Fiction, regardless of genre, is mainly about people—how they treat one another, how they react to crises, how they think about and interact with the world. People are complex, and for that reason are unpredictable, depending on circumstances. Fiction magnifies that unpredictability for dramatic and aesthetic effect. When young David Copperfield first meets Edward Murdstone, the man courting his widowed mother, Murdstone comes across as a perfect gentleman, fooling his impressionable mother. Only after she marries him does his volatile nature surface. (Of course, in true Dickensian style, the name of a character usually hints at his inner nature.)

Let's consider another example, this one from "In the Region of Ice," an award-winning short story by Joyce Carol Oates, which appears in her collection *The Wheel of Love.* Sister Irene, a college professor at a Jesuit University, interacts with Allen, an emotionally unstable student, in her Shakespeare class. Allen's insights into the plays are brilliant: He is able to connect deeply with their profound understanding of human desires and sufferings, but the young man is disruptive in class, and excessively demanding of Sister Irene's attention. The feelings of futility and loneliness that she senses in him are not unlike her own feelings. But how can she help Allen? What does he really want from her?

> He looked at her with his dark intense eyes, and Sister Irene felt them focus upon her. She was terrified at what he was trying to do—he was trying to force her into a human relationship.

The irony here is painful. Because of her religious calling, Sister Irene cannot enter such a relationship—and yet her vocation is all about serving others—at the expense of her own needs.

Setbacks that Threaten to Undo Progress Made

Storytellers must be aware of several kinds of character setbacks: false leads, poor choices, underestimations, misinterpretations, miscalculations, accidents, unforeseen dangers. Think of how unforeseen dangers dominate Homer's *Odyssey*, one of the first great stories in Western literature. To cite just one example, after arriving on the island inhabited by Polyphemus, the Cyclops, Odysseus and his men prepare for a fest of hospitality—but instead, the one-eyed giant grotesquely murders several of Odysseus's men. To make matters worse, as Odysseus and his surviving men make their escape, Odysseus, unable to resist bragging, discloses his identity to Polyphemus, who in turn begs his father, the sea god Poseidon, to wreak havoc on Odysseus as he sails for home—setting the stage for more unexpected calamities.

Let's revisit *The Martian*. After all the ingenious progress Watney has made, his habitat is breached—a less-than-one-millimeter tear in the fabric causes the Hab to depressurize explosively. We wonder, as we did at the opening predicament, how Watney could possibly survive.

> The full force of the Hab's atmosphere rushed through the breach. Within a tenth of a second, the rip was a meter long. It propagated all the way around until it met its starting point. The airlock was no longer attached to the Hab.
>
> The unopposed pressure launched the airlock like a cannonball as the Hab's atmosphere explosively escaped through the breach. Inside, the surprised Watney slammed against the airlock's back door with the force of the expulsion.

Weir's splendid attention to detail—at once technical and accessible to the average reader—reinforces the verisimilitude of this shocking reversal of fortune.

What better genre for inevitable setbacks than mystery novels? Think of Robert B. Parker, whose private detective, Spenser, for all his methodical probing, experiences one setback after another before making a breakthrough in a case. In *School Days*, for example, Spenser takes on a school-shooting case that appears to be a slam-dunk: One shooter was caught red-handed, and the second shooter confessed. But because details in the case don't add up, Spenser digs in. When he questions the shooter, whose grandmother insists is innocent, the teenager only smirks and shrugs.

> "How many did you take out?" I said.
>   He shrugged.
> "Why did they need it?"
> "They were assholes."
> "And you could tell that how?" I said.
> "Whole school was assholes," he said.
>   And smirked.

Later, back in his apartment, he watches his dog, Pearl, sleeping. Her position "had caused her mouth to fall open and her tongue to loll out the left side of it. … 'Yeah,' I said, 'That's about where I am.'"

A Sudden Insight Illuminates a Seemingly Insurmountable Problem

Insights, revelations, epiphanies: These sudden shifts in the fate of your protagonist do not merely arrive out of the blue but are the result of intense probing. Hester Prynne, branded with the scarlet *A* she must always wear in public, gains an existential insight into the human condition, not just her own. Instead of experiencing despair from the el-

---

INCORPORATING SURPRISE

- Before plunging into the task of writing a short story or novel, write a synopsis of the story you want to tell. For a 5,000-word short story, aim for a one-page synopsis. For an 80,000-word novel, aim for ten pages.
- For each of the scenarios that follow, write a one-paragraph synopsis of a story that would incorporate at least three unexpected story-based techniques:
  - An accident causes the protagonist to reassess her relationship with her boyfriend, who may have caused the accident.
  - A long-suppressed memory in one of the characters surfaces as a result of some incident, threatening the well being of those around him and perhaps even himself.
  - A natural disaster sends the protagonist's goal into a tailspin.
  - A long-buried secret about one of the characters is discovered, perhaps by a friend or family member, which results in that character losing her job or good reputation.
  - The protagonist experiences a spiritual transformation as a result of a series of strange encounters.
- Dig out one of your rejected stories and re-energize it by incorporating some of the elements of the unexpected we've discussed.

---

ders' efforts to shame her, she begins to wonder if the scarlet letter has offered her a new perspective.

> She shuddered to believe, yet could not help believing, that it gave her a sympathetic knowledge of the hidden sin in other hearts. … What were they? Could they be other than the insidious whispers of the bad angel … that the outward guise of purity was but a lie, and that if truth were everywhere to be shown, a scarlet letter would blaze forth on many a bosom besides Hester Prynne's.

This sudden insight into the human condition both unsettles and comforts her. It is one thing to be deemed an outcast, a fallen woman amid the saintly, and quite another to suspect that everyone else is just as fallen as she, in one way or another.

In Oates's story discussed earlier, Allen writes Sister Irene a letter (after his father committed him to a mental institution) in which he claims to be resting comfortably— but also asks that she visit his father to explain that what Allen really wishes for is "to an escape to another world." This is followed by a passage from Shakespeare's *Measure for Measure* (the imprisoned Claudio's speech to his sister). Sister Irene suddenly realizes that Allen is obliquely—one might say artistically—expressing his desire to commit suicide.

RHETORICAL ELEMENTS OF THE UNEXPECTED

"He's a grand, ungodly, God-like man," Captain Peleg says of Captain Ahab when Ishmael, the narrator of *Moby-Dick*, inquires about the elusive captain of the Pequod. The oxymoron is both disturbing and refreshing; we aren't used to seeing "God-like" described as "ungodly." Yet in a novel that probes the disparities between appearance and reality on many different levels, the description proves apt.

In *School Days*, when Spenser visits the school where the shooting took place, he reflects wryly on his initial sensory impression of this setting. His reaction is startling—yet like a good poem it rings true.

> It smelled like a school. It was air-conditioned and clean, but the smell of school was adamant. I never knew what the smell was. Youth? Chalk dust? Industrial cleaner? Boredom?

Such descriptions should never be gratuitous. The word *boredom*, for example, resonates with the situation: Could it be, we suddenly wonder, that one of the shooters (a student) had been bored? Parker reinforces this suspicion a few paragraphs later when Spenser, inspecting a classroom, thinks, "I could taste the stiflement, the limitations, the deadly boredom, the elephantine plod of the clock as it ground through the day."

SUGGESTIONS FOR INCORPORATING UNEXPECTED ELEMENTS

There are three ways to energize your story with the unexpected:

1. Plan them as part of the outlining stage.
2. Fly by the seat of your pants and trust your imagination to deliver plot twists and turns as you draft
3. Plow through a first draft without worrying about incorporating unexpected elements, and then insert them during the second draft, when you have a clearer sense of how and where to include them.

These options, of course, are not mutually exclusive. I, for one, prefer to outline with tentative twists and turns included; then draft quickly, staying open to new possibilities; and finally rethink the entire story for a second draft, with new ideas for disrupting the reader's expectations.

If you're new at plotting, I recommend following this plan:

1. Work up a preliminary plotline consisting only of the key story events and/or revelations. Don't worry about incorporating unexpected elements yet.
2. Once you have mapped out the main storyline, determine where complications can plausibly yet unexpectedly occur, and incorporate them.

3. Finally, double-check overall plot integrity for consistency and believability.

Of course, the real challenge lies in coming up with effective devices that will heighten the drama of your story. Be careful that your unexpected elements do not seem contrived or overly formulaic, but arise organically from the characters' natures or from the situation itself.

The art of fiction is largely the art of revelation: What will be revealed next about the principal characters, or about the obstacles standing in the way of the protagonist's goal? Every memorable story, from the *Odyssey* to *The Martian*, is replete with such revelations. The key to ensuring their success lies not only in the verisimilitude of the story but in the surprise elements that keep readers turning pages.

Fred D. White's fiction has appeared in many print and online magazines, including *Aphelion, Atticus Review, Burningword, Confrontation, Limestone, Foliate Oak, Off Course Literary Journal*, and *Praxis*, and as a podcast from *No Extra Words*. His most recent books are *The Writer's Idea Thesaurus* and *Where Do You Get Your Ideas?*, both published by Writer's Digest Books, and *The Well-Crafted Argument*, now in its sixth edition from Cengage Learning. His most recent articles on writing include "Flash Forward" (*Writer's Digest*, March/April 2017). A professor of English Emeritus (Santa Clara University), Fred lives near Sacramento, California, with his wife, Terry Weyna, an attorney and science fiction and fantasy blogger.

UNLEASH YOUR STORYTELLING SUPERPOWER

....

Gabriela Pereira

Some say that at the heart of every story is a compelling character. I agree, but with one crucial caveat: Characters aren't just a necessary ingredient for your story—they *are* your story. Without them you have nothing more than a sequence of plot points. Characters humanize your story and give readers someone to root for. It's one thing to watch a newsreel or read a news report of a dramatic event, but when you experience that story through a character, it suddenly becomes more personal and powerful.

Compare, for example, Stephen Crane's newspaper account "The Sinking of the *Commodore*" (*The New York Press*, 1897) with his short story "The Open Boat," published in *Scribner's* magazine the following year. The former gives a sequence of events summing up what happened and when, who died, and how. The short story puts us in the boat, standing shoulder to shoulder with the desperate men as they bail the rising water and eventually abandon ship. Both accounts are from the same author, who was aboard the ship as it went down, but the short story is far more engaging. In it we see the events unfold as those sailors would have experienced them. When we craft stories around a character, we're not just telling it to our readers. We're showing them what it feels like to be there.

CHARACTER TYPES AND DESIRES

Every writer is drawn to a character archetype that she is particularly adept at bringing to life on the page. When it comes to the protagonist (or main character of your story), there are four such types. But before we dive into the particulars of each one, it's important to understand where these archetypes come from.

The protagonist is the focal point for your story. Who this character is and what she wants will drive the plot from beginning to end. The archetypes for this main character come from the intersection between her personality type and what she wants.

What Is Your Protagonist's Type?

Every character in literature falls into one of two types. No matter how nuanced or multifaceted your protagonist may be, at her most basic she is either an *everyman* or a *larger-than-life hero*.

The everyman protagonist—or what I like to call the ordinary Joe (or Jane)—is a regular guy going about his regular life, until something happens that turns his world upside down. The ordinary Joe is an unlikely hero caught in extraordinary circumstances. Though he is out of his league, he eventually rises beyond his ordinariness and does something astonishing. While at first glance the everyman might not be anything special, with the right motivation he can become a hero.

At the other end of the scale we have the larger-than-life hero. This character is so powerful and amazing, she seems almost perfect. We already know all the incredible things this character can do, so instead the key with bringing this character to life is to show a hint of vulnerability, a chink in the armor. After all, even Superman has his kryptonite.

Keep in mind these two personality types are not separate categories so much as they are opposite ends of the same spectrum. Most characters fall somewhere in the middle of two extremes, and as the story progresses they shift toward the opposite pole. I call this concept the "Opposite is Possible" theory. As writers it is our job to show that our main characters can become the opposite of how they appear at the beginning of the story. This is not about making your protagonist behave in ways that seem outlandish or *out of character*. Rather, the goal is to show the potential for change and plant the right hints, so when your everyman or larger-than-life hero does begin to shift, it doesn't force the reader out of the story. Remember that in every story, your protagonist must change in some way. Regardless of whether this change is extreme or subtle, you need to craft that main character with that possibility for change already baked into the narrative.

What Does Your Character Want?

"Make your character want something!" If you have taken a writing class or read any books about the craft, you have likely heard this advice. But it's not enough to make your protagonist want just anything. It has to be something so important to your character that the pursuit of that desire will keep your story moving. Making your character want a glass of water is not that compelling if he can simply get up and walk to the kitchen. But if your character is stranded on a raft in the middle of the ocean, then a glass of water takes on a whole new level of significance.

Just as there are two types of protagonists, there are also only two fundamental things your character can want. On one hand, your character might want to change something, whether in himself or the world around him. Or his most fervent desire might be the preservation of the status quo. Of course, no story is ever quite that simple, and often your character will want many different, sometimes contradictory things. When you consider all these desires, however, you will usually find that your character leans toward one type over the other. As with the character types, what your character wants exists on a spectrum rather than as two binary extremes.

At this point we have established that the protagonist's personality and desire fall on two distinct spectrums, but what does any of this have to do with us as writers? That's where the concept of the storytelling superpower comes in.

UNDERSTANDING YOUR STORYTELLING SUPERPOWER

When you intersect the protagonist's personality type with what she wants, you get one of four archetypes: the underdog, the disruptor, the survivor, and the protector. The storytelling superpower matrix shows how we get each of these archetypes from looking at character type and desire. The underdog is an everyman character who wants to change something in himself or the world around him. The disruptor also wants to effect change, but in this case the character is in the larger-than-life category. The survivor and protector, on the other hand, both want to preserve something in their lives or their world, with the survivor as the everyman type and the protector as a larger-than-life hero.

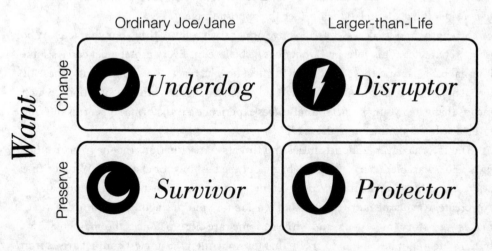

As writers, we each tend to gravitate toward one of these archetypes over the other three. Look at stories you've written or ones you love to read. Chances are, one of these archetypes keeps coming up again and again. Think also about how you view yourself, and it's likely that the archetype you most like to write (or read about) is the one you identify with the most. This is not to say that you never identify with the other types, but it's likely that one of these resonates with you more than the others. I call this preferred archetype your *storytelling superpower*.

Identifying your storytelling superpower isn't meant to set limitations or compartmentalize your creativity. Rather, when you understand your natural tendencies and preferences, it allows you to play to your strengths and stretch yourself beyond your comfort zone. After all, if one archetype tugs at your heartstrings more than the others, you'll likely pour more passion and creative energy into crafting that character, which in turn will make your writing shine.

The Three Layers of Character Development

As you'll soon discover, each archetype has positive qualities as well as weaknesses. Understanding these pros and cons will help you ratchet up the stakes and increase the conflict in your story. You will also learn to identify aspects of your character that can be off-putting to your readers, making them want to stop reading altogether. Training yourself to identify these red flags will help you craft characters and stories your readers can't help but love.

To understand each storytelling superpower archetype, you need to consider three layers of that character: her internal state, her external situation, and how readers will relate to her. In business, a *SWOT analysis* assesses an idea based on its strengths, weaknesses, opportunities, and threats. We'll do a similar analysis here, adding an extra layer to consider the reader relationship. (See the opposite page.)

Strengths and weaknesses are positive or negative traits within your character. Who is your character at his core, and what does he believe in? Every protagonist carries some internal baggage, and these qualities will affect how he reacts to various events. These internal qualities are also somewhat fixed and consistent across different situations, which means that when your character finally *does* experience a transformation at this internal layer, it will feel significant to the reader.

The external layer—opportunities and threats—are situations that happen around or to your character. What scenarios bring out the best in your character? Which situations cause her to misbehave? And, even more interesting, what environments can you create to generate more conflict and tension for your protagonist? Conflict is what makes your story interesting, and while in some rare circumstances the character's internal state might be enough to create that tension, often the juiciest conflict arises from

Character Analysis

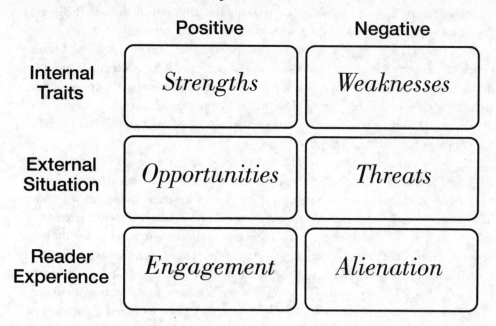

	Positive	Negative
Internal Traits	*Strengths*	*Weaknesses*
External Situation	*Opportunities*	*Threats*
Reader Experience	*Engagement*	*Alienation*

a mismatch between your protagonist's internal qualities and the environment where she finds herself.

Finally, you must also consider the relationship your character has with your reader. Which of your character's internal qualities will your readers find engaging, and which will alienate them? Does the character make choices or react to external situations in ways that resonate with readers, or are his behaviors repellent? There are also certain signature stories (e.g., rags to riches, fish out of water, etc.) that tend to work better with some archetypes than the others. Knowing what these signature stories are will help you determine if you are crafting the best narrative for your character.

MEET THE ARCHETYPES

The Underdog

The quintessential underdog is a relatable character with a deep desire to change something in herself or in the world around her. From Katniss Everdeen in Suzanne Collins's *The Hunger Games* to Marty McFly in the Back to the Future film series, underdogs are regular people caught in extraordinary circumstances but who manage to rise to the occasion and do something heroic. Underdogs have a lot of pluck and determination, and they're not afraid to do whatever it takes to reach their goals. However, these characters may sometimes feel like they have something to prove, so they pick battles they cannot win. And while their "bring it on" attitude might be inspiring and may get them through challenging circumstances, underdogs don't cope well with situations that demand retreat.

In terms of reader engagement, this archetype is one of the most compelling because people love rooting for underdogs. When readers see an underdog come out on top, it makes them think, *If he can do it, maybe I can, too.* But if taken too far, the underdog can seem self-righteous, like they have a chip on their shoulder. And when underdogs stubbornly make bad choices or pick the wrong battles again and again, readers may stop feeling sympathy for the character.

Signature underdog stories include rags-to-riches narratives, epic David-and-Goliath-style battles, and classic comebacks in which a character who used to be on top needs to earn back his former glory. Because the underdog is so relatable and these stories often have such high stakes, underdogs are compelling characters that readers find irresistible.

This is one of the most prevalent archetypes in short fiction, in part because the scope of the short story favors everyman characters over their larger-than-life counterparts. Also, it's easier to convey a character's transformation within a condensed word count if the protagonist is already seeking out change in the first place, as is the case with underdogs. To see the underdog in action, look at Mrs. Mallard in Kate Chopin's "The Story of an Hour," the nameless narrator in "The Yellow Wallpaper" by Charlotte Perkins Gilman, or Pinky in Claire Davis's story "Labors of the Heart."

The Disruptor

Disruptors are larger-than-life characters who rebel against the status quo. They will do whatever it takes to change their societies, overcome all odds, and defeat tyranny. From Elizabeth Bennet in *Pride and Prejudice* by Jane Austen, to the title character in F. Scott Fitzgerald's *The Great Gatsby*, to Tris Prior in Veronica Roth's Divergent series, disruptors take on many different forms. They are charismatic leaders who know how to persuade and inspire the people around them, though they sometimes focus so much on their mission that they wind up hurting the people around them. And, like underdogs, disruptors may concentrate so much on instigating change that despite their larger-than-life qualities they might pick fights they cannot win.

This archetype is especially powerful if you want to infuse your writing with a broader message. Because disruptors possess a strong vision, they can serve as a vessel to communicate your own opinions or ideals from behind the scenes. The danger is that if you make the allegory or satire too heavy-handed, you may end up sounding preachy and alienating your readers. Also, with all that passion and charisma comes narcissism and a lack of empathy. Disruptors don't always play well with others, and there is a fine line between being a rebel and a bully. To make your disruptor a sympathetic or even likable character, you need to make her motivations clear to your readers and have her show at least some vulnerability.

This may be the reason why disruptors are far less common in short stories than in book-length literature. It takes time to tease out a character's motivations and show her weaknesses. Short fiction may not give you the necessary space to give your disruptor the depth she needs to engage your readers. This is where supporting characters can be useful in making a disruptor protagonist seem less bad by comparison. For instance, in Flannery O'Connor's "A Good Man Is Hard to Find," the grandmother is clearly unlikable—at the beginning of the story, it is hard for readers to sympathize with her. But when The Misfit holds the family captive and begins killing people, suddenly the grandmother doesn't seem quite as terrible, and we almost feel sorry for her. Similarly, Neddy Merrill in "The Swimmer" by John Cheever is a vapid, entitled snob, but as we see his life slowly deteriorate, we can't help but feel compassion for him.

The Survivor

Until now, we have looked at characters who want to change something either in themselves or in the world around them. Now we shift gears to archetypes driven by a desire for preservation. True to his name, a survivor character will do whatever it takes to preserve his life as he knows it. This may be a literal battle for survival or simply a desire not to shake up the status quo, but to the character it feels like a life-and-death struggle. Whether he is stranded on a desert island, kidnapped by an evil genius, or fighting to beat a terminal illness, readers will admire a survivor for his pluck, determination, and sheer creative willpower.

Like underdogs, survivors are of the everyman type, so readers see a part of themselves reflected in these characters and feel inspired when they persist against all odds. There is also something inherently hopeful in this archetype. Despite the doom and gloom that often follows these characters, they hold fast and persist even if all seems lost. Taken to the extreme, survivors can become self-reliant to a fault, often isolating themselves and failing to ask for help even when they desperately need it.

As writers, we also need to be careful not to let the character's struggle derail the story and make the issue or problem the story's only raison d'être. It's one thing to craft your narrative around a character who overcomes a trauma, but there has to be more to the story than the trauma alone. A beautiful example is the short story "Everyday Use," in which author Alice Walker explores issues of race, culture, and what it means to honor your heritage. While these themes are very present throughout, this is not a "racial heritage story" but is instead a story in which the theme comes to light in how differently the two main characters interpret and understand their racial heritage, and the conflict that subsequently arises between them.

The Protector

Protectors are larger-than-life heroes. Whether or not they wear capes, boots, and spandex, when the world is in danger, they are compelled to protect it and those they love. As with survivors, protectors are driven by a desire to preserve rather than to shake things up. Whether it's Iron Man, James Bond, or the nerdy and militant Dwight Schrute from the television series *The Office*, protectors show almost superhuman fortitude in their quest to defend what they believe in, prevent disasters, and stand up to the forces of evil.

Protectors are the most popular and prevalent character archetype, in part because heroic characters are powerful and inspiring. With all this power, however, often comes arrogance, and protectors can become obsessed with status and might even misuse their power. Also, these characters do not like to follow rules or be subordinate to someone else, and they detest change, especially if it undermines their authority. As with all larger-than-life characters, the way to make protectors engaging and relatable to readers is to show a hint of vulnerability and imperfection.

Protectors often are more likable than their disruptor counterparts. After all, it's easier for readers to root for a hero who is trying to *save* the world than for one who wants to *take over* the world or *change* it in his favor. However, the horror genre often features a counterexample in which the larger-than-life protector character is extremely unlikable. This can be seen in early classics from Nathaniel Hawthorne and Edgar Allan Poe. Unsympathetic protectors in these works are compelling because readers want to see them suffer. In Hawthorne's "Young Goodman Brown" and "The Birthmark," and in many of Poe's short stories, the appeal of the story isn't that the character succeeds but that he fails. And the best way to make a reader root against a character is to make that character unlikable.

YOUR CHARACTER'S TRANSFORMATION

It's important to remember that these four archetypes are not fixed categories. Remember that change is inherent in any work of fiction; if your character doesn't change in some way, then it's a static dossier, not a story. Keep in mind that this change does not have to be extreme. You do not need to push your character from one pole to its opposite. Instead, it can be a subtle shift.

Remember, too, that the character's desire needs to drive this transformation. In Flannery O'Connor's "A Good Man Is Hard to Find," we see the grandmother change from a narcissistic and manipulative matriarch into a desperate woman begging for her life. The story is so heart wrenching because she starts out trying to control and dominate everyone in her family but ends up losing all control—including over her own life. As you craft your characters, consider not only what they want and how they will transform throughout the story, but also how that desire will affect and support that change.

Your story's resolution hinges on how you resolve your protagonist's quest for what they desire. Does your character get what she wants? If so, does she still want it? The ending will depend on how you answer these two questions, but keep in mind that your character's personality, what she wants, and how she transforms in pursuit of it, are all inextricably linked. The key is to weave these threads together without tying up your story in a neat bow. Often what distinguishes a great story from a mediocre one is the artistry of the ending, which both resolves the character's quest for the thing she wants and also transforms her. When the ending feels unexpected *and* inevitable—surprising but also deeply satisfying to the reader—you know a story is truly exceptional.

Gabriela Pereira is a writer, speaker, and self-proclaimed word nerd who wants to challenge the status quo of higher education. She is the instigator of DIYMFA.com, host of the podcast DIY MFA Radio, and has an MFA in creative writing from The New School. Her book *DIY MFA: Write with Focus, Read with Purpose, Build Your Community* is out now from Writer's Digest Books. To find out your storytelling superpower and learn how to unleash its full potential, take the quiz at DIYMFA.com/STSP.

DERIVING THEME FROM CHARACTER & PLOT

Jack Smith

Any number of stories with different plots may have the same basic theme. We might say, "This story is about courage in the face of adversity." Or "This story is about mercy over justice." Or "This story is about reason gone mad." But does every story need a theme? It probably *will* have one, whether or not you devise it purposefully. Thus, the key to creating an effective theme lies in knowing which story elements contribute to it, and how. Setting, language (especially if it's metaphorical or analogical), and symbolism all contribute to the richness and efficacy of theme, but often the most compelling ones are derived from character and plot. In fact, many writers must develop these elements first and then pull theme from them.

CREATING THEMES AND IDEAS

Let's say you begin your story or novel with a theme or idea in mind, hoping to empower your work with considerable range and depth. You're heavily invested in your thematic idea, and you want to make this theme quite evident so that the reader won't miss it. You're not intending to be didactic—you know good literature isn't—but you do want a work that is more than "a mere story." You want levels of abstraction that make this piece of fiction "real" literature. Should you go for it? Should you attack the creative process with a given theme in mind? Some top literary writers discourage it.

For Walter Cummins, co-publisher of Serving House Books and author of several story collections, this approach "invites the imposition of a heavy hand." Instead, he suggests allowing thematic ideas to come on their own, emerging "from the germ of a situation, character conflicts, and active scenes." When Cummins writes, he focuses on the "dramatic situation" and its resolution, his primary goal being "to come up with the right ending and to make that ending convincing." Once he's able to accomplish this, he states, "Whatever theme emerges from the ending is a shorthand simplification of what the story actually conveys."

Gladys Swan, author of four novels and seven collections of short stories, also avoids approaching her work with a theme in mind. Doing so, she says, "tends to make the story seem contrived or to make the theme obvious." Like Cummins, she believes that themes and ideas must emerge from both characters and plot. First she must come up with the right characters; she doesn't necessarily have them in mind. To get started, she draws inspiration from several things: "an image, an incident, a bit of interesting behavior, a chance remark, all of which I find the need to explore." Characters eventually come, and once they do, Swan says, "I can shape things, selecting what best serves the emerging unity of the piece." From this unity emerge the themes and ideas that inform a given story, but she doesn't try to put them into an abstract statement. They should be apparent to any perceptive reader, she thinks, in the various interstices and dynamics of the story.

For short story writer and novelist Jack Remick, themes must come out of character. Yet he first makes sure he isn't manipulating his characters. Once he has a character in mind, he engages in an exercise he calls "The Time Walk-Back": "I pick up the character, say, five minutes before the story opens. I don't know what the story is yet, but that's okay: [then I look at] my character … one hour before … one week before … one year before … five years before." Doing this exercise allows Remick to discover all kinds of things about his protagonist and other characters—"who they are, what they do, what they want"—before he allows them to speak because, he says, "when they do speak, you're sort of eavesdropping instead of making up stuff." Meanwhile, he interrogates his characters, attempting to discover "what Claude Lévi-Strauss calls 'polarities.'" Polarities include such opposites as: "open/closed; thick/thin; rich/poor; raw/cooked." These polarities, says Remick, serve not only a character-based function but a plot-based one as well: "The polarities lead to story arcs, and story arcs lead to character change and plot tracks. A plot track can be built on a character, an object, or an action." On their own steam, then, Remick's characters lead him to "plot tracks" that hint at one or more possible themes in a story or novel.

Emphasizing character as the locus of theme, Dennis Must, author of two novels and three story collections, states that he follows Faulkner's dictum. Faulkner once advised, "I would say to get the character in your mind. Once he is in your mind, and he is right, and he's true, then he does the work himself." For Must, theme and character are "mutually dependent." The true character, says Must, "invariably carries a story's theme inside his ineluctable heart." But there's more: To avoid the obvious, the writer must be "keenly sensitive to a character's inherent dualities and ambivalence." It's in these dualities that we'll find a theme suggested in Must's work.

Though Stephanie Dickinson, author of several books of fiction, works consciously in the revision stage by "editing and sculpting," she also makes certain that any themes that emerge in her work spring naturally out of the dramatic conflict of characters. For this conflict, she relies on "*hot-button* material or subject matter" about teenage girls, "the impulsive, rebellious years when choices can lead to mistakes that last a lifetime." With this firm foundation in dramatic action, she can avoid being heavy-handed with thematic ideas, no matter how ruthlessly she wields the revision pen. "As many threads as you can pull together," says Dickinson, "with almost the precision of needle-work, the stronger the writing, the more evocative."

Beyond the wellsprings of dramatic conflict, Dickinson also relies on theme for "the textures of place, the light and dark shadings of a scene, in some ways a cinematic approach to thematic concept." With this highly visual method, she depends on specific details as well as the accretion of these details to suggest theme. Dickinson tries to unify the story around a central focus, working to "tie up loose ends or cut them, heightening those perceptions that evoke emotion and meaning."

HANDLING SPECIFIC THEMES IN FICTIONAL WORKS

As we've discussed, it may be risky to begin your fictional process with a given theme in mind. Instead, as you write early drafts, allow your characters and plot to unfold, letting thematic ideas come about naturally. They will certainly come, says Dickinson: "Gurus of how to write well tell us good storytelling will have a theme even if the writer hasn't consciously imposed one." It's a matter of letting it happen. The more you explore your characters and conflict, the more it's bound to happen.

It happened for Dickinson in *Love Highway*. Based loosely on the 2006 Jennifer Moore murder, her novel is a "duet for two voices: two Manhattan girls, one a murder victim and the other a passive perpetrator, each narrating authentically their half of the book." In writing this novel, Dickinson wanted to "explore and somehow understand this collision of the different worlds inhabited by two young women close in age." Of course, real-life events are only the springboard for fiction; it's what the writer does with the material that counts. Using stream of consciousness, Dickinson focused on the interior of her characters, peering deeply into their hearts and minds. As she did so, she discovered compelling intersections between them, suggesting parallel transformations that pointed to levels beyond the surface of character and plot. According to Dickinson, "Those plot-points of transformation where the girls most echoed each other in their perceptions and passions, becoming almost interchangeable, were freighted with thematic meaning." The themes in the novel are many, says Dickinson, dealing with sins of commission as well as omission. It was in the revision process that she felt at liberty to hone these themes: "Some points I emphasized by slowing the pacing of the action. Others I enlarged with dialogue and moments of epiphany, and then I stitched them back into the whole." Though she refined her material, she did stay clear of authorial intrusion: "I wanted to withhold judgment and allow the characters to reveal themselves." For Dickinson, fiction writing is a two-part process: in early drafts, she achieves a firm foundation in dramatic conflict; then, in revision, she refines any suggested ideas or themes.

Also in the revision stage, Dickinson refines theme through her cinematic approach. In *Love Highway*, her chiaroscuro added thematic texture to both characters and setting: "The two girls, victim and perpetrator, were profoundly connected as if Siamese twins caught between the Walks and Don't Walks, the millions of lit windows turning themselves off, letting the warehouses of grimy brick and scarecrow water towers do the looking out." Again, while Dickinson felt at liberty to explore the novel's language for its thematic possibilities, she remained faithful to the characters who had sprung full-blown from the drafting process.

If themes tend to stem naturally from the nexus of character and plot, sometimes a writer must depend on a process of discovery to unveil these two key story elements. In her story "The Old Hotel," Swan had neither characters nor plot in mind. All she had was a basic starting point: a striking image of an elaborate Victorian hotel in New Mexico. When she was thirteen and toured this hotel, it was no longer in use. Thirty years later, says Swan, this hotel "was completely gone from the desert landscape stretching away to the distant mountains." A sense of profound change moved Swan to write about the hotel. She worked with what she had: "I wrote about twenty drafts of a description of the hotel. Then the characters finally appeared." They were occupants of this mysterious hotel, once elaborately furnished: "Jack Whedon, a spineless and incompetent sort slickered into buying the hotel; his wife, Penny, hard-nosed and self-serving; and Jewel, their teenage daughter." Added to this family were two others: "Viny, a childlike, loving young woman, and a former music teacher with a mysterious past, who has come from Europe. Both have come to live at the hotel." Once she became immersed in the storytelling, Jewel became her focus. "The Old Hotel" soon became "a coming-of-age story with the time-honored themes of innocence and experience." But other characters also declared themselves and introduced the theme of illusions, including deception of "both self and others." Swan didn't impose these themes from without—they emerged in the telling. As she states it, "These motifs emerged as I wrote the story, coming from the interactions of the characters, who are not based on anyone I've ever known."

DEVELOPING THEMES IN YOUR OWN WORK: TIPS FROM THE PROS

- **READ WIDELY.** For Gladys Swan, appreciating themes and ideas in literature calls for reading beyond contemporary fiction to the classics, ancient drama, and poetry, as well as nonfiction: "History, psychology, science, and the arts, as well as literature, and whatever else interests you in the world around you."

- **DON'T START WITH SOMETHING TO SAY.** "In my teaching experience," says Walter Cummins, "many beginning writers think they should have something important to say. Few writers do." What makes successful fiction, for Cummins, is not a particular theme but how theme is expressed, which calls for "characters and plots that engage and move us, and provide a sense of the complexity of human existence."

- **FEEL THE PULSE THAT DRAWS YOU IN EMOTIONALLY AS WELL AS INTELLECTU-ALLY.** "As I approach a narrative," says Dennis Must, "its pulse must arouse in me an acute sense of vulnerability or personal risk as to how the work may unfold." On the intellectual level, he says, "I also know that the effort will resolve itself ambiguously."

- **FIND THE SPINE, OR KEY GOVERNING PRINCIPLE OF THE STORY.** "Unfortunately," says Jack Remick, "the spine always comes late in the writing. I would say that the writer has to wait for the story to reveal its spine. Some writers call it the *armature*."

- **WRITE FLASH FICTION TO UNDERSTAND THEME AS A UNIFYING IDEA.** According to Stephanie Dickinson, "View the paragraph as a world-building exercise. It is a perfect structure with a beginning, a middle, and an end."

However you arrive at character, you should consider it, alongside conflict, as the wheelhouse of your story or novel. For Must, it's in the "ineluctable heart" of the protagonist where we find a story's theme and the possibility for universal, existential conflicts. In Must's "Dry Bread and Turnip Soup," the theme turns on the issue of personal identity. The protagonist, Peter Eckerd, is forced to question who he really is when his wife and her male companion strip him of everything that has defined him, including his library full of books, his manuscripts, and his clothes. Though he has admitted to accumulating too much, the wholesale carting away of his familiar possessions has caused him to wonder if he ever existed. By story's end, realizing that he surely must, by now, be a stranger to his wife, he opts for the guestroom. Yet Peter Eckerd soon becomes ambivalent, drawn between two personae. Says Must, the character "felt enlightened, for he realized he'd been an accomplice in perpetuating a static *I*. He'd become prisoner of his dormant self." On the other hand, he wishes to continue being his former self, hoping his wife will invite him back to her bedside. And thus, typical of Must's characters, Peter's duality provokes important existential questions such as "What is the nature of identity?" "What makes us who we are?" "Do we have a fixed or permanent self?" The story's theme is embodied in the questions themselves, not in pat answers.

If theme is not contrived by the author, it can give a work of literature much substance, as it does in Must's story. But it's possible, too, that a particular theme might not be quite as important as the literary devices that develop it. For instance, in Remick's *Gabriela and the Widow*, the theme is a familiar one of character transformation. While an important theme, Remick believes that his literary technique, his "structural scheme of polarities," commands the most attention. The novel's *spine*, as he calls it, is based on certain key polarities—in this case, *thick* versus *thin*. "This polarity," says Remick, "has a multitude of transforms, each transform linked to an object." For example, when Gabriella is first introduced to the reader, she represents *thin*: skinny, barefoot, in indigenous garb. But at the end of the novel she is *thick*, having come into the many material possessions of the rich Widow. Gabriela's plot track, says Remick, is represented by a "clothing arc" that represents her overall "psychological, physical, and financial transformation" in the novel. Remick's character and plot mechanisms gain more prominence than does the theme itself. The theme is important, but it's the symbolic handling of Remick's organizing polarities that mostly, he believes, grabs the reader's attention.

As interesting and compelling as theme can be, a good story, Cummins believes, cannot be reduced to it. There is so much more: all the felt experiences that radiate in it. In one of his recently published stories, "Celebrities," Cummins drew upon memories of a house in Brooklyn Heights where he'd lived as a young man of twenty-one. He recalled three of the tenants: a fledgling actor, a boat design hobbyist, and a young woman who met famous people at airports. "The characters that emerged from these real people were wannabe celebrities," says Cummins. But he went beyond these three characters to invent his protagonist, who "ghost-writes songs for a star and gets no recognition." Given the thrust of the story, Cummins states, "I suppose the theme that emerged was the shallowness of fame. But that is a cliché. Many, perhaps most, themes are. Stories have to be satisfying in themselves, much more interesting than the themes they can be reduced to." Even so, to develop this theme, Cummins says, "I had to invent character conflicts and, after several revisions, developed one between the actor and the protagonist. But what would be the ending, the climactic scene?" The ending scene is what Cummins depends on for his "shorthand simplification" to carry an idea. It has to be believable, convincing. He struck on the following: "I had the others in the building gather to watch the actor's last-minute appearance on a late-night talk show. He makes a fool of himself. Then I had to work out in a much-revised final paragraph how the protagonist reacts to his rival's humiliation. What does his action reveal about his own insight into his relationship with fame?" Cummins sees the theme of shallowness as only part of the story's fictional worth: "The story turns out to be about one man's unique response to that theme, which is more complicated than the theme itself." The story was nominated for a Pushcart.

Theme is the "unifying idea" of a story or novel. But be careful about approaching a work of fiction with a particular unifying idea in mind. You can do so, but as you write, be sure to let it hover somewhere up in the stratosphere, and focus on getting down into the dust of your characters' lives, into everything that makes them fully human. After all, if you want your themes or ideas to hook your reader, they will do so only through lively, flesh-and-blood characters, ones that seem so real they can step right off the page. Abstract ideas, though they can be quite compelling to contemplate, won't drive fiction. It's felt life that does this.

Jack Smith has published four novels: *Miss Manners for War Criminals* (2017), *Being* (2016), *Icon* (2014), and *Hog to Hog*, which won the 2007 George Garrett Fiction Prize and was published by Texas Review Press in 2008. He has published stories in *Southern Review*, *North American Review*, *Texas Review*, *Xconnect*, *In Posse Review*, and *Night Train*. His reviews have appeared in *Ploughshares*, *Georgia Review*, *American Book Review*, *Prairie Schooner*, *Mid-American Review*, *Pleiades*, *The Missouri Review*, and *Xconnect*. He has published a few dozen articles in both *Novel & Short Story Writer's Market* and *The Writer* magazine. His *Write and Revise for Publication: A 6-Month Plan for Crafting an Exceptional Novel and Other Works of Fiction* was published in 2013 by Writer's Digest Books. Besides his writing, Smith was fiction editor of *The Green Hills Literary Lantern*, published by Truman State University, for twenty-five years.

FORESHADOWING & ECHOING

....

Jack Smith

Writing fiction is a juggling act that requires you to keep several elements in the air at once. For instance, in a good work of fiction, characters undergo conflicts and change, developing in different ways and to different degrees. Readers should be able to trace the protagonist's overall character arc over the course of the story. As the plot develops, the short story or novel needs to build toward a final resolution that satisfies the reader and feels inevitable but not predictable.

Along the story's continuum, *foreshadowing* is instrumental in creating believable key events, especially the climactic one. "As a storyteller," says Barry Kitterman, author of *Baker's Boy*, "to make all the events of a story believable, my job is to go back to the early parts of the story and set everything up." Doing so, says Kitterman, avoids a *deus ex machina*, one that brings in "a big dramatic ending that hasn't been sufficiently set up."

While foreshadowing looks forward, *echoing* looks behind and reminds readers of what they've already seen, reinforcing a key element of a plot thread or a thematic idea. Both elements help knit a story together into a well-woven tapestry. Yet knowing the importance of each is one thing; handling them well is quite another. How do you avoid being too obvious? How many instances of foreshadowing or echoing should you include, and where?

BEING TOO OBVIOUS

When either foreshadowing or echoing are too apparent, they function like huge signposts in a piece of fiction. While we may want prominent signs in road travel, the enjoyment of reading a story can diminish when the writer intrudes with such obvious markers. Stephanie Cowell, author of four historical novels, cautions against "hammering it too much into the reader's mind."

Gary Fincke is author of thirty books of fiction, poetry, and nonfiction, including *Sorry I Worried You*, winner of the Flannery O'Connor Award for Short Fiction. About his most recent collection, *The Killer's Dog*, Fincke states that he doesn't think elements of foreshadowing and echoing are readily apparent in many of these stories. "I would like to think it's because they are there but not exposed until a close reading unearths them in the way that we discover significance in our lives." They are part of the overall design of the story, but it takes a critical eye to note and analyze the function of each.

How do you avoid being too obvious? One way, says Kitterman, is to "employ a little misdirection." For instance, in creating a prop detail that will serve a key role in plot development, try using a mix of different details so that, for the time being, the key detail will register "in a quiet corner of the reader's brain" and only be present "when the story requires it." The embedded detail will then make sense later, says Kitterman.

Fantasy writer Janice Hardy sneaks elements into the reader's subconscious "so they anticipate whatever emotion or event I want to prepare them for." At first glance, says Hardy, the reader may not pick up on the clue. "It's a hint of something that seems innocuous when they first see it, but then carries greater meaning or fits perfectly with something later." She cites as an example a scene from her fantasy novel *The Shifter*, in which her protagonist, Nya, returns home from work to discover she's been evicted from her boarding room. Hardy captures the moment in one, succinct line: "My door was pegged shut." This line plants a seed, Hardy believes, that will grow later in the reader's mind: "This one line foreshadows that she's about to lose all sense of safety and a place to run to. She's been kicked out, and no one will help her get back home. As the story continues, the number of 'safe places' for her dwindle."

Dropping in clues lightly, or "casually," as mystery writer Krista Davis puts it, helps avoid intrusive authorial sign posts. She cites an example from her novel *The Diva Serves High Tea*, in which a character is attacked in her home at night. "The victim spends the rest of the night with the protagonist. A friend hears about [the attack], looks around his house for a weapon … and takes a decorative halberd [a combined spear and battle axe] with him to the protagonist's home. Of course, everyone makes fun of the halberd, but in light of the situation, it's soon forgotten." For Davis, it's best that this halberd is forgotten—temporarily, that is. "Because a halberd is unusual," she says, "readers will take note of it, but they're not likely to think about it afterward, as the story progresses. At the end of the book, the halberd makes a reappearance when a boy remembers seeing it and comes to the rescue with it when the protagonist is being attacked."

If you should avoid explicit, heavy-handed foreshadowing, you should do the same with echoing. There's no question that a story or novel ending that provides a well-turned echo has great value, says Kitterman. "Everyone loves a great last line. Everyone loves a final sentence or two that ties the story together, that brings the reader back to a beautiful moment, that moves the writing to the place where the story vibrates and becomes more than a story, becomes truth." But in an effort to end your story with stunning impact, you can overdo it, as Kitterman points out. "The danger here, as my old teacher Bill Kittredge used to say, is that it's easy to hit the nail right on the head and hit it one time too many, really sink[ing] that nail a half inch into the sheetrock so nobody will ever miss what a terrific nail pounder you are." Achieving grandiose utterance comes at a price, then, if the echo comes on too strong. It cheats the reader of a rich sense of felt life. "The harder we strain to come up with the perfect last line—the perfect echo—the greater the danger the ending will feel forced," Kitterman says.

In considering this issue of the well-wrought closing echo, Kitterman looks back to a story he wrote some years ago, "In Dog Years." In this story, a little long-haired dog named Jack London dies midway through the story. "It was this loss," says Kitterman, "that started the main character down a road of a sad string of losses." These are substantive losses: his marriage, his job, and his prominent position in the community. At the end of the story, the protagonist offers a benediction for some young schoolchildren in his small town. Notice how Kitterman's closing line pulls everything together and also works in a subtle echo of the dog Jack London: "He hoped they would live contented and safe, with children of their own and dogs in their homes, celebrating one happy marriage per lifetime." With this "quiet reference to dogs," as Kitterman puts it, he is able to reinforce the role of Jack London, the dog, as emblematic of loss itself.

CHOOSING FORESHADOWING INSTANCES

How many instances of foreshadowing are enough—or too much? Davis holds that one mention is usually sufficient. "If it's something that I feel might have been missed and is absolutely crucial to understanding the plot, then I might repeat it. But when you do that, you take the risk that you're signaling the importance of that item." Too much repetition risks, once again, that authorial signpost. If, in the service of plot, you need to provide this emphasis, do so, says Davis, but you're better off sticking to one mention.

Opinion varies on the ideal number of foreshadowing instances. Cowell says, "I think twice is enough, but it can be three times for foreshadowing. It's amazing how stronger things can register in a novel than they do in life. Since the reader expects everything on the page to have some meaning in the whole book, he or she will take it in and tuck it in her mind." Hardy follows the Rule of Three and says that each element of foreshadowing accomplishes a given goal: "The first mention is small, almost a throwaway detail that introduces the reader to whatever I want to foreshadow. The second mention connects it to the character in some way. The third mention is the payoff." For Hardy it's through these three instances that she can grab her readers emotionally and also assure believability: "I want the device to either create anticipation if I'm building toward an emotional payoff, or create a sense of inevitability if I'm creating a situation that needs to feel plausible." She knows she hasn't prepared her reader enough "when the details don't trigger the emotion I'm looking for in the reader." The number of times, if kept to three, isn't too much, Hardy says, unless one of the instances "shifts from a hint to a big neon sign saying, 'This is going to happen, wait for it.'" And so, a writer can be too obvious in two ways: in the manner of presenting the foreshadowing element, and in creating too many instances of foreshadowing, or, as Cowell puts it, in too obvious *hammering*.

WHERE TO PLACE FORESHADOWING AND ECHOING

How do you determine *where*, exactly, to provide foreshadowing? Cowell uses it when she feels "the present scene is a little low on drama and wonder[s] if the reader's attention will drift." In Davis's murder mysteries, "something significant must happen in the beginning of the book to capture the attention of the reader before the murder." It's a matter of suspense—a mystery novel has to get the reader hooked early on. "That's the perfect time," says Davis, "to set up an incident that foreshadows what is to come. Additionally, you can mention weapons that might be used later or unusual behavior that will make more sense once your sleuth investigates."

Exactly where you put certain foreshadowing details is one question to consider, and the answer undoubtedly depends on the particular story or novel. How you *determine* where to put these foreshadowing details is quite another issue—a process question. Do you know in advance, or do you discover as you write where certain signals need to be placed?

For Kitterman, it's a matter of discovery. "I suppose," he says, "there must be some writers who, from the moment they begin a story, know exactly where it's going to end up." But Kitterman himself doesn't know, and, he says, "Everyone I've ever listened to has told me it's best for the writer *not* to assume she knows the ending of a story before she writes her way to that ending point." In fiction writing, states Kitterman, very little is nailed down, with unpredictable developments as he depends on his creative imagination. "If," as he says, "writing a story is a process of discovery, then any given story will make two or three unexpected moves along the way, and those unexpected moves will require the writer to go back later and do the work of dropping hints, making promises, leaving breadcrumbs for the reader to follow." For Kitterman, it's in the act of revision that one embeds any necessary foreshadowing details.

Hardy's process is akin to Kitterman's. "I don't typically plan my foreshadowing in advance. I let the story unfold during the first draft and then look for potential foreshadowing moments during revisions." For her, those foreshadowing moments tend to crop up in the initial draft, though in the revision stages substantive tweaking may be necessary. "Those elements tend to lurk in my subconscious, so they slip into a first draft all on their own," she says. "However, I *will* go back and revise to strengthen a scene that *would* work to foreshadow something. Often I don't see the perfect moment until I have the entire story written down."

We've already seen that an echo can come at the end of a story, providing a powerful reminder of its basic thrust. For Cowell, certain works may also call for echoing at various intervals to develop the plot as well as the theme: "In my novel *Claude and Camille: A Novel of Monet*, I keep echoing the theme of his water lily paintings and what they mean to him. As the book progresses we know Monet is looking for his wife, who died young in the water lilies. Finally he has a dream that she is *in* the pond, and he goes splashing in it in the middle of the night calling for her. It's a scene I'm proud of in a book that was not easy to write."

Echoing can also serve a third function. In her fantasy novels, Hardy makes use of echoing in creating plot and thematic parallels. Echoing serves as the wheelhouse of the novel, the engine that drives her whole fictional universe, which is characterized by moral ambiguity. "I enjoy playing with ethical questions and gray areas," says Hardy, "and echoes work quite well here. I'll pose an ethical question such as 'How many bad things can you do and still be a good person?' and show how the various characters in the book will answer that question. Those individual choices illustrate how blurry the line is, and how there is no right or wrong answer." Hardy works consciously, but not forcibly, to create these echoes that unify a given fantasy novel, reinforcing examples of the theme and rounding out the emotional notes of the character arcs.

Foreshadowing and echoing are indispensable plot and structure devices. Yet one can overmanage them and turn them into glaring, too-obvious signposts that deny the reader the experience of felt life that fiction should provide. When they are labored or heavy handed, both are akin to the writer addressing the reader directly. As with most other aspects of fiction, subtlety is usually the best approach.

THE DNA OF CHARACTERS

Dialogue, Narrative, and Actions

....

Olivia Markham

Characterization is the creation and convincing representation of fictitious characters (Random House Unabridged Dictionary, 2nd edition). To be convincing, protagonists and villain(s) must be fully developed characters within your story world. Therefore, you must get to know your characters before you start writing, even if the details change as you draft your manuscript. The sketches you develop before you begin writing (character questionnaires, Myers-Briggs assessments, enneagrams, and so on) are like the chromosomes that define basic traits and give a character life.

After that creation comes the "convincing representation of characters" or the creation on the page, since it's the characters' *dialogue*, *narrative*, and *actions*—their *DNA*—that make them truly convincing and unique. And to engage readers emotionally, a character's DNA should generally be balanced within each scene.

DIALOGUE

Including rich details in a character's dialogue can portray a more realistic sense of the fictional world and, thus, more realistic characters. Dialogue isn't just a back-and-forth between characters; it involves what they say and how they say it, their tone and speech cadence, the phrases they use repeatedly, and their physical habits and mannerisms as they talk. These details reveal rich insights about a character: his attitudes, values, worldview, and frame of mind. Dialogue reveals character not only by what is said but *how*. It truly shines when readers can identify the speaker by the words he uses and the way he talks rather than by dialogue tags.

When long narrative passages will slow the pace too much, use dialogue to convey a character's current situation and background—her interests, the work she's doing, and her familial, friendly, and romantic relationships. These elements can flavor her speech.

In Linda Howard's novel *Drop Dead Gorgeous*, protagonist Blair Mallory engages in humorous dialogue to show the current situation and convey something about the characters. In this scene, Blair and her fiancé, Wyatt Bloodsworth, are talking.

> [Wyatt] all but whimpered. "*Please*. Just tell me why you've decided you can't marry me." …
>
> "Because *Blair Bloodsworth* is too cutesy to be bearable!" Oh, God, I was beset by B-words. "People would hear that name and think, okay, she has to be a blond nitwit, one of those people who snaps gum and twirls her finger in her hair. No one would take me seriously!"
>
> He rubbed his forehead as if he were getting a headache. "So all this is because Blair and Bloodsworth both start with a *B*?"
>
> I cast my gaze upward. "The light dawns."
>
> "That's a load of bullshit."
>
> "And the bulb just burned out." Aaargh! When would the avalanche of B-words stop? This always happens to me. When something starts bugging me (aaargh again!) I can't get away from the alliteration.
>
> "Bloodsworth isn't a cutesy name, no matter what the first name is," he said, scowling at me. "It has *blood* in it, for God's sake. As in blood and guts. That isn't cutesy."

Dialogue is also perfect for showing past influences: former relationships, transformative events, socioeconomic and educational backgrounds, and where a character grew up. It can subtly hint at a character's gender, ethnicity, and age, especially with the judicious use of dialect.

Finally, dialogue is an effective tool for creating subtext and foreshadowing. What *isn't* said, what is merely hinted at, what is avoided, and what is lied about—all are elements that generate tension and nuance within scenes.

Dialogue that describes or characterizes the protagonist or other characters can obviously come from POV characters, but it can also come from other characters as they reveal their perceptions in conversation. Opinions expressed by one character about another character can say much about both the speaker and the person being discussed.

This passage from *Pride and Prejudice* by Jane Austen is an example of how characters can reveal information about others and themselves. It also highlights how dialogue can create subtext and foreshadowing by what *isn't* said but merely hinted at. The first speaker is Mrs. Bennett as she talks with her husband.

> "Why, my dear, you must know, Mrs. Long says that Netherfield is taken by a young man of large fortune from the north of England. …"
>
> "Is he married or single?"

> "Oh! Single, my dear, to be sure! A single man of large fortune; four or five thousand a year. What a fine thing for our girls!"
>
> "How so? How can it affect them?"
>
> "My dear Mr. Bennett," replied his wife, "how can you be so tiresome! You must know that I am thinking of his marrying one of them."
>
> "Is that his design in settling here?"
>
> "Design! Nonsense, how can you talk so! But it is very likely that he *may* fall in love with one of them, and therefore you must visit him as soon as he comes."

Good dialogue should be condensed as much as possible. Elmore Leonard omitted nouns at the beginning of sentences, as well as pronouns like *who* and *that* within sentences. His dialogue makes his characters' speech more authentic. His characters speak a kind of shorthand, which helps make the author's dialogue swift and snappy.

Here's an example of Leonard's dialogue from his novel *Pronto*.

> Raylan said … "I'm going to shoot his nose off he don't answer me. What'd you come here for?"
>
> "Talk to her, say hello."
>
> "About what, Harry Arno?"
>
> "About *her*. I see her around. You know, so I want to get to know her."

NARRATIVE

The most useful form of narrative is *interior dialogue*, in which characters, in their own point of view, express opinions internally about their lives or about action as it's happening. Interior dialogue can provide insight into a character's family relations, work life, habits, and values. It can show what she excels at, and how she reacts to bad news or criticism.

Interior dialogue is put to best use when the story is in the intimate and personal first-person point of view. Here's an example from *Drop Dead Gorgeous*, in which Blair Mallory has just been hit by a car in a parking lot.

> Well, for pete's sake, where *was* someone? Were all those people going to stay in the frickin' mall until midnight? How long would I have to lie there before someone saw me and came to help? I'd almost been smashed to a pulp! I needed a little concern here, a little *something*.
>
> I was getting very indignant. Hello … a body lying in the parking lot, and no one notices? Yes, it was night, but the parking lot was lit by those huge vapor lights, and I wasn't lying between two cars or anything. I was … I opened my eyes and tried to get my bearings.
>
> My vision was blurred; all I could see were black shadows and patches of light, and those swam and ran together.

Interior dialogue is also useful for introducing intermediate characters who are neither minor (extras or walk-ons) nor protagonists, such as a sister or best friend whose story affects the protagonist's arc. Examples of intermediates are the hero's sister in Julie

James' *Suddenly One Summer*, and Elizabeth Bennett's best friend, Charlotte, in *Pride and Prejudice*, by Jane Austen. Here's an example from *Suddenly One Summer*. Author Julie James introduces the hero's sister using the hero's interior dialogue, and gives readers another reason to like the guy.

> "Fine. I'm worried about Nicole, too," he admitted, despite being firmly of the belief that his mother didn't need to be thinking about this today.
>
> It wasn't exactly a secret that his twenty-five-year-old sister, Nicole, had been struggling as a single mom ever since giving birth to her daughter, Zoe, four months ago. As a part-time actress and a full-time instructor at a local children's theater, she worked days, evenings, and some weekends, yet still barely made enough to support herself in the city.

Expositional narrative, or summary narrative, on the other hand, should be used somewhat sparingly. In the maxim "Show; don't tell," summary narrative is the telling. Telling is acceptable when it is used to summarize minor events or provide mundane but necessary information. A change of setting can be summarized in this way, and an example of this appears in *Love Irresistibly* by Julie James.

> Promptly at seven a.m. on Sunday morning, Cade, Vaughn, and Huxley rode the elevators that would take them to the entrance of Sogna. A hostess desk, made of dark mahogany wood, stood empty before a set of wide etched glass doors—doors that were open.

Summary narrative can be used to quickly describe or tell readers something without using dialogue or actions. This is illustrated in the chapter-two opening of Linda Howard's novel *Up Close and Dangerous*.

> Cameron Justice gave the small airfield and parking lot a swift, encompassing glance as he pulled his blue Suburban into his allotted slot. Though it wasn't yet six-thirty in the morning, he wasn't the first to arrive. The silver Corvette meant his friend and partner, Bret Larsen—the L. of J&L. Executive Air Limo—was already there, and the red Ford Focus signaled the presence of their secretary, Karen Kaminsky.

Summary narrative can also appear as backstory, which helps readers understand the characters' choices, and as character descriptions, which develop mood, theme, and foreshadowing. Here is an example of minor character description from *Pride and Prejudice*, in which author Jane Austen gives her perspective of how her heroine, Elizabeth Bennett, would assess Mr. Bingley's sisters.

> Elizabeth listened in silence, but was not convinced; [the Bingley's sisters'] behavior at the assembly had not been calculated to please in general; and with more quickness of observation and less pliancy of temper than her sister, and with a judgement too unassailed by any attention to herself, she was very little disposed to approve them. They were in fact very fine ladies; not deficient in good humour when they were pleased, nor in the power of making themselves agreeable when they chose it, but proud and conceited.

> ## THE DNA CHECKLIST
>
> - I've used a balance of dialogue, narrative, and actions to bring the character to life on the page.
> - I've revealed character through the choices they make when they're under pressure—their actions and reactions.
> - I've written rounded, whole main characters rather than characters that fulfill a convenient function or stereotype within the story.
> - My protagonist's characterizations reflect the particular internal issue he is struggling with in the novel. The plot is built around the way the protagonist works through that issue and resolves it.
> - In general, I've used straight exposition less than dialogue or actions, since it invariably slows or kills the pace.
> - I've used dialogue, rather than long passages of summary exposition or description, to convey details, history, and background. Strong details in dialogue give a more realistic sense of the fictional world, and the characters in it.
> - I've omitted from my characters' dialogue any repetitious information (things the characters should already know) and anything unrealistic or unnecessary. Dialogue should not be written as though directed to the readers; it should read as if it is being spoken between the characters within a scene.

However, exposition that appears in scene sequels explains the character's conflicts *after you've dramatized them* and offers a different perspective—on the conflict, on the character's reactions to it, and on the characters involved. When you want to focus on something important, something that is key to the story or the character, you can use narrative-only scenes—or dialogue- or action-only scenes—to direct the readers' attention to specific characteristics, events, or actions.

An excellent example of this kind of scene sequel can be found in James Patterson's novel *1st to Die*. Chapter eleven contains mostly narrative, covering Lindsay Boxer's reactions to some very bad news about her health. This approach allows the reader to stay at a distance as the character comes to terms with the news. Lindsay takes her dog for a walk, thinks about her doctor, showers and assesses herself in the mirror, puts on a CD, cooks dinner, and drinks some wine. She thinks about her divorce, her mother's death, and her father—the few times she's seen him—and then on the terrace, with a view of the bay, she sits down to eat with the dog at her feet. For the second time that day, she realizes she's crying.

In general, straight exposition, or summary exposition, should be used less than dialogue or actions, since it invariably slows or kills the pace. Though sections that contain *only* interior dialogue can be used more in the young adult and romance genres, keep in mind that it can bring the action to a grinding halt.

ACTIONS

The maxim "Show; don't tell," applies chiefly to a character's actions. As the author, you decide which experiences the character will have and how he will grow, but that character is defined by what he chooses to do in the face of the problems you throw at him and based on the background and physical, mental, spiritual, and emotional makeup you've given him. The only way readers can ever fully know a character is through the choices he makes while under pressure. The greater the pressure, the deeper the revelation.

Actions reveal character through what they do, how they do it, and with whom; through how they treat themselves and others; and through physical reactions to obstacles, complications, and reversals—when progress is made but the situation then regresses to a previous status. In real life, how a person reacts to something can reveal quite a lot about who she is and her circumstances. Just as you and I are defined by our reactions to events in our lives, so it is with our characters.

Knowing your characters means you can gauge how they would react when faced with obstacles or frustrations. For instance, does your character react to events with humor, anger, or silence? Actions or reactions reflect decisions, attitudes, goals, background, and experiences—all of which are mirrored in how characters deal with obstacles, other people, and situations. Those actions reflect opinions and interpretations of people and events, as well as their unique worldview. Who they are drives the choices they make when faced with those obstacles. For example, in the novel *The Book Thief*, protagonist Liesel can't read or write. Her fellow students surround her and chant the word *dummkopf* ("stupid head") to mock her. She responds by thoroughly beating up the main instigator, which reveals quite a bit about her character.

In Julie James' *Love Irresistibly*, the protagonist, General Counsel Brooke Parker, decides how she will respond to a request from Assistant U.S. Attorney Cade Morgan.

> He'd come here, to *her* office, to ask for *her* help. Now he was threatening her with obstruction of justice charges—and most annoyingly, he was doing it with a smile.
>
> So she returned the favor. "That is nice, Mr. Morgan. Because in response to your tough-guy speech, I, in turn, would've had to give you my tough-*girl* speech, about where, exactly, federal prosecutors who come to my office looking for assistance can stick their obstruction of justice threats." She smiled ever so charmingly. "So I'm glad we were able to sidestep that whole ugly business. Whew."

Although her attention was focused on Cade, out of the corner of her eye, Brooke could see Agents Huxley and Roberts looking at the wall and ceiling, seemingly trying to hide their smiles.

Whether through dialogue, narrative, or actions, the details you include about your character must serve a purpose. If a character's traits don't imply or reveal an internal issue that drives your plot, she'll be lifeless and uninteresting—merely a list of details. Most character traits are better revealed in scenes that drive the plot forward and appeal to the senses. When you happen upon the right balance of dialogue, narrative, and action, your characters will leap to life, and readers won't be able to resist following them on their journey.

This is **Olivia Markham**'s second article on craft for the Writer's Market series. The first one, "Voice Lessons," appeared in the 2016 edition of *Novel & Short Story Writer's Market*. Olivia welcomes writing projects—articles, books, etc.—and also offers ghostwriting and collaborative writing services for books. She is also a freelance editor. Her website is OliviaMarkham-Editing.com.

STEVE BERRY

Mixing Fact, Fiction, History, and Speculation

....

Janice Gable Bashman

//

Steve Berry's career reads like a parable about persistence. He spent twelve years producing eight manuscripts, and he landed an agent six years into the process. That agent spent
another seven years submitting five different manuscripts to New York publishers; Berry's work received a total of *eighty-five* rejections. Finally, though, his persistence paid
off. Berry is now a *New York Times* and number one internationally best-selling author of
sixteen modern-day suspense thrillers with a historical hook. His Cotton Malone series,
which includes *The Lost Order*, *The 14th Colony*, *The Patriot Threat*, *The Lincoln Myth*, and
The King's Deception, as well as four stand-alone novels, have been translated into forty
languages, with 21 million copies in print. They consistently appear on notable bestseller
lists and receive acclaim from critics and readers alike.

Berry, who was a trial lawyer for thirty years before turning to writing full time, is
also persistent when it comes to his favorite subject: history. He devotes time to History Matters, a historic preservation foundation he started with his wife, Elizabeth, and
he serves on the board of the Smithsonian Libraries. He also uses three hundred to four
hundred sources to research each of his novels, seamlessly blending fact, history, and
speculation into exciting fiction. Here, Berry discusses his experiences with rejection, his
methods for research, and his belief that anyone can learn the craft of writing.

You received a slew of rejections before landing an agent and publishing your
first novel. How did you handle it, and what did you learn from the experience?
It was not pleasant. Nobody likes to be told no over and over. But when I made the
decision to write a novel in 1990, I never thought it would be easy. It was something
I'd thought about for years and finally decided to act on. My first attempt was long
and awful—170,000 words, which tells you how bad it really was. The second and
third attempts weren't much better. It wasn't until the fourth try that I began to ap-

preciate the harsh reality that writing novels is hard. But I kept writing, producing eight manuscripts. Each one was a learning experience. My education was one of trial and error—mainly lots of error. During that time, I attended a writers' group once a week for six years, where the participants would tear apart everything I wrote. Then I'd go home and put it all back together, hopefully a little better than before. Between the writers' group and writing every day, I taught myself the craft.

Not until six years into the process was I fortunate enough to land an agent, Pam Ahearn. God bless her. She kept me around for seven years and eighty-five rejections, until May 2002, when Ballantine Books finally bought *The Amber Room*. On the eighty-sixth attempt, [we found] the right editor at the right time with the right story. … Like I say all the time, "I may or may not know much about writing, but I'm an expert on rejection." Every writer has to be.

You've stated that you believe writing is "an acquired skill" and that anybody can learn it. What are some of the most important aspects of craft that you've learned, and how were you able to apply them to your writing to improve your work?

The sheer volume of what I learned during those twelve years of rejection is too much for this limited response. I actually teach it in a three-hour course that my wife, Elizabeth, and I do for our History Matters foundation. We've taught around three thousand students, and that workshop has helped raise over one million dollars for historic preservation.

The amazing thing about the craft of writing is that it can be acquired by anyone willing to put in the time and effort. It can only be learned by actually doing it, and there are far more failures along that path than successes. No shortcuts exist. None at all. The most important thing I learned, the one thing no writer can ever forget, is that you have to write every day and stick to your routine. Writing is a discipline. You have to set a schedule that works for you, and you have to stick to it. … Even now, I write every day.

You use three hundred to four hundred sources for each novel and often research historical sites in person. It seems like it would be difficult to combine all that information with the fictional elements of your novel. What is that process like for you?

I look for subject matter others have not touched, those historical tidbits that are usually found in the footnotes of a book. Aspects of history that are relatively unknown but, hopefully, readers will want to know more about. I especially do not want to plow a field that others have already worked in fiction. I want something fresh and different. No writer wants to copy someone else. You have to establish your own style.

I realized something early on, though. A lot of people were learning their history from novels like mine. That's not necessarily a good thing since a novel, by definition, is not real. That's why I work hard to keep my stories about 90 percent accurate to reality, [altering] only 10 percent for entertainment value since, after all, that's my main goal—to entertain the reader. It's the niche I found for me. Every writer has to find their niche. It's the only way to survive in today's publishing world.

One final note: I always place a writer's note in the back of each book. … There, I explain what's real and what's not, so there'll be no misunderstandings. That note reflects the research arc that goes into each story. It's also another part of my niche. My readers have come to expect the writer's note.

When blending fact, history, and speculation in fiction, what must you keep in mind to make the story seamless and plausible?

For me, it's keeping [the story] as close to reality as possible—the closer the better. Readers of books like mine want not only to be entertained [but] to learn, to experience. I can't tell you how many e-mails I've received from folks who've ventured off from the novel and read more nonfiction on the subject I explored. It would be far simpler to make it all up, but then the story would also be much less plausible.

[The process] is quite difficult. … My task would be so much easier if I could just make the history up. But finding the right history, and then merging it with my fictional characters, all the while making everything that happens relevant to modern day—that's a difficult assignment.

Here's an example from *The Charlemagne Pursuit*:

> Workers busied themselves. Two bishops watched in silence. The tomb they were about to enter had not been opened since January 29, 814, the day on which the Most Serene Augustus Crowned By God the Great Peaceful Emperor, Governing the Roman Empire, King of the Franks and Lombards Through the Mercy of God, died. By then he was already wise beyond mortals, an inspirer of miracles, the protector of Jerusalem, a clairvoyant, a man of iron, a bishop of bishops. One poet proclaimed that no one would be nearer to the apostolic band than he. In life he had been called Carolus. Magnus first became attached to his name in reference to his great height, but now indicated a more greatness. His French label, though, was the one used most commonly, a merger of Carolus and Magnus into a name presently uttered with heads bowed and voices low, as if speaking of God.
>
> Charlemagne.

There is a lot happening in these two paragraphs. The reader is not only venturing into a mysterious, sealed tomb, but also learning about Charlemagne. The trick with information is to keep it short, interesting, and absolutely relevant to what is happening. I always try to insert information while something else is likewise occurring, thereby making its presence a bit more unnoticeable.

Your novels take place in locations throughout the world, and yet you immerse your readers in these settings, making them feel familiar. What advice can you give to other authors hoping to do the same in their own work?

Visiting the places is not an absolute prerequisite, but it definitely helps. There is no substitute for walking the streets, hearing the sounds, feeling the vibrations, soaking in the atmosphere. It's intoxicating and can send your imagination soaring. I've been to nearly all of the locales I've used [in my novels]. There's no question that you learn so much more on the ground than from books or travel guides. I also try hard to keep those locales intact, changing only a few things here and there, which I point out in the writer's note at the end of the book. Like I said before, keeping real things real is most important. But one caveat: It's not imperative that you visit the sites. Not at all. You can definitely work from books and photographs. As the great thriller writer William Diehl once said, "That's why God made *National Geographic.*"

What do you find most difficult about the process?

Merging information with action is my hardest challenge. I have to constantly tell myself that I'm writing a novel, not a textbook. Its primary purpose is to entertain. When is the right mix achieved between information and action? Unfortunately, there is no magic formula on that. Only trial and error and experience can teach when that balance is achieved. I study novels all the time, watching for that mix, seeing how it's done right and wrong. When is it right? You can tell. It's that feeling when you read something and you think, *That is really smooth. One word led to the other and then to another, effortlessly.* We've all read stuff like that.

Your protagonist, Cotton Malone, is always getting himself into trouble. Which characteristics do you think make readers follow him from book to book?

Cotton popped into my head and was born in Copenhagen while I was sitting at a café in Højbro Plads, a popular Danish square. That's why he owns a bookshop there. I wanted a character with government ties and a background that would make him, if threatened, formidable. But I also wanted him to be human, with flaws. He's not perfect in any way. He makes mistakes, like we all do. Since I love rare books, it was natural that Cotton would, too. So he became a trained Justice Department operative-turned-bookseller who manages, from time to time, to find trouble. I also gave him an eidetic memory, since who wouldn't like one of those? At the same time, Cotton is clearly a man in conflict. His marriage has failed, he maintains a difficult relationship with his teenage son, and he's lousy with women. He's like your neighbor, but a neighbor who can do extraordinary things when necessary. He first sprang from the page in *The Templar Legacy*, and there have been eleven more adventures after that. Along the way he's changed. It's important that a character mature, develop, evolve. You don't want him or her to stay the same. I'm so thrilled that readers have come to like him.

Other than rejection, what are some of the biggest challenges you have experienced as a writer, and what have you learned from them?

The business of writing is so challenging. When I first started out in 2003, the landscape was much simpler. There were hardcovers [and] paperbacks, and books were sold in bookstores, which were everywhere. Of course, that was before the e-revolution of 2008 to 2010, which altered everything irrevocably. [Now] the business of writing changes by the day. A commercial fiction writer who wants to survive has to be schooled in every one of those changes. I spend an enormous amount of time watching the business. You also have to be a skilled marketer and a savvy publicist today. There is so much product out there for sale at a variety of price points. And don't fool yourself—price matters. To make a career as a commercial fiction writer, you have to understand how to make your product stand out among the pack. That comes from cover design, cover copy, tag lines, plots, titles, you name it—it's all important. It's a lot, I know. But it's reality.

With the challenges writers face today, why do you keep writing?

Writers write for one reason and one reason only—we all have a little voice in our head that compels us to write. That little voice drove me crazy in the 1980s. Finally, in the 1990s, I listened to it and started to write. I'm a commercial fiction writer. I'm paid to produce a product. Money is certainly not an unimportant subject … but I write simply because I have to. If I didn't, the little voice would drive me crazy. I used to think I was nuts thinking that way. But I've talked to a lot of writers, and every one of them has that same little voice.

Janice Gable Bashman is the Bram Stoker Award–nominated author of *Predator* and *Wanted Undead or Alive*. She is publisher of *The Big Thrill*, the International Thriller Writers' magazine. Visit Janice at janicegablebashman.com.

LIANE MORIARTY

Walking the Line

....

Jessica Strawser

Liane Moriarty is a tightrope writer—her characters and plotlines striking a near-impossible balance between the likeable-relatable and the magnetic-eccentric, the irresistibly humorous and the unbearably tragic. That she writes from Australia lends a certain exotic quality to her myriad foreign editions (not many American readers have spouses who say things like, "Don't be ridiculous, you goose, you know I'm bloody besotted with you"), but it's the universality of her characters and themes—inherently recognizable neighborhoods and schoolyards plunged into *What would you do?* scenarios—that make her a reader favorite and book club staple worldwide.

Consider how Madeline, a central character in her 2014 smash *Big Little Lies* (which unravels hidden threads connecting three families, with deadly consequences), contemplates turning forty: "She could still feel 'forty' the way it felt when she was fifteen. Such a colorless age. Marooned in the middle of your life. Nothing would matter all that much when you were forty. You wouldn't have real feelings when you were forty, because you'd be safely cushioned by your frumpy forty-ness. *Forty-year-old woman found dead.* Oh dear. *Twenty-year-old woman found dead.* Tragedy! Sadness! Find that murderer!"

Or how Cecilia in the 2013 blockbuster *The Husband's Secret* struggles not to peek at a letter she finds, labeled to be opened upon the death of her husband (who is very much alive): "Perhaps this was a case of that vague anxiety she knew some women experienced. *Other* women. She'd always thought anxious people were cute. Dear little anxious people like Sarah Sacks. She wanted to pat their worry-filled heads."

Such compulsive readability has propelled Moriarty's slow climb to stardom. Her earliest titles, beginning with *Three Wishes* in 2003, made the former advertising copywriter a modestly successful living back in Sydney. But a curious thing happened when the writer found herself an export—sold to more territories than any other author at Curtis Brown Australia. *The Last Anniversary*, *The Hypnotist's Love Story*, and *What Alice Forgot* grew her audience incrementally; *The Husband's Secret* exploded in popularity (as of this printing, boasting more than *eighteen thousand* customer reviews on Amazon—averaging 4.5 stars, no less); *Big Little Lies* debuted at number one on *The New York Times* bestsellers list. At one point she had *three books* on the list at once.

Her latest, *Truly Madly Guilty*, tracing the fallout from one disastrous barbecue, was an instant hit out the gate in the summer of 2016. And February 2017 premiered the *Big Little Lies* HBO miniseries, starring Reese Witherspoon and Nicole Kidman.

Adept as she is at balancing on that tightrope, Moriarty spoke with us with her feet planted firmly on the ground.

Your characters often have unusual occupations or predispositions—in *Truly Madly Guilty,* we meet a professional cellist and a hoarder. How do you know when you've hit on the basis for a truly compelling character?

Well, for example, I've always loved the cello, and I tried to learn as an adult. I wasn't very good—everybody was happy when I gave it up!—but I still love the sound of it. You're always looking for occupations for your characters, because work plays a huge part in our lives. The temptation as writers is often to give them a career that you yourself know about, so you end up having lots of characters in books who work in bookshops and things like that. I try to avoid that.

I'm not that fond of research, but I thought, *Well, I'd love to know more about music as a profession*, so this gave me the opportunity to interview three cellists, two of whom were full-time employees at the Sydney Symphony Orchestra. I've discovered this: You feel like you're asking a huge favor, asking them to talk about their lives and careers, but people enjoy it. They spoke to me at length and let me into the green room after performances. It was wonderful.

The hoarder was inspired by a memoir I read about the daughter of a hoarder. I read some other memoirs and spent a lot of time on the Children of Hoarders website.

Your novel mentions those popular TV shows about hoarders, but the effects on the children are not an aspect they typically show.

No—they make it all seem very simple. I've been doing these [book tour] events, and when I start talking about things that the children of hoarders suffer there's always at least one person nodding in a way that I think, *This person knows exactly what I'm talking about.* It's a terrible way to grow up.

Your characters are described with an incredible level of detail. How much of that development occurs in your mind before or while you write, versus on the page?

I don't plan the characters beforehand. I have a basic sketch in my head, and perhaps one attribute I know they're going to have—so when I start writing, it's difficult. They feel cardboard-like, and I miss the characters from my previous book. But within the writing process and continually thinking about them, I gradually allow myself to understand them. By the time I'm about halfway through, they're moving for me and talking properly, but I always have to go back and rewrite those early scenes once I know them.

Do you keep writing to the end before you go back?

No, I tend to rewrite as I go. I'm a little bit all over the place—I don't have a system. I might sit there one day and see where the document opens and just start rewriting whatever's on the page in front of me.

I'm definitely not one of those who does one full draft and then another full draft. I like to finish that last scene with a feeling as if: *It's done.* I will hold off writing the last [chapter] if I know there are lots of things I need to fix.

Is that process just for the characters, or for the plot, too? Your ends always seem to be so neatly tied up.

I'm also working out the plot as I go—exactly the same as with the characters. I always have a separate document called "Things I Need to Fix" once I've worked out, *Okay, this is what's going to happen, so therefore this character can no longer say this or do this,* or, *I'm going to need to signpost this back in chapter three,* or whatever. By two-thirds of the way in, I know the ending, so that's always my favorite part, because I've finally worked out how it's all going to come together: I've solved all the problems that I set myself.

You must think a lot as you write about what you're revealing to the reader, and how, and when. In *The Hypnotist's Love Story* the key reveal about the antagonist is gradual; in *The Husband's Secret* the big reveal is at the very end; in *Truly Madly Guilty*, it's in the middle, with the buildup determining the structure of the whole book. Can you talk about your approach?

> *Truly Madly Guilty* was different: I didn't want to reveal what happened at the barbecue because I didn't want the reader to judge the reactions of everybody who was there. I wanted them to see the reactions as they were and not be thinking, *Well, they should be reacting in a particular way!*
>
> I think some readers did get impatient, and some admitted to me that they flipped ahead to find out what happened so they could just enjoy the story. You don't want to reveal too late, by which time people are frustrated, but you don't want to reveal it too early because then the suspense drops. This was a particularly tricky book in terms of structure, and who knows if I got it right. I won't do a structure like that again, I don't think.

I can't think of many books aside from *The Husband's Secret* that end with the readers knowing such a big, important thing that the characters will never know. It was brilliant. Did you wrestle with the end?

> I didn't wrestle with that because I really enjoyed that idea myself, as a reader. I *did* wrestle with one of my editors who hated that ending. I felt strongly that I took pleasure in knowing something that the characters didn't. I feel vindicated whenever a reader lets me know, which they often do, how much they loved the ending—although I have also seen reviews saying exactly the same as my editor, that it took them out of the story. It goes to show there's absolutely no right and wrong.

What does that process look like, working with multiple editors in multiple countries?

> I work with three: my editor in the U.K., my editor in Australia, and my editor in America. It does make it hard, because often their editorial reports contradict each other, so in the end I have to make my own decision. Sometimes I love the fact that I'm getting such a broad spectrum of different comments, and other times I wish I only had one editor and it drives me crazy.

Do you turn it in to all of them at the same time?

> Yes, and they all read each other's reports, so they all know that I'm making the decision on what comments I will take out of all three. With *The Husband's Secret* ending, my American editor loved it and my Australian editor folded. I think she even maybe came around to our way of thinking, though it wasn't to her taste. In the end they maybe convince each other, but the final decision rests with me.

A recent article in *The Sydney Morning Herald* claimed that while you're the most successful Australian author ever in the U.S., many Australians have never even heard of you. Surely that's an exaggeration?

I think it was. They actually got a lot of angry letters after that headline appeared, saying, "What are you talking about? We know her!" and how patronizing that was. The comment I think they were trying to make was just that I had bigger success outside of Australia before the books really took off in my home country.

In those years before your breakout, were there any frustrations you think would be inspirational to share?

Well, definitely I'd feel down going to bookshops and not seeing any of my books in stock. I was always grateful just to be published, but certainly it was a bit depressing when you'd see some author getting a huge splash and think, *Gosh, I just have to keep putting these books out*. It took a long time for me to get invited to the Sydney Writers' Festival … though I was being published internationally.

But I also think it's *good* to achieve success a little later. If you achieve huge success with your first book, which of course is your dream, it must be hard to deal with when you come to write your second book, whereas when I came to write my second book I felt quite cheery. I didn't feel the huge weight of expectations.

Was there a turning point where you started to think, *This is definitely a career*?

I felt that way from my first book, really, because I kept getting deals—I could still count it as a job that I'd sit at my desk and write stories. But I did hold onto a lot of my advertising/copywriting clients for a while. It was around the time of *The Husband's Secret* that I thought, *Okay, you can let those go now—there's no need to hold onto them*.

How did copywriting influence your fiction writing?

Perhaps it made me more of a commercial writer than I may otherwise have been: Nobody wants to read advertising copy, so you have to keep your sentences short and sharp and succinct. You have to lead the reader, you have to trick them to keep on reading something they don't really want to read. *Less words*: That was always the thing with advertising copy. The art director always wanted *less, less, less*, so that makes you a punchier writer. But I don't know—maybe I was always going to be this sort of writer!

Your stories address some serious issues: grief, death, infidelity, rape, domestic violence. Are there things you consciously want readers to take away, or is that not something you think about in hitting on a theme?

I prefer *not* to think I'm preaching some particular message. I think you can tell as a reader when a character starts making a statement and you can suddenly hear the author talking. Probably sometimes I'm accidentally guilty of that, but the only message I want somebody to take away from reading my book is that they'd quite like to read another Liane Moriarty book.

Of course, people do take lots of other things from them, sometimes great things which I'm touched by, and other times I might inadvertently offend by things I never meant them to take from the book. I can't get too caught up in that. I just have to focus on the characters and story.

Your sister Jackie is also a novelist, and you've talked a lot about how friendly sibling rivalry was a strong motivator early in your career. Now that you're both such successful authors, in what ways do you continue to influence each other's work?

I have to admit, whenever I read anything Jackie has written I still feel envy, because I think she's a genius. I don't think she's ever written a boring sentence—she's incapable of it. She inspires me to do better all the time. The one thing we're competitive about is family material: If there's a story that somebody's told or that's happened to us, or if Mum rings me up and starts telling me something, I'll say, "Have you told this to anybody else yet? Because I want it!"

How do you think you've grown in your career?

I hope I've just gotten better in general. I *love* it when people say that they liked whatever the most recent book is best and that they can see me evolving as a writer. I definitely took, with *The Husband's Secret*, a more suspenseful, darker turn than in my previous books, but I don't think that necessarily means I'll keep writing darker books. I might go back to more [comedic novels]. I feel very anxious about not feeling that I have to stick to a certain formula. That's on my mind.

Otherwise it's really hard for me to tell how I've evolved. In the end I just have to come back to the story and get back to enjoying writing, sitting down, and making up a story like I did when I was ten years old.

Jessica Strawser is the editorial director of *Writer's Digest* magazine.

SCOTT TUROW

Public Defender

································

Tyler Moss

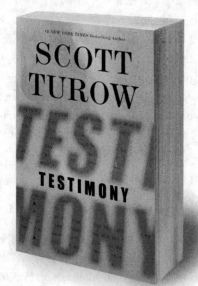

Author, attorney, advocate—Scott Turow's collective roles range in scope and responsibility, yet each is a key exhibit in the mountain of evidence that upholds his position in writing's upper echelon.

Over the past four decades—2017 marks the fortieth anniversary of his acclaimed debut, the law-school memoir *One L*—Turow has published eleven bestsellers (nine of them legal thrillers), served two stints as president of The Authors Guild, and penned op-eds for *The New York Times* and essays for *The Atlantic*, all while continuing to practice law (most of it pro bono) in his hometown of Chicago. When asked why he didn't quit his day job after finding literary success (the way most other lawyers-turned-bestsellers do), his response is firm: "For me, having to produce a book a year would be a form of slavery."

Indeed, it's that kind of conviction that keeps Turow's body of work squarely in the realm of art.

As president of The Authors Guild, he fought relentlessly for writers to receive a fair wage equal to their creative output. His background as a litigator made him an ideal can-

didate for the position, targeting issues such as intellectual property rights and e-book piracy during his tenure.

With one foot in the literary world and the other in law, the twain meet in his novels. All are largely set in Kindle County, a fictional facsimile of Chicago's Cook County, where the Cubs are called the Trappers, the Lake looms large, and the courts are packed with complex cases. It's a setting shaped in his celebrated first novel—1987's *Presumed Innocent*, later made into an eponymous film starring Harrison Ford—in which deputy prosecutor Rusty Sabich is charged with the murder of a beautiful colleague with a mysterious past.

His latest, *Testimony*, Turow's first novel in four years, dropped in May 2017. It's a suspenseful globe-trotter in which middle-aged attorney Bill ten Boom leaves behind his life in Kindle County for a role with the International Criminal Court in The Hague. His new position takes him to Bosnia, where he investigates an alleged genocide, has a fling with a sultry barrister, and becomes involved in the pursuit of a Serbian war criminal. Turow deftly explores identity as a theme both overt and subtle, as ten Boom struggles with a family secret that has roots reaching back to Nazi Germany.

Turow took a short recess from the courthouse and his current work-in-progress to chat with us from his home in the Chicago suburbs.

Between your writing and your legal practice, how in the world do you prioritize your time?

When I'm writing I usually push everything else aside and write in the morning until the early afternoon. Now, that can be interrupted—I've got a court call on Monday, so it's not invariable. Life interferes, which is what you would expect of life.

Wally Stegner, who was one of my teachers at Stanford [University's writing program in the early 1970s, prior to law school], really taught the value of putting your butt in the chair every day, especially if you're trying to write a novel. I've found it a really valuable lesson. He used to say, "It's true the muse may not visit you every day, but you have to sit down and give her a chance to show up." I thought there was great wisdom in that. The writing, now and for many years, has had the first claim on my time.

How do skills honed in practicing law translate to how you approach your writing?

There's a good deal of back and forth between the two callings. I learned in the courtroom a whole lot about being a novelist that I didn't learn during my years as a Stegner Fellow at Stanford. I always thought the ideal would be to write a novel that would be equally appealing to—as I put it in my debates with members of the faculty—a bus driver and an English professor. Certainly, as a prosecutor in a courtroom, you're trying to tell a story to a broad audience.

I learned about being concise because you don't have infinite patience or attention from a jury. I learned that, whatever I had been taught or valued about literary experiments or refinements, sometimes the tried-and-true was a better idea. I certainly came to embrace crime as a subject matter by recognizing how potent the effect was, both on jurors and everybody else watching in the courtroom.

I realized pretty quickly that, without trying to press the metaphor too far, being a prosecutor and being an author were more similar than I would have thought, in the sense that you are telling the jury a story and it's a story about how something that the community regards as evil happened. You tell the story through multiple voices—those voices happen to be called *witnesses* in the courtroom—but if you lose track of the need to be telling a consistent narrative, you're losing your way as a prosecutor. I truly learned a great deal in my first couple of years as a prosecutor that I later turned into the writing of *Presumed Innocent*.

Novels in the milieu of the law trend toward a formula: crime, reveals, resolution. Yet your books manage to shirk the formulaic. What's your secret?

My first secret is … I don't like formulas. [Laughs.] I don't like novels where I know the ending halfway through. It just comes from personal preference. And you're right: The classic detective story has a pretty predictable ending. There's a crime, the detective investigates, the detective solves it, good triumphs over evil, and the guilty get punished. So it's always a variation on that theme. I take a certain amount of god-like pleasure in toying with readers and sort of rubbing my hands and going, *They're never going to figure this one out.*

A hallmark of your novels is the casual reappearance of characters from past books. These relationships between characters seem to extend beyond what's on the page. How extensively do you develop their backstories?

I am deeply struck by the way people move from the background to the foreground in life. I got married again this last summer. The woman I married is someone I met thirty years ago. Twenty-five years later, through a remarkable set of coincidences, we begin pursuing a personal relationship and end up married five years [after that]. I just love that. I love the ironies of it. I love everything it says about the unpredictability of life. So I've built it into the novels.

Will a character in the next book be thinking back to something that happened while Bill ten Boom was U.S. attorney in Kindle County? You can virtually guarantee it. The reflection about ten Boom will be nowhere near as appreciative of ten

Boom as he is of himself. It's like I'm given the opportunity to do further commentary—like when you get a DVD and you've got the outtakes. It's a chance to not only add to the book I'm writing, but to the books I've [already] written.

Your novels proceed at a brisk pace, full of twists and turns. What is your writing process like?

Essentially, I've preserved the writing process that I had in writing *Presumed Innocent*. I was working full time as an assistant U.S. attorney. The job was wonderful but consuming. The only time I had to write was on the morning commuter train, because by the end of the day I was too overwrought with what had gone on in the office. So it was only in the morning, on the thirty-minute train ride, that I could write.

Because I had only thirty minutes, it just didn't seem natural to try to connect things, because there was too much boiling up inside of me that demanded expression. Whatever I was feeling passionate about that I could convert into fodder for the story I was beginning to tell, I'd write down that day—whether it was dialogue, or a particular setting, or the history of a character, a piece of internal reflection about the justice system—I wrote it down and figured I'd someday put it all together. Were it not for the invention of the personal computer, I'm not sure that would've happened. But in 1982 I bought the first of the so-called portable computers, which weighed only forty pounds. I began typing in all these disparate pieces and thinking about how they'd fit together, trying to put them in order. And that's still the process I follow.

For about a year I write [each story] that way. I feel my way along: Who is the main character, what is his family like, what are those relationships like? I know what I want to write about in general, but the specific contours … I've got a lot of thinking to do. Once I'm done with that, I'll begin trying to shape it, and that's just a matter of sitting there and going, "What pieces fit together?" And over the course of the year some sequence would've begun to suggest itself to me. I almost never figure out the ultimate resolution—the whodunit—at that point.

You've served two stints as president of The Authors Guild. What compelled you to take on such a public role in the interest of the greater writing community?

Some of it is natural to somebody who has been, at moments, a lawyer for the downtrodden. I've been unbelievably fortunate in my writing career. I have been deeply conscious of the fact that, for the privileged few of us who can call ourselves best-selling writers, almost everything that's happened in publishing—and there've been tremendous changes since *One L* was published forty years ago—it's worked to our advantage. It's a phenomenon of American society over the last forty years that it's become much more a winner-take-all society. While it's been great for best-selling authors, it hasn't been good for most people in the literary community. The notion that you publish a couple of books and you have a career and a publisher that'll be publishing your books for the rest of your life, that went out the window. People scuffle to make a living.

My perception of that became dramatically exacerbated by the digital revolution. What fundamentally happened is that [up to that point] authors controlled their copyrights so they had control of the intellectual property, and that gave them a certain bargaining position. With the advent of digital, you had a lot of other intellectual property owners, whether Amazon or others. But it's all big capital. All of a sudden big capital is a player, and they're in control in a much different way.

The result has turned into a massive food fight in which all of the various constituencies have decided to improve their position at the expense of authors. I was very proud to be a spokesperson for the American authorial community because, quite frankly, as a general matter, they're getting screwed. There's a lot to complain about—not for me, but for the other 99 percent.

Significant as the digital shift has been, what is the biggest challenge you currently see for writers?

If you look at e-books in the big picture, they have every potential to expand the literary marketplace, and because of that, to expand author's earnings. [But] this becomes an example of everybody [else wanting] to eat lunch at the author's expense. You have publishers who have succeeded in changing the royalty structure from physical books to e-books, so what used to be based on the retail price of a hardcover [is now] based on the net sales. The division of the spoils in the hardcover world is basically 50-50 between author and publisher. The standard e-book royalty is 25 percent of the net, so author's incomes on e-books have essentially been cut in half.

Then you have the entry of Amazon. And Amazon, in my view, is engaged in what when I was in law school was called predatory pricing. They sold e-books for less than they were paying the publishers for them. In my view, the point of this was as a barrier to entry to other people from getting into the e-book market, because how many other companies can afford to enter a market where you're losing two to five bucks every time you sell a book?

The distortions that Amazon was creating in that market ended up coming at the expense of authors. There is absolutely nothing wrong with the e-book as an institution—it's what's come with it that's perilous for authors.

The other thing that concerns me is that as Amazon gets more and more control, they have certainly displayed an attitude of trying to cut down on the share that goes to publishers. If they're ever successful in getting rid of publishers, in my view, the authors are next. There won't be anywhere else to go, and if Amazon says your royalty will be half of what it used to be, then it will be half of what it used to be.

You've written eleven bestsellers over a four-decade writing career. How have you sustained such consistent success?

This process, for me, has not yet become dull. The beginnings with a book require a lot of self-discipline to make myself sit down. But once I'm into it, I get up in the morning really looking forward to writing. And I look forward to what I'm going to discover—and, also, to taking advantage of what I've learned in writing the last book and hopefully not making the same mistakes. Making new mistakes, but not the same mistakes. So to whatever extent I get credit, I think it's because I have not suffered any flagging of interest in what I'm writing. I still love the process. I remind myself all the time: *What a life! You get handsomely rewarded for going upstairs every day and playing with your imaginary friends.*

Tyler Moss is the managing editor of *Writer's Digest* magazine.

JUNOT DÍAZ

Filling the Silence

....

Jessica Strawser

///

"Junot Díaz is known to start conversations some folks would rather not have." So began stalwart journalist Bill Moyers' hourlong "Moyers & Company" episode with Díaz, titled "Rewriting the Story of America." As a Dominican-American who splashed onto the international literary stage with the much-heralded 1997 short story collection *Drown*, which aimed to shine a light into immigrant neighborhoods; an early-career Pulitzer Prize winner for his first novel, 2008's *The Brief Wondrous Life of Oscar Wao*, which found its unforgettable titular character in an overweight, lovesick New Jersey teen who dreams of becoming a Dominican J.R.R. Tolkien; and a Rutgers Master of Fine Arts graduate who has been an outspoken critic of the lack of diversity from creative writing programs to bookshelves (himself co-founding the Voices of Our Nation workshops for writers of color to help combat the problem), Díaz is likely used to others attempting to sum him up for the masses. He accepted Moyers' description in stride.

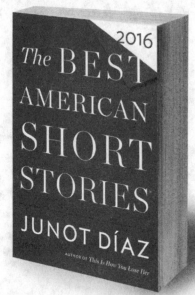

"I find in the culture silences—places people don't want to talk—and I build in them, I work in them," he told Moyers later in the interview. "Because that's what an artist does.

… An artist points their finger in directions that not everyone wants to look."

A 2012 MacArthur "Genius" Fellow who received a National Book Award nomination that same year for his lone *Oscar Wao* follow-up to date, *The New York Times* best-selling novel *This Is How You Lose Her*, Díaz doesn't bow to pressure to write faster or publish broadly, nor does he devote himself narrowly to his craft. He quietly serves as fiction editor at *Boston Review* in addition to his passionate work as a creative writing professor. On *Late Night with Seth Meyers* in 2015, he fielded questions about joining the faculty at the Massachusetts Institute of Technology rather than choosing a school more known for its writing program. "I just like nerds," he joked. But then he turned serious, giving the audience a glimpse of his real drive: "Convincing science, technology, engineering kids that art is important is a battle that I like to fight."

Indeed, Díaz is not overly concerned with being thought of as highbrow. He has praised genre fiction, and is known for teaching dramatic structure to his students using *Star Wars* as a core example. And yet the literary community loves him for it. Most recent in a long line of accolades, he was selected to edit *The Best American Short Stories 2016*.

Díaz is elusive about what readers can expect next from him ("I got nada right now," he tells me, adding, "I'm really sorry"), but took some time away from his coveted summer between semesters to discuss the new anthology, what writing lessons he deems most valuable, and why acknowledgment isn't always a good thing.

What an honor, to have been selected to edit 2016's *Best American Short Stories* anthology. How did this opportunity come about—and did you have any hesitation at all in accepting?

Just a simple e-mail—I wish it was more romantic than that. Certainly I had reservations. I've got so many other commitments on top of my teaching and my writing (what little there is of it) that I feared the anthology would overwhelm everything. And then there was the introduction that would need to be written—I'm a notoriously slow writer, and the thought of being responsible for a ten-pager turned my blood cold. Still, I knew that I owed quite a lot to [the people behind] *Best American Short Stories* and felt that debt keenly. I also understood that selecting the winning stories was an important privilege, one that once extended I could not turn down easily. So I said yes, and it was on.

What was your approach to curating the collection? Can you walk us through the process—the challenges, the highlights?

I got sent a raft of stories in three separate packages. With that much reading coming through, you have to be disciplined, especially if you have your students' papers that need to be returned. (Or maybe that's just me.) I ended up locking myself in the bathroom of my tiny apartment and sitting on the floor and going through the stories. That was the one place I could be guaranteed not to be interrupted. Anytime I encountered a story that had magic in it, I piled it under the sink. Stories that I did not respond to I pushed out the door. Soon enough I had stories everywhere and when my partner and my friends needed to use the bathroom they had to pick their way through mounds of prose.

When I finished the initial reading, I then reread all the stories a second time—starting with the ones that I had pushed out the door. A lot of stories ended up on different sides of the threshold as a consequence.

And then I read all the stories a third time. It was brutal. But I just had to be sure. I didn't want to let anything slip between the cracks. The only reason I was asked to edit this volume was because someone out there in the world was equally conscientious and didn't let *this* nobody writer slip between the cracks.

The biggest challenge was on the second and third readings—trying to read each of the stories fresh, without letting my previous decisions influence my determination. Nearly impossible, but in a few cases I was able to see something in a story that I hadn't noticed on the first two readings.

One of the greatest pleasures, of course, was stumbling onto young literary artists whose work I did not know, whose talents were energizing and breathtaking. For someone who has already been seriously published, [selection for the] *Best American Short Stories* is a welcome honor, but for a young writer it can make all the difference. Still, for all my sympathies, the young writers most certainly had to earn their places. When you have John Edgar Wideman in the mix firing on all cylinders, you have to bring your absolute everything to the work.

What do you think makes the short story form such a rich training ground for great literary writing?

Well, I started out writing novels—I wrote two bad ones before I ever touched a short story. I'm sure I speak for nothing, but *all* writing is great training for writing. Of course one learns specific things writing in a specific genre, and some of those skills carry over from one form to another. Those failed novels taught me an immense amount about focus and about paying attention to my audience—essential skills for writing the short story. Had I not written those bad novels, I doubt I would have ever had any luck with short stories.

As an active participant in the writing community, how does your work as the fiction editor at the *Boston Review* and a writing professor at MIT inform your own writing or further enrich your creative life?

To be honest, I'm a pretty reluctant member of the larger writing community. I'm not an [Association of Writers & Writing Programs] habitué; I can spend weeks without mentioning to anyone that I'm a writer. I'm a minority these days [of this opinion], but I'm not certain it's a good thing for writers to spend a lot of time with other writers. Solidarity and community are essential—I am not arguing against either—but when the majority of your friends are writers … that seems to work for a lot of people, but that shit's just not for me.

The ongoing professionalization of writing, an outcome of our neoliberal moment, has acted centrifugally on writers, clotting them together in ways that are unprecedented. I tend to spend more time with *readers*. What truly enriches my creative life are folks who do anything other than writing, especially Dominicans and other immigrants. And books, of course. I don't need much else to inspire me as long as I have books and Dominicans.

You mentioned being a slow writer. What's your advice to writers struggling to stay true to their own process while holding their own in today's hurry-up publishing climate?

I always urge young writers who feel the pressure to produce to spend more time browsing bookstores. I urge them to check how many books any writer tends to have on the shelf. Ours is a culture where it's lucky for a writer to be remembered for even one book, less three or four. Writing twenty books in your career is wonderful; I wish I had written as much. But ultimately I'd rather write the best book I can write no matter how long it takes me than the best book I can write fast simply because the unrelenting pace of our society demands speed in all things.

Should we be so lucky to be enrolled in one of your creative writing courses for a semester, what would we experience on the first day of class? What about on the last day?

I don't know about that. I'm like most faculty members—excited about the material but wrestling to communicate its value and complexity to my students. I'm fortunate because I teach in a hyperprivileged institution and so at least things are easier in this setting. First day is dull: just getting through the syllabus, making sure the students understand that I mean business when I say I want them off their phones and computers. Hopefully what they'll get a flash of is my enthusiasm for the material. In all honesty I tend to shine more as a professor in the courses where there is more material. I'm pretty basic in a standard creative writing workshop, but in a class like

Apocalyptic Storytelling or World-building where the students study a wide range of texts, that's where I like to imagine I shine.

As for the last day: If you're in my world-building class we always have a party. Students often dress up in costumes referencing some of the texts we engaged. Some students tear up because the class is over, but most are happy they had an opportunity to play hard and think hard with a professor who tends to feed them. At a place like MIT it's not easy being a student; the demands are significant, and a class like mine, where the faculty actually knows your name, is often a sanctuary.

What do you feel is the single most valuable lesson writers can learn early in their development as both artists and professionals?

To resist their deep longing for approval. One needs to write not what a public wants but what it needs. The first kind of work is what your need for approval will generate; the second is what your struggle will bring forth.

How do you feel your own writing has most significantly grown or evolved over the years?

I'm not sure I can say. Maybe I've gotten slower and less showy, but it's really up to readers to decide. We writers fill the pages, sure, but it's other folks who read and evaluate them. To me it's a mystery what kind of writer I am, but readers have the advantage of detachment. And they're the ones who know best.

You won the Pulitzer so early on. What has that early acknowledgment of your writing done for your mind-set in approaching future works? And with the perspective of your own experience, what kind of recognition do you feel can be most helpful and, conversely, most damaging to writers?

I'm not sure the Pulitzer has done much for my work. Perhaps I've slowed down because I need to hear all the more clearly the voices inside of me. … The part of me that writes best is the part of me that only speaks when the voices of popularity and ambition and, yes, approval fall quiet. It's often a struggle to open a space inside myself for that necessary voice to speak.

What can I tell you? Some writers thrive under the public eye; others wilt. Some writers need approval to thrive, and others just do their thing. I imagine it would be nice if a writer had some time to develop their craft and aesthetic before blowing up, but the world doesn't take advice from anyone. What happens, happens. We have very little control in how our work will be received. As artists all we can do is cleave to the work, pursue the love of literature that brought us to the page, and hope that is enough.

You've written and spoken about the lack of diversity in publishing, starting at the academic level—and you helped found The Voices of Our Nation Arts Foundation in hopes of helping to change that. What would you like writers to know about VONA?

> Voices is one of the only multigenre creative writing workshops open to all people of color in the country. Given the current and future demographic of our nation, Voices plays a necessary, almost prophetic, role in our literary industrial complex, which as we all know is overwhelmingly white but which is beginning to wrestle with its own violent lack of diversity.

What can each of us do to help be a part of the change we'd like to see in the industry?

> I wish all of us would read more promiscuously, more transgressively. I wish we read outside our comfort zones. Can't name ten Asian-American writers? Read ten Asian-American writers then. Haven't read a book of poetry in years? Read ten.
>
> I've done plenty of readings, and [do] you know that I've met readers who haven't read anything but white writers for a year or two? That happens more often than some of us would like to believe. That doesn't say great things about our literary culture.
>
> If all readers in the U.S. spent the next five years reading only works by people of color, the entire nation would be in a better place. That's a utopian dream. Still, where would we be without our utopian dreams?

BUSINESS BASICS

Successfully Submit Your
Novels & Short Stories

///

It's true there are no substitutes for talent and hard work. A writer's first concern must always be attention to craft. No matter how well presented, a poorly written story or novel has little chance of being published. On the other hand, a well-written piece may be equally hard to sell in today's competitive publishing market. Talent alone is just not enough.

To be successful, writers need to study the field and pay careful attention to finding the right market. While the hours spent perfecting your writing are usually hours spent alone, you're not alone when it comes to developing your marketing plan. *Novel & Short Story Writer's Market* provides you with detailed listings containing the essential information you'll need to locate and contact the markets most suitable for your work.

Once you've determined where to send your work, you must turn your attention to presentation. We can help here, too. We've included the basics of manuscript preparation, along with information on submission procedures and how to approach markets. We also include tips on promoting your work. No matter where you're from or what level of experience you have, you'll find useful information here on everything from presentation to mailing to selling rights to promoting your work—the "business" of fiction.

APPROACHING MAGAZINE MARKETS

A query letter by itself is usually not required by most magazine fiction editors. If you are approaching a magazine to find out if fiction is accepted, a query is fine, but editors looking for short fiction want to see the actual piece. A cover letter can be useful as a letter of introduction, but the key here is brevity. A successful cover letter is no more than one page (20-lb. bond paper). It should be single-spaced with a double space between paragraphs, proofread carefully, and neatly typed in a standard typeface (not script or italic). The writer's name, address, phone number, and e-mail address must appear at the top, and the letter should be addressed, ideally, to a specific editor. (If the editor's name is unavailable, use "Fiction Editor.")

The body of a successful cover letter contains the name and word count of the story, a brief list of previous publications, if you have any, and the reason you are submitting to this particular publication. Mention that you have enclosed a self-addressed, stamped envelope for reply. Also, let the editor know if you are sending a disposable manuscript (not to be returned; more and more editors prefer disposable manuscripts that save them time and save you postage). Finally, don't forget to thank the editor for considering your story.

Note that more and more publications prefer to receive electronic submissions, both as e-mail attachments and through online submission forms. See individual listings for specific information on electronic submission requirements, and always visit magazines' websites for up-to-date guidelines.

APPROACHING BOOK PUBLISHERS

Some book publishers ask for queries first, but most want a query plus sample chapters or an outline or, occasionally, the complete manuscript. Again, make your letter brief. Include the essentials about yourself: name, address, phone number, e-mail address, and publishing experience. Include a three- or four-sentence "pitch" and only the personal information related to your story. Show that you have researched the market with a few sentences about why you chose this publisher.

BOOK PROPOSALS

A book proposal is a package sent to a publisher that includes a cover letter and one or more of the following: sample chapters, outline, synopsis, author bio, publications list. When asked to send sample chapters, send up to three consecutive chapters. An outline covers the highlights of your book chapter by chapter. Be sure to include details on main characters, the plot, and subplots. Outlines can run up to thirty pages, depending on the length of your novel. The object is to tell what happens in a concise but clear manner. A synopsis is a shorter summary of your novel, written in a way that expresses the emotion of the story in addition to just explaining the essential points. Evan Marshall, literary agent and author of *The Marshall Plan for Getting Your Novel Published* (Writer's Digest Books), suggests you aim for a page of synopsis for every twenty-five pages of manuscript. Marshall also advises you write the synopsis as one unified narrative, without section heads, subheads, or chapters to break up the text. The terms *synopsis* and *outline* are sometimes used interchangeably, so be sure to find out exactly what each publisher wants.

ABOUT OUR POLICIES

We occasionally receive letters asking why a certain magazine, publisher, or contest is not in the book. Sometimes when we contact listings, the editors do not want to be listed because they:

- do not use very much fiction.
- are overwhelmed with submissions.
- are having financial difficulty or have been recently sold.
- use only solicited material.
- accept work from a select group of writers only.
- do not have the staff or time for the many unsolicited submissions a listing may bring.

Some of the listings do not appear because we have chosen not to list them. We investigate complaints of unprofessional conduct in editors' dealings with writers and misrepresentation of information provided to us by editors and publishers. If we find these reports to be true after a thorough investigation, we will delete the listing from future editions.

There is no charge to the companies that list in this book. Listings appearing in *Novel & Short Story Writer's Market* are compiled from detailed questionnaires, phone interviews, and information provided by editors, publishers, and directors of awards and conferences. The publishing industry is volatile, and changes of address, editor, policies, and needs happen frequently. To keep up with the changes between editions of the book, we suggest you check the market information on the Writer's Market website at www.writersmarket.com. Many magazine and book publishers offer updated information for writers on their websites. Check individual listings for those website addresses.

Organization newsletters and small magazines devoted to helping writers also list market information. Several offer online bulletin boards, message centers, and chat lines with up-to-the-minute changes and happenings in the writing community.

We rely on our readers, as well, for new markets and information about market conditions. E-mail us if you have any new information or if you have suggestions on how to improve our listings to better suit your writing needs.

A FEW WORDS ABOUT AGENTS

Agents are not usually needed for short fiction and most do not handle it unless they already have a working relationship with you. For novels, you may want to consider working with an agent, especially if you intend to market your book to publishers who do not look at unsolicited submissions. For more on approaching agents and to read listings of agents willing to work with beginning and established writers, see our **Literary Agents** section. You can also refer to this year's edition of *Guide to Literary Agents*, edited by Chuck Sambuchino.

MANUSCRIPT MECHANICS

A professionally presented manuscript will not guarantee publication. But a sloppy, hard-to-read manuscript will not be read—publishers simply do not have the time. Here's a list of suggested submission techniques for polished manuscript presentation:

- For a short story manuscript, your first page should include your name, address, phone number, and e-mail address (single spaced) in the upper left corner. In the upper right, indicate an approximate word count. Center the name of your story about one-third of the way down the page, skip a line, and center your byline (the byline is optional). Skip four lines and begin your story. On subsequent pages, put your last name and page number in the upper right corner.
- For book manuscripts, use a separate title page. Put your name, address, phone number, and e-mail address in the lower right corner and word count in the upper right. If you have representation, list your agent's name and address in the lower right. (This bumps your name and contact information to the upper left corner.) Center your title and by-line about halfway down the page. Start your first chapter on the next page. Center the chapter number and title (if there is one) one-third of the way down the page. Include your last name and the novel's title in all caps in the upper left header, and put the page number in the upper right header of this page and each page to follow. Start each chapter with a new page.
- Proofread carefully. Keep a dictionary, thesaurus, and stylebook handy and use the spell-check function on your computer.
- Include a word count. Your word processing program can likely give you a word count.
- Suggest art where applicable. Most publishers do not expect you to provide artwork and some insist on selecting their own illustrators, but if you have suggestions, let them know. Magazine publishers work in a very visual field and are usually open to ideas.
- Keep accurate records. This can be done in a number of ways, but be sure to keep track of where your stories are and when you sent them out. Write down submission dates. If you do not hear about your submission for a long time—about one to two months longer than the reporting time stated in the listing—you may want to contact the publisher. When you do, you will need an accurate record for reference.

Electronic Submissions

- If sending electronic submissions via e-mail or online submission form, check the publisher's website first for specific information and follow the directions carefully.

Hard-Copy Submissions

- Many publications no longer accept hard-copy submissions. Make sure to read the submission guidelines carefully.
- Use white 8½" × 11" bond paper, preferably 16- or 20-lb. weight. The paper must be heavy enough not to show pages underneath and strong enough to take handling by several people.
- Type your manuscript on a computer and print it out using a laser or ink-jet printer (or, if you must, use a typewriter with a new ribbon).
- An occasional spot of white-out is okay, but don't send a marked-up manuscript with many typos.
- Always double-space and leave a 1" margin on all sides of the page.
- Don't forget word count. If you are using a typewriter, there are several ways to count the number of words in your piece. One way is to count the words in five lines and divide that number by five to find an average. Then count the number of lines and multiply to find the total words. For long pieces, you may want to count the words in the first three pages, divide by three, and multiply by the number of pages you have.
- Always keep a copy. Manuscripts do get lost. To avoid expensive mailing costs, send only what is required. If you are including artwork or photos but you are not positive they will be used, send photocopies. Artwork is hard to replace.
- Enclose a self-addressed, stamped envelope (SASE) if you want a reply or if you want your manuscript returned. For most letters, a business-size (#10) envelope will do. Avoid using any envelope too small for an 8½" × 11" sheet of paper. For manuscripts, be sure to include enough postage and an envelope large enough to contain it. If you are requesting a sample copy of a magazine or a book publisher's catalog, send an appropriately sized envelope.
- Consider sending a disposable manuscript that saves editors time (this will also save you money).

RIGHTS

The Copyright Law states that writers are selling one-time rights (in almost all cases) unless they and the publisher have agreed otherwise. A list of various rights follows. Be sure you know exactly what rights you are selling before you agree to the sale.

Copyright is the legal right to exclusive publication, sale, or distribution of a literary work. As the writer or creator of a written work, you need simply to include your name and the date on your piece in order to copyright it. Be aware, however, that most editors today consider placing the copyright symbol on your work the sign of an amateur and many are even offended by it.

To get specific answers to questions about copyright (but not legal advice), you can call the Copyright Public Information Office at (202)707-3000 weekdays between 8:30 A.M. and 5 P.M. EST. Publications listed in *Novel & Short Story Writer's Market* are copyrighted unless otherwise stated. In the case of magazines that are not copyrighted, be sure to keep a copy of your manuscript with your notice printed on it. For more information on copyrighting your work, see *The Copyright Handbook: What Every Writer Needs to Know, 11th edition*, by Stephen Fishman (Nolo Press, 2011).

Some people are under the mistaken impression that copyright is something they have to send away for and that their writing is not properly protected until they have "received" their copyright from the government. The fact is, you don't have to register your work with the Copyright Office in order for your work to be copyrighted; all writing is copyrighted the moment it is put to paper.

Although it is generally unnecessary, registration is a matter of filling out an application form (for writers, that's Form TX). The Copyright Office now recommends filing an online claim at www.copyright.gov/forms. The online service carries a basic claim fee of $35. If you opt for snail mail, send the completed form, a nonreturnable copy of the work in question, and a check for $65 to the Library of Congress, Copyright Office-TX, 101 Independence Ave. SE, Washington, DC 20559-6000. If the thought of paying $35 each to register every piece you write does not appeal to you, you can cut costs by registering a group of your works with one form, under one title, for one $65 fee.

Most magazines are registered with the Copyright Office as single collective entities themselves; that is, the individual works that make up the magazine are not copyrighted individually in the names of the authors. You'll need to register your article yourself if you wish to have the additional protection of copyright registration.

For more information, visit the U.S. Copyright Office online at www.copyright.gov.

First Serial Rights

This means the writer offers a newspaper or magazine the right to publish the article, story, or poem for the first time in a particular periodical. All other rights to the material remain with the writer. The qualifier "North American" is often added to this phrase to specify a geographical limit to the license.

When material is excerpted from a book scheduled to be published and it appears in a magazine or newspaper prior to book publication, this is also called first serial rights.

One-Time Rights

A periodical that licenses one-time rights to a work (also known as simultaneous rights) buys the nonexclusive right to publish the work once. That is, there is nothing to stop the author from selling the work to other publications at the same time. Simultaneous sales would typically be to periodicals with different audiences.

Second Serial (Reprint) Rights

This gives a newspaper or magazine the opportunity to print an article, poem, or story after it has already appeared in another newspaper or magazine. Second serial rights are nonexclusive; that is, they can be licensed to more than one market.

All Rights

This is just what it sounds like. All rights means a publisher may use the manuscript anywhere and in any form, including movie and book club sales, without further payment to the writer (although such a transfer, or assignment, of rights will terminate after thirty-five years). If you think you'll want to use the material more than once, you must avoid submitting to such markets or refuse payment and withdraw your material. Ask the editor whether he is willing to buy first rights instead of all rights before you agree to an assignment or sale. Some editors will reassign rights to a writer after a given period, such as one year. It's worth an inquiry in writing.

Subsidiary Rights

These are the rights, other than book publication rights, that should be covered in a book contract. These may include various serial rights; movie, television, audiotape, and other electronic rights; translation rights, etc. The book contract should specify who controls these rights (author or publisher) and what percentage of sales from the licensing of these subrights goes to the author.

Dramatic, Television, and Motion Picture Rights

This means the writer is selling his material for use on the stage, in television, or in the movies. Often a one-year option to buy such rights is offered (generally for 10 percent of the total price). The interested party then tries to sell the idea to actors, directors, studios, or television networks. Some properties are optioned over and over again, but most fail to become dramatic productions. In such cases, the writer can sell his rights again and again—as long as there is interest in the material.

Electronic Rights

These rights cover usage in a broad range of electronic media, from online magazines and databases to interactive games. The editor should state in writing the specific electronic rights he is requesting. The presumption is that the writer keeps unspecified rights.

Compensation for electronic rights is a major source of conflict between writers and publishers, as many book publishers seek control of them and many magazines routinely include electronic rights in the purchase of print rights, often with no additional payment. Writers can suggest an alternative way of handling this issue by asking for an additional

15 percent to purchase first rights and a royalty system based on the number of times an article is accessed from an electronic database.

MARKETING AND PROMOTION

Everyone agrees writing is hard work whether you are published or not. Yet once you achieve publication, the work changes. Now not only do you continue writing and revising your next project, you must also concern yourself with getting your book into the hands of readers. It's time to switch hats from artist to salesperson.

While even best-selling authors whose publishers have committed big bucks to marketing are asked to help promote their books, new authors may have to take it upon themselves to plan and initiate some of their own promotion, usually dipping into their own pockets. While this does not mean that every author is expected to go on tour, sometimes at their own expense, it does mean authors should be prepared to offer suggestions for promoting their books.

Depending on the time, money, and personal preferences of the author and publisher, a promotional campaign could mean anything from mailing out press releases to setting up book signings to hitting the talk-show circuit. Most writers can contribute to their own promotion by providing contact names—reviewers, hometown newspapers, civic groups, organizations—that might have a special interest in the book or the writer.

Above all, when it comes to promotion, be creative. What is your book about? Try to capitalize on it. Focus on your potential audiences and how you can help them connect with your book.

IMPORTANT LISTING INFORMATION

- Listings are not advertisements. Although the information here is as accurate as possible, the listings are not endorsed or guaranteed by the editors of *Novel & Short Story Writer's Market*.
- *Novel & Short Story Writer's Market* reserves the right to exclude any listing that does not meet its requirements.

SELLING YOUR BOOK & YOUR BRAND

Trends in Marketing and Promoting Fiction

....

Jennifer D. Foster

///

To say that the book-publishing landscape has changed dramatically over the last decade is an understatement. The staggering popularity of the e-book, the decline of the bricks-and-mortar bookstore, the merging of major publishers, the waning book-review sections in newspapers and magazines, and the relentless reign of social media have all contributed, in ways large and small, to this monumental shift. The methods for effectively promoting and marketing fiction have followed in suit. Publishers' marketing and publicity budgets and staff have been slashed, and then slashed again. Authors are now working in tandem with publishing houses to get the word out about their books, and increasingly they are expected to take marketing and promotional matters into their own hands.

So what are the most successful ways to drive readership and book sales today? Are staple social media sites like Facebook and Twitter effective? What about Goodreads, the world's largest website for readers and book recommendations? In addition to navigating the buffet of social media platforms, authors have questions about the strategies behind do-it-yourself marketing and promotion. How do you effectively engage an audience? What are the best methods to build an authentic reader community as a first-time or seasoned author? And what's the role of today's publisher in marketing and promoting books?

From blogs and online advertising to author pages and digital giveaways, discover the whys, hows, wheres, and whats from many in the frontlines of today's fluid book publishing industry, giving you the inside track on successfully marketing and promoting your novel.

BOOK PUBLISHING: A FEW STATS

Before looking at current trends in marketing and promoting fiction, it's helpful to understand today's book-publishing world, which is alive and well, albeit in a state of perpetual evolution. The introduction of the e-book and print-on-demand (POD) brought about a seismic shift in publishing formats, including the explosive rise of self-publishing.

And while the popularity of online shopping has fostered the growth of online bookstores (like Amazon) over physical chain bookstores, it seems like some tables (or is that pages?) are now turning—again. Association of American Publishers' stats reveal e-book sales were down 21.8 percent for the first quarter of 2016 versus the same time period in 2015. And according to a January 2017 article in *Publishers Weekly*, "Unit sales of print books were up 3.3 percent in 2016 over 2015. Total print unit sales hit 674 million, marking the third-straight year of growth." *Business Insider* revealed another surprise in the first month of 2017: "The number of independent [book]stores has increased 30 percent since 2009, after seeing one thousand stores shut down between 2000 and 2007. There are now 2,311 independent bookstores in total, as of 2016." This is undeniable evidence that indie bookstores have been enjoying a kind of renaissance, taking advantage of the chasm left by the dwindling number of national chain bookstores.

PUBLISHING IN A DIGITAL WORLD

But what do all these stats mean when it comes to present trends in marketing and promoting fiction? "Gone are the days of an author handing off their cherished manuscript to an editor of a large publishing house, who takes their work and magically transforms it into a best-selling book with a gorgeous cover and worldwide media coverage—all while the author languishes in the background, their job done—except to go on a book tour if the publisher can afford it," says Nina Munteanu, ecologist, writing instructor at the University of Toronto, and author of *Water Is… The Meaning of Water*, *Natural Selection*, and *The Fiction Writer: Get Published, Write Now!* Today, social media reigns supreme, and many authors are taking on some or much of the marketing and promoting role, once the sole job of the publisher.

Alison Morgan, former publisher of Tundra Books and lecturer in the book-publishing program at Ryerson University in Toronto, Ontario, says, "If you think of social media as a medium that encourages self-expression, there is a lot more 'storytelling' going on." She also notes social media has provided a forum for myriad people to talk about books. And because its impact is measurable, social media provides vast opportunities for marketing and promotion. Nick Courage, author of *The Loudness* and a publishing consultant who splits his time between New York and Pittsburgh, says this evolution has created a digital space that "offers publishers incredible agency and agility in terms of reaching potential readers." A budget "that previously went to print advertisements or travel for touring authors is now more likely to be used in targeted online promotions."

For Greg Ioannou, owner and founder of Iguana Books in Toronto, Ontario, freelance editor, and co-founder of PubLaunch.com, this redefinition has brought about "the sidelining of the gatekeepers." With the rise of POD and e-books, self-publishing writers "no longer have to beg agents or publishers to let them through the gates." What's more, the accessibility of self-publishing means "there are far more books out there than ever before, but the number of readers hasn't grown." Translation? The market is heavily saturated, so "effective marketing has become increasingly important for self-publishers, because it's virtually impossible to sell books without it." But that holds true regardless of the publishing route your work takes. And because publishers now have smaller marketing budgets and fewer staff, the margin for error has greatly diminished.

The Key Question: Will It Sell?

Lynn Wiese Sneyd, owner of LWS Literary Services in Tucson, Arizona, says that "if your book is published by a traditional publisher, expect the publicist to be involved for about three to five months." However, she cautions, "Do not expect them to handle all, or even a majority, of marketing activities. That responsibility rests squarely on the author's shoulders." Even the Association of Canadian Publishers clearly states on its "Resources" Web page that "many publishers have a publicity department that will handle this while the book is on the front list. However, once the next season is published, or you have published the book on your own, the job of getting publicity exposure for the book falls to the authors themselves." Publishing houses have become "primarily focused on the question 'Will it sell?' to decide whether or not to publish books," says Ioannou.

According to Marie Lamb, Toronto, Ontario-based freelance editor, Journey Prize-nominated short story writer, and author of *The History of Hilary Hambrushina*, "The role of publishers today seems to be primarily to teach authors how to market their books." In fact, Big Five publishers like Penguin Random House, Simon & Schuster, and HarperCollins now "have sites that offer authors access to sales information, but also information about how to promote their own books: [how to] set up a Facebook [author] page, how to tweet, what kinds of social media are most effective, how often to post, and what kinds of material are most likely to engage readers," explains Morgan.

A Built-In Audience

Trevor Cole, award-winning Canadian author of *The Whisky King* and *Hope Makes Love*, adds that publishers are now quite careful about where they spend their marketing dollars. "I think it's commonly understood that marketing departments have more say now in acquisition decisions—they want to know how to position a book before they buy it, and they want to see solid sales potential in the books they acquire." Geoffrey E. Taylor, director of the International Festival of Authors in Toronto, Ontario, reveals, "The amount of time and effort publishers can place on promoting books is tied to the marketability and sales potential of the book. For an author who spent ten years writing a novel, this isn't necessarily good news, because a publisher isn't spending ten years promoting their book." What's more, says Ioannou, "publishers are increasingly looking for writers with an established platform—a 'built-in' audience—and are increasingly unwilling to take a chance on first-time or unknown authors." Angela Misri, digital journalist, author of the Portia Adams mystery series, journalism instructor at Ryerson University and University of Toronto, and co-founder of ThePlotGoesViral.com, agrees: "If a publisher knows you are going to make an effort in pushing your book out over social media and in creating additional content for websites and campaigns, then you are a more attractive partner in the book industry."

Victoria, British Columbia, author Dawn Green, who's penned *In the Swish* and *How Samantha Smart Became a Revolutionary*, acquiesces: "Publishers are always working on the next thing because that's their business. … A writer needs to take the promotion of their novel into their own hands." Her theory? "No one believes in a story more than the author, so they have to be willing to champion it … market it … create a buzz." And while she stresses that path varies among authors, "at the very least it means talking about your novel, attending conferences, entering contests, and using available online platforms to share your work." Joyce Grant, Toronto, Ontario-based author of the Gabby series and *Tagged Out*, and co-founder of ThePlotGoesViral.com, shares Misri and Green's view, adding that "authors are often encouraged to mention—even in a query letter—if they have an excellent social media presence. Publishers appreciate … how valuable it is … that's a hot audience for [the author's] next book, because they're already part of the author's reading community." Grant adds, "You already possess a key skill necessary to take advantage of social media—the ability to write well and compellingly. All the rest—how to use various apps and social media—you can learn."

Reaching Readers

People spend a staggering amount of time online in our social media-soaked culture, be it via Facebook, Twitter, Instagram, blogging, texting, or watching YouTube. And that's where many readers are! Munteanu believes that "one of the most positive things in this emerging model [of less promotional input from publishers] is the potential empowerment and growing independence of the writer, forced to better understand the industry and their place in it." Munteanu explains it this way: "Authors are now expected, by small and large publishers alike, to own and take command of their brand and know how to market themselves, showing competence in social media and video, a willingness to spend money and time advertising out of their own pocket, and the savvy to find and engage with readers." Courage sees this "author-level promotional agency" as "wildly empowering," with authors having "access to many of the same marketing tools as their publishers … to run an awareness campaign."

Munteanu also says this shift is "less about writing and more about communicating." Green concurs: "Like most authors, I work best when I'm just left to write and work with my story. The marketing and social media world can be daunting, and at times I feel like it is taking time away from my actual writing process … [but] I am beginning to understand how important the marketing side of the writing world is, and I now believe it is as important as creating the story itself."

However, cautions Ioannou, "The thing to think about before getting into [any] marketing tactics is to know who your audience is, where they spend time, what they're interested in, etc. Basically, it's not about what you use, but *how* you use it." Figure out what they want to hear, and then give it to them, he says, stressing that his best tip for engaging new audiences and selling books is to "focus less on the selling and more on building a relationship with your audience."

TAKING COMMAND OF YOUR BRAND

Ready to market and promote your fiction on your own terms? Here are the nuts and bolts.

The Author Platform

Platform building is a key long-term strategy for success. For those starting from scratch, Courage says the first step toward successful cyber marketing and promotion is "to stop and think about the kinds of author promotions that have really worked or resonated with *you*." He suggests finding an author who writes in the same genre and "who is succeeding in the online space. Chances are, you can use that author as a model for some of your own promotional activities." And always keep in mind that your "target market is a fluid and ever-changing stream of old and new customers," says Kim Staflund, publisher and sales coach for authors, Polished Publishing Group (PPG) in Calgary, Alberta.

Next, Ioannou says joining relevant Facebook groups and becoming a "major member by contributing to the discussion in helpful ways" is crucial. "Once you've built those relationships, you can start producing your own content (like a blog or podcast) that would appeal directly to those audiences," inviting them to follow you through Facebook channels. From there, he says, "you're ready to sell your book to an audience who is genuinely interested in what you want to say."

K.M. Weiland, Nebraska-based curator of the award-winning website HelpingWritersBecomeAuthors.com and author of *Outlining Your Novel* and *Storming: A Dieselpunk*

Adventure, adds to Ioannou's directive, stressing that it's genuineness that will initially attract traffic to your platform. "Selling doesn't sell. True marketing these days is about relationships. When you approach your readers as real people, they will in turn see *you* as a real person and relate to the products you're trying to sell not so much as commodities, but as important moments in the life of someone they actually have a stake in caring about." Like Ioannou and Weiland, Misri also believes in becoming a valuable member of the reader community organically and honestly: "I'm suspicious of people who want my attention on social media but add nothing to the discussion. If your only agenda is to get me to give you something or buy something, then I'm not following you." Misri, who writes "Sherlockian pastiche," advises authors to "create content people will want to share rather than content you need to beg people to share over and over again."

In her book *Successful Selling Tips for Introverted Authors*, Staflund calls the Internet "the great equalizer." He explains that Web pages are the "new storefronts" where you must drive traffic on a consistent basis, catching the attention of your customers "in whichever way speaks to them most clearly." And that's why Misri believes "that a central online location like a website or a blog for your book is the most important thing you can do. … That one website is the place everyone can find you and that publishers can use to direct the audience to. It's the spot where you will interact with your readers, both potential and actual, and it's where you have the most control of your message and your brand."

Wiese Sneyd adds that "content marketing, where an author regularly posts a blog and links it to social media, is what continues to drive readers to your website." That's where an author can collect and build an e-mail list, which is how he reaches readers, letting them know about events and new books. According to Barbara Kyle, Guelph, Ontario-based novelist, writing mentor, and author of *Page-Turner: Your Path to Writing a Novel that Publishers Want and Readers Buy*, that e-mail list is the "number one method for driving book sales. The list is golden." Why? "There is no more effective way to motivate your readership than personal interaction with them, made possible by the list." Kyle is amazed when authors sell their books at live events but make no effort to gather e-mail addresses for following up. "After the one-off event, the author has no way of directly contacting these fine people who have already shown they are fans. Talk about a wasted opportunity!"

E-mail Lists and Curated Content

To collect an e-mail address, explains Wiese Sneyd, "an author usually needs to offer something—a chapter from a new book, a free e-book—something of interest to the reader." Morgan says she's "a sucker for an excerpt," often purchasing books based on sample text found online. And Elizabeth Sims, American prizewinning novelist, writing authority, and author of *You've Got a Book in You: A Stress-Free Guide to Writing the Book of Your*

Dreams, notes she always gets a sales spike with the "newschats" she sends out up to four times a year via her list when she's about to release a new book, as well as when she shares news via Facebook. Weiland agrees with Kyle and Wiese Sneyd's sentiments: "Start building an e-mail list as soon as you can, since this will be your only assured direct route to dedicated readers." She says to give readers "content they care about to keep their attention: drawings, freebies, special deals, glimpses into your life." For those doing book launches, Weiland says to "craft them with care, since Amazon's sales algorithms will treat you right if you can prove early on that you can generate sales."

Blogging and Social Media Marketing

Blogs and popular social media sites also have great potential for generating genuine engagement and marketing opportunities. "For the more introverted authors who are uncomfortable with public speaking and bookstore signings or launches, blogging and social media marketing are an absolute godsend," says Staflund. "[Blogging] utilizes the power of keywords to draw people in from anywhere in the world with Internet access," she says. And "there's the benefit of free social media websites to super-charge those blogging campaigns." But perhaps the biggest benefit to blogging and social media marketing is that they are "unobtrusive forms of advertising." Staflund notes, "Blogging appeals to the audience that is already in the market for your products and services." If a reader "is typing those keywords into a search engine to try to find you, it's because he or she is already interested in what you have to offer. All you have to do is be there in the top organic search engine results, and voilà: You've got your prospective customer's attention and hopefully some new business to go with it." Sims's blog *Zestful Writing*, for example, focuses on the writing craft and the writer's life, topics that "seem to do well at keeping me connected with readers and aspiring writers."

Blogging has now gone a step further with author blog tours as the trend du jour. "[They're] just like a real-life tour, except instead of visiting libraries and book clubs in person, the author stops in on various blogs by writing posts," says Grant. She suggests finding blogs that you like and that are relevant to your book. Be sure to offer the blogger something, such as a book giveaway for their readers. And, Grant says, keep the post brief, engaging, and relevant to the intended audience. However, do not tell people to buy your book in the post. "That's an ad, not a blog tour post. Just having an article and credits or links on the blog will take people back to your book and author website," she explains. Grant also advises including a photo of yourself and your book, as well as a short bio. Her best advice for author blog tours? "Social media the heck out of your post. That will help you *and* the blogger. Afterward, continue supporting the blog via social [media]—don't be a fair-weather friend. Generosity always goes a long way, especially in the writing community."

Misri says the social media channels authors use depend on the kind of books they write. For example, for young adult authors, she thinks Snapchat and Instagram are important, whereas for adult nonfiction writers, she thinks Facebook and Quora are best. It also depends on the content being offered. Munteanu sees Twitter and Facebook as "great places to announce a project and build anticipation," and "dramatized videos or trailers further tantalize with sneak peeks." Morgan praises Twitter "for its brevity and the potential it has to lead you to all sorts of information," whereas Sims loathes Twitter: "I see it as a silent scream of hype, and it just makes me nervous on some reptilian level, but I dutifully announce new work and sometimes new blog entries on it. And I respond when someone mentions me." Grant says tweets on a Twitter author page "should drive traffic to your blog, which should ultimately drive sales. That's a synergistic plan." She also stresses the value of well-executed author pages in online bookstores like Amazon and on Goodreads, as does Misri, who believes that author pages "are things you initiate once and basically add to every time you have a new book, so it's a low-maintenance necessity."

Despite this, Grant says many authors don't set up their author page on venues such as Goodreads. "As a reader, I'll click on their name, hoping to get more information, and I find a page with just their name and the book title, sometimes not even a headshot. That's a lost opportunity." Green is just one of many authors taking advantage of both synergy and opportunity with her latest book *How Samantha Smart Became a Revolutionary*. She's hired a graphic designer and has come up with a game plan to create an online persona for the main character that includes a character Instagram account that follows the storyline and an interactive Web page. "As social media plays a large role within the story, this works really well as a tandem project—using the online world in conjunction with the hard-paper written word, allowing the reader to take their experience beyond the page." Green refers to the whole project as "a multimedia dynamic approach to creating a story."

And when it comes to social media interaction versus sales, Grant says to follow the 80/20 rule: "80 percent interacting with your readers about the subject you all share an interest in, and at the most 20 percent on actually 'selling' your book." Clarifies Grant, "Very few of your tweets and posts should be, 'Buy my book.' Use your engagement on social media to become a pillar of that particular reading community. People will get to know and be interested in you, and they'll buy your book after that." Like Misri, Grant says, "No one wants to follow a Twitter account that just pushes a product all the time. That would be like signing up for a string of ads. Be interesting, and people will be interested in being with you—just like in real life."

Digital Giveaways, Online Advertising, Online Book Reviews, and Paid Publicity

Ioannou notes that digital giveaways through services like BookBub and Riffle are gaining popularity. These online services allow writers to offer temporarily discounted or free books to a list of readers. "This can be a great way to get your book into readers' hands and make those impulse purchases happen, especially as a way to hook people into the first part of a series, [ultimately driving] the book up the bestsellers list on Amazon and elsewhere," he contends.

Another marketing trend is online advertising. Kyle says that after the e-mail list, "the number two method to drive sales is with online ads on Facebook that get streamed into people's Facebook news feeds. … Facebook's highly sophisticated algorithms allow you to target incredibly precise audiences, for example readers who are fans of an author in the same genre as yours." Grant adds that "online ads are probably a lot cheaper than many authors might realize. You can get a great, really targeted ad on Facebook for ten dollars. How many books do you have to sell to cover that cost? Not many. It can be a really good bang for the buck." Sims shares Grant's view: "Paid advertising is a much more straightforward way to sell than trying to be everybody's friend on social media."

In a similar vein, authors can pay for professional book reviews via sites such as Kirkus Indie. For $425 to $575, an author can obtain an unbiased, concise review of their book, which they can then decide if they want to publish on KirkusReviews.com, where it can be discovered by consumers, publishers, agents, and others in the industry. Reviews can also be solicited via Amazon and Goodreads, which Munteanu says "have provided excellent validation" for her work. She labels this "seal of approval by a grass roots readership as a critical part of the selling process and worth spending considerable time in acquiring." Her logic? "Reviews recommend your work; they are the last step in the selling process." And, she stresses, "reviews guarantee your product," noting that "we have seen a shift from a reliance on reviews from professional reviewers to the general readership—right on the bookseller site."

Staflund says those authors looking for solid publicity should consider hiring a publicist. Though often expensive, "it's worth the investment when you're working with a reputable firm [that has] developed longstanding relationships with all the 'movers and shakers' in the media," and knows how to format news stories that tie you and your book into current events. Attracting television, radio, and newspaper interviews from the mainstream media creates "a heightened interest in the author, which should boost sales much like advertising does," she says.

CREATING ORDER OUT OF CYBER CHAOS

But how does an author organize all this digital activity, especially before publication day? Misri says to use a calendar, marking down the date of publication and then backtracking to add all physical and virtual plans. For example, if a book launch is scheduled the same week as your book's release, she says to "make sure you're creating content for your blog and images that can be easily shared all over the Internet, promoting your launch." If you're self-publishing, "get some beta readers to write early reviews on Goodreads and run an online contest to amp up the buzz, where you give away a copy of the book." These cross-promotional efforts create strong interest for your book, and if you schedule your digital giveaway before your publication date, Goodreads will let contest entrants know when your book is published. Misri also says to "mark major holidays and come up with ways to feature your books and characters in blogs and social media posts."

Weiland is all about a master plan, too: "Know what you're going to say and why." She likes to break down her social media schedule into different subjects and then brainstorms interesting things to share in each category that relate to her audience. "This makes it so much easier than just sitting down at the computer, trying to come up with a random Facebook status people will actually care about."

Still pondering taking the plunge into the digital marketing and promoting pool? "Think of how much time and toil you put into creating your book, then how much you put into finding the right publisher," says Lamb. "You've attained a mountain summit, and you don't want to suddenly plunge downhill by seeing your book fail to sell many copies. You want to do all you can to support its rise up a higher mountain." So regardless of the digital marketing and promotional roads you take for your fiction, Morgan says regular posting is important, as is offering information that's not available elsewhere. These exclusive elements could include "cover reveals, notes about characters, background information about the book … any extras that make followers feel connected to the author." Munteanu advises to use the social media sites "that suit you best, because these are more likely to be successful for you—if only because you are more likely to persist with them and use them proficiently." Weiland stresses that it's all about having fun: "Don't let marketing be a chore; embrace it as a challenge. Your audience will sense that attitude and respond to it."

GRASS ROOTS MARKETING AND PUBLICITY

Staflund believes marketing and selling are "a marathon, not a sprint." Thus "the more an author or publisher does to promote a book on a consistent basis, the better—using both traditional and online techniques combined." So while social media is often the most successful route to take for author exposure, there are myriad other ways to get your book and brand "out there" that shouldn't be dismissed.

First, don't write off the promotional power of your local library. Wiese Sneyd credits libraries for stepping up to fill the void left by bookstores, and many now regularly host book signings and promote events through their newsletters and websites. And, she says, "The local media is more likely to pick up a story about an author featured at a public library because the library is a community venue." Like Wiese Sneyd, Courage encourages authors to introduce themselves to local booksellers and librarians to see if there are any opportunities to connect with local readers. "You might be surprised at the networks you uncover," he says.

Kevin Morgan Watson, publisher and editor in chief of Press 53 in North Carolina, says that as a small-press publisher, he's always "on the lookout for bookstores with well-cultivated poetry and short fiction sections" because "these stores seem to always have an active staff in touch with the local reading and writing communities, which gives them an edge over online booksellers." His advice to authors publishing with small presses? "Get out there and meet your readers through readings, conferences, and festivals. Social media is overcrowded and extremely loud, so it's difficult to get the word out to a large audience." Taylor agrees, adding that "events like festivals provide an opportunity for audiences to connect directly with authors. They are becoming more important as a marketing tool."

Morgan Watson also suggests collecting e-mail addresses at events and sending thank-you-for-attending notes, later letting attendees know about your next book or next tour, even if it is not in their area—"They probably have friends all around the country." He also suggests writing some shorter pieces to place in magazines and journals. "It's like free advertising and will connect you with other writers, editors, and more readers, who will all become your support team later, when your book is published."

Wiese Sneyd reminds authors to submit their work to book award competitions and contests for increased exposure. And Morgan says covering what she calls "the basics" is essential: using a professional author photo, keeping bookmarks and business cards handy, and seeking professional coaching in preparing for radio and television interviews or speaking engagements. Taylor believes authors also "have to find the secondary markets for their books and expand upon those to reach customers directly." He says, for example, if a book has a niche market, a trade show or a farmers' market may be suitable venues.

Both Taylor and Courage stress the importance of joining or connecting with local writing organizations, groups, and book clubs, which usually hold readings and other networking events. "Authors are often the best readers. Getting other authors to read your work also helps to promote it," says Taylor. However, says Courage, "Ultimately, you'll want to branch out and reach a wider readership online, but it may be more rewarding to create a solid local foundation for your author platform first, if possible."

THE LAST WORD

"I still believe, and will always believe, that the best way to engage a new audience and sell books is to write a great book that people want to read and talk about. That's the writer's first and biggest priority," says Cole. After that, adds Green, authors need to grasp that "the world is becoming more and more driven to their phones and social media," so "all authors need to start getting creative with how we tell stories. Modern literacy is about more than the written word." But, cautions Kyle, realize that marketing and promoting via social media is "a mixed blessing; we love the one-on-one intimacy that it gives us with readers, but keeping current can be a massive time suck—time away from writing."

Sims concurs: "If you try to jump on every marketing and promo bandwagon, you will cut your throat." She maintains that authors educate themselves on what's available and then make choices. "Commit to doing a couple of things well, see how it goes, and then change things up in response to your data, or add things if you feel you can." Munteanu summarizes it this way: "A strong belief in your project is the ultimate goal, and with it will naturally come success. We generally find it much easier to sell something we believe in than to sell ourselves—an idea, a conviction, a brand. This is really at the heart of selling yourself and your brand." And, she asserts, "Nothing is more attractive than demonstrated enthusiasm and passion for something. Communicating from the heart will go a long way in gathering a genuine audience."

Jennifer D. Foster is a Toronto, Canada–based freelance writer, editor, and content strategist. She's been in the writing and editing business for two decades, and her company is Planet Word. Jennifer's clients are from the book and custom publishing, magazine, health, and marketing and communications fields and include the Art Gallery of Ontario, *Quill & Quire*, Greystone Books, *The Globe and Mail*, Upon a Star Books, Dietitians of Canada, Dundurn Press, the Ontario Dental Association, and Firefly Books. When she's not busy spilling ink for her first novel, walking her greyhound (Aquaman), or reading, Jennifer enjoys mentoring novice editors and writers, travelling, antiquing, gardening, and yoga. Jennifer is chair of Editors Toronto and administrative director of Rowers Reading Series in Toronto. Find her online at lifeonplanetword.wordpress.com.

LAUNCH PAD

Could a Serialized Storytelling Community Catapult Your Career?

....

Diane Shipley

Few things strike fear into a writer's heart like the idea of showing an early draft to a friend, let alone millions of strangers. We've been conditioned to believe that giving away work for free is amateurish. And as for inviting comments from the masses? Pure masochism.

But serialized storytelling sites and apps like Fictionpress, Radish, and most notably Wattpad (which has 45 million users) have turned those ideas on their head. They provide spaces for aspiring novelists to share works-in-progress, a chapter at a time, so writers can build an audience, receive constructive criticism, and—if they're lucky—land a book deal. Anna Todd's *After* started as One Direction fanfiction on Wattpad, gained over a billion reads, and launched a seven-book series. Sarah J. Maas wrote the first book in her bestselling Throne of Glass series on Fictionpress. And in 2016, Natasha Preston's young adult thriller *The Cellar*, which started on Wattpad, became a number one *New York Times* bestseller.

There's even a chance that Hollywood could come calling: Streaming service Hulu is turning *Throne of Glass* into a show, *After* has been optioned for film, and Universal Cable Productions signed a deal with Wattpad in late 2016 that will bring some of the site's most popular writers to television.

But not everyone who joins an online storytelling community is looking for fame and fortune. When Rebecca Sky signed up with Wattpad five years ago, it was as a reader, not a writer. Growing up, she'd always enjoyed creating stories for her younger siblings, but lacked confidence in her spelling and grammar skills. The more she read on Wattpad, though, the more she realized writers don't have to be perfect, and that they often improved over time. She decided to try writing a novel as a hobby, posting each chapter to Wattpad. At first, she got some blunt criticism for her English, but she says this

---

THE WRITE FIT

Which storytelling platform is right for you?

WATTPAD (WATTPAD.COM)

- Pros: The ratio of readers to writers (ten-to-one) means the chance to get plentiful, in-depth feedback. You can also be given opportunities to connect with publishers, brands, and studios.
- Cons: The site is increasingly competitive, so it's harder to stand out. Reads and votes don't necessarily equal publishing industry interest—or sales.

INKVITE (INKVITE.ME; IOS)

- Pros: Inkvite is one of the few storytelling communities to focus on short stories, and it offers the chance to collaborate with others.
- Cons: It's only available for Apple devices and not yet well known.

FICTIONPRESS (FICTIONPRESS.COM)

- Pros: It's a low-pressure place to practice writing and receive encouragement from fellow scribes.
- Cons: There are fewer readers to engage with. Writers are unlikely to get spotted by agents or editors. The platform allows users to copy and paste, increasing the risk of plagiarism.

RADISH (RADISHFICTION.COM; IOS AND ANDROID)

- Pros: Radish claims that authors can earn up to $13,000 a month. It's growing fast and just raised $3 million in investment. It's also backed by Amy Tan.
- Cons: Radish isn't a great showcase for your work if you don't write romance. There are far fewer users than Wattpad and no opportunity to chat with readers. It's an app only, making it more difficult to promote stories on social media.

---

forced her to learn quickly from her mistakes. Within a few months, *The Descendants* had racked up 200,000 reads. (*Reads* are the total number of times someone has clicked on any page in the story rather than the number of readers, but this was nonetheless an encouraging start.)

She brainstormed ways to interact more with her readers. "To be able to talk to people who are engaging in your work and enjoying it, or maybe not enjoying it, and to learn and grow and build this community, I find it really exciting," she says. She wrote a new novel, *The Cheater's Club*, and asked readers to vote after every few chapters on what should happen next. Choices ranged from which love interest her main character should go on a date with to which party the character should attend. Her fans loved it, and Sky says it kept her on her toes. "Not a lot of writers get to be playful with their work, and Wattpad allows you to be as creative as you want to be, so I had fun with that."

Three years ago, Wattpad invited her to become part of its Wattpad Stars program, which gives popular writers the chance to work with publishers, movie studios, and brands. As a result, she was invited to write a short story for *Imagines*, a Simon & Schuster collection about celebrity encounters, as well as serialized content for Lay's and Athenos feta cheese. But her biggest success so far has been *The Love Curse*, a paranormal romance that attracted 11.8 million reads and the attention of an agent, who Sky signed with in 2016.

Unlike a lot of writers on Wattpad, Linda Poitevin had already been traditionally published when she joined the site in 2014. She had just gotten back the rights to her romance novel *Gwynneth Ever After*, the story of a Hollywood star who falls in love with a single mom, and published it as an e-book. But it hadn't sold as well as she'd hoped. She started posting it on Wattpad, and it was picked for their Featured List, a staff-curated selection of good stories.

HOW TO WATTPAD

Ready to launch? Keep these tips in mind.

- Make sure your book's a good fit: romance, fantasy, and thrillers are ideal, especially if there's a social media or pop culture angle and the protagonists are under thirty.
- Sign up at Wattpad.com, and fill out your profile with a photo and a brief bio.
- You'll need a catchy title and a professional-looking cover image: Ninety percent of users are scrolling on cell phones, the title and image need to encourage them to read.
- Update your story on a regular schedule (at least once a week), keep chapters under 3,000 words, and end each installment on a cliffhanger to entice readers back.
- Be a good literary citizen: Follow and encourage other writers, and respond to everyone who comments on your story.
- Wattpad's Writer Analytics let you see your readers' genders, ages, and geographical regions, as well as which chapters they liked the most, giving you real-time feedback you can act on.
- If you need to remove your book from the site, leave sample chapters up so you can keep readers interested, and consider adding free content, such as a prequel novella, to reward loyal fans.

Within a month, *Gwynneth* hit number ten in the Featured Romance chart and had 814 votes (the Wattpad version of "likes," which drive the recommendations other users see). Within two months, it had 7,679. When the full story was posted, it had 59,000 votes and more than four million reads. Even better, this popularity translated into sales. Whenever she uploaded a new chapter, readers would comment that they wanted more, so Poitevin posted links to the finished novel's Amazon and iBooks sales pages at the end of each installment. In the ten months before it was on Wattpad, she had sold 314 copies. Nine weeks after, she was selling between one hundred and 350 copies a week.

However, there's no guarantee of success—or of income. Poitevin later uploaded an urban fantasy novel that didn't take off, perhaps because she'd established herself as a romance author. She also points out that because the average user age is twenty, some readers have no option but to wait for each chapter. "There's a tremendous number of young readers who don't have the money, some of them in countries where they have difficulty accessing digital books, so you have to be willing to give your book away for free."

She recently posted a new novel, *Shadow of Doubt*, on Radish, an app-only storytelling platform. Users can wait a week for a new chapter or pay to read it early (two Radish

WATTPAD SUCCESS STORIES

THE DARK HEROINE BY ABIGAIL GIBBS (WILLIAM MORROW, 2013)

The first author to be discovered on Wattpad, she started writing this young adult vampire romance at fifteen and snagged a six-figure book deal at eighteen.

THE KISSING BOOTH BY BETH REEKLES (EMBER, 2013)

A YA love story about a girl in love with her best friend's brother, it racked up 19 million reads and is being made into a movie by Netflix.

THE LOST BOYS BY LILIAN CARMINE (EBURY PRESS, 2013)

After gaining 33 million reads (a record at the time), Carmine landed a three-book deal for the story of a girl who falls in love with a ghost.

LIFE'S A WITCH BY BRITTANY GERAGOTELIS (SIMON & SCHUSTER, 2014)

A paranormal romance set in a coven, Geragotelis's novel was rejected by traditional publishers until Wattpad brought her 19 million reads and a three-book deal.

FOLLOW ME BACK BY AV GEIGER (2017, SOURCEBOOKS FIRE)

The lives of an agoraphobic teenager and the pop star she's obsessed with become enmeshed in this YA thriller, which has 4.1 million reads so far.

coins cost ninety-nine cents and open two chapters; authors get half). But Poitevin still prefers Wattpad because it's easier to chat to readers and get instant feedback. She says she can't see any drawbacks to uploading a story, whether new or previously published. "As a platform for attracting a new readership, it is brilliant."

Taran Matharu joined Wattpad specifically to get a book deal, inspired by the site's first breakout authors, Abigail Gibbs and Beth Reekles. He started posting chapters of his work-in-progress, the epic fantasy *Summoner: The Novice*, in 2014, and racked up 100,000 reads in the first month and one million in three. After an NBC journalist interviewed him for an online story about serialized fiction, an audiobook company offered to buy the rights to his book. Matharu contacted agents to ask for advice, and within twenty-four hours he had six offers of representation. *Summoner: The Novice* and its two sequels all became *New York Times* bestsellers, and he just signed a new six-figure, three-book deal for a series he describes as "*Avatar* meets *The 100* meets *Gladiator*." He's the only male Wattpad author to have made it big, probably because the site has been female-dominated since its early days as a place to find Teen Wolf and One Direction fanfiction.

While he's grateful to Wattpad for kick-starting his career, Matharu wouldn't necessarily recommend it to writers who want to be traditionally published. Most publishers ask that you take down your Wattpad work the minute you sign a contract. Since the best way to communicate with readers is by updating your story, it's difficult to let followers know when the new, edited version goes on sale once you take down the Wattpad version. You could e-mail them from your profile, but many e-mail programs, including Gmail, automatically mark Wattpad messages as spam. "It's a great website for responding to fans and a great place to get your work out but a terrible place to build a following you can actively communicate with," he says. Nor does he think his popularity there boosted his sales: He attributes success to a good story, an eye-catching cover, and publisher-driven promotion, as his pre-order figures were comparable with other first-time novelists.

Literary agent Mandy Hubbard agrees that Wattpad popularity doesn't necessarily translate into commercial success. Writers sometimes query her with books that were written on the site, and while she appreciates proof that they can build an audience, she'd rather see their next novel. She says publishers often treat a book that's been online in its entirety as a reprint, making it hard to get reviews—or respect. She also thinks some online writers are too quick to expect a book deal. She speaks from experience: The author of eleven published books, she started writing on Fictionpress in 2003, where she posted six practice novels in the space of two years. She wrote a couple more offline, landed an agent, and *Prada and Prejudice* was published in 2009. "So many people today are like, 'I'm going to write a book and it's going to be published,' and it's so rare the first thing you write is going to be that one," she says. "I wish more writers would look at it like, 'I'm going to write a book or two and enjoy that process, and *then* query agents.'"

Publishing company Sourcebooks wants to make it easier for authors to bridge the gap between Wattpad and mainstream success. They entered a partnership with the company in 2013 when they agreed to publish polished, edited versions of some of the most popular stories from the site while the original versions remained online. This allowed authors (including Natasha Preston and Ali Novak, whose *My Life with the Walter Boys* has 63 million reads and counting) to become published authors but also stay on Wattpad and keep in touch with their fans.

Sourcebooks vice president and editorial director Todd Stocke says booksellers were initially wary about this new model, but it's been a success. He does have one caveat, though: "It *is* uncommon. There are God knows how many writers on Wattpad, and I publish a handful of them." However, he expects publishers to continue to find talent via Wattpad (and possibly other online storytelling communities) for a long time to come. "It's an incredibly viable resource, and, more importantly, it's a terrific place for writers to work on their craft."

Diane Shipley is a freelance journalist who writes about publishing, pop culture, health, and technology—or any combination of the above. Her bylines include *The Guardian*, *The Washington Post*, *Glamour*, and *Mental Health Today*. She's also a frequent contributor to Twitter (@dianeshipley).

PUBLISHING SHORT STORIES

5 Steps to Lit Mag Success

....

Windy Lynn Harris

When you're ready to submit a short story, it's wise to formulate a plan of action. To find publishing success, you need to send your story to the right editor, include a proper introduction, and format the piece correctly. The thought of submitting your work in a professional manner may seem daunting, but it's easy when you break it down into five steps:

1. Categorize Your Manuscript
2. Study Potential Magazines
3. Write a Cover Letter
4. Format Your Manuscript
5. Press Send with Confidence

1. CATEGORIZE YOUR MANUSCRIPT

Short stories are sold with two basic pieces of information: the word count and the genre. The three main short story categories are all defined by length. *Microfiction* refers to stories up to 100 words long, *flash fiction* describes stories between 100 to 1,000 words, whereas *short stories* are between 1,000 words and 20,000 words.

Next, you must decide whether you wrote a *literary* short story or a *genre* short story, since each type is sold to different magazines. Genre fiction refers to stories that fit the traditional categories of mystery, romance, science fiction, fantasy, and horror. Genre magazines expect high-quality prose and well-developed stories. They want plot-driven tales that reflect the expectations of a specific genre.

Literary fiction, on the other hand, is a bit harder to define. Literary stories embody art on the page. These stories emphasize meaning over entertainment. They are character driven instead of plot-driven, and often experiment with traditional storytelling formats and devices.

If you feel like your story is a blend of both, decide how best to market it by doing some math. If your story is more than 50 percent plot-based action, then your best chance for publishing success is in a genre magazine. If 50 percent or more of your pages are spent on character interiority or highlighting the human experience, send it to a literary magazine. Still not sure? Check the voice. If you've employed a lyrical, original, or daring voice, a literary magazine is the best choice.

2. STUDY POTENTIAL MAGAZINES

Nearly every literary magazine has a page at their website, typically called "Submission Guidelines" or "Writers' Guidelines," that identifies the kind of material they accept. These guidelines tell you everything you need to know about submitting to a publication, including:

- whether they acquire genre stories or literary stories
- an acceptable word count range
- the payment they offer, which could include money, complimentary copies, and/or subscriptions to the magazine
- whether multiple submissions (submitting more than one story at a time) are acceptable
- whether simultaneous submissions (sending the same story to other magazines at the same time) are acceptable
- how to send your submission (by e-mail, snail mail, or an online submissions manager such as Submittable)

It's important to keep in mind that when a magazine offers a contract, they're not buying your short story. They're buying the right to use it for a limited time, in a specific medium (print, electronic, film, etc.). Your rights return to you at the end of a contract period, typically ninety to 120 days after publication. Rights information will be listed in the submission guidelines, too. Make sure you agree with the magazine's terms before submitting your story.

To find a viable match for your work, compare the submission guidelines to the categories you've identified for your story. If the word length and genre are compatible, and you're happy with the terms, check to see if the magazine is currently accepting stories. If they are, continue to Step 3. If the submission window is closed, note the name of the magazine for future reference, and move on to another.

3. WRITE A COVER LETTER

A cover letter is an introduction to you and your story. A cover letter for short stories is much shorter than the one you'd send to a literary agent or a book publisher. It consists of just a few sentences in a one-page business letter.

In the first paragraph, introduce your story with the title and word count. If you're submitting to the magazine for a specific reason, say so. Maybe you liked a certain a piece they published last month, or maybe you know a friend who was published there.

List your writing credentials next. Don't fret if you're early in your career and haven't earned any publishing credits yet. Mention a few writing groups or writing classes you've attended to demonstrate that you take your writing seriously. After you've been published, list your publishing credits instead. Last, thank the editor for her time considering your work.

Format your cover letter using these guidelines:

- Use 12-point Times New Roman, Courier, or similar font.
- Use block paragraphs: single-spaced paragraphs with an extra space between paragraphs and no indents.
- Use 1" to 1.5" margins.
- Address your letter to the proper editor (not "Sir," "Madam," or "To whom it may concern") and spell the name correctly.

If you're sending your cover letter by snail mail, take these additional steps:

- At the top left corner, add your name, address, e-mail address, website, and phone number. These items are single spaced.
- Add the date of submission below your contact information.
- Add the magazine's contact information below the date.
- Leave three extra lines after your salutation so you have room to sign your name.
- Tell the editor what you've sent in a short enclosure line (For example, "Encl: Manuscript and SASE"). *SASE* stands for "Self-Addressed, Stamped Envelope," which you will need to provide with mailed submissions.

Here's an example of a basic, straightforward cover letter.

> Dear Mr. Daniels,
>
> Please consider the following 700-word short story, "Ferris Wheel," for your publication. This story is based on my own memories as a child growing up in a small resort town. I think it would be a good fit with the other nostalgic pieces you print in *American Short Fiction*.
>
> I am a member of AWP and a student at Gotham Writers Workshop.

Thank you for your time considering "Ferris Wheel." I have attached the completed manuscript, per your request.

Sincerely,

Fabulous Writer

Once you create a custom cover letter for a story, you can send that same letter to as many editors as it takes to find your work a home. Just remember to change the editor's name and the magazine information before you send it out the door.

4. FORMAT YOUR MANUSCRIPT

Some publications have very specific guidelines for formatting your short story, and if you're submitting to one of these magazines, follow their instructions to the letter. Use these standard guidelines for any other submissions:

- Print manuscripts on 8.5" × 11" white paper.
- Use 1" to 1.5" margins.
- Use 12-point Times New Roman, Courier, or similar font.
- Make sure your manuscript contains no bad breaks (end-of-the-line hyphenated words), and remove justified right margin.
- Double-space the entire manuscript.
- Indent each paragraph five spaces.
- Don't add additional spacing between paragraphs.

Next, add identifying information, your byline, and the header:

- Type your name, address, phone number, and e-mail in the upper left corner, single spaced. In the upper right corner, type the word count.
- On the first page, type the story's title and center it. Place your byline beneath it. These are double spaced. You can present the title in all caps, or not—your choice.
- On page two and subsequent pages, add a header that includes your title and last name.

5. PRESS SEND WITH CONFIDENCE

Once you have a well-written, properly formatted story, a short query letter, and a few well-researched magazines, you're ready to send out your work. I suggest sending each new story to at least five editors at a time. (Make sure each magazine accepts simultaneous submissions.) For each rejection letter you receive, find a new market and submit that story again until you've made a match.

Keep track of the dates you submit, who you send work to, and the responses you get. As soon as your story is accepted by a magazine, contact the other editors and let them know the story is no longer available. Then celebrate your success!

Windy Lynn Harris is a prolific writer with over seventy bylines in literary, women's, and trade magazines across the U.S. and Canada in places like *The Literary Review*, *34th Parallel*, and *Pithead Chapel*, among many others. She is the founder of Market Coaching for Creative Writers, a mentoring program that teaches writers how to get their short prose published in magazines, and the author of *Writing and Selling Short Stories and Personal Essays: The Essential Guide to Getting Your Work Published*. She is a frequent speaker at literary events. Find her online at www.windylynnharris.com.

CREATING YOUR LITERARY COMMUNITY

Heather Villa

When I wrote feature articles for a business journal, I searched for the *why* behind ingenious products and services. For one assignment, I attended an electric vehicle (EV) gathering, held at a library. This free event, open to the public, was co-sponsored by an EV association and a national laboratory. There, I met an organized group of united enthusiasts, each playing necessary but different roles in the promotion of a revolutionary mode of transportation. Zealous supporters, curious onlookers, and a scientist directly connected to the technology had flocked to the event to discuss their shared passion. More than a dozen EVs lined the patio. Attendees had the chance to see batteries under the hoods and chat with the owners.

In conversing with the various participants, I gained the information I needed to write a compelling article, plus, journalistic objectivity aside, the desire to purchase an EV. But I actually left with something much more valuable: *the* business model for establishing literary success. It doesn't start with tweets, Facebook campaigns, or blog posts. It starts with *community*.

As much as you love the story you've written, your words are still a product. Products need people who believe in the value of innovation, and your writing is no exception. Whether you pen short stories, novels, or experimental flash fiction, to gain influence as an author, you need to target early adopters. Your initial market begins with one passionate supporter, followed by another. As entrepreneur and TED speaker Derek Sivers puts it, "Three is a crowd, and a crowd is news."

Afeez Alade-Kolawole, founder of TryMyEV, a London-based group offering non-EV owners EV driving experiences, explains, "To grow a community you need people who are enlightened and willing to share the solution to a problem, hence creating what then becomes a movement and ultimately a community."

You have the ability to build a literary network that will champion you and your written words. Here's how to do it.

1. BELIEVE IN YOURSELF: ACKNOWLEDGE YOUR POTENTIAL AS A WRITER

Belief in your literary potential is necessary to build a community. Consider what Tesla Inc.'s CEO, Elon Musk, says: "The first step is to establish that something is possible; then probability will occur."

Vulnerability is essential to exposing your aspiration. Avoid the temptation to hide until you think you've perfected your craft. Begin by sharing your writing with someone. Not everyone will be interested in what you write, but someone will.

You should also consider your target market. The idea isn't to write a story with broad appeal, but one that will attract and be accessible to a specific audience.

Similarly, EVs don't appeal to every driver. But here's what I discovered at the EV gathering: The attendees were attracted to alternative transportation, a technology backed by passionate innovators—a technology that evolves as ideas are shared.

When you trust yourself to show your written words to early adopters, you'll gain the support needed to nurture your abilities and foster continued belief in yourself.

2. INTERACT WITH WRITERS: LEARN FROM OTHERS WHO HAVE GONE BEFORE YOU, AND BUILD RELATIONSHIPS

Writers need other writers. As I prepared to pitch my novel to a literary agent at a writers conference, an attendee offered to let me practice with her. Reluctantly, I agreed. *Why would someone want to help me?* I wondered. About twenty seconds into the pitch, the attendee interrupted me and asked, "What would happen if your protagonist acted in the opposite way?" *That would change everything,* I thought to myself. I also realized she was right. The proposed question led to necessary revisions and a friendship with an established author. My new friend and I happened to live in the same city, and we later joined a writers' group that had been promoted at the conference. While the conference was life changing, the group has transformed the way I write. By conversing and sharing ideas with agented and published novelists, I became an active participant. Our confessed struggles were real, but so were our eventual victories.

Trailblazing is a common thread that writers and EV enthusiasts share. Writers must be risk-takers who tirelessly work together in order to gain influence beyond themselves. Alade-Kolawole points out that current EV owners are pioneers, and he extends his vision beyond the United Kingdom.

3. CONSIDER EDITORIAL ADVICE: REFINE YOUR WORK

The vision of a healthy community should include a transformative process. The advancements in EV battery technology, structural design, and even affordability respond to what consumers expect.

The same holds true for written words. That's why it's important to seek feedback from beta readers, critique partners, and editors. The key is to find someone who is immersed in your genre and is bold enough to challenge your work. A word of caution: Revisions may take longer and be more difficult than writing your first drafts, especially if you're simultaneously analyzing someone else's work. But this process also comes with its own rewards: Working alongside someone who understands what you're going through allows you to grow as a writer.

4. SHOW GENEROSITY TO OTHER WRITERS: LEND SUPPORT

If you admire an author, let him or her know—through a heartfelt e-mail, a book review, or a blog post. On social media platforms, tell others about novel or short stories you adore. Public praise highlights the significance of a community, which is much more valuable than a writer's individual promotional efforts for their own work.

As Alade-Kolawole seeks to move EV ownership beyond early adopters, he believes that growth happens through interaction from person to person and adds, "The importance of a community is [that] it facilitates knowledge sharing."

That's why a supportive network working together to promote an idea is essential to the advancement of any movement, including a literary one.

5. EXPRESS GRATITUDE TO PEOPLE WHO BELIEVE IN YOU: REMEMBER THAT SUCCESS IS NEVER A SOLO VENTURE

In the early stages of your writing career, your biggest supporters might include family and friends who respect the time you need to write. As you progress, you will probably add critique partners and beta readers to your network. Later your community may include an agent and editor, followed by a publisher and possibly publicists, librarians, booksellers, and teachers. And, of course, every writer's community includes her readers.

Throughout your literary journey, mail handwritten notes, send e-mails, or make phone calls to express gratitude to your supporters. Furthermore, as you write a novel, make notes of people who champion you. That way you won't forget to thank someone in your book's acknowledgments.

A few days following the EV gathering, I received an e-mail from the president of the organization thanking me for attending and inviting me to the next meeting. While I didn't become an EV club member, I appreciated the gesture.

The life of a writer is often solitary, but relationships are crucial. Building your network and marketing your writing will take time and effort, as it should. But by following these steps, you'll ultimately create an alliance of writers who believe in and *trust* each other, so much so that the energy will be contagious and *your* fan base will extend beyond early adopters. Alade-Kolawole summarizes this idea perfectly: "A community only grows if we all contribute."

Heather Villa is a former cartographer, and she told stories with maps before becoming a freelance writer. Between assignments, she writes fiction. Visit heathervillawrites.com, or say hello on Twitter: @heathervilla1.

LITERARY AGENTS

///

Many publishers are willing to look at unsolicited submissions, but most feel having an agent is in the writer's best interest. In this section we include agents who specialize in or represent fiction.

The commercial fiction field is intensely competitive. Many publishers have small staffs and little time. For that reason, many book publishers rely on agents for new talent. Some publishers even rely on agents as "first readers" who must wade through the deluge of submissions from writers to find the very best. For writers a good agent can be a foot in the door—someone willing to do the necessary work to put your manuscript in the right editor's hands.

It would seem today that finding a good agent is as hard as finding a good publisher. Yet writers who have agents say they are invaluable. Not only can an agent help you make your work more marketable, an agent also acts as your business manager and adviser, protecting your interests during and after contract negotiations.

Still, finding an agent can be very difficult for a new writer. If you are already published in magazines, you have a better chance than someone with no publishing credits. (Some agents read periodicals searching for new writers.) Although many agents do read queries and manuscripts from unpublished authors without introduction, referrals from their writer clients can be a big help. If you don't know any published authors with agents, attending a conference is a good way to meet agents. Some agents even set aside time at conferences to meet new writers.

Almost all the agents listed here have said they are open to working with new, previously unpublished writers as well as published writers. They do not charge a fee to cover the time and effort involved in reviewing a manuscript or a synopsis and chapters, but their time is still extremely valuable. Send an agent your work only when you feel it is as complete and polished as possible.

USING THE LISTINGS

It is especially important that you read individual listings carefully before contacting these busy agents. The first information after the company name includes the address and phone, fax, e-mail address (when available), and website. **Member Agents** gives the names of individual agents working at that company. (Specific types of fiction an agent handles are indicated in parentheses after that agent's name). The **Represents** section lists the types of fiction the agency works with. Reading the **Recent Sales** gives you the names of writers an agent is currently working with and, very important, publishers the agent has placed manuscripts with. **Tips** presents advice directly from the agent to authors.

Also, look closely at the openness to submissions icon that precedes most listings. It indicates how willing an agency is to take on new writers.

THE AHEARN AGENCY, INC.

2021 Pine St., New Orleans LA 70118. (504)861-8395. **Fax:** (504)866-6434. **E-mail:** pahearn@aol.com. **Website:** www.ahearnagency.com. **Contact:** Pamela G. Ahearn. Other memberships include MWA, RWA, ITW. Represents 30 clients.

○ Prior to opening her agency, Ms. Ahearn was an agent for 8 years and an editor with Bantam Books.

REPRESENTS Novels. **Considers these fiction areas:** crime, detective, romance, suspense, thriller.

☛ Handles general adult fiction, specializing in women's fiction and suspense. Does not deal with any nonfiction, poetry, juvenile material or science fiction.

HOW TO CONTACT Query with SASE or via e-mail. Please send a one-page query letter stating the type of book you're writing, word length, where you feel your book fits into the current market, and any writing credentials you may possess. Please do not send ms pages or synopses if they haven't been previously requested. If you're querying via e-mail, send no attachments unless requested. Accepts simultaneous submissions. Responds in 2 months on submissions, 4 months on queries. Obtains most new clients through recommendations from others, solicitations, conferences.

TERMS Agent receives 15% commission on domestic sales; 20% commission on foreign sales. Offers written contract, binding for 1 year; renewable by mutual consent.

RECENT SALES *Black-Eyed Susans* by Julia Heaberlin, *The Art of Sinning* by Sabrina Jeffries, *The Comfort of Black* by Carter Wilson, *Flirting with Felicity* by Gerri Russell, *The Iris Fan* by Laura Joh Rowland, *The Loner* by Kate Moore, *Can't Find My Way Home* by Carlene Thompson.

WRITERS CONFERENCES Romance Writers of America, Thrillerfest, Bouchercon.

TIPS "Be professional! Always send in exactly what an agent/editor asks for—no more, no less. Keep query letters brief and to the point, giving your writing credentials and a very brief summary of your book. If 1 agent rejects you, keep trying—there are a lot of us out there!"

BETSY AMSTER LITERARY ENTERPRISES

6312 SW Capitol Hwy. #503, Portland OR 97239. **E-mail:** b.amster.assistant@gmail.com (for adult titles), b.amster.kidsbooks@gmail.com (for children's and young adult). **Website:** www.amsterlit.com. **Contact:** Betsy Amster (adult), Mary Cummings (children's and young adult). Estab. 1992. Member of AAR. Represents more than 65 clients.

○ Prior to opening her agency, Ms. Amster was an editor at Pantheon and Vintage for 10 years and served as editorial director for the Globe Pequot Press for 2 years. Prior to joining the agency, Mary Cummings served as education director at the Loft Literary Center in Minneapolis for 14 years, overseeing classes, workshops, and conferences. She curated the annual Festival of Children's Literature and selected judges for the McKnight Award in Children's Literature.

REPRESENTS Nonfiction, novels, juvenile books. **Considers these fiction areas:** crime, detective, family saga, juvenile, literary, middle grade, multicultural, mystery, picture books, police, suspense, thriller, women's, young adult.

HOW TO CONTACT "For fiction or memoirs, please embed the first three pages in the body of your e-mail. For nonfiction, please embed the overview of your proposal." For children's and young adult, see submission requirements online. "For picture books, please embed the entire text in the body of your e-mail. For novels, please embed the first 3 pages." Accepts simultaneous submissions. Responds in 1 month to queries. Responds in 2 months to mss. Obtains most new clients through recommendations from others, solicitations, and conferences.

TERMS Agent receives 15% commission on domestic sales. Agent receives 20% commission on foreign sales. Offers written contract, binding for 1 year; three-month notice must be given to terminate contract. Charges for photocopying, postage, messengers, galleys/books used in submissions to foreign and film agents and to magazines for first serial rights. (Please note that it is rare to incur much in the way of expenses now that most submissions are made by e-mail.)

APONTE LITERARY AGENCY

E-mail: agents@aponteliterary.com. **Website:** aponteliterary.com. **Contact:** Natalia Aponte. Member of AAR. Signatory of WGA.

MEMBER AGENTS Natalia Aponte (any genre of mainstream fiction and nonfiction, but she is especially seeking women's novels, historical novels, supernatural and paranormal fiction, fantasy novels, political and science thrillers); Victoria Lea (any category, especially interested in women's fiction, science fiction and speculative fiction).

REPRESENTS Novels. **Considers these fiction areas:** fantasy, historical, paranormal, science fiction, supernatural, thriller, women's.

- Actively seeking women's novels, historical novels, supernatural and paranormal fiction, fantasy novels, political and science thrillers, science fiction and speculative fiction. In nonfiction, will look at any genre with commercial potential.

HOW TO CONTACT E-query. Accepts simultaneous submissions. Responds in 6 weeks if interested.

RECENT SALES *The Nightingale Bones* by Ariel Swan, *An Irish Doctor in Peace and At War* by Patrick Taylor, *Siren's Treasure* by Debbie Herbert.

THE AXELROD AGENCY

55 Main St., P.O. Box 357, Chatham NY 12037. (518)392-2100. **E-mail:** steve@axelrodagency.com. **Website:** www.axelrodagency.com. **Contact:** Steven Axelrod. Member of AAR. Represents 15-20 clients.

- Prior to becoming an agent, Mr. Axelrod was a book club editor.

MEMBER AGENTS Steven Axelrod, representation; Lori Antonson, subsidiary rights.

REPRESENTS Novels. **Considers these fiction areas:** crime, mystery, new adult, romance, women's.

- This agency specializes in women's fiction and romance.

HOW TO CONTACT Query via e-mail. Accepts simultaneous submissions. Obtains most new clients through recommendations from others.

TERMS Agent receives 15% commission on domestic sales; 20% commission on foreign sales. No written contract.

WRITERS CONFERENCES RWA National Conference.

AZANTIAN LITERARY AGENCY

Website: www.azantianlitagency.com. **Contact:** Jennifer Azantian. Estab. 2014.

- Prior to her current position, Ms. Azantian was with Sandra Dijkstra Literary Agency.

REPRESENTS Novels. **Considers these fiction areas:** fantasy, horror, middle grade, science fiction, urban fantasy, young adult.

- Actively seeking fantasy, science fiction, and psychological horror for adult, young adult, and middle-grade readers.

HOW TO CONTACT To submit, send your query letter, 1-2 page synopsis, and first 10-15 pages all pasted in an e-mail (no attachments). Please note in the e-mail subject line if your work was requested at a conference, is an exclusive submission, or was referred by a current client. Accepts simultaneous submissions. Responds within 6 weeks. Check the website before submitting to make sure Ms. Azantian is currently open to queries.

BARONE LITERARY AGENCY

385 North St., Batavia OH 45103. (513)732-6740. **Fax:** (513)297-7208. **E-mail:** baroneliteraryagency@roadrunner.com. **Website:** www.baroneliteraryagency.com. **Contact:** Denise Barone. Estab. 2010. Member of AAR. Signatory of WGA. RWA Represents 10 clients.

REPRESENTS Nonfiction, novels. **Considers these fiction areas:** action, adventure, cartoon, comic books, commercial, confession, contemporary issues, crime, detective, erotica, ethnic, experimental, family saga, fantasy, feminist, frontier, gay, glitz, hi-lo, historical, horror, humor, inspirational, juvenile, lesbian, literary, mainstream, metaphysical, military, multicultural, multimedia, mystery, new adult, New Age, occult, paranormal, plays, police, psychic, regional, religious, romance, satire, science fiction, short story collections, spiritual, sports, supernatural, suspense, thriller, translation, urban fantasy, war, westerns, women's, young adult.

- Actively seeking adult contemporary romance. Does not want textbooks.

HOW TO CONTACT "We are no longer accepting snail mail submissions; send a query letter via e-mail instead. If I like your query letter, I will ask for the first three chapters and a synopsis as attachments." Accepts simultaneous submissions. "I make every effort to respond within 4 weeks." Obtains new clients by queries/submissions via e-mail only.

TERMS Agent receives 15% commission on domestic sales, 20% on foreign sales. Offers written contract.

RECENT SALES *All The Glittering Bones* by Anna Snow (Entangled Publishing), *Devon's Choice* by Cathy Bennett (Clean Reads), *Molly's Folly* by Denise Gwen (Clean Reads), *In Deep* by Laurie Albano (Solstice Publishing).

WRITERS CONFERENCES Lori Foster's Readers and Authors' Get-Together 2016, West Chester, OH; A Weekend with the Authors 2016, Nashville, TN; Willamette Writers' Conference, 2013, Portland, OR.

TIPS "The best writing advice I ever got came from a fellow writer, who wrote, 'Learn how to edit yourself,' when signing her book to me."

THE BENT AGENCY

E-mail: info@thebentagency.com. **Website:** www.thebentagency.com. **Contact:** Jenny Bent, Susan Hawk, Molly Ker Hawn, Gemma Cooper, Louise Fury, Brooks Sherman, Beth Phelan, Victoria Lowes, Heather Flaherty. Estab. 2009. Member of AAR.

○ Prior to forming her own agency, Ms. Bent was an agent and vice president at Trident Media Group.

MEMBER AGENTS Jenny Bent (adult fiction, including women's fiction, romance, and crime/suspense; she particularly likes novels with magical or fantasy elements that fall outside of genre fiction; young adult and middle-grade fiction; memoir; humor); **Susan Hawk** (children's books exclusively, from picture books to young adult, including contemporary, mystery, fantasy, science fiction, historical fiction, and humor); **Molly Ker Hawn** (young adult and middle-grade books, including contemporary, historical, fantasy, science fiction, thrillers, and mystery); **Gemma Cooper** (all ages of children's and young adult books, including picture books; likes historical, contemporary, thrillers, mystery, humor, and science fiction); **Louise Fury** (children's fiction: picture books, literary middle-grade, and all young adult; adult fiction: speculative fiction, suspense/thriller, commercial fiction, and all subgenres of romance including erotic; nonfiction: cookbooks and pop culture); **Brooks Sherman** (speculative and literary adult fiction, select narrative nonfiction; all ages of children's and young adult books, including picture books; likes historical, contemporary, thrillers, humor, fantasy, and horror); **Beth Phelan** (young adult, thrillers, suspense and mystery, romance and women's fiction, literary and general fiction, cookbooks, lifestyle, and pets/animals); **Victoria Lowes** (romance and women's fiction, thrillers and mystery, and young adult); **Heather Flaherty** (young adult and middle-grade fiction: all genres; select adult fiction: upmarket fiction, women's fiction, and female-centric thrillers; select nonfiction: pop culture, humorous, and social media–based projects, as well as teen memoir).

REPRESENTS Nonfiction, novels, short story collections, juvenile books. **Considers these fiction areas:** adventure, commercial, crime, erotica, fantasy, feminist, historical, horror, humor, juvenile, literary, mainstream, middle grade, multicultural, mystery, new adult, picture books, romance, short story collections, suspense, thriller, women's, young adult.

HOW TO CONTACT For Jenny Bent, e-mail queries@thebentagency.com; for Susan Hawk, e-mail kidsqueries@thebentagency.com; for Molly Ker Hawn, e-mail hawnqueries@thebentagency.com; for Gemma Cooper, e-mail cooperqueries@thebentagency.com; for Louise Fury, e-mail furyqueries@thebentagency.com; for Brooks Sherman, e-mail shermanqueries@thebentagency.com; for Beth Phelan, e-mail phelanagencies@thebentagency.com; for Victoria Lowes, e-mail lowesqueries@thebentagency.com; for Heather Flaherty, e-mail flahertyqueries@thebentagency.com. "Tell us briefly who you are, what your book is, and why you're the one to write it. Then include the first 10 pages of your material in the body of your e-mail. We respond to all queries; please resend your query if you haven't had a response within 4 weeks." Accepts simultaneous submissions.

RECENT SALES *Caraval* by Stephanie Garber (Flatiron), *Rebel of the Sands* by Alwyn Hamilton (Viking Children's/Penguin BFYR), *My Perfect Me* by J.M.M. Nuanez (Kathy Dawson Books/Penguin BFYR), *The Square Root of Summer* by Harriet Reuter Hapgood (Roaring Brook/Macmillan), *Dirty Money* by Lisa Renee Jones (Simon & Schuster), *True North* by Liora Blake (Pocket Star).

VICKY BIJUR LITERARY AGENCY

27 W. 20th St., Suite 1003, New York NY 10011. **E-mail:** queries@vickybijuragency.com. **Website:** www.vickybijuragency.com. Estab. 1988. Member of AAR.

○ Vicky Bijur worked at Oxford University Press and with the Charlotte Sheedy Literary Agency. Books she represents have appeared on the *New York Times Bestseller List*, in the *New York Times* Notable Books of the Year, *Los Angeles Times* Best Fiction of the Year, *Washington Post* Book World Rave Reviews of the Year.

MEMBER AGENTS Vicky Bijur; Alexandra Franklin.

REPRESENTS Nonfiction, novels. **Considers these fiction areas:** commercial, literary, mystery, new adult, thriller, women's, young adult, campus novels, coming-of-age.

⊶ "We are not the right agency for screenplays, picture books, poetry, self-help, science fiction, fantasy, horror, or romance."

HOW TO CONTACT "Please send a query letter of no more than 3 paragraphs on what makes your book special and unique, a very brief synopsis, its length and genre, and your biographical information, along with the first 10 pages of your ms. Please let us know in your query letter if it is a multiple submission, and kindly keep us informed of other agents' interest and offers of representation. If sending electronically, paste

the pages in an e-mail as we don't open attachments from unfamiliar senders. If sending by hard copy, please include an SASE for our response. If you want your material returned, include an SASE large enough to contain pages and enough postage to send back to you." Accepts simultaneous submissions. "We generally respond to all queries within 8 weeks of receipt."
RECENT SALES *That Darkness* by Lisa Black, *Long Upon the Land* by Margaret Maron, *Daughter of Ashes* by Marcia Talley.

DAVID BLACK LITERARY AGENCY

335 Adams St., Suite 2707, Brooklyn NY 11201. (718)852-5500. **Fax:** (718)852-5539. **Website:** www.davidblackagency.com. **Contact:** David Black, owner. Member of AAR. Represents 150 clients.
MEMBER AGENTS David Black; Jenny Herrera; Gary Morris; Joy E. Tutela (narrative nonfiction, memoir, history, politics, self-help, investment, business, science, women's issues, GLBT issues, parenting, health and fitness, humor, craft, cooking and wine, lifestyle and entertainment, commercial fiction, literary fiction, MG, YA); Susan Raihofer (commercial fiction and nonfiction, memoir, pop culture, music, inspirational, thrillers, literary fiction); Sarah Smith (memoir, biography, food, music, narrative history, social studies, literary fiction).
REPRESENTS Nonfiction, novels. **Considers these fiction areas:** commercial, literary, middle grade, thriller, young adult.
HOW TO CONTACT "To query an individual agent, please follow the specific query guidelines outlined in the agent's profile on our website. Not all agents are currently accepting unsolicited queries. To query the agency, please send a one- to two-page query letter describing your book, and include information about any previously published works, your audience, and your platform." Do not e-mail your query unless an agent specifically asks for an e-mail. Accepts simultaneous submissions. Responds in 2 months to queries.
RECENT SALES Some of the agency's best-selling authors include: Erik Larson, Stuart Scott, Jeff Hobbs, Mitch Albom, Gregg Olsen, Jim Abbott, and John Bacon.

BOND LITERARY AGENCY

4340 E. Kentucky Ave., Suite 471, Denver CO 80246. (303)781-9305. **E-mail:** queries@bondliteraryagency.com. **Website:** www.bondliteraryagency.com. **Contact:** Sandra Bond.

○ Prior to her current position, Ms. Bond worked with agent Jody Rein.

MEMBER AGENTS Sandra Bond, agent (fiction: adult commercial and literary, mystery/thriller/suspense, women's, historical, young adult; nonfiction: narrative, history, science, business); Becky LeJeune, associate agent (fiction: horror, mystery/thriller/suspense, science fiction/fantasy, historical, general fiction, young adult).
REPRESENTS Nonfiction, novels, juvenile books. **Considers these fiction areas:** commercial, crime, detective, family saga, fantasy, historical, horror, juvenile, literary, mainstream, middle grade, multicultural, mystery, police, science fiction, suspense, thriller, urban fantasy, women's, young adult.

☞ Agency does not represent romance, poetry, young reader chapter books, children's picture books, or screenplays.

HOW TO CONTACT Please submit query by e-mail (absolutely no attachments unless requested). No unsolicited mss. "They will let you know if they are interested in seeing more material. No phone calls, please." Accepts simultaneous submissions.
RECENT SALES *Betrayal at Iga* by Susan Spann, *Border Bandits, Border Raids* by W.C. Jameson, *Among the Lesser Gods* by Margo Catts, *Imagine* by Federico Pena, *The Past is Never* by Tiffany Quay Tyson.

BOOK CENTS LITERARY AGENCY, LLC

364 Patteson Dr., #228, Morgantown WV 26505. **E-mail:** cw@bookcentsliteraryagency.com. **Website:** www.bookcentsliteraryagency.com. **Contact:** Christine Witthohn. Estab. 2005. Member of AAR. RWA, MWA, SinC, KOD
REPRESENTS Novels, juvenile books. **Considers these fiction areas:** commercial, literary, mainstream, multicultural, mystery, new adult, paranormal, romance, suspense, thriller, urban fantasy, women's, young adult.

☞ Actively seeking upmarket fiction, commercial fiction (particularly if it has crossover appeal), women's fiction (emotional and layered), romance (single title or category), mainstream mystery/suspense, thrillers (particularly psychological), and young adult. For a detailed list of what this agency is currently searching for, visit the website. Does not want to receive third party submissions, previously published titles, short stories/novellas, erotica, inspirational, historical, science fiction/fantasy, horror/pulp/slasher thrillers, middle-grade, children's picture books, poetry, or screenplays/ Does not want stories with priests/nuns, religion, abuse of children/animals/elderly, rape, or serial killers.

HOW TO CONTACT Submit via form on website. Does not accept mail or e-mail submissions. Accepts simultaneous submissions.

TIPS Sponsors the International Women's Fiction Festival in Matera, Italy. See www.womensfictionfestival.com for more information. Ms. Witthohn is also the U.S. rights and licensing agent for leading French publisher Bragelonne, German publisher Egmont, and Spanish publisher Edebe. For a list of upcoming publications, leading clients, and sales, visit www.publishersmarketplace.com/members/BookCents.

BOOKENDS LITERARY AGENCY

Website: www.bookendsliterary.com. **Contact:** Jessica Faust, Kim Lionetti, Jessica Alvarez, Moe Ferrara, Tracy Marchini, Beth Campbell. Estab. 1999. Member of AAR. RWA, MWA, SCBWI. Represents 50+ clients.

MEMBER AGENTS Jessica Faust (women's fiction, mysteries, thrillers, suspense, young adult), **Kim Lionetti** (romance, women's fiction, young adult), **Jessica Alvarez** (romance, women's fiction, erotica, romantic suspense), **Beth Campbell** (fantasy, science fiction, young adult, suspense, romantic suspense, and mystery), **Moe Ferrara** (middle-grade, young adult, and adult: romance, science fiction, fantasy, horror), **Tracy Marchini** (picture book, middle-grade, and young adult: fiction and nonfiction).

REPRESENTS Nonfiction, novels, juvenile books. **Considers these fiction areas:** adventure, crime, detective, erotica, fantasy, gay, historical, horror, juvenile, lesbian, mainstream, middle grade, multicultural, mystery, paranormal, picture books, police, romance, science fiction, supernatural, suspense, thriller, urban fantasy, women's, young adult.

➥ "BookEnds is currently accepting queries from published and unpublished writers in the areas of romance, mystery, suspense, science fiction and fantasy, horror, women's fiction, picture books, middle-grade, and young adult. In nonfiction we represent titles in the following areas: current affairs, reference, business and career, parenting, pop culture, coloring books, general nonfiction, and nonfiction for children and teens." BookEnds does not represent short fiction, poetry, screenplays, or techno-thrillers.

HOW TO CONTACT Visit website for the most up-to-date guidelines and current preferences. BookEnds agents accept all submissions through their personal Query Manager forms. These forms are accessible on the agency website under Submissions. Accepts simultaneous submissions. "Our response time goals are 6 weeks for queries and 12 weeks on requested partials and fulls."

THE BOOK GROUP

20 W. 20th St., Suite 601, New York NY 10011. (212)803-3360. **E-mail:** submissions@thebookgroup.com. **Website:** www.thebookgroup.com. Estab. 2015. Member of AAR. Signatory of WGA.

MEMBER AGENTS Julie Barer; Faye Bender; Brettne Bloom (fiction: literary and commercial fiction, select young adult; nonfiction, including cookbooks, lifestyle, investigative journalism, history, biography, memoir, and psychology); Elisabeth Weed (upmarket fiction, especially plot-driven novels with a sense of place); Rebecca Stead (innovative forms, diverse voices, and open-hearted fiction for children, young adults, and adults); Dana Murphy (story-driven fiction with a strong sense of place, narrative nonfiction/essays with a pop-culture lean, and YA with an honest voice).

REPRESENTS **Considers these fiction areas:** commercial, literary, mainstream, women's, young adult. ➥ Please do not send poetry or screenplays.

HOW TO CONTACT Send a query letter and 10 sample pages to submissions@thebookgroup.com, with the first and last name of the agent you are querying in the subject line. All material must be in the body of the e-mail, as the agents do not open attachments. "If we are interested in reading more, we will get in touch with you as soon as possible." Accepts simultaneous submissions.

RECENT SALES *This Is Not Over* by Holly Brown, *Perfect Little World* by Kevin Wilson, *City of Saints & Thieves* by Natalie C. Anderson, *The Runaway Midwife* by Patricia Harman, *Always* by Sarah Jio, *The Young Widower's Handbook* by Tom McAllister.

BOOKS & SUCH LITERARY MANAGEMENT

52 Mission Circle, Suite 122, PMB 170, Santa Rosa CA 95409. **E-mail:** representation@booksandsuch.com. **Website:** www.booksandsuch.com. **Contact:** Janet Kobobel Grant, Wendy Lawton, Rachel Kent, Mary Keeley, Rachelle Gardner. Estab. 1996. CBA, American Christian Fiction Writers Represents 250 clients.

○ Prior to founding the agency, Ms. Grant was an editor for Zondervan and managing editor for

Focus on the Family. Ms. Lawton was an author, sculptor, and designer of porcelain dolls and became an agent in 2005. Ms. Keeley previously was an acquisitions editor for Tyndale publishers. Ms. Kent has worked as an agent for ten years and is a graduate of UC Davis majoring in English. Ms. Gardner worked as an editor at NavPress, at General Publishing Group in rights and marketing, and at Fox Broadcasting Company as special programming coordinator before becoming an agent in 2007.

REPRESENTS Nonfiction, novels, novellas, juvenile books. **Considers these fiction areas:** action, adventure, commercial, crime, family saga, frontier, historical, inspirational, juvenile, literary, mainstream, middle grade, mystery, new adult, religious, romance, spiritual, suspense, women's, young adult.

☛ This agency specializes in general and inspirational fiction and nonfiction, and in the Christian booksellers market. Actively seeking well-crafted material that presents Judeo-Christian values, if only subtly.

HOW TO CONTACT Query via e-mail only; no attachments. Accepts simultaneous submissions. Responds in 1 month to queries. "If you don't hear from us asking to see more of your writing within 30 days after you have sent your e-mail, please know that we have read and considered your submission but determined that it would not be a good fit for us." Obtains most new clients through recommendations from others, conferences.

TERMS Agent receives 15% commission on domestic sales. Agent receives 20% commission on foreign sales. Offers written contract; two-month notice must be given to terminate contract. No additional charges.

RECENT SALES A full list of this agency's clients (and the awards they have won) is on the agency website.

WRITERS CONFERENCES Mount Hermon Christian Writers Conference, American Christian Fiction Writers Conference, San Francisco Writers Conference.

TIPS "Our agency highlights personal attention to individual clients that includes coaching on how to thrive in a rapidly changing publishing climate, grow a career, and get the best publishing offers possible."

BRADFORD LITERARY AGENCY

5694 Mission Center Rd., #347, San Diego CA 92108. (619)521-1201. **E-mail:** queries@bradfordlit.com. **Website:** www.bradfordlit.com. **Contact:** Laura Bradford, Natalie Lakosil, Sarah LaPolla, Monica Odom. Estab. 2001. Member of AAR. RWA, SCBWI, ALA Represents 130 clients.

MEMBER AGENTS Laura Bradford (romance [historical, romantic suspense, paranormal, category, contemporary, erotic], mystery, women's fiction, thrillers/suspense, middle grade & YA); Natalie Lakosil (children's literature [from picture book through teen and New Adult], romance [contemporary and historical], cozy mystery/crime, upmarket women's/general fiction and select children's nonfiction); Sarah LaPolla (YA, middle grade, literary fiction, science fiction, magical realism, dark/psychological mystery, literary horror, and upmarket contemporary fiction); Monica Odom (nonfiction by authors with demonstrable platforms in the areas of: pop culture, illustrated/graphic design, food and cooking, humor, history and social issues; narrative nonfiction, memoir, literary fiction, upmarket commercial fiction, compelling speculative fiction and magic realism, historical fiction, alternative histories, dark and edgy fiction, literary psychological thrillers, and illustrated/picture books).

REPRESENTS Nonfiction, fiction, novels, juvenile books. **Considers these fiction areas:** commercial, crime, ethnic, gay, historical, juvenile, lesbian, literary, mainstream, middle grade, multicultural, mystery, new adult, paranormal, picture books, romance, science fiction, thriller, women's, young adult.

☛ Laura Bradford does not want to receive poetry, screenplays, short stories, westerns, horror, new age, religion, crafts, cookbooks, gift books. Natalie Lakosil does not want to receive inspirational novels, memoir, romantic suspense, adult thrillers, poetry, screenplays. Sarah LaPolla does not want to receive nonfiction, picture books, inspirational/spiritual novels, romance, or erotica. Monica Odom does not want to receive genre romance, erotica, military, poetry, or inspirational/spiritual works.

HOW TO CONTACT Accepts e-mail queries only; For submissions to Laura Bradford or Natalie Lakosil, send to queries@bradfordlit.com. For submissions to Sarah LaPolla, send to sarah@bradfordlit.com. For submissions to Monica Odom, send to Monica@bradfordlit.com. The entire submission must appear in the body of the e-mail and not as an attachment. The subject line should begin as follows: "QUERY: (the title of the ms or any short message that is important should follow)." For fiction: e-mail a query letter along with the first chapter of ms and a synopsis. Include the genre and word count in your query letter. Nonfiction: e-mail full nonfiction proposal including a query letter and a sample chapter. Accepts simultaneous submissions. Responds in 4 weeks to queries; 10 weeks to mss. Obtains most new clients through queries.

TERMS Agent receives 15% commission on domestic sales; 25% commission on foreign sales. Offers written contract. Charges for extra copies of books for foreign submissions.

RECENT SALES Sold 115 titles in the last year, including *Snowed in with Murder* by Auralee Wallace (St. Martin's), *All the Secrets We Keep* by Megan Hart (Montlake), *The Notorious Bargain* by Joanna Shupe (Avon), *Allegedly* by Tiffany Jackson (Katherine Tegen Books), *Wives of War* by Soraya Lane (Amazon), *The Silver Gate* by Kristin Bailey (Katherine Tegen Books), *Witchtown* by Cory Putman Oakes (Houghton Mifflin Harcourt), *Under Her Skin* by Adriana Anders (Sourcebooks), *The Fixer* by HelenKay Dimon (Avon), *Too Hard to Forget* by Tessa Bailey (Grand Central), *In A Daze Work* by Siobhan Gallagher (Ten Speed), *Piper Morgan Makes a Splash* by Stephanie Faris (Aladdin), *The Star Thief* by Lindsey Becker (Little, Brown), *Vanguard* by Ann Aguirre (Feiwel & Friends), *Gray Wolf Island* by Tracey Neithercott (Knopf), *Single Malt* by Layla Reyne (Carina Press), *Whiskey Sharp: Unraveled* by Lauren Dane (HQN).

WRITERS CONFERENCES RWA National Conference, Romantic Times Booklovers Convention.

BRANDT & HOCHMAN LITERARY AGENTS, INC.

1501 Broadway, Suite 2310, New York NY 10036. (212)840-5760. **Fax:** (212)840-5776. **Website:** brandthochman.com. **Contact:** Gail Hochman. Member of AAR. Represents 200 clients.

MEMBER AGENTS Gail Hochman (works of literary fiction, idea-driven nonfiction, literary memoir and children's books); Marianne Merola (fiction, nonfiction and children's books with strong and unique narrative voices); Bill Contardi (voice-driven young adult and middle grade fiction, commercial thrillers, psychological suspense, quirky mysteries, high fantasy, commercial fiction and memoir); Emily Forland (voice-driven literary fiction and nonfiction, memoir, narrative nonfiction, history, biography, food writing, cultural criticism, graphic novels, and young adult fiction); Emma Patterson (fiction from dark, literary novels to upmarket women's and historical fiction; narrative nonfiction that includes memoir, investigative journalism, and popular history; young adult fiction); Jody Kahn (literary and upmarket fiction; narrative nonfiction, particularly books related to sports, food, history, science and pop culture—including cookbooks, and literary memoir and journalism); Henry Thayer (nonfiction on a wide variety of subjects and fiction that inclines toward the literary). The e-mail addresses and specific likes of each of these agents is listed on the agency website.

REPRESENTS Nonfiction, novels. **Considers these fiction areas:** fantasy, historical, literary, middle grade, mystery, suspense, thriller, women's, young adult.

☛ No screenplays or textbooks.

HOW TO CONTACT "We accept queries by e-mail and regular mail; however, we cannot guarantee a response to e-mailed queries. For queries via regular mail, be sure to include a SASE for our reply. Query letters should be no more than 2 pages and should include a convincing overview of the book project and information about the author and his or her writing credits. Address queries to the specific Brandt & Hochman agent whom you would like to consider your work. Agent e-mail addresses and query preferences may be found at the end of each agent profile on the 'Agents' page of our website." Accepts simultaneous submissions. Obtains most new clients through recommendations from others.

TERMS Agent receives 15% commission on domestic sales; 20% commission on foreign sales.

RECENT SALES This agency sells 40-60 new titles each year. A full list of their hundreds of clients is on the agency website.

TIPS "Write a letter which will give the agent a sense of you as a professional writer—your long-term interests as well as a short description of the work at hand."

BARBARA BRAUN ASSOCIATES, INC.

7 E. 14th St., #19F, New York NY 10003. **Fax:** (212)604-9023. **E-mail:** bbasubmissions@gmail.com. **Website:** www.barbarabraunagency.com. **Contact:** Barbara Braun. Member of AAR. Authors Guild, PEN Center USA

REPRESENTS Nonfiction, novels. **Considers these fiction areas:** commercial, historical, literary, multicultural, mystery, thriller, women's, young adult, Art-related fiction.

☛ "Our fiction is strong on stories for women, art-related fiction, historical and multicultural stories, and to a lesser extent mysteries and thrillers. We are interested in narrative nonfiction and current affairs books by journalists, as well as YA literature." Does not represent poetry, science fiction, fantasy, horror, or screenplays.

HOW TO CONTACT "We no longer accept submissions by regular mail. Please send all queries via e-mail, marked 'Query' in the subject line. Your query should include: a brief summary of your book, word count, genre, any relevant publishing experience, and the first 5 pages of your ms pasted into the body of the e-mail. (No attachments—we will not open these.)" Accepts simultaneous submissions.

TERMS Agent receives 15% commission on domestic sales; 20% commission on foreign sales. No reading fees.

TIPS "Our clients' books are represented throughout Europe, Asia, and Latin America by various sub-agents. We are also active in selling motion picture rights to the books we represent, and work with various Hollywood agencies."

BRESNICK WEIL LITERARY AGENCY

115 W. 29th St., Third Floor, New York NY 10001. (212)239-3166. **Fax:** (212)239-3165. **E-mail:** query@ bresnickagency.com. **Website:** bresnickagency.com. **Contact:** Paul Bresnick.

Prior to becoming an agent, Mr. Bresnick spent 25 years as a trade book editor.

MEMBER AGENTS Paul Bresnick; Susan Duff (women's health, food and wine, fitness, humor, memoir); Lisa Kopel (narrative nonfiction, memoir, pop culture, and both commercial and literary fiction); Matthew MiGangi (music, American history, sports, politics, weird science, pop/alternative culture, video games, and fiction).

REPRESENTS Nonfiction, novels. **Considers these fiction areas:** commercial, literary.

Matthew DiGangi does not represent YA, middle grade, or books for children.

HOW TO CONTACT Electronic submissions only. For fiction, submit query and 2 chapters. For nonfiction, submit query with proposal. Accepts simultaneous submissions.

CURTIS BROWN, LTD.

10 Astor Place, New York NY 10003. (212)473-5400. **Fax:** (212)598-0917. **Website:** www.curtisbrown.com. **Contact:** Ginger Knowlton. Member of AAR. Signatory of WGA.

MEMBER AGENTS Noah Ballard (literary debuts, upmarket thrillers and narrative nonfiction, and he is always on the look-out for honest and provocative new writers); Ginger Clark (science fiction, fantasy, paranormal romance, literary horror, and young adult and middle grade fiction); Kerry D'Agostino (a wide range of literary and commercial fiction, as well as narrative nonfiction and memoir); Katherine Fausset (literary fiction, upmarket commercial fiction, journalism, memoir, popular science, and narrative nonfiction); Holly Frederick; Peter Ginsberg, president; Elizabeth Harding, vice president (represents authors and illustrators of juvenile, middle-grade and young adult fiction); Steve Kasdin (commercial fiction, including mysteries/thrillers, romantic suspense—emphasis on the suspense, and historical fiction; narrative nonfiction, including biography, history and current affairs; and young adult fiction, particularly if it has adult crossover appeal; not interested in SF/fantasy, memoirs, vampires and writers trying to capitalize on trends); Ginger Knowlton, executive vice president (authors and illustrators of children's books in all genres); Timothy Knowlton, CEO; Jonathan Lyons (biographies, history, science, pop culture, sports, general narrative nonfiction, mysteries, thrillers, science fiction and fantasy, and young adult fiction); Laura Blake Peterson, vice president (memoir and biography, natural history, literary fiction, mystery, suspense, women's fiction, health and fitness, children's and young adult, faith issues and popular culture); Maureen Walters, senior vice president (working primarily in women's fiction and nonfiction projects on subjects as eclectic as parenting & child care, popular psychology, inspirational/motivational volumes as well as a few medical/nutritional books); Mitchell Waters (literary and commercial fiction and nonfiction, including mystery, history, biography, memoir, young adult, cookbooks, self-help and popular culture); Monika Woods.

REPRESENTS Nonfiction, novels. **Considers these fiction areas:** fantasy, horror, humor, juvenile, literary, mainstream, middle grade, mystery, paranormal, picture books, religious, romance, spiritual, sports, suspense, thriller, women's, young adult.

HOW TO CONTACT Please refer to the "Agents" page on the website for each agent's submission guidelines. Accepts simultaneous submissions. Responds in 3 weeks to queries; 5 weeks to mss. Obtains most new clients through recommendations from others, solicitations, conferences.

TERMS Agent receives 15% commission on domestic sales; 20% on foreign sales. Offers written contract. 75-day notice must be given to terminate contract. Charges for some postage (overseas, etc.).

RECENT SALES This agency prefers not to share information on specific sales.

MARIE BROWN ASSOCIATES, INC.

412 W. 154th St., New York NY 10032. (212)939-9725 for Marie Brown, (678)515-7907 for Janell Walden Agyeman. **Fax:** (212)939-9728. **E-mail:** info@janellwaldenagyeman.com. **Website:** www.janellwaldenagyeman.com. **Contact:** Marie Brown, Janell Walden Agyeman. Estab. 1984. Author's Guild, Independent Book Publishers Association, SCBWI

MEMBER AGENTS Marie Brown, Janell Walden Agyeman (middle-grade, young adult, and new adult fiction featuring multicultural protagonists in contemporary or historical settings; narrative nonfiction that illuminates the experiences of people of color or enlightened responses to the human journey).

REPRESENTS Nonfiction, novels, juvenile books. **Considers these fiction areas:** contemporary issues, ethnic, hi-lo, historical, juvenile, literary, mainstream, middle grade, multicultural, new adult, paranormal, picture books, supernatural, urban fantasy, women's, young adult.

> Ms. Brown's special interests include sports and performing arts. Ms. Agyeman's special interests include spirituality and cultural issues. Actively seeking debut fiction for adults (literary and popular) and for young readers. Ms. Brown does not want to receive genre fiction or poetry. Ms. Agyeman does not want to receive true crime, high fantasy, thrillers, or poetry.

HOW TO CONTACT "We are closed to unsolicited submissions from time to time; check the website to confirm our review status before querying. Marie Brown will consider hard copy materials submitted according to her guidelines (on website). Janell Agyeman welcomes e-mailed queries when she is open to unsolicited submissions. Check the website to know her current submissions review policy before sending queries." Responds within 3 months. Primarily obtains new clients through recommendations and conferences.

TERMS Agent receives 15% commission on domestic sales. Agent receives 20% commission on foreign sales. Offers written contract.

RECENT SALES *The Man in 3B* by Carl Weber, *Pushout* by Monique Morris, *Born Bright* by C. Nicole Mason, *Degree Zombie Zone* by Patrik Henry Bass, *Harlem Renaissance Party* by Faith Ringgold, *Stella by Starlight* by Sharon M. Draper.

TIPS "Have your project professionally edited and/or critiqued before submitting; show us your very best work."

BROWNE & MILLER LITERARY ASSOCIATES

52 Village Place, Hinsdale IL 60521. (312)922-3063. **E-mail:** mail@browneandmiller.com. **Website:** www.browneandmiller.com. **Contact:** Danielle Egan-Miller, president. Estab. 1971. Member of AAR. RWA, MWA, Authors Guild

> Prior to joining the agency as Jane Jordan Browne's partner, Danielle Egan-Miller worked as an editor.

REPRESENTS Nonfiction, novels. **Considers these fiction areas:** commercial, crime, detective, erotica, family saga, historical, inspirational, literary, mainstream, mystery, police, religious, romance, suspense, thriller, women's, Christian/inspirational fiction.

> Browne & Miller is most interested in literary and commercial fiction, women's fiction, women's historical fiction, literary-leaning crime fiction, dark suspense/domestic suspense, romance of most subgenres including time travel, Christian/inspirational fiction by established authors, and a wide range of platform-driven nonfiction by nationally-recognized author-experts. Does not want to receive young adult or middle-grade. "We do not represent picture books, horror, science fiction or fantasy, short stories, poetry, original screenplays, articles, or software."

HOW TO CONTACT Query via e-mail only; no attachments. Do not send unsolicited mss. Accepts simultaneous submissions.

ANDREA BROWN LITERARY AGENCY, INC.

E-mail: andrea@andreabrownlit.com; caryn@andreabrownlit.com; lauraqueries@gmail.com; jennifer@andreabrownlit.com; kelly@andreabrownlit.com; jennL@andreabrownlit.com; jamie@andreabrownlit.com; jmatt@andreabrownlit.com; kathleen@andreabrownlit.com; lara@andreabrownlit.com; soloway@andreabrownlit.com. **Website:** www.andreabrownlit.com. Member of AAR.

> Prior to opening her agency, Ms. Brown served as an editorial assistant at Random House and Dell Publishing and as an editor with Knopf.

MEMBER AGENTS Andrea Brown (president); Laura Rennert (executive agent); Caryn Wiseman (senior agent); Jennifer Laughran (senior agent); Jennifer Rofé (senior agent); Kelly Sonnack (agent); Jamie Weiss Chilton (agent); Jennifer Mattson (agent); Kathleen Rushall (agent); Lara Perkins (associate agent, digital manager); Jennifer March Soloway (assistant agent).

REPRESENTS Nonfiction, fiction, juvenile books. **Considers these fiction areas:** juvenile, picture books, young adult, middle-grade, all juvenile genres..

☛ Specializes in all kinds of children's books—illustrators and authors. 98% juvenile books. Considers: nonfiction, fiction, picture books, young adult.

HOW TO CONTACT For picture books, submit a query letter and complete ms in the body of the e-mail. For fiction, submit a query letter and the first 10 pages in the body of the e-mail. For nonfiction, submit proposal, first 10 pages in the body of the e-mail. Illustrators: submit a query letter and 2-3 illustration samples (in jpeg format), link to online portfolio, and text of picture book, if applicable. "We only accept queries via e-mail. No attachments, with the exception of jpeg illustrations from illustrators." Visit the agents' bios on our website and choose only *1* agent to whom you will submit your e-query. Send a short e-mail query letter to that agent with "QUERY" in the subject field. Accepts simultaneous submissions. "If we are interested in your work, we will certainly follow up by e-mail or by phone. However, if you haven't heard from us within 6 to 8 weeks, please assume that we are passing on your project." Obtains most new clients through referrals from editors, clients and agents. Check website for guidelines and information.

TERMS Agent receives 15% commission on domestic sales. Agent receives 25% commission on foreign sales. Offers written contract.

RECENT SALES *The Scorpio Races* by Maggie Stiefvater (Scholastic), *The Future of Us* by Jay Asher, *Triangles* by Ellen Hopkins (Atria), *Crank* by Ellen Hopkins (McElderry/S&S), *Burned* by Ellen Hopkins (McElderry/S&S), *Impulse* by Ellen Hopkins (McElderry/S&S), *Glass* by Ellen Hopkins (McElderry/S&S), *Tricks* by Ellen Hopkins (McElderry/S&S), *Fallout* by Ellen Hopkins (McElderry/S&S), *Perfect* by Ellen Hopkins (McElderry/S&S), *The Strange Case of Origami Yoda* by Tom Angleberger (Amulet/Abrams), *Darth Paper Strikes Back* by Tom Angleberger (Amulet/Abrams), *Becoming Chloe* by Catherine Ryan Hyde (Knopf), Sasha Cohen autobiography (HarperCollins), *The Five Ancestors* by Jeff Stone (Random House), *Thirteen Reasons Why* by Jay Asher (Penguin), *Identical* by Ellen Hopkins (S&S).

WRITERS CONFERENCES SCBWI, Asilomar; Maui Writers' Conference, Southwest Writers' Conference, San Diego State University Writers' Conference, Big Sur Children's Writing Workshop, William Saroyan Writers' Conference, Columbus Writers' Conference, Willamette Writers' Conference, La Jolla Writers' Conference, San Francisco Writers' Conference, Hilton Head Writers' Conference, Pacific Northwest Conference, Pikes Peak Conference.

SHEREE BYKOFSKY ASSOCIATES, INC.

P.O. Box 706, Brigantine NJ 08203. **E-mail:** shereebee@aol.com. **Website:** www.shereebee.com. **Contact:** Sheree Bykofsky. Estab. 1991. Member of AAR. Author's Guild, Atlantic City Chamber of Commerce, PRC Council Represents 1,000+ clients.

Ō Prior to opening her agency, Sheree Bykofsky served as executive editor of the Stonesong Press and managing editor of Chiron Press. Janet Rosen worked as associate book editor at *Glamour* and as the senior books and fiction editor at *Woman* before turning to agenting at Sheree Bykofsky Associates, where she represents a range of nonfiction and a limited amount of fiction.

MEMBER AGENTS Sheree Bykofsky, Janet Rosen.

REPRESENTS Nonfiction, novels, scholarly books. **Considers these fiction areas:** commercial, contemporary issues, crime, detective, literary, mainstream, mystery, women's.

☛ This agency is seeking nonfiction, both prescriptive and narrative, and some fiction. Prescriptive nonfiction: primarily health and business. Narrative nonfiction: pop culture, biography, history, popular and social science, language, music, cities, medicine, fashion, military, and espionage. Fiction: women's commercial fiction (with a literary quality) and mysteries. Does not want to receive poetry, children's, screenplays, westerns, science fiction, or horror.

HOW TO CONTACT Query via e-mail to submitbee@aol.com. "We only accept e-queries. We respond only to those queries in which we are interested. No attachments, snail mail, or phone calls, please. We do not open attachments." Fiction: one-page query, one-page synopsis, and first three pages of ms in body of the e-mail. Nonfiction: one-page query in the body of the e-mail. Accepts simultaneous submissions. Responds in 1 month to requested mss. Obtains most new clients through referrals but still reads all submissions closely.

TERMS Agent receives 15% commission on domestic sales. Agent receives 15% commission on foreign sales, plus international co-agent receives another 10%. Offers written contract, binding for 1 year. Charges for international postage.

RECENT SALES *Virtual Billions: The Genius, the Drug Lord, and the Ivy League Twins Behind the Rise of Bitcoin* by Eric Geissinger (Prometheus Books), *Thank You, Teacher: Grateful Students Tell the Stories of the Teachers Who Changed Their Lives* by Holly and Bruce Holbert (New World Library), *The Type B Manager: Leading Successfully in a Type A World* by Victor Lipman (Prentice Hall), *Let the Story Do the Work: The Art of Storytelling for Business Success* by Esther Choy (Amacom), *Convicting Avery: The Bizarre Laws and Broken System Behind "Making a Murderer"* by Michael D. Cicchini (Prometheus Books), *The Curious Case of Kiryas Joel: The Rise of a Village Theocracy and the Battle to Defend the Separation of Church and State* by Louis Grumet with John Caher (Chicago Review Press).

WRITERS CONFERENCES Truckee Meadow Community College Keynote, ASJA Writers Conference, Asilomar, Florida Suncoast Writers' Conference, Whidbey Island Writers' Conference, Florida First Coast Writers' Festival, Agents and Editors Conference, Columbus Writers' Conference, Southwest Writers' Conference, Willamette Writers' Conference, Dorothy Canfield Fisher Conference, Maui Writers' Conference, Pacific Northwest Writers' Conference, IWWG.

KIMBERLEY CAMERON & ASSOCIATES

1550 Tiburon Blvd., #704, Tiburon CA 94920. (415)789-9191. **Website:** www.kimberleycameron. com. **Contact:** Kimberley Cameron. Member of AAR. Signatory of WGA.

○ Kimberley Cameron & Associates (formerly The Reece Halsey Agency) has had an illustrious client list of established writers, including Aldous Huxley, Upton Sinclair, William Faulkner, and Henry Miller.

MEMBER AGENTS Kimberley Cameron; Elizabeth Kracht (temporarily closed to submissions); Amy Cloughley (literary and upmarket fiction, women's,

historical, narrative nonfiction, travel or adventure memoir); Mary C. Moore (fantasy, science fiction, upmarket "book club," genre romance, thrillers with female protagonists, and stories from marginalized voices); Lisa Abellera (currently closed to unsolicited submissions); Douglas Lee, douglas@kimberlycameron.com (only accepting submissions via conference and in-person meetings in the Bay Area).

REPRESENTS **Considers these fiction areas:** commercial, fantasy, historical, literary, mystery, romance, science fiction, thriller, women's, young adult, LGBTQ.

☛ "We are looking for a unique and heartfelt voice that conveys a universal truth."

HOW TO CONTACT Prefers queries via site. Only query 1 agent at a time. For fiction, fill out the correct submissions form for the individual agent and attach the first 50 pages and a synopsis (if requested) as a Word doc or PDF. For nonfiction, fill out the correct submission form of the individual agent and attach a full book proposal and sample chapters (includes the first chapter and no more than 50 pages) as a Word doc or PDF. Accepts simultaneous submissions. Obtains new clients through recommendations from others, solicitations.

MARIA CARVAINIS AGENCY, INC.

Rockefeller Center, 1270 Avenue of the Americas, Suite 2915, New York NY 10020. (212)245-6365. **Fax:** (212)245-7196. **E-mail:** mca@mariacarvainisagency.com. **E-mail:** mca@mariacarvainisagency.com. **Website:** www.mariacarvainisagency.com. Estab. 1977. Member of AAR. Authors Guild, Women's Media Group, ABA, MWA, RWA Represents 75 clients.

○ Prior to opening her agency, Ms. Carvainis spent more than 10 years in the publishing industry as a senior editor with Macmillan, Basic Books, Avon Books, and Crown Publishers. Ms. Carvainis has served as a member of the AAR Board of Directors and AAR Treasurer, as well as serving as chair of the AAR Contracts Committee. She presently serves on the AAR Royalty Committee.

MEMBER AGENTS Maria Carvainis, president/literary agent; Elizabeth Copps, associate agent.

REPRESENTS Nonfiction, novels. **Considers these fiction areas:** action, adventure, commercial, contemporary issues, crime, family saga, historical, horror, humor, juvenile, literary, mainstream, middle grade, multicultural, mystery, romance, suspense, thriller, women's, young adult.

☞ The agency does not represent screenplays, children's picture books, science fiction, or poetry.

HOW TO CONTACT If you would like to query the agency, please send a query letter, a synopsis of the work, first 5-10 pages, and note of any writing credentials. Please e-mail queries to mca@mariacarvainisagency.com. All attachments must be either Word documents or PDF files. The agency also accepts queries by mail to Maria Carvainis Agency, Inc., Attention: Query Department. If you want the materials returned to you, please enclose a SASE. Otherwise, please be sure to include your e-mail address. There is no reading fee. Accepts simultaneous submissions. Responds to queries within 1 month. Obtains most new clients through recommendations from others, conferences, query letters.

TERMS Agent receives 15% commission on domestic sales. Agent receives 20% commission on foreign sales. Offers written contract. Charges clients for foreign postage.

RECENT SALES *Someone to Love* by Mary Balogh (Signet), *Sting* by Sandra Brown (Grand Central), *Enraptured* by Candace Camp (Pocket Books), *If You Only Knew* by Kristan Higgins (HQN Books), *Palindrome* by E.Z. Rinsky (Witness Impulse), *Almost Paradise* by Corabel Shofner (Farrar Straus & Giroux Books for Young Readers).

CHALBERG & SUSSMAN

115 W. 29th St., Third Floor, New York NY 10001. (917)261-7550. **Website:** www.chalbergsussman.com. Member of AAR. Signatory of WGA.

◑ Prior to her current position, Ms. Chalberg held a variety of editorial positions, and was an agent with The Susan Golomb Literary Agency. Ms. Sussman was an agent with Zachary Shuster Harmsworth. Ms. James was with The Aaron Priest Literary Agency.

MEMBER AGENTS Terra Chalberg; Rachel Sussman (narrative journalism, memoir, psychology, history, humor, pop culture, literary fiction); Nicole James (plot-driven fiction, psychological suspense, uplifting female-driven memoir, upmarket self-help, and lifestyle books); Lana Popovic (young adult, middle grade, contemporary realism, speculative fiction, fantasy, horror, sophisticated erotica, romance, select nonfiction, international stories).

REPRESENTS Nonfiction, fiction, novels. **Considers these fiction areas:** erotica, fantasy, horror, literary, middle grade, romance, science fiction, suspense, young adult, contemporary realism, speculative fiction.

HOW TO CONTACT To query by e-mail, please contact one of the following: terra@chalbergsussman.com, rachel@chalbergsussman.com, nicole@chalbergsussman.com, lana@chalbergsussman.com. To query by regular mail, please address your letter to 1 agent and include SASE. Accepts simultaneous submissions.

RECENT SALES The agents' sales and clients are listed on their website.

CHASE LITERARY AGENCY

242 W. 38th St., 2nd Floor, New York NY 10018. (212)477-5100. **E-mail:** farley@chaseliterary.com. **Website:** www.chaseliterary.com. **Contact:** Farley Chase.

MEMBER AGENTS Farley Chase.

REPRESENTS Nonfiction, fiction, novels. **Considers these fiction areas:** commercial, historical, literary, mystery.

☞ No romance, science fiction, or young adult.

HOW TO CONTACT E-query farley@chaseliterary.com. If submitting fiction, please include the first few pages of the ms with the query. "I do not response to queries not addressed to me by name. I'm keenly interested in both fiction and nonfiction. In fiction, I'm looking for both literary or commercial projects in either contemporary or historical settings. I'm open to anything with a strong sense of place, voice, and, especially plot. I don't handle science fiction, romance, supernatural or young adult." Accepts simultaneous submissions.

RECENT SALES *Devil in the Grove: Thurgood Marshall, the Groveland Boys, and the Dawn of a New America* by Gilbert King (Harper); *Heads in Beds: A Reckless Memoir of Hotels, Hustles, and So-Called Hospitality* by Jacob Tomsky (Doubleday); *And Every Day Was Overcast* by Paul Kwiatowski (Black Balloon); *The Badlands Saloon* by Jonathan Twingley (Scribner).

CHENEY ASSOCIATES, LLC

78 Fifth Ave., 3rd Floor, New York NY 10011. (212)277-8007. **Fax:** (212)614-0728. **E-mail:** submissions@cheneyliterary.com. **Website:** www.cheneyliterary.com. **Contact:** Elyse Cheney; Adam Eaglin; Alex Jacobs; Alice Whitwham.

◑ Prior to her current position, Ms. Cheney was an agent with Sanford J. Greenburger Associates.

MEMBER AGENTS Elyse Cheney; Adam Eaglin (literary fiction and nonfiction, including history, politics, current events, narrative reportage, biography, memoir, and popular science); Alexander Jacobs (narrative nonfiction [particularly in the areas of history, science, politics, and culture], literary fiction, crime, and memoir); Alice Whitwham (literary and commercial fiction, as well as voice-driven narrative nonfiction, cultural criticism, and journalism).

REPRESENTS Nonfiction, novels. **Considers these fiction areas:** commercial, crime, family saga, historical, literary, short story collections, suspense, women's.

HOW TO CONTACT Query by e-mail or snail mail. For a snail mail responses, include a SASE. Include up to 3 chapters of sample material. Do not query more than 1 agent. Accepts simultaneous submissions.

RECENT SALES *The Love Affairs of Nathaniel P.* by Adelle Waldman (Henry Holt & Co.); *This Town* by Mark Leibovich (Blue Rider Press); *Thunder & Lightning* by Lauren Redniss (Random House).

CK WEBBER ASSOCIATES

E-mail: carlie@ckwebber.com. **Website:** ckwebber. com. **Contact:** Carlisle Webber. Member of AAR. Signatory of WGA.

- Ms. Webber's professional publishing experience includes an internship at Writers House and work with the Roger Williams Agency and the Jane Rotrosen Agency. She is also a graduate of the Columbia Publishing Course and holds a Professional Certificate in Editing from UC Berkeley.

REPRESENTS Novels, juvenile books. **Considers these fiction areas:** action, adventure, commercial, contemporary issues, crime, detective, family saga, fantasy, feminist, horror, literary, mainstream, middle grade, mystery, new adult, romance, science fiction, suspense, thriller, westerns, women's, young adult.

- "We are currently not accepting nonfiction (including memoir), picture books, easy readers, early chapter books, poetry, scripts, novellas, or short story collections."

HOW TO CONTACT Accepts queries via e-mail only. To submit your work for consideration, please send a query letter, synopsis, and the first 30 pages or 3 chapters of your work, whichever is more, to carlie@ ckwebber.com and put the word "query" in the subject line of your e-mail. Please include your materials in the body of your e-mail. Blank e-mails that include an attachment will be deleted unread. Accepts simultaneous submissions.

WM CLARK ASSOCIATES

186 Fifth Ave., Second Floor, New York NY 10010. (212)675-2784. **E-mail:** general@wmclark.com. **Website:** www.wmclark.com. **Contact:** William Clark. Estab. 1997. Member of AAR.

- Prior to opening WCA, Mr. Clark was an agent at the William Morris Agency.

REPRESENTS Nonfiction, novels. **Considers these fiction areas:** contemporary issues, ethnic, historical, literary, mainstream, young adult.

- "It is advised that before querying you become familiar with the kinds of books we handle by browsing our Book List, which is available on our website."

HOW TO CONTACT Accepts queries via online query form only. "We will endeavor to respond as soon as possible as to whether or not we'd like to see a proposal or sample chapters from your ms." Responds in 1-2 months to queries.

TERMS Agent receives 15% commission on domestic sales; 20% commission on foreign sales. Offers written contract.

FRANCES COLLIN, LITERARY AGENT

P.O. Box 33, Wayne PA 19087-0033. **E-mail:** queries@ francescollin.com. **Website:** www.francescollin.com. Estab. 1948. Member of AAR. Represents 50 clients.

- Sarah Yake has been with the agency since 2005 and handles foreign and subrights as well as her own client list. She holds an M.A. in English Literature and has been a sales rep for a major publisher and a bookstore manager. She currently teaches in the Rosemont College Graduate Publishing Program.

MEMBER AGENTS Frances Collin; Sarah Yake.

REPRESENTS Nonfiction, fiction, novels. **Considers these fiction areas:** adventure, commercial, experimental, feminist, historical, juvenile, literary, middle grade, multicultural, science fiction, women's, young adult.

- Actively seeking authors who are invested in their unique visions and who want to set trends not chase them. "I'd like to think that my authors are unplagiarizable by virtue of their distinct voices and styles." Does not want previously self-published work. Query with new mss only, please.

HOW TO CONTACT "We ask that writers send a traditional query e-mail describing the project and copy and paste the first 5 pages of the ms into the body of the e-mail. We look forward to hearing from you at queries@francescollin.com. Please send queries to that e-mail address. Any queries sent to another e-mail address within the agency will be deleted unread." Accepts simultaneous submissions. Responds in 1-3 weeks for initial queries, longer for full mss.

◎ JILL CORCORAN LITERARY AGENCY

2150 Park Place, Suite 100, El Segundo CA 90245. **Website:** jillcorcoranliteraryagency.com. **Contact:** Jill Corcoran. Estab. 2013.

MEMBER AGENTS Jill Corcoran, Adah Nuchi, Silvia Arienti, Eve Porinchak.

REPRESENTS Nonfiction, novels, juvenile books. **Considers these fiction areas:** commercial, crime, juvenile, middle grade, picture books, romance, young adult.

☞ Actively seeking picture books, middle-grade, young adult, crime novels, psyhcological suspense, and true crime. Does not want to receive screenplays, chapbooks, or poetry.

HOW TO CONTACT Please go online to the agency submissions page and submit to the agent you feel would best represent your work. Accepts simultaneous submissions.

CORVISIERO LITERARY AGENCY

275 Madison Ave., at 40th, 14th Floor, New York NY 10016. **E-mail:** query@corvisieroagency.com. **Website:** www.corvisieroagency.com. **Contact:** Marisa A. Corvisiero, senior agent and literary attorney. Member of AAR. Signatory of WGA.

MEMBER AGENTS Marisa A. Corvisiero, senior agent and literary attorney (contemporary romance, thrillers, adventure, paranormal, urban fantasy, science fiction, MG, YA, picture books, Christmas themes, time travel, space science fiction, nonfiction, self-help, science business); Saritza Hernandez, senior agent (all kinds of romance, GLBT, YA, erotica); Doreen Thistle (do not query); Cate Hart (YA, fantasy, magical realism, MG, mystery, fantasy, adventure, historical romance, LGBTQ, erotic, history, biography); Veronica Park (dark or edgy YA/NA, Commercial adult, adult romance and romantic suspense, and funny and/or current/controversial nonfiction); Vanessa Robins (New Adult, human, YA, thrillers, romance, sci-fi, sports-centric plots, memoirs, cultural/ethnic/sexuality, humor, medical narratives); Kelly Peterson (MG, fantasy, paranormal, sci-fi, YA, steampunk, historical, dystopian, sword and sorcery, romance, historical romance, adult, fantasy, romance); Justin Wells; Kaitlyn Johnson.

REPRESENTS Nonfiction, fiction, novels. **Considers these fiction areas:** adventure, erotica, fantasy, gay, historical, lesbian, middle grade, mystery, paranormal, picture books, romance, science fiction, suspense, thriller, urban fantasy, young adult, Magical realism, steampunk, dystopian, sword and sorcery.

HOW TO CONTACT Accepts submissions via e-mail only. Include 5 pages of complete and polished ms pasted into the body of an e-mail, and a 1-2 page synopsis. For nonfiction, include a proposal instead of the synopsis. Put "Query for [Agent]" in the e-mail subject line. Accepts simultaneous submissions.

CREATIVE BOOK SERVICES

111 W. 19th St., Sixth Floor, New York NY 10011. (212)226-1936. **E-mail:** bob.mecoy@gmail.com. **Contact:** Bob Mecoy, owner. Estab. 2001.

REPRESENTS Nonfiction, novels. **Considers these fiction areas:** action, adventure, cartoon, comic books, crime, detective, fantasy, literary, mainstream, mystery, new adult, romance, science fiction, sports, urban fantasy, war.

☞ Actively seeking fiction (literary, crime, science fiction/fantasy, romance), nonfiction (true crime, finance, adventure, memoir, literary), and graphic novels of all stripes.

HOW TO CONTACT Query with sample chapters and synopsis. Accepts simultaneous submissions.

CREATIVE MEDIA AGENCY, INC.

1745 Broadway, 17th Floor, New York NY 10019. (212)812-1494. **E-mail:** paige@cmalit.com. **Website:** www.cmalit.com. **Contact:** Paige Wheeler. Estab. 1997. Member of AAR. WMG, RWA, MWA, Authors Guild Represents about 30 clients.

◎ After starting out as an editor for Harlequin Books in NY and Euromoney Publications in London, Paige repped writers, producers and celebrities as an agent with Artists Agency, until she formed Creative Media Agency in 1997. In 2006, she co-created Folio Literary Management and grew that company for 8 years into a successful mid-sized agency. In 2014 she decided to once again pursue a boutique approach, and she relaunched CMA.

REPRESENTS Nonfiction, fiction, novels. **Considers these fiction areas:** commercial, crime, detective, historical, inspirational, mainstream, middle grade, mystery, new adult, romance, suspense, thriller, women's, young adult, general fiction.

☞ Fiction: All commercial and upscale (think book club) fiction, as well as women's fiction, romance (all types), mystery, thrillers, inspirational/Christian and psychological suspense. "I enjoy both historical fiction as well as contemporary fiction, so do keep that in mind. I seem to be especially drawn to a story if it has a high concept and a fresh, unique voice."

HOW TO CONTACT E-query. Write "query" in your e-mail subject line. For fiction, paste in the first 5 pages of the ms after the query. For nonfiction, paste in an extended author bio as well as the marketing section of your book proposal after the query. Accepts simultaneous submissions. Responds in 4-6 weeks.

D4EO LITERARY AGENCY

7 Indian Valley Rd., Weston CT 06883. (203)544-7180. **Fax:** (203)544-7160. **Website:** www.d4eoliteraryagency.com. **Contact:** Bob Diforio. Estab. 1990.

○ Prior to opening his agency, Mr. Diforio was a publisher.

MEMBER AGENTS Bob Diforio; Joyce Holland; Pam Howell; Quressa Robinson; Kelly Van Sant.

REPRESENTS Nonfiction, novels. **Considers these fiction areas:** adventure, detective, erotica, juvenile, literary, mainstream, middle grade, mystery, new adult, romance, sports, thriller, young adult.

HOW TO CONTACT Each of these agents has a different submission e-mail and different tastes regarding how they review material. See all on their individual agent pages on the agency website. Responds in 1 week to queries if interested. Obtains most new clients through recommendations from others.

TERMS Offers written contract, binding for 2 years; automatic renewal unless 60 days notice given prior to renewal date. Charges for photocopying and submission postage.

LAURA DAIL LITERARY AGENCY, INC.

350 Seventh Ave., Suite 2003, New York NY 10001. (212)239-7477. **E-mail:** ldail@ldlainc.com. **E-mail:** queries@ldlainc.com. **Website:** www.ldlainc.com. Member of AAR.

MEMBER AGENTS Laura Dail; Tamar Rydzinski; Elana Roth Parker.

REPRESENTS Nonfiction, fiction, novels, juvenile books. **Considers these fiction areas:** commercial, crime, detective, fantasy, feminist, historical, juvenile, mainstream, middle grade, multicultural, mystery, thriller, women's, young adult.

☞ Specializes in women's fiction, literary fiction, young adult fiction, as well as both practical and idea-driven nonfiction. "Tamar is interested in everything else that is well-written and has great characters, including graphic novels. Due to the volume of queries and mss received, we apologize for not answering every e-mail and letter. None of us handles children's picture books or chapter books. No New Age. We do not handle screenplays or poetry."

HOW TO CONTACT "If you would like, you may include a synopsis and no more than 10 pages. If you are mailing your query, please be sure to include a self-addressed, stamped envelope; without it, you may not hear back from us. To save money, time and trees, we prefer queries by e-mail to queries@ldlainc.com. We get a lot of spam and are wary of computer viruses, so please use the word 'Query' in the subject line and include your detailed materials in the body of your message, not as an attachment." Accepts simultaneous submissions. Responds in 2-4 weeks.

DARHANSOFF & VERRILL LITERARY AGENTS

133 W. 72nd St., Room 304, New York NY 10023. (917)305-1300. **E-mail:** submissions@dvagency.com. **Website:** www.dvagency.com. Member of AAR.

MEMBER AGENTS Liz Darhansoff; Chuck Verrill; Michele Mortimer; Eric Amling.

REPRESENTS Nonfiction, novels. **Considers these fiction areas:** literary, middle grade, suspense, young adult.

HOW TO CONTACT Send queries via e-mail. Accepts simultaneous submissions.

RECENT SALES A full list of clients is available on their website.

LIZA DAWSON ASSOCIATES

350 Seventh Ave., Suite 2003, New York NY 10001. (212)465-9071. **E-mail:** querycaitie@lizadawsonassociates.com. **Website:** www.lizadawsonassociates.com. **Contact:** Caitie Flum. Member of AAR. MWA, Women's Media Group Represents 50+ clients.

○ Prior to becoming an agent, Ms. Dawson was an editor for 20 years, spending 11 years at William Morrow as vice president and 2 years at Putnam as executive editor. Ms. Blasdell was a senior editor at HarperCollins and Avon. Ms Johnson-Blalock was an assistant at Trident

Media Group. Ms. Flum was the coordinator for the Children's Book of the Month club.

MEMBER AGENTS Liza Dawson, queryliza@lizadawsonassociates.com (plot-driven literary and popular fiction, historical, thrillers, suspense, history, psychology [both popular and clinical], politics, narrative nonfiction, and memoirs); Caitlin Blasdell, querycaitlin@lizadawsonassociates.com (science fiction, fantasy [both adult and young adult], parenting, business, thrillers, and women's fiction; Hannah Bowman, queryhannah@lizadawsonassociates.com (commercial fiction [especially science fiction and fantasy, young adult] and nonfiction in the areas of mathematics, science, and spirituality); Jennifer Johnson-Blalock, queryjennifer@lizadawsonassociates.com (nonfiction, particularly current events, social sciences, women's issues, law, business, history, the arts and pop culture, lifestyle, sports, and food; commercial and upmarket fiction, especially thrillers/mysteries, women's fiction, contemporary romance, young adult, and middle-grade); Caitie Flum, querycaitie@lizadawsonassociates.com (commercial fiction, especially historical, women's fiction, mysteries, crossover fantasy, young adult, and middle-grade; nonfiction in the areas of theater, current affairs, and pop culture).

REPRESENTS Nonfiction, novels. **Considers these fiction areas:** action, adventure, commercial, contemporary issues, crime, detective, ethnic, family saga, fantasy, feminist, gay, historical, horror, humor, juvenile, lesbian, mainstream, middle grade, multicultural, mystery, new adult, police, romance, science fiction, supernatural, suspense, thriller, urban fantasy, women's, young adult.

☛ This agency specializes in readable literary fiction, thrillers, mainstream historicals, women's fiction, young adult, middle-grade, academics, historians, journalists, and psychology.

HOW TO CONTACT Query by e-mail only. No phone calls. Each of these agents has their own specific submission requirements, which you can find online at the agency's website. Obtains most new clients through recommendations from others, conferences, and queries.

TERMS Agent receives 15% commission on domestic sales. Agent receives 20% commission on foreign sales. Offers written contract.

THE JENNIFER DE CHIARA LITERARY AGENCY

299 Park Ave., 6th Floor, New York NY 10171. (212)739-0803. **E-mail:** jenndec@aol.com. **Website:** www.jdlit.com. **Contact:** Jennifer De Chiara. Estab. 2001.

MEMBER AGENTS Jennifer De Chiara, jenndec@aol.com (fiction interests include literary, commercial, women's fiction [no bodice-rippers, please], chick-lit, mystery, suspense, thrillers, funny/quirky picture books, middle-grade, and young adult; nonfiction interests include celebrity memoirs and biographies, LGBT, memoirs, books about the arts and performing arts, behind-the-scenes-type books, and books about popular culture); Stephen Fraser, fraserstephena@gmail.com (one-of-a-kind picture books; strong chapter book series; whimsical, dramatic, or humorous middle-grade; dramatic or high-concept young adult; powerful and unusual nonfiction on a broad range of topics; Marie Lamba, marie.jdlit@gmail.com (young adult and middle-grade fiction, along with general and women's fiction and some memoir; interested in established illustrators and picture book authors); Roseanne Wells, queryroseanne@gmail.com (literary fiction, young adult, middle-grade, narrative nonfiction, select memoir, science (popular or trade, not academic), history, religion (not inspirational), travel, humor, food/cooking, and similar subjects); Victoria Selvaggio, vselvaggio@windstream.net (board books, picture books, chapter books, middle-grade, young adult, new adult, and adult; interested in nonfiction and fiction in all genres); Damian McNicholl, damianmcnichollvarney@gmail.com (accessible literary, historical [except naval, World War II, and romance], legal thrillers, offbeat/quirky, memoir, narrative nonfiction [especially biography, investigative journalism, cultural, legal, and LGBT]); Alexandra Weiss, alexweiss.jdlit@gmail.com (voice-driven young adult stories, especially in contemporary, science fiction, and paranormal genres; quirky and fun middle-grade and children's books; magical realism and literary fiction).

REPRESENTS Nonfiction, novels, juvenile books. **Considers these fiction areas:** commercial, contemporary issues, crime, detective, ethnic, family saga, fantasy, feminist, gay, historical, horror, humor, inspirational, juvenile, lesbian, literary, mainstream, middle grade, multicultural, mystery, new adult, New

Age, paranormal, picture books, science fiction, suspense, thriller, urban fantasy, women's, young adult. **HOW TO CONTACT** Each agent has their own e-mail submission address and submission instructions; check the website for the current updates, as policies do change. Accepts simultaneous submissions. Obtains most new clients through recommendations from others, conferences, query letters.

TERMS Agent receives 15% commission on domestic sales. Offers written contract.

DEFIORE & COMPANY

47 E. 19th St., 3rd Floor, New York NY 10003. (212)925-7744. **Fax:** (212)925-9803. **E-mail:** info@ defliterary.com, submissions@defliterary.com. **Website:** www.defliterary.com. Member of AAR. Signatory of WGA.

○ Prior to becoming an agent, Mr. DeFiore was publisher of Villard Books (1997-1998), editor in chief of Hyperion (1992-1997), editorial director of Delacorte Press (1988-1992), and an editor at St. Martin's Press (1984-88).

MEMBER AGENTS Brian DeFiore (popular nonfiction, business, pop culture, parenting, commercial fiction); Laurie Abkemeier (memoir, parenting, business, how-to/self-help, popular science); Matthew Elblonk (young adult, popular culture, narrative nonfiction); Caryn Karmatz-Rudy (popular fiction, self-help, narrative nonfiction); Adam Schear (commercial fiction, humor, young adult, smart thrillers, historical fiction, quirky debut literary novels, popular science, politics, popular culture, current events); Meredith Kaffel Simonoff (smart upmarket women's fiction, literary fiction [especially debut], literary thrillers, narrative nonfiction, nonfiction about science and tech, sophisticated pop culture/humor books); Rebecca Strauss (literary and commercial fiction, women's fiction, urban fantasy, romance, mystery, young adult, memoir, pop culture, select nonfiction); Lisa Gallagher (fiction and nonfiction); Nicole Tourtelot (narrative and prescriptive nonfiction, food, lifestyle, wellness, pop culture, history, humor, memoir, select young adult and adult fiction); Ashely Collom (women's fiction, children's and young adult, psychological thrillers, memoir, politics, photography, cooking, narrative nonfiction, LGBT issues, feminism, occult); Miriam Altshuler (adult literary and commercial fiction, narrative nonfiction, middle-grade, young adult, memoir, narrative nonfiction, self-help, family sagas, historical novels); Reiko Davis (adult literary and upmarket fiction, narrative nonfiction, young adult, middle-grade, memoir).

REPRESENTS Nonfiction, novels, short story collections, juvenile books, poetry books. **Considers these fiction areas:** comic books, commercial, ethnic, feminist, gay, lesbian, literary, mainstream, middle grade, mystery, paranormal, picture books, poetry, romance, short story collections, suspense, thriller, urban fantasy, women's, young adult.

☛ "Please be advised that we are not considering dramatic projects at this time."

HOW TO CONTACT Query with SASE or e-mail to submissions@defliterary.com. "Please include the word 'query' in the subject line. All attachments will be deleted; please insert all text in the body of the e-mail. For more information about our agents, their individual interests, and their query guidelines, please visit our 'About Us' page on our website." Accepts simultaneous submissions. Obtains most new clients through recommendations from others.

TERMS Agent receives 15% commission on domestic sales. Agent receives 20% commission on foreign sales. Offers written contract; 10-day notice must be given to terminate contract. Charges clients for photocopying and overnight delivery (deducted only after a sale is made).

JOELLE DELBOURGO ASSOCIATES, INC.

101 Park St., Montclair NJ 07042. (973)773-0836. **Fax:** (973)783-6802. **E-mail:** joelle@delbourgo.com. **E-mail:** submissions@delbourgo.com. **Website:** www. delbourgo.com. Member of AAR. Represents more than 500 clients.

○ Prior to becoming an agent, Ms. Delbourgo was an editor and senior publishing executive at HarperCollins and Random House. She began her editorial career at Bantam Books where she discovered the Choose Your Own Adventure series. Joelle Delbourgo brings more than three decades of experience as an editor and agent. Jacqueline Flynn was Executive Editor at Amacom for more than 15 years.

MEMBER AGENTS Joelle Delbourgo; Jacqueline Flynn.

REPRESENTS Nonfiction, fiction, novels. **Considers these fiction areas:** adventure, commercial, contemporary issues, crime, detective, fantasy, feminist, juvenile, literary, mainstream, middle grade, military, mystery, new adult, New Age, romance, science fiction, thriller, urban fantasy, women's, young adult.

☞ "We are former publishers and editors with deep knowledge and an insider perspective. We have a reputation for individualized attention to clients, strategic management of authors' careers, and creating strong partnerships with publishers for our clients." Do not send scripts, picture books, poetry.

HOW TO CONTACT It's preferable if you submit via e-mail to a specific agent. Query 1 agent only. No attachments. Put the word "Query" in the subject line. "While we do our best to respond to each query, if you have not received a response in 60 days you may consider that a pass. Please do not send us copies of self-published books unless requested. Let us know if you are sending your query to us exclusively or if this is a multiple submission. For nonfiction, let us know if a proposal and sample chapters are available. If not, you should probably wait to send your query when you have a completed proposal. For fiction and memoir, embed the *first* 10 pages of ms into the e-mail after your query letter. Please no attachments. If we like your first pages, we may ask to see your synopsis and more ms. Please do not cold call us or make a follow-up call unless we call you." Accepts simultaneous submissions.

TERMS Agent receives 15% commission on domestic sales and 20% commission on foreign sales as well as television/film adaptation. Offers written contract. Charges clients for postage and photocopying.

RECENT SALES *Witness: Lessons from Elie Wiesel's Classroom, Ariel Burger* After Anatevka: A Sequel to Fiddler on the Roof, Alexandra Silber, *UnSelfie: The Habits of Empathy* by Dr. Michele Borba (Touchstone/Simon & Schuster), *The Prisoner* by Ben H. Winters (Mulholland/Little Brown), The Guardian Herd novels by Jennifer Lynn Alvarez.

WRITERS CONFERENCES Unicorn Conference, March 2017.

TIPS "Do your homework. Do not cold call. Read and follow submission guidelines before contacting us. Do not call to find out if we received your material. No e-mail queries. Treat agents with respect, as you would any other professional, such as a doctor, lawyer or financial advisor."

SANDRA DIJKSTRA LITERARY AGENCY

1155 Camino del Mar, PMB 515, Del Mar CA 92014. **E-mail:** elise@dijkstraagency.com. **E-mail:** queries@dijkstraagency.com. **Website:** www.dijkstraagency.com.

Member of AAR. Authors Guild, Organization of American Historians, RWA. Represents 100+ clients.

MEMBER AGENTS President: Sandra Dijkstra (adult only). Acquiring Associate agents: Elise Capron (adult only); Jill Marr (adult only); Thao Le (adult and YA); Roz Foster (adult and YA); Jessica Watterson (subgenres of adult and new adult romance, and women's fiction); Suzy Evans (adult and YA); Jennifer Kim (adult and YA).

REPRESENTS Nonfiction, fiction, novels, short story collections, juvenile books, scholarly books. **Considers these fiction areas:** commercial, contemporary issues, detective, family saga, fantasy, feminist, historical, horror, juvenile, literary, mainstream, middle grade, multicultural, mystery, new adult, romance, science fiction, short story collections, sports, suspense, thriller, urban fantasy, women's, young adult.

HOW TO CONTACT "Please see guidelines on our website, www.dijkstraagency.com. Please note that we only accept e-mail submissions. Due to the large number of unsolicited submissions we receive, we are only able to respond those submissions in which we are interested." Accepts simultaneous submissions. Responds to queries of interest within 6 weeks.

TERMS Works in conjunction with foreign and film agents. Agent receives 15% commission on domestic sales and 20% commission on foreign sales. Offers written contract. No reading fee.

TIPS "Remember that publishing is a business. Do your research and present your project in as professional a way as possible. Only submit your work when you are confident that it is polished and ready for prime-time. Make yourself a part of the active writing community by getting stories and articles published, networking with other writers, and getting a good sense of where your work fits in the market."

DONAGHY LITERARY GROUP

(647)527-4353. **E-mail:** stacey@donaghyliterary.com. **E-mail:** query@donaghyliterary.com. **Website:** www.donaghyliterary.com. **Contact:** Stacey Donaghy.

○ Prior to opening her agency, Ms Donaghy served as an agent at the Corvisiero Literary Agency. And before this she worked in training and education; acquiring and editing academic materials for publication and training. Ms. Noble interned for Jessica Sinsheimer of Sarah Jane Freymann Literary Agency. Ms.

Miller previously worked in children's publishing with Scholastic Canada and also interned with Bree Ogden during her time at the D4EO Agency. Ms. Ayers-Barnett is a former Associate Editor for Pocket Books, Acquisitions Editor for Re.ad Publishing, and a freelance book editor for New York Book Editors. Mr. Franks is a former bookseller and book club collector organizer for The Mysterious Bookshop in New York City, freelance editor for mysteriouspress. com and proofreader for Europa Editions.

MEMBER AGENTS Stacey Donaghy (romantic suspense, LGBTQ, thriller, mystery, contemporary romance, erotic romance and YA); Valerie Noble (historical, science fiction and fantasy [think Kristin Cashore and Suzanne Collins] for young adults and adults); Sue Miller (YA, urban fantasy, contemporary romance); Amanda Ayers Barnett (mystery/thrillers and middle-grade, young adult, new adult and women's fiction); Alex Franks (contemporary fiction, literary fiction, science fiction, espionage, thriller & mystery).

REPRESENTS Fiction. **Considers these fiction areas:** commercial, crime, detective, erotica, ethnic, family saga, fantasy, feminist, gay, historical, horror, juvenile, lesbian, literary, mainstream, middle grade, multicultural, mystery, new adult, paranormal, police, psychic, romance, science fiction, sports, supernatural, suspense, thriller, urban fantasy, women's, young adult.

HOW TO CONTACT Query via e-mail, no attachments. Visit agency website for "submission guidelines" and for "team" to view agent bios. Do not e-mail agents directly. Accepts simultaneous submissions. Responds in 6-8 weeks to queries. Responds within 8-12 weeks to mss. Time may vary during holidays and closures.

TERMS Agent receives 15% commission on domestic sales. Agent receives 20% commission on foreign sales. Offers written contract, 30-day notice must be given to terminate contract.

WRITERS CONFERENCES Romantic Times Booklovers Convention, Windsor International Writers Conference, OWC Ontario Writers Conference, SoCal Writers Conference, WD Toronto Writer's Workshop.

TIPS "Only submit to 1 DLG agent at a time, we work collaboratively and often share projects that may be better suited to another agent at the agency."

JIM DONOVAN LITERARY

5635 SMU Blvd., Suite 201, Dallas TX 75206. **E-mail:** jdliterary@sbcglobal.net. **Contact:** Melissa Shultz, agent. Estab. 1993. Represents 34 clients.

MEMBER AGENTS Jim Donovan (history—particularly American, military and Western; biography; sports; popular reference; popular culture; fiction—literary, thrillers and mystery); Melissa Shultz (all subjects listed above [like Jim], along with parenting and women's issues).

REPRESENTS Nonfiction, fiction, novels. **Considers these fiction areas:** action, adventure, commercial, crime, detective, frontier, historical, mainstream, multicultural, mystery, police, suspense, thriller, war, westerns.

☞ This agency specializes in commercial fiction and nonfiction. "Does not want to receive poetry, children's, sci-fi, fantasy, short stories, memoir, inspirational or anything else not listed above."

HOW TO CONTACT "For nonfiction, I need a well-thought-out query letter telling me about the book: What it does, how it does it, why it's needed now, why it's better or different than what's out there on the subject, and why the author is the perfect writer for it. For fiction, the novel has to be finished, of course; a short (2- to 5-page) synopsis—not a teaser, but a summary of all the action, from first page to last—and the first 30-50 pages is enough. This material should be polished to as close to perfection as possible." Accepts simultaneous submissions. Responds in 2 weeks to queries; 1 month to mss. Obtains most new clients through recommendations from others.

TERMS Agent receives 15% commission on domestic sales. Agent receives 20% commission on foreign sales. Offers written contract, binding for 1 year; 30-day notice must be given to terminate contract. This agency charges for things such as overnight delivery and ms copying. Charges are discussed beforehand.

RECENT SALES *The Road to Jonestown* by Jeff Guinn (S&S), *The Earth Is All That Lasts* by Mark Gardner (HarperCollins), *As Good as Dead* by Stephen Moore (NAL), *James Monroe* by Tim McGrath (NAL), *The Greatest Fury* by William C. Davis (NAL), *The Hamilton Affair* by Elizabeth Cobbs (Arcade), *Resurrection Pass* by Kurt Anderson (Kensington).

TIPS "Get published in short form—magazine reviews, journals, etc.—first. This will increase your credibility considerably, and make it much easier to sell a full-length book."

DUNHAM LITERARY, INC.

110 William St., Suite 2202, New York NY 10038. (212)929-0994. **E-mail:** query@dunhamlit.com. **Website:** www.dunhamlit.com. **Contact:** Jennie Dunham. Estab. 2000. Member of AAR. SCBWI Represents 50 clients.

○ Prior to opening her agency, Ms. Dunham worked as a literary agent for Russell & Volkening. The Rhoda Weyr Agency is now a division of Dunham Literary, Inc.

MEMBER AGENTS Jennie Dunham, Bridget Smith.
REPRESENTS Nonfiction, fiction, novels, short story collections, juvenile books. **Considers these fiction areas:** family saga, fantasy, gay, historical, humor, juvenile, literary, mainstream, middle grade, multicultural, mystery, new adult, picture books, science fiction, short story collections, sports, urban fantasy, women's, young adult.

➣ Westerns, horror, genre romance, poetry.

HOW TO CONTACT E-mail queries preferred, with all materials pasted in the body of the e-mail. Attachments will not be opened. Paper queries are also accepted. Please include a SASE for response and return of materials. If submitting to Bridget Smith, please include the first 5 pages with the query. Accepts simultaneous submissions. Responds in 4 weeks to queries; 2 months to mss. Obtains most new clients through recommendations from others, solicitations.

TERMS Agent receives 15% commission on domestic sales. Agent receives 20% commission on foreign sales.

RECENT SALES Sales include *The Bad Kitty Series* by Nick Bruel (Macmillan), *The Christmas Story* by Robert Sabuda (Simon & Schuster), *The Gollywhopper Games* and Sequels by Jody Feldman (HarperCollins), *First & Then* by Emma Mills (Macmillan), *Learning Not To Drown* by Anna Shinoda (Simon & Schuster), *Gangsterland* by Tod Goldberg (Counterpoint), *A Shadow All of Light* by Fred Chappell (Tor), *Forward From Here* by Reeve Lindbergh (Simon & Schuster).

DUNOW, CARLSON, & LERNER AGENCY

27 W. 20th St., Suite 1107, New York NY 10011. (212)645-7606. **E-mail:** mail@dclagency.com. **Website:** www.dclagency.com. Member of AAR.

MEMBER AGENTS Jennifer Carlson (narrative nonfiction writers and journalists covering current events and ideas and cultural history, as well as literary and upmarket commercial novelists); Henry Dunow (quality fiction–literary, historical, strongly written commercial–and with voice-driven nonfiction across a range of areas–narrative history, biography, memoir, current affairs, cultural trends and criticism, science, sports); Erin Hosier (nonfiction: popular culture, music, sociology and memoir); Betsy Lerner (nonfiction writers in the areas of psychology, history, cultural studies, biography, current events, business; fiction: literary, dark, funny, voice driven); Yishai Seidman (broad range of fiction: literary, postmodern, and thrillers; nonfiction: sports, music, and pop culture); Amy Hughes (nonfiction in the areas of history, cultural studies, memoir, current events, wellness, health, food, pop culture, and biography; also literary fiction); Eleanor Jackson (literary, commercial, memoir, art, food, science and history); Julia Kenny (fiction—adult, middle grade and YA—and is especially interested in dark, literary thrillers and suspense); Edward Necarsulmer IV (strong new voices in teen & middle grade as well as picture books); Stacia Decker; Arielle Datz (fiction—adult, YA, or middle-grade—literary and commercial, nonfiction—essays, unconventional memoir, pop culture, and sociology).

REPRESENTS Nonfiction, fiction, novels, short story collections. **Considers these fiction areas:** commercial, literary, mainstream, middle grade, mystery, picture books, thriller, young adult.

HOW TO CONTACT Query via snail mail with SASE, or by e-mail. E-mail preferred, paste 10 sample pages below query letter. No attachments. Will respond only if interested. Accepts simultaneous submissions. Responds in 4-6 weeks if interested.

RECENT SALES A full list of agency clients is on the website.

DYSTEL, GODERICH & BOURRET LLC

1 Union Square W., Suite 904, New York NY 10003. (212)627-9100. **Fax:** (212)627-9313. **Website:** www.dystel.com. Estab. 1994. Member of AAR. Other membership includes SCBWI. Represents 600+ clients.

MEMBER AGENTS Jane Dystel; Miriam Goderich, miriam@dystel.com (literary and commercial fiction as well as some genre fiction); Stacey Glick, sglick@dystel.com (YA, middle grade, children's nonfiction, and select adult contemporary fiction); Michael Bourret, mbourret@dystel.com (middle grade and young adult fiction, commercial adult fiction); Jim McCarthy, jmccarthy@dystel.com (literary women's fiction, underrepresented voices, mysteries, romance, paranormal fiction); Jessica Papin, jpapin@dystel.com (plot-driven literary and smart commercial fiction); Lauren Abramo, labramo@dystel.com (humorous middle grade and contemporary YA on the children's side, and upmarket commercial fiction and well-paced literary fiction on the adult side); John Rudolph, jrudolph@dystel.com (picture book author/illustrators, middle grade, YA, select commercial fiction); Sharon Pelletier, spelletier@dystel.com (smart commercial fiction, from upmarket women's fiction to domestic suspense to literary thrillers, and strong contemporary romance novels); Michael Hoogland, mhoogland@dystel.com (thriller, SFF, YA, upmarket women's fiction); Erin Young, eyoung@dystel.com (YA/MG, literary and intellectual commercial thrillers); Amy Bishop, abishop@dystel.com (commercial and literary women's fiction, fiction from diverse authors, historical fiction, YA); Kemi Faderin, kfaderin@dystel.com (smart, plot-driven YA, historical fiction, contemporary women's fiction, literary fiction).

REPRESENTS Considers these fiction areas: commercial, ethnic, gay, lesbian, literary, mainstream, middle grade, mystery, paranormal, romance, suspense, thriller, women's, young adult.

☛ "We are actively seeking fiction for all ages, in all genres." No plays, screenplays, or poetry.

HOW TO CONTACT Query via e-mail and put "Query" in the subject line. "Synopses, outlines or sample chapters (say, 1 chapter or the first 25 pages of your ms) should either be included below the cover letter or attached as a separate document. We won't open attachments if they come with a blank e-mail." Accepts simultaneous submissions. Responds in 6 to 8 weeks to queries; within 8 weeks to mss. Obtains most new clients through recommendations from others, solicitations, conferences.

TERMS Agent receives 15% commission on domestic sales; 19% commission on foreign sales. Offers written contract.

WRITERS CONFERENCES Backspace Writers' Conference, Pacific Northwest Writers' Association, Pike's Peak Writers' Conference, Writers League of Texas, Love Is Murder, Surrey International Writers Conference, Society of Children's Book Writers and Illustrators, International Thriller Writers, Willamette Writers Conference, The South Carolina Writers Workshop Conference, Las Vegas Writers Conference, Writer's Digest, Seton Hill Popular Fiction, Romance Writers of America, Geneva Writers Conference.

TIPS "DGLM prides itself on being a full-service agency. We're involved in every stage of the publishing process, from offering substantial editing on mss and proposals, to coming up with book ideas for authors looking for their next project, negotiating contracts and collecting monies for our clients. We follow a book from its inception through its sale to a publisher, its publication, and beyond. Our commitment to our writers does not by any means, end when we have collected our commission. This is one of the many things that makes us unique in a very competitive business."

JUDITH EHRLICH LITERARY MANAGEMENT, LLC

146 Central Park W., 20E, New York NY 10023. (646)505-1570. **Fax:** (646)505-1570. **E-mail:** jehrlich@judithehrlichliterary.com. **Website:** www.judithehrlichliterary.com. Estab. 2002. Member of the Author's Guild and the American Society of Journalists and Authors.

🗩 Prior to her current position, Ms. Ehrlich was a senior associate at the Linda Chester Agency and is an award-winning journalist; she is the co-author of *The New Crowd: The Changing of the Jewish Guard on Wall Street* (Little, Brown).

MEMBER AGENTS Judith Ehrlich, jehrlich@judithehrlichliterary.com (upmarket, literary and quality commercial fiction).

REPRESENTS Nonfiction, fiction, novels, short story collections, juvenile books. **Considers these fiction areas:** adventure, commercial, contemporary issues, crime, detective, family saga, historical, humor, juvenile, literary, middle grade, mystery, picture books, short story collections, suspense, thriller, women's, young adult.

☛ Does not want to receive novellas, poetry, textbooks, plays, or screenplays.

HOW TO CONTACT E-query, with a synopsis and some sample pages. The agency will respond only if interested. Accepts simultaneous submissions.

RECENT SALES *The Bicycle Spy* by Yona Zeldis McDonough (Scholastic), *The House on Primrose Pond* by Yona McDonough (NAL/Penguin), *You Were Meant for Me* by Yona McDonough (NAL/Penguin), *Echoes of Us: The Hybrid Chronicles* Book 3 by Kat Zhang (HarperCollins), *Once We Were: The Hybrid Chronicles* Book 2 by Kat Zhang (HarperCollins).

EINSTEIN LITERARY MANAGEMENT

27 W. 20th St., No. 1003, New York NY 10011. (212)221-8797. **E-mail:** info@einsteinliterary.com. **E-mail:** submissions@einsteinliterary.com. **Website:** einsteinliterary.com. **Contact:** Susanna Einstein. Estab. 2015. Member of AAR. Signatory of WGA.

○ Prior to her current position, Ms. Einstein was with LJK Literary Management and the Einstein Thompson Agency.

MEMBER AGENTS Susanna Einstein, Susan Graham, Shana Kelly.

REPRESENTS Nonfiction, fiction, novels, short story collections, juvenile books. **Considers these fiction areas:** comic books, commercial, crime, fantasy, historical, juvenile, literary, middle grade, mystery, picture books, romance, science fiction, suspense, thriller, women's, young adult.

☛ "As an agency we represent a broad range of literary and commercial fiction, including upmarket women's fiction, crime fiction, historical fiction, romance, and books for middle-grade children and young adults, including picture books and graphic novels. We also handle nonfiction including cookbooks, memoir and narrative, and blog-to-book projects. Please see agent bios on the website for specific information about what each of ELM's agents represents." Does not want poetry, textbooks, or screenplays.

HOW TO CONTACT Please submit a query letter and the first 10 double-spaced pages of your ms in the body of the e-mail (no attachments). Does not respond to mail queries or telephone queries or queries that are not specifically addressed to this agency. Accepts simultaneous submissions. Responds in 6 weeks if interested.

ETHAN ELLENBERG LITERARY AGENCY

155 Suffolk St., No. 2R, New York NY 10002. (212)431-4554. **E-mail:** agent@ethanellenberg.com. **Website:** ethanellenberg.com. **Contact:** Ethan Ellenberg. Estab. 1984. Member of AAR. Science Fiction and Fantasy Writer's of American, SCBWI, RWA, and MWA.

MEMBER AGENTS Ethan Ellenberg, president; Evan Gregory, senior agent; Bibi Lewis, associate agent (YA and women's fiction).

REPRESENTS Nonfiction, fiction. **Considers these fiction areas:** commercial, ethnic, fantasy, literary, middle grade, mystery, picture books, romance, science fiction, thriller, women's, young adult, general.

☛ "We specialize in commercial fiction and children's books. In commercial fiction we want to see science fiction, fantasy, romance, mystery, thriller, women's fiction; all genres welcome. In children's books, we want to see everything: picture books, early reader, middle grade and young adult. We do some nonfiction: history, biography, military, popular science, and cutting edge books about any subject. Does not want to receive poetry, short stories, or screenplays.

HOW TO CONTACT Query by e-mail. Paste all of the material in the order listed. Fiction: query letter, synopsis, first 50 pages. Nonfiction: query letter, book proposal. Picture books: query letter, complete ms, 4-5 sample illustrations. Illustrators: query letter, 4-5 sample illustrations, link to online portfolio. Will not respond unless interested. Accepts simultaneous submissions. Responds in 2 weeks.

EMPIRE LITERARY

115 W. 29th St., 3rd Floor, New York NY 10001. (917)213-7082. **E-mail:** abarzvi@empireliterary.com. **E-mail:** queries@empireliterary.com. **Website:** www. empireliterary.com. Estab. 2013. Member of AAR. Signatory of WGA.

MEMBER AGENTS Andrea Barzvi; Carrie Howland; Kathleen Schmidt; Penny Moore.

REPRESENTS Nonfiction, novels. **Considers these fiction areas:** literary, middle grade, women's, young adult.

HOW TO CONTACT Please only query 1 agent at a time. "If we are interested in reading more we will get in touch with you as soon as possible." Accepts simultaneous submissions.

FELICIA ETH LITERARY REPRESENTATION

555 Bryant St., Suite 350, Palo Alto CA 94301-1700. **E-mail:** feliciaeth.literary@gmail.com. **Website:** eth-literary.com. **Contact:** Felicia Eth. Member of AAR.

REPRESENTS Novels. **Considers these fiction areas:** historical, literary, mainstream, suspense.

☛ This agency specializes in high-quality fiction (preferably mainstream/contemporary) and provocative, intelligent, and thoughtful nonfiction on a wide array of commercial subjects. "The agency does not represent genre ficiton, including romance novels, sci fi and fantasy, westerns, anime and graphic novels, mysteries."

HOW TO CONTACT For fiction: Please write a query letter introducing yourself, your book, your writing background. Don't forget to include degrees you may have, publishing credits, awards and endorsements. Please wait for a response before including sample pages. "We only consider material where the ms for which you are querying is complete, unless you have previously published." For nonfiction: A query letter is best, introducing idea and what you have written already (proposal, ms?). "For writerly nonficiton (narratives, bio, memoir) please let us know if you have a finished ms. Also it's important you include information about yourself, your background and expertise, your platform and notoriety, if any. We do not ask for exclusivity in most instances but do ask that you inform us if other agents are considering the same material." Accepts simultaneous submissions.

TERMS Agent receives 15% commission on domestic sales; 20% commission on foreign and film sales. Charges clients for photocopying and express mail service.

RECENT SALES *Bumper Sticker Philosophy* by Jack Bowen (Random House), *Boys Adrift* by Leonard Sax (Basic Books), *The Memory Thief* by Emily Colin (Ballantine Books), *The World is a Carpet* by Anna Badkhen (Riverhead).

WRITERS CONFERENCES "Wide array—from Squaw Valley to Mills College."

MARY EVANS INC.

242 E. Fifth St., New York NY 10003. (212)979-0880. **Fax:** (212)979-5344. **E-mail:** info@maryevansinc.com. **Website:** maryevansinc.com. Member of AAR.

MEMBER AGENTS Mary Evans (progressive politics, alternative medicine, science and technology, social commentary, American history and culture); Julia Kardon (literary and upmarket fiction, narrative nonfiction, journalism, and history); Tom Mackay (nonfiction that uses sport as a platform to explore other issues and playful literary fiction).

REPRESENTS Nonfiction, novels. **Considers these fiction areas:** literary, upmarket.

No screenplays or stage plays.

HOW TO CONTACT Query by mail or e-mail. If querying by mail, include a SASE. If querying by e-mail, put "Query" in the subject line. For fiction: Include the first few pages, or opening chapter of your novel as a single Word attachment. Accepts simultaneous submissions. Responds within 4-8 weeks.

FAIRBANK LITERARY REPRESENTATION

P.O. Box 6, Hudson NY 12534-0006. (617)576-0030. **Fax:** (617)576-0030. **E-mail:** queries@fairbankliterary.com. **Website:** www.fairbankliterary.com. **Contact:** Sorche Fairbank. Member of AAR.

MEMBER AGENTS Sorche Fairbank (narrative nonfiction, commercial and literary fiction, memoir, food and wine); Matthew Frederick, matt@fairbankliterary.com (scout for sports nonfiction, architecture, design).

REPRESENTS Nonfiction, novels, short story collections. **Considers these fiction areas:** action, adventure, feminist, gay, lesbian, literary, mainstream, mystery, sports, suspense, thriller, women's, Southern voices.

"I tend to gravitate toward literary fiction and narrative nonfiction, with a strong interest in women's issues and women's voices, international voices, class and race issues, and projects that simply teach me something new about the greater world and society around us. We have a good reputation for working closely and developmentally with our authors and love what we do." Actively seeking literary fiction, international and culturally diverse voices, narrative nonfiction, topical subjects (politics, current affairs), history, sports, architecture/design and pop culture. Does not want to receive romance, poetry, science fiction, pirates, vampire, young adult, or children's works.

HOW TO CONTACT Query with SASE. Submit author bio. Accepts simultaneous submissions. Obtains most new clients through recommendations from others, solicitations, conferences, ideas generated in-house.

TERMS Agent receives 15% commission on domestic sales; 20% commission on foreign sales. Offers written contract, binding for 12 months; 45-day notice must be given to terminate contract.

RECENT SALES *When Clowns Attack* by Chuck Sambuchino (Running Press), *101 Things I Learned in School* series by Matthew Fredericks. All recent sales available on website.

TIPS "Be professional from the very first contact. There shouldn't be a single typo or grammatical flub in your query. Have a reason for contacting me about your project other than I was the next name listed on some website. Please do not use form query software! Believe me, we can get a dozen or so a day that look identical—we know when you are using a form. Show me that you know your audience—and your competition. Have the writing and/or proposal at the very,

very best it can be before starting the querying process. Don't assume that if someone likes it enough they'll 'fix' it. The biggest mistake new writers make is starting the querying process before they—and the work—are ready. Take your time and do it right."

LEIGH FELDMAN LITERARY

E-mail: assistant@lfliterary.com. **E-mail:** query@lfliterary.com. **Website:** lfliterary.com. **Contact:** Leigh Feldman. Estab. 2014. Member of AAR. Signatory of WGA.

○ During her 25 years as a literary agent based in New York City, Leigh Feldman has established herself as an invaluable partner to the writers she represents, and is highly respected by her peers in the industry. Her agency, Leigh Feldman Literary, is the culmination of experiences and lessons learned from her 20-plus years at Darhansoff, Verrill, Feldman Literary Agency and Writer's House. In that time, Feldman has represented National Book Award winners and bestsellers of literary fiction, historical fiction, memoir, middle grade, and young adult. No matter the writer or the category, Feldman only represents books she believes in, that captivate her, and that she can best serve with her passion and tenacity. Leigh Feldman Literary is a full service literary agency.

REPRESENTS Nonfiction, fiction, novels, short story collections. **Considers these fiction areas:** contemporary issues, family saga, feminist, gay, historical, lesbian, literary, multicultural, short story collections, women's, young adult.

⌐ Does not want mystery, thriller, romance, paranormal, sci-fi.

HOW TO CONTACT E-query. "Please include 'query' in the subject line. Due to large volume of submissions, we regret that we can not respond to all queries individually. Please include the first chapter or the first 10 pages of your ms (or proposal) pasted after your query letter. I'd love to know what led you to query me in particular, and please let me know if you are querying other agents as well." Accepts simultaneous submissions.

RECENT SALES List of recent sales and best known sales are available on the agency website.

THE FIELDING AGENCY, LLC

1550G Tiburon Blvd., #528, Tiburon CA 94920. **E-mail:** wlee@fieldingagency.com. **Website:** www.fieldingagency.com. **Contact:** Whitney Lee.

REPRESENTS Nonfiction, fiction, juvenile books.

HOW TO CONTACT Accepts simultaneous submissions.

DIANA FINCH LITERARY AGENCY

116 W. 23rd St., Suite 500, New York NY 10011. (917)544-4470. **E-mail:** diana.finch@verizon.net. **E-mail:** diana.finch@verizon.net or via link at the website (preferred). **Website:** dianafinchliteraryagency.blogspot.com ; www.facebook.com/DianaFinchLitAg. **Contact:** Diana Finch. Estab. 2003. Member of AAR. Represents 40 clients.

○ Seeking to represent books that change lives. Prior to opening her agency in 2003, Ms. Finch worked at Ellen Levine Literary Agency for 18 years and started her publishing career in the editorial department at St. Martin's Press.

REPRESENTS Nonfiction, fiction, novels, scholarly books. **Considers these fiction areas:** action, adventure, contemporary issues, crime, detective, ethnic, historical, literary, mainstream, new adult, police, sports, thriller, young adult.

⌐ "Does not want romance, mysteries, or children's picture books."

HOW TO CONTACT This agency prefers submissions via its online form. Accepts simultaneous submissions. Obtains most new clients through recommendations from others.

TERMS Agent receives 15% commission on domestic sales. Agent receives 20% commission on foreign sales. Offers written contract. "I charge for overseas postage, galleys, and books purchased, and try to recoup these costs from earnings received for a client, rather than charging outright."

RECENT SALES *Stealing Schooling* by Professor Noliwe Rooks (The New Press), *Merchants of Men* by Loretta Napoleoni (Seven Stories Press), *Beyond $15* by Jonathan Rosenblum (Beacon Press), *The Age of Inequality* by the Editors of In These Times (Verso Books), *Seeds of Rebellion* by Mark Schapiro (Hot Books/Skyhorse).

WRITERS CONFERENCES Florida Writers Conference 2016; Washington Writers Conference annually; Writers Digest NYC Conference annually; CLMP/New School conference annually, and more.

TIPS "Do as much research as you can on agents before you query. Have someone critique your query letter before you send it. It should be only 1 page and describe your book clearly—and why you are writing it—but also demonstrate creativity and a sense of your writing style."

FINEPRINT LITERARY MANAGEMENT

207 W. 106th St., Suite 1D, New York NY 10025. (212)279-1282. **Website:** www.fineprintlit.com. Estab. 2007. Member of AAR.

MEMBER AGENTS Peter Rubie, CEO, peter@fineprintlit.com (nonfiction interests include narrative nonfiction, popular science, spirituality, history, biography, pop culture, business, technology, parenting, health, self help, music, and food; fiction interests include literate thrillers, crime fiction, science fiction and fantasy, military fiction and literary fiction, middle grade and boy-oriented YA fiction); Stephany Evans, stephany@fineprintlit.com (nonfiction: health and wellness, spirituality, lifestyle, food and drink, sustainability, running and fitness, memoir, and narrative nonfiction; fiction interests include mystery/crime, women's fiction, from literary to commercial to romance); Laura Wood, laura@fineprintlit.com (serious nonfiction, especially in the areas of science and nature, along with substantial titles in business, history, religion, and other areas by academics, experienced professionals, and journalists; select genre fiction only (no poetry, literary fiction or memoir) in the categories of science fiction & fantasy and mystery); June Clark, june@fineprintlit.com (nonfiction projects in the areas of entertainment, self-help, parenting, reference/how-to books, food and wine, style/beauty, and prescriptive business titles); Jacqueline Murphy, jacqueline@fineprintlit.com.

REPRESENTS Nonfiction, fiction, novels, short story collections. **Considers these fiction areas:** commercial, crime, fantasy, historical, literary, mainstream, middle grade, mystery, romance, science fiction, suspense, thriller, women's, young adult.

HOW TO CONTACT E-query. For fiction, send a query, synopsis, bio, and 30 pages pasted into the e-mail. No attachments. For nonfiction, send a query only; proposal requested later if the agent is interested. Accepts simultaneous submissions. Obtains most new clients through recommendations from others, solicitations.

TERMS Agent receives 15% commission on domestic sales; 20% commission on foreign sales.

FLANNERY LITERARY

1140 Wickfield Ct., Naperville IL 60563. **E-mail:** jennifer@flanneryliterary.com. **Website:** flanneryliterary.com. **Contact:** Jennifer Flannery. Estab. 1992. Represents 40 clients.

REPRESENTS Nonfiction, fiction, novels, juvenile books. **Considers these fiction areas:** juvenile, middle grade, new adult, picture books, young adult.

☞ This agency specializes in children's and young adult fiction and nonfiction. It also accepts picture books. 100% juvenile books.

HOW TO CONTACT Query by e-mail only. "Multiple queries are fine, but please inform us. Please no attachments. If you're sending a query about a novel, please include in the e-mail the first 5-10 pages; if it's a picture book, please include the entire text." Accepts simultaneous submissions. Responds in 2 weeks to queries; 1 month to mss. Obtains new clients through referrals and queries.

TERMS Agent receives 15% commission on domestic sales. Agent receives 20% commission on foreign sales. Offers written contract, binding for life of book in print.

TIPS "Write an engrossing, succinct query describing your work. We are always looking for a fresh new voice."

FLETCHER & COMPANY

78 Fifth Ave., 3rd Floor, New York NY 10011. **E-mail:** info@fletcherandco.com. **Website:** www.fletcherandco.com. **Contact:** Christy Fletcher. Estab. 2003. Member of AAR.

MEMBER AGENTS Christy Fletcher (referrals only); Melissa Chinchillo (select list of her own authors); Rebecca Gradinger (literary fiction, up-market commercial fiction, narrative nonfiction, self-help, memoir, Women's studies, humor, and pop culture); Gráinne Fox (literary fiction and quality commercial authors, award-winning journalists and food writers, American voices, international, literary crime, upmarket fiction, narrative nonfiction); Lisa Grubka (fiction—literary, upmarket women's, and young adult; and nonfiction — narrative, food, science, and more); Sylvie Greenberg (literary fiction, business, sports, science, memoir and history); Donald Lamm (history, biography, investigative journalism, politics, current affairs, and business); Todd Sattersten (business books); Eric Lupfer; Sarah Fuentes; Veronica Goldstein; Mink Choi; Erin McFadden.

REPRESENTS Nonfiction, novels. **Considers these fiction areas:** commercial, crime, literary, women's, young adult.

HOW TO CONTACT Send queries to info@fletcherandco.com. Please do not include e-mail attachments with your initial query, as they will be deleted.

Address your query to a specific agent. No snail mail queries. Accepts simultaneous submissions.

RECENT SALES *The Profiteers* by Sally Denton; *The Longest Night* by Andrea Williams; *Disrupted: My Misadventure in the Start-Up Bubble* by Dan Lyons; *Free Refills: A Doctor Confronts His Addiction* by Peter Grinspoon, M.D.; *Black Man in a White Coat: A Doctor's Reflections on Race and Medicine* by Damon Tweedy, M.D.

FOLIO LITERARY MANAGEMENT, LLC

The Film Center Building, 630 Ninth Ave., Suite 1101, New York NY 10036. (212)400-1494. **Fax:** (212)967-0977. **Website:** www.foliolit.com. Member of AAR. Represents 100+ clients.

Prior to creating Folio Literary Management, Mr. Hoffman worked for several years at another agency; Mr. Kleinman was an agent at Graybill & English.

MEMBER AGENTS Claudia Cross (romance novels, commercial women's fiction); Scott Hoffman (literary and commercial fiction, spiritual or religious-themed fiction, sci-fi/fantasy literary fiction); Jeff Kleinman (bookclub fiction [not genre commercial, like mysteries or romances], literary fiction, thrillers and suspense novels); Dado Derviskadic; Frank Weimann (adult and children's fiction); Michael Harriot (fantasy/science fiction); Erin Harris (book club, historical fiction, literary, psychological suspense, young adult); Katherine Latshaw (middle grade); Annie Hwang (literary and upmarket fiction with commercial appeal); Erin Niumata (commercial women's fiction, romance, historical fiction, mysteries, psychological thrillers, suspense); Ruth Pomerance (commercial fiction); Marcy Posner (adult: commercial women's fiction, historical fiction, mystery, biography, history, health, and lifestyle, commercial novels, thrillers, narrative nonfiction; children's: contemporary YA and MG, mystery series for boys, select historical fiction and fantasy); Jeff Silberman (commercial, literary, and book club fiction); Steve Troha; Emily van Beek (YA, MG, picture books), Melissa White (literary and commercial fiction, MG, YA); John Cusick (middle grade, picture books, YA); Jamie Chambliss.

REPRESENTS Nonfiction, novels. **Considers these fiction areas:** commercial, fantasy, horror, literary, middle grade, mystery, picture books, religious, romance, thriller, women's, young adult.

No poetry, stage plays, or screenplays.

HOW TO CONTACT Query via e-mail only (no attachments). Read agent bios online for specific submission guidelines and e-mail addresses, and to check if someone is closed to queries. "All agents respond to queries as soon as possible, whether interested or not. If you haven't heard back from the individual agent within the time period that they specify on their bio page, it's possible that something has gone wrong, and your query has been lost—in that case, please e-mail a follow-up."

TIPS "Please do not submit simultaneously to more than 1 agent at Folio. If you're not sure which of us is exactly right for your book, don't worry. We work closely as a team, and if one of our agents gets a query that might be more appropriate for someone else, we'll always pass it along. It's important that you check each agent's bio page for clear directions as to how to submit, as well as when to expect feedback."

FOUNDRY LITERARY + MEDIA

33 W. 17th St., PH, New York NY 10011. (212)929-5064. **Fax:** (212)929-5471. **Website:** www.foundry-media.com.

MEMBER AGENTS Peter McGuigan, pmsubmissions@foundrymedia.com (smart, offbeat voices in all genres of fiction and nonfiction); Yfat Reiss Gendell, yrgsubmissions@foundrymedia.com (unique commercial fiction, including young adult fiction, that touch on her nonfiction interests, including speculative fiction, thrillers, and historical fiction); Chris Park, cpsubmissions@foundrymedia.com (character-driven fiction); Hannah Brown Gordon, hbgsubmissions@foundrymedia.com (stories and narratives that blend genres including thriller, suspense, historical, literary, speculative); Brandi Bowles, bbsubmissions@foundrymedia.com (high-concept novels that feature strong female bonds and psychological or scientific themes); Kirsten Neuhaus, knsubmissions@foundrymedia.com (smart fiction that appeals to a wide market); Jessica Regel, jrsubmissions@foundrymedia.com (young adult and middle grade books, as well as a select list of adult general fiction, women's fiction); Anthony Mattero, amsubmissions@foundrymedia.com; Peter Steinberg, pssubmissions@foundrymedia.com (commercial and literary fiction, young adult); Roger Freet, rfsubmissions@foundrymedia.com; Adriann Ranta, arsubmissions@foundrymedia.com (accepts all genres and age groups; loves women's fiction and smart, fresh, genre-bending works for children).

REPRESENTS **Considers these fiction areas:** commercial, historical, humor, literary, middle grade, suspense, thriller, women's, young adult.

HOW TO CONTACT Target 1 agent only. Send queries to the specific submission e-mail of the agent. For fiction: send query, synopsis, author bio, first 3 chapters—all pasted in the e-mail. For nonfiction, send query, sample chapters, TOC, author bio (all pasted). "We regret that we cannot guarantee a response to every submission we receive. If you do not receive a response within 8 weeks, your submission is not right for our lists at this time." Accepts simultaneous submissions.

TIPS "Consult website for each agent's submission instructions."

FOX LITERARY

110 W. 40th St., Suite 2305, New York NY 10018. **E-mail:** submissions@foxliterary.com. **Website:** foxliterary.com.

MEMBER AGENTS Diana Fox.

REPRESENTS Nonfiction, fiction, graphic novels. **Considers these fiction areas:** fantasy, historical, romance, science fiction, thriller, young adult, general.

HOW TO CONTACT E-mail query and first 5 pages in body of e-mail. E-mail queries preferred. For snail mail queries, must include an e-mail address for response and no response means no. Do not send SASE. No e-mail attachments. Accepts simultaneous submissions.

SARAH JANE FREYMANN LITERARY AGENCY

(212)362-9277. **E-mail:** sarah@sarahjanefreymann.com. **E-mail:** submissions@sarahjanefreymann.com. **Website:** www.sarahjanefreymann.com. **Contact:** Sarah Jane Freymann, Steve Schwartz.

MEMBER AGENTS Sarah Jane Freymann (nonfiction: spiritual, psychology, self-help, women/men's issues, books by health experts [conventional and alternative], cookbooks, narrative nonfiction, natural science, nature, memoirs, cutting-edge journalism, travel, multicultural issues, parenting, lifestyle, fiction: literary, mainstream YA); Jessica Sinsheimer, jessica@sarahjanefreymann.com; Steven Schwartz, steve@sarahjanefreymann.com (popular fiction [crime, thrillers, and historical novels], world and national affairs, business books, self-help, psychology, humor, sports and travel).

REPRESENTS Nonfiction, fiction, novels. **Considers these fiction areas:** crime, historical, literary, mainstream, thriller, young adult, Popular fiction.

HOW TO CONTACT Query via e-mail. No attachments. Below the query, please paste the first 10 pages of your work. Accepts simultaneous submissions.

TERMS Charges clients for long distance, overseas postage, photocopying. 100% of business is derived from commissions on ms sales.

FREDRICA S. FRIEDMAN AND CO., INC.

857 Fifth Ave., New York NY 10065. (212)639-9455. **E-mail:** info@fredricafriedman.com. **E-mail:** submissions@fredricafriedman.com. **Website:** www.fredricafriedman.com. **Contact:** Ms. Chandler Smith.

Prior to establishing her own literary management firm, Ms. Friedman was the Editorial Director, Associate Publisher and Vice President of Little, Brown & Co., a division of Time Warner, and the first woman to hold those positions.

REPRESENTS Nonfiction, fiction.

Does not want poetry, plays, screenplays, children's picture books, sci-fi/fantasy, or horror.

HOW TO CONTACT Submit e-query, synopsis; be concise, and include any pertinent author information, including relevant writing history. If you are a fiction writer, submit the first 10 pages of your ms. Keep all material in the body of the e-mail. Accepts simultaneous submissions. Responds in 6 weeks.

REBECCA FRIEDMAN LITERARY AGENCY

E-mail: brandie@rfliterary.com. **Website:** www.rfliterary.com. Estab. 2013. Member of AAR. Signatory of WGA.

Prior to opening her own agency in 2013, Ms. Friedman was with Sterling Lord Literistic from 2006 to 2011, then with Hill Nadell Agency.

MEMBER AGENTS Rebecca Friedman (commercial and literary fiction with a focus on literary novels of suspense, women's fiction, contemporary romance, and young adult, as well as journalistic nonfiction and memoir); Susan Finesman, susan@rfliterary.com (fiction, cookbooks, and lifestyle); Abby Schulman, abby@rfliterary.com (YA and nonfiction related to health, wellness, and personal development); Brandie Coonis, brandie@rfliterary.com (writers that defy genre).

REPRESENTS Nonfiction, fiction. **Considers these fiction areas:** commercial, fantasy, literary, mystery, new adult, romance, science fiction, suspense, women's, young adult.

HOW TO CONTACT Please submit your query letter and first chapter (no more than 15 pages, double-spaced).

Accepts simultaneous submissions. Tries to respond in 6-8 weeks.

RECENT SALES A complete list of agency authors is available online.

THE FRIEDRICH AGENCY

19 W. 21st St., Suite 201, New York NY 10010. (212)317-8810. **E-mail:** mfriedrich@friedrichagency.com; lcarson@friedrichagency.com; kwolf@friedrichagency.com. **Website:** www.friedrichagency.com. **Contact:** Molly Friedrich; Lucy Carson; Kent D. Wolf. Estab. 2006. Member of AAR. Signatory of WGA. Represents 50+ clients.

◯　Prior to her current position, Ms. Friedrich was an agent at the Aaron Priest Literary Agency.

MEMBER AGENTS Molly Friedrich, founder and agent (open to queries); Lucy Carson, TV/film rights director and agent (open to queries); Kent D. Wolf, foreign rights director and agent (open to queries).

REPRESENTS Nonfiction, fiction, novels, short story collections. **Considers these fiction areas:** commercial, literary, multicultural, suspense, women's, young adult.

HOW TO CONTACT Query by e-mail only. Please query only 1 agent at this agency. Accepts simultaneous submissions.

RECENT SALES *W Is for Wasted* by Sue Grafton, *Olive Kitteridge* by Elizabeth Strout. Other clients include Frank McCourt, Jane Smiley, Esmeralda Santiago, Terry McMillan, Cathy Schine, Ruth Ozeki, Karen Joy Fowler, and more.

FULL CIRCLE LITERARY, LLC

3268 Governor Dr. #323, San Diego CA 92122. **E-mail:** info@fullcircleliterary.com. **Website:** www.fullcircleliterary.com. **Contact:** Stefanie Von Borstel. Estab. 2005. Member of AAR. Society of Children's Books Writers & Illustrators, Authors Guild. Represents 100+ clients.

MEMBER AGENTS Stefanie Von Borstel; Adriana Dominguez; Taylor Martindale Kean (multicultural voices); Lilly Ghahremani.

REPRESENTS Considers these fiction areas: literary, middle grade, multicultural, picture books, women's, young adult.

☛　Actively seeking nonfiction by authors with a unique voice and strong platform, projects that offer new and diverse viewpoints, and literature with a global or multicultural perspective. "We are particularly interested in books with a Latino or Middle Eastern angle."

HOW TO CONTACT Online submissions only via submissions form online. Please complete the form and submit cover letter, author information and sample writing. For sample writing: fiction please include the first 10 ms pages. For nonfiction, include a proposal with 1 sample chapter. Accepts simultaneous submissions. "Due to the high volume of submissions, please keep in mind we are no longer able to personally respond to every submission. However, we read every submission with care and often share for a second read within the office. If we are interested, we will contact you by e-mail to request additional materials (such as a complete ms or additional mss). Please keep us updated if there is a change in the status of your project, such as an offer of representation or book contract." If you have not heard from us in 6-8 weeks, your project is not right for our agency at the current time and we wish you all the best with your writing. Thank you for considering Full Circle Literary, we look forward to reading! Obtains most new clients through recommendations from others and conferences.

TERMS Agent receives 15% commission on domestic sales; 25% commission on foreign sales. Offers written contract which outlines responsibilities of the author and the agent.

FUSE LITERARY

Foreword Literary, Inc. dba FUSE LITERARY, P.O. Box 258, La Honda CA 94020. **E-mail:** info@fuseliterary.com. **E-mail:** query[firstnameofagent]@fuseliterary.com. **Website:** www.fuseliterary.com. **Contact:** Contact each agent directly via e-mail. Estab. 2013. RWA, SCBWI. Represents 100+ clients.

◯　Each agent at Fuse had a specific set of interests and jobs prior to becoming a member of Team Fuse. Laurie ran a multi-million dollar publicity agency. Michelle was an editor at a St. Martins Press. Emily worked in the contracts department at Simon & Schuster. Gordon ran a successful independent editing business. Tricia worked in the video game industry. Connor worked in talent management. Jennifer was (and is still) a lawyer. Check each agent's bio on our website for more specific information.

MEMBER AGENTS Laurie McLean (only accepting referral inquiries and submissions requested at conferences or online events, with the exception of unsolicited adult and children's science fiction); Gordon Warnock, querygordon@fuseliterary.com (fiction: high-concept commercial fiction, literary fiction

(adults through YA), graphic novels (adults through MG); nonfiction: memoir (adult, YA, NA, graphic), cookbooks/food narrative/food studies, illustrated/art/photography (especially graphic nonfiction), political and current events, pop science, pop culture (especially punk culture and geek culture), self-help, how-to, humor, pets, business and career); Connor Goldsmith, queryconnor@fuseliterary.com (fiction: sci-fi/fantasy/horror, thrillers, and upmarket commercial fiction with a unique and memorable hook; books by and about people from marginalized perspectives, such as LGBT people and/or racial minorities; nonfiction (from recognized experts with established platforms): history (particularly of the ancient world), theater, cinema, music, television, mass media, popular culture, feminism and gender studies, LGBT issues, race relations, and the sex industry); Michelle Richter, querymichelle@fuseliterary.com (primarily seeking fiction, specifically book club reads, literary fiction, and mystery/suspense/thrillers; for nonfiction, seeking fashion, pop culture, science/medicine, sociology/social trends, and economics); Emily S. Keyes, queryemily@fuseliterary.com (young adult, middle grade, and select commercial fiction, including fantasy & science fiction, women's fiction, new adult fiction, pop culture and humor); Tricia Skinner, querytricia@fuseliterary.com (Romance: science fiction, futuristic, fantasy, military/special ops, medieval historical; brand new relationships; diversity); Jennifer Chen Tran, queryjennifer@fuseliterary.com (literary fiction, commercial fiction, women's fiction, upmarket fiction, contemporary romance, mature young adult, new adult, suspense/thriller, select graphic novels (adult, YA, MG); memoir, narrative nonfiction in the areas of adventure, biography, business, current affairs, medical, history, how-to, pop-culture, psychology, social entrepreneurism, social justice, travel, and lifestyle books (home, design, fashion, food).
REPRESENTS Nonfiction, fiction, novels, juvenile books, scholarly books, poetry books. **Considers these fiction areas:** action, adventure, cartoon, comic books, commercial, confession, contemporary issues, crime, detective, erotica, ethnic, experimental, family saga, fantasy, feminist, frontier, gay, glitz, hi-lo, historical, horror, humor, inspirational, juvenile, lesbian, literary, mainstream, metaphysical, middle grade, multicultural, multimedia, mystery, new adult, New Age, occult, paranormal, picture books, plays, poetry, poetry in translation, police, psychic, regional, ro-

mance, satire, science fiction, spiritual, sports, supernatural, suspense, thriller, urban fantasy, westerns, women's, young adult. "We are committed to expanding storytelling into a wide variety of formats other than books, including video games, movies, television shows, streaming videos, enhanced e-books, VR, etc."
HOW TO CONTACT E-query an individual agent. Check the website to see if any individual agent has closed themselves to submissions, as well as each agent's individual submission preferences. (You can find these details by clicking on 'Team Fuse' and then clicking on each agent's photo.) Usually responds in 4-6 weeks, but sometimes more if an agent is exceptionally busy. Check each agent's bio/submissions page on the website. Only accepts e-mailed queries that follow online guidelines.
TERMS "We earn 15% on negotiated deals for books and with our co-agents earn between 20-30% on foreign translation deals depending on the territory; 20% on TV/Movies/Plays; other multimedia deals are so new there is no established commission rate. The author has the last say, approving or not approving all deals." After the initial 90-day period, there is a 30-day termination of the agency agreement clause. No fees.
RECENT SALES Seven-figure deal for *New York Times* bestseller Julie Kagawa (YA); mid-six-figure deal for Michael J. Sullivan (fantasy); quarter-million-dollar deal for Melissa D. Savage (MG); *First Watch* by Dale Lucas (fantasy); *Elektra's Adventures in Tragedy* by Douglas Rees (YA); Runebinder Trilogy by Alex Kahler (YA); *Perceptual Intelligence* by Dr. Brian Boxler Wachler (science); *Game Programming for Artists* by Huntley & Brady (how-to); *Pay Day* by Kellye Garrett (mystery); *Reality Star* by Laura Heffernan (women's fiction); *Everything We Keep, Things We Leave Behind* by Kerry Lonsdale (women's fiction); *Maggie and Abby's Neverending Pillow Fort* by Will Taylor (MG); *The Sky Between You and Me* by Catherine Alene (YA).
WRITERS CONFERENCES Agents from this agency attend many conferences. A full list of their appearances is available on the agency website.

MAX GARTENBERG LITERARY AGENCY
912 N. Pennsylvania Ave., Yardley PA 19067. (215)295-9230. **Website:** www.maxgartenberg.com. **Contact:** Anne Devlin (nonfiction). Estab. 1954. Represents 100 clients.

MEMBER AGENTS Anne G. Devlin (current events, politics, true crime, women's issues, sports, parenting, biography, environment, narrative nonfiction, health, lifestyle, and celebrity).

REPRESENTS Novels.

HOW TO CONTACT Writers desirous of having their work handled by this agency may query by e-mail to agdevlin@aol.com. Accepts simultaneous submissions. Responds in 2 weeks to queries; 6 weeks to mss. Obtains most new clients through recommendations from others, following up on good query letters.

TERMS Agent receives 15% commission on domestic sales; 20% commission on foreign sales.

RECENT SALES *The Enlightened College Applicant* by Andrew Belasco (Rowman and Littlefield); *Beethoven for Kids: His Life and Music* by Helen Bauer (Chicago Review Press); *Portrait of a Past Life Skeptic* by Robert L. Snow (Llewellyn Books); *What Patients Taught Me* by Audrey Young, MD (Sasquatch Books); *Unorthodox Warfare: The Chinese Experience* by Ralph D. Sawyer (Westview Press); *Encyclopedia of Earthquakes and Volcanoes* by Alexander E. Gates (Facts on File); *Starved* by Ann McTiernan, MD, PhD (Central Recovery Press).

TIPS "We have recently expanded to allow more access for new writers."

GELFMAN SCHNEIDER / ICM PARTNERS

850 7th Ave., Suite 903, New York NY 10019. **E-mail:** mail@gelfmanschneider.com. **Website:** www.gelfmanschneider.com. **Contact:** Jane Gelfman, Deborah Schneider. Member of AAR. Represents 300+ clients.

MEMBER AGENTS Deborah Schneider (all categories of literary and commercial fiction and nonfiction); Jane Gelfman; Heather Mitchell (particularly interested in narrative nonfiction, historical fiction and young debut authors with strong voices); Penelope Burns, penelope.gsliterary@gmail.com (literary and commercial fiction and nonfiction, as well as a variety of young adult and middle grade).

REPRESENTS Nonfiction, fiction, juvenile books. **Considers these fiction areas:** commercial, fantasy, historical, literary, mainstream, middle grade, mystery, science fiction, suspense, women's, young adult.

☞ "Among our diverse list of clients are novelists, journalists, playwrights, scientists, activists & humorists writing narrative nonfiction, memoir, political & current affairs, popular science and popular culture nonfiction, as well as literary &

commercial fiction, women's fiction, and historical fiction." Does not currently accept screenplays or scripts, poetry, or picture book queries.

HOW TO CONTACT Query. Check Submissions page of website to see which agents are open to queries and further instructions. Accepts simultaneous submissions.

TERMS Agent receives 15% commission on domestic sales; 20% commission on foreign sales; 15% commission on film sales. Offers written contract. Charges clients for photocopying and messengers/couriers.

THE GERNERT COMPANY

136 E. 57th St., New York NY 10022. (212)838-7777. **E-mail:** info@thegernertco.com. **Website:** www.thegernertco.com. **Contact:** Sarah Burnes. Estab. 1996.

💬 Prior to her current position, Ms. Burnes was with Burnes & Clegg, Inc.

MEMBER AGENTS Sarah Burnes (literary fiction and nonfiction; children's fiction); Stephanie Cabot (represents a variety of genres, including crime/thrillers, commercial and literary fiction, latte lit, and nonfiction); Chris Parris-Lamb (nonfiction, literary fiction); Seth Fishman (looking for the new voice, the original idea, the entirely breathtaking creative angle in both fiction and nonfiction); Logan Garrison Savits (young adult fiction); Will Roberts (smart, original thrillers with distinctive voices, compelling backgrounds, and fast-paced narratives); Erika Storella (nonfiction projects that make an argument, narrate a history, and/or provide a new perspective); Andy Kifer (literary fiction, smart genre fiction (especially sci-fi), and nonfiction by brilliant writers who can make you fall in love with a subject you never knew you cared about); Anna Worrall (smart women's literary and commercial fiction, psychological thrillers, and narrative nonfiction); Ellen Coughtrey (women's literary and commercial fiction, historical fiction, narrative nonfiction and smart, original thrillers, plus. well-written Southern Gothic anything); Jack Gernert (stories about heroes—both real and imagined); Libby McGuire (distinctive storytelling in both fiction and nonfiction, across a wide range of genres). At this time, Courtney Gatewood and Rebecca Gardner are closed to queries. See the website to find out the tastes of each agent.

REPRESENTS Nonfiction, novels. **Considers these fiction areas:** commercial, crime, fantasy, historical, literary, middle grade, science fiction, thriller, women's, young adult.

HOW TO CONTACT Please send us a query letter by e-mail to info@thegernertco.com describing the work you'd like to submit, along with some information about yourself and a sample chapter if appropriate. Please indicate in your letter which agent you are querying. Please do not send e-mails directly to individual agents. It's our policy to respond to your query only if we are interested in seeing more material, usually within 4-6 weeks. See company website for more instructions. Accepts simultaneous submissions. Obtains most new clients through recommendations from others, solicitations.

RECENT SALES *Partners* by John Grisham; *The River Why* by David James Duncan; *The Thin Green Line* by Paul Sullivan; *A Fireproof Home for the Bride* by Amy Scheibe; *The Only Girl in School* by Natalie Standiford.

GHOSH LITERARY

E-mail: submissions@ghoshliterary.com. **Website:** www.ghoshliterary.com. **Contact:** Anna Ghosh. Member of AAR. Signatory of WGA.

○ Prior to opening her own agency, Ms. Ghosh was previously a partner at Scovil Galen Ghosh.

REPRESENTS Nonfiction, fiction.

☛ "Anna's literary interests are wide and eclectic and she is known for discovering and developing writers. She is particularly interested in literary narratives and books that illuminate some aspect of human endeavor or the natural world. Anna does not typically represent genre fiction but is drawn to compelling storytelling in most guises."

HOW TO CONTACT E-query. Please send an e-mail briefly introducing yourself and your work. Although no specific format is required, it is helpful to know the following: your qualifications for writing your book, including any publications and recognition for your work; who you expect to buy and read your book; similar books and authors. Accepts simultaneous submissions.

GLASS LITERARY MANAGEMENT

138 W. 25th St., 10th Floor, New York NY 10001. (646)237-4881. **E-mail:** alex@glassliterary.com; rick@glassliterary.com. **Website:** www.glassliterary.com. **Contact:** Alex Glass or Rick Pascocello. Estab. 2014. Member of AAR. Signatory of WGA.

MEMBER AGENTS Alex Glass; Rick Pascocello.

REPRESENTS Nonfiction, novels.

☛ Represents general fiction, mystery, suspense/thriller, juvenile fiction, biography, history, mind/body/spirit, health, lifestyle, cookbooks, sports, literary fiction, memoir, narrative nonfiction, pop culture. "We do not represent picture books for children."

HOW TO CONTACT "Please send your query letter in the body of an e-mail and if we are interested, we will respond and ask for the complete ms or proposal. No attachments." Accepts simultaneous submissions.

RECENT SALES *100 Days of Cake* by Shari Goldhagen, *The Red Car* by Marcy Dermansky, *The Overnight Solution* by Dr. Michael Breus, *So That Happened: A Memoir* by Jon Cryer, *Bad Kid* by David Crabb, *Finding Mr. Brightside* by Jay Clark, *Strange Animals* by Chad Kultgen.

BARRY GOLDBLATT LITERARY LLC

320 7th Ave. #266, Brooklyn NY 11215. **E-mail:** query@bgliterary.com. **Website:** www.bgliterary.com. **Contact:** Barry Goldblatt. Estab. 2000. Member of AAR. Signatory of WGA.

MEMBER AGENTS Barry Goldblatt; Jennifer Udden, query.judden@gmail.com (speculative fiction of all stripes, especially innovative science fiction or fantasy; contemporary/erotic/LGBT/paranormal/historical romance; contemporary or speculative YA; select mysteries, thrillers, and urban fantasies).

REPRESENTS Fiction. **Considers these fiction areas:** fantasy, middle grade, mystery, romance, science fiction, thriller, young adult.

☛ "Please see our website for specific submission guidelines and information on our particular tastes."

HOW TO CONTACT "E-mail queries can be sent to query@bgliterary.com and should include the word 'query' in the subject line. To query Jen Udden specifically, e-mail queries can be sent to query.judden@gmail.com. Please know that we will read and respond to every e-query that we receive, provided it is properly addressed and follows the submission guidelines below. We will not respond to e-queries that are addressed to no one, or to multiple recipients. While we do not require exclusivity, exclusive submissions will receive priority review. If your submission is exclusive to Barry Goldblatt Literary, please indicate so by including the word 'Exclusive' in the subject line of your e-mail. Your e-query should include the following within the body of the e-mail: your query letter, a synopsis of the book, and the first 5 pages of your ms. We will not open or respond to any e-mails that have attachments. Our response time is 4 weeks on queries, 6-8 weeks on full mss. If you haven't heard from us within that time, feel free to check in via e-mail." Accepts simultaneous submissions. Obtains clients through referrals, queries, and conferences.

TERMS Agent receives 15% commission on domestic sales; 20% on foreign and dramatic sales. Offers written contract. 60 days notice must be given to terminate contract.

RECENT SALES *Other Broken Things* by C. Desir, *Masks and Shadows* by Stephanie Burgis, *Wishing Day* by Lauren Myracle; *Mother-Daughter Book Camp* by Heather Vogel Frederick.

TIPS "We're a hands-on agency, focused on building an author's career, not just making an initial sale. We don't care about trends or what's hot; we just want to sign great writers."

FRANCES GOLDIN LITERARY AGENCY, INC.

214 W. 29th St., Suite 410, New York NY 10001. (212)777-0047. **Fax:** (212)228-1660. **Website:** www. goldinlit.com. Estab. 1977. Member of AAR.

MEMBER AGENTS Frances Goldin, founder/president; Ellen Geiger, vice president/principal (nonfiction: history, biography, progressive politics, photography, science and medicine, women, religion and serious investigative journalism; fiction: literary thriller, and novels in general that provoke and challenge the status quo, as well as historical and multicultural works. Please no New Age, romance, how-to or right-wing politics); Matt McGowan, agent/rights director, mm@goldinlit.com, (literary fiction, essays, history, memoir, journalism, biography, music, popular culture & science, sports [particularly soccer], narrative nonfiction, cultural studies, as well as literary travel, crime, food, suspense and sci-fi); Sam Stoloff, vice president/principal, (literary fiction, memoir, history, accessible sociology and philosophy, cultural studies, serious journalism, narrative and topical nonfiction with a progressive orientation); Ria Julien, agent/counsel; Nina Cochran, literary assistant.

REPRESENTS Nonfiction, novels. **Considers these fiction areas:** historical, literary, mainstream, multicultural, suspense, thriller.

☛ "We are hands on and we work intensively with clients on proposal and ms development." "Please note that we do not handle screenplays, romances or most other genre fiction, and hardly any poetry. We do not handle work that is racist, sexist, ageist, homophobic, or pornographic."

HOW TO CONTACT There is an online submission process you can find online. Responds in 4-6 weeks to queries.

IRENE GOODMAN LITERARY AGENCY

27 W. 24th St., Suite 700B, New York NY 10010. **E-mail:** miriam.queries@irenegoodman.com, barbara. queries@irenegoodman.com, rachel.queries@irene-goodman.com, kim.queries@irenegoodman.com, victoria.queries@irenegoodman.com, irene.que-ries@irenegoodman.com, brita.queries@irenegood-man.com. **E-mail:** submissions@irenegoodman.com. **Website:** www.irenegoodman.com. **Contact:** Brita Lundberg. Estab. 1978. Member of AAR. Represents 150 clients.

MEMBER AGENTS Irene Goodman, Miriam Kriss, Barbara Poelle, Rachel Ekstrom, Kim Perel, Brita Lundberg, Victoria Marini.

REPRESENTS Nonfiction, fiction, novels, juvenile books. **Considers these fiction areas:** action, crime, detective, family saga, historical, horror, middle grade, mystery, romance, science fiction, suspense, thriller, urban fantasy, women's, young adult.

☛ Commercial and literary fiction and nonfiction. No screenplays, poetry, or inspirational fiction.

HOW TO CONTACT Query. Submit synopsis, first 10 pages pasted into the body of the e-mail. E-mail queries only! See the website submission page. No e-mail attachments. Query 1 agent only. Accepts simultaneous submissions. Responds in 2 months to queries. Consult website for each agent's submission guidelines.

TERMS 15% commission.

TIPS "We are receiving an unprecedented amount of e-mail queries. If you find that the mailbox is full, please try again in two weeks. E-mail queries to our personal addresses will not be answered. E-mails to our personal inboxes will be deleted."

SANFORD J. GREENBURGER ASSOCIATES, INC.

55 Fifth Ave., New York NY 10003. (212)206-5600. **Fax:** (212)463-8718. **Website:** www.greenburger.com. Member of AAR. Represents 500 clients.

MEMBER AGENTS Matt Bialer, lribar@sjga.com (fantasy, science fiction, thrillers, and mysteries as well as a select group of literary writers, and also loves smart narrative nonfiction including books about current events, popular culture, biography, history, music, race, and sports); Brenda Bowen, querybb@sjga.com (literary fiction, writers and illustrators of picture books, chapter books, and middle-grade and teen fiction); Faith Hamlin, fhamlin@sjga.com (receives submissions by referral); Heide Lange, queryhl@sjga.com (receives submissions by referral); Daniel Mandel, querydm@sjga.com (literary and commercial fiction, as well as memoirs and nonfiction about business, art, history, politics, sports, and popular culture); Courtney Miller-Callihan, cmiller@sjga.com (YA, middle grade, women's fiction, romance, and historical novels, as well as nonfiction projects on unusual topics, humor, pop culture, and lifestyle books); Nicholas Ellison, nellison@sjga.com; Chelsea Lindman, clindman@sjga.com (playful literary fiction, upmarket crime fiction, and forward thinking or boundary-pushing nonfiction); Rachael Dillon Fried, rfried@sjga.com (both fiction and nonfiction authors, with a keen interest in unique literary voices, women's fiction, narrative nonfiction, memoir, and comedy); Lindsay Ribar, co-agents with Matt Bialer (young adult and middle grade fiction); Bethany Buck querybbuck@sjga.com (middle-grade fiction and chapter books, teen fiction, and a select list of picture book authors and illustrators); Stephanie Delman sdelman@sjga.com (literary/upmarket contemporary fiction, psychological thrillers/suspense, and atmospheric, near-historical fiction); Ed Maxwell emaxwell@sjga.com (expert and narrative nonfiction authors, novelists and graphic novelists, as well as children's book authors and illustrators).

REPRESENTS Nonfiction, fiction, novels, juvenile books. **Considers these fiction areas:** commercial, crime, family saga, fantasy, feminist, historical, literary, middle grade, multicultural, mystery, picture books, romance, science fiction, thriller, women's, young adult.

☛ **No screenplays.**

HOW TO CONTACT E-query. "Please look at each agent's profile page for current information about what each agent is looking for and for the correct e-mail address to use for queries to that agent. Please be sure to use the correct query e-mail address for each agent." Agents may not respond to all queries; will respond within 6-8 weeks if interested. Obtains most new clients through recommendations from others.

TERMS Agent receives 15% commission on domestic sales. Agent receives 20% commission on foreign sales. Charges for photocopying and books for foreign and subsidiary rights submissions.

RECENT SALES *Inferno* by Dan Brown, *Sweet Pea and Friends: A Sheepover* by John Churchman and Jennifer Churchman, *Code of Conduct* by Brad Thor.

KATHRYN GREEN LITERARY AGENCY, LLC

157 Columbus Ave., Suite 510, New York NY 10023. (212)245-4225. **E-mail:** query@kgreenagency.com. **Website:** www.kathryngreenliteraryagency.com. **Contact:** Kathy Green. Estab. 2004. Other memberships include Women's Media Group. Represents approximately 20 clients.

○ Prior to becoming an agent, Ms. Green was a book and magazine editor.

REPRESENTS Nonfiction, fiction, novels, short story collections, juvenile books. **Considers these fiction areas:** commercial, crime, detective, family saga, historical, humor, juvenile, literary, mainstream, middle grade, multicultural, mystery, police, romance, satire, suspense, thriller, women's, young adult.

☛ "Considers all types of fiction but particularly like historical fiction, cozy mysteries, young adult and middle grade. For nonfiction, I am interested in memoir, parenting, humor with a pop culture bent, and history. Quirky nonfiction is also a particular favorite." Does not want to receive science fiction, fantasy, children's picture books, screenplays, or poetry.

HOW TO CONTACT Query by e-mail. Send no attachments unless requested. Do not send queries via regular mail. Responds in 4 weeks. "Queries do not have to be exclusive; however if further material is requested, please be in touch before accepting other representation." Accepts simultaneous submissions. Obtains most new clients through recommendations from others, solicitations, conferences.

TERMS Agent receives 15% commission on domestic sales; 20% commission on foreign sales.

RECENT SALES *Sit.Stay.Heal* by Mel C. Miskimen, *Unholy City* by Carrie Smith.

GREYHAUS LITERARY

3021 20th St., Pl. SW, Puyallup WA 98373. **E-mail:** scott@greyhausagency.com. **E-mail:** submissions@greyhausagency.com. **Website:** www.greyhausagency.com. **Contact:** Scott Eagan, member RWA. Estab. 2003. Member of AAR. Signatory of WGA.

REPRESENTS Novels. **Considers these fiction areas:** new adult, romance, women's.

☛ Greyhaus only focuses on romance and women's fiction. Please review submission information found on the website to know exactly what Greyhaus is looking for. Stories should be 75,000-120,000 words in length or meet the word count requirements for Harlequin found on its website. Does not want fantasy, single title inspirational, young adult or middle grade, picture books, memoirs, biographies, erotica, urban fantasy, science fiction, screenplays, poetry, authors interested in only e-publishing or self-publishing.

HOW TO CONTACT Submissions to Greyhaus can be done through one of these methods: (1) A standard query letter via e-mail. If using this method, do not attach documents or send anything else other than a query letter. (2) Use the Submission Form found on the website on the Contact page. (3) Send a query, the first 3 pages, and a synopsis of no more than 3-5 pages (and SASE), using a snail-mail submission. Accepts simultaneous submissions. Responds in up to 3 months.

JILL GRINBERG LITERARY MANAGEMENT

392 Vanderbilt Ave., Brooklyn NY 11238. (212)620-5883. **E-mail:** info@jillgrinbergliterary.com. **Website:** www.jillgrinbergliterary.com. Estab. 1999. Member of AAR.

◑ Prior to her current position, Ms. Grinberg was at Anderson Grinberg Literary Management.

MEMBER AGENTS Jill Grinberg; Cheryl Pientka; Katelyn Detweiler; Sophia Seidner.

REPRESENTS Nonfiction, fiction, novels. **Considers these fiction areas:** fantasy, historical, juvenile, literary, mainstream, middle grade, picture books, romance, science fiction, women's, young adult.

☛ "We do not accept unsolicited queries for screenplays."

HOW TO CONTACT "Please send queries via e-mail to info@jillgrinbergliterary.com–include your query letter, addressed to the agent of your choice, along with the first 50 pages of your ms pasted into the body of the e-mail or attached as a doc. or docx. file. We also accept queries via mail, though e-mail is preferred. Please send your query letter and the first 50 pages of your ms by mail, along with a SASE, to the attention of your agent of choice. Please note that unless a SASE with sufficient postage is provided, your materials will not be returned. As submissions are shared within the office, please only query 1 agent with your project." Accepts simultaneous submissions.

TIPS "We prefer submissions by electronic mail."

JILL GROSJEAN LITERARY AGENCY

1390 Millstone Rd., Sag Harbor NY 11963. (631)725-7419. **E-mail:** jilllit310@aol.com. **Contact:** Jill Grosjean. Estab. 1999.

◑ Prior to becoming an agent, Ms. Grosjean managed an independent bookstore. She also worked in publishing and advertising.

REPRESENTS Novels. **Considers these fiction areas:** historical, literary, mainstream, mystery, thriller, women's.

☛ Actively seeking literary novels and mysteries. Does not want serial killer, science fiction or YA novels.

HOW TO CONTACT E-mail queries preferred, no attachments. No cold calls, please. Accepts simultaneous submissions, though when ms requested, requires exclusive reading time. Accepts simultaneous submissions. Responds in 1 week to queries; month to mss. Obtains most new clients through recommendations and through recommendations and solicitations.

TERMS Agent receives 15% commission on domestic sales; 20% commission on foreign and film sales.

RECENT SALES *A Murder in Time* by Julie McEwain (Pegasus Books), *A Twist in Time* by Julie McEwain (Pegasus Books), *The Silver Gun* by LA Chandlar (Kensington Books), *The Edison Effect* by Bernadette Pajer (Poison Pen Press), *Threading the Needle* by Marie Bostwick (Kensington Publishing), *Tim Cratchit's Christmas Carol: A Novel of Scrooge's Legacy* by Jim Piecuch (Simon & Schuster).

WRITERS CONFERENCES Thrillerfest, Texas Writer's League, Book Passage Mystery's Writer's Conference.

LAURA GROSS LITERARY AGENCY

E-mail: assistant@lg-la.com. **Website:** www.lg-la.com. Estab. 1988. Represents 30 clients.

◑ Prior to becoming an agent, Ms. Gross was an editor and ran a reading series.

REPRESENTS Nonfiction, novels.

☛ "I represent a broad range of both fiction and nonfiction writers. I am particularly interested in history, politics, and current affairs, and also love beautifully written literary fiction and intelligent thrillers."

HOW TO CONTACT Queries accepted online via online form on LGLA Submittable site. No e-mail queries. "On the submission form, please include a concise but substantive cover letter. You may include the first 6,000 words of your ms in the form as well. We will request further sample chapters from you at a later date, if we think your work suits our list." There may be a delay of several weeks in responding to your query. Accepts simultaneous submissions.

TERMS Agent receives 15% commission on domestic sales; 20% commission on foreign sales. Offers written contract.

HARTLINE LITERARY AGENCY

123 Queenston Dr., Pittsburgh PA 15235-5429. (412)829-2483. **E-mail:** joyce@hartlineliterary.com. **Website:** www.hartlineliterary.com. **Contact:** Joyce A. Hart. Estab. 1992. ACFW Represents 200 clients.

MEMBER AGENTS Joyce A. Hart, principal agent (no unsolicited queries); Jim Hart, jim@hartlineliterary.com; Diana Flegal, diana@hartlineliterary.com; Linda Glaz, linda@hartlineliterary.com; Andy Scheer, andy@hartlineliterary.com; Cyle Young, cyle@hartlineliterary.com.

REPRESENTS Nonfiction, fiction, novels, novellas, juvenile books, scholarly books. **Considers these fiction areas:** contemporary issues, family saga, humor, inspirational, new adult, religious, romance, suspense, women's, young adult.

☞ "This agency specializes in the Christian bookseller market." Actively seeking adult fiction, self-help, nutritional books, Christian living, devotional, and business. Does not want to receive erotica, gay/lesbian, fantasy, horror, etc.

HOW TO CONTACT E-query preferred, USPS to the Pittsburgh office. Target 1 agent only. "All e-mail submissions sent to Hartline Agents should be sent as a MS Word doc (or in rich text file format from another word processing program) attached to an e-mail with 'submission: title, authors name and word count' in the subject line. A proposal is a single document, not a collection of files. Place the query letter in the e-mail itself. Do not send the entire proposal in the body of the e-mail or send PDF files." Further guidelines online. Accepts simultaneous submissions. Responds in 2 months to queries; 3 months to mss. Obtains most new clients through recommendations from others, and at conferences.

TERMS Agent receives 15% commission on domestic sales. Offers written contract.

JOHN HAWKINS & ASSOCIATES, INC.

80 Maiden Ln., Suite 1503, New York NY 10038. (212)807-7040. **E-mail:** jha@jhalit.com. **Website:** www.jhalit.com. **Contact:** Moses Cardona (rights and translations); Annie Kronenberg (permissions); Warren Frazier, literary agent; Anne Hawkins, literary agent. Member of AAR. The Author Guild Represents 100+ clients.

MEMBER AGENTS Moses Cardona, moses@jhalit.com (commercial fiction, suspense, business, science, and multicultural fiction); Warren Frazier, frazier@jhalit.com (fiction; nonfiction, specifically technology, history, world affairs and foreign policy); Anne Hawkins, ahawkins@jhalit.com (thrillers to literary fiction to serious nonfiction; interested in science, history, public policy, medicine and women's issues).

REPRESENTS Nonfiction, fiction, novels, short story collections, novellas. **Considers these fiction areas:** commercial, historical, literary, multicultural, suspense, thriller.

HOW TO CONTACT Query. Include the word "Query" in the subject line. For fiction, include 1-3 chapters of your book as a single Word attachment. For nonfiction, include your proposal as a single attachment. E-mail a particular agent directly if you are targeting one. Accepts simultaneous submissions. Responds in 1 month to queries. Obtains most new clients through recommendations from others.

TERMS Agent receives 15% commission on domestic sales; 20% commission on foreign sales. Charges clients for photocopying.

RECENT SALES *Forty Rooms* by Olga Grushin, *A Book of American Martyrs* by Joyce Carol Oates, *City on Edge* by Stefanie Pintoff, *Cold Earth* by Ann Cleeves, *The Good Lieutenant* by Whitney Terrell, *Grief Cottage* by Gail Godwin.

☺ HELEN HELLER AGENCY INC.

4-216 Heath St. W., Toronto ON M5P 1N7 Canada. (416)489-0396. **E-mail:** info@helenhelleragency.com. **Website:** www.helenhelleragency.com. **Contact:** Helen Heller. Represents 30+ clients.

☺ Prior to her current position, Ms. Heller worked for Cassell & Co. (England), was an editor for Harlequin Books, a senior editor for Avon Books, and editor in chief for Fitzhenry & Whiteside.

MEMBER AGENTS Helen Heller, helen@helenhelleragency.com (thrillers and front-list general fiction); Sarah Heller, sarah@helenhelleragency.com (front list commercial YA and adult fiction, with a particular interest in high concept historical fiction); Barbara Berson, barbara@helenhelleragency.com (literary fiction, nonfiction, and YA).

REPRESENTS Nonfiction, novels. **Considers these fiction areas:** commercial, crime, historical, literary, mainstream, thriller, young adult.

HOW TO CONTACT E-mail info@helenhelleragency.com. Submit a brief synopsis, publishing history, author bio, and writing sample, pasted in the body of the e-mail. No attachments with e-queries. Accepts simultaneous submissions. Responds within 3 months if interested. Accepts simultaneous submissions. Obtains most new clients through recommendations from others, solicitations.

TIPS "Whether you are an author searching for an agent, or whether an agent has approached you, it is in your best interest to first find out who the agent represents, what publishing houses has that agent sold to recently and what foreign sales have been made. You should be able to go to the bookstore, or search online and find the books the agent refers to. Many authors acknowledge their agents in the front or back or their books."

RICHARD HENSHAW GROUP

145 W. 28th St., 12th Floor, New York NY 10001. (212)414-1172. **E-mail:** submissions@henshaw.com. **Website:** www.richardhenshawgroup.com. **Contact:** Rich Henshaw. Member of AAR.

○ Prior to opening his agency, Mr. Henshaw served as an agent with Richard Curtis Associates, Inc.

REPRESENTS Novels. **Considers these fiction areas:** fantasy, historical, horror, literary, mainstream, mystery, police, romance, science fiction, thriller, young adult.

⬥ "We specialize in popular fiction and nonfiction and are affiliated with a variety of writers' organizations. Our clients include *New York Times* bestsellers and recipients of major awards in fiction and nonfiction." "We only consider works between 65,000-150,000 words." "We do not represent children's books, screenplays, short fiction, poetry, textbooks, scholarly works or coffee-table books."

HOW TO CONTACT "Please feel free to submit a query letter in the form of an e-mail of fewer than 250 words to submissions@henshaw.com address." No snail mail queries. Accepts simultaneous submissions. Obtains most new clients through recommendations from others, solicitations, conferences.

TERMS Agent receives 15% commission on domestic sales; 20% commission on foreign sales. No written contract. Charges clients for photocopying and book orders.

TIPS "While we do not have any reason to believe that our submission guidelines will change in the near future, writers can find up-to-date submission policy information on our website. Always include a SASE with correct return postage."

HILL NADELL LITERARY AGENCY

6442 Santa Monica Blvd., Suite 201, Los Angeles CA 90038. (310)860-9605. **E-mail:** queries@hillnadell.com. **Website:** www.hillnadell.com. Represents 100 clients.

MEMBER AGENTS Bonnie Nadell (nonfiction books include works on current affairs and food as well as memoirs and other narrative nonfiction; in fiction, she represents thrillers along with upmarket women's and literary fiction); Dara Hyde (literary and genre fiction, narrative nonfiction, graphic novels, memoir and the occasional young adult novel).

REPRESENTS Nonfiction, novels. **Considers these fiction areas:** literary, mainstream, thriller, women's, young adult.

HOW TO CONTACT Send a query and SASE. If you would like your materials returned, please include adequate postage. To submit electronically: Send your query letter and the first 5-10 pages to queries@hillnadell.com. No attachments. Due to the high volume of submissions the agency receives, it cannot guarantee a response to all e-mailed queries. Accepts simultaneous submissions.

TERMS Agent receives 15% commission on domestic and film sales; 20% commission on foreign sales. Charges clients for photocopying and foreign mailings.

HOLLOWAY LITERARY

P.O. Box 771, Cary NC 27512. **E-mail:** submissions@hollowayliteraryagency.com. **Website:** hollowayliteraryagency.com. **Contact:** Nikki Terpilowski. Estab. 2011. Member of AAR. Signatory of WGA. International Thriller Writers and Romance Writers of America Represents 26 clients.

MEMBER AGENTS Nikki Terpilowski (romance, women's fiction, Southern fiction, historical fiction, cozy mysteries, military/political thrillers, commercial, upmarket/book club fiction, African-American fiction of all types); Rachel Burkot (young adult contemporary, women's fiction, upmarket/book club fiction, contemporary romance, Southern fiction, literary fiction); Michael Caligaris (literary fiction, autobiographical fiction, short story collections or connected stories as a novel, Americana, crime fiction, mystery/noir, dystopian fiction, civil unrest/political uprising/war novels, memoir, new journalism and/or long-form journalism, essay collections, satirical/humor writing, and environmental writing).

REPRESENTS Nonfiction, fiction, movie scripts, feature film. **Considers these fiction areas:** action, adventure, commercial, contemporary issues, crime, detective, ethnic, family saga, fantasy, glitz, historical, inspirational, literary, mainstream, metaphysical, middle grade, military, multicultural, mystery, new adult, New Age, regional, romance, short story collections, spiritual, suspense, thriller, urban fantasy, war, women's, young adult.

☛ "Note to self-published authors: While we are happy to receive submissions from authors who have previously self-published novels, we do not represent self-published works. Send us your unpublished mss only." Does not want horror, true crime or novellas.

HOW TO CONTACT Send query and first 15 pages of ms pasted into the body of e-mail to submissions@hollowayliteraryagency.com. In the subject header write: (Insert Agent's Name)/Title/Genre. Holloway Literary does accept submissions via mail (query letter and first 50 pages). Expect a response time of at least 3 months. Include e-mail address, phone number, social media accounts, and mailing address on your query letter. Accepts simultaneous submissions. Responds in 4-6 weeks. If the agent is interested, he/she'll respond with a request for more material.

RECENT SALES A list of recent sale is available on the website's client news page.

HSG AGENCY

37 W. 28th St., 8th Floor, New York NY 10001. **E-mail:** channigan@hsgagency.com; jsalky@hsgagency.com; jgetzler@hsgagency.com; tprasanna@hsgagency.com; leigh@hsgagency.com. **Website:** hsgagency.com. **Contact:** Carrie Hannigan; Jesseca Salky; Josh Getzler;Tanusri Prasanna; Leigh Eisenman. Estab. 2011. Member of AAR. Signatory of WGA.

○ Prior to opening HSG Agency, Ms. Hannigan, Ms. Salky. and Mr. Getzler were agents at Russell & Volkening.

MEMBER AGENTS Carrie Hannigan; Jesseca Salky (literary and mainstream fiction); Josh Getzler (foreign and historical fiction; both women's fiction, straight-ahead historical fiction, and thrillers and mysteries); Tanusri Prasanna (picture books, children's, MG, YA, select nonfiction); Leigh Eisenman (literary and upmarket fiction, foodie/cookbooks, health and fitness, lifestyle, and select narrative nonfiction).

REPRESENTS Nonfiction, fiction, novels, juvenile books. **Considers these fiction areas:** adventure, commercial, contemporary issues, crime, detective, ethnic, family saga, historical, juvenile, literary, mainstream, middle grade, multicultural, mystery, picture books, thriller, translation, women's, young adult.

HOW TO CONTACT Electronic submissions only. Send query letter, first 5 pages of ms within e-mail to appropriate agent. Avoid submitting to multiple agents within the agency. Picture books: include entire ms. Responds in 4-6 weeks if interested.

RECENT SALES A Spool of Blue Thread by Anne Tyler (Knopf), Blue Sea Burning by Geoff Rodkey (Putnam), The Partner Track by Helen Wan (St. Martin's Press), The Thrill of the Haunt by E.J. Copperman (Berkley), Aces Wild by Erica Perl (Knopf Books for Young Readers), Steve & Wessley: The Sea Monster by Jennifer Morris (Scholastic), Infinite Worlds by Michael Soluri (Simon & Schuster).

INKLINGS LITERARY AGENCY

3419 Virginia Beach Blvd. #183, Virginia Beach VA 23452. (757)340-1070. **Fax:** (904)758-5440. **E-mail:** michelle@inklingsliterary.com. **E-mail:** query@inklingsliterary.com. **Website:** www.inklingsliterary.com. Estab. 2013. RWA, SinC, HRW.

○ "We offer our clients interactive representation for their work, as well as developmental guidance for their author platforms, working with them as they grow. With backgrounds in book selling, business, marketing, publicity, contract negotiation, as well as editing and writing, and script work, we work closely with our clients to build their brands and their careers." The face of publishing is ever-changing, and bending and shifting with the times and staying ahead of the curve are key for Michelle and her agency, Inklings Literary Agency. The agents of Inklings Literary Agency all strictly adhere to the AAR's code of ethics.

MEMBER AGENTS Michelle Johnson, michelle@inklingsliterary.com (in adult and YA fiction, contemporary, suspense, thriller, mystery, horror, fantasy — including paranormal and supernatural elements within those genres), romance of every level, nonfiction in the areas of memoir and true crime); Dr. Jamie Bodnar Drowley, jamie@inklingsliterary.com (new adult fiction in the areas of romance [all subgenres], fantasy [urban fantasy, light sci-fi, steampunk], mystery and thrillers—as well as young adult [all subgenres] and middle grade stories); Margaret Bail, margaret@inklingsliterary.com (romance, science fiction, mystery, thrillers, action adventure, historical fiction, Western, some fantasy, memoir, cookbooks, true crime); Naomi Davis, naomi@inklingsliterary.com (romance of any variety—including paranormal, fresh urban fantasy, general fantasy, new adult and light sci-fi; young adult in any of those same genres; memoirs about living with disabilities, facing criticism, and mental illness); Whitley Abell, whitley@inklingsliterary.com (young adult, middle grade, and select upmarket women's fiction); Alex Barba, alex@inklingsliterary.com (YA fiction).

REPRESENTS Nonfiction, fiction, novels, juvenile books. **Considers these fiction areas:** action, adventure, commercial, contemporary issues, crime, detective, erotica, ethnic, fantasy, feminist, gay, historical, horror, juvenile, lesbian, mainstream, metaphysical, middle grade, military, multicultural, multimedia, mystery, new adult, New Age, occult, paranormal, police, psychic, regional, romance, science fiction, spiritual, sports, supernatural, suspense, thriller, urban fantasy, war, women's, young adult.

HOW TO CONTACT E-queries only. To query, type "Query (Agent Name)" plus the title of your novel in the subject line, then please send your query letter, short synopsis, and first 10 pages pasted into the body of the e-mail to query@inklingsliterary.com. Check the agency website to make sure that your targeted agent is currently open to submissions. Accepts simultaneous submissions. For queries, no response in 3 months is considered a rejection. Yes

TERMS Agent takes 15% domestic, 20% subsidiary commission. Charges no fees.

INKWELL MANAGEMENT, LLC

521 Fifth Ave., Suite 2600, New York NY 10175. (212)922-3500. **Fax:** (212)922-0535. **E-mail:** info@inkwellmanagement.com. **E-mail:** submissions@inkwellmanagement.com. **Website:** www.inkwellmanagement.com. Represents 500 clients.

MEMBER AGENTS Stephen Barbara (select adult fiction and nonfiction); William Callahan (nonfiction of all stripes, especially American history and memoir, pop culture and illustrated books, as well as voice-driven fiction that stands out from the crowd); Michael V. Carlisle; Catherine Drayton (bestselling authors of books for children, young adults and women readers); David Forrer (literary, commercial, historical and crime fiction to suspense/thriller, humorous nonfiction and popular history); Alexis Hurley (literary and commercial fiction, memoir, narrative nonfiction and more); Nathaniel Jacks (memoir, narrative nonfiction, social sciences, health, current affairs, business, religion, and popular history, as well as fiction—literary and commercial, women's, young adult, historical, short story, among others); Jacqueline Murphy; (fiction, children's books, graphic novels and illustrated works, and compelling narrative nonfiction); Richard Pine; Eliza Rothstein (literary and commercial fiction, narrative nonfiction, memoir, popular science, and food writing); David Hale Smith; Kimberly Witherspoon; Jenny Witherell; Charlie Olson; Liz Parker (commercial and upmarket women's fiction and narrative, practical, and platform-driven nonfiction); George Lucas; Lyndsey Blessing; Claire Draper; Kate Falkoff; Claire Friedman; Michael Mungiello; Jessica Mileo; Corinne Sullivan; Maria Whelan.

REPRESENTS Novels. **Considers these fiction areas:** commercial, crime, historical, literary, middle grade, picture books, romance, short story collections, suspense, thriller, women's, young adult.

HOW TO CONTACT "In the body of your e-mail, please include a query letter and a short writing sample (1-2 chapters). We currently accept submissions in all genres except screenplays. Due to the volume of queries we receive, our response time may take up to 2 months. Feel free to put 'Query for [Agent Name]: [Your Book Title]' in the e-mail subject line." Accepts simultaneous submissions. Obtains most new clients through recommendations from others.

TERMS Agent receives 15% commission on domestic sales; 20% commission on foreign sales. Offers written contract.

TIPS "We will not read mss before receiving a letter of inquiry."

INTERNATIONAL TRANSACTIONS, INC.

P.O. Box 97, Gila NM 88038-0097. (845)373-9696. **Fax:** (480)393-5162. **E-mail:** submission-nonfiction@intl-trans.com; submission-fiction@intltrans.com. **Website:** www.intltrans.com. **Contact:** Peter Riva. Estab. 1975.

MEMBER AGENTS Peter Riva (nonfiction, fiction, illustrated; television and movie rights placement); Sandra Riva (fiction, juvenile, biographies); JoAnn Collins (fiction, women's fiction, medical fiction).

REPRESENTS Nonfiction, fiction, novels, short story collections, juvenile books, scholarly books, illustrated books, anthologies. **Considers these fiction areas:** action, adventure, commercial, crime, detective, erotica, experimental, family saga, feminist, gay, historical, humor, inspirational, lesbian, literary, mainstream, middle grade, military, multicultural, mystery, new adult, police, satire, science fiction, spiritual, sports, suspense, thriller, translation, war, westerns, women's, young adult, chick lit.

⌐ "We specialize in large and small projects, helping qualified authors perfect material for publication." Always actively seeking intelligent, well-written innovative material that breaks new ground. Does not want to receive material influenced by TV (too much dialogue); a rehash of previous successful novels' themes, or poorly prepared material.

HOW TO CONTACT First, e-query with an outline or synopsis. E-queries only. Put "Query: [Title]" in the e-mail subject line. Responds in 3 weeks to queries; 5 weeks to mss after request. Obtains most new clients through recommendations from others, solicitations.

TERMS Agent receives 15% (25% on illustrated books) commission on domestic sales; 20% commission on foreign sales and media rights. Offers written contract; 100-day notice must be given to terminate contract. No additional fees, ever.

RECENT SALES Averaging 20+ book placements per year.

JANKLOW & NESBIT ASSOCIATES

285 Madison Ave., 21st Floor, New York NY 10017. (212)421-1700. **Fax:** (212)355-1403. **E-mail:** info@janklow.com. **E-mail:** submissions@janklow.com. **Website:** www.janklowandnesbit.com. Estab. 1989.

MEMBER AGENTS Morton L. Janklow; Anne Sibbald; Lynn Nesbit; Luke Janklow; PJ Mark (interests are eclectic, including short stories and literary novels. His nonfiction interests include journalism, popular culture, memoir/narrative, essays and cultural criticism); Paul Lucas (literary and commercial fiction, focusing on literary thrillers, science fiction and fantasy; also seeks narrative histories of ideas and objects, as well as biographies and popular science); Emma Parry (nonfiction by experts, but will consider outstanding literary fiction and upmarket commercial fiction); Kirby Kim (formerly of WME); Marya Spence; Allison Hunter; Melissa Flashman; Stefanie Lieberman.

REPRESENTS Nonfiction, fiction.

HOW TO CONTACT Query via snail mail or e-mail. Include a cover letter, synopsis and the first 10 pages if sending fiction (no attachments). For nonfiction, send a query and full outline. Address your submission to an individual agent. Accepts simultaneous submissions. Responds in 8 weeks to queries/mss. Obtains most new clients through recommendations from others.

TIPS "Please send a short query with first 10 pages or artwork."

J DE S ASSOCIATES, INC.

9 Shagbark Rd., Norwalk CT 06854. (203)838-7571. **E-mail:** jdespoel@aol.com. **Website:** www.jdesassociates. com. **Contact:** Jacques de Spoelberch. Estab. 1975.

◯ Prior to opening his agency, Mr. de Spoelberch was an editor with Houghton Mifflin. And launched International Literary Management for the International Management Group.

REPRESENTS Novels. **Considers these fiction areas:** crime, detective, frontier, historical, juvenile, literary, mainstream, mystery, New Age, police, suspense, westerns, young adult.

HOW TO CONTACT "Brief queries by regular mail and e-mail are welcomed for fiction and nonfiction, but kindly do not include sample proposals or other material unless specifically requested to do so." Accepts simultaneous submissions. Responds in 2 months to queries. Obtains most new clients through recommendations from authors and other clients.

TERMS Agent receives 15% commission on domestic sales; 20% commission on foreign sales. Charges clients for foreign postage and photocopying.

RECENT SALES Joshilyn Jackson's new novel, *A Grown-Up Kind of Pretty* (Grand Central); Margaret George's final Tudor historical, *Elizabeth I* (Penguin); the fifth in Leighton Gage's series of Brazilian thrillers, *A Vine in the Blood* (Soho); Genevieve Graham's romance *Under the Same Sky* (Berkley Sensation);

Hilary Holladay's biography of the early Beat Herbert Huncke, *American Hipster* (Magnus); Ron Rozelle's *My Boys and Girls Are in There: The 1937 New London School Explosion* (Texas A&M); the concluding novel in Dom Testa's YA science fiction series, *The Galahad Legacy* (Tor); and Bruce Coston's new collection of animal stories, *The Gift of Pets* (St. Martin's Press).

THE CAROLYN JENKS AGENCY

30 Cambridge Park Dr., Cambridge MA 02140. (617)354-5099. **E-mail:** queries@carolynjenksagency.com. **Website:** www.carolynjenksagency.com. **Contact:** Carolyn Jenks. Estab. 1987. Signatory of WGA.
MEMBER AGENTS Carolyn Jenks; see agency website for a list of junior agents.
REPRESENTS Nonfiction, fiction, novels, juvenile books. **Considers these fiction areas:** action, adventure, contemporary issues, crime, ethnic, experimental, family saga, feminist, gay, historical, horror, juvenile, lesbian, literary, mainstream, mystery, new adult, science fiction, thriller, women's, young adult.
HOW TO CONTACT Please submit a one-page query including a brief bio via the form on the agency website. "Due to the high volume of queries we receive, we are unable to respond to everyone. Queries are reviewed on a rolling basis, and we will follow up directly with the author if there is interest in a full ms. Queries should not be addressed to specific agents. All queries go directly to the director for distribution." Obtains new clients by recommendations from others, queries/submissions, agency outreach.
TERMS Offers written contract, 1-3 years depending on the project. Requires 60-day notice before terminating contract. No fees.
RECENT SALES *Snafu* by Miryam Sivan (Cuidano Press), *The Land of Forgotten Girls* by Erin Kelly (HarperCollins), *The Christos Mosaic* by Vincent Czyz (Blank Slate Press), *A Tale of Two Maidens* by Anne Echols (Bagwyn Books), *Esther* by Rebecca Kanner (Simon & Schuster), *Magnolia City* by Duncan Alderson (Kensington Books).
TIPS "Do not make cold calls to the agency. E-mail contact only. Do not query for more than 1 property at a time. If possible, have a professional photograph of yourself ready to submit with your query, as it is important to be media-genic in today's marketplace. Be ready to discuss platform."

JET LITERARY ASSOCIATES

941 Calle Mejia, #507, Santa Fe NM 87501. (505)780-0721. **E-mail:** etp@jetliterary.com. **Website:** www.jetliterary.wordpress.com. **Contact:** Liz Trupin-Pulli. Estab. 1975.
MEMBER AGENTS Liz Trupin-Pulli (adult fiction/nonfiction; romance, mysteries, parenting); Jim Trupin (adult fiction/nonfiction, military history, pop culture).
REPRESENTS Nonfiction, fiction, novels, short story collections.

➤ "JET was founded in New York in 1975, so we bring a wealth of knowledge and contacts, as well as quite a bit of expertise to our representation of writers." JET represents the full range of adult fiction and nonfiction. Does not want to receive YA, sci-fi, fantasy, horror, poetry, children's, how-to or religious books.

HOW TO CONTACT Only an e-query should be sent at first. Accepts simultaneous submissions. Responds in 1 week to queries; 8-12 weeks to mss. Obtains most new clients through recommendations from others, solicitations, conferences.
TERMS Agent receives 15% commission on domestic sales; 10% commission on foreign sales, while foreign agent receives 10%. Offers written agency contract, binding for 3 years. This agency charges for reimbursement of mailing and any photocopying.
TIPS "Do not write cute queries; stick to a straightforward message that includes the title and what your book is about, why you are suited to write this particular book, and what you have written in the past (if anything), along with a bit of a bio."

LAWRENCE JORDAN LITERARY AGENCY

231 Lenox Ave., Suite One, New York NY 10027. (212)662-7871. **Fax:** (212)865-7171. **E-mail:** ljlagency@aol.com. **Contact:** Lawrence Jordan, president.

Prior to opening his agency, Mr. Jordan served as an editor with Doubleday & Co.

REPRESENTS Novels.

➤ This agency specializes in general adult fiction and nonfiction. Handles spiritual and religious books, mystery novels, action suspense, thrillers, biographies, autobiographies, and celebrity books. Does not want to receive poetry, movie scripts, stage plays, juvenile books, fantasy novels, or science fiction.

HOW TO CONTACT Online submissions only. Please note that the agency takes on only a few new clients each year. Accepts simultaneous submissions. **TERMS** Agent receives 15% commission on domestic sales; 20% commission on foreign and film sales. Charges for long-distance calls, photocopying, foreign submission costs, postage, cables, messengers.

KELLER MEDIA INC.

578 Washington Blvd., No. 745, Marina del Rey CA 90292. (800)278-8706. **Website:** www.kellermedia. com. **Contact:** Wendy Keller, senior agent (nonfiction only); Megan Close Zavala, literary agent (nonfiction and fiction); Elise Howard, query manager. Estab. 1989. Member of the National Speakers Association.

○ Prior to becoming an agent, Ms. Keller was an award-winning journalist and worked for PR Newswire. Prior to her agenting career, Ms. Close Zavala read, reviewed, edited, rejected, and selected thousands of book and script projects for agencies, film companies, and publishing companies. She uses her background in entertainment and legal affairs in negotiating the best deals for her clients and in helping them think outside of the box.

REPRESENTS Nonfiction, fiction. **Considers these fiction areas:** action, adventure, commercial, family saga, historical, literary, multicultural, mystery, new adult, police, regional, romance, suspense, thriller, women's.

➥ "All of our authors are highly credible experts, who have or want to create a significant platform in media, academia, politics, paid professional speaking, syndicated columns, and/or regular appearances on radio/TV. For fiction submissions, we are interested in working with authors who have strong, fresh voices and who have unique stories (especially in the mystery/thriller/suspense and literary fiction genres!)." Does not want (and absolutely will not respond to) scripts, teleplays, screenplays, poetry, juvenile, science fiction, fantasy, anything religious or overtly political, picture books, illustrated books, young adult, science fiction, fantasy, first-person stories of mental or physical illness, wrongful incarceration, abduction by aliens, books channeled by aliens, demons, or dead celebrities ("we wish we were kidding!").

HOW TO CONTACT To query, please review our current screening criteria on our website: www.kellermedia.com/our-screening-criteria. "Please do not mail us anything unless requested to do so by a staff member." Accepts simultaneous submissions. Responds in 7 days or less. Obtains most new clients through referrals.

TERMS Agent receives 15% commission on domestic sales; 20% commission on foreign, dramatic, sponsorship, appearance fees, audio, and merchandising deals; 30% on speaking engagements we book for the author.

RECENT SALES Check online for latest sales.

HARVEY KLINGER, INC.

300 W. 55th St., Suite 11V, New York NY 10019. (212)581-7068. **E-mail:** queries@harveyklinger.com. **Website:** www.harveyklinger.com. **Contact:** Harvey Klinger. Estab. 1977. Member of AAR. PEN Represents 100 clients.

MEMBER AGENTS Harvey Klinger; David Dunton (popular culture, music-related books, literary fiction, young adult, fiction, and memoirs); Andrea Somberg (literary fiction, commercial fiction, romance, sci-fi/fantasy, mysteries/thrillers, young adult, middle grade, quality narrative nonfiction, popular culture, how-to, self-help, humor, interior design, cookbooks, health/fitness); Wendy Levinson (literary and commercial fiction, occasional children's YA or MG, wide variety of nonfiction); Rachel Ridout (children's MG and YA).

REPRESENTS Nonfiction, fiction, novels, juvenile books. **Considers these fiction areas:** action, adventure, commercial, contemporary issues, crime, detective, erotica, family saga, fantasy, gay, glitz, historical, horror, juvenile, lesbian, literary, mainstream, middle grade, mystery, new adult, police, romance, suspense, thriller, women's, young adult.

➥ This agency specializes in big, mainstream, contemporary fiction and nonfiction. Great debut or established novelists and in nonfiction, authors with great ideas and a national platform already in place to help promote one's book. No Screenplays, poetry, textbooks or anything too technical.

HOW TO CONTACT Use online e-mail submission form on the website, or query with SASE via snail mail. No phone or fax queries. Don't send unsolicited mss or e-mail attachments. Make submission letter to the point and as brief as possible. Accepts simultaneous submissions. Responds in 2-4 weeks to queries, if interested. Obtains most new clients through recommendations from others.

TERMS Agent receives 15% commission on domestic sales; 25% commission on foreign sales. Offers written contract. Charges for photocopying mss and overseas postage for mss.

RECENT SALES *Land of the Afternoon Sun* by Barbara Wood; *I Am Not a Serial Killer* by Dan Wells; *Me, Myself and Us* by Brian Little; *The Secret of Magic* by Deborah Johnson; *Children of the Mist* by Paula Quinn. Other clients include George Taber, Terry Kay, Scott Mebus, Jacqueline Kolosov, Jonathan Maberry, Tara Altebrando, Alex McAuley, Eva Nagorski, Greg Kot, Justine Musk, Michael Northrup, Nina LaCour, Ashley Kahn, Barbara De Angelis, Robert Patton, Augusta Trobaugh.

KNEERIM & WILLIAMS

90 Canal St., Boston MA 02114. **Website:** www.kwblit.com. Also located in New York and Washington D.C. Estab. 1990.

O   Prior to becoming an agent, Mr. Williams was a lawyer; Ms. Kneerim was a publisher and editor; Mr. Wasserman was an editor and journalist; Ms. Bloom worked in magazines; Ms. Flynn worked in academia.

MEMBER AGENTS Katherine Flynn, flynn@kwblit.com (history, biography, politics, current affairs, adventure, nature, pop culture, science, and psychology for nonfiction and particularly loves exciting narrative nonfiction; literary and commercial fiction with urban or foreign locales, crime novels, insight into women's lives, biting wit, and historical settings); Jill Kneerim, jill@kwblit.com (narrative history; sociology; psychology and anthropology; biography; women's issues; and good writing); Ike Williams, jtwilliams@kwblit.com (biography, history, politics, natural science, and anthropology); Carol Franco, carolfranco@comcast.net (business; nonfiction; distinguished self-help/how-to); Lucy Cleland; Hope Denekamp; Emma Hamilton.

☛   Actively seeking distinguished authors, experts, professionals, intellectuals, and serious writers.

HOW TO CONTACT E-query an individual agent. Send no attachments. Put "Query" in the subject line. Accepts simultaneous submissions. Obtains most new clients through recommendations from others.

THE KNIGHT AGENCY

232 W. Washington St., Madison GA 30650. **E-mail:** deidre.knight@knightagency.net. **E-mail:** submissions@knightagency.net. **Website:** knightagency.net/. **Contact:** Deidre Knight. Estab. 1996. Member of AAR. SCWBI, WFA, SFWA, RWA. Represents 200+ clients.

MEMBER AGENTS Deidre Knight (romance, women's fiction, erotica, commercial fiction, inspirational, m/m fiction, memoir and nonfiction narrative, personal finance, true crime, business, popular culture, self-help, religion, and health); Pamela Harty (romance, women's fiction, young adult, business, motivational, diet and health, memoir, parenting, pop culture, and true crime); Elaine Spencer (romance (single title and category), women's fiction, commercial "book-club" fiction, cozy mysteries, young adult and middle grade material); Lucienne Diver (fantasy, science fiction, romance, suspense and young adult); Nephele Tempest (literary/commercial fiction, women's fiction, fantasy, science fiction, romantic suspense, paranormal romance, contemporary romance, historical fiction, young adult and middle grade fiction); Melissa Jeglinski (romance [contemporary, category, historical, inspirational], young adult, middle grade, women's fiction and mystery); Kristy Hunter (romance, women's fiction, commercial fiction, young adult and middle grade material), Travis Pennington (young adult, middle grade, mysteries, thrillers, commercial fiction, and romance [nothing paranormal/fantasy in any genre for now]).

REPRESENTS Nonfiction, fiction, novels. **Considers these fiction areas:** commercial, crime, erotica, fantasy, gay, historical, juvenile, lesbian, literary, mainstream, middle grade, multicultural, mystery, new adult, paranormal, psychic, romance, science fiction, thriller, urban fantasy, women's, young adult.

☛   Actively seeking Romance in all subgenres, including romantic suspense, paranormal romance, historical romance (a particular love of mine), LGBT, contemporary, and also category romance. Occasionally I represent new adult. I'm also seeking women's fiction with vivid voices, and strong concepts (think me before you). Further seeking YA and MG, and select nonfiction in the categories of personal development, self-help, finance/business, memoir, parenting and health. Does not want to receive screenplays, short stories, poetry, essays, or children's picture books.

HOW TO CONTACT E-queries only. "Your submission should include a one-page query letter and the first five pages of your ms. All text must be contained in the body of your e-mail. Attachments will not be opened nor included in the consideration of your work. Queries must be addressed to a specific agent. Please do not query multiple agents." Accepts simultaneous submissions. Responds in 1-2 weeks on queries, 6-8 weeks on submissions.

TERMS 15% Simple agency agreement with open-ended commitment. 15% commission on all domestic sales, 20% on foreign and film.

STUART KRICHEVSKY LITERARY AGENCY, INC.

6 E. 39th St., Suite 500, New York NY 10016. (212)725-5288. **Fax:** (212)725-5275. **Website:** www.skagency.com. Member of AAR.

MEMBER AGENTS Stuart Krichevsky, query@skagency.com (emphasis on narrative nonfiction, literary journalism and literary and commercial fiction); Ross Harris, rhquery@skagency.com (voice-driven humor and memoir, books on popular culture and our society, narrative nonfiction and literary fiction); David Patterson, dpquery@skagency.com (writers of upmarket narrative nonfiction and literary fiction, historians, journalists and thought leaders); Mackenzie Brady Watson, mbwquery@skagency.com (narrative nonfiction, science, history, sociology, investigative journalism, food, business, memoir, and select up-market and literary YA fiction); Hannah Schwartz, hsquery@skagency; Laura Usselman, luquery@skagency.com.

REPRESENTS Nonfiction, novels. **Considers these fiction areas:** commercial, contemporary issues, literary, young adult.

HOW TO CONTACT Please send a query letter and the first few (up to 10) pages of your ms or proposal in the body of an e-mail (not an attachment) to 1 e-mail address. No attachments. Responds if interested. Accepts simultaneous submissions. Obtains most new clients through recommendations from others, solicitations.

THE LA LITERARY AGENCY

P.O. Box 46370, Los Angeles CA 90046. (323)654-5288. **E-mail:** ann@laliteraryagency.com; maureen@laliteraryagency.com. **Website:** www.laliteraryagency.com. **Contact:** Ann Cashman.

○ Prior to becoming an agent, Eric Lasher worked in broadcasting and publishing in New York and Los Angeles. Prior to opening the agency, Maureen Lasher worked in New York at Prentice-Hall, Liveright, and Random House. Please visit the Agency website (www.laliteraryagency.com) for more information.

MEMBER AGENTS Ann Cashman, Eric Lasher, Maureen Lasher.

REPRESENTS Nonfiction, fiction, novels. **Considers these fiction areas:** action, adventure, commercial, contemporary issues, crime, detective, family saga, feminist, historical, literary, mainstream, mystery, suspense, thriller, women's.

HOW TO CONTACT Nonfiction: query letter and book proposal. Fiction: query letter and full ms as an attachment. Accepts simultaneous submissions.

PETER LAMPACK AGENCY, INC.

The Empire State Building, 350 Fifth Ave., Suite 5300, New York NY 10118. (212)687-9106. **Fax:** (212)687-9109. **E-mail:** andrew@peterlampackagency.com. **Website:** www.peterlampackagency.com. **Contact:** Andrew Lampack.

REPRESENTS Nonfiction, fiction, novels. **Considers these fiction areas:** action, adventure, commercial, crime, detective, literary, mainstream, mystery, police, suspense, thriller.

⌐ "This agency specializes in commercial fiction, and nonfiction by recognized experts." Actively seeking literary and commercial fiction in the following categories: adventure, action, thrillers, mysteries, suspense, and psychological thrillers. Does not want to receive horror, romance, science fiction, westerns, historical literary fiction, or academic material.

HOW TO CONTACT The Peter Lampack Agency no longer accepts material through conventional mail. E-queries only. When submitting, you should include a cover letter, author biography and a 1 or 2 page synopsis. Please do not send more than 1 sample chapter of your ms at a time. "Due to the extremely high volume of submissions, we ask that you allow 4-6 weeks for a response." Accepts simultaneous submissions. Obtains most new clients through referrals made by clients.

TERMS Agent receives 15% commission on domestic sales. Agent receives 20% commission on foreign sales.

RECENT SALES *Built to Thrill* by Clive Cussler, *Frozen Fire* by Clive Cussler and Graham Brown, *Odessa Sea* by Clive Cussler and Dirk Cussler, *The Oregon Files* by Clive Cussler and Boyd Morrison, *Police State:*

How America's Cops Get Away with Murder by Gerry Spence, *The Cutthroat* by Clive Cussler and Justin Scott, *The Pirate* by Clive Cussler and Robin Burcell, *The Schooldays of Jesus* by J.M. Coetzee.

WRITERS CONFERENCES BookExpo America; Mystery Writers of America.

TIPS "Submit only your best work for consideration. Have a very specific agenda of goals you wish your prospective agent to accomplish for you. Provide the agent with a comprehensive statement of your credentials—educational and professional accomplishments."

THE STEVE LAUBE AGENCY

24 W. Camelback Rd., A-635, Phoenix AZ 85013. (602)336-8910. **E-mail:** krichards@stevelaube.com. **Website:** www.stevelaube.com. Estab. 2004. Other memberships include CBA, RWA, Author's Guild, etc. Represents 250+ clients.

○ Prior to becoming an agent, Mr. Laube worked over a decade as a Christian bookseller (named bookstore of the year in 1989) and 11 years as editorial director of nonfiction with Bethany House Publishers (named editor of the year by AWSA). Mrs. Murray was an accomplished novelist and agent for 15 years. Mrs. Ball was an executive editor with Tyndale, Multnomah, Zondervan, and B&H Publishing. Mr. Balow was marketing director for the "Left Behind" series at Tyndale.

MEMBER AGENTS Steve Laube (president), Tamela Hancock Murray, Karen Ball, Dan Balow.

REPRESENTS Nonfiction, fiction, novels. **Considers these fiction areas:** fantasy, inspirational, religious, science fiction.

☛ Primarily serves the Christian market (CBA). Actively seeking Christian fiction and Christian nonfiction. Does not want to receive children's picture books, poetry, or cookbooks.

HOW TO CONTACT Submit proposal package, outline, 3 sample chapters, SASE. For e-mail submissions, attach as Word doc or PDF. Consult website for guidelines, because queries are sent to assistants, and the assistants' e-mail addresses may change. Accepts simultaneous submissions. Responds in 6-8 weeks to queries. Obtains most new clients through recommendations from others, solicitations, conferences.

TERMS Agent receives 15% commission on domestic sales; 20% commission on foreign sales. Offers written contract; 30-day notice must be given to terminate contract.

RECENT SALES Average closing on a new book deal every two business days, often for multiple titles in a contract. Clients include Susan May Warren, Lisa Bergren, Lynette Eason, Deborah Raney, Allison Bottke, H. Norman Wright, Ellie Kay, Karol Ladd, Stephen M. Miller, Judith Pella, Nancy Pearcey, William Lane Craig, Elizabeth Goddard, Pamela Tracy, Kim Vogel Sawyer, Mesu Andrews, Mary Hunt, Hugh Ross, Timothy Smith, Roseanna White, Bill and Pam Farrel, Ronie Kendig.

WRITERS CONFERENCES Mount Hermon Christian Writers' Conference; American Christian Fiction Writers' Conference (ACFW).

LAUNCHBOOKS LITERARY AGENCY

E-mail: david@launchbooks.com. **Website:** www.launchbooks.com. **Contact:** David Fugate. Represents 45 clients.

○ David Fugate has been an agent for over 25 years and has successfully represented more than 1,000 book titles. He left another agency to found LaunchBooks in 2005.

REPRESENTS Nonfiction, fiction, novels. **Considers these fiction areas:** action, adventure, commercial, crime, fantasy, horror, humor, mainstream, military, paranormal, satire, science fiction, sports, suspense, thriller, urban fantasy, war, westerns, young adult.

☛ "We're looking for genre-breaking fiction. Do you have the next *The Martian*? Or maybe the next *Red Rising*, *Ready Player One*, *Ancillary Sword*, or *The Bone Clocks*? We're on the lookout for fun, engaging, contemporary novels that appeal to a broad audience. In nonfiction, we're interested in a broad range of topics. Check www.launchbooks.com/submissions for a complete list."

HOW TO CONTACT Query via e-mail. Accepts simultaneous submissions. Responds in 1 week to queries; 4 weeks to mss. Obtains most new clients through recommendations from others, solicitations.

TERMS Agent receives 15% commission on domestic sales; 25% commission on foreign sales. Offers written contract; 30-day notice to terminate contract. Charges occur very seldom. This agency's agreement limits any charges to $50 unless the author gives a written consent.

RECENT SALES *The Martian* by Andy Weir (Random House); *The Remaining: Allegiance* by DJ Molles

(Orbit); *The Fold* by Peter Clines (Crown); *Faster, Higher, Stronger* by Mark McClusky (Hudson Street Press); *Fluent in Three Months* by Benny Lewis (HarperOne); *Captivate* by Vanessa Van Edwards (Portfolio); *Born for This* by Chris Guillebeau (Crown); *The Art of Invisibility* by Kevin Mitnick (Little, Brown); *Hell Divers* by Nicholas Smith (Blackstone); *A History of the United States in Five Crashes* by Scott Nations (William Morrow); *Level Up Your Life* by Steve Kamb (Rodale).

LEVINE GREENBERG ROSTAN LITERARY AGENCY, INC.

307 Seventh Ave., Suite 2407, New York NY 10001. (212)337-0934. **Fax:** (212)337-0948. **E-mail:** submit@lgrliterary.com. **Website:** www.lgrliterary.com. Member of AAR. Represents 250 clients.

○ Prior to opening his agency, Mr. Levine served as vice president of the Bank Street College of Education.

MEMBER AGENTS Jim Levine (nonfiction, including business, science, narrative nonfiction, social and political issues, psychology, health, spirituality, parenting); Stephanie Rostan (adult and YA fiction; nonfiction, including parenting, health & wellness, sports, memoir); Melissa Rowland; Daniel Greenberg (nonfiction: popular culture, narrative nonfiction, memoir, and humor; literary fiction); Victoria Skurnick; Danielle Svetcov (nonfiction); Lindsay Edgecombe (narrative nonfiction, memoir, lifestyle and health, illustrated books, as well as literary fiction); Monika Verma (nonfiction: humor, pop culture, memoir, narrative nonfiction and style and fashion titles; some young adult fiction (paranormal, historical, contemporary)); Kerry Sparks (young adult and middle grade; select adult fiction and occasional nonfiction); Tim Wojcik (nonfiction, including food narratives, humor, pop culture, popular history and science; literary fiction); Arielle Eckstut (no queries); Sarah Bedingfield (literary and upmarket commercial fiction, Epic family dramas, literary novels with notes of magical realism, darkly gothic stories, psychological suspense).

REPRESENTS Nonfiction, novels. **Considers these fiction areas:** commercial, literary, mainstream, middle grade, suspense, young adult.

HOW TO CONTACT E-query to submit@lgrliterary.com, or online submission form. "If you would like to direct your query to 1 of our agents specifically, please feel free to name them in the online form or in the e-mail you send." Cannot respond to submissions by mail. Do not attach more than 50 pages. "Due to the volume of submissions we receive, we are unable to respond to each individually. If we would like more information about your project, we'll contact you within 3 weeks (though we do get backed up on occasion!)." Accepts simultaneous submissions. Obtains most new clients through recommendations from others.

TERMS Agent receives 15% commission on domestic sales; 20% commission on foreign sales. Offers written contract. Charges clients for out-of-pocket expenses—telephone, fax, postage, photocopying—directly connected to the project.

RECENT SALES *Notorious RBG* by Irin Carmon and Shana Knizhnik, *Pogue's Basics: Life* by David Pogue, *Invisible City* by Julia Dahl, *Gumption* by Nick Offerman, *All the Bright Places* by Jennifer Niven.

WRITERS CONFERENCES ASJA Writers' Conference.

TIPS "We focus on editorial development, business representation, and publicity and marketing strategy."

LIPPINCOTT MASSIE MCQUILKIN

27 West 20th Street, Suite 305, New York NY 10011. **E-mail:** info@lmqlit.com. **Website:** www.lmqlit.com.

MEMBER AGENTS Laney Katz Becker, laney@lmqlit.com (book club fiction, upmarket women's fiction, suspense, thrillers and memoir); Ethan Bassoff, ethan@lmqlit.com (literary fiction, crime fiction, and narrative nonfiction in the areas of history, sports writing, journalism, science writing, pop culture, humor, and food writing); Jason Anthony, jason@lmqlit.com (commercial fiction of all types, including young adult, and nonfiction in the areas of memoir, pop culture, true crime, and general psychology and sociology); Will Lippincott, will@lmqlit.com (narrative nonfiction and nonfiction in the areas of politics, history, biography, foreign affairs, and health); Rob McQuilkin, rob@lmqlit.com (literary fiction; narrative nonfiction and nonfiction in the areas of memoir, history, biography, art history, cultural criticism, and popular sociology and psychology; Rayhane Sanders, rayhane@lmqlit.com (literary fiction, historical fiction, upmarket commercial fiction [including select YA], narrative nonfiction [including essays], and select memoir); Stephanie Abou (literary and upmarket commercial fiction (including select young adult and middle grade), crime fiction, memoir, and narrative nonfiction); Julie Stevenson (literary and upmarket fiction, narrative nonfiction, YA and children's books).

REPRESENTS Nonfiction, novels. **Considers these fiction areas:** commercial, contemporary issues, crime, literary, mainstream, middle grade, suspense, thriller, women's, young adult.

☛ "Lippincott Massie McQuilkin is a full-service literary agency that focuses on bringing fiction and nonfiction of quality to the largest possible audience."

HOW TO CONTACT E-query preferred. Include the word "Query" in the subject line of your e-mail. Review the agency's online page of agent bios (lmqlit. com/contact.html), as some agents want sample pages with their submissions and some do not. If you have not heard back from the agency in 4 weeks, assume they are not interested in seeing more. Accepts simultaneous submissions. Obtains most new clients through recommendations from others, solicitations, conferences.

TERMS Agent receives 15% commission on domestic sales. Agent receives 20% commission on foreign sales. Offers written contract; 30-day notice must be given to terminate contract. Only charges for reasonable business expenses upon successful sale.

RECENT SALES Clients include Peter Ho Davies, Kim Addonizio, Natasha Trethewey, David Sirota, Katie Crouch, Uwen Akpan, Lydia Millet, Tom Perrotta, Jonathan Lopez, Chris Hayes, Caroline Weber.

LITERARY MANAGEMENT GROUP, INC.

P.O. Box 41004, Nashville TN 37204. (615)812-4445. **E-mail:** brucebarbour@literarymanagementgroup.com. **Website:** literarymanagementgroup.com. **Contact:** Bruce R. Barbour. Estab. 1996. Represents 100+ clients.

💬 Prior to becoming an agent, Mr. Barbour held executive positions at several publishing houses, including Revell, Barbour Books, Thomas Nelson, and Random House.

REPRESENTS Nonfiction.

☛ Does not want to receive gift books, poetry, children's books, short stories, or juvenile/ young adult fiction. No unsolicited mss or proposals from unpublished authors.

HOW TO CONTACT E-mail proposal as an attachment. Consult website for submission guidelines. Accepts simultaneous submissions. "We acknowledge receipt and review proposals within 4 weeks."

TERMS Agent receives 15% commission on domestic sales.

STERLING LORD LITERISTIC, INC.

115 Broadway, New York NY 10006. (212)780-6050. **Fax:** (212)780-6095. **E-mail:** info@sll.com. **Website:** www.sll.com. Estab. 1987. Member of AAR. Signatory of WGA.

MEMBER AGENTS Philippa Brophy (represents journalists, nonfiction writers and novelists, and is most interested in current events, memoir, science, politics, biography, and women's issues); Laurie Liss (represents authors of commercial and literary fiction and nonfiction whose perspectives are well developed and unique); Sterling Lord; Peter Matson (abiding interest in storytelling, whether in the service of history, fiction, the sciences); Douglas Stewart (primarily fiction for all ages, from the innovatively literary to the unabashedly commercial); Neeti Madan (memoir, journalism, popular culture, lifestyle, women's issues, multicultural books and virtually any intelligent writing on intriguing topics); Robert Guinsler (literary and commercial fiction (including YA), journalism, narrative nonfiction with an emphasis on pop culture, science and current events, memoirs and biographies); Jim Rutman; Celeste Fine (expert, celebrity, and corporate clients with strong national and international platforms, particularly in the health, science, self-help, food, business, and lifestyle fields); Martha Millard (fiction and nonfiction, including well-written science fiction and young adult); Mary Krienke (literary fiction, memoir, and narrative nonfiction, including psychology, popular science, and cultural commentary); Jenny Stephens (nonfiction: cookbooks, practical lifestyle projects, transportive travel and nature writing, and creative nonfiction; fiction: contemporary literary narratives strongly rooted in place); Alison MacKeen (idea-driven research books: social scientific, scientific, historical, relationships/ parenting, learning and education, sexuality, technology, the life-cycle, health, the environment, politics, economics, psychology, geography, and culture; literary fiction, literary nonfiction, memoirs, essays, and travel writing); John Maas (serious nonfiction, specifically business, personal development, science, self-help, health, fitness, and lifestyle); Sarah Passick (commercial nonfiction in the celebrity, food, blogger, lifestyle, health, diet, fitness and fashion categories).

REPRESENTS Nonfiction, fiction. **Considers these fiction areas:** commercial, juvenile, literary, middle grade, picture books, science fiction, young adult.

HOW TO CONTACT Query via snail mail. "Please submit a query letter, a synopsis of the work, a brief proposal or the first 3 chapters of the ms, a brief bio or resume, and SASE for reply. Original artwork is not accepted. Enclose sufficient postage if you wish to have your materials returned to you. We do not respond to unsolicited e-mail inquiries." Accepts simultaneous submissions.

TERMS Agent receives 15% commission on domestic sales; 20% commission on foreign sales. Offers written contract.

LOWENSTEIN ASSOCIATES INC.

115 E. 23rd St., Floor 4, New York NY 10010. (212)206-1630. **E-mail:** assistant@bookhaven.com. **Website:** www.lowensteinassociates.com. **Contact:** Barbara Lowenstein. Member of AAR.

MEMBER AGENTS Barbara Lowenstein, president (nonfiction interests include narrative nonfiction, health, money, finance, travel, multicultural, popular culture, and memoir; fiction interests include literary fiction and women's fiction); Mary South (literary fiction and nonfiction on subjects such as neuroscience, bioengineering, women's rights, design, and digital humanities, as well as investigative journalism, essays, and memoir).

REPRESENTS Nonfiction, fiction, novels, short story collections. **Considers these fiction areas:** commercial, literary, middle grade, science fiction, women's, young adult.

➥ Barbara Lowenstein is currently looking for writers who have a platform and are leading experts in their field, including business, women's issues, psychology, health, science and social issues, and is particularly interested in strong new voices in fiction and narrative nonfiction. Does not want westerns, textbooks, children's picture books and books in need of translation.

HOW TO CONTACT "For fiction, please send us a 1-page query letter, along with the first 10 pages pasted in the body of the message by e-mail to assistant@bookhaven.com. If nonfiction, please send a 1-page query letter, a table of contents, and, if available, a proposal pasted into the body of the e-mail. Please put the word 'QUERY' and the title of your project in the subject field of your e-mail and address it to the agent of your choice. Please do not send an attachment as the message will be deleted without being read and no reply will be sent." Accepts simultaneous submissions. Responds in 6 weeks to queries. Obtains most new clients through recommendations from others, solicitations, conferences.

TERMS Agent receives 15% commission on domestic sales; 20% commission on foreign sales. Offers written contract. Charges for large photocopy batches, messenger service, international postage.

TIPS "Know the genre you are working in and read!"

DONALD MAASS LITERARY AGENCY

1000 Dean St., Suite 252, Brooklyn NY 11238. (212)727-8383. **Website:** www.maassagency.com. Estab. 1980. Member of AAR. Other memberships include SFWA, MWA, RWA. Represents more than 100 clients.

◐ Prior to opening his agency, Mr. Maass worked as an editor at Dell Publishing (New York) and as a reader at Gollancz (London). He is a past president of the Association of Authors' Representatives, Inc. (AAR).

MEMBER AGENTS Donald Maass (mainstream, literary, mystery/suspense, science fiction, romance); Jennifer Jackson (science fiction and fantasy for both adult and YA markets, thrillers that mine popular and controversial issues, YA that challenges traditional thinking); Cameron McClure (literary, mystery/suspense, urban, fantasy, narrative nonfiction and projects with multicultural, international, and environmental themes, gay/lesbian); Amy Boggs (fantasy and science fiction, YA/MG, historical fiction about eras that aren't well known); Katie Shea Boutillier (women's fiction/book club, edgy/dark, realistic/contemporary YA, commercial-scale literary fiction, and celebrity memoir); Michael Curry (science fiction and fantasy, near future thrillers); Caitlin McDonald (SF/F [YA/MG/Adult], genre-bending/cross-genre fiction, diversity).

REPRESENTS Nonfiction, fiction, novels, juvenile books. **Considers these fiction areas:** contemporary issues, crime, detective, ethnic, fantasy, feminist, gay, historical, horror, juvenile, lesbian, literary, mainstream, middle grade, multicultural, mystery, paranormal, police, regional, romance, science fiction, supernatural, suspense, thriller, urban fantasy, westerns, women's, young adult.

➥ This agency specializes in commercial fiction, especially science fiction, fantasy, thrillers, suspense, women's fiction—for both the adult and YA markets. Does not want poetry, screenplays, picture books.

HOW TO CONTACT Query via e-mail only. All the agents have different submission addresses and instructions. See the website and each agent's online profile for exact submission instructions. Accepts simultaneous submissions.

TERMS Agency receives 15% commission on domestic sales; 20% commission on foreign sales.

RECENT SALES *The Aeronaut's Windlass* by Jim Butcher (Penguin Random House), *City of Blades* by Robert Jackson Bennett (Crown), *I am Princess X* by Cherie Priest (Scholastic), *Treachery at Lancaster Gate* by Anne Perry (Random House), *Marked in Flesh* by Anne Bishop (Penguin Random House), *We Are the Ants* by Shaun David Hutchinson (Simon & Schuster), *The Book of Phoenix* by Nnedi Okorafor (DAW), *Ninefox Gambit* by Yoon Ha Lee (Solaris), *The Far End of Happy* by Kathryn Craft (Sourcebooks), *The Traitor Baru Cormorant* by Seth Dickinson (Tor).

WRITERS CONFERENCES See each agent's profile page at the agency website for conference schedules.

TIPS "We are fiction specialists, also noted for our innovative approach to career planning. We are always open to submissions from new writers." Works with subagents in all principle foreign countries and for film and television.

GINA MACCOBY LITERARY AGENCY

P.O. Box 60, Chappaqua NY 10514. (914)238-5630. **E-mail:** query@maccobylit.com. **Website:** www.publishersmarketplace.com/members/ginamaccoby/. **Contact:** Gina Maccoby. Estab. 1986. Member of AAR. AAR Board of Directors; Royalties and Ethics and Contracts subcommittees; Authors Guild, SCBWI.

REPRESENTS Nonfiction, fiction, novels, juvenile books. **Considers these fiction areas:** crime, detective, family saga, juvenile, literary, mainstream, middle grade, multicultural, mystery, new adult, thriller, women's, young adult.

HOW TO CONTACT Query by e-mail only. Accepts simultaneous submissions. Owing to volume of submissions, may not respond to queries unless interested. Obtains most new clients through recommendations.

TERMS Agent receives 15% commission on domestic sales; 20-25% commission on foreign sales, which includes subagents commissions. May recover certain costs, such as purchasing books, shipping books overseas by airmail, legal fees for vetting motion picture contracts, bank fees for electronic funds transfers, overnight delivery services.

WRITERS CONFERENCES ThrillerFest PitchFest; Washington Independent Writers Conference; Literary Writers Conference New York City.

CAROL MANN AGENCY

55 Fifth Ave., New York NY 10003. (212)206-5635. **Fax:** (212)675-4809. **E-mail:** submissions@carolmannagency.com. **Website:** www.carolmannagency.com. **Contact:** Isabella Ruggiero. Member of AAR. Represents Roughly 200 clients.

MEMBER AGENTS Carol Mann (health/medical, religion, spirituality, self-help, parenting, narrative nonfiction, current affairs); Laura Yorke; Gareth Esersky; Myrsini Stephanides (nonfiction areas of interest: pop culture and music, humor, narrative nonfiction and memoir, cookbooks; fiction areas of interest: offbeat literary fiction, graphic works, and edgy YA fiction); Joanne Wyckoff (nonfiction areas of interest: memoir, narrative nonfiction, personal narrative, psychology, women's issues, education, health and wellness, parenting, serious self-help, natural history; also accepts fiction); Lydia Shamah (edgy, modern fiction and timely nonfiction in the areas of business, self-improvement, relationship and gift books, particularly interested in female voices and experiences); Tom Miller (narrative nonfiction, self-help/psychology, popular culture, body-mind-spirit, wellness, business, and literary fiction).

REPRESENTS Novels. **Considers these fiction areas:** commercial, literary, young adult, graphic works.

☛ Does not want to receive genre fiction (romance, mystery, etc.).

HOW TO CONTACT Please see website for submission guidelines. Accepts simultaneous submissions. Responds in 4 weeks to queries.

TERMS Agent receives 15% commission on domestic sales; 20% commission on foreign sales. Offers written contract.

MARSAL LYON LITERARY AGENCY, LLC

PMB 121, 665 San Rodolfo Dr. 124, Solana Beach CA 92075. **E-mail:** kevan@marsallyonliteraryagency.com. **Website:** www.marsallyonliteraryagency.com. **Contact:** Kevan Lyon, Jill Marsal. Estab. 2009. RWA

MEMBER AGENTS Kevan Lyon (women's fiction, with an emphasis on commercial women's fiction, young adult fiction and all genres of romance); Jill Marsal (all types of women's fiction and all types of romance; mysteries, cozies, suspense, and thrillers; nonfiction in the areas of current events, business, health, self-help, relationships, psychology, parenting, history, science, and narrative nonfiction); Patricia Nelson (literary fiction and commercial fiction, all types of women's fiction, contemporary and historical romance, young adult and middle grade fiction, LGBTQ fiction for both YA and adult); Deborah Ritchkin (lifestyle books, specifically in the areas of food, design and entertaining; pop culture; women's issues; biography; and current events; her niche interest is projects about France, including fiction); Shannon Hassan (literary and commercial fiction, young adult and middle grade fiction, and select nonfiction). **REPRESENTS** Nonfiction, fiction, novels, juvenile books. **Considers these fiction areas:** commercial, juvenile, literary, mainstream, middle grade, multicultural, mystery, paranormal, romance, suspense, thriller, women's, young adult.

HOW TO CONTACT Query by e-mail. Query only 1 agent at this agency at a time. "Please visit our website to determine who is best suited for your work. Write 'query' in the subject line of your e-mail. Please allow up to several weeks to hear back on your query." Accepts simultaneous submissions.

TIPS "Our agency's mission is to help writers achieve their publishing dreams. We want to work with authors not just for a book but for a career; we are dedicated to building long-term relationships with our authors and publishing partners. Our goal is to help find homes for books that engage, entertain, and make a difference."

THE EVAN MARSHALL AGENCY

1 Pacio Ct., Roseland NJ 07068-1121. (973)287-6216. **Fax:** (973)488-7910. **E-mail:** evan@evanmarshallagency.com. **Website:** www.evanmarshallagency.com. **Contact:** Evan Marshall. Estab. 1987. Member of AAR. Novelists, Inc. Represents 50+ clients.

○ Prior to becoming an agent, Evan Marshall held senior editorial positions at Houghton Mifflin, Ariel Books, New American Library, Everest House and Dodd, Mead, where he acquired national and international bestsellers.

REPRESENTS Fiction, novels. **Considers these fiction areas:** action, adventure, crime, detective, erotica, ethnic, family saga, fantasy, feminist, frontier, gay, glitz, historical, horror, humor, inspirational, lesbian, literary, mainstream, military, multicultural, multi-

media, mystery, new adult, New Age, occult, paranormal, police, psychic, regional, religious, romance, satire, science fiction, spiritual, sports, supernatural, suspense, thriller, translation, urban fantasy, war, westerns, women's, young adult, romance (contemporary, gothic, historical, regency).

➛ "We represent all genres of adult and young adult full-length fiction." Actively seeking high-quality adult and young adult fiction in all genres. Does not want articles, children's books, essays, memoirs, nonfiction, novellas, poetry, screenplays, short stories, stage plays.

HOW TO CONTACT Actively seeking new clients. E-mail query letter, synopsis and first 3 chapters of novel within body of e-mail. Accepts simultaneous submissions. Responds in 1 week to queries. Responds in 1 month to mss. Obtains new clients through queries and through recommendations from editors and current clients.

TERMS Agent receives 15% commission on domestic sales; 20% commission on foreign sales. Offers written contract.

RECENT SALES *No Place I'd Rather Be* by Cathy Lamb (Kensington), *A Beau for Katie* by Emma Miller (Love Inspired), *The Bloody Black Flag* by Steve Goble (Seventh Street), *Fortune's Secret Husband* by Karen Rose Smith (Harlequin), *Windigo Moon* by Robert Downes (Blank Slate Press).

THE MARTELL AGENCY

1350 Avenue of the Americas, Suite 1205, New York NY 10019. **Fax:** (212)317-2676. **E-mail:** submissions@themartellagency.com. **Website:** www.themartellagency.com. **Contact:** Alice Martell.

REPRESENTS Nonfiction, novels.

➛ Seeks the following subjects in fiction: literary and commercial, including mystery, suspense and thrillers. Does not want to receive romance, genre mysteries, genre historical fiction, or children's books.

HOW TO CONTACT E-query Alice Martell. This should include a summary of the project and a short biography and any information, if appropriate, as to why you are qualified to write on the subject of your book, including any publishing credits. Accepts simultaneous submissions.

MARGRET MCBRIDE LITERARY AGENCY

P.O. Box 9128, La Jolla CA 92038. (858)454-1550. **E-mail:** staff@mcbridelit.com. **Website:** www.mcbrideliterary.com. Estab. 1981. Member of AAR. Other memberships include Authors Guild.

○ Prior to opening her agency, Ms. McBride worked at Random House and Ballantine Books. Later, she became the Director of Publicity at Warner Books, and Director of Publicity, Promotions and Advertising for Pinnacle Books.

MEMBER AGENTS Margret McBride; Faye Atchison.

REPRESENTS Nonfiction, fiction, novels. **Considers these fiction areas:** action, adventure, comic books, commercial, confession, contemporary issues, crime, detective, family saga, feminist, historical, horror, juvenile, mainstream, multicultural, multimedia, mystery, new adult, paranormal, police, psychic, regional, supernatural, suspense, thriller, young adult.

☞ This agency specializes in mainstream nonfiction and some commercial fiction. Actively seeking commercial nonfiction, business, health, self-help. Does not want screenplays, romance, poetry, or children's.

HOW TO CONTACT Please check our website, as instructions are subject to change. Only e-mail queries are accepted: staff@mcbridelit.com. In your query letter, provide a brief synopsis of your work, as well as any pertinent information about yourself. We recommend that authors look at book jacket copy of professionally published books to get an idea of the style and content that should be included in a query letter. Essentially, you are marketing yourself and your work to us, so that we can determine whether we feel we can market you and your work to publishers. There are detailed nonfiction proposal guidelines on our website. Please note: The McBride Agency will not respond to queries sent by mail, and will not be responsible for the return of any material submitted by mail. Accepts simultaneous submissions. Responds within 8 weeks to queries; 6-8 weeks to requested mss. "You are welcome to follow up by phone or e-mail after 8 weeks if you have not yet received a response."

TERMS Agent receives 15% commission on domestic sales; 25% commission on translation rights sales (15% to agency, 10% to sub-agent). Charges for overnight delivery and photocopying.

RECENT SALES *Nimble* by Baba Prasad (Perigee/Penguin Random House—U.S. and World rights excluding India), *Carefrontation* by Dr. Arlene Drake (Regan Arts/Phaidon), *There Are No Overachievers* by Brian Biro

(Crown Business/Penguin Random House), *Cheech Is Not My Real Name* by Richard Marin (Grand Central Books/Hachette), *Killing It!* by Sheryl O'Loughlin (Harper Business/HarperCollins), *Scrappy* by Terri Sjodin (Portfolio/Penguin Random House).

TIPS E-mail queries only. Please don't call to pitch your work by phone.

SEAN MCCARTHY LITERARY AGENCY

E-mail: submissions@mccarthylit.com. **Website:** www.mccarthylit.com. **Contact:** Sean McCarthy. Estab. 2013.

○ Prior to his current position, Sean McCarthy began his publishing career as an editorial intern at Overlook Press and then moved over to the Sheldon Fogelman Agency.

REPRESENTS Considers these fiction areas: juvenile, middle grade, picture books, young adult.

☞ Sean is drawn to flawed, multifaceted characters with devastatingly concise writing in YA, and boy-friendly mysteries or adventures in MG. In picture books, he looks more for unforgettable characters, off-beat humor, and especially clever endings. He is not currently interested in high fantasy, message-driven stories, or query letters that pose too many questions.

HOW TO CONTACT E-query. "Please include a brief description of your book, your biography, and any literary or relevant professional credits in your query letter. If you are a novelist: Please submit the first 3 chapters of your ms (or roughly 25 pages) and a 1-page synopsis in the body of the e-mail or as a Word or PDF attachment. If you are a picture book author: Please submit the complete text of your ms. We are not currently accepting picture book mss over 1,000 words. If you are an illustrator: Please attach up to 3 JPEGs or PDFs of your work, along with a link to your website." Accepts simultaneous submissions.

MCCORMICK LITERARY

37 W. 20th St., New York NY 10011. (212)691-9726. **E-mail:** queries@mccormicklit.com. **Website:** mccormicklit.com. Member of AAR. Signatory of WGA.

MEMBER AGENTS David McCormick; Pilar Queen (narrative nonfiction, practical nonfiction, and commercial women's fiction); Bridget McCarthy (literary and commercial fiction, narrative nonfiction, memoir, and cookbooks); Alia Hanna Habib (literary fiction, narrative nonfiction, memoir and cookbooks); Edward Orloff (literary fiction and narrative nonfiction, especially cultural history, politics, biography, and the arts); Daniel Menaker; Leslie Falk; Emma Borges-Scott.

REPRESENTS Nonfiction, novels. **Considers these fiction areas:** literary, women's.

HOW TO CONTACT Snail mail queries only. Send an SASE. Accepts simultaneous submissions.

MCINTOSH & OTIS, INC.

353 Lexington Ave., New York NY 10016. (212)687-7400. **Fax:** (212)687-6894. **E-mail:** info@mcintoshandotis.com. **Website:** www.mcintoshandotis.com. **Contact:** Eugene H. Winick, Esq.. Estab. 1928. Member of AAR. Signatory of WGA. SCBWI

MEMBER AGENTS Elizabeth Winick Rubinstein, ewrquery@mcintoshandotis.com (literary fiction, women's fiction, historical fiction, and mystery/suspense, along with narrative nonfiction, spiritual/self-help, history and current affairs); Shira Hoffman, shquery@mcintoshandotis.com (young adult, MG, mainstream commercial fiction, mystery, literary fiction, women's fiction, romance, urban fantasy, fantasy, science fiction, horror and dystopian); Christa Heschke, CHquery@mcintoshandotis.com (picture books, middle grade, young adult and new adult projects); Adam Muhlig, AMquery@mcintoshandotis.com (music–from jazz to classical to punk–popular culture, natural history, travel and adventure, and sports); Eugene Winick.

REPRESENTS Considers these fiction areas: fantasy, historical, horror, literary, middle grade, mystery, new adult, paranormal, picture books, romance, science fiction, suspense, urban fantasy, women's, young adult.

- ☛ Actively seeking "books with memorable characters, distinctive voices, and great plots."

HOW TO CONTACT E-mail submissions only. Each agent has their own e-mail address for subs. For fiction: Please send a query letter, synopsis, author bio, and the first 3 consecutive chapters (no more than 30 pages) of your novel. For nonfiction: Please send a query letter, proposal, outline, author bio, and 3 sample chapters (no more than 30 pages) of the ms. For children's & young adult: Please send a query letter, synopsis and the first 3 consecutive chapters (not to exceed 25 pages) of the ms. Accepts simultaneous submissions. Obtains clients through recommendations from others, editors, conferences and queries.

TERMS Agent receives 15% commission on domestic sales; 20% on foreign sales.

WRITERS CONFERENCES Attends Bologna Book Fair, in Bologna Italy in April, SCBWI Conference in New York in February, and regularly attends other conferences and industry conventions.

ROBIN MIZELL LTD.

1600 Burnside St., Suite 205, Beaufort SC 29902. (614)774-7405. **E-mail:** mail@robinmizell.com. **Website:** www.robinmizell.com. **Contact:** Robin Mizell. Estab. 2008.

REPRESENTS Nonfiction, fiction, novels. **Considers these fiction areas:** action, adventure, contemporary issues, crime, ethnic, family saga, feminist, frontier, gay, historical, humor, lesbian, literary, mainstream, military, multicultural, mystery, new adult, police, suspense, thriller, translation, war, young adult.

- ☛ This agency specializes in prescriptive nonfiction, long-form narrative journalism, neuroscience, psychology, sociology, pop culture, literary and upmarket commercial fiction, and young adult (not children's or middle grade) fiction and nonfiction. Actively seeking psychological suspense.

HOW TO CONTACT E-query with the first 5 pages of your work pasted below in the e-mail. More specific submission instructions can be found on the agency website. Accepts simultaneous submissions. You should receive a response to your e-mail query within 30 days.

TIPS "This agency will not consider a prospective client who does not have an online presence."

HOWARD MORHAIM LITERARY AGENCY

30 Pierrepont St., Brooklyn NY 11201. (718)222-8400. **Fax:** (718)222-5056. **E-mail:** info@morhaimliterary.com. **Website:** www.morhaimliterary.com. Member of AAR.

MEMBER AGENTS Howard Morhaim, howard@morhaimliterary.com; Kate McKean, kmckean@morhaimliterary.com; DongWon Song, dongwon@morhaimliterary.com; Kim-Mei Kirtland, kimmei@morhaimliterary.com.

REPRESENTS Considers these fiction areas: fantasy, historical, literary, middle grade, new adult, romance, science fiction, women's, young adult, LGBTQ young adult, magical realism, fantasy should be high fantasy, historical fiction should be no earlier than the 20th century..

- ☛ Kate McKean is open to many subgenres and categories of YA and MG fiction. Check the website for the most details. Actively seeking fiction, nonfiction, and young adult novels.

HOW TO CONTACT Query via e-mail with cover letter and 3 sample chapters. See each agent's listing for specifics. Accepts simultaneous submissions.

MOVEABLE TYPE MANAGEMENT

244 Madison Ave., Suite 334, New York NY 10016. **E-mail:** achromy@movabletm.com. **Website:** www.movabletm.com. **Contact:** Adam Chromy. Estab. 2002.

REPRESENTS Nonfiction, fiction, novels. **Considers these fiction areas:** action, commercial, crime, detective, erotica, hi-lo, historical, literary, mainstream, mystery, romance, satire, science fiction, sports, suspense, thriller, women's.

➤ Mr. Chromy is a generalist, meaning that he accepts fiction submissions of virtually any kind (except juvenile books aimed for middle grade and younger) as well as nonfiction. He has sold books in the following categories: new adult, women's, romance, memoir, pop culture, young adult, lifestyle, horror, how-to, general fiction, and more.

HOW TO CONTACT E-queries only. Responds if interested. For nonfiction: Send a query letter in the body of an e-mail that precisely introduces your topic and approach, and includes a descriptive bio. For journalists and academics, please also feel free to include a CV. Fiction: Send your query letter and the first 10 pages of your novel in the body of an e-mail. Your subject line needs to contain the word "Query" or your message will not reach the agency. No attachments and no snail mail. Accepts simultaneous submissions.

RECENT SALES *The Wedding Sisters* by Jamie Brenner (St. Martin's Press), *Rage* by (AmazonCrossing), *Sons Of Zeus* by Noble Smith (Thomas Dunne Books), *World Made By Hand and Too Much Magic* by James Howard Kunstler (Grove/Atlantic Press), *Dirty Rocker Boys* by Bobbie Brown (Gallery/S&S).

DEE MURA LITERARY

P.O. Box 131, Massapequa NY 11762. (516)795-1616. **E-mail:** info@deemuraliterary.com. **E-mail:** query@deemuraliterary.com. **Website:** www.deemuraliterary.com. **Contact:** Dee Mura. Signatory of WGA. Women's National Book Association, GrubStreet

💬 Prior to opening her agency, Mura was a public relations executive with a roster of film and entertainment clients. She is the president and CEO of both Dee Mura Literary and Dee Mura Entertainment.

MEMBER AGENTS Dee Mura, Kimiko Nakamura, Kaylee Davis.

REPRESENTS Nonfiction, fiction, novels, short story collections, juvenile books. **Considers these fiction areas:** action, adventure, comic books, commercial, contemporary issues, crime, detective, erotica, ethnic, family saga, fantasy, feminist, frontier, gay, glitz, historical, horror, humor, inspirational, juvenile, lesbian, literary, mainstream, metaphysical, middle grade, military, multicultural, multimedia, mystery, new adult, New Age, occult, paranormal, police, psychic, regional, religious, romance, satire, science fiction, short story collections, spiritual, sports, supernatural, suspense, thriller, translation, urban fantasy, war, westerns, women's, young adult, Espionage, Magical realism, Speculative Fiction, Crossover.

➤ No screenplays, poetry, or children's picture books.

HOW TO CONTACT Query with SASE or e-mail query@deemuraliterary.com (e-mail queries are preferred). Please include the first 25 pages in the body of the e-mail as well as a short author bio and synopsis of the work. Responds to queries in 4-5 weeks. Responds to mss in approximately 8 weeks. Obtains new clients through recommendations, queries, and conferences. Accepts simultaneous submissions. Responds to queries in 3-4 weeks. Responds to mss in approximately 8 weeks. Obtains new clients through recommendations, queries, and conferences.

TERMS Agent receives 15% commission on domestic sales. Agent receives 20% commission on foreign sales. Offers written contract.

RECENT SALES *An Infinite Number of Parallel Universes* by Randy Ribay, *The Number 7* by Jessica Lidh.

WRITERS CONFERENCES BookExpo America, New England Crime Bake, New England SCBWI Agent Day, The Writer's Institute Conference at UW-Madison, Writer's Digest Annual Conference.

TIPS For more information, please visit us online at deemuraliterary.com.

JEAN V. NAGGAR LITERARY AGENCY, INC.

JVNLA, Inc., 216 E. 75th St., Suite 1E, New York NY 10021. (212)794-1082. **Website:** www.jvnla.com. **Contact:** Jennifer Weltz. Estab. 1978. Member of AAR. Other memberships include Women's Media Group,

SCBWI, Pace University's Masters in Publishing Board Member. Represents 450 clients.

MEMBER AGENTS Jennifer Weltz (well researched and original historicals, thrillers with a unique voice, wry dark humor, and magical realism; enthralling narrative nonfiction; voice driven young adult, middle grade); Alice Tasman (literary, commercial, YA, middle grade, and nonfiction in the categories of narrative, biography, music or pop culture); Laura Biagi (literary fiction, magical realism, psychological thrillers, young adult novels, middle grade novels, and picture books).

REPRESENTS Nonfiction, fiction, novels, short story collections, novellas, juvenile books, scholarly books, poetry books.

☞ This agency specializes in mainstream fiction and nonfiction and literary fiction with commercial potential as well as young adult, middle grade, and picture books. Does not want to receive screenplays.

HOW TO CONTACT "Visit our website to send submissions and see what our individual agents are looking for. No snail mail submissions please!" Accepts simultaneous submissions. Depends on the agent. No responses for queries unless the agent is interested.

TERMS Agent receives 15% commission on domestic sales; 20% commission on foreign sales. Offers written contract. Charges for overseas mailing, messenger services, book purchases, photocopying—all deductible from royalties received.

RECENT SALES *Mort(e)* by Robert Repino, *The Paying Guests* by Sarah Waters, *Violent Crimes* by Phillip Margolin, *An Unseemly Wife* by E.B. Moore, *The Man Who Walked Away* by Maud Casey, *Dietland* by Sarai Walker, *In the Land of Armadillos* by Helen Maryles Shankman, *Not If I See You First* by Eric Lindstrom.

TIPS "We recommend courage, fortitude, and patience: the courage to be true to your own vision, the fortitude to finish a novel and polish it again and again before sending it out, and the patience to accept rejection gracefully and wait for the stars to align themselves appropriately for success."

NELSON LITERARY AGENCY

1732 Wazee St., Suite 207, Denver CO 80202. (303)292-2805. **E-mail:** query@nelsonagency.com. **E-mail:** querykristin@nelsonagency.com. **Website:** www.nelsonagency.com. **Contact:** Kristin Nelson, President. Estab. 2002. Member of AAR. RWA, SCBWI, SFWA. Represents 37 clients.

REPRESENTS Fiction, novels, young adult, middle grade, literary commercial, upmarket women's fiction, single-title romance, science fiction, fantasy. **Considers these fiction areas:** commercial, fantasy, historical, horror, literary, mainstream, middle grade, romance, science fiction, suspense, thriller, urban fantasy, women's, young adult.

☞ NLA specializes in representing commercial fiction and high-caliber literary fiction. "We represent many popular genre categories, including historical romance, steampunk, and all subgenres of YA." Regardless of genre, "we are actively seeking good stories well told." Does not want nonfiction, memoir, stage plays, screenplays, short story collections, poetry, children's picture books, early reader chapter books, or material for the Christian/inspirational market.

HOW TO CONTACT "Please visit our website and carefully read our submission guidelines. We do not accept any queries on Facebook or Twitter. Query by e-mail only. Write the word 'Query' in the e-mail subject line along with the title of your novel. Send no attachments, but please paste the first 10 pages of your novel in the body of the e-mail beneath your query letter." Accepts simultaneous submissions. Makes best efforts to respond to all queries within 10 business day. Response to full mss requested can take up to 3 months.

TERMS Agent charges industry standard commission.

TIPS "If you would like to learn how to write an awesome pitch paragraph for your query letter or would like any info on how publishing contracts work, please visit Kristin's popular industry blog Pub Rants: nelsonagency.com/pub-rants/."

NEW LEAF LITERARY & MEDIA, INC.

110 W. 40th St., Suite 2201, New York NY 10018. (646)248-7989. **Fax:** (646)861-4654. **E-mail:** query@newleafliterary.com. **Website:** www.newleafliterary.com. Estab. 2012. Member of AAR.

MEMBER AGENTS Joanna Volpe (women's fiction, thriller, horror, speculative fiction, literary fiction and historical fiction, young adult, middle grade, art-focused picture books); Kathleen Ortiz, Director of Subsidiary Rights and literary agent (new voices in YA and animator/illustrator talent); Suzie Townsend (new adult, young adult, middle grade, romance [all subgenres], fantasy [urban fantasy, science fiction, steampunk, epic fantasy] and crime fiction [mysteries, thrillers]); Pouya Shahbazian, Director of Film and

Television (no unsolicited queries); Janet Reid, janet@newleafliterary.com; Jaida Temperly (all fiction: magical realism, historical fiction; literary fiction; stories that are quirky and fantastical; nonfiction: niche, offbeat, a bit strange; middle grade; JL Stermer (nonfiction, smart pop culture, comedy/satire, fashion, health & wellness, self-help, and memoir).

REPRESENTS Nonfiction, fiction, novels, novellas, juvenile books, poetry books. **Considers these fiction areas:** crime, fantasy, historical, horror, literary, mainstream, middle grade, mystery, new adult, paranormal, picture books, romance, thriller, women's, young adult.

HOW TO CONTACT Send query via e-mail. Please do not query via phone. The word "Query" must be in the subject line, plus the agent's name, i.e.–Subject: Query, Suzie Townsend. You may include up to 5 double-spaced sample pages within the body of the e-mail. No attachments, unless specifically requested. Include all necessary contact information. You will receive an auto-response confirming receipt of your query. "We only respond if we are interested in seeing your work." Responds only if interested. All queries read within 1 month.

RECENT SALES *Carve the Mark* by Veronica Roth (HarperCollins), *Red Queen* by Victoria Aveyard (HarperCollins), *Lobster Is the Best Medicine* by Liz Climo (Running Press), *Ninth House* by Leigh Bardugo (Henry Holt), *A Snicker of Magic* by Natalie Lloyd (Scholastic).

DANA NEWMAN LITERARY

9720 Wilshire Blvd., 5th Floor, Beverly Hills CA 90212. **E-mail:** dananewmanliterary@gmail.com. **Website:** dananewman.com. **Contact:** Dana Newman. Estab. 2009. Member of AAR. California State Bar Represents 28 clients.

○ Prior to becoming an agent, Ms. Newman was an attorney in the entertainment industry for 14 years.

MEMBER AGENTS Dana Newman (narrative nonfiction, business, lifestyle, current affairs, parenting, memoir, pop culture, sports, health, literary, and upmarket fiction).

REPRESENTS Nonfiction, novels, short story collections. **Considers these fiction areas:** commercial, contemporary issues, family saga, feminist, historical, literary, multicultural, sports, women's.

⚷ Ms. Newman has a background as an attorney in contracts, licensing, and intellectual property law. She is experienced in digital content creation and distribution. "We are interested in practical nonfiction (business, health and wellness, psychology, parenting, technology) by authors with smart, unique perspectives and established platforms who are committed to actively marketing and promoting their books. We love compelling, inspiring narrative nonfiction in the areas of memoir, biography, history, pop culture, current affairs/women's interest, sports, and social trends. On the fiction side, we consider a very selective amount of literary fiction and women's upmarket fiction." Does not want religious, children's, poetry, horror, mystery, thriller, romance, or science fiction.

HOW TO CONTACT E-mail queries only. For both nonfiction and fiction, please submit a query letter including a description of your project and a brief biography. "If we are interested in your project, we will contact you and request a full book proposal (nonfiction) or a synopsis and the first 25 pages (fiction)." Accepts simultaneous submissions. "If we have requested your materials after receiving your query, we usually respond within 4 weeks." Obtains new clients through recommendations from others, queries, and submissions.

TERMS Obtains 15% commission on domestic sales; 20% on foreign sales. Offers 1 year written contract. Notice must be given 1 month prior to terminate a contract.

RECENT SALES *Into the Abyss* by Ginger Lerner-Wren (Beacon Press), *Native Advertising* by Mike Smith (McGraw-Hill), *Breakthrough: The Making of America's First Woman President* by Nancy L. Cohen (Counterpoint), *Just Add Water* by Clay Marzo and Robert Yehling (Houghton Mifflin Harcourt), *A Stray Cat Struts* by Slim Jim Phantom (St. Martin's Press), *Tuff Juice* by Caron Butler and Steve Springer (Lyons Press).

PARK LITERARY GROUP, LLC

270 Lafayette St., Suite 1504, New York NY 10012. (212)691-3500. **Fax:** (212)691-3540. **E-mail:** info@parkliterary.com. **E-mail:** queries@parkliterary.com. **Website:** www.parkliterary.com. Estab. 2005.

MEMBER AGENTS Theresa Park (plot-driven fiction and serious nonfiction); Abigail Koons (popular science, history, politics, current affairs and art, and women's fiction); Peter Knapp (children's and YA).

REPRESENTS Nonfiction, novels. **Considers these fiction areas:** juvenile, middle grade, suspense, thriller, women's, young adult.

☛ The Park Literary Group represents fiction and nonfiction with a boutique approach: an emphasis on servicing a relatively small number of clients, with the highest professional standards and focused personal attention. Does not want to receive poetry or screenplays.

HOW TO CONTACT Please specify the first and last name of the agent to whom you are submitting in the subject line of the e-mail. All materials must be in the body of the e-mail. Responds if interested. For fiction submissions, please include a query letter with short synopsis and the first 3 chapters of your work. Accepts simultaneous submissions.

RECENT SALES This agency's client list is on their website. It includes bestsellers Nicholas Sparks, Soman Chainani, Emily Giffin, and Debbie Macomber.

L. PERKINS AGENCY

5800 Arlington Ave., Riverdale NY 10471. (718)543-5344. **E-mail:** submissions@lperkinsagency.com. **Website:** lperkinsagency.com. Estab. 1987. Member of AAR. Represents 150 clients.

◗ Ms. Perkins has been an agent for 25 years. She is also the author of *The Insider's Guide to Getting an Agent* (Writer's Digest Books), as well as 3 other nonfiction books. She has edited 25 erotic anthologies, and is also the founder and publisher of Riverdale Avenue Books, an award-winning hybrid publisher with 9 imprints.

MEMBER AGENTS Tish Beaty, ePub agent (erotic romance–including paranormal, historical, gay/lesbian/bisexual, and light-BDSM fiction; also, she seeks new adult and YA); Sandy Lu, sandy@lperkinsagency.com (fiction: she is looking for dark literary and commercial fiction, mystery, thriller, psychological horror, paranormal/urban fantasy, historical fiction, YA, historical thrillers or mysteries set in Victorian times; nonfiction: narrative nonfiction, history, biography, pop science, pop psychology, pop culture [music/theatre/film], humor, and food writing); Lori Perkins (not currently taking new clients); Leon Husock (science fiction & fantasy, as well as young adult and middle-grade); Rachel Brooks (picture books, all genres of young adult and new adult fiction, as well as adult romance—especially romantic suspense [NOTE: Rachel is currently closed to unsolicited submissions]); Maxi-

milian Ximinez (fiction: science fiction, fantasy, horror, thrillers; nonfiction: popular science, true crime, arts and trends in developing fields and cultures).

REPRESENTS Nonfiction, fiction, novels, short story collections. **Considers these fiction areas:** commercial, crime, detective, erotica, fantasy, feminist, gay, historical, horror, lesbian, literary, middle grade, mystery, new adult, paranormal, picture books, romance, science fiction, short story collections, supernatural, thriller, urban fantasy, women's, young adult.

☛ "Most of our clients write both fiction and nonfiction. This combination keeps our clients publishing for years. The founder of the agency is also a published author, so we know what it takes to write a good book." Actively seeking erotic romance, romance, young adult, middle grade, science fiction, fantasy, memoir, pop culture, thrillers. Does not want poetry, stand alone short stories or novellas, scripts, plays, westerns, textbooks.

HOW TO CONTACT E-queries only. Include your query, a 1-page synopsis, and the first 5 pages from your novel pasted into the e-mail, or your proposal. No attachments. Submit to only 1 agent at the agency. No snail mail queries. "If you are submitting to one of our agents, please be sure to check the submission status of the agent by visiting their social media accounts listed [on the agency website]." Accepts simultaneous submissions. Obtains most new clients through recommendations from others, solicitations, conferences.

TERMS Agent receives 15% commission on domestic sales; 20% commission on foreign sales. No written contract. Charges clients for photocopying.

RECENT SALES *Arena* by Holly Jennings, *Taking the Lead* by Cecilia Tan, *The Girl with Ghost Eyes* by M. H. Boroson, *Silent Attraction* by Lauren Brown.

WRITERS CONFERENCES Romantic Times; Romance Writers of America nationals; Rainbow Book Fair; NECON; Killercon; BookExpo America; World Fantasy Convention.

TIPS "Research your field and contact professional writers' organizations to see who is looking for what. Finish your novel before querying agents. Read my book, *An Insider's Guide to Getting an Agent*, to get a sense of how agents operate. Read agent blogs-agentinthemiddle.blogspot.com and ravenousromance. blogspot.com."

RUBIN PFEFFER CONTENT

648 Hammond St., Chestnut Hill MA 02467. **E-mail:** info@rpcontent.com. **Website:** www.rpcontent.com. **Contact:** Rubin Pfeffer. Estab. 2014. Member of AAR. Signatory of WGA.

○ Rubin has previously worked as the vice-president and publisher of Simon & Schuster Children's Books and as an independent agent at East West Literary Agency.

REPRESENTS Considers these fiction areas: juvenile, middle grade, picture books, young adult.

HOW TO CONTACT Note: This agent accepts submissions by referral only. Specify the contact information of your reference when submitting. Authors/illustrators should send a query and a 1-3 chapter ms via e-mail (no postal submissions). The query, placed in the body of the e-mail, should include a synopsis of the piece, as well as any relevant information regarding previous publications, referrals, websites, and biographies. The ms may be attached as a .doc or a .pdf file. Specifically for illustrators, attach a PDF of the dummy or artwork to the e-mail. If you would like to query Melissa Nasson with your picture book, middle grade, or YA ms, query with the first 50 pages to melissa@rpcontent.com. Accepts simultaneous submissions. Responds within 6-8 weeks.

AARON M. PRIEST LITERARY AGENCY

200 W. 41st St., 21st Floor, New York NY 10036. (212)818-0344. **Fax:** (212)573-9417. **E-mail:** info@aaronpriest.com. **Website:** www.aaronpriest.com. Estab. 1974. Member of AAR.

MEMBER AGENTS Aaron Priest, querypriest@aaronpriest.com (thrillers, commercial fiction, biographies); Lisa Erbach Vance, queryvance@aaronpriest.com (contemporary fiction, thrillers/suspense, international fiction, narrative nonfiction); Lucy Childs, querychilds@aaronpriest.com (literary and commercial fiction, memoir, edgy women's fiction); Mitch Hoffman, queryhoffman@aaronpriest.com (thrillers, suspense, crime fiction, and literary fiction, as well as narrative nonfiction, politics, popular science, history, memoir, current events, and pop culture).

REPRESENTS Considers these fiction areas: commercial, contemporary issues, crime, literary, middle grade, suspense, thriller, women's, young adult.

☞ Does not want to receive poetry, screenplays, horror or sci-fi.

HOW TO CONTACT Query 1 of the agents using the appropriate e-mail listed on the website. "Please do not submit to more than 1 agent at this agency. We urge you to check our website and consider each agent's emphasis before submitting. Your query letter should be about 1 page long and describe your work as well as your background. You may also paste the first chapter of your work in the body of the e-mail. Do not send attachments." Accepts simultaneous submissions. Responds in 4 weeks, only if interested.

TERMS Agent receives 15% commission on domestic sales.

PROSPECT AGENCY

551 Valley Rd., PMB 377, Upper Montclair NJ 07043. (718)788-3217. **Fax:** (718)360-9582. **Website:** www.prospectagency.com. Estab. 2005. Member of AAR. Signatory of WGA. Represents 130+ clients.

MEMBER AGENTS Emily Sylvan Kim, esk@prospectagency.com (romance, women's, commercial, young adult, new adult); Rachel Orr, rko@prospectagency.com (picture books, illustrators, middle grade, young adult); Becca Stumpf, becca@prospectagency.com (young adult and middle grade [all genres, including fantasy/SciFi, literary, mystery, contemporary, historical, horror/suspense], especially MG and YA novels featuring diverse protagonists and life circumstances. Adult SciFi and Fantasy novels with broad appeal, upmarket women's fiction, smart, spicy romance novels); Carrie Pestritto, carrie@prospectagency.com (narrative nonfiction, general nonfiction, biography, and memoir; commercial fiction with a literary twist, women's fiction, romance, upmarket, historical fiction, high-concept YA and upper MG); Linda Camacho, linda@prospectagency.com (middle grade, young adult, and adult fiction across all genres, especially women's fiction/romance, horror, fantasy/sci-fi, graphic novels, contemporary; select literary fiction; fiction featuring diverse/marginalized groups); Kirsten Carleton, kcarleton@prospectagency.com (upmarket speculative, thriller, and literary fiction for adult and YA).

REPRESENTS Nonfiction, fiction, novels, novellas, juvenile books, scholarly books, textbooks. **Considers these fiction areas:** commercial, contemporary issues, crime, ethnic, family saga, fantasy, feminist, gay, historical, horror, humor, juvenile, lesbian, literary, mainstream, middle grade, multicultural, mystery, new adult, picture books, romance, science fiction, suspense, thriller, urban fantasy, women's, young adult.

☛ "We're looking for strong, unique voices and unforgettable stories and characters."

HOW TO CONTACT All submissions are electronic and must be submitted through the portal at prospectagency.com/submissions. We do not accept any submissions through snail mail. Accepts simultaneous submissions. Obtains new clients through conferences, recommendations, queries, and some scouting.

TERMS Agent receives 15% on domestic sales, 20% on foreign sales sold directly and 25% on sales using a subagent. Offers written contract.

○ P.S LITERARY AGENCY

2010 Winston Park Dr., 2nd Floor, Oakville ON L6H 5R7 Canada. **E-mail:** query@psliterary.com. **Website:** www.psliterary.com. **Contact:** Curtis Russell, principal agent; Carly Watters, senior agent; Maria Vicente, associate agent; Kurestin Armada, associate agent; Eric Smith; associate agent. Estab. 2005.

MEMBER AGENTS Curtis Russell (literary/commercial fiction, mystery, thriller, suspense, romance, young adult, middle grade, picture books, business, history, politics, current affairs, memoirs, health/wellness, sports, humor, pop culture, pop science, pop psychology); Carly Watters (upmarket/commercial fiction, women's fiction, book club fiction, literary thrillers, cookbooks, health/wellness, memoirs, humor, pop science, pop psychology); Maria Vicente (young adult, middle grade, illustrated picture books, pop culture, science, lifestyle, design); Kurestin Armada (magic realism, science fiction, fantasy, illustrated picture books, middle grade, young adult, graphic novels, romance, design, cookbooks, pop psychology, photography, nature, science); Eric Smith (young adult, new adult, literary/commercial fiction, cookbooks, pop culture, humor, essay collections).

REPRESENTS Nonfiction, novels, juvenile books. **Considers these fiction areas:** action, adventure, detective, erotica, ethnic, experimental, family saga, fantasy, feminist, gay, historical, horror, humor, juvenile, lesbian, literary, mainstream, middle grade, multicultural, mystery, new adult, picture books, romance, science fiction, sports, thriller, urban fantasy, women's, young adult.

☛ Actively seeking both fiction and nonfiction. Seeking both new and established writers. Does not want to receive poetry or screenplays.

HOW TO CONTACT Query letters should be directed to query@psliterary.com. PSLA does not accept or respond to phone, paper or social media queries. Responds in 4-6 weeks to queries/proposals. Obtains most new clients through solicitations.

TERMS Agent receives 15% commission on domestic sales; 25% commission on foreign sales. "We offer a written contract, with 30-days notice terminate."

TIPS "Please review our website for the most up-to-date submission guidelines. We do not charge reading fees. We do not offer a critique service."

THE PURCELL AGENCY

E-mail: tpaqueries@gmail.com. **Website:** www.thepurcellagency.com. **Contact:** Tina P. Schwartz. Estab. 2012. SCBWI Represents 32 clients.

MEMBER AGENTS Tina P. Schwartz; Kim Blair McCollum.

REPRESENTS Nonfiction, novels, juvenile books. **Considers these fiction areas:** juvenile, middle grade, young adult.

☛ This agency also takes juvenile nonfiction for MG and YA markets. At this point, the agency is not considering fantasy, science fiction or picture book submissions.

HOW TO CONTACT Check the website to see if agency is open to submissions and for submission guidelines. Accepts simultaneous submissions.

RECENT SALES *A Kind of Justice* by Renee James, *Adventures at Hound Hotel* by Shelley Swanson Sateren, *Adventures at Tabby Towers* by Shelley Swanson Sateren, *Keys to Freedom* by Karen Meade.

QUEEN LITERARY AGENCY

30 E. 60th St., Suite 1004, New York NY 10022. (212)974-8333. **Fax:** (212)974-8347. **E-mail:** submissions@queenliterary.com. **Website:** www.queenliterary.com. **Contact:** Lisa Queen.

○ Prior to her current position, Ms. Queen was a former publishing executive and most recently head of IMG Worldwide's literary division.

REPRESENTS Novels. **Considers these fiction areas:** commercial, historical, literary, mystery, thriller.

☛ Ms. Queen's specialties: "While our agency represents a wide range of nonfiction titles, we have a particular interest in business books, food writing, science and popular psychology, as well as books by well-known chefs, radio and television personalities, and sports figures."

HOW TO CONTACT E-query. Accepts simultaneous submissions.

RECENT SALES A full list of this agency's clients and sales is available on their website.

RED SOFA LITERARY

P.O. Box 40482, St. Paul MN 55104. (651)224-6670. **E-mail:** dawn@redsofaliterary.com; jennie@redsofaliterary.com; laura@redsofaliterary.com; bree@redsofaliterary.com; amanda@redsofaliterary.com; stacey@redsofaliterary.com; erik@redsofaliterary.com. **Website:** www.redsofaliterary.com. **Contact:** Dawn Frederick, owner/literary agent; Jennie Goloboy, literary agent; Laura Zats, literary agent; Amanda Rutter, associate literary agent; Bree Ogden, literary agent; Stacey Graham, associate literary agent. Estab. 2008. Authors Guild and the MN Publishers Round Table Represents 125 clients.

MEMBER AGENTS Jennie Goloboy; Laura Zats; Bree Ogden; Amanda Rutter; Stacey Graham; Erik Hane.

REPRESENTS Nonfiction, fiction, novels, juvenile books. **Considers these fiction areas:** action, adventure, commercial, detective, erotica, ethnic, fantasy, feminist, gay, humor, juvenile, lesbian, literary, mainstream, middle grade, mystery, picture books, romance, science fiction, suspense, thriller, urban fantasy, young adult.

Dawn Fredrick: "I am always in search of a good work of nonfiction that falls within my categories (see my specific list at our website). I especially love pop culture, interesting histories, social sciences/advocacy, humor and books that are great conversation starters. As for fiction, I am always in search of good YA and MG titles. For YA I will go a little darker on the tone, as I enjoy a good gothic, contemporary or historical YA novel. For MG, I will always want something fun and lighthearted, but would love more contemporary themes too." Jennie Goloboy: "I mostly represent adult science fiction and fantasy. Within that genre, I'm looking for work that's progressive, innovative, and most of all, fun. I loved Childhood's End, but I'd never want to represent something that bleak." Laura Zats: "Adventurous, fun, STEM-inspired middle-grade fiction. Diverse YA of all kinds, especially the smart, geeky mss. Feminist romance and erotica with high-quality writing and fresh takes on tropes.

Adult science fiction and fantasy that pass the Bechdel Test and/or the Mako Mori Test. Please note that I am actively searching for diverse and feminist books and diverse and feminist authors across all of my representative categories." Amanda Rutter: "Science fiction/fantasy, the non-YA ideas, young adult and middle grade–science fiction/fantasy." Bree Ogden: "Highly artistic picture books (high brow art, think Varmints), young adult–not looking for sci-fi, fantasy, paranormal, or dystopian, New Adult–any genre as long as it has a strong romantic element, adult–Will look at any genre, preferred genres: transgressive, horror, noir, crime, mystery, thriller, bizarro, gothic, romance, erotica, graphic novels, some select nonfiction–no memoir or academia, humor, pop culture, art books." Stacey Graham: "Dark MG, horror, humor and humorous memoir, New Age with a strong platform, history [colonial U.S. and British history are favorites]–fiction and nonfiction for adults or MG, quirky nonfiction—adult and MG/YA." Erik Hane: "Literary fiction, Nonfiction [no memoirs]." Dawn: "Memoirs, it seems everyone ignores this request. I also prefer to represent books that aren't overly sappy, overly romantic, or any type of didactic/moralistic." Laura: "Nonfiction, including memoir. Adult mystery/thriller/literary fiction. Fiction without quirky or distinctive hooks. Books that follow or fit in trends." Amanda: "I am definitely not a nonfiction person. I rarely read it myself, so wouldn't know where to start where to represent! Also, although I enjoy middle grade fiction and would be happy to represent, I won't take on picture books." Bree: "There are not a lot of genres that I completely close myself off to. I won't represent any type of religious fiction or nonfiction. I also won't look at anything with paranormal elements. I'm not extremely keen on high fantasy or hard sci-fi, but if I find the right one." Stacey: "At this time, I do not want to represent YA, fantasy, sci-fi, or romance." Erik: "I definitely don't want to represent fiction that sets out at the start to be 'genre.' I like reading it, but I don't think it's for me as an agent. Bring me genre elements, but I think I'd rather let the classification happen naturally. I also don't want memoir unless you've really, really got something unique and accessible. I also don't want to represent children's lit; that's another thing I really do love and appreciate but don't quite connect with professionally."

HOW TO CONTACT Query by e-mail or mail with SASE. No attachments, please. Submit full proposal (for nonfiction especially, for fiction it would be nice) plus 3 sample chapters (or first 50 pages) and any other pertinent writing samples upon request by the specific agent. Do not sent within or attached to the query letter. Pdf/doc/docx is preferred, no rtf documents please. Accepts simultaneous submissions. Obtains new clients through queries, also through recommendations from others, solicitations.

TERMS Agent receives 15% commission on domestic sales; 20% commission on foreign sales. Offers written contract.

RECENT SALES *Semiosis* by Sue Burke (Tor, 2017); *Welcome Home* edited and authored by Eric Smith (Jolly Fish Press, 2017); *Body Horror: Essays on Misogyny and Capitalism* by Anne Elizabeth Moore (Curbside Splendor, 2017); *Dr. Potter's Medicine Show* by Eric Scott Fischl (Angry Robot Books, 2017); *Play Like a Girl: How a Soccer School in Kenya's Slums Started a Revolution* by Ellie Roscher (Viva Editions, 2017); *Not Now, Not Ever* by Lily Anderson (St. Martin's 2018); *Gunslinger Girl* by Lyndsay Ely (James Patterson Books, 2017); *The Cats of Ulthar*, illustrated by Abigail Larson (One Peace Books, 2016); *Branded* (Book #2 of INKED series) by Eric Smith (Bloomsbury Spark, 2016); *Seeking Mansfield* by Kate Watson (Jolly Fish Press, 2017); *Behind the Books: How Debut Authors Navigate from the Idea to the End* by Chris Jones (University of Chicago Press, 2017); *Ten Years An Orc: A Decade in the World of Warcraft* by Tony Palumbi (Chicago Review Press, 2017); *Bad Bitch* by Christina Saunders (SMP Swerve, 2016); *Alice's Adventures Coloring Book* by Abigail Larson (F+W Media, 2016); *An Accident of Stars* by Foz Meadows (Angry Robot Books, 2016); *Caring for Creation* by Paul Douglas and Rev. Mitch Hescox (Bethany House, 2016); *Crafting With Feminism* by Bonnie Burton (Quirk Books); *Freeze/Thaw* by Chris Bucholz (Apex Books, 2016); *The Stumps of Flattop Hill* by Ken Lamug (One Peace Books, 2016); *Some Hell* by Patrick Nathan (Graywolf, 2018); *Nice Girls Endure* by Chris Struyk-Bonn (Switch Press, 2016); Book 3 of One Night in Sixes by Tex Thompson (Solaris Books, 2017).

WRITERS CONFERENCES Writer's Digest, SDSU Writer's Conference, WorldCon, CONvergence, SCWBI (regional conferences), FWA Conference, DFW Writers Conference, Northern Colorado Writers Conference, Horror World Convention, Loft Literary Conference, Madison Writers Workshop, Emerald City Writers Conference, Missouri Writers Guild, Pike's Peak Conference.

TIPS "Always remember the benefits of building an author platform, and the accessibility of accomplishing this task in today's industry. Most importantly, research the agents queried. Avoid contacting every literary agent about a book idea. Due to the large volume of queries received, the process of reading queries for unrepresented categories (by the agency) becomes quite the arduous task. Investigate online directories, printed guides (like *Writer's Market*), individual agent websites, and more, before beginning the query process. It's good to remember that each agent has a vision of what s/he wants to represent and will communicate this information accordingly. We're simply waiting for those specific book ideas to come in our direction."

REES LITERARY AGENCY

14 Beacon St., Suite 710, Boston MA 02108. (617)227-9014. **E-mail:** lorin@reesagency.com. **Website:** reesagency.com. Estab. 1983. Member of AAR. Represents more than 100 clients.

MEMBER AGENTS Ann Collette, agent10702@aol.com (fiction: literary, upscale commercial women's, crime [including mystery, thriller and psychological suspense], upscale western, historical, military and war, and horror; nonfiction: narrative, military and war, books on race and class, works set in Southeast Asia, biography, pop culture, books on film and opera, humor, and memoir); Lorin Rees, lorin@reesagency.com (literary fiction, memoirs, business books, self-help, science, history, psychology, and narrative nonfiction); Rebecca Podos, rebecca@reesagency.com (young adult and middle grade fiction, particularly books about complex female relationships, beautifully written contemporary, genre novels with a strong focus on character, romance with more at stake than "will they/won't they," and LGBTQ books across all genres).

REPRESENTS Novels. **Considers these fiction areas:** commercial, crime, historical, horror, literary, middle grade, mystery, suspense, thriller, westerns, women's, young adult.

HOW TO CONTACT Consult website for each agent's submission guidelines and e-mail addresses, as they differ. Accepts simultaneous submissions. Obtains most new clients through recommendations from others, conferences, submissions.

TERMS Agent receives 15% commission on domestic sales; 20% commission on foreign sales.

REGAL HOFFMANN & ASSOCIATES LLC

242 W. 38th St., Floor 2, New York NY 10018. (212)684-7900. **Fax:** (212)684-7906. **E-mail:** submissions@rhaliterary.com. **Website:** www.rhaliterary.com. Estab. 2002. Member of AAR. Represents 70 clients.

MEMBER AGENTS Claire Anderson-Wheeler (nonfiction: memoirs and biographies, narrative histories, popular science, popular psychology; adult fiction: primarily character-driven literary fiction, but open to genre fiction, high-concept fiction; all genres of young adult / middle grade fiction); Markus Hoffmann (international and literary fiction, crime, [pop] cultural studies, current affairs, economics, history, music, popular science, and travel literature); Joseph Regal (literary fiction, international thrillers, history, science, photography, music, culture, and whimsy); Stephanie Steiker (serious and narrative nonfiction, literary fiction, graphic novels, history, philosophy, current affairs, cultural studies, biography, music, international writing); Grace Ross (literary fiction, historical fiction, international narratives, narrative nonfiction, popular science, biography, cultural theory, memoir).

REPRESENTS Considers these fiction areas: literary, mainstream, middle grade, thriller, young adult.

⌑   "We represent works in a wide range of categories, with an emphasis on literary fiction, outstanding thriller and crime fiction, and serious narrative nonfiction." Actively seeking literary fiction and narrative nonfiction. Does not want romance, science fiction, poetry, or screenplays.

HOW TO CONTACT Query with SASE or уia e-mail to submissions@rhaliterary.com. No phone calls. Submissions should consist of a 1-page query letter detailing the book in question, as well as the qualifications of the author. For fiction, submissions may also include the first 10 pages of the novel or 1 short story from a collection. Responds if interested. Accepts simultaneous submissions. Responds in 4-8 weeks.

TERMS Agent receives 15% commission on domestic sales; 20% commission on foreign sales. "We charge no reading fees."

RECENT SALES *Wily Snare* by Adam Jay Epstein, *Perfectly Undone* by Jamie Raintree, *A Sister in My House* by Linda Olsson, *This Is How It Really Sounds* by Stuart Archer Cohen, *Autofocus* by Lauren Gibaldi, *We've Already Gone This Far* by Patrick Dacey, *A Fierce and Subtle Poison* by Samantha Mabry, *The Life of the World to Come* by Dan Cluchey, *Willful Disregard* by Lena Andersson, *The Sweetheart* by Angelina Mirabella.

TIPS "We are deeply committed to every aspect of our clients' careers, and are engaged in everything from the editorial work of developing a great book proposal or line editing a fiction ms to negotiating state-of-the-art book deals and working to promote and publicize the book when it's published. We are at the forefront of the effort to increase authors' rights in publishing contracts in a rapidly changing commercial environment. We deal directly with co-agents and publishers in every foreign territory and also work directly and with co-agents for feature film and television rights, with extraordinary success in both arenas. Many of our clients' works have sold in dozens of translation markets, and a high proportion of our books have been sold in Hollywood. We have strong relationships with speaking agents, who can assist in arranging author tours and other corporate and college speaking opportunities when appropriate. We also have a staff publicist and marketer to help promote our clients' and their work."

☺ THE RIGHTS FACTORY

P.O. Box 499, Station C, Toronto ON M6J 3P6 Canada. (416)966-5367. **Website:** www.therightsfactory.com. Estab. 2004. Represents ~150 clients.

MEMBER AGENTS Sam Hiyate (President: fiction, nonfiction and graphic novel); Kelvin Kong (Rights Manager: clients by referral only); Ali McDonald (Kidlit Agent: YA and children's literature of all kinds); Olga Filina (Associate Agent: commercial and historical fiction; great genre fiction in the area of romance and mystery; nonfiction in the field of business, wellness, lifestyle and memoir; and young adult and middle grade novels with memorable characters); Cassandra Rogers (Associate Agent: adult literary and commercial women's fiction; historical fiction; nonfiction on politics, history, science, and finance; humorous, heartbreaking and inspiring memoir); Lydia Moed (Associate Agent: science fiction and fantasy, historical fiction, diverse voices; narrative nonfiction on a wide variety of topics, including history, popular science, biography and travel); Natalie Kimber (Associate Agent: literary and commercial fiction and creative nonfiction in categories such as memoir, cooking, pop-culture, spirituality, and sustainability); Harry Endrulat (Associate Agent: children's literature, especially author/illustrators and Canadian voices); Haskell Nussbaum (Associate Agent: literature of all kinds).

REPRESENTS Nonfiction, fiction, novels, short story collections, novellas, juvenile books. **Considers these fiction areas:** commercial, crime, family saga, fantasy, gay, hi-lo, historical, horror, juvenile, lesbian, literary, mainstream, middle grade, multicultural, mystery, new adult, paranormal, picture books, romance, science fiction, short story collections, suspense, thriller, urban fantasy, women's, young adult.

☛   Plays, screenplays, textbooks.

HOW TO CONTACT There is a submission form on this agency's website. Accepts simultaneous submissions. Responds in 3-6 weeks.

ANGELA RINALDI LITERARY AGENCY

P.O. Box 7875, Beverly Hills CA 90212-7875. (310)842-7665. **Fax:** (310)837-8143. **E-mail:** info@rinaldiliterary.com. **Website:** www.rinaldiliterary.com. **Contact:** Angela Rinaldi. Member of AAR.

○   Prior to opening her agency, Ms. Rinaldi was an editor at NAL/Signet, Pocket Books and Bantam, and the manager of book development for *The Los Angeles Times.*

REPRESENTS Nonfiction, novels, TV and motion picture rights (for clients only). **Considers these fiction areas:** commercial, historical, literary, mainstream, mystery, suspense, thriller, women's, contemporary, gothic, women's book club fiction.

☛   Actively seeking commercial and literary fiction, as well as nonfiction. For fiction, we do not want to receive humor, CIA espionage, drug thrillers, techno thrillers, category romances, science fiction, fantasy, horror/occult/paranormal, poetry, film scripts, magazine articles or religion. For nonfiction, please do not send us magazine articles, celebrity bios, or tell alls.

HOW TO CONTACT E-queries only. Include the word "Query" in the subject line. For fiction, please send a brief synopsis and paste the first 10 pages into an e-mail. Nonfiction queries should include a detailed cover letter, your credentials and platform information as well as any publishing history. Tell us if you have a completed proposal. Accepts simultaneous submissions. Responds in 2-4 weeks.

TERMS Agent receives 15% commission on domestic sales; 25% commission on foreign sales. Offers written contract.

ANN RITTENBERG LITERARY AGENCY, INC.

15 Maiden Lane, Suite 206, New York NY 10038. (212)684-6936. **E-mail:** info@rittlit.com. **Website:** www.rittlit.com. **Contact:** Ann Rittenberg, president. Member of AAR.

REPRESENTS Nonfiction, novels, juvenile books.

☛   Does not want to receive screenplays, poetry, or self-help.

HOW TO CONTACT Query via e-mail or postal mail (with SASE). Submit query letter with 3 sample chapters pasted in the body of the e-mail. "If you query by e-mail, we will only respond if interested." Accepts simultaneous submissions. Obtains most new clients through referrals from established writers and editors.

TERMS Agent receives 15% commission on domestic sales. Agent receives 20% commission on foreign sales. Offers written contract. This agency charges clients for photocopying only.

RECENT SALES *Since We Fell* by Dennis Lehane, *A Wretched and Precarious Situation* by David Welky, *Knife Creek* by Paul Doiron.

RLR ASSOCIATES, LTD.

420 Lexington Ave., Suite 2532, New York NY 10170. (212)541-8641. **E-mail:** website.info@rlrassociates.net. **Website:** www.rlrassociates.net. **Contact:** Scott Gould. Member of AAR. Represents 50 clients.

REPRESENTS Nonfiction, novels. **Considers these fiction areas:** commercial, literary, mainstream, middle grade, picture books, romance, women's, young adult, genre.

☛   "We provide a lot of editorial assistance to our clients and have connections." Does not want to receive screenplays.

HOW TO CONTACT Query by snail mail. For fiction, send a query and 1-3 chapters (pasted). For nonfiction, send query or proposal. Accepts simultaneous submissions. "If you do not hear from us within 3 months, please assume that your work is out of active consideration." Obtains most new clients through recommendations from others.

TERMS Agent receives 15% commission on domestic sales; 20% commission on foreign sales. Offers written contract.

RECENT SALES Clients include Shelby Foote, The Grief Recovery Institute, Don Wade, David Plowden,

Nina Planck, Karyn Bosnak, Gerald Carbone, Jason Lethcoe, Andy Crouch.

TIPS "Please check out our website for more details on our agency."

B.J. ROBBINS LITERARY AGENCY

5130 Bellaire Ave., North Hollywood CA 91607-2908. **E-mail:** robbinsliterary@gmail.com. **Website:** www.publishersmarketplace.com/members/bjrobbins. **Contact:** (Ms.) B.J. Robbins. Estab. 1992. Member of AAR.

○ Prior to becoming an agent, Robbins spent 15 years in publishing, starting in publicity at Simon & Schuster and later as Marketing Director and Senior Editor at Harcourt.

REPRESENTS Nonfiction, fiction. **Considers these fiction areas:** contemporary issues, crime, detective, ethnic, historical, literary, mainstream, multicultural, mystery, sports, suspense, thriller, women's.

☞ "We do not represent screenplays, plays, poetry, science fiction, horror, westerns, romance, techno-thrillers, religious tracts, dating books or anything with the word 'unicorn' in the title."

HOW TO CONTACT E-query with no attachments. For fiction, okay to include first 10 pages in body of e-mail. Accepts simultaneous submissions. Only responds to projects if interested. Obtains most new clients through conferences, referrals.

TERMS Agent receives 15% commission on domestic sales; 20% commission on foreign sales. Offers written contract. No fees.

RECENT SALES *Shoot for the Moon: The Perilous Voyage of Apollo 11* by James Donovan (Little, Brown); *I Was Told There'd Be Sexbots: Travels Through the Future* by J. Maarten Troost (Holt); *Mongrels* by Stephen Graham Jones (William Morrow); *Blood Brothers: The Story of the Strange Friendship between Sitting Bull and Buffalo Bill* by Deanne Stillman (Simon & Schuster); *Reliance, Illinois* by Mary Volmer (Soho Press).

RODEEN LITERARY MANAGEMENT

3501 N. Southport #497, Chicago IL 60657. **E-mail:** info@rodeenliterary.com. **E-mail:** submissions@rodeenliterary.com. **Website:** www.rodeenliterary.com. **Contact:** Paul Rodeen. Estab. 2009. Member of AAR. Signatory of WGA.

○ Paul Rodeen established Rodeen Literary Management in 2009 after 7 years of experience

with the literary agency Sterling Lord Literistic, Inc.

REPRESENTS Nonfiction, novels, juvenile books, illustrations, graphic novels. **Considers these fiction areas:** juvenile, middle grade, picture books, young adult, graphic novels, comics.

☞ Actively seeking "writers and illustrators of all genres of children's literature including picture books, early readers, middle-grade fiction and nonfiction, graphic novels and comic books, as well as young adult fiction and nonfiction." This is primarily an agency devoted to children's books.

HOW TO CONTACT Unsolicited submissions are accepted by e-mail only. Cover letters with synopsis and contact information should be included in the body of your e-mail. An initial submission of 50 pages from a novel or a longer work of nonfiction will suffice and should be pasted into the body of your e-mail. Accepts simultaneous submissions.

THE ROSENBERG GROUP

23 Lincoln Ave., Marblehead MA 01945. (781)990-1341. **Fax:** (781)990-1344. **Website:** www.rosenberggroup.com. **Contact:** Barbara Collins Rosenberg. Estab. 1998. Member of AAR. Recognized agent of the RWA. Represents 25 clients.

○ Prior to becoming an agent, Ms. Rosenberg was a senior editor for Harcourt.

REPRESENTS Nonfiction, novels, textbooks, college textbooks only. **Considers these fiction areas:** romance, women's, chick lit.

☞ Ms. Rosenberg is well-versed in the romance market (both category and single title). She is a frequent speaker at romance conferences. The Rosenberg Group is accepting new clients working in romance fiction (please see my Areas of Interest for specific romance sub-genres); women's fiction and chick lit. Does not want to receive inspirational, time travel, futuristic or paranormal.

HOW TO CONTACT Query via snail mail. Your query letter should not exceed 1 page in length. It should include the title of your work, the genre and/or sub-genre; the ms's word count; and a brief description of the work. If you are writing category romance, please be certain to let her know the line for which your work is intended. Accepts simultaneous submissions. Obtains most new clients through recommendations from others, solicitations, conferences.

TERMS Agent receives 15% commission on domestic and foreign sales. Offers written contract; 1-month notice must be given to terminate contract. Charges maximum of $350/year for postage and photocopying.

RECENT SALES Sold 27 titles in the last year.

WRITERS CONFERENCES RWA National Conference; BookExpo America.

ANDY ROSS LITERARY AGENCY

767 Santa Ray Ave., Oakland CA 94610. (510)238-8965. **E-mail:** andyrossagency@hotmail.com. **Website:** www.andyrossagency.com. **Contact:** Andy Ross. Estab. 2008. Member of AAR. Represents see website for client list clients.

REPRESENTS Nonfiction, fiction, novels, juvenile books, scholarly books. **Considers these fiction areas:** commercial, contemporary issues, historical, juvenile, literary, middle grade, picture books, young adult.

8— "This agency specializes in general nonfiction, politics and current events, history, biography, journalism and contemporary culture as well as literary, commercial, and YA fiction." Does not want to receive poetry.

HOW TO CONTACT Queries should be less than half page. Please put the word "query" in the title header of the e-mail. In the first sentence, state the category of the project. Give a short description of the book and your qualifications for writing. Accepts simultaneous submissions. Responds in 1 week to queries.

TERMS Agent receives 15% commission on domestic sales; 20% commission on foreign sales or other deals made through a sub-agent. Offers written contract.

RECENT SALES See website.

JANE ROTROSEN AGENCY LLC

85 Broad St., 28th Floor, New York NY 10004. (212)593-4330. **Fax:** (212)935-6985. **Website:** www.janerotrosen.com. Estab. 1974. Member of AAR. Other memberships include Authors Guild. Represents more than 100 clients.

MEMBER AGENTS Jane Rotrosen Berkey (not taking on clients); Andrea Cirillo, acirillo@janerotrosen.com (general fiction, suspense, and women's fiction); Annelise Robey, arobey@janerotrosen.com (women's fiction, suspense, mystery, literary fiction, and select nonfiction); Meg Ruley, mruley@janerotrosen.com (commercial fiction, including suspense, mysteries, romance, and general fiction); Christina Ho-

grebe, chogrebe@janerotrosen.com (young adult, new adult, book club fiction, romantic comedies, mystery, and suspense); Amy Tannenbaum, atannenbaum@janerotrosen.com (contemporary romance, psychological suspense, thrillers, and new adult, as well as women's fiction that falls into that sweet spot between literary and commercial, memoir, narrative and prescriptive nonfiction in the areas of health, business, pop culture, humor, and popular psychology); Rebecca Scherer rscherer@janerotrosen.com (women's fiction, mystery, suspense, thriller, romance, upmarket/literary-leaning fiction); Jessica Errera (assistant to Christina and Rebecca).

REPRESENTS Nonfiction, novels. **Considers these fiction areas:** commercial, literary, mainstream, mystery, new adult, romance, suspense, thriller, women's, young adult.

8— Jane Rotrosen Agency is best known for representing writers of commercial fiction: thrillers, mystery, suspense, women's fiction, romance, historical novels, mainstream fiction, young adult, etc. We also work with authors of memoirs, narrative and prescriptive nonfiction.

HOW TO CONTACT Check website for guidelines. Accepts simultaneous submissions. Obtains most new clients through recommendations from others.

TERMS Agent receives 15% commission on domestic sales; 20% commission on foreign sales. Offers written contract, binding for 3 years; 2-month notice must be given to terminate contract. Charges clients for photocopying, express mail, overseas postage, book purchase.

THE RUDY AGENCY

825 Wildlife Ln., Estes Park CO 80517. (970)577-8500. **E-mail:** mak@rudyagency.com; fred@rudyagency.com; claggett@rudyagency.com. **Website:** www.rudyagency.com. **Contact:** Maryann Karinch. Estab. 2004. Adheres to AAR canon of ethics. Represents 24 clients.

◯ Prior to becoming an agent, Ms. Karinch was, and continues to be, an author of nonfiction books—covering the subjects of health/medicine and human behavior. Prior to that, she was in public relations and marketing: areas of expertise she also applies in her practice as an agent.

MEMBER AGENTS Maryann Karinch; Fred Tribuzzo (fiction: thrillers, historical), and Hilary Claggett (selected nonfiction).

REPRESENTS Nonfiction, fiction, novels, short story collections, scholarly books, textbooks, theatrical stage play, stage plays. **Considers these fiction areas:** action, adventure, commercial, crime, erotica, historical, literary, new adult, sports, thriller.

☞ "We support authors from the proposal stage through promotion of the published work. We work in partnership with publishers to promote the published work and coach authors in their role in the marketing and public relations campaigns for the book." Actively seeking projects with social value, projects that open minds to new ideas and interesting lives, and projects that entertain through good storytelling. Does not want to receive poetry, screenplays, novellas, religion books, children's lit, and joke books.

HOW TO CONTACT "Query us. If we like the query, we will invite a complete proposal (or complete ms if writing fiction). No phone queries, please. We won't hang up on you, but it makes it easier if you send us a note first." Accepts simultaneous submissions. Responds in 8 weeks to mss. Obtains most new clients through recommendations from others, solicitations.

TERMS Agent receives 15% commission on domestic sales. Offers written contract, binding for 1 year.

RECENT SALES *Shakespeare's Ear* by Tim Rayborn (Skyhorse), *Science for Fiction* by David Siegel Bernstein (Prometheus), *Sex and Cancer* by Saketh R. Guntupalli (Rowman & Littlefield).

TIPS "Present yourself professionally. I tell people all the time: Subscribe to *Writer's Digest* (I do), because you will get good advice about how to approach an agent."

VICTORIA SANDERS & ASSOCIATES

440 Buck Rd., Stone Ridge NY 12484. (212)633-8811. E-mail: queriesvsa@gmail.com. Website: www.victoriasanders.com. Contact: Victoria Sanders. Estab. 1992. Member of AAR. Signatory of WGA. Represents 135 clients.

MEMBER AGENTS Victoria Sanders, Chris Kepner, Bernadette Baker-Baughman.

REPRESENTS Nonfiction, fiction, novels, juvenile books. **Considers these fiction areas:** action, adventure, cartoon, comic books, contemporary issues, crime, detective, ethnic, family saga, feminist, gay, historical, humor, inspirational, juvenile, lesbian, literary, mainstream, middle grade, multicultural, mul-

timedia, mystery, new adult, picture books, thriller, women's, young adult.

HOW TO CONTACT Authors who wish to contact us regarding potential representation should send a query letter with the first 3 chapters (or about 25 pages) pasted into the body of the message to queriesvsa@gmail.com. "We will only accept queries via e-mail. Query letters should describe the project and the author in the body of a single, 1-page e-mail that does not contain any attached files. Important note: Please paste the first 3 chapters of your ms (or about 25 pages, and feel free to round up to a chapter break) into the body of your e-mail." Accepts simultaneous submissions. Responds in 1-4 weeks, although occasionally it will take longer. "We will not respond to e-mails with attachments or attached files."

TERMS Agent receives 15% commission on domestic sales; 20% commission on foreign/film sales. Offers written contract.

RECENT SALES Sold 20+ titles in the last year.

TIPS "Limit query to letter (no calls) and give it your best shot. A good query is going to get a good response."

SCHIAVONE LITERARY AGENCY, INC.

236 Trails End, West Palm Beach FL 33413-2135. (561)966-9294. Fax: (561)966-9294. E-mail: profschia@aol.com. Website: www.publishersmarketplace.com/members/profschia; www.schiavoneliteraryagencyinc.blogspot.com. Contact: Dr. James Schiavone, CEO, corporate offices in Florida; Jennifer DuVall, president, New York office. Estab. 1996. Other memberships include National Education Association. Represents 40+ clients.

💬 Prior to opening his agency, Dr. Schiavone was a full professor of developmental skills at the City University of New York and author of 5 trade books and 3 textbooks. Jennifer DuVall has many years of combined experience in office management and agenting.

MEMBER AGENTS James Schiavone, profschia@aol.com; Jennifer DuVall, jendu77@aol.com.

REPRESENTS Nonfiction, fiction, novels, scholarly books, We specialize in Celebrity memoirs. **Considers these fiction areas:** literary, mainstream, mystery, romance, suspense, thriller, young adult.

☞ This agency specializes in celebrity biography and autobiography and memoirs. Actively seeking celebrity memoirs. Does not want to receive poetry.

HOW TO CONTACT "One-page e-mail queries only. Absolutely no attachments. Postal queries are not accepted. No phone calls. We do not consider poetry, short stories, anthologies or children's books. Celebrity memoirs only. No scripts or screen plays. We handle dramatic, film and TV rights, options, and screen plays for books we have agented. We are not interested in work previously published in any format (e.g., self-published; online; e-books; Print On Demand). E-mail queries may be addressed to any of the agency's agents." Accepts simultaneous submissions. Responds in 2 weeks to queries; 6 weeks to mss. Obtains most new clients through referrals.

TERMS Agent receives 15% commission on domestic sales; 20% commission on foreign sales. Offers written contract. No fees.

RECENT SALES Check website.

WRITERS CONFERENCES Key West Literary Seminar; South Florida Writers' Conference; Tallahassee Writers' Conference, Million Dollar Writers' Conference; Alaska Writers Conference; Utah writers conference.

TIPS "We prefer to work with established authors published by major houses in New York. We will consider marketable proposals from new/previously unpublished writers."

WENDY SCHMALZ AGENCY

402 Union St., #831, Hudson NY 12534. (518)672-7697. **E-mail:** wendy@schmalzagency.com. **Website:** www.schmalzagency.com. **Contact:** Wendy Schmalz. Estab. 2002. Member of AAR.

REPRESENTS Nonfiction, fiction, novels, juvenile books. **Considers these fiction areas:** literary, mainstream, middle grade, young adult.

- ☛ Not looking for picture books, science fiction or fantasy.

HOW TO CONTACT Accepts only e-mail queries. Paste synopsis into the e-mail. Do not attach the ms or sample chapters or synopsis. Replies to queries only if they want to read the ms. If you do not hear from this agency within 2 weeks, consider that a no. Accepts simultaneous submissions. Obtains clients through recommendations from others.

TERMS Agent receives 15% commission on domestic sales; 20% on foreign sales; 25% for Asian sales.

SUSAN SCHULMAN LITERARY AGENCY LLC

454 W. 44th St., New York NY 10036. (212)713-1633. **E-mail:** susan@schulmanagency.com. **E-mail:** queries@schulmanagency.com. **Website:** www.publishersmarketplace.com/members/schulman/. **Contact:** Susan Schulman. Estab. 1980. Member of AAR. Signatory of WGA. Other memberships include Dramatists Guild, Writers Guild of America, East, New York Women in Film, Women's Media Group, Agents' Roundtable, League of New York Theater Women.

REPRESENTS Nonfiction, fiction, novels, juvenile books, feature film, TV scripts, theatrical stage play. **Considers these fiction areas:** commercial, contemporary issues, juvenile, literary, mainstream, new adult, religious, women's, young adult.

- ☛ "We specialize in books for by and about women and women's issues including nonfiction self-help books, fiction, and theater projects. We also handle the film, television. and allied rights for several agencies as well as foreign rights for several publishing houses." Actively seeking new nonfiction. Considers plays. Does not want to receive poetry, television scripts or concepts for television.

HOW TO CONTACT "For fiction: query letter with outline and three sample chapters, resume and SASE. For nonfiction: query letter with complete description of subject, at least 1 chapter, resume and SASE. Queries may be sent via regular mail or e-mail. Please do not submit queries via UPS or Federal Express. Please do not send attachments with e-mail queries Please incorporate the chapters into the body of the e-mail." Accepts simultaneous submissions. Responds in less than 1 week generally to a full query and 6 weeks to a full ms. Obtains most new clients through recommendations from others, solicitations, conferences.

TERMS Agent receives 15% commission on domestic sales; 20% commission on foreign sales. Offers written contract; 30-day notice must be given to terminate contract.

RECENT SALES Sold 35 titles in the last year; hundreds of subsidiary rights deals.

WRITERS CONFERENCES Geneva Writers' Conference (Switzerland); Columbus Writers' Conference; Skidmore Conference of the Independent Women's Writers Group. Attends Frankfurt Book Fair, London Book Fair, and BEA annually.

TIPS "Keep writing!" Schulman describes her agency as "professional boutique, long-standing, eclectic."

SCOVIL GALEN GHOSH LITERARY AGENCY, INC.

276 Fifth Ave., Suite 708, New York NY 10001. (212)679-8686. **Fax:** (212)679-6710. **E-mail:** info@sgglit.com. **Website:** www.sgglit.com. **Contact:** Russell Galen. Estab. 1992. Member of AAR. Represents 300 clients.

MEMBER AGENTS Russell Galen, russellgalen@sgglit.com (novels that stretch the bounds of reality; strong, serious nonfiction books on almost any subject that teach something new; no books that are merely entertaining, such as diet or pop psych books; serious interests include science, history, journalism, biography, business, memoir, nature, politics, sports, contemporary culture, literary nonfiction, etc.); Jack Scovil, jackscovil@sgglit.com; Anna Ghosh, annaghosh@sgglit.com (nonfiction proposals on all subjects, including literary nonfiction, history, science, social and cultural issues, memoir, food, art, adventure, and travel; adult commercial and literary fiction); Ann Behar, annbehar@sgglit.com (juvenile books for all ages).

HOW TO CONTACT E-mail queries only. Note how each agent at this agency has their own submission e-mail. Accepts simultaneous submissions.

SCRIBE AGENCY, LLC

5508 Joylynne Dr., Madison WI 53716. **E-mail:** whattheshizzle@scribeagency.com. **E-mail:** submissions@scribeagency.com. **Website:** www.scribeagency.com. **Contact:** Kristopher O'Higgins. Represents 11 clients.

🖰 "With more than 15 years experience in publishing, with time spent on both the agency and editorial sides, with marketing experience to boot, Scribe Agency is a full-service literary agency, working hands-on with its authors on their projects. Check the website (scribeagency.com) to make sure your work matches the Scribe aesthetic.".

MEMBER AGENTS Kristopher O'Higgins.

REPRESENTS Novels, anthologies. **Considers these fiction areas:** fantasy, literary, science fiction.

☛ "Scribe is currently closed to nonfiction and short fiction collections, and does not represent humor, cozy mysteries, faith-based fiction, screenplays, poetry, or works based on another's ideas."

HOW TO CONTACT E-queries only: submissions@scribeagency.com. See the website for submission info, as it may change. Responds approximately 6 weeks to queries.

TERMS Agent receives 15% commission on domestic sales. Agent receives 20% commission on foreign sales. Offers written contract. Charges for postage and photocopying.

WRITERS CONFERENCES BookExpo America; WisCon; Wisconsin Book Festival; World Fantasy Convention; WorldCon.

SECRET AGENT MAN

P.O. Box 1078, Lake Forest CA 92609-1078. (949)698-6987. **E-mail:** query@secretagentman.net. **Website:** www.secretagentman.net. **Contact:** Scott Mortenson. Estab. 1999.

REPRESENTS Nonfiction, fiction, novels. **Considers these fiction areas:** action, crime, detective, horror, literary, mainstream, mystery, paranormal, psychic, religious, science fiction, spiritual, supernatural, suspense, thriller, westerns.

☛ Mystery, thriller, suspense, and detective fiction. Select nonfiction projects that are both interesting and thought-provoking. Does not want to receive scripts or screenplays.

HOW TO CONTACT Query via e-mail only; include sample chapters, synopsis and/or outline. Prefers to read the real thing rather than a description, but a synopsis helps with getting an overall feel of the ms. Accepts simultaneous submissions. Responds in 3-6 weeks. Obtains most new clients through recommendations from others.

LYNN SELIGMAN, LITERARY AGENT

400 Highland Ave., Upper Montclair NJ 07043. (973)783-3631. **E-mail:** seliglit@aol.com. **Contact:** Lynn Seligman. Estab. 1986. Women's Media Group Represents 35 clients.

🖰 Prior to opening her agency, Ms. Seligman worked in the subsidiary rights department of Doubleday and Simon & Schuster, and served as an agent with Julian Bach Literary Agency (which became IMG Literary Agency). Foreign rights are represented by Books Crossing Borders, Inc.

REPRESENTS Nonfiction, fiction, novels. **Considers these fiction areas:** commercial, ethnic, fantasy, feminist, historical, horror, humor, literary, mainstream, mystery, new adult, romance, science fiction, women's, young adult.

🗝 "This agency specializes in general nonfiction and fiction. I also do illustrated and photography books and have represented several photographers for books."

HOW TO CONTACT Query with SASE or via e-mail with no attachments. Prefers to read materials exclusively but if not, please inform. Answers written queries, but does not respond to e-mail queries if not appropriate for the agency. Accepts simultaneous submissions. Responds in 2 weeks to queries; 2 months to mss. Obtains new clients through referrals from other writers and editors as well as unsolicited queries.

TERMS Agent receives 15% commission on domestic sales; 25% commission on foreign sales. Charges clients for photocopying, unusual postage, express mail, telephone expenses (checks with author first).

RECENT SALES Sold 10 titles in 2016 including novels by Dee Ernst, Alexandra Hawkins, and Terra Little.

SERENDIPITY LITERARY AGENCY, LLC

305 Gates Ave., Brooklyn NY 11216. **E-mail:** rbrooks@serendipitylit.com; info@serendipitylit.com. **Website:** www.serendipitylit.com; facebook.com/serendipitylit. **Contact:** Regina Brooks. Estab. 2000. Member of AAR. Signatory of WGA. Represents 150 clients.

🔾   Prior to becoming an agent, Ms. Brooks was an acquisitions editor for John Wiley & Sons, Inc. and McGraw-Hill Companies.

MEMBER AGENTS Regina Brooks; Dawn Michelle Hardy (nonfiction, including sports, pop culture, blog and trend, music, lifestyle and social science); Folade Bell (literary and commercial women's fiction, YA, literary mysteries & thrillers, historical fiction, African-American issues, gay/lesbian, Christian fiction, humor and books that deeply explore other cultures; nonfiction that reads like fiction, including blog-to-book or pop culture); Nadeen Gayle (romance, memoir, pop culture, inspirational/ religious, women's fiction, parenting, young adult, mystery and political thrillers, and all forms of nonfiction); Rebecca Bugger (narrative nonfiction, investigative journalism, memoir, inspirational self-help, religion/spirituality, international, popular culture, and current affairs; literary and commercial fiction); Christina Morgan (literary fiction, crime fiction, and narrative nonfiction in the categories of pop culture, sports, current events and memoir); Jocquelle Caiby (literary fiction, horror, middle grade fiction, and children's books by authors who have been published in the adult market, athletes, actors, journalists, politicians, and musicians).

REPRESENTS Nonfiction, fiction, novels. **Considers these fiction areas:** commercial, gay, historical, lesbian, literary, middle grade, mystery, romance, thriller, women's, young adult, Christian.

HOW TO CONTACT Check the website, as there are online submission forms for fiction, nonfiction and juvenile. Website will also state if we're temporarily closed to submissions to any areas. Accepts simultaneous submissions. Obtains most new clients through conferences, referrals.

TERMS Agent receives 15% commission on domestic sales; 20% commission on foreign sales. Offers written contract; 2-month notice must be given to terminate contract. Charges clients for office fees, which are taken from any advance.

TIPS "See the books *Writing Great Books For Young Adults* and *You Should Really Write A Book: How To Write Sell And Market Your Memoir*. We are looking for high concept ideas with big hooks. If you get writer's block try possibiliteas.co, it's a muse in a cup."

THE SEYMOUR AGENCY

475 Miner St., Canton NY 13617. (315)386-1831. **E-mail:** nicole@theseymouragency.com; julie@theseymouragency.com. **Website:** www.theseymouragency.com. Member of AAR. Signatory of WGA. Other memberships include RWA, Authors Guild, HWA.

MEMBER AGENTS Nicole Rescinti, nicole@theseymouragency.com; Julie Gwinn, julie@theseymouragency.com; Tina Wainscott, tina@theseymouragency.com; Jennifer Wills, jennifer@theseymouragency.com.

REPRESENTS Nonfiction, novels. **Considers these fiction areas:** action, fantasy, inspirational, middle grade, mystery, new adult, religious, romance, science fiction, suspense, thriller, young adult.

HOW TO CONTACT Accepts e-mail queries. Check online for guidelines. Accepts simultaneous submissions. Responds in 1 month to queries; 3 months to mss.

TERMS Agent receives 12-15% commission on domestic sales.

DENISE SHANNON LITERARY AGENCY, INC.

20 W. 22nd St., Suite 1603, New York NY 10010. **E-mail:** info@deniseshannonagency.com. **E-mail:** submissions@deniseshannonagency.com. **Website:**

www.deniseshannonagency.com. **Contact:** Denise Shannon. Estab. 2002. Member of AAR.

○ Prior to opening her agency, Ms. Shannon worked for 16 years with Georges Borchardt and International Creative Management.

REPRESENTS Nonfiction, novels. **Considers these fiction areas:** literary.

☛ "We are a boutique agency with a distinguished list of fiction and nonfiction authors."

HOW TO CONTACT "Queries may be submitted by post, accompanied by a SASE, or by e-mail to submissions@deniseshannonagency.com. Please include a description of the available book project and a brief bio including details of any prior publications. We will reply and request more material if we are interested. We request that you inform us if you are submitting material simultaneously to other agencies." Accepts simultaneous submissions.

RECENT SALES *Mister Monkey* by Francine Prose (Harper), *Hotel Solitaire* by Gary Shteyngart (Random House), *White Flights* by Jess Row (Graywolf Press), *The Underworld* by Kevin Canty (Norton).

TIPS "Please do not send queries regarding fiction projects until a complete ms is available for review. We request that you inform us if you are submitting material simultaneously to other agencies."

WENDY SHERMAN ASSOCIATES, INC.

138 W. 25th St., Suite 1018, New York NY 10001. (212)279-9027. **E-mail:** submissions@wsherman.com. **Website:** www.wsherman.com. **Contact:** Wendy Sherman. Estab. 1999. Member of AAR.

○ Prior to opening the agency, Ms. Sherman held positions as vice president, executive director, associate publisher, subsidiary rights director, and sales and marketing director for major publishers including Simon & Schuster and Henry Holt.

MEMBER AGENTS Wendy Sherman (women's fiction that hits that sweet spot between literary and mainstream, Southern voices, historical dramas, suspense with a well-developed protagonist, and writing that illuminates the multicultural experience, anything related to food, dogs, mothers and daughters).

REPRESENTS Nonfiction, fiction, novels. **Considers these fiction areas:** mainstream, Mainstream fiction that hits the sweet spot between literary and commercial..

☛ "We specialize in developing new writers, as well as working with more established writers."

My experience as a publisher has proven to be a great asset to my clients."

HOW TO CONTACT Query via e-mail only. "We ask that you include your last name, title, and the name of the agent you are submitting to in the subject line. For fiction, please include a query letter and your first 10 pages copied and pasted in the body of the e-mail. We will not open attachments unless they have been requested. For nonfiction, please include your query letter and author bio. Due to the large number of e-mail submissions that we receive, we only reply to e-mail queries in the affirmative. We respectfully ask that you do not send queries to our individual e-mail addresses." Accepts simultaneous submissions. Obtains most new clients through recommendations from other writers.

TERMS Agent receives standard 15% commission. Offers written contract.

RECENT SALES *All Is Not Forgotten* by Wendy Walker; *Z, A Novel of Zelda Fitzgerald* by Therese Anne Fowler; *The Charm Bracelet* by Viola Shipman; *The Silence of Bonaventure Arrow* by Rita Leganski; *Together Tea* by Marjan Kamali; *A Long Long Time Ago and Essentially True* by Brigid Pasulka; *Lunch in Paris* by Elizabeth Bard; *The Rules of Inheritance* by Claire Bidwell Smith; *Eight Flavors* by Sarah Lohman; *How to Live a Good Life* by Jonathan Fields.

TIPS "The bottom line is: Do your homework. Be as well prepared as possible. Read the books that will help you present yourself and your work with polish. You want your submission to stand out."

SPEILBURG LITERARY AGENCY

E-mail: info@speilburgliterary.com. **E-mail:** speilburgliterary@gmail.com. **Website:** speilburgliterary.com. **Contact:** Alice Speilburg. Estab. 2012. SCBWI; MWA; RWA

○ Alice Speilburg previously held publishing positions at John Wiley & Sons and Howard Morhaim Literary Agency.

REPRESENTS Nonfiction, fiction, novels. **Considers these fiction areas:** adventure, commercial, detective, fantasy, feminist, historical, horror, mainstream, middle grade, mystery, police, science fiction, suspense, urban fantasy, westerns, women's, young adult.

☛ Does not want picture books; screenplays; poetry; romance novels.

HOW TO CONTACT If you are interested in submitting your ms or proposal for consideration, please e-mail a query letter along with either three sample chapters for fiction, or a TOC and proposal for nonfiction. Accepts simultaneous submissions.

SPENCERHILL ASSOCIATES

8131 Lakewood Main St., Building M, Suite 205, Lakewood Ranch FL 34202. (941)907-3700. **E-mail:** submission@spencerhillassociates.com. **Website:** www.spencerhillassociates.com. **Contact:** Karen Solem, Nalini Akolekar, Amanda Leuck or Sandy Harding. Member of AAR.

○ Prior to becoming an agent, Ms. Solem was editor in chief at HarperCollins and an associate publisher.

MEMBER AGENTS Karen Solem; Nalini Akolekar; Amanda Leuck; Sandy Harding.

REPRESENTS Fiction, novels. **Considers these fiction areas:** commercial, crime, erotica, family saga, gay, historical, inspirational, literary, mainstream, multicultural, mystery, new adult, paranormal, police, romance, thriller, women's, young adult.

☞ "We handle mostly commercial women's fiction, historical novels, romance (historical, contemporary, paranormal, urban fantasy), thrillers, and mysteries. We also represent Christian fiction only—no nonfiction." No nonfiction, poetry, science fiction, children's picture books, or scripts.

HOW TO CONTACT "We accept electronic submissions and are no longer accepting paper queries. Please send us a query letter in the body of an e-mail, pitch us your project and tell us about yourself: Do you have prior publishing credits? Attach the first three chapters and synopsis preferably in .doc, rtf or txt format to your e-mail. Send all queries to submission@spencerhillassociates.com. We do not have a preference for exclusive submissions, but do appreciate knowing if the submission is simultaneous. We receive thousands of submissions a year and each query receives our attention. Unfortunately, we are unable to respond to each query individually. If we are interested in your work, we will contact you within 12 weeks." Accepts simultaneous submissions.

TERMS Agent receives 15% commission on domestic sales; 20% commission on foreign sales. Offers written contract; 3-month notice must be given to terminate contract.

RECENT SALES A full list of sales and clients is available on the agency website.

THE SPIELER AGENCY

27 W. 20 St., Suite 302, New York NY 10011. (212)757-4439, ext. 1. **Fax:** (212)333-2019. **Website:** thespieleragency.com. **Contact:** Joe Spieler. Represents 160 clients.

○ Prior to opening his agency, Mr. Spieler was a magazine editor.

MEMBER AGENTS Victoria Shoemaker, victoria@thespieleragency.com (environment and natural history, popular culture, memoir, photography and film, literary fiction and poetry, and books on food and cooking); John Thornton, john@thespieleragency.com (nonfiction); Joe Spieler, joe@thespieleragency.com (nonfiction and fiction and books for children and young adults); Helen Sweetland, helen@thespieleragency.com (children's from board books through young adult fiction; adult general-interest nonfiction, including nature, green living, gardening, architecture, interior design, health, and popular science).

REPRESENTS Nonfiction, novels, juvenile books. **Considers these fiction areas:** literary, middle grade, New Age, picture books, thriller, young adult.

HOW TO CONTACT "Before submitting projects to the Spieler Agency, check the listings of our individual agents and see if any particular agent shows a general interest in your subject (e.g., history, memoir, YA, etc.). Please send all queries either by e-mail or regular mail. If you query us by regular mail, we can only reply to you if you include a SASE." Accepts simultaneous submissions. Cannot guarantee a personal response to all queries. Obtains most new clients through recommendations, listing in *Guide to Literary Agents.*

TERMS Agent receives 15% commission on domestic sales. Charges clients for messenger bills, photocopying, postage.

WRITERS CONFERENCES London Book Fair.

NANCY STAUFFER ASSOCIATES

P.O. Box 1203, Darien CT 06820. (203)202-2500. **E-mail:** nancy@staufferliterary.com. **Website:** www.publishersmarketplace.com/members/nstauffer. **Contact:** Nancy Stauffer Cahoon. Other memberships include Authors Guild.

○ "Over the course of my more than 20 year career, I've held positions in the editorial, marketing, business, and rights departments of The New York Times, McGraw-Hill, and Doubleday. Before founding Nancy Stauffer Associates, I was Director of Foreign and Performing Rights then Director, Subsidiary Rights, for Doubleday, where I was honored to have worked with a diverse range of internationally known and bestselling authors of all genres.".

REPRESENTS Considers these fiction areas: literary.

☛ Mysteries, romance, action adventure, historical fiction

HOW TO CONTACT Accepts simultaneous submissions. Obtains most new clients through referrals from existing clients.

TERMS Agent receives 15% commission on domestic sales; 20% commission on foreign sales.

RECENT SALES *You Don't Have to Say You Love Me* by Sherman Alexie, *Our Souls At Night* by Kent Haruf, *Bone Fire* by Mark Spragg.

ROBIN STRAUS AGENCY, INC.

Wallace Literary Agency, 229 E. 79th St., Suite 5A, New York NY 10075. (212)472-3282. **Fax:** (212)472-3833. **E-mail:** info@robinstrausagency.com. **Website:** www.robinstrausagency.com. **Contact:** Ms. Robin Straus. Estab. 1983. Member of AAR.

○ Prior to becoming an agent, Robin Straus served as a subsidiary rights manager at Random House and Doubleday. She began her career in the editorial department of Little, Brown.

REPRESENTS Considers these fiction areas: commercial, contemporary issues, literary, mainstream, women's.

☛ Does not represent juvenile, young adult, horror, romance, Westerns, poetry, or screenplays.

HOW TO CONTACT E-query or query via snail mail with SASE. "Send us a query letter with contact information, an autobiographical summary, a brief synopsis or description of your book project, submission history, and information on competition. If you wish, you may also include the opening chapter of your ms (pasted). While we do our best to reply to all queries, you can assume that if you haven't heard from us after six weeks, we are not interested." Accepts simultaneous submissions.

TERMS Agent receives 15% commission on domestic sales; 20% commission on foreign sales. Offers written contract.

THE STRINGER LITERARY AGENCY LLC

P.O. Box 770365, Naples FL 34107. **E-mail:** mstringer@stringerlit.com. **Website:** www.stringerlit.com. **Contact:** Marlene Stringer. Estab. 2008. Member of AAR. Signatory of WGA. RWA, MWA, ITW, SBCWI Represents 50 clients.

REPRESENTS Fiction, novels. **Considers these fiction areas:** commercial, crime, detective, fantasy, historical, horror, mainstream, multicultural, mystery, new adult, paranormal, police, romance, science fiction, suspense, thriller, urban fantasy, women's, young adult, No space opera SF..

☛ This agency specializes in fiction. "We are an editorial agency, and work with clients to make their mss the best they can be in preparation for submission. We focus on career planning, and help our clients reach their publishing goals. We advise clients on marketing and promotional strategies to help them reach their target readership. Because we are so hands-on, we limit the size of our list; however, we are always looking for exceptional voices and stories that demand we read to the end. You never know where the next great story is coming from." This agency is seeking thrillers, crime fiction (not true crime), mystery, women's fiction, single title and category romance, fantasy (all subgenera), earth-based science fiction (no space opera, aliens, etc.), and YA/teen. Does not want to receive picture books, MG, plays, short stories, or poetry. This is not the agency for inspirational romance or erotica. No space opera. The agency is not seeking nonfiction as of this time (2016).

HOW TO CONTACT Electronic submissions through website submission form only. Please make sure your ms is as good as it can be before you submit. Agents are not first readers. For specific information on what we like to see in query letters, refer to the information at www.stringerlit.com under the heading "Learn." Accepts simultaneous submissions. "We strive to respond quickly, but current clients' work always comes first." Obtains new clients through referrals, submissions, conferences.

TERMS Standard commission. "We do not charge fees."

RECENT SALES *The Conqueror's Wife* by Stephanie Thornton; *When I'm Gone* by Emily Bleeker; *Magic Bitter, Magic Sweet* by Charlie N. Holmberg; *Belle Chasse* by Suzanne Johnson; *Chapel of Ease* by Alex Bledsoe; *Wilds of the Bayou* by Susannah Sandlin; *Summit Lake* by Charlie Donlea; The Jane Doe Series by Liana Brooks; *The Mermaid's Secret* by Katie Schickel; *The Sutherland Scandals* by Anna Bradley; *Fly By Night* by Andrea Thalasinos; The Joe Gale Mystery Series by Brenda Buchanan; The Kate Baer Series by Shannon Baker; Los Nephilim Series by T. Frohock;

The Dragonsworn Series by Caitlyn McFarland; *The Devious Dr. Jekyll* by Viola Carr; *The Dragon's Price* by Bethany Wiggins; The Otter Bite Romance Series by Maggie McConnell; *Machinations* by Haley Stone; Film Rights to *Wreckage* by Emily Bleeker.

WRITERS CONFERENCES RWA National and various other conferences each year.

TIPS "If your ms falls between categories, or you are not sure of the category, query and we'll let you know if we'd like to take a look. We strive to respond as quickly as possible. If you have not received a response in the time period indicated on website, please re-query."

THE STROTHMAN AGENCY, LLC

63 E. 9th St., 10X, New York NY 10003. **E-mail:** info@strothmanagency.com. **E-mail:** strothmanagency@gmail.com. **Website:** www.strothmanagency.com. **Contact:** Wendy Strothman, Lauren MacLeod. Member of AAR. Other memberships include Authors' Guild. Represents 50 clients.

○ Prior to becoming an agent, Ms. Strothman was head of Beacon Press (1983-1995) and executive vice president of Houghton Mifflin's Trade & Reference Division (1996-2002).

MEMBER AGENTS Wendy Strothman (history, narrative nonfiction, narrative journalism, science and nature, and current affairs); Lauren MacLeod (young adult fiction and nonfiction, middle grade novels, as well as highly polished literary fiction and narrative nonfiction, particularly food writing, science, pop culture and history).

REPRESENTS Nonfiction, novels, juvenile books. **Considers these fiction areas:** literary, middle grade, young adult.

☛ "The Strothman Agency seeks out scholars, journalists, and other acknowledged and emerging experts in their fields. We specialize in history, science, narrative journalism, nature and the environment, current affairs, narrative nonfiction, business and economics, young adult fiction and nonfiction, middle grade fiction and nonfiction. We are not signing up projects in romance, science fiction, picture books, or poetry."

HOW TO CONTACT Accepts queries only via e-mail. See submission guidelines online. Accepts simultaneous submissions. "All e-mails received will be responded to with an auto-reply. If we have not replied to your query within 6 weeks, we do not feel that it is right for us." Ac-

cepts simultaneous submissions. Obtains most new clients through recommendations from others.

TERMS Agent receives 15% commission on domestic sales; 20% commission on foreign sales. Offers written contract; 30-day notice must be given to terminate contract.

THE STUART AGENCY

260 W. 52 St., #25C, New York NY 10019. (212)586-2711. **E-mail:** andrew@stuartagency.com. **Website:** stuartagency.com. **Contact:** Andrew Stuart. Estab. 2002.

○ Prior to his current position, Mr. Stuart was an agent with Literary Group International for five years. Prior to becoming an agent, he was an editor at Random House and Simon & Schuster.

MEMBER AGENTS Andrew Stuart (history, science, narrative nonfiction, business, current events, memoir, psychology, sports, literary fiction); Christopher Rhodes, christopher@stuartagency.com (literary and upmarket fiction [including thriller and horror]; connected stories/essays [humorous and serious]; memoir; creative/narrative nonfiction; history; religion; pop culture; and art & design); Rob Kirkpatrick, rob@stuartagency.com (memoir, biography, sports, music, pop culture, current events, history, and pop science).

REPRESENTS Nonfiction, novels. **Considers these fiction areas:** horror, literary, thriller.

HOW TO CONTACT Query via online submission form on the agency website. Accepts simultaneous submissions.

SUITE A MANAGEMENT TALENT & LITERARY AGENCY

136 El Camino Dr., Suite 410, Beverly Hills CA 90212. (310)278-0801. **Fax:** (310)278-0807. **E-mail:** suite-a@juno.com. **Contact:** Lloyd Robinson. Estab. 1990. Signatory of WGA. Other memberships include Signatory of WGA, DGA, SAG-A.F.T.R.A. Represents 76 clients.

○ Prior to becoming an agent, Mr. Robinson worked as a talent manager.

MEMBER AGENTS Lloyd Robinson (adaptation of books and plays for development as features or TV MOW).

REPRESENTS Fiction, novels, movie scripts, feature film, TV scripts, TV movie of the week, episodic drama, documentary, miniseries, variety show, theatrical stage play, stage plays, CD-ROM.

☞ "We represent screenwriters, playwrights, novelists, producers and directors."

HOW TO CONTACT Submit synopsis, outline/proposal, logline. Accepts simultaneous submissions. Obtains most new clients through recommendations from others.

TERMS Agent receives 10% commission on domestic and foreign sales. Offers written contract, binding for minimum 1 year. Charges clients for photocopying, messenger, FedEx, postage.

RECENT SALES This agency prefers not to share information on specific sales or client names.

TIPS "We are a talent agency specializing in the copyright business. 50 percent of our clients generate copyright (screenwriters, playwrights and novelists). 50 percent of our clients service copyright (producers and directors). We represent produced, published, and/or WGA writers who are eligible for staff TV positions, as well as novelists and playwrights whose works may be adapted for film or TV."

EMMA SWEENEY AGENCY, LLC

245 E 80th St., Suite 7E, New York NY 10075. **E-mail:** queries@emmasweeneyagency.com. **Website:** www.emmasweeneyagency.com. Estab. 2006. Member of AAR. Other memberships include Women's Media Group. Represents 80 clients.

○ Prior to becoming an agent, Ms. Sweeney was director of subsidiary rights at Grove Press. Since 1990, she has been a literary agent. Ms. Sutherland Brown was an Associate Editor at St. Martin's Press/Thomas Dunne Books and a freelance editor. Ms. Watson attended Hunter College where she earned a BA in English (with a focus on Creative Writing) and a BA in Russian Language & Culture.

MEMBER AGENTS Emma Sweeney, president; Margaret Sutherland Brown (commercial and literary fiction, mysteries and thrillers, narrative nonfiction, lifestyle, and cookbook); Kira Watson (children's literature).

REPRESENTS Nonfiction, fiction, novels, juvenile books. **Considers these fiction areas:** commercial, contemporary issues, crime, historical, juvenile, literary, mainstream, middle grade, mystery, new adult, suspense, thriller, women's, young adult.

☞ Does not want erotica.

HOW TO CONTACT "We accept only electronic queries, and ask that all queries be sent to queries@emmasweeneyagency.com rather than to any agent directly. Please begin your query with a succinct (and hopefully catchy) description of your plot or proposal. Always include a brief cover letter telling us how you heard about ESA, your previous writing credits, and a few lines about yourself. We cannot open any attachments unless specifically requested, and ask that you paste the first 10 pages of your proposal or novel into the text of your e-mail." Accepts simultaneous submissions.

TALCOTT NOTCH LITERARY

31 Cherry St., Suite 104, Milford CT 06460. (203)876-4959. **Fax:** (203)876-9517. **E-mail:** editorial@talcottnotch.net. **Website:** www.talcottnotch.net. **Contact:** Gina Panettieri, President. Represents 150 clients.

○ Prior to becoming an agent, Ms. Panettieri was a freelance writer and editor. Ms. Munier was Director of Acquisitions for Adams Media Corporation and had previously worked for Disney. Ms. Sulaiman holds degrees from Wellesley and the University of Chicago and had completed an internship with Sourcebooks prior to joining Talcott Notch. Mr. Shalabi holds an MS in Neuroscience and had completed internships with Folio and Veritas agencies as well as with Talcott Notch before joining Talcott Notch as a Junior Agent in late 2016.

MEMBER AGENTS Gina Panettieri, gpanettieri@talcottnotch.net (history, business, self-help, science, gardening, cookbooks, crafts, parenting, memoir, true crime and travel, YA, MG and women's fiction, paranormal, urban fantasy, horror, science fiction, historical, mystery, thrillers and suspense); Paula Munier, pmunier@talcottnotch.net (mystery/thriller, SF/fantasy, romance, YA, memoir, humor, pop culture, health & wellness, cooking, self-help, pop psych, New Age, inspirational, technology, science, and writing); Saba Sulaiman, ssulaiman@talcottnotch.net (upmarket literary and commercial fiction, romance [all subgenres except paranormal], character-driven psychological thrillers, cozy mysteries, memoir, young adult [except paranormal and sci-fi], middle grade, and nonfiction humor); Mohamed Shalabi, mshalabi@talcottnotch (upmarket literary and commercial fiction, psychological thrillers, YA [and subgenres except romance and paranormal], MG, adult nonfiction).

REPRESENTS Nonfiction, fiction, novels, short story collections, novellas, juvenile books. **Considers these fiction areas:** action, adventure, commercial, contemporary issues, crime, ethnic, fantasy, feminist, gay, hi-lo, historical, horror, juvenile, lesbian, literary, mainstream, middle grade, multicultural, multimedia, mystery, new adult, New Age, paranormal, police, romance, science fiction, short story collections, suspense, thriller, urban fantasy, women's, young adult.

⛏ "We are most actively seeking projects featuring diverse characters and stories which expand the reader's understanding of our society and the wider world we live in."

HOW TO CONTACT Query via e-mail (preferred) with first 10 pages of the ms pasted within the body of the e-mail, not as an attachment. Accepts simultaneous submissions. Responds in 2 weeks to queries; 6-10 weeks to mss.

TERMS Agent receives 15% commission on domestic sales; 20% commission on foreign sales. Offers written contract, binding for 1 year.

RECENT SALES Agency sold 65 titles in the last year including *The Widower's Wife* by Cate Holahan (Crooked Lane Books); *Tier One* by Brian Andrews and Jeffrey Wilson (Thomas & Mercer) and *Beijing Red*, written as Alex Ryan (Crooked Lane Books); *Firestorm* by Nancy Holzner (Berkley Ace Science Fiction); *The New Jersey Mob* by Scott Deitche (Rowman and Littlefield); *The Homeplace* by Kevin Wolf (St. Martin's Press); *The Goblin Crown* by Robert Hewitt Wolfe (Turner Publishing); *The Unprescription for Autism* by Janet Lintala (Amacom); *Disintegration* by Richard Thomas (Random House/Alibi); *Red Line* by Brian Thiem (Crooked Lane Books); and more.

TIPS "Know your market and how to reach them. A strong platform is essential in your book proposal. Can you effectively use social media/Are you a strong networker: Are you familiar with the book bloggers in your genre? Are you involved with the interest-specific groups that can help you? What can you do to break through the 'noise' and help present your book to your readers? Check our website for more tips and information on this topic."

TESSLER LITERARY AGENCY, LLC

27 W. 20th St., Suite 1003, New York NY 10011. (212)242-0466. **Website:** www.tessleragency.com. **Contact:** Michelle Tessler. Estab. 2004. Member of AAR. Women's Media Group.

🗩 Prior to forming her own agency, Ms. Tessler worked at the prestigious literary agency Carlisle & Company (now Inkwell Management) and at the William Morris Agency.

REPRESENTS Nonfiction, fiction. **Considers these fiction areas:** commercial, literary, women's.

⛏ "Tessler Literary Agency represents a select number of best-selling and emerging authors. Based in the Flatiron District in Manhattan, we are dedicated to writers of high-quality fiction and nonfiction. Our clients include accomplished journalists, scientists, academics, experts in their field, as well as novelists and debut authors with unique voices and stories to tell. We value fresh, original writing that has a compelling point of view. Our list is diverse and far-reaching. In nonfiction, it includes narrative, popular science, memoir, history, psychology, business, biography, food, and travel. In many cases, we sign authors who are especially adept at writing books that cross many of these categories at once. In fiction, we represent literary, women's, and commercial. If your project is in keeping with the kind of books we take on, we want to hear from you." Does not want genre fiction or children's books or anthologies.

HOW TO CONTACT Submit query through online query form only. Accepts simultaneous submissions. New clients by queries/submissions through the website and recommendations from others.

TERMS Receives 15% commission on domestic sales; 20% on foreign sales. Offers written contract.

THOMPSON LITERARY AGENCY

115 W. 29th St., Third Floor, New York NY 10001. (347)281-7685. **E-mail:** submissions@thompsonliterary.com. **Website:** thompsonliterary.com. **Contact:** Meg Thompson, founder. Estab. 2014. Member of AAR. Signatory of WGA.

🗩 Before her current position, Ms. Thompson was with LJK Literary and the Einstein Thompson Agency.

MEMBER AGENTS Cindy Uh, senior agent; John Thorn, affiliate agent; Sandy Hodgman, director of foreign rights.

REPRESENTS Nonfiction, fiction, novels, juvenile books. **Considers these fiction areas:** commercial, contemporary issues, fantasy, historical, juvenile, literary, middle grade, multicultural, picture books, women's, young adult.

- The agency is always on the lookout for both commercial and literary fiction, as well as young adult and children's books. "Nonfiction, however, is our specialty, and our interests include biography, memoir, music, popular science, politics, blog-to-book projects, cookbooks, sports, health and wellness, fashion, art, and popular culture." "Please note that we do not accept submissions for poetry collections or screenplays, and we only consider picture books by established illustrators."

HOW TO CONTACT "For fiction: Please send a query letter, including any salient biographical information or previous publications, and attach the first 25 pages of your ms. For nonfiction: Please send a query letter and a full proposal, including biographical information, previous publications, credentials that qualify you to write your book, marketing information, and sample material. You should address your query to whichever agent you think is best suited for your project." Accepts simultaneous submissions. Responds in 6 weeks if interested.

THREE SEAS LITERARY AGENCY

P.O. Box 444, Sun Prairie WI 53590. (608)834-9317. **E-mail:** queries@threeseaslit.com. **Website:** threeseasagency.com. **Contact:** Michelle Grajkowski, Cori Deyoe. Estab. 2000. Member of AAR. Other memberships include RWA (Romance Writers of America), SCBWI Represents 55 clients.

- Since its inception, 3 Seas has sold more than 500 titles worldwide. Ms. Grajkowski's authors have appeared on all the major lists including *The New York Times*, *USA Today* and *Publishers Weekly*. Prior to joining the agency in 2006, Ms. Deyoe was a multi-published author. She represents a wide range of authors and has sold many projects at auction.

MEMBER AGENTS Michelle Grajkowski (romance, women's fiction, young adult and middle grade fiction, select nonfiction projects); Cori Deyoe (all subgenres of romance, women's fiction, young adult, middle grade, picture books, thrillers, mysteries and select nonfiction); Linda Scalissi (women's fiction, thrillers, young adult, mysteries and romance).

REPRESENTS Nonfiction, novels. **Considers these fiction areas:** middle grade, mystery, picture books, romance, thriller, women's, young adult.

- "We represent more than 50 authors who write romance, women's fiction, science fiction/fantasy, thrillers, young adult and middle grade fiction, as well as select nonfiction titles. Currently, we are looking for fantastic authors with a voice of their own." 3 Seas does not represent poetry or screenplays.

HOW TO CONTACT E-mail queries only; no attachments, unless requested by agents. For fiction, please e-mail the first chapter and synopsis along with a cover letter. Also, be sure to include the genre and the number of words in your ms, as well as pertinent writing experience in your query letter. For nonfiction, e-mail a complete proposal, including a query letter and your first chapter. For picture books, query with complete text. Accepts simultaneous submissions. Obtains most new clients through recommendations from others, conferences.

TERMS Agent receives 15% commission on domestic sales; 20% commission on foreign sales. Offers written contract.

RECENT SALES Represents best-selling authors, including Jennifer Brown, Katie MacAlister, Kerrelyn Sparks, and C.L. Wilson.

TRANSATLANTIC LITERARY AGENCY

2 Bloor St. E., Suite 3500, Toronto ON M4W 1A8 Canada. (416)488-9214. **E-mail:** info@transatlanticagency.com. **Website:** transatlanticagency.com.

MEMBER AGENTS Trena White (upmarket, accessible nonfiction: current affairs, business, culture, politics, technology, and the environment); Amy Tompkins (adult: literary fiction, historical fiction, women's fiction including smart romance, narrative nonfiction, and quirky or original how-to books; children's: early readers, middle grade, young adult, and new adult); Stephanie Sinclair (literary fiction, upmarket women's and commercial fiction, literary thriller and suspense, YA crossover; narrative nonfiction, memoir, investigative journalism and true crime); Samantha Haywood (literary fiction and upmarket commercial fiction, specifically literary thrillers and upmarket mystery, historical fiction, smart contemporary fiction, upmarket women's fiction and cross-over novels; narrative nonfiction, including investigative journalism, politics, women's issues, memoirs, environmental issues, historical narratives, sexuality, true crime; graphic novels (fiction/nonfiction): preferably full length graphic novels, story collections considered, memoirs, biographies, travel narratives); Jesse Finkelstein (nonfiction: current affairs, business, culture, politics, technology, religion, and the environment); Marie Campbell (middle grade fiction); Shaun Bradley (referrals only; adult literary fiction and narrative nonfiction, primarily science and investigative journalism); Sandra Bishop (fiction; nonfiction: biography, memoir, and positive or humorous how-to books on advice/relationships, mind/body/spirit, religion, healthy living, finances, life-hacks, traveling, living a better life); Fiona Kenshole (children's and young adult; only accepting submissions from referrals or conferences she attends as faculty); Lynn Bennett (not accepting submissions or new clients); David Bennett (children's, young adult, adult).

REPRESENTS Nonfiction, novels, juvenile books.

- ☛ "In both children's and adult literature, we market directly into the U.S., the United Kingdom and Canada." Represents adult and children's authors of all genres, including illustrators. Does not want to receive picture books, musicals, screenplays or stage plays.

HOW TO CONTACT Always refer to the website, as guidelines will change, and only various agents are open to new clients at any given time. Obtains most new clients through recommendations from others.

TERMS Agent receives 15% commission on domestic sales; 20% commission on foreign sales. Offers written contract; 45-day notice must be given to terminate contract. This agency charges for photocopying and postage when it exceeds $100.

RECENT SALES Sold 250 titles in the last year.

TRIADA US

P.O. Box 561, Sewickley PA 15143. (412)401-3376. E-mail: uwe@triadaus.com; brent@triadaus.com; laura@triadaus.com; mallory@triadaus.com; lauren@triadaus.com. **Website:** www.triadaus.com. **Contact:** Dr. Uwe Stender, President. Estab. 2004. Member of AAR.

MEMBER AGENTS Uwe Stender; Brent Taylor; Laura Crockett; Mallory Brown; Lauren Spieller.

REPRESENTS Nonfiction, fiction, novels, juvenile books. **Considers these fiction areas:** action, adventure, comic books, commercial, contemporary issues, crime, detective, ethnic, family saga, fantasy, gay, historical, horror, juvenile, lesbian, literary, mainstream, middle grade, multicultural, mystery, new adult, oc-

cult, picture books, police, suspense, thriller, urban fantasy, women's, young adult.

- ☛ Actively seeking fiction and nonfiction across a broad range of categories of all age levels.

HOW TO CONTACT E-mail queries preferred. Please paste your query letter and the first 10 pages of your ms into the body of a message e-mailed to the agent of your choice. Please note: a rejection from a Triada US agent is a rejection from all. Triada US agents personally respond to all queries and requested material and pride themselves on having some of the fastest response times in the industry. Obtains most new clients through submission inbox (query letters and requested mss), client referrals, and conferences.

TERMS Triada US retains 15% commission on domestic sales and 20% commission on foreign and translation sales. Offers written contract; 30-day notice must be given prior to termination.

RECENT SALES *Plants You Can't Kill* by Stacy Tornio (Skyhorse), *Gettysburg Rebels* by Tom McMillan (Regnery), *The Smart Girl's Guide to Polyamory* by Dedeker Winston (Skyhorse), *Raised by Animals* by Jennifer Verdolin (The Experiment), *The Hemingway Thief* by Shaun Harris (Seventh Street), *The Perfect Fit* by Summer Heacock (Mira), *Not Perfect* by Elizabeth LaBan (Lake Union), *The Lighthouse Keeper* by Cynthia Ellingsen (Lake Union), *Sometime After Midnight* by L. Philips (Viking), *The Diminished* by Kaitlyn Sage Patterson (Harlequin Teen), *A Short History of the Girl Next Door* by Jared Reck (Knopf), *Chaotic Good* by Whitney Gardner (Knopf), *Project Pandora* by Aden Polydoros (Entangled Teen), *Who's That Girl* by Blair Thornburgh (HarperTeen), *Timekeeper* by Tara Sim (Sky Pony), *Smoke and Mirrors* by K.D. Halbrook (Paula Wiseman Books), *The Italy List* by Dee Romito (Aladdin), *Don't Solve the Puzzle* by Krista Van Dolzer (Bloomsbury), *Here Comes Trouble* by Kate Hattemer (Knopf), *Fake Blood* by Whitney Gardner (Simon & Schuster), *Alan Cole Is Not a Coward* by Eric Bell (Katherine Tegen Books).

TRIDENT MEDIA GROUP

41 Madison Ave., 36th Floor, New York NY 10010. (212)333-1511. **Website:** www.tridentmediagroup.com. **Contact:** Ellen Levine. Member of AAR.

MEMBER AGENTS Kimberly Whalen, ws.assistant@tridentmediagroup (commercial fiction and nonfiction, including women's fiction, romance, suspense, paranormal, and pop culture); Alyssa Eisner Henkin (picture books through young adult fiction, including mysteries, period pieces, contemporary school-settings, issues of social justice, family sagas, eerie magical realism, and retellings of classics; children's/YA nonfiction: history, STEM/STEAM themes, memoir) Scott Miller, smiller@tridentmediagroup.com (commercial fiction, including thrillers, crime fiction, women's, book club fiction, middle grade, young adult; nonfiction, including military, celebrity and pop culture, narrative, sports, prescriptive, and current events); Melissa Flashman, mflashman@tridentmediagroup.com (nonfiction: pop culture, memoir, wellness, popular science, business and economics, technology; fiction: adult and YA, literary and commercial); Don Fehr, dfehr@tridentmediagroup.com (literary and commercial fiction, young adult fiction, narrative nonfiction, memoirs, travel, science, and health); John Silbersack, silbersack.assistant@tridentmediagroup.com (fiction: literary fiction, crime fiction, science fiction and fantasy, children's, thrillers/suspense; nonfiction: narrative nonfiction, science, history, biography, current events, memoirs, finance, pop culture); Erica Spellman-Silverman; Ellen Levine, levine.assistant@tridentmediagroup.com (popular commercial fiction and compelling nonfiction, including memoir, popular culture, narrative nonfiction, history, politics, biography, science, and the odd quirky book); Mark Gottlieb (fiction: science fiction, fantasy, young adult, graphic novels, historical, middle grade, mystery, romance, suspense, thrillers; nonfiction: business, finance, history, religious, health, cookbooks, sports, African-American, biography, memoir, travel, mind/body/spirit, narrative nonfiction, science, technology); Alexander Slater, aslater@tridentmdiagroup.com (children's, middle grade, and young adult fiction); Amanda O'Connor, aoconnor@tridentmediagroup.com; Tara Carberry, tcarberry@tridentmediagroup.com (women's commercial fiction, romance, new adult, young adult, and select nonfiction); Alexa Stark, astark@tridentmediagroup.com (literary fiction, upmarket commercial fiction, young adult, memoir, narrative nonfiction, popular science, cultural criticism and women's issues).

REPRESENTS Considers these fiction areas: commercial, crime, fantasy, historical, juvenile, literary, middle grade, mystery, new adult, paranormal, picture books, romance, science fiction, suspense, thriller, women's, young adult.

☛ Actively seeking new or established authors in a variety of fiction and nonfiction genres.

HOW TO CONTACT Submit through the agency's online submission form on the agency website. Query only 1 agent at a time. If you e-query, include no attachments. Accepts simultaneous submissions.

TIPS "If you have any questions, please check FAQ page before e-mailing us."

UNION LITERARY

30 Vandam St., Suite 5A, New York NY 10013. (212)255-2112. **E-mail:** info@unionliterary.com. **E-mail:** submissions@unionliterary.com. **Website:** unionliterary.com. Member of AAR. Signatory of WGA.

○ "Prior to becoming an agent, Trena Keating was editor in chief of Dutton and associate publisher of Plume, both imprints of Penguin, senior editor at HarperCollins, and humanities assistant at Stanford University Press.

MEMBER AGENTS Trena Keating, tk@unionliterary.com (fiction and nonfiction, specifically a literary novel with an exotic setting, a YA/MG journey or transformation novel, a distinctly modern novel with a female protagonist, a creepy page-turner, a quest memoir that addresses larger issues, nonfiction based on primary research or a unique niche, a great essayist, and a voicy writer who is a great storyteller or makes her laugh); **Sally Wofford-Girand**, swg@unionliterary.com (history, memoir, women's issues, cultural studies, gripping literary fiction); **Jenni Ferrari-Adler**, jenni@unionliterary.com (fiction, cookbook/food, young adult and middle grade, narrative nonfiction); **Christina Clifford**, christina@unionliterary.com (literary fiction, international fiction, narrative nonfiction, specifically historical biography, memoir, business, and science); **Shaun Dolan,** sd@unionliterary.com (muscular and lyrical literary fiction, narrative nonfiction, memoir, pop culture, and sports narratives).

☛ "Union Literary is a full-service boutique agency specializing in literary fiction, popular fiction, narrative nonfiction, memoir, social history, business and general big idea books, popular science, cookbooks and food writing." The agency does not represent romance, poetry, science fiction or illustrated books.

HOW TO CONTACT Nonfiction submissions: include a query letter, a proposal and a sample chapter. Fiction submissions: should include a query letter, synopsis, and either sample pages or full ms. "Due to the high volume of submissions we receive, we will only be in contact regarding projects that feel like a match for the respective agent." Accepts simultaneous submissions. Accepts simultaneous submissions. Responds in 1 month.

RECENT SALES *The Sunlit Night* by Rebecca Dinerstein, *Dept. of Speculation* by Jenny Offill, *Mrs. Houdini* by Victoria Kelly.

⊙ UNITED TALENT AGENCY

142 W. 57th St., 6th Floor, New York NY 10019. (212)581-3100. **Website:** www.theagencygroup.com. **Contact:** Marc Gerald.

○ Prior to becoming an agent, Mr. Gerald owned and ran an independent publishing and entertainment agency.

MEMBER AGENTS Marc Gerald (no queries); Juliet Mushens, U.K. Literary division, juliet.mushens@unitedtalent.com (high-concept novels, thrillers, YA, historical fiction, literary fiction, psychological suspense, reading group fiction, SF and fantasy); Sasha Raskin, sasah.raskin@unitedtalent.com (popular science, business books, historical narrative nonfiction, narrative and/or literary nonfiction, historical fiction, and genre fiction like sci-fi but when it fits the crossover space and isn't strictly confined to its genre); Sarah Manning, sarah.manning@unitedtalent.com (enjoys crime, thrillers, historical fiction, commercial women's fiction, accessible literary fiction, fantasy and YA); Diana Beaumont, U.K. Literary division, diana.beaumont@unitedtalent.com (accessible literary fiction with a strong hook, historical fiction, crime, thrillers, women's commercial fiction that isn't too marshmallowy, cookery, lifestyle, celebrity books and memoir with a distinctive voice).

REPRESENTS Nonfiction, novels. **Considers these fiction areas:** commercial, crime, fantasy, historical, literary, science fiction, suspense, thriller, women's, young adult.

HOW TO CONTACT To query Juliet: Please send your cover letter, first 3 chapters and synopsis by e-mail. Juliet replies to all submissions, and aims to respond within 8-12 weeks of receipt of e-mail. To query Sasha: e-query. To query Sarah: Please send you cover letter in the body of your e-mail with synopsis and first 3 chapters by e-mail. She responds to all submissions within 8-12 weeks. Accepts simultaneous submissions.

UPSTART CROW LITERARY

244 Fifth Avenue, 11th Floor, New York NY 10001. **E-mail:** danielle.submission@gmail.com. **Website:** www.upstartcrowliterary.com. **Contact:** Danielle Chiotti, Alexandra Penfold. Estab. 2009. Member of AAR. Signatory of WGA.

MEMBER AGENTS Michael Stearns (not accepting submissions); Danielle Chiotti (all genres of young adult and middle grade fiction; adult upmarket commercial fiction [not considering romance, mystery/suspense/thriller, science fiction, horror, or erotica]; nonfiction in the areas of narrative/memoir, lifestyle, relationships, humor, current events, food, wine, and cooking); Ted Malawer (not accepting submissions); Alexandra Penfold (not accepting submissions); Susan Hawk (books for children and teens only).

REPRESENTS Considers these fiction areas: commercial, mainstream, middle grade, picture books, young adult.

HOW TO CONTACT Submit a query and 20 pages pasted into an e-mail. Accepts simultaneous submissions.

VERITAS LITERARY AGENCY

601 Van Ness Ave., Opera Plaza, Suite E, San Francisco CA 94102. (415)647-6964. **Fax:** (415)647-6965. **E-mail:** submissions@veritasliterary.com. **Website:** www.veritasliterary.com. **Contact:** Katherine Boyle. Member of AAR. Other memberships include Author's Guild and SCBWI.

MEMBER AGENTS Katherine Boyle, kboyle@veritasliterary.com (literary fiction, middle grade, young adult, narrative nonfiction/memoir, historical fiction, crime/suspense, history, pop culture, popular science, business/career); Michael Carr, michael@veritasliterary.com (historical fiction, women's fiction, science fiction and fantasy, nonfiction).

REPRESENTS Nonfiction, novels. **Considers these fiction areas:** commercial, crime, fantasy, historical, literary, middle grade, new adult, science fiction, suspense, women's, young adult.

HOW TO CONTACT This agency accepts short queries or proposals via e-mail only. "Fiction: Please include a cover letter listing previously published work, a one-page summary and the first 5 pages in the body of the e-mail (not as an attachment). Nonfiction: If you are sending a proposal, please include an author biography, an overview, a chapter-by-chapter summary, and an analysis of competitive titles. We do our best to review all queries within 4-6 weeks; however, if you have not heard from us in 12 weeks, consider that a no." Accepts simultaneous submissions. If you have not heard from this agency in 12 weeks, consider that a no.

WALES LITERARY AGENCY, INC.

1508 10th Ave. E. #401, Seattle WA 98102. (206)284-7114. **E-mail:** waleslit@waleslit.com. **Website:** www.waleslit.com. **Contact:** Elizabeth Wales; Neal Swain. Estab. 1990. Member of AAR. Other memberships include Authors Guild.

○ Prior to becoming an agent, Ms. Wales worked at Oxford University Press and Viking Penguin.

MEMBER AGENTS Elizabeth Wales; Neal Swain.

REPRESENTS Nonfiction, fiction, novels.

☛ This agency specializes in quality mainstream fiction and narrative nonfiction. "We're looking for more narrative nonfiction writing about nature, science, and animals." Does not handle screenplays, children's picture books, genre fiction, or most category nonfiction (such as self-help or how-to books).

HOW TO CONTACT E-query with no attachments. Submission guidelines can be found at the agency website along with a list of current clients and titles. Accepts simultaneous submissions. Responds in 2 weeks to queries, 2 months to mss.

TERMS Agent receives 15% commission on domestic sales; 20% commission on foreign sales.

RECENT SALES *Mozart's Starling* by Lyanda Lynn Haupt (Little, Brown), *The Witness Tree* by Lynda Mapes (Bloomsbury USA), *Growing a Revolution* by David Montgomery (W.W. Norton), *Victory Parade* by Leela Corman (Grand Central Publishing), *Find the Good* by Heather Lende (Algonquin).

TIPS "We are especially interested in work that espouses a progressive cultural or political view, projects a new voice, or simply shares an important, compelling story. We also encourage writers living in the Pacific Northwest, West Coast, Alaska, and Pacific Rim countries, and writers from historically underrepresented groups, such as gay and lesbian writers and writers of color, to submit work (but does not discourage writers outside these areas). Most importantly, whether in fiction or nonfiction, the agency is looking for talented storytellers."

WAXMAN LEAVELL LITERARY AGENCY, INC.

443 Park Ave. S, Suite 1004, New York NY 10016. (212)675-5556. **Fax:** (212)675-1381. **Website:** www.waxmanleavell.com.

MEMBER AGENTS Scott Waxman (nonfiction: history, biography, health and science, adventure, business, inspirational sports); Byrd Leavell (narrative nonfiction, sports, humor, and select commercial fiction); Holly Root (middle grade, young adult, women's fiction (commercial and upmarket), urban fantasy, romance, select nonfiction); Larry Kirschbaum (fiction and nonfiction; select self-published breakout books); Rachel Vogel (nonfiction: subject-driven narratives, memoirs and biography, journalism, popular culture and the occasional humor and gift book; selective fiction); Taylor Haggerty (young adult, historical, contemporary and historical romance, middle grade, women's, new adult); Cassie Hanjian (new adult novels, plot-driven commercial and upmarket women's fiction, historical fiction, psychological suspense, cozy mysteries and contemporary romance; for nonfiction, mind/body/spirit, self-help, health and wellness, inspirational memoir, food/wine (narrative and prescriptive), and a limited number of accessible cookbooks); Fleetwood Robbins (fantasy and speculative fiction—all subgenres); Molly O'Neill (middle grade and YA fiction and picture book author/illustrators, and—more selectively—narrative nonfiction [including children's/YA/MG, pop science/pop culture, and lifestyle/food/travel/cookbook projects by authors with well-established platforms]).

REPRESENTS Nonfiction, novels. **Considers these fiction areas:** fantasy, historical, literary, mainstream, middle grade, mystery, paranormal, romance, science fiction, suspense, thriller, urban fantasy, women's, young adult.

HOW TO CONTACT To submit a project, please send a query letter only via e-mail to one of the addresses included on the website. Do not send attachments, though for fiction you may include 5-10 pages of your ms in the body of your e-mail. "Due to the high volume of submissions, agents will reach out to you directly if interested. The typical time range for consideration is 6-8 weeks." "Please do not query more than 1 agent at our agency simultaneously." (To see the types of projects each agent is looking for, refer to the Agent Biographies page on website.) Use these e-mails: scottsubmit@waxmanleavell.com; byrdsubmit@waxmanleavell.com; hollysubmit@waxmanleavell.com; rachelsubmit@waxmanleavell.com; and larrysubmit@waxmanleavell.com; taylorsubmit@waxmanleavell.com; cassiesubmit@waxmanleavell.com; mollysubmit@waxmanleavell.com. Accepts simultaneous submissions.

TERMS Agent receives 15% commission on domestic sales; 10% commission on foreign sales. Offers written contract; 2-month notice must be given to terminate contract.

WELLS ARMS LITERARY

New York NY **E-mail:** info@wellsarms.com. **Website:** www.wellsarms.com. Estab. 2013. Member of AAR. SCBWI, Society of Illustrators. Represents 25 clients.

○ Victoria's career began as an editor at Dial Books for Young Readers, then G. P. Putnam's Sons and then as the founding editorial director and Associate Publisher of Bloomsbury USA's Children's Division. She opened the agency in 2013.

REPRESENTS Nonfiction, fiction, novels, juvenile books, children's book illustrators. **Considers these fiction areas:** juvenile, middle grade, new adult, picture books, young adult.

☞ "We focus on books for young readers of all ages: board books, picture books, readers, chapter books, middle grade, and young adult fiction." Actively seeking middle grade, young adult, magical realism, contemporary, romance, fantasy. "We do not represent to the textbook, magazine, adult romance or fine art markets."

HOW TO CONTACT E-query. Put "query" and your title in your e-mail subject line addressed to info@wellsarms.com. Accepts simultaneous submissions. We try to respond in a month's time. If no response, assume it's a no.

✿ WESTWOOD CREATIVE ARTISTS, LTD.

94 Harbord St., Toronto ON M5S 1G6 Canada. (416)964-3302. **E-mail:** wca_office@wcaltd.com. **Website:** www.wcaltd.com. Represents 350+ clients. **MEMBER AGENTS** Jack Babad; Lix Culotti (foreign contracts and permissions); Carolyn Ford (literary fiction, commerical, women's/literary crossover, thrillers, serious narrative nonfiction, pop culture); Jackie Kaiser (president and CEO); Michael A. Levine; Linda McKnight; Hilary McMahon (fiction, nonfiction, children's); John Pearce (fiction and nonfiction); Meg Tobin-O'Drowsky; Bruce Westwood.

REPRESENTS Nonfiction, fiction, novels. **Considers these fiction areas:** commercial, juvenile, literary, thriller, women's, young adult.

☞ "We take on children's and young adult writers very selectively. The agents bring their diverse interests to their client lists, but are generally looking for authors with a mastery of language, a passionate, expert or original perspective on their subject, and a gift for storytelling." "Please note that WCA does not represent screenwriters, and our agents are not currently seeking poetry or children's picture book submissions."

HOW TO CONTACT E-query only. Include credentials, synopsis, and no more than 10 pages. No attachments. Accepts simultaneous submissions.

RECENT SALES *Ellen in Pieces* by Caroline Adderson (HarperCollins), *Paper Swan* by Ann Y.K. Choi (Simon & Schuster), *Hope Makes Love* by Trevor Cole (Cormorant).

TIPS "We will reject outright complete, unsolicited mss, or projects that are presented poorly in the query letter. We prefer to receive exclusive submissions and request that you do not query more than 1 agent at the agency simultaneously. It's often best if you approach WCA after you have accumulated some publishing credits."

WHIMSY LITERARY AGENCY, LLC

49 N. 8th St., 6G, Brooklyn NY 11249. (212)674-7162. **E-mail:** whimsynyc@aol.com. **Website:** whimsyliteraryagency.com/. **Contact:** Jackie Meyer. Represents 30 clients.

○ Prior to becoming an agent, Ms. Meyer was a VP at Warner Books (now Grand Central/Hachette) for 20 years.

MEMBER AGENTS Jackie Meyer; Lenore Skomal (literary fiction accepted).

REPRESENTS Nonfiction, fiction. **Considers these fiction areas:** commercial, glitz, inspirational, literary, mainstream, metaphysical, New Age, paranormal, psychic.

☞ "Whimsy looks for projects that are concept- and platform-driven. We seek books that educate, inspire, and entertain." Actively seeking experts in their field with integrated and established platforms.

HOW TO CONTACT Send your proposal via e-mail to whimsynyc@aol.com (include your media platform, table of contents with full description of each chapter). First-time authors: "We appreciate proposals that are professional and complete. Please consult the many fine books available on writing book proposals. We are not considering poetry, or screenplays. Please Note: Due to the volume of queries and submissions, we are unable to respond unless they are of interest to us." Accepts simultaneous submissions. Responds "quickly, but only if interested" to queries. *Does not accept unsolicited mss.* Obtains most new clients through recommendations from others, solicitations. **TERMS** Agent receives 15% commission on domestic sales; 20% commission on foreign sales. Offers written contract.

WOLF LITERARY SERVICES, LLC

E-mail: queries@wolflit.com. **Website:** wolflit.com. Estab. 2008. Member of AAR. Signatory of WGA. **MEMBER AGENTS** Kirsten Wolf (no queries); Kate Johnson (literary fiction, particularly character-driven stories, psychological investigations, modern-day fables, international tales, magical realism, and historical fiction; nonfiction: food, feminism, parenting, art, travel and the environment, and she loves working with journalists); Allison Devereux (literary and upmarket commercial fiction; nonfiction, including examinations of contemporary culture, pop science, and modern feminist perspectives; humor and blog-to-book; illustrated novels or memoir; and narrative nonfiction that uses a particular niche topic to explore larger truths about our culture).
REPRESENTS Considers these fiction areas: commercial, historical, literary, magical realism.
HOW TO CONTACT To submit a project, please send a query letter along with a 50-page writing sample (for fiction) or a detailed proposal (for nonfiction) to queries@wolflit.com. Samples may be submitted as an attachment or embedded in the body of the e-mail. Accepts simultaneous submissions.
RECENT SALES *A Criminal Magic* by Lee Kelly (Saga Press/Simon & Schuster), *Shallow Graves* by Kali Wallace (Katherine Tegen Books/HarperCollins), *A Hard and Heavy Thing* by Matthew J. Hefti (Tyrus Books), *What Was Mine* by Helen Klein Ross (S&S/Gallery), *The Extra Woman* by Joanna Scutts (Liveright/Norton), *For the Record* by Charlotte Huang (Delacorte).

WOLFSON LITERARY AGENCY

P.O. Box 266, New York NY 10276. **E-mail:** query@wolfsonliterary.com. **Website:** www.wolfsonliterary.com. **Contact:** Michelle Wolfson. Estab. 2007. Adheres to AAR canon of ethics.
Prior to forming her own agency in December 2007, Ms. Wolfson spent 2 years with Artists & Artisans, Inc. and 2 years with Ralph Vicinanza, Ltd.
REPRESENTS Nonfiction, fiction. **Considers these fiction areas:** commercial, mainstream, new adult, romance, thriller, women's, young adult.
Actively seeking commercial fiction: young adult, mainstream, women's fiction, romance. "I am not taking on new nonfiction clients at this time."
HOW TO CONTACT E-queries only. Accepts simultaneous submissions. Responds only if interested. Positive response is generally given within 2-4 weeks. Responds in 3 months to mss. Obtains most new clients through queries or recommendations from others.
TERMS Agent receives 15% commission on domestic sales; 25% commission on foreign sales. Offers written contract; 30-day notice must be given to terminate contract.
TIPS "Be persistent."

WORDSERVE LITERARY GROUP

7061 S. University Blvd., Suite 307, Centennial CO 80122. **E-mail:** admin@wordserveliterary.com. **Website:** www.wordserveliterary.com. **Contact:** Greg Johnson. Represents 100 clients.
Prior to becoming an agent in 1994, Mr. Johnson was a magazine editor and freelance writer of more than 20 books and 200 articles.
MEMBER AGENTS Greg Johnson, Nick Harrison, Sarah Freese.
REPRESENTS Nonfiction, fiction, novels. **Considers these fiction areas:** historical, inspirational, literary, mainstream, religious, spiritual, suspense, thriller, women's, young adult.
Materials with a faith-based angle. No gift books, poetry, short stories, screenplays, graphic novels, children's picture books, science fiction or fantasy. Please do not send mss that are more than 120,000 words.
HOW TO CONTACT E-query admin@wordserveliterary.com. In the subject line, include the word

"query." All queries should include the following three elements: a pitch for the book, information about you and your platform (for nonfiction) or writing background (for fiction), and the first 5 (or so) pages of the ms pasted into the e-mail. Please view our website for full guidelines: www.wordserveliterary.com/submission-guidlines/. Accepts simultaneous submissions. Response within 60 days. Obtains most new clients through recommendations from others.

TERMS Agent receives 15% commission on domestic sales; 10-15% commission on foreign sales. Offers written contract; up to 60-day notice must be given to terminate contract.

TIPS "We are looking for good proposals, great writing and authors willing to market their books. We specialize in projects with a faith element bent. See the website before submitting."

WRITERS HOUSE

21 W. 26th St., New York NY 10010. (212)685-2400. **Fax:** (212)685-1781. **Website:** www.writershouse.com. Estab. 1973. Member of AAR.

MEMBER AGENTS Amy Berkower; Stephen Barr; Susan Cohen; Dan Conaway; Lisa DiMona; Susan Ginsburg; Susan Golomb; Merrilee Heifetz; Brianne Johnson; Daniel Lazar; Simon Lipskar; Steven Malk; Jodi Reamer, Esq.; Robin Rue; Rebecca Sherman; Geri Thoma; Albert Zuckerman; Alec Shane; Stacy Testa; Victoria Doherty-Munro; Beth Miller; Andrea Morrison; Soumeya Roberts.

REPRESENTS Nonfiction, novels. **Considers these fiction areas:** commercial, fantasy, juvenile, literary, mainstream, middle grade, picture books, science fiction, women's, young adult.

☛ This agency specializes in all types of popular fiction and nonfiction, for both adult and juvenile books as well as illustrators. Does not want to receive scholarly, professional, poetry, plays, or screenplays.

HOW TO CONTACT Individual agent e-mail addresses are available on the website. "Please e-mail us a query letter, which includes your credentials, an explanation of what makes your book unique and special, and a synopsis. Some agents within our agency have different requirements. Please consult their individual Publisher's Marketplace (PM) profile for details. We respond to all queries, generally within six to eight weeks." If you prefer to submit my mail, address it to an individual agent, and please include SASE for our reply. (If submitting to Steven Malk: Writers House, 7660 Fay Ave., #338H, La Jolla, CA 92037.) Accepts simultaneous submissions. "We respond to all queries, generally within 6-8 weeks." Obtains most new clients through recommendations from authors and editors.

TERMS Agent receives 15% commission on domestic sales. Agent receives 20% commission on foreign sales. Offers written contract, binding for 1 year. Agency charges fees for copying mss/proposals and overseas airmail of books.

TIPS "Do not send mss. Write a compelling letter. If you do, we'll ask to see your work. Follow submission guidelines and please do not simultaneously submit your work to more than one Writers House agent."

JASON YARN LITERARY AGENCY

3544 Broadway, No. 68, New York NY 10031. **E-mail:** jason@jasonyarnliteraryagency.com. **Website:** www.jasonyarnliteraryagency.com. Member of AAR. Signatory of WGA.

REPRESENTS Nonfiction, fiction. **Considers these fiction areas:** commercial, fantasy, literary, middle grade, science fiction, suspense, thriller, young adult, graphic novels, comics.

HOW TO CONTACT Please e-mail your query to jason@jasonyarnliteraryagency.com with the word "Query" in the subject line, and please paste the first 10 pages of your ms or proposal into the text of your e-mail. Do not send any attachments. "Visit the About page for information on what we are interested in, and please note that JYLA does not accept queries for film, TV, or stage scripts." Accepts simultaneous submissions.

HELEN ZIMMERMANN LITERARY AGENCY

E-mail: submit@ZimmAgency.com. **Website:** www.zimmermannliterary.com. **Contact:** Helen Zimmermann. Estab. 2003.

◯ Prior to opening her agency, Ms. Zimmermann was the director of advertising and promotion at Random House and the events coordinator at an independent bookstore.

REPRESENTS Nonfiction, fiction. **Considers these fiction areas:** literary, mainstream.

☛ "I am currently concentrating my nonfiction efforts in health and wellness, relationships, popular culture, women's issues, lifestyle, sports, and music. I am also drawn to memoirs that speak to a larger social or historical circumstance, or introduce me to a new phenomenon. And I am always looking for a work of fiction that will keep me up at night!"

HOW TO CONTACT Accepts e-mail queries only. "For nonfiction queries, initial contact should just be a pitch letter. For fiction queries, I prefer a summary, your bio, and the first chapter as text in the email (not as an attachment). If I express interest I will need to see a full proposal for nonfiction and the remainder of the ms for fiction." Accepts simultaneous submissions. Responds in 2 weeks to queries, only if interested. Obtains most new clients through recommendations from others, solicitations.

TERMS Agent receives 15% commission on domestic sales. Offers written contract; 30-day notice must be given to terminate contract.

WRITERS CONFERENCES Washington Independent Review of Books Writers Conference; Yale Writers' Conference; American Society of Journalists and Authors Conference; Writer's Digest Conference; La-Jolla Writer's Conference; Gulf Coast Writers Conference; Kansas Writers Association Conference; New York Writers Workshop; Self Publishing Book Expo; Burlington Writers' Conference; Southern Expressions Writers' Conference; Literary Writers' Conference, NYC.

MAGAZINES

//

This section contains magazine listings that fall into one of several categories: literary, consumer, small circulation, and online. Our decision to combine magazines under one section was twofold: All of these magazines represent markets specifically for short fiction, and many magazines now publish both print and online versions, making them more difficult to subcategorize. Below, we outline specifics for literary, online, consumer, and small circulation magazines.

LITERARY MAGAZINES

Although definitions of what constitutes literary writing vary, editors of literary journals agree they want to publish the best fiction they can acquire. Qualities they look for in fiction include fully developed characters, strong and unique narrative voice, flawless mechanics, and careful attention to detail in content and manuscript preparation. Most of the authors writing such fiction are well read and well educated, and many are students or graduates of university creative writing programs.

Stepping Stones to Recognition

Some well-established literary journals pay several hundred or even several thousand dollars for a short story. Most, though, can only pay with contributor's copies or a subscription to their publication. However, being published in literary journals offers the important benefits of experience, exposure, and prestige. Agents and major book publishers regularly read literary magazines in search of new writers. Work from these journals is also selected for inclusion in annual prize anthologies.

You'll find most of the well-known prestigious literary journals listed here. Many, including *The Southern Review* and *Ploughshares*, are associated with universities, while others like *The Paris Review* are independently published.

Selecting the Right Literary Magazine

Once you have browsed through this section and have a list of journals you might like to submit to, read those listings again carefully. Remember, this is information editors provide to help you submit work that fits their needs. Note that you will find some magazines that do not read submissions all year long. Whether limited reading periods are tied to a university schedule or meant to accommodate the capabilities of a very small staff, those periods are noted within listings (when the editors notify us). The staffs of university journals are usually made up of student editors and a managing editor who is also a faculty member. These staffs often change every year. Whenever possible, we indicate this in listings and give the name of the current editor and the length of that editor's term. Also be aware that the schedule of a university journal usually coincides with that university's academic year, meaning that the editors of most university publications are difficult or impossible to reach during the summer.

Furthering Your Search

It cannot be stressed enough that reading the listings for literary journals is only the first part of developing your marketing plan. The second part, equally important, is to obtain fiction guidelines and to read with great care the actual journal you'd like to submit to. Reading copies of these journals helps you determine the fine points of each magazine's publishing style and sensibility. There is no substitute for this type of hands-on research.

Unlike commercial periodicals available at most newsstands and bookstores, it requires a little more effort to obtain some of the literary magazines listed. The super-chain bookstores are doing a better job these days of stocking literaries, and you can find some in independent and college bookstores, especially those published in your area. The Internet is an invaluable resource for submission guidelines, as more and more journals establish an online presence. You may, however, need to send for a sample copy. We include sample copy prices in the listings whenever possible. In addition to reading your sample copies, pay close attention to the **Tips** section of each listing. There you'll often find a very specific description of the style of fiction the editors at that publication prefer.

Another way to find out more about literary magazines is to check out the various prize anthologies and take note of journals whose fiction is being selected for publication in them. Studying prize anthologies not only lets you know which magazines are publishing award-winning work, but it also provides a valuable overview of what is considered to be the best fiction published today. Those anthologies include:

- *Best American Short Stories*, published by Houghton Mifflin Harcourt
- *New Stories from the South: The Year's Best*, published by Algonquin Books of Chapel Hill
- *The O. Henry Prize Stories*, published by Doubleday/Anchor
- *Pushcart Prize: Best of the Small Presses,* published by Pushcart Press

CONSUMER MAGAZINES

Consumer magazines are publications that reach a broad readership. Many have circulations in the hundreds of thousands or millions. And among the oldest magazines listed in this section are ones not only familiar to us, but also to our parents, grandparents, and even great-grandparents: *The Atlantic Monthly* (1857), *Esquire* (1933), and *Ellery Queen's Mystery Magazine* (1941).

Consumer periodicals make excellent markets for fiction in terms of exposure, prestige, and payment. Because these magazines are well known, however, competition is great. Even the largest consumer publications buy only one or two stories an issue, yet thousands of writers submit to these popular magazines.

Despite the odds, it is possible for talented new writers to break into consumer magazines. Your keys to breaking into these markets include careful research, professional presentation, and, of course, top-quality fiction.

SMALL-CIRCULATION MAGAZINES

Small-circulation magazines include general interest, special interest, regional, and genre magazines with circulations under ten thousand. Although these magazines vary greatly in size, theme, format, and management, the editors are all looking for short stories. Their specific fiction needs present writers of all degrees of expertise and interests with an abundance of publishing opportunities. Among the diverse publications in this section are magazines devoted to almost every topic, every level of writing, and every type of writer. Some of these markets publish fiction about a particular geographic area or by authors who live in that locale.

Although not as high-paying as the large-circulation consumer magazines, you'll find some of the publications listed here do pay writers 10–50¢/word or more. Also, unlike the big consumer magazines, these markets are very open to new writers and relatively easy to break into. Their only criterion is that your story be well written, well presented, and suitable for their particular readership.

ONLINE MARKETS

As production and distribution costs go up and the number of subscribers falls, more and more magazines are giving up print publication and moving online. Relatively inexpensive to maintain and quicker to accept and post submissions, online fiction sites are growing fast in numbers and legitimacy. The benefit for writers is that your stories can get more attention in online journals than in small literary journals. Small journals have small print runs—five hundred to one thousand copies—so there's a limit on how many people will read your work. There is no limit when your work appears online.

There is also no limit to the types of online journals being published, offering outlets for a rich and diverse community of voices. These include genre sites, particularly those for science fiction, fantasy, and horror, and mainstream short fiction markets. Online literary journals range from the traditional to those with a decidedly quirkier bent. Writers will also find online outlets for more highly experimental and multimedia work.

While the medium of online publication is different, the traditional rules of publishing apply to submissions. Writers should research the site and archives carefully, looking for a match in sensibility for their work. Follow submission guidelines exactly and submit courteously. True, these sites aren't bound by traditional print schedules, so your work theoretically may be published more quickly. But that doesn't mean online journals have larger staffs, so exercise patience with editors considering your manuscript.

A final note about online publication: Like literary journals, the majority of these markets are either nonpaying or very low paying. In addition, writers will not receive print copies of the publications because of the medium. So in most cases, do not expect to be paid for your exposure.

SELECTING THE RIGHT MARKET

First, zero in on those markets most likely to be interested in your work. Begin by looking at the Category Index. If your work is more general—or conversely, very specialized—you may wish to browse through the listings, perhaps looking up those magazines published in your state or region.

In addition to browsing through the listings and using the Category Index, check the openness icons at the beginning of listings to find those most likely to be receptive to your work. This is especially true for beginning writers, who should look for magazines that say they are especially open to new writers O and for those giving equal weight to both new and established writers ◑. For more explanation about these icons, see the inside back cover of this book.

Once you have a list of magazines you might like to try, read their listings carefully. Much of the material within each listing carries clues that tell you more about the magazine. "How to Use *NSSWM*" describes in detail the listing information common to all the markets in this book.

The physical description appearing near the beginning of the listings can give you clues about the size and financial commitment to the publication. This is not always an indication of quality, but chances are a publication with expensive paper and four-color artwork on the cover has more prestige than a photocopied publication featuring a clip-art cover.

FURTHERING YOUR SEARCH

Most of the magazines listed here are published in the U.S. You will also find some English-speaking markets from around the world. These foreign publications are denoted with a ◐ symbol at the beginning of listings. To make it easier to find Canadian markets, we include a ◑ symbol at the start of those listings.

30 N

North Central College, Naperville IL 60540. **E-mail:** 30north@noctrl.edu. **Website:** 30northblog.wordpress.com. **Contact:** Katie Draves, Crystal Ice. *30 N*, published semiannually, considers work in all literary genres, including occasional interviews, from undergraduate writers globally. The journal's goal is for college-level, emerging creative writers to share their work publicly and create a conversation with each other.

- Contributors must be currently enrolled as undergraduates at a two- or four-year institution at the time of submission. Reads submissions September-March, with deadlines in February and October.

NEEDS Length: up to 5,000 words.

HOW TO CONTACT Submit complete ms via online submissions manager. "You must be a currently enrolled undergraduate at a two- or four-year institution at the time of submission. Please submit using your .edu e-mail address, your institution, and your year." Include brief bio written in third person.

PAYMENT/TERMS Pays 2 contributor's copies.

TIPS "Don't send anything you just finished moments ago—rethink, revise, and polish. Avoid sentimentality and abstraction. That said, *30 N* publishes beginners, so don't hesitate to submit and, if rejected, submit again."

34THPARALLEL MAGAZINE

Reality & Fiction, Paris, France. **E-mail:** 34thparallel@gmail.com. **Website:** www.34thparallel.net. **Contact:** Martin Chipperfield. Estab. 2007. *34thParallel Magazine*, published quarterly in digital and print editions, promotes and publishes the exceptional writing of new and emerging writers.

- "Each writer is paid a proportion of the magazine sales."

NEEDS Submit via online submissions manager (Submittable). Length: 1,500-3,500 words.

PAYMENT/TERMS Pays cash on magazine sales.

TIPS "It's all about getting your story out there: your reality (creative nonfiction), fiction, journalism, essays, screenplays, poetry (writing that isn't prose), hip-hop, art, photography, photo stories or essays, graphic stories, comics, or cartoons."

580 SPLIT, A JOURNAL OF ARTS AND LETTERS

Mills College, Graduate English Department, 5000 MacArthur Blvd., Oakland CA 94613-0982. **E-mail:** five80split@gmail.com. **Website:** www.mills.edu/academics/graduate/eng/about/580_split.php. Estab. 1998. "*580 Split* is an annual journal of arts and literature published by graduate students of the English Department at Mills College. This national literary journal includes innovative and risk-taking fiction, creative nonfiction, poetry, and art and is one of the few literary journals carried by the Oakland Public Library. *580 Split* is also distributed in well-known Bay Area bookstores."

NEEDS Length: up to 5,000 words.

HOW TO CONTACT Submit complete ms via online submissions manager. No e-mailed or mailed submissions are accepted. Please submit as PDF files.

PAYMENT/TERMS Pays 1 contributor's copy.

TIPS "Get a hold of a past issue, read through it, find out what we are about. Check the website for most recent information."

ABLE MUSE

467 Saratoga Ave., #602, San Jose CA 95129-1326. **E-mail:** submission@ablemuse.com. **Website:** www.ablemuse.com. **Contact:** Alex Pepple, editor. Estab. 1999. *Able Muse: A Review of Poetry, Prose & Art*, published twice/year, predominantly publishes metrical poetry complemented by art and photography, fiction, and nonfiction, including essays, book reviews, and interviews with a focus on metrical and formal poetry.

- Sponsors 2 annual contests: The Able Muse Write Prize for Poetry & Fiction and The Able Muse Book Award for Poetry (in collaboration with Able Muse Press at www.ablemusepress.com). See website for details.

NEEDS "Our emphasis is on literary fiction; *Able Muse* is not a venue for fantasy, romance, horror, action-adventure, gratuitous violence, or inspirational/sentimental genres." Length: up to 4,000 words/ms.

HOW TO CONTACT Send up to 2 ms via online submission form or e-mail. "We will consider longer pieces of exceptional merit."

THE ADIRONDACK REVIEW

Stanhope St., Brooklyn NY 11237, United States. **E-mail:** editors@theadirondackreview.com. **Website:** www.theadirondackreview.com; www.theadirondackreview.submittable.com. **Contact:** Angela Leroux-Lindsey, editor in chief; Nicholas Samaras, poetry editor; Giovanni Appruzzese, translations editor; Sarah Escue, associate editor. Estab. 2000. *The Adirondack Review* is an online quarterly literary magazine featuring poetry, fiction, art, photography, and translations.

NEEDS Length: up to 6,000 words.

HOW TO CONTACT Submit via online submissions manager.

TIPS "*The Adirondack Review* accepts submissions all year long, so send us your poetry, fiction, nonfiction, translation, reviews, interviews, and art and photography."

AFRICAN VOICES

African Voices Communications, Inc., 270 W. 96th St., New York NY 10025. (212)865-2982. **E-mail:** africanvoicesart@gmail.com. **Website:** www.africanvoices.com. **Contact:** Mariahadessa Ekere Tallie, poetry editor. Estab. 1992. *African Voices*, published quarterly, is an "art and literary magazine that highlights the work of people of color. We publish ethnic literature and poetry on any subject. We also consider all themes and styles: avant-garde, free verse, haiku, light verse, and traditional. We do not wish to limit the reader or author."

○ *African Voices* is about 48 pages, magazine-sized, professionally printed, saddle-stapled, with paper cover. Receives about 100 submissions/year, accepts about 30%. Press run is 20,000.

NEEDS Length: 500-2,500 words.

HOW TO CONTACT Send complete ms. Include short bio. Accepts submissions by postal mail. Send SASE for return of ms.

PAYMENT/TERMS Pays contributor's copies.

TIPS "A ms stands out if it is neatly typed with a well-written and interesting storyline or plot. Originality is encouraged. We are interested in more horror, erotic, and drama pieces. *AV* wants to highlight the diversity in our culture. Stories must touch the humanity in us all. We strongly encourage new writers/poets to send in their work. Accepted contributors are encouraged to subscribe."

ⓢ AGNI

Boston University, 236 Bay State Rd., Boston MA 02215. **E-mail:** agni@bu.edu. **Website:** www.agnimagazine.org. **Contact:** Sven Birkerts, editor. Estab. 1972. Eclectic literary magazine publishing first-rate poems, essays, translations, and stories.

○ Reading period is September 1-May 31 only. Online magazine carries original content not found in print edition. All submissions are considered for both. Founding editor Askold Melnyczuk won the 2001 Nora Magid Award for Magazine Editing. Work from *AGNI* has been included and cited regularly in the *Pushcart Prize*, *O. Henry*, and *Best American* anthologies.

NEEDS No genre scifi, horror, mystery, or romance.

HOW TO CONTACT Submit online or by regular mail, no more than 1 story at a time. E-mailed submissions will not be considered. Include a SASE or your e-mail address if sending by mail.

PAYMENT/TERMS Pays $20/page up to $300, plus a one-year subscription, and, for print publication, 2 contributor's copies and 4 gift copies.

TIPS "We're also looking for extraordinary translations from little-translated languages. It is important to read work published in *AGNI* before submitting, to see if your own might be compatible."

ⓢ ALASKA QUARTERLY REVIEW

University of Alaska Anchorage, 3211 Providence Dr., Anchorage AK 99508. **E-mail:** uaa_aqr@uaa.alaska.edu. **Website:** www.uaa.alaska.edu/aqr. **Contact:** Ronald Spatz, editor in chief. Estab. 1982. "*Alaska Quarterly Review* is a literary journal devoted to contemporary literary art, publishing fiction, short plays, poetry, photo essays, and literary nonfiction in traditional and experimental styles. The editors encourage new and emerging writers, while continuing to publish award-winning and established writers."

○ Magazine: 6x9; 232-300 pages; 60 lb. Glatfelter paper; 12 pt. C15 black ink or 4-color; varnish cover stock; photos on cover and photo essays. Reads mss August 15-May 15.

NEEDS "Works in *AQR* have certain characteristics: freshness, honesty, and a compelling subject. The voice of the piece must be strong—idiosyncratic enough to create a unique persona. We look for craft, putting it in a form where it becomes emotionally and intellectually complex. Many pieces in *AQR* concern everyday life. We're not asking our writers to go outside themselves and their experiences to the absolute exotic to catch our interest. We look for the experiential and revelatory qualities of the work. We will champion a piece that may be less polished or stylistically sophisticated if it engages me, surprises me, and resonates for me. The joy in reading such a work is in discovering something true. Moreover, in keeping with our mission to publish new writers, we are looking for voices our readers do not know, voices that may not always be reflected in the dominant culture and that, in all instances, have something important to convey." No romance, children's, or inspirational/religious. Length: up to 50 pages.

HOW TO CONTACT Submit complete ms by mail. Include cover letter with contact information and SASE for return of ms.

PAYMENT/TERMS Pays contributor's copies and honoraria when funding is available.

TIPS "Although we respond to e-mail queries, we cannot review electronic submissions."

⚭⊜ ALBEDO ONE

8 Bachelor's Walk, Dublin 1 , Ireland. **E-mail:** bobn@ yellowbrickroad.ie. **Website:** www.albedo1.com. **Contact:** Bob Nielson. Estab. 1993. "We are always looking for thoughtful, well-written fiction. Our definition of what constitutes science fiction, horror, and fantasy is extremely broad, and we love to see material which pushes at the boundaries or crosses between genres."

NEEDS Length: 2,000-8,000 words.

HOW TO CONTACT Submit complete ms by mail or e-mail.

PAYMENT/TERMS Pays €6/1,000 words, to a maximum of 8,000 words, and 1 contributor's copy.

TIPS "We look for good writing, good plot, good characters. Read the magazine, and don't give up."

THE ALEMBIC

Providence College, English Department, ATTN: The Alembic Editors, 1 Cunningham Square, Providence RI 02918-0001. **Website:** www.providence.edu/english/pages/alembic.aspx. **Contact:** Magazine has revolving editor. Editorial term: 1 year. Estab. 1940. "*The Alembic* is an international literary journal featuring the work of both established and student writers and photographers. It is published each April by Providence College in Providence, Rhode Island."

- ◯   Magazine: 6x9, 80 pages. Contains illustrations, photographs.

NEEDS "We are open to all styles of fiction." Does not read December 1-July 31. Published Bruce Smith, Robin Behn, Rane Arroyo, Sharon Dolin, Jeff Friedman, and Khalid Mattawa. Length: up to 6,000 words.

HOW TO CONTACT Send complete ms with cover letter. Include brief bio. Send SASE (or IRC) for return of ms. Does not accept online submissions.

PAYMENT/TERMS Pays 2 contributor's copies.

TIPS "We're looking for stories that are wise, memorable, grammatical, economical, poetic in the right places, and end strongly. Take Heraclitus' claim that 'character is fate' to heart and study the strategies, styles, and craft of such masters as Anton Chekov, J. Cheever, Flannery O'Connor, John Updike, Rick Bass,

Phillip Roth, Joyce Carol Oates, William Treavor, Lorrie Moore, and Ethan Canin."

ALITERATE

Genre, Ltd., P.O. Box 380020, Cambridge MA 02238. **E-mail:** editor@aliterate.org. **E-mail:** submissions@ aliterate.org. **Website:** www.aliterate.org. Estab. 2016. *Aliterate* is a production of Genre, Ltd., a small nonprofit publisher based in Cambridge, Massachusetts. "Much has been said about the gulf between literary and genre literature. *Aliterate* seeks to publish works that span this divide, blending tight prose with the fantastical. *Aliterate* reads during March and April."

NEEDS *Aliterate* is a publisher of literary genre fiction and publishes only science fiction, fantasy, Westerns, pulps, thrillers, horror, romance, etc. "We consider 'comedy' to be a fairly large genre; if you submit a comedy, please ensure it is also falls within another genre." Submissions should be of a 'literary' character, with an emphasis on character and language over clever plotting. Does not want poetry, inspirational, erotica, gore, polemics, fan fiction, or young adult. Length: 3,000-12,000 words.

HOW TO CONTACT Review is conducted by blind jury. Remove all identifying information from your submission. No need to include a cover letter; we'll solicit biographic information on acceptance. The subject line of your e-mail will be used to track your story in our review system. Submit only 1 ms in each reading period. Submission is open to all writers, apart from residents of Crimea, Cuba, Iran, North Korea, Sudan, and Syria.

PAYMENT/TERMS Pays 6¢/word.

TIPS "We've been asked for examples of authors who would fit the tone of *Aliterate*; they include Samuel Delany, Margaret Atwood, and Walter J. Miller Jr. While we love writers like Asimov, *Aliterate* doesn't aim to be a venue primarily for hard science fiction."

THE ALLEGHENY REVIEW

Allegheny College Box 32, 520 N. Main St., Meadville PA 16335. **E-mail:** review@allegheny.edu. **Website:** alleghenyreview.wordpress.com. **Contact:** Senior editor. Estab. 1983. "*The Allegheny Review* is one of America's only nationwide literary magazines exclusively for undergraduate works of poetry, fiction, and nonfiction. Our intended audience is persons interested in quality literature."

- ◯   Annual. Magazine: 6x9; 100 pages; illustrations; photos. Has published work by Dianne Page, Monica Stahl, and DJ Kinney.

NEEDS Receives 50 unsolicited mss/month. Accepts 3 mss/issue. Publishes ms 2 months after deadline. Publishes roughly 90% new writers/year. Also publishes short shorts (up to 20 pages), nonfiction, and poetry. Does not want "fiction not written by undergraduates—we accept nothing but fiction by currently enrolled undergraduate students. We consider anything catering to an intellectual audience." Length: up to 20 pages, double-spaced.

HOW TO CONTACT Submit complete ms via online submissions manager.

PAYMENT/TERMS Pays 1 contributor's copy; additional copies $3. Sponsors awards/contests; reading fee $5.

TIPS "We look for quality work that has been thoroughly revised. Unique voice, interesting topic, and playfulness with the English language. Revise, revise, revise! And be careful how you send it—the cover letter says a lot. We definitely look for diversity in the pieces we publish."

⑤ ALLEGORY

P.O. Box 2714, Cherry Hill NJ 08034. **E-mail:** submissions@allegoryezine.com. **Website:** www.allegoryezine.com. **Contact:** Ty Drago, publisher and managing editor. Estab. 1998. "We are an e-zine by writers for writers. Our articles focus on the art, craft, and business of writing. Our links and editorial policy all focus on the needs of fiction authors."

⊙   *Allegory* (as Peridot Books) won the Page One Award for Literary Contribution.

NEEDS Receives 150 unsolicited mss/month. Accepts 12 mss/issue; 24 mss/year. Agented fiction 5%. Publishes 10 new writers/year. Also publishes literary essays, literary criticism. Often comments on rejected mss. "No media tie-ins (*Star Trek*, *Star Wars*, etc., or space opera, vampires)." Length: 1,500-7,500 words; average length: 2,500 words.

HOW TO CONTACT "All submissions should be sent by e-mail (no letters or telephone calls) in either text or RTF format. Please place 'Submission [Title]-[first and last name]' in the subject line. Include the following in both the body of the e-mail and the attachment: your name, name to use on the story (byline) if different, your preferred e-mail address, your mailing address, the story's title, and the story's word count."

PAYMENT/TERMS Pays $15/story.

TIPS "Give us something original, preferably with a twist. Avoid gratuitous sex or violence. Funny always scores points. Be clever and imaginative, but be able to tell a story with proper mood and characterization. Put your name and e-mail address in the body of the story. Read the site and get a feel for it before submitting."

ALLIGATOR JUNIPER

Prescott College, 220 Grove Ave., Prescott AZ 86301. (928)350-2012. **Website:** alligatorjuniper.org. "*Alligator Juniper* features contemporary poetry, fiction, creative nonfiction, and b&w photography. We encourage submissions from writers and photographers at all levels: emerging, early career, and established." Annual magazine comprised of the winners and finalists of national contests. "All entrants pay an $18 submission fee and receive a complementary copy of that year's issue in the spring. First-place winning writers in each genre receive a $1,000 prize. The first-place winner in photography receives a $500 award. Finalists in writing and images are published and paid in contributor copies. There is currently no avenue for submissions other than the annual contest."

NEEDS "No children's literature or genre work." Length: up to 30 pages, double-spaced.

HOW TO CONTACT Accepts submissions only through annual contest. Submit via online submission form or regular mail. If submitting by regular mail, include $18 entry fee payable to *Alligator Juniper* for each story. Include cover letter with name, address, phone number, and e-mail. Mss should be typed with numbered pages, double-spaced, 12-point font, and 1" margins. Include author's name on first page. "Double-sided submissions are encouraged." No e-mail submissions.

⑨⑤ AMBIT MAGAZINE

Staithe House, Main Rd., Brancaster Staithe, Norfolk PE31 8PB, United Kingdom. **E-mail:** contact@ambitmagazine.co.uk. **Website:** www.ambitmagazine.co.uk; www.ambitmagazine.co.uk/submit. **Contact:** Briony Bax, editor; Ralf Webb, poetry editor; Kate Pemberton, fiction editor: Olivia Bax and Jean Philippe Dordolo, art editors. Estab. 1959. *Ambit Magazine* is a literary and artwork quarterly published in the U.K. and read internationally. *Ambit* is put together entirely from unsolicited, previously unpublished poetry and short fiction submissions.

⊙   "Please read the guidelines on our website carefully concerning submission windows and policies."

NEEDS Length: up to 5,000 words. "We're very enthusiastic about flash and very short fiction, which is under 1,000 words. Stories should not be published elsewhere, including blogs and online."

HOW TO CONTACT Submit complete ms via Submittable. No e-mail submissions.

PAYMENT/TERMS Payment details on website.

TIPS "Read a copy of the magazine before submitting!"

AMERICAN LITERARY REVIEW

University of North Texas, 1155 Union Circle #311307, Denton TX 76203. **E-mail:** americanliteraryreview@gmail.com. **Website:** www.americanliteraryreview.com. **Contact:** Bonnie Friedman, editor in chief. Estab. 1990. "*The American Literary Review* publishes "excellent poetry, fiction, and nonfiction by writers at all stages of their careers." Beginning in fall 2013, *ALR* became an online publication."

Reading period is from October 1-May 1.

NEEDS "We would like to see more short shorts and stylistically innovative and risk-taking fiction. We like to see stories that illuminate the various layers of characters and their situations with great artistry. Give us distinctive character-driven stories that explore the complexities of human existence." Looks for "the small moments that contain more than at first possible, that surprise us with more truth than we thought we had a right to expect." Has published work by Marylee MacDonald, Michael Isaac Shokrian, Arthur Brown, Roy Bentley, Julie Marie Wade, and Karin Forfota Poklen. No genre works. Length: up to 8,000 words.

HOW TO CONTACT Submit 1 complete ms through online submissions manager for a fee of $3. Does not accept submissions via e-mail or mail.

TIPS "We encourage writers and artists to examine our journal."

THE AMERICAN READER

E-mail: fiction@theamericanreader.com; poetry@theamericanreader.com; criticism@theamericanreader.com. **Website:** theamericanreader.com. **Contact:** Uzoamaka Maduka, editor in chief. *The American Reader* is a bimonthly print literary journal. The magazine is committed to inspiring literary and critical conversation among a new generation of readers, and restoring literature to its proper place in American cultural discourse.

NEEDS Does not accept unsolicited novel excerpts.

HOW TO CONTACT Submit by e-mail: fiction@theamericanreader.com.

⑤ AMERICAN SHORT FICTION

Badgerdog Literary Publishing, P.O. Box 301209, Austin TX 78703. **E-mail:** editors@americanshortfiction.org. **Website:** www.americanshortfiction.org. **Contact:** Rebecca Markovits and Adeena Reitberger, editors. Estab. 1991. "Issued triannually, *American Short Fiction* publishes work by emerging and established voices: stories that dive into the wreck, that stretch the reader between recognition and surprise, that conjure a particular world with delicate expertise—stories that take a different way home."

Stories published by *American Short Fiction* are anthologized in *Best American Short Stories*, *Best American Nonrequired Reading*, *The O. Henry Prize Stories*, *The Pushcart Prize: Best of the Small Presses*, and elsewhere.

NEEDS "Open to publishing mystery or speculative fiction if we feel it has literary value." Does not want young adult or genre fiction. Length: open.

HOW TO CONTACT *American Short Fiction* seeks "short fiction by some of the finest writers working in contemporary literature, whether they are established, new, or lesser-known authors." Also publishes stories under 2,000 words online. Submit 1 story at a time via online submissions manager ($3 fee). No paper submissions.

PAYMENT/TERMS Writers receive $250-500, 2 contributor's copies, free subscription to the magazine. Additional copies $5.

TIPS "We publish fiction that speaks to us emotionally, uses evocative and precise language, and takes risks in subject matter and/or form. Try to read a few issues of *American Short Fiction* to get a sense of what we like. Also, to be concise is a great virtue."

⊕⑤ ANALOG SCIENCE FICTION & FACT

Dell Magazines, 44 Wall St., Suite 904, New York NY 10005-2401. **E-mail:** analogsf@dellmagazines.com. **Website:** www.analogsf.com. **Contact:** Trevor Quachri, editor. Estab. 1930. *Analog* seeks "solidly entertaining stories exploring solidly thought-out speculative ideas. But the ideas, and consequently the stories, are always new. Real science and technology have always been important in *ASF,* not only as the foundation of its fiction but as the subject of articles about real research with big implications for the future."

○ Fiction published in *Analog* has won numerous Nebula and Hugo Awards.

NEEDS "Basically, we publish science fiction stories. That is, stories in which some aspect of future science or technology is so integral to the plot that, if that aspect were removed, the story would collapse. The science can be physical, sociological, psychological. The technology can be anything from electronic engineering to biogenetic engineering. But the stories must be strong and realistic, with believable people (who needn't be human) doing believable things—no matter how fantastic the background might be." No fantasy or stories in which the scientific background is implausible or plays no essential role. Length: 2,000-7,000 words for short stories, 10,000-20,000 words for novelettes and novellas, and 40,000-80,000 for serials.

HOW TO CONTACT Send complete ms via online submissions manager (preferred) or postal mail. Does not accept e-mail submissions.

PAYMENT/TERMS Analog pays 8-10¢/word for short stories up to 7,500 words, 8-8.5¢ for longer material, 6¢/word for serials.

TIPS "I'm looking for irresistibly entertaining stories that make me think about things in ways I've never done before. Read several issues to get a broad feel for our tastes, but don't try to imitate what you read."

ANOTHER CHICAGO MAGAZINE

P.O. Box 408439, Chicago IL 60640. **E-mail:** editors@anotherchicagomagazine.net. **Website:** www.anotherchicagomagazine.net. **Contact:** Caroline Eick Kasner, managing editor; Matt Rowan, fiction editor; David Welch, poetry editor; Colleen O'Connor, nonfiction editor. Estab. 1977. "*Another Chicago Magazine* is a biannual literary magazine that publishes work by both new and established writers. We look for work that goes beyond the artistic and academic to include and address the larger world. The editors read submissions in fiction, poetry, and creative nonfiction year round. The best way to know what we publish is to read what we publish. If you haven't read *ACM* before, order a sample copy to know if your work is appropriate." Sends prepublication galleys.

○ Work published in *ACM* has been included frequently in *The Best American Poetry* and *The Pushcart Prize* anthologies. **Charges $3 submissions fee.**

NEEDS Length: up to 7,500 words.

HOW TO CONTACT Submit complete ms via online submissions manager.

TIPS "Support literary publishing by subscribing to at least 1 literary journal—if not ours, another. Get used to rejection slips, and don't get discouraged. Keep introductory letters short. Make sure ms has name and address on every page, and that it is clean, neat, and proofread. We are looking for stories with freshness and originality in subject angle and style, and work that encounters the world."

◐⑤ THE ANTIGONISH REVIEW

St. Francis Xavier University, P.O. Box 5000, 42 West St., Suite 217, Antigonish NS B2G 2W5, Canada. (902)867-3962. **Fax:** (902)867-5563. **E-mail:** tar@stfx.ca. **Website:** www.antigonishreview.com. **Contact:** Bonnie McIsaac, assistant editor. Estab. 1970. *The Antigonish Review*, published quarterly, tries "to produce the kind of literary and visual mosaic that the modern sensibility requires or would respond to."

NEEDS Send complete ms. Accepts submissions by fax. Accepts electronic (disk compatible with Word-Perfect/IBM and Windows) submissions. Prefers hard-copy submissions. No erotica. Length: 500-5,000 words.

HOW TO CONTACT Send complete ms.

PAYMENT/TERMS Pays $50 and 2 contributor's copies for stories.

TIPS "Send for guidelines and/or sample copy. Send ms with cover letter and SASE with submission."

⑤ ANTIOCH REVIEW

P.O. Box 148, Yellow Springs OH 45387-0148. (937)769-1365. **E-mail:** cdunlevy@antiochreview.org. **Website:** www.antiochreview.org. **Contact:** Robert S. Fogarty, editor; Judith Hall, poetry editor. Estab. 1941. Literary and cultural review of contemporary issues and literature for general readership. *The Antioch Review* "is an independent quarterly of critical and creative thought. For well over 70 years, creative authors, poets, and thinkers have found a friendly reception—regardless of formal reputation. We get far more poetry than we can possibly accept, and the competition is keen. Here, where form and content are so inseparable and reaction is so personal, it is difficult to state requirements or limitations. Studying recent issues of *The Antioch Review* should be helpful."

NEEDS Quality fiction only, distinctive in style with fresh insights into the human condition. No science fiction, fantasy, or confessions. Length: generally under 8,000 words.

HOW TO CONTACT Send complete ms with SASE, preferably mailed flat. Fiction submissions are not accepted between June 1-August 31.

PAYMENT/TERMS Pays $20/printed page, plus 2 contributor's copies.

APALACHEE REVIEW

Apalachee Press, P.O. Box 10469, Tallahassee FL 32302. (850)644-9114. **E-mail:** mtrammell@fsu.edu. **E-mail:** arsubmissions@gmail.com (for queries outside the U.S.). **Website:** apalacheereview.org. **Contact:** Michael Trammell, Alicia Casey, and Jenn Bronson, chief editors; Kathleen Laufenberg, nonfiction editor; Mary Jane Ryals, fiction editor; Jay Snodgrass and Chris Hayes, poetry editors. Estab. 1976. "At *Apalachee Review*, we are interested in outstanding literary fiction, but we especially like poetry, fiction, and nonfiction that address intercultural issues in a domestic or international setting or context."

○ *Apalachee Review*, published annually, is 90 pages, digest-sized, professionally printed, perfect-bound, with card cover. Press run is 300-400. Includes photographs. Member CLMP.

NEEDS Receives 60-100 mss/month. Accepts 5-10 mss/issue. Agented fiction: 0.5%. Publishes 1-2 new writers/year. "We prefer fiction that is no longer than 15 pages in length." Has published Lu Vickers, Joe Clark, Joe Taylor, Jane Arrowsmith Edwards, Vivian Lawry, Linda Frysh, Charles Harper Webb, Reno Raymond Gwaltney. Also publishes short shorts. Does not want cliché-filled, genre-oriented fiction. Length: 600-3,300 words; average length: 2,200 words. Average length of short shorts: 250 words.

HOW TO CONTACT Send complete ms with cover letter. Include brief bio, list of publications. Send either SASE (international authors should see website for "international" guidelines: no IRCs, please) for return of ms, or disposable copy of ms and #10 SASE for reply only.

PAYMENT/TERMS Pays 2 contributor's copies.

❸ APEX MAGAZINE

Apex Publications, LLC, P.O. Box 24323, Lexington KY 40524. **E-mail:** lesley@apex-magazine.com. **Website:** www.apexbookcompany.com. **Contact:** Lesley Conner, managing editor. Estab. 2004. "An elite repository for new and seasoned authors with an oth-

er-worldly interest in the unquestioned and slightly bizarre parts of the universe."

○ "We want science fiction, fantasy, horror, and mash-ups of all three of the dark, weird stuff down at the bottom of your little literary heart."

NEEDS Length: 100-7,500 words.

HOW TO CONTACT Send complete ms.

PAYMENT/TERMS Pays 6¢/word.

APPALACHIAN HERITAGE

CPO 2166, Berea KY 40404. **E-mail:** appalachianheritage@berea.edu. **Website:** appalachianheritage.net. **Contact:** Jason Howard, editor. Estab. 1973. "We are seeking poetry, short fiction, literary criticism and biography, book reviews, and creative nonfiction, including memoirs, opinion pieces, and historical sketches. Unless you request not to be considered, all poems, stories, and articles published in *Appalachian Heritage* are eligible for our annual Plattner Award. All honorees are rewarded with a sliding bookrack with an attached commemorative plaque from Berea College Crafts, and first-place winners receive an additional stipend of $200."

○ Submission period: August 15-December 15.

NEEDS "We do not want to see fiction that has no ties to Southern Appalachia." No genre fiction. Length: up to 7,500 words.

HOW TO CONTACT Submit through online submissions manager only.

PAYMENT/TERMS Pays 3 contributor's copies.

TIPS "Sure, we are *Appalachian Heritage* and we do appreciate the past, but we are a forward-looking contemporary literary quarterly, and, frankly, we receive too many nostalgic submissions. Please spare us the 'Papaw Was Perfect' poetry and the 'Mamaw Moved Mountains' mss and give us some hard-hitting prose, some innovative poetry, some inventive photography, and some original art. Help us be the ground-breaking, stimulating kind of quarterly we aspire to be."

☯ APPLE VALLEY REVIEW: A JOURNAL OF CONTEMPORARY LITERATURE

88 South Third St., Suite 336, San Jose CA 95113. **E-mail:** editor@leahbrowning.net. **Website:** www.applevalleyreview.com. **Contact:** Leah Browning, editor. Estab. 2005. *Apple Valley Review: A Journal of Contemporary Literature*, published semiannually online, features "beautifully crafted poetry, short fiction, and essays."

NEEDS Receives 100+ mss/month. Accepts 1-4 mss/issue; 2-8 mss/year. Published Glen Pourciau, Robert Radin, Jessica Rafalko, Thomas Andrew Green, Inderjeet Mani, and Lisa Robertson. Also publishes short shorts/flash. Does not want strict genre fiction, erotica, work containing explicit language, or anything "particularly violent or disturbing." Length: 100-4,000+ words. Average length: 2,000 words. Average length of short shorts: 800 words.

HOW TO CONTACT Send complete ms with cover letter.

ARKANSAS REVIEW: A JOURNAL OF DELTA STUDIES

Department of English and Philosophy, P.O. Box 1890, Office: Humanities and Social Sciences, State University AR 72467-1890. (870)972-3043; (870)972-2210. **Fax:** (870)972-3045. **E-mail:** mtribbet@astate.edu. **E-mail:** jcollins@astate.edu; arkansasreview@astate.edu. **Website:** altweb.astate.edu/arkreview. **Contact:** Dr. Marcus Tribbett, general editor. Estab. 1998. "All material, creative and scholarly, published in the *Arkansas Review* must evoke or respond to the natural and/or cultural experience of the Mississippi River Delta region."

○ *Arkansas Review* is 92 pages, magazine-sized, photo offset-printed, saddle-stapled, with 4-color cover. Press run is 600; 50 distributed free to contributors.

NEEDS Receives 30-50 unsolicited mss/month. Accepts 2-3 mss/issue; 5-7 mss/year. Agented fiction 1%. Publishes 3-4 new writers/year. Has published work by Susan Henderson, George Singleton, Scott Ely, and Pia Erhart. "No genre fiction. Must have a Delta focus." Length: up to 10,000 words.

HOW TO CONTACT Send complete ms.

PAYMENT/TERMS Pays 3 contributor's copies.

TIPS "Immerse yourself in the literature of the Delta, but provide us with a fresh and original take on its land, its people, its culture. Surprise us. Amuse us. Recognize what makes this region particular as well as universal, and take risks. Help us shape a new Delta literature."

○ ARTS & LETTERS JOURNAL OF CONTEMPORARY CULTURE

Georgia College & State University, Milledgeville GA 31061. (478)445-1289. **Website:** al.gcsu.edu. **Contact:** Laura Newbern, editor; Abbie Lahmers, managing editor. Estab. 1999. *Arts & Letters Journal of Contemporary Culture*, published semiannually, is devoted to contemporary arts and literature, featuring ongoing series such as The World Poetry Translation Series

and The Mentors Interview Series. Wants work of the highest literary and artistic quality.

○ Work published in *Arts & Letters Journal* has received the Pushcart Prize.

NEEDS No genre fiction. Length: up to 25 pages typed and double-spaced.

HOW TO CONTACT Submit complete ms via online submissions manager.

PAYMENT/TERMS Pays $10/printed page (minimum payment: $50) and 1 contributor's copy.

○○○ ASIMOV'S SCIENCE FICTION

Dell Magazines, 44 Wall St., Suite 904, New York NY 10005. **E-mail:** asimovs@dellmagazines.com. **Website:** www.asimovs.com. **Contact:** Sheila Williams, editor; Victoria Green, senior art director. Estab. 1977. "Magazine consists of science fiction and fantasy stories for adults and young adults. Publishes the best short science fiction available."

○ Named for a science fiction "legend," *Asimov's* regularly receives Hugo and Nebula Awards.

NEEDS Wants "science fiction primarily. Some fantasy and humor. It is best to read a great deal of material in the genre to avoid the use of some very old ideas." Submit ms via online submissions manager or postal mail; no e-mail submissions. No horror or psychic/supernatural, sword and sorcery, explicit sex or violence that isn't integral to the story. Would like to see more hard science fiction. Length: 750-15,000 words.

PAYMENT/TERMS Pays 8-10¢/word for short stories up to 7,500 words; 8-8.5¢/word for longer material. Works between 7,500-10,000 words by authors who make more than 8¢/word for short stories will receive a flat rate that will be no less than the payment would be for a shorter story.

TIPS "In general, we're looking for 'character-oriented' stories, those in which the characters, rather than the science, provide the main focus for the reader's interest. Serious, thoughtful, yet accessible fiction will constitute the majority of our purchases, but there's always room for the humorous as well."

○ THE ATLANTIC MONTHLY

The Watergate, 600 New Hampshire Ave., NW, Washington DC 20037. (202)266-6000. **Fax:** (202)266-6001. **E-mail:** submissions@theatlantic.com; pitches@theatlantic.com. **Website:** www.theatlantic.com. **Contact:** Scott Stossel, magazine editor; Ann Hulbert, literary editor. Estab. 1857. General magazine for an educated readership with broad cultural and publicaffairs interests. "*The Atlantic* considers unsolicited mss, either fiction or nonfiction. A general familiarity with what we have published in the past is the best guide to our needs and preferences."

NEEDS "Seeks fiction that is clear, tightly written with strong sense of 'story' and well-defined characters." No longer publishes fiction in the regular magazine. Instead, it will appear in a special newsstand-only fiction issue. Receives 1,000 unsolicited mss/month. Accepts 7-8 mss/year. **Publishes 3-4 new writers/year.** Preferred length: 2,000-6,000 words.

HOW TO CONTACT Submit via e-mail with Word document attachment to submissions@theatlantic.com. Mss submitted via postal mail must be typewritten and double-spaced.

PAYMENT/TERMS Payment varies.

TIPS "Writers should be aware that this is not a market for beginner's work (nonfiction and fiction), nor is it truly for intermediate work. Study this magazine before sending only your best, most professional work. When making first contact, cover letters are sometimes helpful, particularly if they cite prior publications or involvement in writing programs. Common mistakes: melodrama, inconclusiveness, lack of development, unpersuasive characters and/or dialogue."

THE AVALON LITERARY REVIEW

CCI Publishing, P.O. Box 780696, Orlando FL 32878. (407)574-7355. **E-mail:** submissions@avalonliteraryreview.com. **Website:** www.avalonliteraryreview.com. **Contact:** Valerie Rubino, managing editor. Estab. 2011. "*The Avalon Literary Review* welcomes work from both published and unpublished writers and poets. We accept submissions of poetry, short fiction, and personal essays. While we appreciate the genres of fantasy, historical romance, science fiction, and horror, our magazine is not the forum for such work." Quarterly magazine.

NEEDS No erotica, science fiction, or horror. Length: 250-2,500 words.

HOW TO CONTACT Submit complete ms. Only accepts electronic submissions.

PAYMENT/TERMS Pays 5 contributor's copies.

TIPS "The author's voice and point of view should be unique and clear. We seek pieces that spring from the author's life and experiences. Fiction submissions that explore both the sweet and bitter of life with a touch of humor, and poetry with vivid imagery, are a good fit for our review."

THE BALTIMORE REVIEW

6514 Maplewood Rd., Baltimore MD 21212. **E-mail:** editor@baltimorereview.org. **Website:** www.baltimorereview.org. **Contact:** Barbara Westwood Diehl, senior editor. Estab. 1996. *The Baltimore Review* publishes poetry, fiction, and creative nonfiction from Baltimore and beyond. Submission periods are August 1-November 30 and February 1-May 31.

NEEDS Length: 100-5,000 words.

HOW TO CONTACT Send complete ms using online submission form. Publishes 16-20 mss (combination of poetry, fiction, and creative nonfiction) per online issue. Work published online is also published in annual anthology.

PAYMENT/TERMS Pays $40.

TIPS "See editor preferences on staff page of website."

BARBARIC YAWP

BoneWorld Publishing, 3700 County Rt. 24, Russell NY 13684. **Website:** www.boneworldpublishing.com. Estab. 1997. "We publish what we like. Fiction should include some bounce and surprise. Our publication is intended for the intelligent, open-minded reader."

○ *Barbaric Yawp*, published quarterly, is digest-sized; 44 pages; matte cover stock.

NEEDS "We don't want any pornography, gratuitous violence, or whining."

HOW TO CONTACT Submit complete ms by mail. Send SASE for reply and return of ms, or send a disposable copy of ms. Accepts simultaneous, multiple submissions, and reprints.

PAYMENT/TERMS Pays 1 contributor's copy; additional copies $3.

TIPS "Don't give up. Read much, write much, submit much. Observe closely the world around you. Don't borrow ideas from TV or films. Revision is often necessary—grit your teeth and do it. Never fear rejection."

● ● ● THE BARCELONA REVIEW

Correu Vell 12-2, Barcelona 08002, Spain. (00 34) 93 319 15 96. **E-mail:** editor@barcelonareview.com. **Website:** www.barcelonareview.com. **Contact:** Jill Adams, editor. Estab. 1997. *The Barcelona Review* is "the Web's first multilingual review of international, contemporary, cutting-edge fiction. *TBR* is actually 3 separate reviews—English, Spanish, and Catalan—with occasional translations from 1 language to another. Original texts of other languages are presented along with English and Spanish translations as available."

○ "We cannot offer money to contributors, but in lieu of pay we can sometimes offer an excellent Spanish translation (worth quite a bit of money in itself). Work is showcased along with 2 or more known authors in a high-quality literary review with an international readership."

NEEDS Length: up to 4,500 words.

HOW TO CONTACT Submit 1 story at a time. To submit via e-mail, send an attached document. Do not send in the body of an e-mail. Include "Submission/Author Name" in the subject box. Accepts hard copies, but they will not be returned. Double-space ms.

TIPS "Send top-drawer material that has been drafted 2, 3, 4 times—whatever it takes. Then sit on it for a while and look at it afresh. Keep the text tight. Grab the reader in the first paragraph and don't let go. Keep in mind that a perfectly crafted story that lacks a punch of some sort won't cut it. Make it new, make it different. Surprise the reader in some way. Read the best of the short fiction available in your area of writing to see how yours measures up. Don't send anything off until you feel it's ready, and then familiarize yourself with the content of the review/magazine to which you are submitting."

BARRELHOUSE

E-mail: yobarrelhouse@gmail.com. **Website:** www.barrelhousemag.com. **Contact:** Dave Housley, Joe Killiany, and Matt Perez, fiction editors; Tom McAllister, nonfiction editor; Dan Brady, poetry editor. Estab. 2004. *Barrelhouse* is a biannual print journal featuring fiction, poetry, interviews, and essays about music, art, and the detritus of popular culture.

○ Stories originally published in *Barrelhouse* have been featured in *The Best American Nonrequired Reading, The Best American Science Fiction and Fantasy*, and the Million Writer's Award.

NEEDS Length: open, but prefers pieces under 8,000.

HOW TO CONTACT Submit complete ms via online submissions manager. DOC or RTF files only.

PAYMENT/TERMS Pays $50 and 2 contributor copies.

BATEAU

105 Eden St., Bar Harbor ME 04609. **E-mail:** dan@bateaupress.org. **Website:** bateaupress.org. **Contact:** Daniel Mahoney, editor in chief. Estab. 2007. "*Bateau*, published annually, subscribes to no trend but serves to represent as wide a cross-section of contemporary writing as possible. For this reason, readers will most likely love and hate at least something in each issue. We consider this a good thing. To us, it means *Bateau* is eclectic, open-ended, and not mired in a particular strain."

○ *Bateau* is around 80 pages, digest-sized, offset print, perfect-bound, with a 100% recycled letterpress cover. Press run is 250.

HOW TO CONTACT Submit via online submissions manager. Brief bio is encouraged but not required.

PAYMENT/TERMS Pays contributor's copies.

TIPS "Send us your best work. Send us funny work, quirky work, outstanding work, work that is well punctuated or lacks punctuation. Fearless work. Work that wants to crash on our sofa."

BAYOU

Department of English, University of New Orleans, 2000 Lakeshore Dr., New Orleans LA 70148. **E-mail:** bayou@uno.edu. **Website:** bayoumagazine.org. **Contact:** Joanna Leake, editor in chief. Estab. 2002. "A nonprofit journal for the arts, each issue of *Bayou* contains beautiful fiction, nonfiction, and poetry. From quirky shorts to more traditional stories, we are committed to publishing solid work, regardless of style. At *Bayou* we are always interested first in a well-told tale. Our poetry and prose are filled with memorable characters observing their world, acknowledging both the mundane and the sublime, often at once and always with an eye toward beauty. *Bayou* is packed with a range of material from established, award-winning authors as well as new voices on the rise. Recent contributors include Eric Trethewey, Virgil Suarez, Marilyn Hacker, Sean Beaudoin, Tom Whalen, Mark Doty, Philip Cioffari, Lyn Lifshin, Timothy Liu, and Gaylord Brewer. In 1 issue every year, *Bayou* features the winner of the annual Tennessee Williams/New Orleans Literary Festival One-Act Play Competition."

○ Accepts submissions on Submittable and by mail. Reads submissions September 1-May 1.

NEEDS "Flash fiction and short shorts are welcome. No novel excerpts, please, unless they can stand alone as short stories." No horror, gothic, or juvenile fiction. Length: up to 7,500 words.

HOW TO CONTACT Send complete ms via online submission system or postal mail.

PAYMENT/TERMS Pays 2 contributor's copies.

TIPS "Do not submit in more than 1 genre at a time. Don't send a second submission until you receive a response to the first."

THE BEAR DELUXE MAGAZINE

Orlo, 240 N. Broadway, #112, Portland OR 97227. **E-mail:** beardeluxe@orlo.org. **Website:** www.orlo.org. **Contact:** Tom Webb, editor in chief; Kristin Rogers Brown, art director. Estab. 1993. "*The Bear Deluxe Magazine* is a national independent environmental arts magazine publishing significant works of reporting, creative nonfiction, literature, visual art, and design. Based in the Pacific Northwest, it reaches across cultural and political divides to engage readers on vital issues effecting the environment. Published twice per year, *The Bear Deluxe* includes a wider array and a higher percentage of visual artwork and design than many other publications. Artwork is included both as editorial support and as stand-alone or independent art. It has included nationally recognized artists as well as emerging artists. As with any publication, artists are encouraged to review a sample copy for a clearer understanding of the magazine's approach. Unsolicited submissions and samples are accepted and encouraged."

NEEDS "We are most excited by high-quality writing that furthers the magazine's goal of engaging new and divergent readers. We appreciate strong aspects of storytelling and are open to new formats, though we wouldn't call ourselves publishers of 'experimental fiction.'" No traditional sci-fi, horror, romance, or crime/action. Length: up to 4,000 words.

HOW TO CONTACT Query or send complete ms. Prefers postal mail submissions.

PAYMENT/TERMS Pays free subscription to the magazine, contributor's copies, and $25-400, depending on piece; additional copies for postage.

TIPS "Offer to be a stringer for future ideas. Get a copy of the magazine and guidelines, and query us with specific nonfiction ideas and clips. We're looking for original, magazine-style stories, not fluff or PR. Fiction, essay, and poetry writers should know we have an open and blind review policy and they should keep sending their best work even if rejected once. Be as specific as possible in queries."

BEATDOM

Beatdom Books, 42/R Gowrie St., Dundee Scotland DD2 1AF, United Kingdom. **E-mail:** editor@beatdom.com. **Website:** www.beatdom.com. **Contact:** David Wills, editor. Estab. 2007. Beatdom is a Beat Generation-themed literary journal that publishes essays, short stories, and poems related to the Beats. "We publish studies of Beat texts, figures, and legends; we look at writers and movements related to the Beats; we support writers of the present who take their influence from the Beats."

NEEDS Length: up to 5,000 words.

HOW TO CONTACT Submit complete ms via e-mail.

PAYMENT/TERMS Pays $50.

BELLEVUE LITERARY REVIEW

NYU Langone Medical Center, Department of Medicine, 550 First Ave., OBV-A612, New York NY 10016. (212)263-3973. **E-mail:** info@blreview.org. **Website:** www.blreview.org. **Contact:** Stacy Bodziak, managing editor. Estab. 2001. *Bellevue Literary Review*, published semiannually, prints "works of fiction, nonfiction, and poetry that touch upon relationships to the human body, illness, health, and healing."

Work published in *Bellevue Literary Review* has appeared in *The Pushcart Prize* and *Best American Short Stories*. Recently published work by Francine Prose, Molly Peacock, and Chard deNiord. Closed to submissions in July and August.

NEEDS *BLR* "seeks character-driven fiction with original voices and strong settings. While we are always interested in creative explorations in style, we do lean toward classic short stories." No genre fiction. Length: up to 5,000 words. Average length: 2,500 words.

HOW TO CONTACT Submit via online submissions manager.

PAYMENT/TERMS Pays 2 contributor's copies, one-year subscription, and one-year gift subscription.

BELLINGHAM REVIEW

Mail Stop 9053, Western Washington University, Bellingham WA 98225. (360)650-4863. **E-mail:** bellingham.review@wwu.edu. **Website:** wwww.bhreview.org. **Contact:** Susanne Paola Antonetta, editor in chief; Dayna Patterson, managing editor. Estab. 1977. Nonprofit magazine published once/year in the spring. Seeks "literature of palpable quality: poems, stories, and essays so beguiling they invite us to touch their essence. *Bellingham Review* hungers for a kind of writing that nudges the limits of form or executes traditional forms exquisitely."

The editors are actively seeking submissions of creative nonfiction, as well as stories that push the boundaries of the form. Open submission period is from September 15-December 1.

NEEDS Does not want anything nonliterary. Length: up to 6,000 words.

HOW TO CONTACT Submit complete ms via on-line submissions manager.

PAYMENT/TERMS Pays as funds allow, plus contributor's copies.

TIPS "The *Bellingham Review* holds 3 annual contests: the 49th Parallel Award for poetry, the Annie Dillard Award for Nonfiction, and the Tobias Wolff Award for Fiction. See the individual listings for these contests under Contests & Awards for full details."

BERKELEY FICTION REVIEW

Berkeley Fiction Review, c/o ASUC Student Union FMO 432 Eshleman, MC 4500, University of California, Berkeley, Berkeley CA 94720, United States. **E-mail:** berkeleyfictionreview@gmail.com. **Website:** berkeleyfictionreview.com. Estab. 1981. "The *Berkeley Fiction Review* is a UC Berkeley undergraduate, student-run publication. We look for innovative short fiction that plays with form and content, as well as traditionally constructed stories with fresh voices and original ideas."

○ *BFR* nominates to O.Henry, *Best American Short Stories* and *Pushcart* prizes. Sponsored by the ASUC.

NEEDS Length: no more than 25 pages.

HOW TO CONTACT Submit via e-mail with "Submission: Name, Title" in subject line. Include cover letter in body of e-mail, with story as an attachment.

PAYMENT/TERMS Pays 1 contributor's copy.

TIPS "Our criteria is fiction that resonates. Voices that are strong and move a reader. Clear, powerful prose (either voice or rendering of subject) with a point. Unique ways of telling stories—these capture the editors. Work hard, don't give up. Ask an honest person to point out your writing weaknesses, and then work on them. We look forward to reading fresh new voices."

○Ⓢ BEYOND CENTAURI

White Cat Publications, LLC, 33080 Industrial Rd., Suite 101, Livonia MI 48150. (734)237-8522. **Fax:** (313)557-5162. **E-mail:** beyondcentauri@whitecatpublications.com. **Website:** www.whitecatpublications.com/guidelines/beyond-centauri. Estab. 2003. *Beyond Centauri*, published quarterly, contains fantasy, science fiction, sword and sorcery, very mild horror short stories, poetry, and illustrations for readers ages 10 and up.

○ *Beyond Centauri* is 44 pages, magazine-sized, offset printed, perfect-bound, with paper cover for color art, includes ads. Press run is 100; 5 distributed free to reviewers.

NEEDS Looks for themes of science fiction or fantasy. "Science fiction and especially stories that take place in outer space will find great favor with us." Length: up to 2,500 words.

HOW TO CONTACT Submit in the body of an e-mail, or as an RTF attachment.

PAYMENT/TERMS Pays $6/story, $3/reprints, and $2/flash fiction (under 1,000 words), plus 1 contributor's copy.

BIG BRIDGE

Big Bridge Press, P.O. 2724, Tallahassee FL 32304. **E-mail:** walterblue@bigbridge.org. **Website:** www.bigbridge.org. **Contact:** Michael Rothenberg and Terri Carrion, editors. "*Big Bridge* is one of the oldest and most respected online literary arts magazines. For over 20 years, *Big Bridge* has published the best in poetry, fiction, nonfiction essays, journalism, and art (photos, line drawings, performance, installations, site-works, comics, graphics)."

HOW TO CONTACT Only accepts electronic submissions. Submit via e-mail.

TIPS "*Big Bridge* publishes 1 very big issue each year. Each issue features an online chapbook. We are interested in anthology concepts and thematic installations as well as individual submissions. Send query to propose installations and anthology ideas for consideration. All individual submissions should include a bio and bio photo."

BIG MUDDY: A JOURNAL OF THE MISSISSIPPI RIVER VALLEY

Southeast Missouri State University Press, One University Plaza, MS 2650, Cape Girardeau MO 63701. (573) 651-2044. **E-mail:** upress@semo.edu. **Website:** www.semopress.com/bigmuddy/. **Contact:** Carrie Walker, Office Manager/Assistant Editor. Estab. 2000. "*Big Muddy* explores multidisciplinary, multicultural issues, people, and events mainly concerning, but not limited to, the 10-state area that borders the Mississippi River. We publish fiction, poetry, historical essays, creative nonfiction, environmental essays, biography, regional events, photography, art, etc."

NEEDS No romance, fantasy, or children's.

HOW TO CONTACT Receives 50 unsolicited mss/month. Accepts 20-25 mss/issue. Accepts multiple submissions.

PAYMENT/TERMS Pays 2 contributor's copies; additional copies $5. Annual short story ($1,000) and flash fiction ($500) contests.

TIPS "We look for clear language, avoidance of clichés except in necessary dialogue, a fresh vision of the theme or issue. Find some excellent and honest readers to comment on your work-in-progress and final draft. Consider their viewpoints carefully. Revise if needed."

⊙ BIG PULP

Exter Press, P.O. Box 92, Cumberland MD 21501. **E-mail:** editors@bigpulp.com. **Website:** www.bigpulp. com. **Contact:** Bill Olver, editor. Estab. 2008. *Big Pulp* defines "pulp fiction" very broadly: It's lively, challenging, thought provoking, thrilling, and fun, regardless of how many or how few genre elements are packed in. It doesn't subscribe to the theory that genre fiction is disposable; a great deal of literary fiction could easily fall under one of their general categories. Places a higher value on character and story than genre elements.

○ "Submissions are only accepted during certain reading periods. Our website is updated to reflect when we are and are not reading, and what we are looking for."

NEEDS Does not want generic slice-of-life, memoirs, inspirational, political, pastoral odes. Length: up to 2,500 words.

HOW TO CONTACT Submit complete ms.

PAYMENT/TERMS Pays $5-25.

TIPS "We like to be surprised, and we have few boundaries. Fantasy writers may focus on the mundane aspects of a fantastical creature's life or the magic that can happen in everyday life. Romances do not have to be requited or have happy endings, and the object of one's obsession may not be a person. Mysteries need not focus on 'whodunit?' We're always interested in science or speculative fiction focusing on societal issues, but writers should avoid being partisan or shrill. We also like fiction that crosses genre; for example, a science fiction romance or a fantasy crime story. We have an online archive for fiction and poetry and encourage writers to check it out. That said, *Big Pulp* has a strong editorial bias in favor of stories with monkeys. Especially talking monkeys."

BILINGUAL REVIEW

Arizona State University, Hispanic Research Center, P.O. Box 875303, Tempe AZ 85287-5303. (480)965-3867. **Fax:** (480)965-0315. **E-mail:** brp@asu.edu. **Web-**site: www.asu.edu/brp/submit. **Contact:** Gary Francisco Keller, publisher. Estab. 1974. *Bilingual Review* is "committed to publishing high-quality writing by both established and emerging writers."

○ Magazine: 7x10; 96 pages; 55 lb. acid-free paper; coated cover stock.

NEEDS Receives 50 unsolicited mss/month. Accepts 3 mss/issue; 9 mss/year. "We do not publish literature about tourists in Latin America and their perceptions of the 'native culture.' We do not publish fiction about Latin America unless there is a clear tie to the U.S."

HOW TO CONTACT Submit via mail. Send 2 copies of complete ms with SAE and loose stamps. Does not usually accept e-mail submissions except through special circumstance/prior arrangement.

PAYMENT/TERMS Pays 2 contributor's copies; 30% discount for additional copies.

THE BITTER OLEANDER

4983 Tall Oaks Dr., Fayetteville NY 13066. **E-mail:** info@bitteroleander.com. **Website:** www.bitteroleander.com. **Contact:** Paul B. Roth, editor and publisher. "We're reading to find a language uncommitted to the commonplace and more integrated with the natural world. A language that helps define the same particulars in nature that exist in us and have not been socialized out of us." Biannual magazine covering poetry and short fiction and translations of contemporary poetry and short fiction.

○ *The Bitter Oleander* is 6x9, 128 pages, 55 lb. paper, 12 pt. CIS cover stock, contains photos.

NEEDS Wants short, imaginative fiction. Does not want family stories with moralistic plots or fantasy that involves hyper-reality of any sort. Length: up to 2,500 words.

HOW TO CONTACT Submit through online submissions manager.

PAYMENT/TERMS Pays 1 contributor's copy.

TIPS "If you are writing poems or short fiction in the tradition of 98% of all journals publishing in this country, then your work will usually not fit for us. If within the first 400 words my mind drifts, the rest rarely makes it. Be yourself, and listen to no one but yourself."

BLACKBIRD

Virginia Commonwealth University Department of English, P.O. Box 843082, Richmond VA 23284. (804)827-4729. **E-mail:** blackbird@vcu.edu. **Website:** www.blackbird.vcu.edu. Estab. 2001. *Blackbird* is published twice a year.

Reading period: November 15-April 15.

NEEDS "We primarily look for short stories, but novel excerpts are acceptable if self-contained."

HOW TO CONTACT Submit using online submissions manager or by mail. Online submission is preferred.

TIPS "We like a story that invites us into its world, that engages our senses, soul, and mind. We are able to publish long works in all genres, but query *Blackbird* before you send a prose piece over 8,000 words or a poem exceeding 10 pages."

BLACK WARRIOR REVIEW

P.O. Box 862936, Tuscaloosa AL 35486. (205)348-4518. **E-mail:** interns.bwr@gmail.com. **Website:** www.bwr.ua.edu. **Contact:** Gail Aronson, editor. Estab. 1974. "We publish contemporary fiction, poetry, reviews, essays, and art for a literary audience. We publish the freshest work we can find."

Work that appeared in the *Black Warrior Review* has been included in the *Pushcart Prize* anthology, *Harper's Magazine, Best American Short Stories, Best American Poetry,* and *New Stories from the South.*

NEEDS "We are open to good experimental writing and short-short fiction. No genre fiction please." Publishes novel excerpts if under contract to be published. Length: up to 7,000 words.

HOW TO CONTACT One story/chapter per envelope. Wants work that is conscious of form and well-crafted.

PAYMENT/TERMS Pays one-year subscription and nominal lump-sum fee.

TIPS "We look for attention to language, freshness, honesty, a convincing and sharp voice. Send us a clean, well-printed, proofread ms. Become familiar with the magazine prior to submission."

BLUE COLLAR REVIEW

Partisan Press, P.O. Box 11417, Norfolk VA 23517. **E-mail:** red-ink@earthlink.net. **Website:** www.partisanpress.org. **Contact:** A. Markowitz, editor; Mary Franke, co-editor. Estab. 1997. *Blue Collar Review (Journal of Progressive Working Class Literature)*, published quarterly, contains poetry, short stories, and illustrations "reflecting the working-class experience—a broad range from the personal to the societal. Our purpose is to promote and expand working-class literature and an awareness of the connections between workers of all occupations and the social context in which we live. Also to inspire the creativity and latent talent in 'common' working people."

Blue Collar Review is 60 pages, digest-sized, offset-printed, saddle-stapled, with colored card cover, includes ads. Receives hundreds of poems/year, accepts about 15%. Press run is 500.

NEEDS Submit ms via mail. Name and address should appear on every page. Cover letter is helpful but not required. Size 10 SASE is required for response. Length: up to 1,000 words.

PAYMENT/TERMS Pays contributor's copies.

BLUELINE

120 Morey Hall, SUNY Potsdam, Potsdam NY 13676. **E-mail:** blueline@potsdam.edu. **Website:** bluelinemagadk.com. **Contact:** Donald J. McNutt, editor and nonfiction editor; Caroline Downing, art editor; Stephanie Coyne-DeGhett, fiction editor; Rebecca Lehmann, poetry editor. Estab. 1979. "*Blueline* seeks poems, stories, and essays relating to the Adirondacks and regions similar in geography and spirit, or focusing on the shaping influence of nature. Submission period is July-November. *Blueline* welcomes electronic submissions as Word document (DOC or DOCX) attachments. Please identify genre in subject line. Please avoid using compression software." Annual literary magazine publishing fiction, poetry, personal essays, book reviews, and quality visual art for those interested in the Adirondacks or well-crafted nature writing in general.

"Proofread all submissions. It is difficult for our editors to get excited about work containing typographical and syntactic errors."

NEEDS Receives 8-10 unsolicited mss/month. Accepts 2-3 mss/issue. Does not read January-June. Publishes 2 new writers/year. Recently published work by Jim Meirose, Amber Timmerman, Gail Gilliland, Matthew J. Spireng, Roger Sheffer, and Mason Smith. No urban stories or erotica. Length: 500-3,000 words. Average length: 2,500 words.

PAYMENT/TERMS Pays 1 contributor's copy; charges $9 each for 3 or more copies.

TIPS "We look for concise, clear, concrete prose that tells a story and touches upon a universal theme or situation. We prefer realism to romanticism but will consider nostalgia if well done. Pay attention to grammar and syntax. Avoid murky language, sentimentality, cuteness, or folksiness. We would like to see more good, creative nonfiction centered on the literature and/or culture of the Adirondacks, Northern New

York, New England, or Eastern Canada. If ms has potential, we work with author to improve and reconsider for publication. Our readers prefer fiction to poetry (in general) or reviews. Write from your own experience, be specific and factual (within the bounds of your story), and if you write about universal features such as love, death, change, etc., write about them in a fresh way. You'll catch our attention if your writing is interesting, vigorous, and polished."

BLUE MESA REVIEW

Department of Language and Literature, Humanities Building, Second Floor, MSC03 2170, 1 University of New Mexico, Albuquerque NM 87131. **Website:** bluemesareview.org. **Contact:** Has rotating editorial board; see website for current masthead. Estab. 1989. "Originally founded by Rudolfo Anaya, Gene Frumkin, David Johnson, Patricia Clark Smith, and Lee Bartlette in 1989, the *Blue Mesa Review* emerged as a source of innovative writing produced in the Southwest. Over the years the magazine's nuance has changed, sometimes shifting towards more craft-oriented work, other times realigning with its original roots."

○ Open for submissions from September 30-March 31. Contest: June 1-August 31. Only accepts submissions through online submissions manager.

NEEDS Length: up to 6,000 words.

HOW TO CONTACT Submit via online submissions manager.

TIPS "In general, we are seeking strong voices and lively, compelling narrative with a fine eye for craft. We look forward to reading your best work!"

BLUESTEM

English Deptartment, Eastern Illinois University, **Website:** www.bluestemmagazine.com. **Contact:** Olga Abella, editor. Estab. 1966. *Bluestem*, formerly known as *Karamu*, produces a quarterly online issue (December, March, June, September) and an annual spring print issue.

○ Only accepts submissions through online submissions manager.

NEEDS Length: up to 5,000 words.

HOW TO CONTACT Submit only 1 short story at a time. Include bio (less than 100 words) with submission. Query if longer than 5,000 words.

PAYMENT/TERMS Pays 1 contributor's copy and discount for additional copies.

BODY LITERATURE

Website: bodyliterature.com. Estab. 2012. *BODY* is an international online literary journal. "We publish the highest-quality poetry and prose from emerging and established writers.

NEEDS Length: up to 10 pages typed and double-spaced.

HOW TO CONTACT Submit through online submissions manager. Include short cover letter and short third-person bio.

BOMBAY GIN

Naropa University, Creative Writing and Poetics Department, 2130 Arapahoe Ave., Boulder CO 80302. **E-mail:** bgin@naropa.edu. **Website:** www.bombayginjournal.com. **Contact:** Jade Lascelles, editor in chief. Estab. 1974. *Bombay Gin*, published annually, is the literary journal of the Jack Kerouac School of Disembodied Poetics at Naropa University. Produced and edited by MFA students, *Bombay Gin* publishes established writers alongside unpublished and emerging writers. We have a special interest in works that push conventional literary boundaries. Submissions of poetry, prose, visual art, translation, and works involving hybrid forms and cross-genre exploration are encouraged. Translations are also considered. Guidelines are the same as for original work. Translators are responsible for obtaining any necessary permissions."

○ *Bombay Gin* is 150-200 pages, digest-sized, professionally printed, perfect-bound, with color card cover. Has published work by Amiri Baraka, Lisa Robertson, CA Conrad, Sapphire, Fred Moten, Anne Waldman, Diane di Prima and bell hooks, among others.

NEEDS Length: up to 15 pages.

HOW TO CONTACT Submit through online submissions manager. Include 100-word bio, e-mail, and mailing address.

⑤ BOMB MAGAZINE

80 Hanson Place, Ste. 703, Brooklyn NY 11217. (718)636-9100. **Fax:** (718)636-9200. **E-mail:** saul@bombsite.com. **Website:** www.bombmagazine.com. **Contact:** Saul Anton, senior editor. Estab. 1981. "Written, edited, and produced by industry professionals and funded by those interested in the arts, *BOMB Magazine* publishes work which is unconventional and contains an edge, whether it be in style or subject matter."

NEEDS No genre fiction: romance, science fiction, horror, western. Length: up to 25 pages.

HOW TO CONTACT *BOMB Magazine* accepts unsolicited poetry and prose submissions for our literary supplement *First Proof* by online submission manager in January and August. Submissions sent outside these months will not be read. Submit complete ms via online submission manager. E-mailed submissions will not be considered.

PAYMENT/TERMS Pays $100 and contributor's copies.

TIPS "Mss should be typed, double-spaced, and proofread, and should be final drafts. Purchase a sample issue before submitting work."

⑤ BOSTON REVIEW

P.O. Box 425786, Cambridge MA 02142. (617)324-1360. **E-mail:** review@bostonreview.net. **Website:** www.bostonreview.net. **Contact:** Deborah Chasman and Joshua Cohen, editors. Estab. 1975. The editors are committed to a society that fosters human diversity and a democracy in which we seek common grounds of principle amidst our many differences. In the hope of advancing these ideals, *Boston Review* acts as a forum that seeks to enrich the language of public debate.

    Boston Review is a recipient of the Pushcart Prize in Poetry.

NEEDS Currently closed to general fiction submissions but assembling a special issue of fiction on global dystopias, edited by Junot Díaz. See submission page for details. Length: up to 5,000 words, but can be much shorter.

HOW TO CONTACT Send complete ms.

PAYMENT/TERMS Pays $100-300 and contributor's copies.

TIPS "The best way to get a sense of the kind of material *Boston Review* is looking for is to read the magazine. It is all available online for free."

⑤ BOULEVARD

Opojaz, Inc., 6614 Clayton Rd., Box 325, Richmond Heights MO 63117. **E-mail:** editors@boulevardmagazine.org. **Website:** www.boulevardmagazine.org; boulevard.submittable.com/submit. **Contact:** Jessica Rogen, editor. Estab. 1985. Hosts the Short Fiction Contest for Emerging Writers. **Prize:** $1,500 and publication in *Boulevard*. **Postmarked deadline**: December 31. **Entry fee:** $15 for each individual story, with no limit per author. Entry fee includes a one-year subscription to *Boulevard* (1 per author). Make check payable to *Boulevard*. For contests, make check payable to *Boulevard* or submit online at boulevard.

submittable.com/submit. "*Boulevard* is a diverse literary magazine presenting original creative work by well-known authors as well as by writers of exciting promise." Triannual magazine featuring fiction, poetry, and essays. Sometimes comments on rejected mss. *Boulevard* has been called "one of the half-dozen best literary journals" by Poet Laureate Daniel Hoffman in *The Philadelphia Inquirer*. "We strive to publish the finest in poetry, fiction, and nonfiction. We frequently publish writers with previous credits, and we are very interested in publishing less experienced or unpublished writers with exceptional promise. We've published everything from John Ashbery to Donald Hall to a wide variety of styles from new or lesser known poets. We're eclectic. We are interested in original, moving poetry written from the head as well as the heart. It can be about any topic."

    Boulevard is 175-250 pages, digest-sized, flat-spined, with glossy card cover. Receives over 600 unsolicited mss/month. Accepts about 10 mss/issue. Publishes 10 new writers/year. Recently published work by Joyce Carol Oates, Floyd Skloot, John Barth, Stephen Dixon, David Guterson, Albert Goldbarth, Molly Peacock, Bob Hicok, Alice Friman, Dick Allen, and Tom Disch.

NEEDS Submit by mail or Submittable. Accepts multiple submissions. Does not accept mss May 1-October 1. SASE for reply. "We do not want erotica, science fiction, romance, western, horror, or children's stories." Length: up to 8,000 words.

PAYMENT/TERMS Pays $50-500 (sometimes higher) for accepted work.

TIPS "Read the magazine first. The work *Boulevard* publishes is generally recognized as among the finest in the country. We continue to seek more good literary or cultural essays. Send only your best work."

THE BRIAR CLIFF REVIEW

3303 Rebecca St., Sioux City IA 51104. (712)279-1651. **E-mail:** tricia.currans-sheehan@briarcliff.edu. **Website:** bcreview.org. **Contact:** Tricia Currans-Sheehan, editor; Jeanne Emmons, poetry editor; Phil Hey, fiction editor; Paul Weber, Siouxland and nonfiction editor. Estab. 1989. *The Briar Cliff Review*, published annually in April, is "an attractive, eclectic literary/art magazine." It focuses on, but is not limited to, "Siouxland writers and subjects. We are happy to proclaim ourselves a regional publication. It doesn't diminish us; it enhances us."

Member: CLMP, Humanities International Complete.

NEEDS Accepts 5 mss/year. **Publishes 10-14 new writers/year.** Publishes ms 3-4 months after acceptance. Recently published work by Leslie Barnard, Daryl Murphy, Patrick Hicks, Siobhan Fallon, Shelley Scaletta, Jenna Blum, Brian Bedard, Rebecca Tuch, Scott H. Andrews, and Josip Novakovich. "No romance, horror, or alien stories." Length: up to 5,000 words.

HOW TO CONTACT Submit by (send SASE for return of ms) or online submissions manager. Does not accept e-mail submissions (unless from overseas). Seldom comments on rejected mss.

PAYMENT/TERMS Pays 2 contributor's copies; additional copies available for $12.

TIPS "So many stories are just telling. We want some action. It has to move. We prefer stories in which there is no gimmick, no mechanical turn of events, no moral except the one we would draw privately."

THE BROADKILL REVIEW

c/o John Milton & Company, 104 Federal St., Milton DE 19968. **E-mail:** linblask@aol.com. **Website:** www.thebroadkillreview.blogspot.com; sites.google.com/site/thebroadkillreview. **Contact:** James C.L. Brown, editor; Scott Whitaker, literary review editor; Linda Blaskey, poetry and interview editor. Estab. 2005.

"*The Broadkill Review* accepts the best fiction, poetry, and nonfiction by new and established writers. We have published Pushcart-nominated fiction and poetry."

NEEDS No erotica, fantasy, science fiction "unless these serve some functional literary purpose; most do not." Length: up to 6,000 words.

HOW TO CONTACT Send complete ms with cover letter through online submissions manager. Include estimated word count, brief bio, list of publications.

PAYMENT/TERMS Pays contributor's copy.

TIPS "Query the editor first. Visit our website to familiarize yourself with the type of material we publish. Request and read a copy of the magazine first!"

BUENOS AIRES REVIEW

E-mail: editors@buenosairesreview.org. **Website:** buenosairesreview.org. *The Buenos Aires Review* presents the best and latest work by emerging and established writers from the Americas, in both Spanish and English. "We value translation and conversation. We're bilingual. And we're passionate about the art and craft that allows us to be, so we provide a dedicated space for translators to discuss their recent projects."

BURNSIDE REVIEW

P.O. Box 1782, Portland OR 97207. **Website:** www.burnsidereview.org. **Contact:** Sid Miller, founder and editor; Dan Kaplan, managing editor. Estab. 2004. *Burnside Review*, published every 9 months, prints "the best poetry and short fiction we can get our hands on. We tend to publish writing that finds beauty in truly unexpected places; that combines urban and natural imagery; that breaks the heart."

Burnside Review is 80 pages, 6x6, professionally printed, perfect-bound. Charges a $3 submission fee to cover printing costs.

NEEDS "We like bright, engaging fiction that works to surprise and captivate us." Length: up to 5,000 words.

HOW TO CONTACT Submit complete ms via online submissions manager.

PAYMENT/TERMS Pays $25 and 1 contributor's copy.

THE CAFE IRREAL

E-mail: editors@cafeirreal.com. **Website:** www.cafeirreal.com. **Contact:** G.S. Evans and Alice Whittenburg, co-editors. Estab. 1998. "Our audience is composed of people who read or write literary fiction with fantastic themes, similar to the work of Franz Kafka, Kobo Abe, or Clarice Lispector. This is a type of fiction (irreal) that has difficulty finding its way into print in the English-speaking world and defies many of the conventions of American literature especially. As a result, ours is a fairly specialized literary publication, and we would strongly recommend that prospective writers look at our current issue and guidelines carefully." Recently published work by Hernán Ortiz, Venita Blackburn, Robert Garner McBrearty, Guido Eekhaut, Cheryl Pallant, JP Briggs and Mark Budman.

NEEDS Accepts submissions by e-mail. No attachments; include submission in body of e-mail. Include estimated word count. Accepts 6-8 mss/issue; 24-32 mss/year. No horror or "slice-of-life" stories; no genre or mainstream science fiction or fantasy. Length: up to 2,000 words.

PAYMENT/TERMS Pays 1¢/word, $2 minimum.

TIPS "Forget formulas. Write about what you don't know, take me places I couldn't possibly go, don't try to make me care about the characters. Read short fiction by writers such as Franz Kafka, Jorge Luis Borges, Donald Barthelme, Magnus Mills, Ana Maria Shua, and Stanislaw Lem. Also read our website and guidelines."

CALLALOO: A JOURNAL OF AFRICAN DIASPORA ARTS & LETTERS

Texas A&M University, 249 Blocker Hall, College Station TX 77843-4212, United States. (979)458-3108. **Fax:** (979)458-3275. **E-mail:** callaloo@tamu.edu. **Website:** callaloo.tamu.edu. Estab. 1976. *Callaloo: A Journal of African Diaspora Arts & Letters*, published quarterly, is devoted to poetry dealing with the African Diaspora, including North America, Europe, Africa, Latin and Central America, South America, and the Caribbean. Features about 15-20 poems (all forms and styles) in each issue along with short fiction, interviews, literary criticism, and concise critical book reviews.

NEEDS Would like to see more experimental fiction, science fiction, and well-crafted literary fiction particularly dealing with the black middle class, immigrant communities, and/or the black South. Accepts 3-5 mss/issue; 10-20 mss/year. **Publishes 5-10 new writers/year.** Recently published work by Charles Johnson, Edwidge Danticat, Thomas Glave, Nallo Hopkinson, John Edgar Wideman, Jamaica Kincaid, Percival Everett, and Patricia Powell. Also publishes poetry. Length: up to 10,000 words excluding title page, abstract, bio, and references.

HOW TO CONTACT Submit ms via online submissions manager: callaloo.expressacademic.org/login. php. All fiction submissions are now limited to 1 ms per submission with a maximum of 3 submissions by a single author per calendar year.

TIPS "We look for freshness of both writing and plot, strength of characterization, plausibility of plot. Read what's being written and published, especially in journals such as *Callaloo.*"

CALYX

P.O. Box B, Corvallis OR 97339. (541)753-9384. **E-mail:** info@calyxpress.org; editor@calyxpress.org. **Website:** www.calyxpress.org. **Contact:** Brenna Crotty, senior editor. Estab. 1976. *"CALYX* exists to publish fine literature and art by women and is dedicated to publishing the work of all women, including women of color, older women, working-class women and other voices that need to be heard. We are committed to discovering and nurturing developing writers."

Annual open submission (poetry and prose) period is October 1-December 31. Lois Cranston Memorial Poetry Prize ($300 cash prize) is open March 1-June 30. Margarita Donnel-

ly Prize for Prose Writing ($500 cash prize) is open July 1-September 30.

NEEDS Length: no more than 5,000 words.

HOW TO CONTACT All submissions should include author's name on each page and be accompanied by a brief (50-word or less) biographical statement, phone number, and e-mail address. Submit using online submissions manager.

PAYMENT/TERMS Pays in contributor's copies and one-volume subscription.

TIPS "A forum for women's creative work—including work by women of color, lesbian and queer women, young women, old women—*CALYX* breaks new ground. Each issue is packed with new poetry, short stories, full-color artwork, photography, essays, and reviews."

CAMAS: THE NATURE OF THE WEST

The University of Montana, Environmental Studies Program, Rankin Hall 1O16, Missoula MT 59812. (406)243-6273. **Fax:** (406)243-6090. **E-mail:** camas@mso.umt.edu. **Website:** www.camasmagazine. org. **Contact:** Co-editor. Estab. 1992. Published biannually in Winter and Summer. *"Camas* seeks to create an evocative space that celebrates, explores, and acknowledges the complex relationship of people and land and environment in the American West."

"Please check our website or Facebook page for theme and submission periods."

NEEDS Length: 500-3,000 words

HOW TO CONTACT Submit online via our website.

PAYMENT/TERMS Pays 1 contributor's copy.

TIPS "Submit work that speaks to contemporary social issues associated with environmental concerns of the American West. The link to the region can be tenuous or subtle."

THE CAPILANO REVIEW

102-281 Industrial Ave., Vancouver British Columbia V6A 2P2, Canada. **E-mail:** contact@thecapilanoreview.ca. **E-mail:** online through submittable. **Website:** www.thecapilanoreview.ca. **Contact:** Matea Kulic, managing editor. Estab. 1972. Triannual visual and literary arts magazine that "publishes only what the editors consider to be the very best fiction, poetry, drama, or visual art being produced. *TCR* editors are interested in fresh, original work that stimulates and challenges readers. Over the years, the magazine has developed a reputation for pushing beyond the boundaries of traditional art and writing. We are interested in work that is new in concept and in execution."

We no longer accept submissions by mail. Please review our submission guidelines on our website and submit online through submittable.

NEEDS No traditional, conventional fiction. Wants to see more innovative, genre-blurring work. Length: up to 5,000 words.

PAYMENT/TERMS Pays $50-150.

ORSON SCOTT CARD'S INTERGALACTIC MEDICINE SHOW

Hatrack River Publications, P.O. Box 18184, Greensboro NC 27419. **Website:** intergalacticmedicineshow.com; oscigms.com. **Contact:** Edmund R. Schubert, editor. Estab. 2005. *"Orson Scott Card's InterGalactic Medicine Show* is an online fantasy and science fiction magazine. We are a bimonthly publication featuring content from both established and talented new authors. In addition to our bimonthly issues, we offer weekly columns and reviews on books, movies, video games, and writing advice."

NEEDS "We like to see well-developed milieus and believable, engaging characters. We also look for clear, unaffected writing." Length: up to 17,000 words.

HOW TO CONTACT Submit via online submission form. Submit only 1 story at a time. Include estimated word count, e-mail address.

PAYMENT/TERMS Pays 6¢/word.

TIPS "Please note: *IGMS* is a PG-13 magazine and website. That means that while stories can deal with intense and adult themes, we will not accept stories with explicit or detailed sex of the sort that would earn a movie rating more restrictive than PG-13; nor will there be language of the sort that earns an R rating."

THE CARIBBEAN WRITER

University of the Virgin Islands, RR 1, P.O. Box 10,000, Kingshill, St. Croix USVI 00850. (340)692-4152. **E-mail:** info@thecaribbeanwriter.org. **Website:** www.thecaribbeanwriter.org. **Contact:** Alscess Lewis-Brown, editor in chief. Estab. 1986. *The Caribbean Writer* features new and exciting voices from the region and beyond that explore the diverse and multi-ethnic culture in poetry, short fiction, personal essays, creative nonfiction, and plays. Social, cultural, economic, and sometimes controversial issues are also explored, employing a wide array of literary devices.

Poetry published in *The Caribbean Writer* has appeared in *The Pushcart Prize*. *The Caribbean Writer* is 300+ pages, digest-sized, handsome-ly printed on heavy stock, perfect-bound, with glossy card cover. Press run is 1,200.

NEEDS Submit complete ms through online submissions manager. Name, address, phone number, e-mail address, and title of ms should appear in cover letter along with brief bio. Title only on ms. All submissions are eligible for the Virgin Islands Daily News Prize ($500) for a fiction or nonfiction essay to an author residing in the U.S. or British Virgin Islands, the David Hough Literary Prize to a Caribbean author ($500), the Canute A. Brodhurst Prize for Fiction ($400), the Cecile Dejongh Literary Prize to an author whose work best expresses the spirit of the Caribbean ($500), and the Marvin Williams Literary Prize for first-time publication in the Caribbean ($500). Length: up to 3,500 words or 10 pages.

PAYMENT/TERMS Pays 1 contributor's copy.

THE CAROLINA QUARTERLY

CB #3520 Greenlaw Hall, University of North Carolina, Chapel Hill NC 27599-3520. (919)408-7786. **E-mail:** carolina.quarterly@gmail.com. **Website:** www.thecarolinaquarterly.com; thecarolinaquarterly.submittable.com/submit. **Contact:** Travis Alexander, nonfiction editor; Laura Broom, fiction editor; Sarah George and Calvin Olsen, poetry editors. Estab. 1948. *The Carolina Quarterly*, published 3 times/year, prints fiction, poetry, reviews, nonfiction, and visual art. No specifications regarding form, length, subject matter, or style. Considers translations of work originally written in languages other than English.

The Carolina Quarterly is about 100 pages, digest-sized, professionally printed, perfect-bound, with glossy cover; includes ads. Press run is 1,000. Accepts submissions September through May.

NEEDS Length: up to 7,500 words.

HOW TO CONTACT Submit 1 complete ms via online submissions manager or postal mail (address submissions to Fiction Editor).

CAVEAT LECTOR

400 Hyde St., #606, San Francisco CA 94109. **E-mail:** caveatlectormagazine@gmail.com. **Website:** www.caveat-lector.org. **Contact:** Christopher Bernard, co-editor. Estab. 1989. *Caveat Lector*, published 2 times/year, is devoted to the arts and cultural and philosophical commentary. As well as literary work, they publish art, photography, music, streaming audio of selected literary pieces, and short films. Poetry, fic-

tion, artwork, music, and short films are posted on the website. "Don't let those examples limit your submissions. Send what you feel is your strongest work, in any style and on any subject."

⭕ All submissions should be sent with a brief bio and SASE, or submitted electronically. (Poetry submissions are only accepted through postal mail.) Reads poetry submissions February 1-June 30; reads all other submissions year round.

NEEDS Accepts prose submissions (short stories, excerpts from longer works) throughout the year. Submit complete ms by e-mail or mail.

PAYMENT/TERMS Pays contributor's copies.

THE CHAFFIN JOURNAL

E-mail: nancy.jensen@eku.edu. **Website:** www.english. eku.edu/chaffin_journal. **Contact:** Nancy Jensen, editor. Estab. 1998; revised and re-established in 2017. *The Chaffin Journal* is a print journal for literary fiction, poetry, and creative nonfiction, published annually through the English Department at Eastern Kentucky University.

⭕ "We value strong voices, freshness of vision, precision in language, and a sense of urgency in the literary fiction, poetry, and creative nonfiction we publish." Online submission period: April 1-June 15. Use the submission link on website. No postal mail or e-mailed submissions will be considered.

NEEDS Wants literary fiction, primarily short stories. Novel excerpts that can stand alone may be considered. No genre fiction, formula fiction, or erotica. Length: up to 6,000 words

HOW TO CONTACT Submit 1 fiction submission per reading period via online submissions manager.

PAYMENT/TERMS Pays 1 contributor's copy.

THE CHARITON REVIEW

Truman State University Press, 100 E. Normal Ave., Kirksville MO 63501. (660)785-7336. **Fax:** (660)785-4480. **E-mail:** chariton@truman.edu. **Website:** tsup. truman.edu/product/chariton-review/. Estab. 1975. *The Chariton Review* is an international literary journal publishing the best in short fiction, essays, poetry, and translations in 2 issues each year.

NEEDS No flash fiction. Length: up to 7,000 words.

HOW TO CONTACT Submit 1 complete ms through online submissions manager. English only.

⑤ THE CHATTAHOOCHEE REVIEW

555 N. Indian Creek Dr., Clarkston GA 30021. **E-mail:** gpccr@gpc.edu. **Website:** thechattahoocheereview.

gpc.edu. **Contact:** Lydia Ship, managing editor. Estab. 1980. *The Chattahoochee Review*, published quarterly, prints poetry, short fiction, essays, reviews, and interviews. "We publish a number of Southern writers, but *The Chattahoochee Review* is not by design a regional magazine. All themes, forms, and styles are considered as long as they impact the whole person: heart, mind, intuition, and imagination."

⭕ Has recently published work by George Garrett, Jim Daniels, Jack Pendarvis, Ignacio Padilla, and Kevin Canty. *The Chattahoochee Review* is 160 pages, digest-sized, professionally printed, flat-spined, with four-color silk-matte card cover. Press run is 1,250; 300 are complimentary copies sent to editors and "miscellaneous VIPs." No e-mail submissions.

NEEDS Length: 500-1,000 words for short shorts; up to 6,000 words for short stories and novellas.

HOW TO CONTACT "*TCR* publishes high-quality literary fiction characterized by interest in language, development of distinctive settings, compelling conflict, and complex, unique characters. Submit 1 story or up to 3 short shorts via online submissions manager.

PAYMENT/TERMS Pays 2 contributor's copies.

CHAUTAUQUA LITERARY JOURNAL

University of North Carolina at Wilmington, Department of Creative Writing, 601 S. College Rd., Wilmington NC 28403. **E-mail:** chautauquajournal@gmail. com; clj@uncw.edu. **Website:** ciweb.org. **Contact:** Jill Gerard and Philip Gerard, editors. Estab. 2003. *Chautauqua*, published annually in June, prints poetry, short fiction, and creative nonfiction. The editors actively solicit writing that expresses the values of Chautauqua Institution broadly construed: a sense of inquiry into questions of personal, social, political, spiritual, and aesthetic importance, regardless of genre. Considers the work of any writer, whether or not affiliated with Chautauqua Institution. Looking for a mastery of craft, attention to vivid and accurate language, a true lyric "ear," an original and compelling vision, and strong narrative instinct. Above all, it values work that is intensely personal, yet somehow implicitly comments on larger public concerns, like work that answers every reader's most urgent question: Why are you telling me this?

⭕ Reads submissions February 15-April 15 and August 15-November 15. Work published in

Chautauqua has been included in *The Pushcart Prize* anthology.

NEEDS "*Chautauqua* short stories, self-contained novel excerpts, or flash fiction demonstrate a sound storytelling instinct, using suspense in the best sense, creating a compulsion in the reader to continue reading. Wants to engage readers' deep interest in the characters and their actions, unsettled issues of action or theme, or in some cases simple delight at the language itself. A superior story will exhibit the writer's attention to language—both in style and content—and should reveal a masterful control of diction and syntax." Length: up to 25 double-spaced pages or 7,000 words.

HOW TO CONTACT Submit through online submissions manager.

PAYMENT/TERMS Pays 2 contributor's copies.

TIPS "*Chautauqua* has added a new section, which celebrates young writers, ages 12-18. Work should be submitted by a teacher, mentor, or parent. Please confirm on the entry that the piece can be classified as a Young Voices entry. We ask that young writers consider the theme. Essays and stories should remain under 1,500 words. For poetry, please submit no more than 3 poems and/or no more than 6 pages."

CHICAGO QUARTERLY REVIEW

517 Sherman Ave., Evanston IL 60202. **E-mail:** cqr@icogitate.com. **Website:** www.chicagoquarterlyreview.com. **Contact:** S. Afzal Haider and Elizabeth McKenzie, senior editors. Estab. 1994. "The *Chicago Quarterly Review* is a nonprofit, independent literary journal publishing the finest short stories, poems, translations, and essays by both emerging and established writers. We hope to stimulate, entertain, and inspire."

○ The *Chicago Quarterly Review* is 6x9; 225 pages; illustrations; photos. Receives 250 unsolicited mss/month. Accepts 10-15 mss/issue; 20-30 mss/year. Agented fiction 5%. **Publishes 8-10 new writers/year.**

NEEDS Length: up to 5,000 words; average length: 2,500 words.

HOW TO CONTACT Submit through online submissions manager only.

PAYMENT/TERMS Pays 2 contributor's copies.

TIPS "The writer's voice ought to be clear and unique and should explain something of what it means to be human. We want well-written stories that reflect an appreciation for the rhythm and music of language, work that shows passion and commitment to the art of writing."

CHICAGO REVIEW

Taft House, 935 E. 60th St., Chicago IL 60637. **E-mail:** editors@chicagoreview.org. **Website:** chicagoreview.org. **Contact:** Eric Powell, managing editor. Estab. 1946. "Since 1946, *Chicago Review* has published a range of contemporary poetry, fiction, and criticism. Each year typically includes 2 single issues and a double issue with a special feature section."

NEEDS "We will consider work in any literary style but are typically less interested in traditional narrative approaches." Length: up to 5,000 words.

HOW TO CONTACT Submit 1 short story or up to 5 short short stories submitted in 1 file. Submit via online submissions manager. Prefers electronic submissions.

PAYMENT/TERMS Pays contributor's copies.

TIPS "We strongly recommend that authors familiarize themselves with recent issues of *Chicago Review* before submitting. Submissions that demonstrate familiarity with the journal tend to receive more attention than those that appear to be part of a carpet-bombing campaign."

CHIRON REVIEW

Chiron, Inc., 522 E. South Ave., St. John KS 67576-2212. **E-mail:** editor@chironreview.com. **Website:** www.chironreview.com. **Contact:** Michael Hathaway, publisher. Estab. 1982 as *The Kindred Spirit. Chiron Review*, published quarterly, presents the widest possible range of contemporary creative writing—fiction and nonfiction, traditional and off-beat—in an attractive, perfect-bound digest, including artwork and photographs. No taboos.

NEEDS Submit complete ms by mail with SASE, or by e-mail as DOC attachment. Length: up to 2,500 words.

PAYMENT/TERMS Pays 1 contributor's copy.

TIPS "Please check our website to see if we are open to submissions. When you do send submissions, please have mercy on the editors and follow the guidelines noted here and on our website."

CIMARRON REVIEW

205 Morrill Hall, English Department, Oklahoma State University, Stillwater OK 74078. **E-mail:** cimarronreview@okstate.edu. **Website:** cimarronreview.okstate.edu. **Contact:** Toni Graham, editor and fiction editor; Lisa Lewis, poetry editor; Sarah Beth Childers, nonfiction editor. Estab. 1967. "One of the oldest quarterlies in the nation, *Cimarron Review* publishes work

by writers at all stages of their careers, including Pulitzer Prize winners, writers appearing in the Best American Series and the Pushcart anthologies, and winners of national book contests. Since 1967, *Cimarron* has showcased poetry, fiction, and nonfiction with a wide-ranging aesthetic. Our editors seek the bold and the ruminative, the sensitive and the shocking, but above all they seek imagination and truth-telling, the finest stories, poems, and essays from working writers across the country and around the world."

○ *Cimarron Review* is 6.5x8.5; 110 pages. Accepts 3-5 mss/issue; 12-15 mss/year. Publishes 2-4 new writers/year. Eager to receive mss from both established and less experienced writers "who intrigue us with their unusual perspective, language, imagery, and character." Has published work by Molly Giles, Gary Fincke, David Galef, Nona Caspers, Robin Beeman, Edward J. Delaney, William Stafford, John Ashbery, Grace Schulman, Barbara Hamby, Patricia Fargnoli, Phillip Dacey, Holly Prado, and Kim Addonizio.

NEEDS "We are interested in any strong writing of a literary variety but are especially partial to fiction in the modern realist tradition and poetry that engages the reader through a distinctive voice—be it lyric, narrative, etc. When submitting fiction, please do not include a summary of your story in the cover letter. Allow the work to stand on its own." No juvenile or genre fiction. "We have no set page lengths for any genre, but we seldom publish short shorts or pieces longer than 25 pages. There are, however, exceptions to every rule. Our guiding aesthetic is the quality of the work itself."

HOW TO CONTACT Send complete ms with SASE, or submit online through submission manager; include cover letter.

PAYMENT/TERMS Pays 2 contributor's copies.

TIPS "All electronic and postal submissions should include a cover letter. Postal submissions must include a SASE. We do not accept submissions by e-mail. Please follow our guidelines as they appear on our website. In order to get a feel for the kind of work we publish, please read several issues before submitting."

⑤ THE CINCINNATI REVIEW

P.O. Box 210069, Cincinnati OH 45221-0069. (513)556-3954. **Fax:** (513)556-3959. **E-mail:** editors@cincinnatireview.com. **Website:** www.cincinnatireview.com. **Contact:** Michael Griffith, fiction editor;

Don Bogen, poetry editor; Kristen Iversen, nonfiction editor. Estab. 2003. A journal devoted to publishing the best new literary fiction, creative nonfiction, and poetry, as well as book reviews, essays, and interviews.

○ *The Cincinnati Review* is 180-200 pages, digest-sized, perfect-bound, with matte paperback cover with full-color art. Press run is 1,000. Reads submissions August 15-March 15.

NEEDS Does not want genre fiction. Length: up to 40 double-spaced pages.

HOW TO CONTACT Submit complete ms via online submissions manager only.

PAYMENT/TERMS Pays $25/page.

TIPS "Each issue includes a translation feature. For more information on translations, please see our website."

☺ THE CLAREMONT REVIEW

1581-H Hillside Ave., Suite 101, Victoria BC V8T 2C1, Canada. **Website:** www.theclaremontreview.ca. **Contact:** Jody Carrow, editor in chief. The editors of *The Claremont Review* publish first-class poetry, short stories, short plays, visual art, and photography by young adults, ages 13-19, from anywhere in the English-speaking world.

○ "We publish anything from traditional to postmodern but with a preference for works that reveal something of the human condition. By this we mean stories that explore real characters in modern settings. Who are we, what are we doing to the planet, what is our relationship to one another, the Earth, or God? Also, reading samples on the website or from past issues will give you a clearer indication of what we are looking for."

NEEDS Submit complete, double-spaced ms by mail. Include cover letter with name, age, mailing address, e-mail address, school, and brief bio. Allows up to 6 items in each submission. Does not want science fiction, fantasy, or romance. Only accepts submissions from writers ages 13-19. Length: up to 5,000 words.

TIPS "Read guidelines before submitting."

CLARK STREET REVIEW

1757 McKenzie Ct., Loveland CO 80537. **E-mail:** clarkreview@earthlink.net. **Contact:** Ray Foreman, editor. Estab. 1998. *Clark Street Review*, published 6 times/year, publishes narrative poetry and gives poets cause to keep writing by publishing their best work. Press run is 200.

○ "Editor reads everything with a critical eye of 30 years experience in writing and publishing small-press work."

NEEDS Wants short shorts. Include SASE for reply. No cover letter. No limit on submissions. Length: up to 1,200 words.

CLOUDBANK: JOURNAL OF CONTEMPORARY WRITING

P.O. Box 610, Corvallis OR 97339. (541)752-0075. **E-mail:** michael@cloudbankbooks.com. **Website:** www.cloudbankbooks.com. **Contact:** Michael Malan, editor. Estab. 2009. Offers *Cloudbank* Contest for $200 prize. **Entry fee:** $15. See website for guidelines. *Cloudbank* publishes poetry, short prose, and book reviews.

○ *Cloudbank* is digest-sized, 92 pages of print, perfect-bound; color artwork on cover, includes ads. Press run is 400. Subscribers: 300; shelf sales: 100 distributed free.

NEEDS Length: up to 500 words.

HOW TO CONTACT Submit flash fiction by mail with SASE.

PAYMENT/TERMS Pays $200 prize for 1 poem or flash fiction piece per issue.

TIPS "Please consider reading a copy of *Cloudbank* before submitting."

○ COAL CITY REVIEW

Coal City Press, English Department, University of Kansas, Lawrence KS 66045. **Website:** coalcitypress.wordpress.com. **Contact:** Brian Daldorph, editor. *Coal City Review*, published annually, usually late in the year, publishes poetry, short stories, reviews: "the best material I can find."

NEEDS Accepts mainly mainstream fiction: "Please don't send 'experimental' work our way." Length: up to 4,000 words.

PAYMENT/TERMS Pays contributor's copies.

COLD MOUNTAIN REVIEW

Department of English, Appalachian State University, ASU Box 32052, Boone NC 28608. **Website:** www.coldmountain.appstate.edu. **Contact:** Kathryn Kirkpatrick, editor; Nathan Poole, managing editor; Betsy Lawson, assistant editor. *Cold Mountain Review*, published twice/year (in spring and fall), features fiction, nonfiction, poetry, and b&w art. "Themed fall issues rotate with general spring issues, but all work is considered beneath our broad ecological–ecojustice umbrella."

○ *Cold Mountain Review* is about 72 pages, digest-sized, perfect-bound, with light cardstock cover. Reading period is August-May.

NEEDS Considers novel excerpts if the submissions is "an exemplary stand-alone piece." Length: up to 6,000 words.

HOW TO CONTACT Submit 1 piece at a time through online submissions manager or by mail.

PAYMENT/TERMS Pays contributor's copies.

THE COLLAGIST

Dzanc Books, **E-mail:** editor@thecollagist.com; poetry@thecollagist.com; bookreviews@thecollagist.com. **Website:** thecollagist.com. **Contact:** Gabriel Blackwell, editor in chief; Marielle Prince, poetry editor; Michael Jauchen, book review editor. Estab. 2009. *The Collagist* is a monthly journal published on the 15th of each month, containing short fiction, poetry, essays, book reviews, and one of more excerpts from novels forthcoming from (mostly) independent presses.

HOW TO CONTACT Submit short stories through online submissions manager.

⑤ COLORADO REVIEW

Center for Literary Publishing, Colorado State University, 9105 Campus Delivery, Fort Collins CO 80523. (970)491-5449. **E-mail:** creview@colostate.edu. **Website:** coloradoreview.colostate.edu. **Contact:** Stephanie G'Schwind, editor in chief and nonfiction editor; Steven Schwartz, fiction editor; Don Revell, Sasha Steensen, and Matthew Cooperman, poetry editors; Harrison Candelaria Fletcher, nonfiction editor; Dan Beachy-Quick, poetry book review editor; Jennifer Wisner Kelly, fiction and nonfiction book review editor. Estab. 1956. Literary magazine published 3 times/year.

○ Work published in *Colorado Review* has been included in *Best American Essays*, *Best American Short Stories*, *Best American Poetry*, *Best New American Voices*, *Best Travel Writing*, *Best Food Writing*, and the *Pushcart Prize Anthology*.

NEEDS No genre fiction. Length: up to 10,000 words.

HOW TO CONTACT Send complete ms. Fiction mss are read August 1-April 30. Mss received May 1-July 31 will be returned unread. Send no more than 1 story at a time.

PAYMENT/TERMS Pays $200.

COLUMBIA: A JOURNAL OF LITERATURE AND ART

Columbia University, New York NY 10027. **E-mail:** info@columbiajournal.org. **Website:** columbiajournal.org. **Contact:** Staff rotates each year. Estab. 1977. *"Columbia: A Journal of Literature and Art* is an annual publication that features the very best in poetry, fiction, nonfiction, and art. We were founded in 1977 and continue to be one of the few national literary journals entirely edited, designed, and produced by students. You'll find that our minds are open, our interests diverse. We solicit mss from writers we love and select the most exciting finds from our virtual submission box. Above all, our commitment is to our readers—to producing a collection that informs, surprises, challenges, and inspires."

Reads submissions March 1-September 15.

NEEDS Accepts all forms of short fiction: short stories, flash fiction, prose poetry. Length: up to 5,000 words.

HOW TO CONTACT Submit complete ms via online submissions manager. Include short bio.

COMMON GROUND REVIEW

Western New England University, H-5132, Western New England University, 1215 Wilbraham Rd., Springfield MA 01119. **E-mail:** editors@cgreview.org. **Website:** cgreview.org. **Contact:** Janet Bowdan, editor. Estab. 1999. *Common Ground Review*, published twice yearly (Spring/Summer, Fall/Winter), prints poetry and 1 short nonfiction piece in the Fall issue and 1 short fiction piece in the Spring issue. Holds annual poetry contest.

NEEDS Length: up to 12 pages double-spaced.

HOW TO CONTACT Submit via online submissions manager or mail.

PAYMENT/TERMS Pays 1 contributor's copy.

TIPS "For poems, use a few good images to ground and convey ideas; take ideas further than the initial thought. Poems should be condensed and concise, free from words that do not contribute. The subject matter should be worthy of the reader's time and should appeal to a wide range of readers. Form should be an extension of content. Sometimes the editors may suggest possible revisions."

CONCEIT MAGAZINE

Perry Terrell Publishing, P.O. Box 884223, San Francisco CA 94188-4223. **E-mail:** conceitmagazine2007@yahoo.com. **Website:** sites.google.com/site/conceitmagazine and conceitmagazine.weebly.com. **Contact:** Perry Terrell, editor. Estab. 2006. We are a literary sharing organization.

Magazine publishes poetry, short stories, articles, cartoons and essays. Very few guidelines—let me see your creative work. We will decide after reading.

NEEDS List of upcoming themes available for SASE and on website. Receives 60-70 mss/month. Accepts 20-30 mss/issue; up to 640+ mss/year. Ms published 3-10 months after acceptance. Publishes 250 new writers/year. Published D. Neil Simmers, Tamara Fey Turner, Eve J. Blohm, Barbara Hantman, David Body, Milton Kerr, and Juanita Torrence-Thompson. Does not want profanity, porn, gruesomeness. Length: 100-4,000 words. Average length: 1,500-2,000 words. Publishes short shorts. Average length of short shorts: 50-500 words.

HOW TO CONTACT Will read and review your books. "Send review copies to Perry Terrell." Query first or send complete ms with cover letter. Accepts submissions by e-mail and snail mail. Include estimated word count, brief bio, list of publications.

PAYMENT/TERMS Pays 1 contributor's copy. Additional copies $4.50. Pay via PayPal to conceitmagazine@yahoo.com. Pays writers through contests. Monthly contests in 2017. Send SASE or check blog on websites for details."

TIPS "We are a 'literary sharing' organization. Uniqueness and creativity make a ms stand out. Be brave and confident. Let me see what you created. Also, PATIENCE is ultimately required."

CONCHO RIVER REVIEW

Angelo State University, ASU Station #10894, San Angelo TX 76909. **E-mail:** ageyer@usca.edu; haleya@acu.edu; jerry.bradley@lamar.edu; roger.jackson@angelo.edu. **Website:** conchoriverreview.org. **Contact:** R. Mark Jackson, general editor and book review editor; Andrew Geyer, fiction editor; Albert Haley, nonfiction editor; Jerry Bradley, poetry editor. Estab. 1987. *"CRR* aims to provide its readers with escape, insight, laughter, and inspiration for many years to come. We urge authors to submit to the journal and readers to subscribe to our publication."

NEEDS "Editors tend to publish traditional stories with a strong sense of conflict, finely drawn characters, and crisp dialogue." Length: 1,500-5,000 words.

HOW TO CONTACT Submit only 1 ms at a time. Electronic submissions preferred. See website for appropriate section editor.

PAYMENT/TERMS Pays 1 contributor's copy.

CONFRONTATION

English Department, LIU Post, Brookville NY 11548. **E-mail:** confrontationmag@gmail.com. **Website:**

www.confrontationmagazine.org. **Contact:** Jonna G. Semeiks, editor in chief; Belinda Kremer, poetry editor; Terry Kattleman, publicity director/production editor. Estab. 1968. "*Confrontation* has been in continuous publication since 1968. Our taste and our magazine is eclectic, but we always look for excellence in style, an important theme, a memorable voice. We enjoy discovering and fostering new talent. Each issue contains work by both well-established and new writers. We read August 16-April 15. Do not send mss or e-mail submissions between April 16 and August 15."

◐ *Confrontation* has garnered a long list of awards and honors, including the Editor's Award for Distinguished Achievement from CLMP (given to Martin Tucker, the founding editor of the magazine) and NEA grants. Work from the magazine has appeared in numerous anthologies, including the *Pushcart Prize*, *Best Short Stories*, and *The O. Henry Prize Stories*. "We also publish the work of 1 visual artist per issue, selected by the editors."

NEEDS "We judge on quality of writing and thought or imagination, so we will accept genre fiction. However, it must have literary merit or must transcend or challenge genre." No "proselytizing" literature or conventional genre fiction. Length: up to 7,200 words.

HOW TO CONTACT Send complete ms.

PAYMENT/TERMS Pays $175-250; more for commissioned work.

TIPS "We look for literary merit. Keep honing your skills, and keep trying."

CONGRUENT SPACES

820 Taylor St. #5, Medford OR 97504. **E-mail:** congruentspacesmag@gmail.com. **Website:** www.congruentspaces.com. **Contact:** Michael Camarata, editor and publisher. Estab. 2011. "*Congruent Spaces* was developed as a common ground for a diverse variety of voices and writing styles within the writing community. In keeping with this sense of community, all submissions are posted directly to the slush pile in our Writer's Lair, where our community of writers and readers come together to read and rate these submissions. For each issue we then select from the top-rated submissions which stories and poems appear within the pages of our magazine. Our magazine covers fantasy, horror, literary/mainstream fiction, poetry, and science fiction."

NEEDS Submit complete ms on website. No erotic/pornographic material. Length: up to 2,500 words.

PAYMENT/TERMS Pays 1 contributor's copy and one-month membership.

TIPS "Don't submit your work unless you truly believe it is ready for publication. Be sure to proof your formatting for readability before posting the ms for our ratings process. The most common error is failing to adequately separate paragraphs after copying and pasting the submission in the submission form. The easier it is to read your ms, the better your chances of receiving a quality rating and being published."

CONNOTATION PRESS

Website: www.connotationpress.com. **Contact:** Ken Robidoux, publisher. *Connotation Press* accepts submissions in poetry, fiction, creative nonfiction, playwriting, screenplay, interview, book review, music review, etc. "Basically, we're looking at virtually every genre or crossover genre you can create."

NEEDS Submit 1 story of any length, a chapter or excerpt from a novel, or 1-5 flash fiction pieces through online submission manager. Include headshot and short bio.

⑤ CONTRARY

The Journal of Unpopular Discontent, P.O. Box 806363, Chicago IL 60616-3299. **E-mail:** chicago@contrarymagazine.com. **Website:** www.contrarymagazine.com. **Contact:** Jeff McMahon, editor; Frances Badgett, fiction editor; Shaindel Beers, poetry editor. Estab. 2003. *Contrary* publishes fiction, poetry, and literary commentary, and prefers work that combines the virtues of all those categories. Founded at the University of Chicago, it now operates independently and not-for-profit on the South Side of Chicago. Quarterly. Member CLMP.

◐ "We like work that is not only contrary in content but contrary in its evasion of the expectations established by its genre. Our fiction defies traditional story form. For example, a story may bring us to closure without ever delivering an ending. We don't insist on the ending, but we do insist on the closure. And we value fiction as poetic as any poem."

NEEDS Receives 650 mss/month. Accepts 6 mss/issue; 24 mss/year. Publishes 14 new writers/year. Has published Sherman Alexie, Andrew Coburn, Amy Reed, Clare Kirwan, Stephanie Johnson, Laurence Davies, and Edward McWhinney. Length: up to 2,000 words. Average length: 750 words. Publishes short shorts. Average length of short shorts: 750 words.

HOW TO CONTACT Accepts submissions through website only: www.contrarymagazine.com/contrary/submissions.html. Include estimated word count, brief bio, list of publications.

PAYMENT/TERMS Pays $20-60.

TIPS "Beautiful writing catches our eye first. If we realize we're in the presence of unanticipated meaning, that's what clinches the deal. Also, we're not fond of expository fiction. We prefer to be seduced by beauty, profundity, and mystery than to be presented with the obvious. We look for fiction that entrances, that stays the reader's finger above the mouse button. That is, in part, why we favor microfiction, flash fiction, and short shorts. Also, we hope writers will remember that most editors are looking for very particular species of work. We try to describe our particular species in our mission statement and our submission guidelines, but those descriptions don't always convey nuance. That's why many editors urge writers to read the publication itself, in the hope that they will intuit an understanding of its particularities. If you happen to write that particular species of work we favor, your submission may find a happy home with us. If you don't, it does not necessarily reflect on your quality or your ability. It usually just means that your work has a happier home somewhere else."

THE COPPERFIELD REVIEW

A Journal for Readers and Writers of Historical Fiction, **E-mail:** copperreview@aol.com. **E-mail:** copperreview@aol.com. **Website:** www.copperfieldreview.com. **Contact:** Meredith Allard, executive editor. Estab. 2000. "We are a quarterly online literary journal that publishes historical fiction, reviews, and interviews related to historical fiction. We believe that by understanding the lessons of the past through historical fiction, we can gain better insight into the nature of our society today, as well as a better understanding of ourselves."

⭘ "Remember that we are a journal for readers and writers of historical fiction. We only consider submissions that are historical in nature."

NEEDS "We will consider submissions in most fiction categories, but the setting must be historical in nature. We don't want to see anything not related to historical fiction." Receives 40 unsolicited mss/month. Publishes 30-40% new writers/year. Publishes short shorts. Length: 500-3,000 words.

HOW TO CONTACT Send complete ms. Name and e-mail address should appear on the first page of the submission. Accepts submissions pasted into an e-mail only. "Do not query first. Send the complete ms according to our guidelines."

TIPS "We wish to showcase the very best in historical fiction. Stories that use historical periods to illuminate universal truths will immediately stand out. We are thrilled to receive thoughtful work that is polished, poised, and written from the heart. Be professional, and only submit your very best work. Be certain to adhere to a publication's submission guidelines, and always treat your e-mail submissions with the same care you would use with a traditional publisher."

COPPER NICKEL

E-mail: wayne.miller@ucdenver.edu. **Website:** copper-nickel.org. **Contact:** Wayne Miller, editor/managing editor; Brian Barker and Nicky Beer, poetry editors; Joanna Luloff, fiction and nonfiction editor; Teague Bohlen, fiction editor. Estab. 2002. *Copper Nickel*—the national literary journal housed at the University of Colorado Denver—was founded by poet Jake Adam York in 2002. When York died in 2012, the journal went on hiatus until its relaunch in 2014.

⭘ Work published in *Copper Nickel* has appeared in *Best American Poetry*, *Best American Short Stories*, and *Pushcart Prize* anthologies. Contributors to *Copper Nickel* have received numerous honors for their work, including the National Book Critics Circle Award; the Kingsley Tufts Poetry Award; the American, California, Colorado, Minnesota, and Washington State Book Awards; the Georg Büchner Prize; the T.S. Eliot and Forward Poetry Prizes; the Anisfield-Wolf Book Award; the Whiting Writers Award; the Alice Fay Di Castagnola Award; the Lambda Literary Award; and fellowships from the National Endowment for the Arts; the Guggenheim, Ingram Merrill, Witter Bynner, Soros, Rona Jaffe, Bush, and Jerome Foundations; the Bunting Institute; Cave Canem; and the American Academy in Rome. Submission period: August 15-April 15.

HOW TO CONTACT Submit 1 story or 3 pieces of flash fiction at a time through online submissions manager.

PAYMENT/TERMS Pays $30/printed page, 2 contributor's copies, and a one-year subscription.

COTTONWOOD

Room 400 Kansas Union, 1301 Jayhawk Blvd., University of Kansas, Lawrence KS 66045. **E-mail:** tlorenz@

ku.edu. **Website:** www2.ku.edu/~englishmfa/cottonwood. **Contact:** Tom Lorenz, fiction editor. Estab. 1965. "Established in the 1960s, *Cottonwood* is the nationally circulated literary review of the University of Kansas. We publish high-quality literary work in poetry, fiction, and creative nonfiction. Over the years authors such as William Stafford, Rita Dove, Connie May Fowler, Virgil Suarez, and Cris Mazza have appeared in the pages of *Cottonwood*, and recent issues have featured the work of Kim Chinquee, Quinn Dalton, Carol Lee Lorenzo, Jesse Kercheval, Joanne Lowery, and Oliver Rice. We welcome submissions from new and established writers. New issues appear once yearly, in the fall."

NEEDS Length: up to 8,500 words.

HOW TO CONTACT Submit with SASE.

PAYMENT/TERMS Pays contributor's copies.

TIPS "We're looking for depth and originality of subject matter, engaging voice and style, emotional honesty, command of the material and the structure. *Cottonwood* publishes high-quality literary fiction, but we are very open to the work of talented new writers. Write something honest and that you care about, and write it as well as you can. Don't hesitate to keep trying us. We sometimes take a piece from a writer we've rejected a number of times. We generally don't like clever, gimmicky writing. The style should be engaging but not claim all the the attention itself."

CRAB CREEK REVIEW

7315 34th Ave. NW, Seattle WA 98117. **E-mail:** crabcreekreview@gmail.com. **Website:** www.crabcreekreview.org. **Contact:** Jenifer Lawrence, editor in chief; Martha Silano, poetry editor. Estab. 1983. *Crab Creek Review* is a 100-page, perfect-bound paperback. "We are a literary journal based in the Pacific Northwest that is looking for poems, stories, and essays that pay attention to craft. We appreciate risk-taking, wild originality, and consummate craftsmanship. We publish established and emerging writers."

◗ Nominates for the Pushcart Prize. Annual *Crab Creek Review* poetry prize: $500.

NEEDS Accepts only the strongest fiction. Prefers shorter work and flash fiction. Has published fiction by Shann Ray, Sharma Shields, Daniel Homan. Length: 3,500 words.

HOW TO CONTACT Send complete ms.

PAYMENT/TERMS Pays 1 contributor's copy.

⑤ CRAB ORCHARD REVIEW

Southern Illinois University Carbondale, Department of English, Faner Hall 2380, Mail Code 4503, 1000 Faner Dr., Carbondale IL 62901. (618)453-6833. **Fax:** (618)453-8224. **E-mail:** jtribble@siu.edu. **Website:** www.craborchardreview.siu.edu. **Contact:** Allison Joseph, editor in chief and poetry editor; Carolyn Alessio, prose editor; Jon Tribble, managing editor. Estab. 1995. "We are a general-interest literary journal published twice/year. We strive to be a journal that writers admire and readers enjoy. We publish fiction, poetry, creative nonfiction, fiction translations, interviews, and reviews."

NEEDS No science fiction, romance, western, horror, gothic, or children's. Wants more novel excerpts that also stand alone. Length: up to 25 pages double-spaced.

HOW TO CONTACT Submit through online submissions manager.

PAYMENT/TERMS Pays $25/published magazine page ($100 minimum), 2 contributor's copies, and one-year subscription.

CRAZYHORSE

College of Charleston, Department of English, 66 George St., Charleston SC 29424. (843)953-4470. **E-mail:** crazyhorse@cofc.edu. **Website:** crazyhorse.cofc.edu. **Contact:** Jonathan Bohr Heinen, managing editor; Emily Rosko, poetry editor; Anthony Varallo, fiction editor; Bret Lott, nonfiction editor. Estab. 1960. "We like to print a mix of writing regardless of its form, genre, school, or politics. We're especially on the lookout for original writing that doesn't fit the categories and that engages in the work of honest communication."

◗ Reads submissions September 1-May 31.

NEEDS "We are open to all narrative styles and forms, and are always on the lookout for something we haven't seen before. Send a story we won't be able to forget." Submit 1 story through online submissions manager. Length: 2,500-8,500 words.

PAYMENT/TERMS Pays $20/page ($200 maximum) and 2 contributor's copies.

TIPS "Write to explore subjects you care about. The subject should be one in which something is at stake. Before sending, ask, 'What's reckoned with that's important for other people to read?'"

CREAM CITY REVIEW

University of Wisconsin-Milwaukee, Department of English, P.O. Box 413, Milwaukee WI 53201. E-

mail: info@creamcityreview.org. **Website:** uwm.edu/creamcityreview. **Contact:** Loretta McCormick, editor in chief; Mollie Boutell, managing editor. Estab. 1975. *Cream City Review* publishes "memorable and energetic fiction, poetry, and creative nonfiction. Features reviews of contemporary literature and criticism as well as author interviews and artwork. We are interested in camera-ready art depicting themes appropriate to each issue."

○ Reading periods: August 1-November 1 for fall/winter issue; January 1-April 1 for spring/summer issue.

NEEDS "We would like to see more quality fiction. No horror, formulaic, racist, sexist, pornographic, homophobic, science fiction, romance." Length: up to 20 pages.

HOW TO CONTACT Submit ms via online submissions manager.

PAYMENT/TERMS Pays one-year subscription beginning with the issue in which the author's work appears.

CRUCIBLE

Barton College, P.O. Box 5000, Wilson NC 27893. **E-mail:** crucible@barton.edu. **Website:** www.barton.edu/crucible. Estab. 1964. *Crucible*, published annually in the fall, publishes poetry and fiction as part of its Poetry and Fiction Contest run each year. Deadline for submissions is May 1.

○ *Crucible* is under 100 pages, digest-sized, professionally printed on high-quality paper, with matte card cover. Press run is 500.

NEEDS Length: up to 8,000 words.

HOW TO CONTACT Submit ms by e-mail. Do not include name on ms. Include separate bio.

PAYMENT/TERMS Pays $150 for first prize, $100 for second prize, contributor's copies.

CUMBERLAND RIVER REVIEW

Trevecca Nazarene University, Department of English, 333 Murfreesboro Rd., Nashville TN 37210. **E-mail:** crr@trevecca.edu. **Website:** crr.trevecca.edu. **Contact:** Graham Hillard, editor; Christian Keen, managing editor. *The Cumberland River Review* is a quarterly online publication of new poetry, fiction, essays, and art. The journal is produced by the department of English at Trevecca Nazarene University and welcomes submissions from both national and international writers and artists.

○ Reading period: September through April.

NEEDS Length: up to 5,000 words.

HOW TO CONTACT Submit 1 story through online submissions manager or mail (include SASE).

CURA: A LITERARY MAGAZINE OF ART AND ACTION

441 E. Fordham Rd., English Department, Dealy 541W, Bronx NY 10548. **E-mail:** curamag@fordham.edu. **Website:** www.curamag.com. **Contact:** Sarah Gambito, editor. Estab. 2011. *CURA: A Literary Magazine of Art and Action* is a multimedia initiative based at Fordham University committed to integrating the arts and social justice. Featuring creative writing, visual art, new media, and video in response to current news, we seek to enable an artistic process that is rigorously engaged with the world at the present moment. *CURA* is taken from the Ignatian educational principle of "cura personalis," care for the whole person. On its own, the word *cura* is defined as guardianship, solicitude, and significantly, written work.

○ Reading period: October 15-March 15.

NEEDS Length: up to 6,000 words.

HOW TO CONTACT Submit complete ms through online submissions manager.

PAYMENT/TERMS Pays 1 contributor's copy.

CURRENT ACCOUNTS

Current Accounts, Apt. 2D, Bradshaw Hall, Hardcastle Gardens, Bolton BL2 4NZ, U.K.. **E-mail:** bswscribe@gmail.com. **E-mail:** fjameshartnell@aol.com. **Website:** sites.google.com/site/bankstreetwriters. **Contact:** Rod Riesco. Estab. 1994. *Current Accounts*, an online publication, prints poetry, drama, fiction, and nonfiction by members of Bank Street Writers, and other contributors.

○ Receives about 200 poems and stories/plays per year; accepts about 5%.

NEEDS Length: up to 1,500 words, and preferably under 1,000 words for short stories. Plays should be 1 act and no longer than 4 minutes read aloud.

HOW TO CONTACT E-mail submissions only. "Stories need to be well-constructed with good believable characters, an awareness of 'show, don't tell' dialogue that is real, a plot that moves along, and an ending that is neither obvious nor ridiculously farfetched. Too many stories are overwritten and leave nothing unexplained for the reader to work out and enjoy. All genres (within the word length) are acceptable. We don't get enough plays."

PAYMENT/TERMS Pays 1 contributor's copy.

TIPS Bank Street Writers meets once/month and offers workshops, guest speakers, and other activities. E-mail for details."We like originality of ideas, images, and use of language. No inspirational or religious verse unless it's also good in poetic terms."

CUTTHROAT, A JOURNAL OF THE ARTS

P.O. Box 2414, Durango CO 81302. (970)903-7914. **E-mail:** cutthroatmag@gmail.com. **Website:** www.cutthroatmag.com. **Contact:** Pamela Uschuk, editor in chief; Beth Alvarado, fiction editor; William Luvaas, online fiction editor; William Pitt Root, poetry editor. Estab. 2005. Sponsors the Rick DeMarinis Short Fiction Prize ($1,250 first prize). See separate listing and website for more information. "We publish only high-quality fiction, creative nonfiction, and poetry. We are looking for the cutting edge, the endangered word, fiction with wit, heart, soul, and meaning." *CUTTHROAT* is a literary magazine/journal and "one separate online edition of poetry, translations, short fiction, essays, and book reviews yearly."

◑ Member CLMP.

NEEDS Send review copies to Pamela Uschuk. List of upcoming themes available on website. Receives 100+ mss/month. Accepts 6 mss/issue; 10-12 mss/year. Does not read October 1-March 1 and June 1-July 15. **Publishes 5-8 new writers/year.** Published Michael Schiavone, Rusty Harris, Timothy Rien, Summer Wood, Peter Christopher, Jamey Genna, Doug Frelke, Sally Bellerose, and Marc Levy. Publishes short shorts and book reviews. Does not want romance, horror, historical, fantasy, religious, teen, or juvenile. Length: 500-5,000 words.

HOW TO CONTACT Submit complete ms through online submissions manager (preferred) or mail (include SASE).

PAYMENT/TERMS Pays contributor copies. Additional copies: $10.

TIPS "Read our magazine, and see what types of work we've published. The piece must have heart and soul, excellence in craft. "

◐ THE DALHOUSIE REVIEW

Dalhousie University, Halifax NS B3H 4R2, Canada. **E-mail:** dalhousie.review@dal.ca. **Website:** dalhousiereview.dal.ca. **Contact:** Lynne Evans, production manager. Estab. 1921. *Dalhousie Review*, published 3 times/year, is a journal of criticism publishing poetry and fiction. Considers works from both new and established writers.

◑ *Dalhousie Review* is 144 pages, digest-sized. Press run is 500.

NEEDS Length: up to 8,000 words.

HOW TO CONTACT Submit by e-mail. Writers are encouraged "to follow whatever canons of usage might govern the particular work in question and to be inventive with language, ideas, and form."

PAYMENT/TERMS Pays 2 contributor's copies.

DARGONZINE

E-mail: dargon@dargonzine.org. **Website:** dargonzine.org. **Contact:** Jon Evans, editor. "*DargonZine* is an e-zine that prints original fantasy fiction by aspiring fantasy writers. The Dargon Project is a shared world anthology whose goal is to provide a way for aspiring fantasy writers to meet and improve their writing skills through mutual contact and collaboration as well as through contact with a live readership via the Internet. Our goal is to write fantasy fiction that is mature, emotionally compelling, and professional. Membership in the Dargon Project is a requirement for publication."

◑ Publishes 1-3 new writers/year.

NEEDS Must be a member of the Dargon Project to submit fiction for publication. See website for details and guidelines.

PAYMENT/TERMS "As a strictly noncommercial magazine, our writers' only compensation is their growth and membership in a lively writing community."

TIPS "The Readers and Writers FAQs on our website provide much more detailed information about our mission, writing philosophy, and the value of writing for *DargonZine*."

⑤ THE DARK

Prime Books, P.O. Box 1152, Germantown MD 20875. **E-mail:** thedarkmagazine@gmail.com. **Website:** www.thedarkmagazine.com. **Contact:** Silvia Moreno-Garcia and Sean Wallace, editors. Estab. 2013.

◑ Stories featured in *The Dark* have appeared in *The Best Horror of the Year*, *The Year's Best Dark Fantasy & Horror: 2016*, and *The Year's Best Weird Fiction*.

NEEDS "Don't be afraid to experiment or to deviate from the ordinary; be different—try us with fiction that may fall out of 'regular' categories. However, it is also important to understand that despite the name, *The Dark* is not a market for graphic, violent horror." Length: 2,000-6,000 words.

HOW TO CONTACT Send complete ms by e-mail attached in Microsoft Word DOC only. No multiple submissions.

PAYMENT/TERMS Pays 3¢/word.

TIPS "All fiction must have a dark, surreal, fantastical bend to it. It should be out of the ordinary and/or experimental. Can also be contemporary."

THE DEADLY QUILL

E-mail: lorne@deadlyquill.com. **E-mail:** submissions@deadlyquill.com. **Website:** deadlyquill.com. **Contact:** Lorne McMillan. Estab. 2015. "We are looking to give an outlet for writers of short fiction in the tradition of *The Twilight Zone*, Alfred Hitchcock, and *The Outer Limits*. Make the story grab you and not let go until the very end."

NEEDS The stories should take the reader by the throat and not let go. Does not want anything that doesn't grab you. No violence for the sake of violence. Length: 2,000-5,000 words.

PAYMENT/TERMS Pays 1 e-pub contributor's copy.

THE DEAD MULE SCHOOL OF SOUTHERN LITERATURE

NC 27889. **E-mail:** deadmule@gmail.com. **E-mail:** submit.mule@gmail.com. **Website:** www.deadmule.com. **Contact:** Valerie MacEwan, publisher and editor. Estab. 1996. The *Mule* sponsors flash fiction contests with no entry fees. See the site for specifics. Chapbooks published by invitation, also short fiction compilations. "No good southern fiction is complete without a dead mule." *The Dead Mule* is one of the oldest, if not *the* oldest, continuously published online literary journals alive today. Publisher and editor Valerie MacEwan welcomes submissions. *The Dead Mule School of Southern Literature* wants flash fiction, visual poetry, essays, and creative nonfiction. Twenty Years Online, 1996-2016. Celebrate With a Dead Mule. 2017 means 21 years online—that's a century in cyber-time.

⊙ "*The Dead Mule School of Southern Literature* Institutional Alumni Association recruits year round. We love reading what you wrote."

NEEDS "We welcome the ingenue and the established writer. It's mostly about you entertaining us and capturing our interest. Everyone is South of Somewhere; go ahead, check us out." No soft porn, no erotica, no ethnic slurs and all that the term implies. The Dead Mule is read in high schools, writers are encouraged to consider the audience when they submit. 2,500 word limit, but we're flexible. We love short fiction, 750 words or less.

HOW TO CONTACT All submissions must be accompanied by a "southern legitimacy statement," details of which can be seen within each page on *The Dead Mule* and within the submishmash entrypage.

PAYMENT/TERMS Pays sporadically "whenever CafePress/*Dead Mule* sales reach an agreeable amount."

TIPS "Read the site to get a feel for what we're looking to publish. Read the guidelines. We look forward to hearing from you. We are nothing if not for our writers. *The Dead Mule* strives to deliver quality writing in every issue. It is in this way that we pay tribute to our authors. Send us something original."

DENVER QUARTERLY

University of Denver, 2000 E. Asbury, Denver CO 80208. (303) 871-2892. **E-mail:** denverquarterly@gmail.com. **Website:** www.du.edu/denverquarterly. **Contact:** Laird Hunt, editor. Estab. 1965. Publishes fiction, articles, and poetry for a generally well-educated audience primarily interested in literature and the literary experience. Audience reads *DQ* to find something a little different from a strictly academic quarterly or a creative writing outlet.

⊙ *Denver Quarterly* received an Honorable Mention for Content from the American Literary Magazine Awards, and selections have been anthologized in the *Pushcart Prize* anthologies. Reads September 15-May 15. Mss submitted between May 15 and September 15 will regretfully be returned unread.

NEEDS "We are interested in experimental fiction (minimalism, magic realism, etc.) as well as realistic fiction and writing about fiction. No sentimental, science fiction, romance, or spy thrillers." Length: up to 15 pages.

HOW TO CONTACT Submit by mail or online submissions manager.

PAYMENT/TERMS Pays 2 contributor's copies.

◐♡ DESCANT: FORT WORTH'S JOURNAL OF POETRY AND FICTION

TCU Department of English, Box 297270, Ft. Worth TX 76129. **E-mail:** descant@tcu.edu. **Website:** www.descant.tcu.edu. **Contact:** Matthew Pitt, editor in chief and fiction editor; Alex Lemon, poetry editor. Estab. 1956. "*descant* seeks high-quality poems and stories in both traditional and innovative form."

⊙ Member CLMP. Magazine: 6x9; 120-150 pages; acid-free paper; paper cover. Reading period: September 1-April 1. Offers 4 annual cash awards for work already accepted for publication in the journal: The $500 Frank O'Connor

Award for the best story in an issue, the $250 Gary Wilson Award for an outstanding story in an issue, the $500 Betsy Colquitt Award for the best poem in an issue, and the $250 Baskerville Publishers Award for outstanding poem in an issue. Several stories first published by *descant* have appeared in *Best American Short Stories*.

NEEDS Receives 20-30 unsolicited mss/month. Accepts 3-5 mss/year. Publishes ms 1 year after acceptance. Publishes 50% new writers/year. Recently published work by William Harrison, Annette Sanford, Miller Williams, Patricia Chao, Vonesca Stroud, and Walt McDonald. No horror, romance, fantasy, erotica. Length: up to 5,000 words.

HOW TO CONTACT Send complete ms through online submissions manager or mail.

PAYMENT/TERMS Pays 2 contributor's copies; additional copies $6.

TIPS "We look for character and quality of prose. Send your best short work."

DIAGRAM

Department of English, University of Arizona, P.O. Box 210067, Tucson AZ 85721-0067. **E-mail:** editor@thediagram.com. **Website:** www.thediagram.com. **Contact:** Ander Monson, editor; T. Fleischmann and Nicole Walker, nonfiction editors; Sarah Blackman and Katie Jean Shinkle, fiction editors; Heidi Gotz and E.A. Ramey, poetry editors. Estab. 2000. "*DIAGRAM* is an electronic journal of text and art, found and created. We're interested in representations, naming, indicating, schematics, labeling and taxonomy of things; in poems that masquerade as stories; in stories that disguise themselves as indices or obituaries. We specialize in work that pushes the boundaries of traditional genre or work that is in some way schematic. We do publish traditional fiction and poetry, too, but hybrid forms (short stories, prose poems, indexes, tables of contents, etc.) are particularly welcome! We also publish diagrams and schematics (original and found)."

○ Publishes 6 new writers/year. Bimonthly. Member CLMP. "We cosponsor a yearly chapbook contest for prose, poetry, or hybrid work with New Michigan Press with a Spring deadline. Guidelines on website."

NEEDS Receives 100 unsolicited mss/month. Accepts 2-3 mss/issue; 15 mss/year. "We don't publish genre fiction unless it's exceptional and transcends the genre boundaries." Length: open.

HOW TO CONTACT Send complete ms. Accepts submissions by online submissions manager; no e-mail. If sending by snail mail, send SASE for return of the ms or send disposable copy of the ms and #10 SASE for reply only.

TIPS "Submit interesting text, images, sound, and new media. We value the insides of things, vivisection, urgency, risk, elegance, flamboyance, work that moves us, language that does something new, or does something old—well. We like iteration and reiteration. Ruins and ghosts. Mechanical, moving parts, balloons, and frenzy. We want art and writing that demonstrates interaction; the processes of things; how functions are accomplished; how things become or expire, move or stand. We'll consider anything."

THE DOS PASSOS REVIEW

Briery Creek Press, Longwood University, Department of English and Modern Languages, 201 High St., Farmville VA 23909. **E-mail:** brierycreek@gmail.com. **E-mail:** dospassosreview@gmail.com. **Website:** brierycreekpress.wordpress.com/the-dos-passos-review. **Contact:** Managing Editor. "We are looking for writing that demonstrates characteristics found in the work of John Dos Passos, such as an intense and original exploration of specifically American themes, an innovative quality, and a range of literary forms, especially in the genres of fiction and creative nonfiction. We are not interested in genre fiction or prose that is experiment for the sake of experiment. We are also not interested in nonfiction that is scholarly or critical in nature. Send us your best unpublished literary prose or poetry."

○ Reading periods: April 1-July 31 for Fall issue; February 1-May 31 for Spring issue.

NEEDS No genre fiction. Length: up to 3,000 words for short stories; up to 1,000 for flash fiction.

HOW TO CONTACT Submit 1 short story or 3 flash fiction pieces by e-mail as attachment. Include cover letter and brief bio.

PAYMENT/TERMS Pays 2 contributor's copies.

DOWN IN THE DIRT

E-mail: dirt@scars.tv. **Website:** www.scars.tv/dirt. **Contact:** Janet Kuypers, editor. Estab. 2000. *Down in the Dirt*, published every other month online and in print issues sold via Amazon.com throughout the U.S., U.K., and continental Europe, prints "good work that makes you think, that makes you feel like you've lived through a scene instead of merely read it." Also considers poems. *Down in the Dirt* is published "electronically as well as in print, either as printed magazines sold through our printer over the Internet, on the Web, or sold through our printer. And for prose, because we get so much of it, all we can suggest is, the shorter the better."

Has published work by Mel Waldman, Ken Dean, Jon Brunette, John Ragusa, and Liam Spencer.

NEEDS No religious, rhyming, or family-oriented material. Average length: 1,000 words. "Contact us if you are interested in submitting very long stories or parts of a novel (if accepted, it would appear in parts in multiple issues)."

HOW TO CONTACT Query editor with e-mail submission. "99.5% of all submissions are via e-mail only, so if you do not have electronic access, there is a strong chance you will not be considered. We recommend you e-mail submissions to us, either as an attachment (TXT, RTF, DOC, or DOCX files, but not PDF) or by placing it directly in the e-mail letter. For samples of what we've printed in the past, visit our website."

DOWNSTATE STORY

1825 Maple Ridge, Peoria IL 61614. (309)688-1409. **E-mail:** ehopkins7@prodigy.net. **Website:** www.downstatestory.com; www.wiu.edu/users/mfgeh/dss. Estab. 1992.

NEEDS Does not want porn. Length: 300-2,000 words.

HOW TO CONTACT Submit complete ms with cover letter and SASE via postal mail.

TIPS "We want more political fiction. We also publish short shorts and literary essays."

DRAMATICS MAGAZINE

Educational Theatre Association, 2343 Auburn Ave., Cincinnati OH 45219. (513)421-3900. **E-mail:** gbossler@schooltheatre.org. **Website:** schooltheatre.org. **Contact:** Gregory Bossler, editor in chief. Estab. 1929. *Dramatics* is for students (mainly high school age) and teachers of theater. The magazine wants student readers to grow as theater artists and become a more discerning and appreciative audience. Material is directed to both theater students and their teachers, with strong student slant. Tries to portray the theater community in all its diversity.

NEEDS Young adults: drama (one-act and full-length plays). "We prefer unpublished scripts that have been produced at least once." Does not want to see plays that show no understanding of the conventions of the theater. No plays for children, no Christmas or didactic "message" plays. Length: 10 minutes to full length.

HOW TO CONTACT Submit complete ms. Buys 5-9 plays/year. Emerging playwrights have better chances with résumé of credits.

PAYMENT/TERMS Pays $100-500 for plays.

TIPS "Obtain our writer's guidelines and look at recent back issues. The best way to break in is to know our audience—drama students, teachers, and others interested in theater—and write for them. Writers who have some practical experience in theater, especially in technical areas, have an advantage, but we'll work with anybody who has a good idea. Some freelancers have become regular contributors."

DRUNKEN BOAT

119 Main St., Chester CT 06412. **E-mail:** editor@drunkenboat.com. **Website:** www.drunkenboat.com. Estab. 1999. *Drunken Boat*, published 2 times/year online, is a multimedia publication reaching an international audience with an extremely broad aesthetic. "*Drunken Boat* is committed to actively seeking out and promoting the work of marginalized and underrepresented artists, including especially people of color, women, queer, differently abled, and gender nonconforming artists." To cover operational costs, charges a $3 fee for each submission.

NEEDS "Please submit 1 story or piece of longer work. We welcome the well-written in every style, from microfiction to hypertext to pieces of novels, original and in translation (with the writer's permission), American and from around the globe."

TIPS "Submissions should be submitted in Word and RTF format only. (This does not apply to audio, visual, and Web work.) Accepts chapbooks. See our submissions manager system."

DUCTS

P.O. Box 3203, Grand Central Station, New York NY 10163. **E-mail:** vents@ducts.org. **Website:** www.ducts.org. **Contact:** Mary Cool, editor in chief; Tim Tomlinson, fiction editor; Lisa Kirchner, memoir editor; Amy Lemmon, poetry editor; Jacqueline Bishop, art editor. Estab. 1999. *Ducts* is a semiannual webzine of personal stories, fiction, essays, memoirs, poetry, humor, profiles, reviews, and art. "*Ducts* was founded in 1999 with the intent of giving emerging writers a venue to regularly publish their compelling, personal stories. The site has been expanded to include art and creative works of all genres. We believe that these genres must and do overlap. *Ducts* publishes the best, most compelling stories, and we hope to attract readers who are drawn to work that rises above."

NEEDS No novel excerpts.

HOW TO CONTACT Submit by e-mail to julie@ducts.org.

PAYMENT/TERMS Pays $20.

TIPS "We prefer writing that tells a compelling story with a strong narrative drive."

ECLECTICA MAGAZINE

E-mail: editors@eclectica.org. **Website:** www.eclectica.org. **Contact:** Tom Dooley, managing editor. Estab. 1996. "A sterling-quality literary magazine on the World Wide Web. Not bound by formula or genre, harnessing technology to further the reading experience and dynamic, and interesting in content. *Eclectica* is a quarterly online journal devoted to showcasing the best writing on the Web, regardless of genre. 'Literary' and 'genre' work appear side-by-side in each issue, along with pieces that blur the distinctions between such categories. Pushcart Prize, National Poetry Series, and Pulitzer Prize winners, as well as Nebula Award nominees, have shared issues with previously unpublished authors."

○ Submission deadlines: December 1 for January/February issue, March 1 for April/May issue, June 1 for July/August issue, September 1 for October/November issue.

NEEDS Needs "high-quality work in any genre." Accepts short stories and novellas. Length: up to 20,000 words for short fiction; longer novella-length pieces accepted.

HOW TO CONTACT Submit via online submissions manager.

TIPS "We pride ourselves on giving everyone (high schoolers, convicts, movie executives, etc.) an equal shot at publication, based solely on the quality of their work. Because we like eclecticism, we tend to favor the varied perspectives that often characterize the work of international authors, people of color, women, alternative lifestylists—but others who don't fit into these categories often surprise us."

ECOTONE, REIMAGINING PLACE

University of North Carolina Wilmington, Department of Creative Writing, 601 S. College Rd., Wilmington NC 28403. **E-mail:** info@ecotonejournal.com. **Website:** www.ecotonemagazine.org. **Contact:** David Gessner, editor in chief. Estab. 2005. "*Ecotone, Reimagining Place* is a literary journal of place seeking to publish creative work that illuminates the edges between science and literature, the urban and rural, and the personal and biological." Semiannual.

○ Literary magazine/journal: 6x9. Reading period: August 15-October 1, December 15-February 1. "*Ecotone* charges a small fee for electronic submissions. If you are unable to pay this fee, please submit by postal mail."

NEEDS Has published Kevin Brockmeier, Michael Branch, Brock Clarke, Daniel Orozco, Steve Almond, and Pattiann Rogers. Does not want genre (fantasy, horror, science fiction, etc.) or young adult fiction. Length: up to 30 pages. "We are now considering shorter prose works (under 2,500 words) as well."

HOW TO CONTACT Submit via online submissions manager or postal mail with SASE. Include brief cover letter, listing both the title of the piece and the word count. Do not include identifying information on or within the ms itself. Also publishes literary essays, poetry.

⑤ ELLIPSIS

Westminster College, 1840 S. 1300 E., Salt Lake City UT 84105. (801)832-2321. **E-mail:** ellipsis@westminstercollege.edu. **Website:** ellipsis.westminstercollege.edu. Estab. 1965. *Ellipsis*, published annually in April, needs good literary poetry, fiction, essays, plays, and visual art.

○ Reads submissions August 1-November 1. Staff changes each year; check website for an updated list of editors. *Ellipsis* is 120 pages, digest-sized, perfect-bound, with color cover. Accepts about 5% of submissions received. Press run is 2,000; most distributed free through college.

NEEDS Length: up to 6,000 words.

HOW TO CONTACT Submit complete ms via online submissions manager. Include cover letter.

PAYMENT/TERMS Pays $50 and 2 contributor's copies.

EMRYS JOURNAL

P.O. Box 8813, Greenville SC 29604. (864)409-3679. **E-mail:** emrys.info@gmail.com. **Website:** www.emrys.org. **Contact:** Lindsey DeLoach Jones, editor. Estab. 1984. *Emrys Journal* publishes fiction, poetry, and creative nonfiction. "We are pleased to have published works of the highest quality from both emerging and established writers."

⬭ Reading period: August 1-November 1.

NEEDS Length: up to 5,000 words.

HOW TO CONTACT Submit complete ms via online submissions manager.

TIPS "Before submitting, please familiarize yourself with our magazine by reading past contributions to the *Emrys Journal*."

EPOCH

251 Goldwin Smith Hall, Cornell University, Ithaca NY 14853-3201. (607)255-3385. **Website:** www.epoch. cornell.edu. **Contact:** Michael Koch, editor; Heidi E. Marschner, managing editor. Estab. 1947. Looking for well-written literary fiction, poetry, personal essays. Newcomers welcome. Open to mainstream and avant-garde writing.

⬭ Magazine: 6x9; 128 pages; good quality paper; good cover stock. Receives 500 unsolicited mss/month. Accepts 15-20 mss/issue. Reads unsolicited submissions September 15-April 15. Publishes 3-4 new writers/year. Has published work by Antonya Nelson, Doris Betts, Heidi Jon Schmidt.

NEEDS No genre fiction. Would like to see more Southern fiction (Southern U.S.).

HOW TO CONTACT Send complete ms. Considers fiction in all forms, short short to novella length.

PAYMENT/TERMS Pay varies; pays up to $150/unsolicited piece.

TIPS "Tell your story, speak your poem, straight from the heart. We are attracted to language and to good writing, but we are most interested in what the good writing leads us to, or where."

EVANSVILLE REVIEW

University of Evansville Creative Writing Department, 1800 Lincoln Ave., Evansville IN 47722. (812)488-1042. **E-mail:** evansvillereview@evansville.edu. **Website:** https://theevansvillereview.submittable.com/submit. **Contact:** Amanda Alexander, editor in chief; Sari Baum, editor in chief; Brittney Kaleri, nonfiction editor; William Capella, fiction editor; Beth Brunmeier, poetry editor. Estab. 1990. "*The Evansville Review* is an annual literary journal published at the University of Evansville. Our award-

winning journal includes poetry, fiction, nonfiction, plays, and interviews by a wide range of authors, from emerging writers to Nobel Prize recipients. Past issues have included work by Joyce Carol Oates, Arthur Miller, John Updike, Joseph Brodsky, Elia Kazan, Edward Albee, Willis Barnstone, Shirley Ann Grau, and X.J. Kennedy."

⬭ Reading period: September 1-October 31.

NEEDS "We are open to a wide range of styles, though our aim is always the highest literary quality. Hit us with your best language, your most compelling characters. Make us remember your story." Does not want erotica, fantasy, experimental, or children's fiction. Submit up to 3 pieces of flash fiction (1,000 words each) or 1 story (up to 9,000 words).

HOW TO CONTACT Submit online at theevansvillereview.submittable.com/submit.

PAYMENT/TERMS Pays contributor's copies.

EVENING STREET REVIEW

Evening Street Press, Inc., 2701 Corabel Ln., #27, Sacramento CA 95821. **E-mail:** editor@eveningstreetpress.com. **Website:** www.eveningstreetpress.com. **Contact:** Barbara Bergmann, managing editor. Estab. 2007. "Intended for a general audience, *Evening Street Press* is centered on Elizabeth Cady Stanton's 1848 revision of the Declaration of Independence: 'that all men and women are created equal,' with equal rights to 'life, liberty, and the pursuit of happiness.' It focuses on the realities of experience, personal and historical, from the most gritty to the most dreamlike, including awareness of the personal and social forces that block or develop the possibilities of this new culture."

HOW TO CONTACT Send complete ms. E-mail submissions preferred.

PAYMENT/TERMS Pays 1 contributor's copy.

TIPS "Does not want to see male chauvinism. Mss are read year round. See website for chapbook and book competitions."

⬤⬭ FAILBETTER.COM

2022 Grove Ave., Richmond VA 23221. **E-mail:** submissions@failbetter.com. **Website:** www.failbetter. com. **Contact:** Thom Didato, editor. Estab. 2000. "We are a quarterly online magazine published in the spirit of a traditional literary journal—dedicated to publishing quality fiction, poetry, and artwork. While the Web plays host to hundreds, if not thousands, of genre-related sites (many of which have merit), we are not one of them."

○ Member CLMP.

NEEDS "If you're sending a short story or novel excerpt, send only 1 at a time. Wait to hear from us before sending another."

HOW TO CONTACT Submit work by pasting it into the body of an e-mail. Must put "Submission" in e-mail's subject line. Do not send attachments. Also accepts postal mail submissions.

TIPS "Read an issue. Read our guidelines! We place a high degree of importance on originality, believing that even in this age of trends it is still possible. We are not looking for what is current or momentary. We are not concerned with length: One good sentence may find a home here, as the bulk of mediocrity will not. Most importantly, know that what you are saying could only come from you. When you are sure of this, please feel free to submit."

FAULTLINE

University of California at Irvine, Department of English, 435 Humanities Instructional Building, Irvine CA 92697. (949)824-1573. **E-mail:** faultline@uci.edu. **Website:** faultline.sites.uci.edu. **Contact:** Stefan Karlsson, poetry editor; Kathleen Mackay, fiction editor. Estab. 1992.

○ Reading period is October 15-February 15. Submissions sent at any other time will not be read. Editors change in September of each year.

NEEDS Length: up to 20 pages.

HOW TO CONTACT Submit complete ms via online submissions manager or mail. "While simultaneous submissions are accepted, multiple submissions are not accepted. Please restrict your submissions to 1 story at a time, regardless of length."

PAYMENT/TERMS Pays contributor copies.

TIPS "Our commitment is to publish the best work possible from well-known and emerging authors with vivid and varied voices."

FEMINIST STUDIES

0103 Taliaferro Hall, University of Maryland, College Park MD 20742. (301)405-7415. **Fax:** (301)405-8395. **E-mail:** info@feministstudies.org; atambe@umd.edu. **E-mail:** kmantilla@feministstudies.org. **Website:** www.feministstudies.org. **Contact:** Ashwini Tambe, editorial director; Karla Mantilla, managing editor. Estab. 1974. Over the years, *Feminist Studies* has been a reliable source of significant writings on issues that are important to all classes and races of women. Those familiar with the literature on women's studies are well aware of the importance and vitality of the journal and the frequency with which articles first published in *Feminist Studies* are cited and/or reprinted elsewhere. Indeed, no less than 4 anthologies have been created from articles originally published in *Feminist Studies*: *Clio's Consciousness Raised: New Perspectives on the History of Women*; *Sex and Class in Women's History*; *U.S. Women in Struggle: A Feminist Studies Anthology*; and *Lesbian Subjects: A Feminist Studies Reader*."

○ "*Feminist Studies* is committed to publishing an interdisciplinary body of feminist knowledge that sees intersections of gender with racial identity, sexual orientation, economic means, geographical location, and physical ability as the touchstone for our politics and our intellectual analysis. Whether work is drawn from the complex past or the shifting present, the articles and essays that appear in *Feminist Studies* address social and political issues that intimately and significantly affect women and men in the United States and around the world."

NEEDS "We are interested in work that addresses questions of interest to the *Feminist Studies* audience, particularly work that pushes past the boundaries of what has been done before." Length: up to 15 pages or 5,500 words.

HOW TO CONTACT Submit May 1-December 1. Submit complete ms by mail or e-mail (creative@feministstudies.org). Has published Meena Alexander, Nicole Brossard, Jayne Cortez, Toi Derricotte, Diane Glancy, Marilyn Hacker, Lyn Hejinian, June Jordan, Audre Lorde, Cherrie Moraga, Sharon Olds, Grace Paley, Ruth Stone, and Mitsuye Yamada.

FICTION

Department of English, City College of New York, Convent Ave. & 138th St., New York NY 10031. **E-mail:** fictionmageditors@gmail.com. **Website:** www.fictioninc.com. **Contact:** Mark J. Mirsky, editor. Estab. 1972. "As the name implies, we publish only fiction; we are looking for the best new writing available, leaning toward the unconventional. *Fiction* has traditionally attempted to make accessible the inaccessible, to bring the experimental to a broader audience." Reading period for unsolicited mss is September 15-June 15.

⚪ Stories first published in *Fiction* have been selected for the *Pushcart Prize: Best of the Small Presses*, *O. Henry Prize Stories*, and *Best American Short Stories*.

NEEDS No romance, science fiction, etc. Length: reads any length, but encourages lengths under 5,000 words.

HOW TO CONTACT Submit complete ms via mail or online submissions manager.

TIPS "The guiding principle of *Fiction* has always been to go to terra incognita in the writing of the imagination and to ask that modern fiction set itself serious questions, if often in absurd and comedic voices, interrogating the nature of the real and the fantastic. It represents no particular school of fiction, except the innovative. Its pages have often been a harbor for writers at odds with each other. As a result of its willingness to publish the difficult, experimental, and unusual, while not excluding the well known, *Fiction* has a unique reputation in the U.S. and abroad as a journal of future directions."

FICTION INTERNATIONAL

San Diego State University, San Diego State University, Department of English and Comp. Lit, 5500 Campanile Dr., San Diego CA 92182-6020. **E-mail:** hjaffe@mail.sdsu.edu. **E-mail:** https://fictioninternational.submittable.com/submit. **Website:** fictioninternational.sdsu.edu. **Contact:** Harold Jaffe, editor. Estab. 1973. "*Fiction International* is the only literary journal in the United States emphasizing formal innovation and social activism. Each issue revolves around a theme and features a wide variety of fiction, nonfiction, indeterminate prose, and visuals by leading writers and artists from around the world."

⚪ Has published works by William Burroughs, Clarice Lispector (Brazil), Robert Coover, Edmund White, Joyce Carol Oates, Walter Abish, and Kathy Acker.

NEEDS Each issue is themed; see website for details. No genre fiction. Length: up to 5,500 words.

HOW TO CONTACT Submit complete ms via online submissions manager.

FICTION TERRIFICA

17 Ninth Ave. NW, Suite C, Glen Burnie MD 21061. 4436941695. **E-mail:** dschaff@fictionterrifica.com; dwest@fictionterrifica.com. **E-mail:** submissions@fictionterrifica.com. **Website:** www.fictionterrifica.com. **Contact:** Destiny West, managing editor. Estab. 2014. "*Fiction Terrifica* is a website/bimonthly e-zine dedicated to helping small press writers and previously unpublished writers publish their mss. We are a royalty-based publishing site. We promote writers on Facebook and Twitter, along with any works they may have currently for sale. Our only requirement for acceptance is that the work be horror, dark fiction, science fiction, or fantasy related. We host links to our authors works available at other sites. We also offer Kindle publishing on a royalty basis."

NEEDS Length: 1,500-10,000 words.

HOW TO CONTACT Query before submitting.

TIPS "The best advice I can give is to write a good story, article, or personal experience publishing piece and submit it. We are always looking to promote new and upcoming writers. Have your piece polished and ready for publication."

⚪⚫ THE FIDDLEHEAD

University of New Brunswick, Campus House, 11 Garland Court, Box 4400, Fredericton NB E3B 5A3, Canada. (506)453-3501. **Fax:** (506)453-5069. **E-mail:** fiddlehd@unb.ca. **Website:** www.thefiddlehead.ca. **Contact:** Kathryn Taglia, managing editor; Ross Leckie, editor; Mark Anthony Jarman and Gerard Beirne, fiction editors; Phillip Crymble, Ian LeTourneau, and Rebecca Salazar, poetry editors; Sabine Campbell and Ross Leckie, reviews editors. Estab. 1945. "Canada's longest living literary journal, *The Fiddlehead* is published 4 times/year at the University of New Brunswick, with the generous assistance of the University of New Brunswick, the Canada Council for the Arts, and the Province of New Brunswick. It is experienced, wise enough to recognize excellence, and always looking for freshness and surprise. *The Fiddlehead* publishes short stories, poems, book reviews, and a small number of personal essays. Our full-color covers have become collectors' items and feature work by New Brunswick artists and from New Brunswick museums and art galleries. The journal is open to good writing in English from all over the world, looking always for freshness and surprise. Our editors are always happy to see new unsolicited works in fiction and poetry. Work is read on an ongoing basis; the acceptance rate is around 1-2%. Apart from our annual contest, we have no deadlines for submissions."

⚪ "No criteria for publication except quality. For a general audience, including many poets and writers." Has published work by George

Elliott Clarke, Kayla Czaga, Daniel Woodrell, and Clea Young. *The Fiddlehead* also sponsors an annual writing contest.

NEEDS Receives 100-150 unsolicited mss/month. Accepts 4-5 mss/issue; 20-40 mss/year. Agented fiction: small percentage. Publishes high percentage of new writers/year. Does not want fiction aimed at children. Length: up to 6,000 words. Rarely publishes flash fiction.

HOW TO CONTACT Send SASE and *Canadian* stamps or IRCs for return of mss. No e-mail or faxed submissions. Simultaneous submissions only if stated on cover letter; must contact immediately if accepted elsewhere.

PAYMENT/TERMS Pays up to $40 (Canadian)/published page and 2 contributor's copies.

TIPS "If you are serious about submitting to *The Fiddlehead*, you should subscribe or read several issues to get a sense of the journal. Contact us if you would like to order sample back issues."

⊘ FILLING STATION

P.O. Box 22135, Bankers Hall RPO, Calgary AB T2P 4J5, Canada. **E-mail:** mgmt@fillingstation.ca. **Website:** www.fillingstation.ca. **Contact:** Paul Zits, managing editor. Estab. 1993. *filling Station*, published 3 times/year, prints contemporary poetry, fiction, visual art, interviews, reviews, and articles. "We are looking for all forms of contemporary writing, but especially that which is innovative and/or experimental."

○ *filling Station* is 64 pages, 8.5x11, perfect-bound, with card cover, includes photos and artwork. Receives about 100 submissions for each issue, accepts approximately 10%. Press run is 700.

NEEDS Length: up to 10 pages (submissions at the upper end of this length spectrum will need to be of exceptional quality to be considered).

HOW TO CONTACT Submit fiction via Submittable.

PAYMENT/TERMS Pays $25 honorarium and three-issue subscription.

TIPS "*filling Station* accepts singular or simultaneous submissions of previously unpublished poetry, fiction, creative nonfiction, nonfiction, or art. We are always on the hunt for great writing!"

⑤ THE FIRST LINE

Blue Cubicle Press, LLC, P.O. Box 250382, Plano TX 75025. (972)824-0646. **E-mail:** submission@thefirst-line.com. **Website:** www.thefirstline.com. **Contact:** Robin LaBounty, ms coordinator. Estab. 1999. "*The First Line* is an exercise in creativity for writers and a chance for readers to see how many different directions we can take when we start from the same place. The purpose of *The First Line* is to jumpstart the imagination—to help writers break through the block that is the blank page. Each issue contains short stories that stem from a common first line; it also provides a forum for discussing favorite first lines in literature."

NEEDS "We only publish stories that start with the first line provided. We are a collection of tales—of different directions writers can take when they start from the same place. " Length: 300-5,000 words.

HOW TO CONTACT Submit complete ms.

PAYMENT/TERMS Pays $25-50.

TIPS "Don't just write the first story that comes to mind after you read the sentence. If it is obvious, chances are other people are writing about the same thing. Don't try so hard. Be willing to accept criticism."

FIVE POINTS

Georgia State University, P.O. Box 3999, Atlanta GA 30302-3999. **Website:** www.fivepoints.gsu.edu. **Contact:** David Bottoms, co-editor. Estab. 1996. *Five Points*, published 3 times/year, is committed to publishing work that compels the imagination through the use of fresh and convincing language.

○ Magazine: 6x9; 200 pages; cotton paper; glossy cover; photos. Has published Alice Hoffman, Natasha Tretheway, Pamela Painter, Billy Collins, Philip Levine, George Singleton, Hugh Sheehy, and others. All submissions received outside of our reading periods are returned unread.

NEEDS Receives 250 unsolicited mss/month. Accepts 4 mss/issue; 15-20 mss/year. Reads fiction August 15-December 1 and January 3-March 31. Publishes 1 new writer/year. Sometimes comments on rejected mss. Sponsors awards/contests. Length: up to 7,500 words.

HOW TO CONTACT Submit through online submissions manager. Include cover letter.

PAYMENT/TERMS Pays $15/page ($250 maximum), plus free subscription to magazine and 2 contributor's copies; additional copies $4.

TIPS "We place no limitations on style or content. Our only criteria is excellence. If your writing has an original voice, substance, and significance, send it to us. We will publish distinctive, intelligent writing that has something to say and says it in a way that captures and maintains our attention."

FLINT HILLS REVIEW

Department of English, Modern Languages, and Journalist, Emporia State University, 1 Kellogg Circle, Emporia KS 66801. **E-mail:** awebb@emporia.edu; krabas@emporia.edu. **E-mail:** bluestem@emporia.edu. **Website:** www.emporia.edu/fhr. **Contact:** Amy Sage Webb and Kevin Rabas, editors. Estab. 1996. *Flint Hills Review*, published annually, is "a regionally focused journal presenting writers of national distinction alongside new authors. *FHR* seeks work informed by a strong sense of place or region, especially Kansas and the Great Plains region. We seek to provide a publishing venue for writers of the Great Plains and Kansas while also publishing authors whose work evidences a strong sense of place, writing of literary quality, and accomplished use of language and depth of character development."

○ Magazine: 6x9; 75-200 pages; perfect-bound; 60 lb. paper; glossy cover; illustrations; photos. Has published work by Julene Bair, Elizabeth Dodd, Dennis Etzel Jr., Patricia Lawson, and Amanda Frost. Reads mss November to mid-March.

NEEDS No religious, inspirational, children's. Wants to see more writing of literary quality with a strong sense of place. Publishes short shorts. Include bio. Length: 1-3 pages for short shorts; 7-25 pages for short stories.

HOW TO CONTACT Submit complete ms by mail or e-mail.

PAYMENT/TERMS Pays 2 contributor's copies; additional copies at discounted price.

TIPS "Submit writing that has strong imagery and voice, writing that is informed by place or region, writing of literary quality with depth of character development. Hone the language to the most literary depiction possible in the shortest space that still provides depth of development without excess length."

THE FLORIDA REVIEW

Department of English, University of Central Florida, P.O. Box 161346, Orlando FL 32816-1346. **E-mail:** flreview@ucf.edu. **Website:** floridareview.cah.ucf.edu. **Contact:** Lisa Roney, editor. Estab. 1972. "*The Florida Review* publishes exciting new work from around the world from writers both emerging and well known. We are not Florida-exclusive, though we acknowledge having a jungle mentality and a preference for grit, and we have provided and continue to offer a home for many Florida writers."

○ Has published work by Gerald Vizenor, Billy Collins, Sherwin Bitsui, Kelly Clancy, Denise Duhamel, Tony Hoagland, Baron Wormser, Marcia Aldrich, and Patricia Foster. Accepts mailed submissions only if author does not have regular access to the Internet.

NEEDS No genre fiction. Length: 3-25 pages.

HOW TO CONTACT Submit complete ms via online submissions manager.

TIPS "We're looking for writers with fresh voices and original stories. We like risk."

FLOYD COUNTY MOONSHINE

720 Christiansburg Pike, Floyd VA 24091. (540)745-5150. **E-mail:** floydshine@gmail.com. **Website:** www.floydcountymoonshine.com. **Contact:** Aaron Lee Moore, Editor in Chief. Estab. 2008. *Floyd County Moonshine*, published biannually, is a "literary and arts magazine in Floyd, Virginia, and the New River Valley. We accept poetry, short stories, and essays addressing all manner of themes; however, preference is given to those works of a rural or Appalachian nature. *Floyd County Moonshine* publishes a variety of home-grown Appalachian writers in addition to writers from across the country. The mission of *Floyd County Moonshine* is to publish thought-provoking, well-crafted, free-thinking, uncensored prose and poetry. Our literature explores the dark and Gothic as well as the bright and pleasant in order to give an honest portrayal of the human condition. We aspire to publish quality literature in the local color genre, specifically writing that relates to Floyd, Virginia, and the New River Valley. Floyd and local Appalachian authors are given priority consideration; however, to stay versatile we also aspire to publish some writers from all around the country in every issue. We publish both well-established and beginning writers."

○ Wants literature addressing rural or Appalachian themes. Has published poetry by Steve Kistulentz, Louis Gallo, Ernie Wormwood, R.T. Smith, Chelsea Adams, and Justin Askins.

NEEDS "Any and all subject matter is welcome, although we gravitate toward Local Color (especially stories set in Floyd, the New River Valley, or a specific rural setting) and the Southern Gothic." Length: up to 8,000 words.

HOW TO CONTACT Accepts e-mail (preferred). Submit a Word document as attachment. Accepts previously published works and simultaneous submissions on occasion. Cover letter is unnecessary. Include brief bio. Reads submissions year round.

PAYMENT/TERMS Pays 1 contributor's copy.

TIPS "If we favor your work, it may appear in several issues, so prior contributors are also encouraged to resubmit. Every year we choose at least 1 featured author for an issue. We also nominate for Pushcart prizes, and we will do book reviews if you mail us the book."

FLYWAY

Department of English, 206 Ross Hall, Iowa State University, Ames IA 50011-1201. **E-mail:** flywayjournal@gmail.com; flyway@iastate.edu. **Website:** www.flyway.org. **Contact:** Zachary Lisabeth, managing editor. Estab. 1995. Based out of Iowa State University, *Flyway: Journal of Writing and Environment* publishes poetry, fiction, nonfiction, and visual art exploring the many complicated facets of the word environment—at once rural, urban, and suburban—and its social and political implications. Also open to all different interpretations of environment.

○ Reading period is October 1-May 1. Has published work by Rick Bass, Jacob M. Appel, Madison Smartt Bell, Jane Smiley. Also sponsors the annual the spring "Sweet Corn Prize in Fiction" short story contest. Details on website.

NEEDS Length: up to 5,000 words. Average length: 3,000 words. Also publishes short shorts of up to 1,000 words. Average length: 500 words.

HOW TO CONTACT Submit mss only via online submission manager. Receives 50-100 mss monthly. Accepts 3-5 stories per issue; up to 10 per year. Also reviews novels and short-story collections. Submit 1 short story or up to 3 short shorts.

PAYMENT/TERMS Pays one-year subscription to *Flyway*.

TIPS "For *Flyway*, there should be tension between the environment or setting of the story and the characters in it. A well-known place should appear new, even alien and strange through the eyes and actions of the characters. We want to see an active environment, too—a setting that influences actions, triggers it's one events."

⑤ FOGGED CLARITY

Fogged Clarity and Nicotine Heart Press, P.O. Box 1016, Muskegon MI 49443-1016. (231)670-7033. **E-mail:** editor@foggedclarity.com; submissions@foggedclarity.com. **Website:** www.foggedclarity.com. **Contact:** Editors. Estab. 2008. "*Fogged Clarity* is an arts review that accepts submissions of poetry, fiction, nonfiction, music, visual art, and reviews of work in all mediums. We seek art that is stabbingly eloquent. Our print edition is released once every year, while new issues of our online journal come out at the beginning of every month. Artists maintain the copyrights to their work until they are monetarily compensated for said work. If your work is selected for our print edition and you consent to its publication, you will be compensated."

○ "By incorporating music and the visual arts and releasing a new issue monthly, *Fogged Clarity* aims to transcend the conventions of a typical literary journal. Our network is extensive, and our scope is as broad as thought itself; we are, you are, unconstrained. With that spirit in mind, *Fogged Clarity* examines the work of authors, artists, scholars, and musicians, providing a home for exceptional art and thought that warrants exposure."

NEEDS Length: up to 8,000 words.

HOW TO CONTACT Submit 1-2 complete ms by e-mail (submissions@foggedclarity.com) as attached DOC or DOCX file. Subject line should be formatted as: "Last Name: Medium of Submission." For example, "Evans: Fiction." Include brief cover letter, complete contact information, and a third-person bio.

TIPS "The editors appreciate artists communicating the intention of their submitted work and the influences behind it in a brief cover letter. Any artists with proposals for features or special projects should feel free to contact Ben Evans directly at editor@foggedclarity.com."

FOLIATE OAK LITERARY MAGAZINE

University of Arkansas-Monticello, Arts & Humanities, 562 University Dr., Monticello AR 71656. **E-mail:** foliateoak@gmail.com. **E-mail:** foliateoakliterary-magazine.submittable.com. **Website:** www.foliateoak.com. **Contact:** Diane Payne, faculty advisor. Estab. 1973. The *Foliate Oak Literary Magazine* is an online student-run magazine accepting hybrid prose, poetry, fiction, flash, creative nonfiction, and artwork.

○ "After you receive a rejection/acceptance notice, please wait 1 month before submitting new work. **Submission Period: August 1-April 24**. We do not read submissions during summer break. If you need to contact us for anything other than submitting your work, please write to foliateoak@gmail.com." No e-mail submissions.

NEEDS Does not want pornographic, racist, or homophobic content. We avoid genre fiction. Length: 200-2,500 words.

HOW TO CONTACT Send complete ms through online submission manager. "Remember to include your brief third-person bio."

TIPS "Please submit all material via our online submission manager. Read our guidelines before submitting. We are eager to include multimedia submissions of videos, music, and collages. Submit your best work."

FOLIO, A LITERARY JOURNAL AT AMERICAN UNIVERSITY

Department of Literature, American University, Washington DC 20016. (202)885-2971. **Fax:** (202)885-2938. **E-mail:** folio.editors@gmail.com. **Website:** www.american.edu/cas/literature/folio. **Contact:** Editor in chief. Estab. 1984. "*Folio* is a nationally recognized literary journal sponsored by the College of Arts and Sciences at American University in Washington, DC. Since 1984, we have published original creative work by both new and established authors. Past issues have included work by Michael Reid Busk, Billy Collins, William Stafford, and Bruce Weigl, and interviews with Michael Cunningham, Charles Baxter, Amy Bloom, Ann Beattie, and Walter Kirn. We look for well-crafted poetry and prose that is bold and memorable."

○ Poems and prose are reviewed by editorial staff and senior editors. Reads submissions in the fall of each year. To submit, please visit: https://foliolitjournal.submittable.com/submit.

NEEDS Length: up to 5,000 words.

HOW TO CONTACT Submit via online submission form at foliolitjournal.submittable.com/submit. Cover letters must contain all of the following: brief bio, e-mail address, snail mail address, phone number, and title(s) of work enclosed.

FOURTEEN HILLS

Department of Creative Writing, San Francisco State University, 1600 Holloway Ave., San Francisco CA 94137. **E-mail:** hills@sfsu.edu. **Website:** www.14hills. net. Estab. 1994. "*Fourteen Hills* publishes the highest-quality innovative fiction and poetry for a literary audience."

○ Semiannual magazine: 6x9; 200 pages; 60 lb. paper; 10-point C15 cover. Reading periods: September 1-December 1 for summer issue; March 1-June 1 for winter issue.

NEEDS Has published work by Susan Straight, Yiyun Li, Alice LaPlante, Terese Svoboda, Peter Rock, Stephen Dixon, and Adam Johnson. Length: up to 6,000 words or 20 pages for short stories; up to 1,000 words or 10 pages each for flash fiction.

HOW TO CONTACT Submit 1 short story or 3 flash fiction pieces via online submissions manager.

PAYMENT/TERMS Pays 2 contributor's copies and offers discount on additional copies.

TIPS "Please read an issue of *Fourteen Hills* before submitting."

THE FOURTH RIVER

Chatham University, Woodland Rd., Pittsburgh PA 15232. **E-mail:** 4thriver@gmail.com. **Website:** thefourthriver.com. Estab. 2005. *The Fourth River*, an annual publication of Chatham University's MFA in Creative Writing Programs, features literature that engages and explores the relationship between humans and their environments. Wants writings that are richly situated at the confluence of place, space, and identity, or that reflect upon or make use of landscape and place in new ways.

○ *The Fourth River* is digest-sized, perfect-bound, with full-color cover by various artists. *The Fourth River*'s contributors have been published in *Glimmer Train*, *Alaska Quarterly Review*, *The Missouri Review*, *The Best American Short Stories*, *The O. Henry Prize Stories*, and *The Best American Travel Writing*. Reading periods: November 1-January 1 (fall online issue) and July 1-September 1 (spring print issue).

NEEDS Length: up to 7,000 words.

HOW TO CONTACT Submit complete ms via online submissions manager.

○ ⑤ FREEFALL MAGAZINE

FreeFall Literary Society of Calgary, 460, 1720 29th Ave. SW, Calgary AB T2T 6T7, Canada. **E-mail:** editors@freefallmagazine.ca. **Website:** www.freefall-magazine.ca. **Contact:** Ryan Stromquist, managing editor. Estab. 1990. Magazine published triannually containing fiction, poetry, creative nonfiction, essays on writing, interviews, and reviews. "We are looking for exquisite writing with a strong narrative."

NEEDS Length: up to 4,000 words.

HOW TO CONTACT Submit via online submissions manager.

PAYMENT/TERMS Pays $10/printed page in the magazine ($100 maximum) and 1 contributor's copy.

TIPS "Our mission is to encourage the voices of new, emerging, and experienced Canadian writers and provide a platform for their quality work."

🐟 FREEXPRESSION

Peter F Pike T/As FreeXpresSion, P.O. Box 4, West Hoxton NSW 2171, Australia. (02)96075559. **E-mail:** editor@freexpression.com.au. **Website:** www.freexpression.com.au. **Contact:** Peter F. Pike, managing editor. Estab. 1993. *FreeXpresSion*, published monthly, contains creative writing, how-to articles, short stories, and poetry, including cinquain, haiku, etc., and bush verse. Open to all forms. "Christian themes OK. Humorous material welcome. No gratuitous sex; bad language OK. We don't want to see anything degrading."

> *FreeXpresSion* also publishes books up to 200 pages **through subsidy arrangements with authors**. Some poems published throughout the year are used in *Yearbooks* (annual anthologies). *FreeXpresSion* is 32 pages, magazine-sized, offset-printed, saddle-stapled, full color. Receives about 3,500 poems/year, accepts about 30%.

HOW TO CONTACT Submit prose via e-mail.

🐟 THE FROGMORE PAPERS

21 Mildmay Rd., Lewes, East Sussex BN7 1PJ, England. **Website:** www.frogmorepress.co.uk. **Contact:** Jeremy Page, editor. Estab. 1983. *The Frogmore Papers*, published semiannually, is a literary magazine with emphasis on new poetry and short stories.

> *The Frogmore Papers* is 42 pages, photocopied in photo-reduced typescript, saddle-stapled, with matte card cover. Accepts 2% of poetry received. Press run is 500. Reading periods: October 1-31 for March issue and April 1-30 for September issue.

NEEDS Length: up to 2,000 words.

HOW TO CONTACT Submit by e-mail or mail (postal submissions only accepted from within the U.K.).

PAYMENT/TERMS Pays 1 contributor's copy.

🟢 FUGUE LITERARY MAGAZINE

200 Brink Hall, University of Idaho, P.O. Box 44110, Moscow ID 83844. **E-mail:** fugue@uidaho.edu. **Website:** www.fuguejournal.com. **Contact:** Alexandra Teague, faculty advisor. Estab. 1990. "Begun in 1990 by the faculty in the Department of English at University of Idaho, *Fugue* has continuously published poetry, plays, fiction, essays, and interviews from established and emerging writers biannually. We take pride in the work we print, the writers we publish, and the presentation of each and every issue. Working in collaboration with local and national artists, our covers display some of the finest art from photography and digital art to ink drawings and oil paintings. We believe that each issue is a print and digital artifact of the deepest engagement with our culture, and we make it our personal goal that the writing we select and presentation of each issue reflect the reverence we have for art and letters."

> Work published in *Fugue* has won the Pushcart Prize and has been cited in *Best American Essays*. Submissions are accepted online only. Poetry, fiction, and nonfiction submissions are accepted September 1-May 1. All material received outside of this period will not be read. $3 submission fee per entry. See website for submission instructions.

HOW TO CONTACT Submit complete ms via online submissions manager. "Please send no more than 2 short shorts or 1 story at a time. Submissions in more than 1 genre should be submitted separately. All multiple submissions will be returned unread. Once you have submitted a piece to us, wait for a response on this piece before submitting again."

PAYMENT/TERMS Pays 2 contributor's copies and additional payment.

TIPS "The best way, of course, to determine what we're looking for is to read the journal. As the name *Fugue* indicates, our goal is to present a wide range of literary perspectives. We like stories that satisfy us both intellectually and emotionally, with fresh language and characters so captivating that they stick with us and invite a second reading. We are also seeking creative literary criticism which illuminates a piece of literature or a specific writer by examining that writer's personal experience."

GARGOYLE

Paycock Press, 3819 13th St. N, Arlington VA 22201. (703)525-9296. **E-mail:** rchrdpeabody9@gmail.com. **Website:** www.gargoylemagazine.com. **Contact:** Richard Peabody, editor; Lucinda Ebersole, co-editor. Estab. 1976. "*Gargoyle* has always been a scallywag magazine, a maverick magazine, a bit too academic for the underground and way too underground for the academics. We are a writer's magazine in that we are read by other writers and have never worried about reaching the masses." Annual.

The submission window opens each year in August and remains open until full. Recently published work by Abdul Ali, Nin Andrews, Claudia Apablaza, Sara Backer, Tina Barr, Stacy Barton, Alessandra Bava, Bill Beverly, Mary Biddinger, Matthew Blasi, Gerri Brightwell, Dana Cann, Michael Casey, Karen Chase, Kelly Cherry, Joan Colby, Katherine Coles, Nicelle Davis, Jennifer K. Dick, Gabriel Don, Lauren Fairbanks, Angela Featherstone, April L. Ford, Thaisa Frank, Myronn Hardy, Lola Haskins, Allison Hedge-Coke, Nancy Hightower, Paul House, Laird Hunt, Gerry LaFemina, Louise Wareham Leonard, Gilles Leroy, Susan Lewis, Peter Tieryas Liu, Duane Locke, Jonathan Lyons, James Magruder, Margaret McCarthy, Dora E. McQuaid, Ana Merino, Joe Mills, Gloria Mindock, Sheryl L. Nelms, Rodney Nelson, Amanda Newell, Rebecca Nison, Kevin O'Cuinn, W.P. Osborn, Abbey Mei Otis, Jose Padua, Theresa Pappas, Kit Reed, Doug Rice, Lou Robinson, Gregg Shapiro, Rose Solari, Marilyn Stablein, Janet Steen, D.E. Steward, Dariel Suarez, Art Taylor, Virgie Townsend, Dan Vera, Elisha Wagman, Vallie Lynn Watson, Tim Wendel, Theodore Wheeler, and Kirby Wright.

NEEDS Wants "edgy realism or experimental works. We run both." Wants to see more Canadian, British, Australian, and Third World fiction. Receives 300 unsolicited mss/week during submission period. Accepts 20-50 mss/issue. Agented fiction 5%. **Publishes 2-3 new writers/year**. Publishes 1-2 titles/year. Format: trade paperback originals. No romance, horror, science fiction. Length: up to 5,000 words. "We have run 2 novellas in the past 40 years."

PAYMENT/TERMS Pays 1 contributor's copy and offers 50% discount on additional copies.

TIPS "We have to fall in love with a particular fiction."

A GATHERING OF THE TRIBES

P.O. Box 20693, Tompkins Square Station, New York NY 10009. (212)777-2038. **E-mail:** gatheringofthetribes@gmail.com. **E-mail:** tribes.editor@gmail.com. **Website:** www.tribes.org. **Contact:** Steve Cannon. Estab. 1992. *A Gathering of the Tribes* is a multicultural and multigenerational publication featuring poetry, fiction, interviews, essays, visual art, and musical scores. The audience is anyone interested in the arts from a diverse perspective."

Magazine: 8.5x10; 130 pages; glossy paper and cover; illustrations; photos. Receives 20 unsolicited mss/month. Publishes 40% new writers/year. Has published work by Carl Watson, Ishle Park, Wang Pang, and Hanif Kureishi. Sponsors awards/contests.

NEEDS "Would like to see more satire/humor. We are open to all work; just no poor writing/grammar/syntax." Length: 2,500-5,000 words.

HOW TO CONTACT Send complete ms by postal mail or e-mail.

PAYMENT/TERMS Pays 1 contributor's copy.

TIPS "Make sure your work has substance."

THE GEORGIA REVIEW

The University of Georgia, Main Library, Room 706A, 320 S. Jackson St., Athens GA 30602. (706)542-3481. **Fax:** (706)542-0047. **E-mail:** garev@uga.edu. **Website:** thegeorgiareview.com. **Contact:** Stephen Corey, editor. Estab. 1947. "*The Georgia Review* is a literary quarterly committed to the art of editorial practice. We collaborate equally with established and emerging authors of essays, stories, poems, and reviews in the pursuit of extraordinary works that engage with the evolving concerns and interests of intellectually curious readers from around the world. Our aim in curating content is not only to elevate literature, publishing, and the arts, but also to help facilitate socially conscious partnerships in our surrounding communities."

$3 online submission fee waived for subscribers. No fees for mss submitted by post. Reading period: August 15-May 15.

NEEDS "We seek original, excellent short fiction not bound by type. Ordinarily we do not publish novel excerpts or works translated into English, and we discourage authors from submitting these."

HOW TO CONTACT Send complete ms via online submissions manager or postal mail.

PAYMENT/TERMS Pays $50/published page.

GERTRUDE

P.O. Box 28281, Portland OR 97228. **E-mail:** editorgertrudepress@gmail.com. **Website:** www.gertrudepress.org. **Contact:** Tammy. Estab. 1999. *Gertrude*, the annual literary arts journal of Gertrude Press, is a "publication featuring the voices and visions of the gay, lesbian, bisexual, transgender, and supportive community."

NEEDS Has published work by Carol Guess, Demrie Alonzo, Henry Alley, and Scott Pomfret. Length: up to 3,000 words.

HOW TO CONTACT Submit 1-2 pieces via online submissions manager, double-spaced. Include word count for each piece in cover letter.

TIPS "We look for strong characterization and imagery, and new, unique ways of writing about universal experiences. Follow the construction of your work until the ending. Many stories start out with zest, then flipper and die. Show us, don't tell us."

THE GETTYSBURG REVIEW

Gettysburg College, Gettysburg College, 300 N. Washington St., Gettysburg PA 17325. (717)337-6770. **E-mail:** mdrew@gettysburg.edu. **Website:** www.gettysburgreview.com. **Contact:** Mark Drew, editor; Jess L. Bryant, managing editor. Estab. 1988. Published quarterly, *The Gettysburg Review* considers unsolicited submissions of poetry, fiction, and essays. "Our concern is quality. Mss submitted here should be extremely well written." Reading period September 1-May 31.

NEEDS Wants high-quality literary fiction. "We require that fiction be intelligent and aesthetically written." No genre fiction. Length: 2,000-7,000 words.

HOW TO CONTACT Send complete ms with SASE.

PAYMENT/TERMS Pays $15/printed page, a one-year subscription, and 1 contributor's copy.

GINOSKO LITERARY JOURNAL

Ginosko, PO Box 246, Fairfax CA 94978. (415)785-3160. **E-mail:** editorginosko@aol.com. **E-mail:** editorginosko@aol.com. **Website:** www.ginoskoliteraryjournal.com. **Contact:** Robert Paul Cesaretti, editor.

Estab. 2002. *Ginosko* Flash Fiction Contest: Deadline is March 1; $5 entry fee; $250 prize. "*Ginosko* (ghin-océ-koe): To perceive, understand, realize, come to know; knowledge that has an inception, a progress, an attainment. The recognition of truth by experience." Accepting short fiction and poetry, creative nonfiction, interviews, social justice concerns, and literary insights for www.ginoskoliteraryjournal.com.

Reads year round. Length of articles flexible; accepts excerpts. Publishing as semiannual e-zine. Print anthology every 2 years. Check downloadable issues on website for tone and style. Downloads free; accepts donations. Member CLMP.

NEEDS Download issue for tone & style. 25-5000

HOW TO CONTACT Submit via postal mail, e-mail (prefers attachments: WPS, DOC, or RTF), or online submissions manager Submittable (ginosko.submittable.com/submit).

TIPS "Read several issues for tone and style."

GLIMMER TRAIN STORIES

Glimmer Train Press, Inc., P.O. Box 80430, Portland OR 97280. **Fax:** (503)221-0837. **E-mail:** eds@glimmertrain.org. **Website:** www.glimmertrain.org. **Contact:** Susan Burmeister-Brown. Estab. 1991. "We are interested in literary short stories, particularly by new and emerging writers."

Recently published work by Benjamin Percy, Laura van den Berg, Manuel Muñoz, Claire Vaye Watkins, Abby Geni, Peter Ho Davies, William Trevor, Thisbe Nissen, and Yiyun Li.

NEEDS Length: 500-20,000 words.

HOW TO CONTACT Submit via the website at www.glimmertrain.org. In a pinch, send a hard copy and include SASE for response. Receives 36,000 unsolicited mss/year. Accepts 15 mss/issue; 45 mss/year. Agented fiction 1%. Publishes 20 new writers/year.

PAYMENT/TERMS Pays $700 for standard submissions, up to $3,000 for contest-winning stories.

TIPS "In the last 2 years, over half of the first-place stories have been their authors' very first publications. See our contest listings in Contests & Awards section."

GRAIN

P.O. Box 3986, Regina SK S4P 3R9, Canada. (306)791-7749. **Fax:** (306)565-8554. **E-mail:** grainmag@skwriter.com. **Website:** www.grainmagazine.ca. Estab. 1973. "*Grain, The Journal of Eclectic Writing* is a literary quarterly that publishes engaging, diverse, and challenging writing and art by some of the best Canadian and international writers and artists. Every issue features superb new writing from both developing and established writers. Each issue also highlights the unique artwork of a different visual artist. *Grain* has garnered national and international recognition for its distinctive, cutting-edge content and design."

○ *Grain* is 112-128 pages, digest-sized, professionally printed. Press run is 1,100. Receives about 3,000 submissions/year. **Submissions are read September 1-May 31 only.** Mss postmarked June 1-August 31 will not be read.

NEEDS No romance, confession, science fiction, vignettes, mystery. Length: up to 3,500 words.

HOW TO CONTACT Postal submissions only. Send typed, unpublished material only (considers work published online to be previously published). Please only submit work in 1 genre at a time.

PAYMENT/TERMS Pays $50/page ($250 maximum) and 3 contributor's copies.

TIPS "Only work of the highest literary quality is accepted. Read several back issues."

⑤ GRASSLIMB

P.O. Box 420816, San Diego CA 92142. **E-mail:** editor@grasslimb.com. **Website:** www.grasslimb.com. **Contact:** Valerie Polichar, editor. Estab. 2002. *Grasslimb* publishes literary prose, poetry, and art. Fiction is best when it is short and avant-garde or otherwise experimental.

NEEDS "Fiction in an experimental, avant-garde, or surreal mode is often more interesting to us than a traditional story." "Although general topics are welcome, we're less likely to select work regarding romance, sex, aging, and children." Length: up to 2,500 words; average length: 1,500 words.

HOW TO CONTACT Send complete ms via e-mail or postal mail with SASE.

PAYMENT/TERMS Pays $10-70 and 2 contributor's copies.

TIPS "We publish brief fiction work that can be read in a single sitting over a cup of coffee. Work is generally 'literary' in nature rather than mainstream. Experimental work welcome. Remember to have your work proofread and to send short work. We cannot read over 3,000 words and prefer under 2,000 words. Include word count."

GREEN HILLS LITERARY LANTERN

Truman State University, Department of English, Truman State University, Kirksville MO 63501. **E-mail:** adavis@truman.edu. **Website:** ghll.truman.edu. **Contact:** Adam Brooke Davis, prose editor, managing editor; Joe Benevento, poetry editor. Estab. 1990. *Green Hills Literary Lantern* is published annually, in June, by Truman State University. Historically, the print publication ran between 200-300 pages, consisting of poetry, fiction, reviews, and interviews. The digital magazine is of similar proportions and artistic standards. Open to the work of new writers, as well as more established writers.

NEEDS "We are interested in stories that demonstrate a strong working knowledge of the craft. Avoid genre fiction or mainstream religious fiction. Otherwise, we are open to short stories of various settings, character conflict, and styles, including experimental. Above all, we demand that work be 'striking.' Language should be complex, with depth through analogy, metaphor, simile, understatement, irony, etc.—but all this must not be overwrought or self-consciously literary. If style is to be at center stage, it must be interesting and provocative enough for the reader to focus on style alone. 'Overdone' writing surely is not either." No word limit.

HOW TO CONTACT Submit complete ms.

GREEN MOUNTAINS REVIEW

Johnson State College, 337 College Hill, Johnson VT 05656. (802)635-1350. **E-mail:** gmr@jsc.edu. **Website:** greenmountainsreview.com. **Contact:** Elizabeth Powell, editor; Jessica Hendry Nelson, nonfiction editor; Jacob White, fiction editor; Ben Aleshire, assistant poetry editor. Semiannual magazine covering poems, stories, and creative nonfiction by both well-known authors and promising newcomers.

○ The editors are open to a wide range of styles and subject matter. Open reading period: September 1-March 1.

NEEDS Recently published work by Tracy Daugherty, Terese Svoboda, Walter Wetherell, T.M. McNally, J. Robert Lennon, Louis B. Jones, and Tom Whalen. Publishes short shorts. Also publishes literary criticism, poetry. Sometimes comments on rejected mss. Length: up to 25 pages, double-spaced.

HOW TO CONTACT Submit ms via online submissions manager.

PAYMENT/TERMS Pays contributor's copies, one-year subscription, and small honorarium, depending on grants.

TIPS "We encourage you to order some of our back issues to acquaint yourself with what has been accepted in the past."

◐◑ THE GREENSBORO REVIEW

MFA Writing Program, 3302 MHRA Building, UNC-Greensboro, Greensboro NC 27402. **E-mail:** jlclark@uncg.edu. **Website:** tgronline.net. **Contact:** Jim Clark, editor. Estab. 1965. "A local lit mag with an international reputation. We've been 'old school' since 1965."

○ Stories for *The Greensboro Review* have been included in *Best American Short Stories, The O. Henry Awards Prize Stories, New Stories from the South* and *Pushcart Prize*. Does not accept e-mail submissions.

NEEDS Length: up to 7,500 words.

HOW TO CONTACT Submit complete ms via online submission form or postal mail. Include cover letter and estimated word count.

PAYMENT/TERMS Pays contributor's copies.

TIPS "We want to see the best being written regardless of theme, subject, or style."

THE GRIFFIN

Gwynedd Mercy University, 1325 Sumneytown Pike, P.O. Box 901, Gwynedd Valley PA 19437-0901. **E-mail:** garber.r@gmercyu.edu. **Website:** www.gmercyu.edu/about-gwynedd-mercy/publications/griffin. **Contact:** Dr. Donna M. Allego, editor. Estab. 1999. Published by Gwynedd Mercy University, *The Griffin* is a literary journal for the creative writer—subscribing to the belief that improving the human condition requires dedication to and respect for the individual and the community. Seeks works which explore universal qualities—truth, justice, integrity, compassion, mercy. Publishes poetry, short stories, short plays, and reflections.

NEEDS All genres considered. No slashers, graphic violence, or sex, however. Length: up to 2,500 words.

HOW TO CONTACT Submit complete ms via e-mail or on disk with a hard copy. Include short author bio.

TIPS "Pay attention to the word length requirements, the mission of the magazine, and how to submit ms as set forth. These constitute the writer's guidelines listed online."

GRIST

English Dept., 301 McClung Tower, Univ. of Tennessee, Knoxville TN 37996-0430. **E-mail:** gristeditors@gmail.com. **Website:** www.gristjournal.com. Estab. 2007. *Grist* is a nationally distributed journal of fiction, nonfiction, poetry, interviews, and craft essays. We seek work of high literary quality from both emerging and established writers, and we welcome all styles and aesthetic approaches.

○ Each issue is accompanied by Grist Online, which features some of the best work we receive during our reading period. In addition to general submissions, *Grist* holds the ProForma Contest every spring, recognizing unpublished creative work that explores the relationship between content and form, whether in fiction, nonfiction, poetry, or a hybrid genre. Throughout the year, we publish interviews, craft essays, and reviews on our blog, The Writing Life.

NEEDS Length: 7,000 words.

HOW TO CONTACT Send complete ms.

TIPS "*Grist* seeks work from both emerging and established writers, whose work is of high literary quality."

GUERNICA MAGAZINE

112 W. 27th St., Suite 600, New York NY 10001. **E-mail:** editors@guernicamag.com; publisher@guernicamag.com. **Website:** www.guernicamag.com. **Contact:** see masthead online for specific editors. Estab. 2004. *Guernica* is called a 'great online literary magazine' by *Esquire*. *Guernica* contributors come from dozens of countries and write in nearly as many languages.

○ Received Caine Prize for African Writing, Best of the Net.

NEEDS *Guernica* strongly prefers fiction with a diverse international outlook—or if American, from an underrepresented or alternative perspective. (No stories about American tourists in other countries, please.) Has published Jesse Ball, Elizabeth Crane, Josh Weil, Justo Arroyo, Sergio Ramírez Mercado, Matthew Derby, E.C. Osondu (Winner of the 2009 Caine Prize for African Writing). No genre fiction or satire. Length: 1,200-4,500 words.

HOW TO CONTACT Submit complete ms via online submissions manager.

TIPS "Please read the magazine first before submitting. Most stories that are rejected simply do not fit our approach. Submission guidelines available online."

GULF COAST: A JOURNAL OF LITERATURE AND FINE ARTS

4800 Calhoun Rd., Houston TX 77204-3013. (713)743-3223. **E-mail:** editors@gulfcoastmag.org. **Website:** www.gulfcoastmag.org. **Contact:** Luisa Muradyan Tannahill, editor; Michele Nereim, managing editor; Georgia Pearle, digital editor; Henk Rossouw, Dan Chu, and Erika Jo Brown, poetry editors; Alex McElroy, Charlotte Wyatt, and Corey Campbell, fiction editors; Alex Naumann and Nathan Stabenfeldt, nonfiction editors; Jonathan Meyer, online fiction editor; Carolann Madden, online poetry editor; Melanie Brkich, online nonfiction editor. Estab. 1986.

Magazine: 7x9; approximately 300 pages; stock paper, gloss cover; illustrations; photos.

NEEDS "Please do not send multiple submissions; we will read only 1 submission per author at a given time, except in the case of our annual contests." No children's, genre, religious/inspirational.

HOW TO CONTACT *Gulf Coast* reads general submissions, submitted by post or through the online submissions manager, September 1-March 1. Submissions e-mailed directly to the editors or postmarked March 1-September 1 will not be read or responded to. "Please visit our contest page for contest submission guidelines." Receives 500 unsolicited mss/month. Accepts 6-8 mss/issue; 12-16 mss/year. Agented fiction: 5%. Publishes 2-8 new writers/year. Recently published work by Alan Heathcock, Anne Carson, Bret Anthony Johnston, John D'Agata, Lucie Brock-Broido, Clancy Martin, Steve Almond, Sam Lipsyte, Carl Phillips, Dean Young, and Eula Biss. Publishes short shorts.

PAYMENT/TERMS Pays $50/page.

TIPS "Submit only previously unpublished works. Include a cover letter. Online submissions are strongly preferred. Stories or essays should be typed, double-spaced, and paginated with your name, address, and phone number on the first page and the title on subsequent pages. Poems should have your name, address, and phone number on the first page of each." The Annual Gulf Coast Prizes award publication and $1,500 each in poetry, fiction, and nonfiction; opens in December of each year. Honorable mentions in each category will receive a $250 second prize. Postmark/online entry deadline: March 22 of each year. Winners and honorable mentions will be announced in May. **Entry fee:** $23 (includes one-year subscription). Make checks payable to *Gulf Coast*. Guidelines available on website.

GULF STREAM MAGAZINE

English Department, FIU, Biscayne Bay Campus, 3000 NE 151 St., AC1-335, North Miami FL 33181. **E-mail:** gulfstreamlitmag@gmail.com. **Website:** www.gulfstreamlitmag.com. **Contact:** Miguel Pichardo, editor in chief. Estab. 1989. "*Gulf Stream Magazine* has been publishing emerging and established writers of exceptional fiction, nonfiction, and poetry since 1989. We also publish interviews and book reviews. Past contributors include Sherman Alexie, Steve Almond, Jan Beatty, Lee Martin, Robert Wrigley, Dennis Lehane, Liz Robbins, Stuart Dybek, David Kirby, Ann Hood, Ha Jin, B.H. Fairchild, Naomi Shihab Nye, F. Daniel Rzicznek, and Connie May Fowler. *Gulf Stream Magazine* is supported by the Creative Writing Program at Florida International University in Miami, Florida. Each year we publish 2 online issues."

NEEDS Does not want romance, historical, juvenile, or religious work.

HOW TO CONTACT "Submit online only. Please read guidelines on website in full. Submissions that do not conform to our guidelines will be discarded. We do not accept e-mailed or mailed submissions. We read from September 1-November 1 and January 1-March 1."

PAYMENT/TERMS Pays contributor's copies.

TIPS "We look for fresh, original writing: well-plotted stories with unforgettable characters, fresh poetry, and experimental writing. Usually longer stories do not get accepted. There are exceptions, however."

HAIGHT ASHBURY LITERARY JOURNAL

558 Joost Ave., San Francisco CA 94127. (415)584-8264. **E-mail:** haljeditor@gmail.com. **Website:** haightashburyliteraryjournal.wordpress.com; www.facebook.com/pages/Haight-Ashbury-Literary-Journal/365542018331. **Contact:** Alice Rogoff and Cesar Love, editors. Estab. 1979. *Haight Ashbury Literary Journal*, publishes well-written poetry and fiction. *HALJ*'s voices are often of people who have been marginalized, oppressed, or abused. *HALJ* strives to bring literary arts to the general public, to the San Francisco community of writers, to the Haight Ashbury neighborhood, and to people of varying ages, genders, ethnic groups, and sexual preferences. The Journal is

produced as a tabloid to maintain an accessible price for low-income people.

NEEDS Submit 1-3 short stories or 1 long story. Submit only once every 6 months. No e-mail submissions (unless overseas); postal submissions only. "Put name and address on every page, and include SASE. No bio." Sometimes publishes theme issues (each issue changes its theme and emphasis).

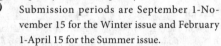 HANGING LOOSE

Hanging Loose Press, 231 Wyckoff St., Brooklyn NY 11217. (347)529-4738. **Fax:** (347)227-8215. **E-mail:** print225@aol.com. **Website:** www.hangingloosepress.com. **Contact:** Robert Hershon and Mark Pawlak, editors. Estab. 1966. *Hanging Loose*, published in April and October, concentrates on the work of new writers. Wants excellent, energetic poems and short stories.

- *Hanging Loose* is 120 pages, offset-printed on heavy stock, flat-spined, with 4-color glossy card cover.

HOW TO CONTACT Submit 1 complete ms by postal mail with SASE.

PAYMENT/TERMS Pays small fee and 2 contributor's copies.

HARPUR PALATE

English Department, Binghamton University, P.O. Box 6000, Binghamton NY 13902-6000. **E-mail:** harpur.palate@gmail.com. **Website:** harpurpalate.com. **Contact:** Liam Meilleur, editor in chief; Carolyn Keller, nonfiction editor; Brian Kelly, poetry editor; Heather Humphrey, fiction editor. Estab. 2000. *Harpur Palate*, published biannually, is "dedicated to publishing the best poetry and prose, regardless of style, form, or genre. We have no restrictions on subject matter or form. Quite simply, send us your highest-quality fiction and poetry."

- Submission periods are September 1-November 15 for the Winter issue and February 1-April 15 for the Summer issue.

NEEDS Receives 400 unsolicited mss/month. Accepts 5-10 mss/issue; 12-20 mss/year. Publishes 5 new writers/year. Has published work by Darryl Crawford and Tim Hedges, Jesse Goolsby, Ivan Faute, and Keith Meatto. Does not accept novel excerpts. Length: up to 6,000 words.

HOW TO CONTACT Prefers submissions through online submissions manager, or send complete ms by

postal mail with SASE. No more than 1 submission per envelope.

PAYMENT/TERMS Pays 2 contributor copies.

TIPS "We are interested in high-quality writing of all genres but especially literary poetry and fiction. We also sponsor a fiction contest for the Summer issue and a poetry and nonfiction contest for the Winter issue with $500 prizes."

HARVARD REVIEW

Lamont Library, Harvard University, Cambridge MA 02138. (617)495-9775. **E-mail:** info@harvardreview.org. **Website:** harvardreview.fas.harvard.edu. **Contact:** Christina Thompson, editor; Suzanne Berne, fiction editor; Major Jackson, poetry editor. Estab. 1992. Semiannual magazine covering poetry, fiction, essays, drama, graphics, and reviews in the spring and fall by an eclectic range of international writers. "Previous contributors include John Updike, Alice Hoffman, Joyce Carol Oates, Miranda July, and Jim Crace. We also publish the work of emerging and previously unpublished writers."

- Does not accept e-mail submissions. Reading period: November 1-May 31.

NEEDS No genre fiction (romance, horror, detective, etc.). Length: up to 7,000 words.

HOW TO CONTACT Submit by online submissions manager or mail (with SASE).

TIPS "Writers at all stages of their careers are invited to apply; however, we can only publish a very small fraction of the material we receive. We recommend that you familiarize yourself with *Harvard Review* before you submit your work."

HAWAI'I PACIFIC REVIEW

1060 Bishop St., Honolulu HI 96813. **Website:** hawaiipacificreview.org. **Contact:** Tyler McMahon, editor; Christa Cushon, managing editor. Estab. 1987. "*Hawai'i Pacific Review* is the online literary magazine of Hawai'i Pacific University. It features poetry and prose by authors from Hawai'i, the mainland, and around the world. *HPR* was started as a print annual in 1987. In 2013, it began to publish exclusively online. *HPR* publishes work on a rolling basis. Poems, stories, and essays are posted 1 piece at a time, several times a month. All contents are archived on the site."

NEEDS Prefers literary work to genre work. Length: up to 4,000 words.

HOW TO CONTACT Submit 1 ms via online submissions manager.

TIPS "We look for the unusual or original plot, and prose with the texture and nuance of poetry. Character development or portrayal must be unusual/original; humanity shown in an original, insightful way (or characters); sense of humor where applicable. Be sure it's a draft that has gone through substantial changes, with supervision from a more experienced writer, if you're a beginner. Write about intense emotion and feeling, not just about someone's divorce or shaky relationship. No soap-opera-like fiction."

HAWAI'I REVIEW

University of Hawaii Board of Publications, 2445 Campus Rd., Hemenway Hall 107, Honolulu HI 96822. (808)956-3030. **Fax:** (808)956-3083. **E-mail:** hawaiireview@gmail.com. **Website:** hawaiireview. org/. Estab. 1973. *Hawai'i Review* is a student-run bi-annual literary and visual arts print journal featuring national and international writing and visual art, as well as regional literature and visual art of Hawai'i and the Pacific.

◯ Accepts submissions online through Submittable only. Offers yearly award with $500 prizes in poetry and fiction.

NEEDS Length: up to 7,000 words for short stories, up to 2,500 words for flash fiction.

HOW TO CONTACT Send 1 short story or 2 pieces of flash fiction via online submission manager.

TIPS "Make it new."

◉◉◉ HAYDEN'S FERRY REVIEW

Arizona State University, c/o Dept. of English,, Arizona State University, P.O. Box 870302, Tempe AZ 85287. **Website:** haydensferryreview.com. **Contact:** Editorial staff changes every year; see website for current masthead. Estab. 1986. "*Hayden's Ferry Review* publishes the best-quality fiction, poetry, and creative nonfiction from new, emerging, and established writers."

◯ Work from *Hayden's Ferry Review* has been selected for inclusion in *Pushcart Prize* anthologies and *Best Creative Nonfiction*. No longer accepts postal mail or e-mail submissions.

NEEDS Word length open, but typically does not accept submissions over 25 pages.

HOW TO CONTACT Send complete ms via online submissions manager.

PAYMENT/TERMS Pays 2 contributor's copies and one-year subscription.

HELIOTROPE

E-mail: heliotropeditor@gmail.com. **Website:** www. heliotropemag.com. Estab. 2006. *Heliotrope* is a quarterly e-zine that publishes fiction, articles, and poetry.

NEEDS "If your story is something we can't label, we're interested in that, too." Length: up to 5,000 words.

HOW TO CONTACT Submit complete ms via e-mail.

PAYMENT/TERMS Pays 10¢/word.

◉ THE HELIX

Central Connecticut State University English Dept., **E-mail:** helixmagazine@gmail.com. **Website:** helix-magazine.org. **Contact:** See masthead online for current editorial staff. "*The Helix* is a Central Connecticut State University publication, and it puts out an issue every semester. It accepts submissions from all over the globe. The magazine features writing from CCSU students, writing from the Hartford County community, and an array of submissions from all over the world. The magazine publishes multiple genres of literature and art, including poetry, fiction, drama, nonfiction, paintings, photography, watercolor, collage, stencil, and computer-generated artwork. It is a student-run publication and is funded by the university."

NEEDS Length: up to 3,000 words.

HOW TO CONTACT Submit complete ms by online submissions manager.

TIPS "Please see our website for specific deadlines, as it changes every semester based on a variety of factors, but we typically leave the submission manager open sometime starting in the summer to around the end of October for the Fall issue, and during the winter to late February or mid-March for the Spring issue. Contributions are invited from all members of the campus community, as well as the literary community at large."

HELLOHORROR

Houston TX (512)537-0504. **E-mail:** info@hellohorror.com. **E-mail:** submissions@hellohorror.com. **Website:** www.hellohorror.com. **Contact:** Brent Armour, editor in chief. Estab. 2012. "*HelloHorror* is an online literary magazine. We are currently in search of literary pieces, photography, and visual art, including film from writers and artists that have a special knack for inducing goose bumps and raised hairs. This genre has become, especially in film, noticeably saturated in gore and high shock-value aspects as a crutch to avoid the true challenge of bringing about real psychological fear to an audience that's persistently more and more numb to its tactics. While we are not opposed to the extreme, blood and guts need bones and cartilage. Otherwise it's just a sloppy mess."

⭕ "Specifically, we are looking for pieces grounded in psychological fear induced by surreal situations unusual to horror rather than gore. We will not automatically pass on a gore-drenched story, but it needs to have its foundations in psychological horror."

NEEDS "We don't want fiction that can in no way be classified as horror. Some types of dark science fiction are acceptable, depending on the story." Length: 6-20 pages for short stories; up to 1,000 words for flash fiction.

HOW TO CONTACT Submit complete ms via e-mail.

TIPS "We like authors that show consideration for their readers. A great horror story leaves an impression on the reader long after it is finished. Consider your reader and consider yourself. What really scares you as opposed to what's stereotypically supposed to scare you? Bring us and our readers into that place of fear with you."

ALFRED HITCHCOCK'S MYSTERY MAGAZINE

Dell Magazines, 44 Wall St., Suite 904, New York NY 10005. **E-mail:** alfredhitchcockmm@dellmagazines.com. **Website:** www.themysteryplace.com/ahmm. Estab. 1956.

NEEDS Wants "original and well-written mystery and crime fiction. Because this is a mystery magazine, the stories we buy must fall into that genre in some sense or another. We are interested in nearly every kind of mystery: stories of detection of the classic kind, police procedurals, private eye tales, suspense, courtroom dramas, stories of espionage, and so on. We ask only that the story be about crime (or the threat or fear of one). We sometimes accept ghost stories or supernatural tales, but those also should involve a crime." No sensationalism. Length: up to 12,000 words.

HOW TO CONTACT Send complete ms.

PAYMENT/TERMS Payment varies.

TIPS "No simultaneous submissions, please. Submissions sent to *Alfred Hitchcock's Mystery Magazine* are not considered for or read by *Ellery Queen's Mystery Magazine*, and vice versa."

HOBART

P.O. Box 1658, Ann Arbor MI 48103. **E-mail:** aaron@hobartpulp.com. **Website:** www.hobartpulp.com. **Contact:** Aaron Burch, editor. Also accepts comics submissions; see online examples. "We tend to like quirky stories like truck driving, mathematics, and vagabonding. We like stories with humor (humorous but engaging, literary but not stuffy). We want to get excited about your story and hope you'll send your best work."

⭕ All submissions must go through online submissions manager. Only accepting submissions for online journal.

NEEDS "We publish nonstuffy, unpretentious, high-quality fiction that never takes itself too serious and always entertains." Length: up to 2,000 words; prefers submissions of about 1,000 words.

HOW TO CONTACT Submit complete ms via online submissions manager.

TIPS "We'd love to receive fewer run-of-the-mill relationship stories and more stories concerning truck drivers, lumberjacks, carnival workers, and gunslingers. In other words, surprise us. Show us a side of life rarely depicted in literary fiction."

HOTEL AMERIKA

Columbia College Chicago, The Department of Creative Writing, 600 S. Michigan Ave., Chicago IL 60605. (312)369-8175. **Website:** www.hotelamerika.net. **Contact:** David Lazar, editor; Jenn Tatum, managing editor. Estab. 2002. *Hotel Amerika* is a venue for both well-known and emerging writers. Publishes exceptional writing in all forms. Strives to house the most unique and provocative poetry, fiction, and non-fiction available.

⭕ Mss will be considered between September 1 and May 1. Materials received after May 1 and before September 1 will be returned unread. Work published in *Hotel Amerika* has been included in *The Pushcart Prize* and *The Best American Poetry*, and featured on *Poetry Daily*.

NEEDS Welcomes submissions in all genres of creative writing, generously defined. Does not publish book reviews as such, although considers review-like essays that transcend the specific objects of consideration.

HOW TO CONTACT Submit complete ms through online submissions manager.

THE HUDSON REVIEW

33 W. 67th St., New York NY 10023. (212)650-0020. **E-mail:** info@hudsonreview.com. **Website:** hudson-review.com. **Contact:** Paula Deitz, editor. Estab. 1948. "Since its beginning, the magazine has dealt with the area where literature bears on the intellectual life of the time and on diverse aspects of American culture. It has no university affiliation and is not committed to any narrow academic aim or to any particular political perspective. The magazine serves as a major forum for the work of new writers and for the exploration of new developments in literature and the arts. It has a distinguished record of publishing little-known or undiscovered writers, many of whom have become major literary figures. Each issue contains a wide range of material including poetry, fiction, essays on literary and cultural topics, book reviews, reports from abroad, and chronicles covering film, theater, dance, music, and art. *The Hudson Review* is distributed in 25 countries."

○ Unsolicited mss are read according to the following schedule: April 1 through June 30 for poetry, September 1 through November 30 for fiction, and January 1 through March 31 for nonfiction.

NEEDS Length: up to 10,000 words.

HOW TO CONTACT Send complete ms by mail or online submissions manager from **September 1 through November 30** only.

TIPS "We do not specialize in publishing any particular 'type' of writing; our sole criterion for accepting unsolicited work is literary quality. The best way for you to get an idea of the range of work we publish is to read a current issue. Unsolicited mss submitted outside of specified reading times will be returned unread. Do not send submissions via e-mail."

⑨ HUNGER MOUNTAIN

Vermont College of Fine Arts, 36 College St., Montpelier VT 05602. (802)828-8517. **E-mail:** hungermtn@vcfa.edu. **Website:** www.hungermtn.org. **Contact:** Katie Stromme, Assistant Editor. Estab. 2002. Accepts high-quality work from unknown, emerging, or successful writers. Publishing fiction, creative nonfiction, poetry, and young adult & children's writing. Four writing contests annually.

○ *Hunger Mountain* is a print and online journal of the arts. The print journal is about 200 pages, 7x9, professionally printed, perfect-bound, with full-bleed color artwork on cover. Press run is 1,000. Over 10,000 visits online monthly. Uses online submissions manager (Submittable). Member: CLMP.

NEEDS "We look for work that is beautifully crafted and tells a good story, with characters that are alive and kicking, storylines that stay with us long after we've finished reading, and sentences that slay us with their precision." No genre fiction, meaning science fiction, fantasy, horror, detective, erotic, etc. Length: up to 10,000 words.

HOW TO CONTACT Submit ms using online submissions manager: https://hungermtn.submittable.com/submit.

PAYMENT/TERMS $50 for general fiction.

TIPS "Mss must be typed, prose double-spaced. Poets submit poems as one document. No multiple genre submissions. Fresh viewpoints and human interest are very important, as is originality and diversity. We are committed to publishing an outstanding journal of the arts. Do not send entire novels, mss, or short story collections. Do not send previously published work."

I-70 REVIEW

Writing from the Middle and Beyond, 913 Joseph Dr., Lawrence KS 66049. **E-mail:** i70review@gmail.com. **Website:** www.fieldinfoserv.com. **Contact:** Gary Lechliter, Maryfrances Wagner, Greg Field, and Jan Duncan-O'Neal, editors. Estab. 1998. *I-70 Review* is an annual literary magazine. "Our interests lie in writing grounded in fresh language, imagery, and metaphor. We prefer free verse in which the writer pays attention to the sound and rhythm of the language. We appreciate poetry with individual voice and a good lyric or a strong narrative. In fiction, we like short pieces that are surprising and uncommon. We want writing that captures the human spirit with unusual topics or familiar topics with different perspective or approaches. We reject stereotypical and clichéd writing, as well as sentimental work or writing that summarizes and tells instead of shows. We look for writing that pays attention to words, sentences, and style. We publish literary writing. We do not publish anything erotic, religious, or political."

○ Open submission period is July 1-December 31.

NEEDS Rejects anything over 1,500 words, unless solicited. Not interested in anything political, religious, spiritual, didactic, or erotic. Accepts mainly flash fiction and very short literary fiction. Pays in contributor copies. Length: up to 1,500 words.

HOW TO CONTACT Submit complete ms by e-mail.

PAYMENT/TERMS Pays contributor copies.

🟢 ICONOCLAST

1675 Amazon Rd., Mohegan Lake NY 10547-1804. **Website:** www.iconoclastliterarymagazine.com. **Contact:** Phil Wagner, editor and publisher. Estab. 1992. *Iconoclast* seeks and chooses the best new writing and poetry available—of all genres and styles and entertainment levels. Its mission is to provide a serious publishing opportunity for unheralded, unknown, but deserving creators, whose work is often overlooked or trampled in the commercial, university, or Internet marketplace.

NEEDS "Subjects and styles are completely open (within the standards of generally accepted taste—though exceptions, as always, can be made for unique and visionary works)." No slice-of-life stories, stories containing alcoholism, incest, and domestic or public violence. Accepts most genres, "with the exception of mysteries."

HOW TO CONTACT Submit by mail; include SASE. Cover letter not necessary.

PAYMENT/TERMS Pays 1¢/word and 2 contributor's copies. Contributors get 40% discount on extra copies.

TIPS "Please don't send preliminary drafts—rewriting is half the job. If you're not sure about the story, don't truly believe in it, or are unenthusiastic about the subject (we will not recycle your term papers or thesis), then don't send it. This is not a lottery (luck has nothing to do with it)."

🟢🟢🟢 THE IDAHO REVIEW

Boise State University, 1910 University Dr., Boise ID 83725. **E-mail:** mwieland@boisestate.edu. **Website:** idahoreview.org. **Contact:** Mitch Wieland, editor. Estab. 1998. *The Idaho Review* is the literary journal of Boise State University.

🟢   Recent stories appearing in *The Idaho Review* have been reprinted in *The Best American Short Stories, The O. Henry Prize Stories, The Pushcart Prize*, and *New Stories from the South*. Reading period: September 15-March 15.

NEEDS No genre fiction of any type. Length: up to 25 double-spaced pages.

HOW TO CONTACT Submit through online submissions manager.

PAYMENT/TERMS Pays $100/story and contributor's copies.

TIPS "We look for strongly crafted work that tells a story that needs to be told. We demand vision and intelligence and mystery in the fiction we publish."

🟢🟢 IDIOM 23

Central Queensland University, P.O. Box 172, 554-700 Yaamba Rd., Rockhampton QLD 4702, Australia. **E-mail:** idiom@cqu.edu.au; n.anae@cqu.edu.au. **Website:** www.cqu.edu.au/idiom23. **Contact:** Nicole Anae, editor. Estab. 1988. *Idiom 23*, published annually, is "named for the Tropic of Capricorn and is dedicated to developing the literary arts throughout the Central Queensland region. Submissions of original short stories, poems, articles, and b&w drawings and photographs are welcomed by the editorial collective. *Idiom 23* is not limited to a particular viewpoint but, on the contrary, hopes to encourage and publish a broad spectrum of writing. The collective seeks out creative work from community groups with as varied backgrounds as possible."

NEEDS Length: up to 3,000 words.

HOW TO CONTACT Submit complete ms via online submissions manager.

ILLUMINATIONS

Department of English, College of Charleston, 66 George St., Charleston SC 29424-0001. (843)953-1920. **E-mail:** illuminations@cofc.edu. **Website:** illuminations.cofc.edu. **Contact:** Simon Lewis, editor. Estab. 1982. "Over these many years, *Illuminations* has remained consistently true to its mission statement to publish new writers alongside some of the world's finest, including Nadine Gordimer, James Merrill, Carol Ann Duffy, Dennis Brutus, Allen Tate, interviews with Tim O'Brien, and letters from Flannery O'Connor and Ezra Pound. A number of new poets whose early work appeared in *Illuminations* have gone on to win prizes and accolades, and we at *Illuminations* sincerely value the chance to promote the work of emerging writers."

🟢   "As a magazine devoted primarily to poetry, we publish only 1-2 pieces of short fiction and/or nonfiction in any given year, and sometimes publish none at all. "

HOW TO CONTACT Submit complete ms by mail, e-mail, or online submissions manager.

PAYMENT/TERMS Pays 2 contributor's copies of current issue and 1 copy of subsequent issue.

🟢 IMAGE

3307 Third Ave. W., Seattle WA 98119. (206)281-2988. **Fax:** (206)281-2979. **E-mail:** image@imagejournal. org. **Website:** www.imagejournal.org. **Contact:** Gregory Wolfe, publisher and editor. Estab. 1989. "*Image* is a unique forum for the best writing and artwork that is informed by—or grapples with—religious faith. We have never been interested in art that merely regurgitates dogma or falls back on easy answers or didacticism. Instead, our focus has been on writing and visual artwork that embody a spiritual struggle, that seek to strike a balance between tradition and a profound openness to the world. Each issue explores this relationship through outstanding fiction, poetry, painting, sculpture, architecture, film, music, interviews, and dance. *Image* also features 4-color reproductions of visual art."

○ Magazine: 7x10; 136 pages; glossy cover stock; illustrations; photos.

NEEDS No sentimental, preachy, moralistic, obvious stories, or genre stories (unless they manage to transcend their genre). Length: 3,000-6,000 words.

HOW TO CONTACT Send complete ms by postal mail (with SASE for reply or return of ms) or online submissions manager. Does not accept e-mail submissions.

PAYMENT/TERMS Pays $10/page ($150 maximum) and 4 contributor's copies.

TIPS "Fiction must grapple with religious faith, though subjects need not be overtly religious."

🟢🟢🟢 INDIANA REVIEW

Ballantine Hall 529, 1020 E. Kirkwood Ave., Indiana University, Bloomington IN 47405. **E-mail:** inreview@indiana.edu. **Website:** indianareview.org. **Contact:** See masthead for current editorial staff. Estab. 1976. "*Indiana Review*, a nonprofit organization run by IU graduate students, is a journal of innovative fiction, nonfiction, and poetry. We're interested in energy, originality, and careful attention to craft. While we publish many well-known writers, we also welcome new and emerging poets and fiction writers."

○ See website for open reading periods.

NEEDS "We look for daring stories which integrate theme, language, character, and form. We like polished writing, humor, and fiction which has conse-

quence beyond the world of its narrator." No genre fiction. Length: up to 8,000 words.

HOW TO CONTACT Submit via online submissions manager.

PAYMENT/TERMS Pays $5/page ($10 minimum), plus 2 contributor's copies

TIPS "We're always looking for nonfiction essays that go beyond merely autobiographical revelation and utilize sophisticated organization and slightly radical narrative strategies. We want essays that are both lyrical and analytical where confession does not mean nostalgia. Read us before you submit. Often reading is slower in summer and holiday months. Only submit work to journals you would proudly subscribe to, then subscribe to a few. Take care to read the latest 2 issues and specifically mention work you identify with and why. Submit work that 'stacks up' with the work we've published."

INTERNATIONAL EXAMINER

409 Maynard Ave. S., #203, Seattle WA 98104. (206)624-3925. **Fax:** (206)624-3046. **E-mail:** editor@ iexaminer.org. **Website:** www.iexaminer.org. **Contact:** Travis Quezon, editor in chief. Estab. 1974. "*International Examiner* is about Asian American issues and things of interest to Asian Americans. We do not want stuff about Asian things (stories on your trip to China, Japanese Tea Ceremony, etc. will be rejected). Yes, we are in English."

NEEDS Asian American authored fiction by or about Asian Americans only.

HOW TO CONTACT Query.

TIPS "Write decent, suitable material on a subject of interest to the Asian American community. All submissions are reviewed; all good ones are contacted. It helps to call and run an idea by the editor before or after sending submissions."

🟢 INTERPRETER'S HOUSE

36 College Bounds, Old Aberdeen Aberdeen AB24 3DS, England. **E-mail:** theinterpretershouse@aol. com. **Website:** www.theinterpretershouse.com. **Contact:** Martin Malone, editor. Estab. 1996. *The Interpreter's House*, published 3 times/year spring, summer, and autumn, prints short stories and poetry.

○ Submission windows: October for the Spring issue, February for the Summer issue, June for the Autumn issue.

NEEDS Length: up to 2,000 words.

HOW TO CONTACT Submit up to 2 short stories by mail (with SASE) or e-mail.

PAYMENT/TERMS Pays contributor's copies.

💲 THE IOWA REVIEW

308 EPB, The University of Iowa, Iowa City IA 52242. (319)335-0462. **E-mail:** iowa-review@uiowa.edu. **Website:** www.iowareview.org. **Contact:** Harilaos Stecopoulos. Estab. 1970. *The Iowa Review*, published 3 times/year, prints fiction, poetry, essays, reviews, and, occasionally, interviews. Receives about 5,000 submissions/year, accepts up to 100. Press run is 2,900; 1,500 distributed to stores.

💬 This magazine uses the help of colleagues and graduate assistants. Its reading period for unsolicited work is September 1 through December 1. From January through April, the editors read entries to the annual Iowa Review Awards competition. Check the website for further information.

NEEDS "We are open to a range of styles and voices and always hope to be surprised by work we then feel we need." Receives 600 unsolicited mss/month. Accepts 4-6 mss/issue; 12-18 mss/year. Does not read mss January-August. Publishes ms an average of 12-18 months after acceptance. Agented fiction less than 2%. **Publishes some new writers/year.** Recently published work by Johanna Hunting, Bennett Sims, and Pedro Mairal.

HOW TO CONTACT Send complete ms with cover letter. Don't bother with queries. SASE for return of ms. Accepts mss by snail mail (SASE required for response) and online submission form at iowareview.submittable.com/submit; no e-mail submissions.

PAYMENT/TERMS Pays 8¢/word ($100 minimum), plus two contributor's copies.

TIPS "We publish essays, reviews, novel excerpts, stories, poems, and photography. We have no set guidelines regarding content but strongly recommend that writers read a sample issue before submitting."

IRIS

E-mail: submissions@creatingiris.org. **E-mail:** editorial@creatingiris.org. **Website:** www.creatingiris.org. Estab. 2014. "*Iris* seeks works of fiction and poetry that speak to LGBT young adults and their allies. We are interested in creative, thoughtful, original work that engages our young readers. We seek writing that challenges them and makes them think. We're looking for stories that capture their imaginations and characters that are relatable. We think there's a need in the young adult literary market for writing that speaks to the everyday experiences of LGBT adolescents: Themes of identity, friendship, coming out, families, etc., are especially welcome. The protagonist need not identify as LGBT, but we do ask that there be some kind of LGBT angle to your story. We welcome all genres of fiction and poetry!"

💬 "Because we publish for a young demographic, work submitted to *Iris* may not include depictions of sex, drug use, and violence. They can certainly be discussed and referenced, but not directly portrayed."

NEEDS Length: up to 3,000 words.

HOW TO CONTACT Submit complete ms via e-mail as attachment. Include cover letter in text of e-mail.

🌀 ISLAND

P.O. Box 4703, Hobart Tasmania 7000, Australia. **E-mail:** admin@islandmag.com. **Website:** www.islandmag.com. **Contact:** Geordie Williamson, editor at large. Estab. 1979. *Island* seeks quality fiction, poetry, and essays. It is "one of Australia's leading literary magazines, tracing the contours of our national, and international, culture while still retaining a uniquely Tasmanian perspective."

💬 Only publishes the work of subscribers; you can submit if you are not currently a subscriber, but if your piece is chosen, the subscription will be taken from the fee paid for the piece.

NEEDS "Although we are not strict about word limits, we tend not to publish flash fiction or microfiction at time. In terms of upper limits, we are less likely to publish works longer than 5,000 words. This is a general guideline: We do not have a formal cut-off for submissions. However, please be aware that if you submit a work longer than 4,000 words, we may not read beyond this length if we feel certain the work is not suited for publication with us."

HOW TO CONTACT Submit 1 piece via online submissions manager.

PAYMENT/TERMS Pay varies.

JABBERWOCK REVIEW

Department of English, Mississippi State University, Drawer E, Mississippi State MS 39762. **E-mail:** jabberwockreview@english.msstate.edu. **Website:** www.jabberwock.org.msstate.edu. **Contact:** Becky Hagenston, editor. Estab. 1979. *Jabberwock Review* is a literary journal published semi-annually by students and faculty of Mississippi State University. The journal consists of poetry, fiction, and nonfiction from around the world. Funding is provided by the Office of the Provost, the College of Arts & Sciences, the Shackouls Honors College, the Department of English, and subscriptions.

○ Submissions accepted August 15-October 20 and January 15-March 15.

NEEDS Does not publish romance or erotica.

HOW TO CONTACT Submit no more than 1 story at a time.

PAYMENT/TERMS Pays contributor's copies.

TIPS "It might take a few months to get a response from us, but your ms will be read with care. Our editors enjoy reading submissions (really!) and will remember writers who are persistent and committed to getting a story 'right' through revision."

JEWISH CURRENTS

P.O. Box 111, Accord NY 12404. (845)626-2427. **E-mail:** editor@jewishcurrents.org. **E-mail:** submissions@jewishcurrents.org. **Website:** www.jewishcurrents.org. **Contact:** Lawrence Bush, editor; Ron Skolnik, associate editor. Estab. 1946. *Jewish Currents*, published 4 times/year, is a progressive Jewish quarterly magazine that carries on the insurgent tradition of the Jewish left through independent journalism, political commentary, and a 'countercultural' approach to Jewish arts and literature.

○ *Jewish Currents* is 80 pages, magazine-sized, offset-printed, saddle-stapled with a full-color arts section, "Jcultcha & Funny Pages." The Winter issue is a 12-month arts calendar.

HOW TO CONTACT Send complete ms with cover letter. "Writers should include brief biographical information."

PAYMENT/TERMS Pays contributor's copies or small honoraria.

J JOURNAL: NEW WRITING ON JUSTICE

524 W. 59th St., Seventh Floor, New York NY 10019. (212)237-8697. **E-mail:** jjournal@jjay.cuny.edu. **E-mail:** submissionsjjournal@gmail.com. **Website:** www.jjournal.org. **Contact:** Adam Berlin and Jeffrey Heiman, editors. Estab. 2008. "*J Journal* publishes literary fiction, creative nonfiction, and poetry on the justice theme—social, political, criminal, gender, racial, religious, economic. While the justice theme is specific, it need not dominate the work. We're inter-

ested in innovative writing that examines justice from all creative perspectives. Tangential connections to justice are often better than direct."

○ Several works from *J Journal* have been recognized in *Pushcart Prize* anthologies.

NEEDS Receives 100 mss/month. Accepts 5-8 mss/issue; 10-16 mss/year. Length: 750-6,000 words. Average length: 4,000 words.

HOW TO CONTACT Send complete ms with cover letter. Include estimated word count, brief bio, list of publications.

PAYMENT/TERMS Pays 2 contributor's copies. Additional copies $10.

TIPS "We're looking for literary fiction, memoir, personal narrative, or poetry with a connection, direct or tangential, to the theme of justice."

◉ THE JOURNAL

The Ohio State University, 164 Annie and John Glenn Ave., Columbus OH 43210. **E-mail:** managingeditor@thejournalmag.org. **Website:** thejournalmag.org. Estab. 1973. "We are interested in quality fiction, poetry, nonfiction, art, and reviews of new books of poetry, fiction, and nonfiction. We impose no restrictions on category, type, or length of submission for fiction, poetry, and nonfiction. We are happy to consider long stories and self-contained excerpts of novels. Please double-space all prose submissions. Please send 3-5 poems in 1 submission. We only accept online submissions and will not respond to mailed submissions."

○ "We're open to all forms; we tend to favor work that gives evidence of a mature and sophisticated sense of the language."

NEEDS No romance, science fiction, or religious/devotional. Length: up to 10,000 words.

HOW TO CONTACT Send full ms via online submissions manager. "Mss are rejected because of lack of understanding of the short story form, shallow plots, undeveloped characters. Cure: Read as much well-written fiction as possible. Our readers prefer 'psychological' fiction rather than stories with intricate plots. Take care to present a clean, well-typed submission."

PAYMENT/TERMS Pays 2 contributor's copies and one-year subscription.

KAIMANA: LITERARY ARTS HAWAI'I

Hawai'i Literary Arts Council, P.O. Box 11213, Honolulu HI 96828. **E-mail:** reimersa001@hawaii.rr.com. **Website:** www.hawaii.edu/hlac. Estab. 1974. *Kaimana: Literary Arts Hawai'i*, published annually, is the magazine of the Hawai'i Literary Arts Council. Wants submissions with "some Pacific reference—Asia, Polynesia, Hawai'i—but not exclusively."

○ *Kaimana* is 64-76 pages, 7.5x10, saddle-stapled, with high-quality printing. Press run is 1,000. "Poets published in *Kaimana* have received the Pushcart Prize, the Hawaii Award for Literature, the Stefan Baciu Award, the Cades Award, and the John Unterecker Award."

HOW TO CONTACT Submit ms with SASE. No e-mail submissions. Cover letter is preferred.

PAYMENT/TERMS Pays 2 contributor's copies.

TIPS "Hawai'i gets a lot of 'travelling regionalists,' visiting writers with inevitably superficial observations. We also get superb visiting observers who are careful craftsmen anywhere. *Kaimana* is interested in the latter, to complement our own best Hawai'i writers."

○⑤ KALEIDOSCOPE

United Disability Services, 701 S. Main St., Akron OH 44311-1019. (330)762-9755. **Fax:** (330)762-0912. **E-mail:** kaleidoscope@udsakron.org. **Website:** www.kaleidoscopeonline.org. **Contact:** Gail Willmott, editor in chief. Estab. 1979. Kaleidoscope magazine creatively focuses on the experiences of disability through literature and the fine arts. As a pioneering literary resource for the field of disability studies, this award-winning publication expresses the diversity of the disability experience from a variety of perspectives including: individuals, families, friends, caregivers, educators, and healthcare professionals, among others."

○ Kaleidoscope has received awards from the Great Lakes Awards Competition and Ohio Public Images; received the Ohioana Award of Editorial Excellence.

NEEDS Wants short stories with a well-crafted plot and engaging characters. No fiction that is stereotypical, patronizing, sentimental, erotic, or maudlin. No romance, religious or dogmatic fiction; no children's literature. Length: up to 5,000 words.

HOW TO CONTACT Submit complete ms by website or e-mail. Include cover letter.

PAYMENT/TERMS Pays $25.

TIPS "The material chosen for Kaleidoscope challenges and overcomes stereotypical, patronizing, and sentimental attitudes about disability. We accept the work of writers with and without disabilities; however

the work of a writer without a disability must focus on some aspect of disability. The criteria for good writing apply: effective technique, thought-provoking subject matter, and, in general, a mature grasp of the art of storytelling. Writers should avoid using offensive language and always put the person before the disability."

KANSAS CITY VOICES

Whispering Prairie Press, P.O. Box 410661, Kansas City MO 64141. **E-mail:** info@wppress.org. **Website:** www.wppress.org. **Contact:** Jessica Conoley, managing editor. Estab. 2003. *Kansas City Voices*, published annually, features an eclectic mix of fiction, poetry, and art. "We seek exceptional written and visual creations from established and emerging voices."

○ Submission period: December 15 through March 15.

NEEDS Length: up to 2,500 words.

HOW TO CONTACT Submit up to 2 complete mss via online submissions manager.

PAYMENT/TERMS Pays small honorarium and 1 contributor's copy.

TIPS "There is no 'type' of work we are looking for, and while we would love for you to read through our previous issues, it is not an indicator of what kind of work we actively seek. Our editors rotate, our tastes evolve, and good work is just *good work*. We want to feel something when we encounter a piece. We want to be excited, surprised, thoughtful, and interested. We want to have a reaction. We want to share the best voices we find. Send us that one."

○ KASMA MAGAZINE

Kasma Publications, **E-mail:** editors@kasmamagazine.com. **Website:** www.kasmamagazine.com. **Contact:** Alex Korovessis, editor. Estab. 2009. Online magazine. "We publish the best science fiction from promising new and established writers. Our aim is to provide stories that are well written, original, and thought provoking."

NEEDS No erotica or excessive violence/language. Length: 1,000-5,000 words.

HOW TO CONTACT Submit complete ms via e-mail.

PAYMENT/TERMS Pays $25 CAD.

TIPS "The type of stories I enjoy the most usually come as a surprise: I think I know what is happening, but the underlying reality is revealed to me as I read on. That said, I've accepted many stories that don't fit this model. Sometimes I'm introduced to a new story structure. Sometimes the story I like reminds me of another story, but it introduces a slightly different spin on it. Other times, the story introduces such interesting and original ideas that structure and style don't seem to matter as much."

THE KELSEY REVIEW

Liberal Arts Division, Mercer County Community College, P.O. Box 17202, Trenton NJ 08690. **E-mail:** kelsey.review@mccc.edu. **Website:** www.mccc.edu/community_kelsey-review.shtml and kelseyreview.com. **Contact:** Jacqueline Vogtman, Editor. Estab. 1988. *The Kelsey Review*, published online quarterly in September, December, March, and June by Mercer County Community College, serves as an outlet for literary talent of people living and working in the larger Mercer County, New Jersey, area.

Submissions are open between January 1 and May 31 via our Submittable site.

NEEDS Has no specifications as to form, subject matter, or style. Length: up to 4,000 words.

HOW TO CONTACT Submit via online submissions manager. Submissions are limited to people who live, work, or give literary readings in Mercer County, New Jersey.

TIPS "See *The Kelsey Review* website for current guidelines. Note: We only accept submissions from the Mercer County, New Jersey, area."

THE KENYON REVIEW

Finn House, 102 W. Wiggin, Gambier OH 43022. (740)427-5208. **Fax:** (740)427-5417. **E-mail:** kenyonreview@kenyon.edu. **Website:** www.kenyonreview.org. **Contact:** Alicia Misarti. Estab. 1939. "An international journal of literature, culture, and the arts, dedicated to an inclusive representation of the best in new writing (fiction, poetry, essays, interviews, criticism) from established and emerging writers."

The Kenyon Review receives about 8,000 submissions/year. Also publishes *KR Online*, a separate and complementary online literary magazine.

NEEDS Receives 800 unsolicited mss/month. Unsolicited mss accepted September 15-November 1 only. Recently published work by Alice Hoffman, Beth Ann Fennelly, Romulus Linney, John Koethe, Albert Goldbarth, and Erin McGraw. Length: 3-15 typeset pages preferred.

HOW TO CONTACT Only accepts mss via online submissions manager; visit website for instructions. Do not submit via e-mail or mail.

PAYMENT/TERMS Pays 8¢/published word of prose (minimum payment $80; maximum payment $450); word count does not include title, notes, or citations.

TIPS "We no longer accept mailed or e-mailed submissions. Work will only be read if it is submitted through our online program on our website. Reading period is September 15 through November 1. We look for strong voice, unusual perspective, and power in the writing."

🌑 LADY CHURCHILL'S ROSEBUD WRISTLET

Small Beer Press, 150 Pleasant St., #306, Easthampton MA 01027. **E-mail:** smallbeerpress@gmail.com. **Website:** www.smallbeerpress.com/lcrw. **Contact:** Gavin Grant, editor. Estab. 1996. *Lady Churchill's Rosebud Wristlet* accepts fiction, nonfiction, poetry, and b&w art. "The fiction we publish tends toward, but is not limited to, the speculative. This does not mean only quietly desperate stories. We will consider items that fall out with regular categories. We do not accept multiple submissions."

Semiannual.

NEEDS Receives 100 unsolicited mss/month. Accepts 4-6 mss/issue; 8-12 mss/year. Publishes 2-4 new writers/year. Also publishes literary essays, poetry. Has published work by Ted Chiang, Gwenda Bond, Alissa Nutting, and Charlie Anders. "We do not publish gore, sword and sorcery, or pornography. We can discuss these terms if you like. There are places for them all; this is not one of them." Length: 200-7,000 words.

HOW TO CONTACT Send complete ms with a cover letter. Include estimated word count. Send SASE (or IRC) for return of ms, or send a disposable copy of ms and #10 SASE for reply only.

PAYMENT/TERMS Pays $25.

TIPS "We recommend you read *Lady Churchill's Rosebud Wristlet* before submitting. You can pick up a copy from our website or from assorted book shops."

LAKE EFFECT: AN INTERNATIONAL LITERARY JOURNAL

School of Humanities & Social Sciences, Penn State Erie, The Behrend College, Erie PA 16563-1501. **E-mail:** gol1@psu.edu; alp248@psu.edu. **Website:** psbehrend.psu.edu/school-of-humanities-social-sciences/academic-programs-1/creative-writing/cw-student-organizations/lake-effect. **Contact:** George Looney, editor in chief. Estab. 1978. *Lake Effect* is a publication of the School of Humanities and Social Sciences at Penn State Erie, The Behrend College.

NEEDS "*Lake Effect* is looking for stories that emerge from character and language as much as from plot. *Lake Effect* does not, in general, publish genre fiction, but literary fiction. *Lake Effect* seeks work from both established and new and emerging writers." Query first for stories longer than 15 pages.

HOW TO CONTACT Submit via online submissions manager.

THE LAND

Free Press Co., P.O. Box 3169, Mankato MN 56002-3169. (507)345-4523. **E-mail:** editor@thelandonline.com. **Website:** www.thelandonline.com. Estab. 1976. "Although we're not tightly focused on any one type of farming, our articles must be of interest to farmers. In other words, will your article topic have an impact on people who live and work in rural areas?" Prefers to work with Minnesota or Iowa writers.

TIPS "Be enthused about rural Minnesota and Iowa life and agriculture, and be willing to work with our editors. We try to stress relevance. When sending me a query, convince me the story belongs in a Minnesota farm publication."

LANDFALL: NEW ZEALAND ARTS AND LETTERS

Otago University Press, P.O. Box 56, Dunedin 9054, New Zealand. (64)(3)479-4155. **E-mail:** landfall.press@otago.ac.nz. **Website:** www.otago.ac.nz/press/landfall. **Contact:** Editor. Estab. 1947. *Landfall: New Zealand Arts and Letters* contains literary fiction and essays, poetry, extracts from works-in-progress, commentary on New Zealand arts and culture, work by visual artists including photographers and reviews of local books. (*Landfall* does not accept unsolicited reviews.)

Deadlines for submissions: January 10 for the May issue, July 10 for the November issue. "*Landfall* is open to work by New Zealand and Pacific writers or by writers whose work has a connection to the region in subject matter or location. Work from Australian writers is occasionally included as a special feature."

NEEDS Length: up to 3,000 words.

HOW TO CONTACT Submit up to 3 pieces at a time. Prefers e-mail submissions. Include cover letter with contact info and bio of about 30 words.

THE LAUREL REVIEW

Northwest Missouri State University, Dept. of Language, Literature, and Writing, 800 University Dr., Maryville MO 64468. (660)562-1739. **Website:** laurel-review.org. **Contact:** John Gallaher and Luke Rolfes, editors; Daniel Biegelson and Richard Sonnenmoser, associate editors. Estab. 1960. "We publish poetry and fiction of high quality, from the traditional to the avant-garde. We are eclectic, open, and flexible. Good writing is all we seek."

Biannual magazine: 6x9; 124-128 pages; good-quality paper. Reading period: September 1-May 1.

HOW TO CONTACT Submit complete ms via online submission manager or postal mail.

PAYMENT/TERMS Pays 2 contributor's copies and one-year subscription.

TIPS "Nothing really matters to us except our perception that the story presents something powerfully felt by the writer and communicated intensely to a serious reader. (We believe, incidentally, that comedy is just as serious a matter as tragedy, and we don't mind a bit if something makes us laugh out loud; we get too little that makes us laugh, in fact.) We try to reply promptly, though we don't always manage that. In short, we want good poems and good stories. We hope to be able to recognize them, and we print what we believe is the best work submitted."

LEADING EDGE MAGAZINE

4087 JKB, Provo UT 84602. **E-mail:** editor@leadingedgemagazine.com; fiction@leadingedgemagazine.com; art@leadingedgemagazine.com; poetry@leadingedgemagazine.com; nonfiction@leadingedgemagazine.com. **Website:** www.leadingedgemagazine.com. **Contact:** Hayley Brooks, editor in chief. Estab. 1981. "*Leading Edge* is a magazine dedicated to new and upcoming talent in the fields of science fiction and fantasy. We strive to encourage developing and established talent and provide high-quality speculative fiction to our readers." Does not accept mss with sex, excessive violence, or profanity.

Accepts unsolicited submissions.

NEEDS Length: up to 15,000 words.

HOW TO CONTACT Send complete ms with cover letter and SASE. Include estimated word count.

PAYMENT/TERMS Pays 1¢/word; $50 maximum.

TIPS "Buy a sample issue to know what is currently selling in our magazine. Also, make sure to follow the writer's guidelines when submitting."

LE FORUM

University of Maine, Franco-American Center, Orono ME 04469-5719. (207)581-3789. **Fax:** (207)581-3791. **E-mail:** lisa_michaud@umit.maine.edu. **Website:** umaine.edu/francoamerican/le-forum. **Contact:** Lisa Desjardins Michaud, editor. Estab. 1972. "We will consider any type of short fiction, poetry, and critical essay having to do with the Franco-American experience. They must be of good quality in French or English. We are also looking for Canadian writers with French-North American experiences."

HOW TO CONTACT Include SASE.

PAYMENT/TERMS Pays 3 contributor's copies.

TIPS "Write honestly. Start with a strongly felt personal Franco-American experience. If you make us feel what you have felt, we will publish it. We stress that this publication deals specifically with the Franco-American experience."

LILITH MAGAZINE: INDEPENDENT, JEWISH & FRANKLY FEMINIST

119 West 57th St., Suite 1210, New York NY 10019. (212)757-0818. **Fax:** (212)757-5705. **E-mail:** info@lilith.org. **Website:** www.lilith.org. **Contact:** Susan Weidman Schneider, editor in chief; Naomi Danis, managing editor. Estab. 1976. *Lilith Magazine: Independent, Jewish & Frankly Feminist*, published quarterly, welcomes submissions of high-quality, lively writing: reportage, opinion pieces, memoirs, fiction, and poetry on subjects of interest to Jewish women.

○ *Lilith Magazine* is 48 pages, magazine-sized, with glossy color cover. Press run is about 10,000 (about 6,000 subscribers). Subscription: $26/year. For all submissions: Make sure name and contact information appear on each page of mss. Include a short bio (1-2 sentences), written in third person. Accepts submissions year round.

NEEDS Length: up to 3,000 words.

HOW TO CONTACT Send complete ms via online submissions form or mail.

TIPS "Read a copy of the publication before you submit your work. Please be patient."

THE LISTENING EYE

Kent State University Geauga Campus, 14111 Claridon-Troy Rd., Burton OH 44021. (440)286-3840. **E-mail:** grace_butcher@msn.com. **E-mail:** Only from other countries. **Contact:** Grace Butcher, editor. Estab. 1970. "We look for powerful, unusual imagery, content, and plot in our short stories. In poetry, we look for tight lines that don't sound like prose, unexpected images or juxtapositions, the unusual use of language, noticeable relationships of sounds, a twist in viewpoint, an ordinary idea in extraordinary language, an amazing and complex idea simply stated, play on words and with words, an obvious love of language. Poets need to read the 'Big Three'—Cummings, Thomas, Hopkins—to see the limits to which language can be taken. Then read the 'Big Two'—Dickinson to see how simultaneously tight, terse, and universal a poem can be, and Whitman to see how sprawling, cosmic, and personal. Then read everything you can find that's being published in literary magazines today, and see how your work compares to all of the above."

○ Magazine: 5.5x8.5; 60 pages; photographs. "We publish the occasional very short stories (750 words/3 pages double-spaced) in any subject and any style, but the language must be strong, unusual, free from cliché and vagueness. We are a shoestring operation from a small campus, but we publish high-quality work." Reads submissions January 1-April 15 only.

NEEDS "Pretty much anything will be considered except porn." Recently published work by Simon Perchik, Lyn Lifshin, and John Hart. Publishes short shorts. Also publishes poetry. Sometimes comments on rejected mss.

HOW TO CONTACT Send SASE for return of ms or disposable copy of ms with SASE for reply only.

LITERAL LATTÉ

200 E. 10th St., Ste. 240, New York NY 10003. (212)260-5532. **Website:** www.literal-latte.com. **Contact:** Jenine Gordon Bockman and Jeffrey Michael Bockman, editors and publishers. Estab. 1994. Bimonthly online publication. Print anthologies featuring the best of the website. "We want great writing in all styles and subjects. A feast is made of a variety of flavors."

NEEDS Accepts all styles and genres. Length: up to 10,000 words.

HOW TO CONTACT Submit via online submissions manager or postal mail.

PAYMENT/TERMS Pays anthology copies.

TIPS "Keeping free thought free and challenging entertainment are not mutually exclusive. Words make a ms stand out, words beautifully woven together in striking and memorable patterns."

LITERARY JUICE

Seattle WA. **E-mail:** info@literaryjuice.com. **Website:** www.literaryjuice.com. **Contact:** Sara Rajan, editor in chief; Andrea O'Connor and Dinesh Rajan, managing editors. Estab. 2011. Bimonthly online literary magazine that publishes original, unpublished works of fiction, poetry, art, and photography. Does not publish works of nonfiction, essays, or interviews.

NEEDS "We do not publish works with intense sexual content." Length: 100-2,000 words.

HOW TO CONTACT Submit complete ms via online submissions manager.

TIPS Looking for works that are not only thought-provoking, but venture into unconventional territory as well. Avoid submitting mainstream stories and poems (stories about zombies or politics fall into this category). Instead, take the reader to a new realm that has yet to be explored.

⊙ LITERARY MAMA

E-mail: lminfo@literarymama.com. **Website:** www.literarymama.com. **Contact:** Karna Converse, editor in chief. Estab. 2003. Online monthly magazine that features writing about the complexities and many faces of motherhood. Departments include columns, creative nonfiction, fiction, literary reflections, poetry, profiles, and book reviews. "We prefer previously unpublished work and are interested in work that offers a fresh perspective."

● "*Literary Mama* is not currently a paying market. We are all volunteers here: editors, writers, and editorial assistants. With the publication of each issue, we make a concerted effort to promote the work of our contributors via Facebook, Twitter, and our newsletter."

NEEDS "We love stories with strong narrative structure, great characters, interesting settings, beautiful language, and complicated themes." Length: up to 5,000 words.

○◌ THE LITERARY REVIEW

285 Madison Ave., Madison NJ 07940. (973)443-8564. **Fax:** (973)443-8364. **E-mail:** info@theliteraryreview.org. **Website:** www.theliteraryreview.org. **Contact:** Minna Proctor, editor. Estab. 1957. *The Literary Review* is published quarterly by Fairleigh Dickinson University.

● Work published in *The Literary Review* has been included in *Editor's Choice*, *Best American Short Stories*, and *Pushcart Prize* anthologies. Uses online submissions manager.

NEEDS Wants works of high literary quality only. Does not want to see "overused subject matter or pat resolutions to conflicts." Length: up to 7,000 words.

HOW TO CONTACT Submit electronically only. Does not accept paper submissions.

PAYMENT/TERMS Pays 2 contributor's copies and a one-year subscription.

TIPS "We want original dramatic situations with complex moral and intellectual resonance and vivid prose. We don't want versions of familiar plots and relationships. Too much of what we are seeing today is openly derivative in subject, plot, and prose style. We pride ourselves on spotting new writers with fresh insight and approach."

LITTLE PATUXENT REVIEW

P.O. Box 6084, Columbia MD 21045. **E-mail:** editor@littlepatuxentreview.org. **Website:** www.littlepatuxentreview.org. **Contact:** Steven Leyva, editor. Estab. 2006. "*Little Patuxent Review* (*LPR*) is a community-based, biannual print journal devoted to literature and the arts, primarily in the Mid-Atlantic region. We profile the work of a major poet or fiction writer and a visual artist in each issue. We celebrate the launch of each issue with a series of readings and broadcast highlights on *LPR*'s YouTube channel. All forms and styles considered. Please see our website for the current theme."

● *LPR* is about 120 pages; digest-sized; 100# finch cover; artwork (varies depending on featured artist). Has published poetry by Lucille Clifton, Martín Espada, Donald Hall, Joy Harjo, Marie Howe, Myra Sklarew, Clarinda Harriss, and Alan King. 2011 Pushcart Prize for "Patronized" by Tara Hart.

NEEDS Length: up to 5,000 words.

HOW TO CONTACT Submit complete ms by online submissions manager; no mail or e-mail submissions. Include word count and 75-word bio.

PAYMENT/TERMS Pays 1 contributor's copy.

TIPS "Please see our website for the current theme. Poetry and prose must exhibit the highest quality to be considered. Please read a sample issue before submitting."

THE LONDON MAGAZINE

11 Queen's Gate, London SW7 5EL, United Kingdom. (44)(0)20 7584 5977. **E-mail:** admin@thelondonmagazine.org. **Website:** www.thelondonmagazine.org. **Contact:** Steven O'Brien, editor. Estab. 1732. "We publish literary writing of the highest quality. We look for poetry and short fiction that startles and entertains us. Reviews, essays, memoir pieces, and features should be erudite, lucid, and incisive. We are obviously interested in writing that has a London focus, but not exclusively so, since London is a world city with international concerns."

NEEDS "Short fiction should address mature and sophisticated themes. Moreover, it should have an elegance of style, structure and characterization. We do not normally publish science fiction or fantasy writing, or erotica." Length: up to 4,000 words.

HOW TO CONTACT Send complete ms. Submit via online submissions manager, e-mail (as an attachment), or postal mail (enclose SASE).

TIPS "Please look at *The London Magazine* before you submit work so that you can see the type of material we publish."

LONG LIFE

Longevity through Technology, The Immortalist Society, 24355 Sorrentino Ct., Clinton Township MI 48035. **E-mail:** info@cryonics.org. **Website:** www.cryonics.org/resources/long-life-magazine. Estab. 1968. "*Long Life* magazine is a publication for people who are particularly interested in cryonic suspension: the theory, practice, legal problems, etc. associated with being frozen when you die in the hope of eventual restoration to life and health. Many people who receive the publication have relatives who have undergone cryonic preparation or have made such arrangements for themselves or are seriously considering this option. Readers are also interested in other aspects of life extension such as anti-aging research and food supplements that may slow aging. Articles we publish include speculation on what the future will be like; problems of living in a future world, and science in general, particularly as it may apply to cryonics and life extension."

NEEDS "We occasionally publish short fiction, but cryonics and life extension should be essential to the story. We are not interested in horror, in stories where the future is portrayed as gloom and doom, end-of-the-world stories, or those with an inspirational theme." Length: up to 2,500 words.

PAYMENT/TERMS Pays 1 contributor's copy.

TIPS "We are a small magazine but with a highly intelligent and educated readership which is socially and economically diverse. We currently don't pay for material but are seeking new authors and provide contributors with copies of the magazine with the contributor's published works. Look over a copy of *Long Life*, or talk with the editor to get the tone of the publication. There is an excellent chance that your ms will be accepted if it is well written and 'on theme.' Pictures to accompany the article are always welcome, and we like to publish photos of the authors with their first ms."

THE LONG STORY

18 Eaton St., Lawrence MA 01843. (978)686-7638. **E-mail:** rpburnham@mac.com. **Website:** www.longstorylitmag.com. **Contact:** R.P. Burnham. Estab. 1983. For serious, educated, literary people. "We publish high literary quality of any kind but especially look for stories that have difficulty getting published elsewhere: committed fiction, working-class settings, left-wing themes, etc."

NEEDS Receives 25-35 unsolicited mss/month. Accepts 6-7 mss/issue. Publishes 90% new writers/year. No science fiction, adventure, romance, etc. Length: 8,000-20,000 words; average length: 8,000-12,000 words.

HOW TO CONTACT Include SASE.

PAYMENT/TERMS Pays 2 contributor's copies; $6 charge for extras.

TIPS "Read us first, and make sure submitted material is the kind we're interested in. Send clear, legible mss. We're not interested in commercial success; rather, we want to provide a place for long stories, the most difficult literary form to publish in our country."

LONG STORY SHORT, AN E-ZINE FOR WRITERS

P.O. Box 475, Lewistown MT 59457. **E-mail:** alongstory_short@aol.com. **Website:** www.alongstoryshort.

net. **Contact:** Anisa Claire, Kim Bussey, editors. Estab. 2003. *Long Story Short, An E-zine for Writers* publishes "the best fiction and poetry from both emerging and established writers.

○ Free newsletter with poetry of the month chosen by poetry editor; includes author's bio and web page listed in the e-zine. Offers light critique of submissions upon request and a free writing forum.

NEEDS Accepts all genres of flash fiction or prose. Length: up to 2,000 words.

HOW TO CONTACT Submit by e-mail; no attachments.

PAYMENT/TERMS Pays $10-15 and 1 contributor's copy for short stories 1,000-2,000 words. Pays 1 contributor's copy for flash fiction.

THE LOS ANGELES REVIEW

P.O. Box 2458, Redmond WA 98073. (626)356-4760. **Fax:** (626)356-9974. **E-mail:** lareview.trager.editor@gmail.com. **Website:** losangelesreview.org. **Contact:** Alisa Trager, managing editor. Estab. 2003.

NEEDS "We're looking for hard-to-put-down shorties under 500 words and lengthier shorts up to 4,000 words—lively, vivid, excellent literary fiction." Does not accept multiple submissions. Does not want pornography. Length: 500-4,000 words.

HOW TO CONTACT "Submishmash, our online submission form, is now our preferred method of submission, though you may still submit through postal mail. Please see our guidelines online."

TIPS "Read a few recent issues to see what we're about. Pay close attention to the submission guidelines. We like cover letters, but please keep them brief."

LOST LAKE FOLK OPERA

Shipwreckt Books Publishing Company, 309 W. Stevens Ave., Rushford MN 55971. **E-mail:** contact@shipwrecktbooks.com. **Website:** www.shipwrecktbooks.com. **Contact:** Tom Driscoll, managing editor. Estab. 2013. *Lost Lake Folk Opera* magazine, published twice annually, accepts submissions of critical journalism, short fiction, poetry, and graphic art.

○ Seeks high-quality submissions. For journalistic pieces, please query first.

NEEDS Length: 250-3,500 words.

HOW TO CONTACT Query with sample.

PAYMENT/TERMS Pays contributor copies; offers 30% discount off cover price.

TIPS "When in doubt, edit and cut. Please remember to read your submission. Don't expect *LLFO* to wash your car and detail it. Send clean copies of your work."

LOUISIANA LITERATURE

SLU Box 10792, Hammond LA 70402. **E-mail:** lalit@selu.edu. **Website:** www.louisianaliterature.org. **Contact:** Jack B. Bedell, editor. Estab. 1984. "Since 1984, *Louisiana Literature* has featured some of the finest writing published in America. The journal has always striven to spotlight local talent alongside nationally recognized authors. Whether it's work from established writers or from first-time publishers, *Louisiana Literature* is always looking to print the finest poetry and fiction available."

○ Biannual magazine: 6x9; 150 pages; 70 lb. paper; card cover; illustrations. Receives 100 unsolicited mss/month. May not read mss June-July. Publishes 4 new writers/year. Publishes theme issues. Has published work by Anthony Bukowski, Aaron Gwyn, Robert Phillips, and R.T. Smith. Work first published in *Louisiana Literature* is regularly reprinted in collections and is nominated for prizes from the National Book Awards for both genres and the Pulitzer. Recently, stories by Aaron Gwyn and Robert Olen Butler were selected for inclusion in *New Stories from the South*.

NEEDS Reviews fiction. "No sloppy, ungrammatical mss." Length: 1,000-6,000 words; average length: 3,500 words.

HOW TO CONTACT Submit ms via online submissions manager. Ms should be double-spaced.

PAYMENT/TERMS Pays 2 contributor's copies.

TIPS "Cut out everything that is not a functioning part of the story. Make sure your ms is professionally presented. Use relevant, specific detail in every scene. We love detail, local color, voice, and craft. Any professional ms stands out."

THE LOUISIANA REVIEW

Louisiana State University Eunice, Division of Liberal Arts, P.O. Box 1129, Eunice LA 70535. (337)550-1315. **E-mail:** bfonteno@lsue.edu. **Website:** web.lsue.edu/la-review. **Contact:** Dr. Billy Fontenot, editor and fiction editor; Dr. Jude Meche, poetry editor; Dr. Diane Langlois, art editor. Estab. 1999. *The Louisiana Review*, published annually during the fall or spring semesters, offers "Louisiana poets, writers, and artists a place to showcase their most beautiful pieces. Others may submit Louisiana- or Southern-related poetry, stories, and art. Publishes photographs. Sometimes publishes nonfiction." Wants "strong imagery, metaphor, and evidence of craft."

○ *The Louisiana Review* is 100 pages, digest-sized, professionally printed, perfect-bound. Press run is 300-600.

NEEDS Receives 25 unsolicited mss/month. Accepts 5-7 mss/issue. Reads year round. Has published work by Ronald Frame, Tom Bonner, Laura Cario, and Sheryl St. Germaine. Also publishes short shorts. No length restrictions.

HOW TO CONTACT Send SASE for return of ms. Accepts multiple submissions.

PAYMENT/TERMS Pays 1 contributor's copy.

TIPS "We do like to have fiction play out visually as a film would rather than be static and undramatized. Louisiana or Gulf Coast settings and themes preferred."

LULLWATER REVIEW

Emory University, P.O. Box 122036, Atlanta GA 30322. **E-mail:** emorylullwaterreview@gmail.com. **Website:** emorylullwaterreview.com. **Contact:** Aneyn M. O'Grady, editor in chief. Estab. 1990. "We're a small, student-run literary magazine published out of Emory University in Atlanta, Georgia, with 2 issues yearly—once in the fall and once in the spring. You can find us in the *Index of American Periodical Verse*, the *American Humanities Index* and as a member of the Council of Literary Magazines and Presses. We welcome work that brings a fresh perspective, whether through language or the visual arts."

NEEDS Recently published work by Greg Jenkins, Thomas Juvik, Jimmy Gleacher, Carla Vissers, and Judith Sudnolt. No romance or science fiction, please. Length: up to 5,000 words.

HOW TO CONTACT Send complete ms via e-mail. *Does not accept postal mail submissions.*

PAYMENT/TERMS Pays 3 contributor's copies.

TIPS "We at the *Lullwater Review* look for clear, cogent writing, strong character development, and an engaging approach to the story in our fiction submissions. Stories with particularly strong voices and well-developed central themes are especially encouraged. Be sure that your ms is ready before mailing it to us. Revise, revise, revise! Be original, honest, and, of course, keep trying."

LUMINA

Sarah Lawrence College, **E-mail:** lumina@gm.slc.edu. **Website:** luminajournal.com. **Contact:** Sarah Dean, editor in chief; Steven Wolf, fiction editor; Melanie Anagnos, nonfiction editor; Marie Marandola, poetry editor. Estab. 2000. "*LUMINA*'s mission is to provide a journal where emerging and established writers and visual artists come together in exploration of the new and appreciation of the traditional. We want to see sonnets sharing space with experimental prose; we want art that pushes boundaries and bends rules with eloquence."

NEEDS Length: up to 5,000 words.

HOW TO CONTACT Submit via online submissions manager. All submissions are read blind; do not include personal information on submission documents.

LUNGFULL!MAGAZINE

316 23rd St., Brooklyn NY 11215. **E-mail:** customerservice@lungfull.org. **Website:** lungfull.org. **Contact:** Brendan Lorber, editor/publisher. Estab. 1994. "*LUNGFULL!* Magazine World Headquarters in Brooklyn is home to a team of daredevils who make it their job to bring you only the finest in typos, misspellings, and awkward phrases. That's because *LUNGFULL!magazine* is the only literary and art journal in America that prints the rough drafts of people's work so you can see the creative process as it happens."

○ *LUNGFULL!* was the recipient of a grant from the New York State Council for the Arts.

NEEDS Publishes rough drafts.

HOW TO CONTACT Submit up to 15 pages of prose. Include cover letter.

⑤ LYRICAL PASSION POETRY E-ZINE

P.O. Box 17331, Arlington VA 22216. **E-mail:** lpezine-submissions@gmail.com. **Website:** lyricalpassionpoetry.yolasite.com. **Contact:** Raquel D. Bailey, founding editor. Estab. 2007. Founded by award-winning poet Raquel D. Bailey, *Lyrical Passion Poetry E-Zine* is an attractive monthly online literary magazine specializing in Japanese short-form poetry. Publishes quality artwork, well-crafted short fiction, and poetry in English by emerging and established writers. Literature of lasting literary value will be considered. Welcomes the traditional to the experimental. Poetry works written in German will be considered if accompanied by translations. Offers annual short fiction and poetry contests.

HOW TO CONTACT Send complete ms, typed and double-spaced. Cover letter preferred.

◐◉⊘ MĀNOA: A PACIFIC JOURNAL OF INTERNATIONAL WRITING

University of Hawaii at Mānoa, English Department, Honolulu HI 96822. **E-mail:** mjournal-l@lists.hawaii. edu. **Website:** manoajournal.hawaii.edu. **Contact:** Frank Stewart, editor. Estab. 1989. *Mānoa* is seeking high-quality literary fiction, poetry, essays, and translations for an international audience. In general, each issue is devoted to new work from an area of the Asia-Pacific region. "We recommend that authors and translators who wish to submit work examine a copy of the journal and review our website carefully. Our thanks for doing so."

NEEDS Query first. No Pacific exotica. Length: 1,000-7,500 words.

HOW TO CONTACT Send complete ms.

PAYMENT/TERMS Pays $100-500 ($25/printed page).

TIPS "Not accepting unsolicited mss at this time because of commitments to special projects. Please query before sending mss as e-mail attachments."

THE MACGUFFIN

Schoolcraft College, 18600 Haggerty Rd., Livonia MI 48152. (734)462-4400, ext. 5327. **E-mail:** macguffin@schoolcraft.edu. **Website:** www.schoolcraft.edu/macguffin. **Contact:** Steven A. Dolgin, editor; Gordon Krupsky, managing editor;. Estab. 1984. "Our purpose is to encourage, support, and enhance the literary arts in the Schoolcraft College community, the region, the state, and the nation. We also sponsor annual literary events and give voice to deserving new writers as well as established writers."

NEEDS Preferences range from flash and experimental to mainstream. Length: up to 5,000 words.

HOW TO CONTACT Submit ms via e-mail or postal mail. Ms should be double-spaced.

PAYMENT/TERMS Pays 2 contributor's copies.

◐ MAD HATTERS' REVIEW: EDGY AND ENLIGHTENED ART, LITERATURE AND MUSIC IN THE AGE OF DEMENTIA

Wales. **E-mail:** askalice@madhatarts.com; marc@madhatarts.com. **Website:** www.madhattersreview.com. **Contact:** Marc Vincenz, publisher and editor

in chief. *Mad Hatters' Review* "seeks to foster the work of writers and poets: explosive, lyrical, passionate, deeply wrought voices and aesthetic experiments that stretch the boundaries of language, narrative, and image, vital and enduring literary voices that sing on the page as well as in the mind. The name of our annual reflects our view of the world as essentially demented and nonsensical, too frequently a nightmare or 'nondream' that needs to be exposed to the light for what it is, as well as what it is not. We're particularly interested in risky, thematically broad (i.e., saying something about the world and its creatures), psychologically and philosophically sophisticated works. Humor, satire, irony, magical realism, and surrealism are welcome. We look for originality, surprise, intellectual and emotional strength, lyricism, and rhythm. We love writers who stretch their imaginations to the limits and challenge conventional notions of reality and style; we care little for categories. We also adore collaborative ventures, between/among writers, visual artists, and composers."

○ *Mad Hatters' Review* has received an Artistry Award from Sixty Plus Design, 2006-2007 Web Design Award from Invision Graphics, and a Gold Medal Award of Excellence for 2006-7 from ArtSpace2000.com. Member: CLMP.

NEEDS Submissions are open briefly for each issue: check guidelines periodically for dates. **Publishes 1 new writer/year.** Has published Alastair Gray, Kass Fleisher, Vanessa Place, Harold Jaffe, Andrei Codrescu, Sheila Murphy, Simon Perchik, Terese Svoboda, Niels Hav, Martin, Nakell, and Juan Jose Millas (translated from the Spanish). Does not want mainstream prose/story that doesn't exhibit a love of language and a sophisticated mentality. No religious or inspirational writings, confessionals, boys sowing oats, sentimental and coming-of-age stories. Length: up to 3,000 words. Average length: 1,500-2,500 words. Publishes short shorts. Average length of short shorts: 500-800 words.

HOW TO CONTACT Submit via online submissions manager.

TIPS "Imagination, skill with and appreciation of language, inventiveness, rhythm, sense of humor/irony/satire, and compelling style make a ms stand out. Read the magazine. Don't necessarily follow the rules you've been taught in the usual MFA program or workshop."

THE MADISON REVIEW

University of Wisconsin, 600 N. Park St., 6193 Helen C. White Hall, Madison WI 53706. **E-mail:** madisonrevw@gmail.com. **Website:** www.english.wisc.edu/madisonreview. **Contact:** Abigail Zemach and John McCracken, fiction editors; Fiona Sands and Kiyoko Reidy, poetry editors. Estab. 1972. *The Madison Review* is a student-run literary magazine that looks to publish the best available fiction and poetry.

○ Does not publish unsolicited interviews or genre fiction. Send all submissions through online submissions manager.

NEEDS Wants well-crafted, compelling fiction featuring a wide range of styles and subjects. Does not read May-September. No genre: horror, fantasy, erotica, etc. Length: 500-30,000 words, up to 30 pages.

HOW TO CONTACT Send complete ms.

PAYMENT/TERMS Pays 2 contributor's copies, $5 for additional copies.

TIPS "Our editors have very eclectic tastes, so don't specifically try to cater to us. Above all, we look for original, high-quality work."

THE MAGAZINE OF FANTASY & SCIENCE FICTION

P.O. Box 3447, Hoboken NJ 07030. (201)876-2551. **E-mail:** fandsf@aol.com. **Website:** www.fandsf.com; submissions.ccfinlay.com/fsf. **Contact:** C.C. Finlay, editor. Estab. 1949. *The Magazine of Fantasy & Science Fiction* publishes various types of science fiction and fantasy short stories and novellas, making up about 80% of each issue. The balance of each issue is devoted to articles about science fiction, a science column, book and film reviews, cartoons, and competitions. Bimonthly.

○ *The Magazine of Fantasy & Science Fiction* is one of the oldest and most prestigious magazines in the field, having published Isaac Asimov, Ray Bradbury, Shirley Jackson, Robert Heinlein, Kurt Vonnegut, Joyce Carol Oates, Harlan Ellison, Samuel R. Delany, James Tiptree Jr., Ursula K. Le Guin, Karen Joy Fowler, Ted Chiang, and many others. Many stories published by *F&SF* receive award nominations and are reprinted in Year's Best anthologies. Alaya Dawn Johnson's "A Guide to the Fruits of Hawai'i" won the Nebula Award for Best Novelet in 2015.

NEEDS *F&SF* has no formula for fiction. The speculative element may be slight, but it should be present. We prefer character-oriented stories, whether it's fantasy, science fiction, horror, humor, or another genre. *F&SF* is open to diverse voices and perspectives, and has published writers from all over the world. Length: up to 25,000 words.

HOW TO CONTACT Send complete ms.

PAYMENT/TERMS Pays 7-12¢/word.

TIPS Good storytelling makes a submission stand out. We like to be surprised by stories, either by the character insights, ideas, plots, or prose. Even though we prefer electronic submissions, we need stories in standard mss format (like that described here: www.sfwa.org/writing/vonda/vonda.htm). Read an issue of the magazine before submitting to get a sense of the range of our tastes and interests.

○ THE MAGNOLIA QUARTERLY

P.O. Box 10294, Gulfport MS 39505. **E-mail:** writerpllevin@gmail.com. **Website:** www.gcwriters.org. **Contact:** Phil Levin, editor. Estab. 1985. *The Magnolia Quarterly* publishes poetry, fiction, nonfiction, and reviews. **For members of GCWA only.**

○ *The Magnolia Quarterly* is 40 pages, pocket-sized, stapled, with glossy cover, includes ads. Editing service offered on all prose.

NEEDS Length: about 700 words.

HOW TO CONTACT E-mail submissions in DOC format as attachments.

PAYMENT/TERMS No payment.

THE MAIN STREET RAG

Douglass-Rausch, Ent. LLC, P.O. Box 690100, Charlotte NC 28227-7001. (704)573-2516. **E-mail:** editor@mainstreetrag.com. **Website:** www.mainstreetrag.com. **Contact:** M. Scott Douglass, Publisher/Managing Editor. Estab. 1996. *The Main Street Rag*, published quarterly, prints "poetry, short fiction, essays, interviews, reviews, photos, and art. We like publishing good material from people who are interested in more than notching another publishing credit, people who support small independent publishers like ourselves." Will consider "almost anything," but prefers "writing with an edge—either gritty or bitingly humorous. Contributors are advised to visit our website prior to submission to confirm current needs."

○ *The Main Street Rag* receives about 5,000 submissions/year; publishes 50+ poems and 3-5 stories per issue, a featured interview, photos, and an occasional nonfiction piece. Press run is about 500 (250 subscribers, 15 libraries). **NEEDS** Length: up to 6,000 words. **HOW TO CONTACT** No hard copy submissions—all electronic. See website for details. **PAYMENT/TERMS** Pays 1 contributor's copy.

◑◐◑⑤ THE MALAHAT REVIEW

The University of Victoria, P.O. Box 1700, STN CSC, Victoria BC V8W 2Y2, Canada. (250)721-8524. **E-mail:** malahat@uvic.ca (for queries only). **Website:** www.malahatreview.ca. **Contact:** John Barton, editor. Estab. 1967. Quarterly magazine covering poetry, fiction, creative nonfiction, and reviews. "We try to achieve a balance of views and styles in each issue. We strive for a mix of the best writing by both established and new writers."

NEEDS Length: up to 8,000 words.

HOW TO CONTACT Submit via online submissions manager: malahatreview.ca/submission_guidelines.html#submittable.

PAYMENT/TERMS Pays $60/magazine page.

TIPS "Please do not send more than 1 submission at a time: 3-5 poems, 1 piece of creative nonfiction, or 1 short story (do not mix poetry and prose in the same submission). See *The Malahat Review*'s Open Season Awards for poetry and short fiction, creative nonfiction, long poem, and novella contests in the Awards section of our website."

◑◐⑤ THE MASSACHUSETTS REVIEW

University of Massachusetts, Photo Lab 309, 211 Hicks Way, Amherst MA 01003. (413)545-2689. **E-mail:** massrev@external.umass.edu. **Website:** www.massreview.org. **Contact:** Emily Wojcik, managing editor. Estab. 1959. Seeks a balance between established writers and promising new ones. Interested in material of variety and vitality relevant to the intellectual and aesthetic questions of our time. Aspire to have a broad appeal.

◑ Does not respond to mss without SASE.

NEEDS Wants short stories. Accepts 1 short story per submission. Include name and contact information on the first page. Encourages page numbers. Has published work by Ahdaf Soueif, Elizabeth Denton, and Nicholas Montemarano. Length: up to 30 pages or 8,000 words.

HOW TO CONTACT Send complete ms.

PAYMENT/TERMS Pays $50 and 2 contributor's copies.

TIPS "No mss are considered May-September. Electronic submission process can be found on website. No fax or e-mail submissions. Shorter rather than longer stories preferred (up to 28-30 pages)." Looks for works that "stop us in our tracks." Mss that stand out use "unexpected language, idiosyncrasy of outlook, and are the opposite of ordinary."

MERIDIAN

University of Virginia, P.O. Box 400145, Charlottesville VA 22904-4145. **E-mail:** meridianuva@gmail.com; meridianpoetry@gmail.com; meridianfiction@gmail.com. **Website:** www.readmeridian.org. Estab. 1998. *Meridian* Editors' Prize Contest offers annual $1,000 award. Submit online only; see website for formatting details. **Entry fee:** $8.50, includes one-year electronic subscription to *Meridian* for all U.S. entries or 1 copy of the prize issue for all international entries. **Deadline:** December or January; see website for current deadline. *Meridian*, published semiannually, prints poetry, fiction, nonfiction, interviews, and reviews. "*Meridian* is interested in writing that is vibrant, moving, and alive, and welcomes contributions from a variety of aesthetic approaches. Has published such poets as Alexandra Teague, Gregory Pardlo, Sandra Meek, and Bob Hicok, and such fiction writers as Matt Bell, Kate Milliken, and Ron Carlson. Has recently interviewed C. Michael Curtis, Ann Beatty, and Claire Messud, among other luminaries. Also publishes a recurring feature called 'Lost Classic,' which resurrects previously unpublished work by celebrated writers and which has included illustrations from the mss of Jorge Luis Borges, letters written by Elizabeth Bishop, Stephen Crane's deleted chapter from *The Red Badge of Courage*, and a letter written by Flannery O'Connor about her novel *Wise Blood*."

◑ *Meridian* is 130 pages, digest-sized, offset-printed, perfect-bound, with color cover. Receives about 2,500 poems/year, accepts about 40 (less than 1%). Press run is 1,000 (750 subscribers, 15 libraries, 200 shelf sales); 150 distributed free to writing programs. Work published in *Meridian* has appeared in *The Best American Poetry* and *The Pushcart Prize Anthology*.

NEEDS Submit complete ms via online submissions manager. Length: up to 6,500 words.

PAYMENT/TERMS Pays 2 contributor's copies (additional copies available at discount).

⑤ MICHIGAN QUARTERLY REVIEW

0576 Rackham Bldg., 915 E. Washington, Ann Arbor MI 48109-1070. (734)764-9265. **E-mail:** mqr@umich. edu. **Website:** www.michiganquarterlyreview.com. **Contact:** Jonathan Freedman, editor; Vicki Lawrence, managing editor. Estab. 1962. *Michigan Quarterly Review* is an eclectic interdisciplinary journal of arts and culture that seeks to combine the best of poetry, fiction, and creative nonfiction with outstanding critical essays on literary, cultural, social, and political matters. The flagship journal of the University of Michigan, *MQR* draws on lively minds here and elsewhere, seeking to present accessible work of all varieties for sophisticated readers from within and without the academy.

○ The Laurence Goldstein Award is a $500 annual award to the best poem published in *MQR* during the previous year. The Lawrence Foundation Award is a $1,000 annual award to the best short story published in *MQR* during the previous year. The Page Davidson Clayton Award for Emerging Poets is a $500 annual award given to the best poet appearing in *MQR* during the previous year who has not yet published a book.

NEEDS "No restrictions on subject matter or language. We are very selective. We like stories that are unusual in tone and structure, and innovative in language. No genre fiction written for a market. Would like to see more fiction about social, political, and cultural matters, not just centered on a love relationship or dysfunctional family." Receives 300 unsolicited mss/month. Accepts 3-4 mss/issue; 12-16 mss/year. Publishes 1-2 new writers/year. Has published work by Rebecca Makkai, Peter Ho Davies, Laura Kasischke, Gerald Shapiro, and Alan Cheuse. Length: 1,500-7,000 words; average length: 5,000 words.

HOW TO CONTACT Send complete ms.

PAYMENT/TERMS Payment varies but is usually in the range of $50-$150.

TIPS "Read the journal and assess the range of contents and the level of writing. We have no guidelines to offer or set expectations; every ms is judged on its unique qualities. On essays, query with a very thorough description of the argument and a copy of the first page. Watch for announcements of special issues, which are usually expanded issues and draw upon a lot of freelance writing. Be aware that this is a university quarterly that publishes a limited amount of fiction and poetry and that it is directed at an educated audience, one that has done a great deal of reading in all types of literature."

MID-AMERICAN REVIEW

Bowling Green State University, Department of English, Bowling Green OH 43403. (419)372-2725. **E-mail:** mar@bgsu.edu. **E-mail:** marsubmissions.bgsu. edu. **Website:** www.bgsu.edu/midamericanreview. **Contact:** Abigail Cloud, editor in chief; Teri Dederer, fiction editor. Estab. 1981. "We aim to put the best possible work in front of the biggest possible audience. We publish contemporary fiction, poetry, creative nonfiction, translations, and book reviews."

○ Contests: The Fineline Competition for Prose Poems, Short Shorts, and Everything In Between (June 1 deadline, $10 per 3 pieces, limit 500 words each); The Sherwood Anderson Fiction Award (November 1 deadline, $10 per piece); and the James Wright Poetry Award (November 1 deadline, $10 per 3 pieces).

NEEDS Publishes traditional, character-oriented, literary, experimental, prose poem, and short-short stories. No genre fiction. Length: up to 6,000 words.

HOW TO CONTACT Submit ms by mail with SASE, or through online submission manager. Agented fiction 5%. Recently published work by Mollie Ficek and J. David Stevens.

TIPS "We are seeking translations of contemporary authors from all languages into English; submissions must include the original and proof of permission to translate. We would also like to see more creative nonfiction."

MIDWAY JOURNAL

77 Liberty Avenue #10, Somerville MA 02144. (763)516-7463. **E-mail:** editors@midwayjournal.com. **Website:** www.midwayjournal.com. **Contact:** Christopher Lowe, nonfiction editor; Ralph Pennel, fiction editor; Paige Riehl, poetry editor. Estab. 2006. "Just off of I-94 and on the border between St. Paul and Minneapolis, the Midway, like any other state fairgrounds, is alive with a mix of energies and people. Its position as mid-way, as a place of boundary crossing, also reflects our vision for this journal. The work here complicates and questions the boundaries of genre, binary, and aesthetic. It offers surprises and ways of re-seeing, re-thinking, and re-feeling: a veritable banquet of literary fare. Which is why, in each new issue, we are honored to present work by both new and established writers alike."

⊙ Member CLMP.

NEEDS No length limit.

HOW TO CONTACT Submit 1 piece of fiction or 2 pieces of flash/sudden fiction via online submissions manager.

TIPS "An interesting story with engaging writing, both in terms of style and voice, make a ms stand out. Round characters are a must. Writers who take chances either with content or with form grab an editor's immediate attention. Spend time with the words on the page. Spend time with the language. The language and voice are not vehicles; they, too, are tools."

MINAS TIRITH EVENING-STAR: JOURNAL OF THE AMERICAN TOLKIEN SOCIETY

American Tolkien Society, P.O. Box 97, Highland MI 48357-0097. **E-mail:** editor@americantolkiensociety.org; americantolkiensociety@yahoo.com. **E-mail:** editor@americantolkiensociety.org. **Website:** www.americantolkiensociety.org. **Contact:** Amalie A. Helms, editor. Estab. 1967. *Minas Tirith Evening-Star: Journal of the American Tolkien Society*, published occasionally, publishes poetry, book reviews, essays, and fan fiction. *Minas Tirith Evening-Star* is digest-sized, offset-printed from typescript, with cartoon-like b&w graphics. Press run is 400. Single copy: $3.50; subscription: $12.50. Sample: $3. Make checks payable to American Tolkien Society.

HOW TO CONTACT Submit complete ms by mail or e-mail.

PAYMENT/TERMS Pays 1 contributor's copy.

THE MINNESOTA REVIEW

Virginia Tech, **E-mail:** editors@theminnesotareview.org. **E-mail:** submissions@theminnesotareview.org. **Website:** minnesotareview.wordpress.com. **Contact:** Janell Watson, editor. Estab. 1960. *The Minnesota Review*, published biannually, is a journal featuring creative and critical work from writers on the rise or who are already established. Each issue is about 200 pages, digest-sized, flat-spined, with glossy card cover. Press run is 1,000 (400 subscribers). Also available online. Subscription: $30 for 2 years for individuals, $60/year for institutions. Sample: $15.

⊙ Open to submissions August 1-November 1 and January 1-April 1.

NEEDS Length: up to 5,000 words for short stories, up to 1,000 words for short shorts or flash fiction.

HOW TO CONTACT Submit up to 1 short story or 4 short shorts or flash fiction pieces per reading period via online submissions manager.

PAYMENT/TERMS Pays 2 contributor's copies.

❶ ⓟ ⑤ THE MISSOURI REVIEW

357 McReynolds Hall, University of Missouri, Columbia MO 65211. (573)882-4474. **Fax:** (573)884-4671. **E-mail:** question@moreview.com. **Website:** www.missourireview.com. Estab. 1978. The William Peden Prize of $1,000 is awarded annually to the best piece of fiction to have appeared in the previous volume year. The winner is chosen by an outside judge. There is no separate application process. Publishes contemporary fiction, poetry, interviews, personal essays, cartoons, special features—such as History as Literature series, Found Text series, and Curio Cabinet art features—for the literary and the general reader interested in a wide range of subjects.

NEEDS Length: No restrictions, but longer mss (9,000-12,000 words) or flash fiction ms (up to 2,000 words) must be truly exceptional to be published.

HOW TO CONTACT Send complete ms.

PAYMENT/TERMS Pays $40/printed page.

TIPS "Send your best work."

MOBIUS: THE JOURNAL OF SOCIAL CHANGE

149 Talmadge St., Madison WI 53704. **E-mail:** fmschep@charter.net. **E-mail:** fmschep@charter.net (fiction); demiurge@fibitz.com (poetry). **Website:** www.mobiusmagazine.com. **Contact:** Fred Schepartz, publisher and executive editor. Estab. 1989. *Mobius: The Journal of Social Change* is an online-only journal, published quarterly in March, June, September, and December. "At *Mobius* we believe that writing is power and good writing empowers both the reader and the writer. We feel strongly that alternatives are needed to an increasingly corporate literary scene. *Mobius* strives to provide an outlet for writers disenfranchised by a bottom-line marketplace and challenging writing for those who feel that today's literary standards are killing us in a slow, mind-numbing fashion."

NEEDS Wants fiction dealing with themes of social change. "We like social commentary, but mainly we like good writing. No porn or work that is racist, sexist or any other kind of -*ist*. No Christian or spirituality proselytizing fiction." Length: up to 5,000 words.

HOW TO CONTACT Submit up to 1 story at a time via e-mail (preferred) or mail.

TIPS "We like high impact. We like plot- and character-driven stories that function like theater of the mind. We look first and foremost for good writing. Prose must be crisp and polished; the story must pique my interest and make me care due to a certain intellectual, emotional aspect. *Mobius* is about social change. We want stories that make some statement about the society we live in, either on a macro or micro level. Not that your story needs to preach from a soapbox (actually, we prefer that it doesn't), but it needs to have something to say."

THE MOCHILA REVIEW

Missouri Western State University, Department of English & Modern Languages, 4525 Downs Dr., St. Joseph MO 64507. **E-mail:** mochila@missouriwestern.edu. **Website:** www.missouriwestern.edu/orgs/mochila/homepage.htm. **Contact:** Dr. Marianne Kunkel, editor in chief. Estab. 2000. "*The Mochila Review* is an annual international undergraduate journal published with support from the English and Modern Languages department at Missouri Western State University. Our goal is to publish the best short stories, poems, and essays from the next generation of important authors: student writers. Our staff, comprised primarily of undergraduate students, understands the publishing challenges that emerging writers face and is committed to helping talented students gain wider audiences in the pages of *The Mochila Review* and on our website."

NEEDS Length: up to 5,000 words.

HOW TO CONTACT Submit complete ms via online submissions manager.

PAYMENT/TERMS Pays contributor's copies.

TIPS "Mss with fresh language, energy, passion, and intelligence stand out. Study the craft, and be entertaining and engaging."

MORPHEUS TALES

E-mail: morpheustales@gmail.com. **Website:** morpheustales.wixsite.com/morpheustales. **Contact:** Adam Bradley, publisher. Estab. 2008. "We publish the best in horror, science fiction, and fantasy—both fiction and nonfiction."

NEEDS Length: 800-3,000 words.

HOW TO CONTACT Send complete ms.

MSLEXIA

Mslexia Publications Ltd., P.O. Box 656, Newcastle upon Tyne NE99 1PZ, United Kingdom. (44)(191)204-8860. **E-mail:** submissions@mslexia.co.uk; postbag@mslexia.co.uk; debbie@mslexia.co.uk. **Website:** www.mslexia.co.uk. **Contact:** Debbie Taylor, editorial director. Estab. 1998. "*Mslexia* tells you all you need to know about exploring your creativity and getting into print. No other magazine provides *Mslexia*'s unique mix of advice and inspiration; news, reviews, interviews; competitions, events, grants; all served up with a challenging selection of new poetry and prose. *Mslexia* is read by authors and absolute beginners. A quarterly master class in the business and psychology of writing, it's the essential magazine for women who write."

This publication accepts e-mail submissions except from U.K. writers submitting to New Writing themed writing.

NEEDS See guidelines on website. "Submissions not on 1 of our current themes will be returned (if submitted with a SASE) or destroyed." Length: 50-2,200 words.

HOW TO CONTACT Send complete ms.

PAYMENT/TERMS Pays £15 per 1,000 words prose plus contributor's copies.

TIPS "Read the magazine; subscribe if you can afford it. *Mslexia* has a particular style and relationship with its readers which is hard to assess at a quick glance. The majority of our readers live in the U.K., so feature pitches should be aware of this. We never commission work without seeing a written sample first. We rarely accept unsolicited mss, but prefer a short letter suggesting a feature, plus a brief bio and writing sample."

MYTHIC DELIRIUM

3514 Signal Hill Ave. NW, Roanoke VA 24017-5148. **E-mail:** mythicdelirium@gmail.com. **Website:** www.mythicdelirium.com. **Contact:** Mike Allen, editor. Estab. 1998. "*Mythic Delirium* is an online and e-book venue for fiction and poetry that ranges through science fiction, fantasy, horror, interstitial, and cross-genre territory—we love blurred boundaries and tropes turned on their heads. We are interested in work that demonstrates ambition, that defies traditional approaches to genre, that introduces readers to the legends of other cultures, that re-evaluates the myths of old from a modern perspective, that twists reality in unexpected ways. We are committed to diversity and are open to and encourage submissions from people of every race, gender, nationality, sexual orientation, political affiliation, and religious belief.

We publish 12 short stories and 24 poems a year. Our quarterly e-books in PDF, EPUB, and MOBI formats, published in July, October, January, and April, each contain 3 stories and 6 poems. We also publish 1 story and 2 poems on our website each month. Check our website for our next reading period."

NEEDS "No unsolicited reprints or multiple submissions. Please use the words 'fiction submission' in the e-mail subject line. Stories should be sent in standard ms format as RTF or DOC attachments." Length: up to 4,000 words (firm).

PAYMENT/TERMS Pays 2¢/word.

TIPS "*Mythic Delirium* isn't easy to get into, but we publish newcomers in every issue. Show us how ambitious you can be, and don't give up."

N+1

The Editors, 68 Jay St., Suite 405, Brooklyn NY 11201. **E-mail:** editors@nplusonemag.com. **E-mail:** submissions@nplusonemag.com. **Website:** www.nplusonemag.com. **Contact:** Nikil Saval and Dayna Tortorici, editors.

NEEDS Submit queries or finished pieces by e-mail.

TIPS "Most of the slots available for a given issue will have been filled many months before publication. If you would like to brave the odds, the best submission guidelines are those implied by the magazine itself. Read an issue or two through to get a sense of whether your piece might fit into *n+1*."

⬤❸ NA'AMAT WOMAN

21515 Vanowen Street, Suite 102, Canoga Park CA 91303. (818)431-2200. **E-mail:** naamat@naamat.org; judith@naamat.org. **Website:** www.naamat.org. **Contact:** Judith Sokoloff, editor. Estab. 1926. "Magazine covering a wide variety of subjects of interest to the Jewish community—including political and social issues, arts, profiles; many articles about Israel and women's issues. Fiction must have a Jewish theme. Readers are the American Jewish community." Circ. 15,000. "Magazine covering a wide variety of subjects of interest to the Jewish community— including political and social issues, arts, profiles; many articles about Israel and women's issues. Fiction must have a Jewish theme. Readers are the American Jewish community."

NEEDS Ethnic/multicultural, historical, humor/satire, literary, novel excerpts, women-oriented. Receives 10 unsolicited mss/month. Accepts 1-3 mss/year. "We want serious fiction, with insight, reflection and consciousness." "We do not want fiction that is mostly dialogue. No corny Jewish humor. No Holocaust fiction." Length: 2,000-3,000 words.

HOW TO CONTACT Query with published clips or send complete mss. Responds in 6 months to queries; 6 months to mss. Sample copy for 9x11½ SAE and $2 postage or look online. Sample copy for $2. Writer's guidelines for #10 SASE, or by e-mail. Query with published clips or send complete ms.

PAYMENT/TERMS Pays 10¢/word and 2 contributor's copies. Pays on publication for first North American serial, first, one time, second serial (reprint) rights, makes work-for-hire assignments. Pays 10-20¢/word for assigned articles and for unsolicited articles.

TIPS "No maudlin nostalgia or romance; no hackneyed Jewish humor."

NARRATIVE MAGAZINE

2443 Fillmore St., #214, San Francisco CA 94115. **E-mail:** contact@narrativemagazine.com. **Website:** www.narrativemagazine.com. **Contact:** Michael Croft, senior editor; Mimi Kusch, managing editor; Michael Wiegers, poetry editor. Estab. 2003. "*Narrative* publishes high-quality contemporary literature in a full range of styles, forms, and lengths. Submit poetry, fiction, and nonfiction, including stories, short shorts, novels, novel excerpts, novellas, personal essays, humor, sketches, memoirs, literary biographies, commentary, reportage, interviews, and short audio recordings of short-short stories and poems. We welcome submissions of previously unpublished mss of all lengths, ranging from short-short stories to complete book-length works for serialization. In addition to submissions for issues of *Narrative* itself, we also encourage submissions for our Story of the Week, literary contests, and Readers' Narratives. Please read our Submission Guidelines for all information on mss formatting, word lengths, author payment, and other policies. We accept submissions only through our electronic submission system. We do not accept submissions through postal services or e-mail. You may send us mss for the following submission categories: General Submissions, Narrative Prize, Story of the Week, Readers' Narrative, iPoem, iStory, Six-Word Story, or a specific Contest. Your ms must be in one of the following file forms: DOC, RTF, PDF, DOCX, TXT, WPD, ODF, MP3, MP4, MOV, or FLV."

⬤ *Narrative* has received recognitions in *New Stories from the South, Best American Mystery*

Stories, O. Henry Prize Stories, Best American Short Stories, Best American Essays, and the *Pushcart Prize Collection.* In an article on the business of books, the National Endowment for the Arts featured *Narrative* as the model for the evolution of both print and digital publishing.

NEEDS Has published work by Alice Munro, Tobias Wolff, Marvin Bell, Jane Smiley, Joyce Carol Oates, E.L. Doctorow, and Min Jin Lee. Publishes new and emerging writers.

HOW TO CONTACT Send complete ms.

PAYMENT/TERMS Pays on publication between $150-1,000, $1,000-5,000 for book length, plus annual prizes of more than $32,000.

TIPS "Log on and study our magazine online. Narrative fiction, graphic art, and multimedia are selected, first and foremost, for quality."

THE NASSAU REVIEW

Nassau Community College, Nassau Community College, English Department, 1 Education Dr., Garden City NY 11530. **E-mail:** nassaureview@ncc. edu. **Website:** www.ncc.edu/nassaureview. **Contact:** Christina M. Rau, editor in chief. Estab. 1964. *The Nassau Review* welcomes submissions of many genres, preferring work that is "innovative, captivating, well-crafted, and unique, work that crosses boundaries of genre and tradition. You may be serious. You may be humorous. You may be somewhere in between. We are looking simply for quality. New and seasoned writers are welcome."

All open submissions are under consideration for the Writer Awards.

NEEDS Accepts simultaneous submissions: "Please let us know they are simultaneous when you submit them." Does not want "children's literature; cliché, unoriginal work; fan fiction." Length: 100-3,000 words.

HOW TO CONTACT Submit via online submissions manager. Include title, word count, and bio of up to 100 words.

PAYMENT/TERMS Pays 1 contributor's copy.

NATURAL BRIDGE

Department of English, University of Missouri-St. Louis, 1 University Blvd., St. Louis MO 63121. **E-mail:** natural@umsl.edu. **Website:** www.umsl. edu/~natural. Estab. 1999. *Natural Bridge,* published biannually in April and December, invites submissions of poetry, fiction, personal essays, and translations.

No longer accepts submissions via e-mail. Accepts submissions through online submission manager and postal mail only.

NEEDS Submit year round; however, "we do not read May 1-August 1." Recently published work by Tayari Jones, Steve Stern, Jamie Wriston Colbert, Lex Williford, and Mark Jay Mirsky. Also publishes literary essays, poetry. Sometimes comments on rejected mss.

HOW TO CONTACT Submit 1 ms through online submissions manager ($3 fee for nonsubscribers) or postal mail (free).

PAYMENT/TERMS Pays 2 contributor's copies and one-year subscription.

NEBO

Arkansas Tech University, Department of English, Russellville AR 72801. **E-mail:** nebo@atu.edu. **E-mail:** nebo@atu.edu. **Website:** www.atu.edu/world-languages/Nebo.php. **Contact:** Editor. Estab. 1983. *Nebo,* published in the spring and fall, publishes fiction, poetry, creative nonfiction, drama, comics, and art from Arkansas Tech students and unpublished writers as well as nationally known writers.

Reads submissions August 15-May 1.

NEEDS Accepts all genres. Length: up to 5,000 words.

HOW TO CONTACT Submit complete ms by e-mail or postal mail.

TIPS "Avoid pretentiousness. Write something you genuinely care about. Please edit your work for spelling, grammar, cohesiveness, and overall purpose. Many of the mss we receive should be publishable with a little polishing. Mss should never be submitted handwritten or on 'onion skin' or colored paper."

NEON MAGAZINE

Neon Books, U.K. **E-mail:** info@neonmagazine.co.uk. **E-mail:** subs@neonmagazine.co.uk. **Website:** www. neonmagazine.co.uk. **Contact:** Krishan Coupland. Quarterly website and print magazine covering alternative work of any form of poetry and prose, short stories, flash fiction, artwork, and reviews. "Genre work is welcome. Experimentation is encouraged. We like stark poetry and weird prose. We seek work that is beautiful, shocking, intense, and memorable. Darker pieces are generally favored over humorous ones."

Neon was previously published as *FourVolts Magazine.*

NEEDS "No nonsensical prose; we are not appreciative of sentimentality." No word limit.

PAYMENT/TERMS Pays royalties.

TIPS "Send several poems, 1-2 pieces of prose, or several images via form e-mail. Include the word 'submission' in your subject line. Include a short biographical note (up to 100 words). Read submission guidelines before submitting your work."

💲 THE NEW CRITERION

900 Broadway, Ste. 602, New York NY 10003. **Website:** www.newcriterion.com. **Contact:** Roger Kimball, editor and publisher; David Yezzi, poetry editor. Estab. 1982. "A monthly review of the arts and intellectual life, *The New Criterion* began as an experiment in critical audacity—a publication devoted to engaging, in Matthew Arnold's famous phrase, with 'the best that has been thought and said.' This also meant engaging with those forces dedicated to traducing genuine cultural and intellectual achievement, whether through obfuscation, politicization, or a commitment to nihilistic absurdity. We are proud that *The New Criterion* has been in the forefront both of championing what is best and most humanely vital in our cultural inheritance and in exposing what is mendacious, corrosive, and spurious. Published monthly from September through June, *The New Criterion* brings together a wide range of young and established critics whose common aim is to bring you the most incisive criticism being written today."

⬤ *The New Criterion* is 90 pages, 7x10, flat-spined. Single copy: $12.

◐⊙ NEW DELTA REVIEW

University of Louisiana English Dept., Baton Rouge LA 70803. **Website:** ndrmag.org. Estab. 1984. "We seek vivid and exciting work from new and established writers. We have published fiction from writers such as National Book Award finalist Patricia Smith, Pushcart Prize winner Stacey Richter, and former poet laureate Billy Collins."

⬤ Semiannual. Editors change every year; check website. Online only. *New Delta Review* also sponsors the Matt Clark Prizes for fiction and poetry, the annual Ryan Gibbs Awards for short fiction and photography, and an annual chapbook contest. Work from the magazine has been included in the *Pushcart Prize* anthology.

NEEDS "We publish fiction in wildly different styles and modes. It's easy to say, "Please read our journal to get a sense of our aesthetic," so we will! After you've read, please send us fiction that is emotionally engaging and structurally sound. We also appreciate (carefully considered) risks with language, content, and form. We also have a special interest in flash fiction, and brief series of flash pieces." "No Elvis stories, overwrought 'Southern' fiction, or cancer stories." Length: up to 3,000 words.

PAYMENT/TERMS Offers no payment, but all published pieces are eligible for yearly editor's prize of $250.

TIPS "Our staff is open-minded and youthful. We base decisions on merit, not reputation. The ms that's most enjoyable to read gets the nod. Be bold, take risks, surprise us."

💲 NEW ENGLAND REVIEW

Middlebury College, Middlebury VT 05753. (802)443-5075. **E-mail:** nereview@middlebury.edu. **Website:** www.nereview.com. **Contact:** Marcia Parlow, managing editor. Estab. 1978. *New England Review* is a prestigious, nationally distributed literary journal. Reads September 1 through May 31 (postmarked dates).

⬤ *New England Review* is 200+ pages, 7x10, printed on heavy stock, flat-spined, with glossy cover with art. Receives 3,000-4,000 poetry submissions/year, accepts about 70-80 poems/year. Receives 550 unsolicited mss/month, accepts 6 mss/issue, 24 fiction mss/year. Does not accept mss June-August. Agented fiction less than 5%.

NEEDS Send 1 story at a time, unless it is very short. Wants only serious literary fiction and novel excerpts. Publishes approximately 10 new writers/year. Has published work by Steve Almond, Christine Sneed, Roy Kesey, Thomas Gough, Norman Lock, Brock Clarke, Carl Phillips, Lucia Perillo, Linda Gregerson, and Natasha Trethewey. Length: not strict on word count.

HOW TO CONTACT Send complete ms via online submission manager. No e-mail submissions. "Will consider simultaneous submissions, but it must be stated as such and you must notify us immediately if the ms is accepted for publication elsewhere."

PAYMENT/TERMS Pays $20/page ($20 minimum), and 2 contributor's copies.

TIPS "We consider short fiction, including short shorts, novellas, and self-contained extracts from novels in both traditional and experimental forms. In nonfiction, we consider a variety of general and literary but not narrowly scholarly essays; we also publish long and short poems, screenplays, graphics, translations, critical reassessments, statements by artists working in various media, testimonies, and letters from abroad. We are committed to exploration of all forms of contemporary cultural expression in the U.S. and abroad. With few exceptions, we print only work not published previously elsewhere."

ⓘⓒⓢ NEW LETTERS

University of Missouri-Kansas City, 5101 Rockhill Rd., Kansas City MO 64110. (816)235-1168. **Fax:** (816)235-2611. **E-mail:** newletters@umkc.edu. **Website:** www.newletters.org. **Contact:** Robert Stewart, editor in chief. Estab. 1934. "*New Letters*, published quarterly, continues to seek the best new writing, whether from established writers or those ready and waiting to be discovered. In addition, it supports those writers, readers, and listeners who want to experience the joy of writing that can both surprise and inspire us all."

Ⓠ   Submissions are not read May 1 through October 1.

NEEDS No genre fiction. Length: up to 5,000 words.

HOW TO CONTACT Send complete ms.

PAYMENT/TERMS Pays $30-75.

TIPS "We aren't interested in essays that are footnoted or essays usually described as scholarly or critical. Our preference is for creative nonfiction or personal essays. We prefer shorter stories and essays to longer ones (an average length is 3,500-4,000 words). We have no rigid preferences as to subject, style, or genre, although commercial efforts tend to put us off. Even so, our only fixed requirement is good writing."

NEW MADRID

Journal of Contemporary Literature, Murray State University, Department of English and Philosophy, 7C Faculty Hall, Murray KY 42071-3341. (270)809-4730. **E-mail:** msu.newmadrid@murraystate.edu. **Website:** newmadridjournal.org. **Contact:** Ann Neelon, editor; Jacque E. Day, managing editor. "*New Madrid* is the national journal of the low-residency MFA program at Murray State University. It takes its name from the New Madrid seismic zone, which falls within the central Mississippi Valley and extends through western Kentucky."

Ⓠ   See website for guidelines and upcoming themes. "We have 2 reading periods, August 15-October 15 and January 15-March 15." Also

publishes poetry and creative nonfiction. Rarely comments on/critiques rejected mss.

NEEDS Length: up to 20 pages double-spaced.

HOW TO CONTACT Accepts submissions by online submissions manager only. Include brief bio, list of publications. Considers multiple submissions.

PAYMENT/TERMS Pays 2 contributor's copies.

TIPS "Quality is the determining factor for breaking into *New Madrid*. We are looking for well-crafted, compelling writing in a range of genres, forms, and styles."

ⓢ NEW OHIO REVIEW

English Department, 360 Ellis Hall, Ohio University, Athens OH 45701. (740)707-3191. **E-mail:** noreditors@ohio.edu. **Website:** www.ohiou.edu/nor. **Contact:** David Wanczyk, editor. Estab. 2007. *New Ohio Review*, published biannually in spring and fall, publishes fiction, nonfiction, and poetry. Member CLMP. Reading period is September 15-December 15 and January 15-April 15. Annual contests, Jan 15th-Apr 15th ($1000 prizes).

NEEDS Considers literary short fiction; no novel excerpts.

HOW TO CONTACT Send complete ms.

PAYMENT/TERMS Pays $30 minimum in addition to 2 contributor's copies and one-year subscription.

ⓢ NEW ORLEANS REVIEW

Box 195, Loyola University, New Orleans LA 70118. (504)865-2295. **E-mail:** noreview@loyno.edu. **Website:** neworleansreview.org. **Contact:** Heidi Braden, managing editor; Mark Yakich, fiction editor. Estab. 1968. *New Orleans Review* is an annual journal of contemporary literature and culture, publishing new poetry, fiction, nonfiction, art, photography, film, and book reviews.

Ⓠ   The journal has published an eclectic variety of work by established and emerging writers, including Walker Percy, Pablo Neruda, Ellen Gilchrist, Nelson Algren, Hunter S. Thompson, John Kennedy Toole, Richard Brautigan, Barry Spacks, James Sallis, Jack Gilbert, Paul Hoover, Rodney Jones, Annie Dillard, Everette Maddox, Julio Cortazar, Gordon Lish, Robert Walser, Mark Halliday, Jack Butler, Robert Olen Butler, Michael Harper, Angela Ball, Joyce Carol Oates, Diane Wakoski, Dermot Bolger, Roddy Doyle, William Kotzwinkle, Alain Robbe-Grillet, Arnost Lustig, Raymond Queneau, Yusef Komunyakaa, Michael Martone, Tess Gallagher, Matthea Harvey, D. A. Powell, Rikki Ducornet, and Ed Skoog.

NEEDS Length: up to 6,500 words.

HOW TO CONTACT Submit complete ms using online submissions manager ($3 fee).

PAYMENT/TERMS Pays 2 contributor's copies.

TIPS "We're looking for dynamic writing that demonstrates attention to the language and a sense of the medium, writing that engages, surprises, moves us. We're not looking for genre fiction or academic articles. We subscribe to the belief that in order to truly write well, one must first master the rudiments: grammar and syntax, punctuation, the sentence, the paragraph, the line, the stanza. We receive about 3,000 mss a year and publish about 3% of them. Check out a recent issue, send us your best, proofread your work, be patient, be persistent."

⊘🟊 THE NEW QUARTERLY

St. Jerome's University, 290 Westmount Rd. N., Waterloo ON N2L 3G3, Canada. (519)884-8111, ext. 28290. **E-mail:** editor@tnq.ca; info@tnq.ca. **Website:** www.tnq.ca. Estab. 1981. "Emphasis on emerging writers and genres, but we publish more traditional work as well if the language and narrative structure are fresh."

◖   Open to Canadian writers only. Reading periods: March 1-August 31; September 1-February 28.

NEEDS *Canadian work only.* We are not interested in genre fiction. We are looking for innovative, beautifully crafted, deeply felt literary fiction."

HOW TO CONTACT Send complete ms with submission cover sheet and bio. Does not accept submissions by e-mail. Accepts simultaneoues submissions if indicated in cover letter.

PAYMENT/TERMS Pays $250/story.

TIPS "Reading us is the best way to get our measure. We don't have preconceived ideas about what we're looking for other than that it must be Canadian work (Canadian writers, not necessarily Canadian content). We want something that's fresh, something that will repay a second reading, something in which the language soars and the feeling is complexly rendered."

NEW SOUTH

Georgia State University, Campus Box 1894, MSC 8R0322 Unit 8, Atlanta GA 30303-3083. **E-mail:** newsoutheditors@gmail.com. **Website:** www.newsouthjournal.com. Estab. 1980. Semiannual maga-zine dedicated to finding and publishing the best work from artists around the world. Wants original voices searching to rise above the ordinary. Seeks to publish high-quality work, regardless of genre, form, or regional ties.

◖   *New South* is 160+ pages. Press run is 2,000; 500 distributed free to students. The *New South* Annual Writing Contest offers $1,000 for the best poem and $1,000 for the best story or essay; one-year subscription to all who submit. Submissions must be unpublished. Submit up to 3 poems, 1 story, or 1 essay on any subject or in any form. Guidelines available online. Competition receives 300 entries. Past judges include Sharon Olds, Jane Hirschfield, Anthony Hecht, Phillip Levine, and Jake Adam York. Winner will be announced in the Fall issue.

NEEDS Receives 200 unsolicited mss/month. Publishes and welcomes short shorts. Length: up to 9,000 words (short stories); up to 1,000 words (short shorts).

HOW TO CONTACT Submit 1 short story or up to 5 short shorts through Submittable.

PAYMENT/TERMS Pays 2 contributor's copies.

TIPS "We want what's new, what's fresh, and what's different—whether it comes from the Southern United States, the South of India, or the North, East or West of Anywhere."

🖙 NEW WELSH REVIEW

P.O. Box 170, Aberystwyth, Ceredigion SY23 1 WZ, United Kingdom. 01970-628410. **E-mail:** editor@newwelshreview.com. **E-mail:** submissions@newwelshreview.com. **Website:** www.newwelshreview.com. **Contact:** Gwen Davies, editor. "*New Welsh Review*, a literary magazine published 3 times/year and ranked in the top 5 British literary magazines, publishes stories, poems, and critical essays. The best of Welsh writing in English, past and present, is celebrated, discussed, and debated. We seek poems, short stories, reviews, special features/articles, and commentary."

HOW TO CONTACT Submit complete ms by e-mail.

PAYMENT/TERMS Pays direct to account or sends check on publication and 1 copy at discounted contributor's rate of £5 inc p&p."

🟊 THE NEW YORKER

1 World Trade Center, New York NY 10007. **E-mail:** themail@newyorker.com. **E-mail:** poetry@newy-

orker.com. **Website:** www.newyorker.com. **Contact:** David Remnick, editor in chief. Estab. 1925. A quality weekly magazine of distinct news stories, articles, essays, and poems for a literate audience.

○ *The New Yorker* receives approximately 4,000 submissions per month.

NEEDS Publishes 1 ms/issue.

HOW TO CONTACT Send complete ms by e-mail (as PDF attachment) or mail (address to Fiction Editor).

PAYMENT/TERMS Payment varies.

TIPS "Be lively, original, not overly literary. Write what you want to write, not what you think the editor would like."

NIMROD: INTERNATIONAL JOURNAL OF PROSE AND POETRY

University of Tulsa, 800 S. Tucker Dr., Tulsa OK 74104-3189. (918)631-3080. **Fax:** (918)631-3033. **E-mail:** nimrod@utulsa.edu. **Website:** www.utulsa.edu/nimrod. **Contact:** Eilis O'Neal, editor in chief; Cassidy McCants, associate editor. Estab. 1956. Since its founding in 1956 at The University of Tulsa, *Nimrod International Journal of Prose and Poetry*'s mission has been the discovery, development, and promotion of new writing. On a national and international scale, *Nimrod* helps new writers find their audiences through publication in our semiannual journal. We offer new and promising work that may be unfamiliar to readers, such as writing from countries not well represented in the American mainstream, writing in translation, and writing from people of under-represented ages, races, and sexual identities. On a personal scale, we continue our longstanding dedication to a full review of every submission to *Nimrod* by at least two readers from our Editorial Board. We also remain committed to responding personally to the hundreds of submissions we receive, often offering direct editorial feedback geared to helping writers expand their craft. *Nimrod* supports and defends the literary tradition of small magazines, spotlighting lesser-known poets and writers and providing foundations for their literary careers. We promote a living literature, believing that it is possible to search for, recognize, and reward contemporary writing of imagination, substance, and skill.

○ Semiannual magazine: 200 pages; perfect-bound; 4-color cover. Receives 300 unsolicited mss/month. **Publishes 50-120 new writers/year.** Reading period: January 1 through November 30. Online submissions accepted at nimrodjournal.submittable.com/submit. Does not accept submissions by e-mail unless the writer is living outside the U.S. and cannot submit using the submissions manager. Poetry published in *Nimrod* has been included in *The Best American Poetry*.

NEEDS Wants "vigorous writing, characters that are well developed, dialogue that is realistic without being banal." Length: up to 7,500 words.

HOW TO CONTACT Submit complete ms by mail or through the online submissions manager. Include SASE for work submitted by mail.

PAYMENT/TERMS Pays 2 contributor's copies.

🌀 NINTH LETTER

Department of English, University of Illinois, 608 S. Wright St., Urbana IL 61801. **E-mail:** info@ninthletter.com; editor@ninthletter.com; fiction@ninthletter.com; poetry@ninthletter.com; nonfiction@ninthletter.com. **Website:** www.ninthletter.com. **Contact:** Editorial staff rotates; contact genre-specific e-mail address with inquiries. "*Ninth Letter* accepts submissions of fiction, poetry, and essays from September 1-February 28 (postmark dates). *Ninth Letter* is published semiannually at the University of Illinois, Urbana-Champaign. We are interested in prose and poetry that experiment with form, narrative, and non-traditional subject matter, as well as more traditional literary work."

○ *Ninth Letter* won Best New Literary Journal 2005 from the Council of Editors of Learned Journals (CELJ) and has had poetry selected for *Best American Poetry*, *The Pushcart Prize*, *Best New Poets*, and *The Year's Best Fantasy and Horror*.

NEEDS Length: up to 8,000 words.

HOW TO CONTACT "Please send only 1 story at a time. All mailed submissions must include an SASE for reply."

PAYMENT/TERMS Pays $25/printed page and 2 contributor's copies.

NITE-WRITER'S INTERNATIONAL LITERARY ARTS JOURNAL

158 Spencer Ave., Suite 100, Pittsburgh PA 15227. **E-mail:** nitewritersliteraryarts@gmail.com. **Website:** sites.google.com/site/nitewriterinternational/home. **Contact:** John Thompson. Estab. 1994. *Nite-Writer's International Literary Arts Journal* is "dedicated to

the emotional intellectual with a creative perception of life."

○ Journal is open to beginners as well as professionals.

NEEDS Length: up to 1,200 words.

HOW TO CONTACT All literary works should be in DOC format in 12-point font.

TIPS "Read a lot of what you write—study the market. Don't fear rejection, but use it as a learning tool to strengthen your work before resubmitting."

THE NORMAL SCHOOL

The Press at the California State University - Fresno, 5245 North Backer Ave., M/S PB 98, Fresno CA 93740-8001. **E-mail:** editors@thenormalschool.com. **Website:** thenormalschool.com. **Contact:** Sophie Beck, managing editor. Estab. 2008. Semiannual magazine that accepts outstanding work by beginning and established writers.

○ Mss are read September 1-December 1 and January 15-April 15. Address submissions to the appropriate editor. Charges $3 fee for each online submission, due to operational costs.

NEEDS "We consider literary short fiction with contemporary themes and styles. We tend to prefer character-driven work and pieces that explore marginalized voices." Does not want any genre writing. Length: up to 7,000 words.

HOW TO CONTACT Submit complete ms via online submissions manager.

PAYMENT/TERMS Pays 2 contributor's copies and one-year subscription.

❸ NORTH AMERICAN REVIEW

University of Northern Iowa, 1222 W. 27th St., Cedar Falls IA 50614. (319)273-6455. **E-mail:** nar@uni.edu. **Website:** northamericanreview.org. Estab. 1815. "The *North American Review* is the oldest literary magazine in America and one of the most respected; though we have no prejudices about the subject matter of material sent to us, our first concern is quality."

○ This is the oldest literary magazine in the country and one of the most prestigious. Also one of the most entertaining—and a tough market for the young writer.

NEEDS Wants to see more "well-crafted literary stories that emphasize family concerns. We'd also like to see more stories engaged with environmental concerns." Reads fiction mss during academic year. **Publishes 2 new writers/year.** Recently published work

by Lee Ann Roripaugh, Dick Allen, and Rita Welty Bourke. "No flat narrative stories where the inferiority of the character is the paramount concern." Length: up to 30 pages.

HOW TO CONTACT Submit ms via online submissions manager.

TIPS "We like stories that start quickly and have a strong narrative arc. Poems that are passionate about subject, language, and image are welcome, whether they are traditional or experimental, whether in formal or free verse (closed or open form). Nonfiction should combine art and fact with the finest writing."

❸ NORTH CAROLINA LITERARY REVIEW

East Carolina University, Mailstop 555 English, Greenville NC 27858-4353. (252)328-1537. **Fax:** (252)328-4889. **E-mail:** nclrsubmissions@ecu.edu; bauerm@ecu.edu. **Website:** www.nclr.ecu.edu. **Contact:** Margaret Bauer. Estab. 1992. "Articles should have a North Carolina slant. Fiction, creative nonfiction, and poetry accepted through yearly contests. First consideration is always for quality of work. Although we treat academic and scholarly subjects, we do not wish to see jargon-laden prose; our readers, we hope, are found as often in bookstores and libraries as in academia. We seek to combine the best elements of a magazine for serious readers with the best of a scholarly journal."

○ Accepts submissions through Submittable.

NEEDS Length: up to 6,000 words.

HOW TO CONTACT Submit fiction for the Doris Betts Fiction Prize competition via Submittable.

PAYMENT/TERMS First-place winners of contests receive a prize of $250. Other writers whose stories are selected for publication receive contributor's copies.

TIPS "By far the easiest way to break in is with special issue sections. We are especially interested in reports on conferences, readings, meetings that involve North Carolina writers, and personal essays or short narratives with a strong sense of place. See back issues for other departments. Interviews are probably the other easiest place to break in; no discussions of poetics/theory, etc., except in reader-friendly (accessible) language. Interviews should be personal, more like conversations, and extensive, exploring connections between a writer's life and his or her work."

NORTH DAKOTA QUARTERLY

University of North Dakota, 276 Centennial Dr. Stop 7209, Merrifield Hall Room 15, Grand Forks ND

58202. (701)777-3322. **E-mail:** ndq@und.edu. **Website:** www.ndquarterly.org. **Contact:** Kate Sweney, managing editor; Gilad Elbom, fiction editor; Heidi Czerwiec, poetry editor; Sharon Carson, book reviews editor. Estab. 1911. "*North Dakota Quarterly* strives to publish the best fiction, poetry, and essays that in our estimation we can. Our tastes and interests are best reflected in what we have been recently publishing, and we suggest that you look at some current issues for guidance."

○ Only reads fiction and poetry September 1-May 1. Work published in *North Dakota Quarterly* was selected for inclusion in *The O. Henry Prize Stories*, *The Pushcart Prize Series*, and *Best American Essays*.

NEEDS No length restrictions.

HOW TO CONTACT Submit complete ms by postal mail.

○ NOTRE DAME REVIEW

University of Notre Dame, B009C McKenna Hall, Notre Dame IN 46556. **Website:** ndreview.nd.edu. Estab. 1995. "The *Notre Dame Review* is an independent, noncommercial magazine of contemporary American and international fiction, poetry, criticism, and art. Especially interested in work that takes on big issues by making the invisible seen, that gives voice to the voiceless. In addition to showcasing celebrated authors like Seamus Heaney and Czelaw Milosz, the *Notre Dame Review* introduces readers to authors they may have never encountered before but who are doing innovative and important work. In conjunction with the *Notre Dame Review*, the online companion to the printed magazine, the *nd[re]view*, engages readers as a community centered in literary rather than commercial concerns, a community we reach out to through critique and commentary as well as aesthetic experience."

○ Does not accept e-mail submissions. Only reads hardcopy submissions September through November and January through March.

NEEDS "We're eclectic. Upcoming theme issues planned. List of upcoming themes or editorial calendar available for SASE." No genre fiction. Length: up to 3,000 words.

HOW TO CONTACT Submit complete ms via online submissions manager.

PAYMENT/TERMS Pays $5-25.

NOW & THEN: THE APPALACHIAN MAGAZINE

East Tennessee State University, Box 70556, Johnson City TN 37614-1707. (423)439-5348. **Fax:** (423)439-7074. **E-mail:** nowandthen@etsu.edu; sandersr@etsu.edu. **Website:** www.etsu.edu/cas/cass/nowandthen. **Contact:** Randy Sanders, managing editor. Estab. 1984. *Now & Then* accepts a variety of writing genres: fiction, poetry, nonfiction, essays, interviews, memoirs, and book reviews. All submissions must relate to Appalachia and to the issue's specific theme. Readership is educated and interested in the region.

○ "At this time, the magazine is in the process of transitioning to an online-only publication. Therefore, we are currently not accepting submissions. Follow our progress by visiting the *Now & Then* website at www.etsu.edu/cas/cass/nowandthen."

NTH DEGREE

1219-M Gaskins Rd., Henrico VA 23238. **E-mail:** submissions@nthzine.com. **Website:** www.nthzine.com. **Contact:** Michael D. Pederson. Estab. 2002. Free online fanzine to promote up-and-coming new science fiction and fantasy authors and artists. Also supports the world of fandom and conventions.

○ No longer accepts hard copy submissions.

NEEDS Length: up to 7,500 words.

HOW TO CONTACT Submit complete ms via e-mail.

PAYMENT/TERMS Pays in contributor's copies.

TIPS "Don't submit anything that you may be ashamed of 10 years later."

NUTHOUSE

P.O. Box 119, Ellenton FL 34222. **Website:** www.nuthousemagazine.com. *Nuthouse*, published every 3 months, uses humor of all kinds, including homespun and political.

○ *Nuthouse* is 12 pages, digest-sized, photocopied from desktop-published originals. Receives about 500 poems/year, accepts about 100. Press run is 100. Subscription: $5 for 4 issues.

NEEDS "We publish all genres, from the homespun to the horrific. We don't automatically dismiss crudity or profanity. We're not prudes. Yet we consider such elements cheap and insulting unless essential to the gag. *NuTHOuSe* seeks submissions that are original, tightly written, and laugh-out-loud funny." Length: up to 1,000 words. "The shorter, the better."

HOW TO CONTACT Send complete ms with SASE and cover letter. Include estimated word count, bio (paragraph), and list of publications. No e-mail submissions.

PAYMENT/TERMS Pays 1 contributor's copy.

OBSIDIAN

Brown University, **E-mail:** obsidianatbrown@gmail.com. **Website:** obsidian-magazine.tumblr.com. **Contact:** Staff rotates each year; see website for current masthead. Estab. 1975. *Obsidian* is a "literary and visual space to showcase the creativity and experiences of black people, specifically at Brown University, formed out of the need for a platform made for us, by us." It is "actively intersectional, safe, and open: a space especially for the stories and voices of black women, black queer and trans people, and black people with disabilities."

NEEDS Length: up to 4,000 words.

HOW TO CONTACT Submit by e-mail as attachment. Include brief bio up to 3 sentences long.

TIPS "Following proper format is essential. Your title must be intriguing and text clean. Never give up. Some of the writers we publish were rejected many times before we published them."

◯ OLD RED KIMONO

Georgia Highlands College, 3175 Cedartown Hwy. SE, Rome GA 30161. **E-mail:** napplega@highlands.edu. **Website:** www.highlands.edu/site/ork. **Contact:** Dr. Nancy Applegate, professor of English; Thomas Dobson, literary editor. Estab. 1972. *Old Red Kimono*, published annually, prints original, high-quality poetry and fiction.

◯   *Old Red Kimono* is 72 pages, magazine-sized, professionally printed on heavy stock, with colored matte cover with art. Receives about 500 submissions/year, accepts about 60-70. Sample: $3.

NEEDS Length: up 1,500 words.

HOW TO CONTACT Submit via mail or e-mail.

PAYMENT/TERMS Pays 2 contributor's copies.

⑤ ONE STORY

232 3rd St., #A108, Brooklyn NY 11215. **Website:** www.one-story.com. **Contact:** Maribeth Batcha, pub-

lisher. Estab. 2002. "*One Story* is a literary magazine that contains, simply, 1 story. Approximately every 3-4 weeks, subscribers are sent *One Story* in the mail. *One Story* is artfully designed, lightweight, easy to carry, and ready to entertain on buses, in bed, in subways, in cars, in the park, in the bath, in the waiting rooms of doctor's offices, on the couch, or in line at the supermarket. Subscribers also have access to a website where they can learn more about *One Story* authors and hear about *One Story* readings and events. There is always time to read *One Story*."

◯   Reading period: September 1-May 31.

NEEDS *One Story* only accepts short stories. Do not send excerpts. Do not send more than 1 story at a time. Length: 3,000-8,000 words.

HOW TO CONTACT Send complete ms using online submission form.

PAYMENT/TERMS Pays $500 and 25 contributor's copies.

TIPS "*One Story* is looking for stories that are strong enough to stand alone. Therefore they must be very good. We want the best you can give."

☼ ON SPEC

P.O. Box 4727, Station South, Edmonton AB T6E 5G6, Canada. (780)628-7121. **E-mail:** onspec@onspec.ca. **Website:** www.onspec.ca. Estab. 1989. "We publish speculative fiction and poetry by new and established writers, with a strong preference for Canadian-authored works."

◯   See website guidelines for submission announcements. "Please refer to website for information regarding submissions, as we are not open year round."

NEEDS No media tie-in or shaggy-alien stories. No condensed or excerpted novels, religious/inspirational stories, fairy tales. Length: 1,000-6,000 words.

HOW TO CONTACT Send complete ms. Electronic submissions preferred.

TIPS "We want to see stories with plausible characters, a well-constructed, consistent, and vividly described setting, a strong plot, and believable emotions; characters must show us (not tell us) their emotional responses to each other and to the situation and/or challenge they face. Also: Don't send us stories written for television. We don't like media tie-ins, so don't watch TV for inspiration! Read instead! Strong preference given to submissions by Canadians."

⊙ ⑤ ON THE PREMISES: A GOOD PLACE TO START

On the Premises, LLC, 4323 Gingham Court, Alexandria VA 22310. **E-mail:** questions@onthepremises.com. **Website:** www.onthepremises.com. **Contact:** Tarl Roger Kudrick or Bethany Granger, co-publishers. Estab. 2006. Stories published in *On the Premises* are winning entries in contests that are held every 6 months. Each contest challenges writers to produce a great story based on a broad premise that our editors supply as part of the contest.*On the Premises* aims to promote newer and/or relatively unknown writers who can write what we feel are creative, compelling stories told in effective, uncluttered, and evocative prose. Entrants pay no fees, and winners receive cash prizes in addition to publication. Also holds four "mini-contests" a year in which authors are asked to write extremely short fiction (50 words or so) in accordance with special challenges.

⊙ Does not read March or September. Receives 50-150 mss/month. Accepts 4-7 mss/issue; 8-14 mss/year. Has published a few well-known authors such as multiple award-winner Ken Liu, as well as dozens of lesser known authors and quite a few first-time fiction sellers. Member Small Press Promotions.

NEEDS Themes are announced the day each contest is launched. List of past and current premises available on website. "All genres considered. All stories must be based on the broad premise supplied as part of the contest. Sample premise, taken from the first issue: 'One or more characters are traveling in a vehicle, and never reach their intended destination. Why not? What happens instead?'" No young adult, children's, or "preachy" fiction. "In general, we don't like stories that were written solely to make a social or political point, especially if the story seems to assume that no intelligent person could possibly disagree with the author. Save the ideology for editorial and opinion pieces, please. But above all, we *never ever* want to see stories that do not use the contest premise! Use the premise, and make it 'clear' and 'obvious' that you are using the premise." Length: 1,000-5,000 words. Average length: 3,500 words.

HOW TO CONTACT Submit stories only via submission form at onthepremises.submittable.com/submit. "We no longer accept e-mailed submissions."
PAYMENT/TERMS Pays $60-220.

TIPS "Make sure you use the premise, not just interpret it. If the premise is 'must contain a real live dog,' then think of a creative, compelling way to use a real dog. Revise your draft, then revise again and again. Remember, we judge stories blindly, so craftsmanship and creativity matter, not how well known you are."

☺ OPEN MINDS QUARTERLY

36 Elgin St., 2nd Floor, Sudbury ON P3C 5B4, Canada. (705)222-6472, ext. 303. **E-mail:** openminds@nisa.on.ca. **Website:** www.openmindsquarterly.com. **Contact:** Sarah Mann, editor. Estab. 1997. *Open Minds Quarterly* provides a venue for individuals who have experienced mental illness to express themselves via poetry, short fiction, essays, first-person accounts of living with mental illness, and book/movie reviews. Wants unique, well-written, provocative work. Does not want overly graphic or sexual violence.

⊙ *Open Minds Quarterly* is 24 pages, magazine-sized, saddle-stapled, with 100 lb. stock cover with original artwork, includes ads. Press run is 550; 150 distributed free to potential subscribers, published writers, NISA members, advertisers, and conferences and events.

NEEDS Length: 1,000-3,000 words.
HOW TO CONTACT Submit through website. Cover letter is required. Information in cover letter: indicate your lived experience with mental illness. Reads submissions year round.
PAYMENT/TERMS Pays contributor's copies.

☻ ORBIS

17 Greenhow Ave., West Kirby Wirral CH48 5EL, United Kingdom. **E-mail:** carolebaldock@hotmail.com. **Website:** www.orbisjournal.com. **Contact:** Carole Baldock, editor; Noel Williams, reviews editor. Estab. 1969. "*Orbis* has long been considered one of the top 20 small-press magazines in the U.K. We are interested in social inclusion projects and encouraging access to the arts, young people, under 20s, and 20-somethings. Subjects for discussion: 'day in the life,' technical, topical."

⊙ Please see guidelines on website before submitting.

NEEDS Submit by postal mail or e-mail (overseas submissions only). Include cover letter. Length: up to 1,000 words.

TIPS "Any publication should be read cover to cover because it's the best way to improve your chances of getting published. Enclose SAE with all correspondence. Overseas: 2 IRCs, 3 if work is to be returned."

OXFORD MAGAZINE

Miami University, Oxford OH 45056. **E-mail:** oxmag@miamioh.edu. **Website:** www.oxfordmagazine.org. Estab. 1984. *Oxford Magazine*, published annually online in May, is open in terms of form, content, and subject matter. "Since our premiere in 1984, our magazine has received Pushcart Prizes for both fiction and poetry and has published authors such as Charles Baxter, William Stafford, Robert Pinsky, Stephen Dixon, Helena Maria Viramontes, Andre Dubus, and Stuart Dybek."

○ Work published in *Oxford Magazine* has been included in the *Pushcart Prize* anthology. Does not read submissions July through August.

NEEDS Length: up to 3,000 words.

HOW TO CONTACT Submit complete ms via online submissions manager.

OYEZ REVIEW

Roosevelt University, Dept. of Literature & Languages, 430 S. Michigan Ave., Chicago IL 60605. **E-mail:** oyezreview@roosevelt.edu. **Website:** oyezreview.wordpress.com. Estab. 1965. Annual magazine of the Creative Writing Program at Roosevelt University, publishing fiction, creative nonfiction, poetry, and art. There are no restrictions on style, theme, or subject matter.

○ Reading period is August 1-October 1. Each issue has 104 pages: 92 pages of text and an 8-page spread of 1 artist's work (in color or b&w). Work by the issue's featured artist also appears on the front and back cover, totaling 10 pieces. The journal has featured work from such writers as Charles Bukowski, James McManus, Carla Panciera, Michael Onofrey, Tim Foley, John N. Miller, Gary Fincke, and Barry Silesky, and visual artists Vivian Nunley, C. Taylor, Jennifer Troyer, and Frank Spidale. Accepts queries by e-mail.

NEEDS "We publish short stories and flash fiction on their merit as contemporary literature rather than the category within the genre." Length: up to 5,000 words.

HOW TO CONTACT Send complete ms via online submissions manager or postal mail.

PAYMENT/TERMS Pays 2 contributor's copies.

OYSTER BOY REVIEW

P.O. Box 1483, Pacifica CA 94044. **E-mail:** email_2016@oysterboyreview.com. **Website:** www.oysterboyreview.com. **Contact:** Damon Sauve, editor/publisher. Estab. 1993. Electronic and print magazine. *Oyster Boy Review*, published annually, is interested in "the underrated, the ignored, the misunderstood, and the varietal. We'll make some mistakes."

NEEDS Wants fiction that revolves around characters in conflict with themselves or each other; a plot that has a beginning, a middle, and an end; a narrative with a strong moral center (not necessarily 'moralistic'); a story with a satisfying resolution to the conflict; and an ethereal something that contributes to the mystery of a question but does not necessarily seek or contrive to answer it. Submit complete ms by postal mail or e-mail. No genre fiction.

PAYMENT/TERMS Pays 2 contributor's copies.

TIPS "Keep writing, keep submitting, keep revising."

PACIFICA LITERARY REVIEW

E-mail: pacificalitreview@gmail.com. **Website:** www.pacificareview.com. **Contact:** Matt Muth, editor in chief; Sarina Sheth and Paul Vega, managing editors. "Pacifica Literary Review is a small literary arts magazine based in Seattle. Our print editions are published biannually in winter and summer and we publish year-round on the web. *PLR* is now accepting submissions of poetry, fiction, creative nonfiction, author interviews, and b&w photography. Submission period: September 15-December 15 and Jan 15-May 15."

NEEDS Wants literary fiction and flash fiction. Length: up to 6,000 words for literary fiction; 300-1,000 words for flash fiction.

HOW TO CONTACT Submit complete ms.

PAYMENT/TERMS 2 copies of issue in which author was published and 1 copy of next issue.

PACIFIC REVIEW

SDSU Press, Dept. of English and Comparative Literature, San Diego State University, 5500 Campanile Dr., MC6020, San Diego CA 92182-6020. **E-mail:** pacrevjournal@gmail.com. **E-mail:** info.pacrev@gmail.com. **Website:** pacificreview.sdsu.edu. **Contact:** Hari Alluri, Editor. Estab. 1977. Pacific Review accepts poems, fiction (short stories, flash fiction and excerpts that stand alone), memoir, creative nonfiction, essays, comics, visual art, photography, documented performance and hybrid.

○ Current theme: Errant Mythologies. For details and to submit, please see our Submittable page - https://pacrev.submittable.com/submit. Simultaneous submissions permitted with immediate notification of acceptance elsewhere.

NEEDS Length: up to 5,000 words.

HOW TO CONTACT Submit ms via online submissions manager. Include cover letter with name, postal address, e-mail addresss, phone number, and short bio.

PAYMENT/TERMS Pays 1 contributor's copy.

TIPS "We welcome all submissions as long as they fit the theme and represent work that the author loves and believes we may love."

PACKINGTOWN REVIEW

111 S. Lincoln St., Batavia IL 60510. **E-mail:** packingtownreview@gmail.com. **Website:** www.packingtownreview.com. Estab. 2008. *Packingtown Review* publishes imaginative and critical prose and poetry by emerging and established writers. Welcomes submissions of poetry, scholarly articles, drama, creative nonfiction, fiction, and literary translation, as well as genre-bending pieces.

○ Literary magazine/journal: 8.5 x 11, 250 pages. Press run: 500.

NEEDS Does not want to see uninspired or unrevised work. Wants to avoid fantasy, science fiction, overtly religious, or romantic pieces. Length: up to 4,000 words.

HOW TO CONTACT Send complete ms as attachment. Include cover letter in body of e-mail.

PAYMENT/TERMS Pays 2 contributor's copies.

TIPS "We are looking for well-crafted prose. We are open to most styles and forms. We are also looking for prose that takes risks and does so successfully. We will consider articles about prose."

⑤ PAINTED BRIDE QUARTERLY

Drexel University, Department of English and Philosophy, 3141 Chestnut St., Philadelphia PA 19104. **E-mail:** info@pbqmag.org. **Website:** pbqmag.org. **Contact:** Kathleen Volk Miller and Marion Wrenn, editors. Estab. 1973. *Painted Bride Quarterly* seeks literary fiction (experimental and traditional), poetry, and artwork and photographs.

NEEDS Publishes theme-related work; check website. Holds annual fiction contests. Length: up to 5,000 words.

HOW TO CONTACT Send complete ms through online submissions manager.

PAYMENT/TERMS Pays $20.

TIPS "We look for freshness of idea incorporated with high-quality writing. We receive an awful lot of nicely written work with worn-out plots. We want quality in whatever—we hold experimental work to as strict standards as anything else. Many of our readers write fiction; most of them enjoy a good reading. We hope to be an outlet for quality. A good story gives, first, enjoyment to the reader. We've seen a good many of them lately, and we've published the best of them."

PANK

PANK, Department of Humanities, 1400 Townsend Dr., Houghton MI 49931-1200. **Website:** www.pankmagazine.com. Estab. 2006. "*PANK* Magazine fosters access to emerging and experimental poetry and prose, publishing the brightest and most promising writers for the most adventurous readers. To the end of the road, up country, a far shore, the edge of things, to a place of amalgamation and unplumbed depths, where the known is made and unmade, and where unimagined futures are born, a place inhabited by contradictions, a place of quirk and startling anomaly. *PANK*, no soft pink hands allowed."

NEEDS "Bright, new, energetic, passionate writing, writing that pushes our tender little buttons and gets us excited. Push our tender buttons, excite us, and we'll publish you."

HOW TO CONTACT Send complete ms through online submissions manager.

PAYMENT/TERMS Pays $20, a one-year subscription, and a *PANK* t-shirt.

TIPS "To read *PANK* is to know *PANK*. Or, read a lot within the literary magazine and small-press universe—there's plenty to choose from. Unfortunately, we see a lot of submissions from writers who have clearly read neither *PANK* nor much else. Serious writers are serious readers. Read. Seriously."

○ PAPERPLATES

19 Kenwood Ave., Toronto ON M6C 2R8, Canada. (416)651-2551. **E-mail:** magazine@paperplates.org. **Website:** www.paperplates.org. **Contact:** Bernard Kelly, publisher. Estab. 1990. *paperplates* is a literary quarterly published in Toronto. "We make no distinction between veterans and beginners. Some of our contributors have published several books; some have never before published a single line."

○ No longer accepts IRCs.

NEEDS Length: no more than 7,500 words.

HOW TO CONTACT Submit by mail or e-mail. "Do not send fiction as an e-mail attachment. Copy the first 300 words or so into the body of your message. If you prefer not to send a fragment, you have the option of using surface mail." Include short bio with submission.

THE PARIS REVIEW

544 West 27th St., New York NY 10001. (212)343-1333. **E-mail:** queries@theparisreview.org. **Website:** www.theparisreview.org. **Contact:** Lorin Stein, editor; Robyn Creswell, poetry editor. *The Paris Review* publishes "fiction and poetry of superlative quality, whatever the genre, style, or mode. Our contributors include prominent, as well as less well-known and previously unpublished writers. The Writers at Work interview series includes important contemporary writers discussing their own work and the craft of writing."

○ Address submissions to proper department. Do not make submissions via e-mail.

NEEDS Study the publication. Annual Plimpton Prize award of $10,000 given to a new voice published in the magazine. Recently published work by Ottessa Moshfegh, John Jeremiah Sullivan, and Lydia Davis. Length: no limit.

HOW TO CONTACT Send complete ms.

PAYMENT/TERMS Pays $1,000-3,000.

PASSAGER

Passager Press, 1420 N. Charles St., Baltimore MD 21201. **E-mail:** editors@passagerbooks.com. **Website:** www.passagerbooks.com. **Contact:** Kendra Kopelke, Mary Azrael, Christine Drawl. Estab. 1990. "*Passager* has a special focus on older writers. Its mission is to encourage, engage, and strengthen the imagination well into old age and to give mature readers opportunities that are sometimes closed off to them in our youth-oriented culture. We are dedicated to honoring the creativity that takes hold in later years and to making public the talents of those over the age of 50." Passager publishes 2 issues/year, an Open issue (fall/winter) and a Poetry Contest issue (spring/summer).

○ Literary magazine/journal. 8.25x8.25, 84 pages, recycled paper, full-color cover.

NEEDS Accepts literary fiction submissions from writers over 50. Length: up to 4,000 words.

HOW TO CONTACT Send complete ms with cover letter, or use Submittable. Check website for guidelines. Include estimated word count, brief bio, list of publications. Send either SASE (or IRC) for return of ms, or disposable copy of ms and #10 SASE for reply only.

PAYMENT/TERMS Pays 1 contributor's copy.

TIPS "Stereotyped images of old age will be rejected immediately. Write humorous, tongue-in-cheek essays. Read the publication, or at least visit the website."

PASSAGES NORTH

English Department, Northern Michigan University, 1401 Presque Isle Ave., Marquette MI 49855. (906)227-1203. **E-mail:** passages@nmu.edu. **Website:** www.passagesnorth.com. **Contact:** Jennifer A. Howard, editor in chief; Jacqueline Boucher & Willow Grosz, managing editors; Matthew Gavin Frank & Rachel May, non-fiction and hybrids editors; Patricia Killelea, poetry editor; Monica McFawn, fiction editor. Estab. 1979. *Passages North*, published annually in spring, prints poetry, short fiction, creative nonfiction, essays, and interviews.

○ Magazine: 7x10; 200-350 pgs; 60 lb. paper. Publishes work by established and emerging writers.

NEEDS "Don't be afraid to surprise us." Length: up to 7,000 words.

HOW TO CONTACT Send 1 short story or as many as 3 short-short stories (paste them all into 1 document).

TIPS "We look for voice, energetic prose, writers who take risks. We look for an engaging story in which the author evokes an emotional response from the reader through carefully rendered scenes, complex characters, and a smart, narrative design. Revise, revise. Read what we publish."

THE PATERSON LITERARY REVIEW

Passaic County Community College, 1 College Blvd., Paterson NJ 07505. (973)684-6555. **Website:** www.patersonliteraryreview.com. **Contact:** Maria Mazziotti Gillan, editor/executive director. *Paterson Literary Review*, published annually, is produced by the The Poetry Center at Passaic County Community College.

○ Work for *PLR* has been included in the *Pushcart Prize* anthology and *Best American Poetry*.

NEEDS "We are interested in quality short stories, with no taboos on subject matter." Receives 60 unsolicited mss/month. Publishes 5% new writers/year. Length: up to 1,500 words.

HOW TO CONTACT Send SASE for reply or return of ms. "Indicate whether you want story returned."
PAYMENT/TERMS Pays contributor's copies.

⊗ THE PEDESTAL MAGAZINE

6815 Honors Court, Charlotte NC 28210. **E-mail:** pedmagazine@carolina.rr.com. **Website:** www.thepedestalmagazine.com. **Contact:** John Amen, editor in chief. Estab. 2000. Committed to promoting diversity and celebrating the voice of the individual.

○ See website for reading periods for different forms. Member: CLMP.

NEEDS "We are receptive to all sorts of high-quality literary fiction. Genre fiction is encouraged as long as it crosses or comments upon its genre and is both character-driven and psychologically acute. We encourage submissions of short fiction, no more than 3 flash fiction pieces at a time. There is no need to query prior to submitting; please submit via online submissions manager—no e-mail to the editor." Length: up to 4,000 words for short stories; up to 1,000 words for flash fiction.

PAYMENT/TERMS Pays 3¢/word.

TIPS "If you send us your work, please wait for a response to your first submission before you submit again."

PENNSYLVANIA ENGLISH

Indiana University of Pennsylvania, Department of English, Indiana University of Pennsylvania, HSS 506A, 981 Grant St., Indiana PA 15705. **E-mail:** mtwill@iup.edu. **Website:** paenglish.submittable.com/submit. **Contact:** Dr. Michael T. Williamson, editor (mtwill@iup.edu); Dr. Michael Cox, creative prose editor (mwcox@pitt.edu); Tony Vallone, MFA, poetry editor (avallone@psu.edu); Dr. John Marsden (marsden@iup.edu) and Dr. Michael T. Williamson, literary criticism editors. Estab. 1985. *Pennsylvania English*, published annually, is "sponsored by the Pennsylvania College English Association. Our philosophy is quality. We publish literary fiction (and poetry and nonfiction). Our intended audience is literate, college-educated people."

○ *Pennsylvania English* is 5.25x8.25, up to 200 pages, perfect -bound, full-color cover featuring the artwork of a Pennsylvania artist. Reads mss during the summer. Publishes 4-6 new writers/year. Has published work by Dave Kress, Dan Leone, Paul West, Liz Rosenberg,

Walt MacDonald, Amy Pence, Jennifer Richter, and Jeff Schiff.

NEEDS No genre fiction or romance.

HOW TO CONTACT Submit via online submissions manager. "For all submissions, please include a brief bio for the contributors' page. Be sure to include your name, address, phone number, e-mail address, institutional affiliation (if you have one), the title of your short story, and any other relevant information. We will edit if necessary for space."

PAYMENT/TERMS Pays 1 contributor's copy.

TIPS "Quality of the writing is our only measure. We're not impressed by long-winded cover letters detailing awards and publications we've never heard of. Beginners and professionals have the same chance with us. We receive stacks of competently written but boring fiction. For a story to rise from the rejection pile, it takes more than the basic competence."

PENNSYLVANIA LITERARY JOURNAL

Anaphora Literary Press, 1898 Athens St., Brownsville TX 78520. (470)289-6395. **E-mail:** director@anaphoraliterary.com. **Website:** anaphoraliterary.com. **Contact:** Anna Faktorovich, editor/director. Estab. 2009. *Pennsylvania Literary Journal* is a printed, peer-reviewed journal that publishes critical essays, book reviews, short stories, interviews, photographs, art, and poetry. Published tri-annually, it features special issues on a wide variety of different fields from film studies to literary criticism to interviews with bestsellers. Submissions in all genres from emerging and established writers are warmly welcomed.

NEEDS Detailed, descriptive, and original short stories are preferred. No word limit.

HOW TO CONTACT Send complete ms via e-mail.

PAYMENT/TERMS Does not provide payment.

TIPS "We are just looking for great writing. Send your materials; if they are good and you don't mind working for free, we'll take it."

PENNY DREADFUL: TALES & POEMS OF FANTASTIC TERROR

P.O. Box 719, Radio City Station, Hell's Kitchen NY 10101-0719. **E-mail:** mmpendragon@aol.com. **Website:** www.mpendragon.com/pennydreadful.html. Estab. 1996. *Penny Dreadful: Tales & Poems of Fantastic Terror*, published irregularly (about once a year), features goth-romantic poetry and prose. Publishes poetry, short stories, essays, letters, listings, reviews, and b&w artwork "which celebrate the darker aspects of Man, the World, and their Creator." Wants "literary horror in the tradition of Poe, M.R. James, Shelley, M.P. Shiel, and LeFanu—dark, disquieting tales and verses designed to challenge the reader's perception of human nature, morality, and man's place within the Darkness. Stories and poems should be set prior to 1910 and/or possess a timeless quality." Does not want "references to 20th- and 21st-century personages/events, graphic sex, strong language, excessive gore and shock elements."

○ "Works appearing in *Penny Dreadful* have been reprinted in *The Year's Best Fantasy and Horror*." *Penny Dreadful* nominates best tales and poems for Pushcart Prizes. *Penny Dreadful* is over 100 pages, digest-sized, desktop-published, perfect-bound. Press run is 200.

NEEDS Length: up to 5,000 words.

HOW TO CONTACT Submit complete ms by mail or e-mail. "Mss should be submitted in the standard, professional format: typed, double-spaced, name and address on the first page, name and title of work on all subsequent pages, etc. Include SASE for reply. Also include brief cover letter with a brief bio and publication history."

PAYMENT/TERMS Pays 1 contributor's copy.

PEREGRINE

Amherst Writers & Artists Press, P.O. Box 1076, Amherst MA 01004. (413)253-3307. **E-mail:** peregrinejournal@gmail.com. **E-mail:** peregrine@amherstwriters.com. **Website:** amherstwriters.info/peregrine. **Contact:** Kate Eliza Frank, managing editor; Milo Muise, fiction editor, Rachelle Parker, poetry editor. Estab. 1983. *Peregrine*, published annually, features poetry and fiction. "*Peregrine* has provided a forum for national and international writers since 1983 and is committed to finding excellent work by emerging as well as established writers. We welcome work reflecting diversity of voice. We like to be surprised. We look for writing that is honest, unpretentious, and memorable. All decisions are made by the editors."

○ Magazine: 6x9; 100+ pages; 60 lb. white offset paper; glossy cover. Member: CLMP. Reading period: March 15-May 15.

NEEDS Length: up to 750 words.

HOW TO CONTACT Submit via e-mail. Include word count on first page of submissions. "Shorter stories have a better chance."

PAYMENT/TERMS Pays 2 contributor's copies.

TIPS "Check guidelines before submitting your work. Familiarize yourself with *Peregrine*. We look for heart and soul as well as technical expertise. Trust your own voice."

PERMAFROST: A LITERARY JOURNAL

America's Farthest North Literary Magazine, **University of Alaska Fairbanks**, c/o English Dept., Univ. of Alaska Fairbanks, P.O. Box 755720, Fairbanks AK 99775. **E-mail:** editor@permafrostmag.com. **Website:** permafrostmag.uaf.edu. Estab. 1977. *Permafrost Magazine*, a literary journal, contains poems, short stories, hybrid pieces, creative nonfiction, b&w drawings, photographs, and prints. We print both new and established writers, hoping and expecting to see the best work out there. We have published work by E. Ethelbert Miller, W. Loran Smith, Peter Orlovsky, Jim Wayne Miller, Allen Ginsberg, and Andy Warhol.

○ *Permafrost* is about 200 pages, digest-sized, professionally printed, flat-spined. Also publishes summer online edition.

NEEDS Length: up to 8,000 words.

HOW TO CONTACT Submit complete ms via online submissions manager at permafrostmag.submittable.com; "e-mail submissions will not be read."

PAYMENT/TERMS Pays 1 contributor's copy. Reduced contributor rate of $5 on additional copies.

PERSPECTIVES

c/o Jason Lief, Dordt College, 498 4th Ave. NE, Sioux Center IA 51250. **E-mail:** editors@perspectivesjournal.org. **E-mail:** submissions@perspectivesjournal.org. **Website:** perspectivesjournal.org. **Contact:** Jason Lief. "*Perspectives* is a journal of theology in the broad Reformed tradition. We seek to express the Reformed faith theologically; to engage issues that Reformed Christians meet in personal, ecclesiastical, and societal life; and thus to contribute to the mission of the church of Jesus Christ. The editors are interested in submissions that contribute to a contemporary Reformed theological discussion. Our readers tend to be affiliated with the Presbyterian Church (USA), the Reformed Church in America, and the Christian Reformed Church. Some of our subscribers are academics or pastors, but we also gear our articles to thoughtful, literate laypeople who want to engage in Reformed theological reflection on faith and culture."

○ *Perspectives* is 24 pages, magazine-sized, Web offset-printed, saddle-stapled, with paper cover containing b&w illustration. Receives about 300 poems/year, accepts 6-20. Press run is 1,575.

NEEDS Length: up to 3,000 words.

HOW TO CONTACT Submit complete ms by e-mail.

PHILADELPHIA STORIES

Fiction/Art/Poetry of the Delaware Valley, 93 Old York Rd., Suite 1/#1-753, Jenkintown PA 19046. **Website:** www.philadelphiastories.org. **Contact:** Christine Weiser, executive director/co-publisher. Estab. 2004. *Philadelphia Stories*, published quarterly, publishes "fiction, poetry, essays, and art written by authors living in, or originally from, Pennsylvania, Delaware, or New Jersey. *Philadelphia Stories* also hosts 2 national writing contests: The Marguerite McGlinn Short Story Contest ($2,000 first-place prize; $500 second-place prize; $250 third-place prize) and the Sandy Crimmins National Poetry Contest ($1,000 first-place prize, 3 $100 runner-up prizes). Visit our website for details." *Philadelphia Stories* also launched a "junior" version in 2012 for Philadelphia-area writers ages 12 and younger and a "teen" version for writers ages 13-18. Visit www.philadelphiastories.org/junior for details.

○ Literary magazine/journal: 8.5x11; 24 pages; 70# matte text, all 4-color paper; 70# matte text cover. Contains illustrations, photographs. Subscription: "We offer $20 memberships that include home delivery." Make checks payable to *Philadelphia Stories*. Member: CLMP.

NEEDS Receives 45-80 mss/month. Accepts 3-4 mss/issue for print, additional 1-2 online; 12-16 mss/year for print, 4-8 online. Publishes 50% new writers/year. Also publishes book reviews; send review queries to info@philadelphiastories.org. "We will consider anything that is well written but are most inclined to publish literary or mainstream fiction. We are *not* particularly interested in most genres (science fiction, fantasy, romance, etc.)." Length: up to 5,000 words; 4,000 words average. Also publishes short shorts; average length: 800 words.

PAYMENT/TERMS Pays $25 honorarium from the Conrad Weiser Author Fund and 2 contributor's copies.

TIPS "We look for exceptional, polished prose, a controlled voice, strong characters and place, and interesting subjects. Follow guidelines. We cannot stress this enough. Read every guideline carefully and thoroughly before sending anything out. Send out only polished material. We reject many quality pieces for various reasons; try not to take rejection personally. Just because your piece isn't right for one publication doesn't mean it's bad. Selection is an extremely subjective process."

PHOEBE: JOURNAL OF LITERATURE AND ART

MSN 2C5, George Mason University, 400 University Dr., Fairfax VA 22030. **Website:** www.phoebejournal.com. **Contact:** Andrew Cartwright and Ryan McDonald, nonfiction editors; Sarah Bates, fiction editor, and Joseph Kuhn, assistant fiction editor; Doug Luman, poetry editor, and Janice Majewski, assistant. Estab. 1971. Publishes poetry, fiction, nonfiction, and online content. "*Phoebe* prides itself on supporting up-and-coming writers, whose style, form, voice, and subject matter demonstrate a vigorous appeal to the senses, intellect, and emotions of our readers."

NEEDS No romance or erotica. Length: up to 4,000 words.

HOW TO CONTACT Submit 1 fiction submission via online submission manager.

PAYMENT/TERMS Pays 2 contributor's copies and $400 for contest winner.

PILGRIMAGE MAGAZINE

Colorado State University-Pueblo, Dept. of English, 2200 Bonforte Blvd., Pueblo CO 81001. **E-mail:** info@pilgrimagepress.org. **Website:** www.pilgrimagepress.org. **Contact:** Juan Morales, editor. Estab. 1976. Serves an eclectic fellowship of readers, writers, artists, naturalists, contemplatives, activists, seekers, adventurers, and other kindred spirits.

NEEDS Length: up to 6,000 words. "Shorter works are easier to include, due to space constraints."

TIPS "Our interests include wildness in all its forms; inward and outward explorations; home ground, the open road, service, witness, peace, and justice; symbols, story, and myth in contemporary culture; struggle and resilience; insight and transformation; wisdom wherever it is found; and the great mystery of it all. We like good storytellers and a good sense of humor. No e-mail submissions, please."

THE PINCH

English Department, University of Memphis, Memphis TN 38152. **E-mail:** editor@pinchjournal.com. **Website:** www.pinchjournal.com. Estab. 1980. Semiannual literary magazine. "We publish fiction, creative nonfiction, poetry, and art of literary quality by both established and emerging artists."

○ "The Pinch Literary Awards in Fiction, Poetry, and Nonfiction offer a $1,000 prize and publication. Check our website for details."

NEEDS Wants "character-based" fiction with a "fresh use of language." No genre fiction. Length: up to 5,000 words.

HOW TO CONTACT Submit complete ms (or up to 3 flash fiction pieces) via online submissions manager.

PAYMENT/TERMS Pays 2 contributor's copies. "One work from each genre will be awarded a $200 Featured Writer award, as determined by the editors."

TIPS "We have a new look and a new edge. We're soliciting work from writers with a national or international reputation as well as strong, interesting work from emerging writers."

THE PINK CHAMELEON

E-mail: dpfreda@juno.com. **E-mail:** dpfreda@juno.com. **Website:** www.thepinkchameleon.com. **Contact:** Dorothy Paula Freda, editor/publisher. Estab. 2000. *The Pink Chameleon*, published annually online, contains family-oriented, upbeat poetry, stories, essays, and articles, any genre in good taste that gives hope for the future.

○ Reading period is February 1 through March 31 and September 1 through October 31.

NEEDS Accepts fiction that follows *The Pink Chameleon* online guidelines. No violence for the sake of violence. No novels or novel excerpts. Length: 500-2,500 words; average length: 2,000 words.

HOW TO CONTACT Send complete ms in the body of the e-mail. No attachments. Accepts reprints. Has published work by Deanne F. Purcell, Martin Green, Albert J. Manachino, James W. Collins, Ron Arnold, Sally Kosmalski, Susan Marie Davniero, and Glenn D. Hayes.

PAYMENT/TERMS No payment.

TIPS Wants "simple, honest, evocative emotion; upbeat fiction and nonfiction submissions that give hope for the future; well-paced plots; stories, poetry, articles, essays that speak from the heart. Read guidelines carefully. Use a good, but not ostentatious, opening hook. Stories should have a beginning, middle, and end that make the reader feel the story was worth his or her time. This also applies to articles and essays. In the latter 2, wrap your comments and conclusions in a neatly packaged final paragraph. Turnoffs include

violence and bad language. Simple, genuine, and sensitive work does not need to shock with vulgarity to be interesting and enjoyable."

PISGAH REVIEW

Division of Humanities, Brevard College, 1 Brevard College Dr., Brevard NC 28712. (828)577-8324. **E-mail:** tinerjj@brevard.edu. **E-mail:** pisgahreview.com. **Website:** www.pisgahreview.com. **Contact:** Jubal Tiner, editor. Estab. 2005. "*Pisgah Review* publishes primarily literary short fiction, creative nonfiction, and poetry. Our only criteria is quality of work; we look for the best."

○ Has published Ron Rash, Thomas Rain Crowe, Joan Conner, Gary Fincke, Steve Almond, and Fred Bahnson.

NEEDS Receives 85 mss/month. Accepts 6-8 mss/issue; 12-15 mss/year. Publishes 5 new writers/year. Does not want genre fiction or inspirational stories. Length: 2,000-7,500 words. Average length: 4,000 words. Average length of short shorts: 1,000 words.

HOW TO CONTACT "Send complete ms to our submission manager on our website."

PAYMENT/TERMS Writers receive 2 contributor's copies. Additional copies $7.

TIPS "We select work of only the highest quality. Grab us from the beginning and follow through. Engage us with your language and characters. A clean ms goes a long way toward acceptance. Stay true to the vision of your work, revise tirelessly, and submit persistently."

●⑤ PLANET: THE WELSH INTERNATIONALIST

Berw Ltd., P.O. Box 44, Aberystwyth Ceredigion SY23 3ZZ, United Kingdom. 01970 622408. **E-mail:** submissions@planetmagazine.org.uk. **Website:** www.planetmagazine.org.uk. **Contact:** Emily Trahair, editor. Estab. 1970. A literary/cultural/political journal centered on Welsh affairs but with a strong interest in minority cultures in Europe and elsewhere. *Planet: The Welsh Internationalist*, published quarterly, is a cultural magazine centered on Wales, but with broader interests in arts, sociology, politics, history, and science.

○ *Planet* is 96 pages, A5, professionally printed, perfect-bound, with glossy colour card cover. Receives about 500 submissions/year, accepts about 5%. Press run is 1,000 (800 subscribers, about 10% libraries, 200 shelf sales).

NEEDS Would like to see more inventive, imaginative fiction that pays attention to language and experiments with form. No magical realism, horror, science fiction. Length: 1,500-2,750 words.

HOW TO CONTACT Submit complete ms via mail or e-mail (with attachment). For postal submissions, no submissions returned unless accompanied by an SASE. Writers submitting from abroad should send at least 3 IRCs for return of typescript; 1 IRC for reply only.

PAYMENT/TERMS Pays £50/1,000 words.

TIPS "We do not look for fiction that necessarily has a 'Welsh' connection, which some writers assume from our title. We try to publish a broad range of fiction, and our main criterion is quality. Try to read copies of any magazine you submit to. Don't write out of the blue to a magazine which might be completely inappropriate for your work. Recognize that you are likely to have a high rejection rate, as magazines tend to favor writers from their own countries."

PLEIADES: LITERATURE IN CONTEXT

University of Central Missouri, Department of English, Martin 336, 415 E. Clark St., Warrensburg MO 64093. (660)543-4268. **E-mail:** clintoncrockettp@gmail.com (nonfiction inquiries); pnguyen@ucmo.edu (fiction inquiries); pleiadespoetryeditor@gmail.com (poetry inquiries). **Website:** www.pleiadesmag.com. **Contact:** Clint Crockett Peters, nonfiction editor; Phong Nguyen, fiction editor; and Jenny Molberg, poetry editor. Estab. 1991. "We publish contemporary fiction, poetry, interviews, literary essays, special-interest personal essays, and reviews for a general and literary audience from authors from around the world." Reads in the months of July for the summer issue and December for the winter issue.

NEEDS Reads fiction year-round. No science fiction, fantasy, confession, erotica. Length: 2,000-6,000 words.

HOW TO CONTACT Send complete ms via online submission manager.

PAYMENT/TERMS Pays $10 and contributor's copies.

TIPS "Submit only 1 genre at a time to appropriate editors. Show care for your material and your readers—submit quality work in a professional format.

Cover art is solicited directly from artists. We accept queries for book reviews."

PLOUGHSHARES

Emerson College, 120 Boylston St., Boston MA 02116. (617)824-3757. **E-mail:** pshares@pshares.org. **Website:** www.pshares.org. **Contact:** Ladette Randolph, editor in chief/executive director; Ellen Duffer, managing editor. Estab. 1971. *Ploughshares*, published 3 times/year, is "a journal of new writing guest-edited by prominent poets and writers to reflect different and contrasting points of view. Translations are welcome if permission has been granted. Our mission is to present dynamic, contrasting views on what is valid and important in contemporary literature and to discover and advance significant literary talent. Each issue is guest-edited by a different writer. We no longer structure issues around preconceived themes." Editors have included Carolyn Forché, Gerald Stern, Rita Dove, Chase Twichell, and Marilyn Hacker. "We now accept electronic submissions—there is a $3 fee per submission, which is waived if you are a subscriber."

Ploughshares is 200 pages, digest-sized. Receives about 11,000 poetry, fiction, and essay submissions/year. Reads submissions June 1-January 15 (postmark); mss submitted January 16-May 31 will be returned unread.

NEEDS Has published work by ZZ Packer, Antonya Nelson, and Stuart Dybek. "No genre (science fiction, detective, gothic, adventure, etc.), popular formula, or commerical fiction whose purpose is to entertain rather than to illuminate." Length: up to 6,000 words

HOW TO CONTACT Submit via online submissions form or by mail.

PAYMENT/TERMS Pays $45/printed page ($90 minimum, $450 maximum); 2 contributor's copies; and one-year subscription.

PMS POEMMEMOIRSTORY

University of Alabama at Birmingham, HB 217, 1530 Third Ave. S., Birmingham AL 35294. (205)934-2641. **Fax:** (205)975-8125. **E-mail:** poemmemoirstory@gmail.com. **Website:** www.uab.edu/cas/englishpublications/pms-poemmemoirstory. **Contact:** Kerry Madden, editor in chief. "*PMS poemmemoirstory* appears once a year. We accept unpublished, original submissions of poetry, memoir, and short fiction during our January 1-March 31 reading period. We accept simultaneous submissions; however, we ask that you please contact us immediately if your piece is published elsewhere so we may free up space for other authors. While *PMS* is a journal of exclusively women's writing, the subject field is wide open."

◎ "*PMS* has gone all-digital on Submittable. There is now a $3 fee, which covers costs associated with our online submissions system. Please send all submissions to poemmemoirstory.submittable.com/submit."

NEEDS Length: up to 15 pages or 4,300 words.

HOW TO CONTACT Submit through online submissions manager.

PAYMENT/TERMS Pays 2 contributor's copies.

TIPS "We strongly encourage you to familiarize yourself with *PMS* before submitting. You can find links to some examples of what we publish in the pages of *PMS 8* and *PMS 9*. We look forward to reading your work."

◎⑤ POCKETS

The Upper Room, P.O. Box 340004, Nashville TN 37203. (615)340-7333. **E-mail:** pockets@upperroom.org. **Website:** pockets.upperroom.org. **Contact:** Lynn W. Gilliam, editor. Estab. 1981. In addition to receiving regular submissions, *Pockets* sponsors a fiction contest each year. Magazine published 11 times/year. "*Pockets* is a Christian devotional magazine for children ages 6-12. All submissions should address the broad theme of the magazine. Each issue is built around a theme with material which can be used by children in a variety of ways. Scripture stories, fiction, poetry, prayers, art, graphics, puzzles and activities are included. Submissions do not need to be overtly religious. They should help children experience a Christian lifestyle that is not always a neatly wrapped moral package but is open to the continuing revelation of God's will. Seasonal material, both secular and liturgical, is desired."

◎ Does not accept e-mail or fax submissions.

NEEDS "Stories should contain lots of action, use believable dialogue, be simply written, and be relevant to the problems faced by this age group in everyday life." Length: 600-1,000 words.

HOW TO CONTACT Submit complete ms by mail. No e-mail submissions.

TIPS "Theme stories, role models, and retold scripture stories are most open to freelancers. Poetry is also open. It is very helpful if writers read our writers' guidelines and themes on our website."

POETICA MAGAZINE, CONTEMPORARY JEWISH WRITING

Mizmor L'David Anthology, 5215 Colley Ave #138, Norfolk VA 23508, U.S,. **E-mail:** poeticapublishing@aol.com. **Website:** www.poeticamagazine.com. Estab. 2002. *Poetica Magazine, Contemporary Jewish Writing*, is the publisher of the annual Mizmor L'David Anthology, offers "an outlet for the many writers who draw from their Jewish background and experiences to create poetry/prose/short stories, giving both emerging and recognized writers the opportunity to share their work with the larger community."

◎ *Poetica* is 120 pages, perfect-bound, full-color cover. Receives about 500 poems/year, accepts about 60%. Press run is 350.

NEEDS Length: up to 4 pages.

HOW TO CONTACT Submit ms through online submissions manager. Include e-mail, bio, and mailing address.

PAYMENT/TERMS Pays 1 contributor's copy.

TIPS "We publish original, unpublished works by Jewish and non-Jewish writers alike. We are interested in works that have the courage to acknowledge, challenge, and celebrate modern Jewish life beyond distinctions of secular and sacred. We like accessible works that find fresh meaning in old traditions that recognize the challenges of our generation. We evaluate works on several levels, including its skillful use of craft, its ability to hold interest, and layers of meaning."

POINTED CIRCLE

Portland Community College, Cascade Campus, SC 206, 705 N. Killingsworth St., Portland OR 97217. **Website:** www.pcc.edu/about/literary-magazines/pointed-circle. **Contact:** Wendy Bourgeois, faculty advisor. Estab. 1980. Publishes "anything of interest to educationally/culturally mixed audience. We will read whatever is sent, but we encourage writers to remember we are a quality literary/arts magazine intended to promote the arts in the community. No pornography, nothing trite. Be mindful of deadlines and length limits." Accepts submissions by e-mail, mail; artwork in high-resolution digital form.

Reading period: October 1-February 7. Magazine: 80 pages; b&w illustrations; photos.

NEEDS Length: up to 3,000 words.

HOW TO CONTACT Submitted materials will not be returned; include SASE for notification only. Accepts multiple submissions.

PAYMENT/TERMS Pays 2 contributor's copies.

THE PORTLAND REVIEW

Portland State University, P.O. Box 751, Portland OR 97207. **E-mail:** editor@portlandreview.org. **Website:** portlandreview.org. **Contact:** Alex Dannemiller, editor-in-chief. Estab. 1956. *Portland Review* has been publishing exceptional writing and artwork by local and international artists since 1956.

NEEDS Publishes 40 mss per year.

PAYMENT/TERMS Pays contributor's copies.

TIPS "Please visit portlandreview.org for access to our submission manager and for more information."

POST ROAD

P.O. Box 600725, Newtown MA 02460. **Website:** www.postroadmag.com. **Contact:** Chris Boucher, managing editor. *Post Road,* published twice yearly, accepts unsolicited poetry, fiction, nonfiction, short plays and monologues, and visual-art submissions. Reads March 1-April 30 for the winter issue and July 1-August 31 for the summer issue.

Work from *Post Road* has received the following honors: honorable mention in the 2001 O. Henry Prize Issue guest-edited by Michael Chabon, Mary Gordon, and Mona Simpson; the Pushcart Prize; honorable mention in *The Best American Nonfiction* series; and inclusion in the *Best American Short Stories* 2005.

HOW TO CONTACT Submit ms via online submission form.

PAYMENT/TERMS Pays 2 contributor's copies.

TIPS "We are looking for interesting narrative, sharp dialogue, and deft use of imagery and metaphor. Be persistent, and be open to criticism."

POTOMAC REVIEW: A JOURNAL OF ARTS & HUMANITIES

Montgomery College, 51 Mannakee St., MT/212, Rockville MD 20850. (240)567-4100. **E-mail:** PotomacReviewEditor@montgomerycollege.edu. **E-mail:** potomacreview.submittable.com. **Website:** blogs.montgomerycollege.edu/potomacreview/. **Contact:** Julie Wakeman-Linn, editor in chief; Kathleen Smith, poetry editor; John W. Wang, fiction editor. Estab.

1994. *Potomac Review: A Journal of Arts & Humanities,* published semiannually in August and February, welcomes poetry and fiction from across the spectrum, both traditional and nontraditional poetry, free verse and in-form (translations accepted). "We like traditional fiction and experimental or meta fiction and flash fiction. Essays and creative nonfiction are also welcome."

Reading period: Year round, although slower in the summer. Has published work by David Wagoner, Ryan Ridge, Sandra Beasley, Marilyn Kallet, Katie Cortese, and Amy Holman.

NEEDS Length: up to 5,000 words.

HOW TO CONTACT Submit electronically through website.

THE PRAIRIE JOURNAL

P.O. Box 68073, 28 Crowfoot Terrace NW, Calgary AB T3G 3N8, Canada. **E-mail:** editor@prairiejournal.org (queries only); prairiejournal@yahoo.com. **Website:** www.prairiejournal.org. **Contact:** Anne Burke, literary editor. Estab. 1983. "The audience is literary, university, library, scholarly, and creative readers/writers."

NEEDS No genre: romance, horror, western—sagebrush or cowboys—erotic, science fiction, or mystery. Length: 100-3,000 words.

HOW TO CONTACT Send complete ms. No e-mail submissions.

PAYMENT/TERMS Pays $10-75.

TIPS "We publish many, many new writers and are always open to unsolicited submissions because we are 100% freelance. Do not send U.S. stamps; always use IRCs. We have poems, interviews, stories, and reviews online (query first)."

PRAIRIE SCHOONER

University of Nebraska–Lincoln, 123 Andrews Hall, Lincoln NE 68588. (402)472-0911. **Fax:** (402)472-1817. **E-mail:** prairieschooner@unl.edu. **Website:** prairieschooner.unl.edu. **Contact:** Ashley Strosnider, managing editor. Estab. 1926. "We look for the best fiction, poetry, and nonfiction available to publish, and our readers expect to read stories, poems, and essays of extremely high quality. We try to publish a variety of styles, topics, themes, points of view, and writers with a variety of backgrounds in all stages of their careers. We like work that is compelling—intellectually or emotionally—either in form, language, or content."

Submissions must be received between September 1 and May 1. Poetry published in *Prairie Schooner* has been selected for inclusion in *The Best American Poetry* and the *Pushcart Prize* anthologies. "All mss published in *Prairie Schooner* will automatically be considered for our annual prizes." These include The Strousse Award for Poetry ($500), the Bernice Slote Prize for Beginning Writers ($500), the Hugh J. Luke Award ($250), the Edward Stanley Award for Poetry ($1,000), the Virginia Faulkner Award for Excellence in Writing ($1,000), the Glenna Luschei Prize for Excellence ($1,500), and the Jane Geske Award ($250). Also, each year 10 Glenna Luschei Awards ($250 each) are given for poetry, fiction, and nonfiction. All contests are open only to those writers whose work was published in the magazine the previous year. Editors serve as judges. Also sponsors The *Prairie Schooner* Book Prize.

NEEDS "We try to remain open to a variety of styles, themes, and subject matter. We look for high-quality writing, 3-D characters, well-wrought plots, setting, etc. We are open to realistic and/or experimental fiction."

HOW TO CONTACT Send complete ms through mail, e-mail, or online submissions manager.

PAYMENT/TERMS Pays 3 copies of the issue in which the writer's work is published.

TIPS "Send us your best, most carefully crafted work, and be persistent. Submit again and again. Constantly work on improving your writing. Read widely in literary fiction, nonfiction, and poetry. Read *Prairie Schooner* to know what we publish."

PREMONITIONS

13 Hazely Combe, Arrenton Isle of Wight PO30 3AJ, United Kingdom. **E-mail:** mail@pigasuspress.co.uk. **Website:** www.pigasuspress.co.uk. **Contact:** Tony Lee, editor. "Science fiction and horror stories, plus genre poetry and fantastic artwork."

NEEDS Wants "original, high-quality SF/fantasy. Horror must have a science fiction element and be psychological or scary, rather than simply gory. Cutting-edge SF and experimental writing styles (cross-genre scenarios, slipstream, etc.) are always welcome." "No supernatural fantasy-horror." Length: 500-6,000 words. Send 1 story at a time.

HOW TO CONTACT Submit via mail and include SAE or IRC if you want material returned. "Use a standard ms format: double-spaced text, no right-justify, no staples." Do not send submissions via e-mail, unless by special request from editor. Include personalized cover letter with brief bio and publication credits.

PAYMENT/TERMS Pays minimum $5 or £5 per 1,000 words, plus copy of magazine.

TIPS "Potential contributors are advised to study recent issues of the magazine."

PRISM INTERNATIONAL

Dept. of Creative Writing, Buch E462, 1866 Main Mall, University of British Columbia, Vancouver British Columbia V6T 1Z1, Canada. (604)822-2514. **Fax:** (604)822-3616. **E-mail:** prismcirculation@gmail.com. **Website:** www.prismmagazine.ca. Estab. 1959. A quarterly international journal of contemporary writing—fiction, poetry, drama, creative nonfiction and translation. *PRISM international* is digest-sized, elegantly printed, flat-spined, with original colour artwork on a glossy card cover. Readership: public and university libraries, individual subscriptions, bookstores—a world-wide audience concerned with the contemporary in literature. "We have no thematic or stylistic allegiances: Excellence is our main criterion for acceptance of mss." Receives 1,000 submissions/year, accepts about 80. Circulation is for 1,200 subscribers. Subscription: $35/year for Canadian subscriptions, $40/year for U.S. subscriptions, $45/year for international. Sample: $13.

NEEDS Experimental, traditional. New writing that is contemporary and literary. Short stories and self-contained novel excerpts (up to 25 double-spaced pages). Works of translation are eagerly sought and should be accompanied by a copy of the original. Would like to see more translations. "No gothic, confession, religious, romance, pornography, or sci-fi." Also looking for creative nonfiction that is literary, not journalistic, in scope and tone. Receives over 100 unsolicited mss/month. Accepts 70 mss/year. "PRISM publishes both new and established writers; our contributors have included Franz Kafka, Gabriel Garciía Maárquez, Michael Ondaatje, Margaret Laurence, Mark Anthony Jarman, Gail Anderson-Dargatz and Eden Robinson." Publishes ms 4 months after acceptance. **Publishes 7 new writers/year.** Recently published work by Ibi Kaslik, Melanie Little, Mark Anthony Jarman. Publishes short shorts. Also publishes poetry. For Drama: one-acts/excerpts of no more than 1500 words preferred. Also interested in seeing dramatic monologues. "New writing that is contemporary and literary. Short stories and self-contained novel excerpts. Works of translation are eagerly sought and should be accompanied by a copy of the original. Would like to see more translations. No gothic, confession, religious, romance, pornography, or science fiction." Length: 25 pages maximum.

HOW TO CONTACT "Keep it simple. U.S. contributors take note: Do not send SASEs with U.S. stamps, they are not valid in Canada. Send International Reply Coupons instead." Responds in 4 months to queries; 3-6 months to mss. Sample copy for $13 or on website. Writer's guidelines online. Send complete ms.

PAYMENT/TERMS Pays $20/printed page of prose, $40/printed page of poetry, and 2 copies of issue. Pays on publication for first North American serial rights. Selected authors are paid an additional $10/page for digital rights. Cover art pays $300 and 2 copies of issue. Sponsors awards/contests, including annual short fiction, poetry, and nonfiction contests. Pays $30/printed page, and 2 copies of issue.

TIPS "We are looking for new and exciting fiction. Excellence is still our No. 1 criterion. As well as poetry, imaginative nonfiction and fiction, we are especially open to translations of all kinds, very short fiction pieces and drama which work well on the page. Translations must come with a copy of the original language work."

PSEUDOPOD

Escape Artists, Inc., P.O. Box 965609, Marietta GA 30066. **E-mail:** editor@pseudopod.org. **Website:** pseudopod.org. **Contact:** Shawn M. Garrett and Alex Hofelich, co-editors. Estab. 2006. "*Pseudopod* is the premier horror podcast magazine. Every week we bring you chilling short stories from some of today's best horror authors, in convenient audio format for your computer or MP3 player."

NEEDS Guidelines available at pseudopod.org/guidelines/. Submit via pseudopod.submittable.com/submit. Length: 2,000-6,000 words (short fiction); 500-1,500 words (flash fiction).

PAYMENT/TERMS Pays 6¢/word for original fiction, $100 for short fiction reprints, $20 for flash fiction.

TIPS "Let the writing be guided by a strong sense of who the (hopefully somewhat interesting) protagonist is, even if zero time is spent developing any other characters. Preferably, tell the story using standard past tense, third person, active voice."

A PUBLIC SPACE

323 Dean St., Brooklyn NY 11217. (718)858-8067. **E-mail:** general@apublicspace.org. **Website:** www.apublicspace.org. **Contact:** Brigid Hughes, founding editor; Anne McPeak, managing editor. *A Public Space*, published quarterly, is an independent magazine of literature and culture. "In an era that has relegated literature to the margins, we plan to make fiction and poetry the stars of a new conversation. We believe that stories are how we make sense of our lives and how we learn about other lives. We believe that stories matter."

Accepts unsolicited submissions from September 15-April 15. Submissions accepted through Submittable or by mail (with SASE).

NEEDS No word limit.

HOW TO CONTACT Submit 1 complete ms via online submissions manager.

PUERTO DEL SOL

New Mexico State University, English Dept., P.O. Box 30001, MSC 3E, Las Cruces NM 88003. **E-mail:** puertodelsoljournal@gmail.com. **Website:** www.puertodelsol.org. **Contact:** Evan Lavender-Smith, editor in chief; Tara Westmor, poetry editor; Allison Field Bell, prose editor. Estab. 1964. Publishes innovative work from emerging and established writers and artists. Wants poetry, fiction, nonfiction, drama, theory, artwork, interviews, reviews, and interesting combinations thereof.

Puerto del Sol is 150 pages, digest-sized, professionally printed, flat-spined, with matte card cover with art. Press run is 1,250 (300 subscribers, 25-30 libraries). Reading period is January 15 through March 31.

NEEDS Accepts 8-12 mss/issue; 16-24 mss/year. Publishes several new writers/year. Has published work by David Trinidad, Molly Gaudry, Ray Gonzalez, Cynthia Cruz, Steve Tomasula, Denise Leto, Rae Bryant, Joshua Cohen, Blake Butler, Trinie Dalton, and Rick Moody.

HOW TO CONTACT Send 1 short story or 2-4 short short stories at a time through online submission manager.

PAYMENT/TERMS Pays 2 contributor's copies.

TIPS "We are especially pleased to publish emerging writers who work to push their art form or field of study in new directions."

QUANTUM FAIRY TALES

E-mail: editorqft@gmail.com. **Website:** quantumfairytales.org. **Contact:** The Gnomies. Estab. October 2012. *Quantum Fairy Tales* is a nonprofit, all-volunteer, all-donation, quarterly e-zine showcasing art, poetry and literature with elements of science fiction, fantasy, and the supernatural, with weekly website articles and author/artist highlights. "The best part about *QFT* is that real, live gnomies reply with feedback to every submission."

NEEDS Prose fiction submissions should be 7,000 words or less. Seeking all varieties of speculative fiction.

HOW TO CONTACT E-mail fiction submissions with type of submission, title, author name, and word count in subject line.

TIPS "Your writing and art work must fall in the category of speculative fiction for us to consider it. Every submission gets a free critique whether published or not. If you do not hear from us within 3 months, please give us a nudge. Thank you!"

QUARTER AFTER EIGHT

Ohio University, 360 Ellis Hall, Athens OH 45701. **E-mail:** editor@quarteraftereight.org. **Website:** www.quarteraftereight.org. **Contact:** Kirk Wisland and Claire Eder, editors. "*Quarter After Eight* is an annual literary journal devoted to the exploration of innovative writing. We celebrate work that directly challenges the conventions of language, style, voice, or idea in literary forms. In its aesthetic commitment to diverse forms, *QAE* remains a unique publication among contemporary literary magazines." Reading period: October 15-April 15.

○ Holds annual short prose (any genre) contest with grand prize of $1,008.15. Deadline is November 30.

HOW TO CONTACT Submit through online submissions manager.

TIPS "We look for prose and poetry that is innovative, exploratory, and—most importantly—well written. Please subscribe to our journal and read what is published to get acquainted with the *QAE* aesthetic."

⑤ QUARTERLY WEST

University of Utah, 255 S. Central Campus Dr., Room 3500, Salt Lake City UT 84112. **E-mail:** quarterlywest@gmail.com. **Website:** www.quarterlywest.com. **Contact:** Sara Eliza Johnson and J.P. Grasser, editors. Estab. 1976. "We publish fiction, poetry, nonfiction, and new media in long and short formats, and will consider experimental as well as traditional works."

○ *Quarterly West* was awarded first place for Editorial Content from the American Literary Magazine Awards. Work published in the magazine has been selected for inclusion in the *Pushcart Prize* anthology, the *Best of the Net* anthology, and *The Best American Short Stories* anthology.

NEEDS No preferred lengths; interested in longer, fuller short stories and short shorts. Accepts 6-10 mss/year. No detective, science fiction, or romance.

HOW TO CONTACT Send complete ms using online submissions manager only.

TIPS "We publish a special section of short shorts every issue, and we also sponsor an annual novella contest. We are open to experimental work—potential contributors should read the magazine! Don't send more than 1 story per submission. Novella competition guidelines available online. We prefer work with interesting language and detail—plot or narrative are less important. We don't do religious work."

○○⑤ QUEEN'S QUARTERLY

144 Barrie St., Queen's University, Kingston ON K7L 3N6, Canada. (613)533-2667. **E-mail:** queens.quarterly@queensu.ca. **Website:** www.queensu.ca/quarterly. **Contact:** Dr. Boris Castel, editor; Joan Harcourt, literary editor. Estab. 1893. *Queen's Quarterly* is "a general-interest intellectual review featuring articles on science, politics, humanities, arts and letters, extensive book reviews, and some poetry and fiction."

○ Has published work by Gail Anderson-Dargatz, Tim Bowling, Emma Donohue, Viktor Carr, Mark Jarman, Rick Bowers, and Dennis Bock.

NEEDS Length: up to 2,500 words.

HOW TO CONTACT Send complete ms with SASE and/or IRC. No reply with insufficient postage. Accepts 2 mss/issue; 8 mss/year. Publishes 5 new writers/year.

PAYMENT/TERMS "Payment to new writers will be determined at time of acceptance."

QUIDDITY INTERNATIONAL LITERARY JOURNAL AND PUBLIC-RADIO PROGRAM

Benedictine University at Springfield, 1500 N. 5th St., Springfield IL 62702. **E-mail:** quidditylit@gmail.com. **Website:** www.quidditylit.com. **Contact:** Joanna Beth Tweedy, founding editor; John McCarthy, managing editor. *Quiddity*, published semiannually, is a print journal and public-radio program featuring poetry, prose, and artwork by new, emerging, and established contributors from around the world. Has published work by J.O.J. Nwachukwu-Agbada, Kevin Stein, Karen An-Hwei Lee, and Haider Al-Kabi.

○ *Quiddity* is 176 pages, 7x9, perfect-bound, with 60 lb. full color cover. Receives about 3,500 poems/year, accepts about 3%. Press run is 1,000. Single copy: $9; subscription: $15/year. Make checks payable to *Quiddity*. Each work selected is considered for public-radio program feature offered by NPR-member station. International submissions are encouraged.

NEEDS Length: 5,000 word-max.

HOW TO CONTACT Send complete ms. Submit online through submissions manager.

THE RAG

P.O. Box 17463, Portland OR 97217. **E-mail:** submissions@raglitmag.com; seth@raglitmag.com. **Website:** raglitmag.com. **Contact:** Seth Porter, managing editor; Dan Reilly, editor. Estab. 2011. *The Rag* focuses on the grittier genres that tend to fall by the wayside at more traditional literary magazines. *The Rag*'s ultimate goal is to put the literary magazine back into the entertainment market while rekindling the social and cultural value short fiction once held in North American literature.

○ Fee to submit online ($3) is waived if you subscribe or purchase a single issue.

NEEDS Accepts all styles and themes. Length: up to 10,000 words.

HOW TO CONTACT Send complete ms.

PAYMENT/TERMS Pays 5¢/word, $250 average/story.

TIPS "We like gritty material: material that is psychologically believable and that has some humor in it, dark or otherwise. We like subtle themes, original characters, and sharp wit."

RALEIGH REVIEW LITERARY & ARTS MAGAZINE

Box 6725, Raleigh NC 27628-6725. **E-mail:** info@raleighreview.org. **Website:** www.raleighreview.org. **Contact:** Rob Greene, editor; Landon Houle, fiction editor; Bryce Emley, poetry editor. Estab. 2010. "*Raleigh Review* is a national nonprofit magazine of poetry, short fiction (including flash), and art. We believe that great literature inspires empathy by allowing us to see the world through the eyes of our neighbors, whether across the street or across the globe. Our mission is to foster the creation and availability of accessible yet provocative contemporary literature. We look for work that is emotionally and intellectually complex.

NEEDS "We prefer work that is physically grounded and accessible, though complex and rich in emotional or intellectual power. We delight in stories from unique voices and perspectives. Any fiction that is born from a relatively unknown place grabs our attention. We are not opposed to genre fiction, so long as it has real, human characters and is executed artfully." Length: 250-7,500 words. "While we accept fiction up to 7,500 words, we are more likely to publish work in the 4,500- to 5,000-word range."

HOW TO CONTACT Submit complete ms.

PAYMENT/TERMS Pays $10 maximum.

TIPS "Please be sure to read the guidelines and look at sample work on our website. Every piece is read for its intrinsic value, so new/emerging voices are often published alongside nationally recognized, award-winning authors."

⑤ RATTAPALLAX

Rattapallax Press, 217 Thompson St., Suite 353, New York NY 10012. **E-mail:** devineni@rattapallax.com. **Website:** www.rattapallax.com. **Contact:** Ram Devineni, founder & president; Flávia Rocha, editor in chief. Estab. 1999. Receives 15 unsolicited mss/month. Accepts 3 mss/issue; 6 mss/year. Agented fiction 15%. Receives about 5,000 poems/year; accepts 2%. Publishes 3 new writers/year. Has published work by Stuart Dybek, Howard Norman, Molly Giles, Rick Moody, Anthony Hecht, Sharon Olds, Lou Reed, Marilyn Hacker, Billy Collins, and Glyn Maxwell. *Rattapallax*, published semiannually, is named for "Wallace Stevens's word for the sound of thunder. The magazine includes a DVD featuring poetry films and audio files. *Rattapallax* is looking for the extraordinary in modern poetry and prose that reflect the diversity of world cultures. Our goals are to create international dialogue using literature and focus on what is relevant to our society."

○ *Rattapallax* is 112 pages, magazine-sized, offset-printed, perfect-bound, with 12-pt. CS1 cover; some illustrations; photos. Press run is 2,000 (100 subscribers, 50 libraries, 1,200 shelf sales); 200 distributed free to contributors, reviews, and promos.

NEEDS Length: up to 2,000 words.

HOW TO CONTACT Submit via online submissions manager at rattapallax.submittable.com/submit.

PAYMENT/TERMS Pays 2 contributor's copies.

RATTLING WALL

c/o PEN USA, 269 S. Beverly Dr. #1163, Beverly Hills CA 90212. **E-mail:** therattlingwall@penusa.org. **Website:** therattlingwall.com. **Contact:** Michelle Meyering, editor. Estab. 2010.

○ Magazine: 6x9, square bound.

NEEDS Length: up to 15 pages.

HOW TO CONTACT Submit 1 complete story; no excerpts. Submissions should be double-spaced. Include cover letter with contact information, brief bio, writing sample.

PAYMENT/TERMS Pays 2 contributor's copies.

THE RAVEN CHRONICLES

A Journal of Art, Literature, & the Spoken Word, 15528 12th Ave. NE, Shoreline WA 98155. (206)941-2955. **E-mail:** editors@ravenchronicles.org. **Website:** www.ravenchronicles.org. **Contact:** Phoebe Bosché, managing editor; Stephanie Lawyer, nonfiction editor; Kathleen Alcalá, fiction editor; Paul Hunter, poetry editor. Estab. 1991. "*The Raven Chronicles* publishes work which reflects the cultural diversity of the Pacific Northwest, Canada, and other areas of America. We promote art, literature, and the spoken word for an audience that is hip, literate, funny, informed, and lives in a society that has a multicultural sensibility. We publish fiction, talk art/spoken word, poetry, essays, reflective articles, reviews, interviews, and contemporary art. We look for work that reflects the author's experiences, perceptions, and insights."

NEEDS "Experimental work is always of interest." Length: up to 4,000 words, or 3 flash fiction/lyric prose fiction. "Check with us for maximum length. We sometimes print longer pieces."

HOW TO CONTACT Submit complete ms via online submissions manager.

THE READER

The Reader Organisation, Calderstones Mansion, Calderstones Park, Liverpool L18 3JB, United Kingdom. **E-mail:** magazine@thereader.org.uk; info@thereader.org.uk. **Website:** www.thereader.org.uk. **Contact:** Andrew Parkinson. Estab. 1997. "*The Reader* is a quarterly literary magazine aimed at the intelligent 'common reader'—from those just beginning to explore serious literary reading to professional teachers, academics, and writers. As well as publishing short fiction and poetry by new writers and established names, the magazine features articles on all aspects of literature, language, and reading; regular features, including a literary quiz and a section on the Reading Revolution, reporting on The Reader Organisation's outreach work; reviews; and readers' recommendations of books that have made a difference to them. *The Reader* is unique among literary magazines in its focus on reading as a creative, important, and pleasurable activity, and in its combination of high-quality material and presentation with a genuine commitment to ordinary but dedicated readers." Also publishes literary essays, literary criticism, poetry.

NEEDS Wants short fiction and (more rarely) novel excerpts. Has published work by Karen King Arbisala, Ray Tallis, Sasha Dugdale, Vicki Seal, David Constantine, Jonathan Meades, and Ramesh Avadhani. Length: 1,000-2,500 words. Average length: 2,300 words. Publishes short shorts. Average length of short shorts: 1,500 words.

HOW TO CONTACT No e-mail submissions. Send complete ms with cover letter. Include estimated word count, brief bio, list of publications.

TIPS "The style or polish of the writing is less important than the deep structure of the story (though, of course, it matters that it's well written). The main persuasive element is whether the story moves us—and that's quite hard to quantify. It's something to do with the force of the idea and the genuine nature of enquiry within the story. When fiction is the writer's natural means of thinking things through, that'll get us. "

REAL: REGARDING ARTS & LETTERS

Stephen F. Austin State University, Nacogdoches TX 75962-3007. **Website:** regardingartsandletters.wordpress.com. **Contact:** Andrew Brininstool, editor. Estab. 1968. "*REAL: Regarding Arts & Letters* was founded in 1968 as an academic journal which occasionally published poetry. Now, it is an international creative magazine dedicated to publishing the best contemporary fiction, poetry, and nonfiction." Features both established and emerging writers.

○ Magazine: semiannual, 120 pages, perfect-bound.

NEEDS "We're not interested in genre fiction—science fiction or romance or the like—unless you're doing some cheeky genre-bending. Otherwise, send us your best literary work." Publishes short shorts. Length: up to 6,000 words.

HOW TO CONTACT Submit via online submissions manager.

PAYMENT/TERMS Pays contributor's copies

TIPS "We are looking for the best work, whether you are established or not."

REDACTIONS: POETRY & POETICS

604 N. 31st Ave., Apt. D-2, Hattiesburg MS 39401. **E-mail:** redactionspoetry@yahoo.com. **E-mail:** redactionspoetry@yahoo.com. **Website:** www.redactions.com. **Contact:** Tom Holmes. Estab. 2002. *Redactions*, released every 9 months, covers poems, reviews of new books of poems, translations, manifestos, interviews, essays concerning poetry, poetics, poetry movements, or concerning a specific poet or a group of poets; and anything dealing with poetry.

○ We no longer publish fiction or creative nonfiction.

TIPS "We ONLY accept submissions by e-mail. We read submissions throughout the year. Email submission as an attachment in ONE Word, RTF, or PDF document, or paste in the body of an e-mail. Include brief bio and your snail-mail address. Emails that have no subject line or have nothing written in the body of the e-mail will be deleted. We do not accept blank e-mails with only an attachment. Query after 90 days if you haven't heard from us. See website (redactions.com/submission-and-ordering.asp) for full guidelines, including for cover artwork."

REDIVIDER

Department of Writing, Literature, and Publishing, Emerson College, 120 Boylston St., Boston MA 02116. **E-mail:** editor@redividerjournal.org. **Website:** www.redividerjournal.org. Estab. 1986. *Redivider*, a journal of literature and art, is published twice a year by graduate students in the Writing, Literature, and Publishing Department of Emerson College. Prints new art, fiction, nonfiction, and poetry from new, emerging, and established artists and writers.

○ Every spring, *Redivider* hosts the Beacon Street Prize Writing Contest, awarding a cash prize and publication to the winning submission in fiction, poetry, and nonfiction categories. Hosts the Blurred Genre Contest each fall, awarding cash prizes and publication for flash fiction, flash nonfiction, and prose poetry. See website for details.

NEEDS Length: up to 8,000 words.

HOW TO CONTACT Submit via online submissions manager.

PAYMENT/TERMS Pays 2 contributor's copies.

TIPS "To get a sense of what we publish, pick up an issue!"

RED ROCK REVIEW

College of Southern Nevada, CSN Department of English, J2A, 3200 E. Cheyenne Ave., North Las Vegas NV 89030. (702)651-4094. **Fax:** (702)651-4455. **E-mail:** redrockreview@csn.edu. **Website:** sites.csn.edu/english/redrockreview. **Contact:** Todd Moffett, senior editor; Erica Vital-Lazare, associate editor. Estab. 1994. Dedicated to the publication of fine contemporary literature. Accepts fine poetry and short fiction year round.

○ *Red Rock Review* is about 130 pages, magazine-sized, professionally printed, perfect-bound, with 10-pt. CS1 cover.

NEEDS "We're looking for the very best literature. Stories need to be tightly crafted, strong in character development, built around conflict." Length: up to 5,000 words.

HOW TO CONTACT Send ms via e-mail as Word, RTF, or PDF file attachment.

PAYMENT/TERMS Pays 2 contributor's copies.

RED WHEELBARROW

De Anza College, 21250 Stevens Creek Blvd., Cupertino CA 95014. **Website:** www.deanza.edu/redwheelbarrow. Estab. 1976 as *Bottomfish*; 2000 as *Red Wheelbarrow*.

○ "We seek to publish a diverse range of styles and voices from around the country and the world." Publishes a student edition and a national edition.

NEEDS Length: up to 4,000 words.

HOW TO CONTACT Send complete ms by mail (include SASE) or e-mail with brief bio.

TIPS "Write freely, rewrite carefully. Resist clichés and stereotypes. We are not affiliated with Red Wheelbarrow Press or any similarly named publication."

REED MAGAZINE

San Jose State University, Dept. of English, One Washington Square, San Jose CA 95192. **E-mail:** mail@reedmag.org; cathleen.miller@sjsu.edu. **Website:** www.reedmag.org. **Contact:** Cathleen Miller, editor in chief. Estab. 1867. *Reed Magazine* is California's oldest literary journal. "We publish works of short fiction, nonfiction, poetry, and art, and offer cash prizes in each category."

Accepts electronic submissions only.

NEEDS Does not want children's, young adult, fantasy, or erotica. Length: up to 5,000 words.

HOW TO CONTACT Submit complete ms via online submissions manager.

PAYMENT/TERMS Contest contributors receive 1 free copy; additional copies: $12.

TIPS "Well-writen, original, clean grammatical prose is essential. We are interested in established authors as well as fresh new voices. Keep submitting!"

RIVER STYX MAGAZINE

Big River Association, 3139A Grand Blvd., Suite 203, St. Louis MO 63118. **E-mail:** bigriver@riverstyx.org. **Website:** www.riverstyx.org. **Contact:** Theresa Brickman, managing editor. Estab. 1975. Sponsors an annual Microfiction Contest, judged by the editors. Deadline: December 31. Guidelines available for SASE or on website. "*River Styx* publishes the highest-quality poetry, fiction, interviews, essays, and visual art. We are an internationally distributed multicultural literary magazine."

Work published in *River Styx* has been selected for inclusion in past volumes of *New Stories from the South, The Best American Poetry, Best New Poets, New Poetry from the Midwest*, and *The Pushcart Prize Anthology*.

NEEDS Recently published work by George Singleton, Philip Graham, Katherine Min, Richard Burgin, Nancy Zafris, Jacob Appel, and Eric Shade. Sponsors an annual microfiction contest. No genre fiction, less thinly veiled autobiography. Length: no more than 23-30 ms pages.

HOW TO CONTACT Send complete ms with SASE.

PAYMENT/TERMS Pays 2 contributor copies, plus one-year subscription. Cash payment as funds permit.

ROANOKE REVIEW

221 College Lane, Miller Hall, Salem VA 24153. **E-mail:** review@roanoke.edu. **Website:** roanokereview.org. Estab. 1967. "The *Roanoke Review* is an online literary journal that is dedicated to publishing accessible fiction, nonfiction, and poetry that is smartly written. Humor is encouraged; humility as well."

Has published work by Siobhan Fallon, Jacob M. Appel, and JoeAnn Hart.

NEEDS Receives 150 unsolicited mss/month. Accepts 30 mss/year. Does not read mss February 1-September 1. Publishes 1-5 new writers/year. Length: 1,000-5,000 words. Average length: 3,000 words.

HOW TO CONTACT Submit via Submittable, e-mail, or send SASE for return of ms, or send a disposable copy of ms and SASE for reply only.

TIPS "Pay attention to sentence-level writing—verbs, metaphors, concrete images. Don't forget, though, that plot and character keep us reading. We're looking for stuff that breaks the MFA story style. Be real. Know rhythm. Concentrate on strong images."

THE ROCKFORD REVIEW

Rockford Writers' Guild, Rockford Writers' Guild, P.O. Box 858, Rockford IL 61105. **E-mail:** editor@rockfordwritersguild.org. **E-mail:** editor@rockfordwritersguild.org. **Website:** www.rockfordwritersguild.org. **Contact:** Connie Kuntz. Estab. 1947. Since 1947, Rockford Writers' Guild has published *The Rockford Review* twice a year. Anyone may submit to the winter-spring edition of *The Rockford Review* from July 15-October 15. If published, payment is one contributor copy of journal and $5 per published piece. We also publish a "Members Only" edition in the summer which is open to members of Rockford Writers' Guild. Anyone may be a member of RWG and we have 170 members from the United States, England, Canada, and Mexico. Members are guaranteed publication at least once a year. Check website for frequent updates at www.rockfordwritersguild.org. Follow us Facebook under Rockford Writers' Guild or Twitter and Instagram @guildypleasures.

Poetry 50 lines or less, prose 1,300 words or less. No racist, supremacist, or sexist content. If published in the winter-spring edition of *The Rockford Review*, payment is 1 copy of magazine and $5 per published piece. Pays on publication. Credit line given. Buys first North American serial rights.

NEEDS Prose should express fresh insights into the human condition. No sexist, pornographic, or supremacist content. Length: no more than 1,300 words.
TIPS "We're wide open to new and established writers alike."

○⑤ ROOM

West Coast Feminist Literary Magazine Society, P.O. Box 46160, Station D, Vancouver BC V6J 5G5, Canada. **E-mail:** contactus@roommagazine.com. **Website:** www.roommagazine.com. Estab. 1975. "*Room* is Canada's oldest feminist literary journal. Published quarterly by a collective based in Vancouver, *Room* showcases fiction, poetry, reviews, artwork, interviews, and profiles by writers and artists who identify as women or genderqueer. Many of our contributors are at the beginning of their writing careers, looking for an opportunity to get published for the first time. Some later go on to great acclaim. *Room* is a space where women can speak, connect, and showcase their creativity. Each quarter we publish original, thought-provoking works that reflect women's strength, sensuality, vulnerability, and wit."

○ *Room* is digest-sized; contains illustrations, photos. Press run is 1,600 (900 subscribers, 50-100 libraries, 100-350 shelf sales).

NEEDS Accepts literature that illustrates the female experience—short stories, creative nonfiction, poetry—by, for, and about women.

HOW TO CONTACT Submit complete ms via online submissions manager.

PAYMENT/TERMS Pays $50-120 CAD, 2 contributor's copies, and a one-year subscription.

ROSEBUD

N3310 Asje Rd., Cambridge WI 53523. (608)423-9780. **Website:** www.rsbd.net. **Contact:** Rod, managing editor. Estab. 1993. *Rosebud*, published 3 times/year in April, August, and December, has presented many of the most prominent voices in the nation and has been listed as among the very best markets for writers.

○ *Rosebud* is elegantly printed with full-color cover. Press run is 10,000.

NEEDS Has published work by Ray Bradbury, X.J. Kennedy, and Nikki Giovanni. Publishes short shorts. Also publishes literary essays. Often comments on rejected mss. "No formula pieces."

HOW TO CONTACT Send up to 3 stories to Roderick Clark by postal mail. Include SASE for return of ms and $1 handling fee.

TIPS "Each issue has 6 or 7 flexible departments (selected from a total of 16 departments that rotate). We are seeking stories; articles; profiles; and poems of love, alienation, travel, humor, nostalgia, and unexpected revelation. Something has to 'happen' in the pieces we choose, but what happens inside characters is much more interesting to us than plot manipulation. We like good storytelling, real emotion, and authentic voice."

●◐ SALMAGUNDI

Skidmore College, 815 N. Broadway, Saratoga Springs NY 12866. **Fax:** (518)580-5188. **E-mail:** salmagun@skidmore.edu. **Website:** www.skidmore.edu/salmagundi. Estab. 1965. "*Salmagundi* publishes an eclectic variety of materials, ranging from short-short fiction to novellas from the surreal to the realistic. Authors include J.M. Coerzee, Russell Banks, Steven Millhauser, Marilynne Robinson, Orlando Patterson, Gordon Lish, Anthony Appiah, Clark Blaise, Henri Cole, Mary Gordon, Frank Bidart, Lousie Gluck, Robert Pinsky, Joyce Carol Oates, Mary Gaiteskill, Amy Hempel, and Cynthia Ozick. Our audience is a generally literate population of people who read for pleasure."

○ Magazine: 8x5; illustrations; photos. *Salmagundi* authors are regularly represented in *Pushcart* collections and *Best American Short Story* collections. Reading period: November 1-December 1.

NEEDS Length: up to 12,000 words.

HOW TO CONTACT Submit hard copy only by snail mail with SASE.

PAYMENT/TERMS Pays 6-10 contributor's copies and one-year subscription.

TIPS "I look for excellence and a very unpredictable ability to appeal to the interests and tastes of the editors. Be brave. Don't be discouraged by rejection. Keep stories in circulation. Of course, it goes without saying: Work hard on the writing. Revise tirelessly. Study other magazines as well as this one, and send only to those whose sensibility matches yours."

SALT HILL JOURNAL

Creative Writing Program, Syracuse University, English Deptartment, 401 Hall of Languages, Syracuse University, Syracuse NY 13244. **Website:** salthilljournal.net. **Contact:** Emma DeMilta and Jessica Poli, editors. "*Salt Hill* is published through Syracuse University's Creative Writing MFA program. We strive to publish a mix of the best contemporary and emerging talent in poetry, fiction, and nonfiction. Your work, if accepted, would appear in a long tradition of exceptional contributors, including Steve Almond, Mary Caponegro, Kim Chinquee, Edwidge Danticat, Denise Duhamel, Brian Evenson, B.H. Fairchild, Mary Gaitskill, Terrance Hayes, Bob Hicok, Laura Kasischke, Etgar Keret, Phil Lamarche, Dorianne Laux, Maurice Manning, Karyna McGlynn, Ander Monson, David Ohle, Lucia Perillo, Tomaž Šalamun, Zachary Schomburg, Christine Schutt, David Shields, Charles Simic, Patricia Smith, Dara Wier, and Raúl Zurita among many others."

○ Only accepts submissions by online submission form; does not accept unsolicited e-mail submissions.

NEEDS Length: up to 30 pages.

HOW TO CONTACT Submit via online submissions manager; contact fiction editor via e-mail for retractions and queries only.

THE SANDY RIVER REVIEW

University of Maine at Farmington, 114 Prescott St., Farmington ME 04938. **E-mail:** srreview@gmail. com. **E-mail:** submissions@sandyriverreview.com. **Website:** sandyriverreview.com. **Contact:** Alexandra Umstadt, editor. "*The Sandy River Review* seeks prose, poetry, and art submissions twice a year for our Spring and Fall issues. Prose submissions may be either fiction or creative nonfiction and should be a maximum of 3,500 words in length, 12-point, Times New Roman font, and double-spaced. Most of our art is published in b&w and must be submitted as 300-dpi quality, CMYK color mode, and saved as a TIFF file. We publish a wide variety of work from students as well as professional, established writers. Your submission should be polished and imaginative with strongly drawn characters and an interesting, original narrative. The review is the face of the University of Maine at Farmington's venerable BFA Creative Writing program, and we strive for the highest quality prose and poetry standard."

NEEDS Submit via e-mail. "The review is a literary journal—please, no horror, science fiction, romance." Length: up to 3,5000 words.

HOW TO CONTACT Send complete ms.

PAYMENT/TERMS Pays 3 contributor's copies.

TIPS "We recommend that you take time with your piece. As with all submissions to a literary journal, submissions should be fully completed, polished fi-

nal drafts that require minimal to no revision once accepted. Double-check your prose pieces for basic grammatical errors before submitting."

SANTA CLARA REVIEW

Santa Clara Review, Santa Clara University, 500 El Camino Real, Box 3212, Santa Clara CA 95053-3212. (408)554-4484. **E-mail:** santaclarareview@gmail. com. **Website:** www.santaclarareview.com. Estab. 1869. "*SCR* is one of the oldest literary publications in the West. Entirely student-run by undergraduates at Santa Clara University, the magazine draws upon submissions from SCU affiliates as well as contributors from around the globe. The magazine is published in February and May each year. In addition to publishing the magazine, the Review staff organizes a writing practicum, open mic nights, and retreats for writers and artists, and hosts guest readers. Our printed magazine is also available to view free online. For contacts, queries, and general info, visit our website. *SCR* accepts submissions year round.

NEEDS Length: up to 5,000 words.

HOW TO CONTACT Submit via online submissions manager or mail (include SASE for return of ms).

SANTA MONICA REVIEW

Santa Monica College, 1900 Pico Blvd., Santa Monica CA 90405. **Website:** www.smc.edu/sm_review. **Contact:** Andrew Tonkovich, editor. Estab. 1988. The *Santa Monica Review*, published twice yearly in fall and spring, is a nationally distributed literary arts journal sponsored by Santa Monica College. It currently features fiction and nonfiction.

NEEDS "No crime and detective, mysogyny, footnotes, TV, dog stories. We want more self-conscious, smart, political, humorous, digressive, meta-fiction."

HOW TO CONTACT Submit complete ms with SASE. No e-mail submissions.

PAYMENT/TERMS Pays contributor's copies and subscription.

THE SARANAC REVIEW

Dept. of English, Champlain Valley Hall, 101 Broad St., Plattsburgh NY 12901. (518)564-2241. **Fax:** (518)564-2140. **E-mail:** saranacreview@plattsburgh. edu. **Website:** www.saranacreview.com. **Contact:** J.L. Torres, executive editor. Estab. 2004. "*The Saranac Review* is committed to dissolving boundaries of all kinds, seeking to publish a diverse array of emerging and established writers from Canada and the U.S. *The Saranac Review* aims to be a textual clearing in which a space is opened for cross-pollination between American and Canadian writers. In this way the magazine reflects the expansive, bright spirit of the etymology of its name, Saranac, meaning 'cluster of stars.'" Published annually.

○ "*The Saranac Review* is digest-sized, with color photo or painting on cover. Publishes both digital and print-on-demand versions. Has published Lawrence Raab, Jacob M. Appel, Marilyn Nelson, Tom Wayman, Colette Inez, Louise Warren, Brian Campbell, Gregory Pardlo, Myfanwy Collins, William Giraldi, Xu Xi, Julia Alvarez, and other fine emerging and established writers.

NEEDS "We're looking for well-crafted fiction that demonstrates respect for and love of language. Fiction that makes us feel and think, that edifies without being didactic or self-indulgent and ultimately connects us to our sense of humanity." No genre material (fantasy, science fiction, etc.) or light verse. Length: up to 7,000 words.

HOW TO CONTACT Submit complete ms via online submissions manager (Submittable).

PAYMENT/TERMS Pays 1 contributor's copies and offers discount on additional copies.

THE SEATTLE REVIEW

Box 354330, University of Washington, Seattle WA 98195. (206)543-2302. **E-mail:** seattlereview@gmail.com. **Website:** www.seattlereview.org. **Contact:** Andrew Feld, editor in chief. Estab. 1978. *The Seattle Review* includes poetry, fiction, and creative nonfiction.

○ *The Seattle Review* will only publish long works. Poetry must be 10 pages or longer, and prose must be 40 pages or longer. *The Seattle Review* is 8x10; 175-250 pages. Receives 200 unsolicited mss/month. Accepts 10-15 mss/issue; 20-30 mss/year. Publishes ms 6 months-1 year after acceptance.

NEEDS Only publishes novellas. "Currently, we do not consider, use, or have a place for genre fiction (science fiction, detective, etc.) or visual art," Length: at least 40 double-spaced pages.

HOW TO CONTACT Send complete ms. Accepts electronic submissions only.

PAYMENT/TERMS Pays 2 contributor's copies and 1-year subscription.

TIPS "Know what we publish; no genre fiction. Look at our magazine and decide if your work might be ap-

preciated. Beginners do well in our magazine if they send clean, well-written mss. We've published a lot of 'first stories' from all over the country and take pleasure in discovery."

SEQUESTRUM

Sequestrum Publishing, 1023 Garfield Ave., Ames IA 50014. **E-mail:** sequr.info@gmail.com. **Website:** www.sequestrum.org. **Contact:** R.M. Cooper, managing editor. Estab. 2014. All publications are paired with a unique visual component. Regularly holds contests and features well-known authors, as well as promising new and emerging voices.

NEEDS Length: up to 12,000 words.

HOW TO CONTACT Submit complete ms via online submissions manager.

PAYMENT/TERMS Pays $10-15/story.

TIPS "Reading a past issue goes a long way; there's little excuse not to. Our entire archive is available online to preview, and subscription rates are variable. Send your best, most interesting work. General submissions are always open, and we regularly hold contests and offer awards which are themed."

THE SEWANEE REVIEW

735 University Ave., Sewanee TN 37383. (931)598-1246. **E-mail:** sewaneereview@sewanee.edu. **Website:** thesewaneereview.com. **Contact:** Adam Ross, editor. Estab. 1892. *The Sewanee Review* is America's oldest continuously published literary quarterly. Publishes original fiction, poetry, essays on literary and related subjects, and book reviews for well-educated readers who appreciate good American and English literature. Only erudite work representing depth of knowledge and skill of expression is published.

○ Does not read mss June 1-August 31.

NEEDS No erotica, science fiction, fantasy, or excessively violent or profane material. Length: up to 10,000 words. No short-short stories.

HOW TO CONTACT Submit complete ms via online submissions manager.

PAYMENT/TERMS Pays $10-12/printed page, plus 2 contributor's copies.

SHENANDOAH

Washington and Lee University, Lexington VA 24450. (540)458-8908. **E-mail:** shenandoah@wlu.edu. **Website:** shenandoahliterary.org. **Contact:** R.T. Smith, editor; William Wright, assistant editor. Estab. 1950. Sponsors the Shenandoah Prize for Fiction, awarded annually to the best story published in a volume year of *Shenandoah*, and the Bevel Summers Prize for the Short Short Story, awarded annually to the best short short story of up to 1,000 words. Prizes for both contests are $1,000. For more than half a century, *Shenandoah* has been publishing splendid poems, stories, essays, and reviews which display passionate understanding, formal accomplishment, and serious mischief.

NEEDS No sloppy, hasty, slight fiction. Length: up to 20 pages.

HOW TO CONTACT Send complete ms via online submissions manager.

PAYMENT/TERMS Pays $25/page ($250 maximum), one-year subscription, and 1 contributor's copy.

SHORT STUFF

Bowman Publications, 2001 I St., #5, Fairbury NE 68352. (402)587-5003. **E-mail:** shortstf89@aol.com. Estab. 1989. "We are perhaps an enigma in that we publish only clean stories in any genre. We'll tackle any subject but don't allow obscene language or pornographic description. Our magazine is for grownups, not X-rated 'adult' fare."

NEEDS Receives 500 unsolicited mss/month. Accepts 9-12 mss/issue; 76 mss/year. Has published work by Bill Hallstead, Dede Hammond, and Skye Gibbons. No erotica; nothing morbid or pornographic. Length: 500-1,500 words.

HOW TO CONTACT Send complete ms.

PAYMENT/TERMS Payment varies.

TIPS "We are holiday oriented; mark on outside of envelope if story is for Easter, Mother's Day, etc. We receive 500 mss each month. This is up about 200%. Because of this, I implore writers to send 1 ms at a time. I would not use stories from the same author more than once an issue, and this means I might keep the others too long. Please don't e-mail your stories! If you have an e-mail address, please include that with the cover letter so we can contact you. If no SASE, we destroy the ms."

SIERRA NEVADA REVIEW

999 Tahoe Blvd., Incline Village NV 89451. **E-mail:** sncreview@sierranevada.edu. **Website:** blog.sierranevada.edu/sierranevadareview. Estab. 1990. "*Sierra Nevada Review*, published annually in May, features poetry, short fiction, and literary nonfiction by new and established writers. Wants "writing that leans toward the unconventional, surprising, and risky."

Reads submissions September 1-February 15 only.

NEEDS Length: up to 4,000 words.

HOW TO CONTACT Submit ms via online submissions manager.

PAYMENT/TERMS Pays 2 contributor's copies.

SINISTER WISDOM

2333 McIntosh Rd., Dover FL 33527. (813)502-5549. **E-mail:** julie@sinisterwisdom.org. **Website:** www.sinisterwisdom.org. Estab. 1976. *Sinister Wisdom* is a quarterly lesbian-feminist journal providing fiction, poetry, drama, essays, journals, and artwork. Past issues include "Lesbians of Color," "Old Lesbians/Dykes," and "Lesbians and Religion."

Sinister Wisdom is 5.5x8.5; 128-144 pages; 55 lb. stock; 10 pt. C1S cover; with illustrations, photos.

NEEDS List of upcoming themes available on website. Receives 30 unsolicited mss/month. Accepts 6 mss/issue; 24 mss/year. Recently published work by Jacqueline Miranda, Amanda Esteva, and Sharon Bridgforth. No heterosexual or male-oriented fiction; no 1970s Amazon adventures; nothing that stereotypes or degrades women. Length: 500-5,000 words; average length: 2,000 words.

HOW TO CONTACT Send complete ms. Strongly prefers submissions through online submissions manager. Publishes short shorts. Also publishes literary essays, literary criticism, poetry. Sometimes comments on rejected mss. Reviews fiction.

PAYMENT/TERMS Pays 1 contributor's copy and one-year subscription.

TIPS *Sinister Wisdom* is "a multicultural lesbian journal reflecting the art, writing, and politics of our communities."

SLOW TRAINS LITERARY JOURNAL

P.O. 4741, Denver CO 80155. **E-mail:** editor@slowtrains.com. **Website:** www.slowtrains.com. **Contact:** Susannah Grace Indigo, editor. Estab. 2000. Looking for fiction, essays, and poetry that reflect the spirit of adventure, the exploration of the soul, the energies of imagination, and the experience of Big Fun. Music, travel, sex, humor, love, loss, art, spirituality, childhood/coming of age, baseball, and dreams, but most of all, *Slow Trains* wants to read about the things you are passionate about.

NEEDS Genre writing is not encouraged. No sci-fi, erotica, horror, romance, though elements of those may naturally be included. Length: up to 5,000 words.
HOW TO CONTACT Submit via e-mail only.

SNREVIEW

197 Fairchild Ave., Fairfield CT 06825-4856. **E-mail:** editor@snreview.org. **Website:** www.snreview.org. **Contact:** Joseph Conlin, editor. Estab. 1999. *SNReview* is a quarterly literary e-zine created for writers of nongenre fiction, nonfiction, and poetry. Quarterly.
NEEDS Receives 300 unsolicited mss/month. Accepts 40+ mss/issue; 150 mss/year. Publishes 75 new writers/year. Has published work by Frank X. Walker, Adrian Louis, Barbara Burkhardt, E. Lindsey Balkan, Marie Griffin, and Jonathan Lerner. "No romance, mystery, science fiction, fantasy, or horror genre fiction." Length: up to 7,000 words.
HOW TO CONTACT Submit via e-mail; label the e-mail "SUB: Name of Story." Copy and paste work into the body of the e-mail. Don't send attachments. Include 100-word bio and list of publications.

SONORA REVIEW

University of Arizona, Department of English, Tucson AZ 85721. **Website:** sonorareview.com/. Estab. 1980. "We look for the highest-quality poetry, fiction, and nonfiction, with an emphasis on emerging writers. Our magazine has a long-standing tradition of publishing the best new literature and writers. Check out our website for a sample of what we publish and our submission guidelines."
NEEDS Length: up to 4,000 words.
HOW TO CONTACT Send complete ms via online submissions manager.
PAYMENT/TERMS Pays 2 contributor's copies.

SO TO SPEAK

George Mason University, 4400 University Dr., MSN 2C5, Fairfax VA 22030. **E-mail:** sotospeak@sotospeakjournal.org. **Website:** sotospeakjournal.org. **Contact:** Kristen Brida, editor in chief. Estab. 1993. *So to Speak*, published semiannually, prints "high-quality work relating to feminism, including poetry, fiction, nonfiction (including book reviews and interviews), photography, artwork, collaborations, lyrical essays, and other genre-questioning texts." Wants "work that addresses issues of significance to women's lives and movements for women's equality. Especially interested in pieces that explore issues of race, class, and sexuality in relation to gender."

So to Speak is 100-128 pages, digest-sized, photo-offset-printed, perfect-bound, with glossy cover; includes ads. Press run is 1,000 (75 subscribers, 100 shelf sales); 500 distributed free to students/contributors. Reads submissions September 15-November 15 for spring issue and January 1-April 15 for fall issue.
NEEDS Receives 100 unsolicited mss/month. Accepts 3-5 mss/issue; 6-10 mss/year. **Publishes 7 new writers/year.** Sponsors awards/contests. No science fiction, mystery, genre romance. Length: up to 4,000 words.
HOW TO CONTACT Submit ms via online submissions manager. Include cover letter.
PAYMENT/TERMS Pays 2 contributor's copies.
TIPS "Every writer has something they do exceptionally well; do that and it will shine through in the work. We look for quality prose with a definite appeal to a feminist audience. We are trying to move away from strict genre lines. We want high-quality fiction, nonfiction, poetry, art, innovative and risk-taking work."

SOUNDINGS EAST

Salem State University, English Department, MH249, 352 Lafayette St., Salem MA 01970. **E-mail:** soundingseast@salemstate.edu. **Website:** www.salemstate.edu/soundingseast. Estab. 1973. *Soundings East* is the literary journal of Salem State University, published annually with support from the Center for Creative and Performing Arts.

Reading period: September 1-Feburary 15.
NEEDS Length: up to 10,000 words.
HOW TO CONTACT Submit ms via online submissions manager or by postal mail.

THE SOUTH CAROLINA REVIEW

Center for Electronic and Digital Publishing, Strode Tower Room 611, Box 340522, Clemson SC 29634-0522. (864)656-5399. **Fax:** (864)656-1345. **E-mail:** eander3@clemson.edu. **Website:** www.clemson.edu/cedp/press/scr/index.htm. **Contact:** Elizabeth Stansell, Production Editor. Estab. 1967. Since 1968, *The South Carolina Review* has published fiction, poetry, interviews, unpublished letters and mss, essays, and reviews from well-known and aspiring scholars and writers.

The South Carolina Review is 6x9; 200 pages; 60 lb. cream white vellum paper; 65 lb. color cover stock. Semiannual. Does not read mss

June-August or December. Receives 50-60 unsolicited mss/month.

NEEDS Submit complete ms. Cover letter is preferred. Ms format should be according to new MLA Stylesheet. Do not submit during June, July, August, or December. Recently published work by Thomas E. Kennedy, Ronald Frame, Dennis McFadden, Dulane Upshaw Ponder, and Stephen Jones. Rarely comments on rejected mss.

SOUTH DAKOTA REVIEW

The University of South Dakota, Dept. of English, 414 E. Clark St., Vermillion SD 57069. (605)677-5184. **E-mail:** sdreview@usd.edu. **Website:** www.usd.edu/sdreview. **Contact:** Lee Ann Roripaugh, editor in chief. Estab. 1963. "*South Dakota Review*, published quarterly, is committed to cultural and aesthetic diversity. First and foremost, we seek to publish exciting and compelling work that reflects the full spectrum of the contemporary literary arts. Since its inception in 1963, *South Dakota Review* has maintained a tradition of supporting work by contemporary writers writing from or about the American West. We hope to retain this unique flavor through particularly welcoming works by American Indian writers, writers addressing the complexities and contradictions of the 'New West,' and writers exploring themes of landscape, place, and/or eco-criticism in surprising and innovative ways. At the same time, we'd like to set these ideas and themes in dialogue with and within the context of larger global literary communities. Single copy: $12; subscription: $40/year, $65/2 years. Sample: $8.

- Writing from *South Dakota Review* has appeared in *Pushcart* and *Best American Essays* anthologies. Press run is 500-600 (more than 500 subscribers, many of them libraries).

NEEDS "Our aesthetic is eclectic, but we tend to favor deft use of language in both our poetry and prose selections, nuanced characterization in our fiction, and either elegantly or surprisingly executed formal strategies. As part of our unique flavor, a small handful works in each issue will typically engage with aspects of landscape, ecocritical issues, or place (oftentimes with respect to the American West)." Length: up to 6,000 words.

HOW TO CONTACT Submit via online submissions manager. Include cover letter.

PAYMENT/TERMS Pays 2 contributor's copies.

THE SOUTHEAST REVIEW

Department of English, Florida State University, Tallahassee FL 32306. **E-mail:** southeastreview@gmail.com. **Website:** southeastreview.org. **Contact:** Alex Quinlan, editor in chief. Estab. 1979. "The mission of *The Southeast Review* is to present emerging writers on the same stage as well-established ones. In each semiannual issue, we publish literary fiction, creative nonfiction, poetry, interviews, book reviews, and art. With nearly 60 members on our editorial staff who come from throughout the country and the world, we strive to publish work that is representative of our diverse interests and aesthetics, and we celebrate the eclectic mix this produces. We receive approximately 400 submissions per month, and we accept less than 1-2% of them."

- Publishes 4-6 new (not previously published) writers/year. Accepts submissions year round, "though please be advised that the response time is slower during the summer months." Has published work by A.A. Balaskovits, Hannah Gamble, Michael Homolka, Brandon Lingle, and Colleen Morrissey.

NEEDS Submit Length: up to 7,500 words.

HOW TO CONTACT Submit complete ms through online submissions manager. "All submissions must be typed (prose should be double-spaced) and properly formatted, then uploaded to our online submissions manager as a DOC or RTF file only. Submission manager restricts you from sending us your work more than twice per year. Please wait until you receive a reply regarding a submission before you upload the next." Does not accept e-mail, paper, or previously published submissions.

PAYMENT/TERMS Pays 2 contributor's copies.

TIPS "Avoid trendy experimentation for its own sake (present-tense narration, observation that isn't also revelation). Fresh stories, moving and interesting characters, and a sensitivity to language are still fiction mainstays. We also publish the winner and runners-up of the World's Best Short Story Contest, Poetry Contest, and Creative Nonfiction Contest."

SOUTHERN HUMANITIES REVIEW

Auburn University, 9088 Haley Center, Auburn University AL 36849. (334)844-9088. **Fax:** (334)844-9027. **E-mail:** shr@auburn.edu. **Website:** www.southernhumanitiesreview.com. **Contact:** Aaron Alford, managing editor. Estab. 1967. *Southern Humanities Review* publishes fiction, nonfiction, and poetry.

SOUTHWESTERN AMERICAN LITERATURE

Center for the Study of the Southwest, Texas State University, Brazos Hall, 601 University Dr., San Marcos TX 78666-4616. (512)245-2224. **Fax:** (512)245-7462. **E-mail:** wj13@txstate.edu. **Website:** www.txstate.edu/cssw/publications/sal.html. **Contact:** William Jensen, editor. Estab. 1971. *Southwestern American Literature* is a biannual scholarly journal that includes literary criticism, fiction, poetry, and book & film reviews concerning the Greater Southwest.

○ We are interested only in material dealing with the Southwest.

NEEDS Fiction must deal with the Southwest. Stories set outside our region will be rejected. We are always looking for stories that examine the relationship between the tradition of Southwestern American literature and the writer's own imagination. We like stories that move beyond stereotype. Length: no more than 6,000 words/25 pages.

HOW TO CONTACT Submit using online submissions manager.

PAYMENT/TERMS Pays 2 contributor's copies.

TIPS "Fiction and poetry must deal with the greater Southwest. We look for crisp language, an interesting approach to material. Read widely, write often, revise carefully. We seek stories that, as William Faulkner noted in his Nobel Prize acceptance speech, treat subjects central to good literature—the old verities of the human heart, such as honor and courage and pity and suffering, fear and humor, love and sorrow."

SOUTHWEST REVIEW

P.O. Box 750374, Dallas TX 75275-0374. (214)768-1037. **Fax:** (214)768-1408. **E-mail:** swr@smu.edu. **Website:** www.smu.edu/southwestreview. **Contact:** Willard Spiegelman, editor in chief. Estab. 1915. The majority of readers are well-read adults who wish to stay abreast of the latest and best in contemporary fiction, poetry, and essays in all but the most specialized disciplines. Published quarterly.

○ Has published work by Alice Hoffman, Sabina Murray, Alix Ohlin. The Elizabeth Matchett Stover Memorial Award presents $250 to the author of the best poem or groups of poems (chosen by editors) published in the preceding year. Also offers The Morton Marr Poetry Prize and the David Nathan Meyerson Prize for Fiction.

NEEDS Publishes fiction in widely varying styles. Prefers stories of character development, of psychological penetration, to those depending chiefly on plot. No specific requirements as to subject matter. Length: 3,500-8,000 words preferred.

HOW TO CONTACT Submissions accepted online for a $2 fee. No fee for submissions sent by mail. Submit one story at a time. Reading period: September 1-May 31.

PAYMENT/TERMS Accepted pieces receive nominal payment upon publication and copies of the issue.

TIPS "Despite the title, we are not a regional magazine. Before you submit your work, it's a good idea to take a look at recent issues to familiarize yourself with the magazine. We strongly advise all writers to include a cover letter. Keep your cover letter professional and concise, and don't include extraneous personal information, a story synopsis, or a résumé. When authors ask what we look for in a strong story submission, the answer is simple regardless of graduate degrees in creative writing, workshops, or whom you know: We look for good writing, period."

SOU'WESTER

Department of English, Box 1438, Southern Illinois University Edwardsville, Edwardsville IL 62026. **Website:** souwester.org. **Contact:** Joshua Kryah, poetry editor; Valerie Vogrin, prose editor. Estab. 1960. *Sou'wester* appears biannually in spring and fall.

○ *Sou'wester* is professionally printed, flat-spined, with textured matte card cover, press run is 300 for 500 subscribers of which 50 are libraries. Open to submissions in mid-August for fall and spring issues.

HOW TO CONTACT Submit 1 piece of prose at a time. Will consider a suite of 2-3 flash fiction pieces.

PAYMENT/TERMS Pays 2 contributor's copies and a one-year subscription.

❺ SPACE AND TIME

458 Elizabeth Ave., Somerset NJ 08873. **Website:** www.spaceandtimemagazine.com. **Contact:** Hildy Silverman, publisher. Estab. 1966. *Space and Time* is the longest continually published small-press genre fiction magazine still in print. We pride ourselves in having published the first stories of some of the great writers in science fiction, fantasy, and horror.

🗨 We love stories that blend elements—horror and science fiction, fantasy with science fiction elements, etc. We challenge writers to try something new and send us their hard to classify works-—what other publications reject because the work doesn't fit in their "pigeon-holes."

NEEDS "We are looking for creative blends of science fiction, fantasy, and/or horror." "Do not send children's stories." Length: 1,000-10,000 words. Average length: 6,500 words. Average length of short shorts: 1,000 words.

HOW TO CONTACT Submit electronically as a Word doc or .rtf attachment ONLY during open reading periods. Anything sent outside those period will be rejected out of hand.

PAYMENT/TERMS Pays 1¢/word.

🗨 STAND MAGAZINE

School of English, University of Leeds, Leeds LS2 9JT, United Kingdom. (44)(113)343-4794. **E-mail:** editors@standmagazine.org. **Website:** www.standmagazine.org. **Contact:** Jon Glover, managing editor. Estab. 1952. *Stand Magazine* is concerned with what happens when cultures and literatures meet, with translation in its many guises, with the mechanics of language, with the processes by which the policy receives or disables its cultural makers. *Stand* promotes debate of issues that are of radical concern to the intellectual community worldwide. U.S. submissions can be made through the Virginia office (see separate listing).

🗨 Does not accept e-mail submissions.

NEEDS Does not want genre fiction. Length: up to 3,000 words.

HOW TO CONTACT Submit ms by mail. Include SASE.

🗨 STEPPING STONES MAGAZINE

P.O. Box 902, Norristown PA 19404-0902. **E-mail:** info@ssmalmia.com. **Website:** ssmalmia.com. **Contact:** Trinae Ross, publisher. Estab. 1996. "*Stepping Stones Magazine* is a not-for-profit organization dedicated to presenting awesome writing and art created by people from all lifestyles." Publishes fiction, nonfiction, and poetry."

🗨 Has published poetry by Richard Fenwick, Karlanna Lewis, and Stephanie Kaylor. Receives about 600 poems/year, accepts about 10-15%.

NEEDS Fiction should be able to hold the reader's interest in the first paragraph and sustain that interest throughout the rest of the story. Length: up to 4,000 words.

HOW TO CONTACT Send up to 3 mss via postal mail, e-mail (fiction@ssmalmia.com), or online submissions manager. Include brief bio.

STILL CRAZY

(614)746-0859. **E-mail:** editor@crazylitmag.com. **Website:** www.crazylitmag.com. **Contact:** Barbara Kussow, editor. Estab. 2008. *Still Crazy*, published bi-annually in January and July, features poetry, short stories, and essays written by or about people over age 50. The editor is particularly interested in material that challenges the stereotypes of older people and that portrays older people's inner lives as rich and rewarding. Wants writing by people over age 50 and writing by people of any age if the topic is about people over 50.

🗨 Accepts 3-4 short stories per issue; 5-7 essays; 12-14 poems. Reads submissions year round.

NEEDS Publishes short shorts. Ms published 6-12 months after acceptance. Sometimes features a "First Story," a story by an author who has not been published before. Does not want material that is "too sentimental or inspirational, 'Geezer' humor, or anything too grim." Length: up to 3,500 words, but stories fewer than 3,000 words are more likely to be published.

HOW TO CONTACT Upload submissions via submissions manager on website. Include estimated word count, brief bio, age of writer or "Over 50."

PAYMENT/TERMS Pays 1 contributor's copy.

TIPS Looking for interesting characters and interesting situations that might interest readers of all ages. Humor and lightness welcomed.

STIRRING: A LITERARY COLLECTION

Sundress Publications, **E-mail:** stirring@sundress-publications.com. **E-mail:** stirring.nonfiction@gmail.com; reviews@sundresspublications.com; stirring.fiction@gmail.com; stirring.poetry@gmail.com; stirring.artphoto@gmail.com. **Website:** www.stirringlit.com. **Contact:** Luci Brown and Andrew Koch, managing editors and poetry editors; Kat Saunders, fiction editor; Donna Vorreyer, reviews editor; Gabe Montesanti, nonfiction editor. Estab. 1999. "*Stirring* is one of the oldest continually published literary journals on the Web. *Stirring* is a monthly literary magazine that publishes poetry, short fiction, creative nonfiction, and photography by established and emerging writers."

NEEDS Length: up to 5,000 words.

HOW TO CONTACT Submit complete ms by e-mail to stirring.fiction@gmail.com

STONE SOUP

The Magazine by Young Writers & Artists, Children's Art Foundation, P.O. Box 83, Santa Cruz CA 95063-0083. (831)426-5557. **E-mail:** editor@stonesoup.com. **Website:** https://stonesoup.com/. **Contact:** Ms. Gerry Mandel, editor. Estab. 1973. *Stone Soup,* available in print and digital formats, is the national magazine of writing and art by kids, founded in 1973. The print edition is 48 pages, 7x10, professionally printed in color on heavy stock, saddle-stapled, with coated cover with full-color illustration. Receives 5,000 poetry submissions/year, accepts about 12. Press run is 12,000. Subscription: $38/year (U.S.). "We have a preference for writing and art based on real-life experiences; no formula stories or poems. We only publish writing by children ages 8 to 13. We do not publish writing by adults."

○ Print subscriptions include digital access, including more than 10 years of back issues at stonesoup.com.

NEEDS "We do not like assignments or formula stories of any kind." Length: 150-2,500 words.

HOW TO CONTACT Send complete ms; no SASE.

PAYMENT/TERMS Pays $25 for stories, a certificate and 2 contributor's copies, plus discounts.

TIPS "All writing we publish is by young people ages 13 and under. We do not publish any writing by adults. We can't emphasize enough how important it is to read a couple of issues of the magazine. You can read stories and poems from past issues online. We have a strong preference for writing on subjects that mean a lot to the author. If you feel strongly about something that happened to you or something you observed, use that feeling as the basis for your story or poem. Stories should have good descriptions, realistic dialogue, and a point to make. In a poem, each word must be chosen carefully. Your poem should present a view of your subject, and a way of using words that are special and all your own."

● ⑤ STORIE

Via Suor Celestina Donati 13/E, Rome 00167, Italy. **E-mail:** info@storie.it. **Website:** www.storie.it/english. Estab. 1986. *Storie* is one of Italy's leading cultural and literary magazines. Committed to a truly cross-over vision of writing, the bilingual (Italian/English) review publishes high-quality fiction and poetry, interspersed with the work of alternative wordsmiths such as filmmakers and musicians. Through writings bordering on narratives and interviews with important contemporary writers, it explores the culture and craft of writing.

HOW TO CONTACT "Mss may be submitted directly by regular post without querying first; however, we do not accept unsolicited mss via e-mail. Please query via e-mail first. We only contact writers if their work has been accepted. We also arrange for and oversee a high-quality, professional translation of the piece."

PAYMENT/TERMS Pays $30-600 and 2 contributor's copies.

TIPS "More than erudite references or a virtuoso performance, we're interested in a style merging news writing with literary techniques in the manner of new journalism. *Storie* reserves the right to include a brief review of interesting submissions not selected for publication in a special column of the magazine."

STORYSOUTH

3302 MHRA Building, UNCG, Greensboro NC 27412. **E-mail:** terry@storysouth.com; fiction@storysouth.com; poetry@storysouth.com;. **Website:** www.storysouth.com. **Contact:** Terry Kennedy, editor; Cynthia Nearman, creative nonfiction editor; Drew Perry, fiction editor; Luke Johnson, poetry editor. Estab. 2001. "*storySouth* accepts unsolicited submissions of fiction, poetry, and creative nonfiction during 2 submission periods annually: May 15-July 1 and November 15-January 1. Long pieces are encouraged. Please make only 1 submission in a single genre per reading period."

NEEDS No word-count limit.

HOW TO CONTACT Submit 1 story via online submissions manager.

TIPS "What really makes a story stand out is a strong voice and a sense of urgency—a need for the reader to keep reading the story and not put it down until it is finished."

THE STORYTELLER

65 Highway 328 West, Maynard AR 72444. (870)647-2137. **E-mail:** storytelleranthology@gmail.com. **Website:** www.thestorytellermagazine.com. **Contact:** Regina Riney (Williams), editor. Estab. 1996. "We are here to help writers however we can and to help start them on their publishing career. Proofread! Make

sure you know what we take and what we don't and also make sure you know the word count."

NEEDS Does not want pornography, erotica, horror, graphic language or violence, children's stories, or anything deemed racial or biased toward any religion, race, or moral preference.

HOW TO CONTACT Send complete ms with cover letter and SASE.

TIPS "*The Storyteller* is one of the best places you will find to submit your work, especially new writers. Our best advice, be professional. You have one chance to make a good impression. Don't blow it by being unprofessional."

THE STRAND MAGAZINE

P.O. Box 1418, Birmingham MI 48012-1418. (800)300-6652. **E-mail:** strandmag@strandmag.com. **Website:** www.strandmag.com. Estab. 1998. "After an absence of nearly half a century, the magazine known to millions for bringing Sir Arthur Conan Doyle's ingenious detective, Sherlock Holmes, to the world has once again appeared on the literary scene. First launched in 1891, *The Strand* included in its pages the works of some of the greatest writers of the 20th century: Agatha Christie, Dorothy Sayers, Margery Allingham, W. Somerset Maugham, Graham Greene, P.G. Wodehouse, H.G. Wells, Aldous Huxley, and many others. In 1950, economic difficulties in England caused a drop in circulation, which forced the magazine to cease publication."

NEEDS "We are interested in mysteries, detective stories, tales of terror and the supernatural as well as short stories. Stories can be set in any time or place, provided they are well written, the plots interesting and well thought." Occasionally accepts short shorts and short novellas. "We are not interested in submissions with any sexual content." Length: 2,000-6,000 words.

HOW TO CONTACT Submit complete ms by postal mail. Include SASE. No e-mail submissions.

PAYMENT/TERMS Pays $25-150.

TIPS "No gratuitous violence, sexual content, or explicit language, please."

STRANGE HORIZONS

Strange Horizons, Inc., P.O. Box 1693, Dubuque IA 52004-1693. **E-mail:** editor@strangehorizons.com; fiction@strangehorizons.com. **Website:** strangehorizons.com. **Contact:** Niall Harrison, editor in chief. Estab. 2000. **E-mail:** fiction@strangehorizons.com.

"*Strange Horizons* is a magazine of and about speculative fiction and related nonfiction. Speculative fiction includes science fiction, fantasy, horror, slipstream, and other flavors of fantastica."

Work published in *Strange Horizons* has been shortlisted for or won Hugo, Nebula, Rhysling, Theodore Sturgeon, James Tiptree Jr., and World Fantasy Awards.

NEEDS "We love, or are interested in, fiction from or about diverse perspectives and traditionally under-represented groups, settings, and cultures, written from a nonexoticizing and well-researched position; unusual yet readable styles and inventive structures and narratives; stories that address political issues in complex and nuanced ways, resisting oversimplification; and hypertext fiction." No excessive gore. Length: up to 10,000 words (under 5,000 words preferred).

HOW TO CONTACT Submit via online submissions manager; no e-mail or postal submission accepted.

PAYMENT/TERMS Pays 8¢/word, $50 minimum.

STRAYLIGHT

UW-Parkside, English Department, University of Wisconsin-Parkside, 900 Wood Rd., Kenosha WI 53141. **E-mail:** submissions@straylightmag.com. **Website:** www.straylightmag.com. Estab. 2005. *Straylight*, published biannually, seeks fiction and poetry of almost any style "as long as it's inventive."

Literary magazine/journal: 6x9, 115 pages, quality paper, uncoated index stock cover. Contains illustrations, photographs.

NEEDS "*Straylight* is interested in publishing high-quality, character-based fiction of any style. We tend not to publish strict genre pieces, though we may query them for future special issues. We do not publish erotica." Publishes short shorts and novellas. Does not read May through August. Agented fiction 10%. Length: 1,000-5,000 words for short stories; under 1,000 words for flash fiction; 17,500-45,000 words for novellas. Average length: 1,500-3,000 words.

HOW TO CONTACT Send complete ms with cover letter. Accepts submissions by online submission manager or mail (send either SASE or IRC for return of ms, or disposable copy of ms and #10 SASE for reply only). Include brief bio, list of publications.

PAYMENT/TERMS Pays 2 contributor's copies.

TIPS "We tend to publish character-based and inventive fiction with cutting-edge prose. We are unimpressed with works based on strict plot twists or novelties. Read a sample copy to get a feel for what we publish."

⬤ STUDIO, A JOURNAL OF CHRISTIANS WRITING

727 Peel St., Albury NSW 2640, Australia. (61)(2)6021-1135. **E-mail:** studio00@bigpond.net.au. **Contact:** Paul Grover, publisher. Estab. 1980. *Studio, A Journal of Christians Writing*, published three times a year, prints poetry and prose of literary merit, offering a venue for previously published, new, and aspiring writers and seeking to create a sense of community among Christians writing. Also publishes occasional articles as well as news and reviews of writing, writers, and events of interest to members. People who send material should be comfortable being published under this banner: *Studio, A Journal of Christians Writing*.

○ *Studio* is 60-80 pages, digest-sized, professionally printed on high-quality paper, saddle-stapled, with matte card cover. Press run is 300 (all subscriptions).

NEEDS Cover letter is required. Include brief details of previous publishing history, if any. SAE with IRC required. "Submissions must be typed and double-spaced on 1 side of A4 white paper. Name and address must appear on the reverse side of each page submitted."

PAYMENT/TERMS Pays 1 contributor's copy.

○⬤⬤ SUBTERRAIN

Strong Words for a Polite Nation, P.O. Box 3008, MPO, Vancouver British Columbia V6B 3X5, Canada. (604)876-8710. **Fax:** (604)879-2667. **E-mail:** subter@portal.ca. **Website:** www.subterrain.ca. **Contact:** Brian Kaufman, editor in chief; Natasha Sanders-Kay, managing editor. Estab. 1988. "*subTerrain* magazine is published 3 times/year from modest offices just off of Main Street in Vancouver, BC. We strive to produce a stimulating fusion of fiction, poetry, photography, and graphic illustration from uprising Canadian, U.S., and international writers and artists."

○ Magazine: 8.5x11; 80 pages; colour matte stock paper; colour matte cover stock; illustrations; photos. "Strong words for a polite nation."

NEEDS Receives 100 unsolicited mss/month. Accepts 4 mss/issue; 10-15 mss/year. Recently published work by J.O. Bruday, Lisa Pike, and Peter Babiak. Does not want genre fiction or children's fiction. **3,000 words max.**

HOW TO CONTACT Send complete ms. Include disposable copy of the ms and SASE for reply only. Accepts multiple submissions.

PAYMENT/TERMS Pays $50/page for prose.

TIPS "Read the magazine first. Get to know what kind of work we publish."

⬤ SUBTROPICS

University of Florida, P.O. Box 112075, 4008 Turlington Hall, Gainesville FL 32611-2075. **E-mail:** subtropics@english.ufl.edu. **Website:** www.english.ufl.edu/subtropics. **Contact:** David Leavitt, editor. Estab. 2005. *Subtropics* seeks to publish the best literary fiction, essays, and poetry being written today, both by established and emerging authors. Will consider works of fiction of any length, from short shorts to novellas and self-contained novel excerpts. Gives the same latitude to essays. Appreciates work in translation and, from time to time, republishes important and compelling stories, essays, and poems that have lapsed out of print by writers no longer living. Member: CLMP.

○ Literary magazine/journal: 9x6, 160 pages. Includes photographs. Submissions accepted from September 1-April 15.

NEEDS Does not read May 1-August 31. Agented fiction 33%. **Publishes 1-2 new writers/year.** Has published John Barth, Ariel Dorfman, Tony D'Souza, Allan Gurganus, Frances Hwang, Kuzhali Manickavel, Eileen Pollack, Padgett Powell, Nancy Reisman, Jarret Rosenblatt, Joanna Scott, and Olga Slavnikova. No genre fiction. Length: up to 15,000 words. Average length: 5,000 words. Average length of short shorts: 400 words.

HOW TO CONTACT Submit complete ms via online submissions manager.

PAYMENT/TERMS Pays $500 for short shorts; $1,000 for full stories; 2 contributor's copies.

TIPS "We publish longer works of fiction, including novellas and excerpts from forthcoming novels. Each issue includes a short-short story of about 250 words on the back cover. We are also interested in publishing works in translation for the magazine's English-speaking audience."

THE SUMMERSET REVIEW

25 Summerset Dr., Smithtown NY 11787. **E-mail:** editor@summersetreview.org. **Website:** www.summersetreview.org. **Contact:** Joseph Levens, editor. Estab.

2002. "Our goal is simply to publish the highest-quality literary fiction, nonfiction, and poetry intended for a general audience. This is a simple online literary journal of high-quality material, so simple you can call it unique."

○ Magazine: illustrations and photographs. Periodically releases print issues. Quarterly.

NEEDS No sci-fi, horror, or graphic erotica. Length: up to 8,000 words; average length: 3,000 words. Publishes short shorts.

HOW TO CONTACT Send complete ms by e-mail as attachment or by postal mail with SASE.

TIPS "Style counts. We prefer innovative or at least very smooth, convincing voices. Even the dullest premises or the complete lack of conflict make for an interesting story if it is told in the right voice and style. We like to find little, interesting facts and/or connections subtly sprinkled throughout the piece. Harsh language should be used only if/when necessary. If we are choosing between light and dark subjects, the light will usually win."

THE SUN

107 N. Roberson St., Chapel Hill NC 27516. (919)942-5282. **Fax:** (919)932-3101. **Website:** www.thesunmagazine.org. **Contact:** Sy Safransky, editor. Estab. 1974. *The Sun* publishes essays, interviews, fiction, and poetry. "We are open to all kinds of writing, though we favor work of a personal nature."

○ Magazine: 8.5x11; 48 pages; offset paper; glossy cover stock; photos.

NEEDS Open to all fiction. Receives 800 unsolicited mss/month. Accepts 20 short stories/year. Recently published work by Sigrid Nunez, Susan Straight, Lydia Peelle, Stephen Elliott, David James Duncan, Linda McCullough Moore, and Brenda Miller. No science fiction, horror, fantasy, or other genre fiction. "Read an issue before submitting." Length: up to 7,000 words.

HOW TO CONTACT Send complete ms. Accepts reprint submissions.

PAYMENT/TERMS Pays $300-1,500 and 1-year subscription.

TIPS "Do not send queries except for interviews. We're open to unusual work. Read the magazine to get a sense of what we're about. Our submission rate is extremely high. Please be patient after sending us your work and include return postage."

SYCAMORE REVIEW

Purdue University Department of English, 500 Oval Dr., West Lafayette IN 47907. (765) 494-3783. **Fax:** (765) 494-3780. **E-mail:** sycamore@purdue.edu. **Website:** www.sycamorereview.com. **Contact:** Anthony Sutton, editor in chief; Bess Cooley, managing editor. *Sycamore Review* is Purdue University's internationally acclaimed literary journal, affiliated with Purdue's College of Liberal Arts and the Dept. of English. Strives to publish the best writing by new and established writers. Looks for well-crafted and engaging work, works that illuminate our lives in the collective human search for meaning. Would like to publish more work that takes a reflective look at national identity and how we are perceived by the world. Looks for diversity of voice, pluralistic worldviews, and political and social context.

○ Reading period: September 1-March 31.

NEEDS No genre fiction.

HOW TO CONTACT Submit complete ms via online submissions manager.

PAYMENT/TERMS Pays in contributor's copies and $50/short story.

TIPS "We look for originality, brevity, significance, strong dialogue, and vivid detail. We sponsor the Wabash Prize for Poetry (deadline: December 1) and Fiction (deadline: April 17), $1,000 award for each. All contest submissions will be considered for regular inclusion in the *Sycamore Review*."

◗◉ TAKAHĒ

P.O. Box 13-335, Christchurch 8141, New Zealand. **E-mail:** admin@takahe.org.nz. **E-mail:** essays@takahe.org.nz; fiction@takahe.org.nz; poetry@takahe.org.nz. **Website:** www.takahe.org.nz. **Contact:** Erin Harrington, essays editor; Jane Seaford and Rachel Smith, fiction editors; Joanna Preston, poetry editor. *Takahē* magazine is a New Zealand-based literary and arts magazine that appears 3 times/year with a mix of print and online issues. It publishes short stories, poetry, and art by established and emerging writers and artists as well as essays, interviews, and book reviews (by invitation) in these related areas. The Takahē Collective Trust is a nonprofit organization that aims to support emerging and published writers, poets, artists, and cultural commentators.

NEEDS "We look for stories that have something special about them: an original idea, a new perspective, an interesting narrative style or use of language, an ability to evoke character and/or atmosphere. Above all, we like some depth, an extra layer of meaning, an insight—something more than just an anecdote or a straightforward narration of events." Length: 1,500-3,000 words, "Stories up to 5,000 words may be considered for publication in the online magazine only."

HOW TO CONTACT E-mail submissions are preferred (fiction@takahe.org.nz). Overseas submissions are only accepted by e-mail.

PAYMENT/TERMS Pays small honorarium to New Zealand authors, or one-year subscription to overseas writers.

TIPS "Editorials, book reviews, artwork, and literary commentaries are by invitation only."

◐ TALKING RIVER

Lewis-Clark State College, 500 Eighth Ave., Lewiston ID 83501. (208)792-2716. **E-mail:** talkingriver@lcmail.lcsc.edu. **Website:** www.lcsc.edu/talking-river. **Contact:** Kevin Goodan, editorial advisor. Estab. 1994. "*Talking River*, Lewis-Clark State College's literary journal, seeks examples of literary excellence and originality. Theme may and must be of your choosing. Send us your mss of poetry, fiction, and creative nonfiction. The journal is a national publication, featuring creative work by some of this country's best contemporary writers."

◖ Reads mss August 1-April 1 only.

NEEDS Wants more well-written, character-driven stories that surprise and delight the reader with fresh, arresting yet un-self-conscious language, imagery, metaphor, revelation. Recently published work by Chris Dombrowski, Sherwin Bitsui, and Lia Purpura, Jim Harrison, David James Duncan, Dan Gerber, Alison Hawthorne Deming. No stories that are sexist, racist, homophobic, erotic for shock value; no genre fiction. Length: up to 4,000 words.

HOW TO CONTACT Send complete ms with cover letter by postal mail. Include estimated word count, two-sentence bio, and list of publications. Send SASE for reply and return of ms, or send disposable copy of ms.

PAYMENT/TERMS Pays contributor's copies; additional copies $6.

TIPS "We look for the strong, the unique; we reject clichéd images and predictable climaxes."

◓ TEARS IN THE FENCE

Portman Lodge, Durweston, Blandford Forum, Dorset DT11 0QA, England. **E-mail:** tearsinthefence@gmail.com. **Website:** tearsinthefence.com. Estab. 1984. *Tears in the Fence*, published 3 times/year, is a "small-press magazine of poetry, prose poetry, creative nonfiction, fiction, interviews, essays, and reviews. We are open to a wide variety of poetic styles and work that shows social and poetic awareness whilst prompting close and divergent readings."

◖ *Tears in the Fence* is 176 pages, A5, digitally printed on 110-gms. paper, perfect-bound, with matte card cover. Press run is 600.

NEEDS Length: up to 3,000 words.

HOW TO CONTACT Submit complete ms via e-mail as attachment.

PAYMENT/TERMS Pays 1 contributor's copy.

TEKKA

134 Main St., Watertown MA 02472. (617)924-9044. **E-mail:** editor@tekka.net. **E-mail:** bernstein@eastgate.com. **Website:** www.tekka.net. **Contact:** Mark Bernstein, publisher. Estab. 2003. "*Tekka* takes a close look at serious ideas that intertwingle computing and expression: hypertext, new media, software aesthetics, and the changing world that lies beyond the new economy. *Tekka* is always seeking new writers who can enhance our understanding, tempt our palate, and help explore new worlds and advance the state of the art. We welcome proposals for incisive, original features, reviews, and profiles from freelance writers. Our rates vary by length, department, and editorial requirements but are generally in line with the best Web magazines. We welcome proposals from scholars as well. We also publish short hypertext fiction, as well as fiction that explores the future of reading, writing, media, and computing. We are probably the best market for Web fiction, but we are extremely selective.

HOW TO CONTACT Query.

PAYMENT/TERMS Pay rates vary.

◐◯ TERRAIN.ORG: A JOURNAL OF THE BUILT + NATURAL ENVIROMENTS

Terrain.org, P.O. Box 19161, Tucson AZ 85731-9161. **E-mail:** contact2@terrain.org. **Website:** www.terrain.org. **Contact:** Simmons B. Buntin, editor in chief. Receives 25 mss/month. Accepts 12-15 mss/year. Agented fiction 5%. **Publishes 1-3 new writers/year.** Published Al Sim, Jacob MacAurthur Mooney, T.R. Healy, Deborah Fries, Andrew Wingfield, Braden Hepner, Chavawn Kelly, Tamara Kaye Sellman. *Terrain.org* is based on, and thus welcomes quality submissions from, new and experienced authors and artists alike.

Our online journal accepts only the finest poetry, essays, fiction, articles, artwork, and other contributions' material that reaches deep into the earth's fiery core, or humanity's incalculable core, and brings forth new insights and wisdom. *Terrain.org* is searching for that interface—the integration among the built and natural environments, that might be called the soul of place. The works contained within *Terrain.org* ultimately examine the physical realm around us and how those environments influence us and each other physically, mentally, emotionally, and spiritually."

Beginning March 2014, publication schedule is rolling; we will no longer be issue-based. Sends galleys to author. Publication is copyrighted. Sponsors *Terrain.org* Annual Contest in Poetry, Fiction, and Nonfiction. **Deadline:** August 1. Submit via online submissions manager.

NEEDS Does not want erotica. Length: up to 6,000 words. Average length: 5,000 words. Publishes short shorts. Average length of short shorts: 750 words.

HOW TO CONTACT Accepts submissions online at sub.terrain.org. Include brief bio. Send complete ms with cover letter. Reads September 1-May 30 for regular submissions; contest submissions open year round.

TIPS "We have 3 primary criteria in reviewing fiction: (1) The story is compelling and well crafted. (2) The story provides some element of surprise; whether in content, form, or delivery we are unexpectedly delighted in what we've read. (3) The story meets an upcoming theme, even if only peripherally. Read fiction in the current issue and perhaps some archived work, and if you like what you read—and our overall enviromental slant—then send us your best work. Make sure you follow our submission guidelines (including cover note with bio), and that your mss is as error-free as possible."

💲 THEMA

Thema Literary Society, P.O. Box 8747, Metairie LA 70011-8747. **E-mail:** thema@cox.net. **E-mail:** Only for writers living outside the U.S. **Website:** themaliterarysociety.com. **Contact:** Virginia Howard, editor; Gail Howard, poetry editor. Estab. 1988. "*THEMA* is designed to stimulate creative thinking by challenging writers with unusual themes, such as 'Drop the Zucchini and Run!' and 'Second Thoughts.' Appeals to writers, teachers of creative writing, artists, photographers, and general reading audience."

THEMA is 100 pages, digest-sized professionally printed, with glossy card cover. Receives about 400 poems/year, accepts about 8%. Press run is 400 (230 subscribers, 30 libraries). Subscription: $30 U.S./$40 foreign. Has published poetry by John Grey, Carol Louis Munn, James B. Nicola, and Dennis Trujillo.

NEEDS All stories must relate to one of *THEMA*'s upcoming themes (**indicate the target theme on submission of ms**). See website for themes. No erotica. Length: 300 to 6,000 words (one to twenty double-spaced pages).

HOW TO CONTACT Send complete ms with SASE, cover letter; include "name and address, brief introduction, **specifying the intended target issue for the mss**." SASE. Accepts simultaneous, multiple submissions, and reprints. Does not accept e-mailed submissions except from non-USA addresses.

PAYMENT/TERMS Payment: $10 for under 1,000 words; $25 for stories over 1,000 words, plus one contributor copy.

THIRD COAST

Western Michigan University, English Department, Kalamazoo MI 49008-5331. **E-mail:** editors@thirdcoastmagazine.com. **Website:** www.thirdcoastmagazine.com. **Contact:** S.Marie LaFata-Clay, editor in chief. Estab. 1995. Sponsors an annual fiction contest. First prize: $1,000 and publication. Guidelines available on website. **Entry fee:** $16, which includes one-year subscription to *Third Coast*. "*Third Coast* publishes poetry, fiction (including traditional and experimental fiction, shorts, and novel excerpts, but not genre fiction), creative nonfiction (including reportage, essay, memoir, and fragments), drama, and translations."

Third Coast is 176 pages, digest-sized, professionally printed, perfect-bound, with 4-color cover with art. Reads mss from September through December of each year.

NEEDS Has published work by Bonnie Jo Campbell, Peter Ho Davies, Robin Romm, Lee Martin, Caitlin Horrocks, and Peter Orner. No genre fiction. Length: up to 7,500 words or 25 pages. Query for longer works.

HOW TO CONTACT Send complete ms via online submissions manager.

PAYMENT/TERMS Pays 2 contributor's copies and one-year subscription.

TIPS "We will consider many different types of fiction and favor those exhibiting a freshness of vision and approach."

THE THREEPENNY REVIEW

P.O. Box 9131, Berkeley CA 94709. (510)849-4545. **E-mail:** wlesser@threepennyreview.com. **Website:** www.threepennyreview.com. **Contact:** Wendy Lesser, editor. Estab. 1980. "We are a general-interest, national literary magazine with coverage of politics, the visual arts, and the performing arts." Reading period: January 1-June 30.

NEEDS No fragmentary, sentimental fiction. Length: 800-4,000 words.

HOW TO CONTACT Send complete ms.

PAYMENT/TERMS Pays $400.

TIPS "Nonfiction (political articles, memoirs, reviews) is most open to freelancers."

TIMBER JOURNAL

University of Colorado Boulder, **E-mail:** timberjournal@gmail.com. **Website:** www.colorado.edu/timberjournal. **Contact:** Staff changes regularly; see website for current staff members. *Timber* is a literary journal run by students in the MFA program at the University of Colorado Boulder and dedicated to the promotion of innovative literature. Publishes work that explores the boundaries of poetry, fiction, creative nonfiction, and digital literatures. Produces both an online journal that explores the potentials of the digital medium and an annual print anthology.

    Reading period: August-March (submit once during this time).

NEEDS Length: up to 4,000 words.

HOW TO CONTACT Submit via online submissions manager. Include 30- to 50-word bio.

PAYMENT/TERMS Pays 1 contributor's copy.

TIPS "We are looking for innovative poetry, fiction, creative nonfiction, and digital lit (screenwriting, digital poetry, multimedia lit, etc.)."

TIN HOUSE

McCormack Communications, P.O. Box 10500, Portland OR 97296. (503)219-0622. **E-mail:** info@tinhouse.com. **Website:** www.tinhouse.com. **Contact:** Cheston Knapp, managing editor; Holly MacArthur, founding editor. Estab. 1999. "We are a general-interest literary quarterly. Our watchword is quality. Our audience includes people interested in literature in all its aspects, from the mundane to the exalted."

    Reading period: September 1-May 31.

NEEDS Length up to 10,000 words.

HOW TO CONTACT Submit via online submissions manager or postal mail. Include cover letter with word count.

PAYMENT/TERMS Pays $200-800.

TOASTED CHEESE

E-mail: editors@toasted-cheese.com. **E-mail:** submit@toasted-cheese.com. **Website:** www.toasted-cheese.com. Estab. 2001. *Toasted Cheese* accepts submissions of previously unpublished fiction, flash fiction, creative nonfiction, poetry, and book reviews. See site for book review requirements and guidelines. "Our focus is on quality of work, not quantity. Some issues will therefore contain fewer or more pieces than previous issues. We don't restrict publication based on subject matter. We encourage submissions from innovative writers in all genres and actively seek diverse voices."

    No simultaneous submissions. Be mindful that final notification of acceptance or rejection may take four months. No chapters or excerpts unless they read as a stand-alone story. No first drafts.

NEEDS Toasted Cheese actively seeks submissions from those with diverse voices. See site for submission guidelines and samples of what Toasted Cheese publishes. No fan fiction. No chapters or excerpts unless they read as a stand-alone story. No first drafts.

HOW TO CONTACT See site for submission guidelines and samples of what Toasted Cheese publishes.

PAYMENT/TERMS Toasted Cheese is a nonpaying market.

TIPS "We are looking for clean, professional work from writers and poets of any experience level. Accepted stories and poems will be concise and compelling with a strong voice. We're looking for writers who are serious about the craft: tomorrow's literary stars before they're famous. Take your submission seriously, yet remember that levity is appreciated. See site for submission guidelines and samples of what Toasted Cheese publishes."

TORCH JOURNAL

Torch Literary Arts, **E-mail:** torchliteraryarts@gmail.com. **E-mail:** torchliteraryarts@gmail.com. **Website:** www.torchliteraryarts.org. **Contact:** Amanda Johnston, Founder / Editor. Estab. 2006. *TORCH Journal*, published semiannually online, provides "a place to publish contemporary poetry, prose, and short stories by experienced and emerging writers alike. We prefer our contributors to take risks, and offer a diverse body of work that examines and challenges preconceived notions regarding race, ethnicity, gender roles, and identity." Has published poetry by Sharon Bridgforth, Patricia Smith, Crystal Wilkinson, Tayari Jones, and Natasha Trethewey. Reads submissions April 15-August 31 only. Sometimes comments on rejected poems. Always sends prepublication galleys. No payment. "Within *TORCH*, we offer a special section called Flame that features an interview, biography, and work sample by an established writer as well as an introduction to their Spark—an emerging writer who inspires them and adds to the boundless voice of creative writing by Black women." A free online newsletter is available; see website.

TRIQUARTERLY

School of Professional Studies, Northwestern University, 339 E. Chicago Ave., Chicago IL 60611. **E-mail:** triquarterly@northwestern.edu. **Website:** www.triquarterly.org. **Contact:** Noelle Havens-Afolabi, Managing Editor. Estab. 1964. "*TriQuarterly*, the literary magazine of Northwestern University, welcomes submissions of fiction, creative nonfiction, poetry, short drama, and hybrid work. We also welcome short-short prose pieces." Reading period: November 15-May 1.

NEEDS Length: up to 5,000 words.

HOW TO CONTACT Submit complete ms via online submissions manager.

PAYMENT/TERMS Pays honoraria.

TIPS "We are especially interested in work that embraces the world and continues, however subtly, the ongoing global conversation about culture and society that *TriQuarterly* pursued from its beginning in 1964."

TULANE REVIEW

Tulane University, Suite G08A Lavin-Bernick Center, Tulane University, New Orleans LA 70118. **E-mail:** litsoc@tulane.edu. **Website:** www.tulane.edu/~litsoc/index.html. Estab. 1988. *Tulane Review*, published biannually, is a national literary journal seeking quality submissions of prose, poetry, and art.

○ *Tulane Review* is the recipient of an AWP Literary Magazine Design Award. *Tulane Review* is 70 pages, 7x9, perfect-bound, with 100# cover with full-color artwork.

NEEDS Length: up to 4,000 words.

HOW TO CONTACT Submit via online submissions manager only. Include a brief biography, an e-mail address, and a return address in cover letter.

PAYMENT/TERMS Pays 2 contributor's copies.

UPSTREET

Ledgetop Publishing, P.O. Box 105, Richmond MA 01254-0105. (413)441-9702. **E-mail:** editor@upstreet-mag.org. **Website:** www.upstreet-mag.org. Estab. 2005.

NEEDS Does not want run-of-the-mill genre, children's, anything but literary. Length: 5,000 words.

HOW TO CONTACT Send complete ms.

TIPS Get sample copy, submit electronically, and follow guidelines.

⑤ U.S. CATHOLIC

Claretian Publications, 205 W. Monroe St., Chicago IL 60606. (312)236-7782. **Fax:** (312)236-8207. **E-mail:** literaryeditor@uscatholic.org. **E-mail:** submissions@claretians.org. **Website:** www.uscatholic.org. Estab. 1935. "*U.S. Catholic* puts faith in the context of everyday life. With a strong focus on social justice, we offer a fresh and balanced take on the issues that matter most in our world, adding a faith perspective to such challenges as poverty, education, family life, the environment, and even pop culture."

○ Please include SASE with written ms.

NEEDS Accepts short stories. "Topics vary, but unpublished fiction should be no longer than 1,500 words and should include strong characters and cause readers to stop for a moment and consider their relationships with others, the world, and/or God. Specifically religious themes are not required; subject matter is not restricted. E-mail submissions@uscatholic.org." Length: 700-1,500 words.

HOW TO CONTACT Send complete ms.

PAYMENT/TERMS Pays minimum $200.

○ VAN GOGH'S EAR: BEST WORLD POETRY & PROSE

French Connection Press, 12 Rue Lamartine, Paris 75009, France. (33)(1)4016-1147. **E-mail:** tinafayeayres@gmail.com. **Website:** www.frenchcx.com/press; theoriginalvangoghsearanthology.com. Estab. 2002. *Van Gogh's Ear*, published annually in April, is an anthology series "devoted to publishing powerful poetry and prose in English and English translations by major voices and innovative new talents from around the globe."

○ *Van Gogh's Ear* is 280 pages, digest-sized, off-set-printed, perfect-bound, with 4-color matte cover with commissioned artwork. Poetry published in *Van Gogh's Ear* has appeared in *The Best American Poetry*.

NEEDS Length: up to 1,500 words.

HOW TO CONTACT Submit up to 2 prose pieces by e-mail. Cover letter is preferred, along with a brief bio of up to 120 words.

PAYMENT/TERMS Pays 1 contributor's copy.

TIPS "As a 501(c)(3) nonprofit enterprise, *Van Gogh's Ear* needs the support of individual poets, writers, and readers to survive. Any donation, large or small, will help *Van Gogh's Ear* continue to publish the best cross-section of contemporary poetry and prose. Because of being an anglophone publication based in France, *Van Gogh's Ear* is unable to get any grants or funding. Your contribution will be tax-deductible. Make donation checks payable to Committee on Poetry-*VGE*, and mail them (donations **only**) to the Allen Ginsberg Trust, P.O. Box 582, Stuyvesant Station, New York NY 10009."

●○ VERANDAH LITERARY & ART JOURNAL

Faculty of Arts, Deakin University, 221 Burwood Hwy., Burwood, Victoria 3125, Australia. (61)(3)9251-7134. **E-mail:** verandah@deakin.edu.au. **Website:** verandahjournal.wordpress.com/. Estab. 1985. *Verandah*, published annually in August, is a high-quality literary journal edited by professional writing students. It aims to give voice to new and innovative writers and artists.

○ Submission period: February 1 through June 5. Has published work by Christos Tsiolka, Dorothy Porter, Seamus Heaney, Les Murray, Ed Burger, and John Muk Muk Burke. *Verandah* is 120 pages, professionally printed on glossy stock, flat-spined, with full-color glossy card cover.

NEEDS Length: 350-2,500 words.

HOW TO CONTACT Submit by mail or e-mail. However, electronic version of work must be available if accepted by *Verandah*. Do not submit work without the required submission form (available for download on website). Reads submissions by June 5 deadline (postmark).

PAYMENT/TERMS Pays 1 contributor's copy, "with prizes awarded accordingly."

VESTAL REVIEW

127 Kilsyth Road, Apt. 3, Brighton MA 02135. **E-mail:** submissions@vestalreview.net. **Website:** www.vestalreview.org. **Contact:** Mark Budman, Editor. Estab. **2000**. Semi-annual print magazine specializing in flash fiction.

○ The oldest magazine of flash fiction. A paying market. Our reading periods are February-May and August-November.

NEEDS Only flash fiction under 500 words. No porn, racial slurs, excessive gore, or obscenity. No children's or preachy stories. Nothing over 500 words. Length: 50-500 words.

HOW TO CONTACT Publishes flash fiction. "We accept submissions only through our submission manager."

PAYMENT/TERMS Pays 3-10¢/word and 1 contributor's copy.

TIPS "We like literary fiction with a plot that doesn't waste words. Don't send jokes masked as stories."

● THE VIRGINIA QUARTERLY REVIEW

VQR, P.O. Box 400223, Charlottesville VA 22904. **E-mail:** editors@vqronline.org. **Website:** www.vqronline.org. **Contact:** Allison Wright, executive editor. Estab. 1925. "*VQR*'s primary mission has been to sustain and strengthen Jefferson's bulwark, long describing itself as 'A National Journal of Literature and Discussion.' And for good reason. From its inception in prohibition, through depression and war, in prosperity and peace, *The Virginia Quarterly Review* has been a haven—and home—for the best essayists, fiction writers, and poets, seeking contributors from every section of the United States and abroad. It has not limited itself to any special field. No topic has been alien: literary, public affairs, the arts, history, the economy. If it could be approached through essay or discussion, poetry or prose, *VQR* has covered it." Press run is 4,000.

NEEDS "We are generally not interested in genre fiction (such as romance, science fiction, or fantasy)." Length: 2,000-10,000 words.

HOW TO CONTACT Accepts online submissions only at virginiaquarterlyreview.submittable.com/submit.

PAYMENT/TERMS Pays $1,000-2,500 for short stories; $1,000-4,000 for novellas and novel excerpts.

●● WEB DEL SOL

Wed del Sol Association, 2020 Pennsylvania Ave. NW, Suite 443, Washington D.C. 20006. **E-mail:** editor@

webdelsol.com. **Website:** www.webdelsol.com. **Contact:** Michael Neff, editor in chief. Estab. 1994. Electronic magazine. "The goal of *Web Del Sol* is to use the medium of the Internet to bring the finest in contemporary literary arts to a larger audience. To that end, *WDS* not only web-publishes collections of work by accomplished writers and poets, but hosts over 25 literary arts publications on the WWW such as *Del Sol Review, North American Review, Global City Review, The Literary Review*, and *The Prose Poem*." Estab. 1994.

NEEDS Literary. "*WDS* publishes work considered to be literary in nature, i.e., nongenre fiction. *WDS* also publishes poetry, prose poetry, essays and experimental types of writing." **Publishes 100-200 new writers/year.**

HOW TO CONTACT "Submissions by e-mail from September through November and from January through March only. Submissions must contain some brief bio, list of prior publications (if any), and a short work or portion of that work, neither to exceed 1,000 words. Editors will contact if the balance of work is required." Sample copy online.

TIPS "*WDS* wants fiction that is absolutely cutting edge, unique and/or at a minimum, accomplished with a crisp style and concerning subjects not usually considered the objects of literary scrutiny. Read works in such publications as *Conjunctions* (www.conjunctions.com) and *North American Review* (webdelsol.com/NorthAmReview/NAR) to get an idea of what we are looking for."

WEST BRANCH

Stadler Center for Poetry, Bucknell University, Lewisburg PA 17837-2029. (570)577-1853. **Fax:** (570)577-1885. **E-mail:** westbranch@bucknell.edu. **Website:** www.bucknell.edu/westbranch. **Contact:** G.C. Waldrep, editor. *West Branch* publishes poetry, fiction, and nonfiction in both traditional and innovative styles.

◑ Reading period: August 15 through April 1. No more than 3 submissions from a single contributor in a given reading period.

NEEDS No genre fiction. Length: no more than 30 pages.

HOW TO CONTACT Send complete ms.

PAYMENT/TERMS Pays 5¢/word, with a maximum of $100.

TIPS "All submissions must be sent via our online submission manager. Please see website for guidelines."

We recommend that you acquaint yourself with the magazine before submitting."

◑ ⑤ WESTERLY MAGAZINE

University of Western Australia, The Westerly Centre (M202), Crawley WA 6009, Australia. (61)(8)6488-3403. **Fax:** (61)(8)6488-1030. **E-mail:** westerly@uwa.edu.au. **Website:** westerlymag.com.au. **Contact:** Catherine Noske, editor. Estab. 1956. *Westerly*, published in July and November, prints quality short fiction, poetry, literary criticism, socio-historical articles, and book reviews with special attention given to Australia, Asia, and the Indian Ocean region. "We assume a reasonably well-read, intelligent audience. Past issues of *Westerly* provide the best guides. Not consciously an academic magazine."

◑ *Westerly* is about 200 pages, digest-sized. Online Special Issues complement the print publication. Subscription information available on website. Deadline for July edition: March 31; deadline for November edition: August 31.

NEEDS Length: up to 3,500 words.

HOW TO CONTACT Submit complete ms by mail, e-mail, or online submissions form.

PAYMENT/TERMS Pays $150 and contributor's copies.

WESTERN HUMANITIES REVIEW

University of Utah, English Department, 255 S. Central Campus Dr., Salt Lake City UT 84112-0494. (801)581-6168. **Fax:** (801)585-5167. **E-mail:** managingeditor.whr@gmail.com. **Website:** www.westernhumanitiesreview.com. **Contact:** Michael Mejia, editor; Tessa Fontaine, managing editor. Estab. 1947. *Western Humanities Review* is a journal of contemporary literature and culture housed in the University of Utah English Department. Publishes poetry, fiction, nonfiction essays, artwork, and work that resists categorization.

◑ Reading period: September 1 through April 15. All submissions must be sent through online submissions manager.

NEEDS Does not want genre (romance, science fiction, etc.). Length: 5,000 words.

HOW TO CONTACT Send complete ms.

PAYMENT/TERMS Pays $5/published page (when funds available).

TIPS "Because of changes in our editorial staff, we urge familiarity with recent issues of the magazine. We do not publish writer's guidelines because we think that the magazine itself conveys an accurate picture of our requirements. Please, no e-mail submissions."

WHISKEY ISLAND MAGAZINE

English Dept., Cleveland State University, 2121 Euclid Ave., Cleveland OH 44115. (216)687-3951. **E-mail:** whiskeyisland@csuohio.edu. **Website:** whiskeyislandmagazine.com. **Contact:** Dan Dorman. *Whiskey Island* is a nonprofit literary magazine that has been published in one form or another by students of Cleveland State University for over 30 years.

 Reading periods: August 15 through November 15 and January 15 through April 15. Paper and e-mail submissions are not accepted. No multiple submissions.

NEEDS No translations, please. Length: 1,500-8,000 words for short stories; up to 1,500 words for flash fiction.

HOW TO CONTACT Submit via online submissions manager.

PAYMENT/TERMS Pays 2 contributor's copies.

WICKED ALICE

Dancing Girl Press & Studio, 410 S. Michigan #921, Chicago IL 60605. **E-mail:** wickedalicepoetry@yahoo.com. **Website:** www.sundresspublications.com/wickedalice. **Contact:** Kristy Bowen, editor. Estab. 2001. "*Wicked Alice* is a women-centered online journal dedicated to publishing quality work by both sexes, depicting and exploring the female experience." Wants "work that has a strong sense of image and music. Work that is interesting and surprising, with innovative, sometimes unusual, use of language. We love humor when done well, strangeness, wackiness. Hybridity, collage, intertexuality."

HOW TO CONTACT Submit complete ms by e-mail.

WILD VIOLET

P.O. Box 39706, Philadelphia PA 19106. **E-mail:** wildvioletmagazine@yahoo.com. **Website:** www.wildviolet.net. **Contact:** Alyce Wilson, editor. Estab. 2001. *Wild Violet*, published weekly online, aims "to make the arts more accessible, to make a place for the arts in modern life, and to serve as a creative forum for writers and artists. Our audience includes English-speaking readers from all over the world who are interested in both 'high art' and pop culture."

NEEDS Receives 30 unsolicited mss/month. Accepts 3-5 mss/issue; 135 mss/year. **Publishes 70 new writers/year.** Recently published work by Bill Gaythwaite, Jonathan Lowe, and Nancy Christie. Also publishes literary essays, literary criticism, poetry. Sometimes comments on rejected mss. "No stories where sexual or violent content is just used to shock the reader. No racist writings." Length: 500-6,000 words; average length: 3,000 words.

HOW TO CONTACT Send complete ms. Accepts submissions by e-mail and postal mail. Include estimated word count and brief bio. Send SASE for return of ms or send a disposable copy of ms and #10 SASE for reply only. Accepts simultaneous, multiple submissions.

PAYMENT/TERMS Writers receive bio and links on contributor's page. Sponsors awards/contests.

TIPS "We look for stories that are well-paced and show character and plot development. Even short shorts should do more than simply paint a picture. Mss stand out when the author's voice is fresh and engaging. Avoid muddying your story with too many characters, and don't attempt to shock the reader with an ending you have not earned. Experiment with styles and structures, but don't resort to experimentation for its own sake."

WILLARD & MAPLE

375 Maple Street, Burlington VT 05401. **E-mail:** willardandmaple@champlain.edu. **Website:** willardandmaple.com. Estab. 1994. *Willard & Maple*, published annually in spring, is a student-run literary magazine from Champlain College's Professional Writing Program that considers short fiction, essays, reviews, fine art, and poetry by adults, children, and teens. Wants creative work of the highest quality.

 Willard & Maple is 200 pages, digest-sized, digitally printed, perfect-bound. Receives about 500 poems/year, accepts about 20%. Press run is 600 (80 subscribers, 4 libraries); 200 are distributed free to the Champlain College writing community.

HOW TO CONTACT Send complete ms via e-mail or postal mail. Send SASE for return of ms or send disposable copy of mss and #10 SASE for reply only.

PAYMENT/TERMS Pays 2 contributor's copies.

TIPS "The power of imagination makes us infinite."

WILLOW REVIEW

College of Lake County Publications, College of Lake County, 19351 W. Washington St., Grayslake IL 60030-1198. (847)543-2956. **E-mail:** com426@clcillinois.edu. **Website:** www.clcillinois.edu/community/willowreview.asp. **Contact:** Michael Latza, editor. Estab. 1969. Prizes totaling $400 are awarded to the best poetry and short fiction/creative nonfiction in each issue. *Willow Review*, published annually, is interested in poetry, creative nonfiction, and fiction of high quality. "We have no preferences as to form, style, or subject, as long as each piece stands on its own as art and communicates ideas."

O The editors award prizes for best poetry and prose in the issue. Prize awards vary contingent on the current year's budget but normally range from $100-400. There is no reading fee or separate application for these prizes. All accepted mss are eligible."*Willow Review* can be found on EBSCOhost databases, assuring a broader targeted audience for our authors' work. *Willow Review* is a nonprofit journal partially supported by a grant from the Illinois Arts Council (a state agency), College of Lake County Publications, private contributions, and sales."

NEEDS Accepts short fiction. Considers simultaneous submissions "if indicated in the cover letter" and multiple submissions.

HOW TO CONTACT Send complete ms with cover letter. Include estimated word count, brief bio, list of publications. Send either SASE (or IRC) for return of ms or disposable copy of ms and #10 SASE for reply only.

PAYMENT/TERMS Pays 2 contributor's copies.

THE WINDHOVER

P.O. Box 8008, 900 College St., Belton TX 76513. (254)295-4563. **E-mail:** windhover@umhb.edu. **Website:** undergrad.umhb.edu/english/windhover-journal. **Contact:** Dr. Nathaniel Hansen, editor. Estab. 1997. "*The Windhover* is dedicated to promoting poetry, fiction and creative nonfiction that considers Christian perspectives and engages spiritual themes."

O Reading periods are 2/1-4/15 & 8/1-10/15.

NEEDS Length: 500-4,000 words. Average length: 3,000 words.

PAYMENT/TERMS Pays 1 contributor's copy.

TIPS "We are looking for writing that avoids the didactic, the melodramatic, the trite, the obvious. Eschew tricks and gimmicks. We want writing that invites rereading."

WITCHES AND PAGANS

BBI Media, Inc., P.O. Box 687, Forest Grove OR 97116. (503)430-8817. **E-mail:** editor2@bbimedia.com. **Website:** www.witchesandpagans.com. **Contact:** Anne Newkirk Niven. Estab. 2002. "Devoted exclusively to promoting and covering contemporary Pagan culture, *W&P* features exclusive interviews with the teachers, writers, and activists who create and lead our traditions, visits to the sacred places and people who inspire us, and in-depth discussions of our ever-evolving practices. You'll also find practical daily magic, ideas for solitary ritual and devotion, God/dess-friendly craft-projects, Pagan poetry and short fiction, reviews, and much more in every 88-page issue. *W&P* is available in either traditional paper copy sent by postal mail or as a digital PDF e-zine download that is compatible with most computers and readers."

NEEDS Does not want faction (fictionalized retellings of real events). Avoid gratuitous sex, violence, sentimentality, and pagan moralizing. Don't beat our readers with the Rede or the Threefold Law. Length: 1,000-5,000 words.

HOW TO CONTACT Send complete ms.

TIPS "Read the magazine, do your research, write the piece, send it in. That's really the only way to get started as a writer; everything else is window dressing."

THE WORCESTER REVIEW

1 Ekman St., Worcester MA 01607. (508)797-4770. **E-mail:** twr.diane@gmail.com. **Website:** www.theworcesterreview.org. **Contact:** Diane Vanaskie Mulligan, managing editor. Estab. 1972. *The Worcester Review*, published annually by the Worcester County Poetry Association, encourages "critical work with a New England connection; no geographic limitation on poetry and fiction." Wants "work that is crafted, intuitively honest and empathetic. We like high-quality, creative poetry, artwork, and fiction. Critical articles should be connected to New England."

O *The Worcester Review* is 160 pages, digest-sized, professionally printed in dark type on quality stock, perfect-bound, with matte card cover. Press run is 600.

NEEDS Accepts about 10% unsolicited mss. Agented fiction less than 10%. Recently published work by Robert Pinsky, Marge Piercy, Wes McNair, and Ed Hirsch. Length: 1,000-4,000 words. Average length: 2,000 words.

HOW TO CONTACT Send complete ms via online submissions manager. "Send only 1 short story—reading editors do not like to read 2 by the same author at the same time. We will use only 1."

PAYMENT/TERMS Pays 2 contributor's copies and honorarium if possible.

TIPS "We generally look for creative work with a blend of craftsmanship, insight, and empathy. This does not exclude humor. We won't print work that is shoddy in any of these areas."

WORD RIOT

P.O. Box 414, Middletown NJ 07748-3143. (732)706-1272. **Fax:** (732)706-5856. **E-mail:** wr.submissions@gmail.com. **Website:** www.wordriot.org. **Contact:** Jackie Corley, publisher; Kevin O'Cuinn, fiction editor; Doug Paul Case, poetry editor; Antonia Crane, creative nonfiction editor. Estab. 2002. "*Word Riot* publishes the forceful voices of up-and-coming writers and poets. We like edgy. We like challenging. We like unique voices. Each month we provide readers with book reviews, author interviews, and, most importantly, writing from some of the best and brightest making waves on the literary scene."

Online magazine. Member CLMP.

NEEDS Accepts 20-25 mss/issue; 240-300 mss/year. Agented fiction 5%. Publishes 8-10 new writers/year. "No fantasy, science fiction, romance." Length: 1,000-6,500 words.

HOW TO CONTACT Submit via online submissions manager at wordriot.submittable.com/submit. Do not send submissions by mail.

TIPS "We're always looking for something edgy or quirky. We like writers who take risks."

THE WRITE PLACE AT THE WRITE TIME

E-mail: questions@thewriteplaceatthewritetime.org. **E-mail:** submissions@thewriteplaceatthewritetime.org. **Website:** www.thewriteplaceatthewritetime.org. **Contact:** Nicole M. Bouchard, editor in chief. Estab. 2008. Online literary magazine, published 3 times/year. Publishes fiction, personal nonfiction, craft essays by professionals, and poetry that "speaks to the heart and mind."

"Our writers come from around the world and range from previously unpublished to having written for *The New York Times*, *Time* magazine, *The New Yorker*, *The Wall Street Journal*, *Glimmer Train*, *Newsweek*, *Business Week*, Random House, and Simon and Schuster. Interview subjects include *NYT* best-selling authors such as Tracy Chevalier, Dennis Lehane, Mona Simpson, Janet Fitch, Alice Hoffman, Joanne Harris, Arthur Golden, Jodi Picoult, and Frances Mayes."

NEEDS Considers literary and most genre fiction if thought-provoking and emotionally evocative. No erotica, explicit horror/gore/violence, political. Length: up to 3,500 words. Average length of stories: 3,000 words. Average length of short-shorts: 1,000 words. "If we feel the strength of the submission merits added length, we are happy to consider exceptions."

HOW TO CONTACT Send complete ms with cover letter by e-mail—no attachments. Include estimated word count and brief bio. Accepts multiple submissions, up to 3 stories at a time. Accepts simultaneous submissions if indicated; other publications must be notified immediately upon acceptance. "If accepted elsewhere, we must be notified." Accepts 90-100 mss/year; receives 500-700 mss/year.

TIPS "Through our highly personalized approach to content, feedback, and community, we aim to give a very human visage to the publishing process. We wish to speak deeply of the human condition through pieces that validate the entire spectrum of emotions and the real circumstances of life. Every piece has a unique power and presence that stands on its own; we've had writers write about surviving an illness, losing a child, embracing a foreign land, learning of their parent's suicide, discovering love, finding humor in dark hours, and healing from abuse. Our collective voice, from our aesthetic to our artwork to the words, looks at and highlights aspects of life through a storytelling lens that allows for or promotes a universal understanding."

WRITER'S BLOC

MSC 162, Fore Hall Rm. 110, 700 University Blvd., Texas A&M University-Kingsville, Kingsville TX 78363. (361)593-2516. **E-mail:** kfmrj00@tamuk.edu; connie.salgado@tamuk.edu. **E-mail:** WritersBloc-LitMag@hotmail.com. **Website:** www.tamuk.edu/artsci/langlit/writers_bloc.html. **Contact:** Dr. Michelle Johnson Vela. *Writer's Bloc*, published annually, prints poetry, short fiction, flash fiction, one-act plays, interviews, and essays. "About half of our pages are devoted to the works of Texas A&M University-Kingsville students and half to the works of writers and artists from all over the world." Wants quality poetry; no restrictions on content or form.

○ *Writer's Bloc* is 96 pages, digest-sized. Press run is 300. Reading period: February through May.

NEEDS Submit via e-mail or postal mail. Include cover letter with contact info, short bio. Accepts about 6 mss/year. Publishes short shorts. Also publishes literary essays, poetry. No pornography, genre fiction, or work by children. Length: up to 3,500 words. Average length is 2,500 words.

PAYMENT/TERMS Pays 1 contributor's copy.

THE WRITING DISORDER

P.O. Box 93613, Los Angeles CA 90093. (323)336-5822. **E-mail:** submit@thewritingdisorder.com. **Website:** www.writingdisorder.com. **Contact:** C.E. Lukather, editor; Paul Garson, managing editor; Julianna Woodhead, poetry editor. Estab. 2009. "*The Writing Disorder* is an online literary journal devoted to literature, art, and culture. Our mission is to showcase new and emerging writers—particularly those in writing programs—as well as established ones. We also feature artwork, photography, and comic art. Although we strive to publish original and experimental work, *The Writing Disorder* remains rooted in the classic art of storytelling."

NEEDS Does not want to see romance, religious, or fluff. Length: 20,000 words maximum.

HOW TO CONTACT Query.

PAYMENT/TERMS Pays contributor's copies.

TIPS "We are looking for work from new writers, writers in writing programs, and students and faculty of all ages."

XAVIER REVIEW

Xavier University of Louisiana, 1 Drexel Dr., Box 89, New Orleans LA 70125-1098. **Website:** www.xula.edu/review. **Contact:** Ralph Adamo, editor. Estab. 1980. "*Xavier Review* accepts poetry, fiction, translations, creative nonfiction, and critical essays. Content focuses on African American, Caribbean, and Southern literature, as well as works that touch on issues of religion and spirituality. We do, however, accept quality work on all themes. (Please note: This is not a religious publication.)"

NEEDS Has published work by Andrei Codrescu, Terrance Hayes, Naton Leslie, and Patricia Smith. Also publishes literary essays and literary criticism.

HOW TO CONTACT Send complete ms. Include 2-3 sentence bio and SASE. "We rarely accepts mss over 20 pages."

PAYMENT/TERMS Pays 2 contributor's copies; offers 40% discount on additional copies.

THE YALE REVIEW

The Yale Review, P.O. Box 208243, New Haven CT 06520-8243. (203)432-0499. **Fax:** (203)432-0510. **Website:** www.yale.edu/yalereview. **Contact:** J.D. McClatchy, editor. Estab. 1911. "Like Yale's schools of music, drama, and architecture, like its libraries and art galleries, *The Yale Review* has helped give the University its leading place in American education. In a land of quick fixes and short view and in a time of increasingly commercial publishing, the journal has an authority that derives from its commitment to bold established writers and promising newcomers, to both challenging literary work and a range of essays and reviews that can explore the connections between academic disciplines and the broader movements in American society, thought, and culture. With independence and boldness, with a concern for issues and ideas, with a respect for the mind's capacity to be surprised by speculation and delighted by elegance, *The Yale Review* proudly continues into its third century."

HOW TO CONTACT Submit complete ms with SASE. All submissions should be sent to the editorial office.

PAYMENT/TERMS Pays $400-500.

THE YALOBUSHA REVIEW

University of Mississippi, **E-mail:** yreditors@gmail.com. **Website:** yr.olemiss.edu. **Contact:** Maggie Woodward and Jeffrey Lance, senior editors. Estab. 1995.

NEEDS Length: up to 5,000 words for short stories; up to 1,000 words for flash fiction.

HOW TO CONTACT Submit 1 short story or up to 3 pieces of flash fiction via online submissions manager.

YEMASSEE

University of South Carolina, Department of English, Columbia SC 29208. **E-mail:** editor@yemasseejournal.com. **Website:** yemasseejournal.com. Estab. 1993. "*Yemassee* is the University of South Carolina's literary journal. Our readers are interested in high-quality fiction, poetry, and creative nonfiction. We have no editorial slant; quality of work is our only concern. We publish in the fall and spring, printing 5-7 stories, 2-3 essays, and 12-15 poems per issue. We tend to solicit reviews, essays, and interviews but welcome unsolicited queries. We do not favor any particular aesthetic or school of writing."

○ "Stories from *Yemassee* have been published in *New Stories From the South*. As of 2012, we only accept submissions through our online submissions manager."

NEEDS "We are open to a variety of subjects and writing styles. Our essential consideration for acceptance is the quality of the work." No romance, religious/inspirational, young adult/teen, children's/juvenile, erotica. Wants more experimental work. Length: up to 5,000 words.

HOW TO CONTACT Send complete ms. Submissions for all genres should include a cover letter that lists the titles of the pieces included, along with your contact information (including author's name, address, e-mail address, and phone number). Yemassee Short Fiction Contest: $750 award. Check website for deadline.

PAYMENT/TERMS Pays 2 contributor's copies.

ZEEK: A JEWISH JOURNAL OF THOUGHT AND CULTURE

125 Maiden Ln., 8th Floor, New York NY 10038. (212)453-9435. **E-mail:** zeek@zeek.net. **Website:** www.zeek.net. **Contact:** Erica Brody, editor in chief. Estab. 2001. *ZEEK* "relaunched in late February 2013 as a hub for the domestic Jewish social justice movement, one that showcases the people, ideas, and conversations driving an inclusive and diverse progressive Jewish community. At the same time, we've reaffirmed our commitment to building on *ZEEK*'s reputation for original, ahead-of-the-curve Jewish writing and arts, culture and spirituality content, incubating emerging voices and artists, as well as established ones." *ZEEK* seeks "great writing in a variety of styles and voices, original thinking, and accessible content. That means we're interested in hearing your ideas for first-person essays, reflections and commentary, reporting, profiles, Q&As, analysis, infographics, and more. For the near future, *ZEEK* will focus on domestic issues. Our discourse will be civil."

NEEDS "Calls for fiction submissions are issued periodically. Follow *ZEEK* on Twitter @ZEEKMag for announcements and details."

ZOETROPE: ALL-STORY

Zoetrope: All-Story, The Sentinel Bldg., 916 Kearny St., San Francisco CA 94133. (415)788-7500. **Website:** www.all-story.com. **Contact:** fiction editor. Estab. 1997. *Zoetrope: All Story* presents a new generation of classic stories.

NEEDS Length: up to 7,000 words. "Excerpts from larger works, screenplays, treatments, and poetry will be returned unread."

HOW TO CONTACT "Writers should submit only 1 story at a time and no more than 2 stories a year. We do not accept artwork or design submissions. We do not accept unsolicited revisions nor respond to writers who don't include an SASE." Send complete ms by mail.

PAYMENT/TERMS Pays up to $1,000.

TIPS "Before submitting, nonsubscribers should read several issues of the magazine to determine if their works fit with *All-Story*. Electronic versions of the magazine are available to read, in part, at the website, and print versions are available for purchase by single-issue order and subscription."

ZYZZYVA

57 Post St., Suite 604, San Francisco CA 94104. (415)757-0465. **E-mail:** editor@zyzzyva.org. **Website:** www.zyzzyva.org. **Contact:** Laura Cogan, editor; Oscar Villalon, managing editor. Estab. 1985. "Every issue is a vibrant mix of established talents and new voices, providing an elegantly curated overview of contemporary arts and letters with a distinctly San Francisco perspective."

○ Accepts submissions January 1-May 31 and August 1-November 30. Does not accept online submissions.

NEEDS Length: no limit.

HOW TO CONTACT Send complete ms by mail. Include SASE and contact information.

PAYMENT/TERMS Pays $50.

TIPS "We are not currently seeking work about any particular theme or topic; that said, reading recent issues is perhaps the best way to develop a sense for the length and quality we are looking for in submissions."

BOOK PUBLISHERS

In this section, you will find many of the "big name" book publishers. Many of these publishers remain tough markets for new writers or for those whose work might be considered literary or experimental. Indeed, some only accept work from established authors, and then often only through an author's agent. Although having your novel published by one of the big commercial publishers listed in this section is difficult, it is not impossible. The trade magazine *Publishers Weekly* regularly features interviews with writers whose first novels are being released by top publishers. Many editors at large publishing houses find great satisfaction in publishing a writer's first novel.

In the References section, you'll find the publishing industry's "family tree," which maps out each of the large book publishing conglomerates' divisions, subsidiaries, and imprints. Remember, most manuscripts are acquired by imprints, not their parent company, so avoid submitting to the conglomerates themselves.

Also listed here are "small presses," which publish four or more titles annually. Included among them are independent presses, university presses, and other nonprofit publishers. Introducing new writers to the reading public has become an increasingly important role of these smaller presses at a time when the large conglomerates are taking fewer chances on unknown writers. Many of the successful small presses listed in this section have built their reputations and their businesses in this way and have become known for publishing prize-winning fiction.

These smaller presses also tend to keep books in print longer than larger houses. And, since small presses publish a smaller number of books, each title is equally important to the publisher and each is promoted in much the same way and with the same commitment. Editors also stay at small presses longer because they have more of a stake in the business—often they own the business. Many smaller book publishers are writers themselves and know firsthand the importance of a close editor-author or publisher-author relationship.

TYPES OF BOOK PUBLISHERS

Large or small, the publishers in this section publish books "for the trade." That is, unlike textbook, technical, or scholarly publishers, trade publishers publish books to be sold to the general consumer through bookstores, chain stores, or other retail outlets. Within the trade book field, however, there are a number of different types of books.

The easiest way to categorize books is by their physical appearance and the way they are marketed. Hardcover books are the more expensive editions of a book, sold through bookstores and carrying a price tag of around $20 and up. Trade paperbacks are softbound books, also sold mostly in bookstores, but they carry a more modest price tag of usually around $10 to $20. Today a lot of fiction is published in this form because it means a lower financial risk than hardcover.

Mass-market paperbacks are another animal altogether. These are the smaller "pocket-size" books available at bookstores, grocery stores, drugstores, chain retail outlets, etc. Much genre or category fiction is published in this format. This area of the publishing industry is very open to the work of talented new writers who write in specific genres such as science fiction, romance, and mystery.

At one time, publishers could be easily identified and grouped by the type of books they produce. Today, however, the lines between hardcover and paperback books are blurred. Many publishers known for publishing hardcover books also publish trade paperbacks and have paperback imprints. This enables them to offer established authors (and a very few lucky newcomers) hard-soft deals in which their book comes out in both versions. Thanks to the mergers of the past decade, too, the same company may own several hardcover and paperback subsidiaries and imprints, even though their editorial focuses may remain separate.

CHOOSING A BOOK PUBLISHER

In addition to checking the bookstores and libraries for books by publishers that interest you, you may want to refer to the Category Index at the back of this book to find publishers divided by specific subject categories. The subjects listed in the index are general. Read individual listings to find which subcategories interest a publisher. For example, you will find several romance publishers listed, but you should read the listings to find which type of romance is considered: gothic, contemporary, regency, futuristic, and so on.

The icons appearing before the names of the publishers will also help you in selecting a publisher. These codes are especially important in this section, because many of the publishing houses listed here require writers to submit through an agent. The ⏃ symbol indicates that a publisher accepts agented submissions only. A ● icon identifies those that mostly publish established and agented authors, while a ⬤ points to publishers most open to new writers. See the inside back cover of this book for a complete list and explanations of symbols used in this book.

IN THE LISTINGS

We include several symbols to help you narrow your search. English-speaking foreign markets are denoted by a ⬤. The maple leaf symbol ⬤ identifies Canadian presses. If you are not a Canadian writer but are interested in a Canadian press, check the listing carefully. Many small presses in Canada receive grants and other funds from their provincial or national government and are, therefore, restricted to publishing Canadian authors.

We also include editorial comments set off by a bullet (⬤) within listings. This is where we include information about any special requirements or circumstances that will help you know even more about the publisher's needs and policies. The ⬤ symbol identifies publishers who have recently received honors or awards for their books. The ☻ denotes publishers who produce comics and graphic novels.

Each listing includes a summary of the houses's editorial mission, an overarching principle that ties together what they publish. Under the heading **Contact** we list one or more editors, often with their specific area of expertise.

Book editors asked us again this year to emphasize the importance of paying close attention to the **Needs** and **How to Contact** subheads of listings for book publishers. Unlike magazine editors, who want to see complete manuscripts of short stories, most of the book publishers listed here ask that writers send a query letter with an outline and/or synopsis and several chapters of their novel. "The Business of Fiction Writing," found earlier in this book, outlines how to prepare work to submit directly to a publisher.

There are no subsidy book publishers listed in *Novel & Short Story Writer's Market*. By subsidy, we mean any arrangement in which the writer is expected to pay all or part of the cost of producing, distributing, and marketing his book. We feel a writer should not be asked to share in any cost of turning his manuscript into a book. All the book publishers listed here told us that they do not charge writers for publishing their work. If any of the publishers listed here ask you to pay any part of publishing or marketing your manuscript, please let us know.

A NOTE ABOUT AGENTS

Some publishers are willing to look at unsolicited submissions, but most feel having an agent is in the writer's best interest. In this section more than any other, you'll find a number of publishers who prefer submissions from agents. That's why we've included a section of agents open to submissions from fiction writers (see the Literary Agents section of the listings). For even more agents, along with a great deal of helpful articles about approaching and working with them, refer to *Guide to Literary Agents*.

If you use the Internet or another resource to find an agent not listed in this book, be wary of any agents who charge large sums of money for reading a manuscript. Reading fees do not guarantee representation. Think of an agent as a potential business partner and feel free to ask tough questions about his or her credentials, experience, and business practices.

ABRAMS

115 W. 18th St., 6th Floor, New York NY 10011. (212)206-7715. **Fax:** (212)519-1210. **E-mail:** abrams@abramsbooks.com. **Website:** www.abramsbooks.com. **Contact:** Managing Editor. Estab. 1951. Publishes hardcover and a few paperback originals.

Ⓞ   Does not accept unsolicited materials.

IMPRINTS Stewart, Tabori & Chang: Abrams Appleseed; Abrams Books for Young Readers; Abrams Image; STC Craft; Amulet Books.

NEEDS Publishes hardcover and "a few" paperback originals. Averages 150 total titles/year.

TIPS "We are one of the few publishers who publish almost exclusively illustrated books. We consider ourselves the leading publishers of art books and high-quality artwork in the U.S. Once the author has signed a contract to write a book for our firm the author must finish the ms to agreed-upon high standards within the schedule agreed upon in the contract."

ACADEMY CHICAGO PUBLISHERS

814 N. Franklin St., Chicago IL 60610. (312)337-0747. **Fax:** (312)337-5985. **Website:** www.chicagoreviewpress.com. **Contact:** Yuval Taylor, senior editor. Estab. 1975. "We publish quality fiction and nonfiction. Our audience is literate and discriminating. No novelized biography, history, or science fiction. No electronic submissions." Publishes hardcover and some paperback originals and trade paperback reprints. Book catalog online. Guidelines online.

NEEDS "We look for quality work, but we do not publish experimental, avant garde, horror, science fiction, thrillers novels."

HOW TO CONTACT Submit proposal package, synopsis, 3 sample chapters, and short bio.

TERMS Pays 7-10% royalty on wholesale price. Responds in 3 months.

TIPS "At the moment, we are looking for good nonfiction; we certainly want excellent original fiction, but we are swamped. No fax queries, no disks. No electronic submissions. We are always interested in reprinting good out-of-print books."

Ⓐ   ACE SCIENCE FICTION AND FANTASY

Imprint of the Berkley Publishing Group, Penguin Group (USA), Inc., 375 Hudson St., New York NY 10014. (212)366-2000. **Website:** www.us.penguingroup.com. Estab. 1953. Ace publishes science fiction and fantasy exclusively. Publishes hardcover, paperback, and trade paperback originals and reprints.

Ⓞ   As imprint of Penguin, Ace is not open to unsolicited submissions.

NEEDS No other genre accepted. No short stories.

HOW TO CONTACT Due to the high volume of mss received, most Penguin Group (USA) Inc. imprints do not normally accept unsolicited mss.

TERMS Pays royalty. Pays advance.

ALGONQUIN BOOKS OF CHAPEL HILL

Workman Publishing, P.O. Box 2225, Chapel Hill NC 27515-2225. (919)967-0108. **Website:** www.algonquin.com. **Contact:** Editorial Department. Algonquin Books publishes quality literary fiction and literary nonfiction. Publishes hardcover originals. Guidelines online.

IMPRINTS Algonquin Young Readers.

HOW TO CONTACT Does not accept unsolicited submissions at this time.

🕮   ALLEN & UNWIN

406 Albert St., East Melbourne VIC 3002, Australia. (61)(3)9665-5000. **E-mail:** fridaypitch@allenandunwin.com. **Website:** www.allenandunwin.com. Allen & Unwin publish over 80 new books for children and young adults each year, many of these from established authors and illustrators. "However, we know how difficult it can be for new writers to get their work in front of publishers, which is why we've decided to extend our innovative and pioneering Friday Pitch service to emerging writers for children and young adults. Guidelines online.

AMBERJACK PUBLISHING

P.O. Box 4668 #89611, New York NY 10163. (888)959-3352. **Website:** www.amberjackpublishing.com. Amberjack Publishing offers authors the freedom to write without burdening them with having to promote the work themselves. They retain all rights. "You will have no rights left to exploit, so you cannot resell, republish or use your story again."

NEEDS Amberjack Publishing is always on the lookout for the next great story. "We are interested in fiction, children's books, graphic novels, science fiction, fantasy, humor, and everything in between."

HOW TO CONTACT Submit via online query form with book proposal and first 10 pages of ms.

ANKERWYCKE

American Bar Association, 321 N. Clark St., Chicago IL 60654. **Website:** www.ababooks.org. Estab. 1878. In 1215, the Magna Carta was signed underneath the ancient Ankerwycke Yew tree, starting the process which led to rule by constitutional law—in effect, giving rights and the law to the people. And today, the ABA's Ankerwycke line of books continues to bring the law to the people. With legal fiction, true crime books, popular legal histories, public policy handbooks, and prescriptive guides to current legal and business issues, Ankerwycke is a contemporary and innovative line of books for everyone from a trusted and vested authority. Publishes hardcover and trade paperback originals. Book catalog and ms guidelines online.

NEEDS "We're actively acquiring legal fiction with extreme verisimilitude."

HOW TO CONTACT Query with cover letter; outline or TOC; and CV/bio including other credits. Include e-mail address for response.

TERMS Responds in 1 month to queries and proposals; 3 months to mss.

ANTARCTIC PRESS

7272 Wurzbach, Suite 204, San Antonio TX 78240. (210)614-0396. **E-mail:** submissions@antarctic-press.com. **Website:** www.antarctic-press.com. **Contact:** David Hutchison. Estab. 1985. "Antarctic Press is a Texas-based company that was started in 1984. Since then, we have grown to become one of the largest publishers of comics in the United States. Over the years we have produced over 850 titles with a total circulation of over 5 million. Among our titles are some of the most respected and longest-running independent series in comics today. Since our inception, our main goal has been to establish a series of titles that are unique, entertaining, and high in both quality and profitability. The titles we currently publish exhibit all these traits, and appeal to a wide audience." "Antarctic Press is among the top 10 publishers of comics in the United States. However, the difference in market shares between the top 5 publishers and the next 5 publishers is dramatic. Most of the publishers ranked above us have a far greater share of the market place. That being the case, we are an independent publisher with a small staff, and many of our employees have multiple responsibilities. Bigger companies would spread these responsibilities out among a larger staff. Additionally, we don't have the same financial power as a larger company. We cannot afford to pay high page rates; instead, we work on an advance and royalty system which is determined by sales or potential sales of a particular book. We pride ourselves on being a company that gives new talent a chance to get published and take a shot at comic stardom."

NEEDS comic books, graphic novels.

TERMS Pays royalty on net receipts; ms guidelines online.

ANVIL PRESS

P.O. Box 3008 MPO, Vancouver BC V6B 3X5, Canada. (604)876-8710. **Fax:** (604)879-2667. **E-mail:** info@anvilpress.com. **Website:** www.anvilpress.com. Estab. 1988. Anvil Press publishes contemporary adult fiction, poetry, and drama, giving voice to up-and-coming Canadian writers, exploring all literary genres, discovering, nurturing, and promoting new Canadian literary talent. Currently emphasizing urban/suburban themed fiction and poetry; de-emphasizing historical novels. Canadian authors only. No e-mail submissions. Publishes trade paperback originals. Book catalog for 9×12 SAE with 2 first-class stamps. Guidelines online.

NEEDS Contemporary, modern literature; no formulaic or genre.

HOW TO CONTACT Query with 20-30 pages and SASE.

TERMS Pays advance. Average advance is $500-2,000, depending on the genre. Responds in 2 months to queries; 6 months to mss.

TIPS "Audience is informed, educated, aware, with an opinion, culturally active (films, books, the performing arts). No U.S. authors. Research the appropriate publisher for your work."

ARCADE PUBLISHING

Skyhorse Publishing, 307 W. 36th St., 11th Floor, New York NY 10018. (212)643-6816. **Fax:** (212)643-6819. **E-mail:** arcadesubmissions@skyhorsepublishing.com. **Website:** www.arcadepub.com. **Contact:** Acquisitions Editor. Estab. 1988. Arcade prides itself on publishing top-notch literary nonfiction and fiction, with a significant proportion of foreign writers. Publishes hardcover originals, trade paperback reprints. Book catalog and ms guidelines for #10 SASE.

NEEDS No romance, historical, science fiction.

HOW TO CONTACT Submit proposal with brief query, 1-2 page synopsis, chapter outline, market analysis, sample chapter, bio.

TERMS Pays royalty on retail price and 10 author's copies. Pays advance. Responds in 2 months if interested.

ARCHAIA

Imprint of Boom! Studios, 5670 Wilshire Blvd., Suite 450, Los Angeles CA 90036. **Website:** www.archaia.com. Use online submission form.

NEEDS Looking for graphic novel submissions that include finished art. "Archaia is a multi-award-winning graphic novel publisher with more than 75 renowned publishing brands, including such domestic and international hits as *Artesia, Mouse Guard*, and a line of Jim Henson graphic novels including *Fraggle Rock* and *The Dark Crystal*. Publishes creator-shared comic books and graphic novels in the adventure, fantasy, horror, pulp noir, and science fiction genres that contain idiosyncratic and atypical writing and art. *Archaia does not generally hire freelancers or arrange for freelance work, so submissions should only be for completed book and series proposals.*"

ARROW PUBLICATIONS, LLC

7716 Bells Mill Rd., Bethesda MD 20817. (301)299-9422. **Fax:** (240)632-8477. **E-mail:** arrow_info@arrowpub.com. **Website:** www.arrowpub.com. **Contact:** Tom King, managing editor. Estab. 1987. No graphic novels until further notice. Guidelines online.

NEEDS "We are looking for outlines of stories heavy on romance with elements of adventure/intrigue/mystery. We will consider other romance genres such as fantasy, western, inspirational, and historical as long as the romance element is strong."

HOW TO CONTACT Query with outline first with SASE. Consult submission guidelines online before submitting.

TERMS Makes outright purchase of accepted completed scripts. Responds in 2 month to queries; 1 month to mss sent upon request.

TIPS "Our audience is primarily women 18 and older. Send query with outline only."

✪ ARSENAL PULP PRESS

#202-211 East Georgia St., Vancouver BC V6A 1Z6, Canada. (604)687-4233. **Fax:** (604)687-4283. **E-mail:** info@arsenalpulp.com. **Website:** www.arsenalpulp.com. **Contact:** Editorial Board. Estab. 1980. "We are interested in literature that traverses uncharted territories, publishing books that challenge and stimulate and ask probing questions about the world around us." Publishes trade paperback originals, and trade paperback reprints. Book catalog for 9×12 SAE with IRCs or online. Guidelines online.

NEEDS No children's books or genre fiction, i.e., westerns, romance, horror, mystery, etc.

HOW TO CONTACT Submit proposal package, outline, clips, 2-3 sample chapters.

TERMS Responds in 2-4 months.

ARTE PUBLICO PRESS

University of Houston, 4902 Gulf Fwy, Bldg 19, Rm 100, Houston TX 77204-2004. **Fax:** (713)743-2847. **E-mail:** submapp@uh.edu. **Website:** artepublicopress.com. Estab. 1979. Arte Publico Press is the oldest and largest publisher of Hispanic literature for children and adults in the United States. "We are a showcase for Hispanic literary creativity, arts and culture. Our endeavor is to provide a national forum for U.S.-Hispanic literature." Publishes hardcover originals, trade paperback originals and reprints. Book catalog available free. Guidelines online.

NEEDS "Written by U.S.-Hispanics."

HOW TO CONTACT Submissions made through online submission form.

TERMS Pays 10% royalty on wholesale price. Provides 20 author's copies; 40% discount on subsequent copies. Pays $1,000-3,000 advance. Responds in 1 month to queries and proposals; 4 months to mss.

TIPS "Include cover letter in which you 'sell' your book—why should we publish the book, who will want to read it, why does it matter, etc. Use our ms submission online form. Format files accepted are: Word, plain/text, rich/text files. Other formats will not be accepted. Ms files cannot be larger than 5MB. Once editors review your ms, you will receive an e-mail with the decision. Revision process could take up to 4 months."

ASABI PUBLISHING

Asabi Publishing, **E-mail:** submissions@asabipublishing.com. **Website:** www.asabipublishing.com. **Contact:** Tressa Sanders, publisher. Estab. 2004. Publishes hardcover, mass market and trade paperback originals. Book catalog online. Guidelines online.

IMPRINTS Solomon Publishing Group-Sweden.

NEEDS Anything religious or spiritual, astrology, ghosts, aliens.

HOW TO CONTACT Submit professional query letter.

TERMS Pays 40% royalty on wholesale or list price. Pays up to $500 advance. Responds in 1 month to queries and proposals, 2-6 months to mss.

AUTUMN HOUSE PRESS

87½ Westwood St., Pittsburgh PA 15211. (412)381-4261. **E-mail:** info@autumnhouse.org. **Website:** www.autumnhouse.org. **Contact:** Christine Stroud, Editor-in-Chief. Estab. 1998. "We are a nonprofit literary press specializing in high-quality poetry, fiction, and nonfiction. Our editions are beautifully designed and printed, and they are distributed nationally. Approximately one-third of our sales are to college litera-ture and creative writing classes." Member CLMP and Academy of American Poets. "We distribute our own titles. We do extensive national promotion through ads, web-marketing, reading tours, book fairs and conferences. We are open to all genres. The quality of writing concerns us, not the genre. You can also learn about our annual Fiction Prize, Poetry Prize, Nonfiction Prize, and Chapbook Award competitions, as well as our online journal, *Coal Hill Review*. (Please note that Autumn House accepts unsolicited mss *only* through these competitions.)" Publishes hardcover, trade paperback, and electronic originals. Format: ac-id-free paper; offset printing; perfect and casebound (cloth) bound; sometimes contains illustrations. Aver-age print order: 1,000. Debut novel print order: 1,000. Catalog online. Guidelines online.

NEEDS Holds competition/award for short stories, novels, story collections, memoirs, nonfiction. *We ask that all submissions from authors new to Autumn House come through one of our annual contests.* See website for official guidelines. Responds to queries in 2 days. Accepts mss only through contest. Never cri-tiques/comments on rejected mss.

HOW TO CONTACT "Submit only through our an-nual contest. The competition is tough, so submit only your best work!"

TERMS Pays 7% royalty on wholesale price. Pays $0-2,500 advance. Responds in 1-3 days on queries and proposals; 3 months on mss.

TIPS "The competition to publish with Autumn House is very tough. Submit only your best work."

AVON ROMANCE

Harper Collins Publishers, 10 E. 53 St., New York NY 10022. **E-mail:** info@avonromance.com. **Website:** www.avonromance.com. Estab. 1941. Avon has been publishing award-winning books since 1941. It is rec-ognized for having pioneered the historical romance category and continues to bring the best of commer-cial literature to the broadest possible audience. Pub-lishes paperback and digital originals and reprints.

HOW TO CONTACT Submit a query and ms via the online submission form.

BAEN BOOKS

P.O. Box 1188, Wake Forest NC 27588. (919)570-1640. **E-mail:** info@baen.com. **Website:** www.baen.com. Estab. 1983. "We publish only science fiction and fan-tasy. Writers familiar with what we have published in

the past will know what sort of material we are most likely to publish in the future: powerful plots with sol-id scientific and philosophical underpinnings are the sine qua non for consideration for science fiction sub-missions. As for fantasy, any magical system must be both rigorously coherent and integral to the plot, and overall the work must at least strive for originality."

NEEDS "Style: Simple is generally better; in our opinion good style, like good breeding, never calls at-tention to itself. Length: 100,000-130,000 words Gen-erally we are uncomfortable with mss under 100,000 words, but if your novel is really wonderful send it along regardless of length."

HOW TO CONTACT "Query letters are not neces-sary. We prefer to see complete mss accompanied by a synopsis. We prefer not to see simultaneous submissions. Electronic submissions are strongly preferred. *We no longer accept submissions by e-mail.* Send ms by using the submission form at: ftp.baen.com/Slush/submit.aspx. No disks unless requested. Attach ms as a Rich Text Format (.rtf) file. Any other format will not be considered."

TERMS Responds to mss within 12-18 months.

BAEN PUBLISHING ENTERPRISES

P.O. Box 1188, Wake Forest NC 27588. (919)570-1640. **E-mail:** info@baen.com; toni@baen.com. **Website:** www.baen.com. Estab. 1983. Publishes hardcover, trade paperback, and mass market paperback origi-nals and reprints. Book catalog available free. Guide-lines online.

HOW TO CONTACT Submit synopsis and complete ms. "Electronic submissions are strongly preferred. Attach ms as a Rich Text Format (.rtf) file. Any other format will not be considered." Additional submission guidelines online. Include estimated word count, brief bio. Send SASE or IRC. Responds in 9-12 months. No simultaneous submissions. Sometimes comments on rejected mss.

TERMS Responds in 9-12 months to mss.

TIPS "Keep an eye and a firm hand on the overall story you are telling. Style is important but less impor-tant than plot. Good style, like good breeding, never calls attention to itself. Read *Writing to the Point*, by Algis Budrys. We like to maintain long-term relation-ships with authors."

Ⓐ BALLANTINE BOOKS

Imprint of Penguin Random House, Inc., 1745 Broad-way, 18th Floor, New York NY 10019. (212)782-9000. **Website:** www.penguinrandomhouse.com. Estab.

1952. Ballantine Bantam Dell publishes a wide variety of nonfiction and fiction. Publishes hardcover, trade paperback, mass market paperback originals. Guidelines online.

HOW TO CONTACT Agented submissions only.

Ⓐ BANCROFT PRESS

P.O. Box 65360, Baltimore MD 21209-9945. (410)358-0658. **Fax:** (410)764-1967. **E-mail:** bruceb@bancroftpress.com. **Website:** www.bancroftpress.com. **Contact:** Bruce Bortz, editor/publisher (memoirs, health, investment, politics, history, humor, literary novels, mystery/thrillers, chick lit, young adult). Estab. 1992. "Bancroft Press is a general trade publisher. Our only mandate is 'books that enlighten.' Our most recent emphasis, with 'The Missing Kennedy' and 'Both Sides of the Line,' has been on memoirs." Publishes hardcover and trade paperback originals as well as e-books and audiobooks. Guidelines online.

HOW TO CONTACT Submit complete ms.

TERMS Pays 8-15% royalty on retail price. Pays $750-2,500 advances. Responds in 6-12 months.

TIPS "We advise writers to visit our website and to be familiar with our previous work. Patience is the number one attribute contributors must have. It takes us a very long time to get through submitted material, because we are such a small company. Also, we only publish 4-6 books per year, so it may take a long time for your optioned book to be published. We like to be able to market our books to be used in schools and in libraries. We prefer fiction that bucks trends and moves in a new direction. We are especially interested in mysteries and humor (especially humorous mysteries)."

Ⓐ BARBOUR PUBLISHING, INC.

P.O. Box 719, Urichsville OH 44683. **E-mail:** submissions@barbourbooks.com. **Website:** www.barbourbooks.com. Estab. 1981. "Barbour Books publishes inspirational/devotional material that is nondenominational and evangelical in nature. We're a Christian evangelical publisher." Specializes in short, easy-to-read Christian bargain books. "Faithfulness to the Bible and Jesus Christ are the bedrock values behind every book Barbour's staff produces."

💬 "We no longer accept unsolicited submissions unless they are submitted through professional literary agencies. For more information, we encourage new fiction authors to join a professional writers organization like American Christian Fiction Writers."

FREDERIC C. BEIL, PUBLISHER, INC.

609 Whitaker St., Savannah GA 31401. (912)233-2446. **E-mail:** fcb@beil.com. **Website:** www.beil.com. **Contact:** Frederic Beil. Estab. 1982. Beil publishes books in the fields of biography, history, and fiction. While under way, Beil has published authors of meaningful works and adhered to high standards in bookmaking craftsman. Publishes original titles in hardcover, softcover, and e-book. Catalog online. Upon agreement with author, Beil will provide guidelines to author.

IMPRINTS The Sandstone Press.

HOW TO CONTACT Query with SASE.

TERMS Pays 7.5% royalty on retail price. Does not pay advance. Responds in 1 week to queries.

TIPS "Our objectives are to offer carefully selected texts, to adhere to high standards in the choice of materials and in bookmaking craftsmanship; to produce books that exemplify good taste in format and design; and to maintain the lowest cost consistent with quality."

BELLEBOOKS

P.O. Box 300921, Memphis TN 38130. (901)344-9024. **Fax:** (901)344-9068. **E-mail:** bellebooks@bellebooks.com. **Website:** www.bellebooks.com. Estab. 1999. BelleBooks began by publishing Southern fiction. It has become a "second home" for many established authors, who also continue to publish with major publishing houses. Guidelines online.

NEEDS "Yes, we'd love to find the next Harry Potter, but our primary focus for the moment is publishing for the teen market."

HOW TO CONTACT Query e-mail with brief synopsis and credentials/credits with full ms attached (RTF format preferred).

TIPS "Our list aims for the teen reader and the crossover market. If you're a 'Southern Louise Rennison,' that would catch our attention. Humor is always a plus. We'd love to see books featuring teen boys as protagonists. We're happy to see dark edgy books on serious subjects."

BELLEVUE LITERARY PRESS

New York University School of Medicine, Dept. of Medicine, NYU School of Medicine, 550 First Avenue, OBV 612, New York NY 10016. (212)263-7802. **E-mail:** blpsubmissions@gmail.com. **Website:** blpress.org. **Contact:** Erika Goldman, publisher/editorial director. Estab. 2005. "Publishes literary and authoritative fiction and nonfiction at the nexus of the arts and the sciences, with a special focus on medicine. As our authors explore cultural and historical representations of the human body, illness, and health, they address the impact of scientific and medical practice on the individual and society."

HOW TO CONTACT Submit complete ms.

TIPS "We are a project of New York University's School of Medicine and while our standards reflect NYU's excellence in scholarship, humanistic medicine, and science, our authors need not be affiliated with NYU. We are not a university press and do not receive any funding from NYU. Our publishing operations are financed exclusively by foundation grants, private donors, and book sales revenue."

Ⓐ BERKLEY

Penguin Group (USA) Inc., 375 Hudson St., New York NY 10014. **Website:** penguin.com. Estab. 1955. The Berkley Publishing Group publishes a variety of general nonfiction and fiction including the traditional categories of romance, mystery and science fiction. Publishes paperback and mass market originals and reprints.

Ⓠ "Due to the high volume of mss received, most Penguin Group (USA) Inc. imprints do not normally accept unsolicited mss. The preferred and standard method for having mss considered for publication by a major publisher is to submit them through an established literary agent."

IMPRINTS Ace; Jove; Heat; Sensation; Berkley Prime Crime; Berkley Caliber.

NEEDS No occult fiction.

HOW TO CONTACT Prefers agented submissions.

BETHANY HOUSE PUBLISHERS

Division of Baker Publishing Group, 6030 E. Fulton Rd., Ada MI 49301. (616)676-9185. **Fax:** (616)676-9573. **Website:** bakerpublishinggroup.com/bethanyhouse. Estab. 1956. Bethany House Publishers specializes in books that communicate Biblical truth and assist people in both spiritual and practical areas of life. Considers unsolicited work only through a professional literary agent or through ms submission services, Authonomy or Christian Manuscript Submissions. Guidelines online. *All unsolicited mss returned unopened.* Publishes hardcover and trade paperback originals, mass market paperback reprints. Book catalog for 9 x 12 envelope and 5 first-class stamps.

TERMS Pays royalty on net price. Pays advance. Responds in 3 months to queries.

TIPS "Bethany House Publishers' publishing program relates Biblical truth to all areas of life—whether in the framework of a well-told story, of a challenging book for spiritual growth, or of a Bible reference work. We are seeking high-quality fiction and nonfiction that will inspire and challenge our audience."

Ⓐ BEYOND WORDS PUBLISHING, INC.

20827 NW Cornell Rd., Suite 500, Hillsboro OR 97124. (503)531-8700. **Fax:** (503)531-8773. **E-mail:** info@beyondword.com. **Website:** www.beyondword. com. **Contact:** Submissions Department (for agents only). Estab. 1984. "At this time, we are not accepting any unsolicited queries or proposals, and recommend that all authors work with a literary agent in submitting their work." Publishes hardcover and trade paperback originals and paperback reprints.

HOW TO CONTACT Agent should submit query letter with proposal, including author bio, 5 sample chapters, complete synopsis of book, market analysis, SASE.

BILINGUAL REVIEW PRESS

Hispanic Research Center, Arizona State University, P.O. Box 875303, Tempe AZ 85287-5303. (480)965-3867. **Fax:** (480)965-0315. **E-mail:** brp@asu.edu. **Website:** www.asu.edu/brp. **Contact:** Gary Francisco Keller, publisher. Estab. 1973. "We are always on the lookout for Chicano, Puerto Rican, Cuban American, or other U.S. Hispanic themes with strong and serious literary qualities and distinctive and intellectually important topics."

HOW TO CONTACT Query with SASE. Query should describe book, plot summary, sample chapter, and any other information relevant to the rationale, content, audience, etc., for the book.

TERMS Responds in 3-4 weeks for queries; 3-4 months on requested mss.

TIPS "Writers should take the utmost care in assuring that their mss are clean, grammatically impeccable, and have perfect spelling. This is true not only of the English but the Spanish as well. All accent marks need to be in place as well as other diacritical marks. When these are missing it's an immediate first indication that the author does not really know Hispanic culture and is not equipped to write about it. We are interested in publishing creative literature that treats the U.S Hispanic experience in a distinctive, creative, revealing way. The kind of books that we publish we keep in print for a very long time irrespective of sales. We are busy establishing and preserving a U.S. Hispanic canon of creative literature."

BKMK PRESS

University of Missouri - Kansas City, 5101 Rockhill Rd., Kansas City MO 64110-2499. (816)235-1168. **Fax:** (816)235-2611. **E-mail:** bkmk@umkc.edu. **Website:** newletters.org. Estab. 1971. "BkMk Press publishes fine literature. Reading period February-June." Publishes trade paperback originals. Guidelines online.

HOW TO CONTACT Query with SASE.

TERMS Responds in 4-6 months to queries.

TIPS "We skew toward readers of literature, particularly contemporary writing. Because of our limited number of titles published per year, we discourage apprentice writers or 'scattershot' submissions."

Ⓢ BLACK LAWRENCE PRESS

E-mail: editors@blacklawrencepress.com. **Website:** www.blacklawrencepress.com. **Contact:** Diane Goettel, executive editor. Estab. 2003. Black Lawrence press seeks to publish intriguing books of literature—novels, short story collections, poetry collections, chapbooks, anthologies, and creative nonfiction. Will also publish the occasional translation from German. Publishes 15-20 books/year, mostly poetry and fiction. Mss are selected through open submission and competition. Books are 20-400 pages, offset-printed or high-quality POD, perfect-bound, with 4-color cover.

HOW TO CONTACT Submit complete ms.

TERMS Pays royalties. Responds in 6 months to mss.

BLACK ROSE WRITING

P.O. Box 1540, Castroville TX 78009. **E-mail:** creator@blackrosewriting.com. **Website:** www.blackrosewriting.com. **Contact:** Reagan Rothe. Estab. 2006. Black Rose Writing is an independent publishing house that strongly believes in developing a personal relationship with their authors. The Texas-based publishing company doesn't see authors as clients or just another number on a page, but rather as individual people. People who deserve an honest review of their material and to be paid traditional royalties without ever paying any fees to be published. Publishes fiction and nonfiction. Catalog online. Guidelines online.

IMPRINTS DigiTerra Publishing, Bookend Design

HOW TO CONTACT "Our preferred submission method is via Authors.me, please click 'Submit Here' on our website."

TERMS Royalties start at 10%, e-book royalties 15% (25-30% net). Responds in 3-6 weeks on queries; 1-2 months on mss.

BLACK VELVET SEDUCTIONS PUBLISHING

E-mail: ric@blackvelvetseductions.com. **E-mail:** submissions@blackvelvetseductions.com. **Website:** www.blackvelvetseductions.com. **Contact:** Richard Savage, CEO. Estab. 2005. "We publish across a wide range of romance sub-genres, from soft sweet romance to supernatural romance, domestic discipline to highly erotic romance stories containing D/s and BDSM relationships. We are looking for authors who take something ordinary and make it extraordinary. We want stories with well-developed multi-dimensional characters with back-stories, a high degree of emotional impact, with strong sexual tension between the heroine and hero, and stories that contain strong internal conflict. We prefer stories told in the third person viewpoint, but will consider first person narratives. We put the emphasis on romance, rather than just the erotic. Although we will consider a high level of erotic content, it needs to be in the context of a romance story line. The plots may twist and turn and be full of passion, but please remember that our audience likes a happy ending. Do not be afraid to approach us with a nontraditional character or plot." Publishes trade paperback and electronic originals and reprints. Catalog free or online. Guidelines online.

NEEDS All stories must have a strong romance element. "There are very few sexual taboos in our erotic line. We tend to give our authors the widest latitude. If it is safe, sane, and consensual we will allow our authors latitude to show us the eroticism. However, we will not consider mss with any of the following: bestiality (sex with animals), necrophilia (sex with dead people), pedophillia (sex with children)."

HOW TO CONTACT Only accepts electronic submissions.

TERMS Pays 10% royalty for paperbacks; 50% royalty for electronic books. Responds as swiftly as possible

TIPS "We publish romance and erotic romance. We look for books written in very deep point of view. Shallow point of view remains the number one reason we reject mss in which the storyline generally works."

JOHN F. BLAIR, PUBLISHER

1406 Plaza Dr., Winston-Salem NC 27103. (336)768-1374. **Fax:** (336)768-9194. **E-mail:** editorial@blairpub.com. **Website:** www.blairpub.com. **Contact:** Carolyn Sakowski, president. Estab. 1954. No poetry, young adult, children's, science fiction. Fiction must be set in southern U.S. or author must have strong Southern connection. Catalog online. Guidelines online.

NEEDS "We specialize in regional books, with an emphasis on nonfiction categories such as history, travel, folklore, and biography. We publish only one or two works of fiction each year. Fiction submitted to us should have some connection with the Southeast. We do not publish children's books, poetry, or category fiction such as romances, science fiction, or spy thrillers. We do not publish collections of short stories, essays, or newspaper columns." Does not want fiction set outside southern U.S.

HOW TO CONTACT Accepts unsolicited mss. Any fiction submitted should have some connection with the Southeast, either through setting or author's background. Send a cover letter, giving a synopsis of the book. Include the first 2 chapters (at least 50 pages) of the ms. "You may send the entire ms if you wish. If you choose to send only samples, please include the projected word length of your book and estimated completion date in your cover letter. Send a biography of the author, including publishing credits and credentials."

TERMS Pays royalties. Pays negotiable advance. Responds in 3-6 months.

TIPS "We are primarily interested in nonfiction titles. Most of our titles have a tie-in with North Carolina or the southeastern United States, we do not accept short story collections. Please enclose a cover letter and outline with the ms. We prefer to review queries before we are sent complete mss. Queries should include an approximate word count."

BLAZEVOX [BOOKS]

131 Euclid Ave., Kenmore NY 14217. **E-mail:** editor@blazevox.org. **Website:** www.blazevox.org. **Contact:** Geoffrey Gatza, editor/publisher. Estab. 2005. "We are a major publishing presence specializing in innovative fictions and wide-ranging fields of innovative forms of poetry and prose. Our goal is to publish works that are challenging, creative, attractive, and yet affordable to individual readers. Articles of submission depend on many criteria, but overall items submitted must conform to one ethereal trait, your work must not suck. This put plainly, bad art should be punished; we will not promote it. However, all submissions will be reviewed and the author will receive feedback. We are human too." Guidelines online.

NEEDS Submit complete ms via e-mail.

TERMS Pays 10% royalties on fiction and poetry books, based on net receipts. This amount may be split across multiple contributors. "We do not pay advances."

TIPS "We actively contract and support authors who tour, read and perform their work, play an active part of the contemporary literary scene, and seek a readership."

BLIND EYE BOOKS

1141 Grant St., Bellingham WA 98225. **E-mail:** editor@blindeyebooks.com. **Website:** www.blindeyebooks.com. **Contact:** Nicole Kimberling, editor. Estab. 2007. "Blind Eye Books publishes science fiction, fantasy and paranormal romance novels featuring gay or lesbian protagonists. We do not publish short story collections, poetry, erotica, horror or nonfiction. We would hesitate to publish any ms that is less than 70,000 or over 150,000 words." Guidelines online.

HOW TO CONTACT Submit complete ms with cover letter. Accepts queries by snail mail. Send disposable copy of ms and SASE for reply only. Does not return rejected mss. Authors living outside the U.S. can e-mail the editor for submission guidelines.

BOA EDITIONS, LTD.

P.O. Box 30971, Rochester NY 14603. (585)546-3410. **Fax:** (585)546-3913. **E-mail:** contact@boaeditions.org. **Website:** www.boaeditions.org. **Contact:** Ron Martin-Dent, Director of Publicity and Production; Peter Conners, Publisher. Estab. 1976. BOA Editions, Ltd., a not-for-profit publisher of poetry, short fiction, and poetry-in-translation, fosters readership and appreciation of contemporary literature. By identifying, cultivating, and publishing both new and established poets and selecting authors of unique literary talent, BOA brings high-quality literature to the public. Publishes hardcover, trade paperback, and digital e-book originals. Book catalog online. Guidelines online.

NEEDS BOA publishes literary fiction through its American Reader Series. While aesthetic quality is subjective, our fiction will be by authors more concerned with the artfulness of their writing than the twists and turns of plot. "Our strongest current interest is in short story collections (and short-short story collections). We strongly advise you to read our published fiction collections." *Temporarily closed to novel/collection submissions.*

TERMS Negotiates royalties. Pays variable advance. Responds in 1 week to queries; 5 months to mss.

BOLD STROKES BOOKS, INC.

P.O. Box 249, Valley Falls NY 12094. (518)677-5127. **Fax:** (518)677-5291. **E-mail:** sandy@boldstrokesbooks.com. **E-mail:** submissions@boldstrokesbooks. com. **Website:** www.boldstrokesbooks.com. **Contact:** Sandy Lowe, senior editor. Estab. 2004. Publishes trade paperback originals and reprints; electronic originals and reprints. Guidelines online.

IMPRINTS BSB Fiction; Victory Editions Lesbian Fiction; Liberty Editions Gay Fiction; Soliloquy Young Adult; Heat Stroke Erotica.

NEEDS "Submissions should have a gay, lesbian, transgendered, or bisexual focus and should be positive and life-affirming." We do not publish any non-LGBTQI focused works.

HOW TO CONTACT Submit completed ms with bio, cover letter, and synopsis—electronically only.

TERMS Sliding scale based on sales volume and format. Pays advance. Responds in 1 month to queries; 2 months to proposals; 4 months to mss.

TIPS "We are particularly interested in authors who are interested in craft enhancement, technical development, and exploring and expanding traditional genre definitions and boundaries and are looking for a long-term publishing relationship. LGBTQ-focused works only."

BOOKFISH BOOKS

E-mail: bookfishbooks@gmail.com. **Website:** book-fishbooks.com. **Contact:** Tammy Mckee, acquisitions editor. BookFish Books is looking for novel lengthed young adult, new adult, and middle grade works in all subgenres. Both published and unpublished, agented or unagented authors are welcome to submit. "Sorry, but we do not publish novellas, picture books, early reader/chapter books or adult novels." Responds to every query. Guidelines online.

HOW TO CONTACT Query via e-mail with a brief synopsis and first 3 chapters of ms.

TIPS "We only accept complete mss. Please do not query us with partial mss or proposals."

❷ BOOKOUTURE

StoryFire Ltd., 23 Sussex Rd., Ickenham UB10 8P, United Kingdom. **Website:** www.bookouture.com. **Contact:** Oliver Rhodes, founder and publisher. Estab. 2012. Publishes mass market paperback and electronic originals and reprints. Book catalog online.

IMPRINTS Imprint of StoryFire Ltd.

NEEDS "We are looking for entertaining fiction targeted at modern women. That can be anything from Steampunk to Erotica, Historicals to thrillers. A distinctive author voice is more important than a particular genre or ms length."

HOW TO CONTACT Submit complete ms.

TERMS Pays 45% royalty on wholesale price. Responds in 1 month.

TIPS "The most important question that we ask of submissions is why would a reader buy the next book? What's distinctive or different about your storytelling that will mean readers will want to come back for more. We look to acquire global English language rights for e-book and Print on Demand."

BOOKS FOR ALL TIMES, INC.

Box 202, Warrenton VA 20188. (540)428-3175. **E-mail:** staff@bfat.com. **Website:** www.bfat.com. **Contact:** Joe David, publisher & editor. Estab. 1981. One-man operation. Publishes paperback originals.

NEEDS literary, mainstream/contemporary, short story collections. "No novels at the moment; hopeful, though, of publishing a collection of quality short stories. No popular fiction or material easily published by the major or minor houses specializing in mindless entertainment. Only interested in stories of the Victor Hugo or Sinclair Lewis quality."

HOW TO CONTACT Query with SASE. Responds in 1 month to queries. Sometimes comments on rejected mss. Joe David, publisher.

TERMS Pays negotiable advance. "Publishing/payment arrangement will depend on plans for the book."

TIPS Interested in "controversial, honest stories which satisfy the reader's curiosity to know. Read Victor Hugo, Fyodor Dostoyevsky and Sinclair Lewis for example."

GEORGE BRAZILLER, INC.

277 Broadway, Suite 708, New York NY 10007. **Website:** www.georgebraziller.com. Publishes hardcover and trade paperback originals and reprints.

NEEDS "We rarely do fiction but when we have published novels, they have mostly been literary novels."

HOW TO CONTACT Submit 4-6 sample chapter(s), SASE. Agented fiction 20%. Responds in 3 months to proposals.

❹ BROADWAY BOOKS

Penguin Random House, 1745 Broadway, New York NY 10019. (212)782-9000. **Fax:** (212)782-9411. **Website:** crownpublishing.com/imprint/broadway-books. Estab. 1995. "Broadway publishes high-quality general interest nonfiction and fiction for adults." Publishes hardcover and trade paperback books.

IMPRINTS Broadway Books; Broadway Business; Doubleday; Doubleday Image; Doubleday Religious Publishing; Main Street Books; Nan A. Talese.

HOW TO CONTACT *Agented submissions only.*
TERMS Pays royalty on retail price. Pays advance.

BRONZE MAN BOOKS

Millikin University, 1184 W. Main, Decatur IL 62522. (217)424-6264. **E-mail:** rbrooks@millikin.edu. **Website:** www.bronzemanbooks.com. **Contact:** Dr. Randy Brooks, editorial board; Edwin Walker, editorial board. Estab. 2006. A student-owned and operated press located on Millikin University's campus in Decatur, Ill., Bronze Man Books is dedicated to integrating quality design and meaningful content. The company exposes undergraduate students to the process of publishing by combining the theory of writing, publishing, editing and designing with the practice of running a book publishing company. This emphasis on performance learning is a hallmark of Millikin's brand of education. Publishes hardcover, trade paperback, literary chapbooks and mass market paperback originals.

NEEDS Subjects include art, graphic design, exhibits, general.

HOW TO CONTACT Submit completed ms.

TERMS Outright purchase based on wholesale value of 10% of a press run. Responds in 1-3 months.

TIPS "The art books are intended for serious collectors and scholars of contemporary art, especially of artists from the Midwestern U.S. These books are published in conjunction with art exhibitions at Millikin University or the Decatur Area Arts Council. The children's books have our broadest audience, and the literary chapbooks are intended for readers of contemporary fiction, drama, and poetry."

◯ THE BRUCEDALE PRESS

P.O. Box 2259, Port Elgin ON N0H 2C0, Canada. (519)832-6025. **E-mail:** info@brucedalepress.ca. **Website:** brucedalepress.ca. Estab. 1994. The Brucedale Press publishes books and other materials of regional interest and merit, as well as literary, historical, and/or pictorial works. Publishes hardcover and trade paperback originals. Book catalog online. "Unless responding to an invitation to submit, query first by Canada Post with outline and sample chapter to book-length mss. Send full mss for work intended for children." Guidelines online.

◯ *Accepts works by Canadian authors only. Book submissions reviewed November to January. Submissions to The Leaf Journal accepted in September and March only. Mss must be in Eng-*

lish and thoroughly proofread before being sent. Use Canadian spellings and style.

TERMS Pays royalty.

TIPS "Our focus is very regional. In reading submissions, I look for quality writing with a strong connection to the Queen's Bush area of Ontario. All authors should visit our website, get a catalog, and read our books before submitting."

BULLITT PUBLISHING

P.O. Box, Austin TX 78729. **E-mail:** bullittpublishing@yahoo.com. **E-mail:** submissions@bullittpublishing.com. **Website:** bullittpublishing.com. **Contact:** Pat Williams, editor. Estab. 2012. "Bullitt Publishing is a royalty-offering publishing house specializing in smart, contemporary romance. We are proud to provide print on demand distribution through the world's most comprehensive distribution channel including Amazon.com and BarnesandNoble.com. Digital distribution is available through the world's largest distibutor of e-books and can be downloaded to reading devices such as the iPhone, Ipod Touch, Amazon Kindle, Sony Reader or Barnes & Noble nook. E-books are distributed to the Apple iBookstore, Barnes & Noble, Sony, Kobo and the Diesel eBook Store. Whether this is your first novel or your 101st novel, Bullitt Publishing will treat you with the same amount of professionalism and respect. While we expect well-written entertaining mss from all of our authors, we promise to provide high-quality, professional product in return." Publishes trade paperback and electronic originals.

IMPRINTS Tempo Romance.

◑ BUSTER BOOKS

16 Lion Yard, Tremadoc Rd., London WA SW4 7NQ, United Kingdom. (020)7720-8643. **Fax:** (022)7720-8953. **E-mail:** enquiries@mombooks.com. **Website:** www.busterbooks.co.uk. **Contact:** Buster Submissions. "We are dedicated to providing irresistible and fun books for children of all ages. We typically publish black & white nonfiction for children aged 8-12 novelty titles-including doodle books."

TIPS "We do not accept picturebook or poetry submissions. Please do not send original artwork as we cannot guarantee its safety." Visit website before submitting.

BY LIGHT UNSEEN MEDIA

325 Lakeview Dr., Winchendon MA 01475. (978)433-8866. **Fax:** (978)433-8866. **E-mail:** vyrdolak@bylightunseenmedia.com. **Website:** bylightunseenmedia.com. **Contact:** Inanna Arthen, owner/editor-in-chief. Estab. 2006. The only small press owned and oper-

ated by a recognized expert in vampire folklore, media and culture, By Light Unseen Media was founded in 2006. "Our mission is to explore and celebrate the variety, imagination and ambiguities of the vampire theme in fiction, history and the human psyche." No other mythic trope remotely approaches the vampire as an ever-changing and evolving mirror of the zeitgeist, deepest fears and most fervent fantasies of each successive generation—and none ever will. Particular trends and treatments rise and fall in popularity, but the vampire will never go out of style. By Light Unseen Media offers fiction and nonfiction that transcends the popular cliches of the day and demonstrates the creative variety and infinite potential of the vampire motif. Publishes hardcover, paperback and electronic originals. Catalog online. Ms guidelines online.

NEEDS "We are a niche small press that *only* publishes fiction relating in some way to vampires. Within that guideline, we're interested in almost any genre that includes a vampire trope, the more creative and innovative, the better. Restrictions are noted in the submission guidelines (no derivative fiction based on other works, such as Dracula, no gore-for-gore's-sake 'splatter' horror, etc.) We do not publish anthologies." Does not want anything that does not focus on vampires as the major theme.

HOW TO CONTACT Submit proposal package including synopsis, 3 sample chapters, brief author bio. "We encourage electronic submissions." *Unsolicited mss will not be considered.*

TERMS Pays royalty of 50-70% on net as explicitly defined in contract. Payment quarterly. No advance. Responds in 3 months.

TIPS "We strongly urge authors to familiarize themselves with the vampire genre and not imagine that they're doing something new and amazingly different just because they're not imitating the current fad."

CALKINS CREEK

Boyds Mills Press, 815 Church St., Honesdale PA 18431. **Website:** www.boydsmillspress.com. Estab. 2004. "We aim to publish books that are a well-written blend of creative writing and extensive research, which emphasize important events, people, and places in U.S. history." Guidelines online.

HOW TO CONTACT Submit outline/synopsis and 3 sample chapters.

TERMS Pays authors royalty or work purchased outright.

TIPS "Read through our recently published titles and review our catalog. When selecting titles to publish, our emphasis will be on important events, people, and places in U.S. history. Writers are encouraged to submit a detailed bibliography, including secondary and primary sources, and expert reviews with their submissions."

CANTERBURY HOUSE PUBLISHING, LTD.

4535 Ottawa Trail, Sarasota FL 34233. (941)312-6912. **Website:** www.canterburyhousepublishing.com. **Contact:** Sandra Horton, editor. Estab. 2009. "Our audience is made up of readers looking for wholesome fiction with good southern stories, with elements of mystery, romance, and inspiration and/or are looking for true stories of achievement and triumph over challenging circumstances. We are very strict on our submission guidelines due to our small staff, and our target market of Southern regional settings." Publishes hardcover, trade paperback, and electronic originals. Book catalog online. Guidelines online.

HOW TO CONTACT Query with SASE and through website.

TERMS Pays 10-15% royalty on wholesale price. Responds in 1 month to queries; 3 months to mss.

TIPS "Because of our limited staff, we prefer authors who have good writing credentials and submit edited mss. We also look at authors who are business and marketing savvy and willing to help promote their books."

CARNEGIE MELLON UNIVERSITY PRESS

5032 Forbes Ave., Pittsburgh PA 15289. (412)268-2861. **Fax:** (412)268-8706. **E-mail:** carnegiemellonuniversitypress@gmail.com. **Website:** www.cmu.edu/universitypress/. **Contact:** Poetry Editor or Nonfiction Editor. Estab. 1972. Publishes hardcover and trade paperback originals. Book catalog and guidelines online.

CAROLINA WREN PRESS

120 Morris St., Durham NC 27701. (919)560-2738. **E-mail:** carolinawrenpress@earthlink.net. **Website:** www.carolinawrenpress.org. **Contact:** Robin Miura, Editor & Director. Estab. 1976. "We publish poetry, fiction, and memoirs by or about people of color, women, gay/lesbian issues, and work by writers from, living in, or writing about the U.S. South." Accepts simultaneous submissions, but "let us know if work has been accepted elsewhere." Guidelines online.

NEEDS "We are no longer publishing children's literature of any topic." Books: 6×9 paper; typeset; various bindings; illustrations. Distributes titles through John F. Blair, Amazon.com, Barnes & Noble, Baker & Taylor, and on their website. "We very rarely accept any un-solicited mss, but we accept submissions for the Doris Bakwin Award for Writing by a Woman in Jan-June of even-numbered years and submissions for the Lee Smith Novel Prize in Jan-June of odd-numbered years."

HOW TO CONTACT "We will accept e-mailed que-ries—a letter in the body of the e-mail describing your project—but please do not send large attachments." All other submissions are accepted via Submittable as part of our annual contests.

TERMS We pay our authors an honorarium. Re-sponds in 3 months to queries; 6 months to mss.

TIPS "Best way to get read is to submit to a contest."

CAVE HOLLOW PRESS

P.O. Drawer J, Warrensburg MO 64093. **E-mail:** gb-crump@cavehollowpress.com. **Website:** www.cave-hollowpress.com. **Contact:** G.B. Crump, editor. Es-tab. 2001. Publishes trade paperback originals. Cata-log online. Guidelines available free.

NEEDS "We publish fiction by Midwestern authors and/or with Midwestern themes and/or settings. Our website is updated frequently to reflect the current type of fiction Cave Hollow Press is seeking."

HOW TO CONTACT Query with SASE.

TERMS Pays 7-12% royalty on wholesale price. Pays negotiable amount in advance. Responds in 1-2 months to queries and proposals; 3-6 months to mss.

TIPS "Our audience varies based on the type of book we are publishing. We specialize in Missouri and Midwest regional fiction. We are interested in talent-ed writers from Missouri and the surrounding Mid-west. Check our submission guidelines on the website for what type of fiction we are interested in currently."

CEDAR FORT, INC.

2373 W. 700 S, Springville UT 84663. (801)489-4084. **Website:** www.cedarfort.com. Estab. 1986. "Each year we publish well over 100 books, and many of those are by first-time authors. At the same time, we love to see books from established authors. As one of the larg-est book publishers in Utah, we have the capability and enthusiasm to make your book a success, whether you are a new author or a returning one. We want to publish uplifting and edifying books that help people think about what is important in life, books people en-joy reading to relax and feel better about themselves, and books to help improve lives. Although we do put out several children's books each year, we are extreme-ly selective. Our children's books must have strong re-ligious or moral values, and must contain outstanding writing and an excellent storyline." Publishes hard-cover, trade paperback originals and reprints, mass market paperback and electronic reprints. Catalog and guidelines online.

IMPRINTS Council Press, Sweetwater Books, Bonnev-ille Books, Front Table Books, Hobble Creek Press, CFI, Plain Sight Publishing, Horizon Publishers, Pioneer Plus.

HOW TO CONTACT Submit completed ms.

TERMS Pays 10-12% royalty on wholesale price. Pays $2,000-50,000 advance. Responds in 1 month on que-ries; 2 months on proposals; 4 months on mss.

TIPS "Our audience is rural, conservative, main-stream. The first page of your ms is very important because we start reading every submission, but good writing and plot keep us reading."

CHANGELING PRESS LLC

315 N. Centre St., Martinsburg WV 25404. **E-mail:** submissions.changelingpress@gmail.com. **Website:** www.changelingpress.com. **Contact:** Margaret Riley, publisher. Estab. 2004. Erotic romance, novellas only (10,000-30,000 words). "We're currently looking for contemporary and futuristic short fiction, single title, series, and serials in the following genres and themes: sci-fi/futuristic, dark and urban fantasy, paranormal, BDSM, action adventure, guilty pleasures (adult con-temporary kink), new adult, menage, bisexual and more, gay, interracial, BBW, cougar (M/F), silver fox (M/M), men and women in uniform, vampires, were-wolves, elves, dragons and magical creatures, other shape shifters, magic, dark desires (demons and hor-ror), and hentai (tentacle monsters)." Publishes e-books. Catalog online. Guidelines online.

IMPRINTS Razor's Edge Press.

NEEDS Please read and follow our submissions guidelines available at changelingpress.com/submis-sions.php. All submissions which do not follow the submissions guidelines will be rejected unread. No lesbian fiction submissions without prior approval, please. Absolutely no lesbian fiction written by men.

HOW TO CONTACT E-mail submissions only. Please read and follow our submissions guidelines available at changelingpress.com/submissions.php. All submissions which do not follow the submissions guidelines will be rejected unread.

TERMS Pays 35% gross royalties on site, 50% gross off site monthly. Does not pay advance. Responds in 1 week to queries.

CHARLESBRIDGE PUBLISHING

85 Main St., Watertown MA 02472. (617)926-0329. **Fax:** (617)926-5720. **E-mail:** tradeeditorial@charlesbridge.com. **E-mail:** yasubs@charlesbridge.com. **Website:** www.charlesbridge.com. Estab. 1980. "Charlesbridge publishes high-quality books for children, with a goal of creating lifelong readers and lifelong learners. Our books encourage reading and discovery in the classroom, library, and home. We believe that books for children should offer accurate information, promote a positive worldview, and embrace a child's innate sense of wonder and fun. To this end, we continually strive to seek new voices, new visions, and new directions in children's literature. As of September 2015, we are now accepting young adult novels for consideration." Publishes hardcover and trade paperback nonfiction and fiction, children's books for the trade and library markets. Guidelines online.

IMPRINTS Charlesbridge Teen: Charlesbridge Teen features storytelling that presents new ideas and an evolving world. Our carefully curated stories give voice to unforgettable characters with unique perspectives. We publish books that inspire teens to cheer or sigh, laugh or reflect, reread or share with a friend, and ultimately, pick up another book. Our mission—to make reading irresistible!

NEEDS Strong stories with enduring themes. Charlesbridge publishes both picture books and transitional bridge books (books ranging from early readers to middle-grade chapter books). Our fiction titles include lively, plot-driven stories with strong, engaging characters. No alphabet books, board books, coloring books, activity books, or books with audiotapes or CD-ROMs.

HOW TO CONTACT Please submit only 1 ms at a time. For picture books and shorter bridge books, please send a complete ms. For fiction books longer than 30 ms pages, please send a detailed plot synopsis, a chapter outline, and 3 chapters of text. If sending a young adult novel, mark the front of the envelope with "YA novel enclosed." Please note, for YA, e-mail submissions are preferred to the following address; yasubs@charlesbridge.com. Only responds if interested. Full guidelines on site.

TERMS Pays royalty. Pays advance. Responds in 3 months.

TIPS "To become acquainted with our publishing program, we encourage you to review our books and visit our website where you will find our catalog."

CHILDREN'S BRAINS ARE YUMMY (CBAY) BOOKS

P.O. Box 670296, Dallas TX 75367. **E-mail:** submissions@cbaybooks.com. **Website:** www.cbaybooks.com. **Contact:** Madeline Smoot, publisher. Estab. 2008. "CBAY Books currently focuses on quality fantasy and science fiction books for the middle grade and teen markets. We are not currently accepting unsolicited submissions. We do not publish picture books." "We are distributed by IPG. Our books can be found in their catalog at www.ipgbooks.com." Brochure and guidelines online.

TERMS Pays authors royalty 10%-15% based on wholesale price. Offers advances against royalties. Average amount $500. Pays advance. Responds in 2 months.

CHRISTIAN FOCUS PUBLICATIONS

Geanies House, Fearn, Tain Ross-shire Scotland IV20 1TW, United Kingdom. (44)1862-871-011. **Fax:** (44)1862-871-699. **E-mail:** submissions@christianfocus.com. **Website:** www.christianfocus.com. **Contact:** Director of Publishing. Estab. 1975. Specializes in Christian material, nonfiction, fiction, educational material.

NEEDS Picture books, young readers, adventure, history, religion. Middle readers: adventure, problem novels, religion. Young adult/teens: adventure, history, problem novels, religion. Average word length: young readers—5,000; middle readers—max 10,000; young adult/teen—max 20,000.

TERMS Responds to queries in 2 weeks; mss in 3-6 months.

TIPS "Be aware of the international market as regards writing style/topics as well as illustration styles. Our company sells rights to European as well as Asian countries. Fiction sales are not as good as they were. Christian fiction for youngsters is not a product that is performing well in comparison to nonfiction such as Christian biography/Bible stories/church history, etc."

CHRONICLE BOOKS

680 Second St., San Francisco CA 94107. **E-mail:** submissions@chroniclebooks.com. **Website:** www.chroniclebooks.com. "We publish an exciting range of books, stationery, kits, calendars, and novelty formats. Our list includes children's books and interactive formats; young adult books; cookbooks; fine art, design, and photography; pop culture; craft, fashion, beauty, and home decor; relationships, mind-body-spirit; innovative formats such as interactive journals, kits, decks, and stationery; and much, much more."

Book catalog for 9x12 SAE and 8 first-class stamps. Ms guidelines for #10 SASE.

NEEDS Only interested in fiction for children and young adults. No adult fiction.

HOW TO CONTACT Submit complete ms (picture books); submit outline/synopsis and 3 sample chapters (for older readers). Will not respond to submissions unless interested. Will not consider submissions by fax, e-mail or disk. Do not include SASE; do not send original materials. No submissions will be returned.

TERMS Generally pays authors in royalties based on retail price, "though we do occasionally work on a flat fee basis." Advance varies. Illustrators paid royalty based on retail price or flat fee. Responds to queries in 1 month.

CITY LIGHTS BOOKS

261 Columbus Ave., San Francisco CA 94133. (415)362-8193. **Fax:** (415)362-4921. **Website:** www.citylights.com. Estab. 1953. Publishes paperback originals. Plans 1-2 first novels this year. Averages 12 total titles, 4-5 fiction titles/year.

NEEDS Fiction, essays, memoirs, translations, poetry and books on social and political issues.

HOW TO CONTACT Submit one-page description of the book and a sample chapter or two with SASE. Does not accept unsolicited mss. Does not accept queries by e-mail. See website for guidelines.

CLEIS PRESS

101 Hudson St., 37th Floor, Suite 3705, Jersey City NJ 07302. **Fax:** (510)845-8001. **Website:** www.cleispress.com. Estab. 1980. Cleis Press publishes provocative, intelligent books in the areas of sexuality, gay and lesbian studies, erotica, fiction, gender studies, and human rights. Publishes books that inform, enlighten, and entertain. Areas of interest include gift, inspiration, health, family and childcare, self-help, women's issues, reference, cooking. "We do our best to bring readers quality books that celebrate life, inspire the mind, revive the spirit, and enhance lives all around. Our authors are practical visionaries; people who offer deep wisdom in a hopeful and helpful manner."

NEEDS "We are looking for high-quality fiction and nonfiction."

HOW TO CONTACT Submit complete ms. Include brief bio, list of publishing credits. Send SASE for return of ms or send a disposable ms and SASE for reply only.

TERMS Responds in 2 month to queries.

TIPS "Be familiar with publishers' catalogs; be absolutely aware of your audience; research potential markets; present fresh new ways of looking at your topic; avoid 'PR' language and include publishing history in query letter."

COACH HOUSE BOOKS

80 bpNichol Ln., Toronto ON M5S 3J4, Canada. (416)979-2217. **Fax:** (416)977-1158. **E-mail:** mail@chbooks.com. **E-mail:** editor@chbooks.com. **Website:** www.chbooks.com. **Contact:** Alana Wilcox, editorial director. Independent Canadian publisher of innovative poetry, literary fiction, nonfiction and drama. Publishes trade paperback originals by Canadian authors. Guidelines online.

HOW TO CONTACT We much prefer to receive electronic submissions. Please put your cover letter and CV into one Word or PDF file along with the ms and e-mail it to editor@chbooks.com. We'd appreciate it if you would name your file following this convention: Last Name, First Name - MS Title. For fiction and poetry submissions, please send your complete ms, along with an introductory letter that describes your work and compares it to at least two current Coach House titles, explaining how your book would fit our list, and a literary CV listing your previous publications and relevant experience.

TERMS Pays 10% royalty on retail price. Responds in 6-8 months to queries.

TIPS "We are not a general publisher, and publish only Canadian poetry, fiction, select nonfiction and drama. We are interested primarily in innovative or experimental writing."

COFFEE HOUSE PRESS

79 13th Ave. NE, Suite 110, Minneapolis MN 55413. (612)338-0125. **Fax:** (612)338-4004. **Website:** www.coffeehousepress.org. Estab. 1984. This successful nonprofit small press has received numerous grants from various organizations including the NEA, the McKnight Foundation and Target. Books published by Coffee House Press have won numerous honors and awards. Example: *The Book of Medicines*, by Linda Hogan won the Colorado Book Award for Poetry and the Lannan Foundation Literary Fellowship. Publishes hardcover and trade paperback originals. Book catalog and ms guidelines online.

NEEDS Seeks literary novels, short story collections and poetry.

HOW TO CONTACT Query first with outline and samples (20-30 pages) during annual reading periods (March 1-31 and September 1-30).

TERMS Responds in 4-6 weeks to queries; up to 6 months to mss.

TIPS "Look for our books at stores and libraries to get a feel for what we like to publish. No phone calls, e-mails, or faxes."

ⒶⓈ CONSTABLE & ROBINSON, LTD.

50 Victoria Embankment, London EC4Y 0DZ, United Kingdom. **E-mail:** info@littlebrown.co.uk. **Website:** https://www.littlebrown.co.uk/ConstableRobinson/about-constable-publisher.page. Publishes hardcover and trade paperback originals. Book catalog available free.

NEEDS Publishes "crime fiction (mysteries) and historical crime fiction." Length 80,000 words minimum; 130,000 words maximum.

HOW TO CONTACT *Agented submissions only.*

TERMS Pays royalty. Pays advance. Responds in 1-3 months.

◎ COTEAU BOOKS

Thunder Creek Publishing Co-operative Ltd., 2517 Victoria Ave., Regina SK S4P 0T2, Canada. (306)777-0170. **Fax:** (306)522-5152. **E-mail:** coteau@coteaubooks.com. **Website:** www.coteaubooks.com. **Contact:** Geoffrey Ursell, publisher. Estab. 1975. "Our mission is to publish the finest in Canadian fiction, nonfiction, poetry, drama, and children's literature, with an emphasis on Saskatchewan and prairie writers. De-emphasizing science fiction, picture books." Publishes chapter books for young readers aged 9-12 and novels for older kids ages 13-15 and for ages 15 and up. Publishes trade paperback originals and reprints. Book catalog available free. Guidelines online.

NEEDS No science fiction. No children's picture books.

HOW TO CONTACT Query.

TERMS Pays 10% royalty on retail price. Responds in 3 months.

TIPS "Look at past publications to get an idea of our editorial program. We do not publish romance, horror, or picture books but are interested in juvenile and teen fiction from Canadian authors. Submissions, even queries, must be made in hard copy only. We do not accept simultaneous/multiple submissions. Check our website for new submission timing guidelines."

COVENANT COMMUNICATIONS, INC.

Deseret Book Company, P.O. Box 416, American Fork UT 84003. (801)756-1041. **Fax:** (801)756-1049. **E-mail:** submissionsdesk@covenant-lds.com. **Website:** www.

covenant-lds.com. **Contact:** Kathryn Gordon, managing editor. Estab. 1958. "Currently emphasizing inspirational, doctrinal, historical, biography, and fiction." Guidelines online.

NEEDS "Mss do not necessarily have to include LDS/Mormon characters or themes, but cannot contain profanity, sexual content, gratuitous violence, witchcraft, vampires, and other such material." We do not accept nor publish young adult, middle grade, science fiction, fantasy, occult, steampunk, or gay/lesbian/bisexual/transgender themes.

HOW TO CONTACT Submit complete ms.

TERMS Pays 6-15% royalty on retail price. Responds in 1 month on queries; 4-6 months on mss.

TIPS "We are actively looking for new, fresh Regency romance authors."

CRAIGMORE CREATIONS

PMB 114, 4110 SE Hawthorne Blvd., Portland OR 97124. (503)477-9562. **E-mail:** info@craigmorecreations.com. **Website:** www.craigmorecreations.com. Estab. 2009.

HOW TO CONTACT Submit proposal package. See website for detailed submission guidelines.

⒮ CRESCENT MOON PUBLISHING

P.O. Box 1312, Maidstone Kent ME14 5XU, United Kingdom. (44)(162)272-9593. **E-mail:** cresmopub@yahoo.co.uk. **Website:** www.crmoon.com. **Contact:** Jeremy Robinson, director (arts, media, cinema, literature); Cassidy Hughes (visual arts). Estab. 1988. "Our mission is to publish the best in contemporary work, in poetry, fiction, and critical studies, and selections from the great writers. Currently emphasizing nonfiction (media, film, music, painting). De-emphasizing children's books." Publishes hardcover and trade paperback originals. Book catalog and ms guidelines free.

IMPRINTS Joe's Press; Pagan America Magazine; Passion Magazine.

NEEDS "We do not publish much fiction at present but will consider high-quality new work."

HOW TO CONTACT Query with SASE. Submit outline, clips, 2 sample chapters, bio.

TERMS Pays royalty. Pays negotiable advance. Responds in 2 months to queries; 4 months to proposals and mss.

TIPS "Our audience is interested in new contemporary writing."

CRESTON BOOKS

P.O. Box 9369, Berkeley CA 94709. **E-mail:** submissions@crestonbooks.co. **Website:** crestonbooks.co.

Estab. 2013. Creston Books is author-illustrator driven, with talented, award-winning creators given more editorial freedom and control than in a typical New York house. Catalog online. Guidelines online.

HOW TO CONTACT Please paste text of picture books or first chapters of novels in the body of e-mail. Words of Advice for submitting authors listed on the site.

TERMS Pays advance.

CRIMSON ROMANCE

Simon & Schuster, Inc., 57 Littlefield St., Avon MA 02322. **E-mail:** editorcrimson@gmail.com. **Website:** crimsonromance.com. **Contact:** Tara Gelsomino, Executive Editor. Estab. 2012. Direct to e-book romance imprint of Simon & Schuster, Inc. Publishes electronic originals and print-on-demand copies. Guidelines online.

NEEDS Crimson seeks submissions featuring strong characters, smart stories, and satisfying romance in 5 popular subgenres: contemporary, historical, paranormal, romantic suspense, and spicy. We're looking for previously unpublished novellas (between 20,000 – 50,000 words) and full-length novels (between 50,000 – 90,000 words). All authors—agented or unagented, beginner or veteran writers—are welcome to submit any works that have not been previously published in whole or in part in any media, including self-publishing (Kindle, CreateSpace, etc.). While your work can include other genre elements, Crimson Romances must focus first and foremost on a couple's emotional journey together towards love. Romances, by nature, must be between consenting adults of any gender, race, creed, etc., and have a happily-ever-after or at least happy-for-now ending. We are strictly a romance publisher and will not look at mss for memoirs or other nonfiction, women's fiction or chick lit, young adult, mysteries and thrillers, horror, or general fiction. We're specifically seeking diverse romances (own voices preferred).

HOW TO CONTACT Please see current submission guidelines online.

TERMS Does not pay advance.

Ⓐ CROWN PUBLISHING GROUP

Penguin Random House, 1745 Broadway, New York NY 10019. (212)782-9000. **Website:** crownpublishing.com. Estab. 1933. Publishes popular fiction and nonfiction hardcover originals. *Agented submissions only.* See website for more details.

IMPRINTS Amphoto Books; Back Stage Books; Billboard Books; Broadway Books; Clarkson Potter; Crown; Crown Archetype; Crown Business; Crown Forum; Harmony Books; Image Books; Potter Craft; Potter Style; Ten Speed Press; Three Rivers Press; Waterbrook Multnomah; Watson-Guptill.

CRYSTAL SPIRIT PUBLISHING, INC.

P.O. Box 12506, Durham NC 27709. **E-mail:** crystalspiritinc@gmail.com. **E-mail:** submissions@crystalspiritinc.com. **Website:** www.crystalspiritinc.com. **Contact:** Vanessa S. O'Neal, Senior Managing Editor. Estab. 2004. "Our readers are lovers of high-quality books that are sold as direct sales, in bookstores, gift shops and placed in libraries and schools. They support independent authors and they expect works that will provide them with entertainment, inspiration, romance, and education. Our audience loves to read and will embrace niche authors that love to write." Publishes hardcover, trade paperback, mass market paperback, and electronic originals. Book catalog and ms guidelines online. Guidelines for submissions are stated on the website.

HOW TO CONTACT Full completed mss can be submitted via the website. Mss submitted by mail must include the cover letter and information as stated in the submission guidelines on the website.

TERMS Pays 20-45% royalty on retail price. Responds in 30-45 days

TIPS "Submissions are accepted for publication throughout the year. Works should be positive and nonthreatening. Typed pages only. Nontyped entries will not be reviewed or returned. Ensure that all contact information is correct, abide by the submission guidelines and do not send follow-up e-mails or calls."

CURIOSITY QUILLS

Whampa, LLC, P.O. Box 2160, Reston VA 20195. (800)998-2509. **Fax:** (800)998-2509. **E-mail:** editor@curiosityquills.com. **E-mail:** acquisitions@curiosityquills.com. **Website:** curiosityquills.com. **Contact:** Alisa Gus. Estab. 2011. Curiosity Quills is a publisher of hard-hitting dark sci-fi, speculative fiction, and paranormal works aimed at adults, young adults, and new adults. Firm publishes sci-fi, speculative fiction, steampunk, paranormal and urban fantasy, and corresponding romance titles under its new Rebel Romance imprint. Catalog available. Guidelines online.

IMPRINTS Curiosity Quills Press, Rebel Romance.

NEEDS Looking for "thought-provoking, mind-twisting rollercoasters—challenge our mind, turn our world upside down, and make us question. Those are the makings of a true literary marauder."

HOW TO CONTACT Submit ms using online submission form or e-mail to acquisitions@curiosity-quills.com.

TERMS Pays variable royalty. Does not pay advance. Responds in 1-6 weeks.

● CURIOUS FOX

Brunel Rd., Houndmills, Basingstoke Hants RG21 6XS, United Kingdom. **E-mail:** submissions@curious-fox.com. **Website:** www.curious-fox.com. "Do you love telling good stories? If so, we'd like to hear from you. Curious Fox is on the lookout for U.K.-based authors, whether new talent or established authors with exciting ideas. We take submissions for books aimed at ages 3-young adult. If you have story ideas that are bold, fun, and imaginative, then please do get in touch!" Guidelines online.

HOW TO CONTACT "Send your submission via e-mail to submissions@curious-fox.com. Include the following in the body of the e-mail, not as attachments: Sample chapters, Résumé, List of previous publishing credits, if applicable. We will respond only if your writing samples fit our needs."

DARK HORSE COMICS, INC.

10956 SE Main St., Milwaukie OR 97222. (503)652-8815. **Fax:** (503)654-9440. **E-mail:** dhcomics@darkhorse.com. **E-mail:** dhsubsproposals@darkhouse.com. **Website:** www.darkhorse.com. "In addition to publishing comics from top talent like Frank Miller, Mike Mignola, Stan Sakai and internationally-renowned humorist Sergio Aragonés, Dark Horse is recognized as the world's leading publisher of licensed comics."

NEEDS Comic books, graphic novels. Published *Astro Boy Volume 10 TPB*, by Osamu Tezuka and Reid Fleming; *Flaming Carrot Crossover #1* by Bob Burden and David Boswell.

HOW TO CONTACT Submit synopsis to dhcomics@darkhorse.com. See website (www.darkhorse.com) for detailed submission guidelines and submission agreement, which must be signed. Include a full script for any short story or single-issue submission, or the first 8 pages of the first issue of any series. Submissions can no longer be mailed back to the sender.

TIPS "If you're looking for constructive criticism, show your work to industry professionals at conventions."

DAW BOOKS, INC.

Penguin Random House, 375 Hudson St., New York NY 10014. (212)366-2096. **Fax:** (212)366-2090. **E-mail:** daw@penguinrandomhouse.com. **Website:** www.dawbooks.com. **Contact:** Peter Stampfel, submissions editor. Estab. 1971. DAW Books publishes science fiction and fantasy. Publishes hardcover and paperback originals and reprints. Guidelines online.

NEEDS "Currently seeking modern urban fantasy and paranormals. We like character-driven books with appealing protagonists, engaging plots, and well-constructed worlds. We accept both agented and un-agented mss."

HOW TO CONTACT Submit entire ms, cover letter, SASE. "Do not submit your only copy of anything. The average length of the novels we publish varies but is almost never less than 80,000 words."

TERMS Pays in royalties with an advance negotiable on a book-by-book basis. Responds in 3 months.

KATHY DAWSON BOOKS

Penguin Random House, 375 Hudson St., New York NY 10014. (212)366-2000. **Website:** kathydawsonbooks.tumblr.com. **Contact:** Kathy Dawson, vice-president and publisher. Estab. 2014. Mission statement: Publish stellar novels with unforgettable characters for children and teens that expand their vision of the world, sneakily explore the meaning of life, celebrate the written word, and last for generations. The imprint strives to publish tomorrow's award contenders: quality books with strong hooks in a variety of genres with universal themes and compelling voices—books that break the mold and the heart. Guidelines online.

HOW TO CONTACT Accepts fiction queries via snail mail only. Include cover sheet with one-sentence elevator pitch, main themes, author version of catalog copy for book, first 10 pages of ms (double-spaced, Times Roman, 12 point type), and publishing history. No SASE needed. Responds only if interested.

TERMS Responds only if interested.

DC UNIVERSE

1700 Broadway, New York NY 10019. **Website:** www.dccomics.com. Imprints: Vertigo, Wildstorm, CMX Manga, DC Direct, Mad, DC Kids, Zuda.

HOW TO CONTACT *No unsolicited submissions.* Recycles unsolicited mss. Artists should contact through Comic Con conventions. See submission guidelines on website for more information. International Comic-Cons.

TERMS Artist's guidelines on website.

ⒶDELACORTE PRESS

an imprint of Random House Children's Books, a division of Penguin Random House LLC, New York, 1745

Broadway, New York NY 10019. (212)782-9000. **Web-site:** randomhousekids.com; randomhouseteens.com. Publishes middle grade and young adult fiction in hard cover, trade paperback, mass market and digest formats.

⬭ All query letters and ms submissions must be submitted through an agent or at the request of an editor.

🅐 DEL REY BOOKS

Penguin Random House, 1745 Broadway, 18th Floor, New York NY 10019. (212)782-9000. **Website:** www.penguinrandomhouse.com. Estab. 1977. Del Rey publishes top level fantasy, alternate history, and science fiction. Publishes hardcover, trade paperback, and mass market originals and mass market paperback reprints.

IMPRINTS Del Rey/Manga, Del Rey/Lucas Books.

HOW TO CONTACT *Agented submissions only.*

TERMS Pays royalty on retail price. Pays competitive advance.

TIPS "Del Rey is a reader's house. Pay particular attention to plotting, strong characters, and dramatic, satisfactory conclusions. It must be/feel believable. That's what the readers like. In terms of mass market, we basically created the field of fantasy bestsellers. Not that it didn't exist before, but we put the mass into mass market."

DIAL BOOKS FOR YOUNG READERS

Imprint of Penguin Group (USA), 345 Hudson St., New York NY 10014. (212)366-2000. **Website:** www.penguin.com/children. Estab. 1961. "Dial Books for Young Readers publishes quality picture books for ages 18 months-6 years; lively, believable novels for middle readers and young adults; and occasional nonfiction for middle readers and young adults." Publishes hardcover originals. Book catalog and guidelines online.

NEEDS Especially looking for lively and well-written novels for middle grade and young adult children involving a convincing plot and believable characters. The subject matter or theme should not already be overworked in previously published books. The approach must not be demeaning to any minority group, nor should the roles of female characters (or others) be stereotyped, though we don't think books should be didactic, or in any way message-y. No topics inappropriate for the juvenile, young adult, and middle grade audiences. No plays.

HOW TO CONTACT Accepts unsolicited queries and up to 10 pages for longer works and unsolicited mss for picture books. Will only respond if interested.

TERMS Pays royalty. Pays varies advance. Responds in 4-6 months to queries.

TIPS "Our readers are anywhere from preschool age to teenage. Picture books must have strong plots, lots of action, unusual premises, or universal themes treated with freshness and originality. Humor works well in these books. A very well-thought-out and intelligently presented book has the best chance of being taken on. Genre isn't as much of a factor as presentation."

DIGITAL MANGA PUBLISHING

1487 West 178th St., Suite 300, Gardenia CA 90248. **Website:** www.dmpbooks.com. "Submissions must be original and not infringe on copyrighted works by other creators. Please note that we are a manga publisher; we do not distribute Western style comics or literary novels. Completed works must contain a minimum of 90 pages of content. Submissions may be in black and white or full color. We accept submissions for all genres of manga which comply to U.S. law and we only accept submissions from persons aged 18 and over. Please do not send your original copies as we cannot return them to you. If your work is published online elsewhere, please feel free to include a link for us to further view your portfolio."

DIVERTIR

P.O. Box 232, North Salem NH 03073. **E-mail:** info@divertirpublishing.com. **E-mail:** query@divertirpublishing.com. **Website:** www.divertirpublishing.com. **Contact:** Kenneth Tupper, Publisher. Estab. 2009. Divertir Publishing is an independent publisher located in Salem, NH. "Our goal is to provide interesting and entertaining books to our readers, as well as to offer new and exciting voices in the writing community the opportunity to publish their work. We seek to combine an understanding of traditional publishing with a unique understanding of the modern market to best serve both our authors and readers." Publishes trade paperback and electronic originals. Catalog online. Guidelines online.

NEEDS "We are particularly interested in the following: science fiction, fantasy, historical, alternate history, contemporary mythology, mystery and suspense, paranormal, and urban fantasy." Does not consider erotica or mss with excessive violence.

HOW TO CONTACT Electronically submit proposal package, including synopsis and query letter with author's bio.

TERMS Pays 10-15% royalty on wholesale price (for novels and nonfiction). Does not pay advance. Responds in 1-3 months on queries; 3-4 months on proposals and mss.

TIPS "Please see our Author Info page (online) for more information."

A◐ DOUBLEDAY CANADA

1 Toronto St., Suite 300, Toronto ON M5C 2V6, Canada. **Website:** www.randomhouse.ca. Random House of Canada, 1 Toronto Street, Suite 300, Toronto ON M5C 2V6 Canada. (416)364-4449. **Website:** www.randomhouse.ca. Publishes hardcover and paperback originals. Averages 50 total titles/year.

HOW TO CONTACT Does not accept unsolicited mss. *Agented submissions only.*

DOWN THE SHORE PUBLISHING

P.O. Box 100, West Creek NJ 08092. **Fax:** (609)812-5098. **E-mail:** info@down-the-shore.com. **Website:** www.down-the-shore.com. **Contact:** Acquisitions Editor. "Bear in mind that our market is regional—New Jersey, the Jersey Shore, the mid-Atlantic, and seashore and coastal subjects." Publishes hardcover and trade paperback originals and reprints. Book catalog online. Guidelines online.

HOW TO CONTACT Query with SASE. Submit proposal package, clips, 1-2 sample chapters.

TERMS Pays royalty on wholesale or retail price, or makes outright purchase. Responds in 3 months to queries.

TIPS "Carefully consider whether your proposal is a good fit for our established market."

◐ DRAGON MOON PRESS

3521 43A Ave., Red Deer AB T4N 3E9, Canada. **Website:** www.dragonmoonpress.com. Estab. 1994. "Dragon Moon Press is dedicated to new and exciting voices in science fiction and fantasy." Publishes trade paperback and electronic originals. Books: 60 lb. offset paper; short run printing and offset printing. Average print order: 250-3,000. **Published several debut authors within the last year.** Plans 5 first novels this year. Averages 4-6 total titles, 4-5 fiction titles/year. Distributed through Baker & Taylor. Promoted locally through authors and online at leading retail bookstores like Amazon, Barnes & Noble, Chapters, etc.

NEEDS "At present, we are only accepting solicited mss via referral from our authors and partners. All mss already under review will still be considered by our readers, and we will notify you of our decision." For solicited submissions: Market: "We prefer mss targeted to the adult market or the upper border of YA.

No middle grade or children's literature, please. Fantasy, science fiction (soft/sociological). No horror or children's fiction, short stories or poetry."

TIPS "First, be patient. Read our guidelines. Not following our submission guidelines can be grounds for automatic rejection. Second, be patient, we are small and sometimes very slow as a result, especially during book launch season. Third, we view publishing as a family affair. Be ready to participate in the process and show some enthusiasm and understanding in what we do. Remember also, this is a business and not about egos, so keep yours on a leash! Show us a great story with well-developed characters and plot lines, show us that you are interested in participating in marketing and developing as an author, and show us your desire to create a great book and you may just find yourself published by Dragon Moon Press."

DUFOUR EDITIONS

P.O. Box 7, 124 Byers Rd., Chester Springs PA 19425. (610)458-5005. **Fax:** (610)458-7103. **Website:** www.dufoureditions.com. Estab. 1948. "We publish literary fiction by good writers which is well received and achieves modest sales. De-emphsazing poetry and nonfiction." Publishes hardcover originals, trade paperback originals and reprints. Book catalog available free.

NEEDS "We like books that are slightly off-beat, different and well-written."

HOW TO CONTACT Query with SASE.

TERMS Pays $100-500 advance. Responds in 3-6 months.

◐ THE DUNDURN GROUP

3 Church St., Suite 500, Toronto ON M5E 1M2, Canada. **Website:** www.dundurn.com. Estab. 1972. Dundurn prefers work by Canadian authors. First-time authors are welcome. Publishes hardcover and trade paperback originals and reprints.

HOW TO CONTACT Query with SASE or submit 3 sample chapter(s), synopsis. Accepts queries by mail. Include estimated word count. Responds in 3-4 months to queries. Accepts simultaneous submissions. No electronic submissions.

A THOMAS DUNNE BOOKS

Imprint of St. Martin's Press, 175 Fifth Ave., New York NY 10010. (212)674-5151. **E-mail:** thomasdunnebooks@stmartins.com. **Website:** www.thomasdunnebooks.com. Estab. 1986. "Thomas Dunne Books publishes popular trade fiction and nonfiction. With an output of approximately 175 titles each year, his group covers a range of genres including commercial and literary fiction, thrillers, biography, politics, sports, popular science, and more. The list is intentionally eclectic and includes a wide range of fiction and nonfiction, from first books to international bestsellers." Publishes hardcover and trade paperback originals, and reprints. Book catalog and ms guidelines free.

HOW TO CONTACT *Accepts agented submissions only.*

Ⓐ DUTTON ADULT TRADE

Penguin Random House, 375 Hudson St., New York NY 10014. (212)366-2000. **Website:** penguin.com. Estab. 1852. "Dutton currently publishes 45 hardcovers a year, roughly half fiction and half nonfiction." Publishes hardcover originals. Book catalog online.

HOW TO CONTACT Agented submissions only. *No unsolicited mss.*

TERMS Pays royalty. Pays negotiable advance.

TIPS "Write the complete ms and submit it to an agent or agents. They will know exactly which editor will be interested in a project."

DYNAMITE ENTERTAINMENT

113 Gaither Dr., Suite 205, Mt. Laurel NJ 8054. **E-mail:** submissions@dynamite.com. **Website:** www.dynamiteentertainment.com.

HOW TO CONTACT Query first. Does not accept unsolicited submissions. Include brief bio, list of publishing credits.

DZANC BOOKS

Dzanc Books, Inc., 2702 Lillian, Ann Arbor MI 48104. **Website:** www.dzancbooks.org.

NEEDS "We're an independent nonprofit publishing literary fiction. We also set up writer-in-residence programs and help literary journals develop their subscription bases." Publishes paperback originals.

HOW TO CONTACT Query with outline/synopsis and 35 sample pages. Accepts queries by e-mail. Include brief bio. Agented fiction: 3%. Accepts unsolicited mss. Considers simultaneous submissions, submissions on CD or disk. Rarely critiques/comments on rejected mss. Responds to mss in 5 months.

TIPS "Every word counts—it's amazing how many submissions have poor first sentences or paragraphs and that first impression is hard to shake when it's a bad one."

Ⓐ THE ECCO PRESS

195 Broadway, New York NY 10007. (212)207-7000. **Fax:** (212)702-2460. **Website:** www.harpercollins.com. Estab. 1970. Publishes hardcover and trade paperback originals and reprints.

NEEDS Literary, short story collections. "We can publish possibly 1 or 2 original novels a year."

HOW TO CONTACT *Does not accept unsolicited mss.*

TERMS Pays royalty. Pays negotiable advance.

TIPS "We are always interested in first novels and feel it's important that they be brought to the attention of the reading public."

☯ EDGE SCIENCE FICTION AND FANTASY PUBLISHING

Hades Publications, Box 1714, Calgary AB T2P 2L7, Canada. (403)254-0160. **Website:** www.edgewebsite.com. **Contact:** Editorial Manager. Estab. 1996. EDGE publishes thought-provoking full length novels and anthologies of Science Fiction, Fantasy and Horror. Featuring works by established authors and emerging new voices, EDGE is pleased to provide quality literary entertainment in both print and pixels. Publishes hardcover, trade paperback and e-book originals. Catalog online. Guidelines online.

IMPRINTS EDGE, EDGE-Lite, Absolute XPress.

NEEDS "We are looking for all types of fantasy, science fiction, and horror - except juvenile, erotica, and religious fiction. Short stories and poetry are only required for announced anthologies." Length: 75,000-100,000/words. Does not want juvenile, erotica, and religious fiction.

HOW TO CONTACT Submit first 3 chapters and synopsis. Check website for guidelines. Include estimated word count.

TERMS Pays 10% royalty on net price. Negotiable advance. Responds in 4-5 months to mss.

WILLIAM B. EERDMANS PUBLISHING CO.

2140 Oak Industrial Dr. NE, Grand Rapids MI 49505. (616)459-4591. **Fax:** (616)459-6540. **E-mail:** info@eerdmans.com. **E-mail:** submissions@eerdmans.com. **Website:** www.eerdmans.com. Estab. 1911. "The majority of our adult publications are religious and most of these are academic or semi-academic in character (as opposed to inspirational or celebrity books), though we also publish general trade books on the Christian life. Our nonreligious titles, most of them in regional history or on social issues, aim, similarly, at an educated audience." Publishes hardcover and paperback originals and reprints. Book catalog and ms guidelines free.

HOW TO CONTACT Query with SASE.

TERMS Responds in 4 weeks.

ELLYSIAN PRESS

E-mail: publisher@ellysianpress.com. **E-mail:** submissions@ellysianpress.com. **Website:** www.ellysianpress.com. **Contact:** Maer Wilson. Estab. 2014. "At Ellysian Press, we seek to create a sense of home for our authors, a place where they can find fulfillment as artists. Just as exceptional mortals once sought a place in the Elysian Fields, now exceptional authors can find a place here at Ellysian Press. We are accepting submissions in the following genres: Fantasy, Science Fiction, Paranormal, Paranormal Romance, Horror, along with Young/New Adult in these genres. Please submit polished mss. It's best to have work read by critique groups or beta readers prior to submission." Publishes fantasy, science fiction, paranormal, paranormal romance, horror, young/new adult in these genres. Catalog online. Guidelines online.

HOW TO CONTACT "We accept online submissions only. Please submit a query letter, a synopsis and the first 10 pages of your ms in the body of your e-mail. The subject line should be as follows: QUERY – Your Last Name, TITLE, Genre." If we choose to request more, we will request the full ms in standard format. This means your ms should be formatted as follows: One inch margins on all sides and a nonjustified right margin, 12-point Times New Roman font, double-spaced, DOC or DOCX. Ensure that your paragraph indentations are done via the ruler. Please DO NOT use the TAB key. There are many online guides that explain how to use the ruler. We accept simultaneous submissions. We accept submissions directly from the author or from an agent. We answer every query and submission. If you do not hear back from us within one week, we most likely did not receive your query. Please feel free to check with us. We are currently accepting the following genres only: Fantasy, Science Fiction, Paranormal, Paranormal Romance, Horror, Young Adult/New Adult in these genres. Please do not submit queries for any genres not listed above. You may e-mail queries to submissions@ellysianpress.com.

TERMS Pays quarterly. Does not pay advance. Responds in 1 week for queries; 4-6 weeks for partials and fulls.

ELM BOOKS

1175 Hwy. 130, Laramie WY 82070. (610)529-0460. **E-mail:** leila.monaghan@gmail.com. **Website:** www.elm-books.com. **Contact:** Leila Monaghan, publisher. "We are eager to publish stories by new writers that have real stories to tell. We are looking for short stories (5,000-10,000 words) with real characters and true-to-life stories. Whether your story is fictionalized autobiography, or other stories of real-life mayhem and debauchery, we are interested in reading them!"

NEEDS "We are looking for short stories (1,000-5,000 words) about kids of color that will grab readers' attentions—mysteries, adventures, humor, suspense, set in the present, near past or near future that reflect the realities and hopes of life in diverse communities." Also looking for middle grade novels (20,000-50,000 words).

HOW TO CONTACT Send complete ms for short stories; synopsis and 3 sample chapters for novels.

TERMS Pays royalties.

ENTANGLED TEEN

Website: www.entangledteen.com. "Entangled Teen and Entangled digiTeen, our young adult imprints publish the swoonworthy young adult romances readers crave. Whether they're dark and angsty or fun and sassy, contemporary, fantastical, or futuristic. We are seeking fresh voices with interesting twists on popular genres."

IMPRINTS Teen Crush; Teen Crave.

NEEDS "We are seeking novels in the subgenres of romantic fiction for contemporary, upper young adult with crossover appeal."

HOW TO CONTACT E-mail using site. "All submissions must have strong romantic elements. YA novels should be 50K to 100K in length. Revised backlist titles will be considered on a case by case basis." Agented and unagented considered.

TERMS Pays royalty.

EYEWEAR PUBLISHING

United Kingdom. **E-mail:** info@eyewearpublishing.com. **Website:** store.eyewearpublishing.com. **Contact:** Dr. Todd Swift, director/editor. Estab. 2012. Eyewear Publishing is an independent press, passionate about producing beautifully designed, fascinating books that remain affordable. "Based in London and New York, we celebrate the best writing in English from the U.K. and abroad." Firm publishes fiction, nonfiction, and poetry. Guidelines online.

IMPRINTS Maida Vale Publishing.

TERMS Royalties vary from 10% to 20% Pays variable advance. Response time varies.

FAMILIUS

1254 Commerce Way, Sanger CA 93657. (559)876-2170. **Fax:** (559)876-2180. **E-mail:** bookideas@familius.com. **Website:** familius.com. **Contact:** Acquisitions. Estab. 2011. Familius is all about strengthening families. Collective, the authors and staff have experienced a wide slice of the family-life spectrum. Some come from broken homes. Some are married and in the throes of managing a bursting household. Some are preparing to start families of their own. Together, they publish books and articles that help families be happy. Publishes hardcover, trade paperback, and electronic originals and reprints. Catalog online and print. Guidelines online.

NEEDS All picture books must align with Familius values statement listed on the website footer.

HOW TO CONTACT Submit a proposal package, including a synopsis, 3 sample chapters, and your author platform.

TERMS Authors are paid 10-30% royalty on wholesale price. Responds in 1 month to queries and proposals; 2 months to mss.

FANTAGRAPHICS BOOKS, INC.

7563 Lake City Way NE, Seattle WA 98115. (206)524-1967. **Fax:** (206)524-2104. **Website:** www.fantagraphics.com. **Contact:** Submissions Editor. Estab. 1976. Publishes comics for thinking readers. Does not want mainstream genres of superhero, vigilante, horror, fantasy, or science fiction. Publishes original trade paperbacks. Book catalog online. Guidelines online.

NEEDS "Fantagraphics is an independent company with a modus operandi different from larger, factory-like corporate comics publishers. If your talents are limited to a specific area of expertise (i.e., inking, writing, etc.), then you will need to develop your own team before submitting a project to us. We want to see an idea that is fully fleshed-out in your mind, at least, if not on paper. Submit a minimum of 5 fully-inked pages of art, a synopsis, SASE, and a brief note stating approximately how many issues you have in mind."

TERMS Responds in 2-3 months to queries.

TIPS "Take note of the originality and diversity of the themes and approaches to drawing in such Fantagraphics titles as *Love & Rockets* (stories of life in Latin America and Chicano L.A.), *Palestine* (journalistic autobiography in the Middle East), *Eightball* (surrealism mixed with kitsch culture in stories alternately humorous and painfully personal), and *Naughty Bits* (feminist humor and short stories which both attack and commiserate). Try to develop your own, equally individual voice; originality, aesthetic maturity, and graphic storytelling skill are the signs by which Fantagraphics judges whether or not your submission is ripe for publication."

FARRAR, STRAUS & GIROUX

18 W. 18th St., New York NY 10011. (646)307-5151. **Website:** us.macmillan.com/fsg. **Contact:** Editorial Department. Estab. 1946. "We publish original and well-written material for all ages." Publishes hardcover originals and trade paperback reprints. Catalog available by request. Guidelines online.

NEEDS Do not query picture books; just send ms. Do not fax or e-mail queries or mss.

HOW TO CONTACT Send cover letter describing submission with first 50 pages.

TERMS Pays 2-6% royalty on retail price for paperbacks, 3-10% for hardcovers. Pays $3,000-25,000 advance. Responds in 2-3 months.

FARRAR, STRAUS & GIROUX FOR YOUNG READERS

Macmillan Children's Publishing Group, 175 Fifth Ave., New York NY 10010. (212)741-6900. **Fax:** (212)633-2427. **E-mail:** childrens.editorial@fsgbooks.com. **Website:** www.fsgkidsbooks.com. Estab. 1946. Book catalog available by request. Ms guidelines online.

NEEDS All levels: all categories. "Original and well-written material for all ages."

HOW TO CONTACT Submit cover letter, first 50 pages by mail only.

TIPS "Study our catalog before submitting."

🦊 FAT FOX BOOKS

The Den, P.O. Box 579, Tonbridge TN9 9NG, United Kingdom. (44)(0)1580-857249. **E-mail:** hello@fatfoxbooks.com. **Website:** fatfoxbooks.com. "Can you write engaging, funny, original and brilliant stories? We are looking for fresh new talent as well as exciting new ideas from established writers and illustrators. We publish books for children from 3-14, and if we think the story is brilliant and fits our list, then as one of the few publishers who accepts unsolicited material, we will take it seriously. We will consider books of all genres." Guidelines online. Currently closed to submissions.

HOW TO CONTACT For picture books, send complete ms; for longer works, send first 3 chapters and estimate of final word count.

Ⓐ FEIWEL AND FRIENDS

Macmillan Children's Publishing Group, 175 Fifth Ave., New York NY 10010. (646)307-5151. **Website:** us.macmillan.com. Feiwel and Friends is a publisher of innovative children's fiction and nonfiction literature, including hardcover, paperback series, and individual titles. The list is eclectic and combines quality and commercial appeal for readers ages 0-16. The imprint is dedicated to "book by book" publishing, bringing the work of distinctive and outstanding authors, illustrators, and ideas to the marketplace. This market does not accept unsolicited mss due to the volume of submissions; they also do not accept unsolicited queries for interior art. The best way to submit a ms is through an agent. Catalog online.

FENCE BOOKS

Science Library 320, Univ. of Albany, 1400 Washington Ave., Albany NY 12222. (518)591-8162. **E-mail:** jessp.fence@gmail.com. **Website:** www.fence-portal.org. **Contact:** Submissions Manager. "Fence Books publishes poetry, fiction, and critical texts and anthologies, and prioritizes sustained support for its authors, many of whom come to us through our book contests and then go on to publish second, third, fourth books." Publishes hardcover originals. Guidelines online.

HOW TO CONTACT Submit via contests and occasional open reading periods.

FILBERT PUBLISHING

Box 326, Kandiyohi MN 56251-0326. **E-mail:** filbertpublishing@filbertpublishing.com. **Website:** filbertpublishing.com. **Contact:** Maurice Erickson, acquisitions. Estab. 2001. "We really like to publish books that creative entrepreneurs can use to help them make a living following their dream. This includes books on marketing, books that encourage living a full life, freelancing, self-help, we'll consider a fairly wide range of subjects under this umbrella. The people who purchase our titles (and visit our website) tend to be in their fifties, female, well-educated; many are freelancers who want to make a living writing. Any well-written ms that would appeal to that audience is nearly a slam dunk to get added to our catalog." Publishes trade paperback and electronic originals and reprints. Catalog online. Guidelines online.

NEEDS "We're thrilled when we find a story that sweeps us off our feet. Fiction queries have been very sparse the last couple of years, and we're keen on expanding our current romance line in the coming year."

HOW TO CONTACT Query via SASE with a proposal package, including a synopsis, 5 sample chapters, information regarding your web platform, and a brief mention of your current marketing plan. If you'd like to submit a query via e-mail, that's fine. However, we get a lot of e-mail and if you don't receive a reply within a couple weeks, don't hesitate to resend.

TERMS Paperback authors receive 10% royalty on retail price. E-books receive 50% net. Responds in 1-2 months.

TIPS "Get to know us. Subscribe to Writing Etc./The Creative Entrepreneur to capture our preferred tone. Dig through our website, you'll get many ideas of what we're looking for. We love nurturing new writing careers and most of our authors have stuck with us since our humble beginning. All new authors begin their journey with us with e-book publication. If that goes well, we move on to print. We love words. We enjoy marketing. We really love the publishing business. If you share those passions, feel free to query."

Ⓢ FLYING EYE BOOKS

62 Great Eastern St., London EC2A 3QR, United Kingdom. (44)(0)207-033-4430. **E-mail:** picturbksubs@no-brow.net. **Website:** www.flyingeyebooks.com. Estab. 2013. Flying Eye Books is the children's imprint of award-winning visual publishing house Nobrow. FEB seeks to retain the same attention to detail and excellence in illustrated content as its parent publisher, but with a focus on the craft of children's storytelling and nonfiction. Guidelines online.

FOLDED WORD

79 Tracy Way, Meredith NH 03253. **Website:** www.foldedword.com. **Contact:** Barbara Flaherty, acquisitions editor. Estab. 2008. Folded Word is a literary micro-press that explores the world, one voice at a time. "Our list includes globally-distributed work by authors from 4 continents. We give individualized attention to the editing and design of each title." Catalog online. Guidelines online.

NEEDS "We are seeking nonformulaic narratives that have a strong sense of place and/or time, especially the exploration of unfamiliar place/time. We are looking for mss that are an escape from the everyday, be it a cleansing laugh, a cathartic cry, a virtual holiday, or even a respite from predictable plots. We are also looking for mss that are ecologically aware.

We enjoy quirky characters, voices that take a chance, humor, and word-play. Please, surprise us."

HOW TO CONTACT "We are only seeking 5,000- to 10,000-word mss that can be published as stand-alone chapbooks and chapbook-length collections of flash fiction. We no longer publish novels."

TERMS Pays royalty. Advance only in rare cases with solicited books. Responds in 60 days for queries. If a full ms is requested, it may take 6 months for a final decision.

TIPS "Please be sure you have read some of our recent titles prior to submitting."

FORWARD MOVEMENT

412 Sycamore St., Cincinnati OH 45202. (513)721-6659; (800)543-1813. **Fax:** (513)721-0729. **E-mail:** editorial@forwardmovement.org. **Website:** www.forwardmovement.org. Estab. 1934. "Forward Movement was established to help reinvigorate the life of the church. Many titles focus on the life of prayer, where our relationship with God is centered, death, marriage, baptism, recovery, joy, the Episcopal Church and more. Currently emphasizing prayer/spirituality." Book catalog free. Guidelines online.

TERMS Responds in 1 month.

TIPS "Audience is primarily Episcopalians and other Christians."

FOUR WAY BOOKS

Box 535, Village Station, New York NY 10014. **E-mail:** editors@fourwaybooks.com. **Website:** www.fourwaybooks.com. Estab. 1993. "Four Way Books is a not-for-profit literary press dedicated to publishing poetry and short fiction by emerging and established writers. Each year, Four Way Books publishes the winners of its national poetry competitions, as well as collections accepted through general submission, panel selection, and solicitation by the editors."

NEEDS Open reading period: June 1-30. Book-length story collections and novellas. Submission guidelines will be posted online at end of May. Does not want novels or translations.

✦ FRANCES LINCOLN CHILDREN'S BOOKS

Frances Lincoln, 74-77 White Lion St., London N1 9PF, United Kingdom. (44)(20)7284-4009. **Website:** www.franceslincoln.com. Estab. 1977. "Our company was founded by Frances Lincoln in 1977. We published our first books two years later, and we have been creating illustrated books of the highest quality ever since, with special emphasis on gardening, walking and the outdoors, art, architecture, design and landscape. In 1983, we started to publish illustrated books for children. Since then we have won many awards and prizes with both fiction and nonfiction children's books."

NEEDS Average word length: picture books—1,000; young readers—9,788; middle readers—20,653; young adults—35,407.

HOW TO CONTACT Query by e-mail.

TERMS Responds in 6 weeks to mss.

FREE SPIRIT PUBLISHING, INC.

6325 Sandburg Rd., Suite 100, Minneapolis MN 55427-3674. (612)338-2068. **Fax:** (612)337-5050. **E-mail:** acquisitions@freespirit.com. **Website:** www.freespirit.com. Estab. 1983. "Free Spirit is the leading publisher of learning tools that support young people's social-emotional health and educational needs. We help children and teens think for themselves, overcome challenges, and make a difference in the world." Free Spirit does not accept general fiction, poetry or storybook submissions. Publishes trade paperback originals and reprints. Book catalog and guidelines online.

NEEDS "Please review catalog and author guidelines (both available online) for details before submitting proposal. If you'd like material returned, enclose a SASE with sufficient postage."

TERMS Responds to proposals in 2-6 months.

TIPS "Our books are issue-oriented, jargon-free, and solution-focused. Our audience is children, teens, teachers, parents and youth counselors. We are especially concerned with kids' social and emotional well-being and look for books with ready-to-use strategies for coping with today's issues at home or in school—written in everyday language. We are not looking for academic or religious materials, or books that analyze problems with the nation's school systems. Instead, we want books that offer practical, positive advice so kids can help themselves, and parents and teachers can help kids succeed."

GERTRUDE PRESS

P.O. Box 28281, Portland OR 97228. (503)515-8252. **E-mail:** editorgertrudepress@gmail.com. **Website:** www.gertrudepress.org. Estab. 2005. "Gertrude Press is a nonprofit organization developing and showcasing the creative talents of lesbian, gay, bisexual, trans, queer-identified and allied individuals. We publish limited-edition fiction and poetry chapbooks plus the biannual literary journal, *Gertrude*." Reads chapbook mss only through contests.

TIPS Sponsors poetry and fiction chapbook contest. Prize is $175 and 50 contributor's copies. Submission guidelines and fee information on website. "Read the journal and sample published work. We are not impressed by pages of publications; your work should speak for itself."

GIVAL PRESS

Gival Press, LLC, P.O. Box 3812, Arlington VA 22203. (703)351-0079. **E-mail:** givalpress@yahoo.com. **Website:** www.givalpress.com. **Contact:** Robert L. Giron, editor-in-chief (area of interest: literary). Estab. 1998. "We publish literary works: fiction, nonfiction (essays, academic), and poetry in English, Spanish, and French." Publishes trade paperback, electronic originals, and reprints. Book catalog online. Guidelines online.

HOW TO CONTACT Always query first via e-mail; provide description, author's bio, and supportive material.

TERMS Pays royalty. Per the contest prize, amount per the content. Outside of contests, yes. Responds in 3-5 months.

TIPS "Our audience is those who read literary works with depth to the work. Visit our website—there is much to be read/learned from the numerous pages."

THE GLENCANNON PRESS

P.O. Box 1428, El Cerrito CA 94530. (510)528-4216. **E-mail:** merships@yahoo.com. **Website:** www.glencannon.com. **Contact:** Bill Harris (maritime, maritime children's). Estab. 1993. "We publish quality books about ships and the sea." Average print order: 500. Member PMA, BAIPA. Distributes titles through Baker & Taylor. Promotes titles through direct mail, magazine advertising and word of mouth. Accepts unsolicited mss. Often comments on rejected mss. Publishes hardcover and paperback originals and hardcover reprints.

IMPRINTS Smyth: perfect binding; illustrations.

HOW TO CONTACT Submit complete ms. Include brief bio, list of publishing credits. Send SASE for return of ms or send a disposable ms and SASE for reply only.

TERMS Pays 10-20% royalty. Responds in 1 month to queries; 2 months to mss.

TIPS "Write a good story in a compelling style."

Ⓐ DAVID R. GODINE, PUBLISHER

15 Court Square, Suite 320, Boston MA 02108. (617)451-9600. **Fax:** (617)350-0250. **E-mail:** info@godine.com. **Website:** www.godine.com. Estab. 1970. "We publish books that matter for people who care." This publisher is no longer considering unsolicited mss of any type. Only interested in agented material.

IMPRINTS Black Sparrow Books, Verba Mundi, Nonpareil.

⊙ GOOSE LANE EDITIONS

500 Beaverbrook Ct., Suite 330, Fredericton NB E3B 5X4, Canada. (506)450-4251. **Fax:** (506)459-4991. **E-mail:** info@gooselane.com. **Website:** www.gooselane.com. Estab. 1954. "Goose Lane publishes literary fiction and nonfiction from well-read and highly skilled Canadian authors." Publishes hardcover and paperback originals and occasional reprints.

NEEDS Our needs in fiction never change: Substantial, character-centered literary fiction. No children's, YA, mainstream, mass market, genre, mystery, thriller, confessional or science fiction.

HOW TO CONTACT Query with SAE with Canadian stamps or IRCs. No U.S. stamps.

TERMS Pays 8-10% royalty on retail price. Pays $500-3,000, negotiable advance. Responds in 6 months to queries.

TIPS "Writers should send us outlines and samples of books that show a very well-read author with highly developed literary skills. Our books are almost all by Canadians living in Canada; we seldom consider submissions from outside Canada. We consider submissions from outside Canada only when the author is Canadian and the book is of extraordinary interest to Canadian readers. We do not publish books for children or for the young adult market."

Ⓐ GRAYWOLF PRESS

250 Third Ave. N., Suite 600, Minneapolis MN 55401. (651)641-0077. **Fax:** (651)641-0036. **Website:** www.graywolfpress.org. Estab. 1974. "Graywolf Press is an independent, nonprofit publisher dedicated to the creation and promotion of thoughtful and imaginative contemporary literature essential to a vital and diverse culture." Publishes trade cloth and paperback originals. Book catalog free. Guidelines online.

NEEDS "Familiarize yourself with our list first." No genre books (romance, western, science fiction, suspense)

HOW TO CONTACT Agented submissions only.

TERMS Pays royalty on retail price. Pays $1,000-25,000 advance. Responds in 3 months to queries.

Ⓐ GREENWILLOW BOOKS

HarperCollins Publishers, 10 E. 53rd St., New York NY 10022. (212)207-7000. **Website:** www.greenwillowblog.com. Estab. 1974. *Does not accept unsolicited mss.* "Unsolicited mail will not be opened and will not be returned." Publishes hardcover originals, paperbacks, e-books, and reprints.

HOW TO CONTACT *Agented submissions only.*

TERMS Pays 10% royalty on wholesale price for first-time authors. Offers variable advance.

Ⓐ GROSSET & DUNLAP PUBLISHERS

Penguin Random House, 345 Hudson St., New York NY 10014. **Website:** www.penguin.com. Estab. 1898. Grosset & Dunlap publishes children's books that show children that reading is fun, with books that speak to their interests, and that are affordable so that children can build a home library of their own. Focus on licensed properties, series and readers. "Grosset & Dunlap publishes high-interest, affordable books for children ages 0-10 years. We focus on original series, licensed properties, readers and novelty books." Publishes hardcover (few) and mass market paperback originals.

HOW TO CONTACT *Agented submissions only.*

TERMS Pays royalty. Pays advance.

Ⓒ GROUNDWOOD BOOKS

128 Sterling Rd., Lower Level, Attention: Submissions, Toronto ON M6R 2B7, Canada. (416)363-4343. **Fax:** (416)363-1017. **E-mail:** submissions@groundwoodbooks.com. **Website:** groundwoodbooks.com. "We are always looking for new authors of novel-length fiction for children of all ages. Our mandate is to publish high-quality, character-driven literary fiction. We do not generally publish stories with an obvious moral or message, or genre fiction such as thrillers or fantasy." Publishes 19 picture books/year; 2 young readers/year; 3 middle readers/year; 3 young adult titles/year, approximately 2 nonfiction titles/year. Visit website for guidelines.

HOW TO CONTACT Submit a cover letter, synopsis and sample chapters via e-mail. "Due to the large number of submissions we receive, Groundwood regrets that we cannot accept unsolicited mss for picture books."

TERMS Offers advances. Responds to mss in 6-8 months.

Ⓐ GROVE/ATLANTIC, INC.

154 W. 14th St., 12th Floor, New York NY 10011. **E-mail:** info@groveatlantic.com. **Website:** www.groveatlantic.com. Estab. 1917. "Due to limited resources of time and staffing, Grove/Atlantic cannot accept mss that do not come through a literary agent. In today's publishing world, agents are more important than ever, helping writers shape their work and navigate the main publishing houses to find the most appropriate outlet for a project." Publishes hardcover and trade paperback originals, and reprints. Book catalog available online.

IMPRINTS Black Cat, Atlantic Monthly Press, Grove Press.

HOW TO CONTACT Agented submissions only.

TERMS Pays 7 ½-12 ½% royalty. Makes outright purchase of $5-500,000. Responds in 1 month to queries; 2 months to proposals; 4 months to mss.

ⒸⓄ GUERNICA EDITIONS

1569 Heritage Way, Oakville ON L6M 2Z7, Canada. (905)599-5304. **Fax:** (416)981-7606. **E-mail:** michaelmirolla@guernicaeditions.com. **Website:** www.guernicaeditions.com. **Contact:** Michael Mirolla, editor/publisher (poetry, nonfiction, short stories, novels). Estab. 1978. Guernica Editions is a literary press that produces works of poetry, fiction and nonfiction often by writers who are ignored by the mainstream. "We also feature a new imprint (MiroLand) which accepts memoirs, how-to books, graphic novels, genre fiction with the possibility of children's and cook books" Publishes trade paperback originals and reprints. Book catalog online. Queries and submissions accepted via e-mail between January 1 and April 30.

IMPRINTS MiroLand

NEEDS "We wish to open up into the fiction world and focus less on poetry. We specialize in European, especially Italian, translations."

HOW TO CONTACT E-mail queries only.

TERMS Pays 8-10% royalty on retail price, or makes outright purchase of $200-5,000. Pays $450-750 advance. Responds in 1 month to queries; 6 months to proposals; 1 year to mss.

HADLEY RILLE BOOKS

P.O. Box 25466, Overland Park KS 66225. **E-mail:** contact@hadleyrillebooks.com. **E-mail:** subs@hadleyrillebooks.com. **Website:** hadleyrillebks.word-press.com. **Contact:** Eric T. Reynolds, editor/publisher. Estab. 2005. Currently closed to submissions. Check website for future reading periods.

TIPS "We aim to produce books that are aligned with current interest in the genres. Anthology markets are somewhat rare in SF these days, we feel there aren't enough good anthologies being published each year and part of our goal is to present the best that we can. We like stories that fit well within the guidelines of the particular anthology for which we are soliciting mss. Aside from that, we want stories with strong characters (not necessarily characters with strong personalities, flawed characters are welcome). We want a sense of wonder and awe. We want to feel the world around the character and so scene description is important (however, this doesn't always require a lot of text, just set the scene well so we don't wonder where the character is). We strongly recommend workshopping the story or having it critiqued in some way by readers familiar with the genre. We prefer clichés be kept to a bare minimum in the prose and avoid re-working old story lines."

HAMPTON ROADS PUBLISHING CO., INC.

65 Parker St, Suite 7, Newburyport MA 01950. **E-mail:** submissions@rwwbooks.com. **Website:** www.red-wheelweiser.com. Estab. 1989. "Our reason for being is to impact, uplift, and contribute to positive change in the world. We publish books that will enrich and empower the evolving consciousness of mankind. Though we are not necessarily limited in scope, we are most interested in mss on the following subjects: Body/Mind/Spirit, Health and Healing, Self-Help. Please be advised that at the moment we are not accepting fiction or novelized material that does not pertain to body/mind/spirit, channeled writing." Publishes and distributes hardcover and trade paperback originals on subjects including metaphysics, health, complementary medicine, and other related topics. Guidelines online.

TERMS Pays royalty. Pays $1,000-50,000 advance. Responds in 2-4 months to queries; 1 month to proposals; 6-12 months to mss.

☺ HARLEQUIN BLAZE

225 Duncan Mill Rd., Don Mills ON M3B 3K9, Canada. (416)445-5860. **Website:** www.harlequin.com. **Contact:** Kathleen Scheibling, senior editor. "Harlequin Blaze is a red-hot series. It is a vehicle to build and promote new authors who have a strong sexual edge to their stories. It is also the place to be for seasoned authors who want to create a sexy, sizzling, longer contemporary story." Publishes paperback originals. Guidelines online.

NEEDS "Sensuous, highly romantic, innovative plots that are sexy in premise and execution. The tone of the books can run from fun and flirtatious to dark and sensual. Submissions should have a very contemporary feel—what it's like to be young and single today. We are looking for heroes and heroines in their early 20s and up. There should be a a strong emphasis on the physical relationship between the couples. Fully described love scenes along with a high level of fantasy and playfulness." Length: 55,000-60,000 words.

TIPS "Are you a *Cosmo* girl at heart? A fan of *Sex and the City*? Or maybe you have a sexually adventurous spirit. If so, then Blaze is the series for you!"

HARLEQUIN DESIRE

233 Broadway, Suite 1001, New York NY 10279. (212)553-4200. **Website:** www.harlequin.com. **Contact:** Stacy Boyd, senior editor. Always powerful, passionate, and provocative. "Desire novels are sensual reads and a love scene or scenes are still needed. But there is no set number of pages that needs to be fulfilled. Rather, the level of sensuality must be appropriate to the storyline. Above all, every Silhouette Desire novel must fulfill the promise of a powerful, passionate and provocative read." Publishes paperback originals and reprints. Guidelines online.

NEEDS Looking for novels in which "the conflict is an emotional one, springing naturally from the unique characters you've chosen. The focus is on the developing relationship, set in a believable plot. Sensuality is key, but lovemaking is never taken lightly. Secondary characters and subplots need to blend with the core story. Innovative new directions in storytelling and fresh approaches to classic romantic plots are welcome." Mss must be 50,000-55,000 words.

TERMS Pays royalty. Offers advance.

☺ HARLEQUIN INTRIGUE

225 Duncan Mill Rd., Don Mills ON M3B 3K9, Canada. **Website:** www.harlequin.com. **Contact:** Denise Zaza, senior editor. Wants crime stories tailored to the series romance market packed with a variety of thrilling suspense and whodunit mystery. Word count: 55,000-60,000. Guidelines online.

HOW TO CONTACT Submit online.

⊕ HARLEQUIN SUPERROMANCE

225 Duncan Mill Rd., Don Mills ON M3B 3K9, Canada. **Website:** www.harlequin.com. **Contact:** Victoria Curran, senior editor. "The Harlequin Superromance line focuses on believable characters triumphing over true-to-life drama and conflict. At the heart of these contemporary stories should be a compelling romance that brings the reader along with the hero and heroine on their journey of overcoming the obstacles in their way and falling in love. Because of the longer length relevant subplots and secondary characters are welcome but not required. This series publishes a variety of story types—family sagas, romantic suspense, Westerns, to name a few—and tones from light to dramatic, emotional to suspenseful. Settings also vary from vibrant urban neighborhoods to charming small towns. The unifying element of Harlequin Superromance stories is the realistic treatment of character and plot. The characters should seem familiar to readers—similar to people they know in their own lives—and the circumstances within the realm of possibility. The stories should be layered and complex in that the conflicts should not be easily resolved. The best way to get an idea of we're looking for is to read what we're currently publishing. The aim of Superromance novels is to produce a contemporary, involving read with a mainstream tone in its situations and characters, using romance as the major theme. To achieve this, emphasis should be placed on individual writing styles and unique and topical ideas." Publishes paperback originals. Guidelines online.

NEEDS "The criteria for Superromance books are flexible. Aside from length (80,000 words), the determining factor for publication will always be quality. Authors should strive to break free of stereotypes, clichés and worn-out plot devices to create strong, believable stories with depth and emotional intensity. Superromance novels are intended to appeal to a wide range of romance readers."

HOW TO CONTACT Submit online.

TERMS Pays royalties. Pays advance.

TIPS "A general familiarity with current Superromance books is advisable to keep abreast of ever-changing trends and overall scope, but we don't want imitations. We look for sincere, heartfelt writing based on true-to-life experiences the reader can identify with. We are interested in innovation."

HARMONY INK PRESS

Dreamspinner Press, 5032 Capital Circle SW, Suite 2 PMB 279, Tallahassee FL 32305. (850)632-4648. **Fax:** (888)308-3739. **E-mail:** submissions@harmonyinkpress.com. **Website:** harmonyinkpress.com. **Contact:** Anne Regan. Estab. 2010. Teen and new adult fiction featuring at least 1 strong LGBTQ+ main character who shows significant personal growth through the course of the story.

NEEDS "We are looking for stories in all subgenres, featuring primary characters across the whole LGBTQ+ spectrum between the ages of 14 and 21 that explore all the facets of young adult, teen, and new adult life. Sexual content should be appropriate for the characters and the story."

HOW TO CONTACT Submit complete ms.

TERMS Pays royalty. Pays $500-1,000 advance.

Ⓐ HARPERCOLLINS

195 Broadway, New York NY 10007. (212)207-7000. **Website:** www.harpercollins.com. HarperCollins, one of the largest English language publishers in the world, is a broad-based publisher with strengths in academic, business and professional, children's, educational, general interest, and religious and spiritual books, as well as multimedia titles. Publishes hardcover and paperback originals and paperback reprints.

NEEDS "We look for a strong story line and exceptional literary talent."

HOW TO CONTACT Agented submissions only. *All unsolicited mss returned.*

TERMS Pays royalty. Pays negotiable advance.

TIPS "We do not accept any unsolicited material."

⊕⊘ HARPERCOLLINS CANADA, LTD.

2 Bloor St. E., 20th Floor, Toronto ON M4W 1A8, Canada. (416)975-9334. **Fax:** (416)975-5223. **Website:** www.harpercollins.ca. Estab. 1989. *HarperCollins Canada is not accepting unsolicited material at this time.*

Ⓐ HARPERCOLLINS CHILDREN'S BOOKS/ HARPERCOLLINS PUBLISHERS

195 Broadway, New York NY 10007. (212)207-7000. **Website:** www.harpercollins.com. HarperCollins, one of the largest English language publishers in the world, is a broad-based publisher with strengths in academic, business and professional, children's, educational, general interest, and religious and spiritual books, as well as multimedia titles. Publishes hardcov-

er and paperback originals and paperback reprints. Catalog online.

IMPRINTS **HarperCollins Australia/New Zealand:** Angus & Robertson, Fourth Estate, HarperBusiness, HarperCollins, HarperPerenniel, HarperReligious, HarperSports, Voyager; **HarperCollins Canada:** HarperFlamingoCanada, PerennialCanada; **HarperCollins Children's Books Group:** Amistad, Julie Andrews Collection, Avon, Joanna Cotler Books, Eos, Laura Geringer Books, Greenwillow Books, HarperAudio, HarperCollins Children's Books, HarperFestival, HarperTempest, HarperTrophy, Rayo, Katherine Tegen Books; **HarperCollins General Books Group:** Access, Amistad, Avon, Caedmon, Ecco, Eos, Fourth Estate, HarperAudio, HarperBusiness, HarperCollins, HarperEntertainment, HarperLargePrint, HarperResource, HarperSanFrancisco, HarperTorch, Harper Design International, Perennial, PerfectBound, Quill, Rayo, ReganBooks, William Morrow, William Morrow Cookbooks; **HarperCollins UK:** Collins Bartholomew, Collins, HarperCollins Crime & Thrillers, Collins Freedom to Teach, HarperCollins Children's Books, Thorsons/Element, Voyager Books; **Zondervan:** Inspirio, Vida, Zonderkidz, Zondervan.

NEEDS "We look for a strong story line and exceptional literary talent."

HOW TO CONTACT Agented submissions only. *All unsolicited mss returned.*

TERMS Negotiates payment upon acceptance. Responds in 1 month, will contact only if interested. Does not accept any unsolicted texts.

TIPS "We do not accept any unsolicited material."

Ⓐ HARPER VOYAGER

Imprint of HarperCollins General Books Group, 195 Broadway, New York NY 10007. (212)207-7000. **Website:** www.harpercollins.com. Estab. 1998. Eos publishes quality science fiction/fantasy with broad appeal. Publishes hardcover originals, trade and mass market paperback originals, and reprints. Guidelines online.

NEEDS No horror or juvenile.

HOW TO CONTACT Agented submissions only. *All unsolicited mss returned.*

TERMS Pays royalty on retail price. Pays variable advance.

Ⓐ HARVEST HOUSE PUBLISHERS

990 Owen Loop, Eugene OR 97402. (541)343-0123. **Fax:** (541)302-0731. **Website:** www.harvesthousepub-lishers.com. Estab. 1974. Publishes hardcover, trade paperback, and mass market paperback originals and reprints.

NEEDS *No unsolicited mss, proposals, or artwork.*

HOW TO CONTACT Agented submissions only.

TERMS Pays royalty.

TIPS "For first time/nonpublished authors we suggest building their literary résumé by submitting to magazines, or perhaps accruing book contributions."

HENDRICK-LONG PUBLISHING CO., INC.

10635 Tower Oaks, Suite D, Houston TX 77070. (832)912-READ. **Fax:** (832)912-7353. **E-mail:** hendrick-long@att.net. **Website:** hendricklongpublishing.com. Estab. 1969. "Hendrick-Long publishes historical fiction and nonfiction about Texas and the Southwest for children and young adults." Publishes hardcover and trade paperback originals and hardcover reprints. Book catalog available. Guidelines online.

HOW TO CONTACT Query with SASE. Submit outline, clips, 2 sample chapters.

TERMS Pays royalty on selling price. Pays advance. Responds in 3 months to queries.

HOLIDAY HOUSE, INC.

425 Madison Ave., New York NY 10017. (212)688-0085. **Fax:** (212)421-6134. **E-mail:** info@holidayhouse.com. **Website:** holidayhouse.com. Estab. 1935. "Holiday House publishes children's and young adult books for the school and library markets. We have a commitment to publishing first-time authors and illustrators. We specialize in quality hardcovers from picture books to young adult, both fiction and nonfiction, primarily for the school and library market." Publishes hardcover originals and paperback reprints. Guidelines for #10 SASE.

NEEDS Children's books only.

HOW TO CONTACT Query with SASE. No phone calls, please.

TERMS Pays royalty on list price, range varies. Responds in 4 months.

TIPS "We need mss with strong stories and writing."

Ⓐ HENRY HOLT

175 Fifth Ave., New York NY 10011. (646)307-5095. **Fax:** (212)633-0748. **Website:** www.henryholt.com. *Agented submissions only.*

HOPEWELL PUBLICATIONS

P.O. Box 11, Titusville NJ 08560. **Website:** www.hopepubs.com. **Contact:** E. Martin, publisher. Estab. 2002. "Hopewell Publications specializes in classic reprints—books with proven sales records that have gone out of print—and the occasional new title of interest. Our catalog spans from 1 to 60 years of publication history. We print fiction and nonfiction, and we accept agented and unagented materials. Submissions are accepted online only." Format publishes in hardcover, trade paperback, and electronic originals; trade paperback and electronic reprints. Catalog online. Guidelines online.

IMPRINTS Egress Books, Legacy Classics.

HOW TO CONTACT Query online using our online guidelines.

TERMS Pays royalty on retail price. Responds in 3 months to queries; 6 months to proposals; 9 months to mss.

HOUGHTON MIFFLIN HARCOURT BOOKS FOR CHILDREN

Imprint of Houghton Mifflin Trade & Reference Division, 222 Berkeley St., Boston MA 02116. (617)351-5000. **Fax:** (617)351-1111. **Website:** www.houghtonmifflinbooks.com. Houghton Mifflin Harcourt gives shape to ideas that educate, inform, and above all, delight. *Does not respond to or return mss unless interested.* Publishes hardcover originals and trade paperback originals and reprints. Guidelines online.

HOW TO CONTACT Submit complete ms.

TERMS Pays 5-10% royalty on retail price. Pays variable advance. Responds in 4-6 months to queries.

HOUSE OF ANANSI PRESS

128 Sterling Rd., Lower Level, Toronto ON M6R 2B7, Canada. (416)363-4343. **Fax:** (416)363-1017. **Website:** www.anansi.ca. Estab. 1967. House of Anansi publishes literary fiction and poetry by Canadian and international writers.

NEEDS Publishes literary fiction that has a unique flair, memorable characters, and a strong narrative voice.

HOW TO CONTACT Query with SASE.

TERMS Pays 8-10% royalties. Pays $750 advance and 10 author's copies.

IDW PUBLISHING

2765 Truxtun Rd., San Diego CA 92106. **E-mail:** letters@idwpublishing.com. **Website:** www.idwpublishing.com. Estab. 1999. IDW Publishing currently publishes a wide range of comic books and graphic novels including titles based on GI Joe, Star Trek, Terminator: Salvation, and Transformers. Creator-driven titles include Fallen Angel by Peter David and JK Woodward, Locke & Key by Joe Hill and Gabriel Rodriguez, and a variety of titles by writer Steve Niles including Wake the Dead, Epilogue, and Dead, She Said. Publishes hardcover, mass market and trade paperback originals.

ILIUM PRESS

2407 S. Sonora Dr., Spokane WA 99037. (509)701-8866. **E-mail:** iliumpress@outlook.com. **Contact:** John Lemon, owner/editor. Estab. 2010. "Ilium Press is a small, 1-person press that I created to cultivate and promote the relevance of epic poetry in today's world. My focus is book-length narrative poems in blank (nonrhyming) metered verse, such as iambic parameter or sprung verse. I am very selective about my projects, but I provide extensive editorial care to those projects I take on." Publishes trade paperback originals and reprints, electronic originals and reprints.

TERMS Pays 20-50% royalties on receipts. Does not pay advance. Responds in 6 months.

IMAGE COMICS

2701 NW Vaughn St., Suite 780, Portland OR 97210. **E-mail:** submissions@imagecomics.com. **Website:** www.imagecomics.com. Estab. 1992. Publishes creator-owned comic books, graphic novels. See this company's website for detailed guidelines. Does not accept writing samples without art.

HOW TO CONTACT Query with 1-page synopsis and 5 pages or more of samples. "We do not accept writing (that is plots, scripts, whatever) samples! If you're an established pro, we might be able to find somebody willing to work with you but it would be nearly impossible for us to read through every script that might find its way our direction. Do not send your script or your plot unaccompanied by art—it will be discarded, unread."

TIPS "We are not looking for any specific genre or type of comic book. We are looking for comics that are well written and well drawn, by people who are dedicated and can meet deadlines."

IMBRIFEX BOOKS

Flattop Productions, Inc., 8275 S. Eastern Ave., Suite 200, Las Vegas NV 89123. (702)309-0130. **E-mail:** acquisitions@imbrifex.com. **Website:** https://imbrifex.com. **Contact:** Mark Sedenquist. Estab. 2016. Based in Las Vegas, Nevada, Imbrifex Books publishes both fiction and nonfiction, with a particular interest in books for road trip aficionados and books that have a connection with Las Vegas and the desert Southwest. Titles are distributed world-wide through Legato Publishers Group, IPS and Audible.com. Guidelines online.

TERMS Pays advance. Responds in 2 months.

○ INSOMNIAC PRESS

520 Princess Ave., London ON N6B 2B8, Canada. (416)504-6270. **Website:** www.insomniacpress.com. Estab. 1992. Publishes trade paperback originals and reprints, mass market paperback originals, and electronic originals and reprints. Guidelines online.

NEEDS "We publish a mix of commercial (mysteries) and literary fiction."

HOW TO CONTACT Query via e-mail, submit proposal.

TERMS Pays 10-15% royalty on retail price. Pays $500-1,000 advance.

TIPS "We envision a mixed readership that appreciates up-and-coming literary fiction and poetry as well as solidly researched and provocative nonfiction. Peruse our website and familiarize yourself with what we've published in the past."

INTERLINK PUBLISHING GROUP, INC.

46 Crosby St., Northampton MA 01060. (413)582-7054. **E-mail:** info@interlinkbooks.com. **E-mail:** submissions@interlinkbooks.com. **Website:** www.interlinkbooks.com. Estab. 1987. Interlink is an independent publisher of general trade adult fiction and nonfiction with an emphasis on books that have a wide appeal while also meeting high intellectual and literary standards. "Our list is devoted to works of literature, history, contemporary politics, travel, art, and cuisine from around the world, often from areas underrepresented in Western media." Publishes hardcover and trade paperback originals. Book catalog and guidelines online.

IMPRINTS Olive Branch Press; Crocodile Books; Interlink Books.

NEEDS "We are looking for translated works relating to the Middle East, Africa or Latin America. The only fiction we publish falls into our 'Interlink World Fiction' series. Most of these books, as you can see in our catalog, are translated fiction from around the world. The series aims to bring fiction from other countries to a North American audience. In short, unless you were born outside the United States, your novel will not fit into the series." No science fiction, romance, plays, erotica, fantasy, horror.

HOW TO CONTACT Query by e-mail. Submit outline, sample chapters.

TERMS Pays 6-8% royalty on retail price. Pays small advance. Responds in 3-6 months to queries.

TIPS "Any submissions that fit well in our publishing program will receive careful attention. A visit to our website, your local bookstore, or library to look at some of our books before you send in your submission is recommended."

INVERTED-A

P.O. Box 267, Licking MO 65542. **E-mail:** Katzaya@gmail.com. **Website:** inverteda.com. **Contact:** Aya Katz, chief editor (poetry, novels, political); Nets Katz, science editor (scientific, academic). Estab. 1985. Books: POD. Distributes through Amazon, Bowker, Barnes Noble. Publishes paperback originals. Guidelines for SASE.

HOW TO CONTACT Does not accept unsolicited mss. Query with SASE. Reading period open from January 2 to March 15. Accepts queries by e-mail. Include estimated word count.

TERMS Pays 10 author's copies. Responds in 1 month to queries; 3 months to mss.

TIPS "Read our books. Read the *Inverted-A Horn*. We are different. We do not follow industry trends."

ITALICA PRESS

595 Main St., Suite 605, New York NY 10044. (917)371-0563. **E-mail:** inquiries@italicapress.com. **Website:** www.italicapress.com. Estab. 1985. "Italica Press publishes English translations of modern Italian fiction and medieval and Renaissance nonfiction." Publishes hardcover and trade paperback originals. Book catalog and guidelines online.

NEEDS "First-time translators published. We would like to see translations of Italian writers who are well-known in Italy who are not yet translated for an American audience."

HOW TO CONTACT Query via e-mail.

TERMS Pays 7-15% royalty on wholesale price; author's copies. Responds in 1 month to queries; 4 months to mss.

TIPS "We are interested in considering a wide variety of medieval and Renaissance topics (not historical fiction), and for modern works we are only interested in translations from Italian fiction by well-known

Italian authors. *Only* fiction that has been previously published in Italian. A *brief* e-mail saves a lot of time. 90% of proposals we receive are completely off base—but we are very interested in things that are right on target."

JOURNEYFORTH

Imprint of BJU Press, 1700 Wade Hampton Blvd., Greenville SC 29614. (864)770-1317. **E-mail:** journeyforth@bjupress.com. **Website:** www.journeyforth.com. **Contact:** Nancy Lohr. Estab. 1974. JourneyForth Books publishes fiction and nonfiction that reflects a worldview based solidly on the Bible and that encourages Christians to live out their faith. JourneyForth is an imprint of BJU Press. Publishes paperback originals. Book catalog available free or online. Guidelines online.

NEEDS "Our fiction is all based on a Christian worldview." Does not want short stories, poetry, picture books, or fiction for the adult market.

HOW TO CONTACT Submit proposal with synopsis, market analysis of competing works, and first 5 chapters.

TERMS Pays royalty. yes Responds in 1 month to queries; 3 months to mss.

TIPS "Study the publisher's guidelines. We are looking for engaging text and a biblical worldview. Will read hard copy submissions, but prefer e-mail queries/proposals/submissions."

JUST US BOOKS, INC.

P.O. Box 5306, East Orange NJ 07019. (973)672-7701. **Fax:** (973)677-7570. **Website:** justusbooks.com. Estab. 1988. "Just Us Books is the nation's premier independent publisher of Black-interest books for young people. Our books focus primarily on the culture, history, and contemporary experiences of African Americans." Guidelines online.

IMPRINTS Marimba Books.

NEEDS Just Us Books is currently accepting queries for chapter books and middle reader titles only. "We are not considering any other works at this time."

TIPS "We are looking for realistic, contemporary characters; stories and interesting plots that introduce both conflict and resolution. We will consider various themes and story-lines, but before an author submits a query we urge them to become familiar with our books."

KAEDEN BOOKS

P.O. Box 16190, Rocky River OH 44116. **Website:** www.kaeden.com. Estab. 1986. "Children's book publisher for education K-3 market: reading stories, fiction/nonfiction, chapter books, science, and social studies materials." Publishes paperback originals. Book catalog and guidelines online.

NEEDS "We are looking for stories with humor, surprise endings, and interesting characters that will appeal to children in kindergarten through third grade." No sentence fragments. Please do not submit: queries, ms summaries, or résumés, mss that stereotype or demean individuals or groups, mss that present violence as acceptable behavior.

HOW TO CONTACT Submit complete ms. "Can be as minimal as 25 words for the earliest reader or as much as 2,000 words for the fluent reader. Beginning chapter books are welcome. Our readers are in kindergarten to third grade, so vocabulary and sentence structure must be appropriate for young readers. Make sure that all language used in the story is of an appropriate level for the students to read independently. Sentences should be complete and grammatically correct."

TERMS Work purchased outright from authors. Pays royalties to previous authors. Responds only if interested.

TIPS "Our audience ranges from kindergarten-third grade school children. We are an educational publisher. We are particularly interested in humorous stories with surprise endings and beginning chapter books."

ⓐ KANE/MILLER BOOK PUBLISHERS

4901 Morena Blvd., Suite 213, San Diego CA 92117. (858)456-0540. **Fax:** (858)456-9641. **E-mail:** submissions@kanemiller.com. **Website:** www.kanemiller.com. **Contact:** Editorial Department. Estab. 1985. "Kane/Miller Book Publishers is a division of EDC Publishing, specializing in award-winning children's books from around the world. Our books bring the children of the world closer to each other, sharing stories and ideas, while exploring cultural differences and similarities. Although we continue to look for books from other countries, we are now actively seeking works that convey cultures and communities within the U.S. We are committed to expanding our picture book list and are interested in great stories with engaging characters, especially those with particularly American subjects. When writing about the experiences of a particular community, we will express a preference for stories written from a firsthand experience." Submission guidelines on site.

NEEDS Picture Books: concept, contemporary, health, humor, multicultural. Young Readers: contemporary, multicultural, suspense. Middle Readers: contemporary, humor, multicultural, suspense. "At this time, we are not considering holiday stories (in any age range) or self-published works."

TERMS If interested, responds in 90 days to queries.

TIPS "We like to think that a child reading a Kane/Miller book will see parallels between his own life and what might be the unfamiliar setting and characters of the story. And that by seeing how a character who is somehow or in some way dissimilar—an outsider—finds a way to fit comfortably into a culture or community or situation while maintaining a healthy sense of self and self-dignity, she might be empowered to do the same."

KAYA PRESS

c/o USC ASE, 3620 S. Vermont Ave. KAP 462, Los Angeles CA 90089. (213) 740-2285. **E-mail:** info@kaya.com. **E-mail:** acquisitions@kaya.com. **Website:** www.kaya.com. Estab. 1994. Kaya is an independent literary press dedicated to the publication of innovative literature from the Asian Pacific diaspora. Publishes hardcover originals and trade paperback originals and reprints. Book catalog available free. Guidelines online.

HOW TO CONTACT Submit 2-4 sample chapters, clips, SASE.

TERMS Responds in 6 months to mss.

TIPS "Audience is people interested in a high standard of literature and who are interested in breaking down easy approaches to multicultural literature."

KELSEY STREET PRESS

Poetry by Women, 2824 Kelsey St., Berkeley CA 94705. **Website:** www.kelseyst.com. Estab. 1974. "A Berkeley, California press publishing collaborations between women poets and artists. Many of the press's collaborations focus on a central theme or conceit, like the sprawl and spectacle of New York in *Arcade* by Erica Hunt and Alison Saar." Hardcover and trade paperback originals and electronic originals.

KENSINGTON PUBLISHING CORP.

119 W. 40th St., New York NY 10018. (212)407-1500. **Fax:** (212)935-0699. **E-mail:** jscognamiglio@kensingtonbooks.com. **Website:** www.kensingtonbooks.com. **Contact:** John Scognamiglio, editorial director, fiction (historical romance, Regency romance, women's contemporary fiction, gay and lesbian fiction and nonfiction, mysteries, suspense, mainstream fiction); Michaela Hamilton, editor-in-chief, Citadel Press (thrillers, mysteries, mainstream fiction, true crime, current events); Selena James, executive editor, Dafina Books (African American fiction and nonfiction, inspirational, young adult, romance); Peter Senftleben, assistant editor (mainstream fiction, women's contemporary fiction, gay and lesbian fiction, mysteries, suspense, thrillers, romantic suspense, paranormal romance). Estab. 1975. "Kensington focuses on profitable niches and uses aggressive marketing techniques to support its books." Publishes hardcover and trade paperback originals, mass market paperback originals and reprints. Book catalog and guidelines online.

NEEDS No science fiction/fantasy, experimental fiction, business texts or children's titles.

HOW TO CONTACT Query.

TERMS Pays 6-15% royalty on retail price. Makes outright purchase. Pays $2,000 and up advance. Responds in 1 month to queries and proposals; 4 months to mss.

TIPS "Agented submissions only, except for submissions to romance lines. For those lines, query with SASE or submit proposal package including 3 sample chapters, synopsis."

DENIS KITCHEN PUBLISHING CO., LLC

P.O. Box 2250, Amherst MA 01004. (413)259-1627. **Fax:** (413)259-1812. **E-mail:** help@deniskitchen.com. **Website:** www.deniskitchen.com. **Contact:** Denis Kitchen, publisher. Publishes hardcover and trade paperback originals and reprints.

◯ This publisher strongly discourages e-mail submissions.

NEEDS "We do not want pure fiction. We seek cartoonists or writer/illustrator teams who can tell compelling stories with a combination of words and pictures." No pure fiction (meaning text only).

HOW TO CONTACT Query with SASE. Submit sample illustrations/comic pages. Submit complete ms.

TERMS Pays 6-10% royalty on retail price. Occasionally makes deals based on percentage of wholesale if idea and/or bulk of work is done in-house. Pays $1-5,000 advance. Responds in 4-6 weeks.

TIPS "Our audience is readers who embrace the graphic novel revolution, who appreciate historical comic strips and books, and those who follow popular and alternative culture. We like to discover new talent. The artist who has a day job but a great idea is encouraged to contact us. The pop culture historian who has a new take on an important figure is likewise encouraged. We have few preconceived notions about mss or ideas, though we are decidedly selective. Historically, we have published many first-time authors and artists, some of whom developed into award-winning creators with substantial followings. Artists or illustrators who do not have confidence in their writing should send us self-promotional postcards (our favorite way of spotting new talent)."

KNOPF

Imprint of Random House, 1745 Broadway, New York NY 10019. **Fax:** (212)940-7390. **Website:** knopfdoubleday.com/imprint/knopf. Estab. 1915. Publishes hardcover and paperback originals.

NEEDS Publishes book-length fiction of literary merit by known or unknown writers. Length: 40,000-150,000 words.

HOW TO CONTACT Usually only accepts mss submitted by agents. However, writers may submit sample 25-50 pages with SASE.

TERMS Royalties vary. Offers advance. Responds in 2-6 months to queries.

KNOX ROBINSON PUBLISHING

Knox Robinson Holdings, LLC, 3104 Briarcliff RD NE #98414, Atlanta GA 30345. (404)478-8696. **E-mail:** info@knoxrobinsonpublishing.com. **Website:** www.knoxrobinsonpublishing.com. Estab. 2010. Knox Robinson Publishing began as an international, independent, specialist publisher of historical fiction, historical romance and fantasy. Now open to well-written literature in all genres. Publishes fiction and nonfiction. Catalog available. Guidelines online.

IMPRINTS Under The Maple Tree Books (Children's Literature), Mithras Books (Young Adult Literature).

NEEDS "We are seeking historical fiction featuring obscure historical figures."

HOW TO CONTACT Submit first 3 chapters and author questionnaire found on website.

TERMS Pays royalty. Responds within 6 months to submissions of first 3 chapters. "We do not accept proposals."

LEAPFROG PRESS

Box 505, Fredonia NY 14063. (508)274-2710. **E-mail:** leapfrog@leapfrogpress.com. **Website:** www.leap-frogpress.com. **Contact:** Rebecca Schwab, acquisitions editor; Layla Al-Bedawi, publicity. Estab. 1996. Guidelines online.

NEEDS "We search for beautifully written literary titles and market them aggressively to national trade and library accounts. We also sell film, translation, foreign, and book club rights." Publishes paperback originals. Books: acid-free paper; sewn binding. Average print order: 3,000. First novel print order: 2,000 (average). Member, Publishers Marketing Association, PEN. Distributes titles through Consortium Book Sales and Distribution, St. Paul, MN. Promotes titles through all national review media, bookstore readings, author tours, website, radio shows, chain store promotions, advertisements, book fairs. "Genres often blur; look for good writing. We are most interested in works that are quirky, that fall outside of any known genre, and of course well written and finely crafted. We are most interested in literary fiction."

HOW TO CONTACT Query by e-mail only. Send letter and first 5-10 ms pages within e-mail message. No attachments. Responds in 2-3 weeks to queries by e-mail; 6 months to mss. May consider simultaneous submissions.

TERMS Pays 10% royalty on net receipts. Average advance: negotiable. Response time varies.

TIPS "We like anything that is superbly written and genuinely original. We like the idiosyncratic and the peculiar. We rarely publish nonfiction. Send only your best work, and send only completed work that is ready. That means the completed ms has already been through extensive editing and is ready to be judged. We consider submissions from both previously published and unpublished writers. We are uninterested in an impressive author bio if the work is poor; if the work is excellent, the author bio is equally unimportant."

LETHE PRESS

118 Heritage Ave., Maple Shade NJ 8052. (609)410-7391. **Website:** www.lethepressbooks.com. Estab. 2001. "Welcomes submissions from authors of any sexual or gender identity." Guidelines online.

NEEDS "Named after the Greek river of memory and forgetfulness (and pronounced Lee-Thee), Lethe Press is a small press devoted to ideas that are often neglected or forgotten by mainstream, profit-oriented publishers." Distributes/promotes titles. Lethe Books are distributed by Ingram Publications and Bookazine, and are available at all major bookstores, as well as the major online retailers. **HOW TO CONTACT** Query via e-mail.

ARTHUR A. LEVINE BOOKS

Scholastic, Inc., 557 Broadway, New York NY 10012. (212)343-4436. **Fax:** (212)343-6143. **Website:** www.arthuralevinebooks.com. Estab. 1996. Publishes hardcover, paperback, and e-book editions. Picture Books: Query letter and full text of pb. Novels: Send Query letter, first 2 chapters and synopsis. Other: Query letter, 10-page sample and synopsis/proposal.

NEEDS "Arthur A. Levine is looking for distinctive literature, for children and young adults, for whatever's extraordinary." Averages 18-20 total titles/year.

HOW TO CONTACT Query.

TERMS Responds in 1 month to queries; 5 months to mss.

LILLENAS PUBLISHING CO.

Imprint of Lillenas Drama Resources, P.O. Box 419527, Kansas City MO 64141. (800)877-0700. **Fax:** (816)412-8390. **E-mail:** drama@lillenas.com. **Website:** www.lillenasdrama.com. "We purchase only original, previously unpublished materials. Also, we require that all scripts be performed at least once before it is submitted for consideration. We do not accept scripts that are sent via fax or e-mail. Direct all mss to the Drama Resources Editor." Publishes mass market paperback and electronic originals. Guidelines online.

NEEDS "Looking for sketch and monologue collections for all ages – adults, children and youth. For these collections, we request 12 - 15 scripts to be submitted at one time. Unique treatments of spiritual themes, relevant issues and biblical messages are of interest. Contemporary full-length and one-act plays that have conflict, characterization, and a spiritual context that is neither a sermon nor an apologetic for youth and adults. We also need wholesome so-called secular full-length scripts for dinner theatres and schools." No musicals.

TERMS Pays royalty on net price. Makes outright purchase. Responds in 4-6 months to material.

TIPS "We never receive too many mss."

Ⓐ LITTLE, BROWN AND CO. ADULT TRADE BOOKS

1290 Avenue of the Americas, New York NY 10104. **Website:** www.littlebrown.com. Estab. 1837. "The general editorial philosophy for all divisions continues to be broad and flexible, with high quality and the promise of commercial success as always the first considerations." Publishes hardcover originals and paperback originals and reprints. Guidelines online.

HOW TO CONTACT *Agented submissions only.*

TERMS Pays royalty. Offer advance.

LITTLE PICKLE PRESS

3701 Sacramento St., #494, San Francisco CA 94118. (415)340-3344. **Fax:** (415)366-1520. **E-mail:** info@march4thinc.com. **Website:** www.littlepicklepress.com. Little Pickle Press is a 21st-century publisher dedicated to helping parents and educators cultivate conscious, responsible little people by stimulating explorations of the meaningful topics of their generation through a variety of media, technologies, and techniques. Submit through submission link on site. Includes YA imprint Relish Media. Uses Author.me for submissions for Little Pickle and YA imprint Relish Media. Guidelines available on site.

TIPS "We have lots of mss to consider, so it will take up to 8 weeks before we get back to you."

Ⓐ LITTLE SIMON

Imprint of Simon & Schuster, 1230 Avenue of the Americas, New York NY 10020. (212)698-1295. **Fax:** (212)698-2794. **Website:** www.simonandschuster.com/kids. "Our goal is to provide fresh material in an innovative format for preschool to age 8. Our books are often, if not exclusively, format driven." Publishes novelty and branded books only.

NEEDS Novelty books include many things that do not fit in the traditional hardcover or paperback format, such as pop-up, board book, scratch and sniff, glow in the dark, lift the flap, etc. Children's/juvenile. No picture books. Large part of the list is holiday-themed.

HOW TO CONTACT *Currently not accepting unsolicited mss.*

TERMS Offers advance and royalties.

LIVINGSTON PRESS

University of West Alabama, 100 N. Washington St., Station 22, University of West Alabama, Livingston AL 35470. **Fax:** (205)652-3717. **E-mail:** jwt@uwa.edu. **Website:** www.livingstonpress.uwa.edu. **Contact:** Joe Taylor, director. Estab. 1974. "Livingston Press, as do all literary presses, looks for authorial excellence in style. Currently emphasizing novels." Reading in June only. Check back for details. Publishes hardcover and trade paperback originals, plus Kindle. Book catalog online. Guidelines online.

IMPRINTS Swallow's Tale Press.

NEEDS "We are interested in form and, of course, style." No genre fiction, please.

TERMS Pays 80 contributor's copies, after sales of 1,000, standard royalty. Responds in 4 months to queries; 6-12 months to mss.

TIPS "Our readers are interested in literature, often quirky literature that emphasizes form and style. Please visit our website for current needs."

LOOSE ID

P.O. Box 806, San Francisco CA 94104. **E-mail:** submissions@loose-id.com. **Website:** www.loose-id.com. **Contact:** Treva Harte, editor-in-chief. Estab. 2004. "*Loose Id* is love unleashed. We're taking romance to the edge." Publishes e-books and some print books. Distributes/promotes titles. "The company promotes itself through web and print advertising wherever readers of erotic romance may be found, creating a recognizable brand identity as the place to let your id run free and the people who unleash your fantasies. It is currently pursuing licensing agreements for foreign translations, and has a print program of 2 to 5 titles per month." Guidelines online.

○ "Loose Id is actively acquiring stories from both aspiring and established authors."

NEEDS Wants nontraditional erotic romance stories, including gay, lesbian, heroes and heroines, multi-culturalism, cross-genre, fantasy, and science fiction, straight contemporary or historical romances.

HOW TO CONTACT Query with outline/synopsis and 3 sample chapters. Accepts queries by e-mail. Include estimated word count, list of publishing credits, and why your submission is love unleashed. "Before submitting a query or proposal, please read the guidelines on our website. Please don't hesitate to contact us by e-mail for any information you don't see there."

TERMS Pays e-book royalties of 40%. Responds to queries in 1 month.

MAGE PUBLISHERS, INC.

1780 Crossroads Dr., Odenton MD 21113. (202)342-1642. **Fax:** (202)342-9269. **E-mail:** as@mage.com. **Website:** www.mage.com. Estab. 1985. Mage publishes books relating to Persian/Iranian culture. Publishes hardcover originals and reprints, trade paperback originals. Book catalog available free. Guidelines online.

NEEDS Must relate to Persian/Iranian culture.

HOW TO CONTACT Submit outline, SASE. Query via mail or e-mail.

TERMS Pays royalty. Responds in 1 month to queries.

TIPS "Audience is the Iranian-American community in America and Americans interested in Persian culture."

MANDALA PUBLISHING

Mandala Publishing and Earth Aware Editions, 800 A St., San Rafael CA 94901. **E-mail:** info@mandalapublishing.com. **Website:** www.mandalaeartheditions.com. Estab. 1989. "In the traditions of the East, wisdom, truth, and beauty go hand in- hand. This is reflected in the great arts, music, yoga, and philosophy of India. Mandala Publishing strives to bring to its readers authentic and accessible renderings of thousands of years of wisdom and philosophy from this unique culture-timeless treasures that are our inspirations and guides. At Mandala, we believe that the arts, health, ecology, and spirituality of the great Vedic traditions are as relevant today as they were in sacred India thousands of years ago. As a distinguished publisher in the world of Vedic literature, lifestyle, and interests today, Mandala strives to provide accessible and meaningful works for the modern reader." Publishes hardcover, trade paperback, and electronic originals. Book catalog online.

HOW TO CONTACT Query with SASE.

TERMS Pays 3-15% royalty on retail price. Responds in 6 months.

○ MANOR HOUSE PUBLISHING, INC.

452 Cottingham Crescent, Ancaster ON L9G 3V6, Canada. (905)648-2193. **E-mail:** mbdavie@manor-house.biz. **Website:** www.manor-house.biz. **Contact:** Mike Davie, president (novels and nonfiction). Estab. 1998. Manor House is currently looking for new fully edited, ready-to-run titles to complete our spring-fall 2017 release lineup. This is a rare opportunity for authors, including self-published, to have existing or ready titles picked up by Manor House and made available to retailers throughout the world, while our network of rights agents provide more potential revenue streams via foreign language rights sales. We are currently looking for titles that are ready or nearly ready for publishing to be released this fall. Such titles should be written by Canadian citizens residing in Canada and should be profitable or with strong market sales potential to allow full cost recovery and

profit for publisher and author. Of primary interest are business and self-help titles along with other nonfiction, including new age. Publishes hardcover, trade paperback, and mass market paperback originals (and reprints if they meet specific criteria - best to inquire with publisher). Book catalog online. Guidelines available.

NEEDS Stories should mainly be by Canadian authors residing in Canada, have Canadian settings and characters should be Canadian, but content should have universal appeal to wide audience. In some cases, we will consider publishing non-Canadian fiction authors - provided they demonstrate publishing their book will be profitable for author and publisher.

HOW TO CONTACT Query via e-mail. Submit proposal package, clips, bio, 3 sample chapters. Submit complete ms.

TERMS Pays 10% royalty on retail price. Queries and mss to be sent by e-mail only. "We will respond in 30 days if interested-if not, there is no response. Do not follow up unless asked to do so."

TIPS "Our audience includes everyone-the general public/mass audience. Self-edit your work first, make sure it is well written and well edited with strong Canadian content and/or content of universal appeal (preferably with a Canadian connection of some kind)."

Ⓐ MARINER BOOKS

222 Berkeley St., Boston MA 2116. (617)351-5000. **Website:** www.hmco.com. Estab. 1997.

Ⓠ Mariner Books' *Interpreter of Maladies*, by debut author Jhumpa Lahiri, won the 2000 Pulitzer Prize for fiction and *The Caprices*, by Sabina Murray, received the 2003 PEN/Faulkner Award. Mariner Books' *Interpreter of Maladies*, by debut author Jhumpa Lahiri, won the 2000 Pulitzer Prize for fiction and *The Caprices*, by Sabina Murray, received the 2003 PEN/Faulkner Award.

NEEDS Literary, mainstream/contemporary. Recently published Timothy Egan, Donald Hall, Amitav Ghosh, and Edna O'Brien.

HOW TO CONTACT *Agented submissions only.* Responds in 4 months to mss.

TERMS Pays royalty on retail price or makes outright purchase. Average advance: variable.

MARTIN SISTERS PUBLISHING COMPANY, INC

P.O. Box 1154, Barbourville KY 40906-1499. **Website:** www.martinsisterspublishing.com. Estab. 2011. Firm/imprint publishes trade and mass market paperback originals; electronic originals. Catalog and guidelines online.

HOW TO CONTACT "Please place query letter, marketing plan and the first 5-10 pages of your ms (if you are submitting fiction) directly into your e-mail." Guidelines available on site.

TERMS Pays 7.5% royalty/max on print net; 35% royalty/max on e-book net. No advance offered. Responds in 1 month on queries, 2 months on proposals, 3-6 months on mss.

MARVEL COMICS

135 W. 50th St., 7th Floor, New York NY 10020. **Website:** www.marvel.com. Publishes hardcover originals and reprints, trade paperback reprints, mass market comic book originals, electronic reprints. Guidelines online.

NEEDS Our shared universe needs new heroes and villains; books for younger readers and teens needed.

HOW TO CONTACT Submit inquiry letter, idea submission form (download from website), SASE.

TERMS Pays on a per page work for hire basis or creator-owned which is then contracted. Pays negotiable advance. Responds in 3-5 weeks to queries.

Ⓢ MAVERICK MUSICALS AND PLAYS

17, Tarnkun St., Alexandra Headlands QLD 4572, Australia. Phone/**Fax:** (61)(7)5448 4093. **E-mail:** tahlia@maverickmusicals.com. **Website:** www.maverickmusicals.com. **Contact:** Tahlia Wilkins. Estab. 1978. Guidelines online.

NEEDS "Looking for two-act musicals and one- and two-act plays. See website for more details."

Ⓒ MCCLELLAND & STEWART, LTD.

The Canadian Publishers, 320 Front St. W., Suite 1400, Toronto ON M5V 3B6, Canada. (416)364-4449. **Fax:** (416)598-7764. **Website:** www.mcclelland.com. Publishes hardcover, trade paperback, and mass market paperback originals and reprints.

NEEDS "We publish work by established authors, as well as the work of new and developing authors."

HOW TO CONTACT Query. *All unsolicited mss* returned unopened.

TERMS Pays 10-15% royalty on retail price (hardcover rates). Pays advance. Responds in 3 months to proposals.

THE MCDONALD & WOODWARD PUBLISHING CO.

695 Tall Oaks Dr., Newark OH 43055. (740)641-2691. **Fax:** (740)641-2692. **E-mail:** mwpubco@mwpubco.com. **Website:** www.mwpubco.com. **Contact:** Jerry N. McDonald, publisher. Estab. 1986. McDonald & Woodward publishes books in natural history, cultural history, and natural resources. Currently emphasizing travel, natural and cultural history, and natural resource conservation. Publishes hardcover and trade paperback originals. Book catalog online. Guidelines free on request; by e-mail.

HOW TO CONTACT Query with SASE.

TERMS Pays 10% royalty. Responds in less than 1 month.

TIPS "Our books are meant for the curious and educated elements of the general population."

Ⓐ MARGARET K. MCELDERRY BOOKS

Imprint of Simon & Schuster Children's Publishing Division, 1230 Sixth Ave., New York NY 10020. (212)698-7200. **Website:** imprints.simonandschuster.biz/margaret-k-mcelderry-books. Estab. 1971. "Margaret K. McElderry Books publishes hardcover and paperback trade books for children from pre-school age through young adult. This list includes picture books, middle grade and teen fiction, poetry, and fantasy. The style and subject matter of the books we publish is almost unlimited. We do not publish textbooks, coloring and activity books, greeting cards, magazines, pamphlets, or religious publications." Guidelines for #10 SASE.

NEEDS *No unsolicited mss.*

HOW TO CONTACT *Agented submissions only.*

TERMS Pays authors royalty based on retail price. Pays illustrator royalty of by the project. Pays photographers by the project. Original artwork returned at job's completion. Offers $5,000-8,000 advance for new authors.

TIPS "Read! The children's book field is competitive. See what's been done and what's out there before submitting. We look for high quality: an originality of ideas, clarity and felicity of expression, a well organized plot, and strong character-driven stories. We're looking for strong, original fiction, especially mysteries and middle grade humor. We are always interested in picture books for the youngest age reader. Study our titles."

MEDALLION PRESS

4222 Meridian Pkwy., Aurora IL 60504. (630)513-8316. **E-mail:** emily@medallionpress.com. **Website:** medallionpress.com. **Contact:** Emily Steele, editorial director. Estab. 2003. "We are an independent, innovative publisher looking for compelling, memorable stories told in distinctive voices." Publishes trade paperback, hardcover, e-book originals. Guidelines online. Currently closed to submissions.

NEEDS Word count: 40,000-90,000 for YA; 60,000-120,000 for all others. No short stories, anthologies, erotica, middle grade, children's fiction.

HOW TO CONTACT Submit first 3 consecutive chapters and a synopsis through our online submission form. Please check if submissions are currently open before submitting.

TERMS Offers advance. Responds in 2-3 months to mss.

TIPS "Please visit our website for the most current guidelines prior to submitting anything to us. Please check if submissions are currently open before submitting."

MELANGE BOOKS, LLC

White Bear Lake MN 55110-5538. **E-mail:** melange-books@melange-books.com. **E-mail:** submissions@melange-books.com. **Website:** www.melange-books.com. **Contact:** Nancy Schumacher, publisher and acquiring editor for Melange and Satin Romance; Caroline Andrus, acquiring editor for Fire and Ice for Young Adult. Estab. 2011. Melange is a royalty-paying company publishing e-books and print books. Publishes trade paperback originals and electronic originals. Send SASE for book catalog. Guidelines online.

IMPRINTS Fire and Ice (young and new adult); Satin Romance.

NEEDS Submit a clean mss by following guidelines on website.

HOW TO CONTACT Query electronically by clicking on "submissions" on website. Include a synopsis and 4 chapters.

TERMS Authors receive a minimum of 20% royalty on print sales, 40% on electronic book sales. Does not offer an advance. Responds in 1 month on queries; 2 months on proposals; 4-6 months on mss.

MERRIAM PRESS

489 South St., Hoosick Falls NY 12090. **E-mail:** ray@merriam-press.com. **Website:** www.merriam-press.com. **Contact:** Ray Merriam, owner. Estab. 1988. Merriam Press specializes in military history, particularly World War II history. We are also branching out into other genres, including fiction, historical fiction, poetry, children. Provide brief synopsis of ms. Never send any files in body of e-mail or as an attachment. Publisher will ask for full ms for review. Publishes hardcover and softcover trade paperback original works and reprints. Titles are also made available in e-book editions. Book catalog available in print and PDF editions. Author guidelines and additional information are available on publisher's website.

○ Publisher requires unformatted mss. Mss must be thoroughly edited and error-free.

NEEDS Especially but not limited to military history.

HOW TO CONTACT Query with SASE or by e-mail first. Do not send ms (in whole or in part) unless requested to do so.

TERMS Pays 10% royalty for printed editions and 50% royalty for eBook editions. Royalty payment is based on the amount paid to the publisher, not the retail or list prices. Does not pay advance. Responds quickly (e-mail preferred) to queries.

TIPS "Our military history books are geared for military historians, collectors, model kit builders, wargamers, veterans, general enthusiasts. We now publish some historical fiction and poetry and will consider well-written books on a variety of nonmilitary topics."

MESSIANIC JEWISH PUBLISHERS

6120 Day Long Ln., Clarksville MD 21029. (410)531-6644. **E-mail:** editor@messianicjewish.net. **Website:** www.messianicjewish.net. Publishes hardcover and trade paperback originals and reprints. Guidelines via e-mail.

NEEDS "We publish very little fiction. Jewish or Biblical themes are a must. Text must demonstrate keen awareness of Jewish culture and thought."

HOW TO CONTACT Query with SASE. Unsolicited mss are not return.

TERMS Pays 7-15% royalty on wholesale price.

⬛ METHUEN PUBLISHING LTD

Editorial Department, 35 Hospital Fields Rd., York YO10 4DZ, United Kingdom. **E-mail:** editorial@metheun.co.uk. **Website:** www.methuen.co.uk. Estab. 1889. Guidelines online.

○ No unsolicited mss; synopses and ideas welcome. Prefers to be approached via agents or a letter of inquiry. No first novels, cookery books or personal memoirs.

NEEDS No first novels.

HOW TO CONTACT Query with SASE. Submit proposal package, outline, outline/proposal, resume, publishing history, clips, bio, SASE.

TERMS Pays royalty.

TIPS "We recommend that all prospective authors attempt to find an agent before submitting to publishers and we do not encourage unagented submissions."

MICHIGAN STATE UNIVERSITY PRESS

1405 S. Harrison Rd., Suite 25, East Lansing MI 48823. (517)355-9543. **Fax:** (517)432-2611. **E-mail:** msupress@msu.edu. **Website:** msupress.org. **Contact:** Alex Schwartz and Julie Loehr, acquisitions. Estab. 1947. Michigan State University Press has notably represented both scholarly publishing and the mission of Michigan State University with the publication of numerous award-winning books and scholarly journals. In addition, they publish nonfiction that addresses, in a more contemporary way, social concerns, such as diversity and civil rights. They also publish literary fiction and poetry. Publishes hardcover and softcover originals. Book catalog and ms guidelines online.

NEEDS Publishes literary fiction.

HOW TO CONTACT Submit proposal.

TERMS Pays variable royalty.

MILKWEED EDITIONS

1011 Washington Ave. S., Suite 300, Minneapolis MN 55415. (612)332-3192. **Fax:** (612)215-2550. **Website:** www.milkweed.org. Estab. 1979. "Milkweed Editions publishes with the intention of making a humane impact on society, in the belief that literature is a transformative art uniquely able to convey the essential experiences of the human heart and spirit. To that end, Milkweed Editions publishes distinctive voices of literary merit in handsomely designed, visually dynamic books, exploring the ethical, cultural, and esthetic issues that free societies need continually to address." Publishes hardcover, trade paperback, and electronic originals; trade paperback and electronic reprints. Book catalog online. Only accepts submissions during open submission periods. See website for guidelines.

NEEDS Novels for adults and for readers 8-13. High literary quality. For adult readers: literary fiction, nonfiction, poetry, essays. Middle readers: adventure, contemporary, fantasy, multicultural, nature/environment, suspense/mystery. Average length: middle readers—90-200 pages. No romance, mysteries, science fiction.

HOW TO CONTACT "Please submit a query letter with 3 opening chapters (of a novel) or three representative stories (of a collection). Publishes YR."

TERMS Pays authors variable royalty based on retail price. Offers advance against royalties. Pays varied advance from $500-10,000. Responds in 6 months.

TIPS "We are looking for excellent writing with the intent of making a humane impact on society. Please read submission guidelines before submitting and acquaint yourself with our books in terms of style and quality before submitting. Many factors influence our selection process, so don't get discouraged. Nonfiction is focused on literary writing about the natural world, including living well in urban environments."

MILKWEED FOR YOUNG READERS

Milkweed Editions, Open Book Building, 1011 Washington Ave. S., Suite 300, Minneapolis MN 55415. (612)332-3192. **Fax:** (612)215-2550. **Website:** www.milkweed.org. Estab. 1984. "We are looking first of all for high-quality literary writing. We publish books with the intention of making a humane impact on society." Publishes hardcover and trade paperback originals. Book catalog for $1.50. Guidelines online.

HOW TO CONTACT "Milkweed Editions now accepts mss online through our Submission Manager. If you're a first-time submitter, you'll need to fill in a simple form and then follow the instructions for selecting and uploading your ms. Please make sure that your ms follows the submission guidelines."

TERMS Pays 7% royalty on retail price. Pays variable advance. Responds in 6 months to queries.

✪ MONDIAL

203 W. 107th St., Suite 6C, New York NY 10025. 212-864-7095. **Fax:** (208)361-2863. **E-mail:** contact@mondialbooks.com. **Website:** www.mondialbooks.com; www.librejo.com. **Contact:** Andrew Moore, editor. Estab. 1996. Mondial publishes fiction and nonfiction in English, Esperanto, and Hebrew: novels, short stories, poetry, textbooks, dictionaries, books about history, linguistics, and psychology, among others. Since 2007, it has been publishing a literary magazine in Es-

peranto. Publishes hard cover, trade paperback originals and reprints. Guidelines online.

HOW TO CONTACT Query through online submission form.

TERMS Pays 10% royalty on wholesale price. Does not pay advance. Responds to queries in 3 months, only if interested.

✪ MONSOON BOOKS

No.1 Duke of Windsor Suite, Burrough Court, Burrough on the Hill Leicestershire LE14 2QS, United Kingdom. **E-mail:** sales@monsoonbooks.co.uk. **Website:** www.monsoonbooks.co.uk. **Contact:** Philip Tatham, Publisher. Estab. 2002. Monsoon Books is a U.K.-based trade publisher of English-language fiction and narrative nonfiction relating to Asia. All titles have an Asian, usually a SE Asian, angle. Guidelines online.

HOW TO CONTACT Query with outline/synopsis and submit complete ms with cover letter. Accepts queries by snail mail, fax, and e-mail (submissions@monsoonbooks.com.sg. Please include estimated word count, brief bio, list of publishing credits, and list of three comparative titles. Send hard copy submissions to: Monsoon Books Pte Ltd, 71 Ayer Rajah Crescent #01-01, Mediapolis Phase, Singapore 139951. We are not able to return hard copy mss. We do not encourage hand deliveries. Agented fiction 20%. Responds in 8 weeks to your submissions. If you do not hear from us by then, e-mail us. Accepts simultaneous submissions, submissions on CD or disk. Rarely comments on rejected mss. Monsoon Books regularly works with literary agents from the U.K. and Australia (such as David Higham Associates in London and Cameron's Management in Sydney) and we are particularly keen to hear from agents with mss set in Southeast or North Asia as well as mss written by authors from this region.

TIPS "Monsoon welcomes unsolicited mss from agented and unagented authors writing books set in Asia, particularly Southeast Asia."

✪ MOODY PUBLISHERS

Moody Bible Institute, 820 N. LaSalle Blvd., Chicago IL 60610. (800)678-8812. **Fax:** (312)329-4157. **Website:** www.moodypublishers.org. **Contact:** Acquisitions Coordinator. Estab. 1894. "The mission of Moody Publishers is to educate and edify the Christian and to evangelize the non-Christian by ethically publishing conservative, evangelical Christian literature and other media for all ages around the world, and to help provide resources for Moody Bible Institute in its training of future Christian leaders." Publishes hardcover, trade, and mass market paperback originals. Book catalog for 9×12 envelope and 4 first-class stamps. Guidelines online.

HOW TO CONTACT *Agented submissions only.*

TERMS Royalty varies. Responds in 2-3 months to queries.

TIPS "In our fiction list, we're looking for Christian storytellers rather than teachers trying to present a message. Your motivation should be to delight the reader. Using your skills to create beautiful works is glorifying to God."

NBM PUBLISHING

160 Broadway, Suite 700, East Bldg., New York NY 10038. **E-mail:** nbmgn@nbmpub.com. **Website:** nbmpub.com. **Contact:** Terry Nantier, editor. Estab. 1976. Publishes graphic novels for an audience of YA/adults. Types of books include fiction, mystery, biographies and social parodies. Catalog online.

TERMS Advance negotiable. Responds to e-mail 1-2 days; mail 1 week.

THOMAS NELSON, INC.

HarperCollins Christian Publishing, Box 141000, Nashville TN 37214. (615)889-9000. **Website:** www.thomasnelson.com. Thomas Nelson publishes Christian lifestyle nonfiction and fiction, and general nonfiction. Publishes hardcover and paperback orginals.

NEEDS Publishes authors of commercial fiction who write for adults from a Christian perspective.

HOW TO CONTACT *Does not accept unsolicited mss.* No phone queries.

TERMS Rates negotiated for each project. Pays advance.

NEW DIRECTIONS

80 Eighth Ave., New York NY 10011. **Fax:** (212)255-0231. **E-mail:** editorial@ndbooks.com. **Website:** www.ndbooks.com. **Contact:** Editorial Assistant. Estab. 1936. "Currently, New Directions focuses primarily on fiction in translation, avant garde American fiction, and experimental poetry by American and foreign authors. If your work does not fall into 1 of those categories, you would probably do best to submit your work elsewhere." Hardcover and trade paperback originals. Book catalog and guidelines online.

NEEDS No juvenile or young adult, occult or paranormal, genre fiction (formula romances, sci-fi or westerns), arts & crafts, and inspirational poetry.

HOW TO CONTACT Brief query only.

TERMS Responds in 3-4 months to queries.

TIPS "Our books serve the academic community."

NEWEST PUBLISHERS LTD.

201, 8540-109 St., Edmonton AB T6G 1E6, Canada. (780)432-9427. **Fax:** (780)433-3179. **E-mail:** info@newestpress.com. **E-mail:** submissions@newestpress.com. **Website:** www.newestpress.com. Estab. 1977. NeWest publishes Western Canadian fiction, nonfiction, poetry, and drama. Publishes trade paperback originals. Book catalog for 9×12 SASE. Guidelines online.

HOW TO CONTACT Submit complete ms.

TERMS Pays 10% royalty. Responds in 6-8 months to queries.

NEW ISSUES POETRY & PROSE

Western Michigan University, 1903 W. Michigan Ave., Kalamazoo MI 49008-5463. (269)387-8185. **E-mail:** new-issues@wmich.edu. **Website:** wmich.edu/newissues. **Contact:** Managing Editor. Estab. 1996. Guidelines online.

HOW TO CONTACT Only considers submissions to book contests.

NEW LIBRI PRESS

4907 Meridian Ave. N., Seattle WA 98103. **E-mail:** query@newlibri.com. **Website:** www.newlibri.com. **Contact:** Michael Muller, editor; Stanislav Fritz, editor. Estab. 2011. "We only accept e-mail submissions, not USPS." Publishes trade paperback, electronic original, electronic reprints. Catalog online. Guidelines online. Electronic submissions only.

NEEDS "Open to most ideas right now; this will change as we mature as a press. As a new press, we are more open than most and time will probably shape the direction. That said, trite as it is, we want good writing that is fun to read. While we currently are not looking for some sub-genres, if it is well written and a bit off the beaten path, submit to us. We are e-book focused. **We may not create a paper version if the e-book does not sell**, which means some fiction may be less likely to currently sell (e.g., picture books are problematic).

HOW TO CONTACT Submit query, synopsis, and full ms (so we don't have to ask for it later if we like it. We will read about 50 pages to start).

TERMS Pays 20-35% royalty on wholesale price. No advance. Responds in 3 months to mss.

TIPS "Our audience is someone who is comfortable reading an e-book,or someone who is tired of the recycled authors of mainstream publishing, but still wants a good, relatively fast, reading experience. The industry is changing, while we accept for the traditional model, we are searching for writers who are interested in sharing the risk and controlling their own destiny. We embrace writers with no agent."

NEW RIVERS PRESS

1104 Seventh Ave. S., Moorhead MN 56563. **Website:** www.newriverspress.com. **Contact:** Nayt Rundquist, managing editor. Estab. 1968. New Rivers Press publishes collections of poetry, novels, nonfiction, translations of contemporary literature, and collections of short fiction and nonfiction. "We continue to publish books regularly by new and emerging writers, but we also welcome the opportunity to read work of every character and to publish the best literature available nationwide. Each fall through the Many Voices Project competition, we choose 2 books: 1 poetry and 1 prose."

NEEDS Sponsors American Fiction Prize to find best unpublished short stories by American writers.

NIGHTSCAPE PRESS

P.O. Box 1948, Smyrna TN 37167. **E-mail:** info@nightscapepress.com. **E-mail:** submissions@nightscapepress.com. **Website:** www.nightscapepress.com. Estab. 2012. Nightscape Press is seeking quality book-length words of at least 50,000 words (40,000 for young adult). Guidelines online. Currently closed to submissions. Will announce on site when they reopen to submissions.

NEEDS "We are not interested in erotica or graphic novels."

HOW TO CONTACT Query.

TERMS Pays monthly royalties. Offers advance.

😀 NORTIA PRESS

Santa Ana CA **E-mail:** acquisitions@nortiapress.com. **Website:** www.nortiapress.com. Estab. 2009. Publishes trade paperback and electronic originals.

NEEDS "We focus mainly on nonfiction as well as literary and historical fiction, but are open to other genres. No vampire stories, science fiction, or erotica, please."

HOW TO CONTACT Submit a brief e-mail query. Please include a short bio, approximate word count of book, and expected date of completion (fiction titles should be completed before sending a query, and should contain a sample chapter in the body of the e-mail). All unsolicited snail mail or attachments will be discarded without review.

TERMS Pays negotiable royalties on wholesale price. Responds in 1 month.

TIPS "We specialize in working with experienced authors who seek a more collaborative and fulfilling relationship with their publisher. As such, we are less likely to accept pitches form first-time authors, no matter how good the idea. As with any pitch, please make your e-mail very brief and to the point, so the reader is not forced to skim it. Always include some biographic information. Your life is interesting."

Ⓐ W.W. NORTON & COMPANY, INC.

500 Fifth Ave., New York NY 10110. (212)354-5500. **Fax:** (212)869-0856. **Website:** www.wwnorton.com. Estab. 1923. "W. W. Norton & Company, the oldest and largest publishing house owned wholly by its employees, strives to carry out the imperative of its founder to 'publish books not for a single season, but for the years' in fiction, nonfiction, poetry, college textbooks, cookbooks, art books and professional books. Due to the workload of our editorial staff and the large volume of materials we receive, *Norton is no longer able to accept unsolicited submissions*. If you are seeking publication, we suggest working with a literary agent who will represent you to the house."

🐦 NOSY CROW PUBLISHING

The Crow's Nest, 10a Lant St., London SE1 1QR, United Kingdom. (44)(0)207-089-7575. **Fax:** (44)(0)207-089-7576. **E-mail:** hello@nosycrow.com. **E-mail:** submissions@nosycrow.com. **Website:** nosycrow.com. "We publish books for children 0-14. We're looking for 'parent-friendly' books, and we don't publish books with explicit sex, drug use or serious violence, so no edgy YA or edgy cross-over. And whatever New Adult is, we don't do it. We also publish apps for children from 2-7, and may publish apps for older children if the idea feels right." Guidelines online.

NEEDS "As a rule, we don't like books with 'issues' that are in any way overly didactic."

HOW TO CONTACT Prefers submissions by e-mail, but post works if absolutely necessary.

TIPS "Please don't be too disappointed if we reject your work! We're a small company and can only publish a few new books and apps each year, so do try other publishers and agents: publishing is necessarily a hugely subjective business. We wish you luck!"

OCEANVIEW PUBLISHING

595 Bay Isles Rd., Suite 120-G, Longboat Key FL 34228. **E-mail:** mail@oceanviewpub.com. **E-mail:** submissions@oceanviewpub.com. **Website:** www.oceanviewpub.com. Estab. 2006. "Independent publisher of nonfiction and fiction, with primary interest in original mystery, thriller and suspense titles. Accepts new and established writers." Publishes hardcover and electronic originals. Catalog and guidelines online.

NEEDS Accepting adult mss with a primary interest in the mystery, thriller and suspense genres—from new and established writers. No children's or YA literature, poetry, cookbooks, technical manuals or short stories.

HOW TO CONTACT Within body of e-mail only, include author's name and brief bio (Indicate if this is an agent submission), ms title and word count, author's mailing address, phone number and e-mail address. Attached to the e-mail should be the following: A synopsis of 750 words or fewer. The first 30 pages of the ms. Please note that we accept only Word documents as attachments to the submission e-mail. Do not send query letters or proposals.

TERMS Responds in 3 months on mss.

OMNIDAWN PUBLISHING

2200 Adeline St., Suite 150, Oakland CA 94607. **Website:** www.omnidawn.com. Estab. 1999. Guidelines online.

TIPS "Check our website for latest information."

ONSTAGE PUBLISHING

190 Lime Quarry Rd., Suite 106-J, Madison AL 35758-8962. (256)542-3213. **Fax:** (256)542-3213. **E-mail:** submissions@onstagepublishing.com. **Website:** www.onstagepublishing.com. **Contact:** Dianne Hamilton, senior editor. Estab. 1999. "At this time, we only produce fiction books for ages 8-18. We have added an e-book only side of the house for mysteries for grades 6-12. See our website for more information. We will not do anthologies of any kind. Query first for nonfiction projects as nonfiction projects must spark our interest. We no longer are accepting written submissions. We want e-mail queries and submissions. For submissions: Put the first 3 chapters in the body of the e-mail. Do not use attachments! We will delete any submission with an attachment without acknowledgment."

Suggested ms lengths: Chapter books: 3,000-9,000 words, Middle Grade novels: 10,000-40,000 words, Young adult novels: 40,000-60,000 words. Guidelines online.

NEEDS Middle readers: adventure, contemporary, fantasy, history, nature/environment, science fiction, suspense/mystery. Young adults: adventure, contemporary, fantasy, history, humor, science fiction, suspense/mystery. Average word length: chapter books—4,000-6,000 words; middle readers—5,000 words and up; young adults—25,000 and up. Recently published *Mission: Shanghai* by Jamie Dodson (an adventure for boys ages 12+); *Birmingham, 1933: Alice* (a chapter book for grades 3-5). "We do not produce picture books."

TERMS Pays authors/illustrators/photographers advance plus royalties. Responds in 1-3 months.

TIPS "Study our titles and get a sense of the kind of books we publish, so that you know whether your project is likely to be right for us."

● OOLICHAN BOOKS

P.O. Box 2278, Lantzville BC V0B 1M0, Canada. (250)423-6113. **E-mail:** info@oolichan.com. **Website:** www.oolichan.com. Estab. 1974. Publishes hardcover and trade paperback originals and reprints. Book catalog online. Guidelines online.

● Only publishes Canadian authors.

NEEDS "We try to publish at least 2 literary fiction titles each year. We receive many more deserving submissions than we are able to publish, so we publish only outstanding work. We try to balance our list between emerging and established writers, and have published many first-time writers who have gone on to win or be shortlisted for major literary awards, both nationally and internationally."

HOW TO CONTACT Submit proposal package, publishing history, clips, bio, cover letter, 3 sample chapters, SASE.

TERMS Pays royalty on retail price. Responds in 1-3 months.

TIPS "Our audience is adult readers who love good books and good literature. Our audience is regional and national, as well as international. Follow our submission guidelines. Check out some of our titles at your local library or bookstore to get an idea of what we publish. Don't send us the only copy of your ms. Let us know if your submission is simultaneous, and inform us if it is accepted elsewhere. Above all, keep writing!"

OOLIGAN PRESS

369 Neuberger Hall, 724 SW Harrison St., Portland OR 97201. (503)725-9410. **E-mail:** acquisitions@ooliganpress.pdx.edu. **Website:** ooligan.pdx.edu. **Contact:** Acquisitions Co-Managers. Estab. 2001. "We seek to publish regionally significant works of literary, historical, and social value.

We define the Pacific Northwest as Northern California, Oregon, Idaho, Washington, British Columbia, and Alaska. We recognize the importance of diversity, particularly within the publishing industry, and are committed to building a literary community that includes traditionally underrepresented voices; therefore, we are interested in works originating from, or focusing on, marginalized communities of the Pacific Northwest." Publishes trade paperbacks, electronic originals, and reprints. Catalog online. Guidelines online.

HOW TO CONTACT Query with SASE. *"At this time we cannot accept science fiction or fantasy submissions."*

TERMS Pays negotiable royalty on retail price. Responds in 3 weeks for queries; 3 months for proposals.

TIPS "Search the blog for tips."

☼○ ORCA BOOK PUBLISHERS

1016 Balmoral Rd., Victoria BC V8T 1A8, Canada. (800)210-5277. **Fax:** (877)408-1551. **E-mail:** orca@orcabook.com. **Website:** www.orcabook.com. **Contact:** Amy Collins, editor (picture books); Sarah Harvey, editor (young readers); Andrew Wooldridge, editor (juvenile and teen fiction); Bob Tyrrell, publisher (YA, teen); Ruth Linka, associate editor (rapid reads). Estab. 1984. Only publishes Canadian authors. Publishes hardcover and trade paperback originals, and mass market paperback originals and reprints. Book catalog for 8½x11 SASE. Guidelines online.

NEEDS Picture books: animals, contemporary, history, nature/environment. Middle readers: contemporary, history, fantasy, nature/environment, problem novels, graphic novels. Young adults: adventure, contemporary, hi-lo (Orca Soundings), history, multicultural, nature/environment, problem novels, suspense/mystery, graphic novels. Average word length: picture books—500-1,500; middle readers—20,000-35,000; young adult—25,000-45,000; Orca Sound-ings—13,000-15,000; Orca Currents—13,000-15,000. No romance, science fiction.

HOW TO CONTACT Query with SASE. Submit proposal package, outline, clips, 2-5 sample chapters, SASE.

TERMS Pays 10% royalty. Responds in 1 month to queries; 2 months to proposals and mss.

TIPS "Our audience is students in grades K-12. Know our books, and know the market."

RICHARD C. OWEN PUBLISHERS, INC.

P.O. Box 585, Katonah NY 10536. (914)232-3903; (800)262-0787. **E-mail:** richardowen@rcowen.com. **Website:** www.rcowen.com. **Contact:** Richard Owen, publisher. Estab. 1982. "We publish child-focused books, with inherent instructional value, about characters and situations with which 5, 6, and 7-year-old children can identify—books that can be read for meaning, entertainment, enjoyment and information. We include multicultural stories that present minorities in a positive and natural way. Our stories show the diversity in America." Not interested in lesson plans, or books of activities for literature studies or other content areas. Submit complete ms and cover letter. Book catalog available with SASE. Ms guidelines with SASE or online.

○ "Due to high volume and long production time, we are currently limiting to nonfiction submissions only."

TERMS Pays authors royalty of 5% based on net price or outright purchase (range: $25-500). Offers no advances. Pays illustrators by the project (range: $100-2,000) or per photo (range: $50-150). Responds to mss in 1 year.

◐ PETER OWEN PUBLISHERS

81 Bridge Rd., London N8 9NP, United Kingdom. (44)(208)350-1775. **Fax:** (44)(208)340-9488. **E-mail:** info@peterowen.com. **Website:** www.peterowen.com. "We are far more interested in proposals for nonfiction than fiction at the moment. No poetry or short stories." Publishes hardcover originals and trade paperback originals and reprints. Book catalog for SASE, SAE with IRC or on website.

NEEDS "No first novels. Authors should be aware that we publish very little new fiction these days."

HOW TO CONTACT Query with synopsis, sample chapters.

TERMS Pays 7½-10% royalty. Pays negotiable advance. Responds in 2 months to queries; 3 months to proposals and mss.

PACIFIC PRESS PUBLISHING ASSOCIATION

Trade Book Division, 1350 N. Kings Rd., Nampa ID 83687. (208)465-2500. **Fax:** (208)465-2531. **Website:** www.pacificpress.com. Estab. 1874. "We publish books that fit Seventh-day Adventist beliefs only. All titles are Christian and religious. For guidance, see www.adventist.org/beliefs/index.html. Our books fit into the categories of this retail site: www.adventistbookcenter.com." Publishes hardcover and trade paperback originals and reprints. Guidelines online.

NEEDS "Pacific Press rarely publishes fiction, but we're interested in developing a line of Seventh-day Adventist fiction in the future. Only proposals accepted; no full mss."

TERMS Pays 8-16% royalty on wholesale price. Responds in 3 months to queries.

TIPS "Our primary audience is members of the Seventh-day Adventist denomination. Almost all are written by Seventh-day Adventists. Books that do well for us relate the Biblical message to practical human concerns and focus more on the experiential rather than theoretical aspects of Christianity. We are assigning more titles, using less unsolicited material—although we still publish mss from freelance submissions and proposals."

PAGESPRING PUBLISHING

P.O. Box 2113, Columbus OH 43221. **E-mail:** sales@pagespringpublishing.com. **E-mail:** submissions@pagespringpublishing.com. **Website:** www.pagespringpublishing.com. **Contact:** Lucky Marble Books Editor or Cup of Tea Books Editor. Estab. 2012. PageSpring Publishing publishes women's fiction under the Cup of Tea Books imprint and YA/middle grade titles under the Lucky Marble Books imprint. Visit the PageSpring Publishing website for submission details. Publishes trade paperback and electronic originals. Catalog online. Guidelines online.

IMPRINTS Cup of Tea Books, Lucky Marble Books.

NEEDS Cup of Tea Books publishes women's fiction. Lucky Marble Books specializes in middle grade and young adult fiction.

HOW TO CONTACT Send submissions for both Cup of Tea Books and Lucky Marble Books to submissions@pagespringpublishing.com. Send a query, synopsis, and the first 30 pages of the ms in the body of the e-mail. please. NO attachments.

TERMS Pays royalty on wholesale price. Endeavors to respond to queries within 3 months.

TIPS Cup of Tea Books would love to see more cozy mysteries and humor. Lucky Marble Books is looking for humor and engaging contemporary stories for middle grade and young adult readers.

PAJAMA PRESS

181 Carlaw Ave., Suite 207, Toronto ON M4M 2S1, Canada. 4164662222. **E-mail:** annfeatherstone@pajamapress.ca. **Website:** pajamapress.ca. **Contact:** Ann Featherstone, senior editor. Estab. 2011. "We publish picture books—both for the very young and for school-aged readers, as well as novels for middle grade readers and contemporary or historical fiction for young adults aged 12+. Our nonfiction titles typically contain a strong narrative element. Pajama Press is also looking for mss from authors of diverse backgrounds. Stories about immigrants are of special interest." Guidelines online.

NEEDS vampire novels; romance (except as part of a literary novel); fiction with overt political or religious messages

TERMS Pays advance. Responds in 6 weeks.

PANTHEON BOOKS

Penguin Random House, 1745 Broadway, New York NY 10019. **Website:** www.pantheonbooks.com. Estab. 1942. Publishes hardcover and trade paperback originals and trade paperback reprints.

Pantheon Books publishes both Western and non-Western authors of literary fiction and important nonfiction. "We only accept mss submitted by an agent."

HOW TO CONTACT *Does not accept unsolicited mss.* Agented submissions only.

PANTS ON FIRE PRESS

2062 Harbor Cove Way, Winter Garden FL 34787. (863)546-0760. **E-mail:** submission@pantsonfirepress.com. **Website:** www.pantsonfirepress.com. **Contact:** Becca Goldman, senior editor; Emily Gerety, editor. Estab. 2012. Pants On Fire Press is an award-winning book publisher of picture, middle-grade, young adult, and adult books. Publishes hardcover originals and reprints, trade paperback originals and reprints, and electronic originals and reprints. Catalog online. Guidelines online.

NEEDS Publishes big story ideas with high concepts, new worlds, and meaty characters for children, teens, and discerning adults. Always on the lookout for action, adventure, animals, comedic, dramatic, dystopian, fantasy, historical, paranormal, romance, sci-fi, supernatural, and suspense stories.

HOW TO CONTACT Submit a proposal package including a synopsis, 3 sample chapters, and a query letter via e-mail.

TERMS Pays 10-50% royalties on wholesale price. Responds in 3 months.

PAPERCUTZ

160 Broadway, Suite 700E, New York NY 10038. (646)559-4681. **Fax:** (212)643-1545. **Website:** www.papercutz.com. Estab. 2004. Publisher of graphic novels for kids and teens. Publishes major licenses and author created comics.

IMPRINTS SuperGenius, Charmz.

NEEDS "Independent publisher of graphic novels based on popular existing properties aimed at the teen and tween market."

TERMS Pays advance. Responds in 2-4 weeks.

TIPS "Be familiar with our titles—that's the best way to know what we're interested in publishing. If you are somehow attached to a successful tween or teen property and would like to adapt it into a graphic novel, we may be interested. We also take submissions for new series preferably that have already a following online."

PARADISE CAY PUBLICATIONS

P.O. Box 29, Arcata CA 95518-0029. (800)736-4509. **Fax:** (707)822-9163. **Website:** www.paracay.com. "Paradise Cay Publications, Inc. is a small independent publisher specializing in nautical books, videos, and art prints. Our primary interest is in mss that deal with the instructional and technical aspects of ocean sailing. We also publish and will consider fiction if it has a strong nautical theme." Publishes hardcover and trade paperback originals and reprints. Book catalog and ms guidelines free on request or online.

IMPRINTS Pardey Books.

NEEDS All fiction must have a nautical theme.

HOW TO CONTACT Query with SASE. Submit proposal package, clips, 2-3 sample chapters.

TERMS Pays 10-15% royalty on wholesale price. Makes outright purchase of $1,000-10,000. Does not normally pay advances to first-time or little-known authors. Responds in 1 month to queries/proposals; 2 months to mss.

TIPS "Audience is recreational sailors. Call Matt Morehouse (publisher)."

PAUL DRY BOOKS

1700 Sansom St., Suite 700, Philadelphia PA 19103. (215)231-9939. **Fax:** (215)231-9942. **E-mail:** editor@pauldrybooks.com. **E-mail:** pdry@pauldrybooks.com. **Website:** pauldrybooks.com. "We publish fiction, both novels and short stories, and nonfiction, biography, memoirs, history, and essays, covering subjects from Homer to Chekhov, bird watching to jazz music, New York City to shogunate Japan." Hardcover and trade paperback originals, trade paperback reprints. Book catalog online.

HOW TO CONTACT "We do not accept unsolicited mss."

TIPS "Our aim is to publish lively books 'to awaken, delight, and educate'—to spark conversation. We publish fiction and nonfiction, and essays covering subjects from Homer to Chekhov, bird watching to jazz music, New York City to shogunate Japan."

PAYCOCK PRESS

3819 N. 13th St., Arlington VA 22201. (703)525-9296. **E-mail:** rchrdpeabody9@gmail.com. **E-mail:** gargoyle@gargoylemagazine.com. **Website:** www.gargoylemagazine.com. **Contact:** Richard Peabody. Estab. 1976. "Too academic for the underground, too outlaw for the academic world. We tend to be edgy and look for ultra-literary work." Publishes paperback originals. Books: POD printing. Average print order: 500. Averages 1 total title/year. Member CLMP. Distributes through Amazon and website.

HOW TO CONTACT Accepts unsolicited mss. Accepts queries by e-mail. Include brief bio. Send SASE for return of ms or send a disposable ms and SASE for reply only.

TERMS Responds to queries in 1 month; mss in 4 months.

TIPS "Check out our website. Two of our favorite writers are Paul Bowles and Jeanette Winterson."

PEACHTREE CHILDREN'S BOOKS

Peachtree Publishers, Ltd., 1700 Chattahoochee Ave., Atlanta GA 30318. (404)876-8761. **Fax:** (404)875-2578. **E-mail:** hello@peachtree-online.com. **Website:** www.peachtree-online.com. **Contact:** Helen Harriss, submissions editor. "We publish a broad range of subjects and perspectives, with emphasis on innovative plots and strong writing." Publishes hardcover and trade paperback originals. Book catalog for 6 first-class stamps. Guidelines online.

NEEDS Looking for very well-written middle grade and young adult novels. No adult fiction. No collections of poetry or short stories; no romance or science fiction.

HOW TO CONTACT Submit complete ms with SASE.

TERMS Pays royalty on retail price. Responds in 6 months and mss.

PEACHTREE PUBLISHERS, LTD.

1700 Chattahoochee Ave., Atlanta GA 30318. (404)876-8761. **Fax:** (404)875-2578. **E-mail:** hello@peachtree-online.com. **Website:** www.peachtree-online.com. Estab. 1977.

NEEDS Picture books, young readers: adventure, animal, concept, history, nature/environment. Middle readers: adventure, animal, history, nature/environment, sports. Young adults: fiction, mystery, adventure. Does not want to see science fiction, romance.

HOW TO CONTACT Submit complete ms or 3 sample chapters by postal mail only.

TERMS Responds in 6-7 months.

✪⊘ PEDLAR PRESS

113 Bond St., St. John's NL A16 1T6, Canada. (709)738-6702. **E-mail:** feralgrl@interlog.com. **Website:** www.pedlarpress.com. **Contact:** Beth Follett, owner/editor. Estab. 1996. Catalog online.

NEEDS Experimental, feminist, gay/lesbian, literary, short story collections. Canadian writers only.

HOW TO CONTACT Query with SASE, sample chapter(s), synopsis.

TERMS Pays 10% royalty on retail price. Average advance: $200-400.

TIPS "I select mss according to my taste, which fluctuates. Be familiar with some if not most of Pedlar's recent titles."

PELICAN PUBLISHING COMPANY

1000 Burmaster St., Gretna LA 70053. (504)368-1175. **Fax:** (504)368-1195. **E-mail:** editorial@pelicanpub.com. **Website:** www.pelicanpub.com. Estab. 1926. " "We believe ideas have consequences. One of the consequences is that they lead to a best-selling book. We publish books to improve and uplift the reader. Currently emphasizing business and history titles." Publishes 20 young readers/year; 1 middle reader/year. "Our children's books (illustrated and otherwise) include history, biography, holiday, and regional.

Pelican's mission is to publish books of quality and permanence that enrich the lives of those who read them." Publishes hardcover, trade paperback and mass market paperback originals and reprints. Book catalog and ms guidelines online.

NEEDS We publish no adult fiction. Young readers: history, holiday, science, multicultural and regional. Middle readers: Louisiana History. Multicultural needs include stories about African-Americans, Irish-Americans, Jews, Asian-Americans, and Hispanics. Does not want animal stories, general Christmas stories, "day at school" or "accept yourself" stories. Maximum word length: young readers—1,100; middle readers—40,000. No young adult, romance, science fiction, fantasy, gothic, mystery, erotica, confession, horror, sex, or violence. Also no psychological novels.

HOW TO CONTACT Submit outline, clips, 2 sample chapters, SASE. Full guidelines on website.

TERMS Pays authors in royalties; buys ms outright "rarely." Illustrators paid by "various arrangements." Advance considered. Responds in 1 month to queries; 3 months to mss. Requires exclusive submission.

TIPS "We do extremely well with cookbooks, popular histories, and business. We will continue to build in these areas. The writer must have a clear sense of the market and knowledge of the competition. A query letter should describe the project briefly, give the author's writing and professional credentials, and promotional ideas."

⤵ PENGUIN GROUP: SOUTH AFRICA

P.O. Box 9, Parklands 2121, South Africa. (27)(11)327-3550. **Fax:** (27)(11)327-3660. **E-mail:** fiction@penguinrandomhouse.co.za. **E-mail:** nonfiction@penguinrandomhouse.co.za. **Website:** www.penguinbooks.co.za. Seeks adult fiction (literary and mass market titles) and adult nonfiction (travel, sports, politics, current affairs, business). No children's, young adult, poetry, or short stories.

HOW TO CONTACT Submit intro letter, 3 sample chapters.

TERMS Pays royalty.

Ⓐ PENGUIN GROUP USA

375 Hudson St., New York NY 10014. (212)366-2000. **Website:** www.penguin.com. General interest publisher of both fiction and nonfiction. *No unsolicited mss.* Submit work through a literary agent. DAW Books is the lone exception. Guidelines online.

Ⓐ PENGUIN RANDOM HOUSE, LLC

Division of Bertelsmann Book Group, 1745 Broadway, New York NY 10019. (212)782-9000. **Website:** www.penguinrandomhouse.com. Estab. 1925. Penguin Random House LLC is the world's largest English-language general trade book publisher. *Agented submissions only. No unsolicited mss.*

IMPRINTS Crown Publishing Group; Knopf Doubleday Publishing Group; Random House Publishing Group; Random House Children's Books; RH Digital Publishing Group; RH International.

THE PERMANENT PRESS

Second Chance Press, Attn: Judith Shepard, 4170 Noyac Rd., Sag Harbor NY 11963. (631)725-1101. **E-mail:** judith@thepermanentpress.com; shepard@thepermanentpress.com. **Website:** www.thepermanentpress.com. **Contact:** Judith and Martin Shepard, acquisitions/co-publishers. Estab. 1978. Mid-size, independent publisher of literary fiction. "We keep titles in print and are active in selling subsidiary rights." Average print order: 1,000-2,500. Averages 16 total titles. Accepts unsolicited mss. Pays 10-15% royalty on wholesale price. Offers $1,000 advance. *Will not accept simultaneous submissions.* Publishes hardcover originals. Catalog available.

NEEDS Promotes titles through reviews. Literary, mainstream/contemporary, mystery. Especially looking for high-line literary fiction, "artful, original and arresting." Accepts any fiction category as long as it is a "well-written, original full-length novel."

TERMS Pays 10-15% royalty on wholesale price. Offers $1,000 advance. Responds in weeks or months.

TIPS "We are looking for good books—be they 10th novels or first ones, it makes little difference. The fiction is more important than the track record. Send us the first 25 pages; it's impossible to judge something that begins on page 302. Also, no outlines—let the writing present itself."

PERSEA BOOKS

277 Broadway, Suite 708, New York NY 10007. (212)260-9256. **Fax:** (212)267-3165. **E-mail:** info@perseabooks.com. **Website:** www.perseabooks.com. Estab. 1975. The aim of Persea is to publish works that endure by meeting high standards of literary merit and relevance. "We have often taken on important books other publishers have overlooked, or have made significant discoveries and rediscoveries, whether of a single work or writer's entire oeuvre. Our books cover a wide range of themes, styles, and genres. We have published poetry, fiction, essays, memoir, biography, titles of Jewish and Middle Eastern interest, women's studies, American Indian folklore, and revived classics, as well as a notable selection of works in translation." Guidelines online.

HOW TO CONTACT Queries should include a cover letter, author background and publication history, a detailed synopsis of the proposed work, and a sample chapter. Please indicate if the work is simultaneously submitted.

TERMS Responds in 8 weeks to proposals; 10 weeks to mss.

Ⓐ PHILOMEL BOOKS

Imprint of Penguin Group (USA), Inc., 375 Hudson St., New York NY 10014. (212)414-3610. **Website:** www.penguin.com. **Contact:** Michael Green, president/publisher. Estab. 1980. "We look for beautifully written, engaging mss for children and young adults." Publishes hardcover originals.

HOW TO CONTACT *No unsolicited mss.*

TERMS Pays authors in royalties. Average advance payment "varies." Illustrators paid by advance and in royalties. Pays negotiable advance.

PIANO PRESS

P.O. Box 85, Del Mar CA 92014. (619)884-1401. **Fax:** (858)755-1104. **E-mail:** pianopress@pianopress.com. **Website:** www.pianopress.com. **Contact:** Elizabeth C. Axford, editor. Estab. 1984. "We publish music-related books, either fiction or nonfiction, music-related coloring books, songbooks, sheet music, CDs, and music-related poetry." Book catalog online.

NEEDS Picture books, young readers, middle readers, young adults: folktales, multicultural, poetry, music. Average word length: picture books—1,500-2,000.

TERMS Pays authors, illustrators, and photographers royalties based on the retail price. Responds if interested.

TIPS "We are looking for music-related material only for the juvenile market. Please do not send non-music-related materials. Query by e-mail first before submitting anything."

Ⓐ💬⊘ PIATKUS BOOKS

Little, Brown Book Group, Carmelite House, 50 Victoria Embankment, London EC4Y 0DZ, United Kingdom. (020)3122-7000. **Fax:** (020)3122-7000. **E-mail:** info@littlebrown.co.uk. **Website:** piatkus.co.uk. Estab. 1979. Publishes hardcover originals, paperback originals, and paperback reprints. Guidelines online.

NEEDS Romance fiction, women's fiction, bookclub fiction.

HOW TO CONTACT *Agented submissions only.*

PICADOR USA

MacMillan, 175 Fifth Ave., New York NY 10010. (212)674-5151. **Website:** us.macmillan.com/picador. Estab. 1994. Picador publishes high-quality literary fiction and nonfiction. "We are open to a broad range of subjects, well written by authoritative authors." Publishes hardcover and trade paperback originals and reprints. Does not accept unsolicited mss. *Agented submissions only.*

TERMS Pays 7-15% on royalty. Advance varies.

PIÑATA BOOKS

Imprint of Arte Publico Press, University of Houston, 4902 Gulf Fwy., Bldg. 19, Room 100, Houston TX 77204-2004. (713)743-2845. **Fax:** (713)743-3080. **E-mail:** submapp@uh.edu. **Website:** www.artepublicopress.com. Estab. 1994. "Piñata Books is dedicated to the publication of children's and young adult literature focusing on U.S. Hispanic culture by U.S. Hispanic authors. Arte Publico's mission is the publication, promotion and dissemination of Latino literature for a variety of national and regional audiences, from early childhood to adult, through the complete gamut of delivery systems, including personal performance as well as print and electronic media." Publishes hardcover and trade paperback originals. Book catalog and guidelines online.

HOW TO CONTACT Submissions made through online submission form.

TERMS Pays 10% royalty on wholesale price. Pays $1,000-3,000 advance. Responds in 2-3 months to queries; 4-6 months to mss.

TIPS "Include cover letter with submission explaining why your ms is unique and important, why we should publish it, who will buy it, etc."

PLAYLAB PRESS

P.O. Box 3701, South Brisbane BC 4101, Australia. **E-mail:** info@playlab.org.au. **Website:** www.playlab.org.au. Estab. 1978. Guidelines online.

HOW TO CONTACT Submit 2 copies of ms, cover letter.

TERMS Responds in 3 months to mss.

TIPS "Playlab Press is committed to the publication of quality writing for and about theatre and performance, which is of significance to Australia's cultural life. It values socially just and diverse publication outcomes and aims to promote these outcomes in local, national, and international contexts."

PLEXUS PUBLISHING, INC.

143 Old Marlton Pike, Medford NJ 08055. (609)654-6500. **Fax:** (609)654-4309. **E-mail:** rcolding@plexus-publishing.com. **Website:** www.plexuspublishing.com. **Contact:** Rob Colding, Book Marketing Manager. Estab. 1977. Plexus publishes regional-interest (southern New Jersey and the greater Philadelphia area) fiction and nonfiction including mysteries, field guides, nature, travel and history. Publishes hardcover and paperback originals. Book catalog and book proposal guidelines for 10x13 SASE.

NEEDS Mysteries and literary novels with a strong regional (southern New Jersey) angle.

HOW TO CONTACT Query with SASE.

TERMS Pays $500-1,000 advance. Responds in 3 months to proposals.

POCKET BOOKS

Simon & Schuster, 1230 Avenue of the Americas, New York NY 10020. (212)698-7000. **Website:** www.simonandschuster.com. Estab. 1939. Pocket Books publishes commercial fiction and genre fiction (WWE, Downtown Press, Star Trek). Publishes paperback originals and reprints, mass market and trade paperbacks. Book catalog available free. Guidelines online.

HOW TO CONTACT *Agented submissions only.*

POCOL PRESS

Box 411, Clifton VA 20124. (703)830-5862. **Website:** www.pocolpress.com. **Contact:** J. Thomas Hetrick, editor. Estab. 1999. "Pocol Press is dedicated to producing high-quality print books and e-books from first-time, nonagented authors. However, all submissions are welcome. We're dedicated to good storytellers and to the written word, specializing in short fiction and baseball. Several of our books have been used as literary texts at universities and in book group discussions around the nation. Pocol Press does not publish children's books, romance novels, or graphic novels. Our authors are comprised of veteran writers and emerging talents." Publishes trade paperback originals. Book catalog and guidelines online.

NEEDS "We specialize in thematic short fiction collections by a single author, westerns, war stories, and baseball fiction. Expert storytellers welcome."

HOW TO CONTACT Does not accept or return unsolicited mss. Query with SASE or submit 1 sample chapter.

TERMS Pays 10-12% royalty on wholesale price. Responds in 1 month to queries; 2 months to mss.

TIPS "Our audience is aged 18 and over. Pocol Press is unique; we publish good writing and great storytelling. Write the best stories you can. Read them to you friends/peers. Note their reaction. Publishes some of the finest fiction by a small press."

THE POISONED PENCIL

Poisoned Pen Press, 6962 E. 1st Ave., Suite 103, Scottsdale AZ 85251. (480)945-3375. **Fax:** (480)949-1707. **E-mail:** info@thepoisonedpencil.com. **E-mail:** ellen@thepoisonedpencil.com. **Website:** www.thepoisonedpencil.com. **Contact:** Ellen Larson, editor. Estab. 2012. Publishes trade paperback and electronic originals. Guidelines online.

○ *Accepts young adult mysteries only.*

NEEDS "We publish only young adult mystery novels, 45,000 to 90,000 words in length. For our purposes, a young adult book is a book with a protagonist between the ages of 13 and 18. We are looking for both traditional and cross-genre young adult mysteries. We encourage off-beat approaches and narrative choices that reflect the complexity and ambiguity of today's world. Submissions from teens are very welcome. Avoid serial killers, excessive gore, and vampires (and other heavy supernatural themes). We only consider authors who live in the U.S. or Canada, due to practicalities of marketing promotion. Avoid coincidence in plotting. Avoid having your sleuth leap to conclusions rather than discover and deduce. Pay attention to the resonance between character and plot; between plot and theme; between theme and character. We are looking for clean style, fluid storytelling, and solid structure. Unrealistic dialogue is a real turn-off."

HOW TO CONTACT Submit proposal package including synopsis, complete ms, and cover letter.

TERMS Pays 9-15% for trade paperback; 25-35% for e-books. Pays advance of $1,000. Responds in 6 weeks to mss.

TIPS "Our audience is made up of young adults and adults who love YA mysteries."

POISONED PEN PRESS

6962 E. 1st Ave., Suite 103, Scottsdale AZ 85251. **E-mail:** submissions@poisonedpenpress.com. **Website:** www.poisonedpenpress.com. **Contact:** Diane DiBi-

ase, Assistant Publisher. Estab. 1997. "Our publishing goal is to offer well-written mystery novels of crime and/or detection where the puzzle and its resolution are the main forces that move the story forward." Publishes hardcover and trade paperback originals, and hardcover and trade paperback reprints. Book catalog and guidelines online.

○ *Not currently accepting submissions. Check website.*

NEEDS Mss should generally be longer than 65,000 words and shorter than 100,000 words. Member Publishers Marketing Associations, Arizona Book Publishers Associations, Publishers Association of West. Distributes through Ingram, Baker & Taylor, Brodart. Does not want novels centered on serial killers, spousal or child abuse, drugs, or extremist groups, although we do not entirely rule such works out.

HOW TO CONTACT Accepts unsolicited mss. Electronic queries only. "Submit clips, first 3 pages. We must receive both the synopsis and ms pages electronically as separate attachments to an e-mail message."

TERMS Pays 9-15% royalty on retail price. Responds in 2-3 months to queries and proposals; 6 months to mss.

TIPS "Audience is adult readers of mystery fiction."

POLIS BOOKS

E-mail: info@polisbooks.com. **E-mail:** submissions@polisbooks.com. **Website:** www.polisbooks.com. Estab. 2013. "Polis Books is an independent publishing company actively seeking new and established authors for our growing list. We are actively acquiring titles in mystery, thriller, suspense, procedural, traditional crime, science fiction, fantasy, horror, supernatural, urban fantasy, romance, erotica, commercial women's fiction, commercial literary fiction, young adult and middle grade books." Guidelines online.

HOW TO CONTACT Query with 3 sample chapters and bio via e-mail.

TERMS Offers advance against royalties. Only responds to submissions if interested

PRESS 53

560 N. Trade St., Suite 103, Winston-Salem NC 27101. (336)770-5353. **E-mail:** editor@press53.com. **Website:** www.press53.com. **Contact:** Kevin Morgan Watson, publisher. Estab. 2005. "Press 53 was founded in October 2005 and quickly began earning a reputation as a quality publishing house of short fiction and poetry

collections." Poetry and short fiction collections only. Catalog online. Guidelines online.

NEEDS "We publish roughly 3-4 short fiction collections each year by writers who are active and earning recognition through publication and awards, plus the winner of our Press 53 Award for Short Fiction." Collections should be between 100 and 250 pages (give or take) with 70% or more of those stories previously published in journals, magazines, anthologies, etc. Does not want novels.

HOW TO CONTACT Finds mss through contest, referrals, and scouting magazines, journals, and contests.

TERMS Pays 10% royalty on gross sales. Pays advance only for contest winners.

TIPS "We are looking for writers who are actively involved in the writing community, writers who are submitting their work to journals, magazines and contests, and who are getting published, building readership, and earning a reputation for their work."

Ⓐ PUFFIN BOOKS

Imprint of Penguin Group (USA), Inc., 375 Hudson St., New York NY 10014. (212)366-2000. **Website:** www.penguin.com. "Puffin Books publishes high-end trade paperbacks and paperback reprints for preschool children, beginning and middle readers, and young adults." Publishes trade paperback originals and reprints.

HOW TO CONTACT *No unsolicited mss. Agented submissions only.*

TIPS "Our audience ranges from little children 'first books' to young adult (ages 14-16). An original idea has the best luck."

Ⓐ G.P. PUTNAM'S SONS HARDCOVER

Imprint of Penguin Group (USA), Inc., 375 Hudson, New York NY 10014. (212)366-2000. **Fax:** (212)366-2664. **Website:** www.penguin.com. Publishes hardcover originals. Request book catalog through mail order department.

HOW TO CONTACT *Agented submissions only.*

TERMS Pays variable royalties on retail price. Pays varies advance.

Ⓐ RANDOM HOUSE PUBLISHING GROUP

Division of Random House, Inc., 1745 Broadway, New York NY 10019. (212)782-9000. **Website:** www.penguinrandomhouse.com. Estab. 1925. Random House is the world's largest English-language general trade book publisher. It includes an array of prestigious imprints that publish some of the foremost writers of our time. Publishes hardcover and paperback trade books.

IMPRINTS Ballantine Books; Bantam; Delacorte; Dell; Del Rey; Modern Library; One World; Presidio Press; Random House Trade Group; Random House Trade Paperbacks; Spectra; Spiegel & Grau; Triumph Books; Villard.

HOW TO CONTACT *Agented submissions only.*

RAZORBILL

Penguin Young Readers Group, 345 Hudson St., New York NY 10014. (212)414-3427. **E-mail:** asanchez@penguinrandomhouse.com; bschrank@penguinrandomhouse.com; jharriton@penguinrandomhouse.com. **Website:** www.razorbillbooks.com. **Contact:** Jessica Almon, executive editor; Casey McIntyre, associate publisher; Deborah Kaplan, vice president and executive art director, Marissa Grossman; assistant editor, Tiffany Liao; associate editor. Estab. 2003. "This division of Penguin Young Readers is looking for the best and the most original of commercial contemporary fiction titles for middle grade and YA readers. A select quantity of nonfiction titles will also be considered."

NEEDS Middle Readers: adventure, contemporary, graphic novels, fantasy, humor, problem novels. Young adults/teens: adventure, contemporary, fantasy, graphic novels, humor, multicultural, suspense, paranormal, science fiction, dystopian, literary, romance. Average word length: middle readers—40,000; young adult—60,000.

HOW TO CONTACT Submit cover letter with up to 30 sample pages.

TERMS Offers advance against royalties. Responds in 1-3 months.

TIPS "New writers will have the best chance of acceptance and publication with original, contemporary material that boasts a distinctive voice and well-articulated world. Check out website to get a better idea of what we're looking for."

Ⓒ REBELIGHT PUBLISHING, INC.

23-845 Dakota St., Suite 314, Winnipeg Manitoba R2M 5M3, Canada. **Website:** www.rebelight.com. **Contact:** Editor. Estab. 2014. Rebelight Publishing is interested in "crack the spine, blow your mind" mss for middle grade, young adult and new adult novels. *Only considers submissions from Canadian writers.* Publishes paperback and electronic originals. Catalog online or PDF available via e-mail request. Guidelines online.

NEEDS All genres are considered, provided they are for a middle grade, young adult, or new adult audience. "Become familiar with our books. Study our website. Stick within the guidelines. Our tag line is 'crack the spine, blow your mind'—we are looking for well-written, powerful, fresh, fast-paced fiction. Keep us turning the pages. Give us something we just have to spread the word about."

HOW TO CONTACT Submit proposal package, including a synopsis and 3 sample chapters. Read guidelines carefully.

TERMS Pays 12-22% royalties on retail price. Does not offer an advance. Responds in 3 months to queries and mss. Submissions accepted via e-mail only.

TIPS "Review your ms for passive voice prior to submitting! (And that means get rid of it.)"

RED DEER PRESS

195 Allstate Pkwy., Markham ON L3R 4TB, Canada. (905)477-9700. **Fax:** (905)477-9179. **E-mail:** rdp@reddeerpress.com. **Website:** www.reddeerpress.com. **Contact:** Richard Dionne, publisher. Estab. 1975. Book catalog for 9 x 12 SASE.

Red Deer Press is an award-winning publisher of children's and young adult literary titles.

NEEDS Publishes young adult, adult science fiction, fantasy, and paperback originals "focusing on books by, about, or of interest to Canadians." Books: offset paper; offset printing; hardcover/perfect-bound. Average print order: 5,000. First novel print order: 2,500. Distributes titles in Canada and the U.S., the U.K., Australia and New Zealand. Young adult (juvenile and early reader), contemporary. No romance or horror.

TERMS Pays 8-10% royalty.

TIPS "We're very interested in young adult and children's fiction from Canadian writers with a proven track record (either published books or widely published in established magazines or journals) and for mss with regional themes and/or a distinctive voice. We publish Canadian authors exclusively."

RED HEN PRESS

P.O. Box 40820, Pasadena CA 91114. (626)356-4760. **Fax:** (626)356-9974. **Website:** www.redhen.org. **Contact:** Mark E. Cull, publisher/executive director. Estab. 1993. "At this time, the best opportunity to be published by Red Hen is by entering 1 of our contests. Please find more information in our award submission guidelines." Publishes trade paperback originals. Book catalog available free. Guidelines online.

HOW TO CONTACT Query with synopsis and either 20-30 sample pages or complete ms using online submission manager.

TERMS Responds in 1-2 months.

TIPS "Audience reads poetry, literary fiction, intelligent nonfiction. If you have an agent, we may be too small since we don't pay advances. Write well. Send queries first. Be willing to help promote your own book."

RED SAGE PUBLISHING, INC.

P.O. Box 4844, Seminole FL 33775. (727)391-3847. **E-mail:** submissions@eredsage.com. **Website:** www.eredsage.com. **Contact:** Alexandria Kendall. Estab. 1995. Publishes books of romance fiction, written for the adventurous woman. Guidelines online and all submissions via e-mail.

HOW TO CONTACT Read guidelines.

TERMS Pays author royalty.

RED TUQUE BOOKS, INC.

477 Martin St., Unit #6, Penticton BC V2A 5L2, Canada. (778)476-5750. **Fax:** (778)476-5651. **E-mail:** dave@redtuquebooks.ca. **E-mail:** Not accepting e-mail submissions. Queries only. **Website:** www.redtuquebooks.ca. **Contact:** David Korinetz, executive editor. Estab. 2009. Red Tuque Books is primarily a book distributor, that also publishes catalogues and anthologies. Interested in Canadian authors only, except for the Annual Canadian Tales Anthology, which will accept stories written about Canada or Canadians by non-Canadians. Publication in the anthology is only through submissions via the Canadian Tales writing contest. See website for details. Contest submissions only.

NEEDS Novels

HOW TO CONTACT Submit a query letter, 1-page synopsis, and first 5 pages only. Include total word count. Accepts ms only by mail. SASE or e-mail address for reply.

TERMS Pays fixed award amount for anthology ($25 to $500). Does not pay advance. Responds in 3-6 weeks.

TIPS "Well-plotted, character-driven stories, preferably with happy endings, will have the best chance of being accepted. Keep in mind that authors who like to begin sentences with 'and, or, and but' are less likely to be considered. Don't send anything gruesome or overly explicit; tell us a good story, but think PG."

ⓐ REVELL

Division of Baker Publishing Group, 6030 E. Fulton Rd., Ada MI 49301. (616)676-9185. **Fax:** (616)676-9573. **Website:** www.bakerbooks.com. Estab. 1870. "Revell publishes to the heart (rather than to the head). For 125 years, Revell has been publishing evangelical books for the personal enrichment and spiritual growth of general Christian readers." Publishes hardcover, trade paperback and mass market paperback originals. Book catalog and ms guidelines online.

◯ *No longer accepts unsolicited mss.*

RIVER CITY PUBLISHING

1719 Mulberry St., Montgomery AL 36106. **E-mail:** fnorris@rivercitypublishing.com. **Website:** www.rivercitypublishing.com. **Contact:** Fran Norris, editor. Estab. 1989. Midsize independent publisher. River City publishes literary fiction, regional, short story collections. No poetry, memoir, or children's books. We also consider narrative histories, sociological accounts, and travel; however, only biographies and memoirs from noted persons will be considered. Publishes hardcover and trade paperback originals.

NEEDS No poetry, memoir, or children's books.

HOW TO CONTACT Send appropriate-sized SASE or IRC, "otherwise, the material will be recycled." Also accepts queries by e-mail. "Please include your electronic query letter as inline text and not an as attachment; we do not open unsolicited attachments of any kind." No multiple submissions. Rarely comments on rejected mss.

TERMS Responds within 9 months.

TIPS "Only send your best work after you have received outside opinions. From approximately 1,000 submissions each year, we publish no more than 8 books and few of those come from unsolicited material. Competition is fierce, so follow the guidelines exactly. First-time novelists are also encouraged to send work."

ⓐ RIVERHEAD BOOKS

Penguin Putnam, 375 Hudson St., New York NY 10014. **Website:** www.penguin.com.

HOW TO CONTACT *Submit through agent only. No unsolicited mss.*

ⓐ ROARING BROOK PRESS

Macmillan Children's Publishing Group, 175 Fifth Ave., New York NY 10010. (646)307-5151. **Website:** us.macmillan.com. Estab. 2000. Roaring Brook Press is an imprint of MacMillan, a group of companies that includes Henry Holt and Farrar, Straus & Giroux. *Roaring Brook is not accepting unsolicited mss.*

NEEDS Picture books, young readers, middle readers, young adults: adventure, animal, contemporary, fantasy, history, humor, multicultural, nature/environment, poetry, religion, science fiction, sports, suspense/mystery.

HOW TO CONTACT *Not accepting unsolicited mss or queries.*

TERMS Pays authors royalty based on retail price.

TIPS "You should find a reputable agent and have him/her submit your work."

◑ RONSDALE PRESS

3350 W. 21st Ave., Vancouver BC V6S 1G7, Canada. (604)738-4688. **Fax:** (604)731-4548. **E-mail:** ronsdale@shaw.ca. **Website:** ronsdalepress.com. **Contact:** Ronald B. Hatch (fiction, poetry, nonfiction, social commentary); Veronica Hatch (YA novels and short stories). Estab. 1988. "Ronsdale Press is a Canadian literary publishing house that publishes 12 books each year, 4 of which are young adult titles. Of particular interest are books involving children exploring and discovering new aspects of Canadian history." Publishes trade paperback originals. Book catalog for #10 SASE. Guidelines online.

NEEDS Young adults: Canadian novels. Average word length: middle readers and young adults—50,000.

HOW TO CONTACT Submit complete ms.

TERMS Pays 10% royalty on retail price. Responds to queries in 2 weeks; mss in 2 months.

TIPS "Ronsdale Press is a literary publishing house, based in Vancouver, and dedicated to publishing books from across Canada, books that give Canadians new insights into themselves and their country. We aim to publish the best Canadian writers."

SADDLEBACK EDUCATIONAL PUBLISHING

3120-A Pullman St., Costa Mesa CA 92626. (888)735-2225. **E-mail:** contact@sdlback.com. **Website:** www.sdlback.com. Saddleback is always looking for fresh, new talent. "Please note that we primarily publish books for kids ages 12-18."

NEEDS "We look for diversity for our characters and content."

HOW TO CONTACT Mail typed submission along with a query letter describing the work simply and where it fits in with other titles.

SAGUARO BOOKS, LLC

16201 E. Keymar Dr., Fountain Hills AZ 85268. **Fax:** (480)284-4855. **E-mail:** mjnickum@saguarobooks.com. **Website:** www.saguarobooks.com. **Contact:** Mary Nickum, CEO. Estab. 2012. Saguaro Books, LLC is a publishing company specializing in middle grade and young adult ficiton by first-time authors. Publishes trade paperback and electronic originals. Catalog online. Guidelines by e-mail.

NEEDS Ms should be well-written; signed letter by a professional editor is required. Does not want agented work.

HOW TO CONTACT Query via e-mail before submitting work. Any material sent before requested will be ignored.

TERMS Pays 20% royalties after taxes and publication costs. Does not offer advance. Responds within 3 months only if we're interested.

TIPS "Visit our website before sending us a query. Pay special attention to the For Authors Only page."

Ⓐ ST. MARTIN'S PRESS, LLC

Holtzbrinck Publishers, 175 Fifth Ave., New York NY 10010. (212)674-5151. **Fax:** (212)420-9314. **Website:** www.stmartins.com. Estab. 1952. General interest publisher of both fiction and nonfiction. Publishes hardcover, trade paperback and mass market originals.

HOW TO CONTACT *Agented submissions only. No unsolicited mss.*

TERMS Pays royalty. Pays advance.

SAKURA PUBLISHING & TECHNOLOGIES

805 Lindaraxa Park North, Alhambra CA 91801. (330)360-5131. **E-mail:** skpublishing124@gmail.com. **Website:** www.sakura-publishing.com. **Contact:** Derek Vasconi, submissions coordinator. Estab. 2007. Visit our website for query guidelines. Mss that don't follow guidelines will not be considered. Sakura Publishing is a traditional, independent book publishing company that seeks to publish Asian-themed books, particularly Asian-Horror, or anything dealing with Japan, Japanese culture, and Japanese horror. Publishes trade paperback, mass market paperback and electronic originals and reprints. Currently accepts only the following genres: Asian fiction, Japanese fiction (in English), Nonfiction, and horror. Please do not send queries for any other genres. Book catalog available for #10 SASE. Guidelines online.

NEEDS Only looking for Asian horror, with preference given to Japanese horror, as well as Japanese fiction, Japanese erotica, Asian erotica. Will consider other types of Asian-centered fiction, but top preference will be on fiction centered in or dealing with Japan or Japanese people living in America.

HOW TO CONTACT Follow guidelines online.

TERMS Royalty payments on paperback, e-book, wholesale, and merchandise Does not pay advance. Responds in 1 week.

TIPS "Please make sure you visit our submissions page at our website and follow all instructions exactly as written. Also, Sakura Publishing has a preference for fiction/nonfiction books specializing in Asian culture."

SALINA BOOKSHELF

1120 W. University Ave., Suite 102, Flagstaff AZ 86001. (877)527-0070. **Fax:** (928)526-0386. **Website:** www.salinabookshelf.com. Publishes trade paperback originals and reprints.

NEEDS Submissions should be in English or Navajo. "All our books relate to the Navajo language and culture."

HOW TO CONTACT Query with SASE.

TERMS Pays varying royalty. Pays advance. Responds in 3 months to queries.

SALVO PRESS

An imprint of Start Publishing, 101 Hudson St., 37th Floor, Suite 3705, Jersey City NJ 07302. **E-mail:** info@salvopress.com. **Website:** www.salvopress.com. Estab. 1998. Salvo Press proudly publishes mysteries, thrillers, and literary books in e-book and audiobook formats. Book catalog and ms guidelines online.

NEEDS "We are a small press specializing in mystery, suspense, espionage and thriller fiction. Our press publishes in trade paperback and most e-book formats."

HOW TO CONTACT Query by e-mail.

TERMS Pays 10% royalty. Responds in 5 minutes to 1 month to queries; 2 months to mss.

SARABANDE BOOKS, INC.

822 E. Market St., Louisville KY 40206. (502)458-4028. **Fax:** (502)458-4065. **E-mail:** info@sarabandebooks.org. **Website:** www.sarabandebooks.org. **Con-**

tact: Sarah Gorham, Editor-in-Chief. Estab. 1994. "Sarabande Books was founded to publish poetry, short fiction, and creative nonfiction. We look for works of lasting literary value. Please see our titles to get an idea of our taste. Accepts submissions through contests and open submissions." Publishes trade paperback originals. Book catalog available free. Contest guidelines for #10 SASE or on website.

○ Charges $15 handling fee with alternative option of purchase of book from website (e-mail confirmation of sale must be included with submission).

NEEDS "We consider novels and nonfiction in a wide variety of genres. We do not consider genre fiction such as science fiction, fantasy, or horror. Our target length is 70,000-90,000 words."

HOW TO CONTACT Queries can be sent via e-mail, fax, or regular post.

TERMS Pays royalty. 10% on actual income received. Also pays in author's copies. Pays $500-1,000 advance.

TIPS "Sarabande publishes for a general literary audience. Know your market. Read-and buy-books of literature. Sponsors contests for poetry and fiction. Make sure you're not writing in a vacuum, that you've read and are conscious of contemporary literature. Have someone read your ms, checking it for ordering, coherence. Better a lean, consistently strong ms than one that is long and uneven. We like a story to have good narrative, and we like to be engaged by language."

SASQUATCH BOOKS

1904 Third Ave., Suite 710, Seattle WA 98101. (206)467-4300. **Fax:** (206)467-4301. **E-mail:** custserv@sasquatchbooks.com. **Website:** www.sasquatchbooks.com. Estab. 1986. "Sasquatch Books publishes books for and from the Pacific Northwest, Alaska, and California is the nation's premier regional press. Sasquatch Books' publishing program is a veritable celebration of regionally written words. Undeterred by political or geographical borders, Sasquatch defines its region as the magnificent area that stretches from the Brooks Range to the Gulf of California and from the Rocky Mountains to the Pacific Ocean. Our top-selling Best Places® travel guides serve the most popular destinations and locations of the West. We also publish widely in the areas of food and wine, gardening, nature, photography, children's books, and regional history, all facets of the literature of place. With more than 200 books brimming with insider information on the West, we offer an energetic eye on the lifestyle, landscape, and worldview of our region. Considers queries and proposals from authors and agents for new projects that fit into our West Coast regional publishing program. We can evaluate query letters, proposals, and complete mss." Publishes regional hardcover and trade paperback originals. Guidelines online.

NEEDS Young readers: adventure, animal, concept, contemporary, humor, nature/environment.

TERMS Pays royalty on cover price. Pays wide range advance. Responds to queries in 3 months.

TIPS "We sell books through a range of channels in addition to the book trade. Our primary audience consists of active, literate residents of the West Coast."

Ⓐ SCHOLASTIC PRESS

Imprint of Scholastic, Inc., 557 Broadway, New York NY 10012. (212)343-6100. **Fax:** (212)343-4713. **Website:** www.scholastic.com. Scholastic Press publishes fresh, literary picture book fiction and nonfiction; fresh, literary nonseries or nongenre-oriented middle grade and young adult fiction. Currently emphasizing subtly handled treatments of key relationships in children's lives; unusual approaches to commonly dry subjects, such as biography, math, history, or science. De-emphasizing fairy tales (or retellings), board books, genre, or series fiction (mystery, fantasy, etc.). Publishes hardcover originals.

NEEDS Looking for strong picture books, young chapter books, appealing middle grade novels (ages 8-11) and interesting and well-written young adult novels. Wants fresh, exciting picture books and novels—inspiring, new talent.

HOW TO CONTACT *Agented submissions only.*

TERMS Pays royalty on retail price. Pays variable advance. Responds in 3 months to queries; 6-8 months to mss.

TIPS "Read *currently* published children's books. Revise, rewrite, rework and find your own voice, style and subject. We are looking for authors with a strong and unique voice who can tell a great story and have the ability to evoke genuine emotion. Children's publishers are becoming more selective, looking for irresistible talent and fairly broad appeal, yet still very willing to take risks, just to keep the game interesting."

SCRIBE PUBLICATIONS

18-20 Edward St., Brunswick VIC 3056, Australia. (61)(3)9388-8780. **E-mail:** info@scribepub.com.au. **E-mail:** submissions@scribepub.com.au. **Website:** www.scribepublications.com.au. **Contact:** Anna Thwaites. Estab. 1976. Scribe has been operating as a wholly independent trade-publishing house for almost 40 years. What started off in 1976 as a desire on publisher Henry Rosenbloom's part to publish 'serious nonfiction' as a one-man band has turned into a multi-award-winning company with 20 staff members in two locations — Melbourne, Australia and London, England — and a scout in New York. Scribe publishes over 65 nonfiction and fiction titles annually in Australia and about 40 in the United Kingdom. "We currently have acquiring editors working in both our Melbourne and London offices. We spend each day sifting through submissions and mss from around the world, and commissioning and editing local titles, in an uncompromising pursuit of the best books we can find, help create, and deliver to readers. We love what we do, and we hope you will, too." Guidelines online.

IMPRINTS Scribble.

HOW TO CONTACT Submit synopsis, sample chapters, CV.

TIPS "We are only able to consider unsolicited submissions if you have a demonstrated background of writing and publishing for general readers."

SCRIBNER

Imprint of Simon & Schuster Adult Publishing Group, 1230 Avenue of the Americas, 12th Floor, New York NY 10020. (212)698-7000. **Website:** www.simonsays.com. Publishes hardcover originals.

HOW TO CONTACT *Agented submissions only.*

TERMS Pays 7-15% royalty. Pays variable advance. Responds in 3 months to queries

SECOND STORY PRESS

20 Maud St., Suite 401, Toronto ON M5V 2M5, Canada. (416)537-7850. **Fax:** (416)537-0588. **E-mail:** info@secondstorypress.ca. **Website:** www.secondstorypress.ca. "Please keep in mind that as a feminist press, we are looking for nonsexist, nonracist and nonviolent stories, as well as historical fiction, chapter books, novels and biography."

NEEDS Considers nonsexist, nonracist, and nonviolent stories, as well as historical fiction, chapter books, picture books.

SEEDLING CONTINENTAL PRESS

520 E. Bainbridge St., Elizabethtown PA 17022. (800)233-0759. **Website:** www.continentalpress.com. "Continental publishes educational materials for grades K-12, specializing in reading, mathematics, and test preparation materials. We are not currently accepting submissions for Seedling leveled readers or instructional materials."

NEEDS Young readers: adventure, animal, folktales, humor, multicultural, nature/environment. Does not accept texts longer than 12 pages or over 300 words. Average word length: young readers—100.

HOW TO CONTACT Submit complete ms.

TERMS Work purchased outright from authors. Responds to mss in 6 months.

TIPS "See our website. Follow writers' guidelines carefully and test your story with children and educators."

SEVEN STORIES PRESS

140 Watts St., New York NY 10013. (212)226-8760. **Fax:** (212)226-1411. **E-mail:** info@sevenstories.com. **Website:** www.sevenstories.com. **Contact:** Acquisitions. Estab. 1995. Founded in 1995 in New York City, and named for the 7 authors who committed to a home with a fiercely independent spirit, Seven Stories Press publishes works of the imagination and political titles by voices of conscience. While most widely known for its books on politics, human rights, and social and economic justice, Seven Stories continues to champion literature, with a list encompassing both innovative debut novels and National Book Award–winning poetry collections, as well as prose and poetry translations from the French, Spanish, German, Swedish, Italian, Greek, Polish, Korean, Vietnamese, Russian, and Arabic. Publishes hardcover and trade paperback originals. Book catalog and ms guidelines free.

HOW TO CONTACT Submit cover letter with 2 sample chapters.

TERMS Pays 7-15% royalty on retail price. Pays advance. Responds in 1 month.

SEVERN HOUSE PUBLISHERS

Salatin House, 19 Cedar Rd., Sutton, Surrey SM2 5DA, United Kingdom. (44)(208)770-3930. **Fax:** (44)(208)770-3850. **Website:** www.severnhouse.com. Severn House is currently emphasizing suspense, romance, mystery. Large print imprint from existing authors. Publishes hardcover and trade paperback originals and reprints. Book catalog available free. **HOW TO CONTACT** *Agented submissions only.* **TERMS** Pays 7-15% royalty on retail price. Pays $750-5,000 advance. Responds in 3 months to proposals.

SHAMBHALA PUBLICATIONS, INC.

4720 Walnut St., Boulder CO 80304. **E-mail:** submissions@shambhala.com. **Website:** www.shambhala.com. Estab. 1969. Publishes hardcover and trade paperback originals and reprints. Book catalog free. Guidelines online.

IMPRINTS Roost Books; Snow Lion.

TERMS Pays 8% royalty on retail price. Responds in 4 months.

SHIPWRECKT BOOKS PUBLISHING COMPANY LLC

309 W. Stevens Ave., Rushford MN 55971. **E-mail:** editor@shipwrecktbooks.com. **E-mail:** contact@shipwrecktbooks.com. **Website:** www.shipwrecktbooks.com. **Contact:** Tom Driscoll, managing editor. Publishes trade paperback originals, mass market paperback originals, and electronic originals. Catalog and guidelines online.

IMPRINTS Rocket Science Press (literary); Up On Big Rock Poetry Series; Lost Lake Folk Art (memoir, biography, essays, fiction and nonfiction).

HOW TO CONTACT E-mail query first. All unsolicited mss returned unopened.

TERMS Authors receive a maximum of 35% royalties. Responds to queries within 6 months.

TIPS "Quality writing. Query first. Development and full editorial services available."

Ⓐ SIMON & SCHUSTER

1230 Avenue of the Americas, New York NY 10020. (212)698-7000. **Website:** www.simonandschuster.com. *Accepts agented submissions only.*

IMPRINTS Aladdin; Atheneum Books for Young Readers; Atria; Beach Lane Books; Folger Shakespeare Library; Free Press; Gallery Books; Howard Books; Little Simon; Margaret K. McElderry Books; Pocket; Scribner; Simon & Schuster; Simon & Schuster Books for Young Readers; Simon Pulse; Simon Spotlight; Threshold; Touchstone; Paula Wiseman Books.

Ⓐ SIMON & SCHUSTER BOOKS FOR YOUNG READERS

Imprint of Simon & Schuster Children's Publishing, 1230 Avenue of the Americas, New York NY 10020.

(212)698-7000. **Fax:** (212)698-2796. **Website:** www.simonsayskids.com. "Simon and Schuster Books For Young Readers is the Flagship imprint of the S&S Children's Division. We are committed to publishing a wide range of contemporary, commercial, award-winning fiction and nonfiction that spans every age of children's publishing. BFYR is constantly looking to the future, supporting our foundation authors and franchises, but always with an eye for breaking new ground with every publication. We publish high-quality fiction and nonfiction for a variety of age groups and a variety of markets. Above all, we strive to publish books that we are passionate about." *No unsolicited mss.* All unsolicited mss returned unopened. Publishes hardcover originals. Guidelines online.

HOW TO CONTACT *Agented submissions only.*

TERMS Pays variable royalty on retail price.

TIPS "We're looking for picture books centered on a strong, fully-developed protagonist who grows or changes during the course of the story; YA novels that are challenging and psychologically complex; also imaginative and humorous middle-grade fiction. And we want nonfiction that is as engaging as fiction. Our imprint's slogan is 'Reading You'll Remember.' We aim to publish books that are fresh, accessible and family-oriented; we want them to have an impact on the reader."

Ⓞ SIMPLY READ BOOKS

501-5525 W. Blvd., Vancouver BC V6M 3W6, Canada. **E-mail:** go@simplyreadbooks.com. **Website:** www.simplyreadbooks.com. Simply Read Books is current seeking mss in picture books, early readers, early chapter books, middle grade fiction, and graphic novels.

HOW TO CONTACT Query or submit complete ms.

SKINNER HOUSE BOOKS

The Unitarian Universalist Association, 24 Farnsworth St., Boston MA 02210. (617)742-2100, ext. 603. **Fax:** (617)948-6466. **E-mail:** bookproposals@uua.org. **Website:** www.uua.org/publications/skinnerhouse. **Contact:** Betsy Martin. Estab. 1975. "We publish titles in Unitarian Universalist faith, liberal religion, history, biography, worship, and issues of social justice. Most of our children's titles are intended for religious education or worship use. They reflect Unitarian Universalist values. We also publish inspirational titles of poetic prose and meditations. Writers should know that Unitarian Universalism is a liberal religious denomination committed to progressive ideals. Currently emphasizing social justice concerns." Publishes trade paperback originals and reprints. Book catalog for 6×9 SAE with 3 first-class stamps. Guidelines online.

NEEDS Only publishes fiction for children's titles for religious instruction.

HOW TO CONTACT Query.

TERMS Responds to queries in 1 month.

TIPS "From outside our denomination, we are interested in mss that will be of help or interest to liberal churches, Sunday School classes, parents, ministers, and volunteers. Inspirational/spiritual and children's titles must reflect liberal Unitarian Universalist values."

SKY PONY PRESS

307 W. 36th St., 11th Floor, New York NY 10018. (212)643-6816. **Fax:** (212)643-6819. **Website:** skyponypress.com. Estab. 2011. Sky Pony Press is the children's book imprint of Skyhorse Publishing. "Following in the footsteps of our parent company, our goal is to provide books for readers with a wide variety of interests." Guidelines online.

NEEDS "We will consider picture books, early readers, midgrade novels, novelties, and informational books for all ages."

HOW TO CONTACT Submit ms or proposal.

SLEEPING BEAR PRESS

2395 South Huron Parkway #200, Ann Arbor MI 48104. (800)487-2323. **Fax:** (734)794-0004. **E-mail:** submissions@sleepingbearpress.com. **Website:** www.sleepingbearpress.com. **Contact:** Manuscript Submissions. Estab. 1998. Book catalog available via e-mail.

NEEDS Picture books: adventure, animal, concept, folktales, history, multicultural, nature/environment, religion, sports. Young readers: adventure, animal, concept, folktales, history, humor, multicultural, nature/environment, religion, sports. Average word length: picture books—1,800.

HOW TO CONTACT Accepts unsolicited queries 3 times per year. See website for details. Query with sample of work (up to 15 pages) and SASE. Please address packages to Manuscript Submissions.

SMALL BEER PRESS

150 Pleasant St., #306, Easthampton MA 01027. (413)203-1636. **Fax:** (413)203-1636. **E-mail:** info@smallbeerpress.com. **Website:** www.smallbeerpress.com. Estab. 2000. Small Beer Press also publishes the zine *Lady Churchill's Rosebud Wristlet.* "SBP's books have recently received the Tiptree and Crawford Awards."

HOW TO CONTACT Does not accept unsolicited novel or short story collection mss. Send queries with first 10-20 pages and SASE.

TERMS Advance and standard royalties.

TIPS "Please be familiar with our books first to avoid wasting your time and ours, thank you. E-mail queries will be deleted. Really."

SMITH AND KRAUS PUBLISHERS, INC.

177 Lyme Rd., Hanover NH 03755. (603)643-6431. **E-mail:** editor@smithandkraus.com. **E-mail:** carolb@smithandkraus.com. **Website:** smithandkraus.com. Estab. 1990. Publishes hardcover and trade paperback originals. Book catalog available free.

NEEDS Does not return submissions.

HOW TO CONTACT Query with SASE.

TERMS Pays 7% royalty on retail price. Pays $500-2,000 advance. Responds in 1 month to queries; 2 months to proposals; 4 months to mss.

SOFT SKULL PRESS INC.

Counterpoint, 2650 Ninth St., Suite 318, Berkeley CA 94710. (510)704-0230. **Fax:** (510)704-0268. **E-mail:** info@counterpointpress.com. **Website:** www.softskull.com. "Here at Soft Skull we love books that are new, fun, smart, revelatory, quirky, groundbreaking, cage-rattling and/or otherwise unusual." Publishes hardcover and trade paperback originals. Book catalog and guidelines online.

NEEDS Does not consider poetry.

HOW TO CONTACT Soft Skull Press no longer accepts digital submissions. Send a cover letter describing your project in detail and a completed ms. For graphic novels, send a minimum of 5 fully inked pages of art, along with a synopsis of your storyline. "Please do not send original material, as it will not be returned."

TERMS Pays 7-10% royalty. Average advance: $100-15,000. Responds in 2 months to proposals; 3 months to mss.

TIPS "See our website for updated submission guidelines."

SOHO PRESS, INC.

853 Broadway, New York NY 10003. (212)260-1900. **E-mail:** soho@sohopress.com. **Website:** www.sohopress.com. **Contact:** Bronwen Hruska, publisher; Mark Doten, senior editor. Estab. 1986. Soho Press

publishes primarily fiction, as well as some narrative literary nonfiction and mysteries set abroad. No electronic submissions, only queries by e-mail. Publishes hardcover and trade paperback originals; trade paperback reprints. Guidelines online.

NEEDS Adventure, ethnic, feminist, historical, literary, mainstream/contemporary, mystery (police procedural), suspense, multicultural.

HOW TO CONTACT Submit 3 sample chapters and cover letter with synopsis, author bio, SASE. *No e-mailed submissions.*

TERMS Pays 10-15% royalty on retail price (varies under certain circumstances). Responds in 3 months.

TIPS "Soho Press publishes discerning authors for discriminating readers, finding the strongest possible writers and publishing them. Before submitting, look at our website for an idea of the types of books we publish, and read our submission guidelines."

SOURCEBOOKS CASABLANCA

Sourcebooks, Inc., 232 Madison Ave., Suite 1100, New York NY 10016. **E-mail:** romance@sourcebooks. com. **Website:** www.sourcebooks.com. **Contact:** Deb Werksman (deb.werksman@sourcebooks.com). "Our romance imprint, Sourcebooks Casablanca, publishes single title romance in all subgenres." Guidelines online.

NEEDS "Our editorial criteria call for: a heroine the reader can relate to, a hero she can fall in love with, a world gets created that the reader can escape into, there's a hook that we can sell within 2-3 sentences, and the author is out to build a career with us."

TERMS Responds in 2-3 months.

TIPS "We are actively acquiring single-title and single-title series romance fiction (90,000-100,000 words) for our Casablanca imprint. We are looking for strong writers who are excited about marketing their books and building their community of readers, and whose books have something fresh to offer in the genre of romance."

SOURCEBOOKS FIRE

1935 Brookdale Rd., Suite 139, Naperville IL 60563. (630)961-3900. **Fax:** (630)961-2168. **E-mail:** submissions@sourcebooks.com. **Website:** www.sourcebooks.com. "We're actively acquiring knockout books for our YA imprint. We are particularly looking for strong writers who are excited about promoting and building their community of readers, and whose books have something fresh to offer the ever-growing young adult audience. We are not accepting any unsolicited or unagented mss at this time. Unfortunately, our staff can no longer handle the large volume of mss that we receive on a daily basis. We will continue to consider agented mss." See website for details.

HOW TO CONTACT Query with the full ms attached in Word doc.

SOURCEBOOKS LANDMARK

Sourcebooks, Inc., Sourcebooks, Inc., 232 Madison Ave., Suite 1100, New York NY 10016. **E-mail:** editorialsubmissions@sourcebooks.com. **Website:** www. sourcebooks.com. "Our fiction imprint, Sourcebooks Landmark, publishes a variety of commercial fiction, including specialties in historical fiction and Austenalia. We are interested first and foremost in books that have a story to tell."

NEEDS "We are actively acquiring contemporary, book club, and historical fiction for our Landmark imprint. We are looking for strong writers who are excited about marketing their books and building their community of readers."

HOW TO CONTACT Submit synopsis and full ms preferred. Receipt of e-mail submissions acknowledged within 3 weeks of e-mail.

TERMS Responds in 2-3 months.

SPENCER HILL PRESS

27 W. 20th St., Suite 1102, New York NY 10011. **Website:** www.spencerhillpress.com. Spencer Hill Press is an independent publishing house specializing in sci-fi, urban fantasy, and paranormal romance for young adult readers. "Our books have that 'I couldn't put it down!' quality." Guidelines online.

NEEDS "We are interested in young adult, new adult, and middle grade sci-fi, psych-fi, paranormal, or urban fantasy, particularly those with a strong and interesting voice."

HOW TO CONTACT Check website for open submission periods.

STERLING PUBLISHING CO., INC.

1166 Avenue of the Americas, 17th Floor, New York NY 10036. (212)532-7160. **Website:** www.sterlingpublishing.com. "Sterling publishes highly illustrated, accessible, hands-on, practical books for adults and children. Our mission is to publish high-quality books that educate, entertain, and enrich the lives of our readers." Publishes hardcover and paperback originals and reprints. Catalog online. Guidelines online.

NEEDS Publishes fiction for children.

HOW TO CONTACT Submit to attention of "Children's Book Editor."

TERMS Pays royalty or work purchased outright. Offers advances (average amount: $2,000).

TIPS "We are primarily a nonfiction activities-based publisher. We have a picture book list, but we do not publish chapter books or novels. Our list is not trend-driven. We focus on titles that will backlist well. "

STONE ARCH BOOKS

1710 Roe Crest Rd., North Mankato MN 56003. **Website:** www.stonearchbooks.com. Catalog online.

NEEDS Imprint of Capstone Publishers.Young readers, middle readers, young adults: adventure, contemporary, fantasy, humor, light humor, mystery, science fiction, sports, suspense. Average word length: young readers—1,000-3,000; middle readers and early young adults—5,000-10,000.

HOW TO CONTACT Submit outline/synopsis and 3 sample chapters. Electronic submissions preferred. Full guidelines available on website.

TERMS Work purchased outright from authors.

TIPS "A high-interest topic or activity is one that a young person would spend their free time on without adult direction or suggestion."

STONE BRIDGE PRESS

P.O. Box 8208, Berkeley CA 94707. **E-mail:** sbp@stonebridge.com. **Website:** www.stonebridge.com. **Contact:** Peter Goodman, publisher. Estab. 1989. "Independent press focusing on books about Asia, primarily Japan and China, in English (business, language, culture, literature, animation)." Publishes hardcover and trade paperback originals. Books: 60-70 lb. offset paper; web and sheet paper; perfect bound; some illustrations. Distributes titles through Consortium. Promotes titles through Internet announcements, special-interest magazines and niche tie-ins to associations. Catalog online.

NEEDS Experimental, gay/lesbian, literary, Asia-themed. "Primarily looking at material relating to Asia, especially Japan and China. "

HOW TO CONTACT Does not accept unsolicited mss. Accepts queries by e -mail.

TERMS Pays royalty on wholesale price. Responds to queries in 4 months; mss in 8 months.

TIPS "Query first before submitting. Research us first and avoid sending mss not in our subject area. Generic and bulk submissions will be ignored. No poetry. Looking also for graphic novels, not manga or serializations."

STONESLIDE BOOKS

Stoneslide Media LLC, P.O. Box 8331, New Haven CT 06530. **Website:** www.stoneslidecorrective.com. Estab. 2012. "We like novels with strong character development and narrative thrust, brought out with writing that's clear and expressive." Publishes trade paperback and electronic originals. Book catalog and guidelines online.

NEEDS "We will look at any genre. The important factor for us is that the story use plot, characters, emotions, and other elements of storytelling to think and move the mind forward."

HOW TO CONTACT Submit proposal package via online submission form including: synopsis and 3 sample chapters.

TERMS Pays 20-80% royalty. Responds in 1-2 months.

TIPS "Read the Stoneslide Corrective to see if your work fits with our approach."

SUBITO PRESS

University of Colorado at Boulder, Dept. of English, 226 UCB, Boulder CO 80309-0226. **E-mail:** subitopressucb@gmail.com. **Website:** www.subitopress.org. Subito Press is a nonprofit publisher of literary works. Each year Subito publishes one work of fiction and one work of poetry through its contest. Publishes trade paperback originals. Guidelines online.

HOW TO CONTACT Submit complete ms to contest.

TIPS "We publish 2 books of innovative writing a year through our poetry and fiction contests. All entries are also considered for publication with the press."

SUNBURY PRESS, INC.

105 S. Market St., Mechanicsburg PA 17055. **E-mail:** info@sunburypress.com. **E-mail:** proposals@sunburypress.com. **Website:** www.sunburypress.com. Estab. 2004. Sunbury Press, Inc., headquartered in Mechanicsburg, PA is a publisher of trade paperback, hard cover and digital books featuring established and emerging authors in many fiction and nonfiction categories. Sunbury's books are printed in the USA and sold through leading booksellers worldwide. "Please use our online submission form." Publishes trade paperback and hardcover originals and reprints; electronic originals and reprints. Catalog and guidelines online.

NEEDS "We are especially seeking climate change / dystopian fiction and books of regional interest."

TERMS Pays 10% royalty on wholesale price. Responds in 3 months.

TIPS "Our books appeal to very diverse audiences. We are building our list in many categories, focusing on many demographics. We are not like traditional publishers—we are digitally adept and very creative. Don't be surprised if we move quicker than you are accustomed to!"

SUNSTONE PRESS

Box 2321, Santa Fe NM 87504. (800)243-5644. **Website:** www.sunstonepress.com. **Contact:** Submissions Editor. Sunstone's original focus was on nonfiction subjects that preserved and highlighted the richness of the American Southwest but it has expanded its view over the years to include mainstream themes and categories—both nonfiction and fiction—that have a more general appeal. Guidelines online.

HOW TO CONTACT Query with 1 sample chapter.

☙ SWEET CHERRY PUBLISHING

Unit 36, Vulcan Business Complex, Vulcan Rd., Leicester Leicestershire LE5 3EF, United Kingdom. **E-mail:** info@sweetcherrypublishing.com. **E-mail:** submissions@sweetcherrypublishing.com. **Website:** www.sweetcherrypublishing.com. Estab. 2011. Sweet Cherry Publishing is an independent publishing company based in Leicester. Our aim is to provide children with compelling worlds and engaging characters that they will want to revisit time and time again. Guidelines online.

NEEDS No erotica.

HOW TO CONTACT Submit a cover letter and a synopsis with 3 sample chapters via post or e-mail. Please note that we strongly prefer e-mail submissions.

TERMS Offers one-time fee for work that is accepted.

TIPS "We strongly prefer e-mail submissions over postal submissions. If your work is accepted, Sweet Cherry may consider commissioning you for future series."

☙ TAFELBERG PUBLISHERS

Imprint of NB Publishers, P.O. Box 879, Cape Town 8000, South Africa. (27)(21)406-3033. **Fax:** (27)(21)406-3812. **E-mail:** engela.reinke@nb.co.za. **Website:** www.tafelberg.com. **Contact:** Engela Reinke. General publisher best known for Afrikaans fiction, authoritative political works, children's/youth literature, and a variety of illustrated and nonillustrated nonfiction.

NEEDS Picture books, young readers: animal, anthology, contemporary, fantasy, folktales, hi-lo, humor, multicultural, nature/environment, scient fiction, special needs. Middle readers, young adults: animal (middle reader only), contemporary, fantasy, hi-lo, humor, multicultural, nature/environment, problem novels, science fiction, special needs, sports, suspense/mystery. Average word length: picture books—1,500-7,500; young readers—25,000; middle readers—15,000; young adults—40,000.

HOW TO CONTACT Submit complete ms.

TERMS Pays authors royalty of 15-18% based on wholesale price. Responds to queries in 2 weeks; mss in 6 months.

TIPS "Writers: Story needs to have a South African or African style. Illustrators: I'd like to look, but the chances of getting commissioned are slim. The market is small and difficult. Do not expect huge advances. Editorial staff attended or plans to attend the following conferences: IBBY, Frankfurt, SCBWI Bologna."

Ⓐ NAN A. TALESE

Imprint of Doubleday, Random House, 1745 Broadway, New York NY 10019. (212)782-8918. **Fax:** (212)782-8448. **Website:** www.nanatalese.com. Nan A. Talese publishes nonfiction with a powerful guiding narrative and relevance to larger cultural interests, and literary fiction of the highest quality. Publishes hardcover originals.

NEEDS Well-written narratives with a compelling story line, good characterization and use of language. We like stories with an edge.

HOW TO CONTACT *Agented submissions only.*

TERMS Pays variable royalty on retail price. Pays varying advance.

TIPS "Audience is highly literate people interested in story, information and insight. We want well-written material submitted by agents only. See our website."

TANTOR MEDIA

Recorded Books, 6 Business Park Rd., Old Saybrook CT 06475. (860)395-1155. **Fax:** (860)395-1154. **E-mail:** rightsemail@tantor.com. **Website:** www.tantor.com. **Contact:** Ron Formica, director of acquisitions. Estab. 2001. Tantor Media, a division of Recorded Books, is a leading audiobook publisher, producing more than 100 new titles every month. We do not publish print or e-books. Publishes audiobooks only. Catalog online. Not accepting print or e-book queries. We only publish audiobooks.

TERMS Responds in 2 months.

TEXAS TECH UNIVERSITY PRESS

1120 Main St., Second Floor, Box 41037, Lubbock TX 79415. (806)742-2982. **Fax:** (806)742-2979. **E-mail:** ttup@ttu.edu. **Website:** www.ttupress.org. Estab. 1971. Texas Tech University Press, the book publishing office of the university since 1971 and an AAUP member since 1986, publishes nonfiction titles in the areas of natural history and the natural sciences; 18th century and Joseph Conrad studies; studies of modern Southeast Asia, particularly the Vietnam War; costume and textile history; Latin American literature and culture; and all aspects of the Great Plains and the American West, especially history, biography, memoir, sports history, and travel. In addition, the Press publishes several scholarly journals, acclaimed series for young readers, an annual invited poetry collection, and literary fiction of Texas and the West. Guidelines online.

NEEDS Fiction rooted in the American West and Southwest, Jewish literature, Latin American and Latino fiction (in translation or English).

☺ THISTLEDOWN PRESS LTD.

410 2nd Ave., Saskatoon SK S7K 2C3, Canada. (306)244-1722. **Fax:** (306)244-1762. **E-mail:** editorial@thistledownpress.com. **Website:** www.thistledownpress.com. **Contact:** Allan Forrie, publisher. Estab. 1975. "Thistledown originates books by Canadian authors only, although we have co-published titles by authors outside Canada. We do not publish children's picture books." Book catalog on website. Guidelines online.

NEEDS Young adults: adventure, anthology, contemporary, fantasy, humor, poetry, romance, science fiction, suspense/mystery, short stories. Average word length: young adults—40,000.

HOW TO CONTACT Submit outline/synopsis and sample chapters. *Does not accept mss.* Do not query by e-mail. "Please note: we are not accepting middle years (ages 8-12) nor children's mss at this time." See Submission Guidelines on Website.

TERMS Pays authors royalty of 10-12% based on net dollar sales. Pays illustrators and photographers by

the project (range: $250-750). Rarely pays advance. Responds to queries in 6 months.

TIPS "Send cover letter including publishing history and SASE."

THUNDERSTONE BOOKS

6575 Horse Dr., Las Vegas NV 89131. **E-mail:** info@thunderstonebooks.com. **Website:** www.thunderstonebooks.com. **Contact:** Rachel Noorda, editorial director. Estab. 2014. "At ThunderStone Books, we aim to publish children's books that have an educational aspect. We are not looking for curriculum for learning certain subjects, but rather stories that encourage learning for children, whether that be learning about a new language/culture or learning more about science and math in a fun, fictional format. We want to help children to gain a love for other languages and subjects so that they are curious about the world around them. We are currently accepting fiction and nonfiction submissions. Picture books without accompanying illustration will not be accepted." Publishes hardcover, trade paperback, mass market paperback, and electronic originals. Catalog available for SASE. Guidelines available.

NEEDS Interested in multicultural stories with an emphasis on authentic culture and language (these may include mythology).

HOW TO CONTACT "If you think your book is right for us, send a query letter with a word attachment of the first 50 pages to info@thunderstonebooks.com. If it is a picture book or chapter book for young readers that is shorter than 50 pages send the entire ms."

TERMS Pays 5-15% royalties on retail price. Pays $300-1,000 advance. Responds in 3 months.

☺⊘ TIGHTROPE BOOKS

#207-2 College St., Toronto ON M5G 1K3, Canada. (416)928-6666. **E-mail:** tightropeasst@gmail.com. **Website:** www.tightropebooks.com. Estab. 2005. Publishes trade paperback originals. Catalog and guidelines online.

☺ Accepting submissions for literary fiction, nonfiction and poetry from Canadian citizens and permanent Canadian residents only.

TERMS Pays 5-15% royalty on retail price. Pays advance of $200-300. Responds if interested.

TIPS "Audience is urban, literary, educated, unconventional."

A TIN HOUSE BOOKS

2617 NW Thurman St., Portland OR 97210. (503)473-8663. **Fax:** (503)473-8957. **E-mail:** masie@tinhouse.com. **Website:** www.tinhouse.com. **Contact:** Masie Cochran, editor; Tony Perez, editor. "We are a small independent publisher dedicated to nurturing new, promising talent as well as showcasing the work of established writers." Distributes/promotes titles through W. W. Norton. Publishes hardcover originals, paperback originals, paperback reprints. Guidelines online.

HOW TO CONTACT *Agented mss only.* "We no longer read unsolicited submissions by authors with no representation. We will continue to accept submissions from agents."

TERMS Responds to queries in 2-3 weeks; mss in 2-3 months.

TITAN PRESS

PMB 17897, Encino CA 91416. **E-mail:** titan91416@yahoo.com. **Website:** https://www.facebook.com/RV-Clef. **Contact:** Romana V. Clef, editor. Estab. 1981. Little literary publisher. Publishes hardcover and paperback originals.

HOW TO CONTACT Does not accept unsolicited mss. Query with SASE. Include brief bio, list of publishing credits.

TERMS Pays 20-40% royalty. Responds to queries in 3 months.

TIPS "Look, act, sound, and *be* professional."

TOR BOOKS

Tom Doherty Associates, 175 Fifth Ave., New York NY 10010. **Website:** www.tor-forge.com. Tor Books is the "world's largest publisher of science fiction and fantasy, with strong category publishing in historical fiction, mystery, western/Americana, thriller, YA." Book catalog available. Guidelines online.

HOW TO CONTACT Submit first 3 chapters, 3-10 page synopsis, dated cover letter, SASE.

TERMS Pays author royalty. Pays illustrators by the project.

TORREY HOUSE PRESS

2806 Melony Dr., Salt Lake City UT 84124. **E-mail:** kirsten@torreyhouse.com. **Website:** torreyhouse.org. **Contact:** Kirsten Allen. Estab. 2010. Torrey House Press is an independent nonprofit publisher promoting environmental conservation through literature.

Publishes hardcover, trade paperback, and electronic originals. Catalog online. Guidelines online.

NEEDS "Torrey House Press publishes literary fiction and creative nonfiction about the world environment and the American West."

HOW TO CONTACT Submit proposal package including: synopsis, complete ms, bio.

TERMS Pays 5-15% royalty on retail price. Responds in 3 months.

TIPS "Include writing experience (none okay)."

☺ TOUCHWOOD EDITIONS

The Heritage Group, 103-1075 Pendergast St., Victoria BC V8V 0A1, Canada. (250)360-0829. **Fax:** (250)386-0829. **E-mail:** edit@touchwoodeditions.com. **Website:** www.touchwoodeditions.com. **Contact:** Renée Layberry, Editor. Publishes trade paperback, originals and reprints. Book catalog and guidelines online.

HOW TO CONTACT Submit bio/CV, marketing plan, TOC, outline, word count.

TERMS Pays 15% royalty on net price. Responds in 6 months to queries.

TIPS "Our area of interest is western Canada. We would like more creative nonfiction and fiction from First Nations authors, and welcome authors who write about notable individuals in Canada's history. Please note we do not publish poetry."

☺ TRADEWIND BOOKS

202-1807 Maritime Mews, Granville Island, Vancouver BC V6H 3W7, Canada. (604)662-4405. **Website:** www.tradewindbooks.com. "Tradewind Books publishes juvenile picture books and young adult novels. Requires that submissions include evidence that author has read at least 3 titles published by Tradewind Books." Publishes hardcover and trade paperback originals. Book catalog and ms guidelines online.

NEEDS Average word length: 900 words.

HOW TO CONTACT Send complete ms for picture books. *YA novels by Canadian authors only. Chapter books by U.S. authors considered.* For chapter books/Middle Grade Fiction, submit the first three chapters, a chapter outline and plot summary.

TERMS Pays 7% royalty on retail price. Pays variable advance. Responds to mss in 2 months.

TRIANGLE SQUARE

Seven Stories Press, 140 Watts St., New York NY 10013. (212)226-8760. **Fax:** (212)226-1411. **E-mail:** info@sevenstories.com. **Website:** https://www.sevenstories.com/imprints/triangle-square. Triangle

Square is a children's and young adult imprint of Seven Story Press.

HOW TO CONTACT Send a cover letter with 2 sample chapters and SASE. Send c/o Acquisitions.

TRISTAN PUBLISHING

2355 Louisiana Ave. N, Golden Valley MN 55427. (763)545-1383. **Fax:** (763)545-1387. **E-mail:** info@tristanpublishing.com; manuscripts@tristanpublishing.com. **Website:** www.tristanpublishing.com. **Contact:** Brett Waldman, publisher. Estab. 2002. Publishes hardcover originals. Catalog and guidelines online.
HOW TO CONTACT Query with SASE; submit completed mss.
TERMS Pays royalty on wholesale or retail price; outright purchase. Responds in 3 months.
TIPS "Our audience is adults and children."

TU BOOKS

Lee & Low Books, 95 Madison Ave., Suite #1205, New York NY 10016. **Website:** www.leeandlow.com/imprints/3. **Contact:** Stacy Whitman, Publisher. Estab. 2010. The Tu imprint spans many genres: science fiction, fantasy, mystery, contemporary, and more. We don't believe in labels or limits, just great stories. Join us at the crossroads where fantasy and real life collide. You'll be glad you did. Young adult and middle grade novels and graphic novels: science fiction, fantasy, contemporary realism, mystery, historical fiction, and more, with particular interest in books with strong literary hooks.

○ For new writers of color, please be aware of the New Visions Award writing contest, which runs every year from June-October. Previously unpublished writers of color and Native American writers may submit their middle grade and young adult novels. See submission guidelines for the contest at https://www.leeandlow.com/writers-illustrators/new-visions-award.

NEEDS At Tu Books, an imprint of Lee & Low Books, our focus is on well-told, exciting, adventurous fantasy, science fiction, and mystery novels and graphic novels starring people of color. We also selectively publish realism that explores the contemporary and historical experiences of people of color. We look for fantasy set in worlds inspired by non-Western folklore or culture, contemporary mysteries and fantasy set all over the world starring people of color, and science fiction that centers the possibilities for people of color in the future. We welcome intersectional narratives that feature LGBTQIA and disabled POC as heroes in their own stories. We are looking specifically for stories for both middle grade (ages 8-12) and young adult (ages 12-18) readers. Occasionally a ms might fall between those two categories; if your ms does, let us know. We are not looking for picture books, chapter books, or short stories at this time. Please do not send submissions in these categories. (See the Lee & Low Books guidelines for books for younger young readers.) Not seeking picture books or chapter books.
HOW TO CONTACT Please include a synopsis and first three chapters of the novel. Do not send the complete ms. Mss should be doubled-spaced. Mss should be accompanied by a cover letter that includes a brief biography of the author, including publishing history. The letter should also state if the ms is a simultaneous or an exclusive submission. "We're looking for middle grade (ages 8-12) and young adult (ages 12 and up) books. We are not looking for chapter books (ages 6 to 9) at this time. Be sure to include full contact information on the first page of the ms. Page numbers and your last name/title of the book should appear on subsequent pages." Unsolicited mss should be submitted online.
TERMS Advance against royalties. Pays advance. Responds only if interested.

TUMBLEHOME LEARNING

P.O. Box 71386, Boston MA 02117. **E-mail:** info@tumblehomelearning.com. **E-mail:** submissions@tumblehomelearning.com. **Website:** www.tumblehomelearning.com. **Contact:** Pendred Noyce, editor. Estab. 2011. Tumblehome Learning helps kids imagine themselves as young scientists or engineeers and encourages them to experience science through adventure and discovery. "We do this with exciting mystery and adventure tales as well as experiments carefully designed to engage students from ages 8 and up." Publishes hardcover, trade paperback, and electronic originals. Catalog available online. Guideliens available on request for SASE.
NEEDS "All our fiction has science at its heart. This can include using science to solve a mystery (see *The Walking Fish* by Rachelle Burk or *Something Stinks!* by Gail Hedrick), realistic science fiction, books in our Galactic Academy of Science series, science-based adventure tales, and the occasional picture book with a science theme, such as appreciation of the stars and constellations in *Elizabeth's Constellation Quilt* by

Olivia Fu. A graphic novel about science would also be welcome."

HOW TO CONTACT Submit completed ms electronically.

TERMS Pays authors 8-12% royalties on retail price. Pays $500 advance. Responds in 1 month to queries and proposals, and 2 months to mss.

TIPS "Please don't submit to us if your book is not about science. We don't accept generic books about animals or books with glaring scientific errors in the first chapter. That said, the book should be fun to read and the science content can be subtle. We work closely with authors, including first-time authors, to edit and improve their books. As a small publisher, the greatest benefit we can offer is this friendly and respectful partnership with authors."

TUPELO PRESS

P.O. Box 1767, North Adams MA 01247. (413)664-9611. **Website:** www.tupelopress.org. **Contact:** Sarah Russell, administrative director. Estab. 2001. "We're an independent nonprofit literary press. We publish book-length poetry, poetry collections, translations, short story collections, novellas, literary nonfiction/memoirs and novels." Guidelines online.

NEEDS "For Novels—submit no more than 100 pages along with a summary of the entire book. If we're interested we'll ask you to send the rest. We accept very few works of prose (3 or 4 per year)."

HOW TO CONTACT Submit complete ms. **Charges a $45 reading fee.**

TERMS Standard royalty contract. Pays advance in rare instances.

✪ TURNSTONE PRESS

Artspace Building, 206-100 Arthur St., Winnipeg MB R3B 1H3, Canada. (204)947-1555. **Fax:** (204)942-1555. **Website:** www.turnstonepress.com. **Contact:** Submissions Assistant. Estab. 1976. "Turnstone Press is a literary publisher, not a general publisher, and therefore we are only interested in literary fiction, literary nonfiction—including literary criticism—and poetry. We do publish literary mysteries, thrillers, and noir under our Ravenstone imprint. We publish only Canadian authors or landed immigrants, we strive to publish a significant number of new writers, to publish in a variety of genres, and to have 50% of each year's list be Manitoba writers and/or books with Manitoba content." Guidelines online.

HOW TO CONTACT "Samples must be 40 to 60 pages, typed/printed in a minimum 12 point serif typeface such as Times, Book Antiqua, or Garamond."

TERMS Responds in 4-7 months.

TIPS "As a Canadian literary press, we have a mandate to publish Canadian writers only. Do some homework before submitting works to make sure your subject matter/genre/writing style falls within the publishers area of interest."

TWILIGHT TIMES BOOKS

P.O. Box 3340, Kingsport TN 37664. **E-mail:** publisher@twilighttimesbooks.com. **Website:** www.twilighttimesbooks.com. **Contact:** Andy M. Scott, managing editor. Estab. 1999. "We publish compelling literary fiction by authors with a distinctive voice." Published 5 debut authors within the last year. Averages 120 total titles; 15 fiction titles/year. Member: AAP, PAS, SPAN, SLF. Guidelines online.

HOW TO CONTACT Accepts unsolicited mss. Do not send complete mss. Queries via e-mail only. Include estimated word count, brief bio, list of publishing credits, marketing plan.

TERMS Pays 8-15% royalty. Responds in 4 weeks to queries; 2 months to mss.

TIPS "The only requirement for consideration at Twilight Times Books is that your novel must be entertaining and professionally written."

TWO DOLLAR RADIO

Website: www.twodollarradio.com. **Contact:** Eric Obenauf, editorial director. Estab. 2005. Two Dollar Radio is a boutique family-run press, publishing bold works of literary merit, each book, individually and collectively, providing a sonic progression that "we believe to be too loud to ignore." Targets readers who admire ambition and creativity. Range of print runs: 2,000-7,500 copies.

HOW TO CONTACT Submit entire, completed ms with a brief cover letter, via Submittable. No previously published work. No proposals. No excerpts. There is a $2 reading fee per submission. Accepts submissions every other month (January, March, May, July, September, November).

TERMS Advance: $500-1,000.

TIPS "We want writers who show an authority over language and the world that is being created, from the very first sentence on."

Ⓐ TYNDALE HOUSE PUBLISHERS, INC.

351 Executive Dr., Carol Stream IL 60188. (800)323-9400. **Fax:** (800)684-0247. **Website:** www.tyndale.com. Estab. 1962. "Tyndale House publishes practical, user-friendly Christian books for the home and family." Publishes hardcover and trade paperback originals and mass paperback reprints. Guidelines online.

NEEDS "Christian truths must be woven into the story organically. No short story collections. Youth books: character building stories with Christian perspective. Especially interested in ages 10-14. We primarily publish Christian historical romances, with occasional contemporary, suspense, or standalones."

HOW TO CONTACT *Agented submissions only. No unsolicited mss.*

TERMS Pays negotiable royalty. Pays negotiable advance.

TIPS "All accepted mss will appeal to Evangelical Christian children and parents."

UNBRIDLED BOOKS

8201 E. Highway WW, Columbia MO 65201. **E-mail:** michalsong@unbridledbooks.com. **Website:** unbridledbooks.com. **Contact:** Greg Michalson. Estab. 2004. "Unbridled Books is a premier publisher of works of rich literary quality that appeal to a broad audience."

HOW TO CONTACT Please query first by e-mail. "Due to the heavy volume of submissions, we regret that at this time we are not able to consider uninvited mss."

TIPS "We try to read each ms that arrives, so please be patient."

UNIVERSITY OF ALASKA PRESS

P.O. Box 756240, Fairbanks AK 99775-6240. (907)474-5831 or (888)252-6657. **Fax:** (907)474-5502. **Website:** www.uaf.edu/uapress. Estab. 1967. "The mission of the University of Alaska Press is to encourage, publish, and disseminate works of scholarship that will enhance the store of knowledge about Alaska and the North Pacific Rim, with a special emphasis on the circumpolar regions." Publishes hardcover originals, trade paperback originals and reprints. Book catalog available free. Guidelines online.

NEEDS Alaska literary series with Peggy Shumaker as series editor. Publishes 1-3 works of fiction/year.

HOW TO CONTACT Submit proposal.

TERMS Responds in 2 months to queries.

TIPS "Writers have the best chance with scholarly nonfiction relating to Alaska, the circumpolar regions and North Pacific Rim. Our audience is made up of scholars, historians, students, libraries, universities, individuals, and the general Alaskan public."

UNIVERSITY OF GEORGIA PRESS

Main Library, Third Floor, 320 S. Jackson St., Athens GA 30602. (706)369-6130. **Fax:** (706)369-6131. **Website:** www.ugapress.org. **Contact:** Mick Gusinde-Duffy, executive editor; Walter Biggins, executive editor; Pat Allen, acquisitions editor; Beth Snead, assistant acquisitions editor. Estab. 1938. University of Georgia Press is a midsized press that publishes fiction only through the Flannery O'Connor Award for Short Fiction competition. Publishes hardcover originals, trade paperback originals, and reprints. Book catalog and guidelines online.

NEEDS Short story collections published in Flannery O'Connor Award Competition.

TERMS Pays 7-10% royalty on net receipts. Pays rare, varying advance. Responds in 2 months to queries.

TIPS "Please visit our website to view our book catalogs and for all ms submission guidelines."

UNIVERSITY OF IOWA PRESS

100 Kuhl House, 119 W. Park Rd., Iowa City IA 52242. (319)335-2000. **Fax:** (319)335-2055. **E-mail:** james-mccoy@uiowa.edu. **Website:** www.uiowapress.org. **Contact:** James McCoy, director. Estab. 1969. The University of Iowa Press publishes both trade and academic work in a variety of fields. Publishes hardcover and paperback originals. Book catalog available free. Guidelines online.

NEEDS Currently publishes the Iowa Short Fiction Award selections. "We do not accept any fiction submissions outside of the Iowa Short Fiction Award. See www.uiowapress.org for contest details."

UNIVERSITY OF MICHIGAN PRESS

839 Greene St., Ann Arbor MI 48106. (734)764-4388. **Fax:** (734)615-1540. **Website:** www.press.umich.edu. **Contact:** Mary Francis, editorial director. "In partnership with our authors and series editors, we publish in a wide range of humanities and social sciences disciplines." Guidelines online.

NEEDS In addition to the annual Michigan Literary Fiction Awards, this publishes literary fiction linked to the Great Lakes region.

HOW TO CONTACT Submit cover letter and first 30 pages.

UNIVERSITY OF TAMPA PRESS

The University of Tampa, 401 W. Kennedy Blvd., Tampa FL 33606. (813)253-6266. **E-mail:** utpress@ut.edu. **Website:** www.ut.edu/tampapress. **Contact:** Richard Mathews, editor. Estab. 1952. "We are a small university press publishing a limited number of titles each year, primarily in the areas of local and regional history, poetry, and printing history. We do not accept e-mail submissions." Publishes hardcover originals and reprints; trade paperback originals and reprints. Book catalog online.

TERMS Does not pay advance. Responds in 3-4 months to queries.

UNIVERSITY OF WISCONSIN PRESS

1930 Monroe St., 3rd Floor, Madison WI 53711. **E-mail:** kadushin@wisc.edu; gcwalker@wisc.edu. **Website:** uwpress.wisc.edu. **Contact:** Raphael Kadushin, executive editor; Gwen Walker, editorial director. Estab. 1937. See submission guidelines on our website.

HOW TO CONTACT Query with SASE or submit outline, 1-2 sample chapter(s), synopsis.

TERMS Pays royalty. Responds in 1-3 weeks to queries; 3-6 weeks to proposals. Rarely comments on rejected work.

TIPS "Make sure the query letter and sample text are well-written, and read guidelines carefully to make sure we accept the genre you are submitting."

ⒶⓈⓄ USBORNE PUBLISHING

83-85 Saffron Hill, London EC1N 8RT, United Kingdom. (44)207430-2800. **Fax:** (44)207430-1562. **E-mail:** mail@usborne.co.uk. **Website:** www.usborne.com. "Usborne Publishing is a multiple-award-winning, worldwide children's publishing company publishing almost every type of children's book for every age from baby to young adult."

NEEDS Young readers, middle readers: adventure, contemporary, fantasy, history, humor, multicultural, nature/environment, science fiction, suspense/mystery, strong concept-based or character-led series. Average word length: young readers—5,000-10,000; middle readers—25,000-50,000; young adult—50,000-100,000.

HOW TO CONTACT *Agented submissions only.*

TERMS Pays authors royalty.

TIPS "Do not send any original work and, sorry, but we cannot guarantee a reply."

Ⓞ VÉHICULE PRESS

P.O.B. 42094 BP Roy, Montreal QC H2W 2T3, Canada. (514)844-6073. **Fax:** (514)844-7543. **E-mail:** sd@vehiculepress.com. **E-mail:** admin@vehiculepress.com. **Website:** www.vehiculepress.com. **Contact:** Simon Dardick, nonfiction; Carmine Starnino, poetry; Dimitri Nasrallah, fiction. Estab. 1973. "Montreal's Véhicule Press has published the best of Canadian and Quebec literature-fiction, poetry, essays, translations, and social history." Publishes trade paperback originals by Canadian authors mostly. Book catalog for 9 x 12 SAE with IRCs.

IMPRINTS Signal Editions (poetry); Esplanade Editions (fiction).

NEEDS No romance or formula writing.

HOW TO CONTACT Query with SASE.

TERMS Pays 10-15% royalty on retail price. Pays $200-500 advance. Responds in 4 months to queries.

TIPS "Quality in almost any style is acceptable. We believe in the editing process."

Ⓞⓔ VERTIGO

DC Universe, Vertigo-DC Comics, 1700 Broadway, New York NY 10019. **Website:** www.vertigocomics.com. At this time, DC Entertainment does not accept unsolicited artwork or writing submissions.

Ⓐ VIKING

Imprint of Penguin Group (USA), Inc., 375 Hudson St., New York NY 10014. (212)366-2000. **Website:** www.penguin.com. Estab. 1925. Viking publishes a mix of academic and popular fiction and nonfiction. Publishes hardcover and originals.

HOW TO CONTACT *Agented submissions only.*

TERMS Pays 10-15% royalty on retail price.

Ⓐ VIKING CHILDREN'S BOOKS

375 Hudson St., New York NY 10014. **Website:** www.penguin.com. "Viking Children's Books is known for humorous, quirky picture books, in addition to more traditional fiction. We publish the highest quality fiction, nonfiction, and picture books for pre-schoolers through young adults." *Does not accept unsolicited submissions.* Publishes hardcover originals.

NEEDS All levels: adventure, animal, contemporary, fantasy, history, humor, multicultural, nature/environment, poetry, problem novels, romance, science fiction, sports, suspense/mystery.

HOW TO CONTACT *Accepts agented mss only.*

TERMS Pays 2-10% royalty on retail price or flat fee. Pays negotiable advance. Responds in 6 months.

TIPS "No 'cartoony' or mass-market submissions for picture books."

Ⓐ VILLARD BOOKS

Penguin Random House, 1745 Broadway, New York NY 10019. (212)572-2600. **Website:** www.penguinrandomhouse.com. Estab. 1983. "Villard Books is the publisher of savvy and sometimes quirky, best-selling hardcovers and trade paperbacks."

NEEDS Commercial fiction.

HOW TO CONTACT *Agented submissions only.*

TERMS Pays negotiable royalty. Pays negotiable advance.

Ⓐ VINTAGE ANCHOR PUBLISHING

Penguin Random House, 1745 Broadway, New York NY 10019. **Website:** www.penguinrandomhouse.com.

HOW TO CONTACT *Agented submissions only.*

TERMS Pays 4-8% royalty on retail price. Average advance: $2,500 and up.

VIVISPHERE PUBLISHING

675 Dutchess Turnpike, Poughkeepsie NY 12603. (845)463-1100, ext. 314. **Fax:** (845)463-0018. **E-mail:** cs@vivisphere.com. **Website:** www.vivisphere.com. **Contact:** Submissions. Estab. 1995. Vivisphere Publishing is now considering new submissions from any genre as follows: game of bridge (cards), nonfiction, history, military, new age, fiction, feminist/gay/lesbian, horror, contemporary, self-help, science fiction and cookbooks. Publishes trade paperback originals and reprints and e-books. Book catalog and ms guidelines online.

◌   "Cookbooks should have a particular slant or appeal to a certain niche. Also publish out-of-print books."

HOW TO CONTACT Query with SASE.

TERMS Pays royalty. Responds in 6-24 months.

WASHINGTON WRITERS' PUBLISHING HOUSE

P.O. Box 15271, Washington DC 20003. **Website:** www.washingtonwriters.org. Estab. 1975. Guidelines online.

NEEDS Washington Writers' Publishing House considers book-length mss for publication by fiction writers living within 75 driving miles of the U.S. Capitol, Baltimore area included, through competition only.

Mss may include previously published stories and excerpts. "Author should indicate where they heard about WWPH."

HOW TO CONTACT Submit an electronic copy by e-mail (use PDF, .doc, or rich text format) or 2 hard copies by snail mail of a short story collection or novel (no more than 350 pages, double or 1-1/2 spaced; author's name should not appear on any ms pages). Include separate page of publication acknowledgments plus 2 cover sheets: one with ms title, poet's name, address, telephone number, and e-mail address, the other with ms title only. Include SASE for results only; mss will not be returned (will be recycled).

TERMS Offers $1,000 and 50 copies of published book plus additional copies for publicity use.

Ⓐ WATERBROOK MULTNOMAH PUBLISHING GROUP

10807 New Allegiance Dr., Suite 500, Colorado Springs CO 80921. (719)590-4999. **Fax:** (719)590-8977. **Website:** www.waterbrookmultnomah.com. Estab. 1996. Publishes hardcover and trade paperback originals. Book catalog online.

HOW TO CONTACT *Agented submissions only.*

TERMS Pays royalty. Responds in 2-3 months.

WHITAKER HOUSE

1030 Hunt Valley Circle, New Kensington PA 15068. **E-mail:** publisher@whitakerhouse.com. **Website:** www.whitakerhouse.com. **Contact:** Editorial Department. Estab. 1970. Publishes hardcover, trade paperback, and mass market originals. Book catalog online. Guidelines online.

NEEDS All fiction must have a Christian perspective.

HOW TO CONTACT Query with SASE.

TERMS Pays 5-15% royalty on wholesale price. Responds in 3 months.

TIPS "Audience includes those seeking uplifting and inspirational fiction and nonfiction."

◍ WHITECAP BOOKS, LTD.

210 - 314 W. Cordova St., Vancouver BC V6B 1 E8, Canada. (604)681-6181. **Fax:** (905)477-9179. **Website:** www.whitecap.ca. "Whitecap Books is a general trade publisher with a focus on food and wine titles. Although we are interested in reviewing unsolicited ms submissions, please note that we only accept submissions that meet the needs of our current publishing program. Please see some of most recent releases to get an idea of the kinds of titles we are interested in."

Publishes hardcover and trade paperback originals. Catalog and guidelines online.

NEEDS No children's picture books or adult fiction.

HOW TO CONTACT See guidelines.

TERMS Pays royalty. Pays negotiated advance. Responds in 2-3 months to proposals.

TIPS "We want well-written, well-researched material that presents a fresh approach to a particular topic."

WHITE MANE KIDS

73 W. Burd St., Shippensburg PA 17257. (717)532-2237. **Fax:** (717)532-6110. **E-mail:** marketing@whitemane.com. **Website:** www.whitemane.com. **Contact:** Harold Collier, acquisitions editor. Estab. 1987. Book catalog and writer's guidelines available for SASE.

IMPRINTS White Mane Books, Burd Street Press, White Mane Kids, Ragged Edge Press.

NEEDS Middle readers, young adults: history (primarily American Civil War). Average word length: middle readers—30,000. Does not publish picture books.

HOW TO CONTACT Query.

TERMS Pays authors royalty of 7-10%. Pays illustrators and photographers by the project. Responds to queries in 1 month, mss in 6-9 months.

TIPS "Make your work historically accurate. We are interested in historically accurate fiction for middle and young adult readers. We do *not* publish picture books. Our primary focus is the American Civil War and some America Revolution topics."

⑤ THE WILD ROSE PRESS

P.O. Box 708, Adams Basin NY 14410-0708. (585)752-8770. **E-mail:** queryus@thewildrosepress.com. **Website:** www.thewildrosepress.com. **Contact:** Rhonda Penders, Editor in Chief. Estab. 2006. Publishes paperback originals, reprints, and e-books in a POD format. Guidelines online.

HOW TO CONTACT *Does not accept unsolicited mss.* Send query letter with outline and synopsis of up to 5 pages. Accepts all queries by e-mail. Include estimated word count, brief bio, and list of publishing credits. Agented fiction less than 1%. Always comments on rejected mss.

TERMS Pays royalty of 7% minimum; 40% maximum. Sends prepublication galleys to author. Responds to queries in 4 weeks; mss in 12 weeks.

TIPS "Polish your ms, make it as error free as possible, and follow our submission guidelines."

Ⓐ WILLIAM MORROW

HarperCollins, 195 Broadway, New York NY 10007. (212)207-7000. **Fax:** (212)207-7145. **Website:** www.harpercollins.com. Estab. 1926. "William Morrow publishes a wide range of titles that receive much recognition and prestige—a most selective house." Book catalog available free.

NEEDS Publishes adult fiction. Morrow accepts only the highest quality submissions in adult fiction. *No unsolicited mss or proposals.*

HOW TO CONTACT *Agented submissions only.*

TERMS Pays standard royalty on retail price. Pays varying advance.

WOODBINE HOUSE

6510 Bells Mill Rd., Bethesda MD 20817. (301)897-3570. **Fax:** (301)897-5838. **E-mail:** info@woodbinehouse.com. **Website:** www.woodbinehouse.com. **Contact:** Acquisitions Editor. Estab. 1985. Woodbine House publishes books for or about individuals with disabilities to help those individuals and their families live fulfilling and satisfying lives in their homes, schools, and communities. Publishes trade paperback originals. Guidelines online.

NEEDS Receptive to stories re: developmental and intellectual disabilities, e.g., autism and cerebral palsy.

HOW TO CONTACT Submit complete ms with SASE.

TERMS Pays 10-12% royalty. Responds in 3 months to queries.

TIPS "Do not send us a proposal on the basis of this description. Examine our catalog or website and a couple of our books to make sure you are on the right track. Put some thought into how your book could be marketed (aside from in bookstores). Keep cover letters concise and to the point; if it's a subject that interests us, we'll ask to see more."

WORLD WEAVER PRESS

Albuquerque NM 87111. **E-mail:** submissions@worldweaverpress.com. **Website:** www.worldweaverpress.com. **Contact:** WWP Editors. Estab. 2012. World Weaver Press publishes digital and print editions of speculative fiction at various lengths for adult, young adult, and new adult audiences. "We believe in great storytelling." Catalog online. Guidelines on website.

NEEDS "We believe that publishing speculative fiction isn't just printing words on the page — it's the act of weaving brand new worlds. Seeking speculative fiction in many varieties: protagonists who have strength, not fainting spells; intriguing worlds with well-developed settings; characters that are to die for (we'd rather find ourselves in love than just in lust)." Full list of interests on website. Does not want giant bugs, ghosts, post-apocalyptic and/or dystopia, angels, zombies, magical realism, surrealism, middle grade (MG) or younger.

HOW TO CONTACT Queries accepted only during February unless otherwise stated on website. Full guidelines will be updates approximately one month before submissions open.

TERMS Average royalty rate of 39% net on all editions. No advance. Responds to query letters within 3 weeks. Responses to mss requests take longer.

TIPS "Use your letter to pitch us the story, not talk about its themes or inception."

WORTHY KIDS/IDEALS BOOKS

6100 Tower Circle, Suite 210, Franklin TN 37067. **Website:** www.idealsbooks.com. Estab. 1944.

NEEDS Picture books: animal, concept, history, religion. Board books: animal, history, nature/environment, religion. Worthy Kids/Ideals publishes for ages birth to 8, no longer than 800 words.

HOW TO CONTACT Submit complete ms.

YELLOW SHOE FICTION SERIES

LSU Press, P.O. Box 25053, Baton Rouge LA 70894. **Website:** www.lsu.edu/lsupress. **Contact:** Michael Griffith, editor. Estab. 2004.

○ "Looking first and foremost for literary excellence, especially good mss that have fallen through the cracks at the big commercial presses. I'll cast a wide net."

HOW TO CONTACT Does not accept unsolicited mss. Accepts queries by mail, Attn: James W. Long.

TERMS Pays royalty. Offers advance.

ZEBRA BOOKS

Kensington, 119 W. 40th St., New York NY 10018. (212)407-1500. **E-mail:** esogah@kensingtonbooks.com. **Website:** www.kensingtonbooks.com. **Contact:** Esi Sogah, senior editor. Zebra Books is dedicated to women's fiction, which includes, but is not limited to romance. Publishes hardcover originals, trade paperback and mass market paperback originals and reprints. Book catalog online.

HOW TO CONTACT Query.

ZUMAYA PUBLICATIONS, LLC

3209 S. Interstate 35, Austin TX 78741. (512)537-3145. **Fax:** (512)276-6745. **E-mail:** business@zumayapublishing.com. **E-mail:** acquisitions@zumayapublications.com. **Website:** www.zumayapublications.com. **Contact:** Rie Sheridan Rose, acquisitions editor. Estab. 1999. Zumaya Publications is a digitally-based micro-press publishing mainly in on-demand trade paperback and e-book formats. "We currently offer approximately 190 fiction titles in the mystery, SF/F, historical, romance, LGBTQ, horror, and occult genres in adult, young adult, and middle reader categories. In 2016, we plan to officially launch our graphic and illustrated novel imprint, Zumaya Fabled Ink. We publish approximately 10-15 new titles annually, at least 5 of which are from new authors. We do not publish erotica or graphic erotic romance at this time. We accept only electronic queries; all others will be discarded unread. A working knowledge of computers and relevant software is a necessity, as our production process is completely digital." Publishes trade paperback and electronic originals and reprints. Guidelines online.

IMPRINTS Zumaya Arcane (New Age, inspirational fiction & nonfiction), Zumaya Boundless (GLBTQ); Zumaya Embraces (romance/women's fiction); Zumaya Enigma (mystery/suspense/thriller); Zumaya Thresholds (YA/middle grade); Zumaya Otherworlds (SF/F/H), Zumaya Yesterdays (memoirs, historical fiction, fiction, western fiction); Zumaya Fabled Ink (graphic and illustrated novels).

NEEDS "We are open to all genres, particularly GLBT and YA/middle grade, historical and western, New Age/inspirational (no overtly Christian materials, please), noncategory romance, thrillers. We encourage people to review what we've already published so as to avoid sending us more of the same, at least, insofar as the plot is concerned. While we're always looking for good mysteries, especially cozies, mysteries with historical settings, and police procedurals, we want original concepts rather than slightly altered versions of what we've already published. We do not publish erotica or graphically erotic romance at this time." Does not want erotica, graphically erotic romance, experimental, literary (unless it fits into one of our established imprints).

HOW TO CONTACT A copy of our rules of submission is posted on our website and can be downloaded. They are rules rather than guidelines and should be read carefully before submitting. It will save everyone time and frustration.

TERMS Pay 20% of net on paperbacks, net defined as cover price less printing and other associated costs; 50% of net on all e-books. Does not pay advance. Responds in 3 months to queries and proposals; 6 months to mss.

TIPS "We're catering to readers who may have loved last year's best seller but not enough to want to read 10 more just like it. Have something different. If it does not fit standard pigeonholes, that's a plus. On the other hand, it has to have an audience. And if you're not prepared to work with us on promotion and marketing, particularly via social media, it would be better to look elsewhere."

CONTESTS & AWARDS

///

In addition to honors and, quite often, cash prizes, contests and awards programs offer writers the opportunity to be judged on the basis of quality alone, without the outside factors that sometimes influence publishing decisions. New writers who win contests may be published for the first time, while more experienced writers may gain public recognition for an entire body of work.

Listed here are contests for almost every type of fiction writing. Some focus on form, such as short stories, novels, or novellas, while others feature writing on particular themes or topics. Still others are prestigious prizes or awards for work that must be nominated.

SELECTING AND SUBMITTING TO A CONTEST

Use the same care in submitting to contests as you would sending your manuscript to a publication or book publisher. Deadlines are very important, and, where possible, we've included this information. For some contests, deadlines were only approximate at our press deadline, so be sure to write, call, or look online for complete information.

Follow the rules to the letter. If, for instance, contest rules require your name on a cover sheet only, you will be disqualified if you ignore this and put your name on every page. Find out how many copies to send. If you don't send the correct amount, by the time you are contacted to send more, it may be past the submission deadline. An increasing number of contests invite writers to query by e-mail, and many post contest information on their websites. Check listings for e-mail and website addresses.

One note of caution: Beware of contests that charge entry fees that are disproportionate to the amount of the prize. Contests offering a $10 prize and charging $7 in entry fees are a waste of your time and money.

24-HOUR SHORT STORY CONTEST

WritersWeekly.com, 5726 Cortez Rd. W., #349, Bradenton FL 34210. 305-768-0261. **Fax:** 305-768-0261. **E-mail:** writersweekly@writersweekly.com. **Website:** www.writersweekly.com/misc/contest.php. **Contact:** Angela Hoy. Popular quarterly contest in which registered entrants receive an assigned topic at start time (usually noon Central Time) and have 24 hours to write and submit a story on that topic. All submissions must be returned via e-mail. Each contest is limited to 500 people. Upon entry, entrant will receive guidelines and details on competition, including submission process. Deadline: Quarterly—see website for dates. Prize: 1st Place: $300; 2nd Place: $250; 3rd Place: $200. There are also 20 honorable mentions and 60 door prizes (randomly drawn from all participants). The top 3 winners' entries are posted on WritersWeekly.com (nonexclusive electronic rights only) and receive a Freelance Income Kit. Writers retain all rights to their work. See website for full details on prizes. Costs: $5. Judged by Angela Hoy (publisher of WritersWeekly.com and Booklocker.com).

AEON AWARD

Albedo One/Aeon Press, Aeon Award, Albedo One, 2 Post Road, Lusk, Dublin , Ireland. (353)(1)873-0177. **E-mail:** fraslaw@yahoo.co.uk. **Website:** www.albedo1.com. **Contact:** Frank Ludlow, event coordinator. Estab. 2004. Prestigious fiction writing competition for short stories in any speculative fiction genre, such as fantasy, science fiction, horror, or anything in-between or unclassifiable. Deadline: November 30. Contest begins January 1. Prize: Grand Prize: €1,000; 2nd Prize: €200; and 3rd Prize: €100. The top three stories are guaranteed publication in *Albedo One*. Costs: €7.50. Judged by Ian Watson, Eileen Gunn, Todd McCaffrey, and Michael Carroll.

AESTHETICA ART PRIZE

Aesthetica Magazine, P.O. Box 371, York YO23 1WL, United Kingdom. **E-mail:** info@aestheticamagazine.com; artprize@aestheticamagazine.com. **Website:** www.aestheticamagazine.com. The Aesthetica Art Prize is a celebration of excellence in art from across the world and offers artists the opportunity to showcase their work to wider audiences and further their involvement in the international art world. There are 4 categories: Photograpic & Digital Art, Three Dimensional Design & Sculpture, Painting & Drawing, Video Installation & Performance. Deadline: August 31. Prizes include: £5,000 main prize courtesy of Hiscox, £1,000 Student Prize courtesy of Hiscox, group exhibition and publication in the Aesthetica Art Prize Anthology. Entry is £15 and permits submission of 2 works in one category. Costs: £10 each category.

AHWA FLASH & SHORT STORY COMPETITION

AHWA (Australian Horror Writers Association), **E-mail:** ahwacomps@australianhorror.com; ahwa@australianhorror.com. **E-mail:** ctrost@hotmail.com. **Website:** www.australianhorror.com. **Contact:** Cameron Trost, Competitions Officer. Competition/award for short stories and flash fiction. Looking for horror stories, tales that frighten, yarns that unsettle readers in their comfortable homes. All themes in this genre will be accepted, from the well-used (zombies, vampires, ghosts etc) to the highly original, so long as the story is professional and well written. Deadline: May 31. Prize: The authors of the winning Flash Fiction and Short Story entries will each receive paid publication in *Midnight Echo*, the Magazine of the AHWA and an engraved plaque. Costs: $5 for flash fiction, $10 for short story; free for AHWA members. Judged by previous winners.

ALABAMA STATE COUNCIL ON THE ARTS INDIVIDUAL ARTIST FELLOWSHIP

201 Monroe St., Suite 110, Montgomery AL 36130. (334)242-4076, ext. 236. **Fax:** (334)240-3269. **E-mail:** anne.kimzey@arts.alabama.gov. **Website:** www.arts.state.al.us. **Contact:** Anne Kimzey, Literary Arts Program Manager. Recognizes the achievements and potential of Alabama writers. Deadline: March 1. Applications must be submitted online by eGRANT. Costs: No entry fee. Judged by independent peer panel. Fellowship recipients notified by mail and announced on website in June.

ALLIGATOR JUNIPER AWARD

Alligator Juniper/Prescott College, 220 Grove Ave., Prescott AZ 86301. (928)350-2012. **Fax:** (928)776-5102. **E-mail:** alligatorjuniper@prescott.edu. **Website:** www.prescott.edu/alligatorjuniper/national-contest/index.html. **Contact:** Skye Anicca, managing editor. Annual contest for unpublished fiction, creative nonfiction, and poetry. Open to all age levels. Each entrant receives a personal letter from staff regarding the status of their submission, as well as minor feedback on the piece. Deadline: October 1. Prize: $1,000 plus publication in all three categories. Finalists in each genre are recognized as such, published, and paid in copies. Costs: $15. Judged by the distinguished writers in each genre and Prescott College writing students enrolled in the Literary Journal Practicum course.

AMERICAN ASSOCIATION OF UNIVERSITY WOMEN AWARD IN JUVENILE LITERATURE

4610 Mail Service Center, Raleigh NC 27699-4610. (919)807-7290. **E-mail:** michael.hill@ncdcr.gov. **Website:** www.ncdcr.gov. **Contact:** Michael Hill, awards coordinator. Annual award. Book must be published during the year ending June 30. Submissions made by author, author's agent or publisher. SASE for contest rules. Recognizes the year's best work of juvenile literature by a North Carolina resident. Deadline: July 15. Prize: Awards a cup to the winner and winner's name inscribed on a plaque displayed within the North Carolina Office of Archives and History. Judged by three-judge panel.

◑   Competition receives 10-15 submissions per category.

THE AMERICAN GEM LITERARY FESTIVAL

FilmMakers Magazine / Write Brothers, FilmMakers Magazine (filmmakers.com), Beverly Hills CA 90210. **E-mail:** info@filmmakers.com. **Website:** filmmakers. com/contests/short_story/. **Contact:** Jennifer Brooks. Estab. 2001. Worldwide contest to recognize excellent short screenplays and short stories. Deadlines: Early: Feb 29; Regular: April 30; Late: June 30; Final: July 31. Prize: Short Script: 1st Place: $1,000. Other cash and prizes to top 5. Costs: Ranges from $19-49, based on number of pages, entry type. Full details via website.

AMERICAN LITERARY REVIEW CONTESTS

American Literary Review, P.O. Box 311307, University of North Texas, Denton TX 76203-1307. (940)565-2755. **E-mail:** americanliteraryreview@gmail.com. **Website:** www.americanliteraryreview.com. Contest to award excellence in short fiction, creative nonfiction, and poetry. Multiple entries are acceptable, but each entry must be accompanied with a reading fee. Do not put any identifying information in the file itself; include the author's name, title(s), address, e-mail address, and phone number in the boxes provided in the online submissions manager. Short fiction: Limit 8,000 words per work. Creative nonfiction: Limit 6,500 words per work. Deadline: October 1. Submission period begins June 1. Prize: $1,000 prize for each category, along with publication in the Spring online issue of the *American Literary Review*. Costs: $15 reading fee for one short story, one creative nonfiction entry, or up to 3 poems.

AMERICAN-SCANDINAVIAN FOUNDATION TRANSLATION PRIZE

The American-Scandinavian Foundation, 58 Park Ave., New York NY 10016. (212)779-3587. **E-mail:** grants@amscan.org; info@amscan.org. **Website:** www.amscan.org. **Contact:** Matthew Walters, director of fellowships & grants. The annual ASF translation competition is awarded for the most outstanding translations of poetry, fiction, drama, or literary prose written by a Scandinavian author born after 1800. Deadline: June 15. Prize: The Nadia Christensen Prize includes a $2,500 award, publication of an excerpt in *Scandinavian Review*, and a commemorative bronze medallion; The Leif and Inger Sjöberg Award, given to an individual whose literature translations have not previously been published, includes a $2,000 award, publication of an excerpt in *Scandinavian Review*, and a commemorative bronze medallion.

SHERWOOD ANDERSON FICTION AWARD

Mid-American Review, Mid-American Review, Dept. of English, Box WM, BGSU, Bowling Green OH 43403. (419)372-2725. **Fax:** (419)372-4642. **E-mail:** mar@bgsu.edu. **Website:** www.bgsu.edu/midamericanreview. **Contact:** Abigail Cloud, editor-in-chief. Offered annually for unpublished mss (6,000 word limit). Contest is open to all writers not associated with a judge or *Mid-American Review*. Deadline: November 1. Prize: $1,000, plus publication in the spring issue of *Mid-American Review*. Four Finalists: Notation, possible publication. Costs: $10. Judged by editors and a well-known writer, i.e., Aimee Bender or Anthony Doerr. Judged by Charles Yu in 2017.

ART AFFAIR SHORT STORY AND WESTERN SHORT STORY CONTESTS

Art Affair - Contest, P.O. Box 54302, Oklahoma City OK 73154, USA. **E-mail:** artaffair@aol.com. **Website:** www.shadetreecreations.com. Estab. 2003. The annual Art Affair Writing Contests include (General) Short Story and Western Short Story categories. See separate listing for Poetry contest. Open to any writer. All short stories must be unpublished. Multiple entries accepted in both categories with separate entry fees for each. Submit original stories on any subject and timeframe for general Short Story category, and submit original western stories for Western Short Story—word limit for all entries is 5,000 words. Guidelines available on website. Deadline: October 1. Prize (in both categories): 1st Place: $50; 2nd Place: $25; 3rd Place: $15. Costs: $5/per story.

○ Stories must be unpublished at time of entry. Entries may be mailed together.

ARTIST TRUST FELLOWSHIP AWARD

1835 12th Ave., Seattle WA 98122. (209)467-8734, ext. 11. **Fax:** (866)218-7878. **E-mail:** info@artisttrust.org. **Website:** www.artisttrust.org. **Contact:** Miguel Guillen, program manager. Fellowships award $7,500 to practicing professional artists of exceptional talent and demonstrated ability. The Fellowship is a merit-based, not a project-based award. Recipients present a Meet the Artist Event to a community in Washington state that has little or no access to the artist and their work. Awards 14 fellowships of $7,500 and 2 residencies with $1,000 stipends at the Millay Colony. Deadline: January 17. Applications available December 3. Prize: $7,500.

ARTS & LETTERS PRIZES

Arts & Letters Journal of Contemporary Culture, Campus Box 89, GC&SU, Milledgeville GA 31061. (478)445-1289. **E-mail:** al.journal@gcsu.edu. **Website:** al.gcsu.edu. **Contact:** The Editors. Offered annually for unpublished work. Deadline: March 31. Prize: $1,000 prize for each of the four major genres. Fiction, poetry, and creative nonfiction winners are published in Fall or Spring issue. The prize-winning one-act play is produced at the Georgia College campus (usually in March). Costs: $20/entry (payable to GC&SU). Judged by the editors (initial screening); see website for final judges and further details about submitting work.

THE ATHENAEUM LITERARY AWARD

The Athenaeum of Philadelphia, 219 S. 6th St., Philadelphia PA 19106-3794. (215)925-2688. **Fax:** (215)925-3755. **E-mail:** jilly@PhilaAthenaeum.org. **Website:** www.philaathenaeum.org/literary.html. **Contact:** Jill LeMin Lee, Librarian. Estab. 1950. The Athenaeum Literary Award was established to recognize and encourage literary achievement among authors who are bona fide residents of Philadelphia or Pennsylvania living within a radius of 30 miles of City Hall at the time their book was written or published. Any volume of general literature is eligible; technical, scientific, and juvenile books are not included. Nominated works are reviewed on the basis of their significance and importance to the general public as well as for literary excellence. Deadline: All nominations must be submitted prior to December 1st of the year of publication. Costs: There is no fee to submit an entry.

⑤ AUTUMN HOUSE POETRY, FICTION, AND NONFICTION PRIZES

P.O. Box 60100, Pittsburgh PA 15211. (412)381-4261. **E-mail:** info@autumnhouse.org. **E-mail:** https://autumnhousepress.submittable.com/submit. **Website:** autumnhouse.org. **Contact:** Christine Stroud, Editor-in-Chief. Estab. 1998. Offers annual prize and publication of book-length ms with national promotion. Submission must be unpublished as a collection, but individual poems, stories, and essays may have been previously published elsewhere. Considers simultaneous submissions. "Autumn House is a nonprofit corporation with the mission of publishing and promoting poetry and other fine literature. We have published books by Chana Bloch, Ellery Akers, Gerald Stern, Ruth L. Schwartz, Ed Ochester, Andrea Hollander, George Bilgere, Ada Limon, and many others." Deadline: June 30. Prize: The winner (in each of three categories) will receive book publication, $1,000 advance against royalties, and a $1,500 travel/publicity grant to promote his or her book. Costs: $30/ms. Judged by Alberto Rios (poetry), Amina Gautier (fiction), and Alison Hawthorne Deming (nonfiction).

AWP AWARD SERIES

Association of Writers & Writing Programs, George Mason University, 4400 University Drive, MSN 1E3, Fairfax VA 22030. **E-mail:** supriya@awpwriter.org. **Website:** www.awpwriter.org. **Contact:** Supriya Bhatnagar, director of publications. AWP sponsors the Award Series, an annual competition for the publication of excellent new book-length works. The competition is open to all authors writing in English regardless of nationality or residence, and is available to published and unpublished authors alike. Offered annually to foster new literary talent. Deadline: Postmarked between January 1 and February 28. Prize: AWP Prize for the Novel: $2,500 and publication by New Issues Press; Donald Hall Prize for Poetry: $5,500 and publication by the University of Pittsburgh Press; Grace Paley Prize in Short Fiction: $5,500 and publication by the University of Massachusetts Press; and AWP Prize for Creative Nonfiction: $2,500 and publication by the University of Georgia Press. Costs: $30 for nonmembers, $20 for members.

BALCONES FICTION PRIZE

Austin Commmunity College, Department of Creative Writing, 1212 Rio Grande St., Austin TX 78701. (512)584-5045. **E-mail:** joconne@austincc.edu. **Website:** www.austincc.edu/crw/html/balconescenter.

html. **Contact:** Joe O'Connell. Awarded to the best book of literary fiction published the previous year. Books of prose may be submitted by publisher or author. Send three copies. Deadline: January 31. Prize: $1,500, winner is flown to Austin for a campus reading. Costs: $30 reading fee.

⑤ THE BALTIMORE REVIEW CONTESTS

The Baltimore Review, 6514 Maplewood Rd., Baltimore MD 21212. **E-mail:** editor@baltimorereview.org. **Website:** www.baltimorereview.org. **Contact:** Barbara Westwood Diehl, senior editor. Estab. 1996. Each summer and winter issue includes a contest theme (see submissions guidelines for theme). Prizes are awarded for first, second, and third place among all categories—poetry, short stories, and creative nonfiction. All entries are considered for publication. Deadline: May 31 and November 30. Prize: 1st Place: $500; 2nd Place: $200; 3rd Place: $100. All entries are considered for publication. Provides a small compensation to all contributors. Costs: $10 entry fee. Judged by the editors of *The Baltimore Review* and a guest, final judge.

BARD FICTION PRIZE

Bard College, P.O. Box 5000, Annandale-on-Hudson NY 12504-5000. (845)758-7087. **Fax:** (845)758-7917. **E-mail:** bfp@bard.edu. **Website:** www.bard.edu/bfp. **Contact:** Irene Zedlacher. Estab. 2001. The Bard Fiction Prize is awarded to a promising, emerging writer who is an American citizen aged 39 years or younger at the time of application. The Bard Fiction Prize is intended to encourage and support young writers of fiction to pursue their creative goals and to provide an opportunity to work in a fertile and intellectual environment. Deadline: June 15. Prize: $30,000 and appointment as writer-in-residence at Bard College for 1 semester. Judged by a committee of 5 judges (authors associated with Bard College).

MILDRED L. BATCHELDER AWARD

50 E. Huron St., Chicago IL 60611-2795. **Website:** www.ala.org/alsc/awardsgrants/. Estab. 1966. The Batchelder Award is given to the most outstanding children's book originally published in a language other than English in a country other than the United States, and subsequently translated into English for publication in the US. The purpose of the award, a citation to an American publisher, is to encourage international exchange of quality children's books by recognizing US publishers of such books in translation. Deadline: December 31.

BELLEVUE LITERARY REVIEW GOLDENBERG PRIZE FOR FICTION

Bellevue Literary Review, NYU Dept of Medicine, 550 First Ave., OBV-A612, New York NY 10016. (212)263-3973. **E-mail:** info@blreview.org; stacy@blreview.org. **Website:** www.blreview.org. **Contact:** Stacy Bodziak, managing editor. The *BLR* prizes award outstanding writing related to themes of health, healing, illness, the mind and the body. Annual competition/award for short stories. Receives about 200-300 entries per category. Send credit card information or make checks payable to Bellevue Literary Review. Guidelines available in February. Accepts inquiries by e-mail, phone, mail. Submissions open in February. Results announced in December and made available to entrants with SASE, by e-mail, on website. Winners notified by mail, by e-mail. Deadline: July 1. Prize: $1,000 and publication in *The Bellevue Literary Review.* Honorable mention winners receive $250 and publication. Costs: $20, or $30 to include 1-year subscription. BLR editors select semi-finalists to be read by an independent judge who chooses the winner. Previous judges include Nathan Englander, Jane Smiley, Francine Prose, and Andre Dubus III.

⑥ GEORGE BENNETT FELLOWSHIP

Phillips Exeter Academy, 20 Main Street, Exeter NH 03833. **E-mail:** teaching_opportunities@exeter.edu. **Website:** www.exeter.edu/bennettfellowship. Annual award for fellow and family to provide time and freedom from material considerations to a person seriously contemplating or pursuing a career as a writer. Applicants should have a ms in progress which they intend to complete during the fellowship period. Ms should be fiction, nonfiction, novel, short stories, or poetry. Duties: To be in residency at the Academy for the academic year; to make oneself available informally to students interested in writing. Committee favors writers who have not yet published a book with a major publisher. Deadline: November 30. A choice will be made, and all entrants notified in mid-April. Prize: Cash stipend (currently $15,260), room and board. Costs: $15 application fee. Application form and guidelines on website. Judged by committee of the English department.

BINGHAMTON UNIVERSITY JOHN GARDNER FICTION BOOK AWARD

Creative Writing Program, Binghamton University, Binghamton University, Department of English, General Literature, and Rhetoric, Library North Room

1149, P.O. Box 6000, Binghamton NY 13902-6000. (607)777-2713. **E-mail:** cwpro@binghamton.edu. **Website:** binghamton.edu/english/creative-writing. **Contact:** Maria Mazziotti Gillan, director. Estab. 2001. Contest offered annually for a novel or collection of fiction published in previous year in a press run of 500 copies or more. Each book submitted must be accompanied by an application form. Publisher may submit more than 1 book for prize consideration. Send 2 copies of each book. Guidelines available on website. Deadline: March 1. Prize: $1,000. Judged by a professional writer not on Binghamton University faculty.

🐍 JAMES TAIT BLACK MEMORIAL PRIZES

University of Edinburgh, School of Literatures, Languages, and Cultures, 50 George Square, Edinburgh EH8 9LH, Scotland. (44-13)1650-3619. **E-mail:** s.strathdee@ed.ac.uk. **Website:** www.ed.ac.uk/events/james-tait-black. Estab. 1919. Open to any writer. Entries must be previously published. Winners notified by phone, via publisher. Contact department of English Literature for list of winners or check website. Accepts inquiries by e-mail or phone. Deadline: December 1. Prize: Two prizes each of £10,000 are awarded: one for the best work of fiction, one for the best biography or work of that nature, published during the calendar year January 1 to December 31. Judged by professors of English Literature with the assistance of teams of postgraduate readers.

🐍 THE BOARDMAN TASKER PRIZE FOR MOUNTAIN LITERATURE

The Boardman Tasker Charitable Trust, 8 Bank View Rd., Darley Abbey Derby DE22 1EJ, UK. 01332 342246. **E-mail:** steve@people-matter.co.uk. **Website:** www.boardmantasker.com. **Contact:** Steve Dean. Offered annually to reward a work with a mountain theme, whether fiction, nonfiction, drama, or poetry, written in the English language (initially or in translation). Subject must be concerned with a mountain environment. Previous winners have been books on expeditions, climbing experiences, a biography of a mountaineer, novels. Guidelines available in January by e-mail or on website. Entries must be previously published. Open to any writer. The award is to honor Peter Boardman and Joe Tasker, who disappeared on Everest in 1982. Deadline: August 1. Prize: £3,000 Judged by a panel of 3 judges elected by trustees.

BOULEVARD SHORT FICTION CONTEST FOR EMERGING WRITERS

Boulevard Magazine, 6614 Clayton Rd., PMB #325, Richmond Heights MO 63117. (314)862-2643. **Website:** www.boulevardmagazine.org. **Contact:** Jessica Rogen, editor. Estab. 1985. Offered annually for unpublished short fiction to a writer who has not yet published a book of fiction, poetry, or creative nonfiction with a nationally distributed press. Holds first North American rights on anything not previously published. Open to any writer with no previous publication by a nationally known press. Guidelines for SASE or on website. Deadline: December 31. Prize: $1,500, and publication in 1 of the next year's issues. Costs: $16 fee/story, includes 1-year subscription to *Boulevard*.

○ THE BRIAR CLIFF REVIEW FICTION, POETRY, AND CREATIVE NONFICTION COMPETITION

The Briar Cliff Review, Briar Cliff University, 3303 Rebecca St., Sioux City IA 51104-0100. **E-mail:** tricia.currans-sheehan@briarcliff.edu (editor); jeanne.emmons@briarcliff.edu (poetry). **Website:** www.bcreview.org. **Contact:** Tricia Currans-Sheehan, editor. Estab. 1989. *The Briar Cliff Review* sponsors an annual contest offering $1,000 and publication to each 1st Prize winner in fiction, poetry, and creative nonfiction. Previous year's winner and former students of editors ineligible. Winning pieces accepted for publication on the basis of first-time rights. Considers simultaneous submissions, "but notify us immediately upon acceptance elsewhere. We guarantee a considerate reading." No mss returned. To reward good writers and showcase quality writing. Deadline: November 1. Prize: $1,000 and publication to each prize winner in fiction, poetry, and creative nonfiction. Costs: $20 per story/creative nonfiction piece or 3 poems. Judged by *Briar Cliff Review* editors.

🐍 BRITISH CZECH AND SLOVAK ASSOCIATION WRITING COMPETITION

24 Ferndale, Tunbridge Wells Kent TN2 3NS, England. **E-mail:** prize@bcsa.co.uk. **Website:** www.bcsa.co.uk/specials.html. Estab. 2002. Annual contest for original writing (entries should be 1,500-2,000 words) in English on the links between Britain and the Czech/Slovak Republics, or describing society in transition in the Republics since 1989. Entries can be fact or fiction. Topics can include history, politics, the sciences, economics, the arts, or literature. Deadline:

June 30. Winners announced in November. Prize: 1st Place: £300; 2nd Place: £100.

THE RBC BRONWEN WALLACE AWARD FOR EMERGING WRITERS

The Writers' Trust of Canada, 460 Richmond St. W., Suite 600, Toronto ON M5C 1P1, Canada. (416)504-8222. **Fax:** (416)504-9090. **E-mail:** info@writerstrust.com. **Website:** www.writerstrust.com. **Contact:** Amanda Hopkins. Presented annually to a Canadian writer under the age of 35 who is not yet published in book form. The award, which alternates each year between poetry and short fiction, was established in memory of Bronwen Wallace. Deadline: March 7. Prize: $10,000. Two finalists receive $2,500 each.

JOHN W. CAMPBELL MEMORIAL AWARD FOR BEST SCIENCE FICTION NOVEL OF THE YEAR

English Department, University of Kansas, Lawrence KS 66045. (785)864-3380. **Fax:** (785)864-1159. **E-mail:** cmckit@ku.edu. **Website:** www.sfcenter.ku.edu/campbell.htm. **Contact:** Chris McKitterick. Estab. 1973. Honors the best science fiction novel of the year. Deadline: Check website. Prize: Campbell Award trophy. Winners receive an expense-paid trip to the university to receive their award. Their names are also engraved on a permanent trophy. Judged by a jury.

CANADIAN AUTHORS ASSOCIATION AWARD FOR FICTION

6 West St. N., Suite 203, Orilla ON L3X 5B8, Canada. **Website:** www.canadianauthors.org. **Contact:** Anita Purcell, executive director. Estab. 1975. Award for full-length, English language literature for adults by a Canadian author. Deadline: January 15. Prize: $1,000. Judging: Each year a trustee for each award appointed by the Canadian Authors Association selects up to 3 judges. Identities of the trustee and judges are confidential.

CANADIAN AUTHORS ASSOCIATION EMERGING WRITER AWARD

6 West St. N., Suite 203, Orilla ON L3X 5B8, Canada. **Website:** www.canadianauthors.org. **Contact:** Anita Purcell, executive director. Estab. 2006. Annual award for a writer under 30 years of age deemed to show exceptional promise in the field of literary creation. Deadline: January 15. Prize: $500. Judging: Each year a trustee for each award appointed by the Canadian Authors Association selects up to 3 judges. Identities of the trustee and judges are confidential.

CASCADE WRITING CONTEST & AWARDS

Oregon Christian Writers, 1075 Willow Lake Road N., Keizer Oregon 97303. **E-mail:** cascade@oregonchristianwriters.org. **E-mail:** cascade@oregonchristianwriters.org. **Website:** oregonchristianwriters.org/. **Contact:** Marilyn Rhoads and Julie McDonald Zander. The Cascade Awards are presented at the annual Oregon Christian Writers Summer Conference (held at the Red Lion on the River in Portland, Oregon, each August) attended by national editors, agents, and professional authors. The contest is open for both published and unpublished works in the following categories: contemporary fiction book, historical fiction book, speculative fiction book, nonfiction book, memoir book, young adult/middle grade fiction book, young adult/middle grade nonfiction book, children's chapter book and picture book (fiction and nonfiction), poetry, devotional, article, column, story, or blog post. Two additional special Cascade Awards are presented each year: the Trailblazer Award to a writer who has distinguished him/herself in the field of Christian writing; and a Writer of Promise Award for a writer who demonstrates unusual promise in the field of Christian writing. For a full list of categories, entry rules, and scoring elements, visit website. Annual multi-genre competition to encourage both published and emerging writers in the field of Christian writing. Deadline: March 31. Submissions period begins February 14. Prize: Award certificate and pin presented at the Cascade Awards ceremony during the Oregon Christian Writers Annual Summer Conference. Finalists are listed in the conference notebook and winners are listed online. Cascade Trophies are awarded to the recipients of the Trailblazer and Writer of Promise Awards. Costs: Published book entry: $35 (OCW member), $45 (nonmember); All other entries: $30 (OCW member), $40 (nonmember). Judged by published authors, editors, librarians, and retail book store owners and employees. Final judging by editors, agents, and published authors from the Christian publishing industry.

KAY CATTARULLA AWARD FOR BEST SHORT STORY

Texas Institute of Letters, P.O. Box 609, Round Rock TX 78680. **E-mail:** tilsecretary@yahoo.com. **Website:** www.texasinstituteofletters.org. Offered annually for work published January 1-December 31 of previous year to recognize the best short story. The story submitted must have appeared in print for the first time to be eligible. Writers must have been born in Texas, must have lived in Texas for at least 2 consecutive years, or the subject matter of the work must be associated with Texas. See website for guidelines. Deadline: January 10. Prize: $1,000.

G. S. SHARAT CHANDRA PRIZE FOR SHORT FICTION

BkMk Press, University of Missouri-Kansas City, BkMk Press, University of Missouri-Kansas City, 5100 Rockhill Rd., Kansas City MO 64110-2499. (816)235-2558. **Fax:** (816)235-2611. **E-mail:** bkmk@umkc.edu; newletters@umkc.edu. **Website:** www.umkc.edu/bkmk. **Contact:** Ben Furnish. Estab. 2002 (Chandra Prize established); 1971 (press established). Offered annually for the best book-length ms collection (unpublished) of short fiction in English by a living author. Translations are not eligible. Initial judging is done by a network of published writers. Final judging is done by a writer of national reputation. Guidelines for SASE, by e-mail, or on website. Deadline: January 15. Prize: $1,000, plus book publication by BkMk Press. Costs: $25 fee, $5 additional for online submission.

⊛◐ PEGGY CHAPMAN-ANDREWS FIRST NOVEL AWARD

P.O. Box 6910, Dorset DT6 9QB, United Kingdom. **E-mail:** info@bridportprize.org.uk. **Website:** www.bridportprize.org.uk. **Contact:** Kate Wilson, Prize Administrator. Estab. 1973. Award to promote literary excellence and new writers. Enter first chapters of novel, up to 8,000 words (minimum 5,000 words) plus 300 word synopsis. Deadline: May 31. Prize: 1st Place: £1,000 plus mentoring & possible publication; Runner-Up: £500. Costs: £20. Judged by Nathan Filer with The Literary Consultancy & A.M. Heath Literary Agents.

CLOUDBANK JOURNAL CONTEST

P.O. Box 610, Corvallis OR 97339. (541)752-0075. **E-mail:** michael@cloudbankbooks.com. **Website:** www.cloudbankbooks.com. **Contact:** Michael Malan. Estab. 2009. Deadline: April 30. Prize: $200 and publication, plus an extra copy of the issue in which the winning poem appears. Two contributors' copies will be sent to writers whose work appears in the magazine. Costs: $15 entry fee. Make check out to *Cloudbank* or pay via Submittable. All writers who enter the contest will receive a 2-issue subscription to *Cloudbank* magazine. Judged by Michael Malan and Peter Sears.

Submissions for contests are accepted via Submittable and by mail. Complete guidelines are available at website. Accept both poetry and flash fiction.

COLORADO BOOK AWARDS

Colorado Humanities & Center for the Book, 7935 E. Prentice Ave., Suite 450, Greenwood Village CO 80111. (303)894-7951. **Fax:** (303)864-9361. **E-mail:** bess@coloradohumanities.org. **Website:** www.coloradohumanities.org. **Contact:** Bess Maher. Estab. 1991. An annual program that celebrates the accomplishments of Colorado's outstanding authors, editors, illustrators, and photographers. Awards are presented in at least ten categories including anthology/collection, biography, children's, creative nonfiction, fiction, history, nonfiction, pictorial, poetry, and young adult. Deadline: January 9.

THE CUTBANK CHAPBOOK CONTEST

CutBank Literary Magazine, *CutBank*, University of Montana, English Dept., LA 133, Missoula MT 59812. **E-mail:** editor.cutbank@gmail.com. **Website:** www.cutbankonline.org. **Contact:** Kate Barrett, editor-in-chief. This competition is open to original English language mss in the genres of poetry, fiction, and creative nonfiction. While previously published stand-alone pieces or excerpts may be included in a ms, the ms as a whole must be an unpublished work. Looking for startling, compelling, and beautiful original work. "We're looking for a fresh, powerful ms. Maybe it will overtake us quietly; gracefully defy genres; satisfyingly subvert our expectations; punch us in the mouth page in and page out. We're interested in both prose and poetry—and particularly work that straddles the lines between genres." Deadline: March 31. Submissions period begins January1. Prize: $1,000 and 25 contributor copies. Costs: $20. Judged by a guest judge each year.

CWW ANNUAL WISCONSIN WRITERS AWARDS

Council for Wisconsin Writers, 4964 Gilkeson Rd, Waunakee WI 53597. **E-mail:** karlahuston@gmail.com. **Website:** www.wiswriters.org. **Contact:** Geoff Gilpin, president and annual awards co-chair; Karla Huston, secretary and annual awards co-chair; Sylvia Cavanaugh, annual awards co-chair; Edward Schultz, annual awards co-chair, Erik Richardson, annual awards co-chair. Estab. 1964. Offered annually for work published by Wisconsin writers during the previous calendar year. Nine awards: Major Achievement (presented in alternate years); short fiction; short non-fiction; nonfiction book; poetry book; fiction book; children's literature; Lorine Niedecker Poetry Award; Christopher Latham Sholes Award for Outstanding Service to Wisconsin Writers (presented in alternate years); Essay Award for Young Writers. Open to Wisconsin residents. Deadline: January 31. Submissions open on November 1. Prizes: First place prizes: $500. Honorable mentions: $50. Costs: $25 nonrefundable fee. List of judges available on website.

DANA AWARDS IN THE NOVEL, SHORT FICTION, AND POETRY

200 Fosseway Dr., Greensboro NC 27445. (336)644-8028. **E-mail:** danaawards@gmail.com. **Website:** www.danaawards.com. **Contact:** Mary Elizabeth Parker, chair. Estab. 1996. Three awards offered annually for unpublished work written in English. Works previously published online are not eligible. The Dana Awards are re-vamping. The Novel Award is now increased to $2,000, based on a new partnership with Blue Mary Books: Blue Mary has agreed to consider for possible publication not only the Novel Award-winning ms, but the top 9 other Novel finalists, as well as the 30 top Novel semifinalists. The Short Fiction and Poetry Awards offer the traditional $1,000 awards each and do not offer a publishing option (currently, Blue Mary publishes only novels). See website for further updates. Purpose is monetary award for work that has not been previously published or received monetary award, but will accept work published simply for friends and family. Deadline: October 31 (postmarked). Prizes: $2,000 for the Novel Award; $1,000 each for the Short Fiction and Poetry awards awards. Costs: $30 per novel entry; $15 per short fiction entry; $15 per 5 poems.

○ The Dana Awards and Blue Mary Books are separate entities. Blue Mary has no part in the reading and judging of mss to determine the Novel Award and the Dana Awards does not advise Blue Mary on publishing. The Dana Awards gives its monetary award only; then, as a further courtesy, will put winner, finalists and semifinalists in touch with Blue Mary. All further agreements and contracts are solely between the authors and Blue Mary.

THE DANAHY FICTION PRIZE

Tampa Review, University of Tampa, 401 W. Kennedy Blvd., Tampa FL 33606. 813-253-6266. **E-mail:** utpress@ut.edu. **Website:** www.ut.edu/TampaReview. Estab.

2006. Annual award for the best previously unpublished short fiction. Deadline: November 30. Prize: $1,000, plus publication in *Tampa Review*. Costs: $20.

THE DEADLY QUILL SHORT STORY WRITING CONTEST

Deadly Quill Magazine, **E-mail:** lorne@deadlyquill.com. **E-mail:** contest@deadlyquill.com. **Website:** www.deadlyquill.com. **Contact:** Lorne McMIllan. Estab. 2015. "We are hoping to give an outlet for short stories that follow the tradition of The Twilight Zone, Alfred Hitchcock, and The Outer Limits." Deadline: August 31. Prizes: $250 first place; $200 second place; $150 third place. Plus, more prizes described online. Costs: $10. Author Edward Willett, Author Lorne McMillan, Author Colin Douglas

○ The stories should reach out and grab you, pull you in, and keep you in. A good ending is crucial.

○ DEAD OF WINTER

E-mail: editors@toasted-cheese.com. **Website:** www.toasted-cheese.com. **Contact:** Stephanie Lenz, editor. Estab. 2001. The contest is a winter-themed horror fiction contest with a new topic/theme each year. Theme and word count parameters announced October 1. Deadline: December 21. Results announced January 31. Winners notified by e-mail. List of winners on website. Prize: Amazon gift certificates and publication in *Toasted Cheese*. Judged by *Toasted Cheese* editors who blind judge each contest. Each judge uses her own criteria to rate entries.

○ Follow contest guidelines

WILLIAM F. DEECK MALICE DOMESTIC GRANTS FOR UNPUBLISHED WRITERS

Malice Domestic, P.O. Box 8007, Gaithersburg MD 20898-8007. **E-mail:** malicegrants@comcast.net. **Website:** www.malicedomestic.org. **Contact:** Harriette Sackler. Estab. 1989. Offered annually for unpublished work in the mystery field. Malice awards one grant to unpublished writers in the Malice Domestic genre at its annual convention in May. The competition is designed to help the next generation of Malice authors get their first work published and to foster quality Malice literature. Malice Domestic literature is loosely described as mystery stories of the Agatha Christie type, i.e., traditional mysteries. These works usually feature no excessive gore, gratuitous violence, or explicit sex. Deadline: November 1. Prize: $2,500, plus a comprehensive registration to the following year's convention and two nights' lodging at the convention hotel.

DIAGRAM/NEW MICHIGAN PRESS CHAPBOOK CONTEST

New Michigan Press, P.O. Box 210067, English, ML 424, University of Arizona, Tucson AZ 85721. **E-mail:** nmp@thediagram.com. **Website:** www.thediagram.com. **Contact:** Ander Monson, editor. Estab. 1999. The annual *DIAGRAM*/New Michigan Press Chapbook Contest offers $1,000, plus publication and author's copies, with discount on additional copies. Deadline: April 28. Prize: $1,000, plus publication. Finalist chapbooks also considered for publication. Costs: $19.

DOBIE PAISANO WRITER'S FELLOWSHIP

The Graduate School, The University of Texas at Austin, Attn: Dobie Paisano Program, 110 Inner Campus Drive Stop G0400, Austin TX 78712-0531. (512)232-3609. **Fax:** (512)471-7620. **E-mail:** gbarton@austin.utexas.edu. **Website:** www.utexas.edu/ogs/Paisano. **Contact:** Gwen Barton. Sponsored by the Graduate School at The University of Texas at Austin and the Texas Institute of Letters, the Dobie Paisano Fellowship Program provides solitude, time, and a comfortable place for Texas writers or writers who have written significantly about Texas through fiction, nonfiction, poetry, plays, or other mediums. The Dobie Paisano Ranch is a very rural and rustic setting, and applicants should read the guidelines closely to insure their ability to reside in this secluded environment. Deadline: January 15. Applications are accepted beginning December 1 and must be post-marked no later than January 15. The Ralph A. Johnston memorial Fellowship is for a period of 4 months with a stipend of $6,250 per month. It is aimed at writers who have already demonstrated some publishing and critical success. The Jesse H. Jones Writing Fellowship is for a period of approximately 6 months with a stipend of $3,000 per month. It is aimed at, but not limited to, writers who are early in their careers. Costs: Application fee: $20 for one fellowship; $30 for both fellowships.

🟢 THE JACK DYER FICTION PRIZE

Crab Orchard Review, Department of English, Mail Code 4503, Faner Hall 2380, Southern Illinois University Carbondale, 1000 Faner Drive, Carbondale IL 62901. (618)453-6833. **Fax:** (618)453-8224. **E-mail:** jtribble@siu.edu. **Website:** www.craborchardreview.siu.edu. **Contact:** Jon C. Tribble, managing editor. Estab. 1995 magazine/1997 fiction prize. Annual award for unpublished short fiction. Entries should consist of 1 story up to 6,000 words maximum in length. *Crab Orchard Review* acquires first North American serial rights to all submitted work. One winner and at least 2 finalists will be chosen. Deadline: May 17. Prize: $2,000, publication and 1-year subscription to *Crab Orchard Review.* Finalists are offered $500 and publication. Costs: $15/entry (up to 3 entries); entrants receive copy of the Winter/Spring issue of *Crab Orchard Review,* which will include the winner and finalists of this competition ($14 value; $1 for Submittable service) sent to a U.S. postal address for your first entry and extend your subscription beyond that according to the number of entries you have. Due to the extremely high cost of International Mail and uncertainty of successful delivery, individuals entering from overseas will need to provide a United States postal address to receive a copy of the issue. Judged by editorial staff (pre-screening); winner chosen by genre editor.

EATON LITERARY AGENCY'S ANNUAL AWARDS PROGRAM

Eaton Literary Agency, P.O. Box 49795, Sarasota FL 34230-6795. (941)366-6589. **Fax:** (941)365-4679. **E-mail:** eatonlit@aol.com. **Website:** www.eatonliterary.com. **Contact:** Richard Lawrence, President. Estab. 1984. Offered biannually for unpublished mss. Entries must be unpublished. Open to any writer. Guidelines available for SASE, by fax, e-mail, or on website. Accepts inquiries by fax, phone, and e-mail. Results announced in April and September. Winners notified by mail. For contest results, send SASE, fax, e-mail, or visit website. Deadline: March 31 (short story); August 31 (book-length). Prize: $2,500 (book-length); $500 (short story). Judged by an independent agency in conjunction with some members of Eaton's staff.

🔵 EMERGING VOICES FELLOWSHIP

PEN Center USA, P.O. Box 6037, Beverly Hills CA 90212, United States. 424 354 0582. **E-mail:** ev@penusa.org. **E-mail:** NA. **Website:** www.penusa.org. **Contact:** Libby Flores. Estab. 1996. Emerging Voices is a literary fellowship based in Los Angeles that aims to provide new writers, who lack access, with the tools they will need to launch a professional writing career. The eight-month fellowship includes the following: PROFESSIONAL MENTORSHIP: Emerging Voices mentors are carefully chosen from PEN Center USA's membership and from professional writers based in Los Angeles. The mentor-fellow relationship is expected to challenge the fellow's work and compel significant creative progress. Mentors will meet and offer written feedback on the Emerging Voices fellows' work in progress. Authors who have been mentors in the past include Ron Carlson, Harryette Mullen, Chris Abani, Jerry Stahl, Ramona Ausubel, Meghan Daum, and Sherman Alexie. CLASSES AT THE UCLA EXTENSION WRITERS' PROGRAM: Participants will attend two free courses (a 12-week writing course and a one-day workshop) at UCLA Extension, donated by the Writers' Program. AUTHOR EVENINGS: Every Monday, fellows will meet with a visiting author, editor or publisher and ask questions about craft. Fellows must read each visiting author's book in advance. Authors who have participated in the past have included Jonathan Lethem, Percival Everett, Maggie Nelson, Cynthia Bond, Aimee Bender, Jerry Stahl, Danzy Senna, and Roxane Gay. MASTER CLASSES: The Master Class is a genre-specific workshop with a professional writer and affords the fellows the opportunity to exchange feedback on their works in progress. Previous Master Class Instructors have included Diana Wagman, Alex Espinoza, and Paul Mandelbaum. VOLUNTEER PROJECT: All Emerging Voices fellows are expected to complete a 25-hour volunteer project that is relevant to the literary community. A few of the organizations that have hosted volunteers included WriteGirl, 826LA, Cedars-Sinai Hospital, and STARS – San Diego Youth Services. VOICE INSTRUCTION CLASS: The Fellowship will provide a one-day workshop with Dave Thomas, a professional voice actor. The Emerging Voices fellows will read their work in a recording studio and receive instruction on reading their work publicly. PUBLIC READINGS: Fellows will participate in three public readings in Los Angeles. STIPEND: The fellowship includes a $1,000 stipend, given in $500 increments. Participants need not be published, but the fellowship is directed toward poets and writers of fiction and creative nonfiction who have clear ideas of what they hope to accomplish through their writing. Each applicant needs to explain how they lack access creatively and/or financially. To provide new writers, who lack access, with the tools they will need to launch a professional writing career. Deadline: August. Costs: $10.

◐ THE FAR HORIZONS AWARD FOR SHORT FICTION

The Malahat Review, University of Victoria, P.O. Box 1700, Stn CSC, Victoria BC V8W 2Y2, Canada. (250)721-8524. **Fax:** (250)472-5051. **E-mail:** malahat@uvic.ca. **E-mail:** horizons@uvic.ca. **Website:** www.malahatreview.ca. **Contact:** Patrick Grace, public-

ity manager. Open to "emerging short fiction writers from Canada, the US, and elsewhere" who have not yet published their fiction in a full-length book (48 pages or more). Deadline: May 1 of odd numbered years Prize: $1,000 CAD, publication in fall issue of *The Malahat Review* (see separate listing in Magazines/Journals). Announced in fall on website, Facebook page, and in quarterly e-newsletter, *Malahat Lite*. Costs: $25 CAD for Canadian entries, $30 USD for US entries; $35 USD from Mexico and outside North America; includes a 1-year subscription to *The Malahat Review* $15 for additional entries, no limit.

THE VIRGINIA FAULKNER AWARD FOR EXCELLENCE IN WRITING

Prairie Schooner, 123 Andrews Hall, University of Nebraska-Lincoln, Lincoln NE 68588-0334. (402)472-0911. **Fax:** (402)472-1817. **E-mail:** PrairieSchooner@unl.edu. **Website:** www.prairieschooner.unl.edu. **Contact:** Kwame Dawes. Offered annually for work published in *Prairie Schooner* in the previous year. Categories: short stories, essays, novel excerpts, and translations. Prize: $1,000. Judged by editorial board.

THE WILLIAM FAULKNER-WILLIAM WISDOM CREATIVE WRITING COMPETITION

Faulkner - Wisdom Competition, Pirate's Alley Faulkner Society, Inc., The Pirate's Alley Faulkner Society, Inc., 624 Pirate's Alley, New Orleans LA 70116-3233. (504)586-1609. **E-mail:** faulkhouse@aol.com. **Website:** www.wordsandmusic.org. **Contact:** Rosemary James, award director. Estab. 1992. See guidelines posted at www.wordsandmusic.org. Deadline: May 15. Prizes: $750-7,500 depending on category. Costs: Charges $10-40, depending on category for entry fees. Judged by established authors, literary agents, and acquiring editors.

SOEURETTE DIEHL FRASER AWARD FOR BEST TRANSLATION OF A BOOK

P.O. Box 609, Round Rock TX 78680. **E-mail:** tilsecretary@yahoo.com. **Website:** texasinstituteofletters.org. Offered every 2 years to recognize the best translation of a literary book into English. Translator must have been born in Texas or have lived in the state for at least 2 consecutive years at some time. Deadline: January 10. Prize: $1,000.

◐ FREEFALL SHORT PROSE AND POETRY CONTEST

Freefall Literary Society of Calgary, 922 9th Ave. SE, Calgary AB T2G 0S4, Canada. **E-mail:** editors@freefallmagazine.ca. **Website:** www.freefallmagazine.ca. **Contact:** Ryan Stromquist, managing editor. Offered annually for unpublished work in the categories of poetry (5 poems/entry) and prose (3,000 words or less). Recognizes writers and offers publication credits in a literary magazine format. Contest rules and entry form online. Acquires first Canadian serial rights; ownership reverts to author after one-time publication. Deadline: December 31. Prize: 1st Place: $500 (CAD); 2nd Place: $250 (CAD); 3rd Place: $75; Honorable Mention: $25. All prizes include publication in the spring edition of *FreeFall Magazine*. Winners will also be invited to read at the launch of that issue, if such a launch takes place. Honorable mentions in each category will be published and may be asked to read. Travel expenses not included. Costs: $25. Judged by current guest editor for issue (who are also published authors in Canada).

GIVAL PRESS NOVEL AWARD

Gival Press, LLC, P.O. Box 3812, Arlington VA 22203. (703)351-0079. **E-mail:** givalpress@yahoo.com. **Website:** www.givalpress.submittable.com. **Contact:** Robert L. Giron. Estab. 2005. Offered every other year for a previously original unpublished novel (not a translation). Guidelines by phone, on website, via e-mail, or by mail with SASE. Results announced late fall of same year. Winners notified by phone. Results made available to entrants with SASE, by e-mail, on website. Purpose is to award the best literary novel. Deadline: May 30. Prize: $3,000, plus publication of book with a standard contract and author's copies. Costs: $50. Final judge is announced after winner is chosen. Entries read anonymously.

O GIVAL PRESS SHORT STORY AWARD

Gival Press, P.O. Box 3812, Arlington VA 22203. (703)351-0079. **E-mail:** givalpress@yahoo.com. **Website:** www.givalpress.submittable.com. **Contact:** Robert L. Giron, publisher. Estab. 2004. Annual literary, short story contest. Entries must be unpublished. Open to anyone who writes original short stories, which are not a chapter of a novel, in English. Receives about 100-150 entries per category. Guidelines available online, via e-mail, or by mail. Results announced in the fall of the same year. Winners notified by phone. Results available with SASE, by e-mail, and on website. Recognizes the best literary short story. Deadline: August 8. Prize: $1,000 and publication on website. Costs: $25 entry fee; make checks payable to Gival Press, LLC. Judged anonymously.

GLIMMER TRAIN'S FAMILY MATTERS CONTEST

Glimmer Train, P.O. Box 80430, Portland OR 97280. (503)221-0836. **Fax:** (503)221-0837. **E-mail:** eds@glimmertrain.org. **Website:** www.glimmertrain.org. **Contact:** Susan Burmeister-Brown. Estab. 1990. This contest is now held once a year, during the months of November and December. Winners are contacted on March 1. Submit online at www.glimmertrain.org. Deadline: December 31. Prize: 1st Place: $2,500, publication in *Glimmer Train Stories*, and 10 copies of that issue; 2nd Place: $500 and consideration for publication; 3rd Place: $300 and consideration for publication. Costs: $18/story. The editors judge.

◖ Represented in recent editions of *The Pushcart Prize*, *New Stories from the Midwest*, *The PEN/O. Henry Prize Stories*, *New Stories from the South*, *Best of the West*, *Best American Mystery Stories*, and *Best American Short Stories Anthologies*.

GLIMMER TRAIN'S FICTION OPEN

Glimmer Train, Inc., Glimmer Train Press, Inc., P.O. Box 80430, Portland OR 97280. (503)221-0836. **Fax:** (503)221-0837. **E-mail:** eds@glimmertrain.org. **Website:** www.glimmertrain.org. **Contact:** Susan Burmeister-Brown. Estab. 1990. Submissions to this category generally range from 3,000-8,000 words, but up to 20,000 is fine. Held twice a year: March 1 - April 30 and July 1 - August 31. Submit online at www.glimmertrain.org. Winners will be called 2 months after the close of the contest. Deadline: April 30 and August 31. Prize: 1st Place: $3,000, publication in *Glimmer Train Stories*, and 10 copies of that issue; 2nd Place: $1,000 and consideration for publication; 3rd Place: $600 and consideration for publication. Costs: $21/story. Judged by the editors.

◖ Represented in recent editions of *The Pushcart Prize*, *New Stories from the Midwest*, *The PEN/O. Henry Prize Stories*, *New Stories from the South*, *Best of the West*, *Best American Mystery Stories*, and *Best American Short Stories Anthologies*.

GLIMMER TRAIN'S SHORT-STORY AWARD FOR NEW WRITERS

Glimmer Train Press, Inc., P.O. Box 80430, Portland OR 97280. (503)221-0836. **Fax:** (503)221-0837. **E-mail:**

eds@glimmertrain.org. **Website:** www.glimmertrain.org. **Contact:** Susan Burmeister-Brown. Estab. 1990. Offered for any writer whose fiction hasn't appeared in a nationally distributed print publication with a circulation over 5,000. Submissions to this category generally range from 1,000–5,000 words, but up to 12,000 is fine. Held three times a year: January 1–February 29, May 1–June 30, September 1–October 31. Submit online at www.glimmertrain.org. Winners will be called 2 months after the close of the contest. Deadline: February 29, June 30, and October 31. Prize: 1st Place: $2,500, publication in *Glimmer Train Stories*, and 10 copies of that issue; 2nd Place: $500 and consideration for publication; 3rd Place: $300 and consideration for publication. Costs: $18/story.

○ Represented in recent editions of *The Pushcart Prize*, *New Stories from the Midwest*, *The PEN/O. Henry Prize Stories*, *New Stories from the South*, *Best of the West*, *Best American Mystery Stories*, and *Best American Short Stories Anthologies*. Pays over $50,000 every year to writers. The prize was increased in 2016.

GLIMMER TRAIN'S VERY SHORT FICTION CONTEST

Glimmer Train Press, Inc., P.O. Box 80430, Portland OR 97280. (503)221-0836. **Fax:** (503)221-0837. **E-mail:** eds@glimmertrain.org. **Website:** www.glimmertrain.org. **Contact:** Susan Burmeister-Brown. Estab. 1990. Offered to encourage the art of the very short story. Word count: 3,000 maximum. Held twice a year: March 1–April 30 and July 1–August 31. Submit online at www.glimmertrain.org. Results announced 2 months after the close of the contest. To encourage the art of the very short story. Deadline: April 30 and August 31. Prize: 1st Place: $2,000, publication in *Glimmer Train Stories*, and 10 copies of that issue; 2nd Place: $500 and consideration for publication; 3rd Place: $300 and consideration for publication. Costs: $16 fee/story. Judged by the editors.

○ Represented in recent editions of *The Pushcart Prize*, *New Stories from the Midwest*, *The PEN/O. Henry Prize Stories*, *New Stories from the South*, *Best of the West*, *Best American Mystery Stories*, and *Best American Short Stories Anthologies*. The prize was just increased in 2016.

☺ GOVERNOR GENERAL'S LITERARY AWARDS

Canada Council for the Arts, 150 Elgin St., P.O. Box 1047, Ottawa ON K1P 5V8, Canada. 1-800-263-5588, ext. 5573. **Website:** ggbooks.ca. Estab. 1937. The Canada Council for the Arts provides a wide range of grants and services to professional Canadian artists and art organizations in dance, media arts, music, theatre, writing, publishing, and the visual arts. The Governor General's Literary Awards are given annually for the best English-language and French-language work in each of 7 categories, including fiction, nonfiction, poetry, drama, children's literature (text), children's literature (illustrated books), and translation. Deadline: Depends on the book's publication date. See website for details. Prize: Each GG winner receives $25,000. Nonwinning finalists receive $1,000. Publishers of the winning titles receive a $3,000 grant for promotional purposes. Evaluated by fellow authors, translators, and illustrators. For each category, a jury makes the final selection.

☻ MARJORIE GRABER-MCINNIS SHORT STORY AWARD

ACT Writers Centre, Gorman House Arts Centre, Ainslie Ave., Braddon ACT 2612, Australia. (61)(2)6262-9191. **Fax:** (61)(2)6262-9191. **E-mail:** admin@actwriters.org.au. **Website:** www.actwriters.org.au. Open theme for a short story with 1,500-3,000 words. Guidelines available on website. Open only to unpublished emerging writers residing within the ACT or region. Deadline: September 18. Submissions period begins in early September. Prize: $600 and publication. Five runners-up receive book prizes. All winners may be published in the ACT Writers Centre newsletter and on the ACT Writers Centre website. Costs: $7.50 for nonmembers; $5 for members.

GREAT LAKES COLLEGES ASSOCIATION NEW WRITERS AWARD

The Great Lakes Colleges Association, 535 W. William, Suite 301, Ann Arbor MI 48103. (734)661-2350. **Fax:** (734)661-2349. **E-mail:** wegner@glca.org. **Website:** glca.org/program-menu/new-writers-award. **Contact:** Gregory R. Wegner, Director of Program Development. Estab. 1970. The Great Lakes Colleges Association (GLCA) is a consortium of 13 independent liberal arts colleges in Ohio, Michigan, Indiana, and Pennsylvania. Deadline: July 25. Prize: Honorarium of at least $500 for winning writers who are invited to give a reading at a member college campus. Each award winner receives invitations from several of the 13 colleges of the GLCA to visit campus. At these campus events an author will give readings, meet students and faculty, and occasionally lead discussions or classes. In addition to an honorarium for each campus visit, travel costs to colleges are paid by GLCA and its member colleges. Judged by professors of literature and writers in residence at GLCA colleges.

⬤ Annual award for a first published volume of poetry, fiction, and creative nonfiction.

GUGGENHEIM FELLOWSHIPS

John Simon Guggenheim Memorial Foundation, 90 Park Ave., New York NY 10016. (212)687-4470. **E-mail:** fellowships@gf.org. **Website:** www.gf.org. Estab. 1925. Often characterized as "midcareer" awards, Guggenheim Fellowships are intended for men and women who have already demonstrated exceptional capacity for productive scholarship or exceptional creative ability in the arts. Fellowships are awarded through two annual competitions: one open to citizens and permanent residents of the United States and Canada, and the other open to citizens and permanent residents of Latin America and the Caribbean. Candidates must apply to the Guggenheim Foundation in order to be considered in either of these competitions. The Foundation receives between 3,500 and 4,000 applications each year. Although no one who applies is guaranteed success in the competition, there is no prescreening: all applications are reviewed. Approximately 200 Fellowships are awarded each year. Deadline: September 15.

🌀 LYNDALL HADOW/DONALD STUART SHORT STORY COMPETITION

Fellowship of Australian Writers (WA), P.O. Box 6180, Swanbourne WA 6910, Australia. (61)(8)9384-4771. **Fax:** (61)(8)9384-4854. **E-mail:** fellowshipaustralianwriterswa@gmail.com. **Website:** www.fawwa.org. Annual contest for unpublished short stories (maximum 3,000 words). Reserves the right to publish entries in a FAWWA publication or on website. Guidelines online or for SASE. Deadline: June 1. Submissions period begins April 1. Prize: 1st Place: $1,00; 2nd Place: $300; 3rd Place: $100. Costs: $10/story (maximum of 3).

HAMMETT PRIZE

International Association of Crime Writers, North American Branch, 243 Fifth Avenue, #537, New York NY 10016. **E-mail:** mfrisque@igc.org. **Website:** www.crimewritersna.org. **Contact:** Mary A. Frisque, executive director, North American Branch. Award for crime novels, story collections, nonfiction by one author. "Our reading committee seeks suggestions from publishers and they also ask the membership for recommendations." Nominations announced in January; winners announced in fall. Winners notified by e-mail or mail and recognized at awards ceremony. For contest results, send SASE or e-mail. Award established to honor a work of literary excellence in the field of crime writing by a US or Canadian author. Deadline: December 15. Prize: Trophy. Judged by a committee of members of the organization. The committee chooses 5 nominated books, which are then sent to 3 outside judges for a final selection. Judges are outside the crime writing field.

WILDA HEARNE FLASH FICTION CONTEST

Big Muddy: A Journal of the Mississippi River Valley, WHFF Contest, Southeast Missouri State University Press, One University Plaza, MS 2650, Cape Girardeau MO 63701. (573) 651-2044. **E-mail:** sswartwout@semo.edu. **Website:** www.semopress.com. **Contact:** Susan Swartwout, publisher. Annual competition for flash fiction, held by Southeast Missouri State University Press. Deadline: October 1. Prize: $500 and publication in *Big Muddy: A Journal of the Mississippi River Valley*. Costs: $15. Semi-finalists will be chosen by a team of published writers. The final ms will be chosen by Susan Swartwout, publisher of the Southeast Missouri State University Press.

DRUE HEINZ LITERATURE PRIZE

University of Pittsburgh Press, 7500 Thomas Blvd., Pittsburgh PA 15260. **Fax:** (412)383-2466. **E-mail:** info@upress.pitt.edu. **Website:** www.upress.pitt.edu. Estab. 1981. Offered annually to writers who have published a book-length collection of fiction or a minimum of 3 short stories or novellas in commercial magazines or literary journals of national distribution. Does not return mss. Deadline: June 30. Open to submissions on May 1. Prize: $15,000. Judged by anonymous nationally known writers such as Robert Penn Warren, Joyce Carol Oates, and Margaret Atwood.

LORIAN HEMINGWAY SHORT STORY COMPETITION

Hemingway Days Festival, P.O. Box 2011 c/o Cynthia. D. Higgs: Key West Editorial, Key West FL 33045. **E-mail:** shortstorykeywest@hushmail.com. **Website:** www.shortstorycompetition.com. **Contact:** Eva Eliot, Editorial Assistant. Estab. 1981. Offered annually for unpublished short stories up to 3,500 words. Guidelines available via mail, e-mail, or online. Award to encourage literary excellence and the efforts of writers whose voices have yet to be heard. Deadline: May 15. Prizes: 1st Place: $1,500, plus publication of his or her winning story in *Cutthroat: A Journal of the*

Arts; 2nd-3rd Place: $500; honorable mentions will also be awarded. Costs: $15/story postmarked by May 1; $20/story postmarked by May 15. Judged by a panel of writers, editors, and literary scholars selected by author Lorian Hemingway. (Lorian Hemingway is the competition's final judge.)

○ HIGHLIGHTS FOR CHILDREN FICTION CONTEST

803 Church St., Honesdale PA 18431-1824. (570)253-1080. **Fax:** (570)251-7847. **E-mail:** eds@highlights-corp.com. **Website:** www.highlights.com. **Contact:** Christine French Cully, editor-in-chief. Stimulates interest in writing for children and rewards and recognizes excellence. Deadline: January 31. Submission period begins January 1. Prize: Three prizes of $1,000 or tuition for any Highlights Foundation Founders Workshop.

TONY HILLERMAN PRIZE

Wordharvest, 1063 Willow Way, Santa Fe NM 87507. (505)471-1565. **E-mail:** wordharvest@wordharvest.com. **Website:** www.wordharvest.com. **Contact:** Anne Hillerman and Jean Schaumberg, co-organizers. Estab. 2006. Awarded annually, and sponsored by St. Martin's Press, for the best first mystery set in the Southwest. Murder or another serious crime or crimes must be at the heart of the story, with the emphasis on the solution rather than the details of the crime. Honors the contributions made by Tony Hillerman to the art and craft of the mystery. Deadline: June 1. Prize: $10,000 advance and publication by St. Martin's Press. Nominees will be selected by judges chosen by the editorial staff of St. Martin's Press, with the assistance of independent judges selected by organizers of the Tony Hillerman Writers Conference (Wordharvest), and the winner will be chosen by St. Martin's editors.

ERIC HOFFER AWARD

Hopewell Publications, LLC, P.O. Box 11, Titusville NJ 08560-0011. **Fax:** (609)964-1718. **E-mail:** info@hope-pubs.com. **Website:** www.hofferaward.com. **Contact:** Christopher Klim, chair. Annual contest for previously published books. Recognizes excellence in independent publishing in many unique categories: Art (titles capture the experience, execution, or demonstration of the arts); Poetry (all styles); Chapbook (40 pages or less, artistic assembly); General Fiction (nongenre-specific fiction); Commercial Fiction (genre-specific fiction); Children (titles for young children); Young Adult (titles aimed at the juvenile and teen markets); Culture (titles demonstrating the human or world experience); Memoir (titles relating to personal experience); Business (titles with application to today's business environment and emerging trends); Reference (titles from traditional and emerging reference areas); Home (titles with practical applications to home or home-related issues, including family); Health (titles promoting physical, mental, and emotional well-being); Self-help (titles involving new and emerging topics in self-help); Spiritual (titles involving the mind and spirit, including relgion); Legacy Fiction and Nonfiction (titles over 2 years of age that hold particular relevance to any subject matter or form); E-book Fiction; E-book Nonfiction. Open to any writer of published work within the last 2 years, including categories for older books. This contest recognizes excellence in independent publishing in many unique categories. Also awards the Montaigne Medal for most though-provoking book, the Da Vinci Eye for best cover, and the First Horizon Award for best new authors. Results published in the US Review of Books. Deadline: January 21. Grand Prize: $2,000; honors in each category, including the Montaigne Medal (most thought-provoking), da Vinci Art (cover art), First Horizon (first book), and Best in Press (small, academic, micro, self-published). Costs: Charges $55; $40 for chapbook.

○ TOM HOWARD/JOHN H. REID FICTION & ESSAY CONTEST

Winning Writers, 351 Pleasant Street, PMB 222, Northampton MA 01060-3961, USA. (866)946-9748. **Fax:** (413)280-0539. **E-mail:** adam@winningwriters.com. **Website:** www.winningwriters.com. **Contact:** Adam Cohen, President. Estab. 1993. Since 2001, Winning Writers has provided expert literary contest information to the public. Sponsors four contests. One of the "101 Best Websites for Writers" (*Writer's Digest*). Open to all writers. Submit any type of short story or essay. Both published and unpublished works are welcome. If you win a prize, requests nonexclusive rights to publish your submission online, in e-mail newsletters, in e-books, and in press releases. Deadline: April 30. Prizes: Two 1st prizes of $1,500 will be awarded, plus 10 honorable mentions of $100 each. Top 12 entries published online. Costs: $18. Judged by Arthur Powers, assisted by Lauren Singer.

THE JULIA WARD HOWE/BOSTON AUTHORS AWARD

The Boston Authors Club, The Boston Authors Club, 36 Sunhill Lane, Newton Center MA 02459. **E-mail:** bostonauthors@aol.com;. **Website:** www.bostonauthorsclub.org. **Contact:** Alan Lawson. Estab. 1900. This annual award honors Julia Ward Howe and her literary friends who founded the Boston Authors Club in 1900. It also honors the membership over 110 years, consisting of novelists, biographers, historians, governors, senators, philosophers, poets, playwrights, and other luminaries. There are 2 categories: trade books and books for young readers (beginning with chapter books through young adult books). Deadline: January 15. Prize: $1,000. Costs: $25/title. Judged by the members.

HENRY HOYNS & POE/FAULKNER FELLOWSHIPS

Creative Writing Program, 219 Bryan Hall, P.O. Box 400121, University of Virginia, Charlottesville VA 22904-4121. (434)924-6675. **Fax:** (434)924-1478. **E-mail:** creativewriting@virginia.edu. **Website:** creativewriting.virginia.edu. **Contact:** Jeb Livingood, associate director. Two-year MFA program in poetry and fiction; all students receive fellowships and teaching stipends that total $18,000 in both years of study. Sample poems/prose required with application. Deadline: December 15.

O L. RON HUBBARD'S WRITERS OF THE FUTURE CONTEST

Author Services, Inc., P.O. Box 1630, Los Angeles CA 90078. (323)466-3310. **Fax:** (323)466-6474. **E-mail:** contests@authorservicesinc.com. **Website:** www. writersofthefuture.com. **Contact:** Joni Labaqui, contest director. Estab. 1983. Foremost competition for new and amateur writers of unpublished science fiction or fantasy short stories or novelettes. Offered to find, reward and publicize new speculative fiction writers so they may more easily attain professional writing careers. Open to writers who have not professionally published a novel or short novel, more than 2 novelettes, or more than 3 short stories. Entry stories must be unpublished. Limit 1 entry per quarter. This is an international contest. Results announced quarterly in e-newsletter. Winners notified by phone. Contest has 4 quarters. There shall be 3 cash prizes in each quarter. In addition, at the end of the year, the 4 first-place, quarterly winners will have their entries rejudged, and a grand prize winner shall be determined. Deadline: December 31, March 31, June 30, September 30. Prize (awards quarterly): 1st Place: $1,000; 2nd Place: $750; and 3rd Place: $500. Annual grand prize: $5,000. Judged by David Farland (initial judge), then by a panel of 4 professional authors.

CAROL OTIS HURST CHILDREN'S BOOK PRIZE

Westfield Athenaeum, 6 Elm St., Westfield MA 01085. (413)568-7833. **Fax:** (413)568-0988. **Website:** www. westath.org. **Contact:** Pamela Weingart. Estab. 2007. The Carol Otis Hurst Children's Book Prize honors outstanding works of fiction and nonfiction, including biography and memoir, written for children and young adults through the age of eighteen that exemplify the highest standards of research, analysis, and authorship in their portrayal of the New England Experience. The prize will be presented annually to an author whose book treats the region's history as broadly conceived to encompass one or more of the following elements: political experience, social development, fine and performing artistic expression, domestic life and arts, transportation and communication, changing technology, military experience at home and abroad, schooling, business and manufacturing, workers and the labor movement, agriculture and its transformation, racial and ethnic diversity, religious life and institutions, immigration and adjustment, sports at all levels, and the evolution of popular entertainment. The public presentation of the prize will be accompanied by a reading and/or talk by the recipient at a mutually agreed upon time during the spring immediately following the publication year. Deadline: December 31. Prize: $500.

INDEPENDENT PUBLISHER BOOK AWARDS

Jenkins Group/Independent Publisher Online, 1129 Woodmere Ave., Ste. B, Traverse City MI 49686. (231)933-0445. **Fax:** (231)933-0448. **E-mail:** jimb@book-publishing.com. **Website:** www.independentpublisher. com. **Contact:** Jim Barnes. Honors the year's best independently published English language titles from around the world. The IPPY Awards reward those who exhibit the courage, innovation, and creativity to bring about change in the world of publishing. Independent spirit and expertise comes from publishers of all areas and budgets, and they judge books with that in mind. Entries will be accepted in over 80 categories, visit website to see details. Open to any published author. Deadline: Late February. Price of submission rises in September and December. Prize: Gold, silver and bronze medals for each category; foil seals available to all. Costs: $75-$95, based on entry date. Judged by a panel of experts representing the fields of design, writing, bookselling, library, and reviewing.

INK & INSIGHTS WRITING CONTEST

Critique My Novel, 2408 W. 8th, Amarillo TX 79106. **E-mail:** contest@InkandInsights.com. **Website:** ink-andinsights.com. **Contact:** Catherine York, contest administrator. Ink & Insights is a writing contest geared toward strengthening the skills of independent writers by focusing on feedback. Each entry is assigned four judges who specialize in the genre of the ms. They read, score, and comment on specific aspects of the segment. The top three mss in the Master and Nonfiction categories move on to the Agent Round and receive a guaranteed read and feedback from a panel of agents. Deadline: April 30 (regular entry), June 30 (late entry). Prize: Prizes vary depending on category. Every novel receives personal feedback from 4 judges. Costs: Early bird entry: $35; Regular entry: $40; Late entry: $45. Judges listed on website, including the agents who will be helping choose the top winners this year.

INTERNATIONAL LITERACY ASSOCIATION CHILDREN'S AND YOUNG ADULT'S BOOK AWARDS

P.O. Box 8139, 800 Barksdale Rd., Newark DE 19714-8139. (302)731-1600, ext. 221. **E-mail:** kbaughman@reading.org. **E-mail:** committees@reading.org. **Website:** www.literacyworldwide.org. **Contact:** Kathy Baughman. The ILA Children's and Young Adults Book Awards are intended for newly published authors who show unusual promise in the children's and young adults' book field. Awards are given for fiction and nonfiction in each of three categories: primary, intermediate, and young adult. Books from all countries and published in English for the first time during the previous calendar year will be considered. Deadline: January 15. Prize: $1,000.

THE IOWA REVIEW AWARD IN POETRY, FICTION, AND NONFICTION

308 EPB, University of Iowa, Iowa City IA 52242. **E-mail:** iowa-review@uiowa.edu. **Website:** www.iowareview.org. *The Iowa Review* Award in Poetry, Fiction, and Nonfiction presents $1,500 to each winner in each genre and $750 to runners-up. Winners and runners-up published in *The Iowa Review*. Deadline: January 31. Submission period begins January 1. Costs: $20. Make checks payable to *The Iowa Review*. Enclose additional $10 (optional) for year-long subscription. Judged by Joyelle McSweeney, Amy Gray, and Charles D'Ambrosio in 2017.

THE IOWA SHORT FICTION AWARD & JOHN SIMMONS SHORT FICTION AWARD

Iowa Writers' Workshop, 507 N. Clinton St., 102 Dey House, Iowa City IA 52242-1000. **Website:** www.uiowapress.org. **Contact:** James McCoy, director. Annual award to give exposure to promising writers who have not yet published a book of prose. Open to any writer. Current University of Iowa students are not eligible. No application forms are necessary. Announcement of winners made early in year following competition. Winners notified by phone. No application forms are necessary. Do not send original ms. Include SASE for return of ms. Deadline: September 30. Submission period begins August 1. Prize: Publication by University of Iowa Press. Judged by senior Iowa Writers' Workshop members who screen mss; published fiction author of note makes final selections.

❸ TILIA KLEBENOV JACOBS RELIGIOUS ESSAY PRIZE CATEGORY

Soul Making Keats Literary Competition, The Webhallow House, 1544 Sweetwood Dr., Broadmoor Village CA 94015-2029. **E-mail:** SoulKeats@mail.com. **Website:** www.soulmakingcontest.us. **Contact:** Eileen Malone. Estab. 2012. Call for thoughtful writings of up to 3,000 words. "No preaching, no proselytizing." Open annually to any writer. Deadline: November 30. Prize: 1st Place: $100; 2nd Place: $50; 3rd Place: $25. Costs: $5.

JESSE H. JONES AWARD FOR BEST WORK OF FICTION

P.O. Box 609, Round Rock TX 78680. **E-mail:** tilsecretary@yahoo.com. **Website:** texasinstituteofletters.org. Offered annually by Texas Institute of Letters for work published January 1-December 31 of year before award is given to recognize the writer of the best book of fiction entered in the competition. Writers must have been born in Texas, have lived in the state for at least 2 consecutive years at some time, or the subject matter of the work should be associated with the state. Deadline: January 10. Prize: $6,000.

JAMES JONES FIRST NOVEL FELLOWSHIP

Wilkes University, Creative Writing Department, Wilkes University, 84 West South Street, Wilkes-Barre PA 18766. (570)408-4547. **Fax:** (570)408-3333. **E-mail:** jamesjonesfirstnovel@wilkes.edu. **Website:** www.wilkes.edu/. Offered annually for unpublished novels (must be works-in-progress). This competition is open to all U.S. citizens who have not previously published novels. The award is intended to honor the spirit of unblinking honesty, determination, and insight into modern culture exemplified by the late James Jones. Deadline: March 15. Submission period begins October 1. Prize: $10,000; 2 runners-up get $1,000 honorarium. Costs: A $30 check/money order, payable to Wilkes University, not to James Jones First Novel Fellowship, must accompany each entry. For online submissions add a $3.00 processing fee.

JUNIPER PRIZE FOR FICTION

University of Massachusetts Press, East Experiment Station, 671 North Pleasant St., Amherst MA 01003. (413)545-2217. **Fax:** (413)545-1226. **E-mail:** info@umpress.umass.edu; kfisk@umpress.umass.edu. **E-mail:** fiction@umpress.umass.edu. **Website:** www.umass.edu/umpress. **Contact:** Karen Fisk, competition coordinator. Estab. 2004. Award to honor and publish outstanding works of literary fiction. Deadline: September 30. Submissions period begins August 1. Winners announced online in April on the press website. Prize: $1,000 cash and publication. Costs: $30.

THE LAWRENCE FOUNDATION AWARD

Prairie Schooner, 123 Andrews Hall, University of Nebraska-Lincoln, Lincoln NE 68588-0334. (402)472-0911. **Fax:** (402)472-9771. **E-mail:** prairieschooner@unl.edu. **Website:** www.prairieschooner.unl.edu. Offered annually for the best short story published in Prairie Schooner in the previous year. Only work published in *Prairie Schooner* in the previous year is considered. Work is nominated by editorial staff. Results announced in the Spring issue. Winners notified by mail in February or March. Prize: $1,000. Judged by editorial staff of *Praire Schooner*.

LAWRENCE FOUNDATION PRIZE

Michigan Quarterly Review, 0576 Rackham Bldg., 915 E. Washington Street, Ann Arbor MI 48109-1070. (734)764-9265. **E-mail:** mqr@umich.edu. **Website:** www.michiganquarterlyreview.com. **Contact:** Vicki Lawrence, managing editor. Estab. 1978. This annual prize is awarded by the *Michigan Quarterly Review* editorial board to the author of the best short story published in *MQR* that year. The prize is sponsored by University of Michigan alumnus and fiction writer Leonard S. Bernstein, a trustee of the Lawrence Foundation of New York. Approximately 20 short stories are published in *MQR* each year. Prize: $1,000. Judged by editorial board.

THE STEPHEN LEACOCK MEMORIAL MEDAL FOR HUMOUR

149 Peter St. N., Orillia ON L3V 4Z4, Canada. (705)326-9286. **E-mail:** bettewalkerca@gmail.com. **Website:** www.leacock.ca. **Contact:** Bette Walker, award committee, Stephen Leacock Associates. The Leacock Associates awards the prestigious Leacock Medal for the best book of literary humor written by a Canadian and published in the current year. The winning author also receives a cash prize of $15,000 thanks to the generous support of the TD Financial Group. 2 runners-up are each awarded a cash prize of $1,500. Deadline: December 31. Prize: $15,000. Costs: $200.

LEAGUE OF UTAH WRITERS CONTEST

The League of Utah Writers, The League of Utah Writers, P.O. Box 64, Lewiston UT 84320. (435)755-7609. **E-mail:** luwcontest@gmail.com; luwriters@gmail.com. **Website:** www.luwriters.org. Open to any writer, the LUW Contest provides authors an opportunity to get their work read and critiqued. Multiple categories are offered; see website for details. Entries must be the original and unpublished work of the author. Winners are announced at the Annual Writers Round-Up in September. Those not present will be notified by e-mail. Deadline: June 15. Submissions period begins March 15. Prize: Cash prizes are awarded. Judged by professional authors and editors from outside the League.

LES FIGUES PRESS NOS BOOK CONTEST

P.O. Box 7736, Los Angeles CA 90007. (323)734-4732. **E-mail:** info@lesfigues.com. **Website:** www.lesfigues.com. **Contact:** Teresa Carmody, director. Les Figues Press creates aesthetic conversations between writers/artists and readers, especially those interested in innovative/experimental/avant-garde work. The Press intends in the most premeditated fashion to champion the trinity of Beauty, Belief, and Bawdry. Deadline: September 15. Prize: $1,000, plus publication by Les Figues Press. Each entry receives LFP book. Costs: $25.

LET'S WRITE LITERARY CONTEST

The Gulf Coast Writers Association, P.O. Box 4808, Biloxi MS 39535. **E-mail:** writerpllevin@gmail.com. **Website:** www.gcwriters.org/contest.html. **Contact:** Philip Levin. The Gulf Coast Writers Association sponsors this nationally recognized contest, which accepts unpublished poems, prose, and short stories from authors all around the US. This is an annual event which has been held for 29 years. Deadline: April 10. Prize: 1st Prize: $80; 2nd Prize: $60; 3rd Prize: $40. Costs: $8 for prose, $8 for 3 poems.

💲 FENIA AND YAAKOV LEVIANT MEMORIAL PRIZE IN YIDDISH STUDIES

Modern Language Association of America, 85 Broad Street, suite 500, New York NY 10004-2434. (646)576-5141. **Fax:** (646)458-0030. **E-mail:** awards@mla.org. **Website:** www.mla.org. **Contact:** Coordinator of book prizes. Offered in even-numbered years for an outstanding English translation of a Yiddish literary work or the publication of a scholarly work. Cultural studies, critical biographies, or edited works in the field of Yiddish folklore or linguistic studies are eligible to compete. See website for details on which they are accepting. Deadline: May 1. Prize: A cash prize, and a certificate, to be presented at the Modern Language Association's annual convention in January.

LITERAL LATTÉ FICTION AWARD

Literal Latté, 200 E. 10th St., Suite 240, New York NY 10003. **E-mail:** litlatte@aol.com. **E-mail:** Link to submittable on www.literal-latte.com. **Website:** www.literal-latte.com. **Contact:** Edward Estlin, contributing editor. Estab. 1994. Award to provide talented writers with 3 essential tools for continued success: money, publication, and recognition. Offered annually for unpublished fiction (maximum 20,000 words). Guidelines online. Open to any writer. Deadline: January 15. Prize: 1st Place: $1,000 and publication in *Literal Latté*; 2nd Place: $300; 3rd Place: $200; also up to 7 honorable mentions. All winners published in *Literal Latté*. Costs: $10 per story; $15 for two.

LITERAL LATTE SHORT SHORTS CONTEST

Literal Latté, 200 E. 10th St., Suite 240, New York NY 10003. **E-mail:** litlatte@aol.com. **E-mail:** Link to submittable on www.literal-latte.com. **Website:** www.literal-latte.com. **Contact:** Jenine Gordon Bockman, editor. Estab. 1994. Keeping free thought free since 1994. Deadline: June 30. Prize: $500. Costs: $10 for up to three shorts. Judged by the editors.

⭕ Annual contest. Send unpublished shorts, 2,000 words max. All styles welcome. Name, address, phone number, e-mail address (optional) on cover page only. Include SASE or e-mail address for reply. All entries considered for publication.

THE HUGH J. LUKE AWARD

Prairie Schooner, 123 Andrews Hall, University of Nebraska-Lincoln, Lincoln NE 68588-0334. (402)472-0911. **Fax:** (402)472-1817. **E-mail:** prairieschooner@unl.edu. **Website:** www.prairieschooner.unl.edu. **Contact:** Kwame Dawes. Offered annually for work published in *Prairie Schooner* in the previous year. Results announced in the Spring issue. Winners notified by mail in February or March. Prize: $250. Judged by editorial staff of *Prairie Schooner*.

THE MARY MACKEY SHORT STORY PRIZE CATEGORY

Soul-Making Keats Literary Competition, The Webhallow House, 1544 Sweetwood Dr., Broadmoor Village CA 94015. **E-mail:** SoulKeats@mail.com. **Website:** www.soulmakingcontest.us. **Contact:** Eileen Malone. Open annually to any writer. Deadline: November 30. Prize: Cash prizes. Costs: $5/entry (make checks payable to NLAPW).

♾️ THE MALAHAT REVIEW NOVELLA PRIZE

The Malahat Review, University of Victoria, P.O. Box 1700 STN CSC, Victoria BC V8W 2Y2, Canada. (250)721-8524. **E-mail:** malahat@uvic.ca. **E-mail:** novella@uvic.ca. **Website:** malahatreview.ca. **Contact:** Patrick Grace, publicity manager. Held in alternate (even numbered) years with the Long Poem Prize. Offered to promote unpublished novellas. Obtains first world rights. After publication rights revert to the author. Open to any writer. Deadline: February 1 (even years). Prize: $1,500 CAD and one year's subscription. Winner published in summer issue of *The Malahat Review* and announced on website, Facebook page, and in quarterly e-newsletter, *Malahat Lite*. Costs: $35 CAD for Canadian entrants; $40 US for American entrants; $45 US for entrants from elsewhere (includes a 1-year subscription to *Malahat*). $15 for additional entries, no limit. Three recognized literary figures are assigned to judge the contest each year.

🔄 THE MAN BOOKER PRIZE

Four Colman Getty PR, 20 St Thomas Street, London SE1 9BF, United Kingdom. (44)(207)697 4200. **Website:** www.themanbookerprize.com. **Contact:** Four Colman Getty PR. Estab. 1968. Books are only accepted through UK publishers. However, publication outside the UK does not disqualify a book once it is published in the

UK. Open to any full-length novel (published October 1-September 30). No novellas, collections of short stories, translations, or self-published books. Open to citizens of the Commonwealth or Republic of Ireland. Deadline: July. Prize: £50,000. Judges appointed by the Booker Prize Management Committee.

☘ MANITOBA BOOK AWARDS

Manitoba Writers' Guild, c/o Manitoba Writers' Guild, 218-100 Arthur St., Winnipeg MB R3B 1H3, Canada. (204)944-8013. **E-mail:** events@mbwriter.mb.ca. **Website:** www.manitobabookawards.com. **Contact:** Ellen MacDonald. Estab. 1983. The awards honor books written by Manitobans, published in Manitoba or about Manitoba. More than $30,000 in prizes is awarded each year to Manitoba writers. The Manitoba Book Awards celebrates literary excellence, originality and diverse talent. Some of Canada's best writers have springboarded to national and international acclaim after winning the Manitoba Book Awards. Previous winners include: Carol Shields (1993), David Bergen (1993,1996, 2009), Miriam Toews (1998, 2000), Margaret Sweatman (1991, 2001), Sandra Birdsell (1992), Jake MacDonald (2002), Allan Levine (2010), Barbara Huck (2014) and Wab Kinew (2016). The 18 awards to be presented at the 29th annual Manitoba Book Awards include Alexander Kennedy Isbister Award for Nonfiction/Prix Alexander-Kennedy-Isbister pour les études et les essais, Beatrice Mosionier Aboriginal Writer of the Year Award /Prix Beatrice-Mosionier pour l'écrivain.e autochtone de l'année (English/Français/Indigenous Languages), Carol Shields Winnipeg Book Award/Prix littéraire Carol-Shields de la ville de Winnipeg, The Chris Johnson Award for Best Play by a Manitoba Playwright /Prix Chris-Johnson pour la meilleure pièce par un dramaturge manitobain, Eileen McTavish Sykes Award for Best First Book, John Hirsch Award for Most Promising Manitoba Writer/Prix John-Hirsch pour l'écrivain manitobain le plus prometteur, Lansdowne Prize for Poetry / Prix Lansdowne de poésie, Le Prix Littéraire Rue-Deschambault, Manuela Dias Book Design and Illustration Awards/Prix Manuela—Dias de conception graphique et d'illustration en édition—4 categories, Margaret Laurence Award for Fiction, Mary Scorer Award for Best Book by a Manitoba Publisher/Prix Mary-Scorer pour le meilleur livre par un éditeur du Manitoba, McNally Robinson Books for Young People Awards—2 categories, McNally Robinson Book of the Year Award, and Lifetime Achievement

Award—English/Français. Deadline: December 1 and January 15. Prize: Several prizes up to $5,000 (Canadian). Costs: $25 per category. Jurors selected by the Manitoba Writers' Guild.

💬 Melanie Matheson, Executive Director of the Manitoba Writers' Guild said, "Manitoba is blessed with an abundance of world class writers and these awards are a tremendous boon to both writers and to the industry. We celebrate that."

🌑 MARSH AWARD FOR CHILDREN'S LITERATURE IN TRANSLATION

The English-Speaking Union, Dartmouth House, 37 Charles St., London En W1J 5ED, United Kingdom. 020 7529 1590. **E-mail:** emma.coffey@esu.org. **Website:** www.marshchristiantrust.org; www.esu.org. **Contact:** Emma Coffey, education officer. Estab. 1996. The Marsh Award for Children's Literature in Translation, awarded biennially, was founded to celebrate the best translation of a children's book from a foreign language into English and published in the UK. It aims to spotlight the high quality and diversity of translated fiction for young readers. The Award is administered by the ESU on behalf of the Marsh Christian Trust.

MARY MCCARTHY PRIZE IN SHORT FICTION

Sarabande Books, 2234 Dundee Rd., Suite 200, Louisville KY 40205. (502)458-4028. **Fax:** (502)458-4065. **E-mail:** info@sarabandebooks.org. **Website:** www.sarabandebooks.org. **Contact:** Sarah Gorham, Editor-in-Chief. Annual competition to honor a collection of short stories, novellas, or a short novel. Deadline: February 15. Submission period begins January 1. Prize: $2,000 and publication (standard royalty contract). Costs: $28.

⊘ THE MCGINNIS-RITCHIE MEMORIAL AWARD

Southwest Review, Southern Methodist University, P.O. Box 750374, Dallas TX 75275-0374. (214) 768-1037. **Fax:** (214) 768-1408. **E-mail:** swr@mail.smu.edu. **Website:** www.smu.edu/southwestreview. **Contact:** Greg Brownderville, editor-in-chief. The McGinnis-Ritchie Memorial Award is given annually to the best works of fiction and nonfiction that appeared in the magazine in the previous year. Mss are submitted for publication, not for the prizes themselves. Guidelines for SASE or online. Prize: $500. Judged by Greg Brownderville.

💲 MCKNIGHT ARTIST FELLOWSHIPS FOR WRITERS, LOFT AWARD(S) IN CHILDREN'S LITERATURE/CREATIVE PROSE/POETRY

The Loft Literary Center, 1011 Washington Ave. S., Suite 200, Open Book, Minneapolis MN 55415. (612)215-2575. **Fax:** (612)215-2576. **E-mail:** loft@loft.org. **Website:** www.loft.org. **Contact:** Bao Phi. "The Loft administers the McKnight Artists Fellowships for Writers. Five $25,000 awards are presented annually to accomplished Minnesota writers and spoken word artists. Four awards alternate annually between creative prose (fiction and creative nonfiction) and poetry/spoken word. The fifth award is presented in children's literature and alternates annually for writing for ages 8 and under and writing for children older than 8." The awards provide the writers the opportunity to focus on their craft for the course of the fellowship year. Prize: $25,000.

MEMPHIS MAGAZINE FICTION CONTEST

Memphis Magazine, co-sponsored by booksellers of Laurelwood and Burke's Book Store, Fiction Contest, c/o *Memphis* magazine, P.O. Box 1738, Memphis TN 38101. (901)521-9000, ext. 451. **Fax:** (901)521-0129. **E-mail:** sadler@memphismagazine.com. **Website:** www.memphismagazine.com. **Contact:** Marilyn Sadler. Annual award for authors of short fiction living within 150 miles of Memphis. Deadline: February 15. Prize: $1,000 grand prize, along with being published in the annual Cultural Issue; two honorable-mention awards of $500 each will be given if the quality of entries warrants. Costs: $20/story.

DAVID NATHAN MEYERSON PRIZE FOR FICTION

Southwest Review, Southern Methodist University, P.O. Box 750374, Dallas TX 75275-0374. (214) 768-1037. **Fax:** (214) 768-1408. **E-mail:** swr@smu.edu. **Website:** www.smu.edu/southwestreview. **Contact:** Greg Brownderville, editor-in-chief. Annual award given to a writer who has not published a first book of fiction, either a novel or collection of stories. All contest entrants will receive a copy of the issue in which the winning piece appears. Deadline: May 1 (postmarked). Prize: $1,000 and publication in the *Southwest Review*. Costs: $25/story.

A MIDSUMMER TALE

E-mail: editors@toasted-cheese.com. **Website:** www.toasted-cheese.com. **Contact:** Theryn Fleming, editor. Estab. 2002. A Midsummer Tale is open to non-genre fiction and creative nonfiction. There is a different theme each year. Entries must be unpublished. Accepts inquiries by e-mail. Deadline: June 21. Results announced on July 31. Winners notified by e-mail. List of winners on website. Prize: Amazon gift certificates and publication in Toasted Cheese. Entries are blind-judged by at least one Toasted Cheese editor

💬 "Nongenre fiction" means literary or mainstream fiction. No science fiction, fantasy, mystery, horror, thriller, romance, western or other genre fiction, please. Follow all contest guidelines.

MILKWEED NATIONAL FICTION PRIZE

1011 Washington Ave. S., Suite 300, Minneapolis MN 55415. (612)332-3192. **Fax:** (612)215-2550. **E-mail:** editor@milkweed.org. **Website:** www.milkweed.org. **Contact:** Patrick Thoman, editor and program manager. Annual award for unpublished works. Mss should be one of the following: a novel, a collection of short stories, one or more novellas, or a combination of short stories and one or more novellas. Deadline: Rolling submissions. Check website for details of when they're accepting mss. Prize: Publication by Milkweed Editions and a cash advance of $5,000 against royalties, agreed upon in the contractual arrangement negotiated at the time of acceptance. Judged by the editors.

MILKWEED PRIZE FOR CHILDREN'S LITERATURE

Milkweed Editions, 1011 Washington Ave. S., Suite 300, Minneapolis MN 55415. (612)332-3192. **Fax:** (612)215-2550. **E-mail:** editor@milkweed.org. **Website:** www.milkweed.org. Milkweed Editions will award the Milkweed Prize for Children's Literature to the best mss for young readers that Milkweed accepts for publication during the calendar year by a writer not previously published by Milkweed. All mss for young readers submitted for publication by Milkweed are automatically entered into the competition. Recognizes an outstanding literary novel for readers ages 8-13 and encourage writers to turn their attention to readers in this age group. Prize: $10,000 cash prize in addition to a publishing contract negotiated at the time of acceptance. Judged by the editors of Milkweed Editions.

MINNESOTA BOOK AWARDS

The Friends of the Saint Paul Public Library, 1080 Montreal Avenue, Suite 2, St. Paul MN 55116. (651)222-3242. **Fax:** (651)222-1988. **E-mail:** mnbookawards@thefriends.org; friends@thefriends.org; info@thefriends.org. **Website:** www.mnbookawards.org. Estab. 1988. A year-round program celebrating and honoring Minnesota's best books, culminating in an annual awards ceremony. Recognizes and honors achievement by members of Minnesota's book and book arts community. Deadline: Nomination should be submitted by 5:00 p.m. on the first Friday in December.

MISSISSIPPI REVIEW PRIZE

Mississippi Review, 118 College Dr., #5144, Hattiesburg MS 39406-0001. (601)266-4321. **Fax:** (601)266-5757. **E-mail:** msreview@usm.edu. **Website:** www.mississippireview.com. Annual contest starting August 1 and running until January 1. Winners and finalists will make up next spring's print issue of the national literary magazine *Mississippi Review*. Each entrant will receive a copy of the prize issue. Deadline: January 1. Prize: $1,000 in fiction and poetry. Costs: $15 mail submission; $16 online submission. Judged by Andrew Malan Milward in fiction, and Angela Ball in poetry.

MONTANA PRIZE IN FICTION

Cutbank Literary Magazine, *CutBank*, University of Montana, English Dept., LA 133, Missoula MT 59812. **E-mail:** editor.cutbank@gmail.com. **Website:** www.cutbankonline.org. **Contact:** Allison Linville, editor-in-chief. The Montana Prize in Fiction seeks to highlight work that showcases an authentic voice, a boldness of form, and a rejection of functional fixedness. Deadline: January 15. Submissions period begins November 9. Prize: $500 and featured in the magazine. Costs: $20. Judged by a guest judge each year.

JENNY MCKEAN MOORE VISITING WRITER

English Department, George Washington University, Rome Hall, 801 22nd St. NW, Suite 760, Washington DC 20052. (202)994-6180. **Fax:** (202)994-7915. **E-mail:** tvmallon@gwu.edu. **Website:** https://english.columbian.gwu.edu/activities-events. **Contact:** Lisa Page, Acting Director of Creative Writing. The position is filled annually, bringing a visiting writer to The George Washington University. During each semester the Writer teaches 1 creative-writing course at the university as well as a community workshop. Seeks someone specializing in a different genre each year—fiction, poetry, creative nonfiction. Annual stipend between $50,000 and $60,000, plus reduced-rent townhouse on campus (not guaranteed). Application deadline: December 12. Annual stipend varies, depending on endowment performance; most recently, stipend was $60,000, plus reduced-rent townhouse (not guaranteed).

THE HOWARD FRANK MOSHER SHORT FICTION PRIZE

Vermont College, 36 College St., Montpelier VT 05602. (802)828-8517. **E-mail:** hungermtn@vcfa.edu. **Website:** www.hungermtn.org. **Contact:** Samantha Kolber, managing editor. Estab. 2002. The Howard Frank Mosher Short Fiction Prize is an annual contest for short fiction. Deadline: March 1 Prize: One first place winner receives $1,000 and publication. Two honorable mentions receive $100 each, and are considered for publication. Costs: $20. Judged by Janet Burroway in 2016 and Caitlyn Horrocks in 2017.

NATIONAL BOOK AWARDS

The National Book Foundation, 90 Broad St., Suite 604, New York NY 10004. (212)685-0261. **E-mail:** nationalbook@nationalbook.org; agall@nationalbook.org. **Website:** www.nationalbook.org. **Contact:** Amy Gall. The National Book Foundation and the National Book Awards celebrate the best of American literature, expand its audience, and enhance the cultural value of great writing in America. The contest offers prizes in 4 categories: fiction, nonfiction, poetry, and young people's literature. Books should be published between December 1 and November 30 of the past year. Deadline: Submit entry form, payment, and a copy of the book by July 1. Prize: $10,000 in each category. Finalists will each receive a prize of $1,000. Costs: $135/title. Judged by a category specific panel of 5 judges for each category.

NATIONAL OUTDOOR BOOK AWARDS

921 S. 8th Ave., Stop 8128, Pocatello ID 83209. (208)282-3912. **E-mail:** wattron@isu.edu. **Website:** www.nobaweb.org. **Contact:** Ron Watters. Nine categories: History/biography, outdoor literature, instructional texts, outdoor adventure guides, nature guides, children's books, design/artistic merit, natural history literature, and nature and the environment. Additionally, a special award, the Outdoor Classic Award, is given annually to books which, over a period of time, have proven to be exceptionally valuable works in the outdoor field. Application forms and eligibility requirements are available online. Applications for the Awards program become available in early June. Deadline: August 24. Prize: Winning books are promoted nationally and are entitled to display the National Outdoor Book Award (NOBA) medallion. Costs: $75.

NATIONAL READERS' CHOICE AWARDS

Oklahoma Romance Writers of America (OKRWA), **E-mail:** nrca@okrwa.com. **Website:** www.okrwa.

com. **Contact:** Kathy L Wheeler. Estab. 1990. "To provide writers of romance fiction with a competition where their published novels are judged by readers." See the website for categories and descriptions. Additional award for best first book. All entries must have an original copyright date during the current contest year. Entries will be accepted from authors, editors, publishers, agents, readers, whoever wants to fill out the entry form, pay the fee, and supply the books. No limit to the number of entries, but each title may be entered only in one category. Open to any writer published by an RWA approved nonvanity/nonsubsidy press. For guidelines, send e-mail or visit website. Deadline: December 1st. Prize: Plaques and finalist certificates awarded at the awards banquet hosted at the Annual National Romance Writers Convention. Costs: $30 per entry, plus $5 for Best First Book Category. Judged by readers.

○ NATIONAL WRITERS ASSOCIATION NOVEL WRITING CONTEST

The National Writers Association, 10940 S. Parker Rd. #508, Parker CO 80134. **E-mail:** natlwritersassn@hotmail.com. **Website:** www.nationalwriters.com. **Contact:** Sandy Whelchel, director. Open to any genre or category. Contest begins December 1. Open to any writer. Annual contest to help develop creative skills, to recognize and reward outstanding ability, and to increase the opportunity for the marketing and subsequent publication of novel mss. Deadline: April 1. Prize: 1st Place: $500; 2nd Place: $250; 3rd Place: $150. Costs: $35. Judged by editors and agents.

NATIONAL WRITERS ASSOCIATION SHORT STORY CONTEST

10940 S. Parker Rd., #508, Parker CO 80134. **E-mail:** natlwritersassn@hotmail.com. **Website:** www.nationalwriters.com. Estab. 1971. The purpose of the National Writers Assn. Short Story Contest is to encourage the development of creative skills, recognize and reward outstanding ability in the area of short story writing. Prize: 1st Prize: $250; 2nd Prize: $100; 3rd Prize: $50; 4th-10th places will receive a book. 1st-3rd place winners may be asked to grant one-time rights for publication in *Authorship* magazine. Honorable Mentions receive a certificate. Costs: $15. Judging will be based on originality, marketability, research, and reader interest. Copies of the judges evaluation sheets will be sent to entrants furnishing an SASE with their entry.

THE NELLIGAN PRIZE FOR SHORT FICTION

Colorado Review/Center for Literary Publishing, Colorado State University, 9105 Campus Delivery, Dept. of English, Colorado State University, Ft. Collins CO 80523-9105. (970)491-5449. **E-mail:** creview@colostate.edu. **Website:** nelliganprize.colostate.edu. **Contact:** Stephanie G'Schwind, editor. Annual competition/award for short stories. Receives approximately 900 stories. All entries are read blind by Colorado Review's editorial staff. Ten to fifteen entries are selected to be sent on to a final, outside judge. Stories must be unpublished and between 10 and 50 pages. "The Nelligan Prize for Short Fiction was established in memory of Liza Nelligan, a writer, editor, and friend of many in Colorado State University's English Department, where she received her master's degree in literature in 1992. By giving an award to the author of an outstanding short story each year, we hope to honor Liza Nelligan's life, her passion for writing, and her love of fiction." Deadline: March 14. Prize: $2,000 and publication of story in *Colorado Review*. Costs: $15, send checks payable to Colorado Review; payment also accepted via our online submission manager link from website. Judged by a different writer each year. 2017 judge is Richard Bausch.

THE NEUTRINO SHORT-SHORT CONTEST

Passages North, Dept. of English, Northern Michigan University, 1401 Presque Isle Ave., Marquette MI 49855. (906)227-1203. **Fax:** (906)227-1096. **E-mail:** passages@nmu.edu. **Website:** www.passagesnorth.com. **Contact:** Jennifer Howard. Offered every 2 years to publish new voices in literary fiction, nonfiction, hybrid-essays and prose poems (maximum 1,000 words). Guidelines available for SASE or online. Deadline: April 15. Submission period begins February 15. Prize: $1,000, and publication for the winner; 2 honorable mentions also published; all entrants receive a copy of *Passages North*. Costs: $15 for up to 3 pieces. Judged by Lindsay Hunter in 2016.

NEW ENGLAND BOOK AWARDS

1955 Massachusetts Ave., #2, Cambridge MA 02140. (617)547-3642. **Fax:** (617)547-3759. **E-mail:** nan@neba.org. **Website:** www.newenglandbooks.org/bookawards. **Contact:** Nan Sorenson, administrative coordinator. Estab. 1990. Annual award. Previously published submissions only. Submissions made by New England booksellers; publishers. Submit written nominations only; actual books should not be sent. Member bookstores receive materials to display winners' books. Award is given to a specific title, fiction, nonfiction, children's. The titles must be either about New England, set in New England or by an author residing in the New England. The titles must be hardcover, paperback original or reissue that was published between September 1 and August 31. Entries must be still in print and available. Deadline: June 10. Prize: Winners will receive $250 for literacy to a charity of their choice. Judged by NEIBA membership.

○ *NEW LETTERS* LITERARY AWARDS

New Letters, University of Missouri-Kansas City, 5101 Rockhill Rd., Kansas City MO 64110-2499, USA. (816)235-1168. **Fax:** (816)235-2611. **Website:** www.newletters.org/writers-wanted/writing-contests. Estab. 1986. Award has 3 categories (fiction, poetry, and creative nonfiction) with 1 winner in each. Offered annually for previously unpublished work. For guidelines, send an SASE to *New Letters*, or visit www.newletters.org/writers-wanted/writing-contests. Deadline: May 18. Prize: 1st place: $1,500, plus publication. Costs: $20 for first entry, $15 for every entry after; add an extra $5 service charge if entering online. Judged by regional writers of prominence and experience. Final judging by someone of national repute. Previous judges include Maxine Kumin, Albert Goldbarth, Charles Simic, and Janet Burroway.

NEW MILLENNIUM AWARDS FOR FICTION, POETRY, AND NONFICTION

New Millennium Writings, 4021 Garden Dr., Knoxville TN 37918. (865)254-4880. **Website:** www.new-millenniumwritings.org. **Contact:** Alexis Williams, Editor and Publisher. Estab. 1996. No restrictions as to style, content or number of submissions. Previously published pieces acceptable if online or under 5,000 print circulation. Simultaneous and multiple submissions welcome. Deadline: Postmarked on or before January 31 for the Winter Awards and July 31 for the Summer Awards. Prize: $1,000 for Best Poem; $1,000 for Best Fiction; $1,000 for Best Nonfiction; $1,000 for Best Short-Short Fiction. Costs: $20.

NEW SOUTH WRITING CONTEST

English Department, Georgia State University, P.O. Box 3970, Atlanta GA 30302-3970. **E-mail:** newsouth@gsu.edu. **Website:** newsouthjournal.com/contest. **Contact:** Stephanie Devine, editor-in-chief. Offered annually to publish the most promising work of up-and-coming writers of poetry (up to 3 poems) and fiction (9,000

word limit). Rights revert to writer upon publication. Guidelines online. Deadline: April 30. Prize: 1st Place: $1,000 in each category; 2nd Place: $250; and publication to winners. Costs: $15. Judged by Anya Silver in poetry and Matthew Salesses in prose.

NORTH CAROLINA ARTS COUNCIL REGIONAL ARTIST PROJECT GRANTS

North Carolina Arts Council, Dept. of Natural and Cultural Resources, MSC #4632, Raleigh NC 27699-4634. (919)807-6512. **Fax:** (919)807-6532. **E-mail:** david.potorti@ncdcr.gov. **Website:** www.ncarts.org. **Contact:** David Potorti, literature and theater director. See website for contact information for the consortia of local arts councils that distribute these grants. Deadline: Dates vary in fall/spring. Prize: $500-3,000 awarded to writers to pursue projects that further their artistic development. These grants are awarded through consortia of local arts councils. See our website for details.

NORTH CAROLINA WRITERS' FELLOWSHIPS

North Carolina Arts Council, North Carolina Arts Council, Writers' Fellowships, Department of Cultural Resources, Raleigh NC 27699-4632. (919)807-6512. **Fax:** (919)807-6532. **E-mail:** david.potorti@ncdcr.gov. **Website:** www.ncarts.org. **Contact:** David Potorti, literature and theater director. The North Carolina Arts Council offers grants to writers, spoken-word artists, playwrights, and screenwriters: fellowships (every other year). Offered every even year to support writers of fiction, poetry, literary nonfiction, literary translation, and spoken word. See website for guidelines and other eligibility requirements. Deadline: November 1 of even-numbered years. Prize: $10,000 grant. Reviewed by a panel of literature professionals (writers and editors).

NORTHERN CALIFORNIA BOOK AWARDS

Northern California Book Reviewers Association, c/o Poetry Flash, 1450 Fourth St. #4, Berkeley CA 94710. (510)525-5476. **E-mail:** ncbr@poetryflash.org; editor@poetryflash.org. **Website:** www.poetryflash.org. **Contact:** Joyce Jenkins, executive director. Estab. 1981. Annual Northern California Book Award for outstanding book in literature, open to books published in the current calendar year by Northern California authors. NCBR presents annual awards to Bay Area (northern California) authors annually in fiction, nonfiction, poetry and children's literature. Encourages writers and stimulates interest in books and reading. Deadline: December 28. Prize: $100 honorarium and award certificate. Judging by voting members of the Northern California Book Reviewers.

○ NOVA WRITES COMPETITION FOR UNPUBLISHED MANUSCRIPTS

Writers' Federation of Nova Scotia, 1113 Marginal Rd., Halifax NS B3H 4P7. (902)423-8116. **Fax:** (902)422-0881. **E-mail:** programs@writers.ns.ca. **Website:** www.writers.ns.ca. **Contact:** Robin Spittal, communications and development officer. Estab. 1975. Annual program designed to honor work by unpublished writers in all 4 Atlantic Provinces. Entry is open to writers unpublished in the category of writing they wish to enter. Prizes are presented in the fall of each year. Categories include: short form creative nonfiction, long form creative nonfiction, novel, poetry, short story, and writing for children/young adult novel. Judges return written comments when competition is concluded. Deadline: December 13. Prizes vary based on categories. See website for details. Costs: $35 fee for novel ($30 for WFNS members); $25 fee for all other categories ($20 for WFNS members).

● SEAN O'FAOLAIN SHORT STORY COMPETITION

The Munster Literature Centre, Frank O'Connor House, 84 Douglas Street, Cork , Ireland. +353-0214319255. **E-mail:** munsterlit@eircom.net. **Website:** www.munsterlit.ie. **Contact:** Patrick Cotter, artistic director. Purpose is to reward writers of outstanding short stories. Deadline: July 31. Prize: 1st prize €2,000; 2nd prize €500. Four runners-up prizes of €100 (approx $146). All six stories to be published in *Southword Literary Journal*. First-Prize Winner offered week's residency in Anam Cara Artist's Retreat in Ireland. Costs: $20.

FRANK O'CONNOR AWARD FOR SHORT FICTION

descant, Texas Christian University's literary journal, TCU Box 298300, Fort Worth TX 76129. **E-mail:** descant@tcu.edu. **Website:** www.descant.tcu.edu. **Contact:** Matthew Pitt, editor. Offered annually for an outstanding story accepted for publication in the current edition of the journal. Publication retains copyright but will transfer it to the author upon request. Deadline: March 31. Open to submissions September 1. Prize: $500.

OHIOANA BOOK AWARDS

Ohioana Library Association, 274 E. First Ave., Suite 300, Columbus OH 43201-3673. (614)466-3831. **Fax:** (614)728-6974. **E-mail:** ohioana@ohioana.org. **Website:** www.ohioana.org. **Contact:** David Weaver, executive director. Estab. 1942. Offered annually to bring national attention to Ohio authors and their books, published in the last year. (Books can only be considered once.) Categories: Fiction, nonfiction, juvenile, poetry, and books about Ohio or an Ohioan. Deadline: December 31. Prize: $1,000 cash prize, certificate, and glass sculpture. Judged by a jury selected by librarians, book reviewers, writers and other knowledgeable people.

OHIOANA WALTER RUMSEY MARVIN GRANT

Ohioana Library Association, 274 E. First Ave., Suite 300, Columbus OH 43201. (614)466-3831. **Fax:** (614)728-6974. **E-mail:** ohioana@ohioana.org. **Website:** www.ohioana.org. **Contact:** David Weaver, executive director. Award to encourage young, unpublished writers 30 years of age or younger. Competition for short stories or novels in progress. Deadline: January 31 Prize: $1,000.

OKLAHOMA BOOK AWARDS

200 NE 18th St., Oklahoma City OK 73105. (405)521-2502. **Fax:** (405)525-7804. **E-mail:** connie.armstrong@libraries.ok.gov. **Website:** www.odl.state.ok.us/ocb. **Contact:** Connie Armstrong, executive director. Estab. 1989. This award honors Oklahoma writers and books about Oklahoma. Awards are presented to best books in fiction, nonfiction, children's, design and illustration, and poetry books about Oklahoma or books written by an author who was born, is living or has lived in Oklahoma. SASE for award rules and entry forms. Winner will be announced at banquet in Oklahoma City. The Arrell Gibson Lifetime Achievement Award is also presented each year for a body of work. Deadline: January 10. Prize: Awards a medal. Costs: $25. Judging by a panel of 5 people for each category, generally a librarian, a working writer in the genre, booksellers, editors, etc.

○ ON THE PREMISES CONTEST

On The Premises, LLC, 4323 Gingham Court, Alexandria VA 22310. **E-mail:** questions@onthepremises.com. **Website:** www.onthepremises.com. **Contact:** Tarl Kudrick or Bethany Granger, co-publishers. *On the Premises* aims to promote newer and/or relatively unknown writers who can write creative, compelling stories told in effective, uncluttered, and evocative prose. Each contest challenges writers to produce a great story based on a broad premise that the editors supply as part of the contest. Deadline: Short story contests held twice a year;

smaller mini-contests held four times a year; check website for exact dates. Prize: 1st Prize: $220; 2nd Prize: $160; 3rd Prize: $120; Honorable Mentions receive $60. All prize winners are published in *On the Premises* magazine in HTML and PDF format. Costs: There are no fees for entering our contests. Judged by a panel of judges with professional editing and writing experience.

☼ OPEN SEASON AWARDS

The Malahat Review, University of Victoria, P.O. Box 1700, Stn CSC, Victoria BC V8V 2Y2, Canada. (250)721-8524. **Fax:** (250)472-5051. **E-mail:** malahat@uvic.ca. **Website:** www.malahatreview.ca. **Contact:** Patrick Grace, publicity manager. The Open Season Awards accepts entries of poetry, fiction, and creative nonfiction. Winners published in spring issue of *Malahat Review* announced in winter on website, facebook page, and in quarterly e-newsletter, *Malahat lite.* Deadline: November 1. Prize: $4,500 over three categories (poetry, fiction, creative nonfiction) and publication in *The Malahat Review* in each category. Costs: $35 CAD for Canadian entries; $40 USD for US entries ($45 USD for entries from Mexico and outside North America). $15 for each additional entry, any genre, no limit to how many times you can send in additional entries. Includes a 1-year subscription to *The Malahat Review.*

OREGON BOOK AWARDS

925 SW Washington St., Portland OR 97205. (503)227-2583. **Fax:** (503)241-4256. **E-mail:** la@literary-arts.org. **Website:** www.literary-arts.org. **Contact:** Susan Denning, director of programs and events. The annual Oregon Book Awards celebrate Oregon authors in the areas of poetry, fiction, nonfiction, drama and young readers' literature published between August 1 and July 31 of the previous calendar year. Awards are available for every category. See website for details. Deadline: August 26. Prize: Grant of $2,500. (Grant money could vary.) Judged by writers who are selected from outside Oregon for their expertise in a genre. Past judges include Mark Doty, Colson Whitehead and Kim Barnes.

OREGON LITERARY FELLOWSHIPS

925 S.W. Washington, Portland OR 97205. (503)227-2583. **E-mail:** susan@literary-arts.org. **Website:** www.literary-arts.org. **Contact:** Susan Moore, Director of programs and events. Oregon Literary Fellowships are intended to help Oregon writers initiate, develop, or complete literary projects in poetry, fiction, literary nonfiction, drama, and young readers literature. Writers in the early stages of their career are encouraged to apply. The awards are merit-based. Deadline: Last Friday in June. Prize: $3,000 minimum award, for approximately 8 writers and 2 publishers. Judged by out-of-state writers

⑤ KENNETH PATCHEN AWARD FOR THE INNOVATIVE NOVEL

Eckhard Gerdes Publishing, 1110 Varsity Blvd., Apt. 221, DeKalb IL 60115. **E-mail:** egerdes@experimental-fiction.com. **Website:** www.experimentalfiction.com. **Contact:** Eckhard Gerdes. This award will honor the most innovative novel submitted during the previous calendar year. Kenneth Patchen is celebrated for being among the greatest innovators of American fiction, incorporating strategies of concretism, asemic writing, digression, and verbal juxtaposition into his writing long before such strategies were popularized during the height of American postmodernist experimentation in the 1970s. Deadline: All submissions must be postmarked between January 1 and July 31. Prize: $1,000 and 20 complimentary copies. Costs: $25 entry fee. Judged by novelist Dominic Ward.

THE PATERSON FICTION PRIZE

The Poetry Center at Passaic Community College, One College Blvd., Paterson NJ 07505. (973)684-6555. **Fax:** (973)523-6085. **E-mail:** mgillan@pccc.edu. **Website:** www.pccc.edu/poetry. **Contact:** Maria Mazziotti Gillan, executive director. Offered annually for a novel or collection of short fiction published the previous calendar year. For more information, visit the website or send SASE. Deadline: February 1. Prize: $1,000.

○ JUDITH SIEGEL PEARSON AWARD

Judith Siegel Pearson Award, c/o Department of English, Wayne State University, Attn: Royanne Smith, 5057 Woodward Ave, Ste. 9408, Detroit MI 48202. **E-mail:** fm8146@wayne.edu. **Website:** https://wsuwritingawards.submittable.com/submit. **Contact:** Donovan Hohn. Offers an annual award for the best creative or scholarly work on a subject concerning women. The type of work accepted rotates each year: drama in 2016, poetry in 2017; nonfiction in 2018; fiction in 2019. Open to all interested writers and scholars. Only submit the appropriate genre in each year. Deadline: February 22. Prize: $500. Judged by members of the writing faculty of the Wayne State University English Department.

WILLIAM PEDEN PRIZE IN FICTION

The Missouri Review, 357 McReynolds Hall, Columbia MO 65211. (573)882-4474. **Fax:** (573)884-4671. E-mail: mutmrcontestquestion@moreview.com. **Website:** www.missourireview.com. **Contact:** Michael Nye, managing editor. Offered annually for the best story published in the past volume year of the magazine. All stories published in *The Missouri Review* are automatically considered. Guidelines online or for SASE. Prize: $1,000 and a reading/reception.

PEN CENTER USA LITERARY AWARDS

PEN Center USA, P.O. Box 6037, Beverly Hills CA 90212. (323)424-4939. **E-mail:** awards@penusa.org. **E-mail:** awards@penusa.org. **Website:** www.penusa.org. Offered for work published or produced in the previous calendar year. Open to writers living west of the Mississippi River. Award categories: fiction, poetry, research nonfiction, creative nonfiction, translation, young adult, graphic literature, drama, screenplay, teleplay, journalism. Deadline: See website for details. Prize: $1,000. Costs: $35 entry fee per submission.

PEN/FAULKNER AWARDS FOR FICTION

PEN/Faulkner Foundation, 201 E. Capitol St. SE, Washington DC 20003. (202)898-9063. **E-mail:** awards@penfaulkner.org. **Website:** www.penfaulkner.org. **Contact:** Emma Snyder, executive director. Offered annually for best book-length work of fiction by an American citizen published in a calendar year. Deadline: October 31. Prize: $15,000 (one Winner); $5,000 (4 Finalists).

PENGUIN RANDOM HOUSE CREATIVE WRITING AWARDS

One Scholarship Way, P.O. Box 297, St. Peter MN 56082. (212)782-9348. **Fax:** (212) 782-5157. **E-mail:** creativewriting@penguinrandomhouse.com. **Website:** www.penguinrandomhouse.com/creativewriting. **Contact:** Melanie Fallon Hauska, director. Offered annually for unpublished work to NYC public high school seniors. 72 awards given in literary and nonliterary categories. Four categories: poetry, fiction/drama, personal essay, and graphic novel. Applicants must be seniors (under age 21) at a New York high school. No college essays or class assignments will be accepted. Deadline: February 3 for all categories. Graphic Novel extended deadline: March 1st. Prize: Awards range from $500-10,000. The program usually awards just under $100,000 in scholarships.

PHOEBE WINTER FICTION CONTEST

Phoebe, MSN 2D6, George Mason University, 4400 University Dr., Fairfax VA 22030. (703)993-2915. E-

mail: phoebe@gmu.edu. **Website:** www.phoebejournal.com/. Offered annually for an unpublished story (25 pages maximum). Guidelines online or for SASE. First serial rights if work is accepted for publication. Purpose is to recognize new and exciting fiction. Deadline: March 19. Prize: $400 and publication in the Spring online issue. Costs: $9. Judged by a recognized fiction writer, hired by *Phoebe* (changes each year). For 2016, the fiction judge will be Patricia Park.

THE PINCH LITERARY AWARDS

Literary Awards, The Pinch, Department of English, The University of Memphis, Memphis TN 38152-6176. (901)678-4591. **Website:** www.pinchjournal.com. Offered annually for unpublished short stories of 5,000 words maximum or up to three poems. Guidelines on website. Cost: $20, which is put toward one issue of *The Pinch*. Deadline: March 15. Prize: 1st place Fiction: $1,500 and publication; 1st place Poetry: $1,000 and publication. Offered annually for unpublished short stories and prose of up to 5,000 words and 1-3 poems. Deadline: March 15. Open to submissions on December 15. Prizes: $1,000 for 1st place in each category. Costs: $20 for initial entry, $10 each for subsequent entries.

PNWA LITERARY CONTEST

Pacifc Northwest Writers Association, PMB 2717, 1420 NW Gilman Blvd., Suite 2, Issaquah WA 98027. (452)673-2665. **Fax:** (452)961-0768. **E-mail:** pnwa@pnwa.org. **Website:** www.pnwa.org. Annual literary contest with 12 different categories. See website for details and specific guidelines. Each entry receives 2 critiques. Winners announced at the PNWA Summer Conference, held annually in mid-July. Deadline: February 20. Prize: 1st Place: $600; 2nd Place: $300; 3rd Place: $100. Costs: $35 for PNWA members; $50 for nonmembers. Judged by an agent or editor attending the conference.

○ POCKETS FICTION-WRITING CONTEST

P.O. Box 340004, Nashville TN 37203-0004. (615)340-7333. **Fax:** (615)340-7267. **E-mail:** pockets@upperroom.org. **Website:** www.pockets.upperroom.org. **Contact:** Lynn W. Gilliam, senior editor. Designed for 6- to 12-year-olds, *Pockets* magazine offers wholesome devotional readings that teach about God's love and presence in life. The content includes fiction, scripture stories, puzzles and games, poems, recipes, colorful pictures, activities, and scripture readings. Freelance submissions of stories, poems, recipes, puzzles and games, and activities are welcome. The primary purpose of *Pockets* is to help children grow in their relationship with God and to claim the good news of the gospel of Jesus Christ by applying it to their daily lives. *Pockets* espouses respect for all human beings and for God's creation. It regards a child's faith journey as an integral part of all of life and sees prayer as undergirding that journey. Deadline: August 15. Submission period begins March 15. Prize: $500 and publication in magazine.

EDGAR ALLAN POE AWARD

1140 Broadway, Suite 1507, New York NY 10001. (212)888-8171. **E-mail:** mwa@mysterywriters.org. **Website:** www.mysterywriters.org. Estab. 1945. Mystery Writers of America is the leading association for professional crime writers in the United States. Members of MWA include most major writers of crime fiction and nonfiction, as well as screenwriters, dramatists, editors, publishers, and other professionals in the field. Purpose of the award: Honor authors of distinguished works in the mystery field. Previously published submissions only. Submissions should be made by the publisher. Work must be published/produced the year of the contest. Deadline: November 30. Prize: Awards ceramic bust of "Edgar" for winner; certificates for all nominees. Judged by active status members of Mystery Writers of America (writers).

THE KATHERINE ANNE PORTER PRIZE FOR FICTION

Nimrod International Journal, The University of Tulsa, 800 S. Tucker Dr., Tulsa OK 74104. (918)631-3080. **Fax:** (918)631-3033. **E-mail:** nimrod@utulsa.edu. **Website:** www.utulsa.edu/nimrod. **Contact:** Eilis O'Neal. Deadline: April 30. Prizes: 1st Place: $2,000 and publication; 2nd Place: $1,000 and publication. Costs: $20, includes a 1-year subscription (2 issues) to *Nimrod*; make checks payable to *Nimrod*. Judged by the *Nimrod* editors, who select the finalists, and a recognized author, who selects the winners.

PRAIRIE SCHOONER BOOK PRIZE

Prairie Schooner and the University of Nebraska Press, Prairie Schooner Prize Series, 123 Andrews Hall, Lincoln NE 68588-0334. (402)472-0911. **E-mail:** PSBookPrize@unl.edu. **Website:** prairieschooner.unl. edu. **Contact:** Kwame Dawes, editor. Annual competition/award for poetry and short story collections. Deadline: March 15. Prize: $3,000 and publication through the University of Nebraska Press. Costs: $25.

PRESS 53 AWARD FOR SHORT FICTION

Press 53, 560 N. Trade St., Suite 103, Winston-Salem NC 27101. (336)770-5353. **E-mail:** kevin@press53. com. **Website:** www.press53.com. **Contact:** Kevin Morgan Watson, Publisher. Estab. 2014. Awarded to an outstanding, unpublished collection of short stories. Deadline: December 31. Submission period begins September 1. Finalists and winner announced no later than May 1. Publication in October. Prize: Publication of winning short story collection, $1,000 cash advance, 1/4-page color ad in *Poets & Writers* magazine, plus 10 copies of the book. Costs: $30 via Submittable or by mail. Judged by Press 53 publisher Kevin Morgan Watson.

PRIME NUMBER MAGAZINE AWARDS

Press 53, 560 N. Trade St., Suite 103, Winston-Salem NC 27101. (336)770-5353. **Fax:** N/A. **E-mail:** kevin@press53. com. **Website:** www.press53.com. **Contact:** Kevin Morgan Watson, Publisher. Awards $1,000 in poetry and short fiction. Deadline: April 15. Submission period begins January 1. Finalists and winners announced by August 1. Winners published in Prime Number Magazine in October. Prize: $1,000 cash. All winners receive publication in Prime Number Magazine online. Costs: $15 via Submittable. Judged by industry professionals to be named when the contest begins.

☼ PRISM INTERNATIONAL ANNUAL SHORT FICTION CONTEST

Creative Writing Program, UBC, Buch. E462 - 1866 Main Mall, Vancouver BC V6T 1Z1, Canada. (604)822-2514. **Fax:** (604)822-3616. **Website:** prismmagazine.ca/contests. **Contact:** Clara Kumagai, executive editor, promotions. Offered annually for unpublished work to award the best in contemporary fiction. Works of translation are eligible. Guidelines by SASE, by e-mail, or on website. Acquires first North American serial rights upon publication, and rights to publish online for promotional or archival purposes. Open to any writer except students and faculty in the Creative Writing Department at UBC, or people who have taken a creative writing course at UBC with the 2 years prior to the contest deadline. Deadline: January 31. Prize: 1st Place: $1,500; 1st Runner-up: $600; 2nd Runner-up: $400; winner is published. Costs: $35 CAD entries; $40 US entries; $45 international entires; $5 each additional entry (outside Canada, pay US currency); includes subscription.

PURPLE DRAGONFLY BOOK AWARDS

Story Monsters LLC, 4696 W Tyson St, Chandler AZ 85226-2903. (480)940-8182. **Fax:** (480)940-8787. **E-mail:** Cristy@StoryMonsters.com; Linda@StoryMonsters.com. **Website:** www.DragonflyBookAwards.com. **Contact:** Cristy Bertini, contest coordinator. The Purple Dragonfly Book Awards are designed with children in mind. Awards are divided into 52 distinct subject categories, ranging from books on the environment and cooking to sports and family issues. The Purple Dragonfly Book Awards are geared toward stories that appeal to children of all ages. Deadline: May 1. Prize: Grand Prize winner receives a $300 cash prize, 100 foil award seals, one hour of marketing consultation from Story Monsters LLC, as well as publicity on Dragonfly Book Awards website and inclusion in a winners' news release sent to a comprehensive list of media outlets. All first-place winners of categories will be put into a drawing for a $100 prize. In addition, each first-place winner in each category receives a certificate commemorating their accomplishment, 25 foil award seals and mention on Dragonfly Book Awards website. All winners are listed in Story Monsters Ink magazine. Costs: $65 for one title in one category, $60 per title when multiple books are entered or $60 per category when one book is entered in multiple categories. Judged by industry experts with specific knowledge about the categories over which they preside.

PUSHCART PRIZE

Pushcart Press, P.O. Box 380, Wainscott NY 11975. (631)324-9300. **Website:** www.pushcartprize.com. **Contact:** Bill Henderson. Estab. 1976. Published every year since 1976, The Pushcart Prize - Best of the Small Presses series "is the most honored literary project in America. Hundreds of presses and thousands of writers of short stories, poetry and essays have been represented in the pages of our annual collections." Little magazine and small book press editors (print or online) may make up to six nominations from their year's publicatoins by the deadline. The nominations may be any combination of poetry, short fiction, essays or literary whatnot. Editors may nominate self-contained portions of books — for instance, a chapter from a novel. Deadline: December 1.

☼ THOMAS H. RADDALL ATLANTIC FICTION AWARD

Writers' Federation of Nova Scotia, 1113 Marginal Rd., Halifax NS B3H 4P7, Canada. (902)423-8116. **Fax:** (902)422-0881. **E-mail:** director@writers.ns.ca. **Website:** www.writers.ns.ca. **Contact:** Nate Crawford, executive director. Estab. 1990. The Thomas Head Raddall Atlantic Fiction Award is awarded for a novel or a book of short fiction by a full-time resident of Atlantic Canada. Deadline: First Friday in December. Prize: Valued at $25,000 for winning title.

DAVID RAFFELOCK AWARD FOR PUBLISHING EXCELLENCE

National Writers Association, 10940 S. Parker Rd., #508, Parker CO 80134. **E-mail:** natlwritersassn@hotmail.com. **Website:** www.nationalwriters.com. **Contact:** Sandy Whelchel. Contest is offered annually for books published the previous year. Published works only. Open to any writer. Guidelines for SASE, by e-mail, or on website. Winners will be notified by mail or phone. List of winners available for SASE or visit website. Purpose is to assist published authors in marketing their works and to reward outstanding published works. Deadline: May 15. Prize: Publicity tour, including airfare, valued at $5,000. Costs: $100.

☻ THE RED HOUSE CHILDREN'S BOOK AWARD

Red House Children's Book Award, 123 Frederick Road, Cheam, Sutton, Surrey SM1 2HT, United Kingdom. **E-mail:** info@rhcba.co.uk. **Website:** www.redhousechildrensbookaward.co.uk. **Contact:** Sinead Kromer, national coordinator. Estab. 1980. The Red House Children's Book Award is the only national book award that is entirely voted for by children. A shortlist is drawn up from children's nominations and any child can then vote for the winner of the three categories: Books for Younger Children, Books for Younger Readers and Books for Older Readers. The book with the most votes is then crowned the winner of the Red House Children's Book Award. Deadline: December 31.

RHODE ISLAND ARTIST FELLOWSHIPS AND INDIVIDUAL PROJECT GRANTS

Rhode Island State Council on the Arts, State of Rhode Island, One Capitol Hill, 3rd Floor, Providence RI 02908. (401)222-3880. **Fax:** (401)222-3018. **E-mail:** Cristina.DiChiera@arts.ri.gov. **Website:** www.arts.ri.gov. **Contact:** Cristina DiChiera, director of individual artist programs. Annual fellowship competition is based upon panel review of poetry, fiction, and playwriting/screenwriting mss. Project grants provide funds for community-based arts projects. Rhode Island artists who have lived in the state for at least 12 consecutive months may apply without a nonprofit sponsor. Applicants for all RSCA grant and award programs must be at least 18 years old and not currently enrolled in an arts-related degree program. Online application and guidelines can be found at www.arts.ri.gov/grants/guidelines/. Deadline: April 1 and October 1. Fellowship awards: $5,000 and $1,000. Grants range from $500-5,000, with an average of around $1,500. Judged by a rotating panel of artists.

HAROLD U. RIBALOW PRIZE

Hadassah Magazine, Hadassah WZOA, 40 Wall Street 8th floor, New York NY 10005. (212) 451-6286. **Fax:** (212) 451-6257. **E-mail:** magtemp3@hadassah.org. **Website:** www.hadassahmagazine.org/. **Contact:** Deb Meisels, coordinator. Offered annually for English-language books of fiction (novel or short stories) on a Jewish theme published the previous year. Books should be submitted by the publisher. Administered annually by *Hadassah Magazine*. Deadline: April 7. Prize: $3,000. The official announcement of the winner will be made in the fall.

✪ THE ROGERS WRITERS' TRUST FICTION PRIZE

The Writers' Trust of Canada, 460 Richmond St. W., Suite 600, Toronto ON M5V 1Y1, Canada. (416)504-8222. **Fax:** (416)504-9090. **E-mail:** info@writerstrust.com. **Website:** www.writerstrust.com. **Contact:** Amanda Hopkins. Awarded annually to the best novel or short story collection published within the previous year. Presented at the Writers' Trust Awards event held in Toronto each fall. Open to Canadian citizens and permanent residents only. Deadline: July 27. Prize: $25,000 and $2,500 to 4 finalists.

🄢 LOIS ROTH AWARD

Modern Language Association, 85 Broad Street, suite 500, New York NY 10004-2434. (646)576-5141. **Fax:** (646)458-0030. **E-mail:** awards@mla.org. **Website:** www.mla.org. Offered in odd-numbered years for an outstanding translation into English of a book-length literary work. Translators need not be members of the MLA. Deadline: April 1. Prize: A cash award and a certificate to be presented at the Modern Language Association's annual convention in January.

ROYAL DRAGONFLY BOOK AWARDS

Story Monsters LLC, 4696 W. Tyson St., Chandler AZ 85226. (480)940-8182. **Fax:** (480)940-8787. **E-mail:** Cristy@StoryMonsters.com; Linda@StoryMonsters.com. **E-mail:** cristy@StoryMonsters.com. **Website:** www. DragonflyBookAwards.com. **Contact:** Cristy Bertini. Offered annually for any previously published work to honor authors for writing excellence of all types of literature—fiction and nonfiction—in 66 categories, appealing to a wide range of ages and comprehensive list of genres. Open to any title published in English. Deadline: October 1. Prize: Grand Prize winner receives a $300 cash prize, 100 foil award seals, one hour of marketing consultation from Story Monsters LLC, as well as publicity on Dragonfly Book Awards website and inclusion in a winners' news release sent to a comprehensive list of media outlets. All first-place winners of categories will be put into a drawing for a $100 prize. In addition, each first-place winner in each category receives a certificate commemorating their accomplishment, 25 foil award seals and mention on Dragonfly Book Awards website. All winners are listed in Story Monsters Ink magazine. Costs: $65 for one title in one category, $60 per title when multiple books are entered or $60 per category when one book is entered in multiple categories.

ERNEST SANDEEN PRIZE IN POETRY AND THE RICHARD SULLIVAN PRIZE IN SHORT FICTION

University of Notre Dame, Dept. of English, 356 O'Shaughnessy Hall, Notre Dame IN 46556-5639. (574)631-7526. **Fax:** (574)631-4795. **E-mail:** creativewriting@nd.edu. **Website:** english.nd.edu/creative-writing/publications/sandeen-sullivan-prizes. **Contact:** Director of Creative Writing. Estab. 1994. The Sandeen & Sullivan Prizes in Poetry and Short Fiction is awarded to the author who has published at least one volume of short fiction or one volume of poetry. Awarded biannually, but judged quadrennially. Submissions Period: May 1 - September 1. Prize: $1,000, a $500 award and a $500 advance against royalties from the Notre Dame Press. Costs: $15.

SANTA FE WRITERS PROJECT LITERARY AWARDS PROGRAM

Santa Fe Writers Project, 369 Montezuma Ave., #350, Santa Fe NM 87501. **E-mail:** info@sfwp.com. **Website:** www.sfwp.com. **Contact:** Andrew Gifford. Estab. 1998. Annual contest seeking fiction and nonfiction of any genre. The Literary Awards Program was founded by a group of authors to offer recognition for excellence in writing in a time of declining support for writers and the craft of literature. Past judges have included Richard Currey, Jayne Anne Phillips, Chris Offutt, Emily St. John Mandel, and David Morrell. Deadline: July 20th. Prize:

$3,300 and publication. Costs: $30. Judged by Benjamin Percy and Mat Johnson in 2017.

SASKATCHEWAN BOOK AWARDS

315-1102 Eighth Ave., Regina SK S4R 1C9, Canada. (306)569-1585. **E-mail:** director@bookawards.sk.ca. **Website:** www.bookawards.sk.ca. **Contact:** Courtney Bates-Hardy, Administrative Director. Estab. 1993. Saskatchewan Book Awards celebrates, promotes, and rewards Saskatchewan authors and publishers worthy of recognition through 14 awards, granted on an annual or semiannual basis. Awards: Fiction, Nonfiction, Poetry, Scholarly, First Book, *Prix du Livre Français*, Regina, Saskatoon, Aboriginal Peoples' Writing, Aboriginal Peoples' Publishing, Publishing in Education, Publishing, Children's Literature/Young Adult Literature, Book of the Year. Deadline: Early November. Prize: $2,000 (CAD) for all awards except Book of the Year, which is $3,000 (CAD). Costs: Costs $50 per award entered. Juries are made up of writing and publishing professionals from outside of Saskatchewan.

Saskatchewan Book Awards is the only provincially focused book award program in Saskatchewan and a principal ambassador for Saskatchewan's literary community. Its solid reputation for celebrating artistic excellence in style is recognized nationally.

THE SATURDAY EVENING POST GREAT AMERICAN FICTION CONTEST

The Saturday Evening Post Society, 1100 Waterway Blvd., Indianapolis IN 46202. **E-mail:** fictioncontest@saturdayeveningpost.com. **Website:** www.saturdayeveningpost.com/fiction-contest. "In its nearly 3 centuries of publication, *The Saturday Evening Post* has included fiction by a who's who of American authors, including F. Scott Fitzgerald, William Faulkner, Kurt Vonnegut, Ray Bradbury, Louis L'Amour, Sinclair Lewis, Jack London, and Edgar Allan Poe. The *Post*'s fiction has not just entertained us; it has played a vital role in defining who we are as Americans. In launching this contest, we are seeking America's next great, unpublished voices." Deadline: July 1. The winning story will receive $500 and publication in the magazine and online. Five runners-up will be published online and receive $100 each. Costs: $10.

ALDO AND JEANNE SCAGLIONE PRIZE FOR A TRANSLATION OF A LITERARY WORK

Modern Language Association, 85 Broad Street, suite 500, New York NY 10004-2434. (646)576-5141. **Fax:** (646)458-0030. **E-mail:** awards@mla.org. **Website:** www.mla.org. **Contact:** Coordinator of Book Prizes. Offered in even-numbered years for an outstanding translation into English of a book-length literary work. Deadline: April 1. Prize: A cash award and a certificate to be presented at the Modern Language Association's annual convention in January.

THE SCARS EDITOR'S CHOICE AWARDS

Scars Publications, **E-mail:** editor@scars.tv. **Website:** scars.tv (contest direct link scars.tv/contests.htm). **Contact:** Janet Kuypers, editor/publisher (whom all reading fee checks need to be made out to). Estab. annually. Award to showcase good writing in an annual book. Prize: Publication of story/essay and 1 copy of the book. Costs: $19/short story and $15/poem.

If you have difficulties sending e-mails through to a scars.tv address, send it to janetkuypers@gmal.com and explain the e-mail problem and specifically what you were writing about.

THE MONA SCHREIBER PRIZE FOR HUMOROUS FICTION & NONFICTION

3940 Laurel Canyon Blvd., #566, Studio City CA 91604. **E-mail:** brad.schreiber@att.net. **Website:** www.bradschreiber.com. **Contact:** Brad Schreiber. Estab. 2000. Established in 2000, to honor Mona Schreiber, a writer and teacher. Entry fees are the same as in 2000 and money from entries helps pay for prizes. The purpose of the contest is to award the most creative humor writing, in any form, under than 750 words, in either fiction or nonfiction, including but not limited to stories, articles, essays, speeches, shopping lists, diary entries, and anything else writers dream up. Complete rules and previous winning entries On website. Deadline: December 1. Prize: 1st Place: $500; 2nd Place: $250; 3rd Place: $100. Costs: $5 fee per entry (checks payable to Mona Schreiber Prize). Foreign entries may include US currency or checks drawn on US banks. Judged by Brad Schreiber, journalist, consultant, instructor, author of among other books, the humor writing how-to *What Are You Laughing At?*

JOANNA CATHERINE SCOTT NOVEL EXCERPT PRIZE CATEGORY

Soul-Making Keats Literary Competition Category, The Webhallow House, 1544 Sweetwood Dr., Broadmoor Village CA 94015-2029. **E-mail:** soulkeats@mail.com. **Website:** www.soulmakingcontest.us. **Contact:** Eileen Malone. Open annually to any writer. Deadline: November 30. Prize: 1st Place: $100; 2nd Place: $50; 3rd Place: $25. Costs: $5/entry (make checks payable to NLAPW).

SCREAMINMAMAS MAGICAL FICTION CONTEST

1911 Cleveland St., Hollywood FL 33020. **E-mail:** screaminmamas@gmail.com. **Website:** www.screaminmamas.com/contests. **Contact:** Darlene Pistocchi, editor/managing director. This contest celebrates moms and the magical spirit of the holidays. If you had an opportunity to be anything you wanted to be, what would you be? Transport yourself! Become that character and write a short story around that character. Can be any genre. Length: 800-3,000 words. Open only to moms. Deadline: June 30. Prize: complementary subscription to magazine, plus publication.

SCREAMINMAMAS VALENTINE'S DAY CONTEST

1911 Cleveland St., Hollywood FL 33020. **E-mail:** screaminmamas@gmail.com. **Website:** www.screaminmamas.com/contests. **Contact:** Darlene Pistocchi, editor/managing director. "Looking for light romantic comedy. Can be historical or contemporary—something to lift the spirits and celebrate the gift of innocent romance that might be found in the everyday life of a busy mom." Length: 600-1,200 words. Open only to moms. Deadline: June 30. Prize: Publication, complementary print copy. Costs: $5.

MARY WOLLSTONECRAFT SHELLEY PRIZE FOR IMAGINATIVE FICTION

Rosebud, ROSEBUD MAGAZINE; ROSEBUD, INC., C/O Rosebud Magazine, N3310 Asje Rd., Cambridge WI 53523, USA. (608)423-9780. **E-mail:** jrodclark@rsbd.net. **Website:** www.rsbd.net. **Contact:** J. Roderick Clark, editor. Estab. 1993. Publishes eclectic mix of poetry, fiction and nonfiction. Genres with a literary feel okay. The Shelley Award is presented for any kind of unpublished imaginative fiction/short stories, 4,000 words or less. Entries are welcome any time. Acquires first rights. Open to any writer. Deadline: June 15 in even years. Prize: Grand Prize: $1,000. 4 runner-ups receive $100. All winners published in *Rosebud*. Costs: $30/story. Judged by editor Rod Clark in 2016.

☉☉ SHORT GRAIN CONTEST

P.O. Box 3986, Regina SK S4P 3R9, Canada. (306)791-7749. **E-mail:** grainmag@skwriter.com. **Website:** www.grainmagazine.ca/short-grain-contest. **Contact:** Jordan Morris, business administrator (inquiries only). The annual Short Grain Contest includes a category for poetry of any style up to 100 lines and fiction of any style up to 2,500 words, offering 3 prizes. Deadline: April 1. Prize: $1,000, plus publication in *Grain Magazine*; 2nd Place: $750; 3rd Place: $500. Costs: $40 CAD; $50 for US and $60 for international entrants, in US or CAD funds; includes 1-year subscription to *Grain Magazine*.

SKIPPING STONES HONOR (BOOK) AWARDS

P.O. Box 3939, Eugene OR 97403, USA. (541)342-4956. **Fax:** (541)342-4956. **E-mail:** editor@skippingstones.org. **Website:** www.skippingstones.org. **Contact:** Arun N. Toké. Estab. 1994. *Skipping Stones* is a well respected, multicultural literary magazine now in its 29th year. Annual award to promote multicultural and/or nature awareness through creative writings for children and teens and their educators. Seeks authentic, exceptional, child/youth friendly books that promote intercultural, international, intergenerational harmony, or understanding through creative ways. Deadline: February 29. Prize: Honor certificates; gold seals; reviews; press release/publicity. Costs: $50. Judged by a multicultural committee of teachers, librarians, parents, students and editors.

THE BERNICE SLOTE AWARD

Prairie Schooner, 123 Andrews Hall, PO Box 880334, Lincoln NE 68588-0334. (402)472-0911. **Fax:** (402)472-1817. **E-mail:** PrairieSchooner@unl.edu. **Website:** www.prairieschooner.unl.edu. **Contact:** Kwame Dawes. Offered annually for the best work by a beginning writer published in *Prairie Schooner* in the previous year. Celebrates the best and finest writing that they have published for the year. Prize: $500. Judged by editorial staff of *Prairie Schooner*.

BYRON CALDWELL SMITH BOOK AWARD

The University of Kansas, Hall Center for the Humanities, 900 Sunnyside Ave., Lawrence KS 66045. (785)864-4798. **E-mail:** vbailey@ku.edu. **Website:** www.hallcenter.ku.edu. **Contact:** Victor Bailey, director. Offered in odd years. To qualify, applicants must live or be employed in Kansas and have written an outstanding book published within the previous 2 calendar years. Translations are eligible. Guidelines for SASE or online. Deadline: March 1. Prize: $1,500.

JEFFREY E. SMITH EDITORS' PRIZE IN FICTION, ESSAY AND POETRY

The Missouri Review, 357 McReynolds Hall, UMC, Columbia MO 65211. (573)882-4474. **Fax:** (573)884-

4671. **E-mail:** contest_question@moreview.com. **Website:** www.missourireview.com. **Contact:** Editor. Offered annually for unpublished work in 3 categories: fiction, essay, and poetry. Guidelines online or for SASE. Deadline: October 15. Prize: $5,000 and publication for each category winner. Costs: $20, includes a 1-year print or digital subscription.

KAY SNOW WRITING CONTEST

Willamette Writers, Willamette Writers, 2108 Buck St., West Linn OR 97068. (503)305-6729. **Fax:** (503)344-6174. **E-mail:** reg@willamettewriters.com. **Website:** www.willamettewriters.org. Willamette Writers is the largest writers' organization in Oregon and one of the largest writers' organizations in the United States. It is a nonprofit, tax-exempt Oregon corporation led by volunteers. Elected officials and directors administer an active program of monthly meetings, special seminars, workshops, and an annual writing conference. Continuing with established programs and starting new ones is only made possible by strong volunteer support. The purpose of this annual writing contest, named in honor of Willamette Writer's founder, Kay Snow, is to help writers reach professional goals in writing in a broad array of categories and to encourage student writers. Deadline: April 23. Submission deadline begins January 15. Prize: One first prize of $300, one second place prize of $150, and a third place prize of $50 per winning entry in each of the six categories. Student first prize is $50, $20 for second place, $10 for third. Costs: $10-$15, no fee for student entries (grades 1-12).

SOCIETY OF MIDLAND AUTHORS AWARD

Society of Midland Authors, Society of Midland Authors, P.O. Box 10419, Chicago IL 60610-0419. **E-mail:** marlenetbrill@comcast.net. **Website:** www.midlandauthors.com. **Contact:** Marlene Targ Brill, awards chair. Since 1957, the Society has presented annual awards for the best books written by Midwestern authors. The Society began in 1915. The Society of Midland Authors (SMA) Award is presented to one title in each of six categories: adult nonfiction, adult fiction, adult biography and memoir, children's nonfiction, children's fiction, and poetry. There may be honor book winners as well. Books and entry forms must be mailed to the 3 judges in each category; for a list of judges and the entry and payment forms, visit the SMA website. Do not mail books to the society's P.O. box. The fee can be sent to the SMA P.P.

box or paid via Paypal. Deadline: January 7. Prize: $500 and a plaque that is awarded at the SMA banquet in May in Chicago. Honorary winners receive a plaque. Costs: $10 entry fee.

⬤🌐 THE ST. LAWRENCE BOOK AWARD

Black Lawrence Press, **E-mail:** editors@blacklawrencepress.com. **Website:** www.blacklawrencepress.com. "Black Lawrence Press is an independent publisher of contemporary poetry, fiction, and creative nonfiction. We also publish the occasional translation from German. Founded in 2004, Black Lawrence became an imprint of Dzanc Books in 2008. In January 2014, we spread our wings and became an independent company in the state of New York. Our books are distributed nationally through Small Press Distribution to Amazon, Barnes & Noble, and various brick and mortar retailers. We also make our titles available through our website and at various conferences and book fairs. Through our annual contests and open reading periods, we seek innovative, electrifying, and thoroughly intoxicating mss that ensnare themselves in our hearts and minds and won't let go." Each year Black Lawrence Press awards The St. Lawrence Book Award for an unpublished first collection of poems or short stories. The St. Lawrence Book Award is open to any writer who has not yet published a full-length collection of short stories or poems. The winner of this contest will receive book publication, a $1,000 cash award, and ten copies of the book. Prizes are awarded on publication. Deadline: August 31. Prize: Publication and $1000. Judged by the Black Lawrence Press editors.

STONY BROOK SHORT FICTION PRIZE

Stony Brook Southampton, 239 Montauk Highway, Southampton NY 11968. **Website:** www.stonybrook.edu/fictionprize. Deadline: March 15. Prize: $1,000.

STORYSOUTH MILLION WRITERS AWARD

E-mail: terry@storysouth.com. **Website:** www.storysouth.com. **Contact:** Terry Kennedy, editor. Estab. 2003. Annual award to honor and promote the best fiction published in online literary journals and magazines during the previous year. Most literary prizes for short fiction have traditionally ignored web-published fiction. This award aims to show that world-class fiction is being published online and to promote to the larger reading and literary community. Deadline: August 15. Nominations of stories begins on March 15. Prize: Prize amounts subject to donation. Check website for details.

THEODORE STURGEON MEMORIAL AWARD FOR BEST SHORT SF OF THE YEAR

Center for the Study of SF, 1445 Jayhawk Blvd, Room 3001, University of Kansas, Lawrence KS 66045. (785)864-2518. **Fax:** (785)864-1159. **E-mail:** cssf@ku.edu. **Website:** sfcenter.ku.edu/sturgeon.htm. **Contact:** Kij Johnson, professor and associate director. Estab. 1987. Award to "honor the best science fiction short story of the year." Prize: Trophy. Winners receive expense-paid trip to the University and have their names engraved on the pernmanent trophy.

♻○ SUBTERRAIN MAGAZINE'S ANNUAL LUSH TRIUMPHANT LITERARY AWARDS COMPETITION

P.O. Box 3008 MPO, Vancouver BC V6B 3X5, Canada. (604)876-8710. **Fax:** (604)879-2667. **E-mail:** subter@portal.ca. **Website:** www.subterrain.ca. Estab. Magazine est. 1988; Lush Triumphant est. 2002. Entrants may submit as many entries in as many categories as they like. Fiction: Max of 3,000 words. Poetry: A suite of 5 related poems (max of 15 pages). Creative Nonfiction (based on fact, adorned with fiction): Max of 4,000 words. Deadline: May 15. Prize: Winners in each category will receive $1,000 cash (plus payment for publication) and publication in the Winter issue. First runner-up in each category will be published in the Spring issue of *subTerrain*. Costs: $27.50/entry includes a 1-year subscription to *subTerrain*.

SYDNEY TAYLOR MANUSCRIPT COMPETITION

Association of Jewish Libraries, Sydney Taylor Manuscript Award Competition, 204 Park St., Montclair NJ 07042-2903. **E-mail:** stmacajl@aol.com. **Website:** www.jewishlibraries.org/main/Awards/SydneyTaylorManuscriptAward.aspx. **Contact:** Aileen Grossberg. Estab. 1985. This competition is for unpublished writers of juvenile fiction. Material should be for readers ages 8-13. The ms should have universal appeal and reveal positive aspects of Jewish life that will serve to deepen the understanding of Judaism for all children. To encourage new fiction of Jewish interest for readers ages 8-13. Deadline: September 30. Prize: $1,000. Judging by qualified judges from within the Association of Jewish Libraries.

THE TEXAS INSTITUTE OF LETTERS LITERARY AWARDS

E-mail: Betwx@aol.com. **Website:** www.texasinstituteofletters.org. Estab. 1936. The Texas Institute of Let-ters gives annual awards for books by Texas authors and writers who have produced books about Texas, including Best Books of Poetry, Fiction, and Nonfiction. Awards are also given for best Short Story, Magazine or Newspaper Article, Essay, and best Books for Children and Young Adults. Work submitted must have been published in the year stipulated, and entries may be made by authors or by their publishers. Complete guidelines and award information is available on the Texas Institute of Letters website.

○ THREE CHEERS AND A TIGER

E-mail: editors@toasted-cheese.com. **Website:** tclj.toasted-cheese.com. **Contact:** Stephanie Lenz, editor. Contestants are to write a short story (following a specific theme) within 48 hours. Contests are held first weekend in Spring (mystery) and first weekend in Fall (science fiction/fantasy). Word limit announced at the start of the contest, 5 pm ET. Contest-specific information is announced 48 hours before the contest submission deadline. Results announced in April and October. Winners notified by e-mail. List of winners on website. Prize: Amazon gift certificates and publication. Costs: Contest is free to enter. Blind-judged by *Toasted Cheese* editors. Each judge uses his or her own criteria to choose entries.

THE THURBER PRIZE FOR AMERICAN HUMOR

77 Jefferson Ave., Columbus OH 43215. **Website:** www.thurberhouse.org. This award recognizes the art of humor writing. Deadline: March 31. Prize: $5,000 for the finalist, noncash prizes awarded to two runners-up. Judged by well-known members of the national arts community.

♻ TORONTO BOOK AWARDS

City of Toronto c/o Toronto Arts & Culture, Cultural Partnerships, City Hall, 9E, 100 Queen St. W., Toronto ON M5H 2N2, Canada. **E-mail:** shan@toronto.ca. **Website:** www.toronto.ca/book_awards. Estab. 1974. The Toronto Book Awards honor authors of books of literary or artistic merit that are evocative of Toronto. Deadline: April 30. Prize: Each finalist receives $1,000 and the winning author receives $10,000 ($15,000 total in prize money available).

STEVEN TURNER AWARD FOR BEST FIRST WORK OF FICTION

6335 W. Northwest Hwy., #618, Dallas TX 75225. **Website:** www.texasinstituteofletters.org. Offered annually for work published January 1-December 31 for the best first book of fiction. Deadline: normally first week in January; see website for specific date. Prize: $1,000.

ANNUAL VENTURA COUNTY WRITERS CLUB SHORT STORY CONTEST

Ventura County Writers Club Short Story Contest, P.O. Box 3373, Thousand Oaks CA 91362. **E-mail:** vcwc.contestchair@gmail.com. **Website:** www.venturacountywriters.com. **Contact:** Contest Chair. Estab. 1999. Annual short story contest for youth and adult writers. High school division for writers still in school. Adult division for those 18 and older. Club membership not required to enter and entries accepted worldwide as long as fees are paid, story is unpublished and in English. Enter through website. Winners get cash prizes and are published in club anthology. Deadline: November 15. Adult Prizes: 1st Place: $500; 2nd Place: $250; 3rd Place: $125. High School Prizes: 1st Place: $100; 2nd Place: $75; 3rd Place: $50. Costs: Submission fee for each story submitted: $15 U.S. for adult VCWC members; $25 U.S. for adult nonmembers; and $10 for high school students. PayPal, credit or debit cards are accepted.

Usually receives less than 500 entries.

WAASNODE SHORT FICTION PRIZE

Passages North, Department of English, Northern Michigan University, 1401 Presque Isle Ave., Marquette MI 49855. (906)227-1203. **Fax:** (906)227-1096. **E-mail:** passages@nmu.edu. **Website:** www.passagesnorth.com. **Contact:** Jennifer Howard. Offered every 2 years to publish new voices in literary fiction (maximum 10,000 words). Guidelines for SASE or online. Submissions accepted online. Deadline: April 15. Submission period begins February 15. Prize: $1,000 and publication for winner; 2 honorable mentions are also published; all entrants receive a copy of *Passages North*. Costs: $15 reading fee/story, make checks payable to Northern Michigan University. Judged by Tiphanie Yanique in 2016.

WABASH PRIZE FOR FICTION

Sycamore Review, Department of English, 500 Oval Dr., Purdue University, West Lafayette IN 47907. **E-mail:** sycamore@purdue.edu; sycamorefiction@purdue.edu. **Website:** www.sycamorereview.com/contest/. **Contact:** Kara Krewer, editor-in-chief. Annual contest for unpublished fiction. Deadline: November 15. Prize: $1,000 and publication. Costs: $20 reading fee; $5 for each additional story.

THE JULIA WARD HOWE AWARD

The Boston Authors Club, 33 Brayton Road, Brighton MA 02135. (617)783-1357. **E-mail:** alan.lawson@bc.edu. **Website:** www.bostonauthorsclub.org. **Contact:** Alan Lawson, president. Julia Ward Howe Prize offered annually in the spring for books published the previous year. Two awards are given: one for adult books of fiction, nonfiction, or poetry, and one for children's books, middle grade and young adult novels, nonfiction, or poetry. No picture books or subsidized publishers. There must be two copies of each book submitted. Deadline: January 15. Prize: $1,000 in each category. Several books will also be cited with no cash awards as Finalists or Highly Recommended. Costs: $25/title.

THE WASHINGTON WRITERS' PUBLISHING HOUSE FICTION PRIZE

Washington Writers' Publishing House, P.O. Box 15271, Washington DC 20003. **E-mail:** wwphpress@gmail.com. **Website:** www.washingtonwriters.org. Fiction writers living within 75 miles of the Capitol are invited to submit a ms of either a novel or a collection of short stories (no more than 350 pages, double-spaced). Deadline: November 15. Submission period begins July 1. Prize: $1,000 and 50 copies of the book. Costs: $25 reading fee.

THE ROBERT WATSON LITERARY PRIZE IN FICTION AND POETRY

The Robert Watson Literary Prizes, *The Greensboro Review*, MFA Writing Program, 3302 MHRA Building, Greensboro NC 27402-6170. (336)334-5459. **E-mail:** jlclark@uncg.edu. **Website:** www.greensbororeview.org. **Contact:** Jim Clark, editor. Offered annually for fiction (up to 25 double-spaced pages) and poetry (up to 10 pages). Entries must be unpublished. Open to any writer. Deadline: September 15. Prize: $1,000 each for best short story and poem. Costs: $14. Judged by editors of *The Greensboro Review*.

WESTERN AUSTRALIAN PREMIER'S BOOK AWARDS

State Library of Western Australia, Perth Cultural Centre, 25 Francis St., Perth WA 6000, Australia. (61)(8)9427-3151. **E-mail:** premiersbookawards@slwa.wa.gov.au. **Website:** pba.slwa.wa.gov.au. **Contact:** Karen de San Miguel. Estab. 1982. Annual competition for Australian citizens or permanent residents of Australia, or writers whose work has Australia as its primary focus. Categories: children's books, digital narrative, fiction, nonfiction, poetry, scripts, writing for young adults, West

Australian history, and Western Australian emerging writers. Deadline: January 31. Prize: Awards $25,000 for Premier's Prize; awards $15,000 each for the Children's Books, Digital Narrative, Fiction, and Nonfiction categories; awards $10,000 each for the Poetry, Scripts, Western Australian History, Western Australian Emerging Writers, and Writing for Young Adults; awards $5,000 for People's Choice Award.

WESTERN HERITAGE AWARDS

National Cowboy & Western Heritage Museum, 1700 NE 63rd St., Oklahoma City OK 73111-7997. (405)478-2250. **Fax:** (405)478-4714. **Website:** www.national-cowboymuseum.org. **Contact:** Jessica Limestall. Estab. 1961. The National Cowboy & Western Heritage Museum Western Heritage Awards were established to honor and encourage the legacy of those whose works in literature, music, film, and television reflect the significant stories of the American West. Accepted categories for literary entries: western novel, nonfiction book, art book, photography book, juvenile book, magazine article, or poetry book. The WHA are presented annually to encourage the accurate and artistic telling of great stories of the West through 16 categories of western literature, television, film and music; including fiction, nonfiction, children's books and poetry. See website for details and category definitions. Deadline: November 30. Prize: Awards a Wrangler bronze sculpture designed by famed western artist, John Free. Costs: $50. Judged by a panel of judges selected each year with distinction in various fields of western art and heritage.

WESTERN WRITERS OF AMERICA

271CR 219, Encampment WY 82325. (307)329-8942. **Fax:** (307)327-5465 (call first). **E-mail:** wwa.moulton@gmail.com. **Website:** www.westernwriters.org. **Contact:** Candy Moulton, executive director. Estab. 1953. Seventeen Spur Award categories in various aspects of the American West. The nonprofit Western Writers of America has promoted and honored the best in Western literature with the annual Spur Awards, selected by panels of judges. Awards, for material published last year, are given for works whose inspirations, image and literary excellence best represent the reality and spirit of the American West. Costs: No fee.

WESTMORELAND POETRY & SHORT STORY CONTEST

Westmoreland Arts & Heritage Festival, 252 Twin Lakes Road, Latrobe PA 15650-9415. (724)834-7474.

Fax: (724)850-7474. **E-mail:** info@artsandheritage.com. **Website:** www.artsandheritage.com. **Contact:** Diane Shrader. Offered annually for unpublished work. Two categories: Poem and Short Story. Short story entries no longer than 4,000 words. Family-oriented festival and contest. Deadline: February 17. Prizes: Award: $200; 1st Place: $125; 2nd Place: $100; 3rd Place: $75. Costs: $10/story or for 2 poems; both categories may be entered for $20.

WILLA LITERARY AWARD

Women Writing the West, 8547 East Arapaho Rd., #J-541, Greenwood Village CO 80112-1436. **E-mail:** Anneschroederauthor@gmail.com. **Website:** www.womenwritingthewest.org. **Contact:** Anne Schroeder. The WILLA Literary Award honors the year's best in published literature featuring women's or girls' stories set in the West. Women Writing the West (WWW), a nonprofit association of writers and other professionals writing and promoting the Women's West, underwrites and presents the nationally recognized award annually (for work published between January 1 and December 31). The award is named in honor of Pulitzer Prize winner Willa Cather, one of the country's foremost novelists. The award is given in 7 categories: historical fiction, contemporary fiction, original softcover fiction, creative nonfiction, scholarly nonfiction, poetry, and children's/young adult fiction/nonfiction. Entry forms available on the website. Deadline: November 1–February 1. Prize: $100 and a trophy. Finalist receives a plaque. Both receive digital and sticker award emblems for book covers. Notice of Winning and Finalist titles mailed to more than 4,000 booksellers, libraries, and others. Award announcement is in early August, and awards are presented to the winners and finalists at the annual WWW Fall Conference. Costs: $50. Judged by professional librarians not affiliated with WWW.

TENNESSEE WILLIAMS/NEW ORLEANS LITERARY FESTIVAL CONTESTS

Tennessee Williams/New Orleans Literary Festival, 938 Lafayette St., Suite 514, New Orleans LA 70113. (504)581-1144. **E-mail:** info@tennesseewilliams.net. **Website:** www.tennesseewilliams.net/contests. **Contact:** Paul J. Willis. Annual contests for: Unpublished One Act, Unpublished Short Fiction, and Unpublished Poem. "Our competitions provide playwrights an opportunity to see their work fully produced before a large audience during one of the largest literary festivals in the nation, and for the festival to showcase the undiscovered talents of poetry and fiction writers." Deadline: November 1 (One Act); November 15 (Poetry); December 1 (Fiction). Prize: One Act: $1,500, staged read at the next festival, full production at the festival the following year, VIP All-Access Festival pass for two years ($1,000 value), and publication in Bayou. Poetry: $1,000, public reading at next festival, publication in Louisiana Cultural Vistas Magazine. Fiction: $1,500, public reading at next festival, publication in Louisiana Literature. Costs: $25 entry fee for One Act and Fiction submissions; $20 entry fee for Poetry submissions. Judged by an anonymous expert panel for One Act contest. Judged by special guest judges, who change every year, for fiction and poetry. See website for full details.

WISCONSIN INSTITUTE FOR CREATIVE WRITING FELLOWSHIP

6195B H.C. White Hall, 600 N. Park St., Madison WI 53706. **E-mail:** rfkuka@wisc.edu. **Website:** creativewriting.wisc.edu/fellowships.html. **Contact:** Sean Bishop, graduate coordinator. Estab. 1986. Fellowship provides time, space and an intellectual community for writers working on first books. Receives approximately 300 applicants a year for each genre. Judged by English Department faculty and current fellows. Candidates can have up to one published book in the genre for which they are applying. Open to any writer with either an M.F.A. or Ph.D. in creative writing. Please enclose a SASE for notification of results. Results announced on website by May 1. Deadline: Last day of February. Open to submissions on December 15. Prize: $30,000 for a 9-month appointment. Costs: $45, payable to the Dept. of English; see website for payment instructions.

THOMAS WOLFE PRIZE AND LECTURE

North Carolina Writers' Network, Thomas Wolfe Fiction Prize, Great Smokies Writing Program, Attn: Nancy Williams, CPO #1860, UNC, Asheville NC 28805. **Website:** englishcomplit.unc.edu/wolfe. Estab. 1999. The Thomas Wolfe Fiction Prize honors internationally celebrated North Carolina novelist Thomas Wolfe. The prize is administered by Tommy Hays and the Great Smokies Writing Program at the University of North Carolina at Asheville. Deadline: January 30. Submissions period begins December 1. Prize: $1,000 and potential publication in *The Thomas Wolfe Review*. Costs: $15 fee for members of the NC Writers' Network, $25 for nonmembers.

TOBIAS WOLFF AWARD FOR FICTION

Bellingham Review, Mail Stop 9053, Western Washington University, Bellingham WA 98225. (360)650-4863. **E-mail:** bellingham.review@wwu.edu. **Website:** www.bhreview.org. **Contact:** Susanne Paola Antonetta, editor-in-chief; Louis McLaughlin, managing editor. Offered annually for unpublished work. Guidelines available on website; online submissions only. Categories: novel exceprts and short stories. Deadline: March 15. Submissions period begins December 1. Prize: $1,000, plus publication and subscription. Costs: $20 entry fee for 1st entry; $10 for each additional entry.

THE WORD AWARDS

The Word Guild, The Word Guild, Suite # 226, 245 King George Rd, Brantford ON N3R 7N7, Canada. 800-969-9010 x 1. **E-mail:** info@thewordguild.com. **E-mail:** info@thewordguild.com. **Website:** www.thewordguild.com. **Contact:** Karen deBlieck. The Word Guild is an organization of Canadian writers and editors who are Christian, and who are committed to encouraging one another and to fostering standards of excellence in the art, craft, practice and ministry of writing. Memberships available for various experience levels. Yearly conference Write Canada (please see website for information) and features keynote speakers, continuing classes and workshops. Editors and agents on site. The Word Awards is for work published in the past year, in almost 30 categories including books, articles, essays, fiction, nonfiction, novels, short stories, songs, and poetry. Please see website for more information. Deadline: January 15. Prize $50 CAD for article and short pieces; $100 CAD for book entries. Finalists book entries are eligible for the $5,000 Grace Irwin prize. Costs: Short Piece Entries: Members: $30 CAD + HST (per short piece entered); Non Members: $60 CAD + HST (per short piece entered). Book Entries: Members: $55 CAD + HST (per title entered); Non Members: $110 + HST (per title entered). Judged by industry leaders and professionals.

WORLD FANTASY AWARDS

P.O. Box 43, Mukilteo WA 98275. **E-mail:** sfexecsec@gmail.com. **Website:** www.worldfantasy.org. **Contact:** Peter Dennis Pautz, president. Offered annually for previously published work in several categories, including life achievement, novel, novella, short story, anthology, collection, artist, special award-pro and special award-nonpro. Works are recommended by attendees of current and previous 2 years' conventions and a panel of judges. Awards to recognize excellence in fantasy literature worldwide. Deadline: June 1. Prize: Trophy. Judged by panel.

WORLD'S BEST SHORT-SHORT STORY CONTEST, NARRATIVE NONFICTION CONTEST & SOUTHEAST REVIEW POETRY CONTEST

The Southeast Review, Florida State University, English Department, Tallahassee FL 32306. **E-mail:** southeastreview@gmail.com. **Website:** www.southeastreview.org. **Contact:** Erin Hoover, editor. Estab. 1979. Annual award for unpublished short-short stories (500 words or less), poetry, and narrative nonfiction (6,000 words or less). Visit website for details. Deadline: March 15. Prize: $500 per category. Winners and finalists will be published in *The Southeast Review*. Costs: $16 reading fee for up to 3 stories or poems, or 1 narrative essay.

WOW! WOMEN ON WRITING QUARTERLY FLASH FICTION CONTEST

WOW! Women on Writing, P.O. Box 41104, Long Beach CA 90853. **E-mail:** contestinfo@wow-womenonwriting.com. **Website:** www.wow-womenonwriting.com/contest.php. **Contact:** Angela Mackintosh, editor. Contest offered quarterly. "We are open to all themes and genres, although we do encourage writers to take a close look at our literary agent guest judge for the season if you are serious about winning." Deadline: August 31, November 30, February 28, May 31. Prize: 1st place: $350 cash prize, $25 Amazon gift certificate, story published on WOW! Women On Writing, interview on blog; 2nd place: $250 cash prize, $25 Amazon gift certificate, story published on WOW! Women On Writing, interview on blog; 3rd place: $150 cash prize, $25 Amazon gift certificate, story published on WOW! Women On Writing, interview on blog; 7 runners up: $25 Amazon gift certificate, story published on WOW! Women on Writing, interview on blog; 10 honorable mentions: $20 gift certificate from Amazon, story title and name published on WOW! Women On Writing. Costs: $10. Judged by a different guest every season, who is either a literary agent, acquiring editor or publisher.

WRITER'S DIGEST ANNUAL WRITING COMPETITION

Writer's Digest, a publication of F+W Media, Inc., 10151 Carver Rd., Suite 200, Cincinnati OH 45242. (715)445-4612, ext. 13430. **E-mail:** writing-competition@fwmedia.com. **Website:** www.writersdigest.com. Writing contest with 10 categories: Inspirational Writing (spiritual/ religious, maximum 2,500 words); Memoir/Personal Essay (maximum 2,000 words); Magazine Feature Article (maximum 2,000 words); Short Story (genre, maximum 4,000 words); Short Story (mainstream/literary, maximum 4,000 words); Rhyming Poetry (maximum 32 lines); Nonrhyming Poetry (maximum 32 lines); Stage Play (first 15 pages and 1-page synopsis); TV/Movie Script (first 15 pages and 1-page synopsis). Entries must be original, in English, unpublished/unproduced (except for Magazine Feature Articles), and not accepted by another publisher/producer at the time of submission. *Writer's Digest* retains one-time publication rights to the winning entries in each category. Deadline: May (early bird); June. Grand Prize: $3,000 and a trip to the Writer's Digest Conference to meet with editors and agents; 1st Place: $1,000 and $100 of Writer's Digest Books; 2nd Place: $500 and $100 of Writer's Digest Books; 3rd Place: $250 and $100 of Writer's Digest Books; 4th Place: $100 and $50 of *Writer's Digest* Books. Costs: $15/first poetry entry; $10/additional poem. All other entries are $25/first ms; $20/additional ms.

○ WRITER'S DIGEST POPULAR FICTION AWARDS

Writer's Digest, 10151 Carver Road, Suite #200, Blue Ash OH 45242. (715)445-4612 ext 13430. **E-mail:** WritersDigestWritingCompetition@fwmedia.com. **Website:** www.writersdigest.com. **Contact:** Nicole Howard, contest administrator. Annual competition/award for short stories. Categories include romance, crime, science fiction, thriller, horror, and young adult. Length: 4,000 words or fewer. Top Award Winners will be notified by mail by December 31. Winners will be listed in the May/ June issue of Writer's Digest, and on writersdigest.com after the issue is published. Early-Bird Deadline: September 16; Final Deadline: October 15. Prizes: Grand Prize: $2,500, a trip to the *Writer's Digest* Conference, $100 off a purchase at writersdigest.com, and the latest edition of *Novel & Short Story Writer's Market*; 1st Place (one for each of 6 categories): $500 cash, $100 off a purchase at writersdigest.com, and the latest edition of *Novel & Short Story Writer's Market*; Honorable Mentions (4 in each of 6 categories): will receive promotion at writersdigest.com and the latest edition of *Novel & Short Story Writer's Market*. Costs: $20 (by September 16); $25 (by October 15).

WRITER'S DIGEST SELF-PUBLISHED BOOK AWARDS

Writer's Digest, 10151 Carver Road, Suite #200, Blue Ash OH 45242. (715)445-4612, ext. 13430. **E-mail:** WritersDigestSelfPublishingCompetition@fwmedia.com. **Website:** www.writersdigest.com. **Contact:** Nicole Howard. Estab. 1992. Contest open to all English-language, self-published books for which the authors have paid the full cost of publication, or the cost of printing has been paid for by a grant or as part of a prize. Categories include: Mainstream/Literary Fiction, Genre Fiction, Nonfiction, Inspirational (spiritual/new age), Life Stories (biographies/autobiographies/family histories/memoirs), Children's Books, Reference Books (directories/encyclopedias/guide books), Poetry, and Middle-Grade/Young Adult Books. Judges reserve the right to re-categorize entries. Judges reserve the right to withhold prizes in any category. All winners will be notified in October. Early bird deadline: April 3. Prizes: Grand Prize: $8,000, a trip to the Writer's Digest Conference, promotion in *Writer's Digest*, 10 copies of the book will be sent to major review houses, and a guaranteed review in *Midwest Book Review*; 1st Place (9 winners): $1,000 and promotion in *Writer's Digest*; Honorable Mentions: $50 worth of Writer's Digest Books and promotion on writersdigest.com. All entrants will receive a brief commentary from one of the judges. Costs: $99; $75/additional entry.

WRITER'S DIGEST SELF-PUBLISHED E-BOOK AWARDS

Writer's Digest, 10151 Carver Road, Suite #200, Blue Ash OH 45242. (715)445-4612, ext. 13430. **E-mail:** WritersDigestSelfPublishingCompetition@fwmedia.com. **Website:** www.writersdigest.com. **Contact:** Nicole Howard. Estab. 2013. Contest open to all English-language, self-published e-books for which the authors have paid the full cost of publication, or the cost of publication has been paid for by a grant or as part of a prize. Categories include: Mainstream/Literary Fiction, Genre Fiction, Nonfiction (includes reference books), Inspirational (spiritual/new age), Life Stories (biographies/autobiographies/family histories/memoirs), Children's Books, Poetry, and Middle-Grade/Young Adult Books. Judges reserve the right to re-categorize entries. Judges reserve the right to withhold prizes in any category. All winners will be notified by December 31. Early bird deadline: August 6; Deadline: September 1. Prizes: Grand Prize: $5,000, promotion in *Writer's Digest*, $200 worth of Writer's Digest Books, and more; 1st Place (9 winners): $1,000 and promotion in *Writer's Digest*; Honorable Mentions: $50 worth of Writer's Digest Books and promotion on writersdigest.com. All entrants will re-

ceive a brief commentary from one of the judges. Costs: $99; $75/additional entry.

WRITER'S DIGEST SHORT SHORT STORY COMPETITION

Writer's Digest, 10151 Carver Road, Suite 200, Blue Ash OH 45242. (715)445-4612; ext. 13430. **E-mail:** WritersDigestShortShortStoryCompetition@fwmedia.com. **Website:** www.writersdigest.com. **Contact:** Nicole Howard. Looking for fiction that's bold, brilliant, and brief. Send your best in 1,500 words or fewer. All entries must be original, unpublished, and not submitted elsewhere at the time of submission. *Writer's Digest* reserves one-time publication rights to the 1st-25th winning entries. Winners will be notified by Feb. 28. Early bird deadline: November 15. Final deadline: December 15. Prize: 1st Place: $3,000 and a trip to the Writer's Digest Conference; 2nd Place: $1,500; 3rd Place: $500; 4th-10th Place: $100; 11th-25th Place: $50 gift certificate for writersdigestshop.com. Costs: $25.

WRITERS-EDITORS NETWORK INTERNATIONAL WRITING COMPETITION

CNW Publishing, P.O. Box A, North Stratford NH 03590-0167. **E-mail:** contestentry@writers-editors.com. **E-mail:** info@writers-editors.com. **Website:** www.writers-editors.com. **Contact:** Dana K. Cassell, executive director. Annual award to recognize publishable talent. New categories and awards for 2016: Nonfiction (unpublished or self-published; may be an article, blog post, essay/opinion piece, column, nonfiction book chapter, children's article or book chapter); fiction (unpublished or self-published; may be a short story, novel chapter, Young Adult [YA] or children's story or book chapter); poetry (unpublished or self-published; may be traditional or free verse poetry or children's verse). Guidelines available online. Deadline: March 15. Prize: 1st Place: $150 plus one year Writers-Editors membership; 2nd Place: $100; 3rd Place: $75. All winners and Honorable Mentions will receive certificates as warranted. Most Promising entry in each category will receive a free critique by a contest judge. Costs: $10 (active or new WEN/FFWA members) or $20 (nonmembers) for each fiction or nonfiction entry; $3 (members) or $5 (nonmembers) for each poem; or $10 for 5 poems (members), $10 for 3 poems (nonmembers). Judged by editors, librarians, and writers.

◎ WRITERS' GUILD OF ALBERTA AWARDS

Writers' Guild of Alberta, Percy Page Centre, 11759 Groat Rd., Edmonton AB T5M 3K6, Canada. (780)422-8174.

Fax: (780)422-2663. **E-mail:** mail@writersguild.ca. **Website:** writersguild.ca. **Contact:** Executive Director. Offers the following awards: Wilfrid Eggleston Award for Nonfiction; Georges Bugnet Award for Fiction; Howard O'Hagan Award for Short Story; Stephan G. Stephansson Award for Poetry; R. Ross Annett Award for Children's Literature; Gwen Pharis Ringwood Award for Drama; Jon Whyte Memorial Essay Award; James H. Gray Award for Short Nonfiction. Deadline: December 31. Prize: Winning authors receive $1,500; short piece prize winners receive $700.

WRITERS' LEAGUE OF TEXAS BOOK AWARDS

Writers' League of Texas, 611 S. Congress Ave., Suite 200A-3, Austin TX 78704. (512)499-8914. **Fax:** (512)499-0441. **E-mail:** sara@writersleague.org. **E-mail:** sara@writersleague.org. **Website:** www.writersleague.org. Open to Texas authors of books published the previous year. Authors are required to show proof of Texas residency (current or past), but are not required to be members of the Writers' League of Texas. Deadline: February 28. Open to submissions October 7. Prize: $1,000 and a commemorative award. Costs: $60/title; $40 for WLT members.

♻ THE WRITERS' TRUST ENGEL/FINDLEY AWARD

The Writers' Trust of Canada, 460 Richmond St. W., Suite 600, Toronto ON M5V 1Y1, Canada. (416)504-8222. **Fax:** (416)504-9090. **E-mail:** info@writerstrust.com. **Website:** www.writerstrust.com. **Contact:** Amanda Hopkins. The Writers' Trust Engel/Findley Award is presented annually at The Writers' Trust Awards Event, held in Toronto each fall, to a Canadian writer for a body of work in hope of continued contribution to the richness of Canadian literature. Open to Canadian citizens and permanent residents only. Prize: $25,000.

LAMAR YORK PRIZE FOR FICTION AND NONFICTION CONTEST

The Chattahoochee Review, Georgia Perimeter College, 2101 Womack Rd., Dunwoody GA 30338-4497. (770)274-5479. **E-mail:** gpccr@gpc.edu. **Website:** thechattahoocheereview.gpc.edu. **Contact:** Anna Schachner, Editor. Offered annually for unpublished creative nonfiction and nonscholarly essays and fiction up to 5,000 words. *The Chattahoochee Review* buys first rights only for winning essay/ms for the purpose of publication in the summer issue. Deadline: January 31. Submission period begins October 1. Prize: 2 prizes of $1,000 each, plus publication. Costs: $15 fee/entry; subscription included in fee. Judged by the editorial staff of *The Chattahoochee Review*.

ZOETROPE ALL STORY SHORT FICTION CONTEST

Zoetrope: All Story, Zoetrope: All-Story, Attn: Fiction Editor, 916 Kearny St., San Francisco CA 94133. (415)788-7500. **E-mail:** contests@all-story.com. **Website:** www.all-story.com. Annual short fiction contest. Considers submissions of short stories and one-act plays no longer than 7,000 words. Excerpts from larger works, screenplays, treatments, and poetry will be returned unread. Deadline: October 1. Submissions period begins July 1. Prizes: 1st place: $1,000 and publication on website; 2nd place: $500; 3rd place: $250. Costs: $20.

ZONE 3 FICTION AWARD

Zone 3, Austin Peay State University, P.O. Box 4565, Clarksville TN 37044. (931)221-7031. **Fax:** (931)221-7149. **E-mail:** wallacess@apsu.edu. **Website:** www.apsu.edu/zone3/contests. **Contact:** Susan Wallace, Managing Editor. Annual contest for unpublished fiction. Open to any fiction writer. Deadline: April 1. Prize: $250 and publication.

CONFERENCES & WORKSHOPS

//

Why are conferences so popular? Writers and conference directors alike tell us it's because writing can be such a lonely business—at conferences writers have the opportunity to meet (and commiserate) with fellow writers, as well as meet and network with publishers, editors, and agents. Conferences and workshops provide some of the best opportunities for writers to make publishing contacts and pick up valuable information on the business, as well as the craft, of writing.

The bulk of the listings in this section are for conferences. Most conferences last from one day to one week and offer a combination of workshop-type writing sessions, panel discussions, and a variety of guest speakers. Topics may include all aspects of writing from fiction to poetry to scriptwriting, or they may focus on a specific type of writing, such as those conferences sponsored by the Romance Writers of America (RWA) for writers of romance or by the Society of Children's Book Writers and Illustrators (SCBWI) for writers of children's books.

Workshops, however, tend to run longer—usually one to two weeks. Designed to operate like writing classes, most require writers to be prepared to work on and discuss their fiction while attending. An important benefit of workshops is the opportunity they provide writers for an intensive critique of their work, often by professional writing teachers and established writers.

Each of the listings here includes information on the specific focus of an event as well as planned panels, guest speakers, and workshop topics. It is important to note, however, some conference directors were still in the planning stages for 2018 when we contacted them. If it was not possible to include 2018 dates, fees, or topics, we provided the most up-to-date information available so you can get an idea of what to expect. For the most current information, it's best to check the conference website or send a self-addressed, stamped envelope to the director in question about three months before the date(s) listed.

FINDING A CONFERENCE

Many writers try to make it to at least one conference a year, but cost and location count as much as subject matter or other considerations when determining which conference to attend. There are conferences in almost every state and province, and even some in Europe are open to North Americans.

To make it easier for you to find a conference close to home—or to find one in an exotic locale to fit into your vacation plans—we've divided this section into geographic regions. The conferences appear in alphabetical order under the appropriate regional heading.

Note that conferences appear under the regional heading according to where they will be held, which is sometimes different from the address given as the place to register or send for information. The regions are as follows:

MULTIPLE U.S. LOCATIONS (PAGE 423)

NORTHEAST (PAGE 423): Connecticut, Maine, Massachusetts, New Hampshire, New York, Rhode Island, Vermont

MIDATLANTIC (PAGE 426): Washington DC, Delaware, Maryland, New Jersey, Pennsylvania

MIDSOUTH (PAGE 428): North Carolina, South Carolina, Tennessee, Virginia, West Virginia

SOUTHEAST (PAGE 429): Alabama, Arkansas, Florida, Georgia, Louisiana, Mississippi, Puerto Rico

MIDWEST (PAGE 430): Illinois, Indiana, Kentucky, Michigan, Ohio

NORTH CENTRAL (PAGE 432): Iowa, Minnesota, Nebraska, North Dakota, South Dakota, Wisconsin

SOUTH CENTRAL (PAGE 433): Colorado, Kansas, Missouri, New Mexico, Oklahoma, Texas

WEST (PAGE 436): Arizona, California, Hawaii, Nevada, Utah

NORTHWEST (PAGE 440): Alaska, Idaho, Montana, Oregon, Washington, Wyoming

CANADA (PAGE 442)

INTERNATIONAL (PAGE 442)

LEARNING AND NETWORKING

Besides learning from workshop leaders and panelists in formal sessions, writers at conferences also benefit from conversations with other attendees. Writers on all levels enjoy sharing insights. A conversation over lunch can reveal a new market for your work or let you know which editors are most receptive to the work of new writers. You can find out about recent editor changes and about specific agents. A casual chat could lead to a new contact or resource in your area.

Many editors and agents make visiting conferences a part of their regular search for new writers. A cover letter or query that starts with "I met you at the Green Mountain Writers Conference," or "I found your talk on your company's new romance line at the Moonlight and Magnolias Writers Conference most interesting ..." may give you a small leg up on the competition.

While a few writers have been successful in selling their manuscripts at a conference, the availability of editors and agents does not usually mean these folks will have the time to read your novel or six best short stories (unless, of course, you've scheduled an individual meeting with them in advance). While editors and agents are glad to meet writers and discuss work in general terms, usually they don't have the time (or energy) to give an extensive critique during a conference. In other words, use the conference as a way to make a first, brief contact.

SELECTING A CONFERENCE

Besides the obvious considerations of time, place, and cost, choose your conference based on your writing goals. If, for example, your goal is to improve the quality of your writing, it will be more helpful to choose a hands-on craft workshop rather than a conference offering a series of panels on marketing and promotion. If, on the other hand, you are a science fiction novelist who would like to meet your fans, try one of the many science fiction conferences or "cons" held throughout the country and the world.

Look for panelists and workshop instructors whose work you admire and who seem to be writing in your general area. Check for specific panels or discussions of topics relevant to what you are writing now. Think about the size—would you feel more comfortable with a small workshop of eight people or a large group of one hundred or more attendees?

If your funds are limited, start by looking for conferences close to home, but you may want to explore those that offer contests with cash prizes—and a chance to recoup your expenses. A few conferences and workshops also offer scholarships, but the competition is stiff and writers interested in these should seek out the requirements early. Finally, students may want to look for conferences and workshops that offer college credit. You will find these options included in the listings here. Again, check the conference website or send a self-addressed, stamped envelope for the most current details.

MULTIPLE U.S. LOCATIONS

ARTIST-IN-RESIDENCE NATIONAL PARKS

E-mail: acadia_information@nps.gov. **Website:** www.nps.gov/subjects/arts/air.htm. **Contact:** Artist-In-Residence Coordinator.

ADDITIONAL INFORMATION See website for contact information for individual parks.

NORTHEAST

⊙ BREAD LOAF ORION ENVIRONMENTAL WRITERS' CONFERENCE

Middlebury College, Middlebury College, Middlebury VT 05753. (802)443-5286. **Fax:** (802)443-2087. **E-mail:** blorion@middlebury.edu. **Website:** www.middlebury.edu/bread-loaf-conferences/blorion. Estab. 2014.

COSTS $2205 for full participants and $1875 for auditors. Both options include room and board.

ACCOMMODATIONS Mountain campus of Middlebury College in Vermont.

ADDITIONAL INFORMATION The event is designed to hone the skills of people interested in producing literary writing about the environment and the natural world. The conference is co-sponsored by the Bread Loaf Writers' Conference, Orion magazine, and Middlebury College's Environmental Studies Program. Application deadline for 2017 conference: February 15. Rolling admissions. Space is limited.

BREAD LOAF WRITERS' CONFERENCE

Middlebury College, Middlebury College, Middlebury VT 05753. (802)443-5286. **Fax:** (802)443-2087. **E-mail:** blwc@middlebury.edu. **Website:** www.middlebury.edu/bread-loaf-conferences/bl_writers. Estab. 1926.

COSTS $3,265 for general contributors and $3,130 for auditors. Both options include room and board.

ACCOMMODATIONS Bread Loaf campus of Middlebury College in Ripton, Vermont.

ADDITIONAL INFORMATION The application deadline for the 2017 event is February 15; there is $15 application fee.

CAPE COD WRITERS CENTER ANNUAL CONFERENCE

P.O. Box 408, Osterville MA 02655. **E-mail:** writers@capecodwriterscenter.org. **Website:** www.capecodwriterscenter.org. **Contact:** Nancy Rubin Stuart, executive director.

COSTS Costs vary, depending on the number of courses selected, beginning at $150. Several scholarships are available.

ACCOMMODATIONS Resort and Conference Center of Hyannis, Massachusetts.

GOTHAM WRITERS' WORKSHOP

writingclasses.com, 555 Eighth Ave., Suite 1402, New York NY 10018. (212)974-8377. **Fax:** (212)307-6325. **E-mail:** contact@gothamwriters.com. **Website:** www.writingclasses.com. Estab. 1993.

ADDITIONAL INFORMATION See the website for courses, pricing, and instructors.

GREEN MOUNTAIN WRITERS CONFERENCE

47 Hazel St., Rutland VT 05701. (802)236-6133. **E-mail:** ydaley@sbcglobal.net. **E-mail:** yvonnedaley@me.com. **Website:** vermontwriters.com. **Contact:** Yvonne Daley, director. Estab. 1998.

💬 "We offer the opportunity to learn from some of the nation's best writers at a small, supportive conference in a lakeside setting that allows one-on-one feedback. Participants often continue to correspond and share work after conferences."

COSTS $525 before April 15; $575 before May 15; $600 before June 1. Partial scholarships are available.

ACCOMMODATIONS Dramatically reduced rates at the Mountain Top Inn and Resort for attendees. Close to other area hotels and bed-and-breakfasts in Rutland County, Vermont.

ADDITIONAL INFORMATION Participants' mss can be read and commented on at a cost. Sponsors contests and publishes a literary magazine featuring work of participants. Brochures available on website or e-mail.

IWWG SPRING BIG APPLE CONFERENCE

International Women's Writing Guild, 5 Penn Plaza, PMB# 19059, New York NY 10001 (917)720-6959. **E-mail:** iwwgquestions@gmail.com. **Website:** www.iwwg.wildapricot.org.

IWWG ANNUAL SUMMER CONFERENCE

(917)720-6959. **E-mail:** iwwgquestions@gmail.com. **Website:** https://iwwg.wildapricot.org/events. **Contact:** Dixie King, executive director. Estab. 1976. 2017 dates: July 7-14. Location: Pennsylvania. More information to come. Average attendance: 500 maximum. Open to all women. Around 65 workshops offered each day.

ACCOMMODATIONS Check website for updated pricing.

ADDITIONAL INFORMATION Choose from 30 workshops in poetry, fiction, memoir and personal narrative, social action/advocacy, and mind-body-spirit. Critique sessions; book fair; salons; open readings. No portfolio required.

JOURNEY INTO THE IMAGINATION: A FIVE-DAY WRITING RETREAT

995 Chapman Rd., Yorktown Heights NY 10598. (914)962-4432. **E-mail:** emily@emilyhanlon.com. **Website:** www.thefictionwritersjourney.com/pendle-hill-spring-writers-retreat.html. **Contact:** Emily Hanlon. Estab. 2004.
COSTS See website for current costs.
ACCOMMODATIONS All rooms are private with shared bath.
ADDITIONAL INFORMATION For brochure, visit website.

KINDLING WORDS EAST

Burlington VT **Website:** www.kindlingwords.org.

THE MACDOWELL COLONY

100 High St., Peterborough NH 03458. (603)924-3886. **Fax:** (603)924-9142. **E-mail:** admissions@macdowellcolony.org. **Website:** www.macdowellcolony.org. Estab. 1907.
COSTS Artists are responsible for travel to and from the Colony. Travel reimbursement and stipends are available for participants of the residency, based on need. There are no residency fees.
ACCOMMODATIONS Exclusive use of a private studio and bedroom are provided for each artist in residence.

MUSE AND THE MARKETPLACE

Grub Street, 162 Boylston St., 5th Floor, Boston MA 02116. (617)695-0075. **E-mail:** info@grubstreet.org. **Website:** museandthemarketplace.com.

The Muse and the Marketplace is designed to give aspiring writers a better understanding of the craft of writing fiction and nonfiction, to prepare them for the changing world of publishing and promotion, and to create opportunities for meaningful networking. On all 3 days, prominent and nationally recognized established and emerging authors lead sessions on the craft of writing—the "muse" side of things—while editors, literary agents, publicists, and other industry professionals lead sessions on the business side—the "marketplace."

ACCOMMODATIONS Boston Park Plaza Hotel.

⊙ ODYSSEY FANTASY WRITING WORKSHOP

P.O. Box 75, Mont Vernon NH 03057. (603)673-6234. **E-mail:** jcavelos@sff.net. **Website:** www.odyssey-workshop.org. **Contact:** Jeanne Cavelos. Estab. 1996.
COSTS $2,025 tuition, $870 housing (double room), $1,740 housing (single room), $40 application fee, $600 food (approximate), $750 optional processing fee to receive college credit.
ADDITIONAL INFORMATION Students must apply and include a writing sample. Application deadline: April 8. Students' works are critiqued throughout the 6 weeks. Workshop information available in October. For brochure/guidelines, send SASE, e-mail, visit website, or call.

RT BOOKLOVERS CONVENTION

81 Willoughby Street, Suite 701, Brooklyn NY 11201. **E-mail:** tere@rtconvention.com. **Website:** rtconvention.com. **Contact:** Tere Michaels.
COSTS $495 for normal registration; $425 for industry professionals (agents, editors). Special discounted rate for readers, $450. Many other pricing options available. See website.
ACCOMMODATIONS Rooms available at the 2017 hotel, the Atlanta Hyatt Regency.

SOUTHMPTON CHILDREN'S LITERATURE CONFERENCE

Stony Brook Southampton MFA in Creative Writing, 239 Montauk Hwy., Southampton NY 11968. (631)632-5007. **Fax:** (631)632-2578. **Website:** www.stonybrook.edu/mfa/clc/. **Contact:** Christian McLean, director of summer and special programs. Estab. 2007. 239 Montauk Hwy., Southampton NY 11968-6700. (631)632-5030. **Fax:** (631)632-2578. **E-mail:** southamptonwriters@notes.cc.sunysb.edu. **Website:** www.stonybrook.edu/writers. Annual conference held in July. "The seaside campus of Stony Brook Southampton is located in the heart of the Hamptons, a renowned resort area only 70 miles from New York City. During free time, participants can draw on inspiration from the Atlantic beaches or explore the charming seaside towns."
COSTS Fees vary. 2017 fees will be available online.
ACCOMMODATIONS On-campus housing, doubles and small singles with shared baths, is modest but comfortable. Supplies list of lodging alternatives.
ADDITIONAL INFORMATION Applicants must complete an application and submit a writing sample

of original, unpublished work. Details available online. Accepts inquiries by e-mail, phone.

THE SOUTHAMPTON WRITERS CONFERENCE

Stony Brook Southampton MFA in Creative Writing Program, 239 Montauk Hwy., Southampton NY 11968. (631)632-5007. **E-mail:** christian.mclean@stonybrook.edu. **Website:** www.stonybrook.edu/southampton/mfa/summer/cwl_home.html. **Contact:** Christian McLean. Estab. 1976.

COSTS 12-day master class: $600 (does not include afternoon faculty-led workshop). 5-day workshop only: $1,395. 5-day workshop plus residency: $1,995 (12 days total). 12-day workshop: $1,995. 12-day residency: $600. (2017 prices not finalized at time of printing.)

ACCOMMODATIONS Participants can stay on campus in air-conditioned dorms.

UNICORN WRITERS CONFERENCE

17 Church Hill Rd., Redding CT 06896, USA. (203)938-7405. **E-mail:** unicornwritersconference@gmail.com. **Website:** www.unicornwritersconference.com. **Contact:** Jan L. Kardys, chair. Estab. 2010.

"The 40 pages for ms reviews are read in advance by your selected agents/editors, but follow the submission guidelines on the website. Check the genre chart for each agent and editor before you make your selection."

COSTS $325 includes all workshops (6 every hour to select on the day of the conference), gift bag, and 3 meals. Additional cost for ms reviews: $60 each.

ACCOMMODATIONS Held at Reid Castle, Purchase, New York. Directions available on event website.

ADDITIONAL INFORMATION The first self-published authors will be featured on the website, and the bookstore will sell their books at the event.

WESLEYAN WRITERS CONFERENCE

Wesleyan University, 294 High St., Room 207, Middletown CT 06459. (860)685-3604. **Fax:** (860)685-2441. **E-mail:** agreene@wesleyan.edu. **Website:** www.wesleyan.edu/writing/conference. **Contact:** Anne Greene, director. Estab. 1956.

ACCOMMODATIONS Meals are provided on campus. Lodging is available on campus or in town.

ADDITIONAL INFORMATION Ms critiques are available but not required.

WRITER'S DIGEST ANNUAL CONFERENCE

F+W Media, Inc., 10151 Carver Rd., Suite 200, Blue Ash OH 45242. (877)436-7764 (option 2). **E-mail:** writersdigestconference@fwmedia.com. **Website:** www.writersdigestconference.com. **Contact:** Taylor Sferra. Estab. 1995.

COSTS Cost varies by location and year. There are typically different pricing options for those who wish attend the pitch slam and those who just want to attend the conference education.

ACCOMMODATIONS A block of rooms at the event hotel is reserved for guests. See the travel page on the website for more information.

WRITERS OMI AT LEDIG HOUSE

55 Fifth Ave., 15th Floor, New York NY 10003. (212)206-6114. **E-mail:** writers@artomi.org. **Website:** www.artomi.org.

ACCOMMODATIONS Residents provide their own transportation. Offers overnight accommodations.

ADDITIONAL INFORMATION "Agents and editors from the New York publishing community are invited for dinner and discussion. Bicycles, a swimming pool, and nearby tennis court are available for use."

YADDO

The Corporation of Yaddo Residencies, P.O. Box 395, 312 Union Ave., Saratoga Springs NY 12866. (518)584-0746. **Fax:** (518)584-1312. **E-mail:** chwait@yaddo.org. **Website:** www.yaddo.org. **Contact:** Candace Wait, program director. Estab. 1900. Two seasons: large season is May-August; small season is October-May (stays from 2 weeks to 2 months; average stay is 5 weeks). Accepts 230 artists/year. Accommodates approximately 35 artists in large season. Those qualified for invitations to Yaddo are highly qualified writers, visual artists (including photographers), composers, choreographers, performance artists and film and video artists who are working at the professional level in their fields. Artists who wish to work collaboratively are encouraged to apply. An abiding principle at Yaddo is that applications for residencies are judged on the quality of the artists' work and professional promise. Site includes four small lakes, a rose garden, woodland, swimming pool, tennis courts. Yaddo's nonrefundable application fee is $30, to which is added a fee for media uploads ranging from $5-10 depending on the discipline. Application fees must be paid by credit card. Two letters of recommendation are requested. Applications are considered by the Admissions Committee and invitations are issued by March 15 (deadline: January 1) and October 1 (deadline: August 1). Information available on website.

COSTS No fee is charged; residency includes room, board, and studio space. Limited travel expenses are available to artists accepted for residencies at Yaddo. **ADDITIONAL INFORMATION** No stipends are offered.

VERMONT STUDIO CENTER

P.O. Box 613, 80 Pearl Street, Johnson VT 05656. (802)635-2727. **Fax:** (802)635-2730. **E-mail:** info@vermontstudiocenter.org. **Website:** www.vermontstudiocenter.org. **Contact:** Gary Clark, writing program director. Estab. 1984. P.O. Box 613, Johnson VT 05656. (802)635-2727. **Fax:** (802)635-2730. **E-mail:** info@vermontstudiocenter.org. **Website:** www.vermontstudiocenter.org. **Contact:** Gary Clark, writing program director. Estab. 1984. Ongoing residencies. Conference duration: From 2-12 weeks. Average attendance: 55 writers and visual artists/month. "The Vermont Studio Center is an international creative community located in Johnson, Vermont, and serving more than 600 American and international artists and writers each year (50 per month). A Studio Center Residency features secluded, uninterrupted writing time, the companionship of dedicated and talented peers, and access to a roster of two distinguished Visiting Writers each month. All VSC Residents receive three meals a day, private, comfortable housing and the company of an international community of painters, sculptors, poets, printmakers and writers. Writers attending residencies at the Studio Center may work on whatever they choose—no matter what month of the year they attend." Visiting writers have included Ron Carlson, Donald Revell, Jane Hirshfield, Rosanna Warren, Chris Abani, Bob Shacochis, Tony Hoagland, and Alice Notley. **COSTS** The cost of a 4-week residency is $3,950. Generous fellowship and grant assistance is available. **ACCOMMODATIONS** Accommodations available on site. "Residents live in single rooms in 10 modest, comfortable houses adjacent to the Red Mill Building. Rooms are simply furnished and have shared baths. Complete linen service is provided. The Studio Center is unable to accommodate guests at meals, overnight guests, spouses, children, or pets." **ADDITIONAL INFORMATION** Fellowships application deadlines are February 15, June 15, and October 1. Writers are encouraged to visit website for more information. May also e-mail, call, fax.

MIDATLANTIC

ALGONKIAN FIVE DAY NOVEL CAMP

2020 Pennsylvania Ave. NW, Suite 443, Washington DC 20006. **E-mail:** info@algonkianconferences.com. **Website:** algonkianconferences.com.

ANTIOCH WRITERS' WORKSHOP

Antioch Writers' Workshop, c/o Antioch University Midwest, 900 Dayton St., Yellow Springs OH 45387. (937)769-1803. **E-mail:** info@antiochwritersworkshop.com. **Website:** www.antiochwritersworkshop.com. **Contact:** Sharon Short, director. Estab. 1986. **ACCOMMODATIONS** Accommodations are available at local hotels and bed-and-breakfasts. **ADDITIONAL INFORMATION** The easiest way to contact this event is through the website's contact form.

BALTIMORE COMIC-CON

Baltimore Convention Center, 1 West Pratt St., Baltimore MD 21201. (410)526-7410. **E-mail:** general@baltimorecomiccon.com. **Website:** www.baltimorecomiccon.com. **Contact:** Marc Nathan. Estab. 1999. **COSTS** General admission, VIP, celebrity, and Harvey Awards tickets are available at baltimorecomiccon.com/tickets. **ACCOMMODATIONS** Does not offer overnight accommodation. Provides list of area hotels and lodging options offering associated discounts. **ADDITIONAL INFORMATION** For brochure, visit website.

BALTIMORE WRITERS' CONFERENCE

English Department, Liberal Arts Bldg., Towson University, 8000 York Rd., Towson MD 21252. (410)704-5196. **E-mail:** prwr@towson.edu. **Website:** baltimorewritersconference.org. Estab. 1994.
◑   This conference has sold out in the past. **ACCOMMODATIONS** Hotels are close by, if required. **ADDITIONAL INFORMATION** Writers may register through the website. Send inquiries via e-mail.

BAY TO OCEAN WRITERS CONFERENCE

P.O. Box 1773, Easton MD 21601. (410)482-6337. **E-mail:** info@baytoocean.com. **Website:** www.baytoocean.com. Estab. 1998. **COSTS** Adults: $100-120. Students: $55. A paid ms review is also available; details on website. Includes continental breakfast and networking lunch.

ADDITIONAL INFORMATION Registration is on website. Pre-registration is required; no registration at door. Conference usually sells out 1 month in advance. Conference is for all levels of writers.

CONFLUENCE

P.O. Box 3681, Pittsburgh PA 15230. **Website:** parsec-sff.org/confluence. Estab. 1996.

HIGHLIGHTS FOUNDATION FOUNDERS WORKSHOPS

814 Court St., Honesdale PA 18431. (877)288-3410. **Fax:** (570)253-0179. **E-mail:** klbrown@highlights-foundation.org. **E-mail:** jo.lloyd@highlightsfoundation.org. **Website:** highlightsfoundation.org. **Contact:** Kent L. Brown, Jr. Estab. 2000.

"Applications will be reviewed and accepted on a first-come, first-served basis. Applicants must demonstrate specific experience in the writing area of the workshop they are applying for—writing samples are required for many of the workshops."

COSTS Prices vary based on workshop. Check website for details.

ACCOMMODATIONS Coordinates pickup at local airport. Offers overnight accommodations. Participants stay in guest cabins on the wooded grounds surrounding Highlights Founders' home adjacent to the house/conference center.

ADDITIONAL INFORMATION Some workshops require pre-workshop assignment. Brochure available for SASE, by e-mail, on website, by phone, by fax. Accepts inquiries by phone, fax, e-mail, SASE. Editors attend conference.

HIGHLIGHTS FOUNDATION WRITERS WORKSHOPS

814 Court St., Honesdale PA 18431. (570)253-1192. **Fax:** (570)253-0179. **E-mail:** jo.lloyd@highlights-foundation.org. **Website:** highlightsfoundation.org. Estab. 1985.

ACCOMMODATIONS Private lodging on-site, included in workshop tuition.

ADDITIONAL INFORMATION Most workshops offer attendees the option of submitting a ms for review at the conference. Workshop brochures/guidelines are available upon request.

JENNY MCKEAN MOORE COMMUNITY WORKSHOPS

English Department, George Washington University, 801 22nd St. NW, Rome Hall, Suite 760, Washington DC 20052. (202)994-6180. **Fax:** (202)994-6637. **E-mail:** lpageinc@aol.com. **Website:** www.gwu.edu/~english/creative_jennymckeanmoore.html. **Contact:** Lisa Page, director of creative writing. Estab. 1976.

ADDITIONAL INFORMATION Admission is competitive and by decided by the quality of a submitted ms.

NEW JERSEY ROMANCE WRITERS PUT YOUR HEART IN A BOOK CONFERENCE

P.O. Box 513, Plainsboro NJ 08536. **Website:** www.njromancewriters.org/conference.html. Estab. 1984.

PENNWRITERS CONFERENCE

P.O. Box 685, Dalton PA 18414. **E-mail:** conference-co@pennwriters.org; info@pennwriters.org. **Website:** pennwriters.org/conference. Estab. 1987.

As the official writing organization of Pennsylvania, Pennwriters has 8 different areas with smaller writing groups that meet. Each of these areas sometimes has their own, smaller event during the year in addition to the annual writing conference.

ACCOMMODATIONS Costs vary. Pennwriters members in good standing get a slightly reduced rate.

ADDITIONAL INFORMATION Sponsors contest. Published authors judge fiction in various categories. Agent/editor appointments are available on a first-come, first-served basis.

PHILADELPHIA WRITERS' CONFERENCE

P.O. Box 7171, Elkins Park PA 19027. (215)619-7422. **E-mail:** info@pwcwriters.org. **Website:** pwcwriters.org. Estab. 1949.

Offers 14 workshops, usually 4 seminars, several "ms rap" sessions, a Friday Roundtable Forum Buffet with speaker, and the Saturday Annual Awards Banquet with speaker. Attendees may submit mss in advance for criticism by the workshop leaders and are eligible to submit entries in more than 10 contest categories. Cash prizes and certificates are given to first and second place winners, plus full tuition for the following year's conference to first place winners.

ACCOMMODATIONS See website for details. Hotel may offer discount for early registration.

ADDITIONAL INFORMATION Accepts inquiries by e-mail. Agents and editors attend the conference. Many questions are answered online.

O SCBWI—NEW JERSEY; ANNUAL SUMMER CONFERENCE

New Jersey NJ **Website:** newjersey.scbwi.org. **Contact:** Cathleen Daniels, regional advisor.

WILLIAM PATERSON UNIVERSITY SPRING WRITER'S CONFERENCE

English Department, Atrium 232, 300 Pompton Rd., Wayne NJ 07470. (973)720-3067. **Fax:** (973)720-2189. **E-mail:** parrasj@wpunj.edu. **Website:** wpunj.edu/cohss/departments/english/writers-conference. **Contact:** John Parras.

COSTS $22-65.

WINTER POETRY & PROSE GETAWAY

Murphy Writing of Stockton University, 35 S. Dr. Martin Luther King Blvd., Atlantic City NJ 08401, USA. (609)626-3596. **E-mail:** info@murphywriting.com. **Website:** www.stockton.edu/wintergetaway. **Contact:** Amanda Murphy. Estab. 1994.

O "At most conferences, writers listen to talks and panels and sit in sessions where previously written work is discussed. At the Getaway, they write. Most workshops are limited to 10 or fewer participants. By spending the entire weekend in one workshop, participants will venture deeper into their writing, making more progress than they thought possible."

COSTS See website or call for current fee information.

ACCOMMODATIONS Room packages at the historic Stockton Seaview Hotel are available.

ADDITIONAL INFORMATION Previous faculty has included Julianna Baggott, Christian Bauman, Laure-Anne Bosselaar, Kurt Brown, Mark Doty (National Book Award winner), Stephen Dunn (Pulitzer Prize winner), Dorianne Laux, Carol Plum-Ucci, James Richardson, Mimi Schwartz, Terese Svoboda, and more.

MIDSOUTH

AMERICAN CHRISTIAN WRITERS CONFERENCES

P.O. Box 110390, Nashville TN 37222. (800)219-7483 or (615)331-8668. **E-mail:** acwriters@aol.com. **Website:** www.acwriters.com. **Contact:** Reg Forder, director. Estab. 1981.

COSTS Costs vary and may depend on type of event (conference or mentoring retreat).

ACCOMMODATIONS Special rates are available at the host hotel (usually a major chain like Holiday Inn).

ADDITIONAL INFORMATION E-mail or call for conference brochures.

CELEBRATION OF SOUTHERN LITERATURE

Southern Lit Alliance, 301 E. 11th St., Suite 301, Chattanooga TN 37403. (423)267-1218. **Fax:** (866)483-6831. **Website:** www.southernlitalliance.org.

CHRISTOPHER NEWPORT UNIVERSITY WRITERS' CONFERENCE & WRITING CONTEST

Life Long Learning Society, CNU's Yoder Barn Theater, 660 Hamilton Dr., Newport News VA 23602 (757)269-4368. **E-mail:** eleanor.taylor@cnu.edu. **Website:** writers.cnu.edu. Estab. 1981.

ACCOMMODATIONS Provides list of area hotels.

HAMPTON ROADS WRITERS CONFERENCE

P.O. Box 56228, Virginia Beach VA 23456. **E-mail:** hrwriters@cox.net. **Website:** hamptonroadswriters.org.

COSTS Costs vary. There are discounts for members, for early bird registration, for students, and more.

HIGHLAND SUMMER CONFERENCE

P.O. Box 7014, Radford University, Radford VA 24142. **E-mail:** tburriss@radford.edu; rbderrick@radford.edu. **Website:** tinyurl.com/q8z8ej9. **Contact:** Dr. Theresa Burriss; Ruth Derrick. Estab. 1978.

JAMES RIVER WRITERS CONFERENCE

2319 E. Broad St., Richmond VA 23223. (804)433-3790. **Fax:** (804)291-1466. **E-mail:** info@jamesriverwriters.org; fallconference@jamesriverwriters.org. **Website:** www.jamesriverwriters.org. Estab. 2003.

COSTS Check website for updated pricing.

⊙ KILLER NASHVILLE

P.O. Box 680759, Franklin TN 37068. (615)599-4032. **E-mail:** contact@killernashville.com. **Website:** www.killernashville.com. Estab. 2006.

COSTS $375 for general registration. Includes network lunches on Friday and Saturday and special sessions with best-selling authors and industry professionals.

ADDITIONAL INFORMATION Additional information about registration is provided online.

NORTH CAROLINA WRITERS' NETWORK FALL CONFERENCE

P.O. Box 21591, Winston-Salem NC 27120. (336)293-8844. **E-mail:** mail@ncwriters.org. **Website:** www.ncwriters.org. Estab. 1985.

COSTS Approximately $250 (includes 4 meals).

ACCOMMODATIONS Special rates are usually available at the conference hotel, but attendees must make their own reservations.

SEWANEE WRITERS' CONFERENCE

735 University Ave., 119 Gailor Hall, Stamler Center, Sewanee TN 37383. (931)598-1654. **E-mail:** swc@sewanee.edu. **Website:** www.sewaneewriters.org. **Contact:** Adam Latham. Estab. 1990.

COSTS $1,100 for tuition, and $700 for room, board, and activity costs.

ACCOMMODATIONS Participants are housed in single rooms in university dormitories. Bathrooms are shared by small groups.

SOUTH CAROLINA WRITERS WORKSHOP

4711 Forest Dr., Suite 3, P.M.B. 189, Columbia SC 29206. **E-mail:** scwwliaison@gmail.com. **Website:** www.myscwa.org. Estab. 1991.

WILDACRES WRITERS WORKSHOP

233 S. Elm St., Greensboro NC 27401. (336)255-8210. **E-mail:** judihill@aol.com. **Website:** www.wildacreswriters.com. **Contact:** Judi Hill, director. Estab. 1985.

COSTS The current price is $830. Check the website for more info.

ADDITIONAL INFORMATION Include a one-page writing sample with registration.

WRITE ON THE RIVER

8941 Kelsey Lane, Knoxville TN 37922. **E-mail:** bob@bobmayer.org. **Website:** www.bobmayer.org. **Contact:** Bob Mayer. Estab. 2002.

COSTS Varies; depends on venue. Please see website for any updates.

ADDITIONAL INFORMATION Limited to 4 participants, and focused on their novel and marketability.

THE WRITERS' WORKSHOP

THE RENBOURNE EDITORIAL AGENCY, 387 Beaucatcher Rd., Asheville NC 28805. (828)254-8111. **E-mail:** writersw@gmail.com. **Website:** www.twwoa.org. Estab. 1985.

"We have exceptional editors on hand to fine-tune your work for publication. We do it all—content, line, and copyediting—with a fine-tooth comb. We accept most genres, and we specialize in novels, memoirs, and creative nonfiction."

COSTS For editorial services: usually $4 per page (double spaced) for a thorough editing, or $3 per page for a read-through and revision suggestions.

ADDITIONAL INFORMATION Also sponsors annual contests in poetry, literary fiction, memoirs, and essay. For guidelines, see website.

SOUTHEAST

ALABAMA WRITERS' CONCLAVE

Website: www.alabamawritersconclave.org. **Contact:** Sue Walker, president. Estab. 1923.

COSTS Previous fees for the conference: $150 for members and $175 for nonmembers. Includes 2 meals. Critique fee: $25 for members and $30 for nonmembers. Membership: $25.

ADDITIONAL INFORMATION "We have major speakers and faculty members who conduct intensive, energetic workshops. Our annual writing contest guidelines and all other information are available online."

ARKANSAS WRITERS' CONFERENCE

1815 Columbia Dr., Conway AR 72034. (501)833-2756. **E-mail:** breannacone1@yahoo.com. **Website:** www.arkansaswritersconference.org.

ATLANTA WRITERS CONFERENCE

Atlanta Writers Club, Westin Atlanta Airport Hotel, 4736 Best Rd., Atlanta GA 30337. **E-mail:** awconference@gmail.com. **Website:** www.atlantawritersconference.com/about. **Contact:** George Weinstein. Estab. 2008.

COSTS Ms critiques are $160 each (2 spots/waitlists maximum). Pitches are $60 each (2 spots/waitlists maximum). There's no charge for waitlists unless a spot opens. Query letter critiques are $60 (1 spot maximum). Other workshops and panels may also cost extra; see website. The "all activities" option is $560 and includes 2 ms critiques, 2 pitches, and 1 of each remaining activity.

ACCOMMODATIONS A block of rooms is reserved at the conference hotel. Booking instructions will be sent in the registration confirmation e-mail.

ADDITIONAL INFORMATION A free shuttle runs between the airport and the hotel.

ASSOCIATION OF WRITERS & WRITING PROGRAMS CONFERENCE & BOOKFAIR

Association of Writers & Writing Programs, George Mason University, 4400 University Dr., MSN 1E3, Fairfax VA 22030. (703)993-4317. **Fax:** (703)993-4302. **E-mail:** conference@awpwriter.org; events@awpwriter.org. **Website:** www.awpwriter.org/awp_conference. Estab. 1973.

ADDITIONAL INFORMATION Upcoming conference locations include Tampa, Florida (March 7-10, 2018).

DRAGON CON

P.O. Box 16459, Atlanta GA 30321. **Website:** www. dragoncon.org.

FLORIDA CHRISTIAN WRITERS CONFERENCE

Word Weavers International, Inc., 504 Spoonbill Court, Winter Springs FL 32708. (386)295-3902. **E-mail:** floridacwc@aol.com. **Website:** floridacwc.net. **Contact:** Eva Marie Everson and Mark T. Hancock. Estab. 1988.

COSTS Ranges: $275 (daily rate—in advance, includes lunch and dinner; specify days) to $1,495 (attendee and participating spouse/family member in same room). Scholarships offered. For more information or to register, go to the conference website.

ACCOMMODATIONS Offers private rooms and double occupancy as well as accommodations for participating and nonparticipating family members. Meals provided, including awards dessert banquet Saturday evening. For those flying into Orlando or Sanford airports, FCWC provides a shuttle to and from the conference center.

FLORIDA ROMANCE WRIITERS FUN IN THE SUN CONFERENCE

Florida Romance Writers, P.O. Box 550562, Fort Lauderdale FL 33355. **E-mail:** frwfuninthesun@yahoo.com. **Website:** frwfuninthesunmain.blogspot.com. Estab. 1986.

MONTEVALLO LITERARY FESTIVAL

Comer Hall, Station 6420, University of Montevallo, Montevallo AL 35115. (205)665-6420. **Fax:** (205)665-6420. **E-mail:** murphyj@montevallo.edu. **Website:** www.montevallo.edu/arts-sciences/college-of-arts-sciences/departments/english-foreign-languages/student-organizations/montevallo-literary-festival. **Contact:** Dr. Jim Murphy, director. Estab. 2003.

MOONLIGHT AND MAGNOLIAS WRITER'S CONFERENCE

Georgia Romance Writers, 3741 Casteel Park Dr., Marietta GA 30064. **Website:** www.georgiaromance-writers.org/mm-conference. Estab. 1982.

OZARK CREATIVE WRITERS, INC. CONFERENCE

P.O. Box 9076, Fayetteville AR 72703. **E-mail:** ozark-creativewriters1@gmail.com. **Website:** www.ozark-creativewriters.com.

A full list of sessions and speakers is online. The conference usually has agents and/or editors in attendance to meet with writers.

SLEUTHFEST

Mystery Writers of America Florida, **E-mail:** sleuth-festinfo@gmail.com. **Website:** sleuthfest.com.

SOUTHEASTERN WRITERS ASSOCIATION— ANNUAL WRITERS WORKSHOP

GA. **E-mail:** purple@southeasternwriters.org. **Website:** www.southeasternwriters.org. Estab. 1975.

Instruction offered for novel writing, nonfiction, young adult, commercial writing, screenwriting, marketing/social media. Includes agent in residence/publisher in residence.

COSTS Cost of workshop: $445 for 4 days or lower prices for daily tuition or early bird special. (See website for tuition pricing.)

ACCOMMODATIONS Lodging at Epworth and throughout St. Simons Island. Visit website for more information.

WRITERS IN PARADISE

Eckerd College, 4200 54th Ave. S., St. Petersburg FL 33711. (727)386-2264. **E-mail:** wip@eckerd.edu. **Website:** writersinparadise.com. Estab. 2005.

ADDITIONAL INFORMATION Application materials are due in November and required of all attendees.

MIDWEST

BACKSPACE AGENT-AUTHOR SEMINAR

P.O. Box 454, Washington MI 48094. (732)267-6449. **Fax:** (586)532-9652. **E-mail:** admin@bksp.org. **Website:** www.backspacewritersconference.com. **Contact:** Christopher Graham and Karen Dionne, organizers. Estab. 2006.

COSTS Each workshop is $225. Attendance limited to 10. Writerws can register for as many workshops as they wish.

BOOKS-IN-PROGRESS CONFERENCE

Carnegie Center for Literacy and Learning, 251 W. Second St., Lexington KY 40507. (859)254-4175. E-mail: ccll1@carnegiecenterlex.org. **Website:** carnegiecenterlex.org. **Contact:** Laura Whitaker, program director. Estab. 2010.

💬 "Personal meetings with faculty (agents and editors) are only available to full conference participants. Limited slots available. Please choose only one agent; only one pitching session per participant."

ACCOMMODATIONS See website for list of area hotels.

CENTRAL OHIO FICTION WRITERS ANNUAL CONFERENCE

Romance Writers of America, P.O. Box 4213, Newark OH 43058. **E-mail:** susan_gee_heino@yahoo.com; msgigimorgan@gmail.com. **Website:** www.cofw.org. **Contact:** Susan Gee Heino, president; Gigi Morgan, conference chair. Estab. 1990.

CHICAGO WRITERS CONFERENCE

E-mail: mare@chicagowritersconference.org. **Website:** chicagowritersconference.org. **Contact:** Mare Swallow. Estab. 2011.

DETROIT WORKING WRITERS ANNUAL WRITERS CONFERENCE

Detroit Working Writers, P.O. Box 82395, Rochester MI 48308. **E-mail:** conference@detworkingwriters. org. **Website:** dww-writers-conference.org. Estab. 1961.

💬 "Detroit Working Writers was founded on June 5, 1900, as the Detroit Press Club, the city of Detroit's first press club. Today, more than a century later, it is a 501(c)(6) organization and the state of Michigan's oldest writers organization."

COSTS Costs vary, depending on early bird registration and membership status within the organization.

FESTIVAL OF FAITH AND WRITING

Department of English, Calvin College, 1795 Knollcrest Circle SE, Grand Rapids MI 49546. (616)526-6770. **E-mail:** ffw@calvin.edu. **Website:** festival.calvin.edu. Estab. 1990.

ACCOMMODATIONS Shuttles are available to and from local hotels. Shuttles are also available for overflow parking lots. A list of hotels with special rates for attendees is available on the conference website. High school and college students can arrange on-campus lodging by e-mail.

INDIANA UNIVERSITY WRITERS' CONFERENCE

464 Ballantine Hall, 1020 E. Kirkwood Ave., Bloomington IN 47405. (812)855-1877. **Fax:** (812)855-9535. **E-mail:** writecon@indiana.edu. **Website:** www.indiana.edu/~writecon. Estab. 1940.

ACCOMMODATIONS Information on accommodations available on website.

ADDITIONAL INFORMATION Follow the conference on Twitter at @iuwritecon.

KENTUCKY WOMEN WRITERS CONFERENCE

University of Kentucky College of Arts & Sciences, 232 E. Maxwell St., Lexington KY 40506. (859)257-2874. **E-mail:** kentuckywomenwriters@gmail.com. **Website:** kentuckywomenwriters.org. **Contact:** Julie Wrinn, director. Estab. 1979.

COSTS $200 for general admission and a workshop and $125 for admission with no workshop.

ADDITIONAL INFORMATION Sponsors prizes in poetry ($200), fiction ($200), nonfiction ($200), playwriting ($500), and spoken word ($500). Winners are also invited to read during the conference. Pre-registration opens May 1.

KENTUCKY WRITERS CONFERENCE

Southern Kentucky Book Fest, Knicely Conference Center, 2355 Nashville Rd., Bowling Green KY 42101. (270)745-4502. **E-mail:** sara.volpi@wku.edu. **Website:** www.sokybookfest.org. **Contact:** Sara Volpi.

💬 Since the event is free, interested attendees are asked to register in advance. Information on how to do so is on the website.

KENYON REVIEW WRITERS WORKSHOP

Kenyon Review, Kenyon College, Gambier OH 43022. (740)427-5208. **Fax:** (740)427-5417. **E-mail:** kenyonreview@kenyon.edu; writers@kenyonreview.org. **Website:** www.kenyonreview.org/workshops. **Contact:** Anna Duke Reach, director. Estab. 1990.

COSTS Fiction, literary nonfiction, poetry, nature writing, translation: $2,295. Teachers: $1,495. All rates include tuition and room and board.

ACCOMMODATIONS The workshop operates a shuttle to and from Gambier and the airport in Columbus, Ohio. Offers overnight accommodations. Participants are housed in Kenyon College student housing.

ADDITIONAL INFORMATION Application includes a writing sample. Admission decisions are made on a rolling basis. Starting in November, workshop information is available online. For a brochure, send e-mail, visit website, call, or fax. Accepts inquiries by SASE, e-mail, phone, fax.

◎ MAGNA CUM MURDER

Magna Cum Murder Crime Writing Festival, E.B. and Bertha C. Ball Center, Ball State University, 400 Minnetrista Pkwy., Muncie IN 47306. (765)285-8975. **Fax:** (765)747-9566. **E-mail:** magnacummurder@yahoo.com;. **Website:** www.magnacummurder.com. Estab. 1994.

COSTS Check website for updates.

MIDWEST WRITERS WORKSHOP

Muncie IN 47306. (765)282-1055. **E-mail:** midwestwriters@yahoo.com. **Website:** www.midwestwriters.org. **Contact:** Jama Kehoe Bigger, director.

COSTS $155-400. Most meals included.

ADDITIONAL INFORMATION Offers scholarships. See website for more information. Keep in touch with the MWW at facebook.com/midwestwriters and twitter.com/midwestwriters.

OHIO KENTUCKY INDIANA CHILDREN'S LITERATURE CONFERENCE

Northern Kentucky University, 405 Steely Library, Highland Heights KY 41099. (859)572-6620. **Fax:** (859)572-5390. **E-mail:** smithjen@nku.edu. **Website:** www.dearbornhighlandsarts.org/oki-conference-registration. **Contact:** Jennifer Smith.

COSTS $85; includes registration/attendance at all workshop sessions, continental breakfast, lunch, and author/illustrator signings. Ms critiques are available for an additional cost. E-mail or call for more information.

SPACE (SMALL PRESS AND ALTERNATIVE COMICS EXPO)

Back Porch Comics, P.O. Box 20550, Columbus OH 43220. **E-mail:** bpc013@gmail.com. **Website:** www.backporchcomics.com/space.htm. **Contact:** Bob Corby, founder.

COSTS Admission is free.

ADDITIONAL INFORMATION For brochure, visit website. Editors participate in conference.

WRITE-TO-PUBLISH CONFERENCE

WordPro Communication Services, 9118 W. Elmwood Dr., Suite 1G, Niles IL 60714. (847)296-3964. **E-mail:** lin@writetopublish.com. **Website:** www.writetopublish.com. **Contact:** Lin Johnson, director. Estab. 1971.

ACCOMMODATIONS Campus residence hall rooms available. See the website for current information and costs.

ADDITIONAL INFORMATION Conference information available in January. For details, visit website, or e-mail brochure@writetopublish.com. Accepts inquiries by e-mail, phone.

NORTH CENTRAL

IOWA SUMMER WRITING FESTIVAL

The University of Iowa, 250 Continuing Education Facility, University of Iowa, Iowa City IA 52242. (319)335-4160. **Fax:** (319)335-4039. **E-mail:** iswfestival@uiowa.edu. **Website:** www.iowasummerwritingfestival.org. Estab. 1987.

ACCOMMODATIONS Accommodations available at area hotels. Information on overnight accommodations available by phone or on website.

ADDITIONAL INFORMATION Brochures are available in February. Inquire via e-mail or on website. "Register early. Classes fill quickly."

GREAT LAKES WRITERS FESTIVAL

Lakeland College, P.O. Box 359, Sheboygan WI 53082. **E-mail:** elderk@lakeland.edu. **Website:** www.greatlakeswritersfestival.org. **Contact:** Karl Elder. Estab. 1991.

COSTS Free and open to the public. Participants may purchase meals and must arrange for their own lodging.

ACCOMMODATIONS Does not offer overnight accommodations. Provides list of area hotels and lodging options.

ADDITIONAL INFORMATION All participants who would like to have their writing considered as an object for discussion during the festival workshops should submit to Karl Elder electronically by October 15. Participants may submit material for workshops in 1 genre only (poetry, fiction, or creative nonfiction). Sponsors contest. Contest entries must contain the writer's name and address on a separate title page, typed, and be submitted as a clear, hard copy on Friday at the festival registration table. Entries may be in each of 3 genres per participant, yet only 1 poem, 1 story, and/or 1 nonfiction piece may be entered. There are 2 categories—high school students and adults—of cash awards for first place in each of the 3 genres. The judges reserve the right to decline to award a prize in 1 or more of the genres. Judges will be the editorial staff of *Seems* (a.k.a. Word of Mouth Books), excluding the festival coordinator, Karl Elder. Information available in September. For brochure, visit website.

GREEN LAKE CHRISTIAN WRITERS' CONFERENCE

W2511 State Rd. 23, Green Lake Conference Center, Green Lake WI 54941. (920)294-3323. **E-mail:** program@glcc.org. **E-mail:** kriswood@glcc.org. **Website:** glcc.org. **Contact:** Kris Wood, conference director. Estab. 1948.

COSTS Check website for updated pricing.

ACCOMMODATIONS Hotels, lodges, and all meeting rooms are air conditioned. Affordable rates, excellent meals.

ADDITIONAL INFORMATION Brochure and scholarship info available online, or contact Kris Wood.

UNIVERSITY OF WISCONSIN AT MADISON WRITERS INSTITUTE

21 N. Park St., Madison WI 53715. (608)265-3972. **E-mail:** laurie.scheer@wisc.edu. **Website:** uwwritersinstitute.wisc.edu. Estab. 1990.

COSTS $195-345, depending on discounts and if you attend one day or multiple days.

SOUTH CENTRAL

AGENTS & EDITORS CONFERENCE, WRITERS LEAGUE OF TEXAS

Writers' League of Texas, 611 S. Congress Ave., Suite 200 A-3, Austin TX 78704. (512)499-8914. **E-mail:** michael@writersleague.org. **E-mail:** michael@writersleague.org. **Website:** www.writersleague.org/38/conference. **Contact:** Michael Noll, program director. Estab. 1982.

COSTS Registration for the 2017 conference opens January 3. Early bird registration: $399 for members and $459 for nonmembers. After April 30, 2017: $439 for members and $499 for nonmembers.

ACCOMMODATIONS Discounted rates are available at the conference hotel.

ADDITIONAL INFORMATION Register before March 15 to receive a free consultation with an agent or editor.

ASPEN SUMMER WORDS LITERARY FESTIVAL & WRITING RETREAT

Aspen Words, 110 E. Hallam St., Suite 116, Aspen CO 81611. (970)925-3122. **Fax:** (970)925-5700. **E-mail:** aspenwords@aspeninstitute.org. **Website:** www.aspenwords.org. **Contact:** Caroline Tory. Estab. 1976.

COSTS $1,375. Includes some meals. Financial aid is available on a limited basis.

ADDITIONAL INFORMATION To apply for a juried workshop, submit up to 10 pages of prose with a $30 application fee by February. Registration to non-juried workshops (Beginning Fiction and Playwriting) is first-come, first-served. Call, e-mail, or visit the website for an application and complete guidelines.

AUSTIN FILM FESTIVAL & CONFERENCE

1801 Salina St., Suite 210, Austin TX 78702. (512)478-4795 or (800)310-3378. **Fax:** (512)478-6205. **Website:** www.austinfilmfestival.com. **Contact:** Conference Director. Estab. 1994.

COSTS Austin Film Festival offers 4 badge levels for entry, and access to the conference depends on the badge level. Go online for offers and to view the different options available with each badge.

CAMPBELL CONFERENCE

University of Kansas Gunn Center for the Study of Science Fiction, Wesoce Hall, 1445 Jayhawk Blvd., Lawrence KS 66045. (785)864-2508. **E-mail:** cmckit@ku.edu; cssf@ku.edu. **Website:** www.sfcenter.ku.edu/campbell-conference.htm. Estab. 1985.

ACCOMMODATIONS Housing information is available. Several airport shuttle services offer reasonable transportation from the Kansas City International Airport to Lawrence.

ADDITIONAL INFORMATION Admission to the workshop is by submission of an acceptable story. Two additional stories are submitted by the middle of June. These 3 stories are distributed to other participants for critiquing and are the basis for the first week of the workshop. One story is rewritten for the second week, when students also work with guest authors. See website for guidelines. This workshop is intended for writers who have just started to sell their work or need that extra bit of understanding or skill to become a published writer.

THE GLEN WORKSHOP

Image Journal, St. John's College, 1160 Camino Cruz Blanca, Santa Fe NM 87505. (206)281-2988. **Fax:** (206)281-2335. **E-mail:** glenworkshop@imagejournal.org. **Website:** glenworkshop.com. Estab. 1995.

COSTS See costs online. "Lodging and meals are included with registration at affordable rates. A low-cost 'commuter' rate is also available for those who wish to camp, stay with friends, or otherwise find their own food and lodging." A limited number of partial scholarships are available.

ACCOMMODATIONS Offers dorm rooms, dorm suites, and apartments.

ADDITIONAL INFORMATION "Like *Image*, the Glen is grounded in a Christian perspective, but its tone is informal and hospitable to all spiritual wayfarers. Depending on the teacher, participants may need to submit workshop material prior to arrival (usually 10-25 pages)."

TONY HILLERMAN WRITERS CONFERENCE
1063 Willow Way, Santa Fe NM 87505. (505)795-1590. **E-mail:** wordharvest@wordharvest.com. **Website:** www.wordharvest.com. **Contact:** Anne Hillerman and Jean Schaumberg, cofounders. Estab. 2004.

COSTS Check website for current pricing.

ACCOMMODATIONS Hilton Santa Fe Historic Plaza.

KINDLING WORDS WEST
Breckenridge CO **Website:** www.kindlingwords.org.

MISSOURI WRITERS' GUILD CONFERENCE
St. Louis MO **E-mail:** mwgconferenceinfo@gmail.com. **Website:** www.missouriwritersguild.org. **Contact:** Tricia Sanders, vice president/conference chair.

ADDITIONAL INFORMATION The primary contact individual changes every year, because the conference chair changes every year. See the website for contact info.

NATIONAL WRITERS ASSOCIATION FOUNDATION CONFERENCE
10940 S. Parker Rd., #508, Parker CO 80138. **E-mail:** natlwritersassn@hotmail.com. **Website:** www.nationalwriters.com. **Contact:** Sandy Whelchel, executive director. Estab. 1926.

ADDITIONAL INFORMATION Awards for previous contests will be presented at the conference. Brochures/guidelines are available online or by SASE.

THE NEW LETTERS WEEKEND WRITERS CONFERENCE
University of Missouri-Kansas City, 5101 Rockhill Rd., Kansas City MO 64110. (816)235-1168. **Fax:** (816)235-2611. **E-mail:** newletters@umkc.edu. **Website:** newletters.org/writers-wanted/nl-weekend-writing-conference. **Contact:** Robert Stewart, director. Estab. 1970s (as The Longboat Key Writers Conference).

COSTS Participants may choose to attend as a noncredit student or they may attend for 1 hour of college credit from the University of Missouri-Kansas City. Conference registration includes Friday evening reception and keynote speaker, and continental breakfast and lunch on Saturday and Sunday.

ACCOMMODATIONS Registrants are responsible for their own transportation, but information on area accommodation is available.

ADDITIONAL INFORMATION Those registering for college credit are required to submit a ms in advance. Ms reading and critique are included in the credit fee. Those attending the conference for noncredit also have the option of having their mss critiqued for an additional fee. Brochures are available for a SASE after March. Accepts inquiries by e-mail and fax.

NETWO WRITERS CONFERENCE
Northeast Texas Writers Organization, P.O. Box 962, Mt. Pleasant TX 75456. (469)867-2624 or (903)573-6084. **E-mail:** jimcallan@winnsboro.com. **Website:** www.netwo.org. Estab. 1987.

COSTS $90 for members before February 29th, and $100 after. $112.50 for nonmembers before February 29th, and $125 after.

ACCOMMODATIONS See website for information on area motels and hotels.The conference is held at the Titus County Civic Center in Mt. Pleasant, Texas.

ADDITIONAL INFORMATION Conference is co-sponsored by the Texas Commission on the Arts. See website for current updates.

NIMROD ANNUAL WRITERS' WORKSHOP
800 S. Tucker Dr., Tulsa OK 74104. (918)631-3080. **E-mail:** nimrod@utulsa.edu. **Website:** www.utulsa.edu/nimrod. **Contact:** Eilis O'Neal, editor in chief. Estab. 1978.

COSTS $60. Lunch provided. Scholarships are available for students.

ADDITIONAL INFORMATION *Nimrod International Journal* sponsors the Katherine Anne Porter Prize for fiction and the Pablo Neruda Prize for poetry. Poetry and fiction prizes: $2,000 each and publication (top prize); $1,000 each and publication (other winners). Deadline: must be postmarked no later than April 30.

NORTHERN COLORADO WRITERS CONFERENCE

407 Cormorant Court, Fort Collins CO 80525. (970)227-5746. **E-mail:** april@northerncoloradowriters.com. **Website:** www.northerncoloradowriters.com. Estab. 2006.

COSTS Prices vary depending on a number of factors. See website for details.

ACCOMMODATIONS Conference hotel may offer rooms at a discounted rate.

PIKES PEAK WRITERS CONFERENCE

Pikes Peak Writers, P.O. Box 64273, Colorado Springs CO 80962. (719)244-6220. **E-mail:** registrar@pikespeakwriters.com. **Website:** www.pikespeakwriters.com/ppwc. Estab. 1993.

COSTS $395-465 (includes all 7 meals).

ACCOMMODATIONS Marriott Colorado Springs holds a block of rooms at a special rate for attendees until late March.

ADDITIONAL INFORMATION Readings with critiques are available on Friday afternoon. Registration forms are online; brochures are available in January. Send inquiries via e-mail.

ROCKY MOUNTAIN FICTION WRITERS COLORADO GOLD CONFERENCE (SEPTEMBER)

Rocky Mountain Fiction Writers, P.O. Box 711, Montrose CO 81402, USA. **E-mail:** conference@rmfw.org. **Website:** www.rmfw.org. Estab. 1982.

COSTS Available on website.

ACCOMMODATIONS Special rates will be available at conference hotel.

ADDITIONAL INFORMATION Editor-conducted critiques are limited to 8 participants, with auditing available. Craft workshops include beginner through professional levels. Pitch appointments and book blurb critiques available at no charge. Also available for an extra charge are master classes, pitch coaching, query letter coaching, special critiques, and more.

ROMANCE WRITERS OF AMERICA NATIONAL CONFERENCE

14615 Benfer Rd., Houston TX 77069. (832)717-5200. **Fax:** (832)717-5201. **E-mail:** info@rwa.org. **Website:** www.rwa.org/conference. Estab. 1981.

COSTS $450-675 depending on your membership status as well as when you register.

ADDITIONAL INFORMATION Annual RTA awards are presented for romance authors. Annual Golden Heart awards are presented for unpublished writers. Numerous literary agents are in attendance to meet with writers and hear book pitches.

SUMMER WRITING PROGRAM

Naropa University, 2130 Arapahoe Ave., Boulder CO 80302. (303)245-4862. **Fax:** (303)546-5287. **E-mail:** swp@naropa.edu. **Website:** www.naropa.edu/swp. **Contact:** Kyle Pivarnik, special projects manager. Estab. 1974.

ADDITIONAL INFORMATION Writers can elect to take the Summer Writing Program for noncredit, graduate credit, or undergraduate credit. The registration procedure varies, so participants should consider which option they are choosing. All participants can elect to take any combination of the first, second, third, and fourth weeks. To request a catalog of upcoming programs or to find additional information, visit the website. Naropa University welcomes participants with disabilities.

TAOS SUMMER WRITERS' CONFERENCE

Department of English Language and Literature, MSC 03 2170, 1 University of New Mexico, Albuquerque NM 87131. (505)277-5572. **E-mail:** nmwriter@unm.edu. **Website:** taosconf.unm.edu. **Contact:** Sharon Oard Warner, founding director. Estab. 1999.

COSTS Week-long workshop registration: $700. Weekend workshop registration: $400. Master classes: $1,350-1,625. Publishing consultations: $175.

WRITING FOR THE SOUL

Jerry B. Jenkins Christian Writers Guild, P.O. Box 88288, Black Forest CO 80908. (866)495-7551. **Fax:** (719)494-1299. **E-mail:** jerry@jerryjenkins.com. **Website:** www.jerryjenkins.com.

THE HELENE WURLITZER FOUNDATION

P.O. Box 1891, Taos NM 87571. (575)758-2413. **Fax:** (575)758-2559. **E-mail:** hwf@taosnet.com. **Website:** www.wurlitzerfoundation.org. **Contact:** Michael A. Knight, executive director. Estab. 1954.

ACCOMMODATIONS Provides individual housing in fully furnished studios/houses (casitas), rent and utility free. Artists are responsible for transportation to and from Taos, their meals, and materials for their work. Bicycles are provided upon request.

WEST

ALTERNATIVE PRESS EXPO (APE)

Comic-Con International, P.O. Box 128458, San Diego CA 92112. (619)491-2475. **Fax:** (619)414-1022. **E-mail:** cci-info@comic-con.org. **Website:** www.alternativepressexpo.com. **Contact:** Eddie Ibrahim, director of programming.

BLOCKBUSTER PLOT INTENSIVE WRITING WORKSHOPS (SANTA CRUZ)

Santa Cruz CA **E-mail:** contact@blockbusterplots.com. **Website:** www.blockbusterplots.com. **Contact:** Martha Alderson (also known as the Plot Whisperer), instructor. Estab. 2000.

COSTS Costs vary based on the time frame of the retreat/workshop.

ACCOMMODATIONS Updated website provides list of area hotels and lodging options.

ADDITIONAL INFORMATION Accepts inquiries by e-mail.

JAMES BONNET'S STORYMAKING: THE MASTER CLASS

Santa Monica CA (310)451-5418. **E-mail:** bonnet@storymaking.com. **Website:** www.storymaking.com. **Contact:** James Bonnet. Estab. 1990.

ACCOMMODATIONS Provides a list of area hotels or lodging options.

ADDITIONAL INFORMATION For brochure, e-mail, visit website, or call. Accepts inquiries by e-mail, phone, and fax. James Bonnet is the author of *Stealing Fire From the Gods: The Complete Guide to Story for Writers and Filmmakers.*

CALIFORNIA CRIME WRITERS CONFERENCE

Sisters in Crime Los Angeles and Southern California Mystery Writers of America, DoubleTree by Hilton Los Angeles—Westside, 6161 W. Centinela Avenue, Culver City CA 90230, USA. **E-mail:** ccwconference@gmail.com. **E-mail:** ccwconference@gmail.com. **Website:** www.ccwconference.org. **Contact:** Rochelle Staab and Sue Ann Jaffarian, 2017 co-chairs. Estab. 1995.

◗   "Sisters in Crime Los Angeles and the Southern California Mystery Writers of America invite emerging and established mystery writers for a weekend of invaluable guidance, insight, and

community. Whether your novel is brewing in your imagination, ready to publish, or you already have several published books under your belt, our workshops, presented by agents, editors, award-winning authors, and crime investigation professionals, are geared to elevate your mystery writing skills and foster relationships on your path to publication and beyond."

COSTS Early bird registration through January 31: $265. Registration February 1-April 30: $300. Registration May 1-31: $335. Onsite registration: $350.

CLARION SCIENCE FICTION AND FANTASY WRITERS' WORKSHOP

Arthur C. Clarke Center for Human Imagination, University of California, San Diego, 9500 Gilman Dr., #0445, La Jolla CA 92093. (858)534-2115. **E-mail:** clarion@ucsd.edu. **Website:** clarion.ucsd.edu. **Contact:** Program Coordinator. Estab. 1968.

COSTS See website for current costs. Application fee is $50 before February 15 and $65 after. "Financial aid is awarded based on a combination of merit, need, and the criteria established by donors for particular funds. They range in size from $100 to over $3000, though most are between $500 and $1500."

ACCOMMODATIONS Participants make their own travel arrangements to and from the campus. Campus residency is required. Participants are housed in semiprivate accommodations (private bedroom, shared bathroom) in student apartments. The workshop fee includes room and board and 3 meals a day at a campus dining facility.

ADDITIONAL INFORMATION "Workshop participants are selected on the basis of their potential for highly successful writing careers. Applications are judged by a review panel composed of the workshop instructors. Applicants submit an application and 2 complete short stories, each between 2,500 words and 6,000 words. The application deadline (typically, March 1) is posted on the Clarion website." Information available in September. For additional information, visit website.

COMMUNITY OF WRITERS AT SQUAW VALLEY

Community of Writers at Squaw Valley, P.O. Box 1416, Nevada City CA 95959. (530)470-8440 or (530)583-5200 (summer). **E-mail:** info@communityofwriters.org. **Website:** www.communityofwriters.org. **Contact:** Brett Hall Jones, Executive Director. Estab. 1969.

Annual conference held in July. Conference duration: 7 days. Average attendance: 124. "Workshops in fiction, nonfiction, and memoir assist talented writers by exploring the art and craft as well as the business of writing." Offerings include daily morning workshops led by writer-teachers, editors, or agents of the staff, limited to 12-13 participants; seminars; panel discussions of editing and publishing; craft colloquies; lectures; and staff readings. Past themes and panels included "The Nation of Narrative Prose: Telling the Truth in Memoir and Personal Essay" and "Anatomy of a Short Story." The workshops are held in a ski lodge at the foot of a ski area. Literary agent speakers have recently included Michael Carlisle, Susan Golomb, Joy Harris, Mary Evans, B.J. Robbins, Janet Silver, and Peter Steinberg. Agents and editors attend/participate.

COSTS Tuition is $1,075, which includes 6 dinners. Limited financial aid is available.

ACCOMMODATIONS The Community of Writers rents houses and condominiums in the Squaw Valley for participants to live in during the week of the conference. Single room (1 participant): $700/week. Double room (twin beds, room shared by conference participant of the same gender): $465/week. Multiple room (bunk beds, room shared with 2 or more participants of the same gender): $295/week. All rooms subject to availability; early requests are recommended. Can arrange airport shuttle pickups for a fee.

INTERNATIONAL COMIC-CON

Comic-Con International, P.O. Box 128458, San Diego CA 92112. (619)491-2475. **Fax:** (619)414-1022. **E-mail:** cci-info@comic-con.org. **Website:** www.comic-con.org/cci. **Contact:** Gary Sassaman, director of print/publications. Comic-Con International, P.O. Box 128458, San Diego, CA 92112-8458. (619)491-2475. **Fax:** (619)414-1022. **E-mail:** cci-info@comic-con.org. **Website:** www.comic-con.org/cci/. Annual. Conference duration: 4 days. Average attendance: 104,000. "The comics industry's largest expo, hosting writers, artists, editors, agents, publishers, buyers and sellers of comics and graphic novels." Site: San Diego Convention Center. "Nearly 300 programming events, including panels, seminars and previews, on the world of comics, movies, television, animation,

art, and much more. We're also, of course, featuring Golden and Silver Age creators, sf/fantasy writers and artists, and longtime Comic-Con friends." Previous special guests included Ray Bradbury, Forrest J. Ackerman, Sergio Aragones, John Romita Sr., J. Michael Straczynski, Daniel Clowes, George Perez.

COSTS Prices vary. Check website for full costs.

ACCOMMODATIONS Does not offer overnight accommodations. Provides list of area hotels or lodging options. Special conference hotel and airfare discounts available. See website for details.

ADDITIONAL INFORMATION For brochure, visit website. Agents and editors participate in conference.

LAS VEGAS WRITER'S CONFERENCE

Henderson Writers' Group, P.O. Box 92032, Henderson NV 89009. (702)953-5675. **E-mail:** info@lasvegaswritersconference.com. **Website:** www.lasvegaswritersconference.com.

COSTS Costs vary depending on the package. See the website. There are early bird rates as well as deep discounts for Clark County high school students.

ADDITIONAL INFORMATION Sponsors contest. Agents and editors participate in conference.

LEAGUE OF UTAH WRITERS' ANNUAL WRITER'S CONFERENCE

Dianne Hardy, League of Utah Writers, 420 W. 750 N., Logan UT 84321. **E-mail:** luwriters@gmail.com. **Website:** www.leagueofutahwriters.org. **Contact:** Tim Keller.

MENDOCINO COAST WRITERS CONFERENCE

1211 Del Mar Dr., P.O. Box 2087, Fort Bragg CA 95437, USA. (707)485-4031. **E-mail:** info@mcwc.org. **Website:** www.mcwc.org. **Contact:** Barbara Lee, registrar; Karen Lewis, executive director. Estab. 1989.

COSTS $575 early bird registration includes morning intensives, afternoon panels and seminars, social events, and most meals. Scholarships available. Opt-in for consultations and Publishing Boot Camp. Early application advised.

ACCOMMODATIONS Many lodging options in the scenic coastal area.

ADDITIONAL INFORMATION "Take your writing to the next level with encouragement, expertise, and inspiration in a literary community where authors are also fantastic teachers." Registration opens March 15.

⊙ MOUNT HERMON CHRISTIAN WRITERS CONFERENCE

P.O. Box 413, Mount Hermon CA 95041. **E-mail:** info@mounthermon.org. **Website:** writers.mounthermon.org. Estab. 1970.

NAPA VALLEY WRITERS' CONFERENCE

Napa Valley College, 1088 College Ave., St. Helena CA 94574. (707)967-2900 ext. 4. **E-mail:** info@napawritersconference.og. **Website:** www.napawritersconference.org. **Contact:** Catherine Thorpe, managing director. Estab. 1981.

On Twitter as @napawriters and on Facebook as facebook.com/napawriters.

COSTS $975; $25 application fee.

PACIFIC COAST CHILDREN'S WRITERS WHOLE-NOVEL WORKSHOP: FOR ADULTS AND TEENS

P.O. Box 244, Aptos CA 95001. **Website:** www.childrenswritersworkshop.com. Estab. 2003.

COSTS Visit website for tiered fees (includes lodging, meals), schedule, and more; e-mail Director Nancy Sondel via the contact form.

SAN DIEGO STATE UNIVERSITY WRITERS' CONFERENCE

SDSU College of Extended Studies, 5250 Campanile Dr., San Diego State University, San Diego CA 92182. (619)594-2099. **Fax:** (619)594-8566. **E-mail:** sdsuwritersconference@mail.sdsu.edu. **Website:** ces.sdsu.edu/writers. Estab. 1984.

COSTS $495-549. Extra costs for consultations.

ACCOMMODATIONS Attendees must make their own travel arrangements. A conference rate for attendees is available at the event hotel (Marriott Mission Valley Hotel).

SAN FRANCISCO WRITERS CONFERENCE

1029 Jones St., San Francisco CA 94109. (415)673-0939. **E-mail:** barbara@sfwriters.org; sfwriterscon@aol.com. **E-mail:** See website for online contest and scholarship submissions and other details. **Website:** sfwriters.org. **Contact:** Barbara Santos, marketing director. Estab. 2003.

Keynoters for 2017: Heather Graham, William Bernhardt, John Perkins. Educational and social sessions featuring more than 120 presenters from the publishing world. Free editorial and PR consults, exhibitor hall, pitching and networking opportunities available throughout the four-day event. Also several free sessions offered to the public. See website for details or sign up for the SFWC Newsletter for updates.

COSTS Full registration is $795 (as of the 2017 event) with early bird registration discounts through February 1.

ACCOMMODATIONS The Intercontinental Mark Hopkins Hotel offers a discounted SFWC rate (based on availability). Call directly: (415)392-3434. The Mark is a historic landmark at the top of Nob Hill in San Francisco. The hotel is located so that everyone arriving at the Oakland or San Francisco airport can take the BART to either the Embarcadero or Powell Street exits, then walk or take a cable car or taxi directly to the hotel.

ADDITIONAL INFORMATION "Present yourself in a professional manner, and the contacts you will make will be invaluable to your writing career. Fliers, details, and registration information are online."

SANTA BARBARA WRITERS CONFERENCE

27 W. Anapamu St., Suite 305, Santa Barbara CA 93101. (805)568-1516. **E-mail:** info@sbwriters.com. **Website:** www.sbwriters.com. Estab. 1972.

COSTS Early conference registration is $575, and regular registration is $650.

ACCOMMODATIONS Hyatt Santa Barbara.

ADDITIONAL INFORMATION Register online or contact for brochure and registration forms.

SCBWI—CENTRAL-COASTAL CALIFORNIA; FALL CONFERENCE

P.O. Box 1500, Simi Valley CA 93062. **E-mail:** cencal@scbwi.org. **Website:** cencal.scbwi.org. **Contact:** Mary Ann Fraser, regional advisor. Estab. 1971.

SCBWI WINTER CONFERENCE ON WRITING AND ILLUSTRATING FOR CHILDREN

4727 Wilshire Blvd #301, Los Angeles CA 90010. (323)782-1010. **Fax:** (323)782-1892. **E-mail:** scbwi@scbwi.org. **Website:** www.scbwi.org. **Contact:** Stephen Mooser. Estab. 2000.

COSTS See website for current cost and conference information.

ADDITIONAL INFORMATION SCBWI also holds an annual summer conference in August in Los Angeles.

THRILLERFEST

P.O. Box 311, Eureka CA 95502. **E-mail:** kimberlyhowe@thrillerwriters.org; infocentral@thrillerwriters.org. **Website:** www.thrillerfest.com. **Contact:** Kimberley Howe, executive director. Estab. 2006.

COSTS $475-1,199, depending on which events are selected. Various package deals are available, and early bird pricing is offered beginning September of each year.

TMCC WRITERS' CONFERENCE

Truckee Meadows Community College, 7000 Dandini Blvd., Reno NV 89512. (775)673-7111. **E-mail:** wdce@tmcc.edu. **Website:** wdce.tmcc.edu. Estab. 1991.

ACCOMMODATIONS Contact the conference manager to learn about accommodation discounts.

ADDITIONAL INFORMATION "The conference is open to all writers, regardless of their level of experience. Brochures are available online and mailed in January. Send inquiries via e-mail."

UCLA EXTENSION WRITERS' PROGRAM

10995 Le Conte Ave., Suite 440, Los Angeles CA 90024. (310)825-9415. **Fax:** (310)206-7382. **E-mail:** writers@uclaextension.edu. **Website:** www.uclaextension.edu/writers. Estab. 1891. 10995 Le Conte Avenue, #440, Los Angeles CA 90024. (310)825-9415. **Fax:** (310)206-7382. **E-mail:** writers@uclaextension.edu. **Website:** www.uclaextension.edu/writers. **Contact:** Cindy Lieberman, program manager. Courses held year-round with one-day or intensive weekend workshops to 12-week courses. Writers Studio held in February. Nine-month master classes are also offered every fall. "The diverse offerings span introductory seminars to professional novel and script completion workshops. The annual Writers Studio and a number of one-, two- and four-day intensive workshops are popular with out-of-town students due to their specific focus and the chance to work with industry professionals. The most comprehensive and diverse continuing education writing program in the country, offering over 550 courses a year, including screenwriting, fiction, writing for the youth market, poetry, nonfiction, playwriting and publishing. Adult learners in the UCLA Extension Writers' Program study with professional screenwriters, fiction writers, playwrights, poets, and nonfiction writers, who bring practical experience, theoretical knowledge, and a wide variety of teaching styles and philosophies to their classes." Site: Courses are offered in Los Angeles on the UCLA campus, in the 1010 Westwood Center in Westwood Village, at the Figueroa Courtyard in downtown Los Angeles, as well as online.

COSTS Depends on length of the course.

ACCOMMODATIONS Students make their own arrangements. Out-of-town students are encouraged to take online courses.

ADDITIONAL INFORMATION Some advanced-level classes have ms submittal requirements; see the UCLA Extension catalog or visit website.

WRITERS STUDIO AT UCLA EXTENSION

1010 Westwood Blvd., Los Angeles CA 90024. (310)825-9415. **E-mail:** writers@uclaextension.edu. **Website:** writers.uclaextension.edu/programs-services/writers-studio. **Contact:** Katy Flaherty. Estab. 1997.

ADDITIONAL INFORMATION For more information, call or e-mail.

WRITERS@WORK WRITING RETREAT

P.O. Box 711191, Salt Lake City UT 84171. (801)996-3313. **E-mail:** jennifer@writersatwork.org. **Website:** www.writersatwork.org. Estab. 1985.

💬 There are several pricing levels for this event, depending on lodging and if the attendee wants a private consultation.

COSTS $650-1,000, based on housing type and consultations.

ACCOMMODATIONS Onsite housing available. Additional lodging information is on the website.

WRITING AND ILLUSTRATING FOR YOUNG READERS CONFERENCE

1480 E. 9400 S., Sandy UT 84093. **E-mail:** staff@wifyr.com. **Website:** www.wifyr.com. Estab. 2000. BYU, conferences and workshops, 348 HCEB, BYU, Provo UT 84602-1532. (801)422-2568. **Fax:** (801)422-0745. **E-mail:** cw348@byu.edu. **Website:** wifyr.byu.edu. **Contact:** Conferences & Workshops. Estab. 2000. Annual. 5-day workshop held in June of each year. The workshop is designed for people who want to write or illustrate for children or teenagers. Participants focus on a single market during daily four-hour morning writing workshops led by published authors or illustrators. Afternoon workshop sessions include a mingle with the authors, editors and agents. Workshop focuses on fiction for young readers: picture books, book-length fiction, fantasy/science fiction, nonfiction, mystery, illustration and general writing. Site: Conference Center at Brigham Young University in the foothills of the Wasatch Mountain range.

💬 Guidelines and registration are on the website.

ACCOMMODATIONS A block of rooms is available at the Best Western Cotton Tree Inn in Sandy, UT, at a discounted rate. This rate is good as long as there are available rooms.

ADDITIONAL INFORMATION There is an online form to contact this event.

NORTHWEST

ALASKA WRITERS CONFERENCE

Alaska Writers Guild, P.O. Box 670014, Chugiak AK 99567. **E-mail:** alaskawritersguild.awg@gmail.com. **Website:** alaskawritersguild.com.

○ Ms critiques available. Note also that the Alaska Writers Guild has many events and meetings each year, not just the annual conference.

CENTRUM'S PORT TOWNSEND WRITERS' CONFERENCE

P.O. Box 1158, Port Townsend WA 98368. (360)385-3102. **E-mail:** info@centrum.org. **Website:** centrum.org/the-port-townsend-writers-conference. **Contact:** Jordan Hartt, director of programs. Estab. 1974. P.O. Box 1158, Port Townsend, WA 98368. (360)385-3102. **Fax:** (360)385-2470. **E-mail:** info@centrum.org; jhartt@centrum.org. **Website:** www.centrum.org. Estab. 1974. Annual. Conference held mid-July. Average attendance: 180. Conference to promote poetry, fiction, and creative nonfiction "featuring many of the nation's leading writers." Two different workshop options: "New Works" and "Works-in-Progress." Site: The conference is held at Fort Worden State Park on the Strait of Juan de Fuca. "The site is a Victorian-era military fort with miles of beaches, wooded trails, and recreation facilities. The park is within the limits of Port Townsend, a historic seaport and arts community, approximately 80 miles northwest of Seattle, on the Olympic Peninsula." Guest speakers participate in addition to full-time faculty.

COSTS Tuition for the conference is $200-700. Admission to afternoon workshops is $200-300. Register online.

ACCOMMODATIONS "Modest room and board facilities on site." Provides list of area lodging options.

ADDITIONAL INFORMATION Brochures/guidelines available for SASE or on website. "The conference focus is on the craft of writing and the writing life, not on marketing."

CLARION WEST WRITERS WORKSHOP

P.O. Box 31264, Seattle WA 98103. (206)322-9083. **E-mail:** info@clarionwest.org. **Website:** www.clarionwest.org. **Contact:** Nelle Graham, workshop director.

○ "Students write their own stories every week while preparing critiques of all the other students' work for classroom sessions. This gives participants a more focused, professional approach to their writing. The core of the workshop remains speculative fiction, and short stories (not novels) are the focus."

COSTS $4,200 (for tuition, housing, most meals). Limited scholarships are available based on financial need. Students can apply by mail or e-mail and must submit 20-30 pages of ms with four-page biography and $60 fee ($35 if received by February 10).

ACCOMMODATIONS Students stay on-site in workshop housing at one of the University of Washington's sorority houses.

ADDITIONAL INFORMATION Conference information available in fall. For brochure/guidelines, send SASE, visit website, e-mail, or call.

EMERALD CITY COMICON

3333 184th St. SW. Suite G, Lynnwood WA 98037. (425)744-2767. **Fax:** (425)675-0737. **E-mail:** info@emeraldcitycomicon.com; ksalierno@reedexpo.com. **Website:** www.emeraldcitycomicon.com. **Contact:** Kristen Salierno, operations manager. Estab. 2002.

COSTS Prices vary based on day.

ACCOMMODATIONS Offers discounted rate at Roosevelt Hotel, Crowne Plaza, and Red Lion in Seattle.

HEDGEBROOK

P.O. Box 1231, Freeland WA 98249. (360)321-4786. **Fax:** (360)321-2171. **Website:** www.hedgebrook.org. **Contact:** Vito Zingarelli, residency director. Estab. 1988.

ADDITIONAL INFORMATION Takes applications 6 months in advance.

KACHEMAK BAY WRITERS' CONFERENCE

Kachemak Bay Campus—Kenai Peninsula College/University of Alaska Anchorage, Kenai Peninsula College—Kachemak Bay Campus, 533 E. Pioneer Ave., Homer AK 99603. (907)235-7743. **E-mail:** iyconf@uaa.alaska.edu. **Website:** writersconf.kpc.alaska.edu.

○ Previous keynote speakers have included Natasha Trethewey, Dave Barry, Amy Tan, Jeffrey Eugenides, and Anne Lamott.

COSTS See the website. Some scholarships available.

ACCOMMODATIONS Homer is 225 miles south of Anchorage, Alaska, on the southern tip of the Kenai

Peninsula and the shores of Kachemak Bay. There are multiple hotels in the area.

IDAHO WRITERS LEAGUE WRITERS' CONFERENCE

601 W. 75 St., Blackfoot ID 83221. (208)684-4200. **Website:** www.idahowritersleague.org. Estab. 1940. **COSTS** Pricing varies. Check website for more information.

JACKSON HOLE WRITERS CONFERENCE

P.O. Box 1974, Jackson WY 83001. (307)413-3332. **E-mail:** connie@blackhen.com. **Website:** jacksonhole-writersconference.com. Estab. 1991.
ADDITIONAL INFORMATION Held at the Center for the Arts in Jackson, Wyoming, and online.

NORWESCON

100 Andover Park W. Suite 150-165, Tukwila WA 98188. (425)243-4692. **E-mail:** info@norwescon.org. **Website:** www.norwescon.org. Estab. 1978.
ACCOMMODATIONS Conference is held at the Doubletree Hotel Seattle Airport.

OREGON CHRISTIAN WRITERS SUMMER CONFERENCE

1075 Willow Lake Rd. N., Keizer OR 97303. **E-mail:** summerconference@oregonchristianwriters.org. **Website:** www.oregonchristianwriters.org. **Contact:** Lindy Jacobs, summer conference director. Estab. 1989.
COSTS $525 for OCW members, $560 for nonmembers. Registration fee includes all classes, workshops, and 2 lunches and 3 dinners. Lodging additional. Full-time registered attendees may also pre-submit 3 proposals for review by an editor (or agent) through the conference, plus sign up for a half-hour mentoring appointment with an author.
ACCOMMODATIONS Conference is held at the Red Lion on the River Hotel. Attendees wishing to stay at the hotel must make a reservation through the hotel. A block of rooms is reserved at a special rate and held until mid-July. The hotel reservation link is posted on the website in late spring. Shuttle bus transportation is provided from Portland Airport (PDX) to the hotel, which is 20 minutes away.
ADDITIONAL INFORMATION Conference details posted online beginning in January. All conferees are welcome to attend the Cascade Awards ceremony, which takes place Wednesday evening during the conference. For more information about the Cascade Writing Contest, please check the website.

OUTDOOR WRITERS ASSOCIATION OF AMERICA ANNUAL CONFERENCE

615 Oak St., Suite 201, Missoula MT 59801. (406)728-7434. **E-mail:** info@owaa.org. **Website:** owaa.org. **Contact:** Jessica Seitz, conference and membership coordinator. Estab. 1927.
COSTS Before April 28, $225 for members and $425 for nonmembers. After April 28, $249 for members and $449 for nonmembers. Single-day rates are also available.

PNWA SUMMER WRITERS CONFERENCE

Writers' Cottage, 317 NW Gilman Blvd. Suite 8, Issaquah WA 98027. (425)673-2665. **E-mail:** pnwa@pnwa.org. **Website:** www.pnwa.org. Estab. 1955.

SITKA CENTER FOR ART AND ECOLOGY

56605 Sitka Dr., Otis OR 97368. (541)994-5485. **Fax:** (541)994-8024. **E-mail:** info@sitkacenter.org. **Website:** www.sitkacenter.org. **Contact:** Mindy Chaffin, program manager. Estab. 1970.
COSTS Workshops are generally $25-505; they do not include meals or lodging.
ACCOMMODATIONS Does not offer overnight accommodations. Provides a list of area hotels or lodging options.
ADDITIONAL INFORMATION Brochure available in February of each year; request a copy by e-mail or phone, or visit website for listing. Accepts inquiries in person or by e-mail, phone, or fax.

SOUTH COAST WRITERS CONFERENCE

Southwestern Oregon Community College, P.O. Box 590, 29392 Ellensburg Ave., Gold Beach OR 97444. (541)247-2741. **Fax:** (541)247-6247. **E-mail:** scwc@socc.edu. **Website:** www.socc.edu/scwriters. **Contact:** Karim Shumaker. Estab. 1996.
COSTS Friday workshop cost is $55. Saturday conference cost is $60 before January 31 and $70 after. Fish fry lunch is $14 if purchased in advance, or $15 at the door.
ACCOMMODATIONS List of local motels that offer discounts to conference participants is available on request.

TIN HOUSE SUMMER WRITERS WORKSHOP

Tin House, 2601 NW Thurman Street, Portland OR 97210. (503)219-0622. **Fax:** (503)222-1154. **E-mail:** lance@tinhouse.com. **Website:** www.tinhouse.com/blog/workshop. **Contact:** Lance Cleland. Estab. 2003.

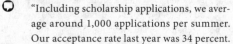 "Including scholarship applications, we average around 1,000 applications per summer. Our acceptance rate last year was 34 percent.

Applications are rolling. Other than for scholarships, there is no firm deadline for applying, though we do tend to start filling up in early May. The average turnaround time for applications is six weeks."

COSTS Tuition: $1,100. Room and board: $650. Mentorships: $750-1,000. Auditing: $300. There is a $40 application fee. Scholarships are available.

ACCOMMODATIONS "The Tin House Summer Writers Workshop is held at Reed College, located on 100 acres of rolling lawns, winding lanes, and magnificent old trees in the southeast area of Portland, Oregon, just minutes from downtown and 12 miles from the airport."

ADDITIONAL INFORMATION Attendees must apply; all information available online.

WRITE ON THE SOUND

WOTS, City of Edmonds Arts Commission, Frances Anderson Center, 700 Main St., Edmonds WA 98020. (425)771-0228. **E-mail:** wots@edmondswa.gov. **Website:** www.writeonthesound.com. **Contact:** Laurie Rose or Frances Chapin. Estab. 1985.

Past attendee says, "I came away from every session with ideas to incorporate into my own writer's toolbox. The energy was wonderful because everyone was there for a single purpose: to make the most of a weekend for writers, whatever the level of expertise. I can't thank all the organizers, presenters, and volunteers enough for a wonderful experience."

COSTS $80-155 (not including optional fees).

ACCOMMODATIONS Best Western Plus/Edmonds Harbor Inn.

ADDITIONAL INFORMATION Schedule posted on website late spring/early summer. Registration opens mid-July. Review the schedule and register early. Attendees are required to select the sessions they wish to attend at the time of registration. Registration fills quickly, and day-of, on-site registration is not available. Waiting lists for conference and ms appointments are available.

CANADA

SAGE HILL WRITING EXPERIENCE

324-1831 College Avenue, Regina Saskatchewan S4P 4V5, Canada. (306)537-7243. **E-mail:** sage.hill@sasktel.net. **Website:** sagehillwriting.ca.

ACCOMMODATIONS Located at Lumsden, 45 kilometers outside Regina.

ADDITIONAL INFORMATION See the website for pricing and current course offerings.

SASKATCHEWAN FESTIVAL OF WORDS

217 Main St. N., Moose Jaw Saskatchewan S6H 0W1, Canada. **E-mail:** amanda@festivalofwords.com. **Website:** www.festivalofwords.com. Estab. 1997.

INTERNATIONAL

ART WORKSHOPS IN GUATEMALA

4758 Lyndale Ave. S., Minneapolis MN 55419. (612)825-0747. **E-mail:** info@artguat.org. **Website:** www.artguat.org. **Contact:** Liza Fourre, director. Estab. 1995.

COSTS See website. Includes tuition, lodging, breakfast, and ground transportation.

ADDITIONAL INFORMATION For brochure/guidelines, visit website, e-mail, or call.

BREAD LOAF IN SICILY WRITERS' CONFERENCE

Middlebury College, Middlebury College, Middlebury VT 05753. (802)443-5286. **Fax:** (802)443-2087. **E-mail:** blsicily@middlebury.edu. **Website:** www.middlebury.edu/bread-loaf-conferences/blsicily. Estab. 2011.

COSTS $3,020. Includes the conference program, transfer to and from Palermo Airport, 6 nights of lodging, 3 meals daily (except for Wednesday), wine reception at the readings, and an excursion to the ancient ruins of Segesta. The charge for an additional person is $1,750. There is a $15 application fee an a $300 deposit.

ACCOMMODATIONS Accommodations are single rooms with private bath. Breakfast and lunch are served at the hotel, and dinner is available at select Erice restaurants. A double room is possible for those who would like to be accompanied by a spouse or significant other.

ADDITIONAL INFORMATION Application deadline for 2017 conference: April 15. Rolling admissions. Space is limited.

BYRON WRITERS FESTIVAL

Northern Rivers Writers' Centre, P.O. Box 1846, Byron Bay New South Wales 2481, Australia. (61)

(02)6685-5115. **Website:** www.byronwritersfestival.com. **Contact:** Edwina Johnson, director. Estab. 1997.
COSTS See website for details. Costs vary for early bird registration, NRWC members, students, and children.

☯ INTERNATIONAL MUSIC CAMP CREATIVE WRITING WORKSHOP

111 11th Ave. SW, Minot ND 58701. (701)838-8472. **Fax:** (701)838-1351. **E-mail:** info@internationalmusiccamp.com. **Website:** www.internationalmusiccamp.com. **Contact:** Christine Baumann and Tim Baumann, camp directors. Estab. 1956.
COSTS Fees vary based on activities. Check website for full details.
ACCOMMODATIONS Airline and depot shuttles are available upon request. Housing is included in the fee.
ADDITIONAL INFORMATION Conference information is available on the website. Welcomes questions via e-mail.

☯◎ INTERNATIONAL WOMEN'S FICTION FESTIVAL

Via Cappuccini 8E, Matera , Italy. (39)0835-312044. **Fax:** (39)333-5857933. **E-mail:** contact@womensfictionfestival.com. **Website:** www.womensfictionfestival.com. **Contact:** Elizabeth Jennings. Estab. 2004.
COSTS Registration costs vary. Check website for full details.
ACCOMMODATIONS The conference is held at Le Monacelle, a restored 17th century convent. Conference travel agency will find reasonably priced accommodation. A paid shuttle is available from the Bari Airport to the hotel in Matera.

☯◎ SALT CAY WRITERS RETREAT

Salt Cay , Bahamas. (732)267-6449. **E-mail:** admin@saltcaywritersretreat.com. **Website:** www.saltcaywritersretreat.com. **Contact:** Karen Dionne and Christopher Graham.

Includes individualized instruction from best-selling authors and top editors and literary agents; dolphin swim; built-in scheduled writing time; evening gatherings with student and author readings; and closing festivities, including authentic Bahamian feast. All sleeping rooms at the retreat hotel are suites. Free or deeply discounted activities for families, including water park, water bikes, kayaks, dolphin and sea lion encounters, snorkeling, scuba-diving, and much more. Complimentary guest access to Atlantis Resort & Casino.
COSTS $2,450 through May 1; $2,950 after.
ACCOMMODATIONS Comfort Suites, Paradise Island, Nassau, Bahamas.

☯ THE UNIVERSITY OF WINCHESTER WRITERS' FESTIVAL

University of Winchester, Winchester Hampshire S022 4NR, United Kingdom. (44)(0)1962-827238. **E-mail:** judith.heneghan@winchester.ac.uk. **Website:** www.writersfestival.co.uk. **Contact:** Judith Heneghan, festival director. Estab. 1980.
COSTS See festival program.
ACCOMMODATIONS On-site student single en-suite accommodation available. Also, a range of hotels and bed and breakfasts nearby in the city.
ADDITIONAL INFORMATION Lunch, and tea/coffee/cake included in the booking cost. Dinner can be booked separately. All dietary needs catered for.

☯ WRITE IT OUT

P.O. Box 704, Sarasota FL 34230. (941)359-3824. **E-mail:** rmillerwio@aol.com. **Website:** www.writeitout.com. **Contact:** Ronni Miller, director. Estab. 1997.
COSTS Costs vary by workshop.
ADDITIONAL INFORMATION Conference information available year round. For brochures/guidelines e-mail, call, or visit website. Accepts inquiries by phone, e-mail.

PUBLISHERS & THEIR IMPRINTS

//

The publishing world is in constant transition. With all the buying, selling, reorganizing, consolidating, and dissolving, it's hard to keep publishers and their imprints straight. To help make sense of these changes, here's a breakdown of major publishers (and their divisions)—who owns whom and which imprints are under each company umbrella. Keep in mind that this information changes frequently. The website of each publisher is provided to help you keep an eye on this ever-evolving business.

HACHETTE BOOK GROUP

www.hachettebookgroup.com

GRAND CENTRAL PUBLISHING
Forever
Forever Yours
Grand Central Life & Style
Twelve
Vision

HACHETTE AUDIO

HACHETTE BOOKS
Black Dog & Leventhal
Jericho Books

HACHETTE NASHVILLE
Center Street
Faith Words

LITTLE, BROWN AND COMPANY
Back Bay Books

Jimmy Patterson

Lee Boudreaux Books

Mulholland Books

LITTLE, BROWN BOOKS FOR YOUNG READERS

LB Kids

Poppy

ORBIT

Redhook

Yen Press

PERSEUS

Avalon Travel

Basic Books

Da Capo

PublicAffairs

Running Press

HARPERCOLLINS

www.harpercollins.com

ADULT

Amistad

Anthony Bourdain Books

Avon

Avon Impulse

Avon Inspire

Avon Red

Bourbon Street Books

Broadside Books

Custom House

Dey Street

Ecco Books

Harper Books

Harper Business

Harper Design

Harper Luxe

Harper Paperbacks

Harper Perennial

Harper Voyager

Harper Wave

HarperAudio

HarperCollins 360

HarperElixir

HarperLegend

HarperOne

William Morrow

William Morrow Paperbacks

Witness

CHILDREN'S

Amistad

Balzer + Bray

Greenwillow Books

HarperAudio

HarperCollins Children's Books

HarperFestival

HarperTeen

HarperTeen Impulse

Katherine Tegen Books

Walden Pond Press

CHRISTIAN PUBLISHING

Bible Gateway

Blink

Editorial Vida

FaithGateway

Grupo Nelson

Nelson Books

Olive Tree

Thomas Nelson

Tommy Nelson

W Publishing Group

WestBow Press

Zonderkidz

Zondervan

Zondervan Academic

HARLEQUIN

Carina Press
Harlequin Books
Harlequin TEEN
HQN Books
Kimani Press
Love Inspired
MIRA Books
Worldwide Mystery

HARPERCOLLINS AUSTRALIA

HARPERCOLLINS CANADA

Collins
Harper Avenue
Harper Perennial
Harper Weekend
HarperCollins Canada
Patrick Crean Editions

HARPERCOLLINS INDIA

HARPERCOLLINS NEW ZEALAND

HARPERCOLLINS UK

4th Estate
Avon
Carina
Collins
Harper Audio
Harper Voyager
Harper360
HarperCollins Children's Books
HarperFiction
HarperImpulse
HarperNonFiction
Mills & Boon
MIRA
MIRA Ink
The Borough Press

Times Books

William Collins

MACMILLAN PUBLISHERS

us.macmillan.com

DISTRIBUTED PUBLISHERS

Bloomsbury USA and Walker & Company

The College Board

Drawn and Quarterly

Entangled Publishing

Graywolf Press

Guinness World Records

Media Lab Books

Page Street Publishing Co.

Papercutz

Rodale

FARRAR, STRAUS AND GIROUX

Faber and Faber Inc.

Farrar, Straus and Giroux Books for Young Readers

FSG Originals

Hill and Wang

North Point Press

Sarah Crichton Books

Scientific American

FIRST SECOND

FLATIRON BOOKS

HENRY HOLT & CO.

Henry Holt Books for Young Readers

Holt Paperbacks

Metropolitan Books

Times Books

MACMILLAN AUDIO

MACMILLAN CHILDREN'S

Farrar, Straus & Giroux for Young Readers

Feiwel & Friends
Henry Holt Books for Young Readers
Imprint
Kingfisher
Macmillan Children's Publishing Group
Priddy Books
Roaring Brook Press
Square Fish
Tor Children's

PICADOR

QUICK AND DIRTY TIPS

ST. MARTIN'S PRESS
Griffin
Let's Go
Minotaur Books
St. Martin's Press Paperbacks
Thomas Dunne Books
Truman Talley Books

TOR/FORGE
Starscape
Tor Teen Books

PENGUIN RANDOM HOUSE

www.penguinrandomhouse.com

CROWN PUBLISHING GROUP
Amphoto Books
Broadway Books
Clarkson Potter
Convergent Books
Crown
Crown Archetype
Crown Business
Crown Forum
Harmony Books
Hogarth

Image Catholic Books

Pam Krauss Books

Potter Craft

Potter Style

Ten Speed Press

Three Rivers Press

Tim Duggan Books

WaterBrook Multnomah

Watson-Guptill

KNOPF DOUBLEDAY PUBLISHING GROUP

Alfred A. Knopf

Anchor Books

Doubleday

Everyman's Library

Nan A. Talese

Pantheon Books

Schocken Books

Vintage Books

Vintage Espanol

PENGUIN

Avery

Berkley

Blue Rider Press

DAW

Dial Books for Young Readers

Dutton

Dutton Children's Books

Firebird

Frederick Warne

G.P. Putnam's Sons

G.P. Putnam's Sons Books for Young Readers

Grosset & Dunlap

InterMix

Kathy Dawson Books

Nancy Paulsen Books

Penguin

Penguin Audio

Peguin Classics

Penguin Press

Penguin Workshop

Penguin Young Readers

Philomel

Plume

Portfolio

Price Stern Sloan

Puffin

Razorbill

Riverhead

Speak

TarcherPerigee

Viking Books

Viking Children's Books

PENGUIN RANDOM HOUSE PUBLISHING GROUP

Alibi

Ballantine Books

Bantam

Delacorte Press

Dell

Del Rey

Del Rey/LucasBooks

The Dial Press

Flirt

Hydra

Loveswept

Lucas Books

One World

The Modern Library

Penguin Random House Trade Group

Penguin Random House Trade Paperbacks

Presidio Press

Random House

Spiegel & Grau

PENGUIN RANDOM HOUSE CHILDREN'S BOOKS

Alfred A. Knopf

Crown

Delacorte Press

Doubleday

Dragonfly Books

Ember

Kids@Random (RH Children's Books)

Golden Books

Laurel-Leaf Books

Now I'm Reading!

The Princeton Review

Random House Books for Young Readers

Schwartz & Wade Books

Sylvan Learning

Wendy Lamb Books

Yearling Books

RANDOM HOUSE AUDIO/LIVING LANGUAGE

Books on Tape

Living Language

Listening Library

Penguin Random House Audio Publishing

RH Large Print

RH INTERNATIONAL

Penguin Random House Australia

The Penguin Random House Group (UK)

Penguin Random House Grupo Editorial (Argentina)

Penguin Random House Grupo Editorial (Chile)

Penguin Random House Grupo Editorial (Colombia)

Penguin Random House Grupo Editorial (Mexico)

Penguin Random House Grupo Editorial (Peru)

Penguin Random House Grupo Editorial (Portugal)

Penguin Random House Grupo Editorial (Spain)

Penguin Random House Grupo Editorial (Uruguay)

Penguin Random House India

Penguin Random House New Zealand

Penguin Random House of Canada

Penguin Random House Struik (South Africa)

Transworld Ireland

Verlagsgruppe Penguin Random House

SIMON & SCHUSTER

www.simonandschuster.com

SIMON & SCHUSTER ADULT PUBLISHING

Adams Media

Atria

Emily Bestler Books

Enliven

Folger Shakespeare Library

Free Press

Gallery

Howard

Jeter Publishing

North Star Way

Pocket

Pocket Star

Scout Press

Scribner

Simon & Schuster

Threshold

Touchstone

SIMON & SCHUSTER CHILDREN'S PUBLISHING

Aladdin

Atheneum

Simon & Schuster Books for Young Readers

Beach Lane Books

Little Simon

Margaret K. McElderry

Paula Wiseman Books

Saga Press

Salaam Reads

Simon Pulse

Simon Spotlight

SIMON & SCHUSTER AUDIO PUBLISHING

Pimsleur

Simon & Schuster Audio

SIMON & SCHUSTER INTERNATIONAL

Simon & Schuster Australia

Simon & Schuster Canada

Simon & Schuster UK

GLOSSARY

ADVANCE. Payment by a publisher to an author prior to the publication of a book, to be deducted from the author's future royalties.

ADVENTURE STORY. A genre of fiction in which action is the key element, overshadowing characters, theme, and setting. The conflict in an adventure story is often man against nature. A secondary plot that reinforces this kind of conflict is sometimes included.

ALL RIGHTS. The rights contracted to a publisher permitting a manuscript's use anywhere and in any form, including movie and book club sales, without additional payment to the writer.

AMATEUR SLEUTH. The character in a mystery, usually the protagonist, who does the detection but is not a professional private investigator or police detective.

ANTHOLOGY. A collection of selected writings by various authors.

ASSOCIATION OF AUTHORS' REPRESENTATIVES (AAR). An organization for literary agents committed to maintaining excellence in literary representation.

AUCTION. Publishers sometimes bid against each other for the acquisition of a manuscript that has excellent sales prospects.

BACKLIST. A publisher's books not published during the current season but still in print.

BIOGRAPHICAL NOVEL. A life story documented in history and transformed into fiction through the insight and imagination of the writer. This type of novel melds the elements of biographical research and historical truth into the framework of a novel, complete with dialogue, drama, and mood. A biographical novel resembles historical fiction, save for one aspect: Characters in a historical novel may be fabricated and then placed into an authentic setting; characters in a biographical novel have actually lived.

BOOK PRODUCER/PACKAGER. An organization that may develop a book for a publisher based upon the publisher's idea or may plan all elements of a book, from its initial concept to writing and marketing strategies, and then sell the package to a book publisher and/or movie producer.

CLIFFHANGER. Fictional event in which the reader is left in suspense at the end of a chapter or episode, so that interest in the story's outcome will be sustained.

CLIP. Sample, usually from a newspaper or magazine, of a writer's published work.

CLOAK-AND-DAGGER. A melodramatic, romantic type of fiction dealing with espionage and intrigue.

COMMERCIAL. Publishers whose concern is salability, profit, and success with a large readership.

CONTEMPORARY. Material dealing with popular current trends, themes, or topics.

CONTRIBUTOR'S COPY. Copy of an issue of a magazine or published book sent to an author whose work is included.

CO-PUBLISHING. An arrangement in which the author and publisher share costs and profits.

COPYEDITING. Editing a manuscript for writing style, grammar, punctuation and factual accuracy.

COPYRIGHT. The legal right to exclusive publication, sale, or distribution of a literary work.

COVER LETTER. A brief letter sent with a complete manuscript submitted to an editor.

"COZY" (OR "TEACUP") MYSTERY. Mystery usually set in a small British town, in a bygone era, featuring a somewhat genteel, intellectual protagonist.

ELECTRONIC RIGHTS. The right to publish material electronically, either in book or short story form.

ELECTRONIC SUBMISSION. A submission of material by e-mail or on computer disk.

ETHNIC FICTION. Stories whose central characters are black, Native American, Italian-American, Jewish, Appalachian, or members of some other specific cultural group.

EXPERIMENTAL FICTION. Fiction that is innovative in subject matter and style; avant-garde, non-formulaic, usually literary material.

EXPOSITION. The portion of the story line, usually the beginning, where background information about character and setting is related.

E-ZINE. A magazine that is published electronically.

FAIR USE. A provision in the copyright law that says short passages from copyrighted material may be used without infringing on the owner's rights.

FANTASY (TRADITIONAL). Fantasy with an emphasis on magic, using characters with the ability to practice magic, such as wizards, witches, dragons, elves, and unicorns.

FANZINE. A noncommercial, small-circulation magazine usually dealing with fantasy, horror or science-fiction literature and art.

FIRST NORTH AMERICAN SERIAL RIGHTS. The right to publish material in a periodical before it appears in book form, for the first time, in the United States or Canada.

FLASH FICTION. *See* short short story.

GALLEY PROOF. The first typeset version of a manuscript that has not yet been divided into pages.

GENRE. A formulaic type of fiction such as romance, western, or horror.

GOTHIC. This type of category fiction dates back to the late eighteenth and early nineteenth centuries. Contemporary gothic novels are characterized by atmospheric, historical settings and feature young, beautiful women who win the favor of handsome, brooding heroes—simultaneously dealing successfully with some life-threatening menace, either natural or supernatural. Gothics rely on mystery, peril, romantic relationships, and a sense of foreboding for their strong, emotional effect on the reader. A classic early gothic novel is Emily Brontë's *Wuthering Heights*.

GRAPHIC NOVEL. A book (original or adapted) that takes the form of a long comic strip or heavily illustrated story of forty pages or more, produced in paperback. Though called a novel, these can also be works of nonfiction.

HARD-BOILED DETECTIVE NOVEL. Mystery novel featuring a private eye or police detective as the protagonist; usually involves a murder. The emphasis is on the details of the crime, and the tough, unsentimental protagonist usually takes a matter-of-fact attitude toward violence.

HARD SCIENCE FICTION. Science fiction with an emphasis on science and technology.

HIGH FANTASY. Fantasy with a medieval setting and a heavy emphasis on chivalry and the quest.

HISTORICAL FICTION. A fictional story set in a recognizable period of history. As well as telling the stories of ordinary people's lives, historical fiction may involve political or social events of the time.

HORROR. Howard Phillips (H.P.) Lovecraft, generally acknowledged to be the master of the horror tale in the twentieth century and the most important American writer of this genre since Edgar Allan Poe, distinguishes horror literature from fiction based entirely on physical fear and the merely gruesome. It is that atmosphere—the creation of a particular sensation or emotional level—that, according to Lovecraft, is the most important element in the creation of horror literature. Contemporary writers enjoying considerable success in horror fiction include Stephen King, Robert Bloch, Peter Straub, and Dean Koontz.

HYPERTEXT FICTION. A fictional form, read electronically, that incorporates traditional elements of storytelling with a nonlinear plot line, in which the reader determines the direction of the story by opting for one of many author-supplied links.

IMPRINT. Name applied to a publisher's specific line (e.g., Owl, an imprint of Henry Holt).

INTERACTIVE FICTION. Fiction in book or computer-software format where the reader determines the path the story will take by choosing from several alternatives at the end of each chapter or episode.

INTERNATIONAL REPLY COUPON (IRC). A form purchased at a post office and enclosed with a letter or manuscript to an international publisher, to cover return postage costs.

JUVENILES, WRITING FOR. This includes works intended for an audience usually between the ages of two and eighteen. Categories of children's books are usually divided in this way: (1) picture books and storybooks (ages two to eight); (2) young readers or easy-to-read books (ages five to eight); (3) middle readers or middle grade (ages nine to eleven); (4) young adult books (ages twelve and up).

LIBEL. Written or printed words that defame, malign, or damagingly misrepresent a living person.

LITERARY AGENT. A person who acts for an author in finding a publisher or arranging contract terms on a literary project.

LITERARY FICTION. The general category of fiction that employs more sophisticated technique, driven as much or more by character evolution than action in the plot.

MAINSTREAM FICTION. Fiction that appeals to a more general reading audience, versus literary or genre fiction. Mainstream is more plot-driven than literary fiction and less formulaic than genre fiction.

MALICE DOMESTIC NOVEL. A mystery featuring a murder among family members, such as the murder of a spouse or a parent.

MANUSCRIPT. The author's unpublished copy of a work, usually typewritten, used as the basis for typesetting.

MASS MARKET PAPERBACK. Softcover book on a popular subject, usually around 4" × 7", directed to a general audience and sold in drugstores and groceries as well as in bookstores.

MIDDLE READER. Also called *middle grade*. Juvenile fiction for readers aged nine to eleven.

MS(S). Abbreviation for *manuscript(s)*.

MULTIPLE SUBMISSION. Submission of more than one short story at a time to the same editor. *Do not make a multiple submission unless requested.*

MYSTERY. A form of narration in which one or more elements remain unknown or unexplained until the end of the story. The modern mystery story contains elements of the mainstream novel: a convincing account of a character's struggle with various physical and psychological obstacles in an effort to achieve his goal, good characterization, and sound motivation.

NARRATION. The account of events in a story's plot as related by the speaker or the voice of the author.

NARRATOR. The person who tells the story, either someone involved in the action or the voice of the writer.

NEW AGE. A term including categories such as astrology, psychic phenomena, spiritual healing, UFOs, mysticism, and other aspects of the occult.

NOIR. A style of mystery involving hard-boiled detectives and bleak settings.

NOM DE PLUME. French for "pen name"; a pseudonym.

NONFICTION NOVEL. A work in which real events and people are written [about] in novel form, but are not camouflaged, as they are in the roman à clef. In the nonfiction novel, reality is presented imaginatively; the writer imposes a novelistic structure on the actual events, keying sections of narrative around moments that are seen (in retrospect) as symbolic. In this way, he creates a coherence that the actual story might not have had. *The Executioner's Song*, by Norman Mailer, and *In Cold Blood*, by Truman Capote, are notable examples of the nonfiction novel.

NOVELLA (ALSO NOVELETTE). A short novel or long story, approximately 20,000–50,000 words.

#10 ENVELOPE. 4" × 9½" envelope, used for queries and other business letters.

OFFPRINT. Copy of a story taken from a magazine before it is bound.

ONETIME RIGHTS. Permission to publish a story in periodical or book form one time only.

OUTLINE. A summary of a book's contents, often in the form of chapter headings with a few sentences outlining the action of the story under each one; sometimes part of a book proposal.

OVER THE TRANSOM. A phrase referring to unsolicited manuscripts, or those that come in "over the transom."

PAYMENT ON ACCEPTANCE. Payment from the magazine or publishing house as soon as the decision to print a manuscript is made.

PAYMENT ON PUBLICATION. Payment from the publisher after a manuscript is printed.

PEN NAME. A pseudonym used to conceal a writer's real name.

PERIODICAL. A magazine or journal published at regular intervals.

PLOT. The carefully devised series of events through which the characters progress in a work of fiction.

POPULAR FICTION. Generally, a synonym for category or genre fiction; i.e., fiction intended to appeal to audiences for certain kinds of novels. Popular, or category, fiction is defined as such primarily for the convenience of publishers, editors, reviewers, and booksellers who must identify novels of different areas of interest for potential readers.

PRINT ON DEMAND (POD). Novels produced digitally one at a time, as ordered. Self-publishing through print on demand technology typically involves some fees for the author. Some authors use POD to create a manuscript in book form to send to prospective traditional publishers.

PROOFREADING. Close reading and correction of a manuscript's typographical errors.

PROOFS. A typeset version of a manuscript used for correcting errors and making changes, often a photocopy of the galleys.

PROPOSAL. An offer to write a specific work, usually consisting of an outline of the work and one or two completed chapters.

PROTAGONIST. The principal or leading character in a literary work.

PSYCHOLOGICAL NOVEL. A narrative that emphasizes the mental and emotional aspects of its characters, focusing on motivations and mental activities rather than on exterior events. The psychological novelist is less concerned about relating what happened than about exploring why it happened. The term is most often used to describe twentieth-century works that employ techniques such as interior monologue and stream of consciousness. Two examples of contemporary psychological novels are Judith Guest's *Ordinary People* and Mary Gordon's *The Company of Women*.

PUBLIC DOMAIN. Material that either was never copyrighted or whose copyright term has expired.

PULP MAGAZINE. A periodical printed on inexpensive paper, usually containing lurid, sensational stories or articles.

QUERY. A letter written to an editor to elicit interest in a story the writer wants to submit.

READER. A person hired by a publisher to read unsolicited manuscripts.

READING FEE. An arbitrary amount of money charged by some agents and publishers to read a submitted manuscript.

REGENCY ROMANCE. A subgenre of romance, usually set in England between 1811 and 1820.

REMAINDERS. Leftover copies of an out-of-print book, sold by the publisher at a reduced price.

REPORTING TIME. The number of weeks or months it takes an editor to report back on an author's query or manuscript.

REPRINT RIGHTS. Permission to print an already published work whose rights have been sold to another magazine or book publisher.

ROMAN À CLEF. French "novel with a key." A novel that represents actual living or historical characters and events in fictionalized form.

ROMANCE NOVEL. A type of category fiction in which the love relationship between a man and a woman pervades the plot. The story is often told from the viewpoint of the heroine, who meets a man (the hero), falls in love with him, encounters a conflict that hinders their relationship, then resolves the conflict. Romance is the overriding element in this kind of story: The couple's relationship determines the plot and tone of the book.

ROYALTIES. A percentage of the retail price paid to an author for each copy of the book that is sold.

SAE. Self-addressed envelope.

SASE. Self-addressed stamped envelope.

SCIENCE FICTION (VS. FANTASY). It is generally accepted that, to be science fiction, a story must have elements of science in either the conflict or setting (usually both).

Fantasy, on the other hand, rarely utilizes science, relying instead on magic, mythological and neomythological beings, and devices and outright invention for conflict and setting.

SECOND SERIAL (REPRINT) RIGHTS. Permission for the reprinting of a work in another periodical after its first publication in book or magazine form.

SELF-PUBLISHING. In this arrangement, the author keeps all income derived from the book, but he pays for its manufacturing, production, and marketing.

SERIAL RIGHTS. The rights given by an author to a publisher to print a piece in one or more periodicals.

SERIALIZED NOVEL. A book-length work of fiction published in sequential issues of a periodical.

SETTING. The environment and time period during which the action of a story takes place.

SHORT SHORT STORY. A condensed piece of fiction, usually under 1,000 words.

SIMULTANEOUS SUBMISSION. The practice of sending copies of the same manuscript to several editors or publishers at the same time. Some editors refuse to consider such submissions.

SLANT. A story's particular approach or style, designed to appeal to the readers of a specific magazine.

SLICE OF LIFE. A presentation of characters in a seemingly mundane situation that offers the reader a flash of illumination about the characters or their situation.

SLUSH PILE. A stack of unsolicited manuscripts in the editorial offices of a publisher.

SOCIAL FICTION. Fiction written with the purpose of bringing positive changes in society.

SOFT/SOCIOLOGICAL SCIENCE FICTION. Science fiction with an emphasis on society and culture versus scientific accuracy.

SPACE OPERA. Epic science fiction with an emphasis on good guys versus bad guys.

SPECULATION (OR SPEC). An editor's agreement to look at an author's manuscript with no promise to purchase.

SPECULATIVE FICTION (SPECFIC). The all-inclusive term for science fiction, fantasy, and horror.

SUBSIDIARY. An incorporated branch of a company or conglomerate (e.g., Alfred Knopf, Inc., a subsidiary of Random House, Inc.).

SUBSIDIARY RIGHTS. All rights other than book publishing rights included in a book contract, such as paperback, book club, and movie rights.

SUBSIDY PUBLISHER. A book publisher who charges the author for the cost of typesetting, printing, and promoting a book. Also called a *vanity publisher*.

SUBTERFICIAL FICTION. Innovative, challenging, nonconventional fiction in which what seems to be happening is the result of things not so easily perceived.

SUSPENSE. A genre of fiction where the plot's primary function is to build a feeling of anticipation and fear in the reader over its possible outcome.

SYNOPSIS. A brief summary of a story, novel or play. As part of a book proposal, it is a comprehensive summary condensed in a page or page and a half.

TABLOID. Publication printed on paper about half the size of a regular newspaper page (e.g., the *National Enquirer*).

TEARSHEET. Page from a magazine containing a published story.

THEME. The dominant or central idea in a literary work; its message, moral, or main thread.

THRILLER. A novel intended to arouse feelings of excitement or suspense. Works in this genre are highly sensational, usually focusing on illegal activities, international espionage, sex, and violence. A thriller is often a detective story in which the forces of good are pitted against the forces of evil in a kill-or-be-killed situation.

TRADE PAPERBACK. A softbound volume, usually around 5" × 8", published and designed for the general public, available mainly in bookstores.

UNSOLICITED MANUSCRIPT. A story or novel manuscript that an editor did not specifically ask to see.

URBAN FANTASY. Fantasy that takes magical characters, such as elves, fairies, vampires, or wizards, and places them in modern-day settings, often in the inner city.

VANITY PUBLISHER. See subsidy publisher.

VIEWPOINT. The position or attitude of the first- or third-person narrator or multiple narrators, which determines how a story's action is seen and evaluated.

WESTERN. Genre with a setting in the West, usually between 1860 and 1890, with a formula plot about cowboys or other aspects of frontier life.

WHODUNIT. Genre dealing with murder, suspense, and the detection of criminals.

WORK-FOR-HIRE. Work that another party commissions you to do, generally for a flat fee. The creator does not own the copyright and therefore cannot sell any rights.

YOUNG ADULT (YA). The general classification of books written for readers twelve and up.

ZINE. A small, noncommercial magazine, often one- or two-person operations run from the home of the publisher/editor. Themes tend to be specialized, personal, experimental, and often controversial.

GENRE GLOSSARY

Definitions of Fiction Subcategories

//

The following were provided courtesy of The Extended Novel Writing Workshop, created by the staff of Writers Online Workshops (www.writersonlineworkshops.com).

MYSTERY SUBCATEGORIES

The major mystery subcategories are listed below, each followed by a brief description and the names of representative authors, so you can sample each type of work. Note that we have loosely classified "suspense/thriller" as a mystery category. While these stories do not necessarily follow a traditional "whodunit" plot pattern, they share many elements with other mystery categories.

AMATEUR DETECTIVE. As the name implies, the detective is not a professional detective (private or otherwise), but is almost always a professional something. This professional association routinely involves the protagonist in criminal cases (in a support capacity), gives him or her a special advantage in a specific case, or provides the contacts and skills necessary to solve a particular crime. (Jonathan Kellerman, Patricia Cornwell, Jan Burke)

CLASSIC MYSTERY (WHODUNIT). A crime (almost always a murder) is solved. The detective is the viewpoint character; the reader never knows any more or less about the crime than the detective, and all the clues to solving the crime are available to the reader.

COURTROOM DRAMA. The action takes place primarily in the courtroom; protagonist is generally a defense attorney out to prove the innocence of his or her client by finding the real culprit.

COZY. A special class of the amateur detective category that frequently features a female protagonist. (Agatha Christie's Miss Marple stories are the classic example.) There is less onstage violence than in other categories, and the plot is often wrapped up in a final scene where the detective identifies the murderer and explains how the crime was solved. In contemporary stories, the protagonist can be anyone from a chronically curious house-wife to a mystery-buff clergyman to a college professor, but he or she is usually quirky, even eccentric. (Susan Isaacs, Andrew Greeley, Lillian Jackson Braun)

ESPIONAGE. The international spy novel is less popular since the end of the Cold War, but stories can still revolve around political intrigue in unstable regions. (John le Carré, Ken Follett)

HEISTS AND CAPERS. The crime itself is the focus. Its planning and execution are seen in detail, and the participants are fully drawn characters that may even be portrayed sympa-thetically. One character is the obvious leader of the group (the "brains"); the other mem-bers are often brought together by the leader specifically for this job and may or may not have a previous association. In a heist, no matter how clever or daring the characters are, they are still portrayed as criminals, and the expectation is that they will be caught and punished (but not always). A caper is more lighthearted, even comedic. The participants may have a noble goal (something other than personal gain) and often get away with the crime. (Eric Ambler, Tony Kenrick, Leslie Hollander)

HISTORICAL. May be any category or subcategory of mystery, but with an emphasis on setting, the details of which must be diligently researched. But beyond the historical de-tails (which must never overshadow the story), the plot develops along the lines of its con-temporary counterpart. (Candace Robb, Caleb Carr, Anne Perry)

JUVENILE/YOUNG ADULT. Written for the 8–12 age group (middle grade) or the 12 and up age group (young adult), the crime in these stories may or may not be murder, but it is serious. The protagonist is a kid (or group of kids) in the same age range as the tar-geted reader. There is no graphic violence depicted, but the stories are scary and the vil-lains are realistic. (Mary Downing Hahn, Wendy Corsi Staub, Cameron Dokey, Norma Fox Mazer)

MEDICAL THRILLER. The plot can involve a legitimate medical threat (such as the outbreak of a virulent plague) or the illegal or immoral use of medical technology. In the former scenario, the protagonist is likely to be the doctor (or team) who identifies the virus and procures the antidote; in the latter he or she could be a patient (or the relative of a victim) who uncovers the plot and brings down the villain. (Robin Cook, Michael Palmer, Mi-chael Crichton, Stanley Pottinger)

POLICE PROCEDURALS. The most realistic category, these stories require the most metic-ulous research. A police procedural may have more than one protagonist since cops rarely work alone. Conflict between partners, or between the detective and his or her superiors, is a common theme. But cops are portrayed positively as a group, even though there may be a couple of bad or ineffective law enforcement characters for contrast and conflict. Jurisdictional disputes are still popular sources of conflict as well. (Lawrence Treat, Joseph Wambaugh, Ridley Pearson, Julie Smith)

PRIVATE DETECTIVE. When described as "hard-boiled," this category takes a tough stance. Violence is more prominent, characters are darker, the detective—while almost always licensed by the state—operates on the fringes of the law, and there is often open resentment between the detective and law enforcement. More "enlightened" male detectives and a crop of contemporary females have brought about new trends in this category. (For female P.I.s: Sue Grafton, Sara Paretsky; for male P.I.s: John D. MacDonald, Lawrence Sanders)

SUSPENSE/THRILLER. Where a classic mystery is always a whodunit, a suspense/thriller novel may deal more with the intricacies of the crime, what motivated it, and how the villain (whose identity may be revealed to the reader early on) is caught and brought to justice. Novels in this category frequently employ multiple points of view and have broader scopes than more traditional murder mysteries. The crime may not even involve murder— it may be a threat to global economy or regional ecology; it may be technology run amok or abused at the hands of an unscrupulous scientist; it may involve innocent citizens victimized for personal or corporate gain. Its perpetrators are kidnappers, stalkers, serial killers, rapists, pedophiles, computer hackers, or just about anyone with an evil intention and the means to carry it out. The protagonist may be a private detective or law enforcement official, but is just as likely to be a doctor, lawyer, military officer, or other individual in a unique position to identify the villain and bring him or her to justice. (James Patterson, John J. Nance)

TECHNO-THRILLER. These are replacing the traditional espionage novel and feature technology as an integral part of not just the setting but the plot as well.

WOMAN IN JEOPARDY. A murder or other crime may be committed, but the focus is on the woman (and/or her children) currently at risk, her struggle to understand the nature of the danger, and her eventual victory over her tormentor. The protagonist makes up for her lack of physical prowess with intellect or special skills and solves the problem on her own or with the help of her family (but she runs the show). Closely related to this category is romantic suspense. But, while the heroine in a romantic suspense is certainly a "woman in jeopardy,'" the mystery or suspense element is subordinate to the romance. (Mary Higgins Clark, Mary Stewart, Jessica Mann)

ROMANCE SUBCATEGORIES

These categories and subcategories of romance fiction have been culled from the *Romance Writer's Sourcebook* (Writer's Digest Books) and Phyllis Taylor Pianka's *How to Write Romances* (Writer's Digest Books). We've arranged the "major" categories below, with the subcategories beneath them, each followed by a brief description and the names of authors who write in each category, so you can sample representative works.

CATEGORY OR SERIES. These are published in "lines" by individual publishing houses (such as Harlequin); each line has its own requirements as to word length, story content, and amount of sex. (Debbie Macomber, Nora Roberts, Glenda Sanders)

CHRISTIAN. With an inspirational Christian message centering on the spiritual dynamic of the romantic relationship and faith in God as the foundation for that relationship; sensuality is played down. (Janelle Burnham, Ann Bell, Linda Chaikin, Catherine Palmer, Dee Henderson, Lisa Tawn Bergen)

GLITZ. So called because they feature generally wealthy characters with high-powered positions in careers that are considered glamorous—high finance, modeling/acting, publishing, fashion—and are set in exciting or exotic (often metropolitan) locales, such as Monte Carlo, Hollywood, London, or New York. (Jackie Collins, Judith Krantz)

HISTORICAL. Can cover just about any historical (or even prehistorical) period. Setting in the historical is especially significant, and details must be thoroughly researched and accurately presented. For a sampling of a variety of historical styles, try Laura Kinsell (*Flowers from the Storm*), Mary Jo Putney (*The Rake and the Reformer*), and Judy Cuevas (*Bliss*). Some currently popular periods/themes in historicals are:

- **GOTHIC:** Historical with a strong element of suspense and a feeling of supernatural events, although these events frequently have a natural explanation. Setting plays an important role in establishing a dark, moody, suspenseful atmosphere. (Phyllis Whitney, Victoria Holt)
- **HISTORICAL FANTASY:** With traditional fantasy elements of magic and magical beings, frequently set in a medieval society. (Amanda Glass, Jayne Ann Krentz, Kathleen Morgan, Jessica Bryan, Taylor Quinn Evans, Carla Simpson, Karyn Monk)
- **EARLY AMERICAN:** Usually Revolution to Civil War, set in New England or the South, but "frontier" stories set in the American West are quite popular as well. (Robin Lee Hatcher, Ann Maxwell, Heather Graham)

- **NATIVE AMERICAN:** Where one or both of the characters are Native Americans; the conflict between cultures is a popular theme. (Carol Finch, Elizabeth Grayson, Karen Kay, Kathleen Harrington, Genell Dellim, Candace McCarthy)
- **REGENCY:** Set in England during the Regency period from 1811 to 1820. (Carol Finch, Elizabeth Elliott, Georgette Heyer, Joan Johnston, Lynn Collum)

MULTICULTURAL. Most currently feature African-American or Hispanic couples, but editors are looking for other ethnic stories as well. Multiculturals can be contemporary or historical and fall into any subcategory. (Rochelle Alers, Monica Jackson, Bette Ford, Sandra Kitt, Brenda Jackson)

PARANORMAL. Containing elements of the supernatural or science fiction/fantasy. There are numerous subcategories (many stories combine elements of more than one) including:
- **TIME TRAVEL:** One or more of the characters travels to another time—usually the past—to find love. (Jude Deveraux, Linda Lael Miller, Diana Gabaldon, Constance O'Day-Flannery)
- **SCIENCE FICTION/FUTURISTIC:** S/F elements are used for the story's setting: imaginary worlds, parallel universes, Earth in the near or distant future. (Marilyn Campbell, Jayne Ann Krentz, J.D. Robb [Nora Roberts], Anne Avery)
- **CONTEMPORARY FANTASY:** From modern ghost and vampire stories to "New Age" themes such as extraterrestrials and reincarnation. (Linda Lael Miller, Anne Stuart, Antoinette Stockenberg, Christine Feehan)

ROMANTIC COMEDY. Has a fairly strong comic premise and/or a comic perspective in the author's voice or the voices of the characters (especially the heroine). (Jennifer Crusie, Susan Elizabeth Phillips)

ROMANTIC SUSPENSE. With a mystery or psychological thriller subplot in addition to the romance plot. (Mary Stewart, Barbara Michaels, Tami Hoag, Nora Roberts, Linda Howard, Catherine Coulter)

SINGLE TITLE. Longer contemporaries that do not necessarily conform to the requirements of a specific romance line and therefore feature more complex plots and nontraditional characters. (Mary Ruth Myers, Nora Roberts, Kathleen Gilles Seidel, Kathleen Korbel)

YOUNG ADULT (YA). Focus is on first love with very little, if any, sex. These can have bittersweet endings, as opposed to the traditional romance happy ending, since first loves are often lost loves. (YA historical: Nancy Covert Smith, Louise Vernon; YA contemporary: Kathryn Makris)

SCIENCE FICTION SUBCATEGORIES

Peter Heck, in his article "Doors to Other Worlds: Trends in Science Fiction and Fantasy," which appears in the 1996 edition of *Science Fiction and Fantasy Writer's Sourcebook* (Writer's Digest Books), identifies some science fiction trends that have distinct enough characteristics to be defined as categories. These distinctions are frequently the result of marketing decisions as much as literary ones, so understanding them is important in deciding where your novel idea belongs. We've supplied a brief description and the names of authors who write in each category. In those instances where the author writes in more than one category, we've included titles of appropriate representative works.

ALTERNATE HISTORY. Fantasy, sometimes with science fiction elements, that changes the accepted account of actual historical events or people to suggest an alternate view of history. (Ted Mooney, *Traffic and Laughter*; Ward Moore, *Bring the Jubilee*; Philip K. Dick, *The Man in the High Castle*)

CYBERPUNK. Characters in these stories are tough outsiders in a high-tech, generally near-future society where computers have produced major changes in the way society functions. (William Gibson, Bruce Sterling, Pat Cadigan, Wilhelmina Baird)

HARD SCIENCE FICTION. Based on the logical extrapolation of real science to the future. In these stories the scientific background (setting) may be as, or more, important than the characters. (Larry Niven)

MILITARY SCIENCE FICTION. Stories about war that feature traditional military organization and tactics extrapolated into the future. (Jerry Pournelle, David Drake, Elizabeth Moon)

NEW AGE. A category of speculative fiction that deals with subjects such as astrology, psychic phenomena, spiritual healing, UFOs, mysticism, and other aspects of the occult. (Walter Mosley, *Blue Light*; Neil Gaiman)

SCIENCE FANTASY. Blend of traditional fantasy elements with scientific or pseudoscientific support (genetic engineering, for example, to "explain" a traditional fantasy creature like the dragon). These stories are traditionally more character driven than hard science fiction. (Anne McCaffrey, Mercedes Lackey, Marion Zimmer Bradley)

SCIENCE FICTION MYSTERY. A cross-genre blending that can either be a more-or-less traditional science fiction story with a mystery as a key plot element, or a more-or-less traditional whodunit with science fiction elements. (Philip K. Dick, Lynn S. Hightower)

SCIENCE FICTION ROMANCE. Another genre blend that may be a romance with science fiction elements (in which case it is more accurately placed as a subcategory within the romance genre) or a science fiction story with a strong romantic subplot. (Anne McCaffrey, Melanie Rawn, Kate Elliott)

SOCIAL SCIENCE FICTION. The focus is on how the characters react to their environments. This category includes social satire. (George Orwell's *1984* is a classic example.) (Margaret Atwood, *The Handmaid's Tale*; Ursula K. Le Guin, *The Left Hand of Darkness*; Marge Piercy, *Woman on the Edge of Time*)

SPACE OPERA. From the term "horse opera," describing a traditional good-guys-versus-bad-guys western, these stories put the emphasis on sweeping action and larger-than-life characters. The focus on action makes these stories especially appealing for film treatment. (The Star Wars series is one of the best examples; also Samuel R. Delany.)

STEAMPUNK. A specific type of alternate-history science fiction set in Victorian England in which characters have access to 20th-century technology. (William Gibson; Bruce Sterling, *The Difference Engine*)

YOUNG ADULT. Any subcategory of science fiction geared to a YA audience (12–18), but these are usually shorter novels with characters in the central roles who are the same age as (or slightly older than) the targeted reader. (Jane Yolen, Andre Norton)

FANTASY SUBCATEGORIES

Before we take a look at the individual fantasy categories, it should be noted that, for purposes of these supplements, we've treated fantasy as a genre distinct from science fiction. While these two are closely related, there are significant enough differences to warrant their separation for study purposes. We have included here those science fiction categories that have strong fantasy elements, or that have a significant amount of crossover (these categories appear in both the science fiction and the fantasy supplements), but "pure" science fiction categories are not included below. If you're not sure whether your novel is fantasy or science fiction, consider this definition by Orson Scott Card in *How to Write Science Fiction and Fantasy* (Writer's Digest Books): "Here's a good, simple, semi-accurate rule of thumb: If the story is set in a universe that follows the same rules as ours, it's science fiction. If it's set in a universe that doesn't follow our rules, it's fantasy. Or in other words, science fiction is about what could be but isn't; fantasy is about what couldn't be."

But even Card admits this rule is only "semi-accurate." He goes on to say that the real boundary between science fiction and fantasy is defined by how the impossible is achieved: "If you have people do some magic, impossible thing [like time travel] by stroking a talisman or praying to a tree, it's fantasy; if they do the same thing by pressing a button or climbing inside a machine, it's science fiction."

Peter Heck, in his article "Doors to Other Worlds: Trends in Science Fiction and Fantasy," which appears in the 1996 edition of the *Science Fiction and Fantasy Writer's Sourcebook* (Writer's Digest Books), does note some trends that have distinct enough characteristics to be defined as separate categories. These categories are frequently the result of marketing decisions as much as literary ones, so understanding them is important in deciding where your novel idea belongs. We've supplied a brief description and the names of authors who write in each category, so you can sample representative works.

ARTHURIAN. Reworking of the legend of King Arthur and the Knights of the Round Table. (T.H. White, *The Once and Future King*; Marion Zimmer Bradley, *The Mists of Avalon*)

CONTEMPORARY (ALSO CALLED "URBAN") FANTASY. Traditional fantasy elements (such as elves and magic) are incorporated into an otherwise recognizable modern setting. (Emma Bull, *War for the Oaks*; Mercedes Lackey, *The SERRAted Edge*; Terry Brooks, the Word & Void series)

DARK FANTASY. Closely related to horror but generally not as graphic. Characters in these stories are the "darker" fantasy types: vampires, witches, werewolves, demons, etc. (Anne Rice; Clive Barker, *Weaveworld*, *Imajica*; Fred Chappell)

FANTASTIC ALTERNATE HISTORY. Set in an alternate historical period (in which magic would not have been a common belief) where magic works, these stories frequently feature actual historical figures. (Orson Scott Card, *Alvin Maker*)

GAME-RELATED FANTASY. Plots and characters are similar to high fantasy, but are based on a particular role-playing game. (Dungeons and Dragons; Magic: The Gathering; World of Warcraft)

HEROIC FANTASY. The fantasy equivalent to military science fiction, these are stories of war and its heroes and heroines. (Robert E. Howard, the Conan the Barbarian series; Elizabeth Moon, *Deed of Paksenarrion*; Michael Moorcock, the Elric series)

HIGH FANTASY. Emphasis is on the fate of an entire race or nation, threatened by an ultimate evil. J.R.R. Tolkien's Lord of the Rings trilogy is a classic example. (Terry Brooks, David Eddings, Margaret Weis, Tracy Hickman)

HISTORICAL FANTASY. The setting can be almost any era in which the belief in magic was strong; these are essentially historical novels where magic is a key element of the plot and/or setting. (Susan Schwartz, *Silk Roads and Shadows*; Margaret Ball, *No Earthly Sunne*; Tim Powers, *The Anubis Gates*)

JUVENILE/YOUNG ADULT. Can be any type of fantasy, but geared to a juvenile (8–12) or YA audience (12–18); these are shorter novels with younger characters in central roles. (J.K. Rowling, Christopher Paolini, C.S. Lewis)

SCIENCE FANTASY. A blend of traditional fantasy elements with scientific or pseudoscientific support (genetic engineering, for example, to "explain" a traditional fantasy creature like the dragon). These stories are traditionally more character driven than hard science fiction. (Anne McCaffrey, Mercedes Lackey, Marion Zimmer Bradley)

HORROR SUBCATEGORIES

Subcategories in horror are less well defined than in other genres and are frequently the result of marketing decisions as much as literary ones. But being familiar with the terms used to describe different horror styles can be important in understanding how your own novel might be best presented to an agent or editor. What follows is a brief description of the most commonly used terms, along with names of authors and, where necessary, representative works.

DARK FANTASY. Sometimes used as a euphemistic term for horror in general, but also refers to a specific type of fantasy, usually less graphic than other horror subcategories, that features more "traditional" supernatural or mythical beings (vampires, werewolves, zombies, etc.) in either contemporary or historical settings. (Contemporary: Stephen King, *Salem's Lot*; Thomas Tessier, *The Nightwalker*. Historical: Brian Stableford, *The Empire of Fear* and *Werewolves of London*)

HAUNTINGS. "Classic" stories of ghosts, poltergeists, and spiritual possessions. The level of violence portrayed varies, but many writers in this category exploit the reader's natural fear of the unknown by hinting at the horror and letting the reader's imagination supply the details. (Peter Straub, *Ghost Story*; Richard Matheson, *Hell House*)

JUVENILE/YOUNG ADULT. Can be any horror style, but with a protagonist who is the same age as, or slightly older than, the targeted reader. Stories for middle grades (8–12 years old) are scary, with monsters and violent acts that might best be described as "gross," but stories for young adults (12–18) may be more graphic. (R.L. Stine, Christopher Pike, Carol Gorman)

PSYCHOLOGICAL HORROR. Features a human monster with horrific, but not necessarily supernatural, aspects. (Thomas Harris, *The Silence of the Lambs*, *Hannibal*; Dean Koontz, *Whispers*)

SPLATTERPUNK. Very graphic depiction of violence—often gratuitous—popularized in the 1980s, especially in film. (*Friday the 13th*, *Halloween*, *Nightmare on Elm Street*, etc.)

SUPERNATURAL/OCCULT. Similar to the dark fantasy, but may be more graphic in its depiction of violence. Stories feature satanic worship, demonic possession, or ultimate evil incarnate in an entity or supernatural being that may or may not have its roots in traditional mythology or folklore. (Ramsey Campbell; Robert McCammon; Ira Levin, *Rosemary's Baby*; William Peter Blatty, *The Exorcist*; Stephen King, *Pet Sematary*)

TECHNOLOGICAL HORROR. "Monsters" in these stories are the result of science run amok or technology turned to purposes of evil. (Dean Koontz, *Watchers*; Michael Crichton, *Jurassic Park*)

PROFESSIONAL ORGANIZATIONS

///

AGENTS' ORGANIZATIONS

ASSOCIATION OF AUTHORS' AGENTS (AAA) Curtis Brown, Haymarket House, 28-29 Haymarket, London SW1Y 4SP. (020)7393-4420. E-mail: wiseoffice@curtisbrown.co.uk. Website: www.agentsassoc.co.uk.

ASSOCIATION OF AUTHORS' REPRESENTATIVES (AAR) 302A West 12th Street, #122, New York, NY 10014. E-mail: administrator@aaronline.org. Website: aaronline.org.

ASSOCIATION OF TALENT AGENTS (ATA) 9255 Sunset Blvd., Suite 930, Los Angeles, CA 90069. (310)274-0628. Fax: (310)274-5063. E-mail: info@agentassociation.com. Website: www.agentassociation.com.

WRITERS' ORGANIZATIONS

ACADEMY OF AMERICAN POETS 75 Maiden Lane, Suite 901, New York, NY 10038. (212)274-0343. Fax: (212)274-9427. E-mail: academy@poets.org. Website: www.poets.org.

AMERICAN CRIME WRITERS LEAGUE (ACWL) E-mail: info@acwl.org. Website: www.acwl.org.

AMERICAN MEDICAL WRITERS ASSOCIATION (AMWA) 30 West Gude Drive, Suite 525, Rockville, MD 20850-4347. (240)238-0940. Fax: (301)294-9006. E-mail: amwa@amwa.org. Website: www.amwa.org.

AMERICAN SCREENWRITERS ASSOCIATION (ASA) E-mail: info@americanscreenwriters.com. Website: www.americanscreenwriters.com.

AMERICAN TRANSLATORS ASSOCIATION (ATA) 225 Reinekers Lane, Suite 590, Alexandria, VA 22314. (703)683-6100. Fax: (703)683-6122. E-mail: ata@atanet.org. Website: www.atanet.org.

EDUCATION WRITERS ASSOCIATION (EWA) 3516 Connecticut Avenue NW, Washington, DC 20008. (202)452-9830. Website: www.ewa.org.

THE ASSOCIATION OF GARDEN COMMUNICATORS (GWA) 355 Lexington Avenue, 15th Floor, New York, NY 10017. (212)297-2198. Fax: (212)297-2149. E-mail: info@gardenwriters.org. Website: www.gardenwriters.org.

HORROR WRITERS ASSOCIATION (HWA) P.O. Box 56687, Sherman Oaks, CA 91413. (818)220-3965. E-mail: hwa.contact@gmail.com. Website: www.horror.org.

THE INTERNATIONAL WOMEN'S WRITING GUILD (IWWG) 5 Penn Plaza, PMB #19059, New York, NY 10001. (917)720-6959. E-mail: iwwgquestions@gmail.com Website: iwwg.wildapricot.org.

MYSTERY WRITERS OF AMERICA (MWA) 1140 Broadway, Suite 1507, New York, NY 10001. (212)888-8171. Fax: (212)888-8107. Website: www.mysterywriters.org.

NATIONAL ASSOCIATION OF SCIENCE WRITERS (NASW) P.O. Box 7905, Berkeley, CA 94707. (510)647-9500. E-mail: editor@nasw.org. Website: www.nasw.org.

ORGANIZATION OF BLACK SCREENWRITERS (OBS) 3010 Wilshire Boulevard, #269, Los Angeles, CA 90010. E-mail: contactus@obswriter.com. Website: www.obswriter.com.

OUTDOOR WRITERS ASSOCIATION OF AMERICA (OWAA) 615 Oak Street, Suite 201, Missoula, MT 59801. (406)728-7434. E-mail: info@owaa.org. Website: www.owaa.org.

POETRY SOCIETY OF AMERICA (PSA) 15 Gramercy Park, New York, NY 10003. (212)254-9628. Website: www.poetrysociety.org.

POETS & WRITERS 90 Broad St., Suite 2100, New York, NY 10004. (212)226-3586. Fax: (212)226-3963. Website: www.pw.org.

ROMANCE WRITERS OF AMERICA (RWA) 14615 Benfer Road, Houston, TX 77069. (832)717-5200. E-mail: info@rwa.org. Website: www.rwa.org.

SCIENCE FICTION AND FANTASY WRITERS OF AMERICA (SFWA) P.O. Box 3238, Enfield, CT 06083-3238. Website: www.sfwa.org.

SOCIETY OF AMERICAN BUSINESS EDITORS AND WRITERS (SABEW) Walter Cronkite School of Journalism and Mass Communication, Arizona State University, 555 North Central Avenue, Suite 406E, Phoenix, AZ 85004-1248 (602)496-7862. E-mail: sabew@sabew.org. Website: www.sabew.org.

SOCIETY OF AMERICAN TRAVEL WRITERS (SATW) 1 Parkview Plaza, Suite 800, Oakbrook Terrace, IL 60181. E-mail: info@satw.org. Website: www.satw.org.

SOCIETY OF CHILDREN'S BOOK WRITERS & ILLUSTRATORS (SCBWI) 4727 Wilshire Boulevard, Suite 301, Los Angeles, CA 90010. (323)782-1010. E-mail: scbwi@scbwi.org. Website: www.scbwi.org.

WESTERN WRITERS OF AMERICA (WWA) E-mail: wwa.moulton@gmail.com. Website: www.westernwriters.org.

INDUSTRY ORGANIZATIONS

AMERICAN BOOKSELLERS ASSOCIATION (ABA) 333 Westchester Avenue, Suite S202, White Plains, NY 10604. (914)406-7500. Fax: (914)417-4013. E-mail: info@bookweb.org. Website: www.bookweb.org.

AMERICAN SOCIETY OF JOURNALISTS & AUTHORS (ASJA) 355 Lexington Avenue, 15th Floor, New York, NY 10017-6603. (212)997-0947. Website: www.asja.org.

THE ASSOCIATION FOR CHRISTIAN RETAIL (CBA) 1365 Garden of the Gods Road, Suite 105, Colorado Springs, CO 80907. (800)252-1950. Fax: (719)272-3510. E-mail: info@cbaonline.org. Website: cbaonline.org.

THE ASSOCIATION FOR WOMEN IN COMMUNICATIONS (AWC) 1717 East Republic Road, Suite A, Springfield, MO 65804. (417)886-8606. Fax: (417)886-3685. E-mail: becky@club-managementservices.com. Website: www.womcom.org.

ASSOCIATION OF AMERICAN PUBLISHERS (AAP) 71 Fifth Avenue, Second Floor, New York NY 10003. (212)255-0200. Fax: (212)255-7007. Or: 455 Massachusetts Avenue NW, Suite 700, Washington, DC 20001. (202)347-3375. Fax: (202)347-3690. Website: publishers.org.

ASSOCIATION OF WRITERS & WRITING PROGRAMS (AWP) George Mason University, 4400 University Drive, MSN 1E3, Fairfax, VA 22030. (703)993-4301. Fax: (703)993-4302. E-mail: awp@awpwriter.org. Website: www.awpwriter.org.

THE AUTHORS GUILD 31 East 32nd Street, Seventh Floor, New York, NY 10016. (212)563-5904. Fax: (212)564-5363. E-mail: staff@authorsguild.org. Website: www.authorsguild.org.

CANADIAN AUTHORS ASSOCIATION (CAA) 6 West Street North, Suite 203, Orilla, ON L3V 5B8 Canada. (705)325-3926. E-mail: admin@canadianauthors.org. Website: www.canadianauthors.org.

DRAMATISTS GUILD OF AMERICA 1501 Broadway, Suite 701, New York, NY 10036. (212)398-9366. Fax: (212)944-0420. Website: www.dramatistsguild.com.

NATIONAL LEAGUE OF AMERICAN PEN WOMEN (NLAPW) Pen Arts Building and Art Museum, 1300 17th St. NW, Washington DC 20036-1973. (202)785-1997. Fax: (202)452-8868. E-mail: contact@nlapw.org. Website: www.nlapw.org.

NATIONAL WRITERS ASSOCIATION (NWA) 10940 South Parker Road, #508, Parker, CO 80134. E-mail: natlwritersassn@hotmail.com. Website: www.nationalwriters.com

NATIONAL WRITERS UNION (NWU) 256 West 38th Street, Suite 703, New York, NY 10018. (212)254-0279. Fax: (212)254-0673. E-mail: nwu@nwu.org. Website: www.nwu.org.

PEN AMERICA 588 Broadway, Suite 303, New York, NY 10012. (212)334-1660. E-mail: info@pen.org. Website: www.pen.org.

PLAYWRIGHTS GUILD OF CANADA (PGC) 401 Richmond Street West, Suite 350, Toronto, ON M5V 3A8 Canada. (416)703-0201. Fax: (416)703-0059. E-mail: info@playwrightsguild.ca. Website: www.playwrightsguild.ca.

VOLUNTEER LAWYERS FOR THE ARTS (VLA) 1 East 53rd Street, New York, NY 10022. (212)319-2787, ext.1. E-mail: vlany@vlany.org. Website: www.vlany.org.

WOMEN IN FILM (WIF) 6100 Wilshire Boulevard, Suite 710, Los Angeles, CA 90048. (323)935-2211. Fax: (323)935-2212. E-mail: info@wif.org. Website: www.wif.org.

WOMEN'S NATIONAL BOOK ASSOCIATION (WNBA) P.O. Box 237, FDR Station, New York NY 10150. (866)610-9622. Fax: (212)208-4629. E-mail: info@wnba-books.org. Website: www.wnba-books.org.

WRITERS' GUILD OF ALBERTA (WGA) Main Floor, Percy Page Centre, 11759 Groat Road NW, Edmonton AB T5M 3K6 Canada. (780)422-8174. Fax: (780)422-2663 (Attn: Writers' Guild of Alberta). E-mail: mail@writersguild.ca. Website: writersguild.ab.ca.

WRITERS GUILD OF AMERICA, EAST (WGA) 250 Hudson Street, Suite 700, New York, NY 10013. (212)767-7800. Fax: (212)582-1909. E-mail: gbynoe@wgaeast.org. Website: www.wgaeast.org.

WRITERS GUILD OF AMERICA, WEST (WGA) 7000 West Third Street, Los Angeles, CA 90048. (323)951-4000, (800)548-4532. Website: www.wga.org.

THE WRITERS' UNION OF CANADA (TWUC) 600-460 Richmond Street West, Toronto, ON M5V 1Y1 Canada. (416)703-8982. Fax: (416)504-9090. E-mail: info@writersunion.ca. Website: www.writersunion.ca.

LITERARY AGENTS SPECIALTIES INDEX

///

ACTION
Barone Literary Agency
Books & Such Literary Management
Carvainis Agency, Inc., Maria
Dawson Associates, Liza
Donovan Literary, Jim
Fairbank Literary Representation
Finch Literary Agency, Diana
Inklings Literary Agency
International Transactions, Inc.
Jenks Agency, The Carolyn
Keller Media Inc.
Klinger, Inc., Harvey
LA Literary Agency, The
Lampack Agency, Inc., Peter
LaunchBooks Literary Agency
Marshall Agency, The Evan
McBride Literary Agency, Margret
Mura Literary, Dee
Sanders & Associates, Victoria
Secret Agent Man
Seymour Agency, The
Triada U.S. Literary Agency, Inc.

ADVENTURE
Barone Literary Agency
Books & Such Literary Management
Carvainis Agency, Inc., Maria
Corvisiero Literary Agency
D4EO Literary Agency
Dawson Associates, Liza
Delbourgo Associates, Inc., Joelle
Donovan Literary, Jim
Ehrlich Literary, Judith
Fairbank Literary Representation
Finch Literary Agency, Diana
HSG Agency
Inklings Literary Agency

International Transactions, Inc.
Jenks Agency, The Carolyn
Keller Media Inc.
Klinger, Inc., Harvey
LA Literary Agency, The
Lampack Agency, Inc., Peter
LaunchBooks Literary Agency
Marshall Agency, The Evan
McBride Literary Agency, Margret
Mura Literary, Dee
Sanders & Associates, Victoria
Triada U.S. Literary Agency, Inc.

COMIC BOOKS
Barone Literary Agency
Mura Literary, Dee
Sanders & Associates, Victoria

COMMERCIAL
Barone Literary Agency
Bent Agency, The
Bijur Literary Agency, Vicky
Black Literary Agency, David
Book Cents Literary Agency, LLC
Book Group, The
Books & Such Literary Management
Braun Associates, Inc., Barbara
Cameron & Associates, Kimberley
Carvainis Agency, Inc., Maria
Chase Literary Agency
Cheney Literary Associates, Elyse
Creative Media Agency, Inc.
Dail Literary Agency, Inc., Laura
Dawson Associates, Liza
DeChiara Literary, Jennifer
DeFiore & Co.
Delbourgo Associates, Inc., Joelle
Dijkstra Literary Agency, Sandra
Donaghy Literary Group

Donovan Literary, Jim
Dunow, Carlson, & Lerner Agency
Dystel & Goderich Literary
Einstein Literary Management
Ellenberg Literary Agency, Ethan
Ehrlich Literary, Judith
FinePrint Literary Management
Fletcher & Company
Folio Literary Management, LLC
Friedrich Agency, The
Greenburger Associates, Sanford J.
Hawkins & Associates, Inc., John
Heller Agency Inc., Helen
HSG Agency
Inklings Literary Agency
InkWell Management, LLC
International Transactions, Inc.
Keller Media Inc.
Klinger, Inc., Harvey
Krichevsky Literary Agency, Stuart
LA Literary Agency, The
Lampack Agency, Inc., Peter
Lippincott Massie McQuilkin
Lowenstein Associates Inc.
Mann Agency, Carol
Marsal Lyon Literary Agency, LLC
McMillan, LLC, Sally Hill
Moveable Type Management
Mura Literary, Dee
Nelson Literary Agency
Priest Literary Agency, Aaron M.
Prospect Agency
Rebecca Friedman Literary Agency
Rees Literary Agency, Helen
Rights Factory, The
Rinaldi Literary Agency, Angela
RLR Associates, Ltd.
Ross Literary Agency, Andy

Barone Literary Agency
Bent Agency, The
Brandt & Hochman Literary Agents
Cameron & Associates, Kimberley
Chalberg & Sussman
Corvisiero Literary Agency
Curtis Brown, Ltd.
Dail Literary Agency, Inc., Laura
Dawson Associates, Liza
DeChiara Literary, Jennifer
Delbourgo Associates, Inc., Joelle
Donaghy Literary Group
Dunham Literary, Inc.
Ellenberg Literary Agency, Ethan
FinePrint Literary Management
Folio Literary Management, LLC
Fox Literary
Greenburger Associates, Sanford J.
Grinberg Literary Management, Jill
Henshaw Group, Richard
Holloway Literary
Inklings Literary Agency
Jenks Agency, The Carolyn
Kidd Agency, Inc., Virginia
Klinger, Inc., Harvey
Laube Agency, The Steve
LaunchBooks Literary Agency
Lowenstein Associates Inc.
Marshall Agency, The Evan
McCarthy Agency, LLC, The
McIntosh & Otis, Inc.
Morhaim Literary Agency, Howard
Mura Literary, Dee
Nelson Literary Agency
New Leaf Literary & Media, Inc.
Prospect Agency
Rebecca Friedman Literary Agency
Red Sofa Literary
Rights Factory, The
Scribe Agency, LLC
Seligman, Literary Agent, Lynn
Seymour Agency, The
Stringer Literary Agency, LLC, The
Talcott Notch Literary
Triada U.S. Literary Agency, Inc.
Trident Media Group
United Talent Agency
Veritas Literary Agency
Waxman Leavell Literary
Webber Associates Literary, CK
Writers House
Yarn Literary Agency, Jason

FEMINIST
Barone Literary Agency
Bent Agency, The
Dail Literary Agency, Inc., Laura
Dawson Associates, Liza
DeChiara Literary, Jennifer
Delbourgo Associates, Inc., Joelle
Fairbank Literary Representation
Greenburger Associates, Sanford J.
Inklings Literary Agency
International Transactions, Inc.

Jenks Agency, The Carolyn
LA Literary Agency, The
Marshall Agency, The Evan
Mura Literary, Dee
Prospect Agency
Red Sofa Literary
Sanders & Associates, Victoria
Seligman, Literary Agent, Lynn

FRONTIER
Barone Literary Agency
Books & Such Literary Management
Donovan Literary, Jim
J de S Associates, Inc.
Jenks Agency, The Carolyn
Marshall Agency, The Evan
Mura Literary, Dee

GAY
Barone Literary Agency
Corvisiero Literary Agency
Dawson Associates, Liza
DeChiara Literary, Jennifer
Donaghy Literary Group
Dystel & Goderich Literary
Fairbank Literary Representation
Inklings Literary Agency
International Transactions, Inc.
Jenks Agency, The Carolyn
Klinger, Inc., Harvey
Marshall Agency, The Evan
Mura Literary, Dee
Prospect Agency
Red Sofa Literary
Rights Factory, The
Serendipity Literary Agency, LLC
Triada U.S. Literary Agency, Inc.

GLITZ
Barone Literary Agency
Holloway Literary
Klinger, Inc., Harvey
Marshall Agency, The Evan
Mura Literary, Dee

HISTORICAL
Aponte Literary Agency
Barone Literary Agency
Bent Agency, The
Books & Such Literary Management
Brandt & Hochman Literary Agents
Braun Associates, Inc., Barbara
Brown Associates, Inc., Marie
Cameron & Associates, Kimberley
Carvainis Agency, Inc., Maria
Chase Literary Agency
Cheney Literary Associates, Elyse
Clark Associates, WM
Corvisiero Literary Agency
Creative Media Agency, Inc.
Dail Literary Agency, Inc., Laura
Dawson Associates, Liza
DeChiara Literary, Jennifer
Donovan Literary, Jim
Dunham Literary, Inc.

Einstein Literary Management
Ehrlich Literary, Judith
Eth Literary Representation, Felicia
Finch Literary Agency, Diana
FinePrint Literary Management
Fox Literary
Freymann Literary, Sarah Jane
Goodman Literary Agency, Irene
Greenburger Associates, Sanford J.
Grosjean Literary Agency, Jill
Hawkins & Associates, Inc., John
Heller Agency Inc., Helen
Henshaw Group, Richard
Holloway Literary
HSG Agency
Inklings Literary Agency
InkWell Management, LLC
International Transactions, Inc.
J de S Associates, Inc.
Jenks Agency, The Carolyn
Keller Media Inc.
Klinger, Inc., Harvey
LA Literary Agency, The
Marshall Agency, The Evan
McBride Literary Agency, Margret
McIntosh & Otis, Inc.
Morhaim Literary Agency, Howard
Mura Literary, Dee
New Leaf Literary & Media, Inc.
Prospect Agency
Rees Literary Agency, Helen
Rights Factory, The
Rinaldi Literary Agency, Angela
Robbins Literary Agency, B.J.
Rudy Agency, The
Seligman, Literary Agent, Lynn
Serendipity Literary Agency, LLC
Speilburg Literary Agency
Stringer Literary Agency, LLC, The
Talcott Notch Literary
Thompson Literary Agency
Triada U.S. Literary Agency, Inc.
Trident Media Group
United Talent Agency
Veritas Literary Agency
Waxman Leavell Literary
Wolf Literary Services
Wordserve Literary Group

HORROR
Azantian Literary Agency
Barone Literary Agency
Bent Agency, The
Carvainis Agency, Inc., Maria
Chalberg & Sussman
Curtis Brown, Ltd.
Dawson Associates, Liza
DeChiara Literary, Jennifer
Dijkstra Literary Agency, Sandra
Folio Literary Management, LLC
Henshaw Group, Richard
Inklings Literary Agency
Jenks Agency, The Carolyn
Klinger, Inc., Harvey

LaunchBooks Literary Agency
Marshall Agency, The Evan
McIntosh & Otis, Inc.
Mura Literary, Dee
New Leaf Literary & Media, Inc.
Prospect Agency
Rees Literary Agency, Helen
Rights Factory, The
Seligman, Literary Agent, Lynn
Stuart Agency, The
Talcott Notch Literary
Triada U.S. Literary Agency, Inc.

HUMOR

Barone Literary Agency
Carvainis Agency, Inc., Maria
Curtis Brown, Ltd.
Dawson Associates, Liza
DeChiara Literary, Jennifer
Dunham Literary, Inc.
Ehrlich Literary, Judith
Hartline Literary Agency
International Transactions, Inc.
Jenks Agency, The Carolyn
Marshall Agency, The Evan
McBride Literary Agency, Margret
Mura Literary, Dee
Prospect Agency
Red Sofa Literary
Seligman, Literary Agent, Lynn

INSPIRATIONAL

Barone Literary Agency
Books & Such Literary Management
Creative Media Agency, Inc.
DeChiara Literary, Jennifer
Hartline Literary Agency
International Transactions, Inc.
Jenks Agency, The Carolyn
Laube Agency, The Steve
Marshall Agency, The Evan
Mura Literary, Dee
Seymour Agency, The
Wordserve Literary Group

JUVENILE

Amster Literary Enterprises, Betsy
Barone Literary Agency
Bent Agency, The
Books & Such Literary Management
Bradford Literary Agency
Brown Associates, Inc., Marie
Carvainis Agency, Inc., Maria
Corcoran Literary Agency, Jill
Curtis Brown, Ltd.
D4EO Literary Agency
Dail Literary Agency, Inc., Laura
Dawson Associates, Liza
DeChiara Literary, Jennifer
Delbourgo Associates, Inc., Joelle
Donaghy Literary Group
Dunham Literary, Inc.
Ehrlich Literary, Judith
Grinberg Literary Management, Jill

HSG Agency
Inklings Literary Agency
J de S Associates, Inc.
Jenks Agency, The Carolyn
Klinger, Inc., Harvey
Maccoby Literary Agency, Gina
Marsal Lyon Literary Agency, LLC
Mura Literary, Dee
Prospect Agency
Red Sofa Literary
Rights Factory, The
Ross Literary Agency, Andy
Rudy Agency, The
Schulman Literary Agency, Susan
Sterling Lord Literistic, Inc.
Thompson Literary Agency
Triada U.S. Literary Agency, Inc.
Trident Media Group
Wells Arms Literary
Writers House

LESBIAN

Barone Literary Agency
Corvisiero Literary Agency
Dawson Associates, Liza
DeChiara Literary, Jennifer
Donaghy Literary Group
Dystel & Goderich Literary
Fairbank Literary Representation
Inklings Literary Agency
International Transactions, Inc.
Jenks Agency, The Carolyn
Klinger, Inc., Harvey
Marshall Agency, The Evan
Mura Literary, Dee
Prospect Agency
Red Sofa Literary
Rights Factory, The
Sanders & Associates, Victoria
Serendipity Literary Agency, LLC

LITERARY

Amster Literary Enterprises, Betsy
Barone Literary Agency
Bent Agency, The
Bijur Literary Agency, Vicky
Black Literary Agency, David
Book Cents Literary Agency, LLC
Book Group, The
Books & Such Literary Management
Brandt & Hochman Literary Agents
Braun Associates, Inc., Barbara
Brown Associates, Inc., Marie
Cameron & Associates, Kimberley
Carvainis Agency, Inc., Maria
Chalberg & Sussman
Chase Literary Agency
Cheney Literary Associates, Elyse
Clark Associates, WM
Curtis Brown, Ltd.
D4EO Literary Agency
Darhansoff & Verrill Literary
DeChiara Literary, Jennifer
DeFiore & Co.

Delbourgo Associates, Inc., Joelle
Dijkstra Literary Agency, Sandra
Dunham Literary, Inc.
Dunow, Carlson, & Lerner Agency
Dystel & Goderich Literary
Einstein Literary Management
Ellenberg Literary Agency, Ethan
Ehrlich Literary, Judith
Eth Literary Representation, Felicia
Fairbank Literary Representation
Finch Literary Agency, Diana
Fletcher & Company
Folio Literary Management, LLC
Freymann Literary, Sarah Jane
Friedrich Agency, The
Full Circle Literary, LLC
Greenburger Associates, Sanford J.
Grinberg Literary Management, Jill
Grosjean Literary Agency, Jill
Hawkins & Associates, Inc., John
Heller Agency Inc., Helen
Henshaw Group, Richard
Hill Nadell Literary Agency
Holloway Literary
HSG Agency
InkWell Management, LLC
International Transactions, Inc.
J de S Associates, Inc.
Jenks Agency, The Carolyn
Keller Media Inc.
Klinger, Inc., Harvey
Krichevsky Literary Agency, Stuart
LA Literary Agency, The
Lampack Agency, Inc., Peter
Levine Greenberg Literary Agency, Inc.
Lippincott Massie McQuilkin
Lowenstein Associates Inc.
Maccoby Literary Agency, Gina
Mann Agency, Carol
Marsal Lyon Literary Agency, LLC
Marshall Agency, The Evan
McBride Literary Agency, Margret
McIntosh & Otis, Inc.
McMillan, LLC, Sally Hill
Morhaim Literary Agency, Howard
Moveable Type Management
Mura Literary, Dee
Nelson Literary Agency
New Leaf Literary & Media, Inc.
Priest Literary Agency, Aaron M.
Prospect Agency
Rebecca Friedman Literary Agency
Red Sofa Literary
Rees Literary Agency, Helen
Regal Hoffman & Associates, LLC
Rights Factory, The
Rinaldi Literary Agency, Angela
RLR Associates, Ltd.
Robbins Literary Agency, B.J.
Robin Mizell Literary Representation
Ross Literary Agency, Andy
Rotrosen Agency LLC, Jane

Trident Media Group
Waxman Leavell Literary

PICTURE BOOKS

Amster Literary Enterprises, Betsy
Bent Agency, The
Bradford Literary Agency
Brown Associates, Inc., Marie
Corcoran Literary Agency, Jill
Corvisiero Literary Agency
Curtis Brown, Ltd.
DeChiara Literary, Jennifer
DeFiore & Co.
Dunham Literary, Inc.
Dunow, Carlson, & Lerner Agency
Ellenberg Literary Agency, Ethan
Ehrlich Literary, Judith
Folio Literary Management, LLC
Full Circle Literary, LLC
Greenburger Associates, Sanford J.
HSG Agency
InkWell Management, LLC
McIntosh & Otis, Inc.
New Leaf Literary & Media, Inc.
Prospect Agency
Rights Factory, The
RLR Associates, Ltd.
Sanders & Associates, Victoria
Spieler Agency, The
Sterling Lord Literistic, Inc.
Thompson Literary Agency
Three Seas Literary Agency
Trident Media Group
Upstart Crow Literary
Wells Arms Literary
Writers House

POLICE

Amster Literary Enterprises, Betsy
Barone Literary Agency
Creative Media Agency, Inc.
Dawson Associates, Liza
Donaghy Literary Group
Donovan Literary, Jim
Finch Literary Agency, Diana
Henshaw Group, Richard
Inklings Literary Agency
International Transactions, Inc.
J de S Associates, Inc.
Keller Media Inc.
Klinger, Inc., Harvey
Lampack Agency, Inc., Peter
Marshall Agency, The Evan
McBride Literary Agency, Margret
Mura Literary, Dee
Speilburg Literary Agency
Stringer Literary Agency, LLC, The
Triada U.S. Literary Agency, Inc.

PSYCHIC

Barone Literary Agency
Donaghy Literary Group
Inklings Literary Agency
Jenks Agency, The Carolyn

Marshall Agency, The Evan
Mura Literary, Dee

REGIONAL

Barone Literary Agency
Holloway Literary
Inklings Literary Agency
Jenks Agency, The Carolyn
Keller Media Inc.
Marshall Agency, The Evan
Mura Literary, Dee

RELIGIOUS

Barone Literary Agency
Books & Such Literary Management
Curtis Brown, Ltd.
Folio Literary Management, LLC
Hartline Literary Agency
Jenks Agency, The Carolyn
Laube Agency, The Steve
Marshall Agency, The Evan
Mura Literary, Dee
Schulman Literary Agency, Susan
Seymour Agency, The

ROMANCE

Ahearn Agency, Inc., The
Axelrod Agency, The
Barone Literary Agency
Bent Agency, The
Book Cents Literary Agency, LLC
Books & Such Literary Management
Bradford Literary Agency
Cameron & Associates, Kimberley
Carvainis Agency, Inc., Maria
Chalberg & Sussman
Corcoran Literary Agency, Jill
Corvisiero Literary Agency
Creative Media Agency, Inc.
Curtis Brown, Ltd.
D4EO Literary Agency
Dawson Associates, Liza
DeFiore & Co.
Delbourgo Associates, Inc., Joelle
Dijkstra Literary Agency, Sandra
Donaghy Literary Group
Dystel & Goderich Literary
Einstein Literary Management
Ellenberg Literary Agency, Ethan
FinePrint Literary Management
Folio Literary Management, LLC
Fox Literary
Goodman Literary Agency, Irene
Greenburger Associates, Sanford J.
Greyhaus Literary
Grinberg Literary Management, Jill
Hartline Literary Agency
Henshaw Group, Richard
Holloway Literary
Inklings Literary Agency
InkWell Management, LLC
Keller Media Inc.
Marsal Lyon Literary Agency, LLC
Marshall Agency, The Evan

McIntosh & Otis, Inc.
Morhaim Literary Agency, Howard
Moveable Type Management
Mura Literary, Dee
Nelson Literary Agency
New Leaf Literary & Media, Inc.
Prospect Agency
Rebecca Friedman Literary Agency
Red Sofa Literary
Rights Factory, The
RLR Associates, Ltd.
Rosenberg Group, The
Rotrosen Agency LLC, Jane
Seligman, Literary Agent, Lynn
Serendipity Literary Agency, LLC
Seymour Agency, The
Spencerhill Associates
Stringer Literary Agency, LLC, The
Talcott Notch Literary
Three Seas Literary Agency
Triada U.S. Literary Agency, Inc.
Trident Media Group
Waxman Leavell Literary
Webber Associates Literary, CK
Wolfson Literary Agency

SATIRE

Barone Literary Agency
International Transactions, Inc.
LaunchBooks Literary Agency
Marshall Agency, The Evan
McBride Literary Agency, Margret
Mura Literary, Dee

SCIENCE FICTION

Aponte Literary Agency
Azantian Literary Agency
Barone Literary Agency
Bradford Literary Agency
Cameron & Associates, Kimberley
Chalberg & Sussman
Corvisiero Literary Agency
Dawson Associates, Liza
Delbourgo Associates, Inc., Joelle
Dijkstra Literary Agency, Sandra
Donaghy Literary Group
Dunham Literary, Inc.
Ellenberg Literary Agency, Ethan
FinePrint Literary Management
Fox Literary
Greenburger Associates, Sanford J.
Grinberg Literary Management, Jill
Henshaw Group, Richard
Inklings Literary Agency
International Transactions, Inc.
Jenks Agency, The Carolyn
Kidd Agency, Inc., Virginia
Laube Agency, The Steve
LaunchBooks Literary Agency
Lowenstein Associates Inc.
Marshall Agency, The Evan
McCarthy Agency, LLC, The
McIntosh & Otis, Inc.
Morhaim Literary Agency, Howard

Moveable Type Management
Mura Literary, Dee
Nelson Literary Agency
Prospect Agency
Rebecca Friedman Literary Agency
Red Sofa Literary
Rights Factory, The
Scribe Agency, LLC
Seligman, Literary Agent, Lynn
Seymour Agency, The
Speilburg Literary Agency
Sterling Lord Literistic, Inc.
Stringer Literary Agency, LLC, The
Talcott Notch Literary
Trident Media Group
United Talent Agency
Veritas Literary Agency
Waxman Leavell Literary
Webber Associates Literary, CK
Writers House
Yarn Literary Agency, Jason

SHORT STORY COLLECTIONS

Cheney Literary Associates, Elyse
DeFiore & Co.
Ehrlich Literary, Judith
InkWell Management, LLC
Mura Literary, Dee
Rights Factory, The

SPIRITUAL

Books & Such Literary Management
Curtis Brown, Ltd.
Inklings Literary Agency
International Transactions, Inc.
Marshall Agency, The Evan
Mura Literary, Dee
Wordserve Literary Group

SPORTS

Barone Literary Agency
Curtis Brown, Ltd.
D4EO Literary Agency
Dawson Associates, Liza
Donaghy Literary Group
Fairbank Literary Representation
Finch Literary Agency, Diana
Inklings Literary Agency
International Transactions, Inc.
Marshall Agency, The Evan
Moveable Type Management
Mura Literary, Dee
Robbins Literary Agency, B.J.

SUPERNATURAL

Aponte Literary Agency
Barone Literary Agency
Brown Associates, Inc., Marie
Inklings Literary Agency
Jenks Agency, The Carolyn
Marshall Agency, The Evan
Mura Literary, Dee

SUSPENSE

Ahearn Agency, Inc., The
Barone Literary Agency
Bent Agency, The
Book Cents Literary Agency, LLC
Books & Such Literary Management
Brandt & Hochman Literary Agents
Carvainis Agency, Inc., Maria
Chalberg & Sussman
Cheney Literary Associates, Elyse
Corvisiero Literary Agency
Creative Media Agency, Inc.
Curtis Brown, Ltd.
Darhansoff & Verrill Literary
Dawson Associates, Liza
DeChiara Literary, Jennifer
DeFiore & Co.
Dijkstra Literary Agency, Sandra
Donaghy Literary Group
Donovan Literary, Jim
Dystel & Goderich Literary
Ehrlich Literary, Judith
Eth Literary Representation, Felicia
Fairbank Literary Representation
FinePrint Literary Management
Hartline Literary Agency
Hawkins & Associates, Inc., John
Inklings Literary Agency
InkWell Management, LLC
International Transactions, Inc.
J de S Associates, Inc.
Keller Media Inc.
Klinger, Inc., Harvey
LA Literary Agency, The
Lampack Agency, Inc., Peter
LaunchBooks Literary Agency
Lippincott Massie McQuilkin
Marsal Lyon Literary Agency, LLC
Marshall Agency, The Evan
McBride Literary Agency, Margret
McIntosh & Otis, Inc.
Moveable Type Management
Mura Literary, Dee
Park Literary Group, LLC
Priest Literary Agency, Aaron M.
Prospect Agency
Rebecca Friedman Literary Agency
Red Sofa Literary
Rees Literary Agency, Helen
Rights Factory, The
Rinaldi Literary Agency, Angela
Robbins Literary Agency, B.J.
Rotrosen Agency LLC, Jane
Secret Agent Man
Seymour Agency, The
Stringer Literary Agency, LLC, The
Talcott Notch Literary
Triada U.S. Literary Agency, Inc.
Trident Media Group
United Talent Agency
Veritas Literary Agency
Waxman Leavell Literary

Webber Associates Literary, CK
Wolfson Literary Agency
Wordserve Literary Group
Yarn Literary Agency, Jason

THRILLER

Ahearn Agency, Inc., The
Aponte Literary Agency
Barone Literary Agency
Bent Agency, The
Bijur Literary Agency, Vicky
Black Literary Agency, David
Book Cents Literary Agency, LLC
Bradford Literary Agency
Brandt & Hochman Literary Agents
Braun Associates, Inc., Barbara
Cameron & Associates, Kimberley
Carvainis Agency, Inc., Maria
Corvisiero Literary Agency
Creative Media Agency, Inc.
Curtis Brown, Ltd.
D4EO Literary Agency
Dail Literary Agency, Inc., Laura
Dawson Associates, Liza
DeChiara Literary, Jennifer
DeFiore & Co.
Delbourgo Associates, Inc., Joelle
Dijkstra Literary Agency, Sandra
Donaghy Literary Group
Donovan Literary, Jim
Dunow, Carlson, & Lerner Agency
Dystel & Goderich Literary
Ellenberg Literary Agency, Ethan
Ehrlich Literary, Judith
Fairbank Literary Representation
Finch Literary Agency, Diana
FinePrint Literary Management
Folio Literary Management, LLC
Fox Literary
Freymann Literary, Sarah Jane
Goodman Literary Agency, Irene
Greenburger Associates, Sanford J.
Grosjean Literary Agency, Jill
Hawkins & Associates, Inc., John
Heller Agency Inc., Helen
Henshaw Group, Richard
Hill Nadell Literary Agency
Holloway Literary
HSG Agency
Inklings Literary Agency
InkWell Management, LLC
International Transactions, Inc.
Jenks Agency, The Carolyn
Keller Media Inc.
Klinger, Inc., Harvey
LA Literary Agency, The
Lampack Agency, Inc., Peter
LaunchBooks Literary Agency
Lippincott Massie McQuilkin
Maccoby Literary Agency, Gina
Marsal Lyon Literary Agency, LLC
Marshall Agency, The Evan
McBride Literary Agency, Margret

Moveable Type Management
Mura Literary, Dee
New Leaf Literary & Media, Inc.
Park Literary Group, LLC
Priest Literary Agency, Aaron M.
Prospect Agency
Red Sofa Literary
Rees Literary Agency, Helen
Regal Hoffman & Associates, LLC
Rights Factory, The
Rinaldi Literary Agency, Angela
Robbins Literary Agency, B.J.
Rotrosen Agency LLC, Jane
Rudy Agency, The
Sanders & Associates, Victoria
Secret Agent Man
Serendipity Literary Agency, LLC
Seymour Agency, The
Speilburg Literary Agency
Spencerhill Associates
Spieler Agency, The
Stringer Literary Agency, LLC, The
Stuart Agency, The
Talcott Notch Literary
Three Seas Literary Agency
Triada U.S. Literary Agency, Inc.
Trident Media Group
United Talent Agency
Waxman Leavell Literary
Webber Associates Literary, CK
Wolfson Literary Agency
Wordserve Literary Group
Yarn Literary Agency, Jason

TRANSLATION
HSG Agency
International Transactions, Inc.
Marshall Agency, The Evan
Mura Literary, Dee

URBAN FANTASY
Barone Literary Agency
Book Cents Literary Agency, LLC
Brown Associates, Inc., Marie
Corvisiero Literary Agency
Dawson Associates, Liza
DeChiara Literary, Jennifer
DeFiore & Co.
Delbourgo Associates, Inc., Joelle
Donaghy Literary Group
Inklings Literary Agency
LaunchBooks Literary Agency
Marshall Agency, The Evan
McIntosh & Otis, Inc.
Mura Literary, Dee
Prospect Agency
Rights Factory, The
Stringer Literary Agency, LLC, The
Talcott Notch Literary
Triada U.S. Literary Agency, Inc.
Waxman Leavell Literary

WAR
Barone Literary Agency
Donovan Literary, Jim

Inklings Literary Agency
International Transactions, Inc.
LaunchBooks Literary Agency
Marshall Agency, The Evan
Mura Literary, Dee

WESTERNS
Barone Literary Agency
Donovan Literary, Jim
International Transactions, Inc.
J de S Associates, Inc.
Jenks Agency, The Carolyn
LaunchBooks Literary Agency
Marshall Agency, The Evan
Mura Literary, Dee
Rees Literary Agency, Helen
Secret Agent Man

WOMEN'S
Ahearn Agency, Inc., The
Amster Literary Enterprises, Betsy
Aponte Literary Agency
Axelrod Agency, The
Barone Literary Agency
Bent Agency, The
Bijur Literary Agency, Vicky
Book Cents Literary Agency, LLC
Book Group, The
Books & Such Literary Management
Bradford Literary Agency
Brandt & Hochman Literary Agents
Braun Associates, Inc., Barbara
Brown Associates, Inc., Marie
Cameron & Associates, Kimberley
Carvainis Agency, Inc., Maria
Cheney Literary Associates, Elyse
Creative Media Agency, Inc.
Curtis Brown, Ltd.
Dail Literary Agency, Inc., Laura
Dawson Associates, Liza
DeChiara Literary, Jennifer
DeFiore & Co.
Delbourgo Associates, Inc., Joelle
Dijkstra Literary Agency, Sandra
Dunham Literary, Inc.
Dystel & Goderich Literary
Einstein Literary Management
Ellenberg Literary Agency, Ethan
Ehrlich Literary, Judith
Fairbank Literary Representation
FinePrint Literary Management
Fletcher & Company
Folio Literary Management, LLC
Full Circle Literary, LLC
Goodman Literary Agency, Irene
Greenburger Associates, Sanford J.
Greyhaus Literary
Grosjean Literary Agency, Jill
Hartline Literary Agency
Hill Nadell Literary Agency
Holloway Literary
HSG Agency
Inklings Literary Agency
InkWell Management, LLC
International Transactions, Inc.

Jenks Agency, The Carolyn
Keller Media Inc.
Klinger, Inc., Harvey
LA Literary Agency, The
Lippincott Massie McQuilkin
Lowenstein Associates Inc.
Marsal Lyon Literary Agency, LLC
Marshall Agency, The Evan
McCarthy Agency, LLC, The
McIntosh & Otis, Inc.
Morhaim Literary Agency, Howard
Moveable Type Management
Mura Literary, Dee
Nelson Literary Agency
New Leaf Literary & Media, Inc.
Park Literary Group, LLC
Priest Literary Agency, Aaron M.
Prospect Agency
Rebecca Friedman Literary Agency
Rees Literary Agency, Helen
Rights Factory, The
Rinaldi Literary Agency, Angela
RLR Associates, Ltd.
Robbins Literary Agency, B.J.
Rosenberg Group, The
Rotrosen Agency LLC, Jane
Schulman Literary Agency, Susan
Seligman, Literary Agent, Lynn
Serendipity Literary Agency, LLC
Speilburg Literary Agency
Straus Agency, Inc., Robin
Stringer Literary Agency, LLC, The
Talcott Notch Literary
Tessler Literary Agency, LLC
Thompson Literary Agency
Three Seas Literary Agency
Triada U.S. Literary Agency, Inc.
Trident Media Group
United Talent Agency
Veritas Literary Agency
Waxman Leavell Literary
Webber Associates Literary, CK
Wolfson Literary Agency
Wordserve Literary Group
Writers House

YOUNG ADULT
Amster Literary Enterprises, Betsy
Azantian Literary Agency
Barone Literary Agency
Bent Agency, The
Bijur Literary Agency, Vicky
Black Literary Agency, David
Book Cents Literary Agency, LLC
Book Group, The
Books & Such Literary Management
Bradford Literary Agency
Brandt & Hochman Literary Agents
Braun Associates, Inc., Barbara
Brown Associates, Inc., Marie
Cameron & Associates, Kimberley
Carvainis Agency, Inc., Maria
Chalberg & Sussman
Clark Associates, WM

Corcoran Literary Agency, Jill
Corvisiero Literary Agency
Creative Media Agency, Inc.
Curtis Brown, Ltd.
D4EO Literary Agency
Dail Literary Agency, Inc., Laura
Darhansoff & Verrill Literary
Dawson Associates, Liza
DeChiara Literary, Jennifer
DeFiore & Co.
Delbourgo Associates, Inc., Joelle
Dijkstra Literary Agency, Sandra
Donaghy Literary Group
Dunham Literary, Inc.
Dunow, Carlson, & Lerner Agency
Dystel & Goderich Literary
Ellenberg Literary Agency, Ethan
Ehrlich Literary, Judith
Finch Literary Agency, Diana
FinePrint Literary Management
Fletcher & Company
Folio Literary Management, LLC
Fox Literary
Freymann Literary, Sarah Jane
Full Circle Literary, LLC
Goodman Literary Agency, Irene
Greenburger Associates, Sanford J.
Grinberg Literary Management, Jill
Hartline Literary Agency
Heller Agency Inc., Helen
Henshaw Group, Richard

Hill Nadell Literary Agency
Holloway Literary
HSG Agency
Inklings Literary Agency
InkWell Management, LLC
International Transactions, Inc.
J de S Associates, Inc.
Jenks Agency, The Carolyn
Klinger, Inc., Harvey
LaunchBooks Literary Agency
Levine Greenberg Literary Agency, Inc.
Lowenstein Associates Inc.
Maccoby Literary Agency, Gina
Mann Agency, Carol
Marsal Lyon Literary Agency, LLC
Marshall Agency, The Evan
McCarthy Agency, LLC, The
McIntosh & Otis, Inc.
Morhaim Literary Agency, Howard
Mura Literary, Dee
Nelson Literary Agency
New Leaf Literary & Media, Inc.
Park Literary Group, LLC
Priest Literary Agency, Aaron M.
Prospect Agency
Rebecca Friedman Literary Agency
Red Sofa Literary
Rees Literary Agency, Helen
Regal Hoffman & Associates, LLC
Rights Factory, The

RLR Associates, Ltd.
Robin Mizell Literary Representation
Ross Literary Agency, Andy
Rotrosen Agency LLC, Jane
Sanders & Associates, Victoria
Schmalz Agency, Wendy
Schulman Literary Agency, Susan
Seligman, Literary Agent, Lynn
Serendipity Literary Agency, LLC
Seymour Agency, The
Speilburg Literary Agency
Spieler Agency, The
Sterling Lord Literistic, Inc.
Stringer Literary Agency, LLC, The
Talcott Notch Literary
Thompson Literary Agency
Three Seas Literary Agency
Triada U.S. Literary Agency, Inc.
Trident Media Group
United Talent Agency
Upstart Crow Literary
Veritas Literary Agency
Waxman Leavell Literary
Webber Associates Literary, CK
Wells Arms Literary
Wolfson Literary Agency
Wordserve Literary Group
Writers House
Yarn Literary Agency, Jason

CATEGORY INDEX

///

BOOK PUBLISHERS

ADVENTURE
Cedar Fort, Inc.
Covenant Communications, Inc.
Dial Books for Young Readers
Divertir Publishing
Frances Lincoln Children's Books
Glencannon Press, The
HarperCollins Children's Books/
    HarperCollins Publishers
Holiday House, Inc.
Hopewell Publications
JourneyForth
Knox Robinson Publishing
Martin Sisters Publishing Company
Melange Books, LLC
Mondial
New Libri Press
PageSpring Publishing
Pants On Fire Press
Piñata Books
Red Tuque Books, Inc.
Salvo Press
Seedling Continental Press
Severn House Publishers
Soho Press, Inc.
Stoneslide Books
Sunbury Press, Inc.
Tor Books
Tu Books
WaterBrook Multnomah Publishing
    Group

CHILDREN'S/JUVENILE
Chronicle Books
Covenant Communications, Inc.
Craigmore Creations

Dial Books for Young Readers
Familius
Farrar, Straus & Giroux
Glencannon Press, The
HarperCollins Children's Books/
    HarperCollins Publishers
Hendrick-Long Publishing Co., Inc.
Holiday House, Inc.
Levine Books, Arthur A.
Mandala Publishing
Pelican Publishing Company
Piano Press
Puffin Books
Salina Bookshelf
Scholastic Press
Tradewind Books
Whitecap Books, Ltd.

COMICS/GRAPHIC NOVELS
Archaia
Image Comics
Insomniac Press
NBM Publishing
Nortia Press
Papercutz
Vertigo

EROTICA
Black Velvet Seductions Publishing
Changeling Press LLC
Crescent Moon Publishing
Guernica Editions
Loose Id
Melange Books, LLC
Mondial
Pedlar Press

ETHNIC/MULTICULTURAL
Arte Publico Press
Bancroft Press
Carolina Wren Press
Charlesbridge Publishing
Coteau Books
Frances Lincoln Children's Books
Gertrude Press
Gival Press
Glencannon Press, The
Interlink Publishing Group, Inc.
Just Us Books, Inc.
Mage Publishers, Inc.
Mondial
Nortia Press
Piano Press
Red Hen Press
River City Publishing
Seedling Continental Press
Soho Press, Inc.
Sunbury Press, Inc.
Tightrope Books
Tor Books
Torch Journal

EXPERIMENTAL
Anvil Press
BlazeVOX
Crescent Moon Publishing
Gertrude Press
Hopewell Publications
Insomniac Press
Livingston Press
New Libri Press
Paycock Press
Pedlar Press
Red Hen Press

Gival Press
Goose Lane Editions
Graywolf Press
Guernica Editions
Hampton Roads Publishing Co., Inc.
HarperCollins Children's Books/
  HarperCollins Publishers
Holiday House, Inc.
Insomniac Press
Knopf
Knox Robinson Publishing
Lethe Press
Little, Brown and Co. Adult Trade
  Books
Livingston Press
Mage Publishers, Inc.
Martin Sisters Publishing Company
Medallion Press
Milkweed Editions
Mondial
New Libri Press
Nortia Press
Oolichan Books
Orca Book Publishers
PageSpring Publishing
Paycock Press
Pedlar Press
Penguin Group: South Africa
Permanent Press, The
Persea Books
Piatkus Books
Picador USA
Pocol Press
Press 53
Red Hen Press
River City Publishing
Riverhead Books
Ronsdale Press
Salvo Press
Sarabande Books, Inc.
Seven Stories Press
Small Beer Press
Soft Skull Press Inc.
Soho Press, Inc.
Stone Bridge Press
Stoneslide Books
Titan Press
Twilight Times Books
Unbridled Books
University of Alaska Press
University of Michigan Press
Vehicule Press
Viking
Vintage Anchor Publishing
Vivisphere Publishing
WaterBrook Multnomah Publishing
  Group
Yellow Shoe Fiction Series

MAINSTREAM
Arcade Publishing
Arte Publico Press
Bancroft Press
Brucedale Press, The

Canterbury House Publishing, Ltd.
Carolina Wren Press
Cave Hollow Press
Cedar Fort, Inc.
Coteau Books
Covenant Communications, Inc.
Divertir Publishing
Gertrude Press
Glencannon Press, The
Holiday House, Inc.
Insomniac Press
Knox Robinson Publishing
Little, Brown and Co. Adult Trade
  Books
Mage Publishers, Inc.
Medallion Press
Mondial
New Libri Press
Orca Book Publishers
Permanent Press, The
Piatkus Books
Pocol Press
Red Hen Press
Riverhead Books
Severn House Publishers
Soft Skull Press Inc.
Soho Press, Inc.
Titan Press
Twilight Times Books
Viking
Villard Books
Vintage Anchor Publishing
WaterBrook Multnomah Publishing
  Group

MILITARY/WAR
Bancroft Press
Glencannon Press, The
Martin Sisters Publishing Company
New Libri Press
Nortia Press
Twilight Times Books
Vivisphere Publishing

MYSTERY/SUSPENSE
Archaia
Avon Romance
Bancroft Press
Brucedale Press, The
Canterbury House Publishing, Ltd.
Coteau Books
Covenant Communications, Inc.
Glencannon Press, The
Harlequin Intrigue
Hopewell Publications
Insomniac Press
JourneyForth
Martin Sisters Publishing Company
Medallion Press
Mondial
Permanent Press, The
Piatkus Books
Poisoned Pen Press
Salvo Press

Severn House Publishers
Soho Press, Inc.
Sunbury Press, Inc.
Tor Books
Tu Books
Twilight Times Books
University of Wisconsin Press
Viking
WaterBrook Multnomah Publishing
  Group

NEW AGE
Bancroft Press
Crescent Moon Publishing
Divertir Publishing
Hampton Roads Publishing Co., Inc.
Twilight Times Books
Psychic/Supernatural
Changeling Press LLC
Hampton Roads Publishing Co., Inc.
Lethe Press
Pants On Fire Press
Twilight Times Books
Write Place At the Write Time, The

REGIONAL
Beil, Publisher, Inc., Frederic C.
Canterbury House Publishing, Ltd.
Cave Hollow Press
Coteau Books
Covenant Communications, Inc.
Nortia Press
Piatkus Books
Plexus Publishing, Inc.
River City Publishing
Twilight Times Books
University of Wisconsin Press
Vehicule Press
Write Place At the Write Time, The

RELIGIOUS
Covenant Communications, Inc.
Divertir Publishing
Mandala Publishing
WaterBrook Multnomah Publishing
  Group
Write Place At the Write Time, The

ROMANCE
Arrow Publications, LLC
Avon Romance
Black Velvet Seductions Publishing
Brucedale Press, The
Bullitt Publishing
Canterbury House Publishing, Ltd.
Changeling Press LLC
Covenant Communications, Inc.
Divertir Publishing
Harlequin Blaze
Harlequin Desire
Harlequin Intrigue
Harlequin Superromance
Knox Robinson Publishing
Loose Id
Medallion Press

Bear Deluxe Magazine, The
Beyond Centauri
Big Pulp
Blackbird
Card's InterGalactic Medicine Show,
   Orson Scott
Conceit Magazine
Congruent Spaces
Dark, The
Down in the Dirt
Downstate Story
Eclectica
First Line, The
Harpur Palate
Literary Juice
Magazine of Fantasy & Science Fic-
   tion, The
Mobius
Nth Degree
On Spec
On the Premises
Pseudopod
Space and Time
Toasted Cheese
Vestal Review
Wild Violet
Witches and Pagans

HUMOR/SATIRE
580 Split
African Voices
Allegheny Review, The
Apalachee Review
Bear Deluxe Magazine, The
Big Muddy
Blackbird
Blueline
Briar Cliff Review, The
Chaffin Journal, The
Conceit Magazine
Congruent Spaces
Cutthroat, A Journal of the Arts
Downstate Story
Ducts
Eclectica
Fiction
First Line, The
Fourteen Hills
Fugue Literary Magazine
Gathering of the Tribes, A
Gertrude
Gettysburg Review, The
Green Mountains Review
Harpur Palate
Hawai'i Pacific Review
Hawai'i Review
Hayden's Ferry Review
Iconoclast
Kenyon Review, The
Literary Juice
London Magazine, The
Lullwater Review
MacGuffin, The

Midway Journal
Missouri Review, The
Mobius
Na'amat Woman
Nassau Review, The
New Letters
Nite-Writer's International Literary
   Arts Journal
North Dakota Quarterly
Now & Then: The Appalachian
   Magazine
Nth Degree
On the Premises
Pink Chameleon, The
Portland Review
Quarter After Eight
Quarterly West
Rockford Review, The
Storyteller, The
Summerset Review, The
Sycamore Review
Talking River
Toasted Cheese
Vestal Review
Wild Violet
Windhover
Witches and Pagans
Word Riot
Write Place At the Write Time, The
Yalobusha Review, The
Yemassee
ZYZZYVA

LESBIAN
Allegheny Review, The
Blackbird
Conceit Magazine
Dos Passos Review, The
Down in the Dirt
Fourteen Hills
Gargoyle
Gertrude
Iris
Kenyon Review, The
Midway Journal
Mobius
Painted Bride Quarterly
Paperplates
Quarter After Eight
Straylight
Toasted Cheese
Wild Violet
Yemassee

LITERARY
580 Split
African Voices
Alaska Quarterly Review
Albedo One
Alembic, The
Allegheny Review, The
American Literary Review
American Short Fiction
Antioch Review

Apalachee Review
Appalachian Heritage
Barbaric Yawp
Bellevue Literary Review
Berkeley Fiction Review
Big Muddy
Blackbird
Black Warrior Review
Blueline
Boston Review
Briar Cliff Review, The
Broadkill Review, The
Chaffin Journal, The
Chicago Quarterly Review
Chicago Review
Coal City Review
Conceit Magazine
Contrary
Crab Orchard Review
Cream City Review
Crucible
Cutthroat, A Journal of the Arts
Dead Mule School of Southern
   Literature, The
descant: Fort Worth's Journal of
   Poetry and Fiction
Diagram
Dos Passos Review, The
Down in the Dirt
Downstate Story
Ducts
Eclectica
Emrys Journal
Epoch
Failbetter.com
Faultline
Fiction
Fiddlehead, The
Florida Review, The
Flyway
Fourteen Hills
Fugue Literary Magazine
Gargoyle
Gathering of the Tribes, A
Gertrude
Gettysburg Review, The
Glimmer Train Stories
Grasslimb
Green Mountains Review
Gulf Coast: A Journal of Literature
   and Fine Arts
Gulf Stream Magazine
Harvard Review
Hawai'i Pacific Review
Hayden's Ferry Review
Iconoclast
Idaho Review, The
Image
Indiana Review
Island
Jabberwock Review
J Journal: New Writing on Justice
Journal, The

Big Muddy
Big Pulp
Bitter Oleander, The
Blackbird
Conceit Magazine
Down in the Dirt
Downstate Story
Eclectica
First Line, The
Grasslimb
Harpur Palate
Hitchcock's Mystery Magazine, Alfred
J Journal: New Writing on Justice
Literary Juice
London Magazine, The
Lullwater Review
Nassau Review, The
On the Premises
Pink Chameleon, The
Storyteller, The
Toasted Cheese
Witches and Pagans

NEW AGE
Allegheny Review, The
Apalachee Review
Blackbird
Conceit Magazine
Down in the Dirt
On the Premises
Toasted Cheese
Wild Violet
Write Place At the Write Time, The

PSYCHIC/ SUPERNATURAL
African Voices
Allegheny Review, The
Barbaric Yawp
Big Pulp
Blackbird
Conceit Magazine
Down in the Dirt
Downstate Story
Eclectica
Magazine of Fantasy & Science Fiction, The
On the Premises
Toasted Cheese
Wild Violet
Write Place At the Write Time, The

REGIONAL
Appalachian Heritage
Barbaric Yawp
Big Muddy
Blackbird
Blueline
Boston Review
Briar Cliff Review, The
Camas: The Nature of the West
Caribbean Writer, The
Chaffin Journal, The

Cream City Review
Crucible
Downstate Story
Eclectica
Flint Hills Review
Gettysburg Review, The
Grasslimb
Gulf Coast: A Journal of Literature and Fine Arts
Hawai'i Pacific Review
Hayden's Ferry Review
Indiana Review
Jabberwock Review
J Journal: New Writing on Justice
Kaimana: Literary Arts Hawai'i
Kelsey Review, The
Landfall: New Zealand Arts and Letters
Louisiana Literature
Louisiana Review, The
North Carolina Literary Review
Now & Then: The Appalachian Magazine
On the Premises
Packingtown Review
Passages North
PMS poemmemoirstory
Portland Review
Prairie Journal, The
Raven Chronicles, The
Rockford Review, The
South Dakota Review
Southwestern American Literature
storySouth
Straylight
Sycamore Review
Talking River
Write Place At the Write Time, The
Xavier Review
Yemassee

RELIGIOUS
African Voices
Allegheny Review, The
Barbaric Yawp
Blackbird
Conceit Magazine
Eclectica
First Line, The
Image
London Magazine, The
Lullwater Review
Nite-Writer's International Literary Arts Journal
Perspectives
Pink Chameleon, The
Pockets
Storyteller, The
Studio, A Journal of Christians Writing
Witches and Pagans
Write Place At the Write Time, The
Xavier Review
Romance

African Voices
Allegheny Review, The
Avalon Literary Review, The
Big Pulp
Conceit Magazine
Copperfield Review, The
Downstate Story
Eclectica
First Line, The
London Magazine, The
Louisiana Review, The
Nite-Writer's International Literary Arts Journal
On the Premises
Pink Chameleon, The
Storyteller, The
Toasted Cheese
Witches and Pagans

SCIENCE FICTION
African Voices
Albedo One
Allegheny Review, The
Allegory
Analog Science Fiction & Fact
Apex Magazine
Barbaric Yawp
Beyond Centauri
Big Pulp
Cafe Irreal, The
Card's InterGalactic Medicine Show, Orson Scott
Conceit Magazine
Congruent Spaces
Down in the Dirt
Downstate Story
Eclectica
First Line, The
Harpur Palate
Kasma Magazine
Lady Churchill's Rosebud Wristlet
Leading Edge
Literal Latté
Lullwater Review
Magazine of Fantasy & Science Fiction, The
Midway Journal
Mobius
Nth Degree
On Spec
On the Premises
Pink Chameleon, The
Premonitions
Rockford Review, The
Space and Time
Toasted Cheese
Wild Violet

THRILLER/ESPIONAGE
Blackbird
Conceit Magazine
Eclectica
First Line, The
Grasslimb

GENERAL INDEX

GENERAL INDEX